WEBSTER'S POCKET DICTIONARY

OF THE ENGLISH LANGUAGE

NICHOLS

Publishing Group

A, a (ā) *n.* The first letter of the English alphabet; the highest grade, meaning excellent or best.

aah (ä) *v.* To exclaim in joy.

aard-vark (ärd´värk˘) *n.* A burrowing African animal, which resembles the anteater and feeds on ants and termites.

a-ba (a bä´) *n.* A striped fabric, woven of goat's or camel's hair; an outer garment made from this fabric or silk, worn by Arabs.

a-ba-ca (ä˘bä kä´) *n.* A plant from the Philippines whose leafstalks are the source of Manila hemp.

a-back (a bak´) *adv.* Unexpectedly; by surprise; startled; confused.

a-bac-te-ri-al (ā bak tir´ ē al) *adj.* Not caused by bacteria.

ab-a-cus (ab´ a kas) *n.* A frame holding parallel rods with beads, used for manual computation, especially by the Chinese.

a-baft (a baft´) *adv.* On or toward the stern, aft, or hind part of a ship.

ab-a-lo-ne (ab˘a lō˘nē) *n.* A member of the genus of gastropod mollusks that will cling to rocks and have a shell which is flat and lined with mother of pearl.

a-ban-don (a ban´don) *v.* To yield utterly; to desert; to forsake; to withdraw protection, support, or help, to give up all rights or interest. **abandonment** *n.*

a-ban-doned (a ban´dond) *adj.* To be deserted; to be forsaken.

a-ban-don-ee (a ban´don ē´) *n.* The person to whom a thing is abandoned.

a-ban-don-ment (a ban´don ment) *n.* The state of being abandoned; or the act of abandoning; to surrender, relinquishment; free from constraint.

a-base (a bās´) *v.* To lower in rank, prestige, position, or estimation; to cast down, to humble.

a-base-ment (a bās´ment) *n.* A state of depression, degradation, or humiliation.

a-bash (a bash´) *v.* To embarrass; to disconcert; to make ashamed or uneasy.

a-bash-ment (a bash´ment) *n.* The state of something being abashed.

a-bate (a bāt´) *v.* To deduct; to make less; to reduce in quantity, value, force, or intensity. **abater** *n.* **abatable** *adj.*

a-bate-ment (a bāt´ment) *n.* The process of abating something; the amount which is abated.

ab-a-tis (ab´a tē) *n.* The collection of felled trees of which the smaller branches have already been cut off.

ab-at-toir (ab´a twär´) *n.* The public slaughterhouse.

ab-ax-i-al (ab ak´sēal) *adj.* To be positioned or situated out of the axis of something.

abb (ab) *n.* A type of low grade wool that

is from the inferior parts of a fleece.

ab-bre-vi-ate (a brē´vē āt´) *v.* To make briefer; to abridge; to shorten; to reduce to a briefer form, as a word or phrase.

ab-bre-vi-a-tion (a brē´vē ā´shan) *n.* A shortened form of a word or phrase, used to represent the full form. **abbreviator** *n.* **abbreviatory** *adj.*

ab-di-cate (ab´di kāt´) *v.* To relinquish power or responsibility formally; to renounce. **abdication** *n.*

ab-do-men (ab´do men) *n.* That part of the human body that lies between the thorax and the pelvis; it contains the stomach, spleen, liver, kidneys, bladder, pancreas, and the intestines.

ab-dom-i-nal (ab dom´i nal) *adj.* Having to do with the abdomen; in, on, or for the abdomen.

ab-dom-i-nous (ab dom´i nus) *adj.* Abdominal; having a large belly.

ab-du-cens nerve *n.* The 6th cranial motor nerves that supply the eye muscles.

ab-du-cent (ab dū´sent) *adj.* Pulling back, or drawing away.

abducent muscles *n.* Muscles that pull back certain parts of the body from the mesial line.

ab-duct (ab dukt´) *v.* To carry away wrongfully, as by force or fraud; to kidnap; to draw aside or away.

ab-duc-tion (ab duk´shan) *n.* An action of abducting. *Med.* Descriptive of the movement of a limb or part of a limb away from the midline of the body.

ab-duc-tor (ab duk´tèr) *n.* A person who or that which abducts; *Med.* muscle that moves certain body parts from the axis of the body.

a-beam (a bēm´) *adv.* At right angles to the keel of a ship.

a-be-ce-dar-i-an (ā˘bē sē dâr´ē an) *n.* A person who teaches the letters of the alphabet, or a person learning the letters. A beginner in any area of learning.

a-be-ce-da-ry (ā˘bē sē´da rē) *adj.* Formed by or pertaining to the letters of the alphabet.

a-bed (a bed´) *adv.* In bed; on a bed; to bed; restricted to bed.

a-bel-mosk (ā˘bel mosk´) *n.* A type of herb which is found in Asia and the East Indies and the musky seeds are used to flavor coffee and for perfumes.

abend In computer science, the termination of processing due to program or system fault; abnormal ending.

ab-er-rant (ab er´ent) *adj.* Straying from the right way or usual course; not being proper or truthful; abnormal or exceptional. **aberrantly** *adv.*

ab-er-ra-tion (ab´er ā´shan) *n.* The disorder of the mind; deviation from a type or standard. **aberrational** *adj*.

a-bet (*a* bet´) *v*. To incite, encourage, or assist by countenance, aid, or approval. **abetment** *n*. **abetter** *n*.

a-bey-ance (*a* bā´ans) *n*. State of expectation, for an occupant or holder; a feeling or state of temporary suspension.

a-bey-ant (*a* bā´ant) *adj*. Temporarily inactive.

ab-hor (ab hor´) *v*. To dislike intensely; to loathe. **abhorrer** *n*. **abhorrence** *n*.

ab-hor-rence (ab hor´rens) *n*. The state of abhorring.

ab-hor-rent (ab hor´ent) *adj*. To be feeling abhorrence; hating; detesting.

a-bid-ance (*a* bīd´ans) *n*. The state of abiding; compliance.

a-bide (*a* bīd´) *v*. To tolerate; to bear; to remain; to last; to conform to; to comply with. **abider** *n*.

a-bid-ing (*a* bī´dïng) *adj*. To be enduring.

ab-i-gail (ab´*e* gāl) *n*. A personal maid of a lady.

-a-bil-i-ty (*e* bïl´et ē) *n*. *suffix* Tendency to act in a specified manner or way.

a-bil-i-ty (*a* bïl´i tē) *n*. State of being able; possession of qualities necessary; competence; skill; a particular talent.

ab-i-o-gen-i-sis (ab´ē ō jen´i sis) *n*. An origination of something living from something that is not living.

abi-o-log-i-cal (ā bī *e* läj i kel) *adj*. Not being made or produced by organisms.

a-bi-otic (ā bī´ät ik) *adj*. Not being biotic.

ab-ir-ri-tant (ab ir´i tant) *n*. A lotion used to reduce irritation.

ab-ject (ab´jekt) *adj*. Sunk to a low condition; mean; despicable; worthless. **abject** *n*. A person who is an outcast.

abjection (ab jek´shan) *n*. A state which is downcast. **abjectness** *n*.

ab-ju-ra-tion (ab´ jü rā´shan) *n*. The process of abjuring.

ab-jure (ab jür´) *v*. To renounce solemnly or on oath; to repudiate; to forswear, to abstain or reject. **-er** *n*.

abl *abbr*. Ablative.

ab-lac-tate (ab lak´tāt) *v*. The act of weaning small infants from the breast.

ab-lac-ta-tion (ab´lak tā´shan) *n*. The weaning from the breast.

ab-late (a blāt´) *v*. To remove something by cutting or erosion.

ab-la-tion (ab lā´shan) *n*. A removal of a part; a process of ablating. *Med*. Removal of a part of the body by surgery

a-blaze (*a* blāz´) *adv*. On fire; brilliantly lighted up; very excited; angry.

a-ble (ā´bl) *adj*. Having sufficient ability; capable or talented. **able** *adj*. *suffix* To be worthy of. **ably** *adv*.

a-ble–bod-ied (ā´bl bod´ēd) *adj*. Having a sound, strong body; competent for

physical service.

a-bloom (a blōm´) *adj*. To be abounding with blooms such as a plant.

ab-lu-ent (ab´lō ent) *adj*. Cleansing by water or liquids. *n*. Something that washes off impurities; detergent or soap.

ab-lut-ed (ab´lōt ed) *adj*. Being washed and clean.

ab-lu-tion (ab lō´shan) *n*. The act of washing, cleansing, or purification by a liquid, usually water; specifically, a washing of the body as a part of religious rites. **ablutionary** *adj*.

a-bly (ā´blē) *adv*. To do something in an able manner.

ab-ne-gate (ab´n*a* gāt´) *v*. To deny; to refuse or renounce; to relinquish or surrender.

ab-ne-ga-tion (ab´ne gā´shan) *n*. The act of relinquishing rights; denial.

ab-ne-ga-tor (ab´na gāt´ẽr) *n*. A person who denies or renounces.

ab-nor-mal (ab nor´mel) *adj*. Descriptive of that which is unusual, not normal; irregular; unnatural. **abnormally** *adv*. **abnormality** *n*.

abnormal psychology *n*. A type of psychology that deals with the behaviors of people.

a-board (*a* bōrd´) *adv*. On board a ship or other vehicle.

a-bode (*a* bōd´) *n*. A dwelling place; home; place of residence; habitation.

a-bol-ish (*a* bol´ish) *v*. To put an end to; to annul; to do away with; nullify; destroy; to put out of existence.

a-bol-ish-a-ble (*a* bol´ish *a* bl) *adj*. Capable of being abolished.

a-bol-ish-er (*a* bol´ish ẽr) *n*. A person who abolishes.

ab-o-li-tion (ab´o lish´an) *n*. The state of being abolished. **abolitionary** *adj*.

ab-o-li-tion-ism (ab´o lish´a niz´um) *n*. The measures that will foster abolition.

ab-o-ma-sum (ab´o mā´sum) *n*. The fourth digestive stomach of the ruminant, lying next to the third stomach or omasum.

a-bom-i-na-ble (a bom´i na bal) *adj*. Detestable; repugnant; loathsome. **abominably** *adv*. **abominableness** *n*.

a-bom-i-nate (a bom´i nāt) *v*. To loathe intensely; to detest; to hate extremely.

ab-o-ral (ab ōr´al) *adj*. To be situated away from the mouth.

ab-o-rig-i-nal (ab´o rij´i nal) *adj*. To be the first in a region; primitive when compared with a more advanced type.

ab-o-rig-i-ne (ab´e rij´i nē) *n*. The first inhabitants of a country; *pl*. original animals and flowers of an area or region.

a-bort (*a* bort´) *v*. To terminate or cause to terminate an operation or procedure before completion; to miscarry in giving birth. In computer science, to terminate a process before completion.

a-bound (*a* bound´) *v*. To have plenty; to exist in large numbers.

a-bout (*a* bout´) *adv*. Approximately; on every side, here and there.

a-bove (*a* buv´) *adv*. Higher or greater than; in or at a higher place.

a-bove–all *adv*. To be before all other considerations.

ab-ra-ca-dab-ra (ab´ra ka dab´ra) *n*. A word believed by some to have magical powers, used in casting spells; nonsense, foolish talk.

a-bra-dant (*a* brăd´ant) *n*. A material used for polishing and grinding, as sand, or glass. **abradant** *adj*. Having an abrasive surface and quality.

a-brade (*a* brād´) *v*. To wear or rub off; to grate off; abrasive, scouring.

a-bra-sion (*a* brā´zhan) *n*. The injury to the skin by scraping the outer layer; any scraped surface; the grinding of a surface using friction.

a-bra-sive (*a* brā´siv) *n*. A substance employed in grinding or abrading. *adj*. to tend to abrade.

ab-re-act (ab´rē akt´) *v*. To release an emotion that is forgotten in psychoanalysis.

ab-re-ac-tion (ab´rē ak´shan) *n*. To eliminate a bad experience by reliving it.

a-breast (*a* brest´) *adv*. Side by side.

a-bri (a brē´) *n*. Place of refuge; shelter.

a-bridge (*a* brij´) *v*. To make smaller, fewer, or shorter while keeping essential contents. **abridger** *n*.

a-bridg-ment (ă brij´ment) *n*. The state of being abridged.

a-broach (*a* brōch´) *adv*. In agitation or action.

a-broad (*a* brod´) *adv*. Widely; in many places; outside one's country; at large.

ab-ro-gate (ab´ro găt´) *v*. To cancel; to put an end to; to repeal. **abrogation** *n*. **abrogable** *adj*. **abrogative** *adj*.

ab-rupt (a brupt´) *adj*. Happening or coming suddenly with no warning; very gruff; steep, craggy of rocks, precipices, etc.; sudden; brusque, without notice to prepare the mind for the event.

ab-rup-tion (a brup´shan) *n*. The sudden breaking away of something.

ab-rupt-ly (*a* brupt´lē) *adv*. In an abrupt manner, sudden and without any notice.

ab-rupt-ness (*a* brupt´nis) *n*. The state or quality of being abrupt; precipitousness; suddenness; unceremonious haste or vehemence.

ab-scess (ab´ses) *n*. An infected place in the body which is sore and swollen, tender or painful, and contains pus, the body's natural response to bacterial infection or an infection. -ed *adj*.

ab-scind (ab sind´) *v*. To cut off; to sever; to pare away; to separate.

ab-scise (ab sīz´) *v*. To part or separate with abscission.

abscisic acid *n*. A type of plant hormone that will promote leaf abscission and dormancy.

ab-scis-sa (ab sis´a) *n*. Any part of the diameter or transverse axis of a conic section, as an ellipse.

ab-scis-sion (ab sizh´an) *n*. A natural separation of fruit, flowers, or the leaves of a plant.

ab-scond (ab skond´) *v*. To run away; to flee from justice. **absconder** *n*.

ab-seil (äp´zīl) *n*. A means of descending from a cliff by securing a line at the peak.

ab-sence (ab´sens) *n*. Being absent, not present; inattention.

ab-sent (ab´sent) *adj*. Not present; away; lacking; nonexistent. **absently** *adv*.

ab-so-lute (ab´so lōt´) *adj*. Unconditional; without restraint; perfect; complete. **absoluteness** *n*. **absolutely** *adv*.

ab-so-lu-tion (ab´sa lō´shan) *n*. The state or act of being absolved; forgiven, discharged.

ab-so-lut-ism (ab´so lō´tiz´um) *n*. The exercise or principle of absolute power in government.

ab-so-lut-ize (ab *solot* iz) *v*. To make something absolute.

ab-sol-u-to-ry (ab sol´ū tōr´ē) *adj*. In an absolving manner; having the capacity to absolve.

ab-solve (ab zolv´) *v*. To set free or release from duties, guilt, debt, or penalty.

ab-so-nant (ab´so nant) *adj*. Contrary, discordant; dissonant; incongruous, abhorrent.

ab-sorb (ab sorb´) *v*. To take in; to take up the full attention; to engage one's whole attention. **absorbable** *adj*.

ab-sorp-tion (ab sorp´shan) *n*. The act of giving full attention or having great interest. *Med*. The process of assimilating food or other substances into the body, which may take place through the gastrointestinal tract, the skin, or the mucous membranes of the eyes, nose, etc.

ab-stain (ab stān´) *v*. To refrain from doing something. **abstainer** *n*.

ab-ste-mi-ous (ab stē´mē us) *adj*. Showing moderation in the use of drink and food. **abstemiousness** *n*. **abstemiously** *adv*.

ab-sten-tion (ab sten´shan) *n*. The act of holding off from using or doing something.

ab-sterge (ab stürj´) *v*. To make clean by wiping; to wash away.

ab-ster-gent (ab stür´jent) *adj*. Having purgative or cleaning properties. *n*. a detergent or anything that aids in cleaning.

ab-stract (ab strakt´) v. To remove material from, to reduce or summarize. **abstractedness** n.

ab-stract-ed (ab strak´tid) adj. Absorbed in thought; absent in mind; inattentive.

ab-strac-tion (ab strak´shan) n. The act of separating, withdrawing; something abstract.

ab-strac-tion-ism (ab strak she nizem) n. Practice of making abstract art.

ab-strac-tive (ab strak´tiv) adj. Having the power or quality of abstracting.

ab-strict (ab strikt) v. To cause an abstraction.

ab-stric-tion (ab strik´shan) adj. A forming of spores with the cutting off of parts of the sporophore.

ab-struse (ab strōs´) adj. Difficult or hard to understand or comprehend. **abstruseness** n. **abstrusely** adv.

ab-surd (ab sürd´) adj. Contrary to reason; clearly untrue or unreasonable. **absurdity** n. **absurdness** n.

ab-surd-ism (ab sürd iz em) n. The philosophy which is based on the idea and belief that man lives in a meaningless universe and the search for order will bring him and the universe into conflict. **absurdist** n.

a-bub-ble (a ´beb el) adj. To be in the process of bubbling.

a-build-ing (a ´bil din) adj. To be in the process of constructing or building.

a-bu-li-a (a bü´lē a) n., Psychol. Form of mental derangement where volition is lost or impaired.

a-bun-dance (a bun´dans) n. Ample supply; plenty; amount more than enough.

a-bun-dant (a bun´dant) adj. Plentiful; sufficient; overflowing, abounding.

a-bun-dant-ly (a bun´dant lē) adv. In sufficient degree; amply; plentifully.

a-buse (a büz´) v. To use in an improper or wrong way. **abuse** n. Improper treatment or employment; improper use or application; misuse. **abuser** n.

a-bu-sive (a bü´siv) adj. Practicing abuse; bad treatment of another. **-ness** n.

a-but (a but´) v. To border; to touch at one end; to be contiguous to; to join at a boundary; to form a point or line of contact, used with on, upon, against.

a-bu-ti-lon (a büt´i lon) n. A member of the genus of mallow family that has lobed leaves and bell-shaped flowers.

a-but-ment (a but´ment) n. Support at the end of an arch or bridge.

a-but-tal (a but´al) n. The bordering part of a piece of land.

a-but-ting (a but´ing) adj. To abut or to serve as an abutment of something.

a-buzz (a buz) adj. To be filled with a buzzing.

a-bys-mal (a biz´mal) adj. Immeasurably deep or low; profound.

a-byss (a bis´) n. A deep crack or gap in the earth. **abyssal** adj.

ac-a-deme (ak´a dēm´) n. The place where instruction is given to pupils.

ac-a-dem-ic (ak´a dem´ik) adj. Higher education; relating to classical or liberal studies, rather than vocational.

a-cad-e-my (a kad´e mē) n., pl. **academies** A private school for special training, as in music, art, or military. A school holding a rank between a college and an elementary school.

a-can-tha (a kan´tha) n. The prickle of a plant; an animal spine; one of the acute processes of the vertebrae of animals.

ac-an-tha-ceous (ak an thā´shus) adj. Armed with prickles.

a-can-thine (a kan´thin) adj. Pertaining to or resembling the plant acanthus.

a-can-tho-ceph-a-la (a kan´tha sef´a la) n. One of the intestinal worms that have a hooked proboscis and will absorb food out of the digestive tract.

a-can-tho-ceph-a-lan (a kan´tha sef´a lan) adj. Having spines or hooks on the head, as certain intestinal worms (the Acanthocephala), which are attached within the bodies of animals.

a cap-pel-la (ä´ka pel´a) adj. Singing without instrumental accompaniment.

ac-a-ri-a-sis (ak´a rī´a sis) n. An infestation that is caused by mites.

ac-a-rid (ak´a rid) n. A member of the order of arachnids that includes ticks and mites.

ac-a-roid (ak´a roid˘) adj. Having the resemblance of a mite.

acaroid resin n. A type of resin that is alcohol soluble and is obtained from the Australian grass trees.

a-car-pel-ous (ā kär´pe lus) adj. To be without carpels.

a-car-pous (ā kär´pus) adj. Barren; not producing fruit.

a-cat-a-lec-tic (ā kat´a lek´tik) adj. Not stopping short; having the complete number of syllables in a line of verse.

a-cau-date (ā kä´dāt) adj. Having no tail.

ac-au-les-cent (ak´a les´ent) adj. Bot. Stemless.

ac-cede (ak sēd´) v. To consent; to agree; to arrive at a certain condition or state.

ac-cel-er-ate (ak sel´a rāt´) v. To make work or run faster; to increase speed; to hasten or quicken; cause to advance faster, to take extra courses. **accelera-tion** n.

ac-cel-er-a-tion (ak sel´a rā´shan) n. The process of accelerating something.

ac-cel-er-a-tive (ak sel´e rā´tiv) adj. To be pertaining to acceleration.

ac-cel-er-a-tor (ak sel´e rā´tor) n. Something that accelerates something else.

ac-cel-er-om-e-ter (ak sel´e rom´i tér) n. An instrument used to measure and record the acceleration of aircraft speed.

ac-cent (ak´sent) n. An effort to make one syllable more prominent than the others.

ac-cen-tu-al (ak sen´chö al) adj. To be pertaining to or having an accent.

accentual verse n. A verse where the accentuation is the basis of the rhythm.

ac-cen-tu-ate (ak sen´chö āt´) v. To make a part more pronounced; to emphasize.

ac-cept (ak sept´) v. To take what is given; to believe to be true; to agree, to receive. accepter n. acceptor n.

ac-cept-able (ak sep´ta bl) adj. Satisfactory; proper; good enough. acceptableness n. acceptability n.

ac-cep-tance (ak sep´tans) n. Approval or belief; an accepting or being accepted.

ac-cept-ant (ak sep´tant) adj. To be willing to accept something.

ac-cep-ta-tion (ak´sep tā´shan) n. The act of receiving; favorable reception.

ac-cept-ed (ak sep´tid) adj. Commonly approved; generally thought of as right or normal; conventional.

ac-cep-tive (ak sep´tiv) adj. Willing to accept or receive.

ac-cess (ak´ses) n. Entrance, admission; near approach; admittance; the state of being approachable; passage that allows communication. In computer science, to call up a program or data.

ac-ces-si-bil-i-ty (ak ses´i bil´i tē) n. The quality of being accessible.

ac-ces-si-ble (ak ses´i bl) adj. Able to be attained or approached; easy of access.

ac-ces-sion (ak sesh´an) n. In Computer Science, the act of obtaining data from storage; the ability to store data.

ac-ces-so-ri-al (ak´si sōr´ē al) adj. To be pertaining to an accessory.

ac-ces-so-ri-ly (ak ses´sa ri lē) adv. An accessory; supplementary; not as principal but as a subordinate.

ac-ces-so-ri-ness (ak ses´sa re nes) n. The state of being accessory, or of being or acting in a secondary character.

ac-ces-so-rize (ak ses´so riz) v. To wear with accessories.

ac-ces-so-ry (ak ses´o rē) adj. Aiding in producing some effect; acting in subordination to the principal agent; contributing to a general effect.

accessory nerves n. The pair of 11th cranial nerves activating the muscles of the chest, shoulders, back, and pharynx.

access code In computer science, the user name or security code required to use a computer, program or certain files.

ac-ciac-ca-tu-ra (ä chä´ka tür´a) n. Music note, a half step below, and struck at the same time as, the main note.

ac-ci-dence (ak´si dens) n. A book that contains the rudiments of grammar; the elementary parts of a subject.

ac-ci-dent (ak´si dent) n. A happening that is not planned or expected.

ac-ci-den-tal (ak´si den´tal) adj. Happening by chance; unexpected.

ac-cip-i-ter (ak sip´i tér) n. A short-winged hawk that has a flight pattern that is darting and low. accipitrine adj.

ac-claim (a klām´) v. To greet with strong approval loud applause; to hail or cheer.

ac-cla-ma-tion (ak´la mā´shan) n. An expression of approval, usually loud.

ac-cli-mate (a klī´mit) v. To get used to a different climate or new surroundings.

ac-cli-ma-ti-za-tion (a klī´ma tī zā´shan) n. The result of acclimatizing.

ac-cli-ma-tize (a klī´ma tīz´) v. To change to or to adapt to a change in altitude, climate, or temperature.

ac-cliv-i-ty (a kliv´i tē) n. An ascending slope.

ac-co-lade (ak´a lād´) n. Award; ceremony used in conferring knight-hood. Arch. A curved molding above an arched opening.

ac-com-mo-date (a kom´a dāt´) v. To give room or lodging; to make fit; to adjust.

ac-com-pa-ni-ment (a kum´pa ni ment) n. Something that goes well with another.

ac-com-pa-ny (a kum´pa nē) v. To be together with; to go along with; to go with or attend as a companion or associate; to go together; to be associated or connected with.

ac-com-plice (a kom´plis) n. Companion who helps another break the law; a partner or partaker in guilt, usually a subordinate.

ac-com-plish (a kom´plish) v. To perform; to carry out; to complete; to do. accomplisher n.

ac-cord (a kord´) n. Harmony; agreement. accord v. To grant or award.

ac-cost (a kost´) v. To come close to and to speak first in an unfriendly manner.

ac-couche-ment (a kösh´mänt) n. Childbirth; confinement.

ac-cou-cheur (ä kö shoer´) n. A surgeon who attends women in childbirth.

ac-cou-cheuse (ä kö shoez´) n. Midwife.

ac-count (a kount´) n. A description; a statement of debts and credits in money transactions; a record; a report.

ac-count-a-ble (a kount´ta bl) adj. Liable to be held responsible; able to be explained. accountably adv.

ac-count-ant (*a* koun´tant) *n*. A person who keeps or examines accounts; a profession.

account executive *n*. Administrator of a client's account; a business service.

ac-count-ing (*a* koun´ting) *n*. A report on how accounts have been balanced; the system of keeping business records or accounts.

ac-cou-tre (*a* kŏ´tĕr) *v*. To give or to provide with furnishings.

ac-cred-it (*a* kred´it) *v*. To authorize someone; to give official power.

ac-cres-cent (*a* kres´ent) *adj*. Increasing; growing.

ac-crete (*a* krēt´) *v*. To grow together or join.

ac-cre-tion (*a* krē´shan) *n*. The process of enlarging something. -ary *adj*.

ac-cru-al (*a* krö´al) *n*. Process or act of accruing; something accrued.

ac-crue (*a* krö´) *v*. To result naturally; to increase at certain times.

acct *abbr*. Account.

ac-cul-tur-a-tion (*a* kul˜cha rā´shan) *n*. The modification of one's culture with a prolonged interaction involving another culture.

ac-cum-ben-cy (*a* kum´ben sē) *n*. State of being accumbent.

ac-cum-bent (*a* kum´bent) *adj*. Leaning or reclining; lying against anything.

ac-cu-mu-late (*a* kū´mya lāt´) *v*. To collect or gather over a period of time; pile up.

ac-cu-ra-cy (ak´yur *a* sē) *n., pl.* **accuracies** Exactness; precision; the fact of being accurate or without mistakes.

ac-cu-rate (ak´yur it) *adj*. Without mistakes or errors; careful and exact; correct. **accurately** *adv*.

ac-curse (*a* kürs´) *v*. To curse.

ac-curs-ed (*a* kür´sid) *adj*. Sure to end badly; under a curse; unpleasant or annoy-ing; very bad. **accursedness** *n*.

ac-cu-sa-tive (*a* kū´za tiv) *adj*. Relating to the direct object of a preposition or of a verb.

ac-cuse (*a* kūz´) *v*. To find fault with; to blame; to charge someone with doing wrong or breaking the law. -er *n*.

ac-cused (*a* kūzd´) *n*. One charged with a crime; a defendant in a court of law.

ac-cus-tom (*a* kus´tom) *v*. To familiarize by habit.

ac-cus-tomed (*a* kus´tomd) *adj*. Often practiced; familiar; usual.

ace (ās) *n*. The face of a die or a playing card marked with one spot; in tennis and some other sports, a score made by a serve that is not returned.

a-ce-di-a (*a* sē´dē *a*) *n*. Loss of interest for living.

a-cel-lu-lar (ā sel´ū lar) *adj*. Having no cells.

a-cen-tric (ā sen´trik) *adj*. To be missing a centromere.

a-ceph-a-lous (ā sef´*a* lus) *adj*. To be without a head.

a-ce-quia (*a* sā´kya) *n*. A type of ditch which can be used for irrigation.

ac-er-ate (as´*e* rāt´) *adj*. Pointed; sharp.

a-cerb (*a* sürb´) *adj*. To be acid in one's mood; critical; bitter, sour, harsh to the taste.

a-cer-bi-ty (*a* sür´bi tē) *n*. Sourness, with roughness of taste.

a-ce-rous (ā sēr´us) *adj*. Without horns.

a-cer-vate (*a* sür´vit) *adj*. To be living or growing in heaps. **acervately** *adv*.

a-ces-cent (*a* ses´ent) *adj*. Slightly sour, turning sour.

ac-e-tab-u-lar-ia (as´i tab´yu lar´ē a) *n*. A type of single-celled alga found in the warm seas which look like mushrooms in shape.

ac-e-tab-u-lum (as´i tab´yu lum) *n*. The socket of the hipbone. **acetabular** *adj*.

ac-e-tal (as´i tal´) *n., Chem*. The liquid formed by imperfect oxidation of alcohol.

ac-et-a-min-o-phen (as *et e* min *e* fen) *n*. A compound which is used for the purpose of relieving pain and fever.

ac-e-tate (as´i tāt´) *n*. Salt formed by union of acetic acid with a base, used in making rayon and plastics.

a-cet-ic (*a* sē´tik) *adj*. To be pertaining to or related to vinegar or acetic acid.

acetic acid (*a* sē´tik as´id) *n*. The main ingredient of vinegar; a sour, colorless liquid that has a sharp smell.

a-ce-ti-fy (*a* set´i fī´) *v*. To change or to turn into acetic acid. **acetification** *n*.

ac-e-tom-e-ter (as´i tom´i tèr) *n*. Instrument for determining the purity or strength or of acetic acid in a solution.

ac-e-to-phe-net-i-din (as´i tō fe net´i din) *n*. A type of compound which is used for relief of pain and fever.

a-cet-y-lene (*a* set´*e* lēn´) *n*. A highly inflammable, poisonous, colorless gas that burns brightly with a hot flame, used in blowtorches for metal working.

ache (āk) *v*. To give or have a dull, steady pain; to want very much; to long for.

a-chene (ā kēn´) *n*. A type of indehiscent one-seeded fruit that has developed from an ovary. **achenial** *adj*.

a-chiev-a-ble (*a* chēv´*a* bl) *adj*. Being capable to be achieved or performed; attainable.

a-chieve (*a* chēv´) *v*. To reach by trying hard; to do; to succeed in doing; to accomplish. **achiever** *n*.

a-chieve-ment (*a* chēv´ ment) *n*. Something achieved by work or skill.

Achilles tendon (*a* kil´ĕz ten´ don) *n*. The tendon that connects the heel bone and calf muscles.

a-chlor-hy-dri-a (ā˝klŏr hī´drē a) *n.* Absence of hydrochloric acid from gastric juices.

a-chon-drite (ā kon drīt) *n.* A type of stony meteorite that does not have rounded grains.

a-chon-dro-pla-sia (ā kon´drọ plā´zhạ) *n.* The failure of the cartilage to develop in a normal manner which results in dwarfism. -plastic *adj.*

ach-ro-mat-ic (ak˝rọ mat´ik) *adj.* The transmitting of light without decomposing it into primary colors.

a-chro-ma-tia (ā krō´ma tin) *n. Biol.* The portion in the nucleus of a cell that is unstainable.

a-chro-ma-tism (ā krō´m a tiz´um) *n.* A quality of giving of images practically free from extraneous colors.

a-chro-ma-tous (ā krō´ma tus) *adj.* Having no color; of a lighter color than is usual or normal.

achy (āk´ē) *adj.* To have aches.

a-cic-u-la (a sik´yu la) *n.* Spine of an animal or plant.

ac-id (as´id) *n.* A chemical compound containing hydrogen that forms a salt when combined with a base, dissolves in water, has a very sour taste, makes litmus paper turn red.

ac-id-fast (as´id fast´) *adj.* Not easily decolorized by acid.

acid head *n.* A user of the drug LSD.

c-id-ic (a sid´ik) *adj. Chem.* Pertaining to acid; to contain a large amount of an acid constituent.

a-cid i fi-er (a sid´i fī´ér) *n.* Any chemical that produces an acid effect.

a-cid-i-fy (a sid´ifī˝) *v.* To make some substance acid.

ac-i-dim-e-ter (as˝i dim´ītėr) *n., Chem.* Instrument used for measuring the amount of acid in a particular volume or weight of a solution.

a-cid-i-ty (a sid´i tē) *n.* Condition or quality of being acid.

ac-I-do-phile (as´i dō fil´) *n., Biol.* Tissue, cell, organism, or substance that shows an affinity towards an acidic environment.

ac-i-do-phil-ic (as˝i dō fil´ik) *adj.* Having the quality to be easily stained with acid; thriving in acid.

ac-i-do-sis (as˝i dō´sis) *n.* The abnormally high concentration of acid in body tissues and blood.

acid rain *n.* Acid precipitation that falls as rain.

acid rock *n.* Lyrics from Rock music that suggest drug-related experiences.

a-cid-u-late (a sij´u lāt´) *v.* To become or make somewhat acid.

a-cid-u-lous (a sij´u lus) *adj.* To be slightly acid in taste.

ac-i-na-ceous (as˝i nā´shus) *adj.* Full of seeds or kernels.

ac-i-nac-i-form (as˝i nas´i form´) *adj.* Formed like or resembling a scimitar sword.

ac-i-nar (as e ner) *adj.* To be pertaining to an acinus.

ac-i-nus (as´i nus) *n.* A sac of a racemose gland which is lined with secreting cells.

ac-know-ledge (ak nol´ij) *v.* To admit the truth, existence or reality.

ac-knowl-edg-ment (ak nol´ij ment) *n.* To acknowledge or own up to something; recognition; confession; something that is given or done in return for a favor.

a-clin-ic (ā klin´ik) *adj.* Applied to an imaginary line that is near the earth's equator where a magnetic needle has no dip. **aclinic line** *n.*

ac-me (ak´mē) *n.* The highest point of attainment; peak.

ac-ne (ak´nē) *n.* An inflammation of the sebaceous or oil-secreting glands of the skin, manifested by eruptions of hard, inflamed pimples. Increased production of androgens, hormones, in both male and female during puberty causes the sebaceous glands to become active and secrete large amounts of sebum, which block the glands and hair follicles.

ac-o-nite (ak´ạ nīt´) *n.* A poisonous plant with flowers resembling hoods; sometimes called monkshood.

a-corn (ā´kọn) *n..* The nut of the oak tree, seated in a woody cup.

a-cot-y-le-don (ā˝kot´ẹ lēd´on) *n.* A plant as a fern or moss, which does not have seed leaves.

a-cous-tic (a kŏ´stik) *adj.* Having to do with sound or the sense of hearing; the sense of sound; absorbing sound. **acoustical** *n.* **acoustically** *adv.*

acoustic nerve *n.* The nerve that serves the ear.

a-cous-tics (a kŏ´stiks) *n.* The scientific study of sound; total effect of sound, especially in an enclosed space.

ac-quaint (a kwant´) *v.* To make familiar; to let know, to make aware; to inform.

ac-quaint-ance (a kwān´tạns) *n.* A person whom one knows but not as a close friend. **acquaintanceship** *n.*

ac-qui-esce (ak˝wē es´) *v.* To agree without arguing; to comply without protest, to comply. **acquiescent** *adj.*

ac-qui-es-cence (ak˝wē es´ens) *n.* The act of giving or acquiescing a quiet; a yielding.

ac-quir-a-ble (a kwī er´ a bl) *adj.* Capable of being acquired.

ac-quire (a kwier´) *v.* To secure control or possession; to become the owner.

acquired immunity *n.* Immunity against disease one develops during a lifetime.

ac-quire-ment (a kwī er´ ment) *n.* The

act of acquiring something, as a skill gained by learning.

ac-qui-si-tion (ak´wĭ zĭsh´an) n. Something that is acquired; the act of acquiring.

ac-quis-i-tive (a kwĭz´ĭ tĭv) adj. Eager to gain and possess things; greedy.

ac-quis-i-tive-ly (a kwĭz´ĭ tĭv lē) adv. An acquisitive manner.

ac-quis-i-tive-ness (a kwĭz´ĭ tĭv nĭs) n. The quality of being acquisitive.

ac-quit (a kwĭt´) v. To rule that a person accused of something is not guilty; to conduct oneself; to behave.

a-cre (ā´kėr) n. A measurement of land that equals 43,560 square feet.

a-cre-age (ā´kėr ĭj) n. The total number of acres in a section of land.

ac-rid (ak´rĭd) adj. Having a sharp, bitter, or irritating taste or smell. **acridity** n. **acridness** n. **acridly** adv.

ac-ri-mo-ni-ous (ak´rĭ mō´nē us) adj. Sharp or bitter in speech or manner.

ac-ri-mo-ny (ak´rĭ mō´nē) n. Sharpness or severity of temper; bitterness of expression.

a-crit-i-cal (ā krĭt´ĭ kal) adj., Med. Not critical.

ac-ro-bat (ak´ro bat´) n. One who is skilled in gymnastic feats. **-ic** adj.

ac-ro-bat-ics (ak´ro bat´ĭks) n. The performance of an acrobat.

ac-ro-car-pous (ak´ro kär´pus) adj., Bot. Applied to mosses whose fruit terminates the growth of a primary root.

ac-ro-cen-tric (ak rō sen trĭk) adj. To have a centromere that is located so one chromosomal arm is longer than the other arm.

ac-ro-dont (ak´ro dont) adj. Having rootless teeth that are joined to the ridges of the upper and lower jaws. n. Animals possessing such teeth.

a-crop-e-tal (a krop´ĭ tal) adj., Bot. Starting at the base and going toward the highest or narrowest point.

ac-ro-pho-bi-a (ak´ro fō´bē a) n. Unusual fear of heights.

ac-ro-spire (ak´ro spĭėr´) n. The first leaf that rises above the ground as grain starts to germinate.

a-cross (a kros´) adv. & prep. From side to side; to one side from the other.

a-cros-tic (a kro´stĭk) n. A series of lines or a poem in which certain letters in each line form a name or motto.

ac-ro-tism (ak´ro tĭz´um) n. The weakness or absence of the pulse.

a-cryl-ic (a krĭl´ĭk) n. Relating to or of acrylic acid or its derivatives.

acrylic fiber n. A fiber which is made of chemicals, used in making fabrics.

ac-ry-lo-ni-trile (ak´rĭ lō nī´trĭl) n. A liquid organic compound used to make acrylic fibers and rubber.

act (akt) n. Doing something; a thing

done; deed; an action; a showing of emotion which is not real or true; a law; decree; one of the main parts of a play, opera, etc.

act (akt) v. To exert power; to produce effects; to be in action or motion; to behave, demean, or conduct oneself; to perform, as an actor; to substitute for; as, to act as captain; to transact; to do or perform; to represent as real; to feign or counterfeit. **act as** To serve as; perform the function or duties of. **act on** To act or obey in accordance with; to affect. **act out** To demonstrate or perform. **act out** Psychol. To express openly subconscious emotions. **act up** To behave in a manner that is unruly or capricious.

act-a-ble (akt´abl) adj. Capable of being acted or performed. **actability** n.

ac-tin (ak´tĭn) n. A type of protein that is in the muscle and becomes active in muscle contractions.

act-ing (ak´tĭng) adj. Temporarily performing the duties, services, or functions of another person.

ac-tin-i-a (ak tĭn´ē a) n. A sea anemone; having a mouth surrounded by tentacles in circle.

ac-tin-ic (ak tĭn´ĭk) adj. Pertaining to rays, esp. the chemical rays of the sun.

ac-tin-i-form (ak tĭn´ĭform´) adj. Bearing a resemblance to an actinia.

ac-tin-ism (ak´tĭ nĭz´um) n. The radiation of heat or light.

ac-tin-o-gen (ak tĭn´o jen´) n. An element which is radioactive.

ac-tin-o-graph (ak tĭn´o graf´) n. Instrument used to measure and register variations of actinic or chemical influence in the solar rays.

ac-ti-nom-e-ter (ak´tĭ nom´ĭtėr) n. An instrument for measuring the intensity of the sun's actinic rays.

ac-ti-no-my-cin (ak´tĭ nōmĭs´ĭn) n. One of the yellow-red or red polypeptide antibiotics that is separated from soil bacteria.

ac-ti-non (ak´tĭ non´) n. A radioactive, gaseous element, existing for only a few seconds, which is isotopic with radon.

ac-tion (ak´shan) n. The process of doing or acting; an effect produced by something; a lawsuit.

ac-tion-able (ak´sha na bl) adj. To be affording ground for a suit at law.

ac-tion-less (ak shen les) adj. To be characterized by inaction and lack of movement.

action painting n. A style of painting where paint is often smeared or dribbled to give a thickly textured surface.

ac-ti-vate (ak´tĭ vāt´) v. To put into action. **activation** n.

ac-tive (ak´tiv) *adj.* Working; full of action; busy; lively; quick, constant. **activeness** *n.* **actively** *adv.*

ac-tiv-ism (ak´ti viz˝um) *n.* A practice based on direct action to affect changes in government and social conditions.

ac-tiv-ity (ak tiv´i tē) *n.* Being active, in motion; normal power of body or mind.

act of God *n.* An unforeseeable, uncontrollable happening caused by nature.

ac-tor (ak´tor) *n.* A person who acts in movies, plays, television shows, etc.

ac-tress (ak´tris) *n.* A female actor.

ac-tu-al (ak´chö al) *adj.* Acting or existing in fact or reality; as it really is; true. **actualness** *n.*

ac-tu-ar-y (ak´chö er´ē) *n.* A person who will figure or calculate insurance.

ac-tu-ate (ak´chö āt´) *v.* To put into motion or action. **actuation** *n.*

ac-tu-a-tor (ak´chö ā´tėr) *n.* Something that will control something else indirectly.

a-cu-i-ty (a kū´i tē) *n.* A sharp perception of something.

a-cu-le-ate (a kū´lē it) *adj.* To have a sting.

a-cu-men (a kū´men) *n.* The quickness of perception; mental acuteness, the keenness of insight.

a-cu-mi-nate (a kū´mi nat´) *adj.* To taper to a point which is slender in shape.

ac-u-punc-ture (ak´ū pungk´chur) *n.* A traditional Chinese means of treating some illnesses or of lessening pain by putting thin needles into certain parts of the body.

a-cute (a kūt´) *adj.* Extremely sensitive; sharp and quick, as pain; shrewd. **acuteness** *n.* **acutely** *adv.*

acute accent *n.* A mark to indicate heavy stress on a syllable.

ADC In computer science, Analog to Digital Converter; a device that converts analog signals to digital data.

ad-age (ad´ij) *n.* A proverb; a wise or true saying.

ad-a-mant (ad a mant) *adj.* Standing firm; not giving in easily; unyielding.

Adams, John *n.* (1735-1826) The second president of the United States from 1797-1801.

Adams, John Quincy *n.* (1767-1848) The sixth president of the United States from 1825-1829.

a-dapt (a dapt´) *v.* To fit or suit; to change oneself so as to adjust to new conditions.

a-dapt-a-ble (adap´ta bl) *adj.* Being capable of adapting; able to adjust oneself without difficulty to new, unfamiliar, or unexpected conditions. **adaptability** *n.*

ad-ax-i-al (ad ak´sē al) *adj.* To be

positioned on one side of the axis.

ADP In computer science, Automatic Data Processing; the manipulation of data with with the use of a computer.

add (ad) *v.* To join or put something with another so that there will be more; to cause an increase. **add up** To make sense; to be reasonable; to arrive or to come to the expected total of a group of numbers. **addable, addible** *adj.*

ad-dend (ad´end) *n.* The number that is added to another number.

ad-den-dum (a den´dum) *n. pl.* **addenda** An addition; an appendix to a book or literacy work; something which is added.

ad-dict (ad´ikt) *n.* A person with a habit so strong that he cannot easily give it up. **addiction** *n.* **addicted** *adj.*

ad-di-tion (adish´an) *n.* An adding of numbers to find their total; the act of joining one thing to another. **-ally** *adv.*

ad-di-tive (ad´i tiv) *n.* A substance added to another in small amounts to alter it.

ad-dress (ad dres´) *v.* To direct or aim; to speak to; to give attention to. **address** *n.* The location to which mail or goods can be sent to a person, business, or organization. In *computer science* the location, in the memory of a computer, where data is kept, to which data is sent, or from where data is drawn.

ad-duce (ad dös´) *v.* To offer as proof or give as a reason. **adducer** *n.*

ad-du-cent (ad dö´sent) *adj.* Bringing together or forward.

ad-duct (ad dukt´) *v.* To move or draw, such as a limb, toward the median axis of the body.

a-demp-tion (a demp´shn) *n., Law* Act of revoking a legacy.

ad-e-ni-tis (ad´e ni tes) *n.* The swelling or inflammation of lymph nodes.

ad-e-nol-dal (ad e noid l) *adj.* To be pertaining to or related to the adenoids.

ad-e-noids (ad´e noid´) *n.* Lymphoid tissue growths in the upper part of the throat behind the nose, that may need to be removed surgically.

ad-e-no-ma (ad´e nō´ma) *n., Pathol.* Benign tumor that originates in a gland.

a-den-o-sine tri-phos-phate (a den´o sēn´ trī fos´fāt) *n.* A nucleotide occurring in all cells, representing the reserve energy of muscle that is important to many biochemical processes that produce or require energy.

adenosis *n.* A disease of a gland, particularly the abnormal development of glandular tissue.

a-dept (ad´ept) *adj.* Highly skilled; expert. **adeptly** *adv.* **adeptness** *n.*

ad-e-qua-cy (ad´e kwa sē) *n.* The state

of being good enough to fill a requirement.

ad-e-quate (ad´e kwit) *adj.* Sufficient; good enough for what is needed. **adequateness** *n.* **adequately** *adv.*

ad eun-dem (ad´ē an´dem) *adj.* To, in, or of the same rank.

ad-here (ad hēr´) *v.* To stay attached; to stick and not come loose; to stay firm in support.

ad-her-ence (ad hēr´ens) *n.* The quality of adhering.

ad-her-end (ad hēr´end) *n.* A surface to which an adhesive is able to adhere.

ad-her-ent (ad hēr´ent) *n.* A person who follows a leader, party, or belief; a believer or supporter.

ad-he-sion (ad hē´zhan) *n.* The act or state of sticking to something or of being stuck together.

ad-he-sive (ad hē´siv) *adj.* Tending to stick and not come loose; having a sticky surface. **adhesiveness** *n.*

adhesive tape *n.* A type of tape that has an adhesive on one side or two sides.

ad hoc (ad hok´) *adv.* For this particular purpose, without larger applications.

ad ho-mi-nem (ad hō´mi nem´) *adj.* Appealing to one's personal feelings and prejudices rather than to intellect and reason.

ad-i-a-bat-ic (ad´ēa bat´ik) *adj.* Referring to physical changes without gain or loss of heat.

ad-i-aph-o-ra (ad ē af´o ra) *n.* Things morally indifferent; matters that have no moral merit or demerit.

a-dieu (a dō´) *interj. & n.* French word for goodby.

ad interim *adj. & adv.* In the meantime.

a-di-os (ä´dē ōs´) *interj.* Spanish word for goodby.

ad-i-pose (ad´i pōs´) *n.* Fat; animal fat stored in the cells of adipose tissue.

adipose tissue *n.* A type of connective tissue where fat is stored in the body, mainly directly under the skin acting as an insulation and a source of energy.

ad-i-po-si-ty (ad´i po´si tē) *n.* Obesity.

ad-ja-cen-cy (a jā´sen sē) *n.* The state of being adjacent.

ad-ja-cent (a jā´sent) *adj.* Nearby; bordering upon; adjoining; neighboring.

ad-jec-ti-val (aj´ik tī´val) *adj.* Belonging to or similar to an adjective.

ad-jec-tive (aj´ik tiv) *n.* A word used to describe a noun or pronoun, indicating which, what kind of, how many, or whose.

ad-join (a join´) *v.* To be next to; to be in or nearly in contact with.

ad-journ (a jern´) *v.* To close a meeting or session for a time; to move from one location to another.

ad-journ-ment (a jern´ment) *n.* The

act of adjourning; the period when a legislature or other public body adjourns its meetings.

ad-judge (a juj´) *v.* To decide by judicial procedure. To pronounce or declare formally by law; to sentence or condemn; to adjudicate upon; to rule upon; to settle.

ad-ju-di-cate (a jö´di kāt´) *v.* To settle a dispute judicially. **adjudicator** *n.*

ad-ju-di-ca-tion (a jö´di kā´shan) *n.* Judicial decision. **adjudicatory** *adj.*

ad-junct (aj´ungkt) *n.* Something less important added to something with more importance. **adjunctive** *adj.*

ad-junc-tion (a jungk´´shan) *n.* Act of adjoining.

ad-jure (ajer´) *v.* To ask urgently; to command solemnly. **adjuration** *n.*

ad-just (ajust´) *v.* To arrange or change; to make work correctly; to regulate.

ad-just-ment (a just´ment) *n.* The act or process of changing; a settlement of a suit or claim.

ad-ju-tan-cy (aj´u tan sē) *n.* The rank of an adjutant.

ad-ju-tant (aj´u tant) *n.* Administrative staff officer who serves as an assistant to the commanding officer.

ad-ju-vant (aj´u vant) *n.* Assistant. *Med.* The substance added to a prescription to aid in the operation of the principal ingredient.

ad-meas-ure (ad mezh´ér) *v.* To judge the dimensions, size, or capacity of something; to measure.

ad-meas-ure-ment (ad mezh´ur ment) *n.* The measure of something, or dimensions ascertained.

ad-min-is-ter (ad min´i stėr) *v.* To direct or manage; to give or carry out instructions. **administrable** *adj.*

ad-min-is-tra-tion (ad min´i strä´shan) *n.* The people who manage a school, company, or organization; the act of administering.

ad-mire (ad mier´) *v.* To hold a high opinion; to regard with wonder, delight, and pleased approval; to regard with admiration. **admiringly** *adv.* **-er** *n.*

ad-mis-si-ble (ad mis´i bl) *adj.* Capable of being admitted, accepted or allowed.

ad-mis-sion (ad mish´an) *n.* The right or act of being admitted; an admitting of the truth of something; a confession.

ad-mit (ad mit´) *v.* To take or accept as being the truth; to permit or give the right to enter.

ad-mit-tance (ad mit´ans) *n.* Permission to enter.

ad-mit-ted-ly (ad mit´id lē) *adv.* By one's own admission or confession.

ad-mix-ture (ad miks´cher) *n.* Blend; mingling.

ad-mon-ish (ad mon´ish) *v.* To warn a person to correct a fault; to criticize in a gentle way. **admonisher** *n.*

ad-mo-ni-tion (ad´mo nish´an) *n.* A mild criticism or warning.

a-do (*a* dō´) *n.* Fuss or trouble.

a-do-be (*a* dō´bē) *n.* A brick or building material made from clay and straw and then dried in the sun.

ad-o-les-cence (a͞d´o les´ans) *n.* Period of physical and psychological development between childhood and adulthood; also known as youth.

ad-o-les-cent (ad´oles´ent) *n.* A person in the transitional period between childhood and adulthood.

a-dopt (adopt´) *v.* To legally take into one's family and raise as one's own.

a-dop-tion (*a* dop´shan) *n.* Act of adopting, or the state of being adopted.

a-dore (*a* dōr´) *v.* To love greatly; to worship or honor; to like very much; to regard with admiration. **adorer** *n.*

a-dorn (*a* dorn´) *v.* To add splendor or beauty.

ad rem *adj.* Relevant to a point at issue.

ad-re-nal (*a* drē´nal) *adj.* Pertaining to the product of the adrenal gland, that is located on or near the kidney.

adrenal gland *n.* A small endocrine gland that consists of a medulla and cortex, located near the kidney.

ad-ren-er-gic (ad´re nėr´jik) *adj.* Med. Liberated or activated by epinephrine or a similar substance.

a-drift (adrift´) *adv.* Drifting; floating freely without being steered; having no clear purpose or aim.

a-droit (*a* droit´) *adj.* Skillful and clever in difficult circumstances. **adroitly** *adv.*

ad-sci-ti-tious (ad´si tish´us) *adj.* Derived from without; adventitious.

ad-script (ad´skript) *adj.* Written to the right of and in line with another letter or symbol.

ad-sorb (ad sorb´) *v.* To collect and hold as molecules of gases, liquids; to become adsorbed. **adsorbable** *adj.*

ad-sorb-ate (ad sor´bāt) *n.* The adsorbed substance in the process of adsorption.

ad-u-late (aj´u lāt´) *v.* To give greater praise or flattery than is proper or deserved.

ad-u-la-tion (aj´u lā´shan) *n.* Praise in excess, or beyond what is merited; high compliment.

a-dult (*a* dult´) *n.* A man or woman who is fully grown; a mature person. **adult** *adj.* Having reached full size and strength. **adulthood** *n.*

a-dul-ter-ate (*a* dul´te rāt´) *v.* To make impure or of less quality by adding improper ingredients.

a-dum-brate (ad um´brāt) *v.* To give a faint shadow or brief outline of; to over-shadow.

a-dust (a dust´) *adj.* Scorched; parched; looking as if burned or scorched.

ad va-lo-rem (ad *va* lōr´um) *adj.* According to value.

ad-vance (ad vans´) *v.* To move ahead; to make or become higher; to increase in value or price. *adj.* Something made or given ahead of time.

ad-vanced (ad vanst´) *adj.* Ahead in time; beyond beginning status.

ad-vance-ment (ad vans´ment) *n.* A promotion in position; progression; money ahead of time.

ad-van-tage (ad van´taj) *n.* A better chance or more forcible position; a condition, thing or event that can help or benefit; the first point, after deuce scored in the game of tennis.

ad-vene (ad vēn´) *v.* To accede or become added to.

ad-vent (ad´vent) *n.* A coming or arrival; the four Sundays before Christmas.

ad-ven-ti-ti-a (ad´ven tish´ē a) *n.* An external connective tissue which covers an organ.

ad-ven-ture (ad ven´chur) *n.* An exciting and dangerous experience; a risky undertaking; an unusual experience; uncertain outcome. **adventure** *v.*

ad-verb (ad´verb) *n.* A word used with a verb, adjective, or another adverb to tell when, where, how, what kind, or how much.

ad ver-bum (ad ver´bum) *adv.* Exactly word for word.

ad-ver-sar-y (ad´ver ser´ē) *n.* An enemy, or a person having hostility toward another person or group of people.

ad-ver-sa-tive (ad ver´sa tiv) *adj.* Expressing difference, or opposition.

ad-verse (ad´vers) *adj.* Opposed; not helpful; against someone or something. **adverseness** *n.* **adversely** *adv.*

ad-ver-si-ty (ad ver´si tē) *n.* Bad luck or misfortune; calamity; bad experience.

ad-vert (ad vert´) *v.* To turn the attention or mind; to regard, notice or observe.

ad-ver-tise (ad´ver tīz´) *v.* To draw public attention to a product you wish to sell, often by printed or broadcast media.

ad-ver-tise-ment (ad´ver tīz´ment) *n.* A public notice designed to advertise something.

ad-vice (ad vīs´) *n.* Suggestion or recommendation regarding a decision or course of action.

ad-vis-a-bil-i-ty (ad vī´za bil´i tē) *n.* Quality of being advisable.

ad-vise (ad vīz´) *v.* To counsel; to inform; to give information to; to give notice.

ad-vised (ad vīzd´) *adj.* Prudent; cautious; informed; thoughtfully considered.

ad-vis-ed-ness (ad vīz´id nis) *n.* The state of being advised; caution.

ad-vise-ment (ad vīz´ment) *n.* Careful

thought and consideration.

ad-vis-er (ad vī´zér) *n.* A person who gives an opinion or advises.

ad-vi-so-ry (ad vī´zo rē) *adj.* Exercising or having the power to advise; giving or containing advice.

ad-vo-ca-cy (ad´vo ka sē) *n.* Act of advocating.

ad-vo-cate (ad´vo kit) *v.* To write or speak in favor of or support.

ad-y-na-mi-a (ad´e nā´mē *a*) *n.* Deficiency of vital power; weakness.

ad-y-tum (ad´i *tum*) *n.* The innermost shrine or sanctuary; in ancient temples, the sanctuary where only priests were permitted to enter.

adz (adz) *n.* An instrument, similar to the ax type, used for chipping timber.

ad-zu-ki bean (ad zö´kē bĕn) *n.* An annual, bushy bean, cultivated in Japan.

a-e-des (ā ē´ dēz) *n.* A mosquito that transmits yellow fever.

ae-gis (ē´jis) *n.* Protection; support or sponsorship.

ae-on (ē´on) *n.* A period of time of indefinite length.

aer-ate (âr´āt) *v.* To purify by exposing to the open air.

aer-a-tor (âr´ā tor) *n.* An apparatus for making carbonated beverages.

aer-i-al (âr´ē al) *adj.* Of or in the air; pertaining to aircraft. *n.* An antenna for television or radio. **aerially** *adv.*

aer-ie (âr´ē) *n.* The nest of a predatory bird, built on a cliff or other high places.

aer-i-form (âr´i form) *adj.* Having the form or nature of air.

aer-i-fy (âr´i fī) *v.* To blow air into; to fill with air; to combine with air.

aer-o (âr´ō) *adj.* Having to do with air, aircraft, or the flying of aircraft.

aer-o-bal-lis-tics (âr´ō ba lis´iks) *n.* The ballistics of projectiles dropped, fired, or launched from aircraft.

aer-o-bics (â rō´ biks) *n.* Strenuous exercise that increases oxygen to the heart and lungs, therefore strengthening them.

aer-o-bi-o-sis (âr´ō bī ō´sis) *n.* Life in an atmosphere of oxygen or air.

aer-o-em-bo-lism (âr´ō em´bo lizm) *n.* Occlusion of blood vessels by nitrogen gas bubbles that form when the body undergoes rapid decrease in air pressure.

aer-og-ra-phy (â rog´rafē) *n.* Description of the air or atmosphere; meteorology.

aer-ol-o-gist (âr ol´o jist) *n.* One who is versed in aerology.

aer-o-nau-tics (âr´o no´tiks) *n.* The science of designing, constructing and operating aircraft. **aeronautic** *adj.*

ae-ron-o-my (â ron´o mē) *n.* Study of chemical and physical phenomena located in the upper regions of the atmosphere.

aer-o-pause (âr´ o poz) *n.* The region in the upper atmosphere where aircraft cannot fly.

aer-o-phore (âr´o fōr´) *n.* Portable equipment for purifying air.

aer-o-plane (âr´o plān) *n.* British word for airplane.

aer-o-sol (âr´o sōl) *n.* A liquid substance under pressure within a metal container.

aer-o-sphere (âr´o sfēr´) *n.* Body of air above the earth's atmosphere.

aer-o-train (är´a trān) *n.* A train which runs at high speed.

Ae-sop (ē´säp) *n.* Greek writer of fables from the sixth century B.C.

aes-thet-ic (es thet´ik) *adj.* Having a love for beauty; pertaining to the sense or study of beauty or taste. **aesthete** *n.*

aes-thet-ics (es thet´iks) *n.* The study of the nature of beauty. **aesthetically** *adv.* **aesthetician** *n.*

a-far (a fär´) *adv.* Far off; far away.

af-fa-ble (af´a bl) *adj.* Good-natured, easy to talk to; friendly. **affably** *adv.*

af-fa-bil-i-ty (af´a bil´i tē) *n.* Quality of being sociable.

af-fair (a fâr´) *n.* An event or happening; matters of business or public concern.

af-fect (a fekt´) *v.* To move emotionally; to influence; to bring about a change in. **affected** *adj.*

af-fec-ta-tion (af ek tā´shan) *n.* Artificial behavior that is meant to impress others. False pretense, artificial show or appearance.

af-fec-tion-ate (a fek´sha nit) *adj.* Loving and gentle. Warmly attached; kind; fond; loving. **affectionately** *adv.* In an affectionate manner; fondly; tenderly; kindly.

af-fen-pin-scher (af´en pin´sher) *n.* A small dog breed with stiff red, black, or gray coat, pointed ears, and shaggy hairs about the eyes, nose, and chin.

af-fi-ance (a fī´ans) *v.* To bind by promise of marriage; to betroth.

af-fi-da-vit (af´i dā´vit) *n.* A written statement by a person swearing that something is the truth.

af-fil-i-ate (a fil´ē āt´) *v.* To join in, connect, or associate with. **-ion** *n.*

af-fine (a fin´) *n.* Relative by marriage.

af-fin-i-ty (a fin´i tē) *n.* A special attraction with kinship; a natural attraction or liking.

af-firm (a ferm´) *v.* To declare positively and be willing to stand by the truth.

af-fir-ma-tion (af´ir mā´shan) *n.* Act of asserting or affirming something as being true; that which is asserted; confirmation; ratification.

af-fix (af´iks) *v.* To attach; to fasten; to add at the end. **affix** *n.* A prefix or suffix added to a word.

af-fla-tus (a flā´tus) *n.* Creative

inspiration.

af-flict (*aflikt´*) *v.* To cause suffering or pain; to cause mental suffering.

af-flic-tion (*aflik´shan*) *n.* A state of distress or acute pain of the body or mind.

af-flu-ence (*af´löens*) *n.* Riches, wealth; abundance; plentiful supply of worldly goods.

af-flu-ent (*af´lö ent*) *adj.* Prosperous; rich; having all the wealth or money needed. **affluently** *adv.*

af-ford (*a förd´*) *v.* To be able to provide; to have enough money to spare.

af-for-est (*a for´ist*) *v.* To turn open land into forest. **afforestation** *n.*

af-fran-chise (*afran´chiz*) *v.* To make free; to grant full citizenship.

af-fray (*a fra´*) *n.* Brawl or noisy fight.

af-freight (*a frāt´*) *v.* To hire, for the transportation of freight or goods.

af-fright (*a frīt´*) *v.* To impress with sudden terror or fear of; to frighten unexpectedly or suddenly.

af-front (*afrunt´*) *v.* To insult one to his face; to confront.

af-fuse (*a füz´*) *adj.* Pour upon; to sprinkle with a liquid.

af-ghan (*af´gan*) *n.* A crocheted or knitted cover in colorful designs.

a-field (*afēld´*) *adv.* Away from home or the usual path.

a-fire (*afīr´*) *adj. & adv.* Burning.

a-flame (*a flām´*) *adj. & adv.* Burning; in flames; glowing.

a-float (*a flōt´*) *adv.* Floating on the surface of water; circulating.

a-flut-ter (*e ´flet er*) *adj.* Nervously excited.

a-foot (*a fet´*) *adj.* In the progress of happening; walking; on foot.

a-fore (*afōr´*) *adv.* Before as in place or time.

a-fore-men-tioned (*a fōr´men´shand*) *adj.* Mentioned before.

a-fore-said (*a fōr´sed´*) *adj.* Having spoken of something before; mentioned previously in the same discourse.

a-fore-thought (*a fōr´thot*) *adj.* Premeditated; planned beforehand; thought of previously.

a-foul (*a foul´*) *adv.* Tangled; entangled in a collision.

a-fraid (*a frād´*) *adj.* Hesitant; filled with fear; reluctant.

a-fresh (*a fresh´*) *adv.* Once more; again; after a pause.

aft (*aft*) *adv.* At, close to, near, or toward the rear of an aircraft or stern of a ship.

af-ter (*af´tēr*) *adv.* In the rear. **after** *prep.* Following; later in time.

af-ter-ef-fect (*af´tēr i fekt´*) *n.* An effect coming after; a delayed effect.

af-ter-thought (*af´tēr thot´*) *n.* An idea occurring later.

af-ter-ward *or* **af-ter-wards** (*af´tēr ward*) *adv.* In later time.

a-gain (*a gen´*) *adv.* Moreover; another time; once more.

a-gainst (*agenst´*) *prep.* In opposition to; in preparation for; in contact with.

a-gape (*a gāp´*) *adv.* With expectation; in wonder; open-mouthed.

ag-ate (*ag´it*) *n.* The type of quartz that has bands of colors.

agate line *n.* Unit of measurement used in classified advertising.

a-ga-ve (*a gā´vē*) *n.* Fleshy-leaved tropical American plant.

age (*āj*) *n.* The length of time from beginning to a certain date; the time of life when a person has full legal rights; the age of 21. **age** *v.* To grow or become old; to mature.

aged (*ā´jid*) *adj.* Grown or become old. **agedness** *n.* **agedly** *adv.*

a-gen-cy (*ā´jen sē*) *n.* A business or service that acts for others; action; active influence; power.

a-gen-da (*a jen´da*) *n.* Program or list of things to be done.

a-gen-e-sis (*ā jen´i sis*) *n. Med.* The lack of, or an imperfect, development.

a-gent (*ā´jent*) *n.* One who acts as the representative of another; one who acts or exerts power.

ag-gior-na-men-to (*e jór ne´men tō*) *n.* Bringing up to date.

ag-glom-er-ate (*a glom´e rāt´*) *v.* To collect; to form into a mass.

ag-glu-ti-nate (*a glöt´i nāt´*) *v.* To join by adhesion; to cause red blood cells to clump together.

ag-glu-ti-nin (*e ´glü n en*) *n.* A substance that causes agglutination; a group or mass formed by the union of separate elements.

ag-grade (*agrād´*) *v.* To raise the level or grade of a river valley.

ag-gran-dize (*ag´ran dīz´*) *n.* To enlarge, to extend; to increase.

ag-gra-vate (*ag´ravāt´*) *v.* To annoy; to make worse.

ag-gra-va-tion (*ag´ra vā´shan*) *n.* Act of making worse or aggravating; irritation, annoyance.

ag-gre-gate (*ag´re git*) *adj.* To gather together into a mass or whole.

ag-gress (*a gres´*) *v.* To commit the first act of offense or hostility.

ag-gres-sion (*a gresh´an*) *n.* Hostile action or behavior; an unprovoked assault.

ag-gres-sive (*a gres´iv*) *adj.* Offensive; distressing; pushy; afflicting.

ag-gres-sor (*agres´ēr*) *n.* An invader.

ag-grieved (*agrēvd´*) *adj.* Wronged or injured.

a-ghast (*agast´*) *adj.* Appalled; struck with amazement.

ag-ile (*aj´il*) *adj.* Marked by the ability to move quickly and easily; nimble.

ag-i-o (aj´ēō´) *n.* The difference in value between one kind of money or another.

ag-i-o-tage (aj´ē *a* tij) *n.* Business of a person who deals in foreign exchange.

ag-i-tate (aj´i tāt´) *v.* To disturb; to upset; to stir or move with violence; to try to arouse the public interest. -ion *n.*

ag-i-ta-tor (aj´i tā´*tor*) *n.* One who or that which stirs up public discontent, agitates, or arouses; a mixing device.

a-gleam (*a* glēm´) *adj.* Gleaming.

ag-let (ag´lit) *n.* A metal tag at the end of a shoelace.

a-gley (aglā´) *adv.* Wrong; awry.

a-glim-mer (*a* glim´ẻr) *adj.* Glimmering.

a-glit-ter (*a* glit´ẻr) *adj.* Glittering.

a-glow (*a* glō´) *adj.* Glowing.

ag-nail (ag´nāl) *n.* Inflammation of a fingernail or toenail; hangnail.

ag-nate (ag´nāt) *n.* Any male relation on the father's side.

ag-no-men (ag nō´men) *n.* An additional word, phrase or nickname, often used to designate a person in place of their real name.

ag-nos-tic (ag nos´tik) *n.* One who doubts that there is a God or life hereafter. agnosticism *n.*

a-go (*a* gō´) *adj.* In the past; gone by.

a-gog (*a* gog´) *adj.* Excited; eagerly expectant.

ag-o-nal (ag´*o* nal) *adj.* Relating to or having the characteristic of agony.

agonic line (ā gä´ik līn) *n.* The imaginary line on the earth's surface that joins places having no magnetic declination and where the magnetic needle points to the true north as well as magnetic north.

ag-o-nize (ag´*o*nīz´) *v.* To afflict with great anguish or to suffer agony. agonized *adj.* agonizing *adj.*

ag-o-ny (ag´*o* nē) *n., pl.* agonies Intense mental distress or physical pain.

ag-o-ra-pho-bi-a (ag´*or a*fō´bē *a*) *n.* Fear of open spaces.

a-graffe (*a* graf´) *n.* The ornamental clasp used for hooking parts of clothing together.

a-gran-u-lo-cy-to-sis (*a* gran¯yu lo sī tō´ sis) *n.* Destructive blood disease that is distinguished by a decrease of the leukocytes.

a-graph-i-a (a graf´ē *a*) *n.* The cerebral disorder in which a patient cannot express ideas by written signs.

a-grar-i-an (agrâr´ē *a*n) *adj.* Pertaining to or of land and its ownership; pertaining to farming; agricultural.

a-grar-i-an-ism (*a* grâr´ē *a* nizm) *n.* The movement and doctrine advocating equal divisions of lands and property.

a-gree (*a* grē´) *v.* To give assent; to consent; to share an understanding or opinion; to be beneficial or suitable; to correspond.

a-gree-a-ble (*a* grē´*a* bl) *adj.* Pleasant; pleasing; willing; ready to consent. agreeableness *n.* agreeably *adv.*

a-gree-ment (*a* grē´ment) *n.* Harmony; concord; state or act of agreeing.

ag-ri-cul-ture (ag´ri kul´chur) *n.* Raising of livestock; farming and cultivating the crops. agriculturalist *n.*

ag-ri-ol-o-gy (ag´rē ol´*o* jē) *n.* The study of human customs, especially those customs of man in a civilization of lesser development.

ag-ro-bi-ol-o-gy (ag´rō bīal´*o* jē) *n.* The science of plant nutrition and life in relation to the production of crops.

a-ground (*a* ground´) *adv.* Stranded; on the ground; to run ashore; beached. aground *adj.* Stranded; on the ground; to run ashore; beached.

a-gue (a´gū) *n.* Fever accompanied by chills or shivering and sweating.

a-head (*a* hed´) *adv.* Before; in advance; to or at the front of something.

a-hoy (*a* hoi´) *interj.* A nautical call or greeting.

aid (ād) *v.* To give help or assistance.

AIDS *n.* Disease that destroys the body's immunological system; Acquired Immune Deficiency Syndrome.

ai-guille (ā gwēl´) *n.* The needle-like tops of rocks and mountain masses.

ail (āl) *v.* To feel sick; to make ill or uneasy.

ail-ment (āl´ment) *n.* A mild illness.

aim (ām) *v.* To direct a weapon; to direct purpose. aim *n.* Intention.

aim-less (ām´lis) *adj.* Lacking of purpose.

ain't (ānt) *contr.* Am not, are not, is not, has not, or have not.

air (âr) *n.* An odorless, tasteless, colorless, gaseous mixture; primarily composed of nitrogen (78%) and oxygen (21%); the sky; a breeze. **on the air** Broadcasting.

air-lift (âr´lift´) *n.* System of transporting supplies or troops by air when ground routes are blocked.

air-plane (âr´plān´) *n.* A vehicle capable of flight, heavier than air, and propelled by jet engines or propellers.

air-wave (âr´wāv´) *n.* The medium of television and radio transmission and communication.

aisle (īl) *n.* Passageway between rows of seats, as in a church, auditorium, or airplane, or meeting place.

a-jar (*a* jär´) *adv. & adj.* Partially opened.

a-kim-bo (*a*kim´bō) *adj. & adv.* Bent; with a crook; arms bent with elbows out, hands on hips.

a-kin (akin´) *adj.* Related, as in family; similar in quality or character.

Alabama *n.* A state located in the southeastern part of the United States, statehood December 14, 1819, state capital Montgomery.

al-a-bas-ter (al´a bas´tẽr) *n.* A dense, translucent, tinted or white, fine-grained gypsum. **alabastrine** *adj.*

a la carte (ä´la kärt´) *adj.* Separate price for each item on the menu.

a-lack (a lak´) *interj.* An exclamation expressive of sorrow.

a-lac-ri-ty (a lak´ri tē) *n.* Readiness; cheerfulness; eagerness; briskness.

a la mode (al´a mōd´) *adj.* Served with ice cream, as pie; fashionable.

a-larm (a lärm´) *n.* A warning of danger; sudden feeling of fear; the bell or buzzer of a clock. **alarm** *v.* To frighten or warn by an alarm. **alarming** *adj.*

a-las (a las´) *interj.* Expressive of anxiety or regret.

Alaska *n.* A state located in the northwestern part of the United States, statehood January 3, 1959, capital Juneau.

a-late *or* **a-lat-ed (ā´lāt, ā´lā ted)** *adj.* Winged; having wings. **alation** *n.*

alb (alb) *n.* White linen robe worn by clergy during Mass.

al-ba-core (al´ba kōr´) *n.* Large marine fish; major source of canned tuna.

al-ba-ta (al bä´ta) *n.* Alloy that consists of a combination of tin, nickel, zinc, and copper.

al-be-do (al bē´dō) *n., Astron.* Measurement of light rays upon a satellite or planet.

al-be-it (ol bē´it) *conj.* Although; even though.

al-bi-no (al bī´nō) *n.* An animal or person with an abnormal whiteness of the skin and hair and pink-colored eyes.

al-bum (al´bum) *n.* A book for photographs, autographs, stamps; a book of collections.

al-bu-men (al bū´men) *n.* White of an egg.

al-bu-min (al bū´men) *n.* Several proteins found in the white of eggs, blood serum, milk, and plant and animal tissue.

al-bu-mi-nu-ri-a (al bū´mi ne´rē a) *n. Pathol.* The condition where the urine contains albumen, that often indicates diseased kidneys.

al-co-hol (al´ko hol´) *n.* Intoxicating liquor containing alcohol; ethanol; a series of related organic compounds.

al-cove (al´kōv) *n.* Recess or partly enclosed extension of a room.

al-de-hyde (al´de hīd´) *n.* Any of a class of highly reactive compounds obtained by oxidation of alcohols.

al-der-man (ol´dẽr man) *n.* Member of a municipal legislative body.

ale (āl) *n.* Beverage similar to, but more bitter than beer, made from malt by fermentation.

a-lee (a lē´) *adv. Naut.* On the sheltered side; opposite of aweather.

a-lem-bic (a lem´bik) *n.* A glass or metal vessel formerly used in distillation.

a-leph-null (ä´lef nul´) *n. Math.* Smallest infinite non-ordinal number.

a-lert (a lert´) *adj.* Vigilant; brisk; watchful; active. **alert** *n.* A danger signal. **alertly** *adv.* **alertness** *n.*

a-lex-in (a lek´sin) *n.* Any of certain substances found in normal blood-serum, capable of destroying bacteria.

a-lex-i-phar-mic (alek´si fär´mik) *adj.* Acting as a means of warding off disease or the effects of poison.

al-fa (al´fa) *n.* A code word in communications to represent the letter A.

al-for-ja (al for´ja) *n.* Leather pouch or saddlebag.

al-fres-co (al fres´kō) *adj. & adv.* In the fresh air; outside..

al-gae (al´jē) *n.* Various primitive, chiefly aquatic, one-celled or multi-cellular plants, as the seaweed.

al-ge-bra (al´je bra) *n.* Generalization of math in which symbols represent members of a specified set of numbers and are related by operations that hold for all numbers in the set. **algebraic** *adj.* **algebraical, algebraically** *adv.*

al-go-pho-bi-a (al´go fō´bē a) *n.* The extreme fear of pain.

algorithm In computer science, precise instructions for performing a specific task.

a-li-as (ā´lē as) *n., pl.* **aliases** Assumed name. **alias** *adv.* Otherwise known as. In computer science, a name assigned to a file or a block of data to address it for processing.

al-i-bi (al´i bī´) *n.* A form of defense, an attempt by a defendant to prove he was elsewhere when a crime was committed; an excuse.

a-li-en (āl´yen) *adj.* Owing allegiance to a government or country, not one's own; unfamiliar; repugnant; from another region or country. **alien** *n.* A stranger; a foreigner.

al-ien-a-ble (āl´ye na bl) *adj.* Able to be transferred to the ownership of another. **alienability** *n.*

al-ien-ate (āl´ye nāt´) *v.* To cause to become indifferent or unfriendly.

al-ien-ist (āl´ye nist) *n.* A psychiatrist accepted by a court as an expert on mental stability.

a-light (a līt´) *v.* To settle; to come down; to dismount. **alight** *adj. & adv.* Burning, lighted.

a-lign *or* **a-line (a līn´)** *v.* To arrange in a line; to take one side of an argument or cause. **aligner** *n.*

a-lign-ment *or* **a-line-ment (a līn´m ent)** *n.* Arrange or position in a straight line.

a-like (a līk´) *adj.* Similar, having close resemblance. **alike** *adv.* In the same manner, way, or degree.

al-i-ment (al´i ment) *n.* Nourishment; food. **alimentation** *n.* **alimental** *adj.*

al-i-men-ta-ry (al´i men´ta rē) *adj.* Pertaining to nutrition or food.

alimentary canal *n.* The tube of the digestive system from the mouth to the anus, including the pharynx, esophagus, stomach, and intestines.

al-i-mo-ny (al´i mō´nē) *n.* Court ordered allowance for support, usually given by a man to his former wife following a divorce or legal separation.

al-i-phat-ic (al´i fat´ik) *adj.* Having to do with organic chemical compounds where the carbon atoms are linked in open chains.

al-i-quant (al´i kwant) *adj.* Applied to a number which will not divide into another number equally.

a-li-un-de (ā´lē un´dē) *adv.* From another source or means.

a-live (a līv´) *adj.* Living; having life; in existence or effect; full of life.

a-li-yah (ā´lē yä) *n.* Immigration of Jews to Israel.

a-liz-a-rin (a liz´ėr in) *n.* A red-orange compound used in dyes.

al-ka-li (al´ka lī´) *n. pl.* **alkalies** *or* **alkalis** A hydroxide or carbonate of an alkali metal, whose aqueous solution is slippery, bitter, caustic, and basic in reactions.

al-ka-lin-ize (al´ka li nīz) *adj.* To make alkaline.

al-ka-loid (al´ka loid) *n.* Any of various nitrogen-containing organic bases obtained from plants. **alkaloidal** *adj.*

al-ka-lo-sis (al´ka lō´sis) *n.* Unusually high alkali content in the blood and tissues.

al-ka-net (al´ka net´) *n.* A plant whose root yields a red dye.

al-kyd res-in (al´kid rez´en) *n.* Group of sticky resins coming from phthalic acid and glycerol, that are used primarily in paints and adhesives.

all (awl) *adj.* Total extent or total entity; being a whole number, amount, or quantity; every.

al-lan-to-is (a lan´tō is) *n.* A sac that is developed from the posterior end of the abdominal cavity in reptiles, birds, and some mammals.

all–a-round (ol´a round´) *n.* Variance of all–round.

al-lay (alā´) *v.* To relieve; to lessen; to calm; to pacify. **allayer** *n.*

al-le-ga-tion (al´e gā´shan) *n.* The act or result of alleging.

al-lege (a lej´) *v.* To affirm; to assert to be true; to declare without proof.

al-le-giance (a lē´jans) *n.* Loyalty to one's nation, cause, or sovereign; obligations of a vassal to an overlord.

al-le-giant (a lē´ja´nt) *n.* A person who owes allegiance.

al-le-go-ry (al´e gōr´ē) *n. pl.* **allegories** A dramatic, literary, or pictorial device in which each object, character, and event symbolically illustrates a religious or moral principle. **allegoric, allegorical** *adj.* **allegorist** *n.*

al-lele (a lēl´) *n.* Any of a group of possible mutational forms of a gene. **allelism** *n.* **allelic** *adj.*

al-le-lu-ia (al´e lōō´ya) *interj.* Expressing praise to God or of thanksgiving.

al-ler-gen (al´ėr jen´) *n.* Substance which causes an allergy. **allergenic** *adj.*

al-ler-gy (al´ėr jē) *n., pl.* **allergies** Pathological or abnormal reaction to environmental substances, as foods, dust, pollens, or microorganisms.

al-le-vi-ate (a lē´vē āt´) *v.* To make more bearable. **alleviation** *n.* **alleviator** *n.*

al-ley (al´ē) *n., pl.* **alleys** A narrow passageway for access between or behind buildings.

al-li-a-ceous (al´ē ā´shus) *adj.* Having the properties of an onion or garlic.

al-li-ance (a lī´ans) *n.* A union, relationship, or connection by kinship, marriage, or common interest; a confederation of nations by a formal treaty; an affinity.

al-lied (a līd´) *adj.* United by agreement, or other means.

al-li-ga-tor (al´i gā´tor) *n.* Large amphibious reptile with very sharp teeth, powerful jaws, and a shorter snout than the related crocodile.

al-lit-er-ate (a lit´e rāt´) *v.* To arrange or form words beginning with the same sound, compose or arrange.

al-lit-er-a-tion (a lit´e rā´shan) *n.* Occurrence of two or more words having the same initial sound.

al-li-um (al´ē um) *n.* Any bulb plant, such as garlic or onion.

al-lo-cate (al´o kāt´) *v.* To assign; to allot.

al-lo-cu-tion (al´o kū´shan) *n.* A formal speech.

al-log-a-mous (a log´amus) *adj.* Having the property of reproduction by cross-fertilization.

al-lo-graph (al´o graf´) *n.* Something written by someone on behalf of another.

al-lo-nym (al´o nim) *n.* The name of another person assumed by an author.

al-lot (a lot´) *v.* To distribute or set aside as a share of something, to divide, assign, or parcel out in parts or portions.

al-lot-ment (a lot´ment) *n.* A shared part, or portion granted or distributed.

al-lo-tropy (al´o trōp ē) *n.* One of two or more existing forms of a chemical element. **allotropic, allotropical** *adj.*

all out (ol´out´) *adv.* With every possible effort or resource.

all-o-ver (ol´ō´vėr) *n.* A design or pattern

that covers the entire surface.

al-low (a lou´) v. To make a provision for, to permit; to permit to have; to admit; to concede. **allowable** adj.

al-low-ance (a lou´ans) n. The act of allowing something, such as a regular amount of money or food; a price discount.

al-loy (aloi´) n. Something that has been added to or reduced in purity or value.

all right adj. Acceptable; meets satisfaction; correct; safe. Slang Good; of sound character; dependable. **all right** adv. Satisfactorily; correctly; unhurt.

all-round (ol´round´) adj. Versatile, including all aspects.

al-lude (a lōd´) v. To refer to something indirectly, to hint at.

al-lure (a lūr´) v. To entice; to tempt. **allure** n. Attraction; charm; enticement; prospect of attracting. **allurement** n. **allurer** n. **alluringly** adv.

al-lu-sion (a lō´zhan) n. The act of referring to something indirectly; a hint.

al-lu-sive (a lō´siv) adj. Reference to something that is not fully expressed. **allusively** adv. **allusiveness** n.

al-lu-vi-um (a lō´vē um) n. Sediment deposited by flowing water as in a river bed. **alluvial** adj.

al-ly (a li´) v. To connect or unite in a formal or close relationship or bond. **ally** n. One united with another in a formal or personal relationship.

alma mater n. College, school, or university one has attended; the anthem of that college, school, or university.

al-ma-nac (ol´ma nak´) n. Annual publication having calendars with weather forecasts, astronomical information, and other useful facts.

al-man-dine (al´man dēn´) n. A name given to the violet variety of the ruby spinel or sapphire; purple Indian garnet.

al-might-y (ol mī´tē) adj. Having absolute power. n. The Almighty God.

al-most (ol´mōst) adv. Not quite; slightly short of.

alms (ämz) n. Goods or money given to the poor in charity.

alms-house (ämz´hous´) n. A poorhouse.

al-ni-co (al´ni kō´) n. A powerful permanent magnet alloy of aluminum, iron, nickel, and other elements.

al-oe (al´ō) n. Any of various mostly African plants having fleshy, spiny-toothed leaves; a cathartic drug made from the juice of the leaves of this plant.

a-loft (a loft´) adv. Toward the upper rigging of a ship; in or into a high place; in the air.

a-lone (a lōn´) adj. Away from other people; single; solitary; excluding anyone or anything else; with nothing further; sole; only; unaccompanied by others. **alone** adv. **aloneness** n.

a-long (a long´) adv. In a line with; following the length or path; in association; together; as a companion.

a-long-shore (along´shōr) adv. Being near, along, or by the shore, either on land or in the water.

a-long-side (a long´sīd´) adv. Along, at, near, or to the side of; side by side with.

a-loof (alōf´) adj. Indifferent; distant. **aloofness** n. **aloofly** adv.

a-loud (a loud´) adv. Orally; audibly.

a-low (a lō´) adv. In a low place, as in the ship's hold.

al-pen-horn (al´pen horn) n. Long curved horn used to send signals.

al-pen-stock (al´pen stok´) n. Long staff with an iron point used by mountain climbers.

al-pes-trine (al pes´trin) adj. Pertaining to mountain regions; growing at very high elevations but not above the timberline.

alpha and omega n. The beginning and the end; the first and last letters of the Greek alphabet.

al-pha-bet (al´fa bet´) n. The letters of a language, arranged in an order fixed by custom.

alpha decay n. Decay of an atomic nucleus as it emits an alpha particle.

alpha ray n. A stream of alpha particles.

al-read-y (ol red´ē) adv. By this or a specified time.

al-sike (al´sik) n. A European perennial clover with white or light pink flowers.

al-so (ol´sō) adv. Likewise; besides; in addition.

al-tar (ol´tēr) n. An elevated structure before which religious ceremonies may be held or sacrifices offered.

al-ter (ol´tēr) v. To make change or become different; to modify; to castrate or spay, as an animal. **alteration** n.

al-ter-a-tive (ol´te rā´tiv) adj. Tending to alter or produce alterations.

al-ter-ca-tion (ol´tēr kā´shan) n. Noisy and heated quarrel.

al-ter-nate (ol´tēr nat´) v. To happen or follow in turn; to occur in successive turns. **alternate** n. Substitute.

alternate key (ALT) In computer science, an alternate shift key used in conjunction with other keys to execute commands.

alternating current n. Electric current that reverses direction at regular intervals.

al-ter-na-tive (ol´tēr´n ativ) n. A choice between two or more possibilities; one of the possibilities to be chosen. **alternative** adj. Allowing a choice.

al-ter-na-tor (ol´tēr nā´tēr) n. Electric generator producing alternating current.

alt-horn (alt´horn´) n. A tenor saxhorn,

often substituted for the French horn in bands.

al-though (ol thō´) *conj.* Even though.

al-tim-e-ter (al tim´i tėr) *n.* Instrument for measuring and indicating altitude.

al-ti-tude (al´ti tūd´) *n.* The height of a thing above a reference level; above the earth's surface; above sea level.

al-to (al´tō) *n.* Low female singing voice; the range between soprano and tenor.

al-to-geth-er (ol´*to* geth´ėr) *adv.* Entirely; with all included or counted.

al-tru-ism (al´trŏ iz´um) *n.* Selfless concern for the welfare of others. **altruist** *n.* **altruistic** *adj.*

ALU In computer science, Arithmetic and Logic Unit; the part of the CPU that performs arithmetic and logic functions.

al-um (al´um) *n.* Any one of several similar double sulfates.

a-lu-mi-na (a lŏ´mi na) *n.* Any of several forms of aluminum oxide.

a-lu-mi-num (a lŏ´mi num) *n.* A silvery-white, ductile metallic element used to form many hard, light, corrosion-resistant alloys.

a-lum-na (a lum´na) *n., pl.* **alumnae** Female graduate or former student of a school, college, or university.

a-lum-nus (a lum´nus) *n. pl.* **alumni** A graduate or former student of a school, college, or university.

al-ve-o-lar (al vē´o lėr) *adj.* Containing or pertaining to sockets, specifically the part of the jaws where the teeth arise.

al-ways (ol´wāz) *adv.* Continuously; forever; on every occasion; at all times.

a-lys-sum (a lis´um) *n.* Herbs of the mustard family bearing small yellow or white racemose flowers with hairy leaves.

am (am) *v.* First person, singular, present tense of the verb to *be*.

AM *abbr.* Ante meridian, Latin for "before noon."

a-mal-gam (a mal´gam) *n.* An alloy of mercury with other metals, as with tin or silver; a blend of diverse elements.

a-mal-ga-mate (a mal´ga māt´) *v.* To mix so as to make a unified whole; to blend. **amalgamation** *n.*

a-man-dine (a man dēn´) *adj.* Made with or garnished with almonds.

am-a-ranth (am´aranth´) *n.* Various weedy plants that have greenish or purplish flowers; an imaginary flower that never fades.

a-mass (a mas´) *v.* To gather a great mass or number of; to accumulate.

am-a-teur (am´a cher´) *n.* One who engages in an activity as a pastime rather than as a profession; one who lacks expertise. **amateurish** *adj.*

am-a-tive (am´a tiv) *adj.* Disposed or

disposing of love; full of love; inclined to love.

am-a-tol (am´a tol´) *n.* An explosive consisting of ammonium nitrate and trinitrotoluene (TNT).

am-a-to-ry (am´a tōr´ē) *adj.* Of or expressive of sexual love.

am-au-ro-sis (am´o rō´sis) *n.* A partial or complete loss of sight due to the loss of power in the optic nerve or retina.

a-maze (amāz´) *v.* To astound; to affect with surprise or wonder. **amazingly** *adv.* **amazedness** *n.* **amazing** *adj.*

a-maze-ment (a māz´ment) *n.* The quality or state of being amazed or astounded.

am-a-zon-ite (am´a zo nīt´) *n.* A semi-precious green variety of microcline found near the Amazon River.

am-bass-a-dor (am bas´a dor) *n.* High ranking official, accredited by one government to another. **ambassadorial** *adj.* **ambassadorship** *n.*

am-ber (am´bėr) *n.* A hard, translucent, yellow, brownish-yellow, or orange fossil resin, used for jewelry and ornaments; medium to dark orange yellow color.

am-ber-gris (am´bėr grēs´) *n.* A waxy, grayish substance produced by sperm whales, and used in making perfumes.

am-bi-dex-trous (am´bi dek´strus) *adj.* Capable of using both the right and left hands with equal facility.

am-bi-ence (am´bēens) *n.* Environment; surrounding atmosphere.

am-bi-ent (am´bē ent) *adj.* Surrounding; on all sides.

am-bi-gu-i-ty (am´bi gū´i tē) *n.* The quality of being obscure or ambiguous.

am-big-u-ous (am big´ū us) *adj.* Doubtful; uncertain, open to interpretation. In computer science, imprecise; of a program command or formula that is stated in such a way that it may yield an undesirable result. **ambiguousness** *n.* **ambiguously** *adv.*

am-bi-tion (am bish´an) *n.* Strong desire to achieve; will to succeed; the goal or object desired.

am-bi-tious (am bish´us) *adj.* Challenging. **ambitiousness** *n.* **ambitiously** *adv.*

am-biv-a-lence (am biv´a lens) *n.* Existence of mutually different feelings about a person or thing.

am-bi-vert (am´bivürt´) *n.* A person having the characteristics of both introvert and extrovert.

am-ble (am´bl) *v.* To move at a leisurely pace. **ambler** *n.*

am-bly-o-pi-a (am´blē ō´pē a) *n.* Dullness or dimness of eyesight without apparent change or defect in the organs.

am-boi-na wood (am boi´na wod) *n.* A curled and mottled wood used in cabinet making.

am-bro-sia (am´brō´zha) n. Food of the Greek Gods and immortals; food having exquisite flavor or fragrance.

am-bu-lance (am´bū lans) n. Vehicle equipped to transport the injured or sick.

am-bu-lant (am´bū lant) adj. To move from one place to another.

am-bu-la-to-ry (am´bū la tŏr´ē) n. Any sheltered part of a building intended as a passageway for walking. adj. Moving about; movable; able to walk.

am-bush (am´bush) n. Surprise attack made from a hidden position. **ambush** v. **ambusher** n. **ambushment** n.

ameba or **amoeba** (a mē´ba) n. A minute single-celled, semi-fluid organism of indefinite, changeable form.

a-mel-io-rate (a měl´ya rāt´) v. To make better or more tolerable; to improve. **ameliorator** n. **ameliorative** adj.

a-men (ā´měn´) interj. Used at the end of a prayer to express solemn approval.

a-me-na-bil-l-ty (a mē´na bil´i tē) n. State of being amenable.

a-me-na-ble (a mē´na bl) adj. Responsive; tractable; accountable.

a-mend (a mend´) v. To correct; to improve; to rectify. **amendable** adj.

a-mend-ment (a mend´ment) n. Correction, reformation or improvement; a legislative bill change or the parliamentary procedure where such alteration is made.

a-mends (a mendz´) n. Compensation for insult or injury.

a-men-i-ty (a měn´i tē) n. pl. **amenities** Agreeableness; means of comfort or convenience.

a-merce (a murs´) v. To punish by a fine decided by the court.

a-merce-ment (a murs´ment) n. Fine imposed on an offender at the discretion of the court.

am-e-thyst (am´i thist) n. Violet or purple form of transparent corundum or quartz, used as a gemstone.

am-e-tro-pi-a (am´i trō´pē a) n. An abnormal condition of the eye where images fail to focus upon the retina.

a-mi-a-ble (ā´mē abl) adj. Friendly and pleasant. **amiableness** n. **amiability** n. **amiably** adv.

am-i-ca-ble (am´i ka bl) adj. Harmonious; friendly; peaceable. **amicability** n. **amicableness** n. **amicably** adv.

a-mi-cus cu-ri-ae (a mī´kus kūr´ē ē´) n. A professional who is asked for or volunteers information on some matter of law that directly affects a particular case.

a-mid (a mid´) prep. In the middle of; surrounded by, among.

a-mid-ships (a mid´ships) adv. Halfway between the bow and the stern.

a-midst (a midst´) prep. In the middle of; surrounded by; during.

a-mi-go (a mē´gō) n. A friend.

a-miss (a mis´) adj. Out of order or place; in an improper or wrong way.

am-i-ty (am´i tē) n. Relationships that are friendly, as between two states.

am-me-ter (am´mē´těr) n. A tool measuring electric current.

am-mo (am´ō) n. Ammunition.

am-mo-nia (a mŏn´ya) n. Colorless, pungent gas.

ammonium hydroxide n. A colorless, basic aqueous solution of ammonia.

am-ne-sia (am nē´zha) n. The partial or complete loss of memory.

am-nes-ty (am´ni stē) n. pl. **amnesties** Pardon for political offenders.

am-ni-on (am´nē on) n. The innermost membrane that surrounds the fetus of birds, mammals, and reptiles.

a-moe-ba Variant of **ameba**.

a-mong (a mung´) prep. In or through the midst of; between one another.

a-mon-til-la-do (a mon´ti lä´dō) n. A pale, dry, sweet sherry.

a-mor-al (ā mor´al) adj. Neither moral nor immoral. **amorality** n.

am-o-rous (am´er us) adj. Inclined to or indicative of sexual love.

a-mor-phous (a mor´fus) adj. Lacking definite form; shapeless; general; vague.

am-or-tize (am´ěr tīz´) v. To liquidate a loan by installment payments; to repay a loan. **amortization** n.

a-mount (a mount´) n. Aggregate, sum or total quantity. **amount** v. To be equivalent.

a-mour (a mur´) n. A forbidden love affair

amour–propre n. Self-respect.

am-pe-lop-sis (am´pe lop´sis) n. Any plant having climbing woody vines or shrubs.

am-per-age (am´pěr ij) n. Strength of an electric current, expressed in amperes.

am-pere (am´pēr) n. Unit of electric current equal to a flow of one amp per second.

am-pere-turn (am´pēr türn´) n. One complete turn or convolution of a conducting coil, through which one ampere of electric current passes.

am-per-sand (am´pěr sand´) n. The character or sign that represents and (&).

am-phet-a-mine (am fet´a mēn´) n. Colorless volatile compound used as a drug.

amphi prefix Around, on both sides, all around on all sides.

am-phib-i-an (am fib´ē an) n. An organism, as a frog or toad, developing from an aquatic state into an air-breathing state; aircraft that can take off and land on land or water; a vehicle that can move on land or water.

am-phi-bole (am´fi bōl´) *n.* A silicate mineral of varying composition, that usually consists of a magnesium, silicate of calcium, and one or more other metals.

am-phi-pod (am´fi pod´) *n.* One of an order of small crustaceous animals having a laterally compressed body and commonly found in fresh and salt water.

am-phi-the-a-ter (am´fi thē´a tèr) *n.* A round or oval building having tiers of seats rising around an arena.

am-pho-ter-ic (am´fo ter´ik) *adj.* Able to react chemically either as an acid or base.

am-ple (am´pel) *adj.* Sufficient; abundant; large. **ampleness** *n.*

am-pli-dyne (am´pli dīn´) *n.* Direct current generator.

am-pli-fi-ca-tion (am´pli fi kā´shan) *n.* An enlargement; an example or product of amplifying.

am-pli-fi-er (am´pli fī´èr) *n.* That which amplifies or enlarges.

am-pli-fy (am´pli fī´) *v.* To make larger, more extended; to explain in greater detail.

am-pli-tude (am´pli tōd) *n.* Maximum value of a periodically varying quantity; greatness of size; fullness.

am-ply (am´plē) *adv.* In sufficient manner.

am-pul *or* **am-pule** (am´pūl) *n.* A small, sealed vial containing a hypodermic injection solution.

am-pu-tate (am´pū tāt´) *v.* To cut off; to remove, as a limb from one's body.

a-muck (a muk´) *adv.* In an uncontrolled manner; a murderous frenzy; out of control.

am-u-let (am´ū lit) *n.* A charm worn as protection against evil or injury.

a-muse (a mūz´) *v.* To entertain in an agreeable, pleasing way. **-ment** *n.*

am-yl-ase (am´elās´) *n.* Any of the enzymes that change starch into sugar.

am-y-lol-y-sis (am´e lol´i sis) *n.* The conversion of starch into soluble products.

a-my-o-to-ni-a (ā´mī o tō´nē) *adj.* Deficiency of muscle tone.

an (an) *adj.* One; one sort of; each; form of "a" used before words beginning with a vowel or with an unpronounced "h" as in elephant or honor.

a-na (ā´na) *n.* A collection of memorable sayings, information, or anecdotes about a person or place.

a-nach-ro-nism (a nak´ro niz´um) *n.* An error in chronology; connecting of a thing, person or happening with another that came later in history;

anything that is out of place in history; any error which implies the misplacing, usually earlier, of person or events in time.

an-a-co-lu-thic (an´a ko lō´ thik) *adj.* Lacking grammatical sequence; inconsistency within a sentence.

an-a-con-da (an´a kon´ da) *n.* A large tropical South American snake which kills its prey by crushing it to death in its coils.

an-a-dem (an´a dem´) *n.* A wreath for the head.

a-nad-ro-mous (a nad´ro mus) *adj.* Migrating up river from the sea to breed in fresh water, as a salmon.

anaemia *n.* Variant of anemia.

an-aes-the-sia (an´is thē´zha) *n.* Variant of anesthesia.

an-a-gram (an´agram´) *n.* Word formed by transposing the letters of another word. **anagrammatical** *adj.*

a-nal (ān´al) *adj.* Of or relating to the anus.

a-nal-cime (a nal´sim) *n.* A white or slightly colored mineral with frequent occurrence in igneous rock masses.

an-a-lects (an´a lekts´) *n.* Selected miscellaneous extracts or small pieces selected from different authors and combined.

an-al-ge-sia (an´al jē´zē a) *n.* Inability to feel pain while awake.

an-al-get-ic (an´al jed´ik) *n.* A remedy or treatment that removes pain.

analog In computer science, description of data represented as a continuous variable, such as sound.

analog computer *n.* A computer which calculates by using physical analogs, where numerical data is represented by measurable quantities as lengths, electrical signals, or voltage.

analog to digital converter In computer science, a device that converts analog data to digital data.

a-nal-o-gous (a nal´o gus) *adj.* Similar; corresponding in certain ways.

an-a-logue (an´a log´) *n.* Something that bears resemblance to something else.

a-nal-o-gy (a nal´o jē) *n. pl.* **analogies** Connection between things that are other-wise dissimilar; a conclusion or opinion that if two things are alike in some respects they must be alike in others.

an-al-pha-bet (an al´fa bet) *n.* A person who is totally illiterate; one who cannot read.

a-nal-y-sis (a nal´i sis) *n.* Breaking up or separation of something into its parts so as to examine them and see how they fit together; result.

an-a-lyst (an´a list) *n.* A person who analyzes or who is skilled in analysis.

analytic geometry *n.* The study of

geometry properties where procedures of algebraic reasoning are applied.

an-a-lyze (an´a līz´) v. To make an analysis of.

an-am-ne-sis (an˝am nē´sis) n. The recalling to mind of things past; recollection; reminiscence.

an-a-pest (an´a pest˝) n. Metrical foot make up of two short syllables followed by one long one. **anapestic** adj.

a-naph-o-ra (a naf´or a) n. The repetition of the same word or words at the beginning of two or more successive clauses or verses.

an-a-plas-ty (an´a plas˝tē) n. Plastic surgery.

an-arch (an´ärk) n. A leader who excites disorder or revolt.

an-ar-chic (an är´kik) adj. Of, like, or promoting confusion or disorder.

an-ar-chism (an´ar kiz˝um) n. Belief that all forms of government act in an unnecessary and unfair way against the liberty of a person and should be done away with.

an-ar-chist (an´ar kist) n. One who rebels with violent revolution against the established order.

an-ar-chy (an´ar kē) n. Lack of political authority, disorder and confusion; the absence of any purpose or standard.

an-as-tig-mat (a nas´tig mat˝) n. System of lenses where astigmatic defects are overcome.

a-nas-to-mo-sis (a nas˝to mō´sis) n. Connection or union of branches, as of rivers, leaf veins, or blood vessels.

a-nas-tro-phe (a nas´tro fē) n. Changing the normal syntactic order of words.

a-nath-e-ma (a nath´a ma) n. Curse; ban; or excommunication

a-nath-e-ma-tize (a nath´e ma tīz) v. To curse; to ban.

a-nat-o-mist (a nat´o mist) n. A person who is skilled in dissection; one who analyzes critically.

a-nat-o-mize (a nat´o mīz´) v. To examine in great detail, to analyze; in biology, to cut in pieces for the purpose of displaying or examining the structure.

a-nat-o-my (a nat´o mē) n. pl. anatomies The branch of morphology dealing with the structure of an organ or organism; a detailed analysis; the art of dissecting or artificially separating the different parts of an organized body, to discover their situation, structure, and function. **anatomical** adj. **anatomic** adj.

an-ces-tor (an´ses tėr) n. A person who comes before one in a family line; someone earlier than a grandparent; forefather. **ancestral** adj.

an-cho-ret (ang´kėr it) or **an-cho-rite** (ang´kė rīt˝) n. A hermit; a recluse; one living in seclusion for religious reasons.

anchor man n. The managing newscaster who coordinates the reports of other participants in a newscast or in live coverage of a news event.

an-cien ré-gime (on sē´an rā jēm´) n. Ancient or old system of government; system no longer prevailing.

an-cient (ān´shent) adj. Anything belonging to the early history of people; very old. **ancientness** n.

an-con (ang´kon) n. The upper end of the ulna or elbow; an architectural support, as a bracket or projection.

and (and) conj. Together with; along with; as well as; added to; as a result; plus; also.

an-dan-te (an dan´tē) adv. Mus. Rather slow in tempo. **andante** adj.

an-dan-ti-no (an˝dan tē´nō) adj. Mus. Slightly faster in tempo than andante.

an-des-ite (an´di zīt˝) n. A dark grayish rock consisting mostly of feldspar.

and-i-ron (and´ī ėrn) n. Heavy metal support for logs or wood in a fireplace.

andr n. The male sex; masculine.

an-dro-gen (an´dro jen) n. Hormone that develops and maintains masculine characteristics. **androgenic** adj.

an-droid (an´droyd) n. In science fiction, a synthetic man made to look like a human.

an-ec-dote (an´ik dōt˝) n. Short account of a story of some happening or about some person. **anecdotal** adj. **anecdotic** adj. **anecdotist** n.

an-e-cho-ic (an´e kō´ik) adj. Neither having nor producing echoes.

a-ne-mi-a (a nē´mē a) n. The condition in which a person's blood does not have enough red corpuscles or hemoglobin and, therefore, does not carry a normal amount of oxygen.

a-ne-mic (a nē´mik) adj. Of or having anemia.

an-e-mom-e-ter (an´e mom´i tėr) n. Instrument for measuring wind force and speed.

an-e-moph-i-lous (an´e mof´i lus) adj. Wind-pollinated.

a-nem-o-scope (a nem´o skōp˝) n. A device that indicates the direction of the wind.

a-nent (a nent´) prep. Regarding; concerning.

an-er-oid (an´e roid˝) adj. Capability to function without fluid.

an-es-the-sia (an˝is thē´zha) n. Condition in which one has no feeling of heat, touch, or pain in all or part of the body.

an-es-the-si-ol-o-gy (an˝is thē´zē ol´o jē) n. The medical study and use of anesthetics. **anesthesiologist** n.

an-es-thet-ic (an˝is thet´ik) adj. Taking away the feeling of pain. **anesthetic** n. Drug, gas, or substance used to bring on anesthesia before surgery.

an-es-the-tize (*a* nes'thi tīz˝) *v*. To bring on unconsciousness by giving anesthetics; to remove the capacity to feel pain in a localized area.

an-eu-rysm (an'yu riz˝um) *n*. A dilation of a blood vessel or artery, that is due to the pressure of blood acting on a part weakened by disease or injury.

a-new (*a* nö') *adv*. Again; once more; in a new way.

an-gel (ān'jel) *n*. An immortal being attendant upon God; a very kind and lovable person; a helping or guiding spirit.

an-ger (ang'gėr) *n*. Feeling of extreme hostility; rage; wanting to fight back.

an-gi-na (an ji'na) *n*. A disease marked by painful choking spasms and attacks of suffocation pain. **anginous** *adj*. **anginose** *adj*. **anginal** *adj*.

an-gi-na pec-to-ris (an ji'na pek'to ris) *n*. Severe pain in the chest, associated with feelings of apprehension and suffocation.

an-gi-ol-o-gy (an˝jē ol'o jē) *n*. The study of blood vessels and lymphatics.

an-gle (ang'gl) *n*. A shape made by two straight lines meeting in a point or two surfaces meeting along a line.

an-gli-cize (ang'gli sīz˝) *v*. To make English in form, idiom, or character.

an-gling (ang'gling) *n*. The act of fishing with a hook and line.

an-go-ra (an gōr'a) *n*. The long silky hair of the Angora rabbit or Angora goat; yarn or fabric made from the hair of an Angora goat or rabbit.

an-gri-ly (ang'gri lē) *adv*. To threaten in an angry manner.

an-gry (ang'grē) *adj*. Feeling or showing anger; having a menacing aspect; inflamed.

an-gu-lar (ang'gū lėr) *adj*. Having angles or sharp corners; measured by an angle or degrees of an arc; forming an angle; gaunt, bony, lean. **angularity** *n*.

an-hy-dride (an hī'drīd) *n*. Chemical compound formed from another by removing the water.

an-hy-drous (an hī'drus) *adj*. Does not contain any water.

an-i-line (an'i lin) *n*. Colorless, oily, poisonous liquid, used to make rubber, dyes, resins, pharmaceuticals, and varnishes.

an-i-mad-vert (an˝i mad vürt') *v*. To make an ill-natured or unfair criticism. **animadversion** *n*. A critical remark

an-i-mal (an'i mal) *n*. Any being other than a human being; any four-footed creature; beast. **animalize** *v*.

an-i-mate (an'i māt˝) *v*. To give liveliness, life or spirit to; to cause to act; to inspire. **animation** *n*.

a-ni-ma-to (ä˝ni mä'tö) *adv*. *Mus*. In a

lively or animated manner; used as a direction.

an-i-ma-tor (an *e* mätėr) *n*. One who animates, such as an artist or technician who produces an animation, as a cartoon or movie film.

an-i-mé (an'i mā˝) *n*. Resin that is exuded from a large tropical tree from which varnish, lacquers, and flavorings are produced.

an-i-mism (an'i miz˝um) *n*. A belief in primitive tribes that natural objects and forces have souls. **animist** *n*.

an-i-mos-i-ty (an˝i mos'i tē) *n. pl*. **animosities** Hostility; bitterness; hatred.

an-i-mus (an'*o* mus) *n*. Feeling of animosity.

an-i-on (an'ī˝on) *n*. An ion with a negative charge that is attracted to an anode; electrolysis.

an-ise (an'is) *n*. A plant with yellowish-white flower clusters and licorice-flavored seeds.

an-i-seed (an'i sēd˝) *n*. Seed used for flavoring and in medicine.

an-i-sette (an˝i set') *n*. Anise-flavored liqueur.

an-kle (ang'kl) *n*. Joint that connects the foot with the leg; slender section of the leg immediately above this joint.

an-ky-lo-sis (ang˝ki lo'sis) *n*. Stiffness, fixation or immovability of a joint, due to a disease or as a result of surgery.

an-la-ge (än'lä ge) *n*. The first recognizable accumulation of cells in a developing organ or part.

an-nals (an'alz) *n. pl*. Descriptive record; history. **annalist** *n*.

an-nat-to (*a* nat'ö) *n*. The red dye made from the pulp from around the seeds of a small tropical American tree.

an-neal (*a* nēl') *v*. To heat and then cool glass slowly to make it less brittle.

an-nex (*a* neks˝) *v*. To add or join a small thing to a larger one. **annexation** *n*.

an-ni-hi-late (*a* nī'i lāt˝) *v*. To destroy completely; totally. **annihilator** *n*.

an-ni-ver-sa-ry (an *i* vür'sa rē) *n., pl*. **anniversaries** The date on which something happened at an earlier time; this event celebrated on this date each year.

an-no-tate (an'ö tāt˝) *v*. To use notes to give one's opinions. **annotator** *n*.

an-no-ta-tion (an˝ö tā'shan) *n*. Critical note on some passage of a book.

an-nounce (*a* nouns˝) *v*. To proclaim; to give notice.

an-noy (*a* noi˝) *v*. To bother; to irritate; to make slightly angry.

an-nu-al (an'ū al) *adj*. Recurring or done at the same time each year; a yearly publication, as a yearbook.

an-nu-i-ty (*a* nö'i tē) *n. pl*. **annuities** Annual payment of an income or allowance.

an-nul (*a* nul´) *v.* To cancel a marriage or a law; to do away with; to put an end to. **annullable** *adj.* **annulment** *n.*

an-nu-lar (an´yu lèr) *adj.* Shaped like or forming a ring. **annularly** *adv.*

an-nun-ci-ate (*a* nun´sē āt´) *v.* To proclaim; to announce.

an-nun-ci-a-tion (*a* nun´sē ā´sh*a*n) *n.* The act of announcing or being announced; an announcement.

an-ode (an´ōd) *n.* Positively charged electrode. **anodic** *adj.* **anodically** *adv.*

an-o-dize (an´o dīz´) *v.* To coat a metallic surface by electrolysis with a protective oxide.

a-noint (*a* noint´) *v.* To apply oil in a religious ceremony. **anointment** *n.*

a-nom-a-ly (*a* nom´a lē) *n., pl.* **anomalies** Anything irregular or abnormal.

a-non (*a* non´) *adv.* Soon; in a short period of time.

a-non-y-mous (*a* non´i mus) *adj.* An unknown or withheld name, agency, lacking a name. **anonymity** *n.*

a-no-rak (ä´no räk) *n.* Parka; a hooded jacket.

an-o-rex-i-a (an´o rek´se *a*) *n.* The loss of appetite that is accompanied by psychotic symptoms.

an-os-mi-a (an oz´mē *a*) *adj.* The loss or deficiency of the sense of smell.

an-oth-er (*a* nuth´ér) *adj.* Additional; one more different, but of the same character.

an-ox-i-a (an ok´sē ä) *n.* Lack of oxygen supply in the body tissue and the complications that result from this lack of oxygen.

an-swer (an´ser) *n.* A written or spoken reply, as to a question; a result or solution, as to a problem. **answer** *v.* To respond; to be responsible for.

an-tag-o-nism (an tag´o niz´um) *n.* Hostility; condition of being against; the feeling of unfriendliness toward.

an-tag-o-nize (an tag´o nīz´) *v.* To arouse hostility; to make an enemy of someone.

ant-arc-tic (ant ärk´tik) *n.* Large area of land completely covered with ice; the South Pole. **antarctic** *adj.*

antarctic circle *n.* An imaginary line parallel to the equator that encircles the antarctic area.

an-te-cede (an´ti sēd´) *v.* To go before; to precede in time.

an-te-ce-dent (an´ti sēd´ent) *adj.* One event that precedes another; previous.

an-te-date (an´ti dāt´) *v.* To precede in time; to give an earlier date than the actual date.

ante meridiem *n.* Time before noon, abbreviated as *a.m.*

an-ten-na (an ten´a) *n.* Feelers on the head of an insect, lobster, crab, etc.; wire or set of wires used in radio and television to send and receive signals.

an-te-ri-or (an tēr´ē or) *adj.* Toward or at the front; coming before; earlier.

an-them (an´them) *n.* Hymn of praise or loyalty; an official song of a country, school, etc.

an-ther (an´thèr) *n.* The part of the flower where the pollen is located at the end of a stamen.

an-thol-o-gy (an thol´o jē) *n.* A collection of stories, poems, or other writings.

an-thra-cite (an´thra sīt´) *n.* Coal with a high carbon content; hard coal.

an-thrax (an´thraks) *n.* The infectious, usually fatal disease found in animals such as cattle and sheep; disease that can be transmitted to man.

an-throp-ic (an throp´ik) *adj.* Relating to man, or to the period of mankind's existence on earth.

an-thro-po-cen-tric (an´thro pō sen´trik) *adj.* To interpret reality in terms of human experience and values.

an-ti (an´tī) *n.* One who opposes a group, policy, practice, or proposal.

an-ti-anx-i-ety (an´tī au´zī et ē) *adj.* Preventing or relieving anxiety.

an-ti-bi-ot-ic (an´tī bī ot´ik) *n.* A substance, as streptomycin or penicillin, effective in the destruction of microorganisms and used widely to prevent or treat diseases.

an-ti-bod-y (an´tī bod´ē) *n.* Substances generated in the blood that react to foreign proteins or carbohydrates, producing immunity against certain microorganisms or their toxins.

an-tic (an´tik) *n.* Mischievous caper or act.

an-tic-i-pate (an tis´i pāt) *v.* To look forward; to act in advance of; to foresee. **anticipatory** *adj.*

an-tic-i-pa-tion (an tis´i pā´shan) *n.* The act of looking forward; expectation of a future event.

an-ti-cli-max (an´tī klī´maks) *n.* A letdown or decline; a commonplace conclusion; a series of significant events followed by a trivial event.

an-ti-co-ag-u-lant (an´tē kō ag´ū lant) *n.* Any agent which hinders the coagulation of the blood.

an-ti-dote (an´ti dōt´) *n.* A substance that counteracts an injury or poison.

an-ti-gen (an´ti jen) *n.* Substance, when introduced into the body, stimulates the production of antibodies.

an-ti-his-ta-mine (an´ti his´ta mēn´) *n.* A drug used to relieve the symptoms of allergies and colds by interfering with the production of histamines.

an-ti-ox-i-dant (an´tē ok´si dant) *n.* A substance that inhibits oxidation.

an-ti-par-ti-cle (an´tē pär´ti kal) *n.*

Identically matched atomic particles, but with exactly opposite electrically charged magnetic properties and spin.

an-tip-a-thy (an tip´a thē) *n., pl.* **antipathies** Feeling of repugnance or opposition. **antipathetic** *adj.*

an-ti-per-spi-rant (an ti per´spe rent) *n.* Substance applied to the underarm to reduce excessive perspiration.

an-ti-phlo-gis-tic (an tē flō jis´tik) *n.* A medicine which counteracts inflammation.

an-ti-pode (an´ti pōd) *n.* A direct opposite. **antipodal** *adj.*

an-ti-pro-ton (an´tē prō´ton) *n.* The antiparticle of a proton.

an-ti-quar-y (an´ti kwer´ē) *n.* A person devoted to the study of rare relics.

an-ti-quate (an´ti kwāt´) *v.* To make old, obsolete or outdated by substituting something new or more practical.

an-ti-quat-ed (an´ti kwā´tid) *adj.* Obsolete; out of style; behind the times.

an-tique (an tēk´) *adj.* Belonging to or of ancient times. *n.* An object that is over 100 years old. **antique** *v.*

an-ti-sep-sis (an´ti sep´sis) *n.* Condition of being free from pathogenic bacteria.

an-ti-sep-tic (an´ti sep´tik) *adj.* Pertaining or capable of producing antisepsis; thoroughly clean.

an-tith-e-sis (an tith´i sis) *n., pl.* **antitheses** Direct opposition or contrast. **antithetical** *adj.*

an-ti-tox-ic (an´ti tok´sik) *adj.* Counteracting poisons or toxic influences.

an-ti-tox-in (an´ti tok´sin) *n.* An antibody formed in the body, capable of neutralizing a specific toxin or infective agent used to produce immunity against infectious diseases.

an-ti-trust (an´tē trust´) *adj.* Having to do with the regulation of trusts, monopolies, and cartels.

an-ti-tus-sive (an´ti tus´iv) *adj.* Capable of controlling or preventing a cough.

an-ti-ven-in (an´tē ven´in) *n.* An antitoxin to a venom, produced by repeated injections of such venom.

anti-virus *n.* In *computer science*, a program designed to detect unauthorized alteration of a computer program.

an-ti-viv-i-sec-tion-ist (an´tē viv i sek´shan ist) *n.* A person opposed to experiments on living animals.

an-to-nym (an´to nim) *n.* A word opposite in meaning to another word.

a-nus (ā´nus) *n.* The lower opening of the alimentary canal.

an-vil (an´vil) *n.* A heavy block of steel or iron on which metal is formed.

anx-i-e-ty (ang zī´i tē) *n.* A state of uncertainty; disturbance of the mind regarding uncertain events.

anx-ious (angk´shus) *adj.* Troubled in mind or worried about some uncertain matter or event. **anxiousness** *n.*

an-y (en´ē) *adj.* One; no matter which; some; every; any quantity or part.

an-y-bo-dy (en´ē bod´ē) *pron.* Anyone; any person.

an-y-how (en´ē hou´) *adv.* By any means; in any way; whatever.

an-y-more (en´ē mōr´) *adv.* At present and from now on.

an-y-one (en´ē wun´) *pron.* Any person; anybody.

an-y-place (en´ē plās´) *adv.* Anywhere.

an-y-thing (en´ē thing´) *pron.* Any occurrence, object or matter.

an-y-time (en ē tim) *adv.* At any time whatever.

an-y-way (en´ē wā´) *adv.* Nevertheless; anyhow; in any manner; carelessly.

an-y-where (en´ē hwâr´) *adv.* In, at, or to any place; to any degree or extent.

a-or-ta (ā or´ta) *n.* Main artery that carries blood away from the heart and distributes blood to all of the body except the lungs. **aortal** *adj.* **aortic** *adj.*

a-pace (a pās´) *adv.* At a rapid or quick pace.

a-part (a pärt´) *adv.* Separate; at a distance; in pieces; to pieces.

a-part-heid (a pärt´hāt) *n.* In the Republic of South Africa, an obsolete policy of discrimination and segregation against non-whites.

a-part-ment (a pärt´ment) *n.* A suite or room in a building equipped for individual living.

ap-a-thy (ap´a thē) *n.* The lack of emotions or feelings. **apathetic** *adj.*

ap-er-ture (ap´ėr chėr) *n.* An opening or open space; a mouth, hole, a passage.

a-pex (ā´peks) *n. pl.* **apexes** *or* **apices** The highest point; tip; top.

a-pha-sia (a fā´zha) *n.* Any partial or total loss of the ability to express ideas, resulting from brain damage. **aphasiac** *n.* **aphasic** *adj.* **aphasic** *n.*

a-phe-li-on (a fē´lē on) *n.* The point in an orbit farthest from the sun.

a-pho-ni-a (ā fō´nē a) *n.* A loss of voice to a whisper.

aph-o-rism (af´o riz´um) *n.* Brief statement of truth or principal.

a-pho-tic (ā fō´tik) *adj.* Without light.

aph-ro-dis-i-ac (af ro diz´ē ak´) *adj.* Increasing or arousing the sexual desire or potency.

a-pi-ar-y (ā´pē er´ē) *n.* Place where bees are kept and raised for their honey.

ap-i-cal (ap´i kal) *adj.* Relating to or formed with the tip of a tongue; belonging to the pointed end of a cone-shaped body.

a-pi-cul-ture (ā´pi kul´chėr) *n.* The keeping of bees; beekeeping.

a-piece (a pēs´) *adv.* For or to each one.

a-pla-sia (a plā´zha) *n.* Defective development of a tissue or organ.

a-plomb (*a* plom´) *n.* Assurance; poise; self-confidence.

a-poc-o-pe (*a* pok´*o* pē) *n.* The loss of the last of one or more sounds, letters, or syllables at the end of a word.

a-poc-ry-phal (*a* pok´ri fal) *adj.* False; of questionable authenticity.

ap-o-gee (ap´*o* jē) *n.* The point most distant from earth in the moon's orbit.

ap-o-graph (ap´*o* graf) *n.* A transcript or copy, as a manuscript.

a-pol-it-i-cal (ā po lit´i kal) *adj.* Having no interest in or involvement in politics.

a-pol-o-get-ic (*a* pol´*o* jet´ik) *adj.* Making an expression of apology. **apologetical** *adj.* **apologetically** *adv.*

a-pol-o-gist (*a* pol´*o* jist) *n.* A person who speaks in defense of a cause, faith or an institution.

a-pol-o-gize (*a* pol´*o* jīz´) *v.* To make an apology.

a-pol-o-gy (*a* pol´*o* jē) *n., pl.* **apologies** A statement expressing regret for an action or fault; a formal justification or defense.

a-poph-y-sis (*a* pof´i sis) *n.* An expanded or projecting part of a bone.

ap-o-plex-y (ap´*o* plek´sē) *n.* Sudden loss of muscular control, consciousness, and sensation resulting from a blockage of the blood vessel in the brain.

a-port (*a* pōrt´) *adv. Naut.* To the left side of a ship.

ap-o-si-o-pe-sis (ap´*o* sī*o* pē´sis) *n.* Sudden stopping short and leaving a thought or statement unfinished for the sake of effect.

a-pos-tate (*a* pos´tat) *n.* One who forsakes his faith or principles.

a-pos-ta-tize (*a* pos´ta tīz´) *v.* To abandon religious faith, principles, or party. **apostasy** *n.*

a-pos-te-ri-o-ri (ā´po stēr´ē ōr´ī) *adj.* Inductive; reasoning from facts to principles or from effect to cause.

a-pos-tro-phe (*a* pos´tro fē) *n.* The mark (´) used to indicate the removal of letters or figures, the plural of letters or figures, and the possessive case; the act of turning away; addressing the usually absent person or a usually personified thing rhetorically.

a-pos-tro-phize (*e*´pas tre fiz) *v.* To make use of apostrophe.

a-poth-e-car-y (*a* poth´e ker´ē) *n., pl.* **apothecaries** A person who prepares and sells drugs for medical uses; a druggist; pharmacist; drugstore.

a-po-the-ci-um (a´ po e thē shē em) *n.* A single-celled structure in many lichens and fungi that consists of a cupped body bearing asci on the exposed flat or concave surface.

ap-o-thegm (ap´*o* them´) *n.* A short, essential, and instructive formulation or saying. **apothegmatic** *adj.*

a-po-the-o-sis (*a* poth´ē ō´sis) *n.* The perfect example; the glorification of a person. **apotheosize** *v.*

ap-pall (*a* pol´) *v.* To overcome by shock or dismay; to overpower with fear; to become pale.

ap-pall-ing (*a* pol´ing) *adj.* Disgusting; dismay or disgust caused by an event or a circumstance. **appallingly** *adv.*

ap-pa-ra-tus (ap´*a* rat´us) *n., pl.* **apparatuses** Appliance or an instrument designed and used for a specific operation.

ap-par-el (*a* par´el) *v.* To dress or put on clothing; to adorn or embellish. **apparel** *n.* Clothing. *Naut.* The sails and rigging of a ship.

ap-par-ent (*a* par´ent) *adj.* Clear and opened to the eye and mind; open to view, visible. **apparently** *adv.*

ap-pa-ri-tion (ap´*a* rish´an) *n.* An unusual or unexpected appearance; the act of being visible; a ghostly figure.

ap-par-i-tor (*a* par´i tor) *n.* An official person sent to carry out the order of a judge, court, or magistrate.

ap-peal (*a* pēl´) *n.* Power to arouse a sympathetic response; an earnest plea; a legal proceeding where a case is brought from a lower court to a higher court for a rehearing. **appeal** *v.* To make a request; to ask another person for corroboration, vindication, or decision on matter of importance.

ap-pear (*a* pēr´) *v.* To come into existence; to come into public view; to come formally before an authorized person.

ap-pear-ance (*a* pēr´ans) *n.* The action or process of appearing; an outward indication of showing.

ap-pease (apēz´) *v.* To give peace; to cause to stop or subside; to calm; to pacify. **appeasement** *n.*

ap-pel-late (*a* pel´it) *adj.* Having the power to hear and review the decisions of the lower courts.

ap-pel-la-tion (ap´*e* lā´shan) *n.* Identifying by a name or title.

ap-pend (*a* pend´) *v.* To add an appendix or supplement, as to a book; to attach.

ap-pend-age (*a* pen´dij) *n.* Something added to something more important or larger; a subordinate or a dependent person.

ap-pen-di-ci-tis (*a* pen´di sī´tis) *n.* Inflammation of the vermiform appendix.

ap-pen-dix (*a* pen´diks) *n., pl.* **appendixes** Supplementary material usually found at the end of something that has been written; *Med.* A small hollow blind process; the vermiform appendix.

ap-per-ceive (ap´er sēv) *v.* To be conscious of perceiving; to have apperception of something.

ap-per-cep-tion (ap´ẽr sep´shan) n. The mental understanding of something perceived in terms of previous experience. **apperceptively** adv. **apperceptive** adj.

ap-per-tain (ap´ẽr tān´) v. To belong to or connect with, as a rightful part.

ap-pe-tence (ap´i tens) n. Appetite; a strong natural craving.

ap-pe-tite (ap´i tīt´) n. The craving or desire for food. **appetitive** adj.

ap-plaud (a plod´) v. To express or show approval by clapping the hands.

ap-plause (a ploz´) n. The expression of public approval. **applausive** adj.

ap-ple (ap´l) n. The round, red, yellow, or green edible fruit of a tree.

ap-pli-ance (a plī ans) n. A piece of equipment or device designed for a particular use.

ap-pli-ca-ble (ap´li ka bl) adj. Appropriate; suitable; capable of being applied.

ap-pli-cant (ap´li kant) n. A person who applies for a job or position.

ap-pli-ca-tion (ap li kā´shan) n. The act of putting something to use; the act of superimposing or administering; request or petition; in computer science, a program designed for a particular use, as a word processor or spreadsheet.

application generator n. In computer science, a program feature to assist in creating custom designed applications.

ap-pli-ca-tive (ap´li kā´tiv) adj. Practical; applied; having an application.

ap-pli-ca-tor (ap´li kā´tor) n. A device used to apply a substance.

ap-plied adj. Putting something to practical use to solve definite problems.

ap-ply (a plī´) v. To make a request using a written application; to put into use for a practical purpose or reason; to put into operation or to bring into action; to employ with close attention.

ap-point (a point´) v. To arrange something; to fix or set officially, designate. **appointed** adj.

ap-point-ment (a point´ment) n. The act of appointing; arrangement for a meeting; a nonelective position or office; an engagement or meeting.

ap-por-tion (a pōr´han) v. To divide and share according to a plan or agreement.

ap-pose (a pōz´) v. To place next to another; to put before. **apposable** adj.

ap-po-site (ap´o zit) adj. Highly appropriate or pertinent; applicable.

ap-po-si-tion (ap´o zish´an) n. A grammatical construction where a noun or noun phrase is followed by another; the explanatory equivalent.

ap-pos-i-tive (a poz´i tiv) adj. Relating to or standing in apposition.

ap-prais-al (a prā´z al) n. The evaluation of property by an authorized person.

ap-praise (a prāz´) v. To estimate the value, worth, or status of an item.

ap-prais-er (a prāz´ẽr) n. One who gives an expert judgment of the value of something.

ap-pre-ci-ate (a prē´shē āt´) v. To recognize the worth, quality, or significance; to value very highly; to be aware of; to realize; to increase in price or value. **appreciatory** adj.

ap-pre-ci-a-tion (a prē´shē ā´shan) n. The expression of admiration, gratitude, or approval; increase in value.

ap-pre-cia-tive (a prē´sha tiv) adj. Having or showing appreciation.

ap-pre-hend (ap´ri hend´) v. To anticipate with anxiety, dread or fear; to recognize the meaning of; to grasp; to understand.

ap-pren-tice (a pren´tis) n. One who is learning a trade, art, or occupation under a skilled worker for a prescribed period of time. **apprentice** v. To work under supervision of a skilled worker.

ap-pressed (a prest´) adj. Pressed close to or lying flat against.

ap-prise (a prīz´) v. To give notice, to inform in verbal or written form.

ap-proach (a prōch´) v. To come near to or draw closer; to be close in appearance. **approach** n. Access to or reaching something.

ap-pro-bate (ap´robāt´) v. To express approval, or satisfaction of; to approve.

ap-pro-ba-tion (ap´ro bā´shan) n. A formal approval.

ap-pro-pri-ate (a prō´prēāt´) v. To take possession of; to take without permission. **appropriate** adj. Suitable for a use or occasion; fitting. **appropriately** adv. **appropriator** n.

ap-pro-pri-a-tion (a prō´prē ā´shan) n. Money set apart for a particular use; the act or instance of appropriating.

ap-prov-able (a prōv´a bl) adj. Something or someone that is capable of being approved. **approvably** adv.

ap-prove (a prōv´) v. To regard or express a favorable opinion; to give formal or official approval.

ap-prox-i-mate (a prok´si māt´) adj. Located close together; almost accurate or exact. **approximate** v. To bring close or near to; approach; estimate; be nearly the same. **approximately** adv.

ap-prox-i-ma-tion (a prok´si mā´sh an) n. An approximate amount or estimate.

ap-pur-te-nance (a pür´te nans) n. Something that belongs with another more important thing.

ap-pur-te-nant (a pür´te nant) adj. Constituting a legal attachment; belonging.

a-prax-ia (a prak´sē a) n. Inability to execute complex coordinated movement. **apractic** adj. **apraxic** adj.

a-pri-cot (ap´ri kot´) n. An oval,

orange-colored fruit resembling the peach and plum in flavor, varying in color, normally a medium orange.

A-pril (ā'prĭl) *n.* The fourth month of the calendar year.

a-pri-o-ri (ā'prī ōr'ī) *adj.* Based on theory rather than personal experience; deductive.

a-pron (ā'prŏn) *n.* A garment used to protect clothing; paved area around an airport terminal building or hangar; waterfront edge of a wharf or pier.

ap-ro-pos (ap'rō pō') *adv.* At a good time; by the way; pertinent.

apse (aps) *n.* A semicircular or polygonal projection of a building or church.

apt (apt) *adj.* Unusually qualified or fitting; appropriate; having a tendency; suitable; quick to understand. **-ly** *adv.*

ap-ti-tude (ap'tǐ tŏŏd') *n.* A natural talent or ability; quickness in learning or understanding.

aq-ua (ak'wa) *n., pl.* **aquae** *or* **aquas** Water; aquamarine.

aq-ua-ma-rine (ak'wa ma rēn') *n.* A color of pale blue to light green; a mineral that is blue, blue-green, or green in color.

aq-ua pu-ra (ak'wa pŭ'ro) *n.* Pure water; distilled water.

aqua regia (ak'wa rē'jē a) *n.* Mixture of hydrochloric and nitric acids that dissolves platinum or gold.

a-quar-i-um (a kwâr'ē um) *n.* An artificial pond where living plants and aquatic animals are maintained.

a-quat-ic (a kwat'ik) *adj.* Anything occurring on or in the water.

aq-ua vi-tae (ak'wa vī'tē) *n.* A very strong liquor; alcohol.

aq-ue-duct (ak'wǐ dŭkt') *n.* A conduit for carrying a large quantity of flowing water; a bridge-like structure supporting a canal over a river.

aq-ue-ous (ā'kwē us) *adj.* Resembling water; dissolved in water; watery.

aqueous humor *n.* The clear fluid in the chamber of the eye between the cornea and lens.

aq-ui-cul-ture *or* **aq-ua-cul-ture** (ak'wǐ kul'chēr) *n.* Breeding fish or produce in natural water; hydroponics.

aq-ui-fer (ak'wǐ fĕr) *n.* The layer of underground gravel, sand, or rocks where water collects.

aq-ui-line (ak'wǐ līn') *adj.* Resembling or related to an eagle; hooked or curved like the beak on an eagle.

a-quiv-er (a kwiv er) *adj.* Trembling.

ar-a-besque (ar'a besk') *n.* An intricate style or design of interwoven leaves, flowers, and geometric forms.

ar-a-ble (ar'a bl) *adj.* Land that is suitable for cultivation by plowing.

a-rach-nid (a rak'nid) *n.* Arthropod that is usually air-breathing, having four

pairs of legs but no antennae; a mite, a spider or scorpions. **arachnid** *adj.*

a-rach-noid (arak'noid) *adj.* Having a covering of loose hair or fibers resembling a spider web.

a-ra-ne-id (a rā'nē id) *n.* A breed of spider.

ar-bi-ter (är'bi tĕr) *n.* A person chosen to decide a dispute, having absolute power of determining and judging.

ar-bi-tra-ble (är'bi tra bl) *adj.* Subject to arbitration.

ar-bi-trar-y (är'bi trer'ē) *adj.* Something based on whim or impulse. **arbitrarily** *adv.* **arbitrariness** *n.*

ar-bi-tra-tion (är'bi trā'shan) *n.* The hearing and determination of a case in controversy, by a person or persons chosen by the parties.

ar-bi-tra-tor (är'bi trā'tor) *n.* A person chosen to settle a dispute or controversy between parties.

ar-bor (är'bor) *n.* A garden shelter that is shady and covered with or made of climbing plants.

Arbor Day *n.* A day assigned as a day for planting trees.

ar-bo-re-al (är bōr'ē al) *adj.* Resembling or related to a tree; living in trees or among trees. **arboreally** *adv.*

ar-bo-re-ous (är bōr'ē us) *adj.* Living in a wooded area; an area surrounded by trees.

ar-bo-re-tum (är'bo rē'tum) *n.* A place for studying and exhibiting trees, shrubs, and plants cultivated for educational and for scientific purposes.

ar-bor-ist (är bo rest) *n.* A specialist in the maintenance and care of trees.

ar-bo-rize (är bo rīz) *v.* To branch repeatedly and freely.

ar-bo-vi-rus (är bo vī res) *n.* Various viruses transmitted by arthropods, including the causative agents for yellow fever and encephalitis.

arc (ärk) *n.* Something that is curved or arched; the luminous discharge of electric current across a gap between two electrodes.

ar-cade (är kad') *n.* An arched covered passageway supported by columns; a long arched gallery or building.

ar-cad-ed (är kād ed) *adj.* Furnished with arcades or arches.

ar-ca-dia (är kā'dē a) *n.* The ancient Greek area usually chosen as background for poetry; region of simple quiet and pleasure.

ar-cane (är kān') *adj.* Secret; hidden; obscure.

arch (ärch) *n.* A structure that spans over an open area and gives support. **archly** *adv.* **archness** *n.*

ar-chae-ol-o-gy (är'kē ol'o jē) *n.* Scientific study of ancient times and ancient peoples. **archaeological** *adj.*

ar-cha-ic (är kā´ik) *adj.* Something that belongs to an earlier time; any word characteristic of an earlier language, now used only in special cases.

ar-cha-ism (är´kē iz˝um) *n.* Something that is outdated or old-fashioned, as an expression or word. **archaistic** *adj.*

arch-er (är´chèr) *n.* A person who is trained in the uses or skill of the bow and arrow.

ar-cher-y (är´che rē) *n.* The practice or art of shooting with a bow and arrow; the equipment used by an archer.

ar-che-spore (är´ki spōer) *n.* A single cell or group of cells from which a mother spore is formed.

ar-che-type (är´ki tîp˝) *n.* An original from which other things are patterned.

arch-fiend (ärch´fēnd˝) *n.* A chief or principal fiend; a person of great wickedness, especially Satan.

ar-chi-pel-a-go (är´ki pel´a gō˝) *n.* Any water space scattered with many islands; a group of islands.

ar-chi-tect (är´ki tekt˝) *n.* A person who may plan, design, and supervise the construction of large structures.

ar-chi-tec-ture (är´ki tek chèr) *n.* The science of designing and building structures; a method or style of construction or building; in *computer science*, the design of a computer that defines such things as type of processor, speed, bus size, etc.

ar-chives (är´kīv) *n.* Public documents or records; the place where archives are kept. **archival** *adj.* **archivist** *n.*

arch-way (ärch´wā˝) *n.* A passage or way under an arch; an arch over a passage.

arc lamp *n.* Electric lamp which produces light when a current passes between two incandescent electrodes.

arc-tic (ärk´tik) *adj.* Extremely cold or frigid; relating to the territory north of the arctic circle. **arctic** *n.* A waterproof, ankle-length boot.

arctic circle *n.* Parallel of the latitude that is approximately 66.5 degrees north of the equator.

ar-dor (är´dèr) *n.* Extreme warmth or passion; emotion; intense heat.

ar-du-ous (är´jū us) *adj.* Taking much effort to bring forth; difficult.

are (är) *v.* First, second, and third person plural and second person singular of the verb "to be."

ar-e-a (âr´ē a) *n.* A flat or level piece of ground. **areal** *adj.*

ar-e-a code (â´ē a) *n.* The three digit number assigned to each telephone area in the United States, used to call.

ar-e-a-way (âr´ē a wā˝) *n.* A sunken space that offers access, light and air to a basement; a sunken area forming a passageway to a basement.

a-re-na (a rē´na) *n.* Enclosed area for public entertainment such as football.

ar-e-na-ceous (ar´e nā´shus) *adj.* Having the properties of sand.

aren't (ärnt) *contr.* Are not.

ar-gon (är´gon) *n.* A colorless, odorless, gaseous element found in the air and in volcanic gases and is used in electric bulbs and electron tubes.

ar-go-sy (är´go sē) *n., pl.* **argosies** A fleet of ships; a large merchant ship.

ar-got (är´gō) *n.* An often secret, specialized vocabulary.

ar-gu-a-ble (är´gū a bl) *adj.* Open to argument; questionable. **arguably** *adv.*

ar-gue (är´gū) *v.* To debate, to offer reason for or against a subject; to dispute, argue, or quarrel; to persuade or influence, to debate over an opinion. **argument** *n.* **arguer** *n.*

ar-gu-men-ta-tive (är´gya men´ta tiv) *adj.* Given to argument; debating or disputing.

a-ri-a (är´ē a) *n.* A vocal piece with accompaniment sung in solo; part of an opera.

a-ri-bo-fla-vin-o-sis (ā´rī bo flā´vi nō´sis) *n. Med.* A vitamin deficiency, in which the mucous membrane of the mouth becomes irritated and some discoloration of the tongue may occur.

ar-id (ar´id) *adj.* Insufficient rain; dry; lacking in interest or feeling; dull.

ar-il (ar´il) *n.* The extra covering of the seed of some plants, such as the nutmeg.

a-rise (a rīz´) *v.* To come from a source; to come to attention; to come into view; to mount; to move to a higher place; to get out of bed.

a-ris-ta (a ris´ta) *n, pl.* **aristae** *or* **aristas** Bristle-like appendage or structure.

ar-is-toc-ra-cy (ar´i stok´ra sē) *n.* A government by select individuals or by a small privileged class; class or group viewed as superior; the hereditary privileged ruling nobility.

a-rith-me-tic (a rith´me tik) *adj.* Branch of math that deals with addition, subtraction, multiplication, division. **arithmetic** *adj.* **arithmetically** *adv.*

arithmetic mean *n.* The number received by dividing the sum of a set of quantities by the number of quantities in the set.

arithmetic progression *n.* A progression in which the difference between any term and the one before or after is constant, as 2,4,6,8, etc.

Arizona *n.* A state located in the southwestern part of the United States, statehood February 14, 1912, capital Phoenix.

Arkansas *n.* A state located in the south-central part of the United States, statehood June 15, 1836, capital Little Rock.

arm (ärm) *n.* The part between the shoulder and the wrist; upper limb of the human body. **arm** *v.* To furnish with protection against danger.

ar-ma-da (är mä′da) *n.* A fleet of warships; a large force of moving things.

Ar-ma-ged-don (är′ma ged′on) *n.* A final battle between the forces of good and evil.

ar-ma-ment (är′ma ment) *n.* Military supplies and weapons; the process of preparing for battle.

ar-ma-ture (är′ma chèr) *n.* The main moving part of an electric device or machine; a piece of soft iron that connects the poles of a magnet.

arm-ful (ärm′fel′) *n. pl.* **armfuls** or **arms-ful** As much as the arm can hold.

arm-hole (ärm′hol′) *n.* The opening in a garment for the arm.

ar-mi-stice (är′mi stis) *n.* The temporary suspension of combat by mutual agreement; truce.

Armistice Day *n.* November 11, 1918 ending of World War I; name of day changed to Veterans Day in 1954.

ar-moire (ärm wär) *n.* A large wardrobe.

ar-mor (är′mor) *n.* Covering used in combat to protect the body, made from a heavy metal. **armor** *v.* **armored** *adj.*

ar-mor-er (är′mor èr) *n.* A person who makes armor; one who assembles, repairs, and tests firearms.

ar-mor-y (är′mo rē) *n, pl.* **armories** The supply of arms for attack or defense; the place where military equipment is stored.

ar-o-mat-ic (ar′o mat′ik) *adj.* Fragrant; giving out an aroma; sweet-scented; pleasant scent.

arm-pit (ärm′pit′) *n.* Hollow area under the arm where it joins the shoulder.

ar-my (är′mē) *n. pl.* **armies** A group of persons organized for a country's protection; the land forces of a country.

a-ro-ma (a rō′ma) *n.* A distinctive fragrance or pleasant odor, fragrance. **aromatical** *adj.* **aromatic** *adj.*

a-round (a round′) *adv. & prep.* To or on all sides; in succession or rotation; from one place to another; in a circle or circular movement.

a-rouse (a rouz′) *v.* To wake up from a sleep; to stir; to excite. **arousal** *n.*

ar-raign (a rān′) *v.* To call before a court to answer a charge or indictment; to accuse of imperfection, inadequacy, or of wrongdoing. **arraignment** *n.*

ar-range (a ränj′) *v.* To put in correct sequence; to prepare for something; to take steps to organize something; to bring about an agreement; to change a musical composition for different instruments or voices.

ar-range-ment (a ränj′ment) *n.* The state

or being arranged; something made by arranging things or parts together.

ar-rant (ar′ant) *adj.* Extreme; being notoriously without moderation.

ar-ras (ar′as) *n.* A screen or wall hanging of tapestry.

ar-ray (a rā′) *v.* To place or set in order; to draw up; to decorate or dress in an impressive attire. **arrayer** *n.*

ar-rears (a rēr′) *n.* The state of being behind something, as an obligation, payment, etc.; an unfinished duty.

ar-rest (a rest′) *n.* To stop or to bring an end to; to capture; to seize; to hold in custody by the authority of law.

ar-rest-ing (a res′ting) *adj.* Very impressive or striking; catching the attention. **arrestingly** *adv.*

ar-rhyth-mi-a (a rith′mē a) *n.* The alteration in rhythm of the heartbeat, either in force or time.

ar-rhyth-mic (a rith′mik) *adj.* Lacking regularity or rhythm.

ar-ris (ar′is) *n.* The line where two meeting surfaces of a body form an angle, as in moldings.

ar-riv-al (a rī′val) *n.* The act of arriving.

ar-rive (a rīv′) *v.* To reach or get to a destination.

ar-ro-gance (ar′o gans) *n.* An overbearing manner, intolerable presumption; an insolent pride.

ar-ro-gant (ar′o gant) *adj.* Overbearing manner; proud and assuming, self-important. **arrogantly** *adv.*

ar-ro-gate (ar′o gāt′) *v.* To demand unduly or presumptuously.

ar-row (ar′o) *n.* A weapon shot from a bow; a sign or mark to show direction.

ar-row-head (ar′ō hed′) *n.* The striking end of an arrow, shaped like a wedge.

ar-row-root (ar′ō rōt′) *n.* A starch-yielding plant of tropical America.

ar-roy-o (a roi′ō) *n.* The dry bed of a stream or creek; a gully or channel.

ar-se-nal (är′se nal) *n.* A collection of weapons; a place where arms and military equipment are manufactured or stored.

ar-se-nic (är′se nik) *n.* A solid, poisonous element, steel-gray in color, used to make insecticide or weed killer. **arsenic** *adj.* **arsenical** *adj.*

ar-son (är′son) *n.* The fraudulent burning of property. **arsonist** *n.* **arsonous** *adj.*

art (ärt) *n.* A human skill of expression of other objects by painting, drawing, sculpture, etc.; a branch of learning.

ar-te-ri-al (är tēr′ē al) *adj.* Having to do with an artery or the oxygenated blood contained in the arteries.

ar-te-ri-og-ra-phy (är tēr′ē og′ra fē) *n.* The visualization of an artery or arterial system after the injection of a radiopaque substance.

ar-te-ri-ole (är tēr′ē ōl′) *n.* One of the

small terminal twigs of an artery that
ends in capillaries.

**ar-te-ri-o-scle-ro-sis (är tēr˝ē ō sklė
rō´sis)** *n.* A disease that causes the
thickening of arterial walls and
impedes circulation of the blood.

ar-ter-y (är´te rē) *n. pl.* arteries A blood
vessel that carries blood from the heart
to the other parts of the body; a major
means for transportation. **arterial** *adj.*

ar-te-sian (är tē´zhun) *adj.* Referring
to a well dug by perpendicular boring
into the ground, at great depths, which
allows water to rise to the surface of
the soil by subterranean pressure.

art-ful (ärt´fel) *adj.* Showing or
performed with skill or art; devious;
cunning. **artfully** *adv.* **artfulness** *n.*

ar-thral-gia (är thral´je) *n.* Pain that
occurs in one or more joints.

ar-thrit-ic (är thrit´ik) *n.* A person who
has arthritis. **arthritic** *adj.*

ar-thri-tis (är thrī´tis) *n.* Inflammation
of body joints.

ar-thro-pod (är´thro pod´) *n.* An animal
with jointed limbs and a segmented
body, as a spider. **arthropodal** *adj.*
arthropodan *adj.* **arthropodous** *adj.*

Arthur, Chester A. *n.* (1829-1886) The
twenty-first president of the United
States from 1881-1885.

ar-ti-ad (är´tē ad´) *n.* An element with
an even atomic number.

ar-ti-cle (är´ti kal) *n.* A term or clause
in a contract; a paragraph or section;
a condition or rule; an object or item.

ar-tic-u-lar (är tik´yu lėr) *adj.* Related
to or of a joint.

ar-tic-u-late (är tik´yu lit) *adj.* Able to
express oneself clearly, effectively,
or readily; speaking in distinct words,
or syllables. **articulate** *v.*

ar-ti-fact (är´ti fakt´) *n.* Something made
by man showing human modification
or workmanship.

ar-ti-fice (är´ti fis) *n.* An artful or clever
skill; ingenuity.

ar-ti-fi-cial (är´ti fish´al) *adj.* Not
genuine; made by man; not found in
nature. **artificially** *adv.*

artificial horizon *n.* The aeronautical
indicator of an airplane designed to
give a surface that is constantly
perpendicular to the vertical and
therefore is parallel to the horizon.

artificial language In *computer science*,
a programming language with a distinct
set of rules and vocabulary.

artificial respiration *n.* A method by
which air is rhythmically forced into
and out of the lungs of a person whose
breathing has ceased.

ar-ti-san (är´ti zan) *n.* A person skilled
in any art or trade.

art-ist (är´tist) *n.* A person who practices
the fine arts of painting, sculpture, etc.

ar-tis-tic (är tis´ik) *adj.* Relating to the
characteristic of an artist or art.

art-ist-ry (är´ti strē) *n.* The artistic
ability or quality of workmanship.

art-less (ärt´lis) *adj.* Lacking knowledge,
art, or skill; crude; natural; simple.

as (az) *adv.* In the manner like; of the
same degree or amount; similar to.

as-bes-tos (as bes´tus) *n.* A non-
combustible, fibrous, mineral form of
magnesium silicate that is used in
insulating and fireproofing.

as-cend (a send´) *v.* To rise up from a
lower level; to climb; to mount; to walk
up. **ascendible** *adj.* **ascendable** *adj.*

as-cen-dant or **as-cen-dent (a sen´dant)**
adj. Rising; moving up.

as-cent (a sent´) *n.* A way up; a slope;
the act of rising.

as-cer-tain (as˝ėr tān´) *v.* To find out
for certain; to make sure, confirm.
ascertainment *n.* **ascertainable** *adj.*

as-cet-ic (a set´ik) *n.* One who retires
from the world and practices strict self-
denial as spiritual discipline; hermit.

as-cet-i-cism (a set´i siz˝um) *n.* The
practice of strict self-denial through
personal and spiritual discipline.

ASCII *abbr.* American Standard Code
for Information Interchange; in
computer science, a standard code for
representing characters in the computer.

ascorbic acid *n.* The anti-scurvy vitamin
present in citrus fruits, tomatoes, and
green vegetables; vitamin C.

as-cot (as´kot) *n.* A scarf or broad tie that
is placed under the chin.

as-cribe (a skrīb´) *v.* To assign or
attribute to something. **ascribable** *adj.*

a-sep-tic (a sep´tik) *adj.* Free or freed
from septic material.

a-sex-u-al (ā sek´shō al) *adj.* Lacking
sexual reproductive organs; without
sex. **asexuality** *n.*

ash (ash) *n.* A type of tree with a hard,
tough elastic wood; the grayish dust
remaining after something has burned.

a-shamed (a shämd´) *adj.* Feeling guilt,
disgrace, or shame; feeling unworthy
or inferior. **ashamedly** *adv.*

a-shore (a shōr´) *adv.* On or to the shore.

a-side (a sīd´) *adv.* Out of the way; to
a side; to one side; something that is
said in an undertone and not meant to
be heard by someone.

ask (ask) *v.* To request; to require or seek
information. **asker** *n.*

a-skance (a skans´) *adv.* With a side
glance; with suspicion or distrust.

a-skew (a skū´) *adv. & adj.* Out of line,
not straight.

a-slant (a slänt´) *adv.* In a slanting
direction.

a-sleep (a slēp´) *adj. & adv.* In a state
of sleep; lacking sensation; not alert.

a-so-cial (ā sō´shal) *adj.* Selfish, not

social; withdrawn.

as-par-a-gus (a spar'a gus) n. A vegetable with tender shoots, very succulent when cooked.

as-pect (as'pekt) n. The situation, position, view, or appearance of something.

aspect ratio n. The ratio of one dimension to another.

as-per-i-ty (a sper'i tē) n., pl. asperities Roughness in manner.

as-per-sion (a sper'zhan) v. False charges or slander; defamation; maligning.

as-phalt (as folt) n. A sticky, thick, blackish mixture of petroleum tar used in paving roads and roofing buildings.

as-phyx-ia (as fik'sē a) n. Lack of oxygen or an excess of carbon dioxide in the system.

as-phyx-i-ate (as fik'sē at') v. To suffocate, to prevent from breathing; choking. **asphyxiation** n.

as-pi-rate (as'pi rāt') v. To give pronunciation with a full breathing sound; to draw out using suction.

as-pire (a spīr') v. To desire with ambition; to strive towards something higher. **aspiringly** adv. **aspirer** n

as-pi-rin (as'pi rin) n. Medication used for the relief of pain and fever.

ass (as) n. A hoofed animal; a donkey; a stupid or foolish person.

as-sail (a sāl') v. To attack violently with words or blows. **assailant** n.

as-sas-sin (a sas'in) n. Murderer, especially one that murders a politically important person either for fanatical motives or for hire.

as-sas-si-nate (a sas'i nāt') v. To murder a prominent person by secret or sudden attack. **assassination** n.

as-sault (a solt') n. A very violent physical or verbal attack on a person.

as-say (a sā') n. To evaluate or to assess; to try; to attempt. **assayer** n.

as-sem-blage (a sem'blij) n. A collection of things or people; artistic composition made from junk and scraps.

as-sem-ble (a sem'bl) v. To put together the parts of something; to come together as a group. **assembly** n.

assembler In *computer science*, a program that translates a programming language into instructions that are understood directly by the computer.

assembly line n. The arrangement of workers, machines, and equipment which allows work to pass from operation to operation in the correct order until the product is assembled.

as-sent (a sent') v. To agree on something. **assenter** n.

as-sert (a sert') v. To declare or state positively, to maintain; to defend.

as-ser-tion (a ser'shan) n. Maintaining claim; the act of affirming.

as-sess (a ses') v. To fix or assign a value to something. **assessor** n.

as-set (as'et) n. A valuable quality or possession; all of the property of a business or a person that can be used to cover liabilities.

as-sid-u-ous (a sij'ö us) adj. Devoted; constant in application; attentive.

as-sign (a sīn') v. To designate as to duty; to give or allot; to attribute; to transfer.

as-sign-ee (a sī nē') n. The person appointed to act for another; the person to whom property or the right to something is legally transferred.

as-sign-ment (a sīn'ment) n. A given amount of work or task to undertake; a post, position, or office to which one is assigned.

as-sim-i-late (a sim'i lāt') v. To take in, to understand; to make similar; to digest or to absorb into the system.

as-sist (a sist') v. To give support, to aid, to give help. **assistant**, **assistance** n.

as-size (a sīz') n. A fixed or customary standard.

as-so-ci-ate (a sō'shē it) v. To connect or join together. n. A partner, colleague, or companion.

as-so-ci-a-tion (a sō'sē ā'shan) n. An organized body of people having a common interest; a society.

as-so-nance (as'o nans) n. The repetition of sound in words or syllables; using the same vowel sound with different consonants. **assonant** adj.

as-sort (a sort') v. To distribute into groups of a classification or kind.

as-sort-ed (a sort'id) adj. Made up of different or various kinds.

as-sort-ment (a sort'ment) n. The act or state of being assorted; a collection of different things.

as-suage (a swäj') v. To quiet, pacify; to put an end to by satisfying.

as-sume (a söm') v. To take upon oneself to complete a job or duty; to take responsibility for; to take for granted.

as-sum-ing (a söm'ing) adj. Putting on airs of superiority, overbearing.

as-sump-tion (a sump shan) n. An idea believed to be true without proof.

as-sur-ance (a sher'ans) n. A statement made to inspire confidence of mind or manner; freedom from uncertainty or self-doubt; self-reliance.

as-sure (a sher') v. To give the feeling of confidence; to make sure or certain.

as-sured (a sherd') adj. Satisfied as to the truth or certainty. **assuredly** adv.

as-sur-er (a sher'ér) n. A person who gives assurance.

as-sur-gent (a ser'jent) adj. Moving or directed upward.

as-ter-isk (as'te risk) n. The character (*) used to indicate letters omitted or as a reference to a footnote.

a-stern (*a* stern´) *adv. & adj.* Toward the rear or back of an aircraft or ship.

as-ter-oid (as´te roid´) *n.* One of thousands of small planets that orbit the sun.

asth-ma (az´ma) *n.* A respiratory disease marked by labored breathing, wheezing, and coughing. **asthmatic** *adj.*

as though *conj.* As if.

a-stig-ma-tism (*a* stig´ma tiz´um) *n.* A defect of the lens of an eye resulting in blurred or imperfect images.

as to *prep.* With reference to or regard to; concerning; according to.

as-ton-ish (*a* ston´ish) *v.* To strike with sudden fear, wonder, or surprise.

as-ton-ish-ment (*a* ston´ish ment) *n.* The state of being amazed or astonished.

as-tound (*a* stound´) *v.* To fill with wonder and bewilderment, amazement. **astounding** *adj.* **astoundingly** *adv.*

as-tral (as´tral) *adj.* Resembling or related to the stars.

a-stray (*a* strā´) *adv.* Away from a proper path or development.

a-stride (*a* strīd´) *prep.* One leg on either side of something; placed or lying on both sides of; extending across or over.

as-trin-gent (*a* strin´jent) *adj.* Able to draw together or to constrict tissues.

as-tro-dome (as´tro dōm´) *n.* A large stadium covered by a dome.

as-trol-o-gy (*a* strol´o jē) *n.* The study of the supposed influences of the planets and stars and their movements and positions on human affairs.

as-tro-naut (as´tro not´) *n.* A person who travels in a spacecraft beyond the earth's atmosphere.

as-tute (*a* stöt´) *adj.* Sharp in discernment; very shrewd; cunning; keen.

a-sun-der (*a* sun´dér) *adv.* Separate into parts or positions apart from each other.

a-sy-lum (*a* sī´lum) *n.* A refuge or institution for the care of the needy or sick; a place of security and retreat.

a-sym-met-ric (ā´sí me´trik) *adj.* Something that is not symmetrical.

a-syn-de-ton (*a* sin´di ton´) *n.* A figure of speech with conjunctions omitted.

at (at) *prep.* To indicate presence, occurrence, or condition; used to indicate time, action, etc.

a-the-ism (ā´thē iz´um) *n.* The disbelief that God exists. **atheist** *n.*

ath-lete (ath´lēt) *n.* A person who participates in exercise or in sports.

a-thwart (*a* thwort´) *adv.* Opposition to the expected or right; from one side to another.

a-tilt (*a* tilt´) *adj. & adv.* Inclined upward or tilted in some way.

at-las (at´las) *n.* A collection or book of maps.

ATM *abbr.* Automatic Teller Machine; a banking terminal that allows a customer to deposit or withdraw money by inserting a card and entering a private number code.

at-mos-phere (at´mos fēr´) *n.* A gaseous mass that surrounds a celestial body, as the earth; a predominant mood.

at-om (at´om) *n.* A tiny particle, the smallest unit of an element.

a-tone (*a* tōn´) *v.* To give satisfaction; to make amends.

a-tone-ment (*a* tōn´ment) *n.* Amends for an injury or a wrong doing; the reconciliation between God and man for sins.

a-tri-um (ā´trē um) *n.* One of the heart chambers; the main hall of a hotel or large house. **atrial** *adj.*

a-tro-cious (*a* trō´shus) *adj.* Extremely cruel or evil, horrible. **atrociously** *adv.*

a-troc-i-ty (*a* tros´i tē) *n. pl.* **atrocities** The condition of being atrocious; horrible; an inhuman, atrocious act.

a-tro-phy (a´trō fē) *v.* To decrease in size; to waste away.

at-tach (*a* tach´) *v.* To bring together; to fasten or become fastened; to bind by personal attachments; to tie together.

at-tack (*a* tak´) *v.* To threaten with force, to assault; to work on with vigor.

at-tain (*a* tān´) *v.* To arrive at or reach a goal, to accomplish; to achieve or obtain by effort. **attainable** *adj.*

at-taint (*a* tānt´) *v.* To disgrace or stain; to find guilty of a crime.

at-tar (at´ar) *n.* The fragrant oil from flowers.

at-tempt (*a* tempt´) *v.* To make an effort to do something. **attempt** *n.*

at-tend (*a* tend´) *v.* To be present; to take charge of or to look after.

at-ten-tion (*a* ten´shan) *n.* Observation, notice, or mental concentration.

at-ten-tive (*a* ten´tiv) *adj.* Observant; paying or giving attention. **attentively** *adv.* **attentiveness** *n.*

at-ten-u-ate (*a* ten´ū āt´´) *v.* To lessen the force, amount or value; to make fine or thin. **attenuation** *n.*

at-test (*a* test´) *v.* To give testimony or to sign one's name as a witness; to declare as truth. **attestation** *n.*

at-ti-tude (at´töd´´) *n.* Mental position; the feeling one has for oneself.

at-tor-ney (*a* ter´nē) *n.* A person with legal training who is appointed by another to transact business for him.

at-tract (*a* trakt´) *v.* To draw by appeal; to cause to draw near by appealing qualities.

at-trac-tion (*a* trak´shan) *n.* The capability of attracting; something that attracts or is meant to attract.

at-trac-tive (*a* trak´tiv) *adj.* Having the power of charming, or quality of attracting. **attractively** *adv.*

at-trib-ute (*a* trib´yöt) *v.* To explain by

showing a cause.

at-trib-ute (*á* trib yūt) *n.* A characteristic of a thing or person. In *computer science*, a characteristic, as of a file that is read-only, archived or hidden.

at-tri-tion (*a* trish´an) *n.* Wearing down by friction; a rubbing against.

at-tune (*a* tūn´) *v.* To bring something into harmony; to put in tune; to adjust.

a-typ-i-cal (ā tip´*i* kal) *adj.* Not conforming to the typical type; different than the usual. **atypically** *adv.*

auc-tion (ok´shan) *n.* A public sale of merchandise to the highest bidder.

au-da-cious (aw dā´shus) *adj.* Bold, daring, or fearless; insolent.

au-di-ble (aw´*di*bl) *adj.* Capable of being heard.

au-di-ence (aw´dē ens) *n.* A group of spectators or listeners; the opportunity to express views; a formal hearing.

au-di-o (aw´dē ō´) *adj.* Of or relating to sound or its high-fidelity reproduction.

au-dit (aw´dit) *n.* Verification or examination of financial accounts or records.

au-di-to-ri-um (aw´di tōr´ē um) *n.* A large room that holds many people.

au-di-to-ry (aw´di tor e) *adj.* Related to the organs or sense of hearing.

aught (awt) *n.* Zero (0).

aug-ment (awg ment´) *v.* To add to or increase; to enlarge; in *computer science*, to expand capabilities, as by increasing speed or memory size.

au jus (ō zhōs´) *adj.* Served in the juices obtained from roasting.

au-ra (or´a) *n.* An emanation said to come from a person's body.

au-ral (or´al) *adj.* Relating to the ear or the sense of hearing. **aurally** *adv.*

au-re-ole (or´ē ōl´) *n.* A halo.

au re-voir (ō´ re vwär´) *interj.* Farewell; goodbye until we meet again.

au-ri-cle (or´i kal) *n.* One of the two upper chambers of the heart; the internal ear.

au-ric-u-lar (o rik´yu lèr) *adj.* Relating to the sense of hearing or of being in the shape of the ear.

au-ric-u-late (o rik´yu lit) *adj.* Shaped like the ear; having ears or some kind of extentions resembling ears.

aus-cul-ta-tion (o´skul tā´shan) *n.* The act of listening to sounds of the internal parts of the body, particularly the chest.

aus-pi-cious (*a* spish´us) *adj.* Indicating success or a favorable outcome.

aus-tere (o stēr´) *adj.* Stern in manner and appearance. **austerity** *n.*

aus-tral (o´stral) *adj.* Southern.

au-then-tic (o then´tik) *adj.* Real; genuine; worthy of acceptance.

au-then-ti-cate (o then´ti kāt´) *v.* To prove something is true or genuine; real; not an imitation. **authenticity** *n.*

au-thor (a´thor) *n.* A person who writes an original literary work. **author** *v.*

au-thor-i-tar-i-an (*a* thor´i târ´ē *an*) *adj.* Demanding blind submission and unquestioned obedience to authority.

au-thor-i-ty (*a* thor´i tē) *n. pl.* **authorities** A group or person with power; a government; an expert.

au-thor-i-za-tion (o´ thor i zā´shan) *n.* The act of authorizing something.

au-thor-ize (o´ tho rīz´) *v.* To give authority, to approve, to justify.

au-tism (o´tiz´um) *n.* Absorption in a self-centered mental state, such as fantasies, daydreams or hallucinations in order to escape from reality.

au-to-bi-og-ra-phy (o´to bī og´ra fē) *n., pl.* **autobiographies** The life story of a person, written by that person.

au-toc-ra-cy (o tok´ra sē) *n.* Government by one person who has unlimited power. **autocrat** *n.* **autocratic** *adj.*

au-to-graph (o´to graf) *n.* A handwritten signature.

au-to-mate (o´to māt´) *v.* To operate by automation; to convert something to automation, to automatize.

au-to-mat-ic (o´to mat´ik) *adj.* Operating with very little control; self-regulating.

automatic backup *n.* In *computer science*, a program that creates a backup copy of files at a set time.

automatic link *n.* In *computer science*, a connection between objects so that the update of one instances will change all occurrences.

automatic load *n.* In *computer science*, a program that is brought on line by a predetermined signal, as of a timer.

au-to-ma-tion (o´to mā´shan) *n.* The equipment and techniques used to make a process or system automatic.

autonomic nervous system *n.* The part of the body's nervous system which is regulated involuntarily.

au-ton-o-mous (o ton´o mus) *adj.* Self-governing; subject to its own laws.

au-ton-o-my (o ton´o mē) *n.* Independence, self-government.

au-top-sy (o´top so) *n., pl.* **autopsies** Postmortem examination; the examination of a body after death to find the cause of death. **autopsic** *adj.*

au-tumn (o´tum) *n.* The season between summer and winter. **autumnal** *adj.*

aux-il-ia-ry (og zil´ya rē) *adj.* Providing help or assistance to someone; giving support.

auxiliary verb *n.* A verb that accompanies a main verb and expresses the mood, voice, or tense.

a-vail (*a* vāl´) *v.* To be of advantage or use; to use. **avail** *n.* The advantage toward attaining a purpose or goal.

a-vail-a-bil-i-ty (*a* vā´la bil´i tē) *n.* The state of being available.

a-vail-a-ble (*a* vā´la bl) *adj.* Ready or present for immediate use; accessible. **availably** *adv.* **availableness** *adj.*

available resources *n.* In *computer science*, all of the processing capacity, memory, storage and peripherals that remains for use after discounting those occupied by primary processing.

a-vant-garde (*a* vänt´gärd´) *n.* The people who apply and invent new ideas and styles in a certain field.

av-a-rice (av´ar is) *n.* One's desire to have wealth and riches.

av-a-ri-cious (av´a rish us) *adj.* Miserly.

a-vast (*a* vast´) *interj. Naut.* A command to stop or cease.

a-ve (ä´vä) *interj.* Farewell; hail.

a-venge (*a* venj´) *v.* To take revenge for something; to vindicate by inflicting pain. **avenger** *n.*

a-ver (*a* ver´) *v.* To be firm and to state positively.

av-er-age (av´êr ij) *n.* Something that is typical or usual, not being exceptional; common.

a-verse (*a* vers´) *adj.* Having a feeling of distaste or repugnance.

a-vert (*a* vert´) *v.* To prevent or keep from happening; to turn aside or away from; to direct away.

a-vi-a-tion (ä´vē ā´shan) *n.* The operation of planes and other aircraft; design and manufacture of planes. **aviator** *n.*

a-vi-cul-ture (ā´vi kul´chur) *n.* Raising and breeding of birds.

av-id (av´id) *adj.* Greedy; eager; enthusiastic. **avidly** *adv.*

a-vi-fau-na (ā´vi fo na) *n.* A name for the birds of a certain period or region.

av-o-ca-tion (av´o kā´ shan) *n.* A pleasurable activity that is in addition to regular work a person must do.

a-void (*a* void´) *v.* To stay away from; to shun; to prevent or keep from happening; to elude. **avoidably** *adv.*

a-void-a-ble (*a* void´*a* bl) *adj.* That which can be avoided; able to get away.

a-void-ance (*a* void´ans) *n.* The act of making something void.

a-vouch (*a* vouch´) *v.* To assert; to guarantee; to vouch for; to admit.

a-vow (*a* vou´) *v.* To state openly on a subject; to confess; to own up to.

a-vow-al (*a* vou´al) *n.* Open declaration; acknowledge frankly.

a-vowed (*a* voud) *adj.* Acknowledged.

a-wait (*a* wāt´) *v.* To wait for something; to expect; to be ready.

a-wake (*a* wāk´) *v.* To wake up; to be alert or watchful.

a-wak-en (*a* wā´ken) *v.* To awake or rouse from sleep.

a-ward (*a* word´) *v.* To give or confer as being deserved, needed, or merited. *n.* A judgment or decision; a prize.

a-ware (*a* wâr´) *adj.* Being conscious or mindful of something; informed.

a-way (*a* wā´) *adv.* At a distance; to another place; apart from.

awe (o) *n.* A feeling of wonder mixed with reverence. **awe** *v.*

a-wea-ry (*a* wē´rē) *adj.* Tired; weary.

a-weigh (*a* wā´) *adj.* To hang just clear of the ground, said of a ship's anchor.

awe-some (o´sum) *adj.* Expressive of awe. **awesomeness** *n.* **awesomely** *adv.*

awe-strick-en (o´strik´en)*adj.* Impressed with awe.

aw-ful (o´ful) *adj.* Very unpleasant or dreadful. **awfully** *adv.*

aw-ful-ness (o´ful nis) *n.* The state or quality of being awful.

a-while (a hwīl´) *adv.* For a short time.

a-whirl (a hwerl´) *adj.* To spin around.

awk-ward (ok´ward) *adj.* Not graceful; clumsy; to cause embarrassment.

awl (ol) *n.* Tool used to make holes in leather.

awn (on) *n.* The part of a piece a grass which resembles a bristle. **awned** *adj.*

awn-ing (o´ning) *n.* Structure that serves as a shelter over a window.

a-wry (*a* rī´) *adj. & adv.* In a twisted or turned position.

ax *or* **axe** (aks) *n.* A tool with a steel head attached to a wooden handle.

ax-il-la (ak sil´a) *n.* The armpit; the area under a bird's wing.

ax-il-lar (ak´si lar) *n.* The underwing, weaker feathers of a bird.

ax-il-lar-y (ak´si ler´ē) *adj.* Growing from the axil of something as a plant.

ax-i-om (ak´sē um) *n.* Statement recognized as being true; something assumed to be true without proof.

ax-i-o-mat-icadj.Obvious; self-evident.

ax-is (ak´sis) *n., pl.* **axes** The line around which an object rotates or may be thought to rotate.

ax-le (ak´sel) *n.* A spindle or shaft around which a wheel or pair of wheels revolve.

ax-le-tree (ak´sel trē´) *n.* A bar which a wheel turns upon.

ax-on (ak´son) *n.* A single, long, nerve cell that carries transmitted nerve impulses away from the body of a cell.

aye (ī) *interj.* Yes, a sound of affirmation; indeed. **aye** *n.* An affirmative vote.

az-i-muth (az´i muth) *n.* Usually recognized as an angle, in air navigation is measured clockwise from the magnetic or true north.

a-zo-ic (*a* zō´ik) *adj.* Time period which occurred before life first appeared on the earth.

az-oth (az´oth) *n.* Mercury, the assumed first principle of all known metals.

AZT *abbr.* Azidothymidine; a drug that relieves the symptoms of AIDS.

az-ure (azh´ur) *n.* The blue color of the sky.

B, b (bē) *n*. The second letter of the English alphabet; a student's grade rating of good, but not excellent.

ba-ba (bä bä) *n*. A rich cake soaked in infant.

ba-bel (bā´bel) *n*. Babbling noise of many people talking at the same time.

ba-biche (*ba* bēsh´) *n*. A thong or lacing made from animal skin; rawhide.

ba-boon (*ba* bön´) *n*. A species of the monkey family with a large body and big canine teeth.

ba-bu (bä´bö) *n*. A Hindu gentleman.

ba-bul (*be* ´bül) *n*. An acacia tree in northern Africa and Asia which yields gum arabic as well as fodder and timber.

ba-bush-ka (*ba* besh´ka) *n*. A kerchief folded into a triangle and worn as a covering on the head.

ba-by (bā´bē) *n., pl.* **babies** A young child; infant. **babyish** *adj*.

baby's breath *n*. A tall herb bearing numerous small, fragrant, white or pink flowers.

baby–sit (bā bē sit) *v*. To assume the responsibility and care for a child or children during the absence of the parents.

bac-ca-lau-re-ate (bak´*a* lor´ē it) *n*. A degree given by universities and colleges; an address given to a graduating class.

bac-ca-rat (bak *e* ´rä bak) *n*. A game of cards played by any number of players betting against a banker.

bac-cha-nal (bak *e* nal) *adj*. Reveling in or characterized by intemperate drinking; riotous; noisy.

bac-cha-na-lia (bak´ *a* nā´lē *a*) *n*. A Roman festival celebrated with dancing and song.

bach (bach) *v. Slang* To live by oneself as does a baohclor.

bach-e-lor (bach´*e* lor) *n*. An unmarried male; the first degree one can receive from a four year university.

ba-cil-lus (ba sil´us) *n., pl,* **bacilli** A rod-like microscopic organism which can cause certain diseases.

bac-i-tra-cin (bas´i trā´sin) *n*. An antibiotic used topically against cocci.

back (bak) *n*. The rear part of the human body from the neck to the end of the spine, also the rear part of an animal; a position in the game of football, in which the player lines up behind the front line of players; the final nine holes of an 18-hole golf course.

back-ward (bak´ward) *adv*. Toward the back; to or at the back; in a reverse order. **backwards** *adv*.

bac-te-ri-cide (bak tēr´i sīd[´) *n*. A substance that kills bacteria.

bac-te-ri-ol-o-gy (bak tēr´ē ol´ *o* jē) *n*. Scientific study of bacteria and its relationship to medicine, etc.

bac-te-ri-o-phage (bak tēr´ē o fāj´) *n*. Any of a group of viruses commonly found in sewage or body products.

bac-te-ri-ol-y-sis (bak tēr´ē o stä´sis) *n*. The process of dissolution or destruction of bacteria.

bac-te-ri-um (bak tēr´ē um) *n., pl.* **bacteria** Any of various forms of numerous unicellular microorganisms that cause disease, some of which are used in industrial work. **bacterial** *adj*.

bad (bad) *adj*. Naughty or disobedient; unfavorable; inferior; poor; spoiled; invalid. **badly** *adv*. **badness** *n*.

badge (baj) *n*. An emblem worn for identification.

badg-er (baj´ēr) *n*. A sturdy burrowing mammal. **badger** *v*. To trouble persistently.

bad-lands (bad´landz¯) *n. pl.* Area with sparse life, peaks, and eroded ridges.

bad-min-ton (bad´min ton) *n*. A court game played with long-handled rackets and a shuttlecock.

baf-fle (baf´fl) *v*. To puzzle; to perplex. **baffle** *n*. A device that checks or regulates the flow of gas, sound, or liquids.

bag (bag) *n*. A flexible container used for holding, storing, or carrying something; a square white canvas container used to mark bases in baseball. **bagful** *n*.

ba-gasse (*ba* gas´) *n*. Plant residue.

bag-a-telle (bag´*a* tel´) *n*. A game played with a cue and balls on an oblong table.

ba-gel (bā´gel) *n*. A hard, glazed, round roll with a chewy texture and a hole in the middle.

bag-gage (bag´ij) *n*. The personal belongings of a traveler.

bag-gy (bag´ē) *adj*. Loose. **baggily** *adv*.

bail-iff (bā´lif) *n*. The officer who guards prisoners and keeps order in a courtroom

bait (bāt) *v*. To lure; to entice. **bait** *n*. Food that is used to catch or trap an animal.

baize (bāz) *n*. A coarse woolen or cotton cloth.

bake (bāk) *v*. To cook in an oven; to harden or dry. **baker** *n*. **baked** adj.

bak-sheesh (bak´shēsh) *n*. A tip or gratuity.

bal-a-lai-ka (bal´*a* lī ka) *n*. A three-stringed musical instrument.

bal-ance (bal´ans) *n*. Device for determining the weight of something; the agreement of totals in the debit and credit records of an account

bal-co-ny (bal´ko nē) *n., pl.* **balconies** Gallery or platform projecting from the wall of a building.

bald (bold) *adj*. Lacking hair on the head. **baldish** *adj*. **baldness** *n*.

bal-da-chin (bal′da kin) *n.* An embroidered fabric of silk and gold used to carry over an important person or sacred object.

bald eagle *n.* The eagle of North America that is dark when young, but has a white head and neck feathers when mature.

bal-der-dash (bol′der dash′) *n.* Nonsense.

bal-dric (bol drik) *n.* A broad belt, stretching from the right or left shoulder diagonally across the body, either as an ornament or to suspend a sword or horn.

bale (bāl) *n.* A large, bound package or bundle.

ba-leen (ba lēn′) *n.* A whalebone.

bale-fire (bāel fier)*n.* A signal fire; an alarm fire.

bale-ful (bāel fel) *adj.* Destructive; deadly; foreboding.

balk (bok) *v.* To refuse to go on; to stop short of something. *n.* A rafter or crossbeam extending from wall to wall. **balky** *adj.*

bal-kan-ize (bol ke nīz) *v.* To partition, as an area, into various small, politically ineffective divisions.

ball (bol) *n.* A round body or mass; a pitched baseball that is delivered outside of the strike zone.

bal-lad (bal′ad) *n.* A narrative story or poem of folk origin; a romantic song.

bal-lade (bol läd′) *n.* A verse form consisting of three stanzas with recurrent rhymes and a refrain for each part.

bal-lad-eer (bal e di er) n. A person who sings ballads.

bal-last (bal′ast) *n.* Heavy material placed in a vehicle to give stability and weight.

ball bearing *n.* A bearing that reduces friction by separating the stationary parts from the moving ones.

bal-le-ri-na (bal′e rē′na) *n.* A female ballet dancer in a company.

bal-let (ba lā′) *n.* An artistic expression of dance by choreographic design.

ballistic missile *n.* A projectile that is self-powered, guided during ascent, and has a free-fall trajectory at descent.

bal-lis-tics (ba lis′tiks) *n.* The science of motion in flight; the firing characteristics of a firearm.

bal-lo-net (bal′o net′) *n.* A compartment within the interior of a balloon or airship to control ascent and descent.

bal-loon (ba lön′) *n.* A bag inflated with gas lighter than air which allows it to float in the atmosphere, often having a basket or compartment for carrying passengers; a bag made of rubber that is used as a child's toy.

bal-lot (bal′ot) *n.* A slip of paper used in secret voting. *v.* To vote by ballot.

bal-lotte-ment (be lät ment) *n.* A method of diagnosing pregnancy, in which a sudden shock is imparted to the fetus, as through the uterine wall, causing it to move suddenly.

ball-park (bol pärk) *n.* A stadium where ball games are played.

ball-point (bol′point′) *n.* A pen that has a small self-inking writing point.

bal-ly-hoo (bal′ē hö′) *n.* Exaggerated advertising.

balm (bäm) *n.* A fragrant ointment that soothes, comforts, and heals.

bal-ne-ol-o-gy (bal nē äl e jē) *n.* The study of the effects of baths employed in therapy.

ba-lo-ney (ba lō′nē) *n., Slang* Nonsense.

bal-sa (bol′sa) *n.* American tree whose wood is very light in weight.

bal-sam (bol′sam) *n.* A fragrant ointment from different trees; a plant cultivated for its colorful flowers.

bal-us-ter (bal′u stėr) *n.* The upright post that supports a handrail.

bal-us-trade (bal e sträd) *n.* A row of small columns or balusters, joined by a rail, serving as an enclosure for altars, balconies, staircases, and terraces.

bam-boo (bam bö′) *n.* Tropical, tall grass with hollow, pointed stems.

bam-boo-zle (bam bö′zl) *v.* To trick or deceive.

ban (ban) *v.* To prohibit; to forbid.

ba-nal (bān′al) *adj.* Trite; lacking freshness.

ba-nan-a (ba nan′a) *n.* The crescent-shaped usually yellow, edible fruit of a tropical plant.

band (band) *n.* A strip used to trim, finish, encircle, or bind; the range of a radio wave length; a group of musicians who join together to play their instruments.

band-age (ban′dij) *n.* A strip of cloth used to protect an injury. **bandage** *v.*

ban-dan-na (ban dan′a) *n.* A brightly colored cotton or silk handkerchief.

ban-deau (ban dō′) *n.* A narrow band worn in the hair; a narrow brassiere.

ban-dit (ban′dit) *n. pl.* bandits, banditti A gangster or robber. **banditry** *n.*

band-mas-ter (band master) *n.* The conductor and trainer of a band or musicians.

ban-do-leer (ban′do lēr′) *n.* A belt worn over the shoulder with pockets for cartridges.

ban-dore (ban dōr′) *n.* A three-stringed instrument resembling a guitar.

band-stand (band′stand′) *n.* A raised platform on which an orchestra or band perform.

ban-dy (ban′dē) *adj.* Bent; crooked; curved outward. **bandy** *v.*

bane (bān) *n.* A cause of destruction or

ruin. **baneful** adj. **banefully** adv.

bang (bang) n. A sudden loud noise; short hair cut across the forehead. **bang** v. To move or hit with a loud noise

ban-gle (bang´gel) n. A bracelet worn around the wrist or ankle.

ban-ish (ban´ish) v. To leave; to drive away; to remove from the mind; to condemn to exile. **banishment** n.

ban-is-ter (ban´i stèr) n. The upright supports of a handrail on a staircase; a handrail.

ban-jo (ban´jō) n. A stringed instrument similar to a guitar. **banjoist** n.

bank (bangk) n. A slope of land adjoining water; an establishment that performs financial transactions.

bank-rupt (bangk´rupt) n. A person who is legally insolvent and whose remaining property is divided among creditors. **bankrupt** v.

ban-ner (ban´ér) n. A piece of cloth, such as a flag, that is used as a standard by a commander or monarch. adj. Outstanding.

ban-nock (ban´ak) n. Unleavened or flat cake made from barley or oatmeal.

banns (banz) n. The announcement of a forthcoming marriage.

ban-quet (bang´kwit) n. An elaborate dinner or feast.

ban-shee (ban´shē) n. A spirit in folklore whose appearance warns a family of approaching death of a member.

ban-ter (bant´er) v. To attack with jokes or jests; to make fun of.

ban-yan (ban´yan) n. A tree from the tropics whose aerial roots grow downward to form additional roots.

bap-tism (bap´tizem) n. A Christian sacrament of spiritual rebirth through the application of water.

bap-tize (bap tīz´) v. To immerse or sprinkle with water during baptism. **baptizer** n.

bar (bär) n. A rigid piece of material used as a support; a barrier or obstacle; a counter where a person can receive drinks. **bar** v. To prohibit or exclude.

barb (bärb) n. A sharp projection that extends backward making it difficult to remove; a breed of horses from Africa noted for their speed and endurance. **barbed** adj.

bar-bar-i-an (bär bâr´ē an) n. A person or culture thought to be primitive and therefore inferior. **barbarous** adj.

bar-be-cue (bär´be kū´) n. An outdoor

bar-bel (bär bel) n. A freshwater fish having four beardlike appendages on its upper jaw.

bar-bell (bär´bel´) n. A bar with weights at both ends, used for exercise.

bar-ber (bär´bér) n. A person whose business is cutting and dressing hair and also shaving and trimming beards.

bar-bette (bär bet´) n. A cylinder protecting a gun turret on a warship.

bar-bi-tal (bär´bi tal´) n. A white hypnotic administered in the form of sodium salt.

bar-bi-tu-rate (bär bich´e ret) n. A derivative of barbituric acid.

bar-ca-role (bär´ka rōl´) n. A Venetian boat song with a strong and weak beat which suggests a rowing rhythm.

bard (bärd) n. A poet; a piece of armor for a horse's neck. **bardic** adj.

bare (bär) adj. Exposed to view; without coloring. **bare** v. **bareness** n.

bare-back (bär´bak´) adv. & adj. Riding a horse without a saddle.

bare-foot (bär fùt) adj. With the feet bare; without shoes or stockings.

ba-rege (be´rezh) n. A sheer fabric for women's clothing.

bare-ly (bär´lē) adv. Sparsely; by a very little amount.

barf (bärf) v. Slang To vomit.

bar-gain (bär´gin) n. A contract or agreement on the purchase or sale of an item; a purchase made at a favorable or good price. **bargain** n. To negotiate over a price of something that is being sold or bought. **bargainer** n.

barge (bärj) n. A flat-bottomed boat. **barge** v. To intrude abruptly.

barge-board (bärj´bôrd´) n. A board which conceals roof timbers that project over gables.

barg-ee (bär´jē) n. One of the crew of a barge or canal boat.

barge-man (bärj´man) n. A deckhand of a barge.

bar graph n. A graphic representation of statistics by means of bars of various, proportionate lengths.

bar-i-tone (bar´i tōn´) n. A male voice in the range between tenor and bass.

bark (bärk) n. The outer protective covering of a tree; the abrupt, harsh sound made by a dog. **bark** v.

bar-ken-tine (bär´ken tēn´) n. A three-masted ship with fore-and-aft rigging.

bar-ker (bär´ker) n. A person in the circus who stands at the entrance and advertises the show.

bar-ley (bär´lē) n. A type of grain used for food and for making whiskey and beer.

bar-low (bär lō) n. A sturdy jackknife.

barm (bärm) n. A yeast which forms on fermenting malt liquors.

bar mitzvah n. A Jewish boy who, having reached the age of 13, assumes the moral and religious duties of an adult; the ceremony that recognizes a boy as a bar mitzvah.

barn (bärn) n. A farm building used to shelter animals and to store farm equipment and products.

bar-na-cle (bär´na kl) n. A fish with a

hard shell that remains attached to an underwater surface.

ba-rom-et-er (ba rom´i tèr) *n.* An instrument that records the weight and pressure of the atmosphere.

bar-on (bar´on) *n.* The lowest rank of nobility in Great Britain. **baroness** *n.*

ba-rong (ba rong´) *n.* A thin-edged knife or sword.

ba-roque (ba rōk´) *adj.* An artistic style characterized by elaborate and ornate forms.

bar-o-tal-gi-a *n.* An ailment of the middle ear resulting from high altitude flying without a pressurized cabin.

ba-rouche (ba rösh´) *n.* A four-wheeled carriage.

bar-rack (bar´ak) *n.* A building for housing soldiers.

bar-ra-cu-da (bar´a kö´da) *n. pl.* **barracuda, barracudas** A fish with a large, narrow body, found in the Atlantic Ocean.

bar-rage (bär´ij) *n.* A concentrated outpouring or discharge of missiles from small arms; an artificial dam to increase the depth of water for use in irrigation or navigation.

bar-ra-tor (bar et er) *n.* One who frequently incites suits at law; an encourager of litigation.

bar-ra-try (bar´a trē) *n.* The unlawful breach of duty by a ship's crew that results in injury to the ship's owner.

barre (bär) *n.* A waist-high bar attached to the walls of a ballet school, used for body support while practicing.

bar-rel (bar´el) *n.* Wooden container with round, flat ends of equal size and sides that bulge.

bar-ren (bar´en) *adj.* Lacking vegetation; sterile.

bar-rette (ba ret´) *n.* A clasp or small bar used to hold hair in place.

bar-ri-cade (bar´i kād´) *n.* Barrier; to stop up, or block off, by a barricade.

bar-ri-er (bar´ē èr) *n.* A structure that restricts or bars entrance.

barrier reef *n.* A coral reef parallel to shore separated by a lagoon.

bar-room (bär´röm´) *n.* A building or room where a person can purchase alcoholic beverages sold at a counter.

bar-row (bar´ō) *n.* A rectangular, flat frame with handles; a wheelbarrow.

bar-tend-er (bär´ten´dèr) *n.* A person who serves alcoholic drinks and other refreshments at a bar.

bar-ter (bär´tèr) *v.* To trade something for something else without the exchange of money; one commodity for another. **bartering, bartered** *v.*

bar-ti-zan (bär´ti zan) *n.* A small structure serving as a lookout.

bar-y-on (bar ē än) *n.* Any of the heavier subatomic particles having

masses greater than a neutron.

basal metabolism *n.* The amount of energy required by a person to maintain minimum vital functions.

ba-salt (bo solt´) *n.* A greenish-black volcanic rock.

base (bās) *n.* The fundamental part; the point from which something begins; headquarters; the lowest part; the bottom. **base** *v.* basely *adv.*

base-ball (bās´bol´) *n.* A game played with a ball and bat; the ball used in a baseball game.

base-ment (bās´ment) *n.* The foundation of a building or home.

base pay *n.* Wages as determined by the amount earned during a given work period exclusive of bonuses, overtime, or other compensation.

base rate *n.* The rate of pay for a stated output or period of labor.

bash (bash) *v.* To smash with a heavy blow; *Slang* A party. **bash** *v.*

bash-ful (bash´ful) *adj.* Socially shy. self-conscious. **bashfully** *adv.*

ba-sic (bā´sik) *adj.* Forming the basis; fundamental. **basically** *adv.*

BASIC *n., Computer Science* A common computer programming language. (Beginner's All-purpose Symbolic Instruction Code.)

ba-sic-i-ty (bā ´sis et ē) *n.* The power of an acid to unite with one or more atoms of a base.

basic skills *n.* A term used in education to denote those skills in any given field which must be acquired as fundamental to further learning.

ba-si-fy (bā se fī) *v.* To cause to become alkaline.

bas-il (baz´il) *n.* An herb used as seasoning in cooking.

bas-i-lisk (bas´i lisk) *n.* A tropical American lizard.

ba-sin (bā´sin) *n.* A sink; a washbowl; a round open container used for washing; an area that has been drained by a river system.

ba-sis (bā´sis) *n., pl.* **bases** The main part; foundation.

bask (bask) *v.* To relax in the warmth of the sun.

bas-ket (bas´kit) *n.* An object made of woven material, as straw, cane, or other flexible items.

bas-ket-ball (bas´kit bol) *n.* A game played on a court with two teams; each team trying to throw the ball through the basketball hoop at the opponents' end of the court.

bas mitzvah *n.* A Jewish girl who, having reached the age of 13, assumes the moral and religious duties of an adult.

ba-so-phil (bā se fil) *n.* A tissue or cell having a natural inclination for basic stains.

bas–re-lief (bä ri lēf) *n.* A mode of sculpturing figures on a flat surface, the figures being raised above the surface.

bass (bas) *n.*, *pl.* **basses** A freshwater fish, one of the perch family.

bass drum *n.* A large drum with a low booming sound.

bass fiddle *n.* The largest, lowest-pitched of the stringed musical instruments.

bass horn *n.* A tuba.

bas-si-net (bas´a net´) *n.* A basket on legs used as an infant's crib; a basket made of wicker with a covering or hood over one end, used as an infant's bed.

bas-soon (ba sön´) *n.* A woodwind instrument with a low-pitched sound.

bast (bast) *n.* The inner bark of exogenous trees, consisting of several layers of fibers.

baste (bāst) *v.* To run a loose stitch to hold a piece of material in place for a short time; to moisten meat while cooking it by pouring on liquids.

bas-tille (ba stēl´) *n.* A tower in France used as a jail.

bas-ti-na-do (bas te nā´ō) *n.* A beating with a stick or cudgel; a mode of punishment in oriental countries.

bast-ing (bā sting) *n.* The long stitches by which pieces of garments are temporarily sewn to each other.

bat (bat) *n.* A wooden stick made from strong wood; a nocturnal flying mammal. **batter** *n.*

batch (bach) *n.* A group of work entered on a computer at one time; a quantity (as of cook-ies, etc.) baked at one time.

bate (bāt) *v.* To abate, lessen, or reduce; to diminish.

ba-teau (ba tō) *n.* A light, broad, and flat-bottomed boat.

batement light *n.* A section of a window having vertical sides and a curved or inclined bottom.

bat-fowl-ing (bat faul-ing) *n.* A mode of catching birds at night by means of a light and nets.

bath (bath) *n.*, *pl.* **baths** The act of washing the body.

bathe (bāth) *v.* To take a bath.

bath-house (bath haus) *n.* A house or building fitted up for bathing; a structure, as at the seaside, serving as a dressing room for bathers; a building for bathing equipped with medical facilities.

ba-thom-e-ter (ba thom´i tér) *n.* An instrument which is used to measure the depth of water.

bath-y-scaphe (bath´i skäf´) *n.* A submersible ship for deep sea exploration.

bath-y-sphere (bath´i sfier) *n.* A diving sphere used for observation of deep sea life.

ba-tik (ba tēk´) *n.* A method of dying fabric, in which parts not to be dyed are coated with wax.

ba-tiste (ba tēst´) *n.* A sheer, soft fabric.

bat-on (be ´tän) *n.* The wand used by a conductor for beating time; the stick used by a band's drum major.

bat-tal-ion (be´tal´yon) *n.* A body of troops; a large group of any kind.

bat-tery (bat´e rē) *n.* A group of heavy guns.

bat-ting (bat´ing) *n.* Cotton wool in rolls or sheets, used as stuffing or lining.

bat-tle (bat´l) *n.* A struggle; combat between opposing forces. **battle** *v.* To engage in a war or battle.

baux-ite (bok sīt) *n.* A mineral consisting essentially of a hydrated aluminum oxide, used as a source of alum and aluminum.

bawd (bod) *n.* A prostitute. **bawdy** *adj.*

bawl (bol) *v.* To cry very loudly.

bay (bā) *n.* The inlet of a body of water; a main division or compartment; an animal that is reddish brown in color.

ba-ya-dere (bī e dif er) *adj.* Stripes on fabrics, running crosswise.

bay antler *n.* The second branch from the base of a stag's horn.

bay-ber-ry (bā´ber´ē) *n.* Evergreen shrub used for decorations and making candles.

bay leaf *n.* The leaf of the bay tree, dried for use as a flavoring in cooking.

bay-o-net (bā´e nit) *n.* A spear-like weapon.

bay-ou (bī´ō) *n.* An arm or outlet of a lake, river.

bay rum *n.* A fragrant liquid from the leaves of the bayberry used in cosmetics and medicine.

bay salt *n.* Coarse-grained salt, especially that obtained by evaporation of seawater.

ba-zaar (ba zär´) *n.* A fair where a variety of items are sold as a money making project for charity, clubs, churches, or other such organizations.

be (hē) *v.* To occupy a position; to exist; used with the present participle of a verb to show action; used as a prefix to construct compound words, as behind, before, because, etc.

beach (bēch) *n.* Pebbly or sandy shore of a lake, ocean, sea, or river.

beach-comb-er (bēch kōmer) *n.* One who earns a living by collecting redeemable wreckage along ocean beaches; a beach-front vagrant.

bea-con (bē´kan) *n.* A coastal guiding or signaling device.

bead (bēd) *n.* A small round piece of material with a hole for threading. **bead** *v.* To adorn with beads. **beading** *n.*

bead-roll (bēd rōl) *n.* A list of persons for whom prayers are to be said.

bead-work (bēd werk) *n*. Ornamental work made with beads.

bea-gle (bē´gl) *n*. A small breed of hunting dog with short legs.

beak (bēk) *n*. The bill of a bird; resembling a beak. **beaked** *adj*.

beak-er (bē´ker) *n*. Large, wide-mouthed cup for drinking; a cylindrical, glass laboratory vessel with a lip for pouring.

beak-i-ron (bēk īern) *n*. The horn or tapering end of an anvil.

beam (bēm) *n*. Large, oblong piece of wood or metal used in construction. **beam** *v*. To shine.

bean (bēn) *n*. An edible seed or seed pod.

bean caper *n*. A small tree growing in warm climates, the flower buds of which are used as capers.

bean curd *n*. A soft vegetable cheese usually found in the Orient.

bear (bâr) *n*. A shaggy, carnivorous mammal. *Slang* A rough or gruff person. **bear** *v*. To endure; to carry; to support. **bearable** *adj*. **bearer** *n*.

bear-cat (bâr´kat) *n*. A panda.

beard (bērd) *n*. Hair growing on the chin and cheeks. **bearded** *adj*.

beast (bēst) *n*. A four-legged animal. *Slang* A brutal person. **beastly** *adj*.

beast of burden *n*. An animal used to perform heavy work and transport heavy materials.

beat (bēt) *v*. To strike repeatedly; to defeat. *adj*. Exhausted, very tired; fatigue. **beat, beater** *n*.

beat-en (bēt´n) *adj*. Made smooth by beating or treading; worn by use; conquered; vanquished.

be-a-tif-ic (bē´a tif´ik) *adj*. Giving or showing extreme bliss or joy.

be-at-i-tude (bē at´i tūd´) *n*. The highest form of happiness; heavenly bliss.

beat-nik (bēt´nik) *n*. A person who lives a nonconformist life; a member of the beat generation.

beau (bō) *n*. Sweetheart; dandy.

beau monde *n*. People of distinguished family, wealth, fame and fashion.

beau-ti-cian (bū tish´an) *n*. One whose business is to improve the appearance of a person's hair, nails, and complexion.

beau-ti-fi-ca-tion (bū´ti fi kā´shon) *n*. The act of beautifying or rendering beautiful; decoration; adornment; embellishment.

beau-ti-ful (būti ful) *adj*. Having the qualities that constitute beauty; highly pleasing to the eye, the ear, or the mind.

beau-ty (bū´tē) *n*. Quality that is pleasing to the eye. **beautifully** *adv*.

beaux arts *n*. The fine arts, as painting and sculpture.

bea-ver (bē´vēr) *n*. A large semiaquatic rodent with webbed feet and flat tail which yields valuable fur for coats, hats, etc.

be-bop (bē´bop´) *n*. *Slang* Jazz music.

be-calm (bē kām´) *v*. To make quiet or calm. **becalming** *v*.

be-cause (bē koz´) *conj*. For a reason; since.

because of *prep*. On account of; as a result of.

bech-a-mel (bā´sha mel´) *n*. A white sauce, seasoned occasionally with onion and nutmeg.

beck (bek) *n*. A summons; a call.

beck-et (bek´it) *n*. A loop for holding something in place.

beck-on (bek´n) *v*. To summon someone with a nod or wave.

be-cloud (bē koud´) *v*. To darken; to obscure; to cause confusion about.

be-come (bē kum´) *v*. To come to be, or to grow. **becoming** *adj*.

be-com-ing (bē kuming) *adj*. Suitable; proper; appropriate; befitting.

bed (bed) *n*. Furniture for sleeping; a piece of planted or cultivated ground. **bedding** *n*. **bed** *v*.

be-daub (bē daub´) *v*. To daub over; to soil with anything thick, slimy, and dirty.

bed-fast (bed´fast´) *adj*. Confined to a bed; bed-ridden.

bed-lam (bed´lam) *n*. A state or situation of confusion.

bee (bē) *n*. A hairy-bodied insect characterized by structures for gathering pollen and nectar from flowers.

beech (bēch) *n*. A tree of light-colored bark, with edible nuts.

beef (bēf) *n., pl.* beefs *or* beeves A cow, steer, or bull that has been fattened for consumption of its meat. **beefy** *adj*.

beef cattle *n*. Cattle raised for food.

beep (bēp) *n*. A warning sound coming from a horn.

beer (bēr) *n*. An alcoholic beverage.

bees-wax (bēz´waks) *n*. The wax from bees that is used for their honeycombs.

beet (bēt) *n*. The root from a cultivated plant that can be used as a vegetable or a source of sugar.

bee-tle (bēt´l) *n*. An insect with modified, horny front wings, which cover the membranous back wings when it is at rest.

be-fall (bi fol´) *v*. To happen or occur to.

be-fit (bi fit´) *v*. To be suitable; appropriate. **befitting** *adj*.

be-fool (bi fōl´) *v*. To make a fool of; to deceive.

be-fore (bi fōr´) *adv*. Earlier; previously. **before** *prep*. In front of.

be-fore-hand (bi fōr´hand´) *adv*. At a time prior to; in advance.

be-foul (bi foul´) *v*. To soil.

be-friend (bi frend´) *v*. To be a friend to someone.

beg (beg) v. To make a living by asking for charity. **beggar** n. **beggarly** adj.

be-gan (bi gan) v. The past tense of begin.

be-get (bi get´) v. To cause or produce; to cause to exist.

be-gin (bi gin´) v. To start; to come into being; to commence. **beginner** n. **beginning** n.

be-gone (bi gon´) interj. Command to go away.

be-go-nia (bi gōn´ya) n. A tropical plant with waxy flowers and showy leaves.

be-grime (bi grīm´) v. To make dirty; to soil with grime.

be-grudge (bi gruj´) v. To envy someone's possessions or enjoyment.

be-guile (bi gīl´) v. To deceive; to delight; to charm.

be-guine (bi gēn´) n. A popular dance of the Caribbean which resembles the rumba.

be-gum (bē´gum) n. A Muslim woman.

be-gun (bi gun) v. The past participle of begin.

be-half (bi haf´) n. The support or interest of another person.

be-have (bi hāv´) v. To function in a certain manner; to conduct oneself in a proper manner.

be-hav-ior (bi hāv´yė) n. Manner of behaving or acting; conduct. **behaviorism** n.

be-head (bi hed´) v. To remove the head from the body; to decapitate.

be-held v. Past participle of behold.

be-hind (bi hīnd´) adv. To or at the back; late or slow in arriving.

be-hold (bi hōld´) v. To look at; to see.

be-hoove (bi hōv´) v. To benefit or give advantage.

beige (bāzh) n. & adj. A light brownish, grey color.

being (bē´ing) n. One's existence.

be-jew-el (bi jö´el) v. To adorn with jewels.

be-la-bor (bi lā´bėr) v. To work on or to discuss beyond the point where it is necessary, to carry to absurd lengths.

be-lat-ed (bi lā´ted) adj. Tardy; late, delayed. **belatedly** adv.

bel canto (bel´ kan tō) n. Operatic singing with rich lyricism and brilliant vocal means.

belch (belch) v. To expel stomach gas through the mouth.

be-lea-guer (bi lē´gėr) v. To surround with an army as to preclude escape; to blockade; to harass.

bel-fry (bel´frē) n., pl. belfries The tower that contains the bell of a church.

be-lief (bi lēf´) n. Something that is trusted or believed.

be-lieve (bi lēv´) v. To accept as true or real; to hold onto religious beliefs. **believable** adj. **believer** n.

be-lit-tle (bi lit´l) v. To think or speak in a slighting manner of someone or something.

bell (bel) n. A metal instrument that gives a ringing sound when struck.

bel-lig-er-ent (be lij´ėr ent) adj. Hostile and inclined to be aggressive. **belligerence, belligerent** n.

bel-low (bel´ō) v. To make a deep, powerful roar like a bull. **bellow** n. **bellowing** adj.

bel-lows (bel´ōz) n. An instrument that produces air in a chamber and expels it through a short tube.

be-long (bi long´) v. To be a part of. **belonging** n.

be-loved (bi luv´id) adj. To be dearly loved.

be-low (bi lō´) adv. At a lower level or place below. prep. To be inferior to.

belt (belt) n. A band worn around the waist; a zone or region that is distinctive in a special way.

belt-way (belt´wā) n. A highway that encircles an urban area.

be-lu-ga (be lö´ga) n. A large white sturgeon whose roe is used to make caviar.

be-moan (bi mōn´) v. To moan or mourn for.

be-muse (bi mūz´) v. To bewilder or confuse; to be lost in thought. -ed adj.

bench (bench) n. A long seat for more than two people; the seat of the judge in a court of law.

bench-er (ben´chėr) n. A person who sits on a bench as a judge or a member of Parliament.

bend (bend) v. To arch; to change the direct course; to deflect. **bending** v.

bends (bendz) n. pl. Stomach and chest pains caused by the reduction of air pressure in the lungs, the result of rising too quickly from deep ocean levels.

beneath (bi nēth´) adv. To be in a lower position; below; underneath.

ben-e-dict (ben´i dikt) n. A previously confirmed bachelor who was recently married.

ben-e-dic-tion (ben´i dik´shan) n. A blessing given at the end of a religious service.

ben-e-fac-tion (ben´e fak´shan) n. A charitable donation; a gift.

ben-e-fice (ben´e fis) n. Fixed capital assets of a church that provide a living.

be-nef-i-cence (be nef´i sens) n. The quality of being kind or charitable.

be-nef-i-cent (be nef´sent) adj. Performing acts of charity and kindness; doing good.

ben-e-fi-cial (ben´e fish´al) adj. Advantageous; helpful; contributing to a valuable end. **beneficially** adv.

ben-e-fi-ci-ar-y (ben´e fish´ē er´ē) n.

The person named to the estate of another in case of death.

ben-e-fit (ben´e fit) *n.* Aid; help; an act of kindness; a social event or entertainment to raise money for a person or cause. **benefit** *v.*

be-nev-o-lence (be nev´o lens) *n.* The inclination to be charitable.

be-nev-o-lent (be nev´o lent) *adj.* Doing good; organized for good works.

ben-ga-line (beng´ga lēn´) *n.* A fabric with narrow transverse cords, usually made of rayon, cotton, or silk and similar to poplin.

be-night-ed (bi nī´tid) *adj.* Overtaken by night.

be-nign (bi nīn´) *adj.* Having a gentle and kind disposition; gracious; not malignant. **benignly** *adv.*

be-nig-nan-cy (be nig´nɑn sē) *n.* The condition of being benevolent, gentle, mild.

be-nig-nant (bi nig´nant) *adj.* Kind; gracious; favorable; beneficial.

ben-i-son (ben´i zen) *n.* A blessing; benediction.

ben-ne (ben´ē) *n.* An East Indian plant known as Sesame, from which edible oil is extracted.

bent (bent) *adj.* Curved, not straight. **bent** *n.* A fixed determination; purpose.

ben-thos (ben´thos) *n.* The whole amount of all organisms that live under water either near the shore or at great depths.

be-numb (bi num´) *v.* To dull; to make numb.

ben-zal-de-hyde (ben zal´de hīd´) *n.* An aromatic liquid used in flavoring and perfumery.

ben-zene (ben´zēn) *n.* A flammable toxic liquid used as a motor fuel.

be-queath (bi kwēth´) *v.* To give or leave to someone by will; to hand down, legacy. **bequeathal** *n.*

be-quest (bi kwest´) *n.* Something that is bequeathed.

be-rate (bi rāt´) *v.* To scold severely.

ber-ceuse (ber suz´) *n.* A lullaby.

bere (bēr) *n.* A barley species.

be-reave (bi rēv´) *v.* To deprive; to suffer the loss of a loved one. **bereft** *adj.* **bereavement** *n.*

be-ret (be rā´) *n.* A round, brimless woolen cap.

berg (berg) *n.* A large mass of ice; iceberg.

ber-ga-mot (bür´ga mot´) *n.* A pear-shaped orange, the rind of which has a fragrant oil used in perfumery.

ber-i-ber-i (ber´ē ber´ē) *n.* Nervous disorder from the deficiency of vitamin B producing partial paralysis of the extremities.

ber-ry (ber´ē) *n., pl.* **berries** An edible fruit, such as a strawberry or black-berry.

ber-serk (bér serk´) *adj.* Destructively violent.

berth (berth) *n.* Space at a wharf for a ship or boat to dock; a built-in bunk or bed on a train or ship.

ber-yl (ber´il) *n.* A mineral composed of silicon, oxygen, and beryllium that is the major source of beryllium; a precious stone which is exceptionally hard.

be-ryl-li-um (bi ril´ē um) *n.* A corrosion-resistant, rigid, lightweight metallic element.

be-seech (bi sēch´) *v.* To ask or request earnestly.

be-set (bi set´) *v.* To set, stud, or surround with something.

be-set-ting (bi set´ing) *adj.* Habitually attacking.

be-show (bi shō´) *n.* An edible fish of the western coast of North America.

be-side (bi sīd´) *prep.* At the side of; next to.

be-sides (bi sīdz´) *adv.* Along the side of; over and above.

be-siege (bi sēj´) *v.* To surround with troops; to harass with requests.

be-smear (bi smir´) *v.* To soil; to smear.

be-smirch (bi smürch´) *v.* To tarnish.

be-som (bē´zum) *n.* A broom made of twigs that are attached to a handle, used to sweep floors.

be-sot (bi sot´) *v.* To make mentally dull, as with drink.

be-spat-ter (bi spat´ėr) *v.* To splash; to soil.

be-speak (bi spēk´) *v.* To indicate; to speak; to foretell. **bespoken** *adj.*

be-sprin-kle (bi spring´kl) *v.* To sprinkle over; to cover by scattering.

best (best) *adj.* Exceeding all others in quality or excellence; most suitable, desirable, or useful. **best** *v.*

bes-tial (bēs´chal) *adj.* Of or relating to an animal; brutish, having the qualities of a beast. **bestially** *adv.* **bestially** *adv.*

bes-tial-i-ty (bes´chē al´i tē) *n.* The quality of a beast; beastliness.

bes-ti-ar-y (bes´chē er´ē) *n.* A medieval collection of fables about imaginary and real animals, each with a moral.

be-stir (bi stėr´) *v.* To rouse into action; to stir; to put into brisk or vigorous action.

best man *n.* The attendant of a bride-groom at a wedding.

be-stow (bi stō´) *v.* To present or to give honor.

be-strew (bi strö´) *v.* To scatter over.

be-stride (bi strid´) *v.* To step over or to straddle.

best seller *n.* A book or an article which has a high volume of sale.

bet (bet) *n.* An amount rised on a stake or wager. **bet** *abbr.* Between.

be-ta (bā´ta) *n.* The second letter of the

Greek alphabet.

be-take (bi tāk´) *v.* To cause oneself to make one's way; move or to go.

beta particle *n.* High–speed positron or electron coming from an atomic nucleus that is undergoing radioactive decay.

be-ta-tron (bā´ta tron´) *n.* Accelerator in which electrons are propelled by the inductive action of a rapidly varying magnetic field.

Bethlehem *n.* The birthplace of Jesus.

be-tide (bi tīd´) *v.* To happen to; to take place.

be-to-ken (bi tō´ken) *v.* To show by a visible sign.

be-tray (bi trā´) *v.* To be disloyal or unfaithful; to indicate; to deceive; treachery. **betrayal** *n.*

be-troth (bi trōth´) *v.* To promise to take or give in marriage. **betrothal** *n.*

be-trothed (bi trōthd´) *n.* A person to whom one is engaged to marry.

bet-ta (bā´t a) *n.* A brightly colored freshwater fish of southeastern Asia.

bet-ter (bet´ẽr) *adj.* More suitable, useful, desirable, or higher in quality. **better** *v.* To improve oneself.

bet-tor, bet-ter (bet´ẽr) *n.* A person who makes bets or wagers.

be-tween (bi twēn´) *prep.* The position or time that separates; in the middle or shared by two.

be-twixt (bi twikst´) *prep.* Not knowing which way one should go; between.

bev-el (bev´el) *n.* The angle at which one surface meets another when they are not at right angles.

bev-er-age (bev´ẽr ij) *n.* A refreshing liquid for drinking other than water.

bev-y (bev´ē) *n., pl.* bevies A collection or group; a flock of birds.

be-wail (bi wāl´) *v.* To express regret or sorrow.

be-ware (bi wâr´) *v.* To be cautious; to be on guard.

be-wilder (bi wil´dẽr) *v.* To confuse; to perplex or puzzle. **bewilderment** *n.*

be-witch (bi wich´) *v.* To fascinate or captivate completely; to cast a spell over. **bewitchment** *n.* **bewitchment** *v.*

bey (bā) *n.* The Turkish title of respect and honor.

be-yond (bē ond´) *prep.* Outside the reach or scope of; something past or to the far side.

bez-el (bez´el) *n.* A flange or groove that holds the beveled edge of an object such as a gem in a ring mounting.

be-zique (be zēk´) *n.* A card game that uses a deck of 64 cards, similar to pinochle.

bhang (bang) *n.* An intoxicant or narcotic obtained from the leaves and flowering tops of hemp used in India for swallowing or smoking.

bi- *pref.* Two; occurring two times; used when constructing nouns.

bi-a-ly (bē ´al ē) *n.* A baked roll with onions on the top.

bi-an-nu-al (bī an´ū al) *adj.* Taking place twice a year; semiannual.

bi-as (bī´as) *n.* A line cut diagonally across the grain of fabric; prejudice. **bias** *v.* To be or to show prejudice.

bi-au-ral (bī or´al) *adj.* Hearing with both ears.

bib (bib) *n.* A cloth that is tied under the chin of small children to protect their clothing; the section of overalls or aprons that is above the waist..

bibb (bib) *n.* A piece of timber bolted to the ship's mast for support.

Bi-ble (bi´bl) *n.* The holy book of Christianity, containing the Old and New Testaments. **Biblically** *adv.*

bib-li-og-ra-phy (bib lē og´ra fē) *n., pl.* bibliographies A list of work by a publisher or writer; a list of sources of information. **bibliographer** *n.*

bib-lio-phile (bib´lē o fīl´) *n.* A person who collects books.

bib-li-ot-ics (bib´lē ot´iks) *n.* The study of handwriting, often used to determine authorship.

bib-u-lous (bib´ya les) *adj.* Inclined to drink; of or related to drinking.

bi-cen-ten-ni-al (bī´sen ten´ē al) *adj.* Happening once every 200 years. **bicentennial** *n.* Anniversary or celebration of 200 years.

bi-ceps (bī´seps) *n.* Large muscle in the front of the upper arm and at the back of the thigh. **bicipital** *adj.*

bick-er (bik´er) *v.* To quarrel or argue. **bicker** *n.*

bi-con-cave (bī kon´kāv) *adj.* Bowing in on two sides.

bi-cul-tur-al (bī kul´chur al) *adj.* Having or containing two distinct cultures.

bi-cus-pid (bī kus´pid) *n.* A tooth with two roots.

bi-cy-cle (bī´si kl) *n.* A two-wheeled vehicle propelled by pedals. **int** *n.*

bid (bid) *v.* To request something; to offer to pay a certain price. *n.* One's intention in a card game. **bidder** *n.*

bid-dy (bid´ē) *n.* A young chicken; hen. *Slang* A fussy woman.

bide (bīd) *v.* To remain; to wait.

bi-det (bi´dā) *n.* A basin for bathing the genital and anal areas.

bi-en-ni-al (bī en´ē el) *adj.* Occurring every two years; lasting or living for only two years.. **biennial** *n.*

bi-en-ni-um (bī en´ē um) *n.* Period of two years.

bier (bēr) *n.* A stand on which a coffin is placed before burial.

bi-fo-cal (bī fō´kal) *adj.* Having two different focal lengths.

bi-fo-cals (bī fō´kal) *n.* Lenses used to

correct both close and distant vision.

bi-fur-cate (bī´fer kāt) v. To divide into two parts. **bifurcation** n. **bifurcate** adj.

bight (bīt) n. The slack in a rope; a bend in the shoreline.

big league n. Major league.

big-ot (big´ot) n. A person who is fanatically devoted to one group, religion, politics, or race. **bigotry** n.

bike (bīk) n. A bicycle. **biker** n. **bike** v.

bi-ki-ni (bi kē´nē) n. A scanty, two-piece bathing suit. **bikinied** adj.

bi-lan-der (bil´an dėr) n. A small merchant vessel having two masts.

bi-lat-er-al (bī lat´er al) adj. Having or relating to two sides. **bilaterally** adv.

bil-bo (bil´bō´) n. An iron bar with sliding shackles to confine prisoners on shipboard.

bile (bīl) n. A brownish-yellow alkaline liquid that is secreted by the liver to help digest fats. **biliary** adj.

bi-lev-el (bī lev el) adj. Divided into two floor levels.

bilge (bilj) n. Lowest inside part of the hull of a ship.

bilge keel n. A projection like a fin along a ship on either side to check rolling.

bi-lin-gual (bī ling´gwal) adj. Able to speak two languages with equal ability.

bil-ious (bil´yus) adj. Suffering gastric distress from a sluggish gallbladder or liver.

bilk (bilk) v. To cheat or swindle.

bill (bil) n. Itemized list of fees for services rendered; a document presented containing a formal statement of a case complaint or petition; the beak of a bird. **biller** n.

bil-la-bong (bil´a bong´) n. A blind channel coming from a river; a dry stream bed which fills up after seasonal rains.

bill-board (bil´bōrd´) n. A place for displaying advertisements.

billed (bild) adj. Having a bill or beak.

bil-let (bil´it) n. An official document which provides a member of the military with board and lodging.

bil-liards (bil´yardz) n. Game played on a table with cushioned edges.

bil-lion (bil´yon) n. A thousand million.

bil-lion-aire (bil´lion-aire) n. A person whose wealth equals at least one billion dollars.

bill of lading n. A form issued by the carrier for promise of delivery of merchandise listed.

Bill of Rights n. The first ten amendments to the United States Constitution.

bill of sale n. A formal instrument for the transfer of personal property.

bil-low (bil´ō) n. Large swell of water or smoke; wave. **billowy** adj.

billy goat n. A male goat.

bi-man-u-al (bī man´ūal) adj. Involving the use of both hands.

bi-met-al-lism (bī met´al iz´um) n. The use of two metals; gold and silver, as legal tenders.

bi-month-ly (bī munth´lē) adj. Occurring every two months.

bin (bin) n. An enclosed place for storage.

bi-na-ry (bī´na rē) adj. Made of two different components or parts.

bind (bīnd) v. To hold with a belt or rope; to bandage; to fasten and enclose pages of a book between covers. **binding** n.

bind-er (bīnd´ėr) n. A notebook for holding paper; payment or written statement legally binding an agreement.

bind-er-y (bīn´da rē) n. pl. **binderies** The place where books are taken to be bound.

binge (binj) n. Uncontrollable self-indulgence; a spree.

bin-na-cle (bin´a kal) n. A place where a ship's compass is contained.

bi-noc-u-lar (bī nok´ū lėr) n. A device designed for both eyes to bring objects that are far away into focus. Also **binoculars**. **binocularity** n.

bi-o-chem-is-try (bī´ō kem´i strē) n. Chemistry of substances and biological processes.

bi-o-de-grad-a-ble (bī di grā e bel) adj. Decomposable by natural processes.

bi-o-feed-back (bio fēd bak) n. The technique of controlling involuntary bodily functions, such as blood pressure and heartbeat.

bi-o-geo-chem-is-try (bī´o jē ō´kem e strē) n. Science dealing with the relation of earth chemicals to plant and animal life.

bi-og-ra-pher (bī og´ra fer) n. The person who writes a biography.

bi-o-haz-ard (bī ō haz erd) n. Biological material that threatens humans, other living beings, or their environment.

biological warfare n. Warfare that uses disease-producing microorganisms to destroy crops, livestock, or human life.

bi-ol-o-gist (bī ol´o jist) n. A person skilled in or who studies biology.

bi-ol-o-gy (bī ol´o jē) n. Science of living organisms and the study of their structure, reproduction, and growth. **biological** adj.

bi-o-med-i-cine (bī´ō med´i sin) n. Medicine that has to do with human response to environmental stress.

bi-on-ics (bī ´än iks) n. Application of biological principles to the study and design of engineering systems, as electronic systems.

bi-o-phys-ics (bī´ō fiz´iks) n. The physics of living organisms. **biophysical** adj.

bi-op-sy (bī´op sē) n., pl. **biopsies** The examination for the detection of a disease in tissues, cells, or fluids removed from a living organism.

bi-ot-ic (bī ot´ik) *adj*. Related to specific life conditions or to life itself.

bi-o-tin (bī´o tin) *n*. Part of the vitamin B complex found in liver, milk, yeast, and egg yolk.

bi-par-ti-san (bī pär´ti zan) *adj*. Supported by two political parties; working together. **bipartisanship** *n*.

bi-ped (bī´ped) *n*. An animal having two feet.

bi-plane (bī´plān˝) *n*. A glider or airplane with wings on two levels.

bi-pod (bī´pod) *n*. Stand supported by two legs.

bi-po-lar (bī pō´lar) *adj*. Having or related to two poles; concerning the earth's North and South Poles.

bi-ra-cial (bī rā´shal) *adj*. Composed of or for members of two races.

bi-ra-mose (bī rā´mōs) *adj*. Having, or consisting of, two branches.

birch (berch) *n*. A tree providing hard, close-grained wood.

bird (berd) *n*. A warm–blooded, egg-laying animal whose body is covered by feathers.

birth (berth) *n*. The beginning of existence.

birth certificate *n*. An official record of a person's date and place of birth.

birth-wort (berth´wert) *n*. An herb with aromatic roots used in medicine to aid in childbirth.

bis (bis) *adv. Mus*. Direction to repeat.

bis-cuit (bis´kit) *n*. Small piece of bread made with baking soda or baking powder; a cookie, or cracker.

bi-sect (bī sekt˝) *v*. To divide or cut into two equal parts. **bisection** *n*.

bi-sex-u-al (bī sek´shö al) *adj*. Sexually relating to both sexes. **bisexuality** *n*. **bisexually** *adv*.

bis-muth (biz´muth) *n*. A white, crystalline metallic element.

bi-son (bī´son) *n*. A large buffalo of northwestern America, with a dark brown coat and short, curved horns.

bisque (bisk) *n*. A creamy soup made from fish or vegetables, unglazed clay.

bis-sex-tile (bī seks´til) *adj*. Related to the extra day occurring in a leap year.

bis-tort (bis´tort) *n*. An American herb with twisted roots used as astringents.

bis-tou-ry (bis´to rē) *n*. A small, narrow surgical knife.

bis-tro (bis´trō) *n., pl*. **bistros** A bar or small nightclub. **bistroic** *adj*.

bit (bit) *n*. A tiny piece or amount of something; a tool designed for boring or drilling, such as drilling for oil; metal mouthpiece of a horse bridle; in *computer science*, either of two characters, as the binary digits zero and one, of a language that has only two characters; a unit of information or storage capacity, as a computer memory.

bite (bīt) *v*. To cut, tear, or crush with the teeth. **bite** *n*. **bitingly** *adv*.

bit-stock (bit´stok˝) *n*. A brace that secures a drilling bit.

bit-ter (bit´ér) *adj*. Having a sharp, unpleasant taste. **bitterness** *n*.

bit-tern (bit´ern) *n*. A small to medium-sized heron with a booming cry.

bit-ter-sweet (bit´ér swēt˝) *n*. A woody vine whose root, when chewed, has first a bitter, then a sweet taste.

bituminous coal *n*. Coal that contains a high ratio of bituminous material and burns with a smoky flame.

bi-valve (bī´valv˝) *n*. A mollusk that has a hinged two-part shell; a clam or oyster.

biv-ou-ac (biv´ö ak˝) *n*. A temporary military camp in the open air. **bivouac** *v*. To camp overnight in the open air.

bi-week-ly (bī wēk´lē) *n*. Occurring every two weeks.

bi-year-ly (bī yér´lē) *n*. Occurring every two years.

bi-zarre (bi zär˝) *adj*. Extremely strange or odd. **bizarrely** *adv*. **bizarreness** *n*.

bi-zon-al (bī´zōn˝al) *adj*. Pertaining to two combined zones.

blab (blab) *v*. To reveal a secret by indiscreetly talking; to gossip.

blab-ber (blab´ér) *v*. To chatter; to blab. **blabber** *n*.

black (blak) *adj*. Very dark in color; depressing; cheerless. **black** *n*. Darkness; the absence of light. **blackly** *adv*.

black-ball (blak´bol) *n*. A vote that prevents a person's admission to an organization or club.

black market (blak´mär´kit) *n*. The illegal buying or selling of merchandise or items.

blad-der (blad´ér) *n*. The expandable sac in the pelvis that holds urine.

blade (blād) *n*. The cutting part of a knife; the leaf of a plant or a piece of grass.

blah (blä) *n*. A feeling of general dissatisfaction.

blame (blām) *v*. To hold someone guilty for something; to find fault. **blameless** *n*. **blamelessly** *adv*. **blamelessness** *n*.

blame-wor-thy (blām´wur´thē) *adj*. Deserving blame.

blanch (blanch) *v*. To remove the color from something, as to bleach; to pour scalding hot water over fresh vegetables.

bland (bland) *adj*. Lacking taste or style. **blandly** *adv*. **blandness** *n*.

blan-dish (blan´dish) *v*. To coax by flattery.

blank (blangk) *adj*. Having no markings or writing; empty; confused, having no interest or emotion on one's face or look. **blankly** *adv*. **blankness** *n*.

blank check n. Carte blanche; freedom of action.

blan-ket (blang´kit) n. A woven covering used on a bed.

blank verse n. A poem of lines that have rhythm but do not rhyme.

blan-quette (blän ket´) n. A stew with a white sauce, usually served with onions or mushrooms.

blare (blâr) v. To make or cause a loud sound.

blar-ney (blär´nē) n. Talk that is deceptive or nonsense; charming or smooth flattery. **blarney** v.

bla-sé (bla zā´) adj. Indifferent to pleasure or excitement; world-weary.

blas-pheme (blas fēm´) v. To speak with irreverence. **blasphemously** adv. **blasphemousness** n.

blas-phem-ous (blas´ fa mus) adj. Containing or exhibiting blasphemy.

blast (blast) n. A strong gust of air; the sound produced when a horn is blown. **blasted** adj.

blast–off (blast´of´) n. The launching of a space ship.

blat (blat) v. To cry, as a calf; to bleat, as a sheep.

bla-tan-cy (blā´tan sē) n. The quality or state of being offensively loud or clamorous.

bla-tant (blāt´ant) adj. Unpleasant; offensively loud; shameless.

blath-er (blath´ẽr) v. To talk without making sense. **blatherer** n.

blath-er-skite (blath´ẽr skīt´) n. One given to voluble, empty talk.

blaze (blāz) n. A bright burst of fire; a sudden outburst of anger; a trail marker; a white mark on an animal's face. **blaze** v.

bla-zer (blā´zẽr) n. A jacket with notched collar and patch pockets.

bla-zon (blāz n) v. To make known; to announce. **blazoner** n.

bldg abbr. Building.

bleach (blēch) v. To remove the color from a fabric; to become white.

bleach-ers (blē´chẽrz) n. Seating for spectators in a stadium.

bleak (blēk) adj. Discouraging and depressing; barren; cold; harsh. **bleakness** n. **bleakly** adv.

blear-y (blēr´ē) adj. Unclearly defined; blurred vision from fatigue or lack of sleep.

bleat (blēt) n. The cry of a sheep or goat.

bleed (blēd) v. To lose blood, as from an injury; to extort money; to mix or allow dyes to run together.

bleep (blēp) n. A signal with a quick, loud sound.

blem-ish (blem´ish) n. A flaw or defect.

blench (blench) v. To turn aside from lack of courage.

blend (blend) v. To mix together smoothly, to obtain a new substance; to combine together. **blender** n.

bless (bles) v. To honor or praise; to confer prosperity or well-being.

bless-ed (bles´id) adj. Holy; enjoying happiness. **blessedly** adv.

bless-ing (bles´ing) n. A short prayer before a meal.

blight (blīt) n. A disease of plants that can cause complete destruction.

blimp (blimp) n. A large aircraft with a non–rigid gas filled hull.

blind (blīnd) adj. Not having eyesight; something that is not based on facts **blind.** n. A shelter that conceals hunters; a window shade.

blink (blingk) v. To squint; to open and close the eyes quickly; to take a quick glance.

blintz (blints) n. A very thin pancake rolled and stuffed with cottage cheese or other fillings.

blip (blip) v. To remove; erase sounds from a recording. **blip** n. The brief interruption as the result of blipping.

bliss (blis) n. To have great happiness or joy. **blissful** adj. **blissfully** adv.

blis-ter (blis´tẽr) n. The swelling of a thin layer of skin that contains a watery liquid. **blister** v. **blisteringly** adj.

blithe (blīth) adj. Carefree or casual. **blithely** adv. **blitheness** n.

blitz (blits) n. A sudden attack; an intensive and forceful campaign.

bliz-zard (bliz´ard) n. A severe winter storm characterized by wind and snow.

blk abbr. Black, block.

bloat (blōt) v. To swell or puff out. **bloat** n. **bloated** adj.

blob (blob) n. A small shapeless mass.

bloc (blok) n. A united group formed for a common action or purpose.

block (blok) n. A solid piece of matter; the act of obstructing or hindering something. **blockage** n.

block-ade (blo käd´) n. The closure of an area. **blockader** n. **blockade** v

block-y (blok´ē) adj. Similar to a block in form; stocky; chunky.

blond (blond) adj. Of a golden or flaxen color; a man with blond hair.

blonde (blond) adj. A woman or girl with blond hair.

blood (blud) n. The red fluid circulated by the heart that carries oxygen and nutrients to all parts of the body.

blood pressure n. A pressure exerted by the blood against the walls of the blood vessels; a measure of heart efficiency.

blood type n. Blood group.

blood vessel n. Any canal in which blood circulates, such as a vein, artery, or capillary.

bloom (blŏm) v. To bear flowers; to flourish; to have a healthy look; radiance. **bloom** n. **blooming** adj.

bloom-ers (blö´mèrz) *n.* Loose pants or trousers that are gathered at the knee or just below.

bloop-er (blö´pèr) *n.* An embarrassing blunder made in public; in baseball, a high pitch lobbed to the batter.

blos-som (blos´om) *n.* A flower or a group of flowers of a plant that bears seeds. **blossom** *v.* To flourish; to grow; to develop. **blossomy** *adj.*

blot (blot) *n.* A spot or stain. **blot** *v.* To dry with an absorbent material.

blotch (bloch) *n.* An area of a person's skin that is discolored; a blemish. **blotchy** *adj.* **blotchily** *adv.*

blot out *v.* To obliterate or obscure; to make unimportant.

blot-ter (blot´èr) *n.* A piece of paper used to blot ink; a book for temporary entries.

blotting paper *n.* A porous paper used to absorb excess ink.

blouse (blous) *n.* A loosely fitting shirt or top.

blow (blö) *v.* To move or be in motion because of a current of air. **blow** *n.* A sudden hit with a hand or fist. **-er** *n.*

blow up *v.* To inflate the truth.

blub-ber (blub´ér) *n.* The fat removed from whales and other marine mammals from which oil comes.

blub-ber-y (blub´a rē) *adj.* Abounding in or resembling blubber.

bludg-eon (bluj´an) *n.* A stick with a loaded end used as a weapon.

blue (blö) *n.* A color the same as the color of a clear sky; the hue that is between violet and green.

bluff (bluf) *v.* To deceive or mislead; to intimidate by showing more confidence than the facts can support. **bluff** *n.* A steep and ridged cliff. **bluffly** *adv.* **bluffness** *n.*

blun-der (blun´dèr) *n.* An error or mistake caused by ignorance. **blunder** *v.* To move clumsily. **blunderer** *n.*

blunt (blunt) *adj.* Frank and abrupt; a dull end or edge. **blunt** *n.* **bluntly** *adv.*

blur (bler) *v.* To smudge or smear; to become hazy. **blur** *n.*

blurt (blert) *v.* To speak impulsively.

blush (blush) *v.* To be embarrassed from modesty or humiliation and to turn red in the face; to feel ashamed. **blush** *n.* Make-up used to give color to the cheekbones. **blushing** *adj.*

blus-ter (blus´tèr) *n.* A violent and noisy wind in a storm. **bluster** *v.* **-erer** *n.*

bo-a (bö´a) *n.* A large nonvenomous snake which coils around prey and crushes it; a long fluffy scarf.

boar (bör) *n.* A male pig; wild pig.

board (börd) *n.* A flat piece of sawed lumber; a flat area on which games are played; a group of people with managerial powers. **board** *v.* To receive lodging, meals or both, usually for pay; to enter a ship, train, or plane.

board-er (börd er) *n.* A person who lives in someone's house and is provided food as well as lodging.

board game *n.* A game played by moving pieces or objects on a board.

board-ing-house (börding haus) *n.* A house in which meals and lodging are provided.

board-walk (börd´wok¯) *n.* A wooden walkway along a beach.

boast (böst) *v.* To brag about one's own accomplishments. **boaster, boastfulness** *n.* **boastful** *adj.* **boastfully** *adv.*

boat (böt) *n.* A small open craft or ship.

bob (bob) *v.* To cause to move up and down in a quick, jerky movement.

bob-bin (bob´in) *n.* A spool that holds thread in a sewing machine.

bob-by (bob´ē) *n.* An English police officer.

bobby socks *n.* Girls' ankle socks.

bob-cat (bob´kat¯) *n.* A wildcat of North America, with reddish-brown fur, small ears, and a short tail.

bo-beche (bö besh´) *n.* A glass collar on a candlestick to catch the wax drippings from the candle.

bob-o-link (bob´a lingk¯) *n.* An American song bird, the male having black, yellowish, and white feathers.

bob-sled (bob´sled¯) *n.* Racing sled which has steering controls on the front runners. **bobsled** *v.* **bobsledder** *n.*

bob-white (bob´hwīt¯) *n.* A game bird of the eastern United States; the common North American quail.

bo-cac-cio (bö kä´chö) *n.* A large rockfish found primarily off the Pacific coast.

bode (böd) *v.* To foretell by omen or sign.

bo-de-ga (bö dä´ga) *n.* A wine shop and grocery store.

bod-ice (bod´is) *n.* The piece of a dress that extends from the shoulder to the waist.

bod-ied (bod´ēd) *adj.* Having a body.

bod-i-less (bod´ē lis) *adj.* Having no body or material form.

bod-kin (bod´kin) *n.* A small instrument with a sharp point for making holes in fabric or leather goods.

bod-y (bod´ē) *n.* The main part of something; the physical part of a person; a human being. **bodily** *adv.*

bodybuilding *n.* The development and toning of the body through diet and exercise. **bodybuilder** *n.*

bog (bog) *n.* A poorly drained, spongy area.

bo-gey (bö´gē) *n.* In golf, one stroke over par for a hole. **bogey** *v.*

bog-gle (bog´l) *v.* To pull away from with astonishment. **boggler** *n.*

bo-gus (bö´gas) *adj.* Not genuine;

counterfeit; worthless in value.

bo-hea (bō hē´) *n.* A black China tea.

boil (boil) *v.* To raise the temperature of water or other liquid until it bubbles; to evaporate; reduce in size by boiling. **boil** *n.* A very painful pus-filled swollen area of the skin caused by bacteria in the skin.

boil-er (boil´ér) *n.* A vessel that contains water and is heated for power.

bois-ter-ous (boi´stèr us) *adj.* Violent, rough and stormy; undisciplined. **boisterously** *adv.* **boisterousness** *n.*

bold (bōld) *adj.* Courageous; showing courage; distinct and clear; conspicuous; confident. **boldly** *adv.* **-ness** *n.*

bold-face (bōld´fās´) *n.* A style of printing type with heavy thick lines.

bole (bōl) *n.* A tree trunk.

bo-le-ro (ba lâr´o) *n.* A short jacket without sleeves, worn open in the front.

boll (bōl) *n.* A rounded capsule that contains seeds, as from the cotton plant.

bol-lard (bōl erd) *n.* A post of wood on a wharf to fasten mooring lines.

boll weevil *n.* A small beetle whose larvae damage cotton bolls.

bo-lo-gna (ba lō´nē) *n.* A seasoned, smoked sausage.

bolo tie *n.* A tie made of cord and fastened with an ornamental clasp.

bol-ster (bōl´stèr) *n.* A long, round pillow.

bolt (bōlt) *n.* A threaded metal pin designed with a head at one end and a removable nut at the other; a thunderbolt; a quick flash of lightning; a large roll of material. **bolt** *v.* To run or move suddenly.

bolt-er *n.* One who bolts.

bomb (bom) *n.* A weapon that is detonated upon impact releasing destructive material as gas or smoke. *Slang* A complete and total failure.

bom-bard (bom bärd´) *v.* To attack repeatedly with missiles or bombs. **bombarder** *n.* **bombardment** *n.*

bom-bar-dier (bom bèr dēr´) *n.* A crew member who releases the bombs from a military aircraft.

bom-ba-zine (bom ba zēn´) *n.* Silk or cotton fabric woven with diagonal ribbing.

bombed *adj. Slang* Drunk.

bomb-er (bom´ér) *n.* A military aircraft that carries and drops bombs.

bona fide *adj.* Performed in good faith; genuine; authentic.

bo-nan-za (ba nan´za) *n.* A profitable pocket or vein of ore; great prosperity.

bon-bon (bon´bon´) *n.* Chocolate or fondant candy with a creamy, fruity, or nutty center.

bond (bond) *n.* Something that fastens or binds together; a duty or binding agreement; an insurance agreement in

which the agency guarantees to pay the employer in the event an employee is accused of causing financial loss.

bond-age (bon´dij) *n.* Slavery; servitude, restraint of a person's freedom.

bond-ed *adj.* Secured by a bond to insure the safety of money or goods.

bond paper *n.* A superior grade of paper used for stationery goods.

bond servant *n.* One who agrees to work without pay.

bonds-man (bondz´man) *n.* One who agrees to provide bond for someone else.

bone (bōn) *n.* The calcified connecting tissue of the skeleton. **bone** *v.*

bone–dry (bōn dir) *adj.* Completely without water.

bone-head (bōn´hed´) *n. Slang* A stupid person. **boneheaded** *adj.*

bon-er (bō´nèr) *n. Slang* A mistake or blunder.

bon-fire (bon´fī´ér) *n.* An open outdoor fire.

bon-go (bong´gō) *n.* A pair of small drums played with the hands.

bon-i-face (bon´a fās´) *n.* The proprietor of a hotel, inn, etc.

bo-ni-to (ba nē´tō) *n.* A game fish related to the tuna.

bon-kers (bän kerz) *adj. Slang* Acting in a crazy fashion.

bon-net (bon´it) *n.* A woman's hat that ties under the chin.

bon-ny (bon´ē) *adj.* Attractive or pleasing; pretty.

bon-sai (bōn´si) *n.* A small ornamental shrub grown in a shallow pot.

bon ton *n.* High style or fashion.

bo-nus (bō´nas) *n., pl.* **bonuses** Something that is given over and above what is expected.

bon vivant *n.* One who lives well or luxuriously.

bon voyage *n.* A farewell wish for a traveler to have a pleasant and safe journey.

bon-y (bō´nē) *adj.* Pertaining to, consisting of, or resembling bone.

boo (bö) *n.* Verbal expression showing disapproval or contempt.

book (bük) *n.* A group of pages fastened along the left side and bound between protective covers; literary work that is written or printed. **Book** The Bible.

book-bind-ing (bük´bīn´ding) *n.* The act or trade of binding books.

book-case (bük´kās´) *n.* A piece of furniture with shelving for storing books.

book-ing (bük´ing) *n.* A scheduled engagement.

book-keep-er (bük´kē´pèr) *n.* A person who keeps accounts and records business.

book-keep-ing (bük´kē´ping) *n.* The

business of recording the accounts and transactions of a business.**-keeper** *n.*

book-let (bŭk´lĭt) *n.* A small book.

book-man (bŭk´mən) *n.* A person interested or versed in books.

book-mark (bŭk´märk´) *n.* Something inserted in a book to mark a place.

book-match (bŭk´mach´) *v.* To match patterns on separate sheets so that they appear to be mirror images of one another.

book of account *n.* A book or records used for recording business transactions.

book re-port (bŭk´rē pōrt´) *n.* A written or oral review of a book, given after reading the book

book review *n.* A critical, usually written, review of a book..

book seller *n.* A person who specializes in selling books.

book shelf *n.* An open shelf area used to display and store books.

book-stall (bŭk´sal´) *n.* A counter or stand where secondhand books are sold.

book-store (bŭk´stōr´) *n.* A place of business that sells reading material, especially books.

book value *n.* The value of something as shown in books about similar businesses.

boom (bōm) *n.* A deep, resonant sound; a long pole extending to the top of a derrick giving support to guide lifted objects. **boom** *v.* To flourish or grow swiftly.

boo-me-rang (bō´mə rang´) *n.* A curved, flat missile that can be thrown so that it returns to the thrower.

boom town *n. Slang* A town with sudden prosperity or growth.

boon (bōn) *n.* Something that is pleasant or beneficial; a blessing; favor.

boon-docks *n. Slang* Backcountry; an out-of-the-way place.

boon-dog-gle (bōn´dog´ul) *n.* A useless activity; a waste of time; a useless article produced with little skill.

boor (bĕr) *n.* A person with clumsy manners and little refinement; rude person. **boorishly** *adv.* **-ness** *n.*

boost (bōst) *v.* To increase; to raise or lift by pushing up from below. **boost** *n.* An increase in something.

booster cable *n.* Electric cables used to jump start a battery from another battery or power source.

boot (bōt) *n.* A protective covering for the foot; any protective sheath or covering. *Computer Science* To load a computer with an operating system or other software.

boot camp *n.* A military training camp for new recruits.

booth (bōth) *n.* A small enclosed compartment or area; an area at trade shows for displaying merchandise for sale; an area in a restaurant with a table and benches.

boot-leg (bōt´leg´) *v. Slang* To sell, make, or transport liquor illegally.

boot-less (bōt´les) *adj.* Without profit or advantage; useless.

booze (bōz) *n. Slang* An alcoholic drink.

bor *abbr.* Borough.

bo-ra (bōr´a) *n.* A cold wind of the Adriatic.

bo-rac-ic (bō ras´ĭk) *adj.* Pertaining to or produced from borax.

bo-rax (bōr´aks) *n.* A crystalline compound used in manufacturing detergents and pharmaceuticals.

bor-der (bor´dĕr) *n.* A surrounding margin or edge; a political or geographic boundary. **border** *v.* To have the edge or boundary adjoining.

bore (bōr) *v.* To make a hole through or in something using a drill; to become tired, repetitious, or dull. **boredom** *n.*

bo-re-al (bōr´ē al) *adj.* Located in or of the north.

bore-dom (bōr´dam) *n.* State of being bored.

bor-er (bōr´ĕr) *n.* A tool used to bore holes.

boric acid *n.* A colorless or white mixture that is used as a preservative and as a weak antiseptic.

bor-ing (bōr´ing) *adj.* That which is tiresome, causes boredom.

born (bôrn) *adj.* Brought into life or being.

bo-ron (bōr´on) *n.* A soft, brown nonmetallic element used in nuclear reactor control elements, abrasives, and flares.

bor-ough (bĕr´ō) *n.* A self-governing incorporated town, found in some United States cities; an incorporated British town that sends one or more representatives to Parliament.

bor-row (bor´ō) *v.* To receive money with the intentions of returning it; to use another's idea as one's own.

borscht (bôrsh) *n.* Hot or cold beet soup.

bor-stal (bor´stal) *n.* An institution for delinquent boys and girls.

bort (bort) *n.* Imperfect diamond fragments used as an abrasive.

bor-zoi (bor´zoi) *n.* A breed of long-haired dogs of the greyhound family.

bosh (bosh) *n.* Foolish talk.

bos-ky (bosk´ē) *adj.* Thickly covered with trees or shrubs; related to a wooded area.

bos-om (bez´am) *n.* The female's breasts; the human chest; the heart or center of something. **bosomy** *adj.*

boss (bos) *n.* An employer or supervisor for whom one works. **boss** *v.* To command or supervise.

bot-a-nist (bot´a nist) *n.* A person skilled

in botany.

bot-a-nize (bot´a nīz) v. To collect and study plants while on a field trip.

bot-a-ny (bot´a nē) n. The science of plants.

botch (boch) v. To ruin something by clumsiness; to repair clumsily. **botch** n. A sore; patchwork. **botcher** n.

both (bōth) adj. & pron. Two in conjunction with one another.

both-er (both´ẽr) v. To pester, harass, or irritate; to be concerned about something. **bothersome** adj.

bot-o-pho-bi-a n. Fear of underground places.

bot-tle (bot´al) n. A receptacle, usually made of glass, with a narrow neck and a top that can be capped or corked; formula or milk that is fed to a baby.

bottle-fed (bot´al fed) adj. Fed from a bottle.

bottle gourd n. A type of gourd.

bot-tle-neck (bot´al nek´) n. A narrow, obstructed passage, highway, road, etc.; a hindrance to progress or production.

bot-tle-nosed dolphin n. A stout-bodied whale having a prominent beak and dorsal fin.

bot-tom (bot´am) n. The lowest or deepest part of anything; the base; underside; the last; the land below a body of water. *Informal* The buttocks. **bottom** adj. **bottomer** n.

bot-tom-less (bot´am lis) adj. Extremely deep; seemingly without a bottom. **bottomlessness** n. **bottomlessly** adv.

bottom line n. The end result; lowest line of a financial statement, showing net loss or gain.

bot-tom-most (bot´om mīst´) adj. Being at the very bottom.

bottom round n. A cut of beef taken above the upper leg and below the rump.

bot-u-lism (boch´a liz´am) n. Food poisoning, often fatal, caused by bacteria that grows in improperly prepared food.

bou-clé (bō klā) n. An uneven yarn which forms loops at different intervals.

bouf-fant (bō fänt´) adj. Full; puffed out.

bou-gain-vil-lae-a (bō¯gan vil´ē a) n. A flower of the 4 o'clock family with purple or red floral flowers.

bough (bou) n. The large branch of a tree.

bou-gie (bō´jē) n. A candle.

bouil-la-baisse (bōl´ya bās´) n. A fish stew using at least two kinds of fish which is highly seasoned.

bouil-lon (bel´yon) n. A clear broth made from meat.

bouillon cube n. A compressed cube of seasoned meat extract.

boul-der (bōl´dẽr) n. A large round rock. **bouldered, bouldery** adj.

boul-e-vard (bül´a värd) n. A broad city street lined with trees.

bou-le-ver-se-ment (bü laver semänt) n. Violent disorder.

bounce (bouns) v. To rebound or cause to rebound; to leap or spring suddenly; to be returned by a bank as being worthless or having no value.

bounce-a-ble (bouns´abl) adj. Capable of bouncing.

bounce back v. To recover rapidly from shock, illness or defeat.

bounc-er (boun´sẽr) n. A person who removes disorderly people from a public place.

bounc-ing (boun´sing) adj. Healthy; vigorous; robust; lively and spirited.

bound (bound) n. Legal or physical restraint. **bound** v. To limit; to be tied.

bound-a-ry (boun´da rē) n., pl. **boundaries** A limit or border.

bound-er (boun´dẽr) n. A vulgar person.

bound-less (bound´lis) adj. Without limits. **boundlessly** adv. **-lessness** n.

boun-te-ous (boun´tē as) adj. Plentiful or generous; giving freely. **bounteously** adv. **bounteousness** n.

boun-ti-ful (boun´ti fal) adj. Abundant; plentiful. **bountifully** adv.

bounty (boun´tē) n. Generosity; an inducement or reward given for the return of something; a good harvest.

bou-quet (bō kā´) n. A group of cut flowers; the aroma of wine; a distinctive fragrance.

bour-bon (ber´bon) n. Whiskey distilled from fermented corn mash.

bour-geois (ber´zhwä) n., pl. **bourgeois** A member of the middle class. **bourgeois** adj.

bout (bout) n. A contest or match; the length of time spent in a certain way.

bou-tique (bō tēk´) n. A small retail shop that sells specialized gifts, accessories, and fashionable clothes.

bou-ton-niere (bōt´o nēr´) n. A flower worn in the buttonhole of a man's jacket.

bou-zou-ki (bō zü kē) n. A long-necked stringed instrument resembling a mandolin.

bo-vine (bō´vīn) adj. Of or relating to an ox or cow. **bovinely** adv.

bowd-ler-ize (bōd´la rīz´) v. To expurgate. **bowdlerization** n.

bow-el (bou´al) n. The digestive tract located below the stomach; the intestines.

box (boks) n. A small container or chest, usually with a lid; a special area in a theater that holds a small group of people; a shrub or evergreen with leaves and hard wood that is yellow in color. v. To fight with the fists.

boy (boi) n. A male youth or child. **boyhood** n. **boyish** adj. **boyishly** adv.

boy-cott (boi´kot) v. To abstain from

dealing with, buying, or using as a means of protest. **boycott** *n*.

boy friend *n*. A male companion.

boy scout *n*. A boy who belongs to a worldwide organization that emphasizes citizenship training and character development; one who gives assistance.

boy-sen-ber-ry (boi´zan ber´ē) *n*. A trailing hybrid which bears fruit developed by crossing blackberries and raspberries.

bra (brä) *n*. Brassiere.

brace (brās) *n*. A device that supports or steadies something. **brace** *v*.

brace-let (brās´lit) *n*. An ornamental band for the wrist.

brac-er (brā´sér) *n*. A person who or that which braces; a tonic or stimulating drink.

bra-ce-ro (brä´serō) *n*. A Mexican laborer.

brack-en (brak´an) *n*. A large species of fern with tough stems and finely divided fronds.

brack-et (brak´it) *n*. A support attached to a vertical surface that projects in order to hold a shelf or other weight. **bracket** *v*. To enclose a word in brackets [ ].

brack-ish (brak´ish) *adj*. Containing salt; distasteful. **brackishness** *n*.

bract (brakt) *n*. A leaf-like plant below a flower cluster or flower. **bracteate, bracteal, bracted** *adj*.

brad (brad) *n*. A nail that tapers to a small head. **brad** *v*.

brad-awl (brad´ol) *n*. A tool used to make holes for brads or screws.

brag (brag) *v*. To assert or talk boastfully. **bragger** *n*. **braggy** *adj*.

brag-ga-do-ci-o (brag´ a dō´rhēō´) *n*. A cockiness or arrogant manner; empty bragging.

brag-gart (brag´art) *n*. A person who brags.

braid (brād) *v*. To interweave three or more strands of something; to plait. **braider, braiding** *n*. **braided** *adj*.

braille (brāl) *n*. A system of printing for the blind, consisting of six dots, two across and four directly under the first two. Numbers and letters are represented by raising certain dots in each group of six.

brain (brān) *n*. The large mass of nerve tissue enclosed in the cranium, responsible for the interpretation of sensory impulses, control of the body, and coordination; the center of thought and emotion in the body. **brain** *v*. *Slang* To hit someone on the head.

brain case *n*. The bony cranium or skull that surrounds the brain.

braise (brāz) *v*. To cook by first browning in a small amount of fat, adding a liquid such as water, and then simmering in a covered container.

brake (brāk) *n*. A device designed to stop or slow the motion of a vehicle or machine. **brake** *v*.

brake fluid *n*. The liquid contained in hydraulic brake cylinders.

brake-man (brāk´man) *n*. A train crew member who assists the conductor; the man who operates the brake on a bobsled.

bram-ble (bram´bl) *n*. A prickly shrub or plant such as the raspberry or blackberry bush.

bran (bran) *n*. The husk of cereal grains that is separated from the flour.

branch (branch) *n*. An extension from the main trunk of a tree. **branch** *v*. To grow out from a main stem in different directions. *Computer Science* To execute a different routine due to a decision statement in the program.

branch office *n*. An office located away from the central location of a business.

brand (brand) *n*. A trademark or label that names a product; a mark of disgrace or shame; a piece of charred or burning wood; a mark made by a hot iron to show ownership. **branch** *v*. **brander** *n*.

bran-dish (bran´dish) *v*. To wave or flourish a weapon.

brand-ling (brand´ling) *n*. A small earthworm.

brand name *n*. A company's trademark.

brand-new (brand´nō´) *adj*. New and unused.

brant (brant) *n*. A wild goose which breeds in the Arctic but migrates southward.

brash (brash) *adj*. Hasty, rash, and unthinking; insolent; impudent.

brass (bras) *n*. An alloy of zinc, copper and other metals in lesser amounts. *Slang* A high-ranking officer in the military.

bras-sard (bras´ärd) *n*. A piece of armor to protect the arm.

brass band *n*. A band with brass and percussion instruments only.

brass-bound (bras´bound´) *adj*. Having a border made of brass or a similar metal.

bras-siere (bra zēr´) *n*. A woman's undergarment with cups to support the breasts.

brass tacks *n*. The details of immediate, practical importance.

brass-y (bras´ē) *adj*. Of or like brass; brazen or impudent.

brat (brat) *n*. An ill-mannered child.

brat-wurst (brat werst) *n*. A fresh pork sausage.

bra-va-do (bra vä´dō) *n*. A false showing of bravery.

brave (brāv) *adj*. Having or displaying courage. **brave** *v*. To face with courage.

brav-er-y (brā'va rē) *n.* The quality of or state of being brave.

bra-vo (brä'vō) *interj.* Expressing approval.

bra-vu-ra (brä vö'ra) *n.* A musical passage which requires exceptional technical skill.

brawl (brol) *n.* A noisy argument or fight. **brawl** *v.* **brawler** *n.*

brawn (brän) *n.* Well-developed and solid muscles. **brawniness** *n.*

brawn-y (brän´ ē) *adj.* Having large strong muscles; strong.

bray (brā) *v.* To make a loud cry like a donkey.

braze (brāz) *v.* To solder using a nonferrous alloy that melts at a lower temperature than that of the metals being joined together.

bra-zen (brā'zan) *adj.* Made of brass; shameless or impudent.

bra-zier (brā'zhēr) *n.* A person who works with brass; a metal pan that holds burning charcoal or coals.

breach (brēch) *n.* Ruptured, broken, or torn condition or area; a break in friendly relations. **breach** *v.* To break the law or an obligation.

breach of promise *n.* The violation of a promise.

bread (bred) *n.* A leavened food made from a flour or meal mixture and baked. *Slang* Money. **bread** *v.* To cover with bread crumbs before cooking.

break (brāk) *v.* To separate into parts with violence or suddenness; to collapse or give way; to change suddenly. *Informal* A stroke of good luck.

break-age (brā'kij) *n.* Things that are broken.

break-a-way (brāk´ a wā´) *n.* A breaking away; a start, as of competitors in a contest.

break-fast (brek'fost) *n.* The first meal of the day.

break-up *n.* A disruption; a dissolution of connection.

breast (brest) *n.* The milk producing glandular organs on a woman's chest; the area of the body from the neck to the abdomen.

breast-bone (brest'bōn´) *n.* The sternum.

breast wall *n.* A retaining wall.

breath (breth) *n.* The air inhaled and exhaled in breathing; a very slight whisper, fragrance or breeze.

breathe (brēth) *v.* To draw air into and then expel it from the lungs; to take a short rest

breech (brēch) *n.* The buttocks; the hind end of the body; the part of a gun or firearm located at the rear of the bore. **breeches** Trousers that fit tightly around the knees.

breed (brēd) *v.* The genetic strain of domestic animals, developed and maintained by mankind. **breeding** *n.*

breeze (brēz) *n.* A slight gentle wind; something that is accomplished with very little effort.

breez-i-ness (brē'zē nes) *n.* The state of experiencing breezes.

breezy *adj.* Brisk, cool.

breve (brēv) *n.* The curved mark over a vowel to indicate a short or unstressed syllable

bre-vet (bra vet´) *n.* A commission giving a military officer a higher rank than the one for which he is being paid.

bre-vi-ar-y (brē'vē er´ē) *n.* A book that contains prayers and psalms for the canonical hours.

brev-i-pen-nate (brev´e pen´āt) *adj.* Having short wings.

brev-i-ros-trate (bre´e ros´trāt) *adj.* Having a short bill or beak.

brev-i-ty (brev´i tē) *n., pl.* **brevities** Of brief duration; concise in expression.

brew (brö) *v.* To make beer from malt and hops by boiling, infusion, and fermentation. **brew** *n.*

brew-age (brö'ij) *n.* Fermented beverage.

brew-er *n.* A person whose occupation is to brew malt liquors.

brew-er-y (brö´a rē) *n.* A building or plant where beer or ale is brewed.

bri-ard (brē är´) *n.* A breed of large strong black dogs of France.

brib-a-ble (brīb´a bl) *adj.* Capable of being bribed.

bribe (brīb) *v.* To influence or induce by giving a token or anything of value for a service. **bribe** *n.*

brib-er-y (brī'ba rē) *n.* The practice of giving or receiving a bribe.

bric-a-brac (brik´a brak´) *n.* A collection of small objects.

brick (brik) *n.* A molded block of baked clay, usually rectangular in shape.

brick-bat (brik´bat´) *n.* A piece of a brick used as a weapon when thrown as a missile.

brick-kiln (brik´kil´) *n.* A furnace in which bricks are baked at a high temperature.

brick-lay-er (brik´lā´ēr) *n.* A person who lays bricks as a profession.

bri-dal (brīd´al) *adj.* Relating to a bride or a nuptial ceremony.

bride (brīd) *n.* A woman just married or about to be married.

bride-groom (brīd´gröm´) *n.* A man just married or about to be married.

brides-maid (brīdz´mād´) *n.* A woman who attends a bride at her wedding.

bridge (brij) *n.* A structure that provides passage over a depression or obstacle; a card game for four players; the platform on a ship from which it is steered.

bri-dle (brīd´al) *n.* A harness used to

restrain or guide a horse. **bridle** v. To restrain or control. **bridler** n.

bridle path n. A path or road used only for riding horseback.

brief (brēf) n. A concise, formal statement of a client's case. **brief** adj. Short in duration. **brief** v. To summarize or inform in a short statement. n.

brief-ing (brē'fing) n. The act of giving essential information.

brief-less (brēf'lis) adj. Having no legal clients.

brief-ly (brēf'lē) adv. In a brief way or short span of time.

bri-er (brī'ér) n. A woody, thorny, or prickly plant. **briery** adj.

brig (brig) n. A prison on a ship; a twinmasted, square-rigged sailing ship.

bri-gade (bri gād') n. A military unit organized for a specific purpose.

brig-a-dier (brig'a dēr') n. An officer in the British army.

brigadier general n. A commissioned officer in the armed forces who ranks above a colonel; insignia is one star.

brig-and (brig'and) n. A person who lives as a robber; bandit.

brig-an-dine (brig'an dēn') n. A medieval body armor.

brig-an-tine (brig'an tēn') n. A square-rigged two-masted ship.

bright (brīt) adj. Brilliant in color; vivid; shining and emitting or reflecting light; happy; cheerful; lovely. **-ness** n.

bright-en (brīt'n) v. To make things brighter. **brightener** n.

bril-liant (bril'yant) adj. Very bright and shiny; sparkling; radiant; extraordinarily intelligent; showing cleverness. **brilliantly** adv.

bril-lian-tine (bril'yan ten') n. A light woven fabric similar to alpaca.

brim (brim) n. The edge or rim of a cup. **brim** v. **brimmed** adj.

brim ful (brim'fċl) adj. Completely full.

brim-mer (brim'ér) n. A cup or other container that is full to the top.

brim-stone (brim'ston') n. Sulfur.

brin-dle (brin'dl) adj. Having dark streaks or flecks on a gray or tawny background.

brine (brīn) n. Water saturated with salt; the water contained in the oceans and seas.

bring (bring) v. To carry with oneself to a certain place; to cause, act, or move in a special direction.

brink (bringk) n. The upper edge or margin of a very steep slope.

bri-oche (brē'ōsh) n. A roll made from flour, eggs, butter, and yeast.

bri-o-lette (brē'a let') n. A pear-shaped diamond cut into facets.

bri-quette (brĭ ket') n. A small brick-shaped piece of charcoal.

brisk (brisk) adj. Moving or acting quickly; being sharp in tone or manner; energetic, invigorating or fresh, pertaining to weather. **briskly** adv.

bris-ket (bris'kit) n. The meat from the lower chest or breast of an animal.

bris-ling (bris'ling) n. A small fish that is processed like a sardine.

bris-tle (bris'al) n. Short, stiff, coarse hair. **bristle** v. To react in angry defiance and manner. **bristly** adv.

britch-es (brich'iz) n. Trousers.

brit-tle (brit'l) adj. Very easy to break; fragile. **brittleness** n.

bro abbr. Brother.

broach (brōch) n. A tapered and serrated tool used for enlarging and shaping a hole. **broach** v.

broad (brod) adj. Covering a wide area; from side to side; clear; bright. **broadly** adv. **broadness** n.

bro-cade (brō kād') n. A silk fabric with raised patterns in silver and gold.

broc-co-li (brok'a lē) n. A green vegetable from the cauliflower family, eaten before the small buds open.

bro-chette (brō shet') n. A skewer used in cooking.

bro-chure (brō sher') n. A booklet or pamphlet.

brock-et (brok'it) n. A small deer of South America.

bro-gan (brō'gan) n. A sturdy oxford shoe.

brogue (brōg) n. A strong regional accent; a heavy shoe with a hobnail sole.

broil (broil) v. To cook by exposure to direct radiant heat.

broil-er (broi'lér) n. A device, usually a part of a stove, that is used for broiling meat; a young chicken.

broke (brōk) adj. Penniless; completely without money.

bro-ken (brō'ken) adj. Separated violently into parts. **brokenly** adv.

bro-ker (brō'kér) n. A person who acts as a negotiating agent for contracts, sales, or purchases in return for payment.

bro-ker-age (brō'kér ij) n. The establishment of a broker.

brome-grass (brōm'gras') n. A type of tall grasses having sagging spikelets.

bro-me-li-ad (brō mē lē ad) n. The family of tropical American plants including the pineapple.

bro-mide (brō'mīd) n. A compound of bromine with other elements; a sedative; a commonplace idea or notion; one who is tiresome.

bro-mine (brō'mēn) n. A nonmetallic element of a deep red, toxic liquid that gives off a disagreeable odor.

bro-mo (brō mō) n. An effervescent mixture used as a sedative or a headache remedy.

headache remedy.

bron-chi-al (brong kē´el)) *adj.* Pertaining to the bronchi or their extensions, through which air flows to reach the lungs. **bronchially** *adv.*

bron-chi-tis (brong kī´tis) *n.* An acute inflammation of the bronchial tubes.

bron-cho-scope (brong´ka skōp´) *n.* A tubular instrument which is illuminated for inspecting the bronchi.

bron-chus (brong´kus) *n., pl.* **bronchi** Either of two main branches of the trachea that lead directly to the lungs.

bron-co (brong´kō) *n.* A wild horse of western North America.

bron-co-bust-er (brong´kō bus´tēr) *n.* The man who breaks wild horses.

bron-to-saur (bron´ta sor´) *n.* A very large dinosaur which grew to a height of 12 feet and a length of over 70 feet.

bronze (bronz) *n.* An alloy of tin, copper, and zinc; moderate olive brown to yellow in color. **bronze** *v.* **bronze** *adj.*

Bronze Age *n.* Human culture between the Iron Age and the Stone Age.

brooch (brōch) *n.* A large decorative pin.

brood (brōd) *n.* The young of an animal; a family of young. **brood** *v.* To produce by incubation; to hatch; to think about at length.

brood-er (brōd er) *n.* An enclosed heated area for raising young chickens.

brook (brek) *n.* A small freshwater stream that contains many rocks.

brook trout *n.* A cold–water fish of eastern North America.

broom (brōm) *n.* A long-handled implement used for sweeping; a shrub with small leaves and yellow flowers.

broth (broth) *n.* The liquid in which fish, meat, or vegetables have been cooked; also called stock.

broth-er (bruth´ér) *n.* A male who shares the same parents as another person.

brough-am (brō´am) *n.* A vehicle without a cover over the driver's seat.

brought *v.* The past tense of bring.

brow (brou) *n.* The ridge above the eye where the eyebrow grows.

brown (broun) *n.* A color between yellow and red; a dark or tanned complexion.

brown-out (broun´out´) *n.* An interruption of electrical power.

browse (brouz) *v.* To look over something in a leisurely and casual way. **browser** *n.*

bruise (brōz) *n.* An injury that ruptures small blood vessels and discolors the skin without breaking it.

brum-by (brem bē) *n.* An unbroken horse.

brum-ma-gem (brum´a jam) *n.* Something inferior.

brunch (brunch) *n.* A combination of a late breakfast and an early lunch.

bru-net *or* **bru-nette** (brō net´) *n.* A person with dark brown hair.

bru-ni-zem (brō¨na zem´) *n.* A dark-colored soil found in some of the areas in the Mississippi Valley.

brunt (brunt) *n.* The principal shock, or force.

brush (brush) *n.* A tool with bristles set into a handle for sweeping, painting, or grooming; a brief encounter.

brush discharge *n.* A discharge of low-intensity electric current with dimly luminous circuit ends.

brusque (brusk) *adj.* Being blunt or short in manner or speech; harsh. **brusquely** *adv.* **brusqueness** *n.*

bru-tal (brōt´al) *adj.* Very harsh or cruel treatment. **brutally** *adv.*

bru-tal-i-ty (brō tal´i tē) *n.* A brutal course of action; ruthless or inhuman behavior.

bru-tal-ize (brō tal īz) *v.* To make inhuman, insensitive.

brute (brōt) *n.* A person characterized by physical power rather than intelligence; a person who behaves like an animal, crude. **brutish** *adj.*

brux-ism (brek´siz em) *n.* The unconscious grinding of the teeth during sleep.

bry-o-ny (brī´a nē) *n.* A vine of the gourd family having large leaves and fruit.

bry-o-phyte (brī´a fīt´) *n.* A division of nonflowering plant which includes the liverworts and mosses.

bub-ble (bub´l) *n.* A small round object, usually hollow; a small body of gas contained in a liquid. **bubble** *v.* To produce bubbles.

bub-bler (bub´lér) *n.* A drinking fountain where water bubbles upward.

bub-bly (bub blē) *adj.* Something containing or full of bubbles. *Slang* Champagne.

bu-bo (bū´bō) *n.* Inflammatory swelling of the lymphatic glands, especially in the area of the groin or armpits.

bubonic plague *n.* The contagious and normally fatal disease that is transmitted by fleas from infected rats, characterized by fever, diarrhea, chills, and vomiting.

Buchanan, James *n.* (1791-1868) The fifteenth president of the United States from 1857-1861.

buck (buk) *n.* The adult male deer; a male animal; the lowest grade in the military category. *Slang* A dollar. **buck** *v.* To arch the back and move so as to throw a rider; to oppose the system.

buck-et (buk´it) *n.* A vessel used to carry liquids or solids; a pail.

bucket brigade *n.* A line of people who pass buckets of water from hand to hand in order to extinguish a fire.

buck-eye (buk´ī) *n*. A tree with flower clusters and glossy brown nuts.

buck-hound (buk´hound´) *n*. A small dog used in hunting deer and other animals.

buckle (buk´l) *v*. To warp, crumple, or bend under pressure. **buckle** *n*. Metal clasp for fastening one end to another..

buckle down *v*. To apply oneself.

bu-col-ic (būkol´ik) *n*. A pastoral poem; someone that is rural or countrified.

bud (bud) *n*. Something that has not developed completely; a small structure that contains flowers or leaves that have not developed.

bud-dy (bud´ē) *n*. A good companion, partner, or friend.

budge (buj) *v*. To give way to; to cause to move slightly.

bud-ger-i-gar (buj´a rē gär´) *n*. A small Australian parrot.

bud-get (buj´it) *n*. The total amount of money allocated for a certain purpose. **budget** *v*.

budg-et-eer (buj´i tēr´) *n*. A person who prepares a budget for someone.

buff (buf) *n*. A leather made mostly from skins of buffalo, elk, or oxen, having the color of light to moderate yellow.

buf-fa-lo (buf´a lō) *n*. A wild ox with heavy forequarters, short horns, and a large muscular hump. **buffalo** *v*. To bewilder, to intimidate.

buf-fet (ba fā´) *n*. A meal placed on a side table so that people may serve themselves; a side table for serving food.

buffet (buf´et) *v*. To strike with the hand; to hit repeatedly.

buffing wheel *n*. The round surface of a wheel covered with cloth used to polish or shine something.

bug (bug) *n*. Any small insect; a concealed listening device. **bug** *v*. To bother or annoy. **buggy** *adj*.

bug-bane (bug´bān) *n*. An herb of the buttercup family with white flowers.

bug-eye (beg´i) *n*. A small boat with a flat bottom.

bug-gy (bug´ē) *n*. A small carriage pulled behind a horse.

bu-gle (bū´gal) *n*. A brass instrument without keys or valves. **bugler** *n*.

buhr-stone (ber´stōn´) *n*. A rock used to make a grinding stone.

build (bild) *v*. To erect by uniting materials into a composite whole; to fashion or create; to develop or add to. **build** *n*. The form or structure of a person.

build-er (bil´dèr) *n*. A person who supervises the construction of a building project.

build-ing (bil´ding) *n*. A roofed and walled structure for permanent use.

build-up (bild´up´) *n*. A collection of materials for a future need.

bulb (bulb) *n*. A rounded underground plant such as a tulip that lies dormant in the winter and blooms in the spring; an incandescent light for electric lamps. **bulbed, bulbaceous** *adj*.

bul-bous (bul´bus) *adj*. Resembling a bulb in shape.

bul-bul (bel´bel) *n*. A songbird often mentioned in poetry.

bulge (bulj) *n*. A swelling of the surface caused by pressure from within.

bul-gur (bul´ger) *n*. Wheat prepared for human consumption.

bu-lim-i-a (bū lim´ēa) *n*. An eating disorder in which a person overeats and then throws up in order to remain thin.

bulk (bulk) *n*. A large mass; anything that has great size, volume, or units.

bulk-age (bulk äg) *n*. A substance that increases the bulk of material in the intestine, thus stimulating peristalsis.

bulk-head (bulk´hed´) *n*. The partition that divides a ship into compartments; a retaining wall along a waterfront.

bulk-y (bul´kē) *adj*. **bulkiness** *n*.

bul-la (bul´a) *n*. A blister or vesicle.

bull-doz-er (bul´dō´zér) *n*. A tractor-like machine with a large metal blade in front for moving earth and rocks.

bul-let (bul´it) *n*. A cylindrical projectile that is fired from a gun.

bul-le-tin (bul´i tan) *n*. A broadcasted statement of public interest; a public notice.

bulletin board *n*. A board on which messages and notices are posted.

bul-rush (bul´rush´) *n*. Tall grass as found in a marsh.

bul-wark (bul´wérk) *n*. A strong protection or support.

bum (bum) *n*. One who begs from others; one who spends time unemployed; one who devotes all his time to fun and recreation. **bum** *v*. To loaf.

bum-ble-bee (bum´bl bē´) *n*. A large hairy bee.

bun (bun) *n*. Any of a variety of plain or sweet small breads; tightly rolled hair that resembles a bun.

bunch (bunch) *n*. A cluster or group of items that are the same.

bun-dle (bun´dl) *n*. Anything wrapped or held together. *Slang* A large amount of money. **bundle** *v*. **bundler** *n*.

bundle up *v*. To dress warmly, usually using many layers of clothing.

bung (bung) *n*. The cork used to plug the bunghole in a large cask.

bun-ga-low (bung´ga lō´) *n*. A small one story cottage.

bung-hole (bung´hōl) *n*. A filling hole in a barrel through which it is filled, which is then closed by a plug.

bun-gle (bung´gl) *v*. To work or act

bun-ion (bun´yan) *n.* An inflamed, painful swelling of the small sac on the first joint of the big toe.

bun-ker (bung´kèr) *n.* A tank for storing fuel on a ship; an embankment or a sand trap creating a hazard on a golf course.

bun-kum (bung´kam) *n.* Meaningless talk.

bunt (bunt) *v.* To tap a pitched ball with a half swing. **bunt** *n.* The center of a square sail.

bunt-ing (bun´ting) *n.* A hooded blanket for a baby; a type of stout-billed bird.

buoy (bō´ē) *n.* A floating object to mark a channel or danger. **buoy** *v.* To stay afloat.

buoy-an-cy (boi´an sē) *n.* The tendency of an object or body to remain afloat in liquid or to rise in gas or air.

buoy-ant (boi ent) *adj.* Having the quality of floating or rising in a fluid.

bur-ble (bür´bl) *n.* A gentle, bubbling flow; a bubbling speech pattern.

bur-bot (ber´bat) *n.* A freshwater fish of the cod family.

bur-den (ber´dan) *n.* Something that is hard to bear; a duty or responsibility; a ship's capacity for carrying cargo. **burden** *v.* **burdensome** *adj.*

bur-dock (ber´dok) *n.* A coarse plant with purplish flowers.

bu-reau (bür´ō) *n., pl.* **bureaus** A low chest for storing clothes; a branch of the government or a subdivision of a department.

bu-reauc-ra-cy (bü rok´ra sē) *n., pl.* **bureaucracies** A body of non-elected officials in a government; the administration of a government through bureaus.

bu-reau-crat (bü´ra krat´) *n.* A government official who has great authority in his own department.

bu-reau-crat-ic (bü´ra krat ic) *adj.*

bu-rette (bü ret´) *n.* A glass tube for measuring quantities of liquid or gas that are discharged or taken in.

burg (berg) *n.* A town or city.

burg-age (ber´gij) *n.* A tenure held under the king for a yearly rent.

bur-geon (ber´jan) *v.* To put forth new life as in leaves, buds, etc.

burg-er (ber´gèr) *n. Slang* A hamburger.

bur-gess (ber´jis) *n.* A representative of the legislature of colonial Maryland and Vir-ginia.

burgh (bürg) *n.* A borough or chartered towns in Scotland.

burgh-er (bür´gèr) *n.* The inhabitant of a borough; a citizen.

bur-glar (ber´glèr) *n.* A person who steals personal items from another person's home.

bur-i-al (ber´ē al) *n.* The process or act of burying, especially the act of burying

a deceased person.

bu-rin (bür´in) *n.* An engraver's cutting tool; a flint tool with a beveled point.

burl (berl) *n.* A woody, often flat and hard, hemispherical growth on a tree.

bur-la-der-o (ber le der´ō) *n.* A wooden barrier to protect the bullfighter from the charge of the bull.

bur-lap (ber´lap) *n.* A coarse cloth woven from hemp or jute.

bur-lesque (bèr lesk´) *n.* Theatrical entertainment with comedy and mocking imitations. **burlesque** *adj.*

bur-ly (ber´lē) *adj.* Very heavy and strong. **burlily** *adv.* **burliness** *n.*

burn (bern) *v.* To be destroyed by fire; to consume fuel and give off heat, char or scorch. **burn** *n.* An injury produced by fire, heat, or steam; the firing of a rocket engine in space. **burning** *adj.*

bur-nish (ber´nish) *v.* To make shiny by rubbing; to polish.

burnt (bernt) *adj.* Scorched or darkened as if by burning.

burp (berp) *n.* A belch. **burp** *v.* To expel gas from the stomach.

burp gun *n.* Small submachine gun.

bur-ro (ber´ō) *n.* A small donkey.

bur-row (ber´ō) *n.* A tunnel dug in the ground by an animal. **burrow** *v.* To construct by tunneling through the earth.

bur-sa (ber´sa) *n.* A sac between the bone and the tendon.

bur-sar (ber´sèr) *n.* The person or official in charge of monies at a college.

bur-sa-ry (ber´sa rē) *n.* The treasury of a college; a grant to a needy student.

burse (bers) *n.* A square cloth used in a Communion service.

bur-si-tis (ber sī´tis) *n.* An inflammation of the small sac between a tendon of the knee, elbow, or shoulder joints.

burst (berst) *v.* To explode or experience a sudden outbreak; to suddenly become visible or audible. **burst** *n.* A sudden explosion or outburst.

bur-ton (ber´ton) *n.* A single or double blocking tackle used for hoisting.

bur-y (ber´ē) *v.* To hide by covering with earth; to inter a body at a funeral service.

bus (bus) *n., pl.* **busses** A large passenger vehicle; a small hand truck; a conductor for collecting electric currents.

bus-by (buz´bē) *n.* A fur hat that is worn in certain regiments of the British Army.

bush (bush) *n.* A low plant with branches near the ground; a dense tuft or growth; land that is covered thickly with undergrowth.

bush basil *n.* A small annual herb.

bush bean *n.* A variety of green beans grown on bushes.

bushed (busht) *adj. Slang* Extremely exhausted; tired.

bush-el (bush´l) *n.* A unit of dry measurement which equals four pecks or 2,150.42 cubic inches; a container that holds a bushel.

bush-fire *n.* A fire burning out of control in the bush.

Bush, George *n.* (1924-) The forty-first president of the United States from 1989-1993.

bush league *n.* An inferior class or team.

bush-y (besh´ē) *adj.* Overgrown with a dense growth of bushes.

bus-i-ly (biz´e lē) *adv.* In a busy manner.

busi-ness (biz´nes) *n.* One's professional dealings or occupation; an industrial or commercial establishment.

busk-er (bes ker) *n.* A person who entertains on the street corner.

bus-kin (bus´kin) *n.* A boot that reaches halfway to the knee; tragedy as that of an ancient Greek drama.

buss (bus) *n.* A kiss.

bust (bust) *n.* A sculpture that resembles the upper part of a human body; the breasts of a woman. **bust** *v.* To break or burst; to become short of money. *Slang* To place a person under arrest.

bus-tle (bus´al) *n.* A padding that gives extra bulk to the back of a woman's skirt. **bustle** *v.* To move energetically; to make a show of being busy.

bus-y (biz´ē) *adj.* Full of activity; engaged in some form of work.

but (but) *conj.* On the contrary to; other than; if not; except for the fact.

bu-tane (bū´tān) *n.* A gas produced from petroleum, used as a fuel refrigerant and aerosol propellant.

butch-er (bech´ú) *n.* One who slaughters animals and dresses them for food.

bu-te-o (bū´tē o´) *n.* Hawks with broad wings and soaring flight.

but-ler (but´lér) *n.* A male servant of a household.

butt (but) *n.* The object of ridicule; the thick large or blunt end of something. **butt** *v.* To hit with horns or the head; to be joined at the end.

butte (būt) *n.* A small mountain with steep precipitous sides with a smaller summit area than a mesa.

but-ter (but´ér) *n.* A fatty substance churned from milk.

but-ter-fly (but´ér flī) *n., pl.* **butterflies** A narrow-bodied insect with four broad, colorful wings; a person occupied with the pursuit of pleasure; a swimming stroke.

but-tocks (but´akz) *n.* The two round fleshy parts of the rump.

but-tress (bu´tris) *n.* A support made of either brick or stone and built against or projecting from a building or wall used for the purpose of giving stability; a support or prop. **buttress** *v.*

butyl alcohol *n.* Chemically related form of alcohol that contains the butyl radical, used in manufacturing perfumes, lacquers and other organic compounds.

bu-tyr-a-ceous (bū´ta rā´shus) *adj.* Having the qualities of butter.

bu-ty-rin (bū´tér in) *n.* A yellowish liquid fat that is present in butter, and is formed from butyric acid.

bux-om (buk´som) *adj.* Lively; full of life; happy; pleasantly plump, cheerful.

bux-om-ly (buk´som lē) *adv.* Vigorously; briskly.

buy (bī) *v.* To purchase in exchange for money; to acquire possession of something.. *n.* Anything that is bought.

buy-er (bī´ér) *v.* A person who buys from a store or an individual; a person employed to make purchases for a company.

buy out *v.* To obtain release from a responsibility, by making a payment; to purchase shares in a business concern or investment.

buy up *v.* To buy extensively or freely.

buzz (buz) *v.* To make a low vibrating sound, as a bee; the continuous humming sound of a bee.

buzz-er (buz´ér) *n.* An electrical signaling device that makes a buzzing sound; one that buzzes.

buzz-word (buz´werd) *n.* An important sounding technical word or phrase, which might have little meaning .

by (bī) *prep.* Up to and beyond; to go past; not later than; next to; according to; beside or near; according to; in relation to.

by and large *adv.* In general.

bye (bī) *n.* A position in which a contestant has no opponent after pairs are drawn for a tournament, and, therefore, advances to the next round; something that is aside from the main consideration or course.

bye-bye (bī bī) *Slang* Farewell.

by-gone (bī gón´) *adj.* Gone by; past; former; departed; out of date..

by-law (bī´lo) *n.* A rule or law governing internal affairs of a group or organization.

by-pass *n.* A secondary route to avoid congested areas; a replacement artery to carry blood past an obstruction.

by-street *n.* A side or secondary street.

byte (bīt) *n.* In *computer science*, a sequence of adjacent binary digits operated on as a unit.

by-way (bī wā) *n.* A secondary or little traveled road; a little known aspect.

by-word (bī werd) *n.* A frequent or commonly used phrase or word; a proverbial saying.

C, c (se) The third letter of the English

C, c (sē) The third letter of the English alphabet; the Roman numeral for 100; *Mus.* The keynote of the C major scale.

cab (kab) *n.* A taxicab; the compartment where a person sits to drive a large truck or machinery.

ca-bal (ka bal´) *n.* A group that conspires against a government or other public institution.

cab-by (kab´ē) *n.* Cab driver.

cab-in (kab´ in) *n.* A small, roughly-built house, especially one made from logs.

ca-ble (kā´bl) *n.* A heavy rope made from fiber or steel; a bound group of insulated conductors; a cablegram.

ca-boo-dle (ka bōd´l) *n. Slang* The entire unit, amount, or collection.

ca-boose (ka bōs´) *n.* The last car of a train that contains the eating and sleeping quarters for the crew.

cab-o-tage (kab´ a tij) *n.* Coastal navigation; the carrying of cargo or passengers within the borders of a nation.

ca-bret-ta (ka bret´a) *n.* Sheepskin used in the making of shoes and gloves.

cab-ri-o-let (kab´ rē o lā) *n.* A lightweight one horse carriage with a single seat and two wheels; a type of automobile similar to a convertible.

ca-ca-o (ka kā´ō) *n.* Any tree of the chocolate family; the dried seed of the cacao tree from which chocolate and cocoa are made.

cach-a-lot (kash´a lot´) *n.* A sperm whale.

cache (kash) *n.* A safe place to hide and conceal goods. **cache** *v.*

ca-chet (ka shā´) *n.* A mark of distinction or authenticity; a seal on a letter or an important document showing that it is official.

cack-le (kak´l) *v.* To laugh with the characteristic shrill noise a hen makes after laying an egg; to talk or laugh with a similar sound. **cackler** *n.*

cac-o-e-thes (kak´ō ē´thēz) *n.* A strong compulsion; a bad habit.

ca-coph-o-ny (ka kof´a nē) *n.* A harsh and disagreeable sound. **cacophonous** *adj.* **cacophonously** *adv.*

cad (kad) *n.* An ungentlemanly man. **caddish** *adj.*

ca-das-tre *or* **ca-das-ter (ka das´tėr)** *n.* An official survey of the value, or worth, and ownership of an area's real estate which is used in assessing taxes.

ca-dav-er (ka dav´ėr) *n.* The body of a person who has died; a corpse.

cad-dis (kad´is) *n.* A woolen fabric; worsted ribbon, yarn or binding.

cad-dish (kad´is) *adj.* Unprincipled; like a cad; ungentlemanly.

cade (kād) *adj.* Of an animal's offspring, abandoned by the mother and brought up by human beings.

ca-delle (ka del´) *n.* A black beetle, that eats stored grain.

ca-dence (kād´ens) *n.* A rhythmic movement or flow.

ca-den-za (ka den´za) *n.* An elaborate ornamental section for a soloist near the end of a concerto.

ca-det (ka det´) *n.* A student in training at a naval or military academy.

cadge (kaj) *v.* To beg or to receive by begging; to mooch. **cadger** *n.*

ca-du-ce-us (ka dō´sē us) *n.* The symbol of the medical profession, a winged staff with two serpents entwined around it.

ca-du-ci-ty (ka dō´si tē) *n.* The tendency to fall; senility; the infirmity of old age.

cae-su-ra (si zher´a) *n.* A pause or break in a line of verse or poetry; a pause or division in a verse; a separation, by the ending of a word or by a pause in the sense, of syllables rhythmically connected.

caf-feine (ka fēn´) *n.* A stimulant found in coffee, tea, and dark colas; a slightly bitter alkaloid used as a stimulant and diuretic.

caf-tan (kaf´tan) *n.* A loose-fitting, full-length garment worn in the Near East.

ca-gey (kā´jē) *adj.* Shrewd, wary, or cautious.

ca-hier (kä yā´) *n.* A number of sheets of paper or leaves of a book placed together, as for binding; a report of the proceedings of any body, as a legislature.

cais-son (kā´san) *n.* A waterproof structure that is used for construction work underwater.

cai-tiff (kā´tif) *n.* A miserable person; a vile person.

ca-jole (ka jōl´) *v.* To wheedle or coax someone into doing something.

cal-a-boose (kal´a bōs´) *n., Slang* A jail.

ca-la-di-um (ka lā´dē um) *n.* Tropical plant having large, beautiful leaves of variegated colors, cultivated as a pot plant for its foliage.

cal-a-man-der (kal´a man´dėr) *n.* A variety of extremely hard wood from an East India tree.

cal-a-mine (kal´a mīn´) *n.* A pink powder of zinc oxide and ferric oxide mixed with mineral oils to form a lotion for skin irritations such as poison ivy.

ca-lam-i-ty (ka lam´i tē) *n., pl.* **calamities** Misfortune or great distress, adversity or mishap; great misery. **calamitous** *adj.* **calamitously** *adv.*

cal-a-mus (kal´amus) *n.* A cane or reed; any palm that yields rattan or canes; the quill of a feather.

ca-lan-do (kä län´dō) *adv. Mus.* Becoming gradually slower and softer in sound; diminishing.

cal-ca-ne-us (kăl kā'nē us) *n.* The largest bone of the tarsus; the heel bone in man.

cal-car (kal'kär) *n.* A spur-like node on the leg of a bird; an oven or reverberating furnace, used in glassworks.

cal-cic (kal' sik) *adj.* Pertaining to lime; containing calcium.

cal-cif-ic (kal sif'ik) *adj.* Forming salts of calcium.

cal-ci-fi-ca-tion (kal'si fi kā'shan) *n.* Process of changing a substance through the deposition of lime.

cal-ci-fuge (kal'si fūj') *n.* A plant that cannot thrive in limestone or in soil saturated with lime.

cal-ci-fy (kal'si fi') *v.* To become or make chalky or stony.

cal-ci-mine (kal'si mīn') *n.* A tinted or white liquid that contains water, glue, coloring matter, and whiting, used to paint walls or ceilings, but which cannot withstand washing.

cal-cine (kal'sīn) *v.* To heat to a high temperature without melting, but causing loss of moisture and reduction.

cal-cite (kal'sīt) *n.* Calcium carbonate mineral, that is found in crystal forms including limestone, chalk and marble.

cal-ci-um (kal'sē um) *n.* The alkaline element that is found in teeth and bones; symbol Ca.

cal-cu-late (kal'kū lāt) *v.* To figure by a mathematical process, to evaluate; to estimate. **calculable** *adj.* **calculably** *adv.* **calculative** *adj.*

cal-cu-lat-ed (kal'kū lā'tid) *adj.* Worked out beforehand with careful estimation, mathematical computation.

cal-cu-lat-ing (kal'kū lā'ting) *adj.* Shrewd consideration of self-interest.

cal-cu-la-tion (kal'kū lā'shan) *n.* The act or the result of mathematical computation.

cal-cu-la-tor (kal'kū lā'tèr) *n.* A machine with a keyboard for automatic mathematical operation.

cal-cu-lus (kal'kū lus) *n.* A stone in the gallbladder or kidneys, the mathematics of integral and differential calculus.

cal-de-ra (kal der'a) *n.* A large crater formed by the collapse of the main part of a volcano, caused by violent volcanic action.

cal-dron (kol'dron) *n.* A large boiler or kettle.

cal-e-fac-to-ry (kal e'fak terē) *n.* A room in a monastery that is heated and used as a sitting room.

cal-en-dar (kal'an dèr) *n.* A system for showing time divisions by years, months, weeks, and days; the twelve months in a year.

cal-ends (kal'endz) *n.* The first day of the month on the Roman calendar.

ca-len-du-la (ka len'ja la) *n.* A marigold; the dried flowers of this plant, used to promote healing.

cal-en-ture (kal'an chèr) *n.* A delirium caused in the tropics by exposure to excessive heat.

ca-les-cence (ka les'ans) *n.* Growing warmth; growing heat.

cal-i-ber (kal'i bèr) *n.* The inner diameter of a tube or gun; the quality or worth of something.

cal-i-brate (kal'ibrāt) *v.* To determine the caliber of; to check or correct the scale of a measuring instrument. **calibration** *n.*

cal-i-co (kal'i kō) *n.* Cotton fabric with figured patterns.

ca-lic-u-lus (ka lik'ya lus) *n.* A small cup-like object.

California *n.* A state located on the western coast of the United States, statehood September 9, 1850, state capital Sacramento.

cal-i-for-nite (kal a for'nīt) *n.* Mineral that resembles jade.

cal-i-per (kal'i pèr) *n.* An instrument with two curved, hinged legs, used to measure inner and outer dimensions.

ca-liph (kā'lif) *n.* A religious and secular head in Islam. **caliphate** *n.*

cal-is-then-ics (kal is then'iks) *n.* Exercises that develop muscular tone and promote good physical condition.

calk (kok) *n.* A projection tilted downward on the shoe of a horse to prevent slipping; a similar device on the sole of a shoe or boot.

call (kol) *v.* To speak to attract attention; to name or designate; to telephone; to pay a short visit; to demand payment; in card games, to demand the opponent show his cards; to stop officially.

cal-la *or* **cal-la lily** (kal'a) *n.* A family of white and yellow flowers enclosing a club-like flower stalk.

cal-lig-ra-pher (ka lig'ra fèr) *n.* A person who writes beautiful handwriting.

cal-lig-ra-phy (ka lig'ra fē) *n.* The art of writing with a pen using different slants and positions, fine penmanship.

call-ing (ko'ling) *n.* The occupation or profession of a person.

cal-li-o-pe (ka lī's pē') *n.* A keyboard musical instrument that is fitted with steam whistles.

Cal-lis-to (ka lis'tō) *n.* The largest of Jupiter's moons.

call money *n.* Money loaned on call or available for call loans.

call off *v.* To cancel, as that which has been planned; to speak or read out loud.

cal-lose (kal'us) *n.* An occasional carbohydrate or periodic component of plant cell walls, which forms the callus at an injury site.

cal-los-i-ty (ka los'i tē) *n.* The condition

of being callous or hardened; abnormal thickness and hardness of the skin and other tissues.

cal-lous (kal′*us*) *adj.* Having calluses; to be without emotional feelings; unfeeling. **callously** *adv.* **-ness** *n.*

call rate *n.* The interest which is charged on a loan repayable on demand.

cal-lus (kal′*us*) *n., pl.* **calluses** A thickening of the horny layer of the skin.

calm (kom) *adj.* Absence of motion; having little or no wind, storms, or rough water.

cal-ma-tive (kal′*ma* tiv) *n.* A tranquilizer.

cal-o-mel (kal′*o* mel′) *n.* A white, tasteless compound used as a purgative.

cal-o-rie (kal′*a* rē) *n.* A measurement of the amount of heat or energy produced by food. **caloric** *adj.*

cal-o-rif-ic (kal *a* rif′ik) *adj.* Capable of producing heat or causing heat.

cal-o-rim-e-ter (kal *o* rim′i tér) *n.* An instrument for measuring heat; any of several apparatuses for measuring quantities of heat absorbed or produced by a body.

ca-lotte (k*a* lot′) *n.* A small domed cap for the skull.

cal-trops (kal′trops) *n.* Plants having spiny heads or fruit.

cal-u-met (kal′ya met′) *n.* A pipe used by the North American Indians during ceremonies; also known as a peace pipe.

ca-lum-ni-ate (k*a* lum′nē āt′) *v.* To slander; to malign.

cal-um-ny (kal′*a*m nē) *n., pl.* **calumnies** A statement that is malicious, false, and damaging to someone's reputation.

cal-va-dos (kal′va dōs′) *n.* An applejack; brandy, distilled from hard apple cider.

Cal-va-ry (kal′va rē) *n.* The location where Jesus Christ was crucified.

calve (kav) *v.* To give birth to a calf.

calx (kalks) *n.* The oxide or ashy residue that remains after metals or minerals have been subjected to combustion.

ca-lyp-so (k*a* lip′sō) *n. pl.* **calypsos** Improvised ballad of the West Indies with lyrics on topical or humorous subjects.

ca-lyp-tra (k*a* lip′tra) *n.* A hood-like part connected with the organs of fructification in flowering plants.

ca-lyx (kā′liks) *n., pl.* **calyxes** The outer cover of a flower.

cam (kam) *n.* A curved wheel used to produce a reciprocating motion.

ca-ma-ra-de-rie (kä′ma rä′de rē) *n.* Good will among friends.

cam-a-ril-la (kam′a ril′a) *n.* A group of private unofficial secret counselors or advisers.

cam-ber (kam′bèr) *n.* A slight curve upward in the middle.

cam-bist (kam′bist) *n.* A person who is well versed in the science of monetary exchange; a dealer in bills of exchange.

cam-bi-um (kam′bē *u*m) *n.* The layer of soft cellular tissue between the bark and wood in trees and shrubs responsible for secondary growth.

cam-bric (kām′brik) *n.* A cotton fabric or white linen.

cambric tea *n.* A mixture of hot water and milk, with sugar and a little tea.

came (kām) *n.* A grooved lead bar that is used to hold together the panes of glass in lattice work or stained-glass windows. *v.* Past tense of to come.

cam-el (kam′el) *n.* An animal used as a beast of burden in desert regions, having either one or two humps on its back.

ca-mel-lia (k*a* mēl′ya) *n.* A greenhouse shrub with shiny green leaves and various colored flowers, used in corsages.

ca-mel-o-pard (k*a* mel′*o* pärd) *n.* A giraffe.

camel's hair *n.* The cloth made of camel's hair.

cam-e-o (kam′ē ō′) *n.* A gem usually cut with one layer contrasting with another serving as a background; a brief appearance by a famous performer in a single scene on a television show or in a movie.

cam-er-a (kam′er a) *n.* An apparatus for taking photographs in a lightproof enclosure with an aperture and shuttered lens through which the image is focused and recorded on photosensitive film.

cam-er-al (kam′ér al) *adj.* Pertaining to public revenues or finances.

camino real *n.* Highway; main road.

cam-i-on (kam′ē an) *n.* A sturdy cart for transporting heavy loads.

ca-mise (k*a* mēz′) *n.* A loose smock or shirt.

cam-i-sole (kam′i sōl′) *n.* A woman's short, sleeveless undergarment.

cam-let (kam′lit) *n.* A rich fabric made from goat's hair, a durable waterproof cloth.

cam-o-mile (kam′a mīl) *n.* Herb with strongly scented flowers that are used medicinally.

cam-ou-flage (kam′a fläzh′) *v.* To disguise by creating the effect of being part of the natural surroundings.

camp (kamp) *n.* A temporary lodging or makeshift shelter.

cam-paign (kam pān′) *n.* An organized operation designed to bring about a particular political, commercial, or social goal. **campaigner** *n.*

cam-pa-ni-le (kam′pa nē′lē) *n.* A free standing bell tower.

cam-pan-u-late (kam pan´ya lit) *adj.* Shaped like a bell, usually as a description for flower petals.

cam-pes-tral (kam pes´tral) *adj.* Relating to the fields or country settings.

camp-ground (kamp graund) *n.* A specially prepared area for camping.

cam-phor (kam´fĕr) *n.* A crystalline compound used as an insect repellent.

cam-pim-e-ter (kam pim´i tĕr) *n.* An apparatus used to measure color range of sensitivity of the retina.

campo santo *n.* A burial ground; a cemetery.

camp-site (kamp sīt) *n.* The area used for camping.

cam-pus (kam´pus) *n.* The buildings and grounds of a college, school, or university.

cam-shaft (kam´shaft´) *n.* The shaft of an engine that is fitted with cams.

can (kan) *v.* To know how to do something; to be physically or mentally able; to have the ability to do something; to preserve fruit or vegetables by sealing in an airtight container. **can** *n.* An airtight container.

ca-nal (ka nal´) *n.* A man-made water channel for irrigating land.

can-a-lic-u-lus *n.* A tubular or canal-like passage or channel, as in a bone.

ca-nal-ize (ka nal´īz) *v.* To convert into canals; to make new canals.

ca-nard (ka närd´) *n.* An untrue story circulated as true; a hoax.

ca-nar-y (ka nâr´ē) *n. pl.* -ies A green or yellow songbird which is popular as a caged bird.

can-cel (kan´sel) *v.* To invalidate or annul; to cross out; to neutralize; in mathematics, to remove a common factor from the numerator and the denominator of a fraction; in computer science, to abort or stop a procedure or program. **cancellation** *n.*

can-cel-la-tion (kan´sa lā´shan) *n.* The act of making void, or invalid; a mark used to cancel something.

can-cer (kan´sel) *n.* A malignant tumor that invades healthy tissue and spreads to other areas; the disease marked by such tumors. **cancerous** *adj.*

can-cri-zans *adj.* Going or moving backward.

can-de-la-bra (kan´de lä´bra) *n. pl.* candelabrum A decorative candlestick with several branching arms for candles.

can-did (kan´did) *adj.* Free from bias, malice, or prejudice; honest and sincere.

can-di-date (kan´di dāt´) *n. pl.* A person who aspires to or is nominated or qualified for a membership, award, or office. **candidacy** *n.*

can-died (kan´dēd) *adj.* Preserved; encrusted with sugar.

can-dle (kan´dl) *n.* A slender, cylindrical mass of wax or tallow containing a linen or cotton wick which is burned to produce light. *v.* To hold something between the eye and a light, as to test eggs for blood clots, growths, or fertility. **candler** *n.*

can-dor (kan´dĕr) *n.* Straightforwardness; frankness of expression.

cane (kān) *n.* A pithy or hollow, flexible, jointed stem of bamboo or rattan that is split for basketry or wicker work; a walking stick. **cane** *v.*

cane-brake (kān´brāk) *n.* A thick growth of cane.

ca-nel-la (ka nel´a) *n.* The cinnamon-like bark from a tree of a West Indian, used as medicine and a condiment.

can-er (kā´nĕr) *n.* A person who weaves cane, especially for chair seats and backs.

cane sugar *n.* Sugar obtained from the sugar cane, sucrose.

ca-nine (kā´nīn) *adj.* Relating to or resembling a dog; of the dog family.

Canis Major (kā nis ma´jĕr) *n.* A constellation in the Southern Hemisphere that contains the Dog Star.

can-ker (kang´kĕr) *n.* An ulcerated sore in the mouth.

can-na (kan´a) *n.* Tropical plant with large leaves and showy flowers.

can-na-bin (kan´a bin) *n.* A poisonous resin that comes from Indian hemp.

can-ni-kin (kan´i kin) *n.* A small can; a cup.

can-nu-la (kan´ya la) *n.* A small tube of metal or the like which draws off fluid or injects medicine into the body.

can-ny (kan´ē) *adj.* Thrifty; careful; cautious; shrewd. **cannily** *adv.*,

can-not (kan´ot) *v.* Can not.

ca-noe (ka nö´) *n.* A lightweight, slender boat with pointed ends which moves by paddling. **canoe** *v.* **canoeist** *n.*

can-on (kan´ĕn) *n.* The laws established by a church council; a priest serving in a collegiate church or cathedral; clergyman. **canonical** *adj.*

can-on-i-cal (ka non´i kal) *n.* The most convenient and simplest form of an equation.

can-on-i-za-tion (kan´a ni zā´shan) *n.* Process of being named to sainthood.

can-on-ize (ka nīz´) *v.* To officially declare a deceased person a saint; to place in the catalogue of the saints; to glorify.

can-o-py (kan´o pē) *n., pl.* canopies A cloth covering used as an ornamental structure over a bed; the supporting surface of a parachute; the transparent cover over the cockpit of an airplane.

cant (kant) *n.* The external angle of a

building. *v.* To throw off by tilting.

can't (kant) *contr.* Can not.

can-ta-bi-le (kän tä'bi lā') *n.* A lyrical, flowing style of music.

can-ta-loupe (kan'ta lōp') *n.* A sweet-tasting, orange-colored muskmelon.

can-tan-ker-ous (kan tang'kėr us) *adj.* Bad-tempered and argumentative. **cantankerously** *adv.*

can-ta-ta (kan tä'ta) *n.* A drama that is sung but not acted.

can-ta-trice (kän'tä trē'che) *n.* A professional female singer.

can-thar-is (kan thar'is) *n.* A preparation obtained from dried, crushed blister beetles, used in medicine.

can-thus (kan'thus) *n.* The angle formed by the junction of the upper and lower eyelids.

can-ti-cle (kan'ti kl) *n.* A hymn or chant sung in church.

can-ti-lev-er (kan'ti lev'ėr) *n.* A long structure, such as a beam, supported only at one end.

can-ton (kan'ton) *n.* A small area of a country divided into parts.

can-ton-ment (kan ton'ment) *n.* One or more temporary billets for troops.

can-tor (kan'tėr) *n.* The chief singer in a synagogue.

can-tus (kan'tus) *n.* A church song or melody.

can-vas (kan'vas) *n.* A heavy fabric used in making tents and sails for boats; a piece of canvas used for oil paintings.

can-vass (kan'vas) *v.* To travel through a region to solicit opinions or votes; to take a poll or survey. **canvasser** *n.*

can-yon (kan'yun) *n.* A deep and narrow gorge with steep sides.

cap (kap) *n.* A covering for the head, usually brimless and made of a soft material; the final or finishing touch to something; a small explosive charge that is used in cap guns.

ca-pa-ble (kā'pa bl) *adj.* Having the ability to perform in an efficient way; qualified. **capability** *n.* **capably** *adv.*

ca-pa-cious (ka pā'shus) *adj.* Having a lot of room or space.

ca-pac-i-tance (ka pas'i tans) *n.* The property of a body or circuit which allows it to store an electrical charge.

ca-pac-i-tate (ka pas'i tāt') *v.* To make capable; to qualify.

ca-pa-ci-tive (ka pas'i tiv) *adj.* Coupling or connector that joins circuits by means of a condenser.

ca-pac-i-tor (ka pas'i tėr) *n.* The circuit element composed of metallic plates that are separated by a dielectric and are used to store a charge temporarily.

ca-pac-i-ty (ka pas'i tē) *n., pl.* **capacities** The ability to contain, receive, or absorb; having the aptitude or ability to do something; the maximum

production or output; in *computer science*, the total amount of data or information that can be processed, stored, or generated.

cap-e-lin (kap'a lin) *n.* A small edible fish, allied to the smelt; codfish.

ca-per (kā'pėr) *n.* A prank; antic.

cap-er-cail-lie (kap'ėr käl'yē) *n.* The largest wood grouse of the Old World.

cape-skin (kāp skin) *n.* A light flexible leather made from the skins of goats from which gloves are frequently made.

ca-pi-as (kā pē as) *n.* An arrest warrant authorizing the act of taking a person or possessions into custody.

cap-il-lar-i-ty (kap'i lar'i tē) *n.* The action of molecules on the surface of a liquid in contact with a solid.

cap-il-lary (kap'i ler'ē) *n. pl.* **-ies** Any of the small vessels that connect the veins and arteries. *adj.* Having a hair-like bore; very fine or small in size.

cap-il-lar-y at-trac-tion *n.* The apparent attraction between a liquid and a solid in capillarity.

cap-i-tal (kap'i tal) *n.* The town or city that is designated as the seat of government for a nation or state; material wealth in the form of money or property that is used to produce more wealth; funds that are contributed to a business by the stockholders or owners; net worth of a company or business.

capital account *n.* An account that shows an individual person or shareholder's financial interest in a business.

capital assets *n.* Business assets that are of a fixed, or permanent nature and not commonly bought and sold.

capital gain *n.* The gains from the sale of capital assets.

cap-i-tal-ism (kap'i ta liz'um) *n.* The economic system in which the means of distribution and production are privately own-ed and operated for private profit.

capital levy *n.* Levy put on capital assets apart from the income tax.

capital punishment *n.* The death penalty.

cap-i-ta-tion (kap'i tā'shan) *n.* A census or tax of equal amount for each person.

cap-i-tol (kap'i tol) *n.* The building used for meetings of the state legislative body; the building in Washington DC where the United States congress meets.

ca-pit-u-late (ka pich'u lāt') *v.* To surrender under terms of an agreement. **capitulator** *n.* **capitulatory** *adj.*

ca-pit-u-lum (ka pich'u lum) *n.* The rounded part of a bone; a rounded or flattened cluster of flowers.

ca-pote (ka pōt') *n.* A long hooded cloak with a close-fitting cap-like bonnet worn by women and children.

capric acid *n.* A fatty acid, found in coconut oil, used for synthetic dyes, perfumes and flavorings.

ca-price (kə prēs´) *n.* A sudden change of action or mind without adequate reason; a whim; an impulse **capricious** *adj.* **capriciousness** *n.*

ca-pri-cious (kə prish´us) *adj.* Apt to change opinions unpredictably; subject to change.

cap-ri-fig (kap´ri fig´) *n.* Uncultivated form of the common fig.

cap-ri-ole (kap´rē ōl´) *n.* A spring or standing still leap given by a horse in exhibitions; a playful leap.

cap-size (kap´sīz) *v.* To overturn in a boat.

cap-stan (kap´stan) *n.*, *Naut.* A drum-like apparatus rotated to hoist weights by winding in a cable on a ship or boat.

cap-su-late (kap´sə lāt´) *adj.* Formed into a capsule.

cap-su-lated (kap´sə lā´tid) *adj.* Formed or in a capsule-like state.

cap-sule (kap´sul) *n.* A small gelatinous case for a dose of oral medicine; a fatty sac that surrounds an organ of the body, as the kidney, and protects it; a summary in a brief form. **sular** *adj.*

cap-tion (kap´shən) *n.* A subtitle; a description of an illustration or picture.

cap-tious (kap´shus) *adj.* Deceptive; critical.

cap-ti-vate (kap´ti vāt´) *v.* To hold the attention, fascinate, or charm a person or group of people. **captivation** *n.*

cap-tive (kap´tiv) *n.* A person being held as a prisoner.

cap-tiv-i-ty (kap tiv´i tē) *n.* The period of being captive.

cap-ture (kap´cher) *v.* To take something or someone by force. **capturer** *n.*

ca-puche (kə pōsh) *n.* A hood or cowl.

cap-y-ba-ra (kap´i bär´a) *n.* A rodent that lives in rivers of South America, and feeds on vegetables and fish.

car (kär) *n.* An automobile; an enclosed vehicle, as a railroad car.

ca-ra-ca-ra (kär a kär a) *n.* Various vulture-like birds of the falcon family.

car-ack (kar´ak) *n.* A large, merchant vessel, of the 15th and 16th centuries.

car-a-cole (kar´a kōl´) *n.* A half turn to the right or left executed by a trained saddle horse.

ca-rafe (kə raf´) *n.* A glass bottle for serving wine or water.

car-a-mel (kar´a mel) *n.* A chewy substance primarily composed of sugar, butter, and milk.

car-a-mel-ize (kar´a ma līz) *v.* To make into caramel.

car-a-pace (kar´a pās´) *n.* The hard, bony shield covering an animal's back, as a turtle's shell.

car-at (kar´at) *n.* The unit of weight for gems that equals 200 milligrams.

car-a-way (kar´a wā´) *n.* An aromatic seed used in cooking.

car-ba-mate (kär´ba māt´) *n.* A salt of carbamic acid.

car-ba-zole (kär´ba zōl´) *n.* A white, basic cyclic compound, found in coal tar, used in making dyes, explosives, insecticides and lubricants.

car-bide (kär´bīd) *n.* A carbon compound with a more electropositive element.

car-bi-nol *n.* Methyl alcohol, or similar alcohol, such as isopropyl alcohol.

carbocyclic compound *n.* Organic compounds having a ring formation made up of carbon atoms, as benzene.

car-bo-hy-drate (kär´bō hī´drāt) *n.* A group of compounds, including starches, celluloses, and sugars that contain carbon, hydrogen, and oxygen.

car-bo-late (kär´bo lāt) *n.* A carbolic acid salt.

car-bo-lat-ed (kär´bo lā´tid) *adj.* Containing carbolic acid.

car-bon (kär´bon) *n.* A nonmetallic element that occurs as a powdery noncrystalline solid; the element symbolized by C. **carbonization** *n.* **carbonize** *v.* **carbonous** *n.*

car-bo-na-do (kär´bo nä´dō) *n.* A piece of meat that has been scored before cooking or grilling.

carbon dating *n.* Process that determines the age of old materials such as archeological and geological specimens.

carbonic acid *n.* A weak dibasic acid, that reacts with bases to form carbonates, and decomposes into water plus carbon dioxide.

carbonium ion *n.* An organic ion having a positive charge at a carbon position.

car-bon-ize (kär´bo nīz´) *v.* To change into carbon or a carbonic residue, as by partial combustion.

carbon monoxide *n.* An odorless, colorless very toxic gas, formed by the incomplete combustion of carbon, burns with a blue flame; highly poisonous when inhaled.

car-cass (kär´kas) *n.* The dead body of an animal; something that no longer has life.

car-cin-o-gen (kär sin´o jen) *n.* A substance or agent that produces cancer.

car-ci-no-ma (kär´si nō´ma) *n.* A malignant tumor; cancer.

car-ci-no-ma-to-sis *n.* A state in which multiple carcinomas develop at the exact same time.

car-di-ac (kär´dē ak´) *adj.* Relating to the heart.

car-di-o-gram (kär´dē o gram´) *n.* The curve or tracing made by a cardiograph and used in the diagnosis of heart defects; the record of a heart's action made by a cardiograph.

cardiopulmonary resuscitation *n.* A procedure used to restore normal breathing after cardiac arrest by using mouth-to-mouth resuscitation, clearing the air passages to the lungs, heart massage by chest compressions and if necessary the use of drugs.

car-di-tis (kär dī´tis) *n.* Inflammation of the heart muscles.

care (kâr) *n.* A feeling of concern, anxiety, or worry; guardianship or custody. *v.* To show interest or regard.

ca-reen (ka rēn´) *v.* To lurch or twist from one side to another while moving rapidly.

ca-reer (ka rēr´) *n.* The profession or occupation a person takes in life.

care-ful (kâr´ful) *adj.* Exercising care; cautious; watchful.

care-less (kâr´lis) *adj.* Not showing or receiving care; being heartless; lacking in consideration.

ca-ress (ka res´) *v.* To gently show affection by touching or stroking. **caress** *n.*

care-tak-er (kâr´tā˝kėr) *n.* One who takes care of land or maintains a building in the owner's absence.

care-worn (kâr´wōrn˝) *adj.* Showing the effects of anxiety; drained due to prolonged overwork.

car-fare (kär´fār˝) *n.* Passenger fare on a public vehicle, such as a bus.

car-go (kär´gō) *n.* Freight; the goods and merchandise carried on a ship, plane, or other vehicle.

car-hop (kär´hop´) *n.* A person who waits on customers at a drive-in restaurant.

Caribbean Sea *n.* An arm of the Atlantic Ocean bounded by the coasts of South and Central America and the West Indies.

car-i-bou (kar´i bö˝) *n.* A large antlered deer of northern North America.

car-i-ca-ture (kar´a ka chėr) *n.* An exaggerated representation, picture or description, in which peculiarities or defects of person or thing are ridiculously exaggerated. **caricature** *v.* To make a caricature of; to represent in a ridiculous and exaggerated fashion.

car-ies (kâr´ēz) *n.* The decay of a bone or tooth.

car-il-lon (kar´i lon) *n.* A set of tuned bells in a tower, that are usually played by a keyboard.

car-i-o-ca (kar´ē ō´ka) *n.* A South American dance and its accompanying music, variation of the samba.

car-min-a-tive (kär min´a tiv) *adj.* Expelling gas from the body.

car-mine (kär min) *n.* A vivid red color; crimson; deep purplish red.

car-nage (kär´nij) *n.* A bloody slaughter; war; massacre.

car-nal (kär´nal) *adj.* Relating to sensual desires. **carnality** *n.* **carnally** *adv.*

car-nall-ite (kär´na līt˝) *n.* A mineral consisting of a hydrous potassium-magnesium chloride which provides a valuable source of potassium.

car-nas-si-al (kär nas´ē al) *adj.* Of or pertaining to teeth of a carnivore adapted for cutting rather than tearing flesh.

car-na-tion (kär nā´shan) *n.* A fragrant perennial flower in a variety of colors.

carnauba wax *n.* Wax obtained from the Brazilian wax palm, and used as a base in polishes.

car-nel-ian (kär nēl´yan) *n.* A clear red chalcedony that is used as a gem.

car-ni-val (kär´ni val) *n.* A traveling amusement show with side shows, a Ferris wheel, and merry-go-rounds; any kind of a happy celebration; the period of festivity preceding Lent.

car-ni-vore (kär´ni vōr˝) *n.* A flesh-eating animal. **carnivorous** *adj.*

car-ob (kar´ob) *n.* A Mediterranean tree, the pods of which, are known as locust beans, contains a sweet pulp.

car-ol (kar´ol) *n* A song to celebrate joy or praise. **caroler** *n.* **carol** *v.*

car-o-tene (kar´o tēn˝) *n.* Pigment of orange or red found in some vegetable and animal fats, can be turned into vitamin A.

ca-rot-i-noid (ka rot´e noid˝) *n.* Red and yellow pigments found in plants, and animals.

ca-rouse (ka rouz´) *v.* To be rowdy and to be in a drunken state. **carouser** *n.*

carp (kärp) *v.* To find unreasonable fault with something or someone; to complain unduly. **carp** *n.* A freshwater fish that contains many small bones but can be eaten with caution.

car-pal (kär´pal) *adj.* Pertaining to the wrist and the bones in the wrist.

car-pel (kär´pel) *n. Bot.* A seed vessel or pistil.

car-pen-ter (kär´pen tėr) *n.* A person who builds and repairs wooden structures. **carpentry** *n.*

car-pet (kär´pit) *n.* A thick, woven or felt floor covering that helps to insulate the floors. **carpet** *n.*

car-pet-ing (kär´pit ing) *n.* Material for carpets; carpets in general.

car-pol-o-gy *n.* The division of botany relating to the structure of seeds and seed vessels.

car-port (kär´pōrt) *n.* A roof attached to the side of a building to give shelter for a vehicle.

car-pus (kär´pus) *n.* The bones of the wrist or the wrist itself.

car-riage (kar´ij) *n*. A horse-drawn cart for passengers.

carron oil *n*. Ointment composed of equal parts of limewater and olive oil, used as a treatment for burns and scalds.

car-rot (kar´ot) *n*. An orange vegetable that is an edible root.

car-rou-sel (kar´a sel´) *n*. A merry-go-round.

car-ry (kar´ē) *v*. To transport from one place to another; to bear the burden, weight, or responsibility of; to keep or have available for sale; to maintain on business books for future settlement.

car-ry-all (kar´ē ol´) *n*. A capacious bag or suitcase for carrying items.

carrying charge *n*. The amount charged over the regular price a merchandise sold on installments.

carry on *n*. Luggage carried on an airplane by passengers.

car sickness *n*. Nausea caused by motion.

cart (kärt) *n*. A two-wheeled vehicle for moving heavy goods; a small lightweight vehicle that can be moved around by hand. **carter** *n*.

carte blanche *n*. Unrestricted authority to make decisions.

car-tel (kär tel´) *n*. A group of independent companies that have organized to control prices, production, etc.

Carter, James Earl Jr. (Jimmy) *n*. (1924-) The thirty-ninth president of the United States from 1977-1981.

car-ti-lage (kär´ti lij) *n*. A tough, elastic substance of connective tissue attached to the surface of bones near the joints. **cartilaginous** *adj*.

car-ti-lag-i-nous (kär´ti laj´i nus) *adj*. Having or resembling cartilage.

car-to-gram (kär´to gram) *n*. A map giving simplified statistical information by using shading.

car-tog-ra-pher (kär tog´ra fèr) *n*. One who makes and or publishes maps.

car-tog-ra-phy (kär tog´ra fē) *n*. The art of developing charts and maps. **cartographer** *n*. **cartographic** *adj*.

car-ton (kär´ ton) *n*. A container made from cardboard.

car-tridge (kär´trij) *n*. A case made of metal, pasteboard, etc., that contains a charge of powder; the primer and shot or projectile for a firearm.

cartridge paper *n*. A durable, strong paper used for making cartridges.

car-tu-lar-y *n*. A record or register of title deeds and other documents; the keeper of such a records or archives.

car-va-crol *n*. A thick, colorless oil.

carve (kärv) *v*. To slice meat or poultry; to cut into something; to create, as sculpture. **carver** *n*.

cary-at-id (kar´ē at´id) *n*. A supporting column sculptured in the form of a female figure.

car-y-op-sis (kar´ē op´ss) *n*. A small, one-seeded, dry, indehiscent fruit in which the seed and fruit fuse in a single grain.

ca-sa-ba (ka sä´ba) *n*. A sweet, edible winter melon having a yellow skin.

cas-cade (kas kād´) *n*. A waterfall that flows over steep rocks.

cas-ca-ril-la (kas´ka ril´a) *n*. The bitter aromatic bark of a West Indian shrub used for making incense and as a tonic.

case (kās) *n*. A particular occurrence or in- stance; an injury or disease; an argument, supporting facts, or reasons that justify a situation; a box or housing to carry things in, as a briefcase; in the law, a suit of action brought against a person.

ca-se-a-tion (kā´sē ā´shan) *n*. The separation of casein from coagulating milk, to form a soft cheesy substance or curd.

case-book (kās´buk´) *n*. A book containing detailed records of cases, that is used for reference and instruction in law, psychology, sociology, and medicine.

case history *n*. A factual information about an individual's personal history.

ca-sein (kā´sēn) *n*. A dairy protein that is used in foods and in manufacturing adhesives and plastics.

case law *n*. Law made by decided cases that serve as precedents.

case system *n*. A method of teaching law based primarily on reported cases instead of textbooks.

case-work *n*. Social work with direct contact and consideration of a patient, his family, and their problems.

cash *n*. Money, or an equivalent, as a check, paid at the time of making a purchase.

cash flow *n*. Reported net income after taxes; the liquidity of a corporation plus amounts charged off plus noncash charges.

cash-ier (ka shēr´) *n*. An employee who handles cash as part of his job description; an officer in a bank in charge of receiving or distributing money.

cashier's check *n*. A check drawn by a bank upon its own funds and signed by its cashier.

cash items *n*. Items such as, government bonds, bank deposits, securities, and the like that are considered equivalent to cash in a corporate statement.

cash-mere (kazh´mēr) *n*. The wool from the Kashmir goat; the yarn made from this wool.

cas-ing (kās ing) *n*. A protective covering; a supporting frame as used around a door or window.

ca-si-no (ka sē´nō) *n*.,k *pl*. **casinos** A

public establishment open especially for gambling.

cask (kask) *n.* A large wooden vessel or barrel; the quantity that a cask will hold.

cas-ket (kas´kit) *n.* A coffin; a small chest or box.

cas-que (kask) *n.* A helmet. **casqued** *adj.*

cas-sa-va (ka sä´va) *n.* A slender erect shrub grown in the tropics.

cas-se-role (kas´e rōl) *n.* A dish in which the food is baked and also served; food cooked and served in this manner.

cas-sette (ka set´) *n.* A cartridge of magnetic tape used in tape recorders to play and record.

cas-sit-er-ite (ka sit´a rīt) *n.* A brown or black mineral that consists of tin dioxide, the chief source of metallic tin.

cas-sock (kas´ok) *n.* A close-fitting garment worn by members of the clergy.

cas-so-war-y (kas´o wer˘ē) *n.* A large, three-toed, flightless ratite bird; closely related to emu.

cast (kast) *v.* To hurl or throw with force.

cast-a-way (kast´a wā) *adj.* Throw away. **castaway** *n.* One who is shipwrecked or discarded.

caste (kast) *n.* A social separation based on a profession, hereditary, or financial hierarchy.

cas-tel-lat-ed (kas´te lā´tid) *adj.* Adorned by battlements and turrets.

cast-er (kas´tér) *n.* A small set of swiveling rollers that are fastened under pieces of furniture and the like.

cas-ti-gate (kas´ti gāt) *v.* To punish or criticize severely. **castigation** *n.*

cast-ing (kas´ting) *n.* The act of one that casts.

casting vote *n.* A deciding vote cast by a president or chairman to break a tie.

cast iron *n.* A hard, brittle, commercial alloy of iron, carbon, and silicon that is cast into a mold.

cas-tle (kas´el) *n.* A fort or fortified dwelling for nobility; any large house or place of refuge; a stronghold.

cast-off (kas tof) *adj.* Discarded; thrown away; thrown to the side.

cas-tor (kas ter) *n.* A beaver; a beaver hat, or a hat that resembles one.

cas-trate (kas´trāt) *v.* To remove the testicles; to remove the ovaries; to spay, to remove something from. -**tion** *n.*

ca-su-al (kazh´ö al) *adj.* Informal; occurring by chance; uncertain. **casually** *adv.* **casualness** *n.*

cas-u-al-ism (kazh´ö a liz˝um) *n.* The state of things where chance prevails; the belief that all things exist or are governed by chance or accident.

ca-su-al-ty (kazh´ö al tē) *n.*, *pl.* **casualties** One who is injured or killed

in an accident. *Milit.* One who is killed, wounded, taken prisoner by the enemy, or missing in action.

cas-u-ist (kazh´ö ist) *n.* A person who studies and resolves cases of conscience or conduct.

ca-tab-o-lism (ka tab´o liz˝um) *n.* In living organisms, a breaking down of more complex molecules into simpler ones, involving the release of energy.

cat-a-chre-sis (kat´a krē´sis) *n.* Misuse of a word context.

cat-a-clysm (kat´a kliz um) *n.* A sudden and violent event; an extensive flood; a deluge. **cataclysmic** *adj.*

cat-a-comb (kat´a kōm´) *n.* An underground passage with small rooms for coffins.

ca-tad-ro-mous (ka tad´ro mus) *adj.* Of fish living in freshwater and going down to the sea to spawn.

cat-a-falque (kat´a falk´) *n.* The structure that supports a coffin during a state funeral.

cat-a-lep-sy (kat´a lep´sē) *n.* A condition in which there is a rigidity of the muscles, causing the patient to remain in a fixed position or posture.

cat-a-log (kat´a log) *n.* A publication containing a list of names, objects, etc.

ca-tal-pa (katal´pa) *n.* A hardy, small ornamental tree found in Asia and America and noted for its heart-shaped leaves and pale showy flowers.

cat-a-lyst (kat´a list) *n.*, *Chem.* Any substance that alters and decreases the time it takes a chemical reaction to occur.

cat-a-ma-ran (kat´a ma ran´) *n.* A boat with twin hulls.

cat-am-ne-sis (kat´am nē´sis) *n.* The medical history of a patient taken during, or after recovering from, an illness.

cat-a-mount (kat´amount´) *n.* A wild cat; as the cougar or lynx.

cat-a-pla-sia (kat´a plā´zha) *n.* The reverting of cells or tissues to an earlier or more primitive stage.

cat-a-plex-y (kat´a plek sē) *n.* A sudden loss of muscle power caused by a strong emotional shock.

cat-a-pult (kat´a pult´) *n.* An ancient military device for throwing arrows or stones; a device for launching aircraft from the deck of a ship, such as a aircraft carrier.

cat-a-ract (kat´a rakt´) *n.* A large waterfall or downpour. *Pathol.* A disease of the lens of the eye, causing total or partial blindness.

ca-tarrh (ka tär´) *n.*, *Pathol.* Inflammation of the nose and throat. -**al** *adj.*

ca-tas-ta-sis (ka tas´ta sis) *n.* The climax of a play.

ca-tas-tro-phe (ka tas´tro fē) *n.* A

terrible and sudden disaster; a calamity.

catastophic *adj.* **catastrophically** *adv.*

cat-a-to-ni-a (kat´a tō´nē a) *n.* The state of suspended animation and the loss of voluntary motion.

ca-taw-ba (ka tô´ba) *n.* A pale red native American grape that is cultivated into a wine of the same name.

catch (kach) *v.* To take; to seize or capture; to reach in time; to intercept; to become entangled or fastened.

catch-all (kach´ol´) *n.* A container or bag for odds and ends.

catch-ment (kach´ment) *n.* The act of catching water; a drainage system that catches water, as a reservoir.

catch on *v.* To understand, learn; to become popular.

catch-word *n.* A word or phrase often repeated; an expression repeated until it represents an idea, party, school, or product.

cat-e-chize (kat´a kiz´) *v.* To teach or instruct orally by means of questions and answers.

cat-e-chu *n.* Any of several dry, earthy, or resinous astringent substances obtained from the wood of tropical plants of Asia and used for medicine, dyeing, or tanning.

cat-e-gor-i-cal (kat´a gor´i kal) *adj.* Absolute; certain; related to or included in a category without qualification.

cat-e-go-rize (kat´a go riz´) *v.* To place in categories.

cat-e-go-ry (kat´a gôr´ē) *n. pl.* -ries A general group to which something belongs.

cat-e-nate (kat´e nāt´) *v.* To connect in a series; links; to concatenate.

ca-ter (kā´tėr) *v.* To provide a food service; to act deferentially toward.

cat-er-pil-lar (kat´a pil´er) *n.* The very fuzzy, worm-like, brightly-colored spiny larva of a moth or butterfly.

cat-gut (kat´gut´) *n.* A thin, tough cord made from the fried intestines of sheep.

ca-the-dral (ka thē´dral) *n.* A large and important church, containing the seat of a bishop.

cath-e-ter (kath´i tėr) *n., Med.* A thin, flexible tube that is inserted into the body cavity for drainage and to draw urine from the bladder. **catheterize** *v.*

ca-thex-is *n.* The channeling of psychic energy in an object.

cath-ode (kath´ōd) *n.* The negatively charged electrode which receives positively charged ions during electrolysis.

cathode ray *n.* A stream of electrons projected from the heated cathode of a vacuum tube under the propulsion of a very strong electric field.

cathode ray tube *n.* The vacuum tube on which images are found, used in a computer screen.

ca-thol-i-con (ka thol´ kon) *n.* A remedy for all diseases; cure-all.

cat-i-on (kat´ī´on) *n.* A positively charged ion that is attracted in electrolytes to a negative electrode.

cat-kin (kat´kin) *n.* The spike-like blossom of the willow, birch trees that resemble a cat's tail.

cat-nap (kat´nap´) *n.* A short nap.

cat-o'-nine-tails (kat´o nīn´tālz´) *n.* A hand-made whip with nine knotted cords fastened to a handle.

ca-top-tric (ka top´trik) *adj.* Pertaining or relating to a reflected light or a mirror.

ca-top-trics (ka top´trik) *n.* The branch of optics that relates to a mirror or reflected light.

cat rig *n.* A rig consisting of a single mast set well forward and carrying one large sail extended by a long boom and gaff.

CAT scan *n.* A cross-sectional picture produced by a scanner, used to x-ray the body by using computerized axial tomography.

CAT scanner *n.* The machine used to produce a cross-sectional picture of the body.

cat-sup (kat´sup) *n. Variation of* ketchup. A condiment made from tomatoes, water, sugar, and other spices.

cat-tle (kat´al) *n. pl.* Farm animals raised for meat and dairy products.

cat-tle-man (kat´al man) *n.* A person in the business of raising or tending cattle.

cat-ty (kat´ē) *adj.* Malicious or spiteful. **cattily** *adv.* **cattiness** *n.*

cat-ty--cor-nered (kat´ē kor´nėrd) *adj.* Not straight; sitting at an angle.

cat-walk (kat´wok´) *n.* Any very narrow path, as along-side a bridge.

Cau-ca-sian (ko kā´ zhan) *n.* An inhabitant of Caucasus. **Caucasian** *adj.* Relating to a major ethnic division of the human race; of or relating to the white race.

cau-cus (ko´kus) *n.* A meeting of a political party to make policy decisions and to select candidates. **caucus** *v.*

cau-dal (kod´al) *adj.* Toward the tail or posterior end of the body.

caudal anesthesia *n.* Insensibility to pain in the lower portion of the body, due to the injection of an anesthetic drug into the caudal part of the spinal canal.

cau-dex (ko´deks) *n.* The woody base of a perennial plant, including roots and stem.

cau-dle (kod´al) *n.* A warm drink usually made of spices, ale, bread, eggs, and sugar.

caught *v.* Past tense of catch.

caul-dron (kol´dron) *n.* A large metal kettle or boiler.

caulk (kok) *v.* To seal seams and edges against leakage of water and air with some substance. **caulker** *n.*

caus-al (ko´zal) *adj.* Relating to or constituting a cause or causes; implying, involving, or expressing a cause or causes.

cau-sa-tion (ko zā´shan) *n.* The act or process of causing or producing an effect.

cause (koz) *v.* To produce a result, consequence, or effect. *n.* A goal, principle; a reason; motive. **causer** *n.*

cau-se-rie (kō´za rē´) *n.* A short informal conversation or chat.

cause-way (koz´wā´) *n.* A paved highway through a marsh tract; raised road over water.

caus-tic (ko´stik) *n.* A curve to which all light rays originating from a point and reflected by a curved surface are tangent.

cau-ter-ize (ko´ta rīz´) *v.* To sear or burn with a hot blade or instrument or fire, as in dead tissue, a hot iron.

cau-ter-y (ko´ta rē) *n.* A very hot instrument used to destroy tissue that does not seem normal.

cau-tion (ko´shan) *n.* A warning; careful planning. **cautionary** *adj.*

cau-tious (ko´shus) *adj.* Very careful.

cav-al-cade (kav´al kād´) *n.* A group of horse-drawn carriages or riders, forming a procession.

cav-a-lier (kav´a lēr´) *n.* A very gallant gentleman; a knight.

cav-al-ry (kav´al rē) *n., pl.* **cavalries** Army troops trained to fight on horseback or in armored vehicles. **cavalryman** *n.*

ca-vate (kā´vāt) *adj.* Hollowed or dug out; giving the appearance of a cave.

cav-a-ti-na (kav´a tē´na) *n.* A simple operatic song or solo.

cave (kāv) *n.* An underground tomb or chamber with an opening at the ground surface.

ca-ve-at (kā´vē at´) *n.* A formal legal notice to stop the proceedings until both sides have a hearing; a warning or caution.

cave dweller *n.* A person, as a prehistoric man, who lives in caves.

cave–in *n.* The action of collapsing or caving in; a place where the ground has fallen in.

cave-man (kāv man) *n.* A person who lives in caves; especially of the Stone Age; a person who acts in a very rough primitive manner.

ca-vern (kav´ern) *n.* A very large underground cave. **cavernous** *adj.*

cav-i-ar *or* **cav-i-are (kav´ē är´)** *n.* The eggs of large fish, eaten as an appetizer.

cav-il (kav´il) *v.* To raise captious and trivial objections; to find fault without good reason.

cav-i-ty (kav´i tē) *n., pl.* **cavities** A decayed place in a tooth; a hollow or hole.

cay (kā) *n.* A range or reef of sand or coral a lying near the surface of the water.

cay-man (kā´mam) *n.* A tropical American crocodile which is fundamentally similar to the alligator.

cay-use (kī ūs´) *n.* A small native range horse of the western United States.

CD *abbr.* Compact disk; civil defense; certificate of deposit.

cease (sēs) *v.* To come to an end or put an end to; to stop.

cease-fire (sēs´fī´er) *v.* To stop fighting, usually as a result of a truce.

cease-less (sēs´lis) *adj.* Endless; without a stop or pause; continual; without intermission. **ceaselessly** *adv.*

ce-cum (se´kum) *n.* The pouch where the large intestine begins.

ce-dar (se´dėr) *n.* An evergreen tree with fragrant, red wood.

cede (sēd) *v.* To formally resign and surrender to another, usually by treaty.

ce-dil-la (si dil´a) *n.* A diacritical mark placed under the letter c (ç) in the French vocabulary to indicate a modification or alteration of the usual phonetic sound.

ceil-ing (sē´ling) *n.* The overhead covering of a room; the maximum limit to some-thing; the maximum height for visibility under specified conditions for aircraft.

ceiling unlimited *n.* A cloudless or almost cloudless sky.

ceiling zero *n.* A cloud ceiling at a height of 50 feet or lower.

ceil-om-e-ter (sē lom´i tėr) *n. Meteor.* A photoelectric instrument for measuring and recording the height of a cloud ceiling.

cel-a-don (sel´a don´) *n.* A pale green ceramic glaze, used in Chinese porcelains and stonewares.

cel-an-dine (sel´an dīn´) *n.* A biennial herb of the poppy family which emits a bright orange-colored juice when its leaves or stems are crushed. The juice from this plant is used in medicine as a diuretic, purgative and fungicide.

cel-e-brate (sel´e brāt´) *v.* To observe with ceremonies, rejoicing, or festivity. **celebration** *n.*

cel-e-brat-ed (sel´e brā´tid) *adj.* Famous, well-known.

cel-e-bra-tion (sel e´brā shen) *n.* The act of celebrating; to demonstrate satisfaction in a festive way.

cel-leb-ri-ty (se leb´ri tē) *n. pl.* **-ies** A famous person.

ce-ler-i-ac (se ler´ē ak) *n.* A variety of celery, grown for its knobby edible turnip-like root.

ce-ler-i-ty (se ler'i tē) n. Swiftness; speed; rapid motion.

cel-er-y (sel'e rē) n. A green vegetable with an edible stalk.

ce-les-ta (se les'ta) n. A musical instrument which produces bell-like tones when the keyboard and metal plates are struck by hammers.

ce-les-tial (se les'chel) adj. Heavenly; spiritual.

celestial body n. Any body of matter in the universe, such as a planet, star, or comet.

celestial equator n. The great circle of the celestial sphere, midway between the celestial poles, assumed to be the extension of the plane of the earth's equator.

celestial navigation n. Navigation by which a geographical location is determined by the position of celestial bodies.

celestial pole n. The two points on the celestial sphere around which the stars appear to revolve.

ce-li-ac (sē'lē ak')adj. Relating or pertaining to the cavity of the abdomen.

celiac disease n. A chronic nutritional disease of young children, common in the tropics, characterized by anemia, sore tongue, and diarrhea.

cel-i-bate (sel'a bit) n. A person who remains unmarried because of religious vows; one who is sexually abstinent. celibacy n. celibate adj.

cell (sel) n. A prison; a small room; the smallest unit of any organism that is cap-able of independent function, is composed of a small mass of cyto-plasm, usually encloses a central nucleus, and is surrounded by a membrane or a rigid cell wall; a cavity of an ovary or pericarp that is seed-bearing. Electr. The part of a battery that generates the electricity; in computer science, the location in memory that holds a single unit of information; a byte.

cel-lar (sel'er) n. An underground area, beneath a building, used for storage.

cel-lar-ette (sel'a ret') n. A cabinet or case for holding bottles of liquors or wines.

cell division n. The process of dividing both the cytoplasm and nucleus of a cell into two, in the process of reproduction.

cel-list (chel'ist) n. A person who plays the cello.

cell membrane n. The thin membrane enclosing the protoplasmic material of the cell; the cell wall.

cel-lo (chel'ō) n. A base instrument of the violin family. list n.

cel-lo-phane (sel'e fān') n. A transparent paper–like material made from treated cellulose that has been processed in thin, clear strips.

cel-lu-lar (sel'ya lēr) adj. Consisting of cells.

cel-lu-lase (sel'ya lās') n. An enzyme that hydrolyzes cellulosic; obtained from a fungus, and used in medicine, septic systems, and brewing.

cel-lu-lite (sel ye līt) n. A fatty deposit or area under the skin found in the hips, thighs, and buttocks.

cel-lu-lose (sel'ya lōs') n. A carbohydrate that is insoluble in ordinary solvents and forms the fundamental material for the structure of plants.

cell wall n. The definite boundary, formed by the protoplasm, that surrounds a biological cell.

ce-men-tum (si men'tum) n. The external layer of bony tissue that forms the outer surface of a tooth within the gum.

cem-e-ter-y (sem'i ter'ē) n. pl. -ies The place for burying the dead.

ce-no-bite (sē'no bīt') n. One of the religious groups that live in a convent or community.

ce-nog-a-my (sē nog'amē) n. The practice of having spouses in common, as primitive tribes.

cen-ser (sen'sēr) n. A vessel or container for burning incense.

cen-sor (sen'sēr) n. A person who examines films and printed materials to determine what might be objection-able and offensive. censorship n.

cen-sor-ship (sen'sēr ship') n. The practice of censoring; the authority of a censor.

cen-sure (sen'shur) n. An expression of criticism and disapproval.

cen-sus (sen'sus) n. An official count of the population.

cent (sent) n. One; one hundredth of a dollar.

cen-tare (sen'târ) n. A square meter.

cen-taur (sen'tor) n. In Greek mythol-ogy, a monster that has a man's arms, head, and trunk, but a horse's body and legs.

cen-te-nar-i-an (sen'te nâr'ē an) n. A person who has reached the age of 100 or more.

cen-te-na-ry (sen'te ner'ē) n. A period or age of 100 years; a century.

cen-ter (sen'tēr) n. The place of equal distance from all sides; the heart; in sports, a person who holds the middle position, as in the forward line.

cen-tile (sen'tīl) n. A scale of comparison from lowest to highest, derived at by dividing into 100 ranks with the lowest as the first.

centile rank n. A score that shows percent of a total distribution is below a certain score.

cen-ti-me-ter (sen´ti mē´tèr) *n.* A metric system of measurement; hundredth part of a meter; slightly more than 0.39 of an inch.

cen-ti-pede (sen´ti pēd´) *n.* A flat arthropod with numerous body segments and legs.

cen-to (sen´tō) *n.* A literary or musical composition made up of parts from other sources.

cen-tral (sen´tral) *adj.* In, near, or at the center; of primary importance. **centrally** *adv.* **centralize** *v.*

cen-tral-i-za-tion (sen´tra li zā´shan) *n.* The concentration of authority within any groups or organizations.

central nervous system *n.* The nervous system that consists of the spinal cord and the brain.

cen-trif-u-gal (sen trif´ū gal) *adj.* Moving or directing away from a center location.

cen-tri-fuge (sen´tri fūj´) *n.* A machine for inducing artificial gravity, used to test the ability of flying personnel, animal subjects, and equipment to withstand the above normal gravitational forces.

cen-tro-bar-ic (sen´tro bar´ik) *adj.* Having to do with the center of gravity; possessing a center of gravity.

cen-tro-sphere (sen´tro sfēr´) *n.* The thick material in the central part of the earth.

cen-tu-ry (sen´cha rē) *n.*, *pl.* **centuries** A period consisting of 100 years.

ceph-a-lal-gia (sef a lal´ja) *n.* Headache.

ceph-a-li-za-tion (sef a li zā´shan) *n.* An evolutionary tendency in the development of animals to localization of sensory and neural organs or parts in or near the head.

ceph-a-lo-pod (sef´a lo pod´) *n.* Any class of mollusks, including the octopus, cuttlefish, and squids, having a tubular siphon under the head.

ceph-a-lo-tho-rax (sef´a lō thōr´aks) *n.* The outer division of the body in crustaceans, spiders, etc. which consists of the united head and thorax.

ce-ram-ic (se ram´ik) *adj.* Of or relating to a brittle material made by firing a nonmetallic mineral, such as clay.

ceramics (se ram´iks) *n.* The art of making a ceramic piece.

cer-a-mist (ser´a mist) *n.* A person who works with ceramics.

ce-rar-gy-rite (se rär´jē rīt´) *n.* Native chloride of silver, having the appearance of horn, and forms an important ore of silver.

ce-rate (sēr´āt) *n.* A thick ointment made by mixing oils with wax, resin, and medicinal ingredients.

cer-car-i-a (sèr kâr´ē a) *n.* A larval stage of worms, characterized by an oval or tadpole shape.

cere (sēr) *n.* A protuberance or wax-like skin growth that contains the nostrils, located at the base of the bill of a bird.

ce-re-al (sēr´ē al) *n.* An edible grain eaten as a breakfast food.

cer-e-bel-lum (ser´e bel´um) *n. pl.* **-bellums** The part of the brain responsible for the coordination of voluntary muscular movements.

cerebral (ser´e bral) *adj.* Pertaining to the cerebrum or brain; relating to intellect.

cerebral hemisphere *n.* The two convoluted lateral halves into which the cerebrum is divided.

cerebral hemorrhage *n.* The rupture of a blood vessel or artery in the brain, therefore allowing blood to escape.

cerebral palsy *n.* A disability that usually occurred at birth and impairs motor function and speech; paralysis, due to brain damage prior to birth or during delivery.

cer-e-brate (ser´e brāt´) *v.* To have or exhibit brain action; to think; to use the mind.

cer-e-brum (ser´e brum) *n. pl.* **-brums** *or* **-bra** The brain structure that is divided into two cerebral hemispheres and occupies most of the cranial cavity.

cere-ment (sēr´ment) *n.* A shroud for wrapping a corpse; any burial cloth.

cer-e-mo-ni-al (ser´e mō´nē al) *adj.* Mark by or relating to a ceremony for a particular occasion.

cer-e-mo-ny (ser´e mō´nē) *n. pl.* **-ies** A ritual or formal act performed in a certain manner. **ceremonious** *adj.*

ce-rise (se rēs´) *n.* The color of deep purplish red.

ce-rite (sēr´īt) *n.* A rare mineral, of a pale rose-red color.

cer-met (sür´met) *n.* A strong heat-resistant compound, made by bonding a metal and a ceramic substance.

ce-ro (sēr´ō) *n.* Either of two large sport and food fishes of the mackerel family, found in the warmer parts of the western Atlantic ocean.

ce-ro-plas-tic (sēr´o plas´tik) *adj.* Pertaining to art modeling in wax.

cer-tain (sèr´tan) *adj. pl.* **-ties** Being very sure of something; without any doubt; inevitable; not mentioned but assumed. **tainly** *adv.* **certainty** *n.*

cer-tif-i-cate (sèr tif´i kāt´) *n.* A document stating the truth or accuracy of something; a document that certifies fulfillment of duties or requirements, as of a course of study.

cer-tif-i-ca-tion (ser´ti fi kā´shan) *n.* A certified statement.

certified check *n.* A check certified as good for payment by the bank upon which it is drawn.

certified mail *n.* First-class mail accompanied by a receipt to be signed by the addressee and returned to the sender.

certified public accountant *n.* A public accountant who has met the requirements of state government and has been granted a certificate from the state in which he/she works or practices.

cer-ti-fy (sĕr´ti fī´) *v.* To testify in writing that something is true or a fact.

cer-ti-o-ra-ri (sĕr´shē o râr´ē) *n.* A writ from a superior court to call up the records of an inferior court for trial or review.

cer-ti-tude (sĕr´ti tŏd´) *n.* Certainty; state of being or feeling certain.

ce-ruse (sēr´ös) *n.* White lead as a pigment, used in painting and cosmetics.

cer-ve-lat (sĕr´ve lat´)*n.* A kind of highly seasoned, dry sausage, usually of young pork salted.

cer-vi-cal (sĕr´vi kal) *adj.* Relating to the neck of the cervix.

cer-vi-ci-tis (sĕr´vi sī´tis) *n.* Inflammation of the uterine cervix.

cer-vix *n.* The neck, esp. the back of the neck; the narrow outer end of the uterus.

ce-sar-ean (si zâr´ē an) *n.* A surgical operation which involves cutting through the abdomen and the uterus to remove a baby when normal delivery is not advisable.

ce-si-um (sē´zē um) *n.* An electro-metal, white in color, from the alkali group, used in photoelectric cells.

ces-sa-tion (se sā´shan) *n.* The act of stopping or ceasing.

ces-sion (sesh´on) *n.* The act of giving up territory or rights to another.

cess-pool (ses´pöl´) *n.* A pit or hole for the collection of drainage from toilets, and sinks and other waste water.

ces-tode (ses´tŏd) *adj.* Belonging to the class or group of internally parasitic flatworms, including the tapeworm.

cet-rus (ses´tus) *n.* A leather hand covering, often loaded with lead or iron, worn by gladiators.

ce-ta-cean (si tā´shan) *n.* Marine mammals that include whales, dolphins, and porpoises.

ce-tane (sē´tān) *n.* A colorless, oily hydrocarbon liquid, used as an additive to improve diesel fuel.

cetane number *n.* The measure of diesel fuel ignition; rating similar to the octane number rating for gasoline.

chafe (chāf) *v.* To become sore by rubbing; to irritate.

chaff (chaf) *n.* The husks of corn and other debris separated from the corn by thrashing, sifting; straw or hay cut up as for food for cattle.

chaf-fer (chā´fĕr) *v.* To bargain; to haggle.

cha-grin (sha grin´) *n.* A feeling of distress caused by disappointment, failure, or humiliation. **chagrin** *v.*

chain (chān) *n.* A connection of several links; anything that confines or restrains. **chain gang** Prisoners that are chained together.

chain reaction *n.* Series of events each of which is initiated by the preceding one.

chair-person (châr´per´san) *n.* The person presiding over a committee, board, or other meeting.

chaise (shāz) *n.* A one horse vehicle for two people.

chaise lounge (shāz´long´) *n.* A chair that reclines and gives support for a person's legs and feet; a kind of reclining-chair with an elongated seat.

chal-ced-o-ny (kal sed´o nē) *n.* A translucent quartz, often pale blue or grayish with a waxlike shine.

chal-co-cite (kal´ko sīt´) *n.* Native sulfide of copper, a mineral having a dark-gray to black color and a metallic shine, occurring in crystals, and forms an important ore of copper.

cha-let (sha lā´) *n.* A cottage that has a gently sloping and overhanging roof.

chal-ice (chal´īs) *n.* A drinking goblet or cup.

chalk (chok) *n.* A soft mineral made from fossil seashells, used for marking on a sur- face, such as a slate board.

chalk-board (chok bōerd) *n.* A blackboard made from slate.

chalk-stone (chok´stōn´) *n.* A chalk-like mass in the small joints of person affected with gout.

chalk up *v.* To credit or attribute to.

chal-lah or **cha-lah** (käl e) *n.* A loaf of leavened white bread that is usually braided and eaten by Jews on holidays and the Sabbath.

chal-lenge (chal´inj) *n.* A demand for a contest; a protest. **challenge** *v.* To call into question. **challenger** *n.*

chal-lis (shal´ē) *n.* A lightweight printed cloth in rayon, cotton, or wool.

chal-one (kā lōn) *n.* A secretion of endocrine origin which inhibits bodily activity.

cha-lu-meau (shal´ū mō) *n.* Woodwind instrument having the lowest register of the clarinet.

cha-lyb-e-ate (ka lib´ē it) *n.* Water or medicine that contains iron.

cham-ber (chăm´bĕr) *n.* A bedroom in a large private home; a judge's office; a meeting place or hall for a legislative body; the compartment of a gun that holds the charge.

cham-ber-lain (chăm´bĕr lin) *n.* The high ranking official of a royal court; an officer charged with the direction and management of the private apartments of a monarch or nobleman..

cham-ber of commerce *n.* Organization of business people and merchants who meet in an effort to promote and regulate commercial and industrial interests in their area.

cham-fer (cham´fer) *n.* A small gutter cut in wood or other hard materials; a beveled edge.

champ (champ) *v.* To crush with the teeth; to chew vigorously or noisily; to show impatience in waiting.

cham-pagne (sham pān´) *n.* A white sparkling wine.

cham-per-ty (cham pert e) *n.* An illegal proceeding whereby a person not concerned in a lawsuit bargains to aid a plaintiff or defendant in consideration of a share of any proceeds gained from the suit.

cham-pi-gnon (sham´pin yen) *n.* The common edible meadow mushroom.

cham-pi-on (cham´pē an) *n.* The holder of first place in a contest; one who defends another person.

cham-pi-on-ship (cham´pē an ship´) *n.* The competition that determines a winner.

chance (chans) *n.* The random existence of something happening; a gamble or a risk, unexpected. **chance** *v.*

chance-ful (chans´ful) *adj.* Eventful; full of chances or accidents; hazardous.

chan-cel (chan´sel) *n.* The area of a church that contains the altar and choir.

chance--med-ley (chans´med´lē) *n.* A sudden, accidental homicide; a violent altercation; haphazard action.

chan-cer-y (chan´se rē) *n.* The office for the safekeeping of official records.

chan-cre (shang´kėr) *n.* A lesion that is the first indication of syphilis.

chan-croid (shang´kroid) *n.* A sore or lesion in the genital area that is similar to a chancre, but does not involve syphilis.

chanc-y (chan´sē) *adj.* Risky; dangerous.

chan-de-lier (shan´de lēr´) *n.* A light fixture with many branches for lights that is suspended from the ceiling.

chan-dler (chand´lėr) *n.* A person who makes and sells candles.

change (chānj) *v.* To become or make different; to alter; to put with another; to use to take the place of another; to freshen a bed by putting clean coverings on. **change** *n.* Coins; money given back when the payment exceeds the bill. **changer** *n.*

change-a-ble (chān je bel) *adj.* Liable or capable to change; subject to alteration; unstable. **changeably** *adv.* **changeability** *n.*

change of life *n.* The process of menopause for women, when they stop

having regular monthly periods.

chan-nel (chan´el) *n.* The deepest part of a stream, river, or harbor; the course that anything moves through or past; a groove. **channel** *v.*

chant (chant) *n.* A melody in which all words are sung on the same note. **chant** *v.* To celebrate with a song.

chan-teuse (shan tōs´) *n.* A professional female singer and entertainer, one who performs in cabarets or nightclubs.

chan-ti-cleer (chan´ti klēr´) *n.* A rooster.

Cha-nu-kah (chä´ne kä´) *n.* Variation of *Hanukkah.*

cha-os (kā´os) *n.* Total disorder. **chaotic** *adj.* **chaotically** *adv.*

chap (chap) *n., Slang* A fellow; a man. *v.* To dry and split open from the cold and wind.

chap-ar-ral (chap´a ral´) *n.* A thicket of low growing evergreen oaks.

chap-book (chap´būk´) *n.* A small book which contains poems, popular stories, fairy tales, ballads, or songs.

chap-el (chap´el) *n.* A place to worship, usually contained in a church.

chap-er-on *or* **chap-er-one (shap´e rōn´)** *n.* An older person who supervises younger people.

chap-fall-en (chap fo´len) *adj.* Having the lower jaw depressed and hanging loosely from exhaustion or humiliation.

chap-i-ter (chap´i tėr) *n.* The upper part or capital of a column.

chap-lain (chap´lin) *n.* A clergyman who conducts religious services for a group.

chap-let (chap´lit) *n.* A garland for the head; a string of beads.

chap-ter (chap´tėr) *n.* One division of a book; a branch of a fraternity, religious order, or society.

cha-que-ta (chä ke´tä) *n.* A leather jacket worn by cowboys of western United States.

char *or* **charr (chär)** *n.* Name given to a species of scaled trouts.

char-a-cin (kar´a sin) *n.* A member of the family of freshwater fishes, brightly colored for use in aquariums.

char-ac-ter (kar´ik tėr) *n.* A quality or trait that distinguishes an individual or group; a person that is portrayed in a play; a distinctive quality or trait. *adj.* Distinctive; peculiar.

char-ac-ter-i-za-tion (kar´ik tė i zā´shan) *n.* The act of characterizing; portrayal; description; artistic representation.

char-ac-ter-ize (kar´ik te rīz´) *v.* To describe the character or quality of; to be characteristic of.

cha-rade (sha rād´) *n.* A game in which words are represented or acted out by pantomime, and the other players must guess the word or phrase.

char-coal (chär´kōl´) *n.* A carbonaceous

material resulting from the imperfect combustion of organic matter, such as wood; material used to draw pictures.

chard (chärd) *n*. On edible white beet with large, succulent leaves.

charge (chärj) *v*. To give responsibility; to ask a price; to accuse; to impute something to; to command; to record a debt owed. *n*. Management; custody; supervision; an expense or price. *Slang* A thrill; excited. **chargeable** *adj*.

charge account *n*. A credit arrangement account where a customer may make im-mediate purchases and delay payment.

charge d'affaires *n*. A subordinate official who is in charge of diplomatic business during the temporary absence of an ambassador or minister.

charg-er (chär´jèr) *n*. An apparatus for recharging a battery.

char-i-ot (chär´ē ot) *n*. An ancient horse-drawn vehicle used to fight battles. **charioteer** *n*.

char-i-ot-eer (chär´ē o tēr) *n*. One who drives a chariot.

char-i-ta-ble (chár´l ta bl) *adj*. Pertaining to or characterized by good will or tenderness toward others; benevolent and kind to the poor.

char-i-ty (char´i tē) *n*. Money or help given to aid the needy; an organization, fund, or institution whose purpose is to aid those in need.

cha-ri-va-ri (sha riv´a rē) *n*. A mock serenade to newlyweds, performed with horns, tin pans, etc.

char-kha (chär´ka) *n*. A spinning wheel used in India for spinning cotton.

char-la-tan (shär´la tan) *n*. One who falsely claims to possess knowledge or a skill he does not have; impostor.

char-lock (chär lok) *n*. The wild mustard, often troublesome in grainfields.

char-lotte (shär´lot) *n*. A dessert consisting of fruit, custard, or whipped cream and cake or ladyfingers.

charm (chärm) *n*. The ability to delight or please; a small ornament that has a special meaning, usually worn on a bracelet.

char-meuse (shär möz´) *n*. A soft, variety of satin.

char-nel (chär´nel) *n*. A special room or building that contains the bones or bodies of the dead.

char-qui (chär´kē) *n*. Jerked beef; beef dried by exposure to the sun.

chart (chärt) *n*. A map, graph, or table that gives information in a form that is easy to read. **chart** *v*.

char-ta-ceous *adj*. Resembling paper: applied to the paper-like texture of leaves or bark.

char-ter (chär´tèr) *n*. An official document that grants certain privileges and rights. *v*. To lease or hire a vehicle or aircraft.

char-tist (chär´tist) *n*. An analyst of stock market prices, whose predictions are based on charts and graphics of past performance and information.

char-treuse (shär tröz´) *n*. A light yellowish green.

char-y (chär´ē) *adj*. Wary; cautious; not wasting time, resources, or money. **charily** *adv*. **chariness** *n*.

chase (chās) *v*. To follow quickly; to pursue; to run after. **chaser** *n*.

chasm (kaz´um) *n*. A very deep crack in the earth's surface.

chas-sis (shas´ē) *n*. The rectangular framework that supports the body and engine of a motor vehicle.

chaste (chāst) *adj*. Morally pure; modest; not guilty of participating in sexual intercourse.

chas-ten *v*. To inflict suffering upon for purposes of moral improvement; discipline or subdue, as by adversity.

chas-tise (chas tīz´) *v*. To severely reprimand; to punish by beating; as flogging. **chastisement** *n*

chas-u-ble (chaz´ū bl) *n*. The vestment without sleeves worn over the alb by a priest when celebrating mass.

chat (chat) *v*. To converse in a friendly manner.

cha-toy-ant (sha toi´ant) *adj*. Having a changeable undulating luster or color. **chatoyant** *n*. Any gem, as a cat's-eye, which is cut in a cabochon and reflects a single band of light.

chat-tel (chatel) *n*. An item of tangible movable personal property.

chauf-feur (shō´fèr) *n*. A person who is hired to drive an automobile for another person.

chaus-sure (shō syr´) *n*. A boot, shoe, slipper; a foot covering.

chau-vin (shō´vin) *n*. Anyone possessed by an absurdly enthusiasm for a cause.

chau-vin-ism (shō´ ve nizem) *n*. Unreasonable belief in the superiority of one's own group or organization. **chauvinist** *n*. **chauvinistic** *adj*.

chaw (cho) *v*. To chew; to chew tobacco.

cheap (chēp) *adj*. Inexpensive; low in cost; of poor quality. **cheap** *adv*. **cheaply** *adv*. **cheapness** *n*.

cheapen (chē´pen) *v*. To lessen the value; to make cheap.

cheap-skate (chēp´skāt´) *n*. A person who is very cheap and refuses to spend money.

cheat (chēt) *v*. To deprive of by deceit; to break the rules. **cheater** *n*.

check (chek) *v*. To control or restrain; to examine for correctness or condition. **check** *n*. The act of verifying, comparing, or testing; a bill one receives at a restaurant; a written order on one's bank to pay money from funds on deposit; the act of comparing item to item; a move in chess which threatens a king and which forces the opponent to move the king to safety.

check-book (chek´bek´) *n.* A book containing blank checks for a checking account.

checking account *n.* A bank account by which the depositor can draw checks.

check list *n.* An alphabetical or systematic list of names of persons or things, intended for purposes of reference.

check-point (chek´point) *n.* A point where inspections are made.

check-up (chek´up´) *n.* A complete physical examination.

ched-dar (ched´ér) *n.* A firm, smooth cheese which ranges in flavor from mild to sharp.

cheek (chēk) *n.* The fleshy part of the face just below the eye and above and to the side of the mouth.

cheek-bone (chēk´bōn´) *n.* The facial bone below the eyes.

cheeky (chē´kē) *adj.* Insolent; impudent.

cheep (chēp) *n.* To utter high-pitched sounds.

cheer (chēr) *v.* To give courage to; to instill with courage or hope.

cheese (chēz) *n.* A food made from the curd of milk that is seasoned and aged.

cheese-par-ing (chēz´pâr´ing) *n.* Something worthless and insignificant.

chee-tah (chē´ta) *n.* A swift-running, long-legged African wildcat.

chef (shef) *n.* A male cook who manages a kitchen; the head cook.

che-la (kē´la) *n.* The pincer-like claw of an arachnid.

che-lo-ni-an (ki lō´nē an) *n.* Tortoise; the tortoise family.

chem-i-cal (kem´i kal) *adj.* Of or related to chemistry. **chemically** *adv.*

chemical engineering *n.* A branch of chemistry that deals with the industrial application of chemistry.

chem-i-lum-i-nes-cence (kem´i lö¨mi nes´ans) *n.* Light produced due to chemical reactions at low temperatures.

chemin de fer *n.* A card game similar to baccarat.

che-mise (she mēz´) *n.* A woman's loose undergarment which resembles a slip; a loose-fitting dress that hangs straight down from the shoulders.

chem-i-sorp-tion (kem´e sorp´shan) *n.* Adsorption during a reaction between two or more chemicals.

chem-ist (kem´ist) *n.* A person who is versed in chemistry.

chem-is-try (kem´i strē) *n.* The scientific study of the composition, structure, and properties of substances and their react-ions.

chem-o-pro-phy-lax-is (kem´ō prō´fa lak´sis) *n.* The prevention of infectious disease by the use of chemical drugs or agents.

chem-os-mo-sis (kem´oz mō´sis) *n.* The chemical action between substances that occurs through an intervening membrane.

chem-o-syn-the-sis (kem´o sin´thi sis) *n.* The process by which organic compounds are formed from organic components by energy derived from chemical reactions.

chem-o-tax-is (kem´o tak´sis) *n.* The orientation or movement of a cell or organism toward or away from a chemical stimulus.

che-mo-ther-a-py (kem´o ther´a pē) *n.* The treatment of a disease, such as cancer, with chemicals.

che-mot-ro-pism (ki mo´tro piz¨um) *n.* The turning or bending of a plant or other organism in relation to chemical stimuli.

chem-ur-gy (kem´ü jē) *n.* A branch of applied chemistry dealing with industrial utilization of organic raw materials, especially from farm products.

cher-ish (cher´ish) *v.* To treat with love; to hold dear.

che-root (she rŏt´) *n.* A cigar that is cut off square at both ends.

cher-ry (cher´ē) *n., pl.* **cherries** A fruit tree bearing a small, round, red, or purplish red fruit with a small, hard stone.

cher-so-nese (kür´so nēz¨) *n.* A peninsula.

chert (chürt) *n.* A compact siliceous rock resembling flint and composed essentially of chalcedonic or opaline silica, either alone or in combination.

cher-ub (cher´ub) *n.* A beautiful young child; a representation of an angel resembling a child with a rosy face and wings.

cher-vil (chür´vil) *n.* An aromatic herb of the carrot family, leaves of which are used in soups and salads.

chest (chest) *n.* The part of the upper body that is enclosed by the thorax; the ribs; a box usually having a hinged lid, used for storage.

cheval glass *n.* A full-length mirror that may be tilted.

chew (chö) *v.* To crush or grind with the teeth; to masticate. **chew** *n.* The act of chewing. **chewer** *n.* **chewy** *adj.*

chi-an-ti (kē än´tē) *n.* A dry red or white wine from Italy.

chi-a-ro-scu-ro (kē är´o sker´ō) *n.* The distribution of shade and light in a picture.

chi-cane (shi kān´) *v.* To quibble over.

chick (chik) *n*. A young chicken or bird. *Slang* A young woman.

chick-en (chik´en) *n*. A domestic fowl; the edible meat of a chicken. *Slang* Cowardly; afraid; losing one's nerve.

chicken pox *n*. A contagious childhood disease, characterized by skin eruptions and fever.

chic-o-ry (chik´o rē) *n. pl.* -ies An herb with blue flowers used in salads, the dried, roasted roots of which are used as a coffee substitute.

chide (chīd) *v*. To scold or find fault, rebuke. **chider** *n*.

chief (chēf) *n*. The person of highest rank. *Slang* Boss. **chiefly** *adj*.

chief-ly (chēf´lē) *adv*. For the most part; mostly; most importantly.

chief-tain (chēf´tan) *n*. The head of a group, clan, or tribe.

chif-fon (shi fon´) *n*. A sheer fabric made from rayon or silk. *adj*. In cooking, having a fluffy texture.

chif-fo-nier (shif ə nēr´) *n*. A tall chest of drawers with a mirror at the top.

chig-ger (chig´ér) *n*. A mite that attaches itself to the skin and causes intense itching.

chi-gnon (shēn´yon) *n*. A roll of hair worn at the back of the neck; a large roll, knot, or twist of hair worn at the back of the head.

chig-oe (chig´ō) *n*. A tropical flee that closely resembles the common flea.

chil-blain (chil´blān´) *n*. An inflammation of the hands and feet caused by exposure to cold.

child (chīld) *n. pl.* **children** A young person of either sex; adolescent; a person between infancy and youth.

child abuse *n*. Sexual or physical mistreatment of a child by a parent, guardian, or other adult.

child-birth (chīld´berth´) *n*. The act of giving birth.

child-hood (chīld´hed) *n*. The time or period of being a child.

child like (chīld´līk´) *adj*. Characteristic of a child.

chil-i (chilē) *n*. A hot pepper; a thick sauce made of meat and chili powder.

chil-i-ad (kil´ē ad´) *n*. A group of one thousand; a period of 1000 years.

chill (chil) *v*. To be cold, often with shivering; to reduce to a lower temperature. *n*. A feeling of cold.

chime (chīm) *n*. A group or set of bells tuned to a scale. *v*. To announce on the hour, by sounding a chime.

chi-me-ra (ki mēr´a) *n*. An absurd fantasy; an imaginary monster with a goat's body, a lion's head, and a serpent's tail.

chi-mer-ic (ki mer´ik) *adj*. Pertaining to or being chimera; unreal; imaginary.

chin (chin) *n*. The lower part of the face.

v. To lift oneself up while grasping an overhead bar until the chin is level with the bar.

chi-na (chī´na) *n*. An earthenware or porcelain made in China.

chi-na-ware (chī´na wâr´) *n*. Tableware made of china or porcelain.

chine (chīn) *n*. The spine or backbone of animals.

chink (chingk) *n*. A narrow crack.

chi-no (chē´nō) *n*. A heavy cotton twill used for military uniforms.

chi-noi-se-rie (shēn woz´e rē) *n*. A style of Chinese art and ornamentation that reflects Chinese qualities, characterized by intricate patterns and motifs.

chintz (chints) *n*. A printed cotton fabric which is glazed.

chintz-y (chint´sē) *adj*. Cheap.

chip (chip) *n*. A small piece that has been broken or cut from another source; a disk used in the game of poker; in *computer science*, an integrated circuit engraved on a silicone substrate.

chip-per (chip´ér) *adj*. Cheerful; happy.

chi-rog-ra-phy (kī rog´ra fē) *n*. Penmanship; handwriting.

chi-ro-man-cy (kī´ro man sē) *n*. The ability of foretelling one's fortune by reading the lines of his hand.

chi-rop-o-dist (kī rop´o dist) *n*. One who treats ailments and irregularities of both the hands and feet.

chi-ro-prac-tic (kī´ro prak´tik) *n*. A method of therapy in which the body is manipulated to adjust the spine. **chiropract** *n*.

chirp (cherp) *n*. The high-pitched sound made by a cricket or certain small birds.

chirr (chür) *v*. To make a short vibrant or trilling sound, as a grasshopper.

chis-el (chiz´el) *n*. A tool with a sharp edge which is used to shape and cut metal, wood, or stone.

chis-eled (chiz´eld) *adj*. Formed or shaped with a chisel.

chit (chit) *n*. A voucher indicating the amount owed for food or drink; a lively girl.

chi-tin (kī´tin) *n*. The substance that forms the hard outer cover of insects.

chit-ter-lings (chit´ér ling) *n. pl.* The small intestines of a pig, used as food.

chiv-al-ry (shiv´al rē) *n. pl.* -ies The brave and courteous qualities of an ideal knight.

chive (chīv) *n*. An herb used as flavoring in cooking.

chlo-ral (klôral) *n*. A pungent colorless oily liquid first prepared from chlorine and alcohol; used in making DDT.

chlo-ral-ose (klôr´a lōs´) *n*. A crystalline compound of combining chloral dextrose, used in medicine as a hypnotic.

chlo-rate (klōr´āt) *n*. A chloric acid salt.

chlo-ride (klōr´īd) *n.* A compound of chlorine with a double positive element.

chlo-rin-ate (klō´i nāt´) *v.* To combine or treat with chlorine or a chlorine compound; to disinfect.

chlo-rine (klōr´ēn) *n.* A greenish-yellow compound used to purify water, bleach, and disinfectant.

chlo-rite (klōr´īt) *n.* A name for a group of usually green minerals, hydrous silicates of aluminum, ferrous iron, and magnesium.

chlo-ro-form (klōr´i form´) *n.* A colorless, volatile liquid of an agreeable smell and taste; used as a veterinary anesthetic.

chlo-ro-phyll (klōr´a fil) *n.* The green pigment that is found in photosynthetic organisms.

chlo-ro-pic-rin (klō´o pik´rin) *n.* A slightly oily, colorless, poisonous liquid that causes vomiting and tears used as a soil fumigant.

chlo-ro-sis (kla rō´sis) *n.* Iron-deficiency in a plant, from lack of iron in the soil or other causes.

chlor-prop-amide (klōr prōp´ amīd) *n.* An oral drug used to lower blood sugar, used to treat mild diabetes.

chock (chok) *n.* A wedge or block placed under a wheel to prevent motion.

choc-o-late (cho´ko lit) *n.* A preparation of ground and roasted cacao nuts that is usually sweetened; a candy or beverage made from chocolate. **chocolaty** *adj.*

choice (chois) *n.* To select or choose; the opportunity, right, or power to choose.

choir (kwīr) *n.* An organized group of singers that usually perform in a church.

choir-mas-ter (kwī´mas´tèr) *n.* The director of a choir, a conductor.

choke (chōk) *v.* To stop normal breathing by an obstruction in the windpipe; to strangle.

chok-er (chō´kèr) *n.* A necklace that fits tightly around the neck.

chol-e-cys-tec-to-my (kol´i si stek´to mē) *n.* The surgical removal of the gall bladder.

chol-er (kol´èr) *n.* Anger, wrath; the state of easily provoked anger.

chol-er-a (kol´èr a) *n.* Any of several infectious diseases of man and domestic animals usually showing signs of severe gastrointestinal symptoms.

chol-er-ic (kol´èr ik) *adj.* Easily irritated; hot tempered; inclined to excessive anger.

cho-les-ter-ol (ka les´te rōl´) *n.* A fatty crystalline substance that is derived from bile and is present in most gallstones, the brain, and blood cells.

cho-line (kō´lēn) *n.* A basic substance that occurs in many animal and plant products and is a member of the vitamin-B complex essential to the function of the liver.

chol-la (chōl´yä) *n.* A very spiny, treelike cacti of southwestern United States and Mexico.

choose (chōz) *v.* To select or pick out; to prefer; to make a choice. **choosy** *or* **chosen** *adj.* **choosey** *adj.*

choos-y (chō´zē) *adj.* Hard to please; particular, selective.

chop (chop) *v.* To cut by making a sharp downward stroke; to cut into bits or small pieces.

cho-ral (kōr´al) *adj.* Pertaining to, written for, or sung by a choir or chorus, adapted. **chorally** *adv.*

cho-rale (ko ral´) *n.* A Protestant hymn with a simple melody, sung in unison.

chord (kord) *n.* The sounding of three or more musical notes simultaneously.

chord-al (kor´dial) *adj.* Relating to music characterized by harmony rather than by counterpoint.

chore (chōr) *n.* A daily task; a task that becomes unpleasant or burdensome.

cho-re-a (ka rē´a) *n.* An acute nervous disease especially of children, marked by irregular and uncontrollable movement of muscles.

cho-re-og-ra-phy (kōr´ē og´ra fē) *n.* The creation of a dance routine for entertainment. **choreographic** *adj.*

cho-ri-o-al-lan-to-is (kōr´ē ō a lan´tō is) *n.* Vascular fetal membrane formed in the fetal tissue of birds, reptiles, and some mammals.

chor-is-ter (kor´i stèr) *n.* A choirboy or a member of a choir; a singer in a choir.

cho-rog-ra-phy (ko rog´ra fē) *n.* The art of mapping, or of describing particular regions, countries, or districts.

cho-rus (kōr´us) *n.* *pl.* **-ses** A group of people who sing together; the repeated verses of a song.

chose (shōz) *v.* The past tense of choose.

cho-sen (chō´zen) *adj.* Selected or preferred above all.

chow-der (chou´dèr) *n.* A soup dish made with fish or clams, often having a milk base.

Christ (krīst) *n.* Jesus; The Messiah; God's son who died to save Christians from sin.

chris-ten (kris´n) *v.* To baptize; to give a Christian name at baptism; to use for the first time. **christening** *n.*

Chris-tian (kris´chan) *n.* A believer and follower of the teachings of Jesus. **Christianly** *adv.* **Christianity** *n.*

Christ-mas (kris´mas) *n.* December 25th, the anniversary of the birth of Jesus Christ, observed as a holiday or holy day.

chro-ma (krō'ma) *n.* The purity or quality of a color, that combines hue and saturation.

chro-mat-ic (krō mat'ik) *adj.* Relating to color.

chrome alum *n.* A dark-violet salt in dyeing, tanning, and photography.

chro-mo-lith-o-graph(krō'mŏli thog'ra fē) *n.* A picture printed in colors by means of the lithographic process.

chro-mo-plast (krō'mo plast') *n.* A plastid, or mass of protoplasm, containing red or yellow pigment.

chro-mo-pro-tein (krō'mo prō'tēn) *n.* A protein compound, as hemoglobin, with a metal-containing pigment or a carotenoid.

chro-mo-some (krō'mə sōm') *n.* One of several small bodies in the nucleus of a cell, containing genes responsible for the determination and transmission of hereditary characteristics.

chro-mo-sphere (krō'mo sfēr') *n.* A gaseous layer surrounding the sun above the photosphere, consisting primarily of hydrogen.

chron-ic (kron'ik) *adj.* Long duration; frequently recurring; continuing for long periods of time; suffering from a disease for a long time.

chron-i-cle (kron'i kal) *n.* A record of events written in the order in which they occurred. **chronicle** *v.* **-er** *n.*

chron-o-graph (kron'o graf') *n.* An astronomical instrument for recording the exact instant of occurrences.

chro-nol-o-gy (krə nol'o jē) *n.* The science of measuring times, periods or years when past events or transactions took place, and arranging them in order of occurrence.

chron-o-scope (kron'o skōp') *n.* An instrument for precise measuring of extremely short-lived phenomena.

chrys-a-lis (kris'a lis) *n.* *pl.-* **ses** The enclosed pupa from which a moth or butterfly develops.

chry-san-the-mum (kri san'the mum) *n.* A cultivated plant having large, showy flowers.

chrys-o-ber-yl (kris'o ber'il) *n.* A mineral, usually of a yellow or greenish color, sometimes used as a gem.

chrys-o-lite (kris'o lit') *n.* A native silicate that varies from yellow to green in color, and in some forms used as a gem.

chtho-ni-an (thō'nē an) *adj.* Dwelling beneath the surface of the earth.

chub (chub) *n.* A freshwater fish related to the carp.

chub-by (chub'ē) *adj.* Plumb; rounded. **chubbiness** *n.*

chuck (chuk) *v.* To tap or pat affectionately under the chin. *Slang* To throw out or to throw away; to quit; to give up. **chuck** *n.* A cut of beef extending from the neck to the ribs.

chuck-hole (chuk'hōl) *n.* A hole in the street or the pavement.

chuck-le (chuk'ul) *v.* To laugh quietly with satisfaction. **chuckler** *n.*

chug (chug) *n.* A short, dull, explosive noise, as from a malfunctioning engine.

chuk-ka (chuk'a) *n.* An ankle-length of boot often made of leather, and laced through pairs of eyelets or a buckle.

chum (chum) *n.* A close friend or pal.

chunk (chungk) *n.* A thick piece of anything; a large quantity of something; a lump.

church (cherch) *n.* A building for Christian worship; a congregation of public Christian worship.

churl (cherl) *n.* A rude or rustic person. **churlish** *adj.* **churlishness** *n.*

churr (chür) *n.* The vibrant or whirring noise made by insects and some birds, such as a partridge.

chute (shōt) *n.* An incline passage through which water, coal, etc., may travel to a destination. *Slang* A parachute.

chut-ney (chut'nē) *n.* An agreeable condiment of fruit, spices, and herbs.

chyme (kīm) *n.* The semi-liquid mass into which food is expelled and converted by gastric secretion during digestion.

ci-ca-da (si kā da) *n.* The popular and generic name of insects with a stout body, large transparent wings and a wide blunt head.

ci-der (sī'dēr) *n.* The juice from apples.

ci-gar (si gär') *n.* Rolled tobacco leaves used for smoking.

cig-a-rette (sig'a ret') *n.* A small amount of tobacco rolled in thin paper for smoking.

cil-i-a (sil'ē a) *n.* The hairs that grow from the edge of the eyelids; eyelashes.

cil-i-ar-y (sil'ē er'ē) *adj.* Pertaining to the eyelids or eyelashes.

cil-ice (sil'is) *n.* A stiff undergarment made of horse or camel hair, formally worn by monks.

cinch (sinch) *n.* The strap for holding a saddle. *v.* To assure. *Slang* Something easy to do.

cin-cho-na (sin kō'na) *n.* A tree in South America whose bark yields quinine.

cin-chon-ism (sin'ko niz'um) *n.* A disorder of the body characterized by dizziness, ear ringing, temporary deafness, and headache, the result of overdoses of cinchona or its alkaloids.

cinc-ture (singk'chēr) *n.* A belt or cord to put around the waist. *v.* To encircle or sur-round with a cincture.

cin-der (sin'dēr) *n.* A piece of something that is partially burned. **cindery** *adj.*

cin-e-ma (sin'a ma) *n.* A motion picture;

a motion picture theater; the business of making a motion picture.

cin-e-mat-o-graph (sin´e mat´o graf´) *n.* A movie projector or camera.

cin-e-ma-tog-ra-phy (sin´e ma tog´ra fē) *n.* The art of photographing a motion picture. **cinematographer** *n.*

cin-e-rar-i-um (sin´a râ´ē um) *n.* A place for receiving the ashes of the dead after cremation.

ci-ne-re-ous (si nēr´ē us) *adj.* Resembling the color of wood ashes.

cin-na-bar (sin´a bär´) *n.* A mineral which is the principal source of mercury.

cin-na-mon (sin´a mon) *n.* The aromatic inner bark of a tropical Asian tree, used as a spice, reddish brown in color.

ci-pher (sī´fêr) *n.* The symbol for the absence of quantity; O; secret writing that has a prearranged key or scheme.

cir-cle (ser´kl) *n.* A process that ends at its starting point; a group of people having a common interest or activity.

cir-cuit (ser´kit) *n.* The closed path through which an electric current flows.

circuit breaker *n.* A switch that automatic-ally interrupts the flow of an electric current in an overloaded circuit.

circuit court *n.* The lowest court of record, located in two or more locations within one jurisdiction.

cir-cuit-ry (sür´ki trē) *n.* The arrangement or detailed plan of an electric circuit.

cir-cu-lar (ser´kū lêr) *adj.* Moving in a circle or round-like fashion; relating to something in a circle; having free motion, as the air. **circularity** *n.*

cir-cu-late (ser´kū lāt´) *v.* To pass from place to place or person to person; to distribute in a wide area. **circulation** *n.* **culator** *n.* **circulatory** *adj.*

cir-cu-la-tion (sür´kū lā´shan) *n.* The movement, or flow of blood through the vessels by the pumping action of the heart; the passing or transmission from one person to another.

cir-cum-cise (ser´kum sīz´) *v.* To remove the foreskin on the male penis, sometimes as a religious rite. **circumcision** *n.*

cir-cum-fer-ence (ser kum´fêr ens) *n.* The perimeter or boundary of a circle. **circumferential** *adj.*

cir-cum-flex (ser´kum fleks´) *n.* A mark indicating the quality or sound of vowels as they appear in words.

cir-cum-gy-ra-tion (sêr´kym jī rā´shan) *n.* A movement in a circular course.

cir-cum-ja-cent (sêr´kum jā´sent) *adj.* Bordering on all sides; surrounding.

cir-cum-lo-cu-tion (sêr´kum lō kū´shan) *n.* The use of more or unnecessarily large words to express an idea.

cir-cum-lu-nar (sür´cum lö´nêr) *adj.* Revolving about or surrounding the moon.

cir-cum-scribe (ser´kum skrīb´) *v.* To confine something within drawn boundaries; to surround.

cir-cum-spect (sür´kum spekt´) *adj.* Examining carefully all circumstances and possible consequences.

cir-cum-stance (ser´kum stans´) *n.* A fact or condition that must be considered when making a decision.

cir-cum-stan-tial (ser´kum stan´shal) *adj.* Incidental; not essential; dependent on circumstances.

cir-cum-stan-ti-ate (ser´kum stan´shē āt) *adj.* Providing support or circumstantial evidence.

cir-cum-vent (ser´kum vent´) *v.* To outwit or gain advantage; to avoid or go around. **circumvention** *n.*

cir-cum-vo-lu-tion (sür´kum vo lö´shan) *n.* The act or rolling or turning around an axis; a single complete turn.

cir-cum-volve (sür´kum volv´) *v.* To revolve about.

cir-cus (ser´kus) *n. pl.* **-cuses** Entertainment featuring clowns, acrobats, and trained animals.

cirque (sürk) *n.* A deep steep-walled circular space, a natural amphitheater.

cir-rho-sis (si rō´sis) *n.* A liver disease that is ultimately fatal. **cirrhotic** *adj.*

cir-ro-cu-mu-lus (sir´ō kū´mū lus) *n.* A cloud of high altitude, consisting of small white rounded masses.

cir-ro-stra-tus (sir´ō strā´tus) *n.* A whitish fairly uniformed layer of cloud or haze.

cir-rus (sir´us) *n. pl.* **cirri** A high altitude, white, wispy cloud.

cis-co (sis´kō) *n.* Any of various species of whitefish found in the Great Lakes area.

cis-tern (sis´têrn) *n.* A man-made tank or artificial reservoir for holding rain water.

cis-tron (sis´tron) *n.* The segment of DNA; the smallest single functional unit of genetic substance, considered equivalent to a gene in molecular biology.

cit-a-del (sit´a del) *n.* A fortress commanding a city; a stronghold.

ci-ta-tion (sī tā´shan) *n.* An official summons from a court; a quotation used in literary or legal material; an honor.

cite (sīt) *v.* To bring forward as proof; to summon to action; to rouse; to summon to appear in court.

cit-i-zen (sit´i zen) *n.* A resident of a town or city; a native or naturalized person entitled to protection from a government; a native or naturalized, as opposed to alien, member of a state or nation. **citizenry, citizenship** *n*.

citizen's band *n*. A two-way radio frequency band for private use.

cit-ral (si´tral) *n*. A liquid aldehyde with a strong lemon odor, obtained from oils of lemons or oranges, or synthetically manufactured, and used in perfumery and flavoring.

cit-ric a-cid (si´trik) *n*. A colorless acid found in lime, lemon, and other juices; the acid derived from lemons and similar fruits or obtained by the fermentation of carbohydrates, and used to flavor foods, beverages, and pharmaceuticals.

cit-ri-cul-ture (si´tri kul˘chĕr) *n*. The cultivation of citrus fruits.

cit-ron-el-la (si˘tra nel´a) *n*. A fragrant grass of southern Asia, found in many oils and used in making insect repellant, liniment, perfume, and soap.

cit-rus (sit´rus) *n. pl.* **citrus, citruses** Any of a variety of trees bearing fruit with thick skins, as limes, oranges, lemons, and grapefruits.

cit-tern (sit´ern) *n*. An ancient stringed instrument, somewhat resembling a guitar but with a more flat pear-shaped body.

cit-y (sit´ē) *n*. A place larger than a town.

city council *n*. The legislative body of a municipality or city with administrative and legislative power.

civ-et (siv´it) *n*. A cat-like mammal that secretes a musky fluid from the genital glands, which is used in perfumery.

civ-ic (siv´ik) *adj*. Relating to or of a citizen, city, or citizenship.

civ-ics (siv´iks) *n*. The social or political science of the rights and duties of citizens.

civ-il (siv´il) *adj*. Relating to citizens; relating to the legal proceedings concerned with the rights of private individuals.

civil aviation *n*. Aviation by commercial or private concerns as separated from military aviation.

civil defense *n*. A civilian program of volunteers ready to provide protection in case of a natural disaster, invasion, or enemy attack.

ci-vil-ian (si vil´yen) *n*. A person not serving in the military, as a firefighter, or as a policeman.

civ-i-li-za-tion (siv´i li zā´shan) *n*. A high level of social, cultural, and political development.

civ-i-lize (siv´i līz´) *v*. To bring out of a state of savagery into one of education and refinement.

civil rights *n. pl.* The nonpolitical rights guaranteed to citizens; the rights provided by the 13th and 14th amendments of the United States Constitution.

civil service *n*. The administrative or executive service of a government or international agency separate from the armed forces.

clack (klak) *n*. A sharp, abrupt sound, continuous talk; chatter.

clack valve *n*. A hinged valve in pumps with a single flap, that permits the flow of fluid in one direction only.

claim (klām) *v*. To ask for one's due; to hold something to be true; to make a statement that something is true; to demand. **claim** *n*. **claimant** *n*.

clair-voy-ance (klâr voi´ans) *n*. The ability to visualize in the mind distant objects or objects hidden from the senses; a mesmeric state.

clam (klam) *n*. Any of various marine and freshwater bivalve mollusks. *Slang* To become silent; to clam up.

clam-my (klam´ē) *adj*. Damp, cold, and sticky. **clammily** *adv*. **clamminess** *n*.

clam-or (klam´ĕr) *n*. A loud noise or outcry; a vehement protest or demand. **clamourous** *adj*. **clamorously** *adv*.

clamp (klamp) *n*. A device designed for holding or fastening things together.

clamp down *v*. The action of making or increasing restrictions or regulations.

clam-shell (klam´shel´) *n*. The shell of a clam; a dredging bucket having two hinged jaws.

clan (klan) *n*. A large group of people who are related to one another by a common ancestor. **clannish** *adj*.

clan-des-tine (klan des´tin) *adj*. Kept or done in secrecy for a purpose.

clang (klang) *v*. To cause or make a loud, ringing, metallic sound.

clan-gor (klang´ĕr) *n*. A loud series of clangs.

clank (klangk) *n*. A sharp, quick, metallic sound.

clap (klap) *v*. To applaud; to strike the hands together with an explosive sound.

clap-board (klab´ord) *n*. A narrow board with one end thicker than the other, used to cover the outside of buildings so as to weatherproof the inside.

claque (klak) *n*. A group hired to attend and applaud at a performance.

clar-en-don (klar´en don) *n*. A condensed style of printing type, similar to roman but with thicker lines.

clar-et (klar´it) *n*. A red Bordeaux table wine; similar red wines produced elsewhere.

clar-i-fy (klar´i fī´) *v*. To become or make clearer. **clarification** *n*.

clar-i-net (klar´i net´) *n*. A woodwind instrument with a single reed. **clarinetist** *n*.

clar-i-ty (klar´i tē) *n*. The state or quality of being clear.

clark-i-a (klär´kē a) *n*. A flowering annual herb of the evening primrose family.

cla-ro (klä´ō) *n.* A light-colored and typically mild cigar.

clar-y (klâr´ē) *n.* An aromatic mint herb used as a potherb and for medicinally.

clash (klash) *v.* To bring or strike together; to collide; to conflict.

clasp (klasp) *n.* A hook to hold parts of objects together; a grasp or grip of the hands. **clasp** *v.*

class (klas) *n.* A group or set that has certain social or other interests in common; a group of students who graduate at the same time.

clas-sic (klas´ik) *adj.* Belonging in a certain category of excellence; having a lasting artistic worth.

clas-si-cal (klas´i kal) *adj.* Relating to the style of the ancient Roman or Greek classics; standard and authoritative, not experimental or new.

clas-si-cism (klas´i siz´um) *n.* A belief in the esthetic principles of ancient Rome and Greece.

clas-si-cist (klas´i sist) *n.* A classical scholar; a follower of classicism.

clas-si-fi-ca-tion (klas´i fi kā´shan) *n.* The act of classifying; to systematically bring together those things which most resemble each other; arrange in categories.

clas-si-fied (klas´i fīd) *adj.* Arranged or divided into classes; withheld from the general public; confidential; secret.

clas-si-fy (klas´i fī´) *v.* To arrange or assign items, people, etc., into the same class or category. **classification** *n.*

class-mate (klas´māt´) *n.* A member of the same class in a school or college.

class-room (klas´rōm´) *n.* A room where students meet for classes and to study.

clas-tic (klas´tik) *adj.* Breaking up or made of fragments or parts.

clat-ter (klat´er) *v.* To make or to cause a rattling sound. **clatter** *n.*

clause (klos) *n.* A group of words which are part of a simple compound, or complex sentence, containing a subject and predicate.

claus-tro-pho-bia (klo´stro fō´bē a) *n.* A fear of small or enclosed places.

cla-ve (klä´vä) *n.* One of a pair of cylindrical hardwood sticks or blocks of wood, held in the hands and clicked together to the rhythm of music.

clav-i-chord (klav´i kord´) *n.* A keyboard instrument which is one step down from the piano.

clav-i-cle (klav´i kl) *n.* The bone that connects the breastbone and the shoulder blade.

cla-vier (kla vēr´) *n.* An instrument with a keyboard, such as the harpsichord.

claw (klo) *n.* A sharp, curved nail on the foot of an animal; the pincer of certain crustaceans, such as crab, lobster, etc.

clay (klā) *n.* A fine-grained, pliable earth that hardens when fired, used to make pottery, bricks, and tiles.

clean (klēn) *adj.* Free from impurities, dirt, or contamination; neat in habits.

clean-cut *n.* Distinctly outlined or defined; cut so the surface or edge is smooth and clean; a wholesome and neat appearance.

clean out *v., Slang* To empty, as a store; to deprive of resources.

cleanse (klenz) *v.* To make pure or clean. **cleanser** *n.*

clean-up (klēn´up´) *n.* An act or instance of cleaning; *Slang* A large profit on a bet or investment.

clear (klēr) *adj.* Free from precipitation and clouds; able to hear, see, or think easily; distinctly, free from doubt or confusion; free from a burden, obligation, or guilt. **clearly** *adv.*

clearance (klēr´ans) *n.* The distance that one object clears another by; a permission to proceed.

clear-head-ed (klēr´hed´id) *adj.* Having a clear understanding of something.

clearing house *n.* Stock Exchange and the Board of Trade, similar clearing houses exist for the facilitation of trading in stocks, grain, or other commodities.

cleat (klēt) *n.* A metal projection that provides support, grips, or prevents slipping.

cleav-a-ble (klē´va bl) *adj.* Capable of being separated or divided.

cleav-age (klē´vij) *n.* The process, act, or result of splitting; the cleft a woman displays in low-cut clothes.

cleave (klēv) *v.* To divide or split by a cutting blow, along a natural division line, as the grain of wood; split; to penetrate or pass through.

cleav-er (klē´vér) *n.* A knife used by butchers.

cleek (klēk) *n.* A large iron hook, used to suspend a pot over a fire.

clef (klef) *n.* A symbol indicating which pitch each line and space represents on a musical staff.

cleft (kleft) *n.* A space or opening made by partially splitting; a crevice.

clem-ent (klem´ent) *adj.* Merciful; mild.

clench (klench) *v.* To clinch; to hold firmly, as with the hands or teeth, close tightly.

clep-sy-dra (klep´si dra) *n.* A name for common devices used for measuring time by the regulated discharge of water; a water clock.

clep-to-ma-ni-a *n.* Compulsive stealing.

cler-gy (klér´jē) *n.* The group of men and women who are ordained as religious leaders and servants of God.

cler-ic (klér´ik) *adj.* Pertaining to the clergy; clerical.

cler-i-cal (kler´i kəl) *adj.* Trained to handle office duties.

clerk (klork) *n.* A worker in an office who keeps accounts, records, and correspondence up to date; a person who works in the sales department of a store.

Cleveland, Stephen Grover *n.* (1837-1908) The twenty-second and twenty-fourth president of the United States, from 1885-1889 and 1893-1897.

clev-er (klev´ẽr) *adj.* Mentally quick; showing dexterity and skill. **cleverly** *adv.* **cleverness** *n.*

clev-is (klev´is) *n.* A piece of metal, usually U-shaped, having a pin or bolt that connects the two sides; shackle.

clew (klō) *n.* A ball of thread, cord, or yarn; a lower corner or loop of a sail.

click (klik) *n.* To make a small sharp sound; to move, strike or produce with a click.

cli-ent (klī´ent) *n.* A person who secures the professional services of another.

cli-en-tele (klī´en tel´) *n.* A collection of patients, customers, or clients.

cliff (klif) *n.* A high, steep edge or face of a rock.

cliff-hanger (klif´hang´ẽr) *n.* Anything which causes suspense and anticipation until the final outcome is known.

cli-mate (klī´mit) *n.* The weather conditions of a certain region generalized or averaged over a period of years; the prevailing atmosphere. **climatic** *adj.* **climatically** *adv.*

cli-ma-tol-o-gy (klī´ma tol´o jē) *n.* The science that deals with climates, an investigation of their phenomena.

cli-max (klī´maks) *n.* The point of greatest intensity and fullest suspense; the culmination.

climb (klīm) *v.* To move to a higher or lower location; to advance in rank or status. **climbable** *adj.* **climber** *n.*

clinch (klinch) *v.* To secure; to fasten; to settle definitively. **clinch** *n.*

cling (kling) *v.* To hold fast to; to grasp or stick, to hold on and resist emotional separation. **clinger** *n.*

clin-ic (klin´ik) *n.* A medical establishment connected with a hospital; a center that offers instruction or counseling.

clinical thermometer *n.* An instrument used in medical practice to measure the body temperature.

cli-ni-cian (kli nish´an) *n.* A physician or one qualified in clinical method skills.

clink (klingk) *v.* To cause a light ringing sound.

clink-er (kling´ker) *n.* An over baked, hard yellowish Dutch brick used for paving. *n., Slang* A blunder; a flop.

clink-er—built *adj.* Having external plates

overlapping one another; as the clapboards of a house.

clin-quant (kling´kant) *adj.* Glittering with tinsel or gold.

Clinton, William *n.* (1946-) The forty-second president of the United States from 1993-.

clip (klip) *v.* To cut off; to curtail; to cut short. *n.* Something that grips, holds, or clasps articles together.

clip artist *n., Slang* A person who makes a profession of robbing or swindling.

clip-board (klip´bôrd´) *n.* A small writing board, having a spring clip, usually at the top, to hold sheets of paper.

clip-per (klip´ẽr) *n.* A sailing vessel that travels at a high rate of speed.

clip-per (klip´ẽr) *n.* A tool used for cutting.

clique (klēk) *n.* A small and exclusive group of people.

cloak (klōk) *n.* A loose outer garment that conceals or covers.

clob-ber (klob´ẽr) *v., Slang* To hit repeatedly and violently.

cloche (klōsh) *n.* A bell-shaped, close-fitting hat.

clock (klok) *n.* An instrument that measures time. **clock** *v.* To time with a watch, clock, stopwatch, etc.

clock-wise (klok´wīz´) *adv.* In the direction the hands of a clock rotate.

clod (klod) *n.* A large piece or lump of earth; a stupid, ignorant person.

clog (klog) *v.* To choke up. *n.* A shoe with a wooden sole.

clois-ter (klol´stẽr) *v.* To confine or seclude in a cloister or convent.

clone (klōn) *n.* An identical reproduction grown from a single cell of the original.

clop (klŏp) *v.* To produce a hollow sound, as if done by a horse's hoof or wooden shoe.

close (klōs) *adj.* Near, as in time, space, or relationship; nearly even, as in competition; fitting tightly. *v.* To shut.

closed (klōzd) *adj.* Forming a self-contained barrier, limited as to season for hunting or fishing.

closed circuit *n.* An unbroken circuit permitting a signal to be transmitted by wire to a limited number of receivers.

close—out (klōz´out´) *n.* A clearance sale of merchandise usually at a reduced price.

close shave *n., Slang* A narrow escape.

clos-et (kloz´it) *n.* A small cabinet, compartment, or room for storage.

close-up (klōs´up´) *n.* A picture taken at close range; a close view or examination of something.

clo-sure (klō´zhẽr) *n.* The act or condition of being closed; an end or conclusion.

clot (klot) *n*. A thick or solid mass, as of blood. **clot** *v*.

cloth (kloth) *n*. *pl*. **cloths** A knitted, woven, or matted piece of fabric, used to cover a table; the professional clothing of the clergy.

clothe (klōth) *v*. To provide clothes; to cover with clothes; to wrap.

clothes (klōz) *n*. Cloth items of a person that can be worn and are washable; dress.

cloth-ing (klō thing) *n*. Garments in general; clothes.

clo-ture (klō shér) *n*. A parliamentary action that calls for an immediate vote.

cloud (kloud) *n*. A visible body of water or ice particles floating in the atmosphere; something that obscures; a cloud of dust or smoke. **cloudy** *adj*.

cloud-i-ly (kloud i lē) *adv*. In an obscure or cloudy manner.

clout (klout) *n*. A heavy blow with the hand. *Slang* The amount of influence or pull a person may have. **clout** *v*.

clove (klōv) *n*. A spice from an evergreen tree; a small bud that is part of a larger group, as a clove of garlic.

clo-ver (klō vér) *n*. A plant that has a dense flower and trifoliolate leaves.

cloy (kloi) *v*. To make one sick or disgusted with too much sweetness.

club (klub) *n*. A heavy wooden stick, used as a weapon; a group of people who have organized themselves with or for a com-mon purpose.

clue (klōō) *n*. Reliable information that leads to the solution of a problem, crime or mystery.

clump (klump) *n*. A group of things in a cluster or group; a shapeless mass. *v*. To plant or place in a clump.

clum-sy (klum zē) *adj*. Lacking coordination, grace, or dexterity; not tactful or skillful. **clumsily** *adv*.

clus-ter (klus tér) *n*. A bunch; a group.

clutch (kluch) *v*. To seize or attempt to seize and hold tightly. *n*. A tight grasp; a device for connecting and disconnecting the engine and the drive shaft in an automobile or other mechanism.

clut-ter (klut ér) *n*. A confused mass of disorder.

coach (kōch) *n*. An automobile that is closed and usually has four doors and four wheels; a trainer or director of athletics, drama, etc.

coach-man (kōch mam) *n*. A man employed to drive a carriage or coach.

co-ad-ju-tor (kō aj u tér) *n*. An assistant.

co-ag-u-la-bil-i-ty (kō ag u la bil i tē) *n*. The capacity of being coagulated.

co-ag-u-lant (kō ag u lant) *n*. A substance that causes coagulation.

co-ag-u-late (kō ag u lāt) *v*. To clot or congeal. **coagulation** *n*.

coal (kōl) *n*. A mineral widely used as a natural fuel; an ember.

coal-er (kō lér) *n*. A person who sells or provides coal; something used to haul or transport coal.

co-a-lesce (kō a les) *v*. To come together or to grow as one.

co-ali-tion (kō a lish an) *n*. A temporary alliance.

co-apt (kō apt) *v*. To fit together and make fast, as in the setting of broken bones.

co-arc-tate (kō ärk tāt) *adj*. Pressed together; compressed; enclosed in a rigid case.

coarse (kōrs) *adj*. Lacks refinement; of inferior or low quality; having large particles; harsh. **coarseness** *v*.

coast (kōst) *v*. To move without propelling oneself; to use the force of gravity alone; to slide or glide along. *n*. The land bordering the sea.

coat (kōt) *n*. An outer garment with sleeves, worn over other clothing; a layer that covers a surface.

co-au-thor (kō o thér) *n*. A person who writes with the assistance of one or more other authors.

coax (kōks) *v*. To persuade by tact, gentleness, or flattery. **coaxingly** *adv*.

co-ax-i-al (kō ak sē al) *adj*. Having common coincident axes.

coaxial cable *n*. A transmission cable consisting of two or more insulated conductors capable of transmitting television, telegraph, signals of high frequency.

cob (kob) *n*. A male swan; a corncob; a thick-set horse that has short legs.

co-balt (kō bolt) *n*. A hard, lustrous metallic element that resembles iron and nickel.

cob-ble (kob l) *v*. To make or repair shoes; to make or put together roughly. **cobbler, cobble** *n*.

CO-BOL (kō bōl) *n*. In Computer Science, computer programming that is simple and based on English.

cob-web (kob web) *n*. The fine thread from a spider which is spun into a web and used to catch prey.

ce-caine (kō kān) *n*. An alkaloid used as an anesthetic and narcotic.

ce-cain-ism (kō kā niz um) *n*., *Pathol*. The addiction to the use of cocaine.

coc-cyx (kok siks) *n*. The small bone at the bottom of the spinal column.

coch-i-neal (koch i nēl) *n*. A brilliant scarlet dye prepared from the dried, pulverized bodies of certain female insects of tropical America.

coch-le-a (kok lē a) *n*. The spiral tube of the inner ear, forming an essential part for hearing.

cock (kok) *n*. The adult male in the domestic fowl family; the rooster; the hammer of a firearm and the readiness for firing. *v.* To raise in preparation for hitting; to ready a firearm for firing.

cock-ade (ko kād´) *n.* A knot of ribbon or something similar worn on a hat as a badge.

cock-eyed (kok´īd) *adj., Slang* Absurdly wrong; slightly crazy; foolishly twisted to one side.

cock-i-ly (kok´i lē) *adv.* In a cocky manner.

cock-loft (kok´loft) *n.* A small loft in the top of a house; a small garret.

cock-pit (kok´pit´) *n.* The compartment of an airplane where the pilot and the crew sit.

cock-roach (kok´rōch´) *n.* A flat-bodied, fast running, chiefly nocturnal insect, many of which are household pests.

cock-sure (kok´shür´) *adj.* Perfectly sure or certain; sometimes on inadequate grounds.

co-co (kō´kō) *n.* The fruit obtained from the coconut palm.

co-coa (kō´kō) *n.* The powder from the roasted husked seed kernels of the cacao.

cocoa butter *n.* A pale fatty substance obtained from cacao beans, used in cosmetics and lotions.

co-co-nut (kō´ko nut) *n.* The nut of the coconut palm, having a hard shell, with a white edible meat, and contains a milky liquid.

co-coon (ko kōn´) *n.* The protective fiber or silk pupal case that is spun by insect larvae.

cod (kod) *n.* A large fish of the North Atlantic important as food.

cod-dle (kod´el) *v.* To cook just below the boiling point; to simmer.

code (kōd) *n.* A system of set rules, a set of secret words, numbers, or letters used as a means of communication; in *Computer Science*, the method of representing information or data by using a set sequence of characters, symbols, or words. **code** *v.*

code conversion *n., Computer* The conversion of information from one code to another.

co-de-fend-ant (kō´di fen´dant)) *n.* One or more defendants in a legal action; a joint defendant.

co-dex (kō´deks) *n.* An ancient manuscript of the classics or Scriptures.

codg-er (koj´ėr) *n.* An odd or eccentric old man.

cod-i-fy (kod´i fī) *v.* To reduce to a code.

co-ed (kō´ed´) *adj.* For, open to or including both men and women; to include both sexes.

co—ed-u-ca-tion (kō´ej e kā´shan) *n.* An educational system for both men and women at the same institution. **coeducational** *adj.*

co-e-qual (kō ē´kwal) *adj.* Equal with

one another, person or thing.

co-erce (kō ėrs´) *v.* To restrain or dominate with force; to compel by law, authority, fear, or force.

co-e-ta-ne-ous (kō´i tā´nē us) *adj.* Beginning to grow or exist at the same time.

co-e-ter-nal (kō´i tür´nal) *adj.* Equally or jointly eternal with another.

co-e-val (kō ē´val) *adj.* Of the same time period. **coeval** *n.*

co-ex-ec-u-tor (kō´ig zek´ū tėr) *n.* A joint executor of a will.

co-ex-ist (kō´ig zist´) *v.* To exist at the same time or together; the ability to live peaceably with others in spite of differences. **coexistence** *n.*

co-ex-ten-sive (kō´ik sten´siv) *adj.* Having the same boundaries.

cof-fee (ko´fē) *n.* A beverage prepared from ground beans of the coffee tree.

cof-fer (ko´fėr) *n.* A strongbox or chest made for valuables.

cof-fin (ko´fin) *n.* A box in which a corpse is buried.

cog (kog) *n.* A tooth or one of a series of teeth on the rim of a wheel in a machine or a mechanical device.

co-gent (kō´jent) *adj.* Compelling; forceful; convincing.

cog-i-tate (koj´i tāt´) *v.* To think carefully about or to ponder; give thought to. **cogitation** *n.* **cogitative** *adj.*

co-gnac (kōn´yak) *n.* A fine brandy made in France.

cog-nate (kog´nāt) *adj.* From a common ancestor; identical or similar in nature; related

cog-na-tion (kog nā´shan) *n.* Relationship by blood.

cog-ni-za-ble (kog´ni za bl) *adj.* Capable of being noticed or observed.

cog-ni-zance (kog´ni zans) *n.* Perception of fact; awareness; recognition; observation.

cog-ni-zant (kog´ni zant) *adj.* Obtained knowledge through personal experiences.

cog-nize (kog nīz´) *v.* To recognize as an object of thought; to perceive; understand.

cog-no-men (kog nō´men) *n. pl.* **cognomens** A person's surname; nickname.

cog-nos-ci-ble (kog nos´ibl) *adj.* Capable of being known; knowable.

cog-wheel (kog´hwēl) *n.* A wheel with cogs or teeth; a gear wheel.

co-hab-it (kō hab´it) *v.* To live together as husband and wife.

co-heir (kō âr´) *n.* A joint heir; a person who shares an inheritance with another.

co-here (kō hēr´) *v.* To stick or hold together.

co-her-ent (kō hēr´ent) *adj.* Sticking together; consistent; to remain united.

co-he-sion (kō hē´zhan) *n.* The act or

state of sticking together.

co-he-sive (kō hē´siv) *adj.* Sticking together.

co-hort (kō´hort) *n.* A group of people who are united in one effort; an accomplice.

coif (koif) *n.* A close-fitting hat that is worn under a nun's veil.

coif-feur (kwä fyür´) *n.* A male hairdresser.

coil (koil) *n.* A series of connecting rings. *v.* To wind in spirals.

coin (koin) *n.* A flat, rounded piece of metal used as money. *v.* To invent or make a new phrase or word.

co-in-cide (kō´in sīd´) *v.* To happen at the same time; to agree exactly.

co-in-ci-dence (kō in´si dens) *n.* Two events happening at the same time by accident but appearing to have some connection.

co-in-ci-dent (kō in´si dent) *adj.* Occupying the same place, position or time simultaneously.

co-in-ci-den-tal (kō in´si den´tal) *adj.* Involving or resulting from a coincidence; happening or existing at the same time.

co-in-her-it-ance (kō´in her´i tans) *n.* Joint inheritance.

co-in-stan-ta-ne-ous (kō´in stan tā´nē us) *adj.* Happening at the same time or instant.

co-in-sur-ance (kō´in shür´ans) *n.* Insurance jointly assumed by another or others.

co-in-sure (kō´in shür´) *v.* To insure jointly with another.

co-i-tus (kō´i tus) *n.* Physical union of male and female sexual organs; sexual intercourse.

coke (kōk) *n.* A solid, carbonaceous fuel made by heating soft coal until some of its gases have been removed. *Slang* Cocaine.

co-l-an-der (kul´an der) *n.* A utensil with a perforated bottom, used for washing or draining food and straining liquids.

cold (kōld) *adj.* Having a low temperature; feeling uncomfortable; without sufficient warmth; lacking in affection or sexual desire; frigid. *n.* An infection of the upper respiratory tract resulting in coughing, sneezing, etc. **-ness** *n.*

cold boot *n., Computer Science* The boot performed when power is turned on for the first time each day.

cole (kōl) *n.* A plant such as the cabbage or a vegetable of the same family.

co-lec-to-my (kō lek´to mē) *n., Surg.* Complete or partial removal of the colon or large intestine.

col-ic (kol´ik) *n.* A sharp pain in the abdomen caused by muscular cramps or spasms, occurring most often in very young babies.

col-i-se-um (kol´i sē´um) *n.* A large amphitheater used for sporting games.

co-lit-is (ko lī´tis) *n., Pathol.* Inflammation of the colon.

col-lab-o-rate (ko lab´o rāt´) *v.* To cooperate or work with another person. **collaboration** *n.* **collaborator** *n.*

col-lapse (ko laps´) *v.* To fall; to give way; to fold and assume a smaller size; to lose all or part of the air in a lung.

col-lar (kol´er) *n.* The upper part of a garment that encircles the neck and is often folded over.

col-lar-bone (kol´er bōn´) *n., Anat.* The clavicle, located near the neck.

col-lard (kol´ard) *n.* A smooth-leaved vegetable of the kale family.

col-late (ko lāt´) *v.* To compare in a critical fashion; to assemble in correct sequence or order.

col-lat-er-al (ko lat´er al) *adj.* Serving to support; guaranteed by stocks, property, bonds, etc.

col-league (kol´ēg) *n.* Someone who works in the same profession or official body.

col-lect (ko lekt´) *v.* To gather or assemble; to gather donations or payments. **collectible** *n.* **collection** *n.*

col-lec-tion (ko lek´shan) *n.* The act or process of collecting or gathering.

col-lec-tive (ko lek´tiv) *adj.* Formed by a number of things or persons.

col-lec-tiv-i-ty (kol´ek tiv´i tē) *n.* Collective character; the state of being collective.

col-lege (kol´ij) *n.* An institution of higher education which grants a bachelor's degree; a school of special instruction or special fields.

col-le-gian (ko lē´jan) *n.* A student or graduate of a college.

col-lide (ko līd´) *v.* To come together with a direct impact; to clash; to come into conflict.

col-li-mate (kol´i māt) *v.* To adjust or to bring into line; make parallel.

col-lin-e-ar (ko lin´ē ar) *adj.* Lying in or passing through the same straight line.

col-li-sion (ko lizh´on) *n.* The act of striking or colliding together.

col-lo-cate (kol´o kāt´) *v.* To compare facts and arrange in correct order; to set or place with, or in relation to.

col-lo-di-on (ko lō´dē on) *n.* A highly flammable spray solution used to protect wounds and used for photographic plates.

col-loid (kol´oid) *n.* A glue-like substance, such as gelatin, that cannot pass through animal membranes.

col-lo-quy (kol´o kwē) *n. pl.* **-quies** A formal conversation or conference.

col-lude (ko lōd´) *v.* To act together through a secret understanding.

col-lu-sion (ko lō´zhon) *n.* A secret agreement between two or more people for an illegal purpose.

co-logne (ko lōn´) *n.* A perfumed substance of fragrant oils and alcohol.

co-lon (kō´lon) *n.* A punctuation mark (:) used to introduce an example or series; used to separate words and numbers; the section of the large intestine that extends from the cecum to the rectum. **colonic** *adj.*

colo-nel (ker´nel) *n.* An officer in the armed forces that ranks above a lieutenant colonel and below a brigadier general.

co-lo-ni-al (ko lō´nē al) *adj.* Pertaining to a colony or colonies.

co-lo-ni-al-ism (ko lō´nē a līz˝um) *n.* The colonial system; the control over an area of people; a policy based on such control.

col-o-ny (kol´o nē) *n. pl* -ies A group of emigrants living in a new land away from, but under the control of, the parent country; a group of insects, as ants.

col-o-phon (kol´o fon´) *n.* The inscription at the end of a book that gives the publication facts.

col-or (kul´ér) *n.* The aspect of things apart from the shape, size, and solidity; a hue or tint that is caused by the different degrees of light that are reflected or emitted by them. **colored** *adj.* **colorful** *adj.* **coloring** *n.*

Col-o-ra-do *n.* A state located in the western central part of the United States, statehood August 1, 1876, state capital Denver.

col-or-a-tion (kul´o rā´shan) *n.* The arrangement of different colors or shades.

col-or-bear-er (kul´ê bâr´ér) *n.* The person in charge of carrying the colors, as of a military formation.

col-or-blind (kul´ér blind´) *adj.* Unable to distinguish colors, either totally or partially.

col-or-cast (kul´ér kâst´) *n.* A television broadcast or program presented in color.

col-or-fast (kul´ér fast´) *adj.* Color that will not run or fade with washing or wearing. **colorfastness** *n.*

color guard *n.* A person in charge of the colors, the flag, as of a military unit.

col-or-ist (kul´ér ist) *n.* A person who colors or works with colors.

col-or-less (kul´ér lis) *adj.* Destitute or lacking color; washed-out.

co-los-sal (ko los´al) *adj.* Very large or gigantic in degree or size.

co-los-sus (ko los´us) *n.* Something that is very large, as a huge state, thing, or person.

col-por-teur (kol´pōr˝tér) *n.* A person who travels from place to place distributing or peddling religious materials and Bibles.

colt (kōlt) *n.* A very young male horse.

col-umn (kol´um) *n.* A decorative and or supporting pillar used in construction; a vertical division of typed or printed lines on paper.

co-lum-nar (ko lum´nér) *adj.* Of, pertaining to, or relating to columns.

col-lum-ni-a-tion (ko lum˝nē ā´shan) *n.* The arrangement of columns in a structure.

col-um-nist (kol´um nist) *n.* A person who writes a newspaper or magazine column.

co-ma (kō´ma) *n.* A deep sleep or unconsciousness caused by an illness or injury.

co-ma-tose (kom´a tōs´) *adj.* Unconscious.

comb (kōm) *n.* A toothed instrument made from a material such as plastic used for smoothing and arranging the hair; the fleshy crest on the head of a fowl.

com-bat (kom bat´) *v.* To fight against; to oppose; to contend. *n.* A struggle; a fight or contest especially with armed conflict, as a battle, war with others.

com-ba-tive (kom bat´iv) *adj.* Marked by eagerness to fight.

comb-er (kō´mér) *n.* A machine or person that combs wool or cotton.

com-bin-a-ble (kom bī´na bl) *adj.* That which may be combined.

com-bi-na-tion (kom˝bi nā´shan) *n.* The process of combining or the state of being combined; a series of numbers or letters needed to open certain locks.

com-bine (kom bin´) *v.* To unite; to merge. *n.* A farm machine that harvests by cutting, threshing, and cleaning the grain.

com-bo (kom´bō) *n.* A small jazz group of three or four musicians who dances.

com-bust (kom bust´) *adj.* To burn up.

com-bus-ti-bil-i-ty (kom bus´ti bil´i tē) *n.* The state of being combustible.

com-bus-ti-ble (kom bus´ti bl) *adj.* Having the capability of burning. *n.* A combustible material as paper or wood.

com-bus-tion (kom bus´chan) *n.* The chemical change that occurs rapidly and pro-duces heat and light; a burning; fire **combustive** *adj.*

come (kum) *v.* To arrive; to approach; to reach a certain position, state, or result; to appear; to come into view.

come about *v.* To come to pass.

come across *v.* To find by chance; to produce an impression

come along *v.* To improve.

come back *v.* To return to health or to a former position or success.

co-me-di-an (ko mē'dē an) *n.* An actor of comedy.

come down *v.* To be humbled; to lose rank or position.

com-e-dy (kom'i dē) *n. pl.* **-ies** A humorous, entertaining performance with a happy ending; a real-life comical situation. **comedic** *adj.*

come in *v.* To enter; to become fashionable; to be brought into use.

co-mes-ti-ble (ko mes'ti bl) *n.* Something that is fit to eat. *adj.* Fit to eat.

com-et (kom'it) *n.* A celestial body that moves in an orbit around the sun, consisting of a solid head that is surrounded by a bright cloud with a long, vaporous tail.

com-fort (kum'fèrt) *v.* To console in time of grief or fear; to make someone feel better; to help; to assist, to have relief or satisfaction; solace. *n.*

com-fort-a-ble (kumf'ta bl) *adj.* In a state of comfort; financially secure, content and happy. **comfortably** *adv.*

com-ic (kom'ik) *adj.* Characteristic of comedy. *n.* A comedian; comic book. **Comics** Comic strips.

com-i-cal (kom'i kal) *adj.* Amusing; humorous.

comic strip *n.* Narrative cartoons appearing in sequence, usually found in newspapers.

com-ing (kum'ing) *n.* Approach; instance of arriving.

com-ma (kom'a) *n.* The punctuation mark (,) used to indicate separation of ideas or a series in a sentence.

com-mand (ko mand') *v.* To rule; to give orders; to dominate. *n., Computer Science* The instruction given that specifies an operation to be performed.

com-man-deer (kom'an dèr') *v.* To force into active military service; to seize.

com-mand-er (kom'an dèr') *n.* The person authorized to command; a leader or chief officer.

com-mand-ment (ko mand'ment) *n.* The act, or power of commanding; a command or mandate.

com-mem-o-rate (ko mem'o rāt) *v.* To honor the memory of; to create a memorial to. **commemorative** *n.* **commemoration** *n.* **commemorator** *n.*

com-mence (ko mens') *v.* To begin; to start.

com-mence-ment (ko mens'ment) *n.* A graduation ceremony.

com-mend (ko mend') *v.* To give praise; to applaud. **commendable** *adj.* **commendably** *adv.* **commendation** *n.*

com-men-da-tion (kom'en dā'shan) *n.* The act of commending; praise; a favorable representation in words that commends.

com-men-su-rate (ko men'sèr it) *adj.*

Equal in duration, extent, or size. **commensuration** *n.*

com-ment (kom'ent) *n.* A statement of criticism, analysis, or observation.

com-men-tar-y (kom'en ter'ē) *n.* A series of comments.

com-mer-cial (ko mer'shal) *adj.* Of or relating to a product; supported by advertising. *n.* An advertisement on radio or television.

com-mer-cial-ize (ko mŭr'sha līz') *v.* To render commercial in character, methods, or spirit; to exploit for profit.

com-min-gle (ko ming'gel) *v.* To mix together; to mingle in one mass; to blend thoroughly.

com-mi-nute (kom'i nöt') *v.* To make small or fine; to reduce to minute particles; to pulverize.

com-mis-er-ate (ko miz'e rat') *v.* To display or feel sympathy for someone.

com-mis-sar (kom'i sär') *n.* An official of the Communist Party whose duties include the enforcement of party loyalty and political indoctrination.

com-mis-sar-i-at (kom'i sâr'ē at) *n.* The department of an army which supplies food for the troops.

com-mis-sar-y (kom'i ser'ē) *n. pl.* **-ies** A store that sells food and supplies on a military base.

com-mis-sion (ko mish'on) *n.* The percentage of the money received from a total, that is paid to a person for his service in the area of sales.

com-mis-sure *n.* A joint, or line of union; the junction between two anatomical parts.

com-mit (ko mit) *v.* To put in trust or charge; consign for safe-keeping or preservation.

com-mit-ment (ko mit'ment) *n.* The act of committing; the agreement to do something in the future.

com-mit-tal (ko mit'al) *n.* Commitment.

com-mit-tee (k o mit'ē) *n.* A group of persons appointed or elected to perform a particular task or function. **committeeman** *n.* **committeewoman** *n.*

com-mode (ko mōd') *n.* A movable washstand with storage underneath; a toilet; a low chest of drawers or bureau.

com-mo-di-ous (ko mō'dē us) *adj.* Roomy; spacious. **modiously** *adv.*

com-mod-i-ty (ko mod'i tē) *n.* Something valuable or useful.

com-mon (kom'on) *adj.* Having to do with, belonging to, or used by an entire community or public; vulgar; unrefined.

com-mon-age (kom'o nij) *n.* Community property; anything in common.

com-mon-al-ty (kom'o nal tē) *n.* The common people; general group.

common denominator *n.* The number

that can be divided evenly by all denominators of a number of fractions.

com-mon-er (kom´o nè) n. Common people.

common fraction n. A fraction where both the denominator and numerator are whole numbers.

common law n. Unwritten law based on judicial decisions, customs, and usages.

common multiple n., Math. A multiple of each of two or more numbers, quantities, or expressions.

com-mon-place (kom´on plās´) n. A trite or obvious observation; something easily taken for granted.

common sense n. Sound practical judgment; but often unsophisticated.

common touch n. The personal quality of appealing to common people.

com-mon-weal-th (kom´on welth´) n. The common good of the whole group of people.

com-mo-tion (ko mō´shan) n. Disturbance; mental excitement; total confusion.

com-move (ko mŏv´) v. To move violently; to excite.

com-mu-nal (ko mŭn´al) adj. Relating to a community; characterized by common sharing or collective ownership by members of a community.

com-mu-nal-i-ty (kom´ŭ nal´it ē) n. Group solidarity; communal character; similar opinions of a group.

com-mune (ko mūn´) v. To converse; to talk together; discuss; to exchange ideas. n. A small rural community.

com-mu-ni-ca-ble (ko mū´ni ka bl) adj. Capable of being transmitted, as with a disease. communicability n.

com-mu-ni-cate (ko mū´ni kāt´) v. To make known; to cause others to partake or share something.

com-mu-ni-ca-tion (ko mū´ni kā´shan) n. The act of transmitting ideas through writing or speech; the means to transmit messages between person or places.

com-mu-ni-ca-tive (ko mū´ni kā´tiv) adj. Inclined to communicate; talkative.

com-mun-ion (ko mūn´yan) n. The mutual sharing of feelings and thoughts; a religious fellowship between members of a church.

com-mun-ion (ko mūn´yan) n. A sacrament in which bread and wine are consumed to commemorate the death of Christ.

com-mu-nism (kom´ū niz´um) n. A system of government in which goods and production are commonly owned; the theory of social change and struggle toward communism through revolution.

com-mu-ni-ty (ko mū´ni tē) n. pl. -ies A group of people living in the same area and under the same government; a class or group having common interests and likes; the state of being held in common; common possession, enjoyment, liability, etc.; common character; agreement; identity.

community property n. Jointly held property by both husband and wife.

com-mu-nize (kom´ū nīz´) v. To transfer individual ownership to community or state owned.

com-mut-a-ble (ko mū´ta bl) adj. Exchangeable.

com-mu-ta-tive (ko mū´ ta tiv) adj. Of or pertaining to commutation.

com-mute (ko mūt´) v. To travel a long distance to one's job each day; to exchange or to substitute.

com-muter (ko mū´tér) n. One who travels a long distance on a regular basis.

com-pact (kom pakt´) adj. Packed together or solidly united; firmly and closely united.

com-pact-i-ble (kom pakt´i bl) adj. Having the qualities for being compacted.

com-pac-tor (kom pak tŏr) n. A device for compressing trash into a small mass for disposal.

com-pan-ion (kom pan´yon) n. An associate; a person employed to accompany or assist another; one hired to travel or live with another.

com-pan-ion-a-ble (kom pan´yo na bl) adj. Friendly; sociable. -iy adv.

com-pan-ion-ate (kom pan´yo ult) adj. Of or relating to companions.

com-pan-ion-way (kom pan´yon wā´) n., Naut. A stairway leading from a ship's deck to the cabin below.

com-pa-ny (kum´pa nē) n. pl. -ies The gathering of persons for a social purpose; a number of persons who are associated for a common purpose, as in business; a business.

com-pa-ra-ble (kom´par a bl) adj. Capable of comparison; worthy of comparison; similar. comparability n. comparably adv. comparable adj.

com-pare (kom pâr´) v. To speak of or represent as similar or equal to; to note the similarities or likenesses of.

com-par-i-son (kom par´i son) n. Likeness; similarity. Gram. Modification of a verb or adjective that indicates the positive, comparative, or superlative degree.

com-part (kom pärt´) v. To divide into parts according to a plan.

com-part-ment (kom pärt´ment) n. One of the sections into which an enclosed area is divided.

com-pass (kum´pas) n. An instrument used to determine geographic direction; an enclosed area or space; the extent of reach of something; range or area; scope; a device shaped like a V that is used for drawing circles.

com-pas-sion (kom pash′on) *n.* Sympathy for a person who is suffering or distressed in some way.

com-pa-thy (kom′pa thē) *n.* Feelings of grief or joy shared with another.

com-pat-i-ble (kom pat′I bl) *adj.* Able to function, exist, or live together harmoniously. **compatibility** *n.*

com-pa-tri-ot (kom pā′trēot) *n.* A person of the same country.

com-peer (kom pēr′) *n.* A person that is a peer or equal.

com-pel (kom pel′) *v.* To urge or force action.

com-pel-la-tion (kom′pe lā′shan) *n.* The act of addressing someone.

com-pen-di-ous (kom pen′dē us) *adj.* Containing the substance of a comprehensive subject in a brief form.

com-pen-dium (kom pen′dēum) *n. pl.* **-diums** A short summary.

com-pen-sa-ble (kom pen′sa bl) *adj.* That is or is entitled to compensation.

com-pen-sate (kom′pen sāt′) *v.* To make up for; to make amends; to pay; to neutralize or counter balance. **compensation** *n.* **compensatory** *adj.*

com-pete (kom pēt′) *v.* To contend with others; to engage in a contest or competition.

com-pe-tent (kom′pi tent) *adj.* Having sufficient ability; being capable. **competence** *n.* **competency** *n.*

com-pe-ti-tion (kom′pi tish′an) *n.* The act of rivalry or competing; a trial of skill or ability; a contest between teams or individuals. **competitive** *adj.*

com-pet-i-tor (kom pet′i tèr) *n.* One who competes against another.

com-pi-la-tion (kom′pi lā′shan) *n.* The act or process of collecting or compiling.

com-pile (kom pīl′) *v.* To put together material gathered from a number of sources; in Computer Science, to convert our language into machine language. **compilation** *n.*

com-pla-cence (kom plā′sens) *n.* A feeling of secure self-satisfaction.

com-pla-cent (kom plā′sent) *adj.* Pleased with one's merits or advantages; self-satisfied.

com-plain (kom plān′) *v.* To express grief, pain, uneasiness, or discontent.

com-plain-ant (kom plā′nant) *n.* A person filing a formal charge.

com-plaint (kom plānt′) *n.* An expression of pain, dissatisfaction, or resentment; a cause or reason for complaining; a grievances.

com-plai-sance (kom plā′sans) *n.* The willingness to please, to oblige, to help. **complaisant** *adj.*

com-plai-sant (kom plā′sant) *adj.* Marked by a need to please; obliging; gracious.

com-ple-ment (kom′ple ment) *n.* Something that perfects, completes, or adds to. **complementary** *adj.*

com-ple-men-tal (kom′ple men′tal) *adj.* Relating to or forming a complement.

complementary colors *n. pl.* Primary or secondary colors in the spectrum, when combined produce a neutral color.

com-plete (kom plēt′) *adj.* Having all the necessary parts; whole; concluded. **completion** *n.*

com-ple-tion (kom plē′shan) *n.* The process or act of completing.

com-plex (kom pleks′) *adj.* Consisting of various intricate parts. **complexity** *n.* **complexly** *adv.*

com-plex-ion (kom plek′shan) *n.* The natural color and texture of the skin, also the disposition of the mind and body. **complexioned** *adj.*

com-plex-i-ty *n.* The state or quality of being complex; intricacy; something complex.

com-pli-ance (kom plī′ans) *n.* The act of agreeing passively to a request, rule, or demand; the tendency to yield to others. **compliant compliancy** *n.*

com-pli-ant (kom plī′ant) *adj.* Ready to comply; yielding; obliging.

com-pli-cate (kom′pli kāt′) *v.* To make or become involved or complex.

com-pli-ca-tion (kom′pli kā′shan) *n.* The situation of complicating or the state of being complicated; entanglement; complexity; something complicated.

com-plic-i-ty (kom plis′i tē) *n.* An involvement or association with a crime.

com-pli-er (kom plī′ér) *n.* One who complies.

com-pli-ment (kom′pli ment) *n.* An expression of praise or admiration.

com-pli-men-ta-ry (kom′pli men′ta rē) *adj.* Conveying a compliment.

com-ply (kom plī′) *v.* To agree, to consent to, or obey a command or wish; requirements. **complier** *n.*

com-po-nent (kom pō′nent) *n.* A constituent part.

com-port (kom pōrt′) *v.* To behave or conduct oneself in a certain way.

com-port-ment (kom pōrt′ment) *n.* Behavior; demeanor; deportment.

com-pose (kom pōz′) *v.* To make up from elements or parts; to produce or create a song; to arrange, as to typeset; artistic composition. **composer** *n.*

com-posed (kom pōzd′) *adj.* Calm.

com-pos-er (kom pō′zér) *n.* One who composes; a person who writes an original work.

com-pos-ite (kom poz′it) *adj.* Made up

from separate elements or parts; combined or compounded. Characteristic of a plant with densely clustered flowers.

com-po-si-tion (kom´po zish´on) n. The act of putting together artistic or literary work; a short essay written for an assignment in school.

com-post (kom´pōst) n. A fertilizing mixture that consists of decomposed vegetable matter.

com-po-sure (kom pō´zhèr) n. Tranquility; calm self-possession.

com-pote (kom´pōt) n. Fruit that is preserved or stewed in syrup; a dish used for holding fruit, candy, etc.

com-pound (kom´pound) n. The combination of two or more parts, elements, or ingredients; In grammar, a new word that is composed of two or more words joined with a hyphen or written as a solid word. Chem. A definite substance that results from combining specific radica n. Elements in certain or fixed proportions. v. To combine; to increase.

compound fracture n. A broken bone that breaks and protrudes through the skin.

compound interest n. Interest computed on the original principal plus accrued interest.

compound sentence n. A sentence compiled of two or more independent clauses.

compound word n. A word made up of two or more words that retain their separate form and signification.

com-pre-hend (kom´pri hend´) v. To perceive, to grasp mentally, or to understand fully; to comprise; to include. comprehension n.

com-pre-hen-si-ble (kom´pri hen´si bl) adj. Capable of being understood. comprehensibility n. -hensibly adv.

com-pre-hen-sion (kom´pri hen´shan) n. The act of understanding or comprehending; the knowledge gained.

com-pre-hen-sive (kom´pri hen´slv) adj. Large in content or scope.

com-press (kom´pres) v. To press together into a smaller space; to condense. n. A soft pad sometimes medicated, for applying cold, heat, moisture, or pressure to a part of the body. compression, compressibility adj. compressible adj.

compressed air n. Air that is under greater pressure than the atmosphere.

com-pres-sive (kom pres´iv) adj. Having the power to compress; tending to compress.

com-pres-sor (kom pres´èr) n. Something that compresses; a machine that is used for compressing air to utilize its expansion.

com-prise (kom prīz´) v. To consist of; to be made up of. comprisable adj.

com-pro-mise (kom´pro mīz´) n. The process of settling or the settlement of differences between opposing sides, with each side making concessions. compromiser n. compromise v.

comp-trol-ler (kon trō´lèr) n. A person appointed to examine and verify accounts.

com-pul-sion (kom pul´shan) n. The act or state of being compelled; an irresistible urge or impulse to act irrationally.

compulsive (kom pul´siv) adj. An act or state of being compelled.

com-pul-so-ry (kom pul´so rē) adj. Enforced, mandatory.

com-punc-tion (kom pungk´shan) n. Anxiety arising from guilt or awareness.

com-pur-ga-tion (kom´pèr gā´shan) n. The clearing of an accused person by the oaths of persons who swear his innocence.

com-put-a-ble (kom pūt´a bl) adj. Capable of being computed.

com-pu-ta-tion (kom´pū tā´shan) n. The action or act of computing. The operation of a computer.

com-pute (kom pūt´) v. To ascertain or determine by the use of mathematics; to determine something by the use of a computer. computability n. computation n. computable adj.

com-put-er (kom pū´tòr) n. A person who computes; a high speed, electronic machine which performs logical calculations, processes, stores, and retrieves programmed information.

com-put-er-ese (kom pū´trēz) n. The jargon used by computer technologists.

com-put-er-i-za-tion (kom pū´te rī zā´ shan) n. The operation or procedure of computerizing.

com-puter-ize (kom pū´te rīz´) v. To process or store information on a computer; to switch from manual operations to computers.

computer language n. The various codes and information that are used to give data and instructions to computers.

computer program n. A system used to find and correct a problem on a computer.

com-rade (kom´rad) n. An associate, friend, or companion who shares one's interest or occupation. -ship n.

con (kon) v. To study carefully. Slang To swindle or trick.

co-na-tus (kō nā´tus) n. A natural impulse, tendency or striving.

con brio (kon brē´ō) adv. In a brisk or vigorous manner.

conc abbr. Concentrated; concentration or concentrate.

con-cat-e-nate (kon kat´e nāt´) v. To join, connect, or link together. concatenate adj. con-catenation n.

con-cave (kon´kāv) adj. Hollowed and curved inward. concavely adv.

con-cav-i-ty (kon kav´i tē) n. A concave surface; quality of being concave.

con-ceal (kon sēl´) v. To keep from disclosure, sight, or knowledge; to hide or withhold. concealable adj. concealer n. concealment n.

con-cede (kon sēd´) v. To grant or yield to a right or privilege; to acknowledge as true. conceder n. conceded adj.

con-ceit (kon sēt´) n. An exaggerated personal opinion of one's own importance.

con-ceit-ed (kon sē´tid) adj. Having an exaggerated or excessively high opinion of oneself.

con-ceive (kon sēv´) v. To become pregnant; to create a mental image. conceivability n. conceivable adj.

con-cen-ter (kon sen´tér) v. To converge or draw to a common center.

con-cen-trate (kon´sen trāt´) v. To give intense thought to; to draw to a common point; to intensify by removing certain elements; to become compact. concentrative adj.

con-cen-tra-tion (kon´sen trā´shan) n. The state of being concentrated or the act of concentrating; the process or act of giving complete attention to a certain problem or task.

concentration camp n. An enclosed camp or prison where political prisoners, aliens, or prisoners of war are confined.

con-cen-tric (kon sen´trik) adj. Having a common center, as circles or spheres.

con-cept (kon´sept) n. A generalized idea formed from particular occurrences or instances; an opinion.

con-cep-tion (kon sep´shon) n. The union of sperm and egg; a mental thought or plan.

con-cern (kon sérn´) n. Something to consider; sincere interest; something that affects one's business or affairs. v. To be interested in; to be involved with. concerned adj.

con-cern-ing (kon sürn´ning) prep. Relating to; regarding.

con-cern-ment (kon sürn´ment) n. Relation or bearing; something in which one is interested or concerned.

con-cert (kon´sért) n. A musical performance for a group of people; agreement in purpose, action, or feeling. v. To act or plan together. concerted adj.

con-cer-ti-no (kon´cher tē´nō) n. A short concerto.

con-cer-to (kon cher´tō) n. pl. -tos, -ti A composition that features one or more solo instruments.

con-ces-sion (kon sesh´an) n. The act of conceding; something that has been conceded; a tract of land that is granted by a government for a particular use.

con-ces-sion-aire (kon sesh´o nâr´) n. The operator or holder of a concession.

con-ces-sive (kon ses´iv) adj. Tending or serving to concede; making for a concession.

conch (kongk) n. A tropical marine mollusk having a large spiral shell and flesh that is edible.

con-chol-o-gy (kong kol´o jē) n. The study of mollusks and shells. conchological adj. conchologist n.

con-cil-i-ar (kon sil´ēêr) adj. Pertaining to, or issued by a council.

con-cil-i-ate (k on sil´ē āt´) v. To win over or to gain a friendship. conciliation n. conciliator n. conciliatory adj.

con-cin-ni-ty (kon sin´i tē) n. Harmonious adaptation of parts to a whole.

con-cise (kon sīs´) adj. Short and to the point.

con-ci-sion (kon sizh´on) n. Concise quality or state.

con-clave (kon´klāv) n. A private or secret meeting; the private meeting of the Roman Catholic cardinals to elect a new pope.

con-clude (kon klöd´) v. To close or bring to an end; to bring about an agreement; to arrive at a decision; to resolve.

con-clu-sion (kon klö´zham) n. The close or end; the final decision, the last main division of a discourse.

con-clu-sive (kon klö´siv) adj. Putting an end to any questions or doubt.

con-coct (kon kokt´) v. To make by combining ingredients; to devise or to plan. concoction n.

con-com-i-tant (kon kom´i tant) adj. Accompanying. concomitance n. .

con-cord (kon´kord) n. Accord; harmony; friendly and peaceful relationships.

con-cor-dance (kon kor´dans) n. A condition of concord or agreement; the alphabetical index of major words used by an author, listed in the order of use in a book.

con-cor-dant (kon kor´dant) adj. Exist in agreement; harmonious.

con-cor-dat (kon kor´dat) n. An agreement between a pope and a government; a compact.

con-course (kon´kōrs) n. A large, open space for the assembling or passage of crowds.

con-cres-cence (kon kres´ens) n. Increase by the addition of particles; growing together.

con-crete (kon´krēt) adj. Pertaining to a specific instance or thing; naming a specific class of things. n. A construction material made from sand, gravel, and cement. v. To bring together in one body or mass. **concretely** adv.

con-cre-tion (kon krē´shan) n. The act or process of concreting; the state of being concreted; something concreted.

con-cu-bine (kong´kū bīn´) n. A woman living with a man and not being legally married to him. **concubinage** n.

con-cu-pis-cence (kon kū´pi sens) n. A strong sexual desire; lust.

con-cur (kon kėr´) v. To agree or express approval; to cooperate; to happen at the same time; to coincide.

con-cur-rence (kon kėr´ans) n. The act of concurring; a agreement in opinion simultaneous happening in time and place.

con-cur-rent (kon kėr´ant) adj. Referring to an event that happens at the same time as another; acting together.

con-cuss (kon kus´) v. To affect with a concussion.

con-cus-sion (kon kush´on) n. A sudden and violent jolt; a violent injury to an organ, especially the brain.

con-demn (kon dem´) v. To find to be wrong; to show the guilt; to announce judgment upon; to officially declare unfit for use. **condemnable** adj. **condemnatory** adj. **condemnation** n.

con-den-sate (kon den´sāt) n. A product of condensation, water from steam.

con-den-sa-tion (kon´den sā´shan) n. The act of condensing.

con-dense (kon dens´) v. To make more dense, concentrated or compact. **condensability** n. **condensation** n. **condenser** n. **condensable** adj.

con-de-scen-sion (kon´di sen´shan) n. The act of condescending; a patronizing behavior.

con-dign (kon dīn´) adj. Well deserved; appropriate.

con-di-ment (kon´di ment) n. A relish, spice, or sauce used to season food.

con-dis-ci-ple (kon´di sī´pl) n. A fellow student.

con-di-tion (kon dish´on) n. The mode or state of existence of a thing or person; a circumstance that is found to be necessary to the occurrence of another; a provision in a contract or will that leaves room for modification or changes at a future date. Slang A sickness or ailment.

con-di-tion-al (kon dish´a nal) adj. Tentative; depending on a condition; implying or expressing a condition. Gram. A mood, clause, tense, or condition. **conditionality** n.

con-di-tion-ed (kon dish´ond) adj. Prepared for a certain process or action by past experience.

con-do (kon dō) n. Slang Condominium.

con-dole (kon dōl´) v. To express sympathetic sorrow at the loss or misfortunes of another.

con-dom (kon´dom) n. A thin rubber sheath used to cover the penis, serving as an anti-venereal or contraceptive purpose during sexual intercourse.

con-do-min-i-um (kon´do min´ē um) n. A joint ownership; an apartment in which all units are owned separately; a building in which the units are owned by each tenant.

con-do-na-tion (kon´dō nā´shan)n. The pardoning of a wrong act.

con-done (kon dōn´) n. To overlook; to forgive; to disregard. **condoner** n.

con-dor (kon´dor) v. One of the largest flying birds, with a bare head and a white downy neck. A very large American vulture with a bare neck and head with dull black plumage and white patches on the wings and neck.

con-du-cive (kon dō´siv) adj. Contributing towards or promotion; helpful.

con-duct (kon dukt´) v. To lead and direct a performance of a band or orchestra; to guide or show the way; to lead; to direct or control the course of; to transmit heat, electricity, or sound. n. Behavior. **conductibility** n.

con-duc-tiv-i-ty (kon´duk tiv´i tē) n. The quality of conducting heat, sound or electricity.

con-duit (kon´dwit) n. A pipe used to pass electric wires or cable through; a channel or pipe that water passes through.

con-du-pli-cate (kon dō´pli kit) adj. Doubled or folded lengthwise.

cone (kōn) n. A solid body that is tapered evenly to a point from a base that is circular; a wafer that is cone-shaped and used for holding ice cream.

cone-nose (kōn´nōz´) n. A large blood-sucking insect, a species of assassin bug infesting houses in the southern and western United States.

con-fab (kon´fab) n. Discussion.

con-fab-u-late (kon fab´u lāt´) v. To chat or speak informally. **confabulation** n. **confabulator** n. **confabulatory** adj.

con-fec-tion-er-y (kon fek´sha ner´ē) n. Candy and sweets as a whole; a store that sells candy and sweets.

con-fec-tion-a-ry (kon fek´sha ner´ē) adj. Of or pertaining to confections or their making; sweets.

con-fec-tion-er (kon fek´sha nėr) n. A person who manufactures or sells candies and other sweets.

con-fed-er-a-cy (kon fed´ėr a sē) n. pl. -ies The union of eleven southern states that seceded from the United States during the Civil War of 1861-1865 and established the Confederate State of America.

con-fed-er-ate (kon fed´ĕr ĭt) n. An ally or friend; a person who supports the Confederacy. **confederate** v.

con-fed-er-a-tion (kon fed´e rā´shan) n. An act of confederating; the state of being confederated.

con-fer (kon fer´) v. To consult with another; to hold a conference; to give or grant. **conferment** n. **conferral** n. **conferrer** n. **conferrable** adj.

con-fer-ence (kon´fĕr ens) n. A formal meeting for discussion; a league of churches, schools, or athletic teams.

con-fess (kon fes´) v. To disclose or admit to a crime, fault, sin, or guilt; to tell a priest or God of one's sins.

con-fes-sion (kon fesh´on) n. The act of confessing.

con-fes-sion-al (kon fesh´o nal) n. The small enclosure where a priest hears confessions.

con-fes-sor (kon fes´ĕr) n. A person who confesses; one who acknowledges a fault.

con-fet-ti (kon fet´ē) n. Small pieces of paper thrown during a celebration.

con-fide (kon fīd´) v. To entrust a secret to another. **confider** n. **confiding** adj.

con-fi-dence (kon´fĭ dens) n. A feeling of self-assurance; a feeling of trust in a person; reliance; good faith.

con-fi-den-tial (kon´fĭ den´shal) adj. Hold as a secret; having another's entrusted confidence on spoken or written matters. **confidentiality** n. **confidentially** adv.

con-fid-ing (kon´fĭd ing) adj. Trusting; reposing confidence; trustful.

con-fig-u-ra-tion (kon fig´ŭ rā´shan) n. An arrangement of parts or things; the arrangement of elements.

con-fig-ure (kon fig´ūr) v. To make or arrange for operation in a certain form or particular way.

con-fine (kon fīn´) v. To keep within a certain boundary or limits. **confines** n. **confinement** n. **confiner** n.

con-firm (kon fĕrm´) v. To establish or support the truth of something; to make stronger; to ratify and bind by a formal approval. **confirmable** adj.

con-fir-ma-tion (kon´fĕr mā´shan) n. The act of confirming to show proof; a religious rite that admits a person to full membership in a church.

con-fir-ma-to-ry (kon fĕr´ma tŏr´ē) adj. Giving additional strength; serving to confirm.

con-firm-ed (kon fĕrmd´) adj. Fixed.

con-fis-cate (kon´fĭ skāt´) v. To seize for public use; to officially seize. **confiscation** n. **confiscator** n.

con-fla-gra-tion (kon´fla grā´shan) n. A large fire, or the burning of a large mass of combustibles.

con-flate (kon´flāt) v. To combine two different ideas into a whole.

con-fla-tion (kon flā´shan) n. The result of merging various elements; blend.

con-flict (kon flikt´) n. A battle; clash; a disagreement of ideas, or interests, opposition. **conflict** v. **conflictive** adj.

conflict of interest n. The conflict when the private financial interests of a public officer stand to benefit by the influence from this position.

con-flu-ence (kon´flō ens) n. The flowing together of two streams or rivers; the point where the two join. **confluent** n. **confluently** adv.

con-flu-ent (kon´flō eny) adj. Flowing or coming together; run together.

con-flux (kon´fluks) n. A flowing together; a meeting or joining; a crowd.

con-fo-cal (kon fō´kal) adj. Of the same focus.

con-form (kon form´) v. To be similar in form or character; to adhere to prevailing customs or modes. **conformable** adj. **conformably** adv.

con-form-a-ble (kor´ma bl) adj. Corresponding in form, manners, or opinions.

con-for-ma-tion (kon´for mā´shan) n. The manner in which something is shaped, structured, or arranged.

con-form-i-ty (kon for´mi tē) n. Likeness; harmony; accordance.

con-found (kon found´) v. To amaze, confuse, or perplex; to confuse one thing for another.

con-found-ed (kon foun´ded) adj. Annoying bothersome.

con-fra-ter-ni-ty (kon´fra tĕr´ni tē) n. A brotherhood society devoted to a purpose.

con-frere (kon´frâr) n. A fellow colleague; a fraternity or profession.

con-front (kon frunt´) v. To put or stand face to face with defiance; to face; to stand or be in front of, providing resistance, as an obstacle; to meet in hostility; to oppose. **confrontation** n.

con-fuse (kon fūz´) v. To mislead or bewilder; to jumble or mix up. **confusedness** n. **confusingly** adv.

con-fu-sion (kon fū´zhan) n. The state of being confused.

con-fu-ta-tion (kon´fū tā´shan) n. The disproving, or proving to be false or invalid.

con-fute (kon fūt´) v. To prove to be invalid or false. **confutable** adj. **confutation** n. **confutative** adj.

con-geal (kon jēl´) v. To jell; to solidify; to change from a liquid to a solid form.

con-ge-la-tion (kon´je lā´shan) n. That which is congealed or solidified or the state of being congealed.

con-ge-ner (kon ´je nĕr) n. A member of the same genus as another plant or animal.

con-gen-ial (kƏn jēn´yƏl) *adj.* Having similar character habits, or tastes; sociable; friendly. **congeniality** *n.*

con-gen-i-tal (kƏn jen´i tal) *adj.* Existing from the time of birth, but not from heredity.

conger eel *n.* A large scaleless eel used for food along the coasts of Europe.

con-gest (kƏn jest´) *v.* To enlarge with an excessive accumulation of blood; to clog. **congestion** *n.* **congestive** *adj.*

con-glo-bate (kƏn glō´bāt) *v.* To form or gather into a ball or small spherical body.

con-glo-ba-tion (kƏn˝glō bā´shƏn) *n.* The act of or gathering into a ball; a round body.

con-glom-er-ate (kƏn glom´ér it) *n.* A business consisting of many different companies; gravel that is embedded in cement material.

con-gou (kong´gö) *n.* A black tea from China.

con-grat-u-late (kƏn grach´u lāt´) *v.* To acknowledge an achievement with praise. **congratulator** *n.*

con-grat-u-la-tions (kƏn grach˝lā´shƏns) *n. pl.* The expression of or the act of congratulating.

con-grat-u-la-to-ry (kƏn grach´u la tōr´ē) *adj.* Expressing congratulations.

con-gre-gate (kong´grƏ gāt´) *v.* To assemble together in a crowd.

con-gre-ga-tion (kong´grƏ gā´shƏn) *n.* A group of people meeting together for worship.

con-gre-ga-tion-al (kong´grƏ gā´shƏl) *adj.* Of or pertaining to a congregation; recognizing the importance and governing power of the congregation.

Con-gress (kong´gris) *n.* The United States legislative body, consisting of the Senate and the House of Represen-tatives. **Congressional** *adj.*

con-gru-ent (kong´grö ent) *adj.* Agreeing to conform; in mathematics, having exactly the same size and shape.

con-gru-ous (kong´grö us) *adj.* Being in agreement, appropriate or fitting.

con-ic *or* **con-i-cal (kon´ik) (kon´i kƏl)** *adj.* Related to and shaped like a cone.

co-nid-i-um (kō nid´ē um) *n.* A propagative body or cell, asexual in its origin and functions.

co-ni-fer (kōni fér) *n.* Evergreen trees and shrubs, that include the pine, fir, spruce, and other conebearing trees.

co-ni-ine (kō´nē ēn´) *n.* A highly poisonous alkaloid found in hemlock.

conj *abbr.* Conjunction.

con-jec-ture (kƏn jek´chér) *n.* A guess or conclusion based on incomplete evidence. **conjecturable, conjectural** *adj.* **conjecture** *v.*

con-join (kƏn join´) *v.* To unite; join together.

con-ju-gal (kon´ju gal) *adj.* Pertaining to the relationship or marriage of husband and wife.

con-ju-gate (kon´ju git) *adj.* To change the form of a verb; to join in pairs. **conjugately** *adv.* **conjugative** *adj.* **conjuga-tor** *n.*

con-junct (kƏn jungkt´) *adj.* Combined; joined together.

con-junc-tion (kƏn jungk´shƏn) *n.* The act of joining; the state of being joined. *Gram.* A word used to join or connect other words, phrases, sentences, or clauses.

con-junc-ti-va (kon´jungk tī´vƏ) *n. pl.* **-vas, -vae** The membrane lining of the eyelids.

con-junc-tive (kƏn jungk´tiv) *adj.* Connective; joining. *Gram.* Serving as a conjunction.

con-junc-ti-vi-tis (kon jungk´ti vī´tis) *n., Pathol.* Inflammation of the membrane that lines the eyelids.

con-jur-a-tion (kon´ju rā´shƏn) *n.* The act of binding by an oath; a solemn appeal.

con-jure (kon´jér) *v.* To bring into the mind, to appeal or call on solemnly; to practice magic.

con man *n., Slang.* A confidence man; a swindler.

con-nate (kon´āt) *adj.* Existing from birth; born or originating together.

con-nect (kƏ nekt´) *v.* To join; to unite; to associate, as to relate. **connectedly** *adv.* **connector** *n.* **connecter** *n.*

con-nect-ed (kƏ nek´tid) *adj.* Linked, bound or fastened together; joined in order or sequence.

Con-nect-i-cut *n.* A state located in the north eastern part of the United States; statehood January 9, 1788; state capital Hartford.

con-nec-tion (kƏ nek´shƏn) *n.* An association of one person or thing to another; a union, link, or bond; an influential group of friends or associates.

con-nec-tive (kƏ nek´tiv) *adj.* Capable of connecting; tending to connect. *n.* something that connects as a word

connective tissue *n.* Tissue which connects, supports, or surrounds other tissues or organs.

con-nip-tion (kƏ nip´shƏn) *n.* A fit of alarm or hysterical excitement.

con-nive (kƏ nīv´) *v.* To ignore a known wrong, therefore implying sanction; to conspire; to cooperate in secret.

con-nois-seur (kon´o ser´) *n.* A person whose expertise in an area of art or taste allows him to be a judge; an expert. **connoisseurship** *n.*

con-no-ta-tion (kon´o tā´shƏn) *n.* The associative meaning of a word in addition to the literal meaning.

con-note (ko nōt´) v. To imply along with the literal meaning.

con-nu-bi-al (ko nö´bē al) adj. Having to do with marriage or the state of marriage. **connubiality** n. **-ly** adv.

con-quer (kong´kėr) v. To subdue; to win; to overcome by physical force.

con-quest (kon´kwest) n. The process or act of conquering; acquisition by force.

con-qui-an n. A card game for two players with 40 cards; the game from which all rummy games originate.

con-quis-ta-dor (kon kwis´ta dor´) n. pl. **-dors** A Spanish conqueror of the sixteenth century.

con-san-guin-e-ous (kon´sang gwin´ē us) adj. Having the same blood; descended from the same ancestor. **consanguineously** adv.

con-science (kon´shens) n. The ability to recognize right and wrong regarding one's own behavior.

conscience clause n. A clause inserted in a law, that relieves persons whose religious beliefs forbid their compliance.

con-sci-en-tious (kon´shē en´shus) adj. Honest; scrupulous; careful.

con-scious (kon´shus) adj. Aware of one's own existence and environment; aware of facts or objects.

con-script (kon´skript) n. One who is drafted or forced to enroll for a service or a job.

con-se-crate (kon´se krāt´) v. To declare something to be holy; to dedicate to sacred uses.

con-se-cra-tion (kon˝se krā´shan) n. The act or state of consecrating.

con-se-cu-tion (kon˝se kū´shan) n. Sequence; succession; logical sequence.

con-sec-u-tive (kon sek´ū tiv) adj. Following in uninterrupted succession. **consecutively** adv. **-tiveness** n.

con-sen-sus (kon sen´sus) n. A general agreement; a collective opinion.

con-sent (kon sent´) v. To agree; an acceptance. **consenter** n.

con-se-quence (kon´se kwens´) n. The natural result from a preceding condition or action; the effect.

con-se-quent (kon´se kwent´) adj. Following as a natural result or effect logical conclusion. **consequently** adv.

con-se-quen-tial (kon´se kwen´shal) adj. Having or showing self-importance. **consequentially** adv.

con-serv-a-tive (kon sėr´va tiv) adj. Opposed to change; desiring the preservation of the existing order of things; moderate; cautious; wanting to conserve. **conservatively** adv. .

con-ser-va-tor (kon´sėr vā tor) n. A person who preserves; a person or

institution responsible for protecting another's interests.

con-ser-va-to-ry (kon sėr´va tōr´ē) n. pl. **-ries** A school of dramatic art or music; a greenhouse.

con-serve (kon sėrv´) v. To save something from decay, loss, or depletion; to maintain; to preserve fruits with sugar. n. A mixture of several fruits cooked together with sugar and sometimes raisins or nuts. **conservable** adj. **conserver** n.

con-sid-er (kon sid´ėr) v. To seriously think about; to examine mentally; to believe or hold as an opinion; to deliberate.

con-sid-er-a-ble (kon sid´ėr a bl) adj. Large in amount or extent; important; worthy of consideration. **-ly** adv.

con-sid-er-a-tion (kon sid´e rā´shan) n. The taking into account of circumstance before forming an opinion; care and thought; a kind or thoughtful treatment or feeling. **considering** prep.

con-sign (kon sīn´) v. To commit to the care of another; to deliver or forward, as merchandise; to put aside, as for specific use. **consignee** n. **consignable** adj. **consignor** n. **consignment** n.

con-sign-ee (kon˝sī nē´) n. The person to whom goods are consigned.

con-sign-ment n. The act of consigning; goods sent or delivered to an agent for sale.

con-sist (kon sist´) v. To be made up of.

con-sis-ten-cy (kon sis´ten sē) n. pl. **-cies** Agreement or compatibility among ideas, events, or successive acts; the degree of texture, viscosity, or density; coherence. **consistent** adj.

con-so-ci-ate (kon sō´shē āt´) v. To bring together or into association.

con-so-ci-a-tion (kon sō˝sē ā´shan) n. Association in; fellowship; an association or union of churches.

con-so-la-tion (kon˝so lā´shan) n. Comfort; the act of consoling; a person who offers consolation.

con-sole (kon sōl´) v. To give comfort to someone. **consolable** adj. **consolation** n. **consolingly** adv.

console table n. A table fixed to a wall by consoles or brackets wall.

con-sol-i-date (kon sol´i dāt´) v. To combine in one or to form a union of; to form a compact mass. **consolidation** n. **consolidator** n.

consolidated school n. A public school, formed by combining schools from several districts.

con-som-mé (kon´so mā´) n. A strong, clear soup made from the stock of meat.

con-so-nant (kon´so nant) n. A sound produced by complete or partial blockage of the air from the mouth, as the sound of b, f, k, s, t; the letter of the alphabet that represents such a sound. *adj.* In agreement. **consonantal** *adj.* **consonantly** *adv.*

con-sort (kon´sort) *n.* A spouse; companion or partner. *v.* To unite or keep in company.

con-sor-ti-um (kon sor´shē um) *n. pl.* **-tia** An association with banks or corporations that require vast resources.

con-spe-cif-ic (kon´spi sif´ik) *adj.* Of the same species.

con-spec-tus (kon spek´tus) *n.* A general summary; a digest; a resume.

con-spic-u-ous (kon spik´ū us) *adj.* Noticeable. **conspicuously** *adv.*

con-spir-a-cy (kon spir´a sē) *n. pl.* **-ies** A plan or act of two or more persons to do an evil act.

con-spir-a-tor-ial (kon spir´a tōr´ē al) *adj.* Relating to a conspiracy or conspirators.

con-spire (kon spīr´) *v.* To plan a wrongful act in secret; to work or act together, to plot against others.

con-sta-ble (kon´sta bl) *n.* A peace officer.

con-stab-u-lar-y (kon stab´ū ler´ē) *adj.* Relating to the jurisdiction of a constable.

con-stant (kon´stant) *adj.* Faithful; unchanging; steady in action, purpose, and affection. *Math.* A quantity that remains the same throughout a given problem. **constancy, constantly** *adv.*

con-ster-na-tion (kon´stėr nā´shan) *n.* Sudden confusion or amazement.

con-sti-pa-tion (kon´sti pā´shan) *n.* A condition of the bowels characterized by difficult or infrequent evacuation.

con-stit-u-en-cy (kon stich´ō en sē) *n. pl.* **-cies** A group of voters that is represented by an elected legislator.

con-stit-u-ent (kon stich´ō ent) *adj.* Having the power to elect a representative. *n.* A necessary element or part.

con-sti-tu-tion (kon´sti tō´shan) *n.* The fundamental laws that govern a nation; structure or composition. **constitutional** *adj.* **constitutionality** *n.*

con-sti-tu-tion-al (kon´sti tō´sha nal) *adj.* Pertaining or relating to the composition of a thing; essential. *n.* Exercise taken to benefit one's health.

con-sti-tu-tion-al-ism (kon´sti tō´sha na liz´um) *n.* The adherence, theory or principle of constitutional rule or authority.

con-sti-tu-tive (kon´sti tō´tiv) *adj.* Having the power to form, compose, enact, or establish.

con-strain (kon strān´) *v.* To restrain by physical or moral means.

con-straint (kon strānt´) *n.* The threat or use of force; confinement; restriction.

con-strict (kon strikt´) *v.* To squeeze, compress, or contract. **constriction** *n.* **constrictive** *adj.* **constrictively** *adv.*

con-stric-tor (kon strik´tėr) *n.* One that constricts; a snake that crushes its prey in its coils.

con-struct (kon strukt´) *v.* To create, make, or build. **constructor** *n.*

con-struc-tion (kon struk´shan) *n.* The act of constructing or building something. *Gram.* The arrangement of words in a meaningful clause or sentence. **constructional** *adj.*

con-struc-tive (kon struk´tiv) *adj.* Useful; helpful; building, advancing, or improving; resulting in a positive conclusion.. **constructiveness** *n.*

con-strue (kon strö´) *v.* To interpret; to translate; to analyze grammatical structure.

con-sul (kon´sul) *n.* An official that resides in a foreign country and represents his or her government's commercial interests and citizens.

con-sul-ate (kon´su lit) *n.* The official premises occupied by a consul.

con-sult (kon sult´) *v.* To seek advice or information from; to compare views. **consultant** *n.* **consultation** *n.*

con-sult-ant (kon sul´tant) *n.* A person who consults; one who offers professional advice or services for a fee.

con-sume (kon sōm´) *v.* To ingest; to eat or drink; to destroy completely; to absorb; to engross. **consumable** *n.*

con-sum-er (kon sō´mėr) *n.* A person who buys services or goods.

con-sum-mate (kon´su māt´) *v.* To conclude; to make a marriage complete by the initial act of sexual intercourse.

con-sump-tion (kon sump´shan) *n.* Fulfillment; the act of consuming; the quantity consumed; tuberculosis.

con-sump-tive (kon sump´tiv) *adj.* Tending to destroy or waste away; affected with or pertaining to pulmonary tuberculosis. **consumptively** *adv.* **consumptiveness** *n.*

con-tact (kon´takt) *n.* The place, spot, or junction where two or more surfaces or objects touch; the connection between two electric conductors. **contacts** Contact lens; thin lens of plastic or glass with an optical prescription, worn directly on the cornea of the eye.

contact lens *n.* A prescription lens for correcting vision, which is applied directly to the cornea of the eye.

con-ta-gion (k on tā´jon) *n.* The transmitting of a disease by contact. **contagious** *adj.* **contagiously** *adv.*

con-ta-gi-um *n.* A virus by which a contagious disease is communicated.

con-tain (kon tān´) *v.* To include or enclose; to restrain or hold back. **containable** *adj.* **containment** *n.*

con-tain-er (kon tā´nėr) v. Something that holds or carries, as a box or can.

con-tain-er-i-za-tion (kon tā˜nėr i zā´shan) n. The procedure of shipping a large amount of goods in one container.

container ship n. A ship that is designed to carry containerized cargo.

con-tam-i-nate (kon tam´i nāt´) v. To pollute or make inferior by adding undesirable elements; to taint; to infect; to make dirty or to soil. **contaminant** n. **contamination** n.

con-tam-i-na-tion (kon tam˜i nā´shan) n. The act or state of contaminating, or of being contaminated.

con-temn (kon tem´) v. To scorn or despise.

con-tem-plate (kon´tem plāt´) v. To look over; to ponder; to consider thoughtfully. **contemplative, -tion** n.

con-tem-pla-tion (kon˜tem plā´shan) n. The act of serious contemplating; thoughtful; attentive consideration.

con-tem-po-ra-ne-ous (kontem´porā´nē us) adj. Occurring or living at the same time; contemporary. **contemporaneously** adv. **contemporaneousness** n.

con-tempt (kon tempt´) n. The act of viewing something as mean, vile, or worthless scorn; legally, the willful disrespect or disregard of authority. **contemptible** adj.

con-tempt-i-ble (kon temp´ti bl) adj. Worthy of contempt; deserving scorn.

con-temp-tu-ous (kon temp´chö us) adj. Feeling or showing contempt. **-ly** adv.

con-tend (kon tend´) v. To dispute; to fight; to debate; to argue. **-er** n.

con-tent (kon´tent) n. Something contained within; the subject matter of a book or document; the proportion of a specified part. adj. Satisfied. **contentment** n. **-edly** adv. **-ed** adj.

con-tent-ed (kon ten´tid) adj. Satisfied with one's circumstances, possessions, or status.

con-ten-tion (kon ten´shan) n. Competition; rivalry; controversy; argument. **contentious** adj. **contentiously** adv.

con-tent-ment (kon tent´ment) n. Feeling of or being contented; a satisfaction of mind.

con-ter-mi-nous (kon tėr´mi nus) adj. Having the same or common boundaries or limits.

con-test (kon´test) n. A competition; strife; conflict. v. To challenge. **contestable** adj. **contestant** n.

con-text (kon´tekst) n. A sentence, phrase, or passage so closely connected to a word or words that it affects their meaning; the environment in which an event occurs.

con-tex-ture (kon teks´chėr) n. The act of interweaving several parts into a whole.

con-tig-u-ous (k on tig´ū us) adj. Situated next to or near in time; meeting or joining at the surface or border.

con-ti-nent (kon´ti nent) n. One of the seven large masses of the earth: Asia; Africa; Australia; Europe; North America; South America; and Antarctica.

con-ti-nen-tal (kon´ti nen´tal) adj. Of or characteristic of a continent.

continental divide n. A divide separating rivers or streams that flow to opposite sides of a continent.

con-tin-gent (kon tin´jent) adj. Likely to happen; happening by chance.

con-tin-u-al (kon tin´u al) adj. Continuing indefinitely; proceeding without interruption; not intermittent.

con-tin-u-a-tion (kon tin´ū ā´shan) n. The act of continuing or prolonging; extension or carrying on after an interruption.

con-tin-ue (kon tin´ū) v. To maintain without interruption a course or condition; to resume; to postpone or adjourn a judicial proceeding. **continuance** n. **continuer** n.

continued fraction n. A fraction with a denominator which contains a fraction and a numerator which contains a fraction.

con-tin-u-ing (kon tin´ū ing) adj. Enduring or lasting; continuous.

con-ti-nu-i-ty (kon´ti nö´i tē) n. pl. **-ties** The quality of being continuous.

con-tin-u-ous (kon tin´ū us) adj. Uninterrupted. **continuously** adv.

con-tort (kon tort´) v. To severely twist out of shape.

con-tor-ted (kon tor´tid) adj. Twisted to an extreme degree or violent manner.

con-tor-tion-ist (kon tor´sha nist) n. An acrobat who exhibits unnatural body positions.

con-tour (kon´tur) n. The outline of a body, figure, or mass.

contour line n. A line on a map carried along the surface connecting points that have the same elevation.

contour map n. A topographic map where with contour lines are shown by the relative spacing of lines known as contour intervals.

con-tra-band (kon´tra band´) n. Illegal or prohibited traffic; smuggled goods.

con-tra-bass (kon´tra bäs´) n. A double bass, also called a contrabassoon.

con-tra-cep-tion (kon´tra sep´shan) n. The voluntary prevention of impregnation. **contraceptive** n.

con-tract (kon´trakt) n. A formal agreement between two or more parties to perform the duties as stated; an oral, written, or implied agreement between two or more persons.

con-trac-tile (kon trak´til) *adj.* Having the power to contract.

con-trac-tion (kon trak´shan) *n.* The act of contracting; a shortening of a word by omitting a letter or letters and replacing it with an apostrophe (').

con-trac-tor (kon´trak tér) *n.* A person who contracts to perform work at a certain price or rate.

con-trac-ture (kon trak´chér) *n.* A permanent shortening of a muscle or tendon producing deformity.

con-tra-dict (kon´tra dikt´) *v.* To express the opposite side or idea; to be inconsistent. **contradictable** *adj.* **contradictory** *adj.* **contradicter** *n.*

con-tra-dic-tion (kon´tra dik´shan) *n.* A statement that implies by the truth and falseness about something; direct opposition.

con-tra-dic-to-ry (kon´tra dik´to ré) *adj.* Opposite; being inconsistent with one another; opposite.

con-trail (kon´trál) *n.* The visible water vapor left in the sky by a plane.

con-tral-to (kon tral´tō) *n. pl.* -tos The lowest female singing voice.

con-trap-tion (kon trap´shan) *n.* A gadget.

con-tra-puntal (kon´tra pun´tal) *adj.* Relating to counterpoint.

con-tra-ri-wise (kon´trer é wiz´) *adv.* In a contrary manner; vice versa; on the contrary.

con-trar-y (kon´trer é) *adj.* Unfavorable; incompatible with another. **contrarily** *adv.* **contrariness** *n.*

con-trast (kon trast´) *v.* To note the differences between two or more people, things, or any item. **con-trastable** *adj.*

con-tra-vene (kon´tra vén´) *v.* To be contrary; to violate; to oppose; to go against.

con-tre-danse (kon´tri dans´) *n.* A graceful folk dance, in which the partners stand opposite one another in two lines.

con-trib-ute (kon trib´ūt) *v.* To give something to someone; to submit for publication. **contribution** *n.* **contributor** *n.* **contributive** *adj.* **contributory** *adj.* **contributively** *adv.*

con-tri-bu-tion (kon´tri bū´shan) *n.* The act of contributing or something contributed.

con-trib-u-to-ry (kon trib´ū tōr´é) *adj.* Contributing to a common fund; furnishing something toward a result.

con-trite (kon trit´) *adj.* Grieving for sin or shortcoming. **contritely** *adv.*

con-triv-ance (kon tri´vans) *n.* The act of or thing contriving, devising, or planning.

con-trol (kon trōl´) *v.* To have the authority or ability to regulate, direct, or dominate a situation. **-able** *adj.*

con-trol-ler (kon trō lér) *n.* The chief accounting officer of a business, also called the comptroller.

controlling interest *n.* The majority stock ownership in a corporation, which exerts control over policy.

control tower *n.* A lookout tower at an airfield or airport having the necessary equipment and personnel to direct air and ground traffic in takeoffs and landings.

con-tro-ver-sy (kon´tro vér´sé) *n.* A dispute; a debate; a quarrel **controversial** *adj.*

con-tro-vert (kon´tro vert´) *v.* To contradict.

con-tu-ma-cy (kon´tu ma sé) *n.* Stubborn rebelliousness to authority.

con-tu-me-li-ous (kon´tu mé´lé us) *adj.* Indicating or expressing humiliation.

con-tu-me-ly (kon´tu me lé) *n. pl* -lies Rude treatment. **contumelious** *adj.*

con-tuse (kon tōz´) *v.* To injure the body without breaking the flesh.

con-tu-sion (kon tō´zhen) *n.* A severe bruise or injury to the body; without breaking of the skin.

co-nun-drum (ko nun´drum) *n.* A riddle with an answer that involves a pun; a question or problem with only a surmise for an answer.

con-va-lesce (kon´va les´) *v.* To grow strong after a long illness, recovery time. **convalescence** *n.*

con-va-les-cence (kon´va les´ens) *n.* Gradual recovery of health and strength after a sickness.

con-vect (kon vekt´) *v.* To move or transfer heat by convection.

con-vec-tion (kon vek´shan) *n.* The transfer of heat by the movement of air, gas, or heated liquid between areas of unequal density, upward flow of warm air. **convectional** *adj.*

con-vec-tor (kon vek´tér) *n.* A heating unit for circulating heat by convection.

con-vene (kon vén´) *v.* To meet or assemble formally; meeting.

con-ven-ience (kon vén´yans) *n.* The quality of being convenient or suitable.

con-ve-nient (kon vé´nyant) *adj.* Suitable and agreeable to the needs or purpose.

con-vent (con´vent) *n.* A local house or community of a religious order, a home for nuns.

con-ven-ti-cle (kon ven´ti kl) *n.* A secret meeting for religious study or worship.

con-ven-tion (kon ven´shan) *n.* A formal meeting; a regulatory meeting between people, states, or nations on matters that affect all of them.

con-ven-tion-al (kon ven´sha nal) *adj.* Commonplace, ordinary.

con-ven-tu-al (kon ven´chō al) *n.* A

member of a conventual community or monastery.

con-verge (kon vėrj´) v. To come to a common point. **convergence** n.

con-vers-a-ble (kon vėr´sa bl) adj. Pleasant and easy to talk to.

con-ver-sa-tion (kon´vėr sā´shan) n. An informal talk, verbal discussion with someone or a group of people, oral communication. **conversational** adj. **conversationally** adv.

converse (kon vėrs´) v. To involve oneself in conversation with another.

con-ver-sion (kon vėr´zhan) n. The act or state of changing to adopt new opinions or beliefs; a formal acceptance of a different religion. **-al** adj.

con-vert-er (kon vėr´tėr) n. One who converts; a machine or device that accepts in-formation in one form and converts to another.

con-vert-i-ble (kon vėr´ti bl) adj. A car with a top that folds back or can be removed completely.

convertible life insurance n. A limited type of life insurance, such as group or term that allows the policy holder to change the policy into an expanded or more permanent form.

convertible stock n. Preferred stock which may upon exercise of the owner's option, be exchanged for common stock

con-vex (kon´veks) adj. Curved outward like the outer surface of a ball.

con-vex-o-con-cave (kon veksō kon kāv´) adj. Convex on one side greater than on the other side, as an eyeglass lens.

con-vey (kon vā´) v. To transport; to pass information on to someone else; to conduct. **conveyable** adj.

con-vey-ance (kon vā´ans) n. The action of conveying; the legal transfer of property or the document effecting it.

con-vict (kon vikt´) v. To prove someone guilty. n. A prisoner.

con-vic-tion (kon vik´shan) n. The act of being convicted.

con-vince (kon vins´) v. To cause to believe without doubt. **-ingly** adv.

con-viv-i-al (kon viv´ē al) adj. Relating to entertainment and good company.

con-vo-ca-tion (kon´vo kā´shan) n. A formal or ceremonial assembly or meeting.

con-voke (kon vōk´) v. To call together for a formal meeting.

con-vo-lute (kon´vo lōt´) adj. Twisted; rolled up together.

con-vo-lu-tion (kon´vo lō´shan) n. A rolling, folding or coiling together; a rolled up or coiled condition.

con-voy (kon´voi) n. A group of cars, trucks, etc., traveling together. v. To escort or guide.

con-vulse (kon vuls´) v. To move or shake violently. **convulsive** adj.

con-vul-sion (kon vul´shan) n. A violent involuntary muscular contraction.

cook (kuk) v. To apply heat to food before eating; to prepare food for a meal. n. A person who prepares food.

cook-book (kuk´buk´) n. A book containing directions for preparing and cooking food.

cook-ie (kuk´ē) n. A sweet, flat cake.

cool (kōl) adj. Without warmth; indifferent or unenthusiastic. Slang First-rate; composure.

cool-ant (kō´lant) n. The cooling agent that circulates through a machine.

Coolidge, John Calvin n. (1872-1933) The thirtieth president of the United States from 1923-1929.

coon (kōn) n., Informal A raccoon.

coop (kōp) n. A cage or enclosed area to contain animals, as chickens.

co-op (kō´op) n. A cooperative.

co-op-er-ate (kō op´e rāt´) v. To work together toward a common cause. **cooperation** n. **cooperator** n.

co-op-er-a-tion n. The action of cooperating; the combination of persons for purposes of production, or distribution for their joint benefit and success; a common effort.

co-op-er-a-tive (kō op´e rā´tiv) adj. Willing to cooperate in working with others. **cooperatively** adv. **cooperativeness** n.

co-opt (kō opt´) v. To elect or choose as a new member.

co-or-di-nate (kō or´di nāt´) v. To be equal in rank, importance, or degree; to plan a wardrobe or outfit so that it goes well together. n. Any of a set of numbers which establishes position on a graph, map, chart, etc. **coordinately** adv. **coordinator** n.

co-or-di-na-tion (kō or´di nā´shan) n. The state of being coordinated.

coot (kōt) n. A short-winged bird. Slang A silly old man.

coot-ie (kō´tē) n., Slang A body louse.

cop (kop) n., Informal A police officer.

co-pal (kō´pal) n. A hard, fossil resin from various tropical trees, used in making varnishes.

co-par-ce-nar-y (kō pär´se nėr´ē) n. Joint ownership; joint heirship.

co-part-ner (kō pärt´nėr) n. A partner with others; a sharer.

cope (kōp) v. To strive; to struggle or contend with something. n. The long cape worn by a priest on special ceremonial occasions.

cop-ier (kop´ē ėr) n. A machine that makes copies of original material.

co-pi-lot (kō pī´ot) n. The assistant pilot on an aircraft.

co-pi-ous adj. Yielding something in

large quantity; abundant. **copiously**
adv.

cop–out *n. Slang* A way to avoid
responsibility; a person who cops out.

cop-per (kop´ér) *n.* A metallic element
that is a good conductor of electricity
and heat, reddish-brown in color.

cop-per-plate (kop´ér plāt) *n.* A copper
plate on which something is engraved.

cop-ra (kop´ra) *n.* Dried coconut meat
that yields coconut oil.

copse (kops) *n.* A thicket made up of
trees or small bushes.

cop-ter (kop´tér) *n., Slang* A helicopter.

cop-u-la (kop´ū la) *n., Gram.* A word
or words which connect a subject and
predicate.

cop-u-late (kop´ū lāt) *v.* To have sexual
intercourse. **copulation** *n.*

copy (kop´ē) *v. pl. -ies* To reproduce
an original. *n.* A single printed text.

cop-y-boy (kop´ē boi´) *n.* A person,
usually employed in a newspaper
office, who carries copy and runs
errands.

copy edit *v.* To edit and correct a written
copy for publication. **copy editor** *n.*

copy-right (kop´ē rīt´) *n.* The statutory
right to sell, publish, or distribute a
literary or artistic work.

co-quette (kō ket´) *n.* A woman who
flirts. **coquettish** *adj.*

co-qui-na (kō kē´na) *n.* A small clam
used for making broth or chowder.

cor-a-cle (kor´a kl) *n.* A small boat made
by covering a wicker frame with hide
or leather.

cor-a-coid (kor´a koid´) *adj.* Relating
or referring to a bony process or
cartilage in various vertebrates, as birds
and reptiles.

cor-al (kor´al) *n.* The stony skeleton of
a small sea creature, often used for
jewelry.

coral reef *n.* A marine mound formed
chiefly of broken pieces and grains of
coral that have become a hard mass.

cor-beil (kor´bel) *n.* A sculptured basket
of flowers and fruits

cor-bi-na *n.* A spotted whiting fish of
the California coast.

cord (cord) *n.* A string or twine; an
insulated wire used to supply electricity
to another source; a measurement for
firewood that equals 128 cubic feet;
a raised rib of fabric, as corduroy.
corder *n.*

cord-age (kor´dij) *n.* Cords or ropes used
on the rigging of ship.

cor-dial (kor´jal) *adj.* Warm-hearted and
sincere. *n.* A liqueur. **cordiality** *n.*

cor-di-er-ite (kor´dē e rīt´) *n.* A silicate
of aluminum, iron, and magnesium in
shades of blue, having a vitreous luster.

cor-di-form (kor´di form´) *adj.* Heart-
shaped.

cord-ing (kor´ding) *n.* A heavy cord used
for ornamental purposes.

cord-ite (kor´dīt) *n.* A smokeless
gunpowder.

cor-don (kor´don) *n.* A circle of men
or ships positioned to guard or enclose
an area; an ornamental ribbon or braid
worn as an insignia of honor.

cor-du-roy (kor´du roi´) *n.* A durable
cotton fabric which has a ribbed pile.

core (kōr) *n.* The innermost or central
part of something; the inedible center
of a fruit that contains the seeds. *v.* To
remove the core from a piece of fruit.

co-re-op-sis (kōr´ē op´sis) *n.* A familiar
garden herb grown for its showy
flowers.

co-re-spon-dent (kō´ri spon´dent) *n.*
A person charged with having committed adultery with the defendant in
a divorce case.

co-ri-a-ceous (kōr´ē ā´shus) *adj.*
Consisting of or resembling leather.

co-ri-an-der (kōr´ē an´dér) *n.* A herb
plant of the carrot family.

co-ri-um (kor´e um) *n.* The vascular
layer of the skin beneath the epidermis.

cork (kork) *n.* The elastic bark of the
oak tree used for bottle stoppers and
craft projects.

cork-age (kor´kij) *n.* The fee that must
be paid when one consumes a bottle
of liquor not purchased on the
premises.

cork-screw (kork´skrō´) *n.* A pointed
metal spiral attached to a handle used
for removing corks from bottles.

cork-wood (kork´wüd) *n.* The light and
porous wood of certain trees and shrubs
of the southeastern United States.

cor-mo-rant (kor´mér ant) *n.* Any bird
of the voracious water birds having
a long neck, webbed feet, and a pouch
under the mouth for holding and
catching fish.

corn (korn) *n.* An American cultivated
cereal plant bearing seeds on a large
ear or cob; the seed of this plant; a
horny thickening of the skin, usually
on the toe.

cor-na-ceous (kor nā´shus) *adj.* A family
of plants, mostly trees and shrubs that
include the dogwood and the tupelo.

cor-ne-a (kor´nē a) *n.* The transparent
membrane of the eyeball. **corneal** *adj.*

cor-ner (kor´nér) *n.* The point formed
when two surfaces or lines meet and
form an angle; the location where two
streets meet.

corner-stone (kor´nér stōn´) *n.* A stone
that forms part of the corner of a
building, usually laid in place with a
special ceremony.

cor-net (kor net´) *n.* A three valved, brass
musical instrument. **cornetist** *n.*

cor-nice (kor´nis) *n.* The horizontal

projecting molding which finishes a wall or building.

cor-niche (kor'nish) n. A road built along the edge of a cliff.

cor-nu (kor'nū) n. A horn-shaped structure.

cor-nu-co-pi-a (kor'nu kō'pē a) n. A curved goat's horn overflowing with flowers, fruit, and corn to signify prosperity.

cor-nute (kor nōt') adj. Having horns; horn-shaped.

cor-ol-lary (kor'oler'ē) n. pl. -ies Something that naturally or incidentally follows or accompanies.

cor-o-nar-y (kor'o ner'ē) adj. Of or relating to the two arteries that supply blood to the heart muscles.

coronary thrombosis n. A blocking of the coronary artery of the heart.

cor-o-ner n. A public officer, of a county or municipality, whose chief function is to investigate, any death not clearly due to natural causes.

cor-o-net (kor' o nit) n. A small, lessor, or inferior crown.

co-ro-no-graph (ka rō'no graf) n. A telescope used for observing and photographing the corona of the sun.

cor-po-ral (kor'pēr al) n. The lowest non-commissioned officer. adj. Relating to or affecting the body.

cor-po-rate (kor'pēr it) adj. Combined into one joint body; relating to a corporation.

cor-po-ra-tion (kor'po rā'shan) n. A group of merchants united in a trade guild; any group or persons that act as one.

cor-po-re-al (kor pōr'ē al) adj. Of a physical nature.

corps (kōrps) n. pl. **corps** A branch of the armed forces; the body of persons under common direction.

corpse (korps) n. A dead body.

cor-pu-lent (kor'pū lent) adj. Having a large or bulky body.

corpus callosum n. The large band of nervous tissue uniting the two cerebral hemispheres in the brain of man and other mammals.

cor-pus-cle (kor'pu sel) n. A minute particle or living cell, especially as one in the blood. **corpuscular** adj.

corpus delicti (kor'pus di lik'tī) n. The essential evidence pertaining to a crime.

cor-rade (ka rād') v. To rub together; to wear away by abrasion.

cor-ral (ka ral') n. An enclosure for containing animals. v., Slang To take possession of.

cor-rect (ka rekt') v. To make free from fault or mistakes. **corrective** n.

cor-re-spond (kor'i spond') v. To communicate by letter or written words; to be harmonious, equal or similar.

correspondingly adv.

cor-re-spond-ent (kor'i spond') n. Something that corresponds to something else; a person who has regular business dealings with another.

cor-ri-dor (kor'i dėr) n. A long hall with rooms on either side; a piece of land that forms a passage through a foreign land.

cor-ri-gen-dum (kor'i jen'dum) n. pl. -da An error in print that is accompanied by its correction.

cor-ri-gi-ble (kor'i ji bl) adj. Able to correct; capable of being corrected.

cor-ri-val (ka rī'val) n. A competitor.

cor-rob-o-rate (k o rob'o rāt') v. To support a position or statement with evidence. **corroboration** n.

cor-rode (ka rōd') v. To eat away through chemical action. **corrosive** n. **corrodible** adj. **corrosion** n.

cor-ro-sion (ka rō'zhan) n. The process of corroding, eating, or wearing away; the chemical effect of acids on metals.

cor-ro-sive (ka rō'siv) n. That which has the power or quality of wearing away gradually.

cor-ru-gate (kor'u gāt') v. To form, draw or bend into folds or alternate grooves and ridges.

corrugated iron n. Galvanized sheet iron or sheet steel, shaped and strengthened by bending into equal parallel grooves and ridges.

cor-rupt (ka rupt') adj. Dishonest; evil. v. To become or make corrupt.

cor-rup-tion (ka rup'shan) n. Impaired of integrity.

cor-sage (kor säzh') n. A small bouquet of flowers worn on a woman's shoulder or wrist.

cor-sair (kor'sâr) n. A pirate; a fast moving vessel.

cor-set (kor'sit) n. An undergarment that is tightened with laces and reinforced with stays, worn to give shape and support to a woman's body.

cor-tege (kor tezh') n. A ceremonial procession; a funeral procession.

cor-tex (kor'teks) n. pl. -tices The external layer of an organ, especially the gray matter that covers the brain; the bark of trees and the rinds of fruits.

cor-ti-sone (kor'ti sōn') n. A hormone produced by the adrenal cortex, used in the treatment of rheumatoid arthritis.

co-run-dum (ka run'dum) n. An aluminum oxide used as an abrasive.

cor-us-cate (kor'u skāt') v. To sparkle. **coruscation** n.

cor-vette (kor vet') n. An armed warship smaller than a destroyer, used as an escort vessel.

cor-vine (kor'vīn) n. Birds including and resembling the crow, and ravens.

co-ry-za (ka rī'za) n. An acute inflamma

tion of the upper respiratory system.

co-sign (kō sig´n) v. To sign a document jointly.

co-sig-na-to-ry (kō sig´na tōr´ē) n. pl. **-ies** One who jointly cosigns a document.

cos lettuce n. A kind of lettuce; romaine.

cos-met-ic (koz met´ik) n. A preparation designed to beautify the face.

cos-mic (koz´mik) adj. Of or relating to cosmos; forming a part of the material universe.

cosmic dust n. Very fine particles existing in or of the universe.

cosmic ray n. An extremely high frequency and energy content that comes from outer space and bombards the atoms of the earth's atmosphere.

cos-mog-o-ny (koz mog´o nē) n. The creation of the universe.

cos-mog-ra-phy n. The general science description of the heavens and the earth, dealing with the whole makeup of nature.

cos-mo-naut (koz mo not) n. A Soviet astronaut.

cos-mop-o-lis (koz mop´o lis) n. A city inhabited by people from many lands.

cos-mo-pol-i-tan (koz´mo pol´i tan) adj. Being at home anywhere in the world.

cos-mop-o-lite (koz mop´o līt) n. A cosmopolitan person.

cos-mos (koz´mos) n. An orderly and harmoniously systematic universe.

cos-set (kos´it) v. To pamper; pet.

cost (kost) n. The amount paid or charged for a purchase. **cost** v. **costly** adj.

cos-ta (kos´ta) n. A part of a leaf or the interior wing of an insect that most resembles a rib.

cos-tive (kos´tiv) adj. Affected with or causing constipation.

cost-mar-y (kost´mâr´ē) n. A perennial plant, with fragrant leaves, used as a pot-herb, in salads.

cos-tume (kos´tōm) n. A suit, dress, or set of clothes characteristic of a particular season or occasion; clothes worn by a person playing a part or dressing up in a disguise.

cot (kot) n. A small, often collapsible bed.

cote (kōt) n. A shelter for small animals as a coop or shed.

co-til-lion (kō til´yan) n. A dance that consists of beautiful and intricate patterns.

cot-tage (kot´lj) n. A small house, usually for vacation use.

cot-ton (kot´on) n. A plant or shrub cultivated for the fiber surrounding its seeds; a fabric created by the weaving of cotton fibers; yarn spun from cotton fibers.

cotton candy n. Spun sugar candy.

cot-ton-seed (kot´on sēd´) n. The seed

of the cotton plant, the oil of which can be used as a substitute for olive oil and in cooking.

couch (kouch) n. A piece of furniture, such as a sofa or bed on which one may sit or recline for rest or sleep. v. To phrase in a certain manner; to lie in ambush.

cou-gar (kö´gèr) n. A large brown cat, also called a mountain lion, panther, and puma.

cough (kof) v. To suddenly expel air from the lungs with an explosive noise.

could (kůd) v. Past tense of can.

could-n't (kůd´ent) contr. Could not.

cou-lisse (kö lēs´) n. A piece of wood, with a groove in which something slides.

cou-loir (köl wär´) n. A gully or mountainside gorge.

cou-lomb (kö´lom) n. The unit of quantity used to measure electricity; the amount conveyed by one ampere in one second.

cou-ma-rone n. A colorless liquid compound, found in coal tar and used to form thermoplastic resins used in printing inks, and adhesives.

coun-cil (koun´sil) n. A group of people assembled for consultation or discussion; an official legislative or advisory body. **councilman**, n.

coun-sel (koun´sel) n. Professional advice given through consultation; a lawyer en-gaged in a trial or management of a court case.

coun-sel-ing (koun´se ling) n. The act or process of giving professional advice.

coun-sel-or (koun´se lèr) n. One who gives advice; a lawyer.

count (kount) v. To name or number so as to find the total number of units involved; to name numbers in order; to take account of in a tally or reckoning; to rely or depend on something or someone; to have significance. n. A nobleman found in various countries throughout Europe, having rank corresponding to that of a British earl; a tally.

count-down (kount´doun´) n. An audible counting in descending order to mark the time remaining before an event.

coun-te-nance (koun´te nans) n. The face as an indication of mood or character; bearing or expression that would suggest approval or sanction.

coun-ter (koun´tèr) n. A level surface over which transactions are conducted, on which food is served, or on which articles are displayed; a person or device that counts to determine a number or amount. v. To move or act in a contrary, or opposing direction or wrong way.

coun-ter-act (koun´tĕr akt´) v. To oppose and, by contrary action, make ineffective.

coun-ter-attack (koun´tĕr a tak´) n. An attack made in response to an enemy attack. **counterattack** v.

coun-ter-bal-ance (koun´tĕr bal´ans) n. A force or influence that balances another; a weight that balances another.

coun-ter-bore (koun´tĕr bōr´) v. To bore out a hole for creating a flat-bottomed enlargement for the head of a screw.

coun-ter-claim (koun´tĕr klām´) n. A contrary claim made to offset another.

coun-ter-clock-wise (koun´tĕr klok´wĭz´) adj. & adv. In a direction contrary to that in which the hands of a clock move.

coun-ter-cul-ture (koun´tĕr kul´chĕr) n. A culture with values opposite those of traditional society.

coun-ter-es-pi-o-nage (koun´tĕr es´pē o näzh´) n. Espionage aimed at discovering and thwarting enemy espionage.

coun-ter-feit (koun´tĕr fĭt) v. To closely imitate or copy with the intent to deceive; to forge. adj. Marked by false pretense. n. Something counterfeit.

coun-ter-foil (koun´tĕr foil´) n. A stub, as on a check or ticket, usually serving as a record of the transaction.

coun-ter-in-tel-ligence (koun´tĕr in tel´i jens) n. An intelligence agency function designed to block information, deceive the enemy, prevent sabotage, and gather military and political material and information.

coun-ter-ir-ri-tant (koun´tĕr ir´i tant) n. An irritation that diverts attention from another. **counterirritant** adj.

coun-ter-man (koun´tĕr man) n. One who works at a counter.

coun-ter-mand (koun´tĕr mand´) v. To reverse or revoke a command by issuing a contrary order. n. An order which reverses or contradicts a previous order.

coun-ter-of-fensive (koun´tĕr o fen´siv) n. A military offensive designed to thwart an enemy attack.

coun-ter-pane (koun´tĕr pān´) n. A covering.

coun-ter-part (koun´tĕr pärt´) n. One that matches or complements another.

coun-ter-plea (koun´tĕr plē) n. A plea made in answer to a previous plea.

coun-ter-plot (koun´tĕr plot´) n. A plot that prevents another from occurring.

coun-ter-point (koun´tĕr point´) n., Mus. The combining of melodies into a harmonic relationship while retaining the linear character.

coun-ter-poise (koun´tĕr poiz´) n. An equal and opposing force or power.

coun-ter-pose (koun´tĕr pōz´) v. To

place in opposition.

coun-ter-pro-duc-tive (koun´tĕr pro duk´tiv) adj. Tending to hinder rather than aid in the attainment of a goal.

coun-ter-pro-pos-al (koun´tĕr pro pō´zal) n. A return proposal for one that has been rejected.

coun-ter-punch (koun´tĕr punch) n. A punch given in quick retaliation, as a boxing punch.

coun-ter-re-vo-lu-tion (koun´tĕr rev´o lō´shan) n. A revolution designed to overthrow a government previously seat-ed by a revolution.

coun-ter-shaft (koun´tĕr shaft´) n. A shaft driven by a belt or gearing from a main shaft and transmits motion to a working part.

coun-ter-sign (koun´tĕr sīn´) n. A signature confirming the authenticity of a document already signed by another; a sign or signal given in response to another. **countersign** v.

coun-ter-spy (koun´tĕr spī´) n. A spy against the espionage actions of a country.

coun-ter-ten-or (koun´tĕr tĕn´ĕr) n. An adult tenor with a very high range, and able to sing in an alto range.

coun-tri-fy (kun´tri fī´) v. To imply country life; rustic; unsophisticated.

coun-try (kun´trē) n. pl. -ies A given area or region; the land of one's birth, residence, or citizenship; a state, nation, or its territory.

coun-try-man (kun´trē man) n. A compatriot; one living in the country or having country ways.

country music n. Music derived from the folk style of the southern United States and from the cowboy.

coun-try-side (kun´trē sīd´) n. A rural area or its inhabitants.

coun-ty (koun´tē) n. pl. -ies A territorial division for local government within a state.

coup (kö) n. A brilliant, sudden move that is usually highly successful.

cou-ple (kup´l) n. A pair; something that joins two things together; a few. v. To join in marriage or sexual union.

cou-pler (kup´lĕr) n. One who or that which couples; a device that transfers electrical energy from one circuit to another.

cou-plet (kup´lĭt) n. Two rhyming lines of poetry in succession.

cou-pling (kup´ling) n. A mechanical devices for uniting or connecting parts or things.

cou-pon (kō´pon) n. A statement of interest due, to be removed from a bearer bond and presented for payment when it is payable; a form surrendered to obtain a product, service, or discount on same; a form to be clipped from a magazine or paper and mailed for discounts or gifts.

cour-age (kûr´ij) *n.* Mental or moral strength to face danger without fear. **courageous** *adj.* **courageously** *adv.*

cou-ri-er (kûr´ē ér) *n.* A messenger; a person who carries contraband for another.

course (kōrs) *n.* The act of moving in a path from one point to another; the path over which something moves; a period of time; a series or sequence; a series of studies.

court (kōrt) *n.* The residence of a sovereign or similar dignitary; a sovereign's family and advisors; an assembly for the transaction of judicial business; a place where trials are conducted; an area marked off for game playing. *v.* To try to win favor or dispel hostility.

cour-te-ous (kėr´tē us) *adj.* Marked by respect for and consideration of others.

cour-te-san (kōr´ti zan) *n.* A prostitute; one who associates with or caters to high-ranking or wealthy men.

cour-te-sy (kėr´ti sē) *n. pl.* -ies Courteous behavior; general allowance despite facts.

court-house (kōrt´hous´) *n.* A building for holding courts of law.

court-i-er (kōr´tē ér) *n.* One in attendance at a royal court.

court-ly (kōrt´lē) *adj.* Dignified; elegant; polite.

court of appeals *n.* A court that hears appeals from a lower court.

court-room (kōrt´rōm´) *n.* A room for holding a court of law.

court-ship (kōrt´ship) *n.* The act or period of courting.

court-yard (kōrt´yärd´) *n.* An open space enclosed by walls.

cous-in (kuz´in) *n.* A child of one's uncle or aunt; a member of a culturally similar race or nationality.

couth (kōth) *adj.* Having breeding, polish, or refinement.

cou-ture (kü tûr´) *n.* The business of designing and selling women's clothing; dressmaker.

covalent bond *n.* The nonionic chemical bond produced by the sharing of an electron pair by two atoms in a chemical process.

cove (kōv) *n.* A small inlet or bay, generally sheltered; a deep recess or small valley in the side of a mountain.

cov-e-nant (kuv´e nant) *n.* A formal, binding agreement; a promise or pledge.

cov-er (kuv´ér) *v.* To place something on or over; to lie over; to spread over; concealment, to guard from attack; to hide or conceal, book binding. *Slang* To be all-encompassing; to act as a

stand-in during another's absence; to have within one's gun sights.

cov-er-age (kuv´ér ij) *n.* A provision for something by contract; that which is covered.

cov-er-all (kuv´ér al´) *n.* A loose one-piece outer garment used to cover other clothing.

cover charge *n.* A charge, at night clubs or restaurants, in addition to the bill for food and drink, used to pay for the entertainment.

cover crop *n.* A crop planted to prevent soil erosion.

covered wagon *n.* A canvas covered wagon with high curved hoops supported by bowed strips of metal or wood.

cov-er-let (kuv´ér lit) *n.* A bedspread.

cov-et (kuv´it) *v.* To wish for enviously; to crave possession of that which belongs to someone else.

cov-ey (kuv´ē) *n.* A small group of birds, especially quail or partridges.

cow (kou) *n. pl.* **cows** The mature female of cattle or of any species when the adult male is referred to as a bull.

cow-ard (kou´ard) *n.* One who shows great fear or timidity. **cowardice** *n.*

cow-bane (kou´bān´) *n.* Any of several poisonous parsley-like plants, as the water hemlock.

cow-boy (kou´boi) *n.* A man who tends cows and horses on a large ranch or farm and does this work while on horseback.

cow-hide (kou´hīd´) *n.* The hide of a cow from which leather is made.

cowl (koul) *n.* A hood or long hooded cloak such as that of a monk; a covering for a chimney that is designed to improve the air draft; the top portion at the front of an automobile where the windshield and dashboard are attached.

cow-lick (kou´lik´) *n.* A lock of hair growing in a different direction than the other hair.

cowl-ing (kou´ling) *n.* A removable metal covering for an engine.

cox-a (kok´sa) *n.* The joint of the hip.

cox-comb (koks´kōm) *n.* A conceited foolish person.

cox-swain (kok´san) *n.* One who steers a boat or racing shell.

coy (koi) *adj.* Quieting or shy, or to pretending to be so. **coyness** *n.*

coy-o-te (kī ō´tē) *n.* A small wolf-like animal that is native to North America.

co-yo-til-lo (kō´yō tēl´yō) *n.* A small shrub of the southwestern United States and Mexico, bearing poisonous fruit.

coy-pu (koi´pö) *n.* A beaver-like, semiaquatic mammal, valued for its soft brown fur.

coz-en (kuz´en) *v.* To swindle, cheat, deceive, win over, or induce to do something by coaxing or trickery.

co-zy (kō´zē) *adj*. Comfortable and warm; snug. **cozy** *n*. A cover placed over a teapot to retain the warmth. **cozily** *adv*.

crab (krab) *n*. *pl*. **crabs** Any one of numerous chiefly marine crustaceans with a short, broad shell, four pairs of legs, and one pair of pincers; sideways motion of an airplane headed into a crosswind. **crabs** Infestation with crab lice.

crab-bed (krab´id) *adj*. Morose or peevish; difficult to read or understand. **crabbedly** *adv*. **crabbedness** *n*.

crab-by (krab bē) *adj*. Cross and ill-tempered.

crab-grass (krab gras) *n*. A grass with stems that root freely and is often a weedy pest in lawns.

crack (krak) *v*. To make a loud explosive sound; to break, snap, or split apart; to break without completely separating; to go at a good speed; to break with a sudden, sharp sound; to solve; to reduce petroleum compounds to simpler forms by heating. *n*. A sharp, witty remark; a weakness caused by decay or age; an attempt or try. *Slang* A highly dangerous and addictive form of cocaine.

crack down *n*. The sudden act of disciplinary actions.

crack-le (krak´el) *v*. To make sharp, sudden, repeated noises; to develop a network of fine cracks.

crack-pot (krak´pot˝) *n*., *Slang* An eccentric person.

crack–up (krak´up˝) *n*. A breakdown of a person's health, especially mental and emotional.

cra-dle (krād´el) *n*. A small bed for infants, usually on rockers or rollers.

craft (kraft) *n*. A special skill or ability; a trade that requires dexterity or artistic skill.

cram (kram) *v*. To pack tightly or stuff; to thrust in a forceful manner; to eat in a greedy fashion; to prepare hastily for an exam.

cram-bo (kram´bō) *n*. A game in which one person gives a word or a line of verse to which another finds a rhyme.

cramp (kramp) *n*. A painful involuntary contraction of a muscle; sharp abdominal pain.

cram-pon (kram´pon) *n*. A hooked apparatus used to raise objects.

cran-age (krā´nij) *n*. To load or unload goods from a ship by using a crane.

cran-dall (kran´dal) *n*. A hammer-like tool for working with soft stone.

crane (krān) *n*. A large bird with long legs and a long neck; a machine used for lifting or moving heavy objects. *v*. To strain or stretch the neck.

cranial index *n*. The ratio multiplied by 100 of the full breadth of the skull to its maximum or full length.

cranial nerve *n*. Any of the nerves that originate in the lower part of the brain and come through openings in the skull.

cra-ni-ol-o-gy (krā˝nē ol´o jē) *n*. The science that deals with the size, shape, and other characteristics of human skulls.

cra-ni-um (krā´nē um) *n*. *pl*. **crania** The skull, especially the part in which the brain is enclosed. **cranial** *adj*.

crank (krangk) *n*. An arm bent at right angles to a shaft and turned to transmit motion; an eccentric person; a bad-tempered person; a grouch. *v*. To operate or start by crank.

crank-case (krangk´kās˝) *n*. The housing of a crankshaft.

crank-shaft (krangk´shaft´) *n*. A shaft propelled by a crank.

crank-y (krang´kē) *adj*. Grouchy, irritable.

cran-ny (kran´ē) *n*. *pl*. **-ies** A small break or crevice; an obscure nook or corner.

crap-pie (krap´ē) *n*. A small sunfish of the central parts of the United States.

craps (kraps) *v*. A gambling game played with two dice.

crap-shoot-er (krap´shō˝tèr) *n*. A person who plays craps.

crap-u-lous *adj*. Associated with drunkenness, sick from excessive consumption of liquor.

crass (kras) *adj*. Insensitive and unrefined.

crate (krāt) *n*. A container, usually made of wooden slats, for protection during ship-ping or storage. **crate** *v*.

cra-ter (krā´tèr) *n*. A bowl-shaped depression at the mouth of a volcano; a depression formed by a meteorite; a hole made by an explosion.

cra-vat (kra vat´) *n*. A necktie.

crave (krāv) *v*. To desire intensely.

cra-ven (krā´ven) *adj*. Completely lacking courage.

crav-ing (krāv ing) *n*. A great desire; an intense longing.

craw (kro) *n*. The crop of a bird; the stomach of a lower animal.

craw-fish (kro´fish´) *n*. A crayfish.

crawl (krol) *v*. To move slowly by dragging the body along the ground in a prone position; to move on hands and knees; to progress slowly.

cray-on (krā´on) *n*. A stick of white or colored chalk or wax used for writing or drawing.

craze (krāz) *v*. To make insane or as if insane; to become insane; to develop a fine mesh of narrow cracks. *n*. Something that lasts for a short period of time; a fad.

cra-zy (krā´zē) *adj*. Insane; impractical;

unusually fond. **craziness** *n*.

crazy bone *n*. The elbow; the funny bone.

crazy quilt *n*. A patch quilt without a particular pattern.

creak (krēk) *v*. A squeaking or grating noise. **creaky** *adj*. **creakily** *adv*.

crease (krēs) *n*. A line or mark made by folding and pressing a pliable substance. **crease** *v*.

creas-er (krēs'ėr) *n*. A sewing machine attachment for creasing leather or cloth.

cre-ate (krē āt') *v*. To bring something into existence; to give rise to.

cre-a-tion (krē ā'shan) *n*. The act of creating; something that is created; the universe.

cre-a-tive (krē ā'tiv) *adj*. Marked by the ability to create; inventive; imaginative. **creatively** *adv*. **creativeness** *n*.

crea-tor (krē ā'tėr) *n*. One that creates. **Creator**. God.

crea-ture (krē'chėr) *n*. Something created; a living being.

cre-dence (krēd'ens) *n*. Belief.

cre-den-dum (kri den'dum) *n*. Something to be believed; an article of faith.

cre-den-za (kri den'za) *n*. A buffet or sideboard, usually without legs.

cred-i-ble (kred'i bl) *adj*. Offering reasonable grounds for belief, confidence in truth and reliance. **credibility** *n*. **credibly** *adv*.

cred-it (kred'it) *n*. An amount at a person's disposal in a bank; recognition by name for a contribution; acknowledgment; recognition by a learning institution that a student has completed a requirement leading to a degree.

cred-u-lous (krej'u lus) *adj*. Gullible; ready to believe on slight or uncertain evidence, easily deceived.. **credulously** *adv*. **credulousness** *n*.

creed (krēd) *n*. A brief authoritative statement of religious belief.

creek (krēk) *n*. A narrow stream. **up the creek** In a difficult or perplexing situation.

creel (krēl) *n*. A wicker basket for holding fish.

creep (krēp) *v*. To advance at a slow pace; to go timidly or cautiously; to grow along a surface, clinging by means of tendrils or aerial roots.

cre-mate (krē'māt) *v*. To reduce to ashes by burning.

cre-ma-tor (krē'mā tėr) *n*. A person who cremates; the furnace where bodies are cremated.

cre-o-sol (krē'o līzd') *n*. A colorless oily liquid from wood tar and guaiacum resin.

cre-o-sote (krē'o sōt') *n*. An oily liquid mixture obtained by distilling coal tar, used especially as a wood preservative.

crepe paper *n*. A decorative paper, with a puckered or wrinkled texture.

crepe rubber *n*. A synthetic rubber in the form of crinkled sheets used for shoe soles.

crept *v*. The past tense of creep.

cre-pus-cu-lar (kri pus'kū lėr) *adj*. Of, resembling, or relating to twilight.

cre-pus-cule (kri pus'kūl) *n*. Pertaining to twilight; glimmering; dusk.

cre-scen-do (kri shen'dō) *adv*. In music, gradually increasing in loudness.

cres-cent (kres'ent) *n*. The shape of the moon in its first and fourth quarters, defined with a convex and a concave edge.

cres-cive (kres'iv) *adj*. Increasing or growing.

cress (kres) *n*. Any of numerous plants with sharp-tasting edible leaves.

cres-set (kres'it) *n*. A lamp or fire pan mounted as a torch or carried on a pole as a lantern.

crest (krest) *n*. A tuft or comb on the head of a bird or animal; the top line of a mountain or hill.

crest-fall-en (krest'fo'len) *adj*. Dejected; discouraged; having a hanging head.

cre-ta-ceous (kri tā'shus) *adj*. Composed of, or having the qualities of chalk.

cre-tin (krē'tin) *n*. One afflicted with cretinism; a person with marked mental deficiency.

cre-tin-ism (krēt'e niz'um) *n*. A condition marked by physical stunting and mental deficiency.

cre-tonne (kri ton') *n*. A strong cotton or linen cloth, used especially for curtains and upholstery, a cotton cloth with various textures of surface printed with pictorial and other patterns.

cre-vasse (kre vas') *n*. A deep crack or crevice.

crev-ice (krev'is) *n*. A narrow crack.

crew (krö) *n*. A group of people that work together; the whole company belonging to an aircraft or ship.

crew-el (krö'el) *n*. Slackly twisted worsted yarn, used in embroidery.

crib (krib) *n*. A small bed with high sides for an infant; a feeding bin for animals.

crib-bage (krib'ij) *n*. A game of cards, for two, three or four players.

crib-ri-form (krib'ri form') *adj*. Having the form of a sieve; pierced with many small openings.

crick (krik) *n*. A painful muscle spasm condition of the neck or back.

cri-er (krī'ėr) *n*. One who calls out public notices.

crime (krīm) *n*. An act or the commission of an act that is forbidden by law.

crim-i-nal (krim'i nal) *adj*. Relating to a crime. *n*. A person who commits a crime.

criminal law *n*. The law of crimes and punishment.

crim-i-nate (krim´ĭnāt´) v. To involve in a crime.

crim-i-nol-o-gy (krim´i nol´o jē) n. Scientific study of crime.

crimp (krimp) v. To cause to become bent or crinkled; to pinch in or together.

crim-son (krim´zon) n. A deep purplish color. v. To make or become crimson.

cringe (krinj) v. To shrink or recoil in fear.

crin-kle (kring´kl) v. To wrinkle. crinkle n. crinkly adj.

crin-o-line (krin´o lin) n. An open-weave fabric used for lining and stiffening garments.

cri-o-sphinx (krī´o sfingks´) n. A sphinx with the head of a ram.

crip-ple (krip´l) n. One who is lame or partially disabled; something flawed or imperfect. adj. Being a cripple. v. To deprive one of the use of a limb or limbs.

cri-sis (krī´sis) n. pl. crises An unstable or uncertain time or state of affairs, the outcome of which will have a major impact; the turning point for better or worse in a disease or fever, hectic situation.

crisp (krisp) adj. Easily broken; brittle; brisk or cold; sharp; clear. v. To make or become crisp. crisply adv. -ness n.

cri-te-ri-on (krī tēr´ē on) n. pl. criteria A standard by which something can be judged.

crit-ic (krit´ik) n. A person who is critical; a person who examines a subject and expresses an opinion as to its value; a person who judges or evaluates art or artistic creations, as a theatre critic.

crit-i-cal (krit´i kal) adj. Very important, as a critical decision; tending to criticize harshly. critically adv.

crit-i-cism (krit´i siz´um) n. The act of criticizing, usually in a severe or negative fashion.

crit-i-cize (krit´i siz´) v. To be a critic; to find fault with; to judge critically; to blame.

cri-tique (kri tēk´) n. A written estimate of the merits of a performance.

croak (krōk) n. A hoarse, raspy cry such as that made by a frog. v. To utter a croak. Slang To die.

cro-chet (krō shā´) n. The needlework achieved by looping thread with a hooked needle.

crock (krok) n. An earthenware pot or jar most often used for cooking or storing food.

crock-et (krok´it) n. An ornament in the form of curved and bent foliage.

croc-o-dile (krok´o dīl´) n. Any of various large, thick-skinned, long-bodied reptiles of tropical and subtropical regions.

crocodile tears n. Insincere or false grief.

cro-cus (krō´kus) n. pl. crocuses A plant having solitary, long-tubed flowers and slender, linear leaves.

croft (kroft) n. A small piece of ground or farm worked by the tenant who lives on the property.

crois-sant (krwä sän´) n. A crescent-shaped roll of flaky bread dough.

crone (krōn) n. A witch-like, withered old woman.

cro-ny (krō´nē) n. pl. cronies A close friend.

crook (krük) n. A bent or hooked implement; a bend or curve; a person given to dishonest acts. crook v. To bend or curve.

crook-ed (krük´id) adj. Dishonest; bent; not straight; deformed.

croon (krōn) v. To sing in a gentle, low voice; to make a continued moaning sound.

crop (krop) n. A plant which is grown and then harvested for use or for sale; a riding whip. v. To cut off short; to appear unexpectedly.

cro-quet (krō kā´) n. An outdoor game played by driving wooden balls through hoops with long-handled mallets.

cro-quette (krō ket´) n. A small patty or roll of minced food that is breaded and deep fried.

cro-qui-gnole (krō´ki nōl) n. A method of styling the hair by winding the hair toward the head on curlers, in a circular style.

cross-current (kros´kèr´ent) n. A current flowing against another; a conflicting tendency.

crotch (kroch) n. The angle formed by the junction of two parts, such as branches, part of the human body where the legs join, a pair of pants where the legs meet. crotched adj.

crotch-et (kroch´it) n. A peculiar opinion or preference.

crouch (krouch) v. To bend at the knees and lower the body close to the ground.

croup (krōp) n. A spasmodic laryngitis, especially of children, marked by a loud, harsh cough and difficulty in breathing. croupy adj.

crou-pi-er (krō´pē èr) n. One who collects and pays bets at a gambling table.

crous-tade (krō städ´) n. A crisp shell, either fried or baked, in which to serve foods.

crou-ton (krō´ton) n. A small piece of toasted or fried bread.

crow (krō) n. A large, black bird. crow v. To brag; to boast.

crow-bar (krō´bär) n. A steel or iron bar with a forked end, used as a lever.

crowd (kroud) n. A large group of people gathered together. v. To assemble in large numbers; to press close.

cru-cial (krō´shal) *adj.* Extremely important; critical.

cru-ci-ble (krō´si bl) *n.* A vessel used for melting and calcining materials at high temperatures; a severe or hard test of someone.

cru-ci-fy (krō´si fī´) *v.* To put to death by nailing to a cross; to treat cruelly; to torment.

crude (krōd) *adj.* Unrefined; lacking refinement or tact; haphazardly made. *n.* Unrefined petroleum. **crudely** *adv.*

cruel (krō´el) *adj.* Inflicting suffering; causing pain. **cruelly** *adv.* **cruelty** *n.*

cru-et (krō´it) *n.* A small glass bottle normally used as a container for oil or vinegar.

cruise (krōz) *v.* To drive or sail about for pleasure; to move about the streets at leisure; to travel at a speed that provides maximum efficiency.

crul-ler (krul´ér) *n.* A light, sweet cake cut in a twisted circular form and fried in deep fat.

crumb (krum) *n.* A small fragment of material, particularly bread.

crum-ble (krum´bl) *v.* To break into small pieces. **crumbly** *adj.*

crump (krump) *v.* To crunch with the teeth. *n.* A crunching sound

crum-ple (krum´pel) *v.* To bend or crush out of shape; to cause to collapse; to be crumpled.

crunch (krunch) *v.* To chew with a crackling noise; to run, walk, etc., with a crushing noise. **crunch** *n.*

cru-ral (krür´al) *adj.* Pertaining to the thigh or leg.

crus (krus) *n.* The part of the leg or hind limb between the femur or thigh and the ankle.

cru-sade (krō sād´) *n.* Any of the military expeditions undertaken by Christian leaders during the 11th, 12th, and 13th centuries to recover the Holy Land from the Moslems. **crusade** *v.*

crush (krush) *v.* To squeeze or force by pressure so as to damage or injure.

crust (krust) *n.* The hardened exterior or surface of bread; a hard or brittle surface layer.

crus-ta-cean (kru stā´shan) *n.* Any one of a large class of aquatic arthropods, including lobsters and crabs, with a segmented body and paired, jointed limbs.

crutch (kruch) *n.* A support usually designed to fit in the armpit and to be used as an aid in walking; any support or prop.

crux (kruks) *n.* An essential or vital moment; a main or central feature.

cry (krī) *v.* To shed tears; to call out loudly; to utter a characteristic call or sound; to proclaim publicly.

cry-o-gen (krī´ō jen) *n.* A substance for producing or obtaining low temperatures.

cry-o-lite *n.* A fluoride of sodium-aluminum and used to make aluminum and soda.

cry-om-e-ter (krī om´i tér) *n.* A thermometer for measuring low temperatures.

cry-o-phyte (krī´ō fīt) *n.*, *Bot.* A plant that grows on snow and ice, usually an alga, but sometimes a moss, or fungus.

crypt (kript) *n.* An underground chamber or vault primarily used to bury the dead.

crypt-a-nal-y-sis (krip´ta nal´i sis) *n.* The study of solving written codes or ciphers.

cryp-tic (krip´tik) *adj.* Intended to be obscure; serving to conceal.

cryp-tog-ra-phy (krip tog´ra fē) *n.* The writing and deciphering of messages in secret code. **cryptographer** *n.*

crys-tal (kris´tal) *n.* Quartz that is transparent or nearly transparent; a body that is formed by the solidification of a chemical element; a clear, high-quality glass. **crystalline** *adj.*

crystal ball *n.* A glass globe foretell the future.

crys-tal-lize (kris´ta līz´) *v.* To cause to form crystals or assume crystalline form; to cause to take a definite form; to coat with crystals, especially sugar crystals.

cten-o-phore (ten´o fōr´) *n.* Any of the free-swimming aquatic animals.

cub (kub) *n.* The young of the lion, wolf, or bear; an awkward child or youth.

cu-ba-ture (ku ba chér) *n.* The determination of the cubic contents.

cub-by-hole (kub´ē hōl´) *n.* A small enclosed area.

cube (kūb) *n.* A regular solid with six equal squares, having all its angles right angles.

cu-beb (kū´beb) *n.* The spicy fruit or dried unripe berry of an East Indian climbing shrub of the pepper family.

cube root *n.* A number whose cube is a given number.

cubic (kū´bik) *adj.* Having the shape of a cube; having three dimensions; having the volume of a cube with the edges of a specified unit.

cu-bi-cle (kū´bi kl) *n.* A small partitioned area.

cu-bit (kū´bit) *n.* An ancient unit of measurement that equals approximately eighteen to twenty inches.

cu-cu-li-form (kū kū´li form) *adj.* Pertaining to birds, which includes road runners and cuckoos.

cu-cum-ber (kū´kum bèr) *n.* A fruit with a green rind and white, seedy flesh.

cu-cur-bit (kū kėr´bit) *n.* A plant from the gourd family.

cud (kud) *n.* Food forced up into the mouth of a ruminating animal from the first stomach and chewed again.

cud-dle (kud´l) *v.* To caress fondly and hold close; to snuggle. **cuddle** *n.*

cudg-el (kuj´el) *n.* A short, thick stick; a heavy club.

cue (kū) *n.* A signal given to an actor or someone making a speech, letting him know it is his turn; a long rod for playing pool and billiards.

cues-ta (kwes´ta) *n.* A hill with a gradual incline on one face and a steep incline on the other.

cuff (kuf) *n.* The lower part of a sleeve; the part of the pant legs which is turned up. *v.* To strike someone.

cuffs (kufs) *n.* Handcuffs.

cui-rass (kwi ras´) *n.* A piece of armor for the breast and back, used for protection.

cui-sine (kwi zēn´) *n.* A style of cooking and preparing food; the food prepared.

cu-let (kū´lit) *n.* The small flat facet forming the bottom of a gem.

cu-lex (kū´leks) *n.* A large group of mosquitoes found in North America and Europe.

cu-li-nar-y (kū´li ner´ē) *adj.* Relating to cooking.

cull (kul) *v.* To select the best from a group, to gather only the best.

culm (kulm) *n.* Coal dust or refuse coal; slack.

cul-mi-nate (kul´mi nāt´) *v.* To reach or rise to the highest point. **culmination** *n.*

cu-lotte (kō lot´) *n.* A woman's full pants made to look like a skirt.

cul-pa-ble (kul´pa bl) *adj.* Meriting blame. **culpability** *n.*

cul-prit (kul´prit) *n.* A person guilty of a crime.

cult (kult) *n.* A group or system of religious worship. **cultic** *adj.*

cul-ti-vate (kul´ti vāt´) *v.* To improve land for planting by fertilizing and plowing; to improve by study; to encourage. **cultivatable** *adj.* **cultivation** *n.* **cultivator** *n.*

cul-ture (kul´chėr) *n.* The act of developing intellectual ability with education; a form of civilization, particularly the beliefs, arts, and customs. *Biol.* The growth of living material in a prepared nutrient media. **culture** *v.*

cul-vert (kul´vėrt) *n.* A drain that runs under a road or railroad.

cum-ber (kum´bėr) *v.* To burden someone.

cum-ber-some (kum´bėr sum) *adj.* Clumsy; awkward. **cumbersomely** *adv.* **cumbersomeness** *n.*

cum-in (kum´im) *n.* A small plant of the parsley family cultivated for its aromatic.

cum-mer-bund (kum´ėr bund´) *n.* A wide sash worn by men in formal attire.

cu-mu-late (kū´mū lāt´) *v.* To heap or build up; amass; accumulate.

cu-mu-la-tive (kū´mū lā´tiv) *adj.* Increasing by successive additions.

cu-mu-lus (kū´mū lus) *n.* *pl.* **cumuli** A white, fluffy cloud with a rounded top and a flat base.

cu-ne-ate (kū´nē it) *adj.* Narrowly triangular and tapering to a point at the base.

cu-ne-i-form (kū nē´i form´) *n.* Wedge-shaped characters used in ancient Babylonian, Assyrian, and Sumerian writing.

cun-ning (kun´ing) *adj.* Crafty; sly.

cup (kup) *n.* A small, open container with a handle, used for drinking; a measure of capacity that equals 1/2 pint, 8 ounces, or 16 tablespoons.

cu-pel (kū´pel) *n.* A small, cup-like porous vessel, usually made of bone ash, used in assaying, to separate gold and silver from lead.

cu-pid-i-ty (kū pid´i tē) *n.* An excessive desire for material gain.

cu-po-la (kū´po la) *n.* A rounded roof; a small vaulted structure that usually rises above a roof.

cu-pre-ous (kū´prē us) *adj.* Consisting of copper.

cur (kūr) *n.* A mongrel; a dog of mixed breeds.

cu-rate (kūr´it) *n.* A member of the clergy that assists the priest.

cu-ra-tor (kū rā´tėr) *n.* A person in charge of a museum.

curb (kūrb) *n.* Something that restrains or controls; the raised border along the edge of a street. **curb** *v.*

curd (kūrd) *n.* The coagulated portion of milk used for making cheese.

cure (kūr) *n.* Recovery from a sickness; a medical treatment; the process of preserving food with the use of salt, smoke, or aging.

cur-few (kūr´fū) *n.* An order for people to clear the streets at a certain hour; the hour at which an adolescent has been told to be home by his or her parents.

cu-ri-o (kūr´ē ō´) *n.* An unusual or rare object.

cu-ri-o-sa (kūr´ē ō´sa) *n.* Books written on unusual or erotic subjects.

cu-ri-os-i-ty (kūrē os´i tē) *n.* The strong desire to know something; something that arouses interest.

cu-ri-ous (kūr´ē us) *adj.* Questioning; inquisitive; eager for information. **curious-ity** *n.* **curiously** *adv.*

cu-ri-um (kūr´ē um) *n.* An artificially

produced radioactive trivalent element.

curl (kürl) *v.* To twist into curves; shape like a coil. *n.* A ringlet of hair. **curler** *n.* **curliness** *n.* **curly** *adj.*

cur-lew (kür´lö) *n.* A migratory bird with long legs and a long slender curved bill.

cur-mudg-eon (kèr muj´on) *n.* An ill-tempered person.

curn (kürn) *n.* A grain; a small quantity.

cur-rant (kür´ant) *n.* A small seedless raisin.

cur-ren-cy (kür´en sē) *n. pl.* **currencies** Money in circulation.

cur-rent (kür´ent) *adj.* Belonging or occurring in the present time. *n.* Water or air that has a steady flow in a definite direction. **currently** *adv.*

current assets *n.* The assets of a company that can be readily converted to cash.

current liabilities *n.* Debts of a business or corporation.

cur-ri-cle (kèr´i kl) *n.* A two-wheeled carriage, drawn by two horses.

cur-ric-u-lum (ku rik´ū lum) *n. pl.* -la, -lums The courses offered in a school.

curse (kürs) *n.* A prayer or wish for harm to come to someone or something. **cursed** *adj.* **curse** *v.*

cur-sive (kèr´siv) *n.* A flowing writing in which the letters are joined together.

cur-sor (kür´sor) *n.* In computer science, the flashing square, underline, or other indicator on the CRT screen of a computer that shows where the next character will be deleted or inserted.

cur-so-ry (kür´so rē) *adj.* Rapidly done, often without care and not paying attention to details.

curt (kèrt) *adj.* Abrupt; rude, as in manner or speech. **curtly** *adv.*

cur-tail (kèr´tāl´) *v.* To shorten.

cur-tain (kür´tan) *n.* A piece of material that covers a window and can be either drawn to the sides or raised.

cur-tate (kür´tāt) *adj.* Shortened or reduced; abbreviated.

cur-ti-lage (kür´ti lij) *n.* The piece of land occupied by a house and its yard.

curt-sy (kürt´sē) *n. pl.* -sies A respectful gesture made by bending the knees and lowering the body. **curtsy** *v.*

curve (kürv) *n.* A continuously curved line without angles.

cush-ion (küsh´on) *n.* A pillow with a soft filling. *v.* To absorb the shock or effect.

cus-pid (kus´pid) *n.* A pointed canine tooth, cuspidate tooth.

cus-pi-dor (kus´pi dor´) *n.* A spittoon.

cuss (kus) *v.* To use profanity.

cus-tard (kus´tèrd) *n.* A mixture of milk, eggs, sugar, and flavoring that is baked.

cus-to-dy (kus´to dē) *n. pl.* -dies The act of guarding; the care and protection of a minor.

cus-tom (kus´tom) *n.* An accepted practice of a community or people; the usual manner of doing something. **customs** The tax one must pay on imported goods. **customary** *adj.*

cut (kut) *v.* To penetrate with a sharp edge, as with a knife; to omit or leave something out; to reap or harvest crops in the fields. *Slang* To cut class; to share in the profits.

cute (kūt) *adj.* Attractive in a delightful way.

cu-vette (kö vet´) *n.* A small vessel or tube used in a laboratory.

cy-cla-mate (si´kle māt) *n.* A sweetener used as a substitute for sugar, based on salts of calcium or sodium.

cyc-la-men (sik´la men) *n.* A plant with red, white, or pink flowers.

cy-cle (sī´kl) *n.* A recurring time in which an event occurs repeatedly; a bicycle or motorcycle. **cyclical** *adj.*

cy-clist (sī´klist) *n.* A person who rides a cycle.

cy-clone (sī´klōn) *n.* A storm with wind rotating about a low pressure center, accompanied by destructive weather.

cy-clo-tron (sī´klo tron´) *n.* Machine that obtains high-energy electrified particles by whirling at a high speed in a strong magnetic field.

cyg-net (sig´nit) *n.* A young swan.

cyl-in-der (sil´in dèr) *n.* A long, round body that is either hollow or solid.

cym-bal (sim´bal) *n.* A pair of brass plates which produce a clashing tone when struck together.

cyn-ic (sin´ik) *n.* One who believes that all people have selfish motives. **cynical** *adj.* **cynicism** *n.*

cy-no-sure (sī´no shör´) *n.* A person or object that attracts admiration and interest.

cyst (sist) *n.* An abnormal sac or vesicle which may collect and retain fluid.

cystic fibrosis *n.* A congenital disease, that usually develops in childhood and results in disorders of the lungs and pancreas.

cys-ti-tis (si stī´tis) *n.* An inflammation of the bladder.

cy-to-gen-e-sis (sī´to jen´i sis) *n.* The origin, development, and changes of cells in animal and vegetable structures.

cy-tol-o-gy (sī tol´o jē) *n.* The scientific study of cell formation, function, and structure, life cycle of a cell. **cytological** *adj.* **cytologic** *adj.* **cytologist** *n.*

cy-tol-y-sis (sī tol´i sis) *n.* The degeneration of cells.

cy-to-plasm (sīto plaz˝um) *n.* The living substance or protoplasm of a cell external to the nuclear membrane.

czar (zär) *n.* An emperor or king or one of the former emperors or kings of Russia. *Slang* One who has authority.

D, d (dē) The fourth letter of the English alphabet; the Roman numeral for 500.

dab (dab) v. To touch quickly with light, short strokes. **dab** n.

dab-ble (dab'l) v. To play in a liquid, as water, with the hands; to work in or play with in a minor way.

dace (dās) n. A small freshwater fish.

dachs-hund (daks'hend) n. A small dog with very short legs, drooping ears, and a long body.

dac-ty-lol-o-gy (dak'ti lol'o jē) n. The art of communicating thoughts or ideas by using the hands and fingers; the language of the deaf.

dad (dad) n., pl. **dads** Father.

dae-dal (dēd'al) adj. Having and showing artistic skill.

daf-fo-dil (daf'o dil) n. A bulbous plant with solitary yellow flowers.

daft (daft) adj. Insane; crazy, or mad; foolish. **daftly** adv. **daftness** n.

da-guerre-o-type (da ger'o tīp') n. A very early photographic process which used silver-coated metallic plates that were sensitive to light.

dah (dä) n. The dash used in the code of telegraphy or radio, represented by a tone interval approximately three times as long as the dot.

dai-ly (dā'lē) adj. To occur, appear, or happen every day of the week. **daily** n. A newspaper which is published daily.

dain-ty (dān'tē) adj. Having or showing refined taste; delicately beautiful. **daintily** adv. **daintiness** n.

dai-qui-ri (dī'ki rē) n. A cocktail made with rum and lime juice.

dair-y (dâr'ē) n., pl. **dairies** A commercial establishment which processes milk for resale.

dale (dāl) n. A small valley.

dal-ly (dal'ē) v. To waste time; to dawdle; to flirt. **dallier** n. **dalliance** n.

dal-ton-ism (dal'to niz″um) n. Color blindness; unable to differentiate between red and green.

dam (dam) n. A barrier constructed for controlling or raising the level of water; female animal who has had offspring.

dam-age (dam'ij) n. An injury to person or property; in law, the compensation given for loss or injury. **damage** v. **damageable** adj. **damagingly** adv.

dam-an (dam'an) n. A small, rabbit-like animal.

dam-a-scene (dam'a sēn') v. To form designs in metal, by inlaying with gold or other precious metals, or by etching.

dam-ask (dam'ask) n. An elaborately patterned, reversible fabric, originally made of silk.

dame (dām) n. A mature woman or matron. *Slang* A woman. **Dame** *Brit.* A title given to a woman, the female equivalent of a British Lord.

dam-mar (dam'ér) n. A resin from various coniferous trees which is used for making colorless varnish.

damp (damp) adj. Between dry and wet; of or relating to poisonous gas or foul air found in a mine. **dampish** adj.

dam-sel (dam'zel) n. A maiden; a young unmarried woman.

dance (dans) v. To move rhythmically to music using improvised or planned steps and gestures. **dancer** n.

dan-dle (dan'dl) v. To move a child or infant up and down on the knees or in the arms with a gentle movement.

dan-ger (dān'jér) n. An exposure to injury, evil, or loss.

dan-ger-ous (dān'jér us) adj. Unsafe. **dangerously** adv. **dangerousness** n.

dan-gle (dang'gl) v. To hang loosely and swing to and fro; to have an unclear grammatical relation in a sentence.

dank (dangk) adj. Uncomfortably damp; wet and cold. **-ly** adv. **dankness** n.

dan-seuse (dän soez') n., pl. **danseuses** A female ballet dancer.

dap-per (dap'ér) adj. Stylishly dressed.

dap-ple (dap'l) v. To make variegated or spotted in color.

dar-by (där'bē) n. A tool for leveling a plaster surface.

dare (dâr) v. To have the boldness or courage to undertake an adventure; to challenge a person as to show proof of courage. **dare** n. **daring** adj.

dark (därk) adj. Dim; to have little or no light; to be difficult to comprehend; of a deep shade of color, as black or almost black. **in the dark** Done in secret; in a state of ignorance. **-ly** adv.

Dark Ages n. The early part of the Middle Ages from about 476 to 1000 A.D.

dar-kle (där'kl) v. To darken or grow dark.

dar-ling (där'ling) n. A favorite person; someone who is very dear; a person tenderly loved. **darlingly** adv.

darn (därn) v. To mend a hole by filling the gap with interlacing stitches.

dart (därt) n. A pointed missile either shot or thrown. **darts** pl. The game of throwing darts at a usually round target.

dash (dash) n. A punctuation mark setting apart a separate thought or dividing a compound word. v. To break or shatter with a striking violent blow; to move quickly; to rush; to finish or perform a duty in haste. **dasher** n.

das-tard (das'térd) n. A coward; a sneak. **dastardliness** n. **dastardly** adj.

da-ta (dā'ta) n., pl. of **datum** Figures or facts from which conclusions may be drawn. In *computer science*, information processed by the computer.

data bank n. In *computer science*, the

location in a computer where information is stored.

database *n.* In *computer science*, a collection of related information.

database file *n.* In *computer science*, a file comprised of records of information in distinct, related fields.

data block *n.* In *computer science*, a selection of data based on a specific search criterion.

data conversion *n.* In *computer science*, an altering of selected data for transfer to a different program or format, as from a database file to a spreadsheet file.

data entry *n.* In *computer science*, the recording or updating of information in a computer file.

data field *n.* In *computer science*, any of the areas in a database dedicated to a particular item of information, as a date or name.

data format *n.* In *computer science*, the type of data acceptable in a particular field, as date, number, or alphameric.

data link *n.* In *computer science*, a connection between computer systems that allow information sharing; a validation formula in a spreadsheet or database that limits entry of data into cell or field base on a previous entry; a link between documents containing similar information that automatically updates all documents when one is changed.

data management *n.* In *computer science*, the process of recording and manipulating data in the conduct of a business.

data parsing *n.* In *computer science*, breaking a data string down to its basic elements for conversion to another file format, as from database fields to spreadsheet cells.

data processing *n.* In *computer science*, the business of handling and storing information using computer hardware and software.

data record *n.* In *computer science*, the set of fields that compromise a unique entry in a database file.

data transmission *n.* In *computer science*, the transfer of information through a computer system or between computer systems.

date (dāt) *n.* A particular point in time; a day, month, or year; the exact time at which something happens; a social engagement; a person's partner on such an occasion.

date-line (dāt´līn´) *n.* The line or phrase at the beginning of a periodical giving the date and place of publication; **date line** the 180th meridian on a map or globe which is where a day begins.

date number *n.* In *computer science*, the

numeric value for a specific date, as by the number of the day, month, and year or the number of days from a base date.

date palm *n.* A palm that bears dates.

da-tum (dā´tum) *n., pl.* **data** A single piece of information.

daub (dob) *v.* To coat or smear with grease, plaster, or an adhesive substance; to defile; to put on without taste. **dauber** *n.*

daugh-ter (do´tèr) *n.* The female offspring of a man or woman; a female descendant of any age. **daughterly** *adj.*

daughter–in–law *n.* A son's wife.

daunt (dont) *v.* To intimidate or discourage.

dav-en-port (dav´en pōrt´) *n.* A large sofa or couch.

dav-it (dav´it) *n.* A small crane on the side of a ship, for lifting its boats.

da-vy (dā´vē) *n.* A miner's lamp.

daw-dle (dod´l) *v.* To waste time; to take more time than is needed. **dawdler** *n.*

dawn (don) *n.* The beginning of a new day; to begin to understand, expand, or develop; to grow lighter. **-ing** *n.*

day (dā) *n.* The period of time that falls between dawn and nightfall; the time that is represented by one rotation of the earth upon its axis, twenty-four hours; the large portion of a day spent in a particular way.

day-care (dā´kâr) *n.* A service provided for working mothers and fathers, offering daytime supervision, training, and safekeeping for their children while they work.

Day of Atonement *n.* Yom Kippur.

daze (dāz) *v.* To bewilder or stun with a heavy blow or shock. **dazedly** *adv.*

DCA *abbr.* In *computer science*, Document Content Architecture; a word processing file format.

dea-con (dē´kon) *n.* The clergy person who ranks immediately below a priest **deaconry** *n.* **deaconship** *n.*

de-ac-ti-vate (dē ak´ti vāt´) *v.* To cause to become inactive.

dead (ded) *adj.* Without life; no longer in existence or use; dormant; quiet; in law, no longer in force.

deaf (def) *adj.* Totally or partially unable to hear; refusing or unwilling to listen.

deal (dēl) *v.* To distribute or pass out playing cards; to be occupied or concerned with a certain matter; to discuss, consider, or take affirmative action. *n.* An indefinite amount; a business transaction. **dealer** *n.*

dean (dēn) *n.* The head administrator of a college, high school, or university supervising students. **deanship** *n.*

dear (dēr) *adj.* Greatly cherished; loved. **dearly** *adv.* **dearness** *n.*

death (deth) *n.* Termination; permanent

cessation of all vital functions.

deb (deb) *n.* A debutante.

de-ba-cle (dā bä´kl) *n.* A sudden downfall, failure, or collapse.

de-bar (di bär´) *v.* To bar from a place; to preclude; to prohibit.

de-bark (di bärk´) *v.* To disembark.

de-base (di bās´) *v.* To lower in character or value; demean. **debasement** *n.*

de-bate (di bāt´) *v.* To discuss or argue opposing points; to consider; to deliberate. **debate** *n.* **debatable** *adj.* **debatably** *adv.* **debater** *n.*

de-bauch (di boch´) *v.* To lead away from morality; to corrupt or pervert **de-bauchery** *n.* **debauchment** *n.*

de-bauch-er-y *n.* The excessive indulgence in sensual pleasures.

de-ben-ture (di ben´chèr) *n.* A voucher given as an acknowledgment of debt.

de-bil-i-tate (di bil´i tāt´) *v.* To make feeble or weak. **debilitation** *n.*

deb-it (deb´it) *n.* A debt or item recorded in an account *v.* To enter a debt in a ledger; to charge someone with a debt.

deb-o-nair (deb´o når´) *adj.* Characterized by courtesy and charm.

dé-bride-ment (di brēd´ment) *n.* Removal of contaminated tissue from a wound in order to prevent the spread of infection.

de-brief (dē brēf´) *v.* To interrogate or question in order to obtain information.

de-bris (*de* brē´) *n.* Scattered or discarded remains or waste.

debt (det) *n.* That which someone owes, as money, services, or goods; an obligation to pay or render something to another.

debt-or (det´ér) *n.* A person owing a debt to another.

de-bug (dē bug) *v.* To find and remove a concealed electronic listening device; in computer science, to remove errors in a computer program. In *computer science,* to find and correct errors in a computer program or the operation of a piece of equipment.

de-bunk (di bungk´) *v.* To expose false pretensions, to show the error in false opinions, statements or claims.

de-but (dā bū´) *n.* A first public appearance; the formal introduction to society; the beginning of a new career. **debut** *v.*

deb-u-tante (deb´ū tänt´) *n.* A young woman making her debut in society.

dec-ade (dek´ād) *n.* A period of ten years; a set or group of ten.

de-ca-dence (dek´a dens) *n.* A process of decay or deterioration; a period or condition of decline, as in morals.

dec-a-dent (dek´a dent) *adj.* Deteriorating; being in a state of decline. *n.* One who is decadent.

dec-a-gon (dek´a gon´) *n. Geom.* A polygon with ten sides and ten angles. **decagonal** *adj.* **decagonally** *adv.*

dec-a-gram *or* **dek-a- gram** (dek´a gram´) *n.* In the metric system, a measure of weight equal to 10 grams.

de-cal (dē´kal) *n.* A design or picture transferred by decalcomania.

de-cal-co-ma-nia (di kal´ko mā´nē a) *n.* The process of transferring pictures or designs printed on special paper to glass, wood, and other materials.

dec-a-li-ter *or* **dek-a-li-ter** (dek´a lē´tér) *n.* In the metric system, a measure of capacity equal to 10 liters.

dec-a-logue *or* **dec-a-log** (dek´a log´) *n.* The Ten Commandments.

dec-a-me-ter *or* **dek-a-me-ter** (dek´a mē´ tèr) *n.* In the metric system, a measure of length equal to 10 meters.

de-cam-e-ter (de kam´et èr) *n.* A line of verse or consisting of ten metrical feet.

de-camp (di kamp´) *v.* To break camp; to leave or depart suddenly.

de-cant (di cant´) *v.* To pour off liquid with-out disturbing the sediments; to pour from one container to another.

de-cap-i-tate (di kap´i tāt´) *v.* To cut off the head; to behead **decapitation** *n.*

de-car-bon-ize (dē kär´bo nīz) *v.* To remove carbon from a substance or motor.

de-cath-lon (di kath´lon) *n.* An athletic event with ten different track and field events in all of which each contestant participates; an Olympic event.

de-cay (di kā´) *v.* To decline in quantity or quality; to rot. *Phys.* To diminish or disintegrate by radioactive decomposition.

de-cease (di sēs´) *v.* To die; to reach life's end.

de-ceit (di sēt´) *n.* Deception; falseness; the quality of being deceptive; concealment. **deceitful** *adj.* **-fully** *adv.*

de-ceive (di sēv´) *v.* To mislead by falsehood; to lead into error; to delude. **deceivable** *adj.* **deceiver** *n.*

de-cel-er-ate (dē sel´e rät) *n.* To decrease in velocity. **deceleration** *n.*

De-cem-ber (di sem´bér) *n.* The twelfth month of the year, having 31 days.

de-cen-ni-al (di sen´ē al) *adj.* Happening once every 10 years; continuing for ten years. **decennially** *adv.*

de-cent (dē´sent) *adj.* Adequate; satisfactory; kind; generous; characterized by propriety of conduct, speech, or dress; respectable. *Informal* Properly or adequately clothed; respectable. **decently** *adv.* **-ness** *n.*

de-cen-tral-ize (dē sen´tra līz´) *v.* To divide the administrative functions of a central authority among several local authorities; to reorganize into smaller and more dispersed parts. **-ation** *n.*

de-cep-tion (di sep´shan) *n*. The act of deceiving; the fact or state of being deceived; anything which deceives or deludes.

de-cep-tive (di sep´tiv) *adj*. Having the tendency or power to deceive. **deceptively** *adv*. **deceptiveness** *n*.

dec-i-are (des´ē âr´) *n*. In the metric system, ten square meters.

de-ci-bel (des´i bl´) *n*. A measurement of sound; one tenth of a bel.

de-cide (di sīd´) *v*. To settle; to determine, as a controversy or contest; to determine the conclusion or issue of; to make up one's mind. **decider** *n*.

de-cid-ed *adj*. Definite or unquestionable; exhibiting determination, resolute. **decidedly** *adv*. **decidedness** *n*.

de-cid-u-ous (di sij´ö us) *adj*. *Biol*. Shedding or falling off at maturity or at a certain season, such as fruit, leaves, petals, antlers, or snake skins.

dec-i-gram (des´i gram´) *n*. In the metric system, the tenth part of a gram.

dec-i-li-ter (des´i lē´tér) *n*. In the metric system, the tenth part of a liter.

de-cil-lion (di sil´yon) *n*. In the U.S., the cardinal number written as one followed by thirty-three zeros.

dec-i-mal (des´i mal) *n*. A proper fraction based on the number 10 and indicated by the use of a decimal point; every decimal place indicating a multiple of a power of 10; a number with a decimal point; a decimal fraction or one of its digits.

decimal number In *computer science*, a value represented in a base 10.

decimal point *n*. A period placed to the left of a decimal fraction.

dec-i-mate (des´i māt´) *v*. To destroy or kill a large proportion of something; to select by lot and kill one out of every ten. **decimation** *n*.

dec-i-meter (des´i mē´tér) *n*. In the metric system, the tenth part of a meter.

de-ci-pher (di sī´fér) *v*. To determine the meaning of something obscure, as a poor handwriting; to translate from code or cipher into plain text; to decode.

de-ci-sion (di sizh´an) *n*. The act of deciding; a judgment or conclusion reached by deciding.

de-ci-sive (di sī´siv) *adj*. Ending uncertainty or dispute; conclusive; characterized by firmness; unquestionable; unmistakable. **decisively** *adv*.

dec-i-stere (des´i stēr´) *n*. In the metric system, a cubic decimeter, or the tenth part of a stere.

de-claim (di klām´) *v*. To speak or deliver loudly and rhetorically; to give a formal speech; to attack verbally. **declamation** *n*. **declamatory** *adj*.

de-clar-ant (di klâr´ant) *n*. One who

makes a declaration.

de-clare (di klâr´) *v*. To make known or clear; to state formally or officially; to say emphatically; to avow; to assert; to make full claim to, as goods liable to duty; to proclaim an opinion or choice for or against something. **declarer, declaration** *n*.

de-class (dē klas´) *v*. To remove from one's class; to lose standing.

de-clas-si-fy (dē klas´i fī) *v*. To remove the security classification of a document, information considered important to national security of a nation. **declassification** *n*.

de-clen-sion (di klen´shan) *n*. A descent; a sloping downward; a decline; a deviation, as from a belief. *Gram*. The inflection of nouns, pronouns, and adjectives according to case, number, and gender **declensional** *adj*.

dec-li-nate (dek´li nāt) *adj*. Bending downward.

dec-li-na-tion (dek´li nā´shan) *n*. The act of bending downward or inclining; deviation, as in conduct or direction; the angle formed between the direction of a compass needle and the true north; a polite refusal.

de-cline (di klīn´) *v*. To reject or refuse something; to grow frail gradually, as in health; to bend or incline to the side or downward; to refuse politely. *Gram*. To give the inflected forms of a noun, pronoun, or adjective. **decline** *n*. The act or result of deterioration, a decline in heath. **declinable** *adj*. **declination** *n*. **decliner** *n*.

de-cliv-i-ty (di kliv´i te) *n., pl*. **declivities** A steep downward slope or surface. **declivitous** *adj*.

de-coct (di kokt´) *v*. To extract by boiling; to condense. **decoction** *n*.

de-code (dē kōd´) *v*. To convert from a coded message into plain language. **decoder** *n*.

de-col-or-a-tion (de kul´ér a´shan) *n*. The removal or loss of color.

de-com-pen-sa-tion (dē´kom pen sā´shan) *n*. The inability of the heart to sustain a constant heart beat.

de-com-pose (dē´kom pōz´) *v*. To decay; to separate into constituent parts. **decomposable** *adj*. **decomposer** *n*.

de-com-pound (dē´kom pound´) *adj*. Having compound parts.

de-com-press (dē´kom pres´) *v*. To relieve of pressure; to bring persons back to normal air pressure, as divers or caisson workers or high-altitude flyers.

de-con-ges-tant (dē´kon jes tant´) *n*. An agent that relieves congestion.

de-con-tam-i-nate (dē´kon tam´i nāt) *v*. To make free of contamination by destroying or neutralizing poisonous chemicals, radioactivity, or other harmful elements. **decontamination** *n.* **decontaminator** *n.*

de-con-trol (dē'kon trōl') *v.* To free from the control of, especially from governmental control.

de-cor (dā kor') *n.* The style of decorating a room, office, or home.

dec-o-rate (dek'o rāt') *v.* To adorn or furnish with fashionable or beautiful things; to confer a decoration or medal upon. **decorator** *n.*

dec-o-rous (dek'ér us) *adj.* Marked by decorum; seemly; proper, as dress or speech. **decorously** *adv.* -ness *n.*

de-cor-ti-cate (dē kor'ti kāt') *v.* To strip or remove the bark; to peel.

de-co-rum (di kōr'um) *n.* Proper behavior; good or fitting conduct.

de-crease (di krēs') *v.* To grow or cause to grow gradually less or smaller; to diminish. *n.* The process or act of decreasing or the resulting state; a decline.

de-cree (di krē) *n.* An authoritative and formal order or decision; a judicial judgment. **decree** *v.*

dec-re-ment (dek're ment) *n.* The process or act of decreasing; the amount lost by gradual waste or diminution.

de-crep-it (di krep'it) *adj.* Broken down or worn out by old age or excessive use. **decrepitly** *adv.* **decrepitude** *n.*

de-cre-scen-do (dē'kri shen'dō) *n., pl.* **decrescendos** *Music* A gradual decrease in force or loudness.

de-crim-i-nal-ize (dē'krim inal īz) *v.* To remove the criminal classification of; to no longer prohibit.

de-cry (di krī') *v.* To disparage or condemn openly; to denounce.

de-cum-bent (di kum'bent) *adj.* Lying down; reclining.

dec-u-ple (dek'ü pel) *adj.* Tenfold; containing groups of ten.

de-curved (dē kürvd') *adj.* Bent or curved downward.

de-cus-sate (di kus'āt) *v.* To arrange in pairs at acute angles; X-shaped.

de-dans (de däns) *n.* The open gallery for spectators' viewing, as provided to view a tennis match.

ded-i-cate (ded'i kāt') *v.* To set apart, as for sacred uses; to set apart for special use, duty, or purpose; to address or inscribe a work of literature, art or music to someone; to commit oneself to a certain cause, course of action, or thought; to unveil or open to the public, a book inscribed to a person or cause.

ded-i-ca-tion (ded'i kā'shan) *n.* The act of dedicating or devotion to a sacred use or meaning.

de-duce (di dös') *v.* To derive a conclusion by reasoning.

de-duct (di dukt') *v.* To subtract or take away from; to subtract or separate, in numbering, estimating, or calculating;

de-duc-tion (di duk'shan) *n.* The act of deducing or subtracting; an amount that is or may be deducted; the process or act of deducting. **deductive** *adj.* **deductively** *adv.*

deed (dēd) *v.* To judge or consider. Anything performed or done; a notable achievement or feat; in law, a legal document, especially one relating to the transference of property. **deedless** *adj.*

deem (dēm) *v.* To judge or consider.

de-es-ca-late (dē es'ka lāt) *v.* To decrease or be decreased gradually, as in intensity, scope, or effect.

de-face (di fās') *v.* To spoil or mar the appearance or surface of something.

de fac-to (dē fak'tō) *adj.* Really or actually exercising authority.

de-fal-cate (di fal'kāt) *v.* To embezzle; to misuse funds. **defalcation** *n.*

def-a-ma-tion (def*a* mā'sham) *n.* The publishing of slanderous words in order to injure someone's reputation.

de-fame (di fām') *v.* To slander or libel. **defamation** *n.* **defamatory** *n.*

de-fault (di folt') *v.* To neglect to fulfill an obligation or requirement, as to pay money due or to appear in court; to forfeit by default. *n.* The failure to participate or compete in a competition. In *computer science*, the preset action for a function key or command.

de-fea-sance (di fē'zans) *n.* A condition of rendering null or void.

de-feat (di fēt') *v.* To win a victory; to beat; to prevent the successful outcome of; to frustrate; to baffle; in law, to make void; to annul. **defeat** *n.*

def-e-cate (def*e* kāt') *v.* To discharge feces from the bowels. **defecation** *n.*

de-fect (dē'fekt) *n.* The lack of something desirable or necessary for completeness or perfection; a fault or imperfection. **defector** *n.*

de-fend (di fend') *v.* Protect.

de-fend-ant (di fen'dant) *n.* The person charged in a criminal or civil lawsuit.

de-fense (di fens) *n.* The action of defending against attack.

de-fer (di fer') *v.* To delay or postpone, to put off doing. **deferment** *n.*

de-fer-ves-cence (dē'fér ves'ens) *n.* A reducing of fever.

de-fi-ance (di fī'ans) *n.* The instance or act of defying; a challenge. **defiant** *adj.*

deficiency disease *n.* A disease due to the lack of dietary elements, such as vitamins or minerals.

de-fi-cient (di fish'ent) *adj.* Lacking in a necessary element.

def-i-cit (def'i sit) *n.* Shortage in amount.

deficit spending *n.* The practice of spending public funds beyond income.

de-file (di fīl´) v. To soil or make unclean; violate one's reputation.

de-fine (di fīn´) v. To identify the essential qualities; to make clear. In computer science, to set a value for a symbol or variable.

de-fin-i-en-dum (di fin´ē en´dum) n. The term or expression to be defined, defining as in a dictionary entry.

de-fin-i-ens (di fin´ē enz) n. A description, expression or statement that defines something.

def-i-nite (def´i nit) adj. Clearly defined; having distinct limits; not vague or general.

de-fin-i-tive (di fin´i tiv) adj. Serving to provide a final solution.

def-i-nit-ize (def´i ni tīz´) v. To make final or definite.

def-la-grate (def´le grāt´) v. To set fire to; to cause to burn rapidly with intense heat.

de-flate (di flāt´) v. To cause to collapse by removing gas or air; to remove self-esteem or conceit. To reduce or restrict money or spending so that prices decline. deflation n.

de-flect (di flekt´) v. To turn aside; to swerve from a course. deflective adj. deflection, deflector n.

de-flow-er (di flou´ér) v. To rob of one's virginity; to violate; to rob of charm or beauty.

de-form (di form´) v. To distort the form of; to be distorted; to mar the beauty or excellence of; to spoil the natural form of. deformative adj. -ity n.

de-fraud (de frod´) v. To cheat; to swindle. defrauder n.

de-fray (di frā´) v. To provide for or to make payment on something. defrayable adj. defrayal n.

de-frock (dē frok´) v. To deprive a priest or minister of the right to practice the functions of his office.

deft (deft) adj. Skillful and neat in one's actions. deftly adv. deftness n.

de-funct (di fungkt´) adj. Deceased; dead; no longer in use. -ness n.

de-fuse (dē fūz) v. To remove the fuse from; to make less dangerous or hostile.

de-fy (di fī´) v. To confront or resist boldly and openly; to challenge someone to do, or not to do, something; to dare, to provoke. defier n.

de-gauss (dē gous´) v. To neutralize the magnetic field of something.

de-gen-er-ate (di jen´e rāt´) v. To decline in quality, value, or desirability; to deteriorate; to become worse. adj. Morally depraved or sexually deviant. degenerative adv. degeneracy n.

de-glu-ti-tion (dē´glü tish´an) n. The act or process of swallowing.

de-grade (dē grād´) v. To reduce in rank, status, or grade; to demote; to reduce in quality or intensity. degraded adj. degradedly adv. degradedness n.

de-gree (di grē´) n. One of a succession of stages or steps; relative manner, condition or respect; the academic title given by an institution of learning upon completion of a course of study or as an honorary distinction; a unit on a temperature or thermometer scale; in law, a measure of severity, as murder in the first degree. Gram. A form used in the comparison of adjectives and adverbs. by degrees Little by little. to a degree Somewhat.

de-hisce (di his´) v. To open, along a natural line, as the capsules or seedpods of a plant.

de-horn (dē horn) v. To remove the horns from an animal.

de-hu-man-ize (dē hū´ma nīz´) v. To deprive of human qualities, especially to make mechanical and routine.

de-hu-mid-i-fy (dē´hū mid´i fī) v. To re-move moisture from.

de-hy-drate (dē hī´drāt) v. To cause to lose moisture or water.

de-hyp-no-tize v. To bring out of the hypnotic state.

de-ice (dē īs´) v. To rid of or keep free of ice. deicer n.

deic-tic (dīk´tik) adj. Demonstrating or pointing out directly.

de-i-fy (dē´i fī´) v. To glorify or idealize; to raise in high regard; to worship as a god or a divine being. -ication n.

deign (dān) v. To think it barely worthy of one's dignity; to condescend.

Dei gratia adv. By the grace of God.

de-ism (dē´iz um) n. A belief in the existence of God but a denial of the validity of revelation.

de-ist (dē´ist) n. One who believes in the existence of God.

de-i-ty (dē´i tē) n. The essential nature or rank of a god; divine character.

dek-a-stere n. In the metric system, a measure of volume equal to 10 steres.

del abbr. Delete.

de-lam-i-nate (dē lam´i nāt´) v. To split into thin layers.

Del-a-ware (del´a wâr´) n. A state located on the eastern coast of the United States, statehood December 7, 1787, state capital Dover.

de-lay (di lā´) v. To put off until a later time; to defer; to cause to be late or detained; to linger; to waste time; to procrastinate. **delay** n.

de-le (dē´lē) n., Printing A mark in typesetting which indicates something is to be deleted or taken out of the manuscript.

de-lec-ta-ble (di lek´ta bl) adj. Giving great pleasure; delightful; savory; delicious. **delectability.** n.

de-lec-ta-tion (dē´ lek tā´shan) n. Enjoyment or pleasure.

del-e-gate (del´e git) n. A person with the power to act as a representative for another; a deputy or agent; a person appointed or elected to represent a territory in the House of Representatives, where he may speak but not vote; a member of the lower legislature in Maryland, Virginia, and West Virginia. v. To entrust and commit to another.

de-lete (di lēt´) v. To cancel; to take out, eliminate, to mark out. **deletion** n.

del-e-te-ri-ous (del´i tēr´ē us) adj. Causing moral or physical injury; harmful. **deleteriously** adv.

delft (delft) n. A glazed earthenware, usually blue and white in color, originating in Delft, Holland, in 1653.

de-li (del ē) n. Slang A delicatessen.

de-lib-er-ate (di lib´e rāt´) v. To say or do something intentionally; to plan in advance; to hold formal discussions. **deliberate**adj.Premeditated;leisurely or slow in manner or motion. **deliberately** adv. **deliberateness** n.

de-lib-er-a-tion (di lib´e rā´shan)n. The act of careful consideration before making a decision. **deliberative** adj.

del-i-ca-cy (del´i ka sē) n., pl. **delicacies** A select or choice food; the quality or state of being delicate; sensitiveness.

del-i-cate (del´i kit) adj. Pleasing to the senses; exquisite and fine in workmanship, texture, or construction; pleasing, as in color, taste, or aroma; sensitive and subtle in perception, feeling, or expression; frail in constitution; easily broken or damaged; considerate of the feelings of others. **delicately** adv.

de-li-cious (di lish´us) adj. Extremely enjoyable and pleasant to the taste. **deliciously** adv. **deliciousness** n.

de-li-cious (di lish´us) n. A variety of red, sweet apples.

de-lict (di likt´) n. An offense; a misdemeanor.

de-light (di līt´) n. A great joy or pleasure. v. To give or take great pleasure; to rejoice; to gratify or please highly. **delighted** adj. **delightedly** adv.

de-light-ful (di līt´ful) adj. Extremely pleasing. **delightfully** adv.

de-lim-it (di lim´it) v. To give or prescribe the limits of.

de-lin-e-ate (di lin´ē āt) v. To represent by a drawing; to draw or trace the outline of something; to sketch; to represent in gestures or words.

de-lin-quent (di ling´kwent) adj. Neglecting to do what is required by obligation or law; falling behind in a payment. n. A juvenile who is out of control, as violating the law.

de-lir-i-ous (di lēr´ē us) adj. Having the characteristic of or pertaining to delirium.

de-lir-i-um (di lēr´ē um) n. A temporary or sporadic mental disturbance associated with fever, shock, or intoxication and marked by excitement, incoherence, and hallucination; uncontrolled excitement and emotion.

de-liv-er (di liv´ér) v. To surrender; to hand over; to set free; to liberate; to give or send forth; to assist in the birth of an offspring; to do what is expected or desired; to take to the intended recipient. To give a speech. **-er** n.

de-louse (dē lous´) v. To free from parasitic lice.

delta ray n. An electron ejected by an ionizing particle as it passes through matter.

de-lude (di lōd´) v. To mislead the mind or judgment; to deceive; to cause to be deceived.

del-uge (del´ūj) v. To flood with water; to overwhelm; to destroy. **deluge** n. A great flood.

de-lu-sion (di lō´zhan) n. A false, fixed belief held in spite of contrary evidence; false impression. **-al** adj.

de luxe or de-luxe (de leks´) adj. High elegance or luxury.

delve (delv) v. To search for information with careful investigation.

de-mag-net-ize (dē mag´ni tīz´) v. To remove the magnetic properties of. **demagnetization, demagnetizer** n.

dem-a-gogue (dem´a gog´) n. A person who leads the populace by appealing to emotions and prejudices. **demagoguery** n. **demagogy** n.

de-mand (di mand´) v. To ask for in a firm tone; to claim as due; to have the need or requirement for; in law, to summon to court; to make a formal claim to property. Econ. The ability and desire to purchase something; the quantity of merchandise wanted at a certain price. **in demand** Sought after; desired. **on demand** On request or presentation; a note payable whenever the lender demands it.

de-mar-cate (di mär´kāt) v. To set boundaries or limits; to separate or limit.

de-mar-ca-tion (dē´mär kā´shan) n. The act of defining the limits or boundaries of something.

de-mean (di mēn´) v. To behave or conduct oneself in a particular manner; to degrade; to humble oneself or another.

de-mean-or (di mē ner) n. A person's conduct toward others; a person's general behavior.

de-ment-ed (di men´tid) adj. Insane.

de-men-tia (di men´sha) n. A deterioration of intellectual faculties.

de-mer-it (dē mer´ĭt) n. A fault; a defect; a mark against one's record, especially for bad conduct in school.

de-mise (di mīz´) n. Death; in law, a transfer of an estate by lease or will.

de-mis-sion (di mish´an) n. Resignation or relinquishment.

dem-o (dem´ō) n., pl. demos Slang A demonstration to show product use and purpose of an item.

de-mo-bi-lize (dē mō´bi līz´) v. To disband; to release from military service.

de-moc-ra-cy (di mok´ra sē) n., pl. democracies A form of government exercised either directly by the people or through their elected representatives; rule by the majority; the practice of legal, political, or social equality.

de-mod-ed (dē mō´did) adj. Out of fashion.

de-mod-u-late (dē moj´u lāt´) v. To detect or intercept a modulated signal.

de-mog-ra-phy (di mog´ra fē) n. Study of the characteristics of human population, such as growth, size, and vital statistics. **demographic** adj. **demographically** adv.

de-mol-ish (di mol´ish) v. To tear down; to raze, to completely do away with; to end. **demolishment** n.

dem-o-li-tion (dem´o lish´an) n. The process of demolishing, especially destruction with explosives.

de-mon (dē´mon) n. An evil spirit; a devil. Informal A person of great skill or zeal..

de-mon-e-tize (dē mon´i tīz´) v. To deprive the currency of its standard value; to withdraw currency from use.

de-mo-ni-ac (di mō´ne ak´) adj. Like or befitting a demon; to be influenced or possessed by or as by demons; of, resembling, or suggestive of a demon.

de-mon-ol-o-gy (dē´mo nol´o jē) n. The belief in or study of demons.

de-mon-stra-ble (di mon´stra bl) adj. Obvious or apparent, proven. **demonstrability** n. **demonstrably** adv.

dem-on-strate (dem´on strāt´) v. To show or prove by reasoning or evidence; to teach by using examples and exhibits; to make a public protest; to march or picket to seek public attention; to prove beyond doubt.

de-mor-al-ize (di mor´a līz´) v. To undermine the morale or confidence of someone; to degrade; to corrupt. **demoralization** n. **demoralizer** n.

de-mote (di mōt´) v. To reduce in rank, grade, or position. **demotion** n.

de-mount v. To remove from its mounting, setting, or place of support.

de-mul-cent (di mul´sent) n. A soothing substance; any medicine which lessens the effects of irritation, as mucilaginous substances,. **demulcent** adj.

de-mur (di mėr´) v. To take issue; to object. **demurral** n.

de-mure (di mūr) adj. Reserved and modest; coy. **demurely** adv.

de-murrer (di mėr´ér) n. In law, a plea to dismiss a lawsuit on the grounds that the plaintiff's statements are insufficient to prove claim.

den (den) n. The shelter for a wild animal; a small room in a home used for private study or relaxation.

den-a-ry (den´arē) adj. Pertaining to the number ten.

de-na-tion-al-ize (dē nash´a na līz´) v. To deprive a person of national status, attachments or characteristics.

de-na-ture (dē nā´chér) v. To change the nature or natural qualities of, especially to make unfit for consumption, without impairing its usefulness. **denaturant** n. **denaturation** n.

den-dri-form adj. Having the form or appearance of a tree.

den-drite (den´drīt) n. Physiol. The branching process of a nerve cell which conducts impulses toward the cell body. **dendritic** adj. **dendritically** adv.

den-drol-o-gy (den drol´o jē) n. Bot. The study of trees.

de-ne-go-ti-ate (dē´ni gō´shē ãt´) v. To negotiate the ending of agreements of an economic or political nature.

den-gue (deng´gä) n., Pathol. An infectious tropical disease transmitted by mosquitoes, characterized by severe joint pains and fever.

de-ni-al (di nī´al) n. A refusal to comply with a request; refusal to acknowledge the truth of a statement; abstinence; self-denial.

den-i-grate (den´i grāt´) v. To slander; to defame, to degrade.

den-i-zen (den´i zen) n. An inhabitant or a person who frequents a place.

de-no-ta-tion (dē´nō tā´shan) n. The meaning of, or the object or objects designated by a word; an indication, as a sign. **denotative** adj.

de-note (di nōt´) v. To make known; to point out; to indicate; to signify; to designate; to mean, said of symbols or words. **denotative** adj.

de-nounce (di nouns´) v. To attack or condemn openly and vehemently; to accuse formally; to announce the ending of something in a formal way.

dense (dĕns) *adj.* Compact; thick; as in a forest or jungle; close; slow to understand; stupid; hardheaded. **densely** *adv.* **denseness** *n.*

den-si-tom-e-ter (dĕn´si tom´ĭte) *n.* An instrument for determining optical or photographic density.

dent (dĕnt) *n.* A small surface depression made by striking or pressing. **dent** *v.* To put a dent in something; to make meaningful progress or headway.

den-tal (dĕn´tal) *adj.* Pertaining to the teeth; of or pertaining to dentistry.

den-ti-cle (dĕn´ti kl) *adj.* Having a small pointed projection.

den-ti-frice (dĕn´ti fris) *n.* A preparation in powder or paste form for cleaning the teeth.

den-ti-lin-gual (dĕn´ti ling´gwal) *adj.* Of speech sounds that are uttered with the cooperation of the tongue and teeth.

den-tine *or* **den-tin** (dĕn´tĭn) *n.* The hard, calcified part of the tooth beneath the enamel, containing the pulp chamber and root canals.

den-tist (dĕn´tĭst) *n.* A licensed person whose profession is the diagnosis, treatment, and prevention of diseases of the gums and teeth.

den-tist-ry (dĕn´tĭ strē) *n.* The profession of a dentist, one that deals with the diagnosis, prevention, and treatment of the teeth and malformations of the mouth and gums.

den-ti-tion (dĕn tĭsh´an) *n.* The kind, number, and arrangement of teeth, as in humans and other animals; the process of cutting teeth.

den-ture (dĕn´chĕr) *n.* A set of artificial teeth either partial or full; also called a dental plate.

de-ny (di nī´) *v.* To declare untrue; to refuse to acknowledge or recognize; to withhold; to refuse to grant. **deny oneself** To refuse oneself something desired; self-denial.

de-o-dar (dē´o dä) *n.* A species of an East Indian cedar tree valued for its wood.

de-o-dor-ant (dē ō´dĕr ant) *n.* A product designed to prevent, mask, or destroy unpleasant odors.

de-o-dor-ize (dē ō´do rīz´) *v.* To destroy, modify, or disguise the odor of. **deodorization** *n.* **deodorizer** *n.*

de-on-tol-o-gy (dē´on tol´o jē) *n.* The study of moral obligation.

de-ox-i-dize (dē ok´si dīz´) *v.* To remove the oxygen from; to reduce from the state of an oxide. **deoxidization** , **deoxidate** *n.* **deoxidizer** *n.*

de-ox-y-ri-bo-nu-cle-ic a-cid (dē ok´sirī´bō nō klē´ik as´id) *n.* A nucleic acid which forms a principal constituent of the genes and is known to play a role of importance in the

genetic action of the chromosomes, also known as DNA.

dep *abbr.* Depart; deposit; deputy.

de-part (di pärt´) *v.* To leave; to go away; to deviate; to die. **departed** *adj.*

de-par-ture (di pär´chĕr) *n.* The act of taking leave or going away; a divergence; a deviation; the act of starting out on a new course of action or going on a trip.

de-paup-er-ate (di po´pĕr ĭt) *adj.* Poorly developed in physical form or size.

de-pend (di pend´) *v.* To rely on; to trust with responsibilities; to be determined or conditioned.

de-pict (di pikt´) *v.* To represent in a sculpture or a picture; to describe or represent in words. **depiction** *n.*

dep-i-late (dep´i lāt´) *v.* To remove the hair from. **depilation** *n.* **depilator** *n.*

de-pil-a-to-ry (di pil´a tōr´ē) *n.* A chemical which removes hair.

de-plane (dē plān´) *v.* To disembark or leave an aircraft.

de-plete (di plēt´) *v.* To exhaust, empty, or use up a supply of something.

de-plor-a-ble (di plōr´a bl) *adj.* Grievous; lamentable; very bad; wretched, **deplorability** *n.*

de-plore (di plōr´) *v.* To have, show, or feel great disapproval of something.

de-ploy (di ploi´) *v.* To spread out; to place or position according to plans.

de-plume (dē plōm´) *v.* To deprive of feathers or plumage; to pluck.

de-pone (di pōn´) *v.* To testify; depose.

de-po-nent (di pō´nent) *n.* A person who testifies under oath giving sworn testimony, especially in writing.

de-pop-u-late (dē pop´ū lāt´) *v.* To quickly remove or lower the population greatly, as by massacre or disease.

de-port (di pōrt´) *v.* To banish or expel someone from a country; to behave in a specified manner. **deportation** *n.*

de-pose (di pōz´) *v.* To remove from a powerful position or office; in law, to declare or give testimony under oath. **deposable** *adj.* **deposal** *n.*

de-pos-it (di poz´ĭt) *v.* To put, place, or set something down; to entrust money to a bank; to put down in the form of a layer, as silt; to give as security or partial payment, mineral masses, such as oil, coal or ores. **depositor** *n.*

de-pot (dē´pō) *n.* A railroad station; a warehouse or storehouse. *Milit.* The place where military materials are manufactured, stored, and repaired; an installation for processing personnel.

dep-ra-va-tion (dep´ra vā´shan) *n.* The act of corrupting; state of being depraved.

de-prave (di prāv´) *v.* To render bad or worse; in morals, to corrupt or pervert. **depraved** *adj.* **depravity** *n.*

dep-re-cate (dep´re kāt´) v. To express regret for or disapproval of; to belittle. **deprecatingly** adv. **deprecation** n.

de-pre-ci-ate (di prē´shē āt´) v. To lessen in value or price. **depreciator** n. **depreciative** adj. **depreciatory** adj.

de-pre-ci-a-tion (di prē´shē āt´) n. A loss in efficiency or value resulting from age or usage; the decline in the purchasing value of money.

de-press (di pres´) v. To make gloomy; to lower the spirits of; to lessen in energy or vigor; to press down; to lower; to diminish in value or price.

de-pres-sion (di presh´an) n. The state of being or the act of depressing; a severe decline in business, accompanied by increasing unemployment and falling prices. Psych. A condition of deep dejection characterized by lack of response to stimulation and withdrawal.

dep-ri-va-tion (dep´ri vā´shan) n. The act or state of being deprived.

de-prive (di prīv´) v. To take something away from; to keep from using, acquiring, or enjoying. **deprivable** adj.

depth (depth) n. The degree or state of being deep; the distance or extent backward, downward, or inward; the most intense part of something; intensity or richness of sound or color; the range of one's comprehension. **depths** pl. A deep part or place; an intense state of feeling or being.

dep-u-ta-tion (dep´ū tā´shan) n. A person or persons who are acting for another or others; the act of deputing or the state of being deputed.

de-pute (de pūt´) v. To appoint as a deputy, an agent, or other figure of authority; to delegate; to transfer.

de-rac-in-ate (di ras´i nāt´) v. To uproot. **deracination.** n.

de-rail (dē rāl´) v. To run off the rails; to cause a train to run off the rails. Slang To change a plan or program.

de-range (di rānj´) v. To disturb the arrangement or normal order of; to unbalance the reason; to make insane.

de-reg-u-late (dē´reg ye lāt´) v. To decontrol or remove from regulation or control.

der-e-lict (der´e likt) adj. Neglectful of obligations; remiss. n. Abandoned or deserted, as a ship at sea; a vagrant; a social outcast.

der-e-lic-tion (der´e lik´shan) n. Voluntary neglect, as of responsibility; the fact or state of being abandoned.

de-ride (di rīd´) v. To ridicule; to treat with scornful mirth. **derider** n. **derision** n. **deridingly** adv. **derisive** adj.

de ri-gueur (de ri ger´) adj. Prescribed or required by manners, custom, or fashion.

der-i-va-tion (der´i vā´shan) n. The act of or process of deriving; the process used to form new words by the addition of affixes to roots, stems, or words.

de-rive (di rīv´) v. To receive or obtain from a source. Chemical To produce a compound from other substances by chemical reaction.

der-mal (der´mel) adj. Relating to or of the skin.

der-ma-ti-tis (der´ma tī´tis) n., Pathol. An inflammation of the skin.

der-mat-o-gen (der mat´o jen) n. The cellular layer at the tip of a plant root where the epidermis is produced.

der-ma-tol-o-gy (der´ma tol´o jē) n. The medical study of the skin and the diseases related it. **dermatologist** n.

der-ma-to-sis (dür´ma tō´sis) n. A disease of the skin or skin tissue.

der-o-gate (der´o gāt´) v. To take or cause to take away from; to detract; to cause to become inferior.

de-rog-a-tory (di rog´a tōr´ē) adj. Having the effect of belittling; lessening. **derogatorily** adv.

der-ri-ere (der´ē ār) n. The buttocks.

der-ring-do (der´ing dö´) n. A courageous or daring action or spirit.

der-ris (der´is) n. An East Indian plant that is the source of an insecticide.

de-salt (dēsot´) v. To remove the salt from sea or saline water.

des-cant (des´kant) v. To play or sing a varied melody.

de-scend (di send´) v. To move from a higher to a lower level; to pass through inheritance; to come from a particular family; to sink in status; to worsen in condition or reputation.

descending sort In computer science, an alphabetical or numerical arrangement from highest to lowest.

de-scent (di sent´) n. A slope; lowering or decline, as in level or status.

de-scribe (di skrīb´) v. To explain in written or spoken words; to draw or trace the figure of. **describable** adj.

de-scrip-tion (di skrip shan) n. The technique or act of describing; an account or statement that describes. **descriptive** adj.

de-scry (di skrī´) v. To catch sight of; to discover by observation.

des-e-crate (des´e krāt´) v. To violate something sacred, turning it into something common or profane.

de-seg-re-gate (dē seg´re gāt´) v. To remove or eliminate racial segregation in work, school, and other activities. **desegregation** n.

de-sen-si-tize (dē sen´si tīz´) v. To make less sensitive; to eliminate the sensitivity of an individual, tissue, or organ to an allergen.

des-ert (de sert´) v. To abandon or

forsake. *Milit.* To be absent without leave with the plan of not returning, AWOL. **desert** (des´ert) *n.* A dry, barren region incapable of supporting any considerable population or vegetation without an artificial water supply.

de-serve (di zerv´) *v.* To be worthy of or entitled to.

des-ic-cant (des´i kant) *n.* A silica gel used to absorb moisture; any material used to that has drying qualities.

des-ic-cate (des´i kāt´) *v.* To preserve by drying, such as food; dehydrate. **desiccation** *n.* **desiccative** *adj.*

de-sid-er-a-tum (di sid´e rā´tum) *n. pl.*-ta A desired and necessary thing.

de-sign (di zīn´) *v.* To draw and sketch preliminary outlines; to invent or create in the mind; to have as an intention or goal. **design** *n.* An artistic or decorative piece of work; a project; a plan; a well thought out intention.

des-ig-nate (dez´ig nāt´) *v.* To assign a name or title to; to point out; to specify; to appoint or select, as to an office, to set apart. **designative** *adj.* **-ion** *n.*

des-i-nence *n.* Termination or ending, as of a line of verse.

de-sir-a-ble (di zīer´a bl) *adj.* Pleasing, attractive, or valuable; worthy of desire. **desirability** *n.* **desirableness** *n.*

de-sire (di zīer´) *v.* To long for; to wish; to crave; to request or ask for; to have sexual appetite.

de-sir-ous (di zīer´us) *adj.* Having a craving or strong desire.

de-sist (di zist´) *v.* To stop doing something; to cease to act.

desktop computer In *computer science,* a personal or micro computer, designed to fit on a desk.

desktop publishing In *computer science,* creation of type and graphics on a desktop computer.

des-mid (des´mid) *n.* Microscopic, unicellular freshwater green algae.

des-o-late (des´o lit) *adj.* Made unfit for habitation; useless; forlorn; forsaken.

des-o-la-tion (des´o la´shan) *n.* A wasteland; the condition of being ruined or deserted; loneliness.

de-spair (di spâr´) *v.* To lose or give up hope; to abandon all purpose. **despair** *n.* **despairing** *adj.* **despairingly** *adv.*

des-per-ate (des´pêr it) *adj.* Rash, violent, reckless, and without care, as from despair; intense; overpowering.

des-per-a-tion (des´pe rā´shan) *n.* The state of being desperate.

des-pi-ca-ble (des´pi ka bl) *adj.* Deserving scorn or contempt. **-bly** *adv.*

de-spise (di spīz´) *v.* To regard with contempt or as worthless. **despiser** *n.*

de-spite (di spīt´) *prep.* Not withstanding; in spite of.

de-spite-ful *adj.* Full of spite; malicious.

de-spoil (di spoil´) *v.* To rob; to strip of property or possessions by force. **despoiler** *n.* **despoilment** *n.*

de-spond (di spond´) *v.* To lose hope, courage, or spirit. **despondently** *adv.*

de-spon-den-cy (di spon´den sē) *n.* A dejection of spirits from loss of courage or hope.

de-spond-ent (di spon´dent) *adj.* Having the feeling of extreme discouragement.

des-pot (des´pot) *n.* An absolute ruler; a tyrant. **despotic** *adj.* **despotically** *adv.*

des-pot-ism (des´po tiz´um) *n.* A system where a ruler has unlimited power or authority.

des-qua-mate (des´kwa māt´) *v.* To come off in scales, as the epidermis in certain diseases; to peel off.

des-sert (di zert´) *n.* A serving of sweet food, as pastry, ice cream, or fruit, as the last course of a meal.

des-ti-na-tion (des´ti nā´shan) *n.* The point or place to which something or someone is directed; the purpose or end for which something is created or intended. In computer science, the file, computer, or peripheral to which data is being transmitted.

des-tine (des´tin) *v.* To be determined in advance; to design or appoint a distinct purpose.

des-ti-ny (des´ti nē) *n., pl.* **destinies** The inevitable fate to which a person or thing is destined; fate; a predetermined course of events.

des-ti-tute (des´ti töt´) *adj.* Extremely poor; utterly impoverished; not having; without the necessities of life.

de-stroy (di stroi´) *v.* To ruin; to tear down; to demolish; to kill; to make useless or ineffective.

de-struct (di strukt´) *n., Aeron.* The deliberate destruction of a defective or dangerous missile or rocket after launch.

des-ue-tude (des´wi töd´) *n.* A condition or state of disuse.

des-ul-to-ry (des´ul tōr´ē) *adj.* Something that occurs by chance; lacking continuity; aimless.

de-tach (di tach´) *v.* To unfasten, disconnect, or separate; to extricate oneself; to withdraw.

de-tail (di tāl) *n.* A part or item considered separately. *Milit.* Military personnel selected for a particular duty.

de-tain (di tān´) *v.* To stop; to keep from proceeding; to delay.

de-tect (di tekt´) *v.* To find out or perceive; to expose or uncover, as a crime. **detectible** *adj.* **detection** *n.*

de-tec-tive (di tek´tiv) *n.* A person whose work is to investigate crimes, discover evidence, and capture criminals.

de-tent (di tent´) *n.* A pawl; a lock.

de-ten-tion (di ten´sh*a***n)** *n.* The act of or state of being detained; in law, a time or period of temporary custody which precedes disposition by a court.

de-ter (di ter´) *v.* To prevent or discourage someone from acting by arousing fear, uncertainty, intimidation, or other strong emotion. **determent** *n.*

de-terge (di terj´) *v.* To cleanse; to wash or clear away unclean or offending matter from.

de-te-ri-o-rate (di tēr´ē *o* **rāt´)** *v.* To worsen; to depreciate, to reduce in quality and value, degenerate or decompose. **deterioration** *n.*

de-ter-mi-na-ble (di tür´mi na bl) *adj.* Capable of being determined, definitely decided. **determinably** *adv.*

de-ter-mi-nate (di ter´mi nit) *adj.* Definitely fixed or limited; conclusive. *Bot.* Terminating in a bud or flower, often at each axis of an inflorescence.

de-ter-mi-na-tion (di tür´mi nā´sh*a***n)** *n.* The act of deciding definitely; a firm resolution; adherence to purposes or aims.

de-ter-mine (di ter´min) *v.* To settle or decide conclusively or authoritatively; to limit to extent or scope; to fix or ascertain; to give direction or purpose to; to come to a conclusion after investigation; *law* to bring to an end.

de-ter-rent (di ter´ent) *n.* Something which deters. *adj.* Serving to deter; restrain from doing. **deterrently** *adv.*

de-test (di test´) *v.* To dislike strongly. **detestable** *adj.* **detestably** *adv.*

de-tes-ta-tion (dē´te stā´sh*a***n)** *n.* Extreme dislike or hatred; abhorrence.

de-throne (di thrōn´) *v.* To remove from the throne, to depose, as a king.

det-i-nue (det´l nō) *n.* The unlawful detention of a person's property, or a common-law action to recover the personal property so detained.

det-o-nate (det´*o* **nat´)** *v.* To explode suddenly and violently.

det-o-na-tor (det´*o* **nā´tėr)** *n.* The device, such as a fuse or percussion cap, used to detonate an explosive.

de-tour (dē´tėr) *n.* A road used temporarily instead of a main road; a deviation from a direct route or course of action.

de-tox-i-fy (dē tok´si fī´) *v.* To free one from dependence on drugs or alcohol, to remove poisonous effects from one's system. **detoxification** *n.*

de-tract (di trakt´) *v.* To take away from; to diminish; to divert. **detraction** *n.* **detractor** *n.* **detractive** *adj.*

de-train (dē trān´) *v.* To leave or cause to leave a railroad train. **-ment** *n.*

det-ri-ment (de´tri ment) *n.* Damage; injury; loss; something which causes damage, injury, or loss. **detrimental** *adj.* **detrimentally** *adv.*

de-tri-tus (di trī´tus) *n.* Loose fragments or particles formed by erosion, glacial action, and other forces; debris.

de-trun-cate (di trung´kāt) *v.* To cut off; to shorten.

deuce (dōs) *n.* Two; a playing card or the side of a die with two spots or figures; in tennis, a tie in which each side has a score of 40 points. *Informal* The devil, bad luck, or a mild oath.

De-us *n.* God.

deu-te-ri-um (dō tēr´ē um) *n.* The isotope of hydrogen which has twice the mass of ordinary hydrogen.

de-val-u-ate (dē val´ū āt´) *v.* To reduce or lessen the value of. **devaluation** *n.*

dev-as-tate (dev´*a* **stāt´)** *v.* To destroy; to ruin; to overwhelm; to overpower. **devastation** *n.*

de-vel-op (di vel´up) *v.* To bring out or expand the potentialities; to make more elaborate; to enlarge; to evolve; to advance from a lower to a higher stage or from an earlier to a later stage of maturation. *Photog.* To process an image upon a sensitized plate that has been exposed to light. **developer** *n.* **developmental** *adj.*

de-vest (di vest´) *v.* To deprive of a right; to take away; divest.

de-vi-ate (dē´vē āt´) *v.* To turn away from a specified prescribed behavior or course, to be different from the normal patterns of a person or thing.

de-vi-a-tion (dē´vē ā´shan) *n.* The act of turning aside from the right way or course; variation from a standard..

de-vice (di vīs´) *n.* Something constructed and used for a specific purpose, as a machine; a crafty or evil scheme or plan; an ornamental design; a motto or an emblem. In computer science, any component or peripheral that is a part of a computer system.

device driver In *computer science*, a program that interprets instructions for the operation of a peripheral, such as a printer.

dev-il or **Devil (dev´il)** *n.* The spirit of evil, the ruler of Hell, Satan, a wicked or malevolent person; a daring, clever, and energetic person; a printer's apprentice, also called a printer's devil.

de-vi-ous (dē´vē us) *adj.* Leading away from the straight, regular, or direct course; rambling; straying from the proper way; tricky; underhanded. **deviously** *adv.* **deviousness** *n.*

de-vise (di vīz´) *v.* To form in the mind; to contrive; to plan; to invent; in law, to transmit or give by will. **devise** *n.* The act of bequeathing lands; a clause in a will conveying real estate.

de-vi-see (di vī zē´) *n.* In law, the person to whom a devise is made.

de-vi-sor (di vī´zėr) *n.* In law, the person

who devises property.

de-vi-tal-ize (dē vīt´*a* līz´) *v.* To make weak; to destroy the vitality.

de-void (di void´) *adj.* Empty; utterly lacking; without.

de-voir (d*e* vwär´) *n.* The act or expression of courtesy or respect; duty or responsibility.

dev-o-lu-tion (dev´*o* lō´sh*a*n) *n.* The act of devolving; passage onward from stage to stage; the passing of property by succession or inheritance.

de-volve (di volv´) *v.* To pass duty or authority on to a successor.

de-vote (di vōt´) *v.* To apply time or oneself completely to some activity, purpose, or cause.

de-vour (di vour´) *v.* To destroy or waste; to eat up greedily; to engulf.

de-vout (di vout´) *adj.* Extremely and earnestly religious; showing sincerity; displaying piety or reverence, a devotion to religion and religious activities. **devoutly** *adv.*

dew (dō) *n.* Moisture condensed from the atmosphere in minute drops onto cool surfaces; something which is refreshing or pure. **dewy** *adj.*

dew point *n.* The temperature at which condensation of vapor occurs.

dex-ter (dek´stĕr) *adj.* Pertaining to or situated on the right side.

dex-ter-i-ty (dek stĕr´i tē) *n.* Proficiency or skill in using the hands or body; cleverness.

dex-ter-ous *or* **dex-trous** (dek´strus) *adj.* Skillful or adroit in the use of the hands, body, or mind. **dexterously** *adv.*

dex-tran (dek´str*a*n) *n.* A white gum-like substance, produced by bacterial action and used as a plasma substitute.

dex-trin (dek´strin) *n.* A group of water soluble gummy substances obtained from starch by the action of heat or weak acids and used as an adhesive.

dex-trose (dek´strōs) *n.* Sugar found in animal blood and in plant tissue and derived synthetically from starches.

di-a-base (dī´*a* bās´) *n.* A minor intrusive rock.

di-a-be-tes (dī´*a* bē´tis) *n., Pathol.* A metabolic disorder characterized by deficient insulin secretion, leading to excess sugar in the urine and blood, extreme hunger, and thirst.

di-a-bet-ic (dī´*a* bet´ik) *adj., Med.* Pertaining to, or affected with diabetes.

di-a-bol-ic *or* **di-a-bol-i-cal** (dī´*a* bol´ik) *adj.* Wicked; proceeding from the devil; satanic or infernal. **diabolically** *adv.* **diabolicalness** *n.*

di-a-chron-ic (dī´*a* kron´ik) *adj.* Dealing with the phenomena or study of language changes over a period of time.

di-a-crit-ic (dī´*a* krit´ik) *n.* A mark near or through a phonetic character or combination of characters, to indicate a special phonetic value or to distinguish words otherwise graphically identical. **diacritical** *adj.* **diacritic** *adj.*

di-a-dem (dī´*a* dem´) *n.* A crown or headband worn to symbolize or indicate royalty or honor.

di-ag-no-sis (dī´ag nō´sis) *n. pl.* **diagnoses** An analysis and examination to identify a disease; the conclusion reached. **diagnostician** *n.*

di-ag-nos-tics *adj.* Branch of medicine dealing with diagnosis.

di-ag-nos-tic (dī´ag nos´tik) *adj.* A symptom by which a disease is known. In computer science, a description of a system to detect and isolate errors or malfunction in programs or equipment.

diagnostic message *n.* In *computer science*, an error message that describes the source of the error.

di-ag-o-nal (dī ag´*o* n*a*l) *adj.* In mathematics, joining two opposite corners of a polygon which are not adjacent. *n.* A diagonal or slanting plane or line; in a diagonal pattern.

di-a-gram (dī´*a* gram´) *n.* A sketch, plan, drawing, or outline designed to demonstrate or clarify the similarity among parts of a whole or to illustrate how something works. **diagram** *v.,* **diagrammatic, diagrammatical** *adj.*

di-a-lect (dī´*a* lekt´) *n.* Manner of speaking; a form of a language prevailing in a particular region or area.

di-a-lec-tic (dī´*a* lek´tik) *n.* The act or practice of argument or exposition in which the conflict between contradictory facts or ideas is resolved. **dialectic** *adj.* **dialectically** *adv.*

di-a-lec-tol-o-gy (dī´*a* lek tol´*o* jē) *n.* The systematic study of dialects.

di-a-logue *or* **di-a-log** (dī´*a* log´) *n.* A conversation involving two or more persons; a conversational passage in a literary work.

dialog box In *computer science*, a panel that appears on screen as a part of a program to furnish instructions, information or to request user input.

di-al-y-sis (dī al´i sis) *n. pl.* **-ses** The separation of substances in solution, which is accomplished by passing them through membranes or filters. **dialysis** A form of *dialysis* used to cleanse the blood of impurities and wastes when the kidneys are unable to perform this function.

di-a-mag-net-ic (dī´*a* mag net´ik) *adj.* Pertaining to a class of substances which are slightly repelled by a magnet.

di-am-e-ter (di am´i tĕr) *n.* In mathematics, a straight line which passes through the center of a circle or sphere and stops at the circumference or surface;

a measurement of that distance.

di-a-pa-son (dī´*a* pā´z*o*n) *n.* The full range of a voice or an instrument; in a pipe organ, either of two principal stops which form the tonal basis for the entire scale.

di-a-pe-de-sis (dī´*a* pī dē´sis) *n.* The passage of blood cells through the capillary walls into the tissues.

di-a-per (dī´pér) *n.* A folded piece of soft, absorbent material placed between a baby's legs and fastened at the waist. *v.* To put a diaper on.

di-aph-a-nous (dī af´*a* nus) *adj.* Of such fine texture as to be transparent or translucent; delicate; almost totally transparent. **diaphanously** *adv.*

di-a-phone (dī´*a* fōn´) *n.* A low-pitched fog horn, that produces a blast of two tones, the sound of which can be heard from a distance.

di-a-phragm (dī´*a* fram´) *n. Anat.* The muscular wall which separates the chest and abdominal cavities; a dividing membrane. A contraceptive device usually made of rubber-like material shaped like a cap to cover the uterine cervix. *Photog.* The disk with an adjustable aperture that can control the amount of light which passes through the lens of a telescope, camera, etc.

di-a-pos-i-tive (dī´*a* poz´i tiv) *n.* A transparent photograph.

di-a-rist (dī´*a* rist) *n.* A person who keeps a diary.

di-ar-rhe-a *or* **di-ar-rhoe-a** (dī´arē´*a*) *n.* A disorder of the intestines causing frequent, loose bowel movements.

di-ar-thro-sis (dī är thrō´sis) *n.* A freely movable joint in which the bones revolve in every direction, as in the shoulder or hip joint.

di-a-ry (dī´*a* rē) *n.* *pl.* -ries A daily record, especially a personal record of one's activities, experiences, or observations; a journal; a book for keeping such records.

di-as-ta-sis (dī as´ta sis) *n.* Dislocation of bones without a fracture.

di-as-to-le (dī as´to lē) *n. Physiol.* The normal rhythmic dilatation of the heart cavities during which they fill with blood. **diastolic** *adj.*

di-as-tro-phism (dī as´tro fiz´*u*m) *n. Geol.* Any process through which the earth's crust is changed into formations such as mountains and continents.

di-a-ther-my (dī´*a* thér´mē) *n.* *pl.* **diathermies** *Med.* The generation of heat in body tissues by high-frequency electromagnetic waves; the application of electric current to produce heat in tissues below the skin for therapeutic purposes. **diathermic** *adj.*

di-ath-e-sis (dī ath´i sis) *n.* Predisposition toward a condition or certain diseases

rather than to others.

di-a-tom (dī´*a* tom) *n.* Any of various tiny planktonic algae whose walls contain silica.

di-a-tom-ic (dī´*a* tom´ik) *adj.* Having two atoms in a molecule.

di-a-ton-ic (dī´*a* ton´ik) *adj., Music* Relating to a standard major or minor scale of eight tones without the chromatic intervals.

di-a-tribe (dī´*a* trīb´) *n.* A bitter, often malicious criticism or denunciation.

di-chot-o-mous (di kot´o mus) *adj.* Dividing into two parts.

di-chot-o-my (di kot´o mē) *n., pl.* **dichotomies** Division into two mutually exclusive subclasses. *Bot.* The branching of something in which each successive axis forks into two equally developed branches.

di-cot-y-le-don (di kot´*a* lēd´*o*n) *n.* A plant which has two seed leaves. **dicotyledonous** *adj.*

di-crot-ic (dī krot´ik) *adj.* Having a double arterial beat for one heartbeat.

dic-tate (dik´tāt) *v.* To read or speak aloud for another to record or transcribe; to give commands, terms, rules, or other orders with authority. **dictate** *n.* A directive or guiding principle.

dic-ta-tor (dik´tā tér) *n.* A person having absolute authority and supreme governmental powers; one who dictates. **dictatorship** *n.*

dic-tion-ar-y (dik´sha ner´ē) *n., pl.* **dictionaries** A reference book or data base containing alphabetically arranged words together with their definitions and usages.

dic-tum (dik´tum) *n., pl.* **dictums** *or* **dicta** An authoritative or positive utterance; a pronouncement; a saying.

did (did) *v.* Past tense of do.

di-dac-tic *or* **didactical** (dīdak´ti k*a*l) *adj* Being inclined to teach or moralize excessively. **didacticism** *n.*

did-dle (did l) *v.* To cheat; to swindle; to waste valuable time.

did-n't (did´*a*nt) *contr.* Did not.

did-y-mous (did´i mus) *adj.* Produced in pairs; twin.

die (dī) *v.* To expire; to stop living; to cease to exist; to fade away; to cease operation or functioning, as an engine. **die hard** To resist defeat or death to the end; to be determined not to give up. **die off** To be removed one after another by death. **die out** To become extinct.

diel-drin (dēl´drin) *n.* A highly toxic chlorinated compound which is used as an insecticide.

di-e-lec-tric (dī´i lek´trik) *n. Elect.* A non−conductor of electricity.

di-er-e-sis (dī er´i sis) *n., pl.* -ses The

mark over a vowel indicating that it is to be pronounced in a separate syllable.

die-sel (dē´zel) *n.* A diesel engine or a vehicle driven by a diesel engine.

di-et (dī´it) *n.* A regulated selection of food and drink, especially one followed for medical or hygienic reasons; something that is taken or provided regularly; an assembly or legislature.

dif-fer (dif´ẽr) *v.* To have different opinions; to disagree; to be unlike.

dif-fer-ence (dif´ẽr ens) *n.* The quality, state, or degree of being different or unlike; a controversy or cause for a disagreement; in mathematics, the amount by which a number or quantity is less or greater than another.

dif-fer-ent (dif´ẽr ent) *adj.* Not the same; separate; other; marked by a difference; unlike; differing from the ordinary. differently *adv.* differentness *n.*

dif-fer-en-tia (dif´e ren´shē a) *n. pl.*-tiae A specific difference; something that distinguishes a species from others of the same genus.

dif-fer-en-tial (dif´e ren´shal) *adj.* Relating to or showing a difference or differences. *n.* The amount or degree to which similar things differ.

differential calculus *n.* In mathematics, the difference or variation of a function with respect to changes in independent variables.

dif-fi-cult (dif´i kult´) *adj.* Hard to do, deal with, or accomplish; hard to please.

dif-fi-dence (dif´i dens) *n.* Lack of self-confidence.

dif-fi-dent (dif´i dent)*adj.* Lacking confidence in oneself; unsure; unassertive. diffidence *n.* diffidently *adv.*

dif-flu-ent (dif´lō ent) *adj.* Having the tendency to flow away.

dif-fuse (di füz´) *v.* To pour out and spread freely in all directions; to scatter.

dig (dig) *v.* To turn up, break up, or remove the earth with a shovel; to discover or learn by investigation or research. *Slang* To understand, like, appreciate or enjoy. *Informal* To work intensively.

dig-a-my (dig´a mē) *n.* Second marriage; the act of marrying after the first marriage has been legally ended.

di-gas-tric (dī gas´trik) *n.* A double muscle separated by a median tendon, that pulls the lower jaw downward and backward.

di-gest (di jest´) *v.* To change ingested food into usable form; to mentally assimilate; to endure; to tolerate patiently; to decompose or soften with moisture or heat. digestibility *n.* digestible *adj.* digestive *adj.*

dig-it (dij´it) *n.* A toe or finger; the Arabic numerals 0 through 9. In computer science, a symbol representing an integer in a numbering system, as 0-9 in decimal notation or 0-F in hexadecimal.

dig-i-tal (dij´i tal) *adj.* Pertaining to or like the fingers or digits; expressed in digits, especially for computer use; reading in digits, as a clock. In computer science, represented by a distinct value.

digital camera In *computer science,* a camera that records images in digital format for downloading and viewing on a computer screen.

digital computer *n.* In *computer science,* a computer using data that is represented as digits to perform operations.

digital data In *computer science,* information recorded in a system of numbers, as binary for the computer.

digital recording In *computer science,* sounds recorded as discrete values.

dig-i-tal-is (dij´i tal´ is) *n.* The foxglove plant; a drug prepared from dried leaves of foxglove, used as a heart stimulant.

di-glot (dī´glot) *adj.* Using two languages; bilingual.

dig-ni-fied (dig´ni fīd´) *adj.* Showing or possessing dignity; poised.

dig-ni-fy (dig´ni fī´) *v.* To give dignity or distinction to something.

dig-ni-tary (dig´ni ter´ē) *n., pl.* dignitaries A person of high rank, notability, and influence.

dig-ni-ty (dig´ni tē) *n., pl.* dignities The quality or state of being excellent; the quality of being poised or formally reserved in appearance and demeanor; a high rank, office, or title.

di-graph (dī´graf) *n.* A pair of letters, as the *ea* in seat or *oa* in boat, that represent a single sound.

di-gress (di gres´) *v.* To turn away from the main subject in a discourse; to wander. digression *n.* digressive *adj.*

dik–dik (dik´dik´) *n.* A very small African antelope.

dike (dīk) *n.* An embankment made of earth, built to hold and control flood waters, also known as a levee; also used in irrigation of crops.

di-lap-i-date (di lap´i dāt´) *v.* To cause to decay or fall into partial ruin through neglect.

di-lap-i-dat-ed (di lap´i dā´tid) *adj.* Being in a state of decay or disrepair.

dil-a-ta-tion (dił´a tā shan) *n.* The state of being expanded or distended; something which is dilated. *Med.* Enlargement of a passageway for medical examination.

di-late (dī lāt´) *v.* To become or make enlarged; to expand; extend in all directions. dilatable *adj.* dilation *n.*

di-lat-ed (dī lā´tid) *adj.* Expanded in all directions; broadened.

dil-a-tom-e-ter (dil´a tom´i tėr)- *n.* An instrument for measuring thermal expansion of substances.

dil-a-to-ry (dil´a tōr´ē) *adj.* Tending to cause delay; slow; tardy. **dilatorily** *adv.*

di-lem-ma (di lem´a) *n.* A predicament requiring a choice between equally undesirable alternatives.

dil-et-tante (dil´i tan´tē) *n., pl.* **dilettantes** One who has an amateurish and superficial interest in something.

dil-i-gence (dil´i jens) *n.* The constant effort to accomplish what is undertaken.

dil-i-gent (dil´i jent) *adj.* Showing painstaking effort and application in whatever is undertaken; industrious; constant in effort to accomplish what is undertaken. **diligently** *adv.*

dill (dil) *n.* An herb with aromatic leaves and seeds used as seasoning.

dil-ly (dil´ē) *n., pl.* **dillies** *Slang* Someone or something that is remarkable or extraordinary.

dil-ly-dal-ly (dil´ē dal´ē) *v.* To waste time with indecision or hesitation.

di-lute (di lōt´) *v.* To weaken, thin, or reduce the concentration of by adding a liquid; reduce strength. **dilution** *n.*

dim (dim) *adj.* Dull; lacking sharp perception or clarity of understanding.

dime (dīm) *n.* A United States coin worth ten cents or one tenth of a dollar.

dime novel *n.* A melodramatic paperback novel.

di-men-sion (di men´shan) *n.* A measurable extent, as length, thickness, or breadth. **dimensions** *pl.* The magnitude or scope of something. **dimensional** *adj.* **dimensionality** *n.*

dim-er-ous (dim´ėr us) *adj.* Consisting of two parts.

di-min-ish (di min´ish) *v.* To become or make smaller or less; to reduce in power, rank, or authority; to decrease; to taper. **diminishment** *n.*

dim-in-ished (di min´isht) *adj.* Reduced; lessened.

di-min-u-en-do (di min´ū en´do) *adj. & adv.* Gradually lessening in volume. **diminuendo** *n.*

di-min-u-tive (di min´ū tiv) *adj.* Very small; tiny.

dim-is-so-ry (dim´i sōr´ē) *adj.* Granting leave to depart.

dim-mer (dim´ėr) *n.* A rheostat used to reduce the intensity of an electric light.

dim-wit (dim´wit) *n.* A simple-minded or stupid person. **dimwitted** *adj.* **dimwittedly** *adv.* **dimwittedness** *n.*

din (din) *n.* A loud, confused, harsh noise.

dine (dīn) *v.* To eat dinner.

ding (ding) *v.* To sound as a bell when struck; to make a ringing sound.

ding-a-ling *n., Slang* A silly person.

din-ghy (ding´gē) *n., pl.* **dinghies** A small rowboat; an inflatable rubber raft.

din-ner (din´ėr) *n.* The main meal of the day; a formal meal honoring someone.

di-no-saur (dī´no sor´) *n. Paleontology* A group of extinct reptiles from the Mesozoic period; some were the largest land animals known to exist.

di-no-there (dī´no thėr´) *n.* A huge, extinct, two-tusked mammal closely associated with the elephant.

dint (dint) *n.* Means; force; effort. **dint** *v.* To drive with force.

di-ode (dī´ōd) *n.* An electron tube which permits electrons to pass in only one direction, used as a rectifier.

di-o-ra-ma (dī´o ram´a) *n.* A miniature scene in three dimensions.

dip (dip) *v.* To let or put down into a liquid momentarily; to lift up and out by scooping or bailing; to make candles by repeatedly immersing wicks in wax or tallow; to sink or go down suddenly. **dip** *n.* A downward motion; a sauce made of liquid, into which something is to be dipped; a depression or hollow. *Slang* A silly person.

diph-the-ri-a (dif thėr´ē a) *n. Pathol.* An acute contagious disease caused by bacillus and characterized by formation of a false membrane in the throat and accompanied by weakness and by fever.

diph-thong (dif´thong) *n.* A blend of a single speech sound which begins with one vowel sound and moves to another in the same syllable, as *oi* in oil and coil or *oy* in boy and toy.

diph-y-o-dont (dif´ē o dont´) *adj.* Having the successive development of two sets of teeth; as humans do.

di-plex (dīpleks) *adj.* Pertaining to sending two simultaneous signals over the same communications path.

di-plo-ma (di plō´ma) *n.* A document issued by a college, school, or university testifying that a student has earned a degree or completed a course of study.

di-plo-ma-cy (di plō´ma sē) *n., pl.* **diplomacies** The practice of conducting international negotiations; skill and tact in dealing with people.

dip-ter-ous (dip´tėr us) *adj.* Pertaining to animals having a single pair of wings such as the fly, gnat, and mosquito.

dire (dīr) *adj.* Dreadful or terrible; threatening disastrous consequence. **direly** *adv.* **direfully** *adv.* **direness** *n.*

di-rect (di rekt´) *v.* To control or regulate the affairs of; to command or order; to or tell someone the way; to cause something to move in a given course; to indicate the destination of a letter;

to supervise or instruct the performance of a job; to move or lie in a straight line; to do something immediate. **direct** *adj.* Without compromise; absolute; in the exact words of a person, as a direct quote; straightforward; referring to the shortest, least complicated route..

di-rec-tion (di rek´shan) *n.* The act of directing; an order or command; the path or line along which something points, travels or lies. **directional** *adj.*

di-rec-tive (di rek´tiv) *n.* A regulation or order from someone with authority.

di-rect-ly (di rekt´lē) *adv.* Immediately; at once; in a direct manner or line; doing without an agent or go-between.

di-rec-tor (di rek´tér) *n.* A person who manages or directs; one of a group of persons who supervises the affairs of an institute, corporation or business.

di-rec-to-ry (di rek´to rē) *n., pl.* **directories** A book listing data, alphabetically or classified, containing the names and addresses of a specific group, persons, organizations, inhabitants, or businesses. In computer science, in the hierarchical file structure, a division that holds related program or data files and sub-directories.

direct tax *n.* A tax which is charged directly to the taxpayer.

dirge (dérj) *n.* A slow mournful song; a funeral hymn.

dir-i-gi-ble (dir´i ji bl) *n.* A lighter-than-air plane which may be steered by means of its own motor power.

dirk (dérk) *n.* A dagger.

dirn-dl (dérn´dl) *n.* A lady's full-skirted dress with a gathered waistband.

dirt (dért) *n.* Soil or earth; obscene or profane language; scandalous or hateful gossip.

dis-a-bil-i-ty (dis´a bil´i tē) *n.* The condition or state of being mentally or physically disabled or unable.

dis-a-ble (dis ā bl) *v.* To make powerless or incapacitate; to disqualify legally.

dis-a-buse (dis´a būz´) *v.* To free from misunderstanding, misconception, or delusion.

dis-ac-cord *n.* Disagreement.

dis-ad-van-tage (dis´ad van´tij) *n.* A circumstance that is unfavorable; loss or damage; detriment.

dis-af-fect (dis´a fekt´) *v.* To weaken or destroy the affection or loyalty of. **disaffection** *n.* **disaffected** *adj.*

dis-af-firm (dis´a fêrm´) *v.* To deny; to refuse to confirm.

dis-af-for-est (dis´a fot´ist) *v.* To strip trees from the forest.

dis-a-gree (dis´a grē´) *v.* To vary in opinion; to differ; to argue; to quarrel; to be unfavorable or unacceptable.

dis-a-gree-able (dis´a grē´a bl) *adj.* Offensive or unpleasant.

dis-al-low (dis´a lou´) *v.* To refuse to allow; to reject as invalid or untrue.

dis-ap-pear (dis´a pēr´) *v.* To vanish; to drop from sight. **disappearance** *n.*

dis-ap-point (dis´a point´) *v.* To fail to satisfy the desires, hopes, or expectations of. **disappointing** *adj.*

dis-ap-pro-ba-tion (dis´ap ro bā´shan) *n.* Disapproval; condemnation.

dis-ap-prove (dis´a prōv´) *v.* To refuse to approve; to reject; to condemn.

dis-arm (dis ärm´) *v.* To make harmless; to deprive or take away the weapons or any means of attack or defense.

dis-ar-range (dis´a ränj´) *v.* To disturb the order of something.

dis-ar-ray (dis´a rā´) *n.* A state of confusion or disorder; an upset or turmoil.

dis-as-sem-ble (dis´a sem´bl) *v.* To take apart.

dis-as-so-ci-ate (dis´a sō´shēāt´) *v.* To break away from or to detach oneself from an association. **-ion** *n.*

dis-as-ter (di zas´tér) *n.* An event that causes great ruin or distress; a sudden and crushing misfortune. **-ous** *adj.*

dis-a-vow (dis´a vou´) *v.* To disclaim or deny any responsibility for or knowledge of. **disavowal** *n.*

dis-band (dis band´) *v.* To disperse; to break up. **disbandment** *n.*

dis-bar (dis bär´) *v.* In law, to expel officially from membership in the bar or the legal profession. **-ment** *n.*

dis-be-lieve (dis´bi lēv´) *v.* To refuse to believe in something. **disbelief** *n.*

dis-burse (dis bêrs´) *v.* To pay out; to give out; to spread out. **-ment** *n.*

disc *or* **disk (disk)** *n. Informal* A phonograph record.

dis-card (di skärd´) *v.* To remove a playing card from one's hand; to throw out. **discard** *n.* The act of discarding; something which is rejected or cast aside. **discarder** *n.* **discardable** *adj.*

dis-cern (di sérn´) *v.* To detect differences visually or with other senses or the intellect; to perceive as separate and distinct. **discerner** *n.* **discernment** *n.* **discernible** *adj.*

dis-cerp-ti-ble *adj.* Capable of being torn apart; divisible.

dis-charge (dis chärj´) *v.* To relieve of a charge, duty, load, or burden; to release as from confinement, custody, care, or duty; to dismiss from employment; to send forth; to shoot or fire a weapon; to get rid of; to release from service or duty; to fulfill an obligation, duty, or debt. **discharge** *n.* The act of discharging or the condition of being discharged.

dis-ci-ple (di sī´pl) *n.* One who accepts and assists in spreading doctrines of another. **Disciple** One of Christ's followers.

dis-ci-pline (dis´i plin) n. Training which corrects, molds, or perfects the mental faculties or moral character; behavior which results from such training; obedience to authority or rules; punishment meant to correct poor behavior. **discipline** v. To train or develop by teaching and by control; to bring order to; to penalize.

dis-claim (dis klām´) v. To disavow any claim to or association with; to deny the authority of ; to renounce or give up a claim on. **disclaimer** n.

dis-close (dis klōz´) v. To make known; to bring into view. **disclosure** n.

dis-co (dis kō) n., pl. discos Discotheque; a nightclub for dancing.

dis-cog-ra-phy (dis kog´ra fē) n. A systematic and descriptive list of phonograph records; as to the performer and date released.

dis-coid (dis´koid) adj. Having the form of or related to a disk, flat and circular.

dis-color (dis kul´ẽr) v. To alter or change the color of. **discoloration** n.

dis-com-fit (dis kum´fit) v To defeat in battle; to make upset or uneasy.

dis-com-fort (dis kum´fẽrt) n. Physical or mental uneasiness; pain; an inconvenience. **discomfort** v. To make uncomfortable.

dis-com-mend (dis´ko mend) v. To blame; to cause to be viewed unfavorably.

dis-com-mode (dis´ko mōd´) v. To inconvenience.

dis-com-pose (dis´kom pōz´) v. To disrupt the composure or serenity of; to unsettle; to destroy the order of. **discomposure** n.

dis-con-cert (dis´kon sẽrt´) v. To upset; to discompose; to perturb.

dis-con-nect (dis´ko nekt´) v. To sever or break the connection of or between, to detach. **disconnection** n.

dis-con-nect-ed (dis´kon nek´tid) adj. Not connected; separate.

dis-con-so-late (dis kon´so lit) adj. Without consolation; dejected; cheerless; sorrowful. **disconsolately** adv.

dis-con-tent (dis´kon tent´) n. Lack of contentment; dissatisfaction. **discontent** v. To make unhappy. **discontentedly** adv. **discontentment** n.

dis-con-tent-ed (dis´kon ten´tid) adj. Not pleased with one's circumstances.

dis-con-tin-ue (dis´kon tin´ū) v. To come or bring to an end; to break the continuity of; to interrupt; to stop trying, taking, or using.

dis-cord (dis´kord) n. Lacking accord or harmony; a harsh combination of musical sounds. **discordant** adj.

dis-cord-ance n. Disagreement;

opposition.

dis-co-theque (dis´kō tek´) n. A nightclub where music is provided for dancing.

dis-count (dis´kount) v. To sell or offer for sale at a price lower than usual; to leave out of account; to disregard.

dis-cour-age (di skẽr´ij) v. To deprive or be deprived of enthusiasm or courage; to hinder by disfavoring; deterring or dissuading. **-ment** n.

dis-course (dis´kōrs) n. A conversation; a formal and lengthy discussion of a subject. v. To write or converse extensively. **discourser** n.

dis-cour-te-ous (dis kẽr´tē us) adj. Lacking consideration or courteous manners. **discourtesy** n.

dis-cov-er (di skuv´ẽr) v. To make known or visible; to observe or learn of for the first time; to explore. **discoverable** adj. **discovery** n.

dis-cred-it (dis kred´it) v. To mar the reputation of or disgrace someone or something; to injure the reputation of. **discredit** n. Loss of credit or reputation; doubt; disbelief. **discreditable** adj. **discreditably** adv.

dis-creet (di skrēt´) adj. Tactful; careful of appearances; modest. **discreetly** adv.

dis-crep-an-cy (di skrep´an sē) n., pl. **discrepancies** A difference in facts.

dis-crete (di skrēt´) adj. Separate; made up of distinct parts.

dis-cre-tion (di skresh´shan) n. The quality or act of being discreet; the ability to make responsible choices; power to decide; the result of separating or distinguishing.

dis-crim-i-nate (di skrim´i nāt´) v. To distinguish or differentiate between someone or something on the basis of race, sex, class, or religion; to detect differences.

dis-cus (dis´kus) n. A heavy disk made of wood, rubber, or metal, which is hurled for distance in athletic competitions; a brightly-colored, disk-shaped freshwater fish of South America.

dis-cuss (di skus´) v. To investigate by argument or debate; to consider or examine something through discourse.

dis-cus-sant (di skus´ant) n. A participant in a discussion.

dis-cus-sion (di skush´an) n. The act of discussing between two or more people about a subject that they may or may not agree on.

dis-dain (dis dān´) v. To treat contemptuously; to look on with scorn.

dis-ease (di zēz´) n. A condition of the living animal, plant body, or any parts which impairs normal functioning; a condition of ill health. **diseased** adj.

dis-em-bark (dis´em bärk´) v. To go

or put ashore from a ship; unload.

dis-em-bod-y (dis´em bod´ē) v. To release or free the soul from physical existence.

dis-em-bow-el (dis´em bou´el) v. To remove the bowels or entrails; to eviscerate. **disembowelment** n.

dis-en-chant (dis´en chant´) v. To free from false beliefs or enchantment. **disenchanting** adj.

dis-en-cum-ber (dis´en kum´bér) v. To relieve of hardships; to free from encumbrance; unburden.

dis-en-gage (dis´en gäj´) v. To free from something that holds or otherwise engages; to set free. **-ment** n.

dis-en-tan-gle (dis´en tang´gl) v. To relieve of entanglement, confusion, etc; unravel. **disentanglement** n.

dis-e-qui-lib-ri-um (dis ē̄ kwi lib´rē um) n. The lack of balance.

dis-es-tab-lish (dis´e stab´lish) v. To deprive of the privileges of an establishment; bring about the end.

dis-es-teem (dis´e stēm´) v. To regard with little esteem. n. Lack of esteem.

dis-fa-vor (dis fā´vér) n. Disapproval; the state of being disliked.

dis-fig-ure (dis fig´ūr) v. To mar, deface, or deform the appearance of something or someone. **disfigurement** n.

dis-grace (dis grās´) n. The state of having lost grace, favor, respect, or honor; something that disgraces.

dis-grun-tle (dis grun´tl) v. To make dissatisfied or discontented.

dis-gust (dis gust´) v. To affect with nausea, repugnance, or aversion; to cause one to become impatient or lose attention. n. A marked aversion to something distasteful; repugnance.

dis-ha-bille (dis´a bēl´) n. The state of being carelessly dressed; undress.

dis-har-mo-ny (dis här´mo nē) n. Lack of harmony or agreement; discord.

di-shev-el (di shev´el) v. To mess up or disarrange; to throw into disorder or disarray.

dis-hon-est (dis on´ist) adj. Lack of honesty; arising from or showing fraud or falseness. **dishonesty** n.

dis-hon-or (dis on´ér) n. The deprivation of honor; disgrace; the state of one who has lost honor; a cause of disgrace; failure to pay a financial obligation. **dishonor** v. To bring disgrace on something or someone; to fail to pay.

dis-il-lu-sion (dis´i lö´zhan) v. To deprive of illusion; to disenchant.

dis-in-cline (dis´in klin´) v. To make unwilling; to cause to be not interested.

dis-in-fect (dis´in fekt´) v. To cleanse and make free from infection, especially by destroying harmful microorganisms; to sterilize. **disinfection** n.

dis-in-gen-u-ous (dis´in jen´ū us) adj. Lacking frankness, sincerity, or simplicity; crafty; not straightforward.

dis-in-her-it (dis´in her´it) v. To deliberately deprive of inheritance; to depose of previously held privileges.

dis-in-te-grate (dis in´te grāt´) v. To break or reduce into separate elements, parts, or small particles; to destroy the unity or integrity of; to explode; to undergo a change in structure, as an atomic nucleus. **disintegration** n. **disintegrator** n.

dis-in=ter (dis´in tèr) v. To exhume or dig up something buried; to bring to light, disclose, uncover, or expose.

dis-in-ter-est-ed (dis in´tèr ist ed) adj. The state of being unbiased, impartial, unselfish, or not interested; free from selfish motive or interest. **disinterest** n. **disinterestedly** adv.

dis-join (dis join´) v. To end the joining of; to become detached; to disconnect.

dis-junct (dis jungkt´) adj. Disjoined; separated; discontinuous.

disk or **disc** (disk) n. A thin, flat, circular object. In computer science, a round, flat plate coated with a magnetic substance on which data for a computer is stored; a fairly flat, circular, metal object used to break up soil; the implement employing such tools.

disk crash n. In computer science, the destruction of a disk and the data it holds as a result of the read/write head coming in contact with the surface of the disk; any disk failure, sometimes recoverable.

disk drive n. Computer hardware on which files are stored; **hard disk** is storage within the computer and floppy disk is any storage medium external to the computer.

diskette n. In computer science, a floppy or removable disk.

disk formatting n. In computer science, a series of reference points recorded on a disk that allow orderly storage and retrieval of data.

disk fragmentation n. In computer science, a condition that occurs after many reads and writes to a disk in that data for a single file is scattered throughout the disk rather than being stored in contiguous sectors.

disk operating system n. In computer science, the software which controls the computer operations, disk drives and disk accessing; abbreviated as DOS.

disk sector n. In computer science, a section of a disk track.

disk tracks n. In computer science, concentric circles of a disk or a diskette where data is stored.

dis-like (dis līk´) v. To regard with

aversion or disapproval. *n.* Distaste.

dis-lo-cate (dis'lō kāt') *v.* To put out of place or proper position. *Medical* To displace a bone from a socket or joint.

dis-lodge (dis loj') *v.* To remove or drive out from a dwelling or position; to force out of a settled position.

dis-loy-al (dis loi'al) *adj.* Not loyal; untrue to personal obligations or duty. **disloyally** *adv.* **disloyalty** *n.*

dis-mal (diz'mal) *adj.* Causing gloom or depression; depressing; lacking in interest or merit. **dismalness** *n.*

dis-may (dis mā') *v.* To deprive or be deprived of courage or resolution through the pressure of sudden fear or anxiety. **dismay** *n.* **dismayingly** *adv.*

dis-mem-ber (dis mem'bèr) *v.* To cut, pull off or disjoin the limbs, members, or parts of. **dismemberment** *n.*

dis-miss (dis mis') *v.* To discharge or allow to leave; to remove from position or service as an employee; to bar from attention or serious consideration; in law, to disallow or reject any further judicial consideration on a claim or action. **dismissal** *n.* **dismissive** *adj.*

dis-o-bey (dis'o bā') *v.* To refuse or fail to obey; to be rebellious. **disobedient** *adj.* **disobediently** *adv.*

dis-or-gan-ize (dis or'ga nīz') *v.* To destroy or break up the organization, unity, or structure of.

dis-o-ri-ent (dis ōr'ē ent) *v.* To cause to lose one's bearings.

dis-own (dis ōn') *v.* To refuse to acknowledge or claim as one's own.

dis-par-age *v.* To bring reproach or discredit upon; lower the estimation of.

dis-pa-rate (dis'pèr it) *adj.* Altogether dissimilar; unequal. **disparately** *adv.*

dis-par-i-ty (di spar'i tē) *n.* Inequality; difference in condition or excellence.

dis-pas-sion-ate (dis pash'o nit) *adj.* Free from bias or passion; impartial.

dis-pel (di spel') *v.* To drive off or away.

dis-pen-sa-ble (di spen'sa bl) *adj.* Capable of being dispensed; not essential.

dis-pen-sa-ry (di spen'sa rē) *n.* A place where medicine is dispensed.

dis-pense (di spens') *v.* To give out; to distribute; to administer; to let go or exempt. **dispense with** To get rid of; to forgo. **dispensation** *n.* **-er** *n.*

dis-place (dis plās) *v.* To change the position of; to take the place of; to discharge from an office; to cause a physical displacement. **-ment** *n.*

dis-play (di splā') *v.* To put forth or spread; to put in view; to show off. **display** *n.* The content of a display. In *computer science*, a device which gives information in a visual form such as a computer screen or a cathode-ray

tube (CRT).

dis-please (dis plēz') *v.* To cause the disapproval or annoyance of; to cause displeasure. **displeasure** *n.*

dis-pose (di spōz') *v.* To put in place; to finally settle or come to terms. **dispose of** To get rid of; to attend to or settle; to transfer or part with, as by selling. **disposal** *n.* **disposable** *adj.*

dis-po-si-tion (dis'po zish'an) *n.* Prevailing mood, temper or emotion; final arrangements.

dis-pos-sess (dis'po zes') *v.* To deprive of possession or ownership of land, property, or other possessions.

dis-prove (dis prōv') *v.* To prove to be false or erroneous.. **disprovable** *adj.*

dis-put-a-ble (di spū'ta bl) *adj.* Capable of being disputed. **disputably** *adv.*

dis-pu-ta-tion (dis'pū tā'shan) *n.* The act of disputing; a debate.

dis-pute (di spūt') *v.* To debate or argue; to question the validity of; to strive against or to resist. **dispute** *n.* A verbal controversy; a quarrel. **disputant** *n.*

dis-qual-i-fy (dis kwol'i fī') *v.* To deprive of the required properties or conditions; to deprive of a power or privilege; to make ineligible for a prize or further competition. **disqualification** *n.*

dis-qui-si-tion (dis'kwi zish'on) *n.* A formal inquiry into or discussion of a subject.

dis-re-gard (dis'ri gärd') *v.* To ignore; to neglect; to pay no attention to; to treat without proper attention. **disregard** *n.* **disregardful** *adj.*

dis-re-la-tion (dis'ri lā'shan) *n.* The lack of a fitting or suitable connection.

dis-re-pair (dis'ri pâr') *n.* The state of being in need of repair.

dis-re-pute (dis'ri pūt') *n.* A state of being held in low esteem; loss of a good reputation; disgrace. **-able** *adj.*

dis-re-spect (dis'ri spekt') *n.* Lack of respect or reverence. **disrespect** *v.*

dis-re-spect-ful *adj.* Displaying a lack of respect. **disrespectfully** *adv.*

dis-robe (dis rōb') *v.* To undress.

dis-rupt (dis rupt') *v.* To throw into disorder or confusion; upset; to cause to break down. **disrupter, disruption** *n.* **disruptive** *adj.*

dis-sat-is-fac-tion (dis'sat is fak'shan) *n.* The feeling of discontent; a lack of satisfaction.

dis-sect (di sekt') *v.* To cut into pieces; to expose the parts of something, such as an animal, for examination; to analyze in detail. **dissection** *n.*

dis-sem-ble (di sem'bl) *v.* To conceal or hide the actual nature of; to put on a false appearance; to conceal facts, intentions or motives. **dissembler** *n.*

dis-sem-i-nate (di sem'i nāt') *v.* To scatter or spread, as if by sowing, over a wide area. **dissemination** *n.* **disseminator** *n.*

dis-sem-i-nule (di sem´i nūl´) *n.* The regenerative part of a plant.

dis-sen-sion (di sen´shan) *n.* Difference of opinion; discord; strife.

dis-sent (di sent´) *v.* To differ in opinion or thought. **dissent** *n.* Difference of opinion; refusal to go along with an established church.

dis-sep-i-ment (di sep´i ment) *n.* A partition between cells of animals and plants.

dis-ser-ta-tion (dis´ėr tā´shan) *n.* A formal written discourse or treatise, especially one submitted for a doctorate.

dis-serv-ice (dis sėr´vis) *n.* An ill turn; an ill service, injury, or harm.

dis-sev-er (di sev´ėr) *v.* To sever; to divide; to separate. **disseverance** *n.*

dis-si-dent (dis´i dent) *adj.* Strong and open difference with an opinion or group. **dissident** *n.* **dissidence** *n.*

dis-sil-i-ent (di sil´ēent) *adj.* Bursting open with force.

dis-sim-i-lar (di sim´i lėr) *adj.* Different; not the same; unlike. **dissimilarity** *n.*

dis-si-mil-i-tude (dis´si mil´i töd´) *n.* Lack of resemblance; unlikeness.

dis-sim-u-late (di sim´ū lāt´) *v.* To conceal under a false appearance; to dissemble.

dis-si-pate (dis´i pāt´) *v.* To disperse or drive away; to squander or waste; to separate into parts and scatter or vanish; to become dispersed; to lose irreversibly. **dissipation** *n.*

dis-so-ci-ate (di sō´shē āt´) *v.* To break from the association with another person or organization.

dis-sol-u-ble (di sol´ū bl) *adj.* Capable of being dissolved.

dis-so-lute (dis´o löt´) *adj.* Loose in morals; lacking moral restraint. **dissolutely** *adv.* **dissoluteness** *n.*

dis-so-lu-tion (dis´o lö´shan) *n.* The act or process of changing from a solid to a fluid form; termination of a business; the separation of body and soul; death.

dis-solve (di zolv´) *v.* To pass into solution, such as dissolving sugar in water; to overcome, as by emotion; to fade away; to become decomposed; to terminate. **dissolvable** *adj.*

dis-so-nance (dis´o nans) *n.* Lack of agreement; a conflict. *Music* A harsh or disagreeable combination of sounds; discord. **dissonant** *adj.*

dis-tal (dis´tal) *n.* Relatively remote from the point of attachment or origin; farthest from the center. **distally** *adv.*

dis-tance (dis´tans) *n.* Separation in time or space; the degree of separation between two points; the space that

separates any two specified points in time; the quality or state of being distant; aloofness. **distance** *v.* To put space between; to keep at a distance.

dis-tant (dis´tant) *adj.* Apart or separated by a specified amount of time or space; coming from, going to, or located at a distance; remotely related. **distantly,**

dis-tend (di stend´) *v.* To expand from internal pressure; to swell. **distensible** *adj.* **distention** *n.*

dis-tich (dis´tik) *n.* A couplet; a few lines of poetic verse that make sense alone.

dis-til-la-tion (dis´til lā´shan) *n.* The act or process of heating a liquid or other substance until it sends off a gas or vapor and then cooling the gas of vapor until it returns to a liquid or solid form, thus separating impurities.

dis-tinct (di stingkt´) *adj.* Distinguished from all others; separated or distinguished by some feature; not the same in number or kind; different; clearly seen; unquestionable; one of a kind.

dis-tin-guish (di sting´gwish) *v.* To recognize as being different; to discriminate; to make something different or noticeable. **distinguishable** *adj.* **distinguished** *adj.*

dis-tort (di stort´) *v.* To twist or bend out of shape; to twist the true meaning of; to give a misleading account of. *Slang* Blow out of shape. **-ion** *n.*

dis-tract (di strakt´) *v.* To draw or divert one's attention away from something; to cause one to feel conflicting emotions. **distract** *n.*

dis-trac-tion (di strak´shan) *n.* The act of distracting; that which distracts.

dis-trait (di strā´) *adj.* Absent-minded.

dis-traught (di strot´) *adj.* Deeply agitated with doubt or anxiety; crazed.

dis-tress (di stres´) *v.* To cause suffering of mind or body. **distress** *n.* Pain or suffering; severe physical or mental strain; a very painful situation.

dis-trib-ute (di strib´ūt) *v.* To divide among many; to deliver or give out; to classify. **distribution** *n.*

dis-trib-u-tor (di strib´ūt ėr) *n.* One who distributes, as a wholesaler; a device that directs electrical current to spark plugs of an engine.

dis-trict (dis´trikt) *n.* An administrative or political section of a territory; a distinctive area. **district** *v.*

district attorney *n.* The public prosecuting officer of a judicial district.

District of Columbia *n.* The capital of the United States of America; the only part of the continental United States which is not a state, is not part of a state, and does not have a voting congress person in the House of Representatives or an elected senator.

dis-trust (dis trust´) *n.* Suspicion; doubt. **distrust** *v.* To doubt; to suspect; to question someone or thing. **distrustful** *adj.* **distrustfully** *adv.*

dis-turb (di stěrb´) *v.* To destroy the tranquillity or composure of; to unsettle mentally or emotionally; to interrupt or interfere with; to bother. **-er** *n.*

dis-un-ion (dis ūn´yon) *n.* The termination of a union; separation.

dis-u-nite (dis´ū nīt´) *v.* To divide or separate.

dis-u-ni-ty (dis´ū nit´ē) *n.* Discord; lack of unity.

dis-use (dis ūs´) *n.* The state of not using; out of use.

dis-u-til-i-ty (dis´ū til´i tē) *n.* The state of causing inconvenience or fatigue; harm; counterproductive.

di-syl-la-ble (dī´sil a bl) *n.* A word having two syllables.

dith-er (dith´ěr) *n.* A state of nervousness or indecision; commotion.

dit-to (dit´ō) *n., pl.* **dittos** An exact copy; the same as stated before. **ditto mark** The pair of marks (") used to substitute for the word *ditto*. **ditto** *adv.*

dit-ty (dit´ē) *n.* A short, simple song.

ditty bag *n.* A small bag used by sailors to hold small articles, such as thread, buttons, and other small personal effects.

di-u-ret-ic (dī´ū ret´ik) *adj.* Tending to cause an increase in the flow of urine. **diuretic** *n.* A drug given to increase the amount of urine produced.

di-ur-nal (dīer´nal) *adj.* Having a daily cycle or recurring every day; of, relating to, or occurring in the daytime; opening in the daytime and closing at night.

di-va (dē´vä) *n., pl.* **divas** *or* **dive** A prima donna; a female opera star.

di-van (di van´) *n.* A long, backless and armless sofa or couch.

di-var-i-cate (dī var´i kat) *v.* To spread apart; branch off.

di-verge (di věrj´) *v.* To move or extend in different directions from a common point; to differ in opinion or manner. **divergence** *n.* **divergent** *adj.*

di-vers (dī´věrz) *adj.* Various; several.

di-verse (dī´vers´) *adj.* Different; unlike in characteristics; having various forms or qualities. **diversely** *adv.*

di-ver-si-fy (di ver´si fī´) *v.* To give variety to something; to engage in varied operations; to distribute over a wide range of types or classes. .

di-ver-sion (di ver´zhan) *n.* The act of diverting from a course, activity or use; something that diverts or amuses. **diversionary** *adj.*

di-ver-sion-ist *n.* A person characterized by political deviation; one engaged in diversionary activities.

di-ver-si-ty (di ver´si tē) *n., pl.* **diversities** A difference; variety; unlikeness.

di-vert (di vert´) *v.* To turn from a set course; to give pleasure by distracting the attention from something that is burdensome or oppressive. **diverting** *adj.* **divertingly** *adv.*

di-vest (di vest´) *v.* To undress or strip, especially of clothing or equipment; to deprive or dispossess of property, authority, or title; to take away from a person. **divestment** *n.*

di-vide (di vīd´) *v.* To separate into parts, areas, or groups; to separate into pieces or portions and give out in shares; to cause to be apart; in mathematics, to perform mathematical division on a number. **divide** *n.* An act of dividing; a dividing ridge between drainage areas. **dividable** *adj.*

div-i-dend (div´i dend´) *n.* An individual share of something distributed; a bonus; a number to be divided; a sum or fund to be divided and distributed.

div-i-na-tion (div´i nā´shan) *n.* The act or practice of foretelling future events, or discovering obscure things.

di-vine (di vīn´) *adj.* Of, relating to, preceding from, or pertaining to God. *Informal* Extremely pleasing. **divine** *n.* A clergyman or theologian. **divine** *v.* To foretell. **divinely** *adv.*

di-vi-sion (di vizh´on) *n.* Separation; something which divides, separates, or marks off; the act, process, or instance of separating or keeping apart, the condition or an instance of being divided in opinion; in mathematics, the process of discovering how many times one quantity is contained in another. *Military* A self-sufficient tactical unit capable of independent action.

di-vi-sive (di vī´siv) *adj.* Tending to create dissension or disunity. **divisiveness** *n.*

di-vi-sor (di vī´zěr) *n.* In mathematics, the number by which a dividend is to be divided.

di-vorce (di vōrs´) *n.* The legal dissolution of a marriage; the complete separation of things. **divorce** *v.* **divorce** *n.* Divorced man. **divorcee** *n.* Divorced woman.

di-vulge (di vulj´) *v.* To reveal or make known; to disclose; to reveal a secret.

di-vul-sion (di vul´shan) *n.* The act of pulling apart; violent separation.

di-zy-got-ic (dī´zī got´ik) *adj.* Describing fraternal twins.

do (dö) *v.* To bring to pass; to bring about; to perform or execute; to put forth; to exert; to bring to an end. **do** *n.* A festive get-together; a command to do something. *Mus.* The first tone of a scale. **do away with** To destroy; to kill. **do in** To tire completely; to kill. **do up** To adorn or dress lavishly; to wrap and tie.

do-cent (dō´sent) *n.* A teacher at a college or university; a guide or lecturer in a museum.

doc-ile (dos´il) *adj.* Easily led, taught, or managed. **docility** *n.*

dock-et (dok´it) *n.* A brief written summary of a document; an agenda; an identifying statement about a document placed on its cover.

doc-tor (dok´tér) *n.* A person trained and licensed to practice medicine, such as a physician, surgeon, veterinarian, or dentist; a person holding the highest degree offered by a university. **doctor** *v.* To restore to good condition; to practice medicine; to administer medical treatment; to tamper with; to alter for a desired end and self gain. **doctoral** *adj.*

doc-tor-ate (dok´tér it) *n.* The degree, status, or title of a doctor.

doc-tri-naire (dok´tri när´) *n.* One who tries to put something into effect with little regard to practical difficulties.

doc-trine (dok´trin) *n.* Something taught as a body of principles; a statement of fundamental government policy, esp. in international relations.

doc-u-ment (dok´ū ment) *n.* An official paper utilized as the basis, proof, or support of something. **document** *v.* To furnish documentary evidence of; to prove with, support by, or provide by documents.

doc-u-men-ta-ry (dok´ū men´ta rē) *adj.* Relating to or based on documents; an artistic way of presenting facts.

doc-u-men-ta-tion (dok´ū men tā´shan) *n.* The act or use of documentary evidence. In *computer science,* information or instructions relating to a program, procedure, etc.

document retrieval In *computer science,* a system for identifying and retrieving data stored in the computer.

dod-der (dod´ér) *v.* To tremble, shake, or totter from weakness or age. **dodder** *n.* *Bot.* A parasitic, twining vine.

do-dec-a-gon (dō dek´agon) *n.* A polygon with twelve sides and twelve angles.

does-n't (duz´ent) *contr.* Does not.

dog-ma (dog´ma) *n.* A rigidly held doctrine proclaimed to be true by a religious group; a principle or idea considered to be the absolute truth.

dog-mat-ic (dog mat´ik) *adj.* Marked by an authoritative assertion of unproved or unprovable principles.

dol-drums (dōl´drumz) *n.* A period of listlessness or despondency. *Naut.* The ocean region near the equator where

there is very little wind.

dole (dōl) *n.* The distribution of food, money, or clothing to the needy; a grant of government funds to the unemployed; something portioned out and distributed bit by bit. **dole** *v.*

dole-ful (dōl´ful) *adj.* Filled with grief or sadness. **dolefully** *adv.*

dol-er-ite (dol´e rīt´) *n.* An igneous rock, similar to basalt, whose composition cannot be determined without a microscope.

dol-i-cho-ce-phal-ic (dol´i kō se fal´ik) *adj.* Having a long head; with the width of the skull small in proportion to the length from back to front.

dol-lar (dol´ér) *n.* A coin, note, or token representing 100 cents; the standard monetary unit of the United States.

dol-lop (dol´op) *n.* A lump or blob of a semi-liquid substance; an indefinite amount or form.

dol-men (dōl´man) *n.* A prehistoric monument made up of a huge stone set on upright stones.

do-lor-ous (dol´ér us) *adj.* Marked by grief or pain; sad; mournful. **dolorously** *adv.* **dolorousness** *n.*

dolt (dōlt) *n.* A stupid person.

do-main (dō mān´) *n.* A territory under one government; a field of activity or interest.

dome (dōm) *n.* A roof resembling a hemisphere; something suggesting a dome.

do-mes-tic (do mes´tik) *adj.* Of or relating to the home, household or family life; interested in household affairs and home life; tame or domesticated; of or relating to policies of one's country; originated in a particular country. **domestic** *n.* A household servant. **domestically** *adv.*

dom-i-cile (dom´i sīl´) *n.* A dwelling place, house, or home; residence. **domicile** *v.* **domiciliary** *adj.*

dom-i-nant (dom´i nant) *adj.* Having the most control or influence; most over-whelming; in genetics, producing a typical effect even when paired with an unlike gene for the same characteristic. **dominance** *n.* **dominantly** *adv.*

do-min-ion (do min´yan) *n.* The power of supreme authority; controlling.

domino theory *n.* The theory that if a certain event occurs, a series of similar events will follow.

do-na-tion (dō nā´shan) *n.* The act of giving or bestowing a gift especially to needy or to charity. **donate** *v.*

done (dun) *adj.* Completely finished or through; doomed to failure, defeat, or death; cooked adequately.

do-nee (dō nē´) *n.* A recipient of a gift.

done for *adj.* Mortally stricken; doomed; left with no opportunity for recovery;

ruined.

don't (dōnt) *contr.* Do not.

dood-le (dōd*e*l) *v.* To scribble, design, or sketch aimlessly, especially when preoccupied. **doodle** *n.*

doom (dōm) *n.* A pronounced judgment, particularly an official condemnation to a severe penalty or death; an unhappy destiny. **doom** *v.* To condemn; to make certain the destruction of.

dor-mant (dor´ma*nt*) *adj.* Asleep; in a state of inactivity or rest.

dor-mi-to-ry (dor´mi tōr´ē) *n.* A large room that contains a number of beds, as at a college.

dor-nick (dor´nik) *n.* A small stone, or a chunk of rock.

dor-sal (dor´sal) *adj.* Of, relating to, or situated on or near the back.

dor-si-ven-tral (dor´si ven˝tral) *adj.* Having distinct differences in the dorsal and ventral surfaces.

dor-sum (dor´sum) *n.* The back; the whole surface of an animal's back.

do-ry (dōr´ē) *n., pl.* **dories** A small flat-bottomed boat with high, flaring sides and a sharp bow.

DOS *abbr. & n.* Disk operating system; a program that controls all of the basic operations of the computer.

dos-age (dō´sij) *n.* The administration of medicine in a measured dose; the amount administered.

dose (dōs) *n.* The measured quantity of a therapeutic agent to be taken at one time or at stated intervals. *Med.* The prescribed amount of radiation to which a certain part of the body is exposed.

dos-si-er (dos´ē ā´) *n.* A complete file of documents or papers giving detailed information about a person or affair.

dot (dot) *n.* A small round spot; a mark made by or as if by a writing implement; a small round mark used in punctuation, a precise moment in time, a short click or buzz forming a letter or part of a letter in the Morse code.

dot-age (dō´tij) *n.* Feebleness or imbecility, especially in old age.

dot matrix In computer science, printing in which characters are formed by numerous dots arranged according to the pattern established for the character.

dote (dōt) *v.* To show excessive affection or fondness; to exhibit mental decline, especially as a result of senility. **doter** *n.* **doting** *adj.* **dotingly** *adv.*

dou-ble (dub´l) *adj.* Twice as much; composed of two like parts; designed for two. *Bot.* Having more than the usual number of petals. **double** *n.* An actor who takes the place of another for scenes calling for special skill; in baseball, a two-base hit. **double** *v.* In baseball, to make a double; to make or become twice as great; to fold in

two; to turn and go back; to serve an additional purpose. **doubly** *adv.*

double click In *computer science,* pressing and releasing a button of a mouse twice in succession, used to activate a selection in some programs.

double density disk In *computer science,* a diskette on which data is packed in order to double its capacity.

double-sided disk In *computer science,* a diskette on which data is stored on both sides.

doubt (dout) *v.* To be uncertain or mistrustful about something; to distrust. **doubt** *n.* **doubter** *n.* **doubtful** *adj.*

dour (der) *adj.* Stern and forbidding; morose and ill-tempered.

douse (dous) *v.* To plunge into liquid; to throw water on; to drench; to extinguish. **douser** *n.*

dove (duv) *n.* Any of numerous pigeons; a gentle, innocent person. **dovish** *adj.*

dow-el (dou´el) *n.* A round wooden pin which fits tightly into an adjacent hole to fasten together the two pieces.

download In *computer science,* the transfer or data to another computer or peripheral device.

downer *n.* A depressant or sedative drug; a barbiturate; something depressing.

dow-ry (dou´rē) *n.* The money, goods, or estate which a woman brings to her husband in marriage; a gift.

dowse (douz) *v.* To search for with a divining rod to find underground water or minerals. **dowser** *n.*

dpi *abbr. & n.* In *computer science,* dots per inch; a measure of the quality of image from scanner or printer' the more dots per inch, the finer the image appears to the eye.

drab (drab) *adj.* Of a light, dull brown or olive brown color; commonplace or dull. **drabness** *n.*

draft (draft) *n.* A current of air, a sketch or plan of something to be made; a note for the transfer of money; the depth of water a ship draws with a certain load. *Milit.* A mandatory selection of men for service. **draft** *v.* To draw a tentative plan or sketch. **draft** *adj.* The drawing of a liquid from a keg or tap.

drag (drag) *v.* To pull along or haul by force; to move with painful or undue slowness; to bring by force; to proceed slowly; to lag behind; to trail on the ground. **drag** *n.* Something which retards motion or action; a tool used under water to detect or collect objects; something which is boring or dull. *Slang* Someone or something that is boring or bothersome; a street; a race. In computer science, to press and hold the mouse button down while moving the cursor, thereby moving the image under the cursor. **dragger** *n.*

drag-on-et (drag'e net') *n.* A little dragon; any small, brightly colored marine fish found in shallow tropical waters.

drain (drān) *n.* To draw off liquid; to use up; to exhaust physically or emotionally; to flow off gradually. **drain** *n.* A means, such as a trench or channel, by which liquid matter is drained; something which causes depletion. **drainer** *n.*

drainage *n.* A system, process or act of draining.

drainpipe *n.* A pipe for draining.

drake (drāk) *n.* A male duck.

DRAM *abbr. & n.* In *computer science,* Dynamic Random Access Memory; memory that must be constantly refreshed to be retained and that is erased when the power is off.

dram (dram) *n.* A small drink; a small portion; a measurement equaling approximately .06 ounces.

dra-ma (drä'me) *n.* A composition in prose or verse, especially one to be presented on the stage, recounting a serious story; a play. **dramatic** *adj.*

dra-mat-ics (dre mat'iks) *n.* Amateur theatrical productions; the study of theatrical arts; excessive emotional behavior.

dram-a-tist (dram'a tist) *n.* Playwright.

drank *v.* Past tense of drink.

drape (drāp) *v.* To cover or adorn with something; to arrange or hang in loose folds. **drape** *n.* The manner in which a cloth hangs or falls; curtain or drapery.

dras-tic (dras'tik) *adj.* Being extremely harsh or severe. **drastically** *adv.*

draught (draft) *n. v.* A variation of draft.

draughts (drafts) *n.* British term for the game of checkers.

draw-er (dror) *n.* One that draws pictures; a sliding box or receptacle in furniture. **drawers** *n.* An article of clothing for the lower body.

drawl (draul) *v.* To speak slowly with prolonged vowels.

drawn *adj.* Haggard.

dray (drā) *n.* A low, heavy cart without sides, used for hauling.

dread (dred) *v.* To fear greatly; to anticipate with alarm, anxiety, or reluctance. **dread** *n.* A great fear.

dread-ful (dred'ful) *adj.* Inspiring dread; very distasteful or shocking; awful. **dreadfully** *adv.* **dreadfulness** *n.*

dream (drēm) *n.* A series of thought images, or emotions which occur during the rapid eye movement or REM state of sleep; an experience in waking life that has the characteristics of a dream; a daydream; something notable for its beauty or enjoyable quality; something that is strongly desired; something that fully satisfies a desire. **dreamy** *adj.* **dreamily** *adv.*

drea-ry (drēr'ē) *adj.* Bleak and gloomy; dull. **drearily** *adv.* **dreariness** *n.*

dredge (drej) *n.* An apparatus used to remove sand or mud from the bottom of a body of water; a boat or barge equipped with a dredge. **dredge** *v.* To dig, gather, or deepen with a dredging machine; to use a dredge; in cooking, to coat with a powdered substance, especially flour or cornmeal.

dregs (dregz) *n.* The sediment of a liquid; the least desirable part.

drench (drench) *v.* To wet thoroughly; to throw water on. **drencher** *n.*

dress (dres) *n.* An outer garment for women and girls; covering or appearance appropriate to a particular time. **dress** *v.* To set straight; to put clothes on; to arrange in a straight line at proper intervals; to provide with clothing; to kill and prepare for market; to put on or wear formal clothes.

dressmaker *n.* A person who makes or alters women's clothing.

dress rehearsal *n.* A rehearsal, complete with costumes and stage props.

drew *v.* Past tense of draw.

drib-ble (drib'l) *v.* To drip; to slobber or drool; to bounce a ball repeatedly; to move in short bounces. **dribbler** *n.*

dried—up (drīd'up') *adj.* Lacking moisture; wrinkled and shriveled.

drink (dringk) *v.* To take liquid into the mouth and swallow; to take in or suck up; to receive into one's consciousness; to partake of alcoholic beverages. **drink** *n.* A liquid suitable for swallowing; alcoholic beverages; a sizable body of water. **drinkable** *adj.* **drinker** *n.*

drip (drip) *v.* To fall in drops. **drip** *n.* Liquid or moisture that falls in drops; the sound made by falling drops. *Slang* A dull or unattractive person.

drive designation In *computer science,* the letter assigned to a drive in order to identify it for sourcing.

driv-el (driv'el) *v.* To slobber; to talk nonsensically. **drivel** *n.*

driver In *computer science,* a program or routine that translates and conveys messages between a computer and a peripheral.

driz-zle (driz'el) *n.* A fine, quiet, gentle rain. **drizzle** *v.*

droit (droit) *n.* A legal right or claim.

droll (drōl) *adj.* Whimsically comical.

drone (drōn) *n.* A male bee, especially a honey bee, which has no sting, performs no work, and produces no honey; a person who depends on others for his survival.

drool (drōl) *v.* To let saliva dribble from the mouth. *Slang* To make an exaggerated expression of desire.

droop (drŏp) *v.* To hang or bend downward; to become depressed. **droop** *n.* **droopingly** *adv.* **droopy** *adj.*

drop (drop) *n.* A tiny, pear-shaped or rounded mass of liquid; a small quantity of a substance; the smallest unit of liquid measure; the act of falling; a swift decline; the vertical distance from a higher to a lower level; a delivery of something by parachute. **drop** *v.* To fall in drops; to descend from one area or level to another; to fall into a state of collapse or death; to pass into a given state or condition; to end or terminate an association or relationship with; to deposit at a specified place. **drop behind** To fall behind. **drop by** To pay a brief visit. **drop out** To quit school without graduating; to withdraw from society.

drop-sy (drop′sē) *n. Med.* A diseased condition in which large amounts of fluid collect in the body tissues and cavities.

dross (dros) *n.* An impurity which forms on the surface of molten metal; inferior, trivial, or worthless matter.

drought (drowt) *n.* A prolonged period of dryness that affects crops; a chronic shortage of something.

drove (drōv) *n.* A herd being driven in a body; a crowd in motion. **drove** *v.* Past tense of drive.

drown (drown) *v.* To kill or die by suffocating in a liquid; to overflow; to cause not to be heard by making a loud noise; to drive out.

drowse (drouz) *v.* To doze. **drowse** *n.*

drows-y (drou′zē) *adj.* Sleepy; tending to induce sleep. **drowsiness** *n.*

drub (drub) *v.* To hit with a stick; to abuse with words; to defeat decisively.

drudge (druj) *n.* A person who does tiresome or menial tasks. **drudgeries,** **drudgery** *n.* **drudge** *v.*

drug (drug) *n.* A substance used in the treatment of disease or illness; a narcotic. **drug** *v.* To take drugs for narcotic effect; to mix or dose with drugs. **drugged** *adj.*

drug-get (drug′it) *n.* A durable cloth of wool and other fibers used chiefly as a floor covering.

drug-gist (drug′ist) *n.* A pharmacist; the owner or operator of a drugstore.

drunk (drungk) *adj.* Intoxicated with alcohol which impairs the physical and mental faculties of a person; overwhelmed by strong feeling or emotion. **drunk** *n.* A drunkard.

drunk-ard (drungk′kėrd) *adj.* A person who is often intoxicated by liquor.

drunk-om-e-ter (drung kom′i tėr) *n.* An instrument for measuring the alcoholic content in the bloodstream by testing the breath.

drupe (drŏp) *n.* A fruit, as the peach, usually having one large pit or seed.

du-al (dō′al) *adj.* Made up or composed of two parts; having a double purpose.

dub (dub) *v.* To confer knighthood upon; to nickname; to give a new sound track to; to add to a film, radio, or television production; to transfer sound already recorded. **dub** *n.* **dubber** *n.*

du-bi-ous (dō′bē us) *adj.* Causing doubt; unsettled in judgment; reluctant to agree; questionable as to quality or validity; verging on impropriety. **dubiousness** *n.* **dubiously** *adv.*

du-cal (dō′kal) *adj.* Pertaining to a duke or dukedom.

duch-ess (duch′is) *n.* The wife or widow of a duke; a female holding a ducal title in her own right.

duct (dukt) *n.* A bodily tube or canal, especially one carrying a secretion; a tubular passage through which something flows.

duc-tile (duk′til) *adj.* Capable of being drawn into a fine strand or wire; easily influenced or persuaded.

dud (dud) *n. Informal* A bomb, shell, or explosive round which fails to detonate; something which turns out to be a failure. **duds** *Slang* Clothing; personal belongings.

dude (dōd) *n. Informal* A city person vacationing on a ranch; a man who is a fancy dresser. *Slang* A fellow.

dudg-eon (duj′on) *n.* A sullen, displeased, or indignant mood.

due (dō) *adj.* Owed; payable; owed or owing as a natural or moral right; scheduled or expected to occur. **due** *n.* Something that is deserved or owed. **dues** A fee or charge for membership.

du-el (dō′el) *n.* A premeditated combat between two people, usually fought to resolve a point of honor; a struggle which resembles a duel. **duelist** *n.*

du-et (dō et′) *n.* A musical composition for two performers or musical instruments.

duff (duf) *v.* To manipulate so as to make anything pass for something new or different; misrepresent.

duf-fel (duf′el) *n.* A coarse woolen material with a thick nap.

duffer *n.* An incompetent or clumsy person; something counterfeit or worthless.

dug (dug) *n.* The nipple of a female mammal.

duke (dōk) *n.* A noble ranking below a prince and above a marquis. **dukes** *pl. Slang* The fists. **dukedom** *n.*

dul-cet (dul′sit) *adj.* Melodious; pleasing to the ear; having an agreeable, soothing quality.

dul-ci-mer (dul′si mėr) *n.* A musical stringed instrument played with two small hammers or by plucking.

dun (dun) v. To press a debtor for payment. **dun** n. A brownish gray to dull grayish brown color. **dun** adj.

dunce (duns) n. A slow-witted person.

dune (dūn) n. A ridge or hill of sand that has been blown or drifted by the wind.

dung (dung) n. The excrement of animals; manure.

dun-ga-ree (dun´ga rē´) n. A sturdy, coarse, cotton fabric, especially blue denim; pants or overalls made from this material.

dun-geon (dun´jon) n. A dark, confining, underground prison chamber.

dunk (dungk) v. To dip a piece of food into liquid before eating; to submerge someone in a playful fashion.

du-o (dö´ō) n., pl. **duos** A musical duet; two people in close association.

du-o-de-num (dū´o dē´num) n., pl. **duodena** or **duodenums** The first portion of the small intestine, extending from the lower end of the stomach to the jejunum. **duodenal** adj

du-pli-cate (dö´pli kit) adj. Identical with another; existing in or consisting of two corresponding parts. **duplicate** n. Either of two things which are identical; an exact copy of an original. **duplicate** v. To make an exact copy of. **duplication** n.

du-plic-i-ty (dö plis´i tē) n. The practice of contradictory speech or thoughts with the intent to deceive; double-dealing.

du-ra-ble (der´a bl) adj. Able to continue for a prolonged period of time without deterioration; long-lasting.

du-ra ma-ter (dor´a mā´tér) n. The tough fibrous membrane that covers the brain and spinal cord.

du-ra-tion (de rā´shan) n. The period of time during which something exists or lasts; continuance in time.

du-ress (de res´) n. Constraint by fear or force; in law, coercion illegally applied; forced restraint.

dur-ing (dur´ing) prep. Throughout the time of; within the time of.

du-ty (dö´tē) n. pl. **duties** Something which a person must or ought to do; a moral obligation; a service, action, or task assigned to one, especially in the military; a government tax on imports. **dutiful** adj.

dwell (dwel) v. To live, as an inhabitant; to continue in a given place or condition; to focus one's attention on.

dwin-dle (dwin´dl) v. To waste away; to become steadily less.

dye (dī) v. To fix a color in or to stain materials; to color with or become colored by a dye. **dye** n. A color imparted by a dye; a coloring matter or material.

dy-ing (dī´ing) adj. Coming to the end of life; about to die.

dy-nam-ic (dī nam´ik) adj. Marked by energy and productive activity or change; of or relating to energy, motion, or force. **dynamically** adv.

dy-nam-ics (dī nam´iks) n. The part of physics which deals with force, energy, and motion and the relationship between them.

dy-na-mism (dī´na miz´um) n. A kind of theory that explains the universe in terms of forces. **dynamist** n. **dynamistic** adj.

dy-na-mite (dī´na mīt´) n. An explosive composed of nitroglycerin and an absorbent material, often packaged in stick form. **dynamite** v. To blow up with or as if with dynamite.

dy-na-mo (dī´na mō´) n. A person who is very energetic; a generator.

dy-na-mom-e-ter (dī´no mom´i tér) n. A type of device that is used for the purpose of measuring mechanical force. **dy-namometric** adj.

dy-na-mo-tor (dī´na mō´tér) n. A combined electrical motor and generator.

dy-nap-o-lis (dī nap´ō lis) n. A type of city that has been planned for orderly growth along a traffic artery.

dy-nas-ty (dī´na stē) n., pl. **dynasties** A succession of rulers from the same family; a family or group which maintains great power, wealth, or position for many years. **dynastic** adj.

dys-cra-sia (dis krā´zha) n. A condition of the body that is abnormal.

dys-en-ter-y (dis´en ter´ē) n. An infection of the lower intestinal tract which produces pain, fever, and severe diarrhea. **dysenteric** adj.

dys-func-tion (dis fungk´shan) n. An abnormal functioning; not working proper. **dysfunctional** adj.

dys-gen-e-sis (dis´jen e sis´) n. The defective development of the gonads of one's body such as in Turner's syndrome.

dys-gen-ic (dis´jen ik) adj. Being biologically defective.

dys-lex-i-a (dis lex´ēa) n. An impairment in one's ability to read; unable to read.

dys-men-or-rhea (dis´men or ē´a) n. Abnormal, painful menstruation. **dysmenorrheic, dysmenorrheal** adj.

dys-pep-sia (dis pep´sha) n. Indigestion. **dyspeptic** adj.

dys-pro-si-um (dis prō´sē um) n. A metallic element used in nuclear research, symbolized by Dy.

dys-tro-phy (is´tro fē) n. Atrophy of muscle tissue; any of various neuromuscular disorders, especially muscular dystrophy. **dystrophic** adj.

dz abbr. Dozen.

E, e (ē) The fifth letter of the English alphabet. *Mus.* The third tone in the natural scale of C.

each (ēch) *adj.* Everyone of two or more considered separately. **each** *adv.* To or for each; apiece. **each** *pron.* Each one.

each other *pron.* Each in reciprocal action or relation; one another.

ea-ger (ē'gèr) *adj.* Marked by enthusiastic interest or desire; having a great desire or wanting something very much; earnest. **eagerly** *adv.*

ear (ēr) *n. Anat.* The hearing organ in vertebrates, located on either side of the head; any of various organs capable of detecting vibratory motion; the ability to hear keenly; attention; something that resembles the external ear. **be all ears** Listen closely. **play by ear** Play without reference to written music.

earn (ern) *v.* To receive payment in return for work done or services rendered; to gain as a result of one's efforts. **earner** *n.*

ear-nest (er'nist) *n.* A serious mental state; payment in advance to bind an agreement; a pledge. *adj.* Characterized by an intense and serious state of mind; having serious intent. **earnestly** *adv.*

earth (erth) *n.* The third planet from the sun, on which there is life; the outer layer of the world; ground; soil; dirt.

earth-quake (erth'kwāk) *n.* A trembling or violent shaking of the crust of the earth.

ease (ēz) *n.* A state of being comfortable; freedom from pain, discomfort, or care; freedom from labor or difficulty; an act of easing or a state of being eased. **ease** *v.* To free from pain or discomfort; to lessen the pressure or tension; to make less difficult; to move or pass with freedom. **at ease** Standing silently with the feet apart, as in a military formation.

ea-sel (ē'æel) *n.* A frame used by artists to support a canvas or picture.

eas-i-ly *adv.* Without difficulty.

east (ēst) *n.* The direction opposite of west; the direction in which the sun rises. **eastward** *adv. & adj.*

Easter (ē'stèr) *n.* A Christian festival celebrating the resurrection of Christ, observed the first Sunday after the full moon on or next after March 21st.

ea-sy (ē'zē) *adj.* Capable of being accomplished with little difficulty; free from worry or pain; not hurried or strenuous; something readily obtainable. **easily** *adv.* **easiness** *n.*

eat (ēt) *v.* To chew and swallow food; to erode; to consume with distress or agitation; to take a meal. **eat crow** To accept what one has been fighting

against. **eat one's heart out** To grieve bitterly. **eat one's words** To retract what has been said. **one's** *n.* **eater** *n.*

eave (ēvz) *n.* The overhanging edge of a roof.

EBCDIC *abbr. & n.* In *computer science*, Extended Binary Coded Decimal Interchange Code; a standard code for numeric representation of alphanumeric characters.

ebb (eb) *n.* The return of the tide towards the sea; a time of decline. *v.* To recede, as the tide does; to fall or flow back; to weaken.

eb-bet *n.* A type of green newt.

ebb tide *n.* The tide while at ebb; a period of decline.

eb-o-nite (eb'o nīt') *n.* A type of hard rubber.

eb-o-ny (eb'o nē) *n., pl.* **ebonies** The dark, hard, colored wood from the center of the ebony tree of Asia and Africa. **ebony** *adj.* Resembling ebony; black.

e-bul-lient (i bul'yent) *adj.* Filled with enthusiasm. **ebullience** *n.*

eb-ul-li-tion (eb'u lish'an) *n.* The process of boiling or bubbling; a sudden release of emotion.

ec-cen-tric (ik sen'trik) *adj.* Differing from an established pattern or accepted norm; deviating from a perfect circle; not located at the geometrical center. **eccentric** *n.* An odd or erratic person; a disk or wheel with its axis not situated in the center. **eccentricity** *n.*

ec-chy-mo-sis *n.* The escaping of blood into the surrounding tissues.

ec-cle-si-as-ti-cal (i klē'zē as'tik) *n.* A clergyman; a person officially serving a church. *adj.* Of or relating to a church.

ec-cle-si-ol-o-gy (i klē'zē ol'a jē) *n.* A study of the architecture of a church.

ec-crine *adj.* To be producing a fluid secretion which does not remove cytoplasm for the secreting cell.

eccrine gland *n.* A sweat gland that produces an eccrine secretion.

ec-dy-sis (ek'di sis) *n.* The act of shedding the outer cuticular layer such as occurs in the insects.

e-ce-sis (i sē'sis) *n.* An establishment of animals in a new habitat.

e-chid-na (i kid'na) *n.* A type of toothless spiny-coated nocturnal mammal found in Australia that feeds mainly on ants.

e-chi-no-derm (i kī'no dèrm') *n.* A member of the phylum Echinodermata having a radially symmetrical shape such as the starfish.

ech-o (ek'ō) *n., pl.* **echoes** Repetition of a sound by reflecting sound waves from a surface; the sound produced by such a reflection; a repetition; reflection of transmitted radar signals by an object.

echo *v.* To repeat or be repeated by; to imitate. In *computer science*, in a DOS program, command or information lines that are displayed on the screen.

ec-lamp-si-a (i klamp´sē a) *n.* A form of toxemia marked by convulsions, often happening during pregnancy.

ec-lec-tic (i klek´tik) *adj.* Having components from diverse sources or styles. eclectically *adv.* eclectic *n.*

e-clipse (i klips´) *n.* A total or partial blocking of one celestial body by another. eclipse *v.* To fall into obscurity or decline; to cause an eclipse of; to overshadow.

e-clip-tic (i klip´tik) *n. Astron.* The circle formed by the intersection of the plane of the earth's orbit and the celestial sphere.

ec-logue (ek´log) *n.* A short pastoral poem in the form of a dialogue.

e-clo-sion (i klō´zhan) *n.* The act of hatching from an egg of a larva.

ec-o-cide *n.* The deliberate destruction of the natural environment by pollutants.

e-col-o-gy (i kol´o jē) *n.* The branch of science studying the relationship between living organisms and their environments. ecological, ecologic *adj.* ecologically *adv.* ecologist *n.*

ec-o-nom-ic (ē´ko nom´ik) *adj.* Relating to the development, production, and management of material wealth; relating to the necessities of life.

ec-o-nom-i-cal (ē´ko nom´i kal) *adj.* Not wasteful; frugal; operating with little waste. economically *adv.*

e-con-o-my (i kon´o mē) *n., pl.* economies Careful management of money, materials, and resources; a reduction in expenses; a system or structure for the management of resources and production of goods and services. economy *adj.*

e-co-sphere (ek´ō sfēr´) *n.* The parts of the universe habitable by living beings.

ec-o-tone *n.* A transition area between two adjacent plant communities where organisms of both communities compete for dominance.

ec-ru (ek´rö) *n.* A light yellowish brown, as the color of unbleached linen.

ec-sta-sy (ek´sta sē) *n., pl.* ecstasies The state of intense joy or delight. ecstatic *adj.* ecstatically *adv.*

ec-to-derm (ek´to dērm´) *n.* The outer cellular membrane of a jellyfish.

ec-to-morph (ek´to morf´) *n.* A body structure, characterized by angularity and leanness. ectomorphic *adj.*

ec-to-par-a-site *n.* An external parasite.

ec-top-ic (ek´top ik) *adj.* Occurring in an abnormal place or position.

ec-to-therm *n.* An animal which is classified as cold-blooded.

ec-ze-ma (ek´se ma) *n.* A noncontagious inflammatory skin condition, marked by itching and scaly patches.

e-daph-ic (i daf´ik) *adj.* Pertaining to or relating to the soil. edaphically *adv.*

ed-dy (ed´ē) *n., pl.* eddies A current, as of water, running against the direction of the main current, especially in a circular motion. eddy *v.*

e-e-ma (i dē´ma) *n.* An accumulation of serous fluid in the connective tissue that is abnormal. edematous *adj.*

e-den-tate (ē den´tāt) *n.* Any of the mammals that have few or no teeth, such as the anteater or sloth.

e-den-tu-lous (ē den´che lus) *adj.* Without teeth; toothless..

edge (ej) *n.* The thin, sharp, cutting side of a blade; keenness; sharpness; the border where an object or area begins or ends; an advantage. edge *v.* To furnish with an edge or border; to sharpen; to move gradually. on edge Tense.

e-dict (ē´dikt) *n.* A public decree; an order or command officially proclaimed.

ed-if-i-ca-to-ry *adj.* To be suitable for improvement in mind or morals.

ed-i-fice (ed´i fis) *n.* A massive building or structure.

ed-i-fy (ed´i fī´) *v.* To benefit and enlighten, morally or spiritually. edification *n.*

ed-it (ed´it) *v.* To prepare, alter, and correct anything for presentation, such as a publication, a speech, or a film; to compile for an edition. In *computer science*, to make changes, as additions or deletions, to a file or document.

edit commands *n.* In *computer science*, commands in a program that facilitate the process of editing, such as *move, copy, paste,* etc.

e-di-tion (i dish´an) *n.* The form in which a book is published; the total number of copies printed at one time; one similar to, but altered from, an earlier version.

edit key *n.* In *computer science*, any of the special keyboard keys, such as insert, or delete, used to edit text.

ed-i-tor *n.* A person who edits or prepares literary matter as a profession.

ed-i-to-ri-al (ed´i tōr´ē al) *n.* An article in a newspaper or magazine which expresses the opinion of a publisher or editor. editorial *adj.* Of or relating to an editor or an editor's work; being or resembling an editorial.

ed-u-ca-ble *adj.* Capable of being educated.

ed-u-cate (ej´e kāt´) *v.* To provide with training; to teach; to supervise the mental or moral growth of.

ed-u-ca-tion (ej´e kā´shan) *n.* The

process of educating or of being educated; the knowledge resulting from the process; the field of study of methods of teaching.

e-duce (i dōs´) v. To call forth or bring out; to develop from given facts.

e-dul-co-rate (i dul´ko rāt´) v. To make something pleasant; to remove acid.

eel (ēl) n. A snake-like fish without scales or pelvic fins.

ee-rie or **ee-ry** (ēr´ē) adj. Suggesting the supernatural or strange; weird; frightening. **eerily** adv. **eeriness** n.

ef-face (i fās´) v. To remove or rub out. **effacer** n. **effacement** n.

ef-fect (i fekt´) n. Something produced by a cause; the power to produce a desired result; the reaction something has on an object; a technique which produces an intended impression. **take effect** To become operative.

ef-fec-tive (i fek´tiv) adj. Producing an expected effect or proper result.

ef-fem-i-nate (i fem´i nit) adj. Having woman-like qualities unsuitable to a man. **effeminacy** n. **effeminately** adv.

ef-fen-di (i fend´ē) n. A man who has an education or property.

ef-fer-ent (ef´ėr ent) adj. Physiol. Carrying outward from a central organ or part; conveying nervous impulses to an effector. **efferent** n. **efferently** adv.

ef-fer-vesce (ef´ėr ves´) v. To foam and hiss as gas escapes; to exhibit liveliness or exhilaration. **effervescently** adv. **effervescence** n. **effervescent** adj.

ef-fete (i fēt´) adj. Exhausted of effectiveness or force; worn-out; decadent.

ef-fi-ca-cious (ef´i kā´shus) adj. Producing an intended effect. **-ly** adv.

ef-fi-cien-cy (i fish´en sē) n. The quality or degree of being efficient.

ef-fi-cient (i fish´ent) adj. Adequate in performance with a minimum of waste or effort; productive without waste.

ef-fi-gy (ef´i jē) n., pl. **effigies** A life-size sculpture or painting representing a crude image or dummy of a hated person.

ef-flo-resce (ef´lo res´) v. To become covered by a powdery crust; to bloom.

ef-flo-res-cence (ef´lo res´ens) n. A time of flowering; fullness of development; powdery crust. **efflorescent** adj.

ef-flu-ence (ef´lö ens) n. An act of flowing out; something that flows out or forth. **effluent** n.

ef-flu-vi-um (i flö´vē um) n., pl. **effluvia** or **effluviums** An unpleasant vapor from something. **effluvial** adj.

ef-flux (ef´luks) n. Something passing away or expiring. **effluxion** n.

ef-fort (ef´ėrt) n. Voluntary exertion of physical or mental energy; a difficult exertion; a normally earnest attempt or achievement; something done

through exertion. Phys. A force applied against inertia.

ef-fron-ter-y (i frun´te rē) n., pl. **effronteries** Shameless boldness; impudence.

ef-ful-gent adj. Shining brilliantly; radiant. **effulgence** n. **effulge** v.

ef-fuse (i füz´) v. To give off; to pour out.

ef-fu-sion (i fü´zhan) n. A flow of liquid or gas through a small opening; an unrestrained outpouring of feeling. **effusive** adj. **effusively** adv.

EGA In computer science, Enhanced Graphics Adapter; a standard for the display on a color monitor screen.

e-gad Interj. An exclamation expressing surprise.

egal-i-tar-i-an (i gal´i târ´ē an) adj. Exhibiting belief in human equality. **egalitarian** n. **egalitarianism** n.

egest (ē jest´) v. To defecate; to rid the body of waste. **egestion** n.

egg (eg) n. The hard-shelled reproductive cell of female animals, especially one produced by a chicken, used as food; the reproductive ovum of an animal. **egg on** v. To incite to action.

eg-lan-tine (eg´lan tin´) n. The sweetbrier, a type of rose.

e-go (ē´gō) n. The self thinking, feeling, and acting distinct from the external world. Psychology The conscious aspect that most directly controls behavior and is most in touch with reality.

e-go-cen-tric (ē´gō sen´trik) adj. Thinking, observing, and regarding oneself as the center of all experiences; self-centered. **egocentric** n.

ego-de-fense n. A mechanism that is psychological and protects the self-image.

e-go-ma-ni-a (ē´gō mā´nē a) n. Self obsession. **egomaniacal** adj.

e-gre-gious (i grē´jus) adj. Outstandingly or remarkably bad; flagrant. **egregiously** adv. **egregiousness** n.

e-gress (ē´gres) n. The act of coming out; emergence; a means of departing; exit.

e-gret (ē´grit) n. Any of several species of white wading birds having long, drooping plumes.

eh interj. An utterance used to ask for confirmation of something just spoken.

ei-det-ic (ī det´ik) adj. Involving vivid recall.

ei-do-lon (ī dō´lon) n. An image that is unsubstantial.

eight (āt) n. The cardinal number equal to 7 + 1; the symbol 8. **eight** adj.

ein-korn n. The type of wheat that can be grown in Europe and has one grain.

ein-stein-i-um (īn stī´nē um) n. A synthetic, radioactive, metallic element.

Eisenhower, Dwight David n. (1890-

the United States from 1953-1961.

ei-ther (ē´thėr) *pron.* One or the other.
either *conj.* Used before the first of two or more alternatives linked by or.
either *adj.* One or the other of two.
either *adv.* Likewise; also.

e-jac-u-late (i jak´ū lāt´) *v.* To eject abruptly, usually referring to a bodily fluid; to utter suddenly and briefly; to exclaim. **ejaculation** *n.*

e-ject (i jekt´) *v.* To throw out; to expel. **ejection** *n.* **ejectable** *adj.*

e-ject-ment (i jekt´ment) *n.* An act for a recovery of possession of real property.

eke out (ēk´ out) *v.* To obtain with great effort; to make do.

e-kis-tics (i´kis tiks) *n.* The science which deals with the settlements of humans.

e-lab-o-rate (i lab´o rāt´) *adj.* Planned or done with great detail; very complex; intricate. **elaborate** *v.* To work out or complete with great detail; to give more detail. **elaboration** *n.*

e-lapse (i laps´) *v.* To slip or glide away; to pass away silently.

e-las-tase *n.* The enzyme in the pancreatic juice which will digest elastin.

e-las-tic (i las´tik) *adj.* Adapting with changing circumstances; capable of easy expansion and contraction. **elastic** *n.* A rubber fabric; a rubber band.

elas-tin (i las´tin) *n.* A type of protein which is similar to collagen.

elas-to-mer (i las´tamėr) *n.* Any elastic substance which resemble rubber.

e-late (i lāt´) *v.* To make proud; to bring joy. **elated** *adj.* **elatedly** *adv.*

el-a-ter (el´a tėr) *n.* Structure of a plant which aids in the distribution of spores.

e-lat-er-ite (i lat´erīt´) *n.* A rubberlike mineral resin which is dark brown and occurs in flexible masses.

e-la-tion *n.* A quality or state of exaltation or joy; a feeling of great happiness.

E layer *n.* The layer in the ionosphere above the earth that is able to reflect radio waves.

el-bow (el´bō) *n.* A sharp turn, as in a river or road, which resembles an elbow. *Anat.* The outer joint of the arm between the up-per arm and forearm. **elbow** *v.* To push or shove aside with the elbow.

eld-er (el´dėr) *adj.* Older. *n.* One who is older than others; a person of great influence; an official of the church. *Bot.* A shrub bearing red or purple fruit.

e-lect (i lekt´) *v.* To choose or select by vote, as for an office; to make a choice. **elect** *adj.* Singled out on purpose; elected but not yet inaugurated. **elect** *n.* One chosen or set apart, especially for spiritual salvation.

e-lec-tric *or* **e-lec-tri-cal** (i lek´trik) *adj.* Relating to electricity; emotionally exciting. **electrically** *adv.*

e-lec-tri-fy (i lek´tri fī´) *v.* To charge something or someone with electricity; to supply with electric power; to excite intensely, as if with an electric shock.

e-lec-tro-a-nal-y-sis *n.* The chemical analysis by electrolysis.

e-lec-tro-car-di-o-gram (i lek´trō kär´dēo gram´) *n.* The record produced by an electrocardiograph; EKG.

e-lec-tro-cute (i lek´tro kūt´) *v.* To kill or execute by the use of electric current or shock. **electrocution** *n.*

e-lec-trode (i lek´trōd) *n.* A conductor

e-lec-tro-dy-na-mom-e-ter *n.* Instrument used to measure electric currents.

e-lec-tro-mag-net (i lek´trō mag´nit) *n.* A magnet consisting of a soft iron core magnetized by an electric current passing through a wire which is coiled around the core.

e-lec-tron (i lek´tron) *n.* *Elect.* A sub-atomic particle with a negative electric charge found outside of an atom nucleus.

electronic bulletin board In *computer science*, a computer message center.

electronic mail In *computer science*, messages exchanged with the use of a computer through an internal network or the services of an outside vendor.

electronic spreadsheet In *computer science*, a computer version of a worksheet with data organized in rows and columns.

e-lec-tron-ics *n.* The branch of physics that deals with the behavior and effects of the flow of electrons in vacuum tubes, gases, and semiconductors.

e-lec-tro-va-lence (i lek´trō vā´lens) *n.* The number of charges transferred in an atom that result in the formation of ions. **electrovalent** *adj.*

el-e-doi-sin *n.* A protein that comes from the salivary glands of the octopus.

el-ee-mos-y-nar-y (el´e mos´i ner´ē) *adj.* Pertaining to or contributed as charity.

el-e-gance (el´e gans) *n.* Refinement in appearance, movement, or manners; elegant quality.

el-e-gant *adj.* Marked by elegance; tasteful or luxurious in dress or manners; gracefully refined, in habits, tastes, or a literary style.

e-le-git *n.* The writ of execution by which any or all of a defendant's goods or property are held by his creditor until the debt is paid.

el-e-gy (el´i jē) *n., pl.* **elegies** A poem expressing sorrow and lamentation for one who is dead.

el-e-ment (el´e ment) *n.* A constituent part. *Chem. & Phys.* A substance not separable into less complex substances by chemical means. **elements** The conditions of the weather.

el-e-men-ta-ry (el'e men'ta rē) *adj.* Fundamental, essential; referring to elementary school, the first introduction of fundamental principles.

el-e-mi (el'emē) *n.* A fragrant oleoresin which is obtained from tropical trees and is used in inks and varnishes.

e-len-chus *n.* An argument which contradicts another argument by proving the contrary to its conclusion.

el-e-phant (el'e fant) *n.* A large mammal having a long, flexible trunk and curved tusks.

el-e-vate (el'e vāt') *v.* To lift up or raise; to promote to a higher rank.

el-e-vat-ed (el'e vā'tid) *adj.* Exalted; above something such as the ground; elated.

elf (elf) *n., pl.* **elves** An imaginary being with magical powers, often mischievous; a small, mischievous child.

e-lic-it (l lis'it) *v.* To bring or draw out; to evoke.

e-lide (i līd') *v.* To omit, especially to slur over in pronunciation, as a vowel, consonant, or syllable. **elidible** *adj*

el-i-gi-ble (el'l ji bl) *adj.* Worthy of being chosen. **eligibility** *n.*

e-lim-i-nate (i lim'i nāt') *v.* To get rid of, remove; to leave out, to omit; to excrete, as waste. **elimination** *n.* **eliminator** *n.* **eliminative** *adj.*

e-li-sion *n.* The act of omitting something, such as an unstressed vowel or syllable in pronunciation or verse.

e-lite (i lēt') *n.* The choice part; a small, powerful group; a type size yielding twelve characters to the inch. **elite** *adj.*

e-lix-ir (i lik'sèr) *n.* A sweetened aromatic liquid of alcohol and water, used as a vehicle for medicine; a medicine regarded as a cure-all; a sovereign remedy.

ell (el) *n.* An extension of a building at right angles to the main structure.

el-lipse (i lips') *n.* A closed curve, somewhat oval in shape.

el-lip-sis (i lip'sis) *n.* An omission of a few words which are obviously understood in a sentence; a mark that indicates an ellipsis, such as ... or ***.

el-o-cu-tion (el'o kū'shan) *n.* The art of effective public speaking. **elocutionary** *adj.* **elocutionist** *n.*

e-lon-gate (i long'gāt) *v.* To stretch out in length; to extend.

e-lon-ga-tion *n.* State of being elongated or stretched out in length; an extension.

e-lope (i lōp') *v.* To run away, especially in order to get married. **elopement** *n.*

el-o-quence *n.* The practice of using language with fluency.

el-o-quent (el'o kwent) *adj.* Having the ability to speak fluently and persuasively; vividly expressive. **eloquence** *n.* **eloquently** *adv.*

else (els) *adj.* Different; other; more; additional. *adv.* Otherwise; besides.

else-where (els'hwâr') *adv.* To or in another place.

e-lu-ci-date (i lū'si dāt') *v.* To make clear, to clarify; to explain. **elucidator** *n.* **elucidation** *n.* **elucidative** *adj.*

e-lu-cu-brate (i lu'kya brāt) *v.* To work something out with studious effort.

e-lude (i lūd') *v.* To evade or avoid; to escape understanding.

e-lu-sive (i lū'siv) *adj.* Tending to evade something or someone. **elusively** *adv.*

e-lute (ē lūt') *v.* *Chem.* To remove material from what has absorbed it with the use of a solvent. **elution** *n.*

e-lu-tri-ate (i lū'trē āt') *v.* To remove or separate by washing. **elutriator** *n.*

e-lu-vi-al *adj.* Related to eluviation.

e-lu-vi-a-tion (i lū'vēā'shan) *n.* Shifting of dissolved material that is in the soil by the movement of water.

e-lu-vi-um *n.* Rock debris produced by the decomposition and weathering of rock; fine sand or soil deposited by the wind.

em *n.* *Printing* A unit of measure for printed matter that is equal to the width of the letter M.

e-ma-ci-ate (i mā'shē āt') *v.* To become or cause to become extremely thin. **emaciated** *adj.* **emaciation** *n.*

e—mail *n.* Electronic mail; messages sent over the Internet or a network.

em-a-nate (em'a nāt') *v.* To come out from a source; to emit. **emanation** *n.*

e-man-ci-pate (i man'si pāt') *v.* To set free from bondage; to liberate. **emancipation** *n.* **emancipator** *n.*

e-mar-gin-ate (i mär'ji nāt) *adj.* To have a notched margin; having a shallow notch at the apex. **emargination** *n.*

e-mas-cu-late (i mas'kū lāt') *v.* To castrate; to deprive of masculine vigor. **emasculation** *n.* **emasculator** *n.*

em-balm (em bäm') *v.* To treat a corpse with preservatives in order to protect it from decay. **embalmer** *n.*

em-bar-go (em bär'gō) *n., pl.* **embargoes** A prohibition or restraint on trade, as a government order forbidding the entry or departure of merchant vessels; for example, .the oil embargo of 1973.

em-bark (em bärk') *v.* To board a ship; to start a venture. **embarkation** *n.*

em-bar-rass (em bar'as) *v.* To cause to feel self-conscious; to confuse; to burden with financial or other difficulties.

em-bas-sage *n.* The commission which has been entrusted to an ambassador.

em-bat-tle (em bat'l) *v.* To prepare or arrange in order for battle.

em-bay (em bā´) v. To shelter.

em-bay-ment n. The formation of a bay.

em-bed (em bed´) v. To fix or enclose tightly in a surrounding mass.

embedded commands In *computer science*, program instructions that establish and maintain the appearance, position and special characteristics of a text or graphics element.

embedded object In *computer science*, a drawing, chart, sound recording, etc. that is fixed in a text or graphics element.

em-bel-lish (em bel´ish) v. To adorn or make beautiful with ornamentation; to decorate; to heighten attractiveness with ornamentation. **-ment** n.

em-ber (em´bèr) n. A small piece of glowing coal or wood, as in a dying fire. **embers** pl. The smoldering ashes or remains of a fire.

em-bez-zle (em bez´l) v. To take money or other items fraudulently.

em-bit-ter (em bit´ér) v. To arouse bitter or hostile feelings. **embitterment** n.

em-blaze (em blāz´) v. To set something ablaze; to provide light with a fire.

em-bla-zon (em blā´zon) v. To decorate in bright colors or with heraldic signs.

em-blem (em´blem) n. A symbol of something; a distinctive design; anything used as an identifying mark. **emblematic** adj. **emblematical** adj.

em-bod-y (em bod´ē) v. To give a bodily form to; to personify. **embodiment** n.

em-bold-en (em bōl´den) v. To encourage; to make bold.

em-bo-lism (em´bo liz´um) n. The blockage of a blood vessel, as by an air bubble or a detached clot.

em-bo-lus n. An abnormal particle such as an air bubble that circulates in the bloodstream.

em-bos-om v. To enclose; to shelter closely; to cherish.

em-boss (em bos´) v. To shape or decorate in relief; to represent in relief.

em-bou-chure (äm´be sher´) n. Mus. The mouthpiece of a wind instrument; the position of the lips used to produce a musical tone.

em-bowed adj. Bent or curved outward.

em-brace (em brās´) v. To clasp or hold in the arms; to hug; to surround; to take in mentally or visually. n. The act of embracing; a hug. **embraceable** adj.

em-brac-er-y n. An attempt to influence or corrupt a jury by bribes or promises.

em-bran-gle v. To entangle; to confuse.

em-bro-cate (em´brō kāt´) v. To moisten and rub an injured part of the body with a liquid medicine. **embrocation** n.

em-broi-der (em broi´dèr) v. To decorate with ornamental needlework; to add fictitious details. **embroidery** n.

em-broil (em broil´) v. To involve in contention or violent actions; to throw into confusion. **embroilment** n.

em-bry-o (em´brē ō´) n.,pl. embryos An organism in its early developmental stage before it has a distinctive form; in the human species, the first eight weeks of development; a young plant within the seed; a rudimentary stage.

em-cee (em´sē´) n. Informal A master of ceremonies. **emcee** v.

e-mend (i mend´) v. To correct or remove faults. **emendation** n. **emender** n.

em-er-ald (em´ér ald) n. A bright-green, transparent variety of beryl, used as a gemstone.

e-merge (i mérj´) v. To rise into view; to come into existence.

e-mer-gen-cy (i mér´jen sē) n., pl. **emergencies** A sudden and unexpected situation requiring prompt action.

e-mer-gent adj. Emerging; unexpected; rising into view.

e-mersed adj. Standing out of or rising above the surrounding water surface.

em-er-y (em´e rē) n. A grainy, mineral substance having impure corundum, used for polishing and grinding.

e-met-ic (e met´ik) adj. A medicine used to induce vomiting. **emetic** n.

em-e-tine n. An alkaloid that is extracted from the ipecac root used as an expectorant.

em-i-grate (em´i grāt´) v. To move from one country or region to settle elsewhere. **emigrant** n. **emigration** n.

e-mi-gré (em´i grā´) n. A refugee.

em-i-nent (em´i nent) adj. High in esteem, rank, or office; conspicuous; outstanding. **eminently** adv.

eminent domain n. The right of a government to take or control property for public use.

em-is-sar-y (em´i ser´ē) n., pl. emissaries A person sent out on a mission.

e-mis-sion n. The act of emitting; something emitted.

e-mit (i mit´) v. To send forth; to throw or give out. **emitter** n.

e-mol-lient (i mol´yent) n. A substance for the soothing and softening of the skin. **emollient** adj.

e-mol-u-ment (i mol´ū ment) n. Profit; returns arising from employment; compensation, as a salary or perquisite.

e-mote (i mōt´) v. To show emotion, as in acting.

e-mo-tion (i mō´shan) n. A strong surge of feeling; any of the feelings of fear, sorrow, joy, hate, or love; physical and psychological reaction to feelings.

em-pa-thy (em´pa thē) n. Psychol. Identification with and understanding of the feelings of another person. **empathetic** adj. **empathic** adj.

em-pha-sis (em´fa sis) n., pl. emphases Significance or importance attached to anything.

em-phat-ic (em fat´ik) *adj.* Expressed or spoken with emphasis. **-ally** *adv.*

em-phy-se-ma *n.* A condition characterized by air-filled expansions of tissues of the body; a lung condition that can result in heart impairment.

em-pire (em´pïèr) *n.* The territories or nations forming a political unit governed by a single supreme authority.

em-pir-ic (em pir´i k) *n.* One who relies on practical experience.

em-pir-i-cal (em pir´i kal) *adj.* Depending on or gained from observation or experiment rather than from theory and science. **empirically** *adv.*

em-place *v.* To put into place or position.

em-place-ment *n.* A platform for guns or military equipment.

em-ploy (em ploi´) *v.* To engage the service or use of; to devote time to an activity.

em-ploy-ee *or* **em-ploy-e (em ploi´ē)** *n.* A person who works for another in return for salary or wages.

em-poi-son *v.* To embitter.

em-po-ri-um (em pōr´ē um) *n , pl.* **emporiums** *or* **emporia** A large store which carries general merchandise.

em-pow-er (em pou´ér) *v.* To authorize; to delegate; to license.

emp-ty (emp´tē) *adj.* Containing nothing; vacant; lacking substance. **empty** *v.* To empty. **emptily** *adv.* **emptiness** *n.*

em-py-e-ma (em´pi ē ma) *n.* The collection of pus in a body cavity.

em-py-re-an (em´pirē´an) *n* Pertaining to the highest part of heaven; the sky.

em-u-late (em´u lāt´) *v.* To strive to equal, especially by imitating.

e-mul-sion (i mul´shan) *n. Chem.* A suspended mixture of small droplets, one liquid within the other. *Photog.* A light-sensitive coating on photographic paper, film, or plates.

en-a-ble (en ā´bl) *v.* To supply with adequate opportunity, knowledge, or power; to give legal power to another. In computer science, allowing to operate, as by computer command.

en-act (en akt´) *v.* To make into law; to decree. **enactment** *n.*

e-nam-el (i nam´el) *n.* A decorative or protective coating fused on a surface, as of pottery; a paint that dries to a hard, glossy surface; the hard outermost covering of a tooth. **enamel** *v.* To apply, inlay, or decorate with enamel.

en-am-or (en am´ér) *v.* To inflame with love; to charm.

en-an-ti-o-morph (i nan´tē o morf´) *n.* A pair of chemical compounds having molecular structures that are mirror images.

en-cap-su-late (en kap´su lāt´) *v.* To enclose or encase in a capsule.

en-cap-su-lat-ed *adj.* Surrounded with a membranous envelope.

en-case (en kās´) *v.* To close within a case.

en-ceinte *n.* A wall or enclosure around a town.

en-ce-phal-ic (en´se fal´ik) *adj.* Pertaining to the brain.

en-ceph-a-li-tis (en sef´a lī´tis) *n. Pathol.* Inflammation of the brain.

en-ceph-a-log-ra-phy *n.* The technique or act of taking X-ray photographs of the brain after replacing the spinal fluid with a gas.

en-ceph-a-lo-my-eli-tis (en sef´a lō mī e lī´tis) *n.* The inflammation of the spinal cord and the brain.

en-chant (en chant´) *v.* To put under a spell; to bewitch; to charm; to delight greatly. **enchanter** *n.*

en-chase (en chās´) *v.* To carve a relief into something; to set a gem in an ornamental setting.

en-chi-rid-i-on (en´kī rid ē en) *n.* A handbook; a manual.

en-ci-pher (en sī´fér) *v.* To convert anything such as a message into a cipher.

en-cir-cle (en sèr´kl) *v.* To form a circle around; surround. **encirclement** *n.*

en-clasp (en klasp´) *v.* To hold onto someone or something.

en-clave (en´klāv) *n.* A country surrounded by a foreign country; a cultural group living within a larger group.

en-clit-ic *adj.* Pertaining to a word connected to a preceding word, and so closely related that it has no independent accent; such as the word *cannot.*

en-close (en klōz´) *v.* To surround on all sides; to put in the same envelope or package with something else.

en-clo-sure *n.* The action of enclosing something; state of being enclosed; the item that is enclosed.

en-code (en kōd´) *v.* To convert or change a message into a code. **encoder** *n.*

en-co-mi-ast (en kō´mē ast´) *n.* A person who praises. **encomiastic** *adj.*

en-com-pass (en kum´pas) *v.* To surround; to form a circle; to enclose.

en-core (äng´kōr) *n.* An audience's demand for a repeat performance; a performance in response to an encore. **encore** *v.* To call for an encore.

en-coun-ter (en koun´tèr) *n.* An unplanned or unexpected meeting or conflict. **encounter** *v.* To come upon unexpectedly; to confront in a hostile situation.

en-cour-age (en kèr´ij) *v.* To inspire with courage or hope; to support. **encouraging** *adj.* **encouragingly** *adv.*

en-croach (en krōch´) *v.* To intrude upon

the rights or possessions of another.
encroacher *n.* **encroachment** *n.*

en-crust (en krust´) *v.* To cover with a crust; to form a crust. **-ation** *n.*

encryption In *computer science*, jumbling or coding of sensitive data for security purposes.

en-cum-ber (en kum´bĕr) *v.* To hinder or burden with difficulties or obligations.

en-cy-clo-pe-di-a (en sī´klo pē´dēa) *n.* A comprehensive work with articles covering a broad range of subjects.

en-cyst (en sist´) *v.* To become enclosed in a sac. **encystment** *n.*

end (end) *n.* A part lying at a boundary; the terminal point at which something concludes; the point in time at which something ceases; a goal; a fragment; a remainder; in football, either of the players in the outermost positions on the line of scrimmage. **end** *v.* To come or bring to a termination; to stop; to ruin or destroy; to die. In computer science, a program code indicating that final command.

en-dam-age (en dam´ij) *v.* To cause damage to something or to someone.

en-da-moe-ba (en´da mē´ba) *n.* Member of the genus that contains amoebas that are parasitic in the intestines.

en-dan-ger (en dān´jĕr) *v.* To expose to danger; to imperil.

end-ar-ter-ec-to-my *n.* The removal of the inner layer of an artery with surgery.

en-deav-or (en dev´ĕr) *n.* An attempt to attain or do something.

en-dem-ic (en dem´ik) *adj.* Peculiar to a particular area or people.

en-der-mic (en dĕr´mik) *adj.* To act through the skin. **endermically** *adv.*

end-ex-ine *n.* A membranous inner layer of the spores of the exine.

end key In *computer science*, a cursor movement key that sends the cursor to the end of a line of text and, used in conjunction with other keys, to the bottom right of the screen, the bottom of the page or the end of a file.

en-do-bi-ot-ic (en´dō bī´t´ik) *adj.* To be living within the host's tissues.

en-do-car-di-um (en´dō kär´dē um) *n.* The membrane lining the cavities of the heart.

en-do-carp *n.* Inner layer of a fruit wall.

en-do-chon-dral *adj.* Occurring in the cartilage of the body.

en-do-crine (en´do krin) *adj.* Making secretions which are distributed in the body by the blood or lymph.

en-do-derm (en´do dĕrm´) *n.* The innermost germ layer in an embryo that becomes the epithelium of the digestive tract.

en-do-der-mis (en´do dĕr´mis) *n.* The

most inner layer in the cortex of a plant.

en-do-en-zyme (en´dō en´zīm) *n.* A kind of enzyme which functions inside the cell.

en-do-er-gic *adj.* To be absorbing energy.

en-dog-a-my (en dog´a mē) *n.* The marriage custom that requires choosing a mate from within a specific group.

en-dog-e-nous (en doj´e nus) *adj. Biol.* Originating or growing from within the cell. **endogeny** *n.*

en-do-lymph *n.* A clear watery fluid in the labyrinth of the ear.

en-do-me-tri-um *n.* The membrane that lines the woman's uterus.

en-dor-phin *n.* Hormones with pain-killing and tranquilizing capabilities secreted by the brain.

en-dorse (en dors´) *v.* To write one's signature on a document, such as the back of a check to obtain the cash indicated on the front, or on the back of a deed or car title, so as to show transfer of ownership; to publicly endorse a person or a thing. **-ment** *n.*

en-do-scope (en´do skōp´) *n. Med.* An instrument used to examine a bodily canal or hollow organ. **endoscopic** *adj.*

en-do-skel-e-ton (en´dō skel´i ton) *n.* A skeleton which is on the inside of one's body.

en-do-tox-in (en´dō tok´sin) *n.* A kind of poisonous substance found in bacteria.

en-do-tra-che-al *adj.* Located within the trachea of the body.

en-dow-ment (en dou´) *v.* The income of an institution derived form donations; a natural ability or capacity.

en-due (en dö´) *v.* To provide; to put on.

en-dure (en der´) *v.* To undergo; to sustain; to put up with; to tolerate; to bear.

en-dur-ing *adj.* Lasting.

en-e-ma (en´e ma) *n.* The injection of a liquid into the rectum for cleansing; the liquid injected.

en-e-my (en´e mē) *n., pl.* **enemies** One who seeks to inflict injury on another; a foe; a hostile force or power.

en-er-gy (en´ĕr jē) *n., pl.* **energies** Vigor; strength; capacity or tendency for working or acting; vitality of expression. *Phys.* The capacity for doing work; usable heat or electric power.

en-er-vate (en´ĕr vāt´) *v.* To deprive of vitality or strength; to weaken.

en-fee-ble (en fē´bl) *v.* To weaken; to make feeble. **enfeeblement** *n.*

en-fet-ter (en fet´ĕr) *v.* To tie up in fetters.

en-fi-lade (en´fi lād´) *n.* An arrangement of things where they are in parallel and opposite rows such as rooms off a hall.

en-fleu-rage (än floe räzh´) *n.* The process used to extract perfumes from flowers.

en-fold (en fōld´) v. To enclose; to wrap in layers; to embrace.

en-force (en fōrs´) v. To compel obedience; to impose by force. **enforceable** *adj.* **enforcement** *n.* **enforcer** *n.*

en-fran-chise (en fran´chīz) v. To grant civil rights, as the right to vote; to give a franchise to. **enfranchisement** *n.*

en-gage (en gāj´) v. To employ or hire; to secure or bind, as by a contract; to pledge oneself, especially to marry; to undertake conflict; to participate. *Mech.* To interlock.

en-gen-der (en jen´dèr) v. To give rise to; to exist; to cause.

en-gild (in gild´) v. To make something bright with light.

en-gine (en´jin) n. A machine which converts energy into mechanical motion; a mechanical instrument; a locomotive. **engine** v.

en-gi-neer (en´ji nēr´) n. Person who works in the field of engineering.

en-gird v. To encompass.

en-gla-cial *adj.* To be frozen or embedded within a glacier.

en-glut v. To gulp or swallow down.

en-gorge (en gorj´) v. To swallow greedily. *Pathol.* To fill an artery with blood. **engorgement** *n.*

en-graft (en graft´) v. *Bot.* To join or fasten, as if by grafting.

en-grail v. To decorate or indent the edge of something with concave curves or notches. **engrailed** *adj.*

en-grav-ing (en grā´ving) n. Technique or act of one who engraves; impression printed from an engraved plate.

en-gross (en grōs´) v. To occupy the complete attention of; to copy or write in a large, clear hand. **engrossing** *adj.*

en-gulf (en gulf´) v. To enclose completely; to submerge; to swallow.

en-hance (en hans´) v. To make greater; to raise to a higher degree.

e-nig-ma (e nig´ma) n. One that baffles; anything puzzling; a riddle; something difficult to explain. **enigmatic** *adj.*

en-isle v. To make an island of; to isolate.

en-jamb-ment *or* **en-jambe-ment** (en jam´ ment) n. Construction of a sentence flowing from one line of a poem to the next, allowing related words to fall on different lines.

en-join (en join´) v. To command to do something; to prohibit, especially by legal action. **enjoiner** *n.*

en-joy (en joi´) v. To feel joy or find pleasure in; to have the use or possession of. **enjoyable** *adj.* **enjoyably** *adv.* **enjoyment** *n.*

en-kin-dle v. To kindle; to set on fire; to make bright.

en-lace v. To encircle; to entwine.

en-large (en lärj´) v. To make larger; to speak or write in greater detail. **enlargeable** *adj.* **enlarger** *n.*

en-light-en (en līt´en) v. To give broadening or revealing knowledge; to give spiritual guidance or light to.

en-list (en list´) v. To secure the help or active aid of. *Milit.* To sign up for service with the armed forces.

en-liv-en (en lī´ven) v. To make livelier, cheerful or vigorous.

en masse (än mas´) *adv.* All together; in a group.

en-mi-ty (en´mi tē) n., pl. **enmities** Deep hatred; hostility.

en-ne-ad n. A collection or group of nine.

en-ne-a-gon (en´ē a gon´) n. A closed plane figure having nine angles and nine sides.

en-ne-a-he-dron (en´ē a hē´dron) n. A solid figure with nine faces.

en-nui (än wē´) n. Boredom; weariness.

e-nol-o-gy n. The science that deals with wine and wine making.

e-nor-mi-ty (i nor´mi tē) n., pl. **enormities** Excessive wickedness; an outrageous offense or crime; the state of being huge.

e-nor-mous (i nor´mus) *adj.* Very great in size or degree. **enormously** *adv.*

e-nough (i nuf´) *adj.* Adequate to satisfy demands or needs. **enough** *adv.* To a satisfactory degree. **enough** *n.* A sufficient amount.

en-quire (en kwēr´) v. Variation of inquire.

en-rage (en rāj´) v. To put or throw into a rage.

en-rap-ture (en rap´chèr) v. To transport into a state of rapture; to delight.

en-rich (en rich´) v. To make rich or richer; to make more productive.

en-roll *or* **en-rol** (en rōl´) v. To enter or write a name on a roll, register, or record; to place one's name on a roll, register, or record. **enrollment** *n.*

en route *adv.* On or along the way.

en-sconce (en skons´) v. To settle securely; to shelter.

en-scroll v. To write or record on a scroll.

en-sem-ble (än säm´bl) n. A group of complementary parts that are in harmony; a coordinated outfit of clothing; a group of people performing together; music for two or more performers.

en-shrine (en shrīn´) v. To place in a shrine; hold sacred. **enshrinement** *n.*

en-shroud (en shroud´) v. To cover with a shroud.

en-slave (en slāv´) v. To make a slave of; to put in bondage. **enslavement** *n.*

en-snare (en snâr´) v. To catch; to trap.

en-snarl v. To tangle or involve in a snarl.

en-sphere (en sfēr´) v. To enclose in or make into a sphere.

en-sue (en sö´) v. To follow as a

consequence.

en-sure (en sher´) *v.* To make certain of.

en-ta-ble-ment *n.* A platform that supports a statue above a pedestal.

en-tail (en tāl´) *v.* To have as a necessary accompaniment or result; to restrict the inheritance of property to a certain line of heirs. **entailment** *n.*

en-tan-gle (en tang´gl) *v.* To tangle; to complicate; to confuse; to involve in a tangle. **entanglement** *n.*

en-tente (än tänt´) *n.* A mutual agreement between governments for cooperative action; the parties to an entente.

en-ter (en´tér) *v.* To go or come into; to penetrate; to begin; to become a member of or participant in; to make a record of; to join in a competition. In *computer science*, to add information, as text to a document, records to a database, etc.

enter key In *computer science*, a function key used to signal the end of a block of copy or enable a selected command; also expressed as CR or carriage return or Return.

en-ter-prise (en´tér prīz´) *n.* A large or risky undertaking; a business organization; boldness and energy in practical affairs.

en-ter-tain (en´tér tān´) *v.* To harbor or give heed to; to accommodate; receive as a guest; to amuse. **entertainer** *n.*

en-ter-tain-ment *n.* The act of entertaining; the accommodating of guests.

en-thrall (en throl´) *v.* To fascinate; to captivate. **enthrallment** *n.*

en-throne (en thrōn´) *v.* To place on a throne. **enthronement** *n.*

en-thuse *v.* To arouse enthusiasm; to exhibit enthusiasm.

en-thu-si-asm (en thö´zē az´um) *n.* Intense feeling for a cause; eagerness; zeal; keen interest.

en-tice (en tīs´) *v.* To attract by arousing desire. **enticer** *n.* **enticement** *n.*

en-tire (en tīer´) *adj.* Having no part left out; whole; complete. **entirely** *adv.*

en-ti-tle (en tī´tl) *v.* To give a name to; to furnish with a right. **entitlement** *n.*

en-ti-ty (en´ti tē) *n., pl.* **entities** The fact of real existence; something that exists alone.

en-to-mos-tra-can *adj.* A subclass of crustaceans which have a moderately simple organization.

en-tou-rage *n.* One's associates; retinue.

en-to-zo-on *n.* An internal parasite; an intestinal worm.

en-trails (en´trālz) *pl. n.* Internal organs of humans or animals.

en-trance (en trans´) *v.* To fascinate; enchant. **entrancement** *n.*

en-trance (en´trans) *n.* The act of

entering; the means or place of entry; the first appearance of an actor in a play; the act of entering into a place; the power or liberty of entering; admission. **entranceway** *n.*

en-trant (en´trant) *n.* One beginning a new course in life; one becoming a new member of an association.

en-trap (en trap´) *v.* To catch in a trap.

en-treat (en trēt´) *v.* To make an earnest request of or for. **entreaty** *n.*

en-trée (än´trā) *n.* A dish served as the main course.

en-tre-mets *n.* A side dish served at the table.

en-trench (en trench´) *v.* To dig a trench, as for defense; to fix or set firmly; to fortify. **entrenchment** *n.*

en-tre-pre-neur (än´tre pre nèr´) *n.* A person who launches or manages a business venture. **entrepreneurial** *adj.*

en-tre-sol *n.* One lower story positioned between two others of greater height.

en-trust (en trust´) *v.* To transfer to another for care or performance; to give as a trust or responsibility.

en-try (en trē´) *n., pl.* **entries** An opening or place for entering; an item entered in a book, list, register, or computer.

en-twine (en twīn´) *v.* To twine about or twist together.

e-nu-mer-ate (i nö´me rāt´) *v.* To count off one by one. **enumeration** *n.*

e-nun-ci-ate (i nun´sē āt´) *v.* To pronounce with clarity; to announce; to proclaim; to declare.

en-u-re-sis *n.* Incontinence; the involuntary discharge of urine.

en-vel-op (en vel´up) *v.* To cover, as by wrapping or folding; to enwrap or wrap up; to surround entirely.

en-ve-lope (en´ve lōp´) *n.* Something that covers or encloses; a paper case, especially for a letter, having a flap for sealing; the bag on an air balloon.

en-ven-om (en ven´om) *v.* To make poisonous; to embitter.

en-vi-a-ble (en´vē a bl) *adj.* Highly desirable. **enviably** *adv.*

en-vi-ron *v.* To surround; to encircle.

en-vi-ron-ment (en vī´ron ment) *n.* The surroundings; the combination of external conditions which affect the development and existence of an individual, group, or organism. In *computer science*, the operating system, the peripherals and programs that make up a computer system. **environmental** *adj.* **environmentally** *a*

en-vi-rons (en vī´ronz) *n., pl.* A surrounding region; a place; outskirts, especially of a city; the vicinity.

en-vis-age (en vīz´ij) *v.* To have or form a mental image of; to visualize.

en-vi-sion (en vizh´an) *v.* To picture in one's mind, or to one's self.

en-voy (en´voi) *n.* A messenger or agent; a diplomatic representative who is dispatched on a special mission.

en-vy (en´vē) *n., pl.* **envies** A feeling of discontent or resentment over someone else's possessions or advantages; any object of envy. **envy** *v.* To feel envy or jealousy about.

en-wind (en wīnd´) *v.* To coil about.

en-wreathe (en rēth´) *v.* To encircle.

en-zo-ot-ic (en´zō ot´ik) *n.* A disease affecting the animals of an area.

en-zyme (en´zīm) *n. Biochem.* A protein produced by living organisms that functions as a biochemical catalyst in animals and plants. **enzymatic** *adj.*

E-o-cene (ē´o sēn) *adj.* Pertaining to the epoch of Tertiary which is between the Oligocene and the Paleocene time periods.

e-o-li-an (ē ō´lē an) *adj.* Caused by or transmitted by the wind.

e-o-lith (ē´o lith) *n.* A kind of flint which is very crudely chipped.

e-on (ē´on) *n.* An indefinitely long period of time.

e-o-sin (ē´o sin) *n.* A type of red dye that is obtained with the action of bromine on fluorescein.

e-o-sin-o-phil (ē´o sin´o fil) *n.* A type of leukocyte which has cytoplasmic inclusions.

e-o-sin-o-phil-i-a *n.* An abnormal increase in the number of eosinophils of the blood that can be caused by an allergic state or infection.

e-pact (ē´pakt) *n.* A period of time which has been added to harmonize the lunar with the solar calendar.

ep-ar-chy (ep´är kē) *n.* The diocese of the Eastern church.

ep-ei-rog-e-ny (ep´i roj´e nē) *n.* A deformation in the crust of the earth which causes the broader features of relief to form.

e-pen-the-sis (e pen´thi sis) *n.* An insertion of a sound into the body of a word.

e-pergne (i pern´) *n.* An ornamental centerpiece for holding flowers or fruit, used on a dinner table.

ep-ex-e-ge-sis (ep ek´si jē´sis) *n.* The additional explanatory matter.

e-phah *n.* The ancient Hebrew unit of dry measure, equal to a little over a bushel.

e-phebe (i-fēb´) *n.* A youth, especially one entering manhood.

e-phem-er-al (i fem´ėr al) *adj.* Referring to something that lasts for a very short time. **ephemerally** *adv.*

e-phem-er-al-it-y (i fem´ėr al´it ē) *n.* The state of being ephemeral.

e-phem-er-id (i fem´ėr id) *n.* A short-lived insect; a mayfly.

e-phem-er-is (i fem´ėr is) *n.* A statement of the positions of a celestial body at regular intervals.

eph-or (ef´ėr) *n.* A Spartan magistrate who had power over the king.

epi- *prefix* Attached to; upon.

ep-i-blast (ep´i blast´) *n.* The layer which is the outside of the blastoderm.

e-pib-o-ly (i pib´o lē) *n.* The process of one part growing around another part.

ep-ic (ep´ik) *n.* A long narrative poem in dignified style that reports the deeds and adventures of a legendary or historical hero; a book or play resembling an epic. **epic** *adj.* Resembling an epic; extending beyond the ordinary in size or scope. **epical** *adj.*

ep-i-ca-lyx (ep´i kā´liks) *n.* An involucre which resembles the calyx.

ep-i-can-thic fold (ep´e kan´thik fōld) *n.* A fold of the upper eyelid skin over the inner angle or both angles of the eye.

ep-i-car-di-um (ep´i kär´dē um) *n.* The visceral part of the pericardium that closely covers the heart. **-ial.** *adj.*

ep-i-cene (ep´i sēn) *adj. Gram.* Of a noun that has only one form to indicate either sex. Having the characteristics that are typical of the other sex.

ep-i-cen-ter (ep´i sen´tėr) *n.* The part of the earth's surface directly above the focus of an earthquake.

ep-i-chlo-ro-hy-drin *n.* A toxic liquid that has a chloroform odor.

ep-i-con-ti-nen-tal *adj.* Being located on a continent or a continental shelf.

ep-i-cot-yl *n.* The part of a seedling stem that lies immediately above the first leaves.

ep-i-cure (ep´i kūr´) *n.* One having refined tastes, esp. in food and wine.

ep-i-cur-ism *n.* The taste of an epicure.

ep-i-cy-cle (ep´i sī´kal) *n.* The path or circle in which a plane will move; a small circle, the center of which moves around in the circumference of a larger circle.

ep-i-dem-ic (ep´i dem´ik) *adj.* Breaking out suddenly and affecting many individuals at the same time in a particular area, especially referring to a contagious disease; alluding to anything that is temporarily widespread, as a fad. **epidemic** *n.*

ep-i-de-mi-ol-o-gy (ep´i dē´mē ol´o jē) *n.* The science concerned with the control and study of epidemic diseases.

ep-i-den-drum (ep´e den´drum) *n.* A member of the genus that contains the tropical American orchids.

ep-i-der-mis (ep´i dėr´mis) *n. Anat.* The outer, nonvascular layer of the skin of a vertebrate. **epidermal** *adj.*

e-pi-der-moid *adj.* Being similar to the

epidermal cells.

e-pi-dia-scope (ep'i dīa skōp') *n.* Projector which is used for opaque objects or transparencies.

ep-i-did-y-mis (ep'i did'i mis) *n.* The convoluted efferent tubes at the back of the testis.

ep-i-dote (ep'dōt') *n.* A green mineral which occurs in metamorphic rock and is sometimes used as a gem.

ep-i-du-ral *adj.* Being outside the dura mater.

ep-i-fau-na *n.* The benthic fauna which live on the sea floor.

ep-i-fo-cal *adj.* Directly above the true center of disturbance of an earthquake.

ep-i-gas-tric (ep'i gas'trik) *adj.* Being over the stomach.

ep-i-ge-al (ep i jē'al) *adj.* Growing above the surface of the ground.

ep-i-gene *adj.* Formed on the surface of the earth.

ep-i-ge-net-ic (ep'i je net'ik) *adj.* Being formed after the laying of rock due to outside influences.

ep-i-glot-tis (ep'i glot'is) *n. Anat.* The leaf-shaped, elastic cartilage at the base of the tongue that covers the windpipe during the act of swallowing.

ep-i-gone (ep'i gōn') *n.* An imitative follower. **epigonic** *adj.*

ep-i-gram (ep'i gram') *n.* A clever, brief, pointed remark or observation; a terse, witty poem or saying.

ep-i-gram-ma-tize (ep'i gram'a tīz') *v.* To make or create an epigram.

ep-i-graph (ep'i graf') *n.* An inscription on a tomb, monument, etc.; a motto or quotation placed at the beginning of a literary work.

e-pig-ra-phy (i pig'ra fē) *n.* The study and interpretation of inscriptions.

e-pig-y-nous *adj. Bot.* Being attached to the ovary surface and appearing to grow from the top.

ep-i-la-tion *n.* The removal of hair.

ep-i-lep-sy (ep'i lep'sē) *n. Pathol.* A nervous disorder marked by attacks of unconsciousness with or without convulsions. **epileptic** adj.

ep-i-lep-ti-form (ep'i lep'ti form') *adj.* To be resembling epilepsy.

ep-i-lep-to-gen-ic *adj.* Tending to be able to induce epilepsy.

ep-i-lep-toid (ep'ilep'toid) *adj.* Showing symptoms of epilepsy.

ep-i-logue *or* **ep-i-log** (ep'i log') *n.* A short speech given by an actor to the audience at the end of a play; an appended chapter placed at the end of a novel or book, etc.

ep-i-mor-pho-sis *n.* A type of regeneration, in invertebrate animals, which involves cell proliferation and subsequent differentiation.

e-pi-my-si-um (ep'i miz'ē um) *n.* The connective tissue sheath of a muscle.

e-pi-nas-ty (ep'i nas'tē) *n.* A movement where the leaf of a plant is bent down and outward.

ep-i-neph-rine *or* **ep-i-neph-rin** (ep'i nef'rin) *n.* A hormone secreted by the adrenal medulla of the adrenal glands that raises the blood pressure and quickens the pulse, used in synthesized form as a cardiovascular stimulant.

e-pi-neu-ri-um (ep'i ner'ē um) *n.* The connective sheath of a nerve trunk.

ep-i-phan-ic (ep i fan'ik) *adj.* To have the character of an epiphany.

e-piph-a-ny (i pif'a nē) *n.* The Christian festival held on January 6th, celebrating the manifestation of Christ to the Gentiles as represented by the Magi; also known as the Twelfth Day; appearance of a divine being.

ep-i-phe-nom-e-nal (ep'ē fe nom'i nal) *adj.* Pertaining to a secondary event accompanying or caused by another.

e-piph-o-ra (e pif'ēr a) *n.* The excessive flow of tears due to a disorder of the lacrimal glands.

e-piph-y-se-al (ep'i fiz'ē al) *adj.* Of or pertaining to an epiphysis.

e-piph-y-sis (i pif'i sis) *n.* A part or section of a bone which is separated from the main body of the bone by a layer of cartilage, and which later becomes united with the bone through further ossification.

ep-i-scope *n.* The projector which is used for items that are opaque.

ep-i-sode (ep'i sōd') *n.* A section of a poem, novel, film, or other narrative that is complete in itself; an occurrence; an incident. **episodic** *adj.*

ep-i-some *n.* The gene that can replicate autonomously in the bacterial cytoplasm. or as an integral part of the chromosomes.

e-pi-ster-num (ep'i stėr'num) *n.* An anterior part of the sternum.

ep-i-taph (ep'i taf') *n.* An inscription, as on a tomb or gravestone, in memory of a deceased person.

e-pit-a-sis (i pit'a sis) *n.* The portion of a play that develops the main action and leads it to a catastrophe.

ep-i-tha-la-mi-um (ep'e tha lā'mē um) *n.* A song or poem in the honor of the groom and the bride.

ep-i-the-li-o-ma (ep'i thē'lē ō'ma) *n.* A tumor either malignant or benign that is derived from epithelial tissue.

ep-i-the-li-um (ep'i thē'lē um) *n., pl.* **epitheliums** *or* **epithelia** *Biol.* The thin, membranous tissue consisting of one or more layers of cells, forming the covering of the outer bodily surface and most of the internal surfaces and organs. **epithelial** *adj.* **epithelioid** *adj.*

ep-i-the-lize *v.* To convert to epithelium.

ep-i-thet (ep´*i* thet´) *n*. A term, word, or phrase used to characterize a person or thing; an abusive phrase or word.

e-pit-o-me (i pit´*o* mē) *n*. A concise summary, as of a book; a typical or ideal example.

e-pit-o-mize (i pit´*o* mīz´) *v*. To serve as a perfect example.

ep-och (ep´ok) *n*. A point in time marking the beginning of a new era; a division of time. **epochal** *adj*.

ep-ode (ep´ōd) *n*. Type of lyric poem.

ep-o-nym (ep´*o* nim) *n*. The person that something is named for. **eponymic** *adj*.

ep-o-pee (ep´*o* pē´) *n*. A type of epic poem.

ep-ox-ide *n*. A kind of epoxy compound.

ep-ox-dize *v*. To change something into an epoxide.

ep-ox-y (e pok´sē) *n*., *pl*. **epoxies** *Chem*. A durable, corrosion-resistant resin used especially in surface glues and coatings. **epoxy** *v*.

ep-si-lon (ep´si lon´) *n*. The fifth letter of the Greek alphabet.

eq-ua-ble (ek´wa bl) *adj*. Not changing or varying; free from extremes; evenly proportioned; uniform; not easily upset.

e-qual (ē´kwal) *adj*. Of the same value, measurement, or quantity as another; having the same privileges or rights of others. **equal** *v*. To be equal to another; to match.

e-qual-i-tar-i-an *n*. A person who adheres to the doctrine of equality for all men.

e-qua-nim-i-ty (ē´kwa nim´i tē) *n*. Composure; calmness under stress.

e-quate (i kwāt´) *v*. To consider or make equal.

e-qua-tion (i kwā´zhan) *n*. The act or process of being equal; a mathematical statement expressing the equality of two quantities, usually shown as (=). In computer science, an expression of equality, as in a spreadsheet formula.

e-qua-tion-al *adj*. To be involving an equation. **equationally** *adv*.

e-qua-tor (i kwā´tér) *n*. The great imaginary circle around the earth; a line lying in a plane perpendicular to the earth's polar axis and dividing the earth's surface into the northern and southern hemispheres. **equatorial** *adj*.

equatorial plane *n*. The plane in a cell which is perpendicular to a spindle of a cell and between the poles when it is dividing.

e-ques-tri-an (i kwes´trē an) *adj*. Relating or pertaining to horsemanship. **equestrian** *n*. The person who rides or performs on a horse.

e-qui-an-gu-lar (ē´kwē ang´gū lér) *adj*. *Geom*. Having all angles equal.

e-qui-ca-lor-ic (ē´kwi *ka* lor´ik) *adj*. Able to yield equal amounts of energy in the body.

e-qui-dis-tant (ē´kwi dis´tant) *adj*. Being equal distances from some point. **equidistance** *n*. **equidistantly** *adv*.

e-qui-lat-er-al (ē´kwi lat´ér al) *adj*. Having all sides equal.

e-qui-lat-er-al hy-per-bo-la *n*. A type of hyperbola, which is a plane curve, that has the straight lines associated with the curve at right angles.

e-quil-i-brant (i kwil *i* brant) *n*. A system of forces that counterbalance to produce equilibrium.

e-quil-i-brate (i kwil´*i* brāt´) *v*. To keep something in equilibrium.

e-qui-li-brist (i kwil´*i* brist) *n*. A person who can balance himself in positions which are unnatural and dangerous.

e-qui-lib-ri-um (ē´kwi lib´rē um) *n*., *pl*. **equilibriums** *Phys*. The state of balance between two opposing influences or forces; any state of compromise, adjustment, or balance.

e-qui-mol-al (ē´kwi mō´lal) *adj*. To have an equal concentration of moles.

e-qui-mo-lar *adj*. Pertaining to an equal amount or number of moles.

e-quine (ē´kwīn) *adj*. Pertaining to or like a horse. **equine** *n*.

e-qui-nox (ē´kwi noks´) *n*. Either of the two times a year when the sun crosses the celestial equator and the days and nights are equal in time.

e-quip (i kwip´) *v*. To furnish or fit with whatever is needed for any undertaking or purpose; to dress for a certain purpose or reason.

e-quip-ment (i kwip´ment) *n*. The state or act of being equipped; the material one is provided with for a special purpose.

e-qui-poise (e´kwi poiz´) *n*. A state of balance.

e-qui-pol-lence (ē´kwi pol´ens) *n*. Equality of power or force.

e-qui-pol-lent (ē´kwi pol´ent) *adj*. To have the same effect. **equipollent** *n*.

e-qui-pon-der-ant *adj*. To be balanced equally.

e-qui-po-tent (ē wi pol´ent) *adj*. To have equal effects for development of something. **equipotential** *n*.

e-qui-prob-a-ble *adj*. To have the same degree of mathematical probability.

e-qui-se-tum (ēk´wi sē *tum*) *n*. A type of perennial plant which can spread by creeping rhizomes, such as the scouring rush.

eq-ui-ta-ble (ek´wi ta bl) *adj*., *pl*. **equitabilities** Being impartial in treatment or judgment. **equitableness** *n*. **equitably** *adv*.

eq-ui-tant (ek´wi tant) *adj*. Of leaves, overlapping one another at the base, such as is seen in the iris.

eq-ui-ta-tion (ek´wi tā´shan) *n*. The art or act of horse riding.

eq-ui-ty (ek'wi tē) *n., pl.* **equities** Fairness or impartiality; the value of property beyond a mortgage or liability; in law, justice based on the concepts of fairness and ethics.

e-quiv-a-lent (i kwiv'a lent) *adj.* Being equal or virtually equal, as in effect or meaning. **equivalence** *n.* **equivalency** *n.* **equivalent** *n.*

e-quiv-o-cal (i kwiv'o kal) *adj.* Ambiguous; questionable; doubtful; signification. **equivocally** *adv.*

e-quiv-o-cate (i kwiv'o kāt') *v.* To intentionally use evasive or vague language. **equivocation** *n.*

e-qui-voque (ek'wi vōk") *n.* A double meaning.

-er *suff.* A thing or person that performs the action of the root verb; a person concerned with a trade or profession, as a banker, teacher, etc.; one who lives in or comes from a certain area, as a northerner, mid-westerner, etc.; used to form the comparative usage degree of adverbs and adjectives.

e-ra (ēr'a) *n.* An extended period of time that is reckoned from a specific date or point in the past and used as the basis of a chronology; a period of time with distinctive characteristics, such as the Victorian era..

e-rad-i-cate (i rad'i kāt') *v.* To destroy utterly; to remove by the roots. **eradicator** *n.* **eradication** *n.* **-able** *adj.*

e-rase (i rās') *v.* To remove something written; to rub or scratch out. *Slang* To kill. **erasable** *adj.* In computer science, to delete, as a block of copy or a file, from storage.

e-ras-er *n.* An implement, such as a piece of cloth or rubber, used to erase or remove writing or other marks.

er-bi-um (er bē um) *n. Chem.* A soft, metallic, silvery, rare-earth element, symbolized by Er.

ere (âr) *prep.* Prior to; before.

e-rect (i rekt') *adj.* In a vertical position; standing up straight. *Physiol.* Being in a state of erection, as through an influx of blood. **erect** *v.* To construct; to build. **erectly** *adv.* **erectness** *n.* **erector** *n.* **erection** *n.*

ere-long (âr long') *adv. Archaic* Before long.

er-e-mite (er'em mīt') *n.* A hermit.

e-rep-sin *n.* A proteolytic mixture that contains peptidases and is found in intestinal secretions.

er-e-thism *n.* The abnormal irritability in any organ or tissue.

erg (erg) *n. Phys.* A unit of work.

er-go (er'gō) *conj. & adv.* Consequently; therefore.

er-go-graph *n.* An implement used to measure and record muscular work completed.

er-gos-ter-ol (er gos'te rōl') *n. Biochem.* A steroid alcohol synthesized by yeast from sugars, converted under ultraviolet radiation to vitamin D.

er-got (er'got) *n.* The disease of rye and other cereal plants; a drug used to contract involuntary muscles and to control hemorrhage.

er-got-a-mine *n.* An alkaloid extracted from ergot, used in treating migraines and stimulating labor contractions.

er-got-ism (er'go tiz'um) *n.* The toxic condition that is produced by eating grain products or grasses that have been infected with ergot fungus.

er-is-tic *adj.* Pertaining to controversy; controversial.

e-rode (i rōd) *v.* To wear away gradually by constant friction; to corrode; to eat away.

e-rog-e-nous (i roj'e nus) *adj.* Responsive to sexual stimulation.

e-ro-sion (i rō'zhan) *n.* The state or process of being eroded. **erosional** *adj.*

e-ro-sive (i rō'siv) *adj.* Eroding or tending to erode. **erosiveness** *n.*

e-rot-ic (i rot'ik) *adj.* Pertaining to or promoting sexual desire.

err (er) *v.* To make a mistake; to sin.

er-rand (er'and) *n.* A short trip to carry a message or to perform a specified task, usually for someone else.

er-rant (er'ant) *adj.* Wandering or traveling about in search of adventure; straying from what is proper or customary. **errantry** *n.*

er-rat-ic (i rat'ik) *adj.* Lacking a fixed course. *Med.* Irregular; inconsistent.

er-ra-tum (i rā'tum) *n., pl.* **errata** An error in printing or writing.

er-ro-ne-ous (e rō'nē us) *adj.* To have or contain an error. **erroneously** *adv.*

er-ror (er'or) *n.* Something said, believed, or done incorrectly; a mistake; the state of being wrong or mistaken; in baseball, a misplay by a team member who is not batting.

errorlevel In *computer science*, in a program or batch file, a value that is tested to signal a branch.

error message in *computer science*, a message from an operating system or program displayed on the monitor or printer indicating that an error in processing has occurred, of citing the source of the error.

er-satz (er'zäts) *adj.* A substitute that is usually inferior; artificial.

erst-while (êrst'hwīl') *adj. Archaic* Former.

er-u-bes-cence *n.* The instance of turning red; blushing.

e-ruct (i rukt') *v.* To belch.

e-ruc-tate *n.* The act of belching wind from the stomach.

er-u-dite (er'ū dīt') *adj.* Scholarly.

er-u-di-tion (er´ū dish´an) *n.* Great learning.

e-rum-pent *adj.* Bursting forth.

e-rupt (i rupt´) *v.* To burst forth violently and suddenly; to explode with steam, lava, etc., as a volcano or geyser; to break out in a skin rash or pimples.

-ery *n. suff.* A business, or a place where something is performed or done, as a bakery; the collection of things; practice or act of something; the qualities or characteristics of something; as slavery.

e-ryn-go *n.* The genus of coarse herbs having toothed or spiny leaves.

er-y-sip-e-las (er´i sip´e las) *n.* An acute, inflammatory, and very uncomfortable skin disease resulting from streptococcus.

e-ryth-ro-cyte (i rith´ro sīt´) *n.* A disk-shaped blood cell that contains hemoglobin and is responsible for the red color of blood.

es-ca-lade (es´ka lād´) *n.* A scaling or mounting by means of ladders.

es-ca-late (es´ka lāt´) *v.* To intensify, increase, or enlarge. **escalation** *n.*

es-ca-la-tor (es´ka lā´tér) *n.* A moving stairway with steps attached to an endless belt.

es-cal-lop (e skol´op) *n. & v.* Variation of scallop.

es-ca-pade (es´ka pād´) *n.* Reckless or playful behavior; a prankish trick.

es-cape (e skāp´) *v.* To break free from capture, confinement, restraint, etc; to fade from the memory; to enjoy temporary freedom from unpleasant realities. In *computer science*, to discontinue processing or to return to a previous menu or operating level. **escape** *n.* **escapee** *n.*

escape hatch *n.* Emergency exit.

escape key (Esc) In *computer science*, a function key that triggers the escape command.

es-cape-ment (e skāp´ment) *n. Mech.* A device used in timepieces to control the movement of the wheel and supply energy impulses to a pendulum or balance; a typewriter mechanism that controls the horizontal movement of the carriage.

escape velocity *n. Phys.* The minimum velocity that a rocket or any body must attain to escape or overcome the earth's gravitational field.

es-carp-ment (e skärp´ment) *n.* A steep slope or drop; a long cliff formed by erosion.

-escence *n. suff.* Process of becoming, as in phosphorescence.

-escent *adj. suff.* Beginning to be; giving off light in a special way, as in phosphorescent.

es-chew (es chö´) *v.* To shun or avoid.

es-cort (es´kort) *n.* A group or individual person accompanying another so as to give protection or guidance; a male who accompanies a female in public.

es-cri-toire (es´kri twär´) *n.* A writing desk.

es-crow (es´krō) *n.* In law, a written deed, contract, or money placed in the custody of a third party until specified conditions are met.

es-cu-lent (es´kū lent) *adj.* Fit for eating.

es-cutch-eon (e skuch´on) *n.* A shield-shaped surface with an emblem bearing a coat of arms; a protective plate, as for a keyhole.

-ese *n. & adj. suff.* An inhabitant or native of; in the language or style of.

E-SIGN *n.* Electronic Signatures in Global and National Commerce; Act of Congress establishing a standard for electronic signatures so that they are valid under the law, passed in 1999.

e-soph-a-gus (i sof´a gus) *n., pl.* **esophagi** *Anat.* The muscular, membranous tube through which food passes on the way from the mouth to the stomach. **esophageal** *adj*

es-o-ter-ic (es´o ter´ĭk) *adj.* Confidential; kept secret; understood or meant for only a particular, often very small, group

es-par-to *n.* Any of two or three types of grass used to make cord and paper.

es-pe-cial (e spesh´al) *adj.* Having a very special place; apart from or above others; exceptional. **especially** *adv.*

es-pi-al (e spī´al) *n.* Observation; discovery.

es-pi-o-nage (es´pē o nazh´) *n.* The act of spying or the hiring of spies to obtain secret information about a competing company or a foreign government.

es-pla-nade (es´pla näd´) *n.* A flat, open stretch of land along a shoreline.

es-pou-sal (e spou´zal) *n.* Support or adoption, as of a cause; a wedding

es-pouse (e spouz´) *v.* To make something one's own; to take as a spouse; to marry; to give in marriage.

es-prit (e sprē´) *n.* Spirit; wit; mental liveliness.

es-prit de corps (e sprē´ de kor´) *n.* A group's spirit of enthusiasm and devotion to the common goals of the group.

es-py (e spī) *v.* To catch a quick view or sight of.

-esque *adj. suff.* Resembling.

es-quire (e skwier´) *n.* A title of courtesy or respect; sometimes written as Esq. be-hind a man's last name.

-ess *n. suff.* Female.

es-say (es´ā) *n.* A short composition that deals with a single topic and expresses the author's viewpoint on a subject;

an effort or attempt. **essayer** *n.*

es-sence (es´ens) *n.* The real nature of something; the most important element; an immaterial spirit; being; a perfume.

es-sen-tial (*e* sen´shal) *adj.* Necessary; indispensable; containing, of, or being an essence. **essential** *n.* **essentiality** *n.* **essentialness** *n.* **essentially** *adv.*

es-sen-tial-ism *n.* The theory that there are definite traditional concepts, standards, and procedures that are indispensable to a society.

es-so-nite *n.* A yellow to brown gem.

est *abbr.* Established; estimate.

-est *adj. & adv. suff.* Used to form the superlative degree of adverbs and adjectives.

es-tab-lish (*e* stab´lish) *v.* To make permanent, stable, or secure; to install; to create or find; to cause to be accepted or recognized; to prove.

es-tab-lish-ment (*e* stab´lish ment) *n.* The state of being established; a place of business or residence; those collectively who occupy positions of influence and status in a society.

es-tate (*e* stāt´) *n.* A usually large or extensive piece of land containing a large house; in law, the nature, degree, and extent of ownership or use of property.

es-teem (*e* stēm´) *v.* To regard with respect.

es-ter (es´tèr) *n. Chem.* Any of a class of organic compounds formed by the reaction of an acid with an alcohol.

es-the-sia (es thē´zha) *n.* Sensibility; feeling.

es-thet-ic (es thet´ik) *adj.* Variation of aesthetic.

es-ti-ma-ble (es´ti ma bl) *adj.* Worthy of respect or admiration. **estimableness** *n.* **estimably** *adv.*

es-ti-mate (es´ti māt´) *v.* To form or give an approximate opinion or calculation. **estimate** *n.* A preliminary opinion or statement of the approximate cost for certain work. **estimator** *n.*

es-ti-ma-tion (es´ti mā´shan) *n.* Judgment; the act of estimating or appraising something.

es-ti-val (es´ti val´) *adj.* Pertaining to or of summer.

es-ti-vate (es´ti vāt´) *v.* To pass the summer in a state of dormancy.

es-trange (*e* stranj´) *v.* To arouse hatred or indifference where there had been love and caring; to disassociate or remove oneself. **estrangement** *n.*

es-tro-gen (es´tro jen) *n. Biochem.* Any of various steroid hormones that regulate female reproductive functions and secondary sex characteristics.

es-tu-ar-y (es´chö er´ē) *n., pl.* estuaries The wide mouth of a river where the current meets the sea and is influenced by tides.

et al *abbr.* And others.

et-a-mine *n.* A lightweight fabric of cotton, silk, or wool.

etc *abbr.* And so forth.

etch (ech) *v.* To engrave or cut into the surface by the action of acid; to sketch or outline by scratching lines with a pointed instrument. **etcher** *n.*

e-ter-nal (i tèr´nal) *adj.* Existing without beginning or end; unending; meant to last indefinitely. **eternalness** *n.*

e-ter-ni-ty (i tèr´ni tē) *n., pl.* eternities Existence without beginning or end; forever; the immeasurable extent of time; the endless time after a person dies.

eth-ane (eth´ān) *n. Chem.* An odorless, colorless, gaseous hydrocarbon from the methane series that is contained in crude petroleum and in natural gas.

eth-a-nol (eth´a nōl´) *n. Chem.* The alcohol obtained after the distillation of certain fermented sugars or starches; the intoxicant in liquors, wines, and beers; alcohol.

e-ther (ē´thèr) *n. Chem.* A highly flammable liquid compound with a characteristic odor, used as a solvent and an anesthetic; the clear upper regions of space.

e-the-re-al (i thèr´ē al) *adj.* Very airy and light; highly refined; delicate; heavenly. **ethereally** *adv.*

eth-ic (eth´ik) *n., pl.* ethics The system of moral values; the principle of right or good conduct.

eth-i-cal (eth´i kal) *adj.* Relating to or of ethics; conforming to right principles of conduct as accepted by a specific profession, as medicine. **ethically** *adv.*

eth-moid (eth´moid) *adj.* Pertaining to a bone of the skull located at the root of the nose, containing a number of perforations for the filaments of the olfactory nerve.

eth-nic (eth´nik) *adj.* Relating to or of a national, cultural, or racial group.

eth-no-cen-tric (eth´nō sen´trik) *adj.* Pertaining to the belief that a person's own culture is better than other ethnic groups.

e-thos *n.* The characteristic spirt of people; character or disposition.

eth-yl (eth´il) *n. Chem.* An organic radical occurring in ether and alcohol; a univalent hydrocarbon radical; any gasoline that is treated with tetraethyl lead to reduce engine knock.

eth-yl-ene (eth´i lēn´) *n. Chem.* A colorless, flammable gas refined from natural gas and petroleum and used as a fuel.

et-i-quette (et´i kit) *n.* The prescribed rules, forms and practices, established for behavior in polite society or in official or professional life.

-ette *n. suff.* Small; female.

e-tui (ā twē´) *n.* A small ornamental case holding pins or other small articles.

et-y-mol-o-gy (et´i mol´o jē) *n., pl.* **etymologies** The history of a word as shown by breaking it down into basic parts, tracing it back to the earliest known form, and indicating its changes in form and meaning; the branch of linguistics that deals with etymologies. **etymological** *adj.* **etymologist** *n.*

et-y-mon (et´i mon´) *n., pl.* **etymons** *or* **etyma** The earlier form of a word in the same language or in the ancestral language.

eu-di-om-e-ter *n.* An instrument used in the analysis and volume measurement of gases.

eu-di-om-e-try *n.* The measurement and analysis of gases using a eudiometer.

eu-gen-ics (ū jen´iks) *n.* The science of improving the physical and mental qualities of human beings through genetics. **eugenic** *adj.* **eugenicist** *n.*

eu-gle-na *n.* Microscopic green protozoa having a single flagellum and a red eyespot, having both animal and plant traits and used in biological research.

eu-la-mel-li-branch (ū´la mel´i brank) *n.* Bivalve mollusk, such as the clam, oyster, and fresh-water mussel.

eu-lo-gize (ū´lo jīz´) *v.* To deliver a eulogy for; to speak in commendation of another. **eulogist** *n.* **eulogizer** *n.*

eu-lo-gy (ū´lo jē) *n., pl.* **eulogies** A speech that honors a person or thing, usually delivered at a funeral; high praise. **eulogistic** *adj.*

eu-nuch (ū´nuk) *n.* A castrated man.

eu-pep-sia *n.* Good digestion.

eu-phe-mism (ū´fe miz´um) *n.* A substitution for a word or expression that is thought to be too strong, blunt, or painful for another person. **euphemistic** *adj.* **euphemistically** *adv.*

eu-pho-ni-um *n.* A musical instrument that resembles the baritone tuba, but has a higher range and mellower tone.

eu-pho-ny (ū´fo nē) *n., pl.* **euphonies** The agreeable sound of spoken words. **euphonious** *adj.* **euphoniously** *adv.*

eu-pho-ri-a (ū fōr´ē a) *n.* A very strong feeling of elation or well-being.

eu-phu-ism (ū´fū iz´um) *n.* An ornate style of writing with frequent use of alliteration, antitheses, and mythological similes.

eu-re-ka (ū rē´ka) *interj.* An expression of triumph or achievement.

eu-rhyth-mics *n.* The art of graceful bodily movements in harmony with music, often improvisational.

eu-ri-pus *n.* An area where the tide flows with dangerous and violent force.

eu-ry-therm *n.* An organism with the ability to adjust physically to widely varying degrees of heat and cold.

eu-sta-chian tube (ū stā´shan tōb) *n. Anat.* The passage between the middle ear and the pharynx that equalizes the air pressure between the tympanic cavity and the atmosphere.

eu-tha-na-sia (u´tha nā´zha) *n.* The act or practice of putting to death painlessly a person suffering from an incurable disease; also called mercy killing.

eu-then-ics (ū then´iks) *n.* The study of improving the physical and mental qualities of human beings by controlling the environmental factors.

eu-the-ri-an *adj.* Referring to a large group.

eu-tro-phy *n.* Healthful, normal nutrition.

e-vac-u-ate (i vak´ū āt´) *v.* To leave a threatened area, town, building, etc.; to empty; to remove the contents. *Physiol.* To discharge or eject, as from the bowels. **evacuative** *adj.*

e-vac-u-a-tion (i vak´ū ā´shan) *n.* The process of evacuating.

e-vac-u-ee (i vak´ū ē´) *n.* A person who is evacuated from a hazardous place.

e-vade (i vād´) *v.* To baffle; to elude; to get away from by using cleverness or tricks.

e-val-u-ate (i val´ū āt´) *v.* To examine carefully; to determine the value of; to appraise. **evaluation** *n.*

ev-a-nesce (ev´a nes´) *v.* To disappear; to fade away.

ev-a-nes-cent (ev´a nes´ent) *adj.* Vanishing or passing quickly; fleeting. **evanescence** *n.* **evanescently** *adv.*

e-van-gel-ist *or* **Evangelist (i van´je list)** *n.* One of four writers of the New Testament Gospels: Matthew, Mark, Luke, and John; a zealous Protestant preacher or missionary.

e-van-ish *v.* To vanish.

e-vap-o-rate (i vap´o rat´) *v.* To convert into vapor; to remove the liquid or moisture from fruit, milk, etc., so as to concentrate or dry it; to vaporize. *adj.* **evaporate** *or* **dry** *n.* **evaporation** *n.*

e-vap-o-tran-spi-ra-tion *n.* The process by which the earth's surface loses moisture by evaporation.

e-va-sion (i vā´zhan) *n.* The act or means of evading.

e-va-sive (i vā´siv) *adj.* Being intentionally vague; equivocal. **evasively** *adv.*

eve (ēv) *n.* The evening before a special day or holiday; the period immediately preceding some event; evening.

e-vec-tion (i vek´shan) *n.* The perturbation of the orbital motion of the moon that is caused due to the attraction of the sun.

e-ven (ē´ven) *adj.* Having a flat, smooth, and level surface; having no irregularities; smooth; on the same line or plane; equally matched; not owing or having anything owed to one; exactly divisible by 2; opposed to odd. **even** *v.* To make even. **break even** *Informal* To end with neither profit or loss, as in business. **get even** Get one's full measure of revenge. **evenly** *adv.*

eve-ning (ēv´ning) *n.* The time between sunset and bedtime.

e-vent (i vent´) *n.* A significant occurrence; something that takes place; the actual or possible set of circumstances; a real or contingent situation; the final outcome; one of the parts of a sports program. **eventfulness** *n.*

e-vent-ful (i vent´ful) *adj.* Momentous; full of events.

e-ven-tide (ē´ven tīd´) *n.* Evening.

e-ven-tu-al (i ven´chŏ al) *adj.* Happening or expected to happen in due course of time. **eventually** *adv.*

e-ven-tu-al-i-ty (i ven´chŏ al´i tē) *n., pl.* **eventualities** A likely or possible occurrence; the conceivable outcome.

e-ven-tu-ate (i ven´chŏ āt´) *v.* To result ultimately; to come out eventually.

ev-er (ev´ėr) *adv.* At any time; on any occasion; by any possible chance or conceivable way; at all times; throughout the entire course of time.

ev-er-more (ev´ėr môr´) *adv. Poet.* For all time to come; always.

e-vert (i vėrt´) *v.* To turn inside out or outward.

e-ver-tor *n.* A muscle that causes an outward rotation of a part.

eve-ry *adj.* Referring to each part of a group without exception. **every which way** *adv. Informal* In every way or direction and with very little order.

eve-ry-bod-y (ev´rē bod´ē) *pron.* Every person.

eve-ry-day (ev´rē dā´) *adj.* Happening every day; daily; suitable for ordinary days.

eve-ry-one (ev´rē wun´) *pron.* Everybody; every person.

eve-ry-place *adv.* Everywhere.

eve-ry-thing (ev´rē thing´) *pron.* All things; whatever exists; whatever is needed, relevant, or important; the essential thing; the only thing that really matters.

eve-ry-where (ev´rē hwâr´) *adv.* In, at, or to everyplace.

e-vict (i vikt´) *v.* To put out or expel a tenant by legal process. **eviction** *n.*

ev-i-dence (ev´i dens) *n.* Signs or facts on which a conclusion can be based; that which makes evident an indication of something. **evidence** *v.* To indicate clearly; to offer evidence.

ev-i-dent (ev´i dent) *adj.* Easily understood or seen; obvious.

e-vil (ē´vil) *adj.* Morally bad or wrong;

causing injury or any other undesirable result; marked by misfortune or distress; low in public esteem. **Evil One** Satan.

e-vince (i vins´) *v.* To demonstrate or indicate clearly; to give an outward sign of having a quality or feeling.

e-vis-cer-ate (i vis´e rāt´) *v.* To remove the vital part of something; to remove the entrails. **evisceration** *n.*

e-voke (i vōk´) *v.* To call or summon forth; to draw forth or produce a reaction; to summon up the spirits by or as by incantations. **evocation** *n.* **evocative** *adj.* **evocatively** *adv.*

ev-o-lu-tion (ev´o lō´shan) *n.* The gradual process of development or change. *Biol.* The theory that all forms of life originated by descent from earlier forms. **evolutionary** *adj.* **evolutionism** *n.* **evolutionist** *n.*

e-volve (i volv´) *v.* To develop or change gradually. *Biol.* To be developed by evolutionary processes; to develop or work out. **evolvement** *n.*

e-vul-sion *n.* The act of pulling out.

ewe (ū) *n.* A female sheep.

ex *n.* The letter x. *Slang* A former spouse. *abbr.* Example; exchange.

ex- (eks) *pref.* Out of; former.

ex-ac-er-bate (ig zas´ėr bāt´) *v.* To make more severe or worse; to aggravate.

ex-act (ig zakt´) *adj.* Perfectly complete and clear in every detail; accurate in every detail with something taken as a model; similar. **exact** *v.* To be demanding about accuracy and detail; to force unjustly for the payment of something; to insist upon as a strict right or obligation; to call for or require. **exactness** *n.* **exactly** *adv.*

ex-ac-tion *n.* Extortion; fees, or contributions levied with injustice.

ex-act-i-tude (ig zak´ti tŏd´) *n.* The quality of being exact.

ex-ag-ger-ate (ig zaj´e rāt´) *v.* To look upon or to represent something as being greater than it really is; to make greater in intensity or size than would be normal or expected. **exaggerated** *adj.* **exaggerative** *adj.* **exaggerator** *n.*

ex-alt (ig zolt´) *v.* To raise in character, honor, rank, etc.; to praise or glorify; to increase the intensity of. **exalted** *adj.* **exalter** *n.* **exaltation** *n.*

ex-am (ig zam´) *n. Slang* An examination.

ex-am-i-na-tion (ig zam´i nā´shan) *n.* A test of skill or knowledge; the act of examining or the state of being examined; medical testing and scrutiny.

ex-am-ine (ig zam´in) *v.* To observe or inspect; to test by questions or exercises, as to fitness or qualification. **examinee** *n.* **examiner** *n.*

ex-ample (ig zam´pl) *n.* One that is

representative as a sample; one worthy of imitation; an object or instance of punishment, reprimand, etc.; a previous instance or case that is identical with or similar to something that is under consideration; a problem or exercise in algebra, arithmetic, etc. **set an example** *v.* To act in such a way as to arouse others to imitation.

ex-an-the-ma *n.* An eruption or rash on the skin; one with fever.

ex-as-per-ate (ig zas´pe rāt´) *v.* To make frustrated or angry; to irritate. **exasperatingly** *adv.* **exasperation** *n.*

ex-ca-vate (eks´ka vāt´) *v.* To dig a hole or cavity; to form or make a tunnel, hole, etc., by digging, scooping, or hollowing out; to remove or uncover by digging; to unearth. **excavation** *n.*

ex-ceed (ik sēd´) *v.* To surpass in quality or quantity; to go beyond the limit; to be superior.

ex-ceed-ing *adj.* Great in extent, quantity, or degree..

ex-cel (ik sel´) *v.* To surpass or to do better than others.

ex-cel-lence (ek´se lens) *n.* The state or quality of being superior or excellent; a superior trait or quality.

ex-cel-lent (ek´se lent) *adj.* The best quality; exceptionally good. **-ly** *adv.*

ex-cept (ik sept´) *prep.* With the omission or exclusion of; aside from; not including; leaving out.

ex-cept-ing (ik sep´ting) *prep.* With the exception that.

ex-cep-tion (ik sep´shan) *n.* The act of or state of being excepted; something that is excluded from or does not conform to a general class, rule, or principle; criticism or objection.

ex-cep-tion-a-ble (ik sep´sha nal) *adj.* Open to objection or exception. **exceptionability** *n.* **exceptionably** *adv.*

ex-cep-tion-al (ik sep´sha nal) *adj.* Being an exception to the rule; unusual, well above average. **exceptionally** *adv.*

ex-cerpt (ik sėrpt´) *n.* A passage from a book, speech, etc. **excerpt** *v.* To select and cite; to take extracts from..

ex-cess (ik ses´) *n.* The amount or condition of going beyond what is necessary, usual, or proper; overindulgence, as in drink or food.

ex-ces-sive (ik ses´iv) *adj.* Exceeding what is usual, necessary, or proper; extreme. **excessiveness** *n.*

exch *abbr.* Exchange.

ex-change (iks chānj) *v.* To give in return for something else; to trade; to return as unsatisfactory and get a replacement. **exchange** *n.* The substitution of one thing for another; a place where brokers meet to buy, sell, or trade; the mutual receiving and giving of equal sums or money. **exchangeable** *adj.*

exchange rate *n.* The value of the currency from one country to another.

ex-cheq-uer (eks´chek ėr) *n.* The treasury of a nation or organization; financial resources; funds. *Slang* One's total financial resources.

ex-cide (ik sīd´) *v.* To cut out.

ex-cip-i-ent *n.* Inert substance, as sugar or jelly, used as a vehicle for an active medicine.

ex-cise (ek´ sīz) *n.* The indirect or internal tax on the production, consumption, or sale of a commodity, such as liquor or tobacco, that is produced, sold, and used or transported within a country.

ex-cise (ik sīz´) *v.* To remove surgically.

ex-cit-a-ble (ik sī´ta bl) *adj.* Reacting to a stimulus; easily excited. **excitably** *adv.* **excitability** *n.* **excitableness** *n.*

ex-cit-ant *n.* A stimulant.

ex-ci-ta-tion *n.* The act of exciting.

ex-cit-a-tive *adj.* Having power to excite; tending to excite.

ex-cite (ik sīt´) *v.* To stir up strong feeling, action, or emotion; to stimulate the emotions of; to bring about; to induce. **excitement** *n.* **excitingly** *adv.*

ex-cit-ed *adj.* Emotionally stimulated; having strong feelings. **excitedly** *adv.*

ex-cit-ing *adj.* Producing excitement; thrilling.

ex-claim (ik sklām´) *v.* To cry out abruptly; to utter suddenly, as from emotion.

ex-cla-ma-tion (ek´skla mā´shan) *n.* An abrupt or sudden forceful utterance.

exclamation point *n.* A punctuation mark (!) used after an interjection or exclamation.

ex-clo-sure *n.* An area closed off; a fenced area.

ex-clude (ik sklōd´) *v.* To keep out; to omit from consideration; to put out.

ex-clu-sion (ik sklō´shan) *n.* Excluding or the state of being excluded; that which is excluded or expelled.

ex-clu-sive (ik sklō´siv) *adj.* Intended for the sole use and purpose of a single individual or group; intended for or possessed by a single source; having no duplicate; the only one; complete; undivided. **exclusively** *adv.* **exclusiveness** *n.* **exclusivity** *n.*

ex-cog-i-tate (eks koj´i tāt) *v.* To contrive; devise.

ex-com-mu-ni-cate (eks´ka mū´nikāt´) *v.* To deprive of the right of church membership. **excommunication** *n.*

ex-co-ri-ate (ik skōr´ē āt´) *v.* To tear the skin or wear off; to censure harshly.

ex-cre-ment (ek´skre ment) *n.* Bodily waste, especially feces.

ex-cres-cent (ik skres´ent) *adj.* Growing abnormally out of something else.

ex-cre-ta (ik skrē´ta) *n.* Excretions from the body such as sweat, urine, etc.

ex-cru-ci-ate v. To cause extreme pain to.

ex-cru-ci-at-ing (ik skrö´shē ā´ting) adj. Intensely painful; agonizing.

ex-cul-pate (ek´skul pāt´) v. To free from wrongdoing; to prove innocent of guilt. exculpation n. exculpatory adj.

ex-cur-sion (ik sker´zhan) n. A short trip, usually made for pleasure; a trip available at a special reduced fare. Phys. The oscillating movement between two points; also, the total distance traveled. excursionist n.

ex-cur-sive (ik sker´siv) adj. To go in one direction and then another; rambling; digressive.

ex-cus-a-to-ry adj. Making an excuse.

ex-cuse (ik skūz´) v. To ask forgiveness or pardon for oneself; to grant pardon or forgiveness; to overlook or accept; to apologize for; to justify; to allow one to leave; to release. excuse n. A reason, justification, or explanation. poor excuse Informal An inferior example for something. excusable adj.

ex-ec (ig zek´) abbr. Executive; executor.

ex-e-cra-ble (ek´si kra bl) adj. Extremely bad; detestable; revolting.

ex-e-crate (ek´si krāt´) v. To detest; to feel or express detestation for; to abhor. execration n. execrator n.

ex-e-cute (ek´se kūt´) v. To carry out; to put into effect; to validate, as by signing; to carry out what has been called for in a will; to put to death by the legal authority. In computer science, to carry out an instruction or set of instructions.

ex-ec-u-tive (ig zek´ū tiv) n. A manager or administrator in an organization; the branch of the government responsible for activating or putting the laws of a country into effect and for carrying out plans or policies.

ex-ec-u-tor (ĭg zek´yu tèr) n. The person appointed to carry out the reading and execution of a will. executorial adj.

ex-ec-u-to-ry adj. Executive; pertaining to what is yet to be performed.

ex-e-ge-sis (ek si jē´sis) n., pl. exegeses An interpretation or explanation of a text. exegetic adj. exegetically adv.

ex-e-get-ics n. The science that lays down the principles and art of scriptural interpretation.

ex-em-plar (ig zem´plèr) n. Something that serves as a worthy model for imitation; a typical example.

ex-em-plum n. An anecdote or story narrated to illustrate a moral.

ex-empt (ig zempt´) v. To free or excuse from an obligation or duty to which others are subject. exemption n.

ex-en-ter-ate (ek sen´te rāt´) v. To surgically remove the contents of a body cavity.

ex-er-cise (ek´sèr sīz´) n. The act of performing drills; the act of training or developing oneself; something that is done to maintain or increase a skill, such as practice on the piano. exercises A ceremony, such as a graduation. exercise v. exerciser n.

ex-ert (ig zèrt´) v. To put into action, as influence or force; to put oneself through a strenuous effort. -ion n.

ex-ha-la-tion n. The process of exhaling; that which is exhaled or emitted.

ex-hale (eks hāl´) v. To breathe out; the opposite of inhale; to breathe forth or give off, as air, vapor, or aroma.

ex-haust (ig zost´) v. To make extremely tired; to drain oneself of resources, strength, etc.; to eliminate all possibilities exhaust n. The escape or discharge of waste gases, working fluid, etc.; the waste gases, etc. that escape; the device through which waste gases are released or expelled. exhaustible adj.

ex-haust-ed adj. Completely consumed; tired.

ex-haus-tion n. Extreme fatigue.

ex-haus-tive (ig zos´tiv) adj. Tending to exhaust or that which exhausts; thoroughly analyzed. exhaustively adv.

ex-hib-it (ig zib´it) v. To display, as to put up for public view; to bring documents or evidence into a court of law. exhibit n. The presentation of something for public viewing. exhibition n. exhibitor, exhibiter n.

ex-hil-a-rate (ig zil´a rāt´) v. To elate, make cheerful, or refresh. exhilaration n. exhilarative adj.

ex-hort (ig zort´) v. To urge by earnest appeal or argument; to advise or recommend strongly. exhortatory n.

ex-hume (ig zöm´) v. To dig up and remove from a grave; to disinter.

ex-i-gen-cy (ek´si jen sē) n., pl. exigencies The quality or state of being urgent. usually pl. A pressing need or needs. exigence n.

ex-i-gent (ek´si jent) adj. Urgent; demanding prompt attention or action.

ex-ig-u-ous (ig zig´ū us) adj. Extremely small; scanty. exiguity n.

ex-ile (eg´zīl) n. The separation by necessity or choice from one's native country or home; banishment; one who has left or been driven from his or her country. exile v. To banish or expel from one's native country or home.

ex-ist (ig zist´) v. To have actual being or reality; to live.

ex-is-tence (ig zis´tens) n. The fact or state of existing, living, or occurring; the manner of existing. existent adj.

ex-is-ten-tial (eg´zi sten´shal) adj. Based on experience; of or relating to existentialism. existentially adv.

ex-is-ten-tial-ism (eg´zi sten´sha liz´um)

n. A philosophy that stresses the active role of the will rather than of reason in facing problems posed by a hostile universe. **existentialist** *n.*

ex-it (eg´zit) *n.* A way or passage out; the act of going away or out; the departure from a stage, as in a play. **exit** *v.* In computer science, a program branch that returns control to the next higher level; to leave a subroutine and return to the main application program or to leave an application and return to the operating system.

ex-o-bi-ol-o-gy (ek´sō bī ol´o jē) *n.* The search for and study of extraterrestrial life and environments.

ex-o-crine *adj.* Secreting externally through a duct.

ex-o-don-tia *n.* The branch of dentistry that deals with tooth extraction.

ex-o-dus (ek´so dus) *n.* A going forth; a departure of large numbers of people, as that of Moses and the Israelites as described in Exodus, the second book of the Old Testament.

ex-o-en-zyme (ek´sō en´zīm) *n.* The enzyme that performs its function outside the cell which produced it.

ex officio (eks o fish´ē ō´) *adj. & adv.* By virtue of or because of office or position.

ex-og-e-nous (ek soj´e nus) *n.* Biol. Growing by additions on the outside.

ex-on-er-ate (ig zon´e rāt´) *v.* To free or clear one from accusation or blame; to relieve or free from responsibility.

ex-or-bi-tant (ig zor´bi tant) *adj.* Beyond usual and proper limits, as in price or demand. **exorbitance** *n.*

ex-or-cise (ek´sor sīz´) *v.* To cast out or expel an evil spirit by prayers or incantations; to free from an evil spirit. **exorciser** *n.* **exorcism** *n.* **exorcist** *n.*

ex-or-di-um (ig zor´dē um) *n.* The beginning of anything, such as a speech.

ex-o-skel-e-ton *n.* An external protective covering, as the shell of crustaceans, the carapace of turtles, and the scales and plates of fish.

ex-o-sphere (ek´sō sfēr´) *n.* Meteor. The outermost region of the earth's atmosphere starting about 400 miles up.

ex-o-ter-ic (ik´so ter´ik) *adj.* Pertaining only to the external; not belonging to the inner or select circle.

ex-o-ther-mic (ek´sō ther´mik) *adj.* Releasing rather than absorbing heat.

ex-ot-ic (ig zot´ik) *adj.* Belonging by nature or origin to another part of the world; foreign; strange, different, and fascinating. **exotically** *adv.*

ex-ot-i-cism *n.* The tendency to adopt what is exotic.

exp *abbr.* Expenses; export; express;

experience..

ex-pand (ik spand´) *v.* To increase the scope, range, volume, or size; to open up or spread out; to develop more fully in form or details. **expandable** *adj.* .

ex-panse (ik spans´) *n.* A wide, open stretch; something spread out over a wide area.

ex-pan-sion (ik span´shan) *n.* The act of or state of being expanded; the amount of increase in range, size, or volume.

expansion card In computer science, a board that is installed in the computer to provide additional memory or functions.

expansion slots In computer science, positions in the computer reserved for the installation of expansion or control boards.

ex-pan-sive (ik span´siv) *adj.* Capable of expanding or inclined to expand; characterized by expansion; broad and extensive; open and generous; outgoing. **expansively** *adv.*

ex parte (eks pär´tē) *adj. & adv.* In law, giving only one side or point of view.

ex-pa-ti-ate (ik spā´shē āt´) *v.* To elaborate; to talk or write at length.

ex-pect (ik spekt´) *v.* To look forward to something as probable or certain; to look for as proper, right, or necessary; to presume or suppose.

ex-pec-ta-tion (ek´spek tā´shan) *n.* The state or act of expecting; something that is expected and looked forward to; something looked forward to in the future; anticipation.

ex-pec-to-rant (ik spek´to rant) *adj.* Helping to promote the discharge of mucus from the respiratory tract. **expectorant** *n.* Any medicine that is used to promote expectoration.

ex-pe-di-en-cy (ik spē´dē en sē) *n. pl.* **expediencies** The state or quality of being expedient.

ex-pe-di-ent (ik spē´dē ent) *adj.* Promoting narrow or selfish interests; pertaining to or prompted by self-interest rather than by what is right.

ex-pe-dite (ek´spi dīt´) *v.* To speed up the progress or process of something; to facilitate; to do with quick efficiency. **expediter** *n.*

ex-pe-di-tion (ek´spi dish´an) *n.* A journey of some length for a definite purpose; the person or group and equipment that engage in such a journey; efficient promptness.

ex-pe-di-tion-ar-y *adj.* Relating to an expedition; sent on military service abroad.

ex-pe-di-tious (ek´spi dish´us) *adj.* Quick; speedy. **expeditiousness** *n.*

ex-pel (ik spel´) *v.* To drive out, as to

dismiss from a school; to force out, as gas from a well. **expellable** *adj.*

ex-pend (ik spend´) *v.* To consume; to pay out or use up.

ex-pend-a-ble (ik spen´da bl) *adj.* Available for spending. **expendables** *Milit.* Equipment or supplies that can be sacrificed. **expendability** *n.*

ex-pen-di-ture (ik spen´di chĕr) *n.* An amount spent; the act or process of expending.

ex-pense (ik spens´) *n.* The outlay or consumption of money; the amount of money required to buy or do something. **expenses** The funds that have been allotted or spent to cover incidental costs; the charges incurred by an employee while at work or necessary to work; the reimbursement for such charges incurred.

ex-pen-sive (ik spen´siv *adj.* Costing a lot of money; high-priced.

ex-pe-ri-ence (ik spēr´ē ens) *n.* The actual participation in something or the direct contact with; the knowledge or skill acquired from actual participation or training in an activity or event; one's total judgments or reactions based on one's past learning.

ex-per-i-ment (ik sper´i ment) *n.* The act or test performed to demonstrate or illustrate a truth. **experiment** *v.* To conduct tests or to perform operations to examine proposed truths or theories. **experimental** *adj.*

ex-pert (ik spert´) *n.* A person having great knowledge, experience, or skill in a certain field. **expert** *adj.* Skilled as the result of training or experience.

ex-per-tise (ek´spĕr tēz´) *n.* A specialized knowledge, ability, or skill in a particular area.

ex-pi-ate (ek´spē āt´) *v.* To atone for; to make amends for. **expiation** *n.* **expiator** *n.* **expiatory** *adj.*

ex-pi-ra-tion *n.* The act of breathing out; emission of breath; exhalation.

ex-pire (ik spīer´) *v.* To come to an end; to die; to breathe out, as from the nose or mouth; to exhale. **expiration** *n.*

ex-plain (ik splān´) *v.* To make understandable; to clarify; to give reasons for; to account for; to give an explanation; to interpret. **explainable** *adj.* **explanatory** *adj.* **explainer** *n.*

ex-pla-na-tion *n.* The act of explaining; the clearing up of a misunderstanding.

ex-plant *v.* To transfer, as live fragments of plant or animal tissue, to a nutrient material for tissue culture.

ex-ple-tive (ek´sple tiv) *n.* An exclamation, often profane, such as *oh!*; a word added merely to fill out a sentence.

ex-pli-ca-ble (ek´spli ka bl) *adj.* Capable of explanation.

ex-pli-cate (ek´spli kāt´) *v.* To clear up

the meaning of. **explication** *n.*

ex-plic-it (ik splis´it) *adj.* Plainly expressed; specific; unreserved in expression; straightforward. **explicitly** *adv.* **explicitness** *n.*

ex-plode (ik splōd´) *v.* To cause to burst or blow up violently with a loud noise; to increase rapidly without control; to show to be false.

ex-ploit (ek´sploit) *n.* A deed or act that is notable. **exploit** *v.* To use to the best advantage of; to make use of in a selfish or unethical way. **exploitable** *adj.* **exploitative** *adj.* **exploitation** *n.*

ex-plo-ra-tion *n.* Travel for purposes of discovery; a systematic search for facts or reasons to aid understanding..

ex-plore (ik splōr´) *v.* To examine and investigate in a systematic way; to travel in unfamiliar territory.

ex-plor-er *n.* One who explores unknown areas.

ex-plo-sion (ik splō´zhan) *n.* A sudden, violent release of energy; the sudden, violent outbreak of personal feelings.

ex-plo-sive (ik splō´siv) *adj.* Marked by or pertaining to an explosion. *n.* A chemical preparation that explodes. **explosively** *adv.* **explosiveness** *n.*

ex-po-nent (ik spō´nent) *n.* A person who represents or speaks for a cause or group. *Mathematics* A number that indicates the number of times a factor is to be multiplied by itself.

ex-port (ik spōrt´) *v.* To carry or send merchandise or raw materials to other countries for resale or trade. **export** *n.* A commodity exported.

ex-por-ta-tion *n.* The conveying of gods and commodities abroad.

ex-pose (ik spōz´) *v.* To lay open, as to criticism or ridicule; to lay bare and uncovered; to reveal the identity of someone; to deprive of the necessities of heat, shelter, and protection. *Photog.* To admit light to a sensitized film or plate. **exposer** *n.*

ex-po-sé (ek´spō zā´) *n.* The reporting of something discreditable or shameful.

ex-po-si-tion (ek´spo zish´an) *n.* A statement of intent or meaning; a detailed presentation of subject matter; a commentary or interpretation; a large public exhibition. **expository** *adj.*

ex-pos-i-tor *n.* A person who explains.

ex post facto (eks´ pōst´fak´tō) *adj.* After the fact and retroactive.

ex-pos-tu-late (ik spos´cha lāt´) *v.* To reason earnestly with someone in an effort to dissuade that person from certain actions or to correct previous actions. **expostulatory** *adj.*

ex-po-sure (ik spō´zhĕr) *n.* The act or state of being exposed; an indication of which way something faces, such as a direction. *Photog.* The act of exposing a sensitive plate or film; the time required for the film or plate to be exposed to develop a picture.

ex-pound (ik spound´) v. To give a detailed statement of something; to explain the meaning at length.

ex-press (ik spres´) v. To formulate in words; to verbalize; to state; to communicate through some medium other than words or signs; to squeeze or press out, as juice from fruit; to send something by a fast or rapid means of delivery. **express** adj. Explicit; precise; fast. **expressly** adv.

ex-pres-sion (ik spresh´an) n. Communication of opinion, thought, or feeling; the outward indication or manifestation of a condition, feeling, or quality; a particular phrase or word from a certain region of the country; a facial aspect or look that conveys a feeling; in mathematics, a symbol, sign, or set that indicates something meaningful. In computer science, a symbol or symbols that describe a mathematical operation.

ex-pres-sive (ik spres´iv) adj. Of or characterized by expression; serving to indicate or express; full of expression. **expressively** adv.

ex-pro-pri-ate (eks pró´prē āt´) v. To transfer or take property from the owner for public use; to deprive a person of property or ownership.

ex-pul-sion (ik spul´shan) n. The act of expelling or the state of being expelled.

ex-punge (ik spunj´) v. To delete or remove; to erase. **expunger** n.

ex-pur-gate (ek´spér gat´) v. To remove obscene or objectionable material from a play, book, etc., before it is available to the public. **expurgation** n.

ex-qui-site (ek´skwi zit) adj. Delicately or intricately beautiful in design or craftsmanship; highly sensitive; keen or acute, as in pain or pleasure. **exquisitely** adv. **exquisiteness** n.

ex-san-gui-nate (eks sang´gwa nāt´) v. To remove the blood from.

ex-scind v. To cut off.

ex-sert-ed adj. Standing out, projected, beyond an encompassing part.

ext abbr. Exterior; external; extention.

ex-tant (ek´stant) adj. Still in existence; not lost or destroyed; surviving.

ex-tem-po-ra-ne-ous (ik stem´po rā´nē us) adj. Acting or performing with little or no advance preparation; delivering carefully prepared material without using notes or exact memorization.

ex-tem-po-rize (ik stem´po rīz´) v. To make, do, or perform with little or no advance preparation; to improvise to meet circumstances.

ex-tend (ik stend´) v. To stretch or open to full length; to make longer, broader, or wider; to continue; to prolong; to

put forth or hold out, as the hand; to exert to full capacity; to offer something.

ex-ten-sion (ik sten´shan) n. The act or state of being extended; an agreement with a creditor that allows a debtor further time to pay a debt. Phys. The property whereby matter occupies space.

ex-tent (ik stent´) n. The degree, dimension, or limit to which anything is extended; the area over which something extends; the size.

ex-ten-u-ate (ik sten´ū āt´) v. To minimize the seriousness of something as a crime or fault. **extenuation** n.

ex-te-ri-or (ik stēr´ē ér) adj. Pertaining to or of the outside; the outer layer.

ex-te-ri-or-ize v. To expose, as an internal organ from the body for surgery.

ex-ter-mi-nate (ik stér´mi nāt´) v. To annihilate; to destroy completely. **extermination** n. **exterminator** n.

ex-tern or **externe** (ek´stérn) n. A person that is associated with but not officially residing in a hospital or an institution.

ex-ter-nal (ik stér´nal) adj. For, of, or on the outside; acting from the outside; pertaining to foreign countries; outside; exterior. **externals** Outward or superficial circumstances. **externally** adv.

ex-tinct (ik stingk´) adj. Inactive; no longer existing; extinguished.

ex-tinc-tion n. The act of extinguishing; a coming to an end.

ex-tine n. The outer coat of a pollen grain.

ex-tin-guish (ik sting´gwish) v. To put an end to; to put out; to make extinct. **extinguishable** adj. **extinguisher** n.

ex-tir-pate (ek´stér pāt´) v. To pull up by the roots; to destroy wholly, completely. **extirpation** n.

ex-tol or **ex-toll** (ik stō´) To praise highly. **extoller** n. **extolment** n.

ex-tort (ik stort´) v. To obtain money from a person by threat, oppression, or abuse of authority. **extortionist** n.

ex-tor-tion n. The practice of extorting money, illegal compulsion to pay money.

ex-tra (ek´stra) adj. Over and above what is normal, required, or expected. **extra** n. A special edition of a newspaper that covers news of special importance; a performer hired for a small part in a movie.

ex-tract (ik strakt´) v. To pull or draw out by force; to obtain in spite of resistance; to obtain from a substance as by pressure or distillation. Mathematics To determine the root of a number. **extract** n. A passage taken from a larger work; a concentrated substance used in cooking. **extractable**, **extractible** adj. **extractor** n.

ex-trac-tion (ik strak´shan) n. The

process or act of extracting; that which is extracted; one's origin or ancestry.

ex-trac-tive *n.* That which may be extracted.

ex-tra-cur-ric-u-lar (ek'stra ka rik'ūlêr) *adj.* Pertaining to activities not directly a part of the curriculum of a school or college; outside the usual duties.

ex-tra-dite (ek'stra dīt') *v.* To obtain or surrender by extradition.

ex-tra-di-tion (ek'stra dish'an) *n.* The legal surrender of an alleged criminal to the jurisdiction of another country, government, or state for trial.

ex-tra-dos (ek'stra dos') *n., pl.* **extrados** *or* **extradoses** The exterior or upper curve of an arch.

ex-tra-ga-lac-tic (ek'stra ga lak'tik) *adj.* Coming from beyond the galaxy; situated beyond the Milky Way.

ex-tra-ju-di-cial *adj.* Out of the ordinary course of a legal procedure.

ex-tra-mu-ral (ek'stra mūr'al) *adj.* Taking place outside of an educational building or institution; involving teams from different schools.

ex-tra-ne-ous (ik strā'ne us) *adj.* Coming from without; foreign; not vital or essential. **extraneously** *adv.*

ex-tra-or-di-nar-y (ik stror'di ner'ē) *adj.* Beyond what is usual or common; remarkable. **extraordinarily** *adv.*

ex-trap-o-late (ik strap'o lāt') *v.* To infer the possibility beyond the strict evidence of a series of events, facts, or observations. *Mathematics* To infer the unknown information by projecting or extending known information. **extrapolation** *n.* **extrapolative** *adj.*

ex-tra-sen-so-ry (ek'stra sen'so rē) *adj.* Beyond the ordinary senses.

extrasensory perception *n.* The ability to foresee something before it actually happens; the ability to know something without any factual knowledge.

ex-tra-ter-res-tri-al (ek'stra te res'trē al) *adj.* Occurring or originating outside the earth or its atmosphere.

ex-tra-ter-ri-to-ri-al (ek'stra ter'itōr'ē al) *adj.* Outside of the jurisdiction of a territory, such as one's country of residence..

ex-tra-ter-ri-to-ri-al-i-ty *n.* An exemption from local legal jurisdiction, as that extended to foreign diplomats.

ex-trav-a-gant (ik strav'a gant) *adj.* Overly lavish in expenditure; wasteful; exceeding reasonable limits; immoderate; unrestrained. **extravagance** *n.*

ex-tra-vas-cu-lar *adj.* Outside of the blood vessels or the vascular system.

ex-tra-ve-hic-u-lar (ek'stra vē hik'ūlar) *adj.* Occurring or done outside a vehicle, especially a spacecraft in flight.

ex-treme (ik strēm') *adj.* Greatly exceeding; going far beyond the bounds of moderation; exceeding what is considered moderate, usual, or reasonable; final; last; of the highest or utmost degree; one of the two ends of farthest limits of anything; a drastic measure. *Mathematics* The first or last term of a proportion or series. **extremely** *adv.* **extremeness** *n.*

ex-trem-ist *n.* A person who advocates or resorts to extreme measures or holds extreme views. **extremism** *n.*

ex-trem-i-ty (ik strem'i tē) *n., pl.* **extremities** The utmost or farthest point; the greatest degree of distress or peril; an extreme measure; an appendage or limb of the body; a hand or foot.

ex-tri-cate (ek'stri kāt') *v.* To free from hindrance, entanglement, or difficulties; to disengage. **extrication** *n.*

ex-trin-sic (ik strin'sik) *adj.* Not inherent; outside the nature of something; from the outside; external. **extrinsically** *adv.*

ex-trorse *adj. Bot.* Facing outward, or directed away from the axis.

ex-tro-vert *or* **extravert** (ek'strō vêrt') *n. Psychol.* A person who is more interested in people and things outside himself than in his own private feelings and thoughts. **extroversion** *n.*

ex-trude (ik strōd') *v.* To push or thrust out; to shape by forcing through dies under pressure; to project or protrude. **extrusion** *n.* **extrusive** *adj.*

ex-u-ber-ance *n.* An expression in speech of being enthused or exuberant.

ex-u-ber-ant (ig zō'bêr ant) *adj.* Full of high spirits, vitality, vigor, and joy; plentiful; abundant. **exuberantly** *adv.*

ex-ude (ig zōd') *v.* To give off; to ooze or trickle forth, as sweat.

ex-ult (ig zult') *v.* To be jubilant; to rejoice greatly. **exultant** *adj.*

ex-ur-bi-a (eks êr'bē a) *n.* The often well-to-do residential area outside the suburbs of a large city. **exurbanite** *n.*

ey-as (ī'as) *n.* A type of bird which is unfledged.; a nestling hawk

eye (ī) *n.* An organ of sight consisting of the cornea, iris, pupil, retina, and lens; a look; gaze; the ability to judge, perceive, or discriminate; the center part. **eye of the storm** *Meteor.* The central area of a hurricane or cyclone. **eye of the wind** *Naut.* The direction from which the wind blows. **eye** *v.* To watch closely. **see eye to eye** To be in complete agreement.

eye-sight (ī'sīt') *n.* The faculty or power of sight; the range of vision.

eye-tooth (ī'tōth') *n., pl.* **eyeteeth** One of the canine teeth of the upper jaw.

eye-wit-ness (ī'wit'nis') *n.* A person who has seen something and can testify to it as a firsthand witness.

F, f (ef) The sixth letter of the English alphabet; in music, the fourth tone in the scale of C major; a failing grade.

fa-ba-ceous adj. Related to or belonging to the bean family of plants.

fa-ble (fā´bl) n. A brief, fictitious story embodying a moral and using persons, animals, or in animate objects as characters; a falsehood; a lie.

fab-ric (fab´rik) n. A cloth produced by knitting, weaving, or spinning fibers; a structure or framework, as the social fabric.

fab-ri-cate (fab´ri kāt´) v. To make or manufacture; to build; to construct by combining or assembling parts; to make up in order to deceive; to invent, as a lie or story. **fabrication** n. **-or** n.

fab-u-lous (fab´ya lus) adj. Past the limits of belief; incredible. *Slang* Very successful or pleasing. **fabulously** adv.

fa-cade (fa säd´) n., *Arch.* The face or front of a building; an artificial or false appearance.

face (fās) n. The front surface of the head from ear to ear and from forehead to chin; external appearance, look, or aspect; the value written on the printed surface of a note or bond; the principal, front, finished, or working surface of anything; the most prominent or significant surface of an object. v. To confront with awareness. **face up** To recognize the existence of something and confront it bravely. **facing** v.

fac-et (fas´it) n. One of the flat, polished surfaces cut upon a gemstone; the small, smooth surface on a bone or tooth; a phase, aspect, or side of a person or subject.

fa-ce-ti-ae (fa sē´shē ē´) n. Humorous or witty writings or remarks.

fa-ce-tious (fa sē´shus) adj.. Given to or marked by playful jocularity; humorous. **facetiously** adv.

face value n. The apparent value of something; the value printed on the face of a bill or bond.

fa-cial (fā´shal) adj. Near, of, or for the face, a massage or other cosmetic treatment for the face. **facially** adv.

fac-ile (fas´il) adj. Requiring little effort; easily achieved or performed; arrived at without due care, effort, or examination; superficial. **facilely** adv.

fa-cil-i-tate (fa sil´i tāt´) v. To make easier. **facilitation** n. **facilitator** n.

fa-cil-i-ty (fa sil´i tē) n. pl. **-ies** Ease in performance, moving, or doing something; something that makes an operation or action easier.

fac-ing (fā´sing) n. The lining or covering sewn to a garment; any outer protective or decorative layer applied to a surface.

fac-sim-i-le (fak sim´i lē) n. An exact copy, as of a document; the method of transmitting drawings, messages, or such by an electronic method.

fact (fakt) n. Something that actually occurred or exists; something that has real and demonstrable existence; actuality.

fac-tion (fak´shan) n. A group or party within a government that is often self-seeking and usually in opposition to a larger group; conflict within a party; discord. **factional** adv.

fac-ti-tious (fak tish´us) adj. Produced artificially; lacking authenticity or genuineness. **factitiously** adv.

fac-tor (fak´tér) n. One who transacts business for another person on a commission basis; one of the elements or causes that contribute to produce the result; in mathematics, one of two or more quantities that when multiplied together give or yield a given product; in biology, a gene. **factorship** n. **factorable** adj. **factorage** n.

fac-to-ry (fak´to rē) n. pl. **-ies** An establishment where goods are manufactured; a plant.

fac-to-tum (fak tō´tum) n. An employee who performs all types of work.

fac-tu-al (fak´chö al) adj. Containing or consisting of facts, literal and exact.

fac-tu-al-ism n. An adherence to factual evidence; a theory that places great emphasis on fact.

fac-u-la n. Any bright patch on the sun's surface.

fac-ture (fak´chér) n. The process, manner or act of construction; making.

fac-ul-ty (fak´ul tē) n. pl. **-ies** A natural ability or power; the inherent powers or capabilities of the body or mind; the complete teaching staff of a school or any other educational institution.

fad (fad) n. A temporary fashion adopted with wide enthusiasm. **faddish** adj. **faddishness** n. **faddist** n.

fade (fād) v. To lose brightness, brilliance, or loudness gradually; to vanish slowly; to lose freshness, vigor, or youth; to disappear gradually.

fa-er-ie (fā´e rē) n., *variation of* fairy.

fag-ot-ing (fag´o ting) n. A method of ornamenting cloth by pulling out horizontal threads and tying the remaining vertical threads into hourglass-shaped bunches.

Fahr-en-heit (far´en hīt´) adj. Of or relating to the temperature scale in which the freezing point of water is 32 degrees and the boiling point of water is 212 degrees under normal atmospheric pressure.

fa-ience (fī äns´) n. Earthenware that is decorated with a colorful opaque glaze.

fail (fāl) v. To be totally ineffective, unsuccessful; to go bankrupt; to receive an academic grade below the acceptable standards; to issue such a grade; to omit or neglect. **failing, failed** *v.*

faille (fīl) *n.* A ribbed material of cotton, silk, or rayon.

fail-safe (fāl´sāf´) *adj.* Of or relating to a system designed to prevent equipment failure or to compensate automatically for a mechanical failure; guaranteed not to fail.

fail-ure (fāl´yėr) *n.* The fact or state of failing; a breaking down in health, action, strength, or efficiency; a situation in which a business becomes insolvent or bankrupt; in school, a failing grade.

faint (fānt) *adj.* Having little strength or vigor; feeble; lacking brightness or clarity; dim. *n.* A sudden, temporary loss of consciousness; a swoon. **faintly** *adv.* **faintness** *n.*

fair (fâr) *adj.* Visually light in coloring; pleasing to the eye; beautiful; impartial; free from blemish or imperfection; moderately large or good; not stormy; without precipitation. *n.* A periodic gathering for the buying and selling of goods and merchandise; a competitive exhibit of agricultural products, livestock, machinery, and other goods; a fund-raising event for a charity.

fairy tale *n.* An incredible or fictitious tale of fanciful creatures; a tale about fairies.

fait accompli *n.* An accomplished fact or deed that is irreversible.

faith (fāth) *n.* A belief in the value, truth, or trust worthiness of someone or something; belief and trust in God, the Scriptures, or other religious writings; a system of religious beliefs.

faith-ful (fāth´ful) *adj.* True and trustworthy in the performance of duty, the fulfillment of promises or obligations, etc. **faithfully** *adv.*

fake (fāk) *adj.* Having a false or misleading appearance; not genuine. *v.* To make a brief, deceptive movement in order to mislead one's opponent in certain sports. **faker** *n.* **fakery** *n.*

fal-cate *adj.* Hooked like a sickle; curved.

fal-chion *n.* A broad, short and slightly curved sword used in medieval times.

fall (fol) *v.* To drop down from a higher place or position due to the removal of support or loss of hold or attachment; to collapse; to become less in rank or importance; to drop when wounded or slain; to be overthrown by another government; to come as though descending as night falls; to pass into a specified condition, as to fall asleep; to cut down or fell, as a tree; to surrender, as a city or fort. **on** To recede; to retreat. **on** To fail in. **for** To be deceived by. **in** the military, to meet and go along with. **out** In the mil-

itary, to leave ranks. **of** To fail to meet a standard or to reach a particular place. **under** To be classified, as to be included. **man** The disobedience of Adam and Eve that began or resulted in original sin. A moral lapse or loss of innocence; autumn. **fall back** *n.* **fall down** *n.* **short** *n.*

fal-la-cious (fa la´shus) *adj.* Containing or based on fundamental errors in reasoning; deceptive; misleading. **fallaciousness** *n.* **fallaciously** *adv.*

fal-la-cy (fal´a sē) *n. pl.* **fallacies** A deception; an error.

fal-li-ble (fal´i bl) *adj.* Capable of making an error; liable to be deceived or misled; apt to be erroneous.

fal-lo-pi-an tube (fa lō´pē an) *n.* One of a pair of long, slender ducts serving as a passage for the ovum from the ovary to the uterus.

fal-low (fal´ō) *n.* Ground that has been plowed but left unseeded during the growing season. *adj.* Light yellowish-brown in color. **fallowness** *n.*

false (fols) *adj.* Contrary to truth or fact; incorrect; deliberately untrue or deceptive; treacherous; unfaithful; not natural or real; artificial; in music, an incorrect pitch. *adv.* Faithless in manner. **falsely** *adv.* **falseness** *n.*

fal-set-to (fol set´ō) *n.* A high singing voice, usually male, that is artificially high. **falsetto** *adv.*

fal-si-fy (fol´si fī´) *v.* To give an untruthful account of; to misrepresent; to alter or tamper with in order to deceive; to forge. **falsifying, falsified** *v.* **falsifier** *n.*

fal-ter (fol´tėr) *v.* To be uncertain or hesitant in action or voice; to waver; to move with unsteadiness.

fame (fām) *n.* Public esteem; a good reputation. **famed** *adj.*

fa-mil-iar (fa mil´yėr) *adj.* Being well-acquainted with; common; having good and complete knowledge of something; unconstrained or informal. *n.* A close friend or associate.

fam-i-ly (fam´i lē) *n. pl.* **-ies** Parents and their children; a group of people connected by blood or marriage and sharing common ancestry; the members of a household; a group or class of like things; in science, a taxonomic category higher than a genus and below an order.

fam-ine (fam´in) *n.* A widespread scarcity of food; a drastic shortage of or scarcity of anything; severe hunger; starvation.

fam-ish (fam´ish) *v.* To starve or cause to starve. **famished** *adj.*

fa-mous (fā´mus) *adj.* Well-known; renowned. **Slang** Excellent; admirable. **famously** *adv.* **famousness** *n.*

fan (fan) *n.* A device for putting air into motion, especially a flat, lightweight, collapsible, wedge-like shape; a machine that rotates thin, rigid vanes. *Slang* An enthusiastic devotee or admirer of a sport, celebrity, diversion, etc. **fan** *v.* To move or stir up air with a fan; to direct air upon; to cool or refresh with or as with a fan; to spread like a fan; in baseball, to strike out.

fa-nat-ic (fa nat´ik) *n.* One who is moved by a frenzy of enthusiasm or zeal. **fanatical** *adj.* **fanaticism** *n.*

fa-nat-i-cism *n.* Excessive vigor, behavior marked by such zeal or enthusiasm.

fan-cy (fan´sē) *n., pl.* **fancies** Imagination of a fantastic or whimsical nature; a notion or idea not based on evidence or fact; a whim or caprice; judgment or taste in art or style **fancy** *adj.* Adapted to please the fancy; highly decorated. **fancy** *v.* To imagine; to visualize; to believe without proof or conviction; to suppose; to breed animals for unconventional traits.

fan-ta-sia (fan´tä´zha) *n.* A composition structured according to the composer's fancy and not observing any strict musical form.

fan-ta-sied *adj.* Present only in one's imagination.

fan-ta-size *v.* To create mental fantasies; to imagine or indulge in fantasies. **fantasizing, fantasized** *v.*

fan-tas-tic (fan tas´tik) *adj.* Existing only in the fancy; unreal; wildly fanciful or exaggerated; impulsive or capricious; coming from the imagination or fancy. *Slang* Superb; wonderful.

fan-ta-sy (fan´ta sē) *n., pl.* **fantasies** A creative imagination; a creation of the fancy; an unreal or odd mental image; a whimsical or odd notion; a highly or ingeniously imaginative creation; in psychology, the sequence of pleasant mental images fulfilling a wish.

far (fär) *adv.* From, to, or at a considerable distance; to or at a certain distance, degree, or point; very remote in time, quality or degree. **far** *adj.& adv.* Remote in space or time; extending widely or at great lengths; extensive or lengthy. **far and away** Decidedly. **far and wide** Everywhere. **far be it from me** Having no audacity or desire. **in so far as** To the extent that. **to go far** To accomplish a lot; to have success; to last a long time or to cover a great extent.

farce (färs) *n.* A theater comedy employing exaggerated or ludicrous situations; a ridiculous situation or action; a seasoned stuffing.

far-cy *n.* A disease of the lymphatic glands and skin, affecting horses and cattle.

fare (fâr) *v.* To be in a specific state; to turn out. **fare** *n.* A fee paid for hired transportation; food or a variety of foods.

fa-ri-na (fa rē´na) *n.* A fine meal obtained chiefly from nuts, cereals, potatoes, or Indian corn, used as a breakfast food or in puddings.

far-i-na-ceous (far´i nā´shus) *adj.* Made from or rich in starch; mealy.

far-off (fär´of´) *adj.* Distant; remote.

far-out *adj. Slang* Very unconventional.

far-a-go (fa rä´gō) *n., pl.* **faragoes** A confused mixture.

far-ther (fär´thẻr) *adv.* To or at a more distant point. **farther** *adj.* More remote or distant.

far-ther-most *adj.* Most distant; farthest.

far-thest (fär´thist) *adj.* To or at the greatest distance.

fas-ci-cle *n.* A small bundle; a single part of a book published in installments.

fas-ci-nate (fas´i nāt´) *v.* To attract irresistibly, as by beauty or other qualities; to captivate; to hold motionless; to spellbind. **fascinating** *adj.* **fascinatingly** *adv.* **fascination** *n.*

fas-cism (fash´iz um) *n.* A one-party system of government marked by a centralized dictatorship, stringent social and economic controls, and often belligerent nationalism. **fascist** *n.,*

fash-ion (fash´an) *n.* The mode or manner of dress, living, and the style that prevails in society, especially in high society; good form or style; current style or custom; a piece of clothing made up in the current style. **fashion** *v.* To make into a given shape or form; to make fitting. **fashionable** *adj.* **fashionably** *adv.*

fast (fäst) *adj.* Swift; rapid; performed quickly; constant; steadfast; firmly secured; sound or deep, as sleep; permitting or suitable for quick movement, requiring rapidity of motion or action; acting or moving quickly. **fast** *v.* To give up food, especially for a religious reason. **fast** *n.* A period prescribed for fasting.

fas-tid-i-ous (fa stid´ē us) *adj.* Exceedingly delicate or refined; hard to please in matters of taste.

fas-tig-i-ate (fas tig´i āt) *adj.* Pointed at the top; tapering upward to a point.

fat (fat) *adj.* Having superfluous flesh or fat; obese; plump; containing much fat or oil; rich or fertile; as land; abundant; plentiful; profitable; thick; broad. **a fat chance** *Slang* Very little or no chance at all. *n.* Any of a large class of yellowish to white, greasy liquid or solid substances that are widely distributed in animal and plant tissues; consisting of various fatty acids and glycerol, generally odorless, tasteless, and colorless, the richest or most desirable part. **fatty** *adj.*

fat-al (fāt´al) *adj.* Causing death; deadly; bringing ruin or disaster; destructive; decisively important; fateful; brought about by fate; destined; inevitable.

fa-tal-ism (fāt´a liz´um) *n.* The belief that events or things are predetermined by fate and cannot be altered. **fatalist** *n.* **fatalistic** *adj.* **fatalistically** *adv.*

fa-tal-i-ty (fā tal´i tē) *n., pl.* **fatalities** Death caused by a disaster or accident; the capability of causing death or disaster; the quality or state of being subject to or determined by fate.

fate (fāt) *n.* The force or power held to predetermine events; fortune; inevitability; the final result or outcome; unfortunate destiny; doom. **fated** *adj.* **fateful** *adj.* Determining destiny; governed by fate; bringing death or disaster. **fatefully** *adv.* .

fa-ther (fā´thĕr) *n.* The male parent; any male forefather; ancestor; a male who establishes or founds something. **Father** A priest; one of the early Christian writers who formulated doctrines and codified observances. To beget; to act as a father toward. **fatherhood** *v.* **fatherly** *adj.*

fath-om (fath´om) *n.* A unit of length that is equal to six feet or approximately 1. 83 m., used mostly in measuring marine depths. **fathom** *v.* To understand fully.

fath-om-less *adj.* Too deep to measure; too difficult to understand.

fa-tigue (fa tēg´) *n.* The state or condition of extreme tiredness or weariness from prolonged physical or mental exertion. **fatigues** Military clothes for heavy work and field duty. **fatigue** *v.* To become or make tired; to exhaust.

fats-hed-era *n.* An ornamental foliage plant with glossy leaves.

fat-sol-u-ble *adj.* Pertaining to something soluble in fat or oil.

fa-tu-i-ty (fa tŏ´i tē) *n.* Stupidity; foolishness.

fat-u-ous (fach´ö us) *adj.* Silly and foolish in a self-satisfied way. **fatuously** *adv.* **fatuousness** *n.*

fau-ces *n.* The passage at the back of the mouth to the pharynx, formed by the membranous, muscular arches extending downward from each side of the soft palate. **faucial** *adj.*

fau-cet (fo´sit) *n.* A fixture with an adjustable valve used to draw liquids from a pipe or cask.

faugh (fo) *interj.* An exclamation of contempt or disgust.

fault (folt) *n.* An impairment or defect; a weakness; a minor offense or mistake; a break in the earth's crust allowing adjoining surfaces to shift in a direction parallel to the crack; a bad serve, as in tennis. *v.* To criticize. **at fault** Open to blame; in the wrong. **faultily** *adv.* **faultless** *adj.* **faulty** *adj.*

faux pas (fō pä´) *n.* A false step; a social blunder.

fa-vor (fā´vĕr) *n.* A helpful or considerate act; the attitude of friendliness or approbation; the condition of being held in high regard; approval or support. **favors** Consent to sexual intimacy, especially as granted by a woman; a token of love or remembrance; a small gift given to each guest at a party. **favor** *v.* To benefit; to give advantage; to prefer or like one more than another; to support or approve; to look like or resemble; to treat with special care. **favorer** *n.*

fa-vor-ite (fā´vĕr it) *n.* Anything regarded with special favor or preferred above all others; in sports, the contestant considered to be the most likely winner.

fa-vus *n.* A fungus that attacks the scalp of humans and the skin of fowls and mammals.

fax *n.* In *computer science*, a facsimile, a copy of a document sent to a remote terminal by a fax machine or computer over telephone lines; a facsimile machine. **fax** *v.* To send a fax copy.

fay (fā) *n.* A fairy or elf.

faze (fāz) *v.* To worry; to disconcert.

fe-al-ty (fē´al tē) *n., pl.* **fealties** The obligation of allegiance owed to a feudal lord by his vassal or tenant; faithfulness; loyalty.

fear (fēr) *n.* An agitated feeling caused by the anticipation or realization of danger; uneasy feeling that something might happen contrary to one's hopes; a feeling of deep, reverential awe and dread. **fear** *v.* To be apprehensive; to suspect. **fearfulness** *n.* **fearful** *adj.* **fearfully** *adv.*

fea-si-ble (fē´zi bl) *adj.* Capable of being put into effect or accomplished; practical. **feasibility** *n.*

feast (fēst) *n.* A delicious meal; a banquet; a day or days of celebration set aside for a religious purpose or in honor of some person, event, or thing. **feast** *v.* To provide with pleasure.

feat (fēt) *n.* A notable act or achievement.

fea-ture (fē´chér) *n.* The appearance or shape of the face; the main presentation at a movie theater; a special article in a magazine or newspaper that is given special prominence. **feature** *v.*

feb-ri-fuge (feb´ri füj´) *n.* A medicine used to reduce fever.

feb-rile (fē´bril) *adj.* Feverish.

Feb-ru-ary (feb´rö er´ē) *n.*. The second month of the year, having 28 days or, in a leap year, 29 days.

fe-ces (fē´sēz) *pl. n.* Waste that is excreted

from the bowels; excrement. **fecal** *adj.*

fe-cund (fē´kund) *adj.* Fruitful; productive. **fecundity** *n.*

fe-cun-date (fē´kun dāt´) *v.* To make fertile. **fecundation** *n.*

fed *v.* Past tense of feed.

fed *v. abbr.* Federal, federated.

fed-er-al (fed´ér al) *adj.* Of, relating to, or formed by an agreement between two or more states or groups in which each retains certain controlling powers while being united under a central authority; of or pertaining to the United States central government. **Federal** Pertaining to or of the central government of Canada; of or supporting the Union in the American Civil War.

fed-er-ate (fed´e rāt´) *v.* To unite in a federal union or alliance.

fe-do-ra (fi dōr´a) *n.* A soft hat with a low crown creased lengthwise and a brim that can be turned up or down.

fee (fē) *n.* A fixed charge, compensation, or payment for something; a charge for professional services; an inherited estate in land.

fee-ble (fē´bl) *adj.* Very weak; lacking in strength; lacking force; ineffective. **feebleness** *n.* **feebly** *adv.*

feed (fēd) *v.* To supply with food; to consume food; to keep supplied, as with fuel for a fire; to draw support or encouragement. In *computer science*, to enter data into a computing machine. **feed** *n.* The mechanical part, as of a sewing machine, that keeps supplying material to be worked on. *Slang* A meal.

feed-back (fēd´bak´) *n.* The return to the input of a portion of the output of a machine; the return of data for corrections or control.

feel (fēl) *v.* To examine, explore, or perceive through the sense of touch; to perceive as a physical sensation; to believe; to consider; to be aware of; to be emotionally affected by; to think; to suppose; to judge; to experience the full force or import of; to produce the sensory impression of being soft, hard, hot or cold; to produce an indicated overall condition, impression, or reaction. **feeling** *n.*

feet *n.* The plural of foot.

feign (fān) *v.* To make a false show of; to dream up a false story and tell it as the truth; to fabricate; to imitate so as to deceive. **feigned** *adj.*

feint (fānt) *n.* A deceptive or misleading movement intended to draw defensive action away from the real target.

feist *n.* A small dog.

feist-y *adj.* Excited; agitated; frisky and exuberant; quarrelsome.

feld-spar (feld´spär´) *n.* Any of a large group of crystalline materials largely made up of silicates of aluminum.

fe-lic-i-tate (fi lis´i tāt´) *v.* To congratulate; to wish happiness.

fe-lic-i-tous (fi lis´i tus) *adj.* Most appropriate; well chosen; pertinent or effective in manner or style.

fe-lic-i-ty (fi lis´i tē) *n., pl.* **felicities** Happiness; bliss; an instance or source of happiness; an agreeably pertinent or effective style.

fe-line (fē´līn) *adj.* Of or relating to cats, including wild and domestic cats; resembling a cat, as in stealth or agility. **feline** *n.* **felinely** *adv.*

fell (fel) *v.* Past tense of fall; to strike or cause to fall down; to finish a seam with a flat, smooth strip made by joining edges, then folding under and stitching flat. **fell** *n.* Timber cut down during one season; an animal's hide; pelt. *adj.* Cruel and fierce; lethal.

fel-lah (fel´a) *n. pl.* **fellahin** or **fellaheen** An Arab peasant or laborer.

fel-low (fel´ō) *n.* A boy or man; an associate, comrade; the counterpart; one of a pair. *Informal* A boyfriend.

fel-low-ship (fel´ō ship´) *n.* A friendly relationship; the condition or fact of having common interests, ideals, or experiences; the status of being a fellow at a college or university, also the financial grant made to a fellow.

fel-ly (fel´ē) *n. pl.* **fellies** The rim of a wooden wheel, into which spokes are inserted.

fel-on (fel´on) *n.* A person who has committed a felony; an inflammation in the terminal joint or at the cuticle of a finger or toe.

felt (felt) *v.* Past tense of feel. *n.* An unwoven fabric made from pressed animal fibers, as wool or fur; a piece of fabric or material made of felt.

fe-male (fē´māl) *n.* The sex that produces ova or bears young; a plant with a pistil but no stamen, which is capable of being fertilized and producing fruit. **female** *adj.* Of or relating to the sex that produces ova or bears young; suitable to this sex; having a bore, slot, or hollow part designed to receive a projecting part, as a plug or prong.

fem-i-nine (fem´i nin) *adj.* Pertaining to or of the female sex; female; characterized by qualities generally attributed to women; lacking in manly qualities. *Gram.* Applicable to females only or to persons or things classified as female. **feminist** *n.*

fe-mur (fē´mèr) *n., pl.* **femurs** or **femora** The bone extending from the pelvis to the knee. **femoral** *adj.*

fen (fen) *n.* A low, marshy land; a bog.

fend (fend) *v.* To ward off or to keep off; to offer resistance. **fending** *v.*

fe-nes-tra *n.* A natural hole in the bone

between the tympanum and the inner ear; a small transparent area often found in wings of butterflies.

fen-es-tra-tion (fen´i strā´shǝn) n. The design and position of doors and windows in a building.

fe-ral (fēral) adj. Not tame nor domesticated; returned to a wild state; existing in an untamed state.

fer-ment (fer ment´) n. Any substance or agent producing fermentation, as yeast, mold, or enzyme; excitement; unrest; agitation. **fermentable** adj.

fer-men-ta-tion (fe´men tā´shǝn) n. The decomposition of complex organic compounds into simpler substances; the conversion of glucose into ethyl alcohol through the action of zymase; great agitation; commotion.

fer-mi-on n. An artificially produced radioactive metallic element.

fer-mi-um (fer´mē ǝm) n. A metallic radioactive element, symbolized by Fm.

fe-ro-cious (fe rō´shǝs) adj. Extremely savage, fierce, cruel, or blood thirsty. *Slang* Very intense. **ferociously** adv. **ferociousness** n. **ferocity** n.

fer-ret (fer´it) n. A small, red-eyed polecat of Europe, often domesticated and trained to hunt rodents or rabbits. **ferret** v. To search out by careful investigation; to drive out of hiding.

fer-ric (fer´ik) adj. Pertaining to or containing iron.

ferric oxide n. A dark compound that occurs as hematite ore and rust.

fer-rif-er-ous adj. Producing or containing iron.

fer-ro-con-crete n. A building material made of concrete and embedded steel rods.

fer-ro-mag-net-ic (fer´ō mag net´ik) adj. Relating to or being typical of substances, as iron and nickel, that are readily magnetized.

fer-rous (fer´us) adj. Pertaining to or containing iron.

fer-tile (fer´til) adj. Biol. Having the ability to reproduce; rich in material required to maintain plant growth. **fertility** n. **fertileness** n.

fer-til-iz-er (fer´ti lī´zėr) n. A material that fertilizes, such as nitrates or manure which enriches soil.

fer-ule (fer´ul) n. A flat stick sometimes used to punish children. **ferule** v.

fer-vent (fer´vent) adj. Passionate; ardent; very hot. **fervency** n.

fer-vid (fer´vid) adj. Fervent to an extreme degree; impassioned; very hot; burning. **fervidly** adv. **fervidness** n.

fer-vor (fer´vėr) n. Great emotional warmth or intensity.

fes-cue (fes´kū) n. A type of tough grass, often used as pasturage.

fes-tal (fes´tal) adj. Pertaining to or typical of a festival, holiday, or feast.

fes-ter (fes´tėr) v. To develop or generate pus; to be a constant source of irritation or resentment.

fes-ti-val (fes´ti val) n. A particular holiday or celebration; a regularly occurring occasion. **festive** adj.

fe-tal (fēt´al) adj. Relating to or like a fetus.

fetch (fech) v. To go after and return with; to draw forth; to elicit; to bring as a price; to sell for; to strike a blow. **fetching** adj. **fetcher** n.

fete (fāt) n. A festival or feast; a very elaborate outdoor celebration. **fete** v.

fet-e-ri-ta n. A grain sorghum with compact heads of large white seeds, raised in the U.S. for grain and forage.

fet-id (fet´id) adj. Having a foul odor; stinking. **fetidly** adv. **fetidness** n.

fet-ish (fet´ish) n. An object that is regarded as having magical powers; something that one is devoted to excessively or irrationally. *Psychiatry* A nonsexual object that arouses or gratifies sexual desires. **fetishist** n.

fet-lock (fet´lok´) n. A tuft of hair that grows just above the hoof at the back of the leg of a horse.

fe-tol-o-gy n. The medical study of a fetus. **fetologist** n.

fet-ter (fet´ėr) n. A chain or other bond put around the ankles to restrain movement, preventing escape; anything that prevents free movement.

fet-tle (fet´l) n. State; the condition of something.

fe-tus (fē´tus) n. The individual unborn organism carried within the womb from the time major features appear; in humans, the unborn young after the eighth week of development.

feud (fūd) n. A bitter quarrel between two families, usually lasting over a long period of time. **feud** v.

feu-dal (fūd´al) adj. Relating to or characteristic of feudalism. **feudalism** n. **feudally** adv.

fe-ver (fē´vėr) n. Abnormally high body temperature and rapid pulse; a craze; a heightened emotion or activity. **feverish** adj. **feverishly** adv.

fever blister n. A cold sore.

few (fū) adj. Small in number; not many. n. A select or limited group.

few-er adj. Pertaining to a smaller number.

fey (fā) adj. Seemingly spellbound; having clairvoyance; acting as if under a spell.

fi-an-ce (fē´än sā´) n. A man to whom a woman is engaged to be married.

fi-as-co (fē as´kō) n. pl. fiascoes A complete or total failure.

fi-at (fī´at) n. A positive and authoritative

order or decree.

fib (fib) *n.* A trivial lie. **fibber** *n.*

fi-ber (fī´bĕr) *n.* A fine, long, continuous piece of natural or synthetic material made from a filament of asbestos, spun glass, textile, or fabric; internal strength; character. **fibrous** *adj.*

fi-ber-glass (fī´bĕr glas´) *n.* A flexible, nonflammable material of spun glass used for textiles, insulation, and other purposes.

fiber optics *n. pl.* Light optics transmitted through very fine, flexible glass rods by internal reflection. **fiber optic** *adj.*

fi-bril *n.* A very fine filament.

fi-bril-lar *adj.* Pertaining to fibers

fib-ril-la-tion (fī´bri lā´shan) *n. Pathol.* Rapid and uncoordinated contraction of the muscle fibers of the heart.

fi-brin (fī´brin) *n. Biochem.* An insoluble protein that promotes the clotting of blood. **fibrinous** *adj.*

fi-brin-o-gen (fī brin´o jen) *n. Biochem.* A complex blood plasma protein that is converted to fibrin during the process of blood clotting.

fi-broid (fī´broid) *adj.* Made up or resembling fibrous tissue.

fi-bro-vas-cu-lar *adj.* Composed of a fibrous conductive tissue which conveys fluid from one part to another.

fib-u-la (fib´ū la) *n. Anat.* The outer and smaller bone of the lower limb or hind leg, in humans located between the knee and ankle.

-fic *adj. suffix* Making; causing; rendering.

-fication *n. suffix* Making; production.

fick-le (fik´l) *adj.* Inconstant in purpose or feeling; changeable. **fickleness** *n.*

fic-tile *adj.* Capable of being molded; relating to soft clay or earthenware.

fic-tion (fik´shan) *n.* Something that is created or imaginary; a literary work that is produced by the imagination and not based on fact. **fictional** *adj.*

fic-tion-al-i-za-tion *n.* The procedure of narrating an actual event in a fictional form.

fic-tion-eer *n.* An author who writes inferior fiction in large quantities.

fic-ti-tious (fik tish´us) *adj.* Nonexistent; imaginary; not genuine; false; not real. **fictitiously** *adv.* **fictitiousness** *n.*

fid-dle (fid´l) *n.* A violin. **fiddle** *v.* To play the violin; to fidget or make nervous or restless movements; to spend time in a careless way. *Naut.* A rack used at the table to prevent things from sliding off. **fit as a fiddle** To enjoy good or perfect health. **second fiddle** In a position subordinate to that of another. **fiddler** *n.*

fi-de-ism *n.* A tenet that certain premises, as of religion and philosophy, need no rational explanation but should be accepted on faith.

fi-del-i-ty (fi del´l tē) *n., pl.* **fidelities** Faithfulness or loyalty to obligations, vows, or duties. *Elect.* The degree to which a phonograph, tape recorder, or other electronic equipment receives and transmits input signals without distortion.

fidg-et (fij´it) *v.* To move nervously or restlessly. **fidgets** *n. pl.* The condition of being nervous or restless. **fidgeter** *n.* **fidgetiness** *n.* **fidgety** *adj.*

fi-du-ci-ary (fi dū´shē er´ē) *adj.* Relating to or pertaining to the holding of something in trust. *n.* An agent; a trustee.

fie (fī) *interj.* An expression of disgust or impatience in response to an unpleasant surprise.

fief (fēf) *n.* A feudal estate in land.

field (fēld) *n.* A piece of land with few or no trees; a cultivated piece of land devoted to the growing of crops; an area in which a natural resource such as oil is found.

fiend (fēnd) *n.* An evil spirit or demon; a person who is totally engrossed in something. *Slang* An addict. **fiendish** *adj.* **fiendishly** *adv.* **fiendishness** *n.*

fierce (fērs) *adj.* Savage and violent in nature. *Slang* Disagreeable or very difficult. **fiercely** *adv.* **fierceness** *n.*

fier-y (fīer´ē) *adj.* Containing or composed of fire; brightly glowing; blazing; hot and inflamed; full of spirit or intense with emotion. **fieriness** *n.*

fi-es-ta (fē es´ta) *n.* A religious holiday or festival.

fife (fīf) *n.* A small, shrill-toned instrument similar to a flute.

fifth (fifth) *n.* The ordinal of five; one of five equal parts. *Mus.* The space between a tone and another tone five steps from it. **fifth** *adj. & adv.*

Fifth Amendment *n.* An amendment to the United States Constitution, ratified in 1791, guaranteeing due process of law and that no person "shall be forced to testify against himself."

fig (fig) *n.* A tree or shrub bearing a sweet, pear-shaped, edible fruit; the fruit of the fig tree.

fight (fīt) *v.* To struggle against; to quarrel; to argue; to make one's way by struggling; to participate in wrestling or boxing until a final decision is reached. *n.* A physical battle; struggle; strife; conflict; combat.

fig-ment (fig´ment) *n.* An invention or fabrication.

fig-ur-a-tion *n.* The process of shaping into a particular figure; the resulting figure or shape.

fig-u-ra-tive (fig´ūr a tiv) *adj.* Based on, like, or containing a figure of speech; metaphorical; representing by means figure   168   film

of a figure or symbol. -ly *adv.*

fig-ure (fig´ūr) *n.* A symbol or character that represents a number; anything other than a letter; the visible form, silhouette, shape, or line of something; the human form or body; an individual, especially a prominent one; the impression or appearance that a person makes; a design or pattern, as in a fabric; a figure of speech; a series of movements, as in a dance. **figures** In mathematics, calculations; an amount shown in numbers. **figure** *v.* To represent; to depict; to compute.

fig-ure-head (fig´ūr hed´) *n.* A person with nominal leadership but no real power; a carved figure on a ship's bow.

figure of speech *n.* An expression, as a metaphor or hyperbole, where words are used in a more forceful, dramatic, or illuminating way.

fil-a-ment (fil´a ment) *n.* A very thin, finely spun fiber, wire, or thread; the fine wire enclosed in an electric lamp bulb which is heated electrically to incandescence. **filamentous** *adj.*

fi-lar *adj.* Of or pertaining to a thread; *Optics* Having threads across the field of vision.

fil-a-ture *n.* The act of forming into threads; the reeling of silk cocoons; a reel for drawing off silk from cocoons; an establishment for reeling silk.

fil-bert (fil´bèrt) *n.* The edible nut of the hazel tree or the tree it grows on.

filch (filch) *v.* To steal. **filcher** *n.*

file (fil) *n.* A device for storing papers in proper order; a collection of papers so arranged; a line of persons, animals, or things placed one behind another; a hard, steel instrument with ridged cutting surfaces, used to smooth or polish. In *computer science,* a set of related information, as spreadsheets, databases, etc., identified by name and manipulated as a unit. **file** *v.* To march as soldiers; to submit documents.

file attributes *n.* In *computer science,* special nature of a file for identification or protection, such as read-only, archived or hidden.

file conversion In *computer science,* the transfer of a file's formatting codes to allow access by another program.

file maintenance *n.* In *computer science,* correcting and updating files and directories to reflect the most recent data available and purging the system of outdated files.

file management In *computer science,* the organization and tracking of files by the operating system and the user.

file manager *n.* In *computer science,* a software utility designed to simplify the task of locating and organizing files.

file name *n.* In *computer science,* the designation that identifies a data file.

file name extension *n.* In *computer science,* a tag of up to three characters following a file name that aids in identification by the operating system, a program or the user.

file protection *n.* In *computer science,* a file attribute that identifies a data file as read-only; a device on a floppy disk that can be set to make the files on the disk read-only.

file server *n.* In *computer science,* a computer that stores a library of program and data files for a number of users in a network.

fi-let (fi lā´) *n.* A filet of meat or fish; lace or net with a pattern of squares.

fil-i-al (fil´ē al) *adj.* Of or relating to a son or daughter; pertaining to the generation following the parents.

fil-i-buster (fil´i bus´tèr) *n.* An attempt to prolong, prevent, or hinder legislative action by using delaying tactics such as long speeches; using time. **filibuster** *v.* **filibusterer** *n.*

fil-i-gree (fil´i grē´) *n.* Delicate, lace-like ornamental work made of silver or gold intertwisted wire. **filigree** *v. & adj.*

fil-ing (fi´ling) *n. also* **filings** Particles removed by a file.

fill-er (fil´èr) *n.* Something that is added to increase weight or bulk or to take up space; a material used to fill cracks, pores, or holes in a surface before it is completed.

fil-let *or* **fi-let** (fil´it) *n.* A narrow ribbon or band for holding the hair; a strip of boneless fish or meat. **fillet** *v.* To slice, bone, or make into fillets.

fill-in *n.* A person or thing that fills the place of another; a review usually, orally of important information.

fil-lip (fil´ip) *n.* A snap of the finger that has been pressed down by the thumb and then suddenly released; something that arouses or excites. **fillip** *v.*

fil-lis-ter *n.* A plane for grooves; a groove on a window sash that holds the glass and putty.

Fillmore, Millard *n.* (1800-1874) The thirteenth president of the United States from 1850-1853.

fil-ly (fil´ē) *n.* A young female horse less than four years of age; a young girl.

film (film) *n.* A thin covering, layer, or membrane. *Photog.* A photosensitive strip or sheet of flexible cellulose material that is used to make photographic negatives or transparencies; the film containing the pictures projected on a large screen; the motion picture itself. **film** *v.* To cover with or as if with a film; to make a movie; to record on film.

film-dom (film´dom) *n.* The movie industry or business.

film-strip (film´strip´) *n.* A strip of film containing graphic matter for still projection on a screen.

fil-ose *adj.* Threadlike.

fil-ter (fil´tèr) *n.* A device, as cloth, paper, charcoal, or any other porous substance, through which a liquid or gas can be passed to separate out suspended matter. *Photog.* A colored screen that controls the kind and intensity of light waves in an exposure.

filth (filth) *n.* Anything that is dirty or foul; something that is considered offensive.

fil-trate (fil´trāt) *v.* To pass or cause to pass through something. **filtrate** *n.* Anything which has passed through the filter. **filtration** *n.*

fin (fin) *n.* A thin membranous extension of the body of a fish or other aquatic animal, used for swimming and balancing. *Slang* A five dollar bill.

fi-na-gle (fi nā´gl) *v. Slang* To get something by trickery or deceit. **finagling** *adj.* **finagler** *n.*

fi-nal (fin´al) *adj.* Pertaining to or coming to the end; last or terminal. **finality** *n.*

finals *n.* Something decisively final, as the last of a series of athletic contests; the final academic examination.

fi-nal-ize (fin´a līz´) *v.* To put into final and complete form. **finalization** *n.*

fi-nance (fi nans´) *n.* The science of monetary affairs. **finances** Monetary resources; funds. **finance** *v.* To supply the capital or funds for something; to sell or provide on a credit basis. **financial** *adj.* **financially** *adv.*

fin-an-cier (fin an sēr´) *n.* An expert who deals with large-scale financial affairs; one who makes loans.

find (find) *v.* To come upon unexpectedly; to achieve; to attain; to ascertain; to determine; to consider; to regard; to recover or regain something; to detect the true identity or nature of something or someone.

fine (fin) *adj.* Superior in skill or quality; very enjoyable and pleasant; light and delicate in workmanship, texture, or structure; made up or composed of very small parts. *Slang* To be in good health; very well. **fine** *n.* The sum of money required as the penalty for an offense. **fineness** *n.* **fine** *v.* **finely** *adj.*

fi-ne (fē´na) *n., Mus.* The end.

fi-nesse (fi nes´) *n.* A highly refined skill; the skillful handling of a situation.

fin-ger (fing´gèr) *n.* One of the digits of the hand, usually excluding the thumb; that part of a glove made to fit the finger; anything resembling the finger. *Mus.* The use of the fingers in playing an instrument. **finger** *v.*

fin-i-al (fin´ē al) *n.* The ornamental projection or terminating part, as on a lamp shade.

fin-i-cal *adj.* Finicky.

fin-ick-y (fin´i kē) *adj.* Hard to please; choosy. **finickiness** *n.*

fi-nis (fin´is) *n.* The end.

fin-ish (fin´ish) *v.* To bring to an end; to conclude; to reach the end; to consume all. *Slang* To kill or destroy. **finish** *n.* The last stage or conclusion of anything; the perfection or polish in manners, speech, or education; the surface quality or appearance of paint, textiles, or other materials. **finish** *adj.* Having a glossy polish.

fi-nite (fi´nit) *adj.* Having bounds or limits; of or relating to a number which can be determined, counted, or measured. **finitely** *adv.* **finiteness** *n.*

fink (fingk) *n. Slang* A person that breaks a strike; an unsavory person.

fin-ny (fin´ē) *adj.* Having or suggesting fins or fin-like extensions.

fire (fīèr) *n.* The chemical reaction of burning, which releases heat and light. **fire** *v.* To inspire enthusiasm; to ignite or cause to become ignited; to bake in a kiln; to discharge a firearm or explosive; to let a person go from a job; to dismiss. **firing** *adj.*

fire escape *n.* A structure, often metal, used as an emergency exit from a building.

fire-man (fīèr´man) *n., pl.* **firemen** A person employed to prevent or extinguish fires; one who tends fires.

fire station *n.* A building used to house firefighting equipment and firemen.

fire-works (fīèr´werks´) *n.* Explosives used to generate colored lights, smoke, and noise for entertainment and celebrations.

firm (ferm) *adj.* Relatively solid, compact, or unyielding to pressure or touch; steadfast and constant; strong and sure. *n.* A partnership of two or more persons for conducting a business. *v.* To become or make firm or firmer.

fir-ma-ment (fer´ma ment) *n.* The expanse of the heavens; the sky.

firn (firn) *n.* Snow that is partially consolidated by thawing and freezing but has not converted to glacial ice.

first (ferst) *adj.* Preceding all others in the order of numbering; taking place or acting prior to all others; earliest; ranking above all in importance or quality; foremost. **first** *adv.* Above or before all others in time, order, rank, or importance; for the very first time. **first** *n.* The ordinal number that matches the number 1 in a series, symbol 1st; the lowest transmission gear in an automotive vehicle.

first aid *n.* The emergency care given

to a person before full treatment and medical care can be obtained.

First Amendment *n.* The amendment to the Constitution of the United States which forbids Congress to interfere with religion, free speech, free press, the right to assemble peaceably, or the right to petition the government, ratified in 1791.

first-hand (ferst´hand´) *adj.* Coming directly from the original source.

firth (ferth) *n.* A narrow inlet of the sea.

fis-cal (fis´kal) *adj.* Relating to or of the finances or treasury of a nation or a branch of government; financial.

fish (fish) *n., pl.* **fish** *or* **fishes** An aquatic animal having fins, gills for breathing, and usually scales; the flesh of fish used as food. **like a fish out of water** Not at ease or comfortable. **fish** *v.* To try to catch fish; to seek or find one's way; to grope; to try and obtain something in an artful or indirect way.

fis-sile (fis´il) *adv.* Capable of being separated or split in the direction of the grain. *Physics* Fissionable.

fis-sion (fish´an) *n.* The process or act of splitting into parts. *Physics* The exploding of the nucleus of an atom that leads to the formation of more stable atoms and the release of large quantities of energy. **fissionable** *adj.*

fis-si-ped (fis´i ped´) *adj.* Having toes that are separated.

fis-sure (fish´er) *n.* A narrow opening, crack, or cleft in a rock. **fissure** *v.*

fist (fist) *n.* The hand closed tightly with the fingers bent into the palm.

fis-tu-la (fis´che la) *n. pl.* **fistulas** *or* **fistulae** *Pathol.* A duct or other passage formed by the imperfect closing of a wound or abscess and leading either to the body surface or to another hollow organ. **fistulous** *adj.*

fit (fit) *v.* To be the proper size and shape; to be in good physical condition; to possess the proper qualifications; to be competent; to provide a time or place for something; to belong. *adj.* Adapted or adequate for a particular circumstance or purpose. *Med.* A convulsion; an impulsive and irregular exertion or action. **fitter, fitness** *n.*

fitch (fich) *n.* The polecat of the Old World or its fur.

fit-ful (fit´ful) *adj.* Characterized by irregular actions; capricious; restless.

five (fiv) *n.* The cardinal number equal to 4 + 1; any symbol of this number, as 5; anything with five units, parts, or members. **five** *adj.*

fix (fiks) *v.* To make stationary, firm, or stable; to direct or hold steadily; to place or set definitely; to make rigid; to arrange or adjust; to prepare, as a meal. **fix** *n.* A position of difficulty or

embarrassment. *Naut.* The position of a ship determined by observations, radio, or bearings. *Slang* The injection of a narcotic such as heroin.

fix-a-tion (fik sā´shan) *n.* The act or state of being fixed; a strong, often unhealthy preoccupation. **fixate** *v.*

fixed disk *n.* In *computer science*, a computer disk that is permanently mounted in its drive.

fixed asset *n.* An item of value having a relatively permanent nature, used in operating a business, but not intended to be converted to cash

fix-i-ty (fik´si tē) *n.* The quality or state of being fixed or stable.

fix-ture (fiks´chēr) *n.* Anything that is fixed or installed, as an appendage of a house; any article of personal property affixed to realty to become a part of and be governed by the law of real property.

fizz (fiz) *n.* A hissing or bubbling sound; effervescence; tiny gas bubbles.

fiz-zle (fiz´l) *v.* To fail after making a promising start. **fizzle** *n.* A hissing or sputtering sound.

flab (flab) *n.* Excessive, loose, and flaccid body tissue. **flabby** *adj.* **flabbiness** *n.*

flac-cid (flak´sid) *adj.* Lacking resilience or firmness. **flaccidity** *n.* **flaccidly** *adv.*

flac-on (flak´on) *n.* A small, stoppered decorative bottle.

flag (flag) *n.* A piece of cloth, usually oblong, bearing distinctive colors and designs to designate a nation, state, city, or organization. *Bot.* Any of various iris or cattail plants with long blade-shaped leaves. **flag** *v.* To adorn with flags for identification or ornamentation; to grow weak or tired.

Flag Day *n.* June 14, 1777, the day on which Congress proclaimed the Stars and Stripes the national standard of the United States.

flag-el-lant (flaj´e lant) *n.* One who whips himself or has himself whipped by another for religious motives or for sexual excitement. **flagellation** *n.*

flag-el-late (flaj´e lāt´) *v.* To punish by whipping; to scourge.

flag-eo-let (flaj´o let´) *n.* A small flute-like wind instrument, with a tubular mouthpiece and six or more holes.

flag-on (flag´on) *n.* A vessel or container with a handle, spout, and hinged lid, used for holding wines or liquors.

fla-grant (flā´grant) *adj.* Obvious; glaring; disgraceful; notorious; outrageous. **flagrantly** *adv.*

flair (flâr) *n.* An aptitude or talent for something; a dashing style.

flak (flak) *n.* Antiaircraft fire; abusive or excessive criticism.

flake (flāk) *n.* A small, flat, thin piece which has split or peeled off from a

surface. *Slang* Odd-ball; eccentric.
flake *v.* **flakily** *adv.* **flakiness** *n.* **-y** *adj.*

flam-boy-ant (flam boi´ant) *adj.*
Extravagantly ornate; showy; florid;
brilliant and rich in color. **flamboyance**
n. **flamboyancy** *n.* **flamboyantly** *adv.*

flame (flām) *n.* A mass of burning vapor
or gas rising from a fire, often having
a bright color and forming a tongue-
shaped area of light; something that
resembles a flame in motion, intensity,
or appearance; a bright, red-yellow
color; violent and intense emotion.
Slang A sweetheart. **flame** *v.*

fla-men-co (flä meng´kō) *n.* A fiery
percussive dance of the Andalusian
gypsies with strong and often
improvised rhythms.

flam-ma-ble (flam´a bl) *adj.* Capable
of being easily ignited and burning
rapidly. **flammability** *n.*

flange (flanj) *n.* A projecting rim or collar
-used to strengthen or guide a wheel
or other object, keeping it on a fixed
track.

flank (flangk) *n.* The fleshy part between
the ribs and the hip on either side of
the body of an animal or human being;
the lateral part of something. *Milit.* The
right or left side of a military bastion
or formation. *v.* To be stationed at the
side of something. **flanker** *n.*

flan-nel (flan´el) *n.* A woven fabric made
of wool or a wool, cotton, or synthetic
blend.

flan-nelet-te *n.* Cotton flannel.

flap (flap) *v.* To move up and down; to
cause to swing or sway loosely, as in
the wind; to strike with something
flexible; to flutter; to beat or strike a
blow with something broad and
flexible. **flap** *n.* Something that hangs
loose or swings freely.

flare (flâr) *v.* To blaze up or burn with
a bright light; to break out suddenly
or violently, as with emotion or action;
to open or spread outward.

flash (flash) *v.* To burst forth repeatedly
or suddenly into a brilliant fire or light;
to occur or appear briefly or suddenly.
flash *n.* A short and important news
break or transmission. **flashy** *adj.*

flash-o-ver (flash´ō´vėr) *n.* A disruptive
abnormal electrical discharge through
the air or around the surface of a liquid.

flask (flask) *n.* A small container made
of glass and used in laboratories.

flat (flat) *adj.* Extending horizontally
with no curvature or tilt; stretched out
level, prostrate or prone; lacking flavor
or zest; deflated. *Mus.* Below the
correct pitch. **flat** *n.* An apartment that
is entirely on one floor of a building.
flat broke Having little or no money.
fall flat Fail to achieve. **flatly** *adv.*

flat-ter (flat´ėr) *v.* To praise extrava-

gantly, especially without sincerity;
to gratify the vanity of; to portray
favorably; to show as more attractive.
flatterer *n.* **flattering** *adj.*

flat-ter-y (flat´e rē) *n.* Excessive, often
insincere compliments.

flat-u-lent (flach´u lent) *adj.* Marked
by or affected with gases generated in
the intestine or stomach; pretentious
without real worth or substance.
flatulence *n.* **flatulently** *adv.*

flaunt (flont) *v.* To display showily.

flau-tist (flo´tist) *n.* A flutist.

fla-vor (flā´vėr) *n.* A distinctive element
in the taste of something; a distinctive,
characteristic quality; a flavoring. *v.*
To impart flavor to. **flavorful** *adj.*

fla-vor-ing (flā´vėr ing) *n.* A substance,
as an extract or something else that is
used to increase the flavor.

flaw (flo) *n.* A defect or blemish that is
often hidden and that may cause failure
under stress; a weakness in character;
a fault in a legal paper that may nullify
it. **flaw** *v.*

flax (flaks) *n.* A plant with blue flowers
and seeds that yield linseed oil and
slender stems from which a fine textile
fiber is derived.

flay (flā) *v.* To remove the skin of; to
scold harshly.

flea (flē) *n.* A small, wingless, bloodsucking, parasitic jumping insect; a parasite
of warm-blooded animals.

fleam (flēm) *n., Surg.* A sharp instrument
used in surgery for opening veins.

flea market *n.* A place where antiques
and used items and goods are sold.

fleck (flek) *n.* A tiny spot or streak; a
small flake or bit. **fleck** *v.* To mark with
flecks.

fledg-ling *or* **fledge-ling (flej´ling)** *n.*
A young bird with newly acquired
feathers; a person who is inexperienced;
a beginner.

flee (flē) *v.* To run away; to move swiftly
away. **fleer** *n.*

fleece (flēs) *n.* A coat of wool covering
a sheep; the soft wool covering a
sheep. **fleece** *v.* To shear the fleece
from; to swindle; to cover with fleece.
fleeciness *n.* **fleecily** *adv.* **fleecy** *adj.*

fleer (flēr) *v.* To laugh or grimace in a
coarse or mocking manner; jeer.

fleet (flēt) *n.* A number of warships
operating together under the same
command; a number of vehicles, as
taxicabs or fishing boats, operated
under one command. **fleet** *adj.* Moving
rapidly or nimbly. **fleetly** *adv.*

flesh (flesh) *n.* Soft tissue of the body
of a human or animal, especially
skeletal muscle; the meat of animals
as distinguished from fish or fowl; the
pulpy substance of a fruit or vegetable;
the body as opposed to the mind or

soul; mankind in general; one's family.

flesh *v.* To arouse the hunting instinct of dogs by feeding fresh meat.

flew *v.* Past tense of *fly*.

flex (fleks) *v.* To bend the arm repeatedly; to contract a muscle.

flex-i-ble (flek´si bl) *adj.* Capable of being bent or flexed; pliable; responsive to change; easily yielding. **flexibility** *n.* **flexibly** *adv.*

flex-or (flek´sér) *n.* A muscle that serves to bend a body joint.

flex time *n.* A system which allows employees to set their own work schedules within a wide range of hours.

flex-ure (flek´shér) *n.* The state of being flexed or bent; a bent part.

flick (flik) *n.* A light, quick snapping movement or the sound accompanying it. *Slang* A movie. **flick** *v.* To strike or hit with a quick, light stroke; to cause to move with a quick movement.

flick-er (flik´ér) *v.* To burn or shine unsteadily, as a candle. **flicker** *n.* A wavering or unsteady light; a North American woodpecker having a brownish back and a spotted breast.

fli-er *or* **fly-er (flī´ér)** *n.* One who or that which flies, especially an aviator; a daring or risky venture; a printed advertisement or handbill for mass distribution.

flight (flīt) *n.* The act or manner of flying; a scheduled airline trip; a group that flies together; a swift or rapid passage or movement, as of time; a group of stairs leading from one floor to another; an instance of fleeing.

flim-flam (flim´flam´) *n.* *Slang* A swindle; trick; hoax. **flimflam** *v.*

flim-sy (flim´zē) *adj.* Lacking in physical strength or substance; unconvincing. **flimsiness** *n.* **flimsily** *adv.*

flinch (flinch) *v.* To wince or pull back, as from pain; to draw away.

flin-ders *n.* Fragments; splinters.

fling (fling) *v.* To throw or toss violently; to throw oneself completely into an activity. **fling** *n.* An act of casting away; a casual attempt; a period devoted to self-indulgence; unrestraint.

flint (flint) *n.* A hard quartz that produces a spark when struck by steel; an implement used by primitive man; an alloy used in lighters to ignite the fuel.

flip (flip) *v.* To turn or throw suddenly with a jerk; to strike or snap quickly and lightly. *Slang* To go crazy; to become upset or angry; to react enthusiastically. **flip** *n.* **flipper** *n.*

flirt (flert) *v.* To make teasing romantic or sexual overtures; to act so as to attract attention; to dart. **flirt** *n.* A person who flirts; a snappy, quick, jerky movement. **flirtation, flirtatiousness** *n.* **flirtatious** *adj.*

flit (flit) *v.* To move rapidly or abruptly.

flit-ter (flit´ér) *v.* To flutter. **flitter** *n.*

float (flōt) *n.* An act or instance of floating; something that floats on the surface of or in a liquid; a device used to buoy the baited end of a fishing line; a floating platform anchored near a shoreline, used by swimmers or boats; a vehicle with a platform used to carry an exhibit in a parade; a drink consisting of ice cream floating in a beverage. **float** *v.* To be or cause to be suspended within or on the surface of a liquid; to be or cause to be suspended in or move through the air as if supported by water; to drift randomly from place to place; to move lightly and easily; to place a security on the market; to obtain money for the establishment or development of an enterprise by issuing and selling securities. **floating** *adj.*

flock (flok) *n.* A group of animals of all the same kind, especially birds, sheep, geese, etc., living, feeding or kept together; a group under the direction of a single person, especially the members of a church; a large number. **flock** *v.* To travel as if in a flock.

floe (flō) *n.* A large, flat mass of floating ice or a detached part of such a mass.

flog (flog) *v.* To beat hard with a whip or stick. **flogger** *n.*

flood (flud) *n.* The great deluge depicted in the Bible; an overflow of water onto land that is normally dry; an overwhelming quantity. **flood** *v.* To overwhelm with or as if with a flood; to fill abundantly or overwhelm; to supply the carburetor of an engine with an excessive amount of fuel; in football, to send more than one pass receiver into the same defensive area.

floor (flōr) *n.* The level base of a room; the lower inside surface of a structure; a ground surface; the right, as granted under parliamentary rules, to speak to a meeting or assembly; an area dividing a building into stories. **floor** *v.* To cover or furnish with a floor; to knock down; to overwhelm; to puzzle; to press the accelerator of a vehicle to the floorboard.

floo-zy (flō´zē) *n., pl.* **floozies** *Slang* A sleazy, loose woman; a prostitute.

flop (flop) *v.* To fall down clumsily; to move about in a clumsy way. *Slang* To completely fail; to go to bed.

flop-py (flop´ē) *adj.* Flexible and loose. **floppily** *adv.* **floppiness** *n.*

floppy disk *n.* In *computer science*, a flexible plastic disk coated with magnetic material, used to record and store computer data.

flo-ra (flōr´a) *n., pl.* **floras** *or* **florae** Plant life growing in a specific region, season, or historic period.

flo-ral (flōr´al) *adj.* Of or pertaining to flowers.

flo-res-cence (flō res´ens) *n.* A state or process of flourishing. **florescent** *adj.*

flor-id (flōr´id) *adj.* Flushed with a rosy color or redness; ornate. **floridness** *n.*

Flor-id-a *n.* A state located on the southeastern coast of the United States, statehood March 3, 1845, state capital Tallahassee.

flo-rif-er-ous *adj.* Producing flowers; blooming.

flo-rist (flōr´ist) *n.* One who grows or sells live flowers and artificial ones made of silk or silk-like fibers.

flo-ris-tics *n.* A branch of the science dealing with the distribution and study of plants upon the earth.

floss (flos) *n.* A loosely twisted embroidery thread; a soft, silky fiber, such as the tassel on corn; a thread, for dental hygiene. **floss** *v.* To clean between the teeth with dental floss.

flo-ta-tion (flō tā´shan) *n.* The act or state of floating.

flot-sam (flot´sam) *n.* Any goods remaining afloat after a ship has sunk.

flounce (flouns) *n.* A gathered piece of material attached to the upper edge of another surface, as on a curtain. **flounce** *v.* To move with exaggerated tosses of the body. **flouncy** *adj.*

floun-der (floun´dėr) *v.* To struggle clumsily, as to gain footing; to act or speak in a confused way. **flounder** *n.* Any of various edible marine flatfish.

flour-ish (fler´ish) *v.* To thrive; to fare well; to prosper and succeed. **flourish** *n.* A decorative touch or stroke, especially in handwriting; a dramatic act or gesture; a musical fanfare, as of trumpets.

flout (flout) *v.* To have or show open contempt for. **floutingly** *adv.*

flow (flō) *v.* To move freely, as a fluid; to circulate, as blood; to proceed or move steadily and easily; to rise; to derive; to be abundant in something; to hang in a loose, free way. **flow** *n.*

flow-age (flō´ij) *n.* An overflowing; a flooded condition; flood water.

flow chart *n.* A diagram that shows the progress of a series of operations on a particular project.

flow-ing (flō´ing) *adj.* Moving at a smooth steady pace; moving with ease, smoothly and gracefully; having a bountiful supply. **flowingly** *adv.*

flu (flö) *n. Informal* Influenza.

flub (flub) *v.* To bungle or botch; to make a mess of. **flub** *n.*

fluc-tu-ant *adj.* Unstable; moving in waves; fluctuating. *Med.* Of a boil or abscess, having a compressible semi-liquid center which requires lancing.

fluc-tu-ate (fluk´chö āt´) *v.* To shift irregularly; to change; to undulate.

flue (flö) *n.* A conduit or passage through which air, gas, steam, or smoke can pass.

flu-ent (flö´ent) *adj.* Having an understanding of a language use; flowing smoothly and naturally; flowing or capable of flowing. **fluency** *n.* **fluently** *adv.*

flu-id (flö´id) *n.* A substance, as water or gas, capable of flowing. **fluid** *adj.* Changing readily, as a liquid. **fluidity, fluidness** *n.* **fluidly** *adv.*

fluid ounce *n.* A United States unit of liquid capacity that is equal to one-sixteenth pint.

fluke (flök) *n.* A flatfish, especially a flounder; a flattened, parasitic trematode worm; the triangular head of an anchor at the end of either of its arms; a barb or point on an arrow; an unexpected piece of good luck.

flung *v.* Past tense of fling.

flunk (flungk) *v. Slang* To fail in, as an examination or course; to give a failing grade to.

flu-o-res-cence (flö´o res´ens) *n. Chem. & Phys.* Emission of electromagnetic radiation, usually as visible light, resulting from and occurring during the absorption of radiation from another source; the radiation emitted. **fluoresce** *v.* **fluorescent** *adj.*

fluor-i-date *v.* To add a fluoride to water in order to prevent tooth decay.

fluor-i-da-tion (flür´i dā´shan) *n.* The addition of fluoride to drinking water to help prevent tooth decay.

flu-o-ride (flö´o rid´) *n.* A compound of fluorine with another element or a radical.

flu-o-rine (flö´o rēn´) *n.* A pale yellow, corrosive, and extremely reactive gaseous element, symbolized by F.

flur-ry (flur´ē) *n., pl.* **flurries** A sudden gust of wind; a brief, light fall of snow or rain, accompanied by small gusts; a sudden burst of activity or commotion. **flurry** *v.* To cause to become agitated.

flush (flush) *v.* To flow or rush out suddenly and abundantly; to become red in the face; to blush; to glow with a reddish color; to purify or wash out with a brief, rapid gush of water; to cause to flee from cover, as a game animal or bird. **flush** *n.* Glowing freshness or vigor; a hand in certain card games, as poker, in which all the cards are the same suit. **flush** *adj.* Having a heightened reddish color; abundant; affluent; prosperous; having surfaces that are even; arranged with adjacent sides close together; having margins aligned with no indentations.

flush *adv*. In an even position with another surface; in a direct way, as a direct blow.

flus-ter (flŭs´tẽr) *v*. To make or become nervous or confused.

flute (flŏt) *n*. A high-pitched, tubular woodwind instrument equipped with finger holes and keys; a decorative groove in the shaft of a column; a small grooved pleat, as in cloth. **fluting** *n*.

flut-ist *n*. A flute player.

flut-ter (flut´ẽr) *v*. To flap or wave rapidly and irregularly; to fly as with a light, rapid beating of the wings; to beat erratically, as one's heart; to move about in a restless way. **flutter** *n*.

flutter kick *n*. An alternate kicking motion in swimming.

flux (flŭks) *n*. A flowing or discharge; a constant flow or movement; a state of constant fluctuation or change; a substance that promotes the fusing of metals and prevents oxide formation. **flux** *v*. To make fluid; to melt; to apply a flux to.

fly (flī) *v*. To move through the air on wings or wing-like parts; to travel by air; to float or cause to float in the air; to escape; to flee; to pass by swiftly or quickly; to hit a fly ball. **fly** *n*. A folded piece of cloth that covers the fastening of a garment, especially trousers; a fly ball one has batted over the field; any of numerous winged insects, including the housefly and the tsetse; a fishing lure that resembles an insect. **fly off the handle** To react explosively.

fly-by-night (flī´bī nīt´) *adj*. Unstable or temporary; financially unsound.

flying saucer *n*. An unidentified disk-shaped or saucer-shaped flying object reported as being seen in the air.

foal (fōl) *n*. The young animal, as a horse, especially one under a year old. **foal** *v*. To give birth to a foal.

foam (fōm) *n*. A mass of bubbles produced on the surface of a liquid by agitation; froth; a firm, spongy material used especially for insulation and upholstery. **foam** *v*. To cause to form foam. **foam at the mouth** To be very angry.

foam rubber *n*. A spongy rubber, of fine texture which is whipped prior to vulcanization, used in pillows and mattresses.

fob (fŏb) *n*. A chain or ribbon attached to a pocket watch and worn dangling from a pocket; an ornament or seal worn on a fob. **fob** *v*. To dispose of by fraud, deceit, or trickery; to put off by excuse.

focal infection *n*. *Pathol*. A persistent bacterial infection, localized in an area or organ which may enter the bloodstream and cause symptoms in other parts of the body.

focal length *n*. The distance to the focus from a lens surface or concave mirror.

fo-cus (fō´kus) *n*., *pl*. **focuses** *or* **foci** A point in an optical system at which rays converge or from which they appear to diverge; the clarity with which an optical system delivers an image; adjustment for clarity; a center of activity or interest **focus** *v*. To produce a sharp, clear image of; to adjust a lens in order to produce a clean image; to direct; to come together at a point of focus. **focal** *adj*. **focally** *adv*.

fod-der (fŏd´ẽr) *n*. A coarse feed for livestock, made from chopped stalks of corn and hay.

foe (fō) *n*. An enemy in war; an opponent or adversary.

foe-tal (fēt´al) *adj*. *Var*. of fetal.

foe-tus (fē´tus) *n*. *Var*. of fetus.

fog (fog) *n*. A vapor mass of condensed water which lies close to the ground; a state of mental confusion or bewilderment. **fog** *v*. To obscure or cover over, as if with fog. **foggily** *adv*. **foggy** *adj*.

foi-ble (foi´bl) *n*. A minor flaw, weakness, or failing.

foil (foil) *v*. To prevent from being successful; to thwart. **foil** *n*. A very thin, flexible sheet of metal; one that serves as a contrast; a fencing sword having a light, thin, flexible blade and a blunt point.

foist (foist) *v*. To pass off something as valuable or genuine.

fold (fōld) *v*. To double or lay one part over another; to bring from an opened to a closed position; to put together and intertwine; to envelop or wrap; to blend in by gently turning one part over another. *Slang* To give in; to stop production; to fail in business. **fold** *n*. A line, layer, pleat or crease formed by folding; a folded edge; an enclosed area for domestic animals; a flock of sheep; a people united by common aims and beliefs; a church and its members.

fol-de-rol (fol´de ro˝) *n*. Nonsense; a pretty but useless ornament.

folding door *n*. A door made of hinged sections that can be folded together.

fo-li-age (fō´lē ij) *n*. The leaves of growing plants and trees; a cluster of flowers and branches.

fo-li-o (fō´lē ō˝) *n*. A large sheet of paper folded once in the middle; a folder for loose papers; a book that consists of folios; a page number.

folk (fōk) *n*., *pl*. **folk** *or* **folks** An ethnic group of people forming a nation or tribe; people of a specified group; a person's parents, family, or relatives.

folk tale *n*. A traditional, anonymous

legend originating and passed down orally from one generation to another.

fol-li-cle (fol´i kl) n. A small anatomical cavity or sac.

fol-low (fol´ō) v. To proceed or come after; to pursue; to follow the course of; to obey; to come after in time or position; to ensue; to result; to attend to closely; to understand the meaning of. **follower** n.

follow out v. To carry to a conclusion; to follow to the end.

follow through v. To extend or carry through, as the part of the stroke after the ball has been hit; to pursue an activity, especially to completion.

follow-up n. The act of following up; a letter sent to enhance a previous communication or notice. **follow up** v. To pursue closely to a conclusion.

fol-ly (fol´ē) n., pl. **follies** Lack of good judgment; an instance of foolishness; an excessively costly and often unprofitable undertaking.

fo-ment (fō ment´) v. To rouse; to incite; to treat therapeutically with moist heat. **foment, fomentation** n.

fond (fond) adj. Affectionate liking; cherished with great affection; deeply felt. **fondness** n.

fon-dant (fon´dant) n. A sweet, soft preparation of sugar used in candies and icing; a candy made chiefly of fondant.

fon-dle (fon´dl) v. To stroke, handle, or caress affectionately and tenderly.

fond-ly (fond´lē) adv. In an affectionately manner.

fon-due (fon dö) n. A preparation of melted cheese, with white wine; a dish consisting of small pieces of food dipped into hot liquid.

font (font) n. A receptacle in a church that holds baptismal or holy water; an assortment of printing type of the same size and face. In computer science, traditionally descriptive of one type face and style in one size; with the introduction of scalable fonts, one font often refers to a type face in a single style in a wide range of sizes.

food (fōd) n. A substance consisting essentially of carbohydrates and protein used to sustain life and growth in the body of an organism; nourishment, as in solid form; something that sustains or nourishes. **food for thought** Something to think about, something to ponder.

food chain n. A sequence of plants and animals in which each uses the next usually smaller or lower member as a food source.

food poisoning n. An acute gastrointestinal ailment caused by bacteria or toxic products produced by the bacteria that contaminate food.

food-stuff (fōd´stuff´) n. A substance having food value.

fool (föl) n. One lacking good sense or judgment; one who can easily be tricked or made to look foolish. **fool** v. To dupe; to act in jest; to joke. *Slang* To amuse oneself.

fool-er-y (fö´le rē) n. Foolish conduct; a foolish action.

fool-ish (fö´lish) adj. Marked by a lack of good sense; unwise. **foolishly** adv. **foolishness** n.

fool-proof adj. Infallible.

foot (füt) n., pl. **feet** The lower extremity of the vertebrate leg upon which one stands; a unit of measurement equal to 12 inches; a basic unit of verse meter that consists of a group of syllables; the end lower or opposite the head; the lowest part. **foot** v. To go on foot; to walk or run. **foot the bill** To pay for all. **on foot** Walking rather than riding.

foot-age n. Length expressed in feet, as the footage of a film; the total number of running feet; as board footage.

foot–and–mouth disease n. A highly contagious febrile virus disease of cattle and other hoofed animals marked by ulcerating blisters in the mouth, around the hooves, and on the udder.

foot-ball (füt´bol) n. A game played by two teams on a long rectangular field having goals at either end whose object is to get the ball over a goal line or between goal posts by running, passing or kicking; the oval ball used in the game of football.

foot-board (füt´bōrd´) n. A small platform to support the feet; a board forming the upright piece across the foot of a bed.

foot-bridge (füt´brij´) n. A bridge for pedestrians.

foot-ed (füt´id) adj. Having a foot or feet; having a certain number of feet: often used in compound words, as a four-footed animal.

foot-fall (füt´fol´) n. A footstep; the sound of a footstep.

foot-gear (füt´gēr´) n. Articles used to cover and protect the feet, as shoes or boots.

foot-hill (füt´hil´) n. A low hill at or near the foot of a mountain or a higher hill.

foot-hold (füt´hōld´) n. A place providing support for the foot, as in climbing; a position usable as a base for advancement.

foot-ing (füt´ing) n. Secure and stable position for placement of the feet; a foundation.

foot-less adj. Without feet.

foot-lights n., pl. *Theater* A row of lights positioned across the front of a stage; the theater as a profession.

foot-lock-er (fŭt´lok˘ĕr) n. A small trunk for personal belongings, designed to be placed at the foot of a bed.

foot-loose (fŭt´lös˘) adj. Free to move as one pleases; having no ties.

foot-note (fŭt´nöt˘) n. A note of reference, explanation, or comment usually below the text on a printed page; a commentary. **footnote** v.

foot-pace (fŭt´pās˘) n. A walking pace; a platform or stair landing.

foot-pad (fŭt´pad˘) n. A person who goes on foot and robs other pedestrians.

foot-path (fŭt´path˘) n. A narrow path for people on foot.

foot-print (fŭt´print˘) n. The outline or impression of the foot on a surface; the area within which a spacecraft is expected to land.

foot-rest (fŭt´rest˘) n. A support for the feet used for resting the feet.

foot soldier n. An infantryman.

foot-sore (fŭt´sōr˘) adj. Having sore or tender feet.

foot-stalk (fŭt´stok˘) n. Zool. A supportive structure that resembles a stalk. Bot. A stem.

foot-step (fŭt´step˘) n. A footprint; the distance covered by a step.

foot-stool (fŭt´stöl˘) n. A low stool for resting the feet.

foot-wear (fŭt´wâr˘) n. Articles, as shoes or boots, worn on the feet.

foot-work (fŭt´werk˘) n. The use of the feet, as in boxing.

fop (fop) n. A man unduly concerned with his clothes or appearance; a dandy. **foppery, foppishness** n. **foppish** adj.

for (for) prep. Used to indicate the extent of something; used to indicate the number or amount of; considering the usual characteristics of; on behalf of someone; to be in favor of. **for** conj. Because; in as much as; with the purpose of.

for-age (for´ij) n. Food for cattle or other domestic animals; a search for supplies or food. **forage** v. To make a raid so as to find supplies; to plunder or rummage through, especially in search of provisions.

for-as-much as conj. In view of the fact that; since.

for-ay (for´ā) n. A raid to plunder; act of war. **foray** v.

for-bade or **for-bad** v. Past tense of forbid.

for-bear (for´bâr˘) v. To refrain from; to use self-restraint; to be patient.

for-bear-ance (for bâr´ans) n. The act of forbearing; a refraining from something, as a debt or obligation.

for-bid (fer bid´) v. To command someone not to do something; to prohibit by law; to prevent.

for-bid-den adj. Prohibited; not permitted.

forbidden fruit n. Bib. Fruit of the tree of knowledge of good and evil in the Garden of Eden which Adam and Eve ate although it was forbidden; an illegal pleasure or immoral indulgence.

forbidding (fer bid´ing) adj. Very difficult; disagreeable.

force (fōrs) n. Energy or power; strength; the use of such power; intellectual influence; a group organized for a certain purpose. Phys. Something that changes the state of rest or the body motion or influence. **force** v. To compel to do something or to act; to obtain by coercion; to bring forth, as with effort; to move or drive against resistance; to break down by force; to press or impose, as one's will. **in force** In large numbers; in effect. **forceful** adj. **forcer** n. **forcefully** adv.

force–feed v. To force food by employing force; to force to take.

force-meat (fōrs´mēt˘) n. Finely ground meat, fish, or poultry, used in stuffing or served separately.

for-ceps (for´seps) n., pl. An instrument resembling a pair of tongs used for manipulating, grasping or extracting, especially in surgery.

force pump n. A pump which draws and forces a liquid by means of pressure or force directly applied, in contrast to a lift pump.

forc-i-ble (fōr´si bl) adj. Accomplished or achieved by force; marked by force. **forcibly** adv.

ford (fōrd) n. A shallow place in a body of water that can be crossed without a boat. **ford** v. To wade across a body of water. **fordable** adj.

Ford, Gerald Rudolph n. (1913-) The thirty-eighth president of the United States from 1974-1977.

Ford, Henry n. (1863-1947) American automobile maker.

for-do, fore-do (for dö) v. To overpower or destroy; to overcome with fatigue.

fore (fōr) adj. & adv. Situated in, at, or toward the front; forward. **fore** n. The front of something. **fore** interj. A cry used by a golfer to warn others that a ball is about to land in their direction.

fore–and–aft (fōr´and aft˘) adj. Lying or going lengthwise on a ship; from stem to stern.

fore-arm (fōr ärm˘) v. To prepare in advance, as for a battle. **forearm** n. The part of the arm between the elbow and the wrist.

fore-bear or **for-bear** (fōr´bâr˘) n. An ancestor.

fore-bode (fōr böd´) v. To give an indication or warning in advance; to have a premonition of something evil. **foreboding** n. **forebodingly** adv.

fore-brain (fōr'brān') *n. Anat.* The anterior of the three primary divisions of the developing vertebrate brain, or the corresponding segments of the adult vertebrate brain.

fore-cast (fōr'kast') *v.* To estimate or calculate in advance, especially to predict the weather. **forecaster** *n.*

fore-cas-tle (fōk'sal) *n.* The part of a ship's upper deck located forward of the foremast; living quarters for the crew at the bow of a merchant ship.

fore-close (fōr klōz') *v.* To recall a mortgage in default and take legal possession of the mortgaged property; to exclude or shut out. **foreclosure** *n.*

fore-go (fōr gō') *v.* To go before; to precede in time, place, etc. **-going** *adj.*

foregone conclusion *n.* An inevitable result; a conclusion determined before argument or consideration of evidence.

for-eign (for'in) *adj.* Situated outside one's native country; belonging to; located in or concerned with a country or region other than one's own; involved with other nations; occurring in a place or body in which it is not normally located. **foreigner** *n.*

foreign affairs *n.* Diplomatic, commercial, or other matters having to do with international relations.

fore-knowl-edge (fōr'nol'ij) *n.* Prior knowledge of something; knowledge beforehand.

fore-most (fōr'mōst') *adj. & adv.* First in rank, position, time, or order.

fo-ren-sic (fo ren'sik) *adj.* Of, relating to, or used in courts of justice or formal debate. **forensically** *adv.*

forensic medicine *n.* A science dealing with the application of medicine in legal problems.

fore-or-dain (fōr'or dān') *v.* Appoint or dispose of in advance; predestine.

fore-quar-ter *n.* The front portion of the body of an animal, as of lamb or beef.

fore-short-en (fōr'shor'ten) *v.* To shorten parts of an object in order to give the illusion of depth.

fore-sight (fōr'sīt') *n.* The act or capacity of foreseeing; the act of looking forward; concern for the future; prudence. **foresighted** *adj.*

fore-skin (fōr'skin') *n.* A fold of skin that covers the glans of the penis.

for-est (for'ist) *n.* A large tract of land covered with trees.

fore-stall (fōr stol') *v.* To exclude, hinder, or prevent by prior measures.

fore-tell (fōr tel') *v.* To tell about in advance; to predict. **foreteller** *n.*

fore-thought (fōr'thot') *n.* Prior thought or planning; a plan for the future.

fore-to-ken (fōr tō'ken) *v.* To warn beforehand. **foretoken** *n.*

for-ev-er (for ev'ér) *adv.* For eternity; without end.

fore-warn (fōr worn') *v.* To warn in advance.

fore-word (fōr'werd) *n.* Preface.

for-feit (for'fit) *n.* Something taken away as punishment; a penalty; something that is placed in escrow and redeemed on payment of a fine; a forfeiture. **forfeit** *v.* To lose or give up the right to by some offense or error.

for-fei-ture *n.* The act of forfeiting; something forfeited; a penalty.

for-gath-er (for gath'ér) *v.* To come together; to convene; to assemble.

forge (fōrj) *n.* A furnace where metals are heated and wrought; a smithy; a workshop that produces wrought iron. **forge** *v.* To form by heating and hammering; to give shape to; to imitate falsely; to advance slowly but steadily; to defraud; to counterfeit. **forger,** **forgery** *n.*

for-get (fér get') *v.* To lose the memory of; to fail to become mindful or aware of at the right time. **forgetful** *adj.* **forgettable** *adj.* **forgetfulness** *n.*

for-give (fér giv') *v.* To pardon; to give up resentment of; to cease to feel resentment against. **forgiveness** *n.*

for-giv-ing *adj.* Disposed to forgive; inclined to overlook offenses; compassionate.

for-go *or* **fore-go** (for gō') To give up or refrain from. **forgoer** *n.*

for-lorn (for lorn') *adj.* Abandoned or left in distress; hopeless; being in a poor condition. **forlornly** *adv.*

form (form) *n.* The shape or contour of something; a body of a living being; the basic nature of or particular state of something; the way in which something exists; variety; manner, as established by custom or regulation; the style or manner determined by etiquette or custom; performance according to established criteria; fitness with regard to training or health; procedure of words, as in a ceremony; a document having blanks for insertion of information; style in musical or literary composition; the design or style of a work of art. In *computer science,* a document designed for the orderly entry of data; the configuration or arrangement of data in a report. **form** *v.* To construct or conceive in the mind. **form** *suffix* Having the form or shape of; cuneiform

for-mal (for'mal) *adj.* Of or pertaining to the outward aspect of something; relating to or concerned with the outward form of something; adhering to convention, rule, or etiquette; based on accepted conventions. **formally** *adv.*

for-mal-de-hyde (for mal'de hīd) *n.* A colorless, gaseous chemical used chiefly as a preservative and disinfectant in synthesizing other compounds.

for-mal-i-ty *n.* The condition or state of being formal; an established form that is required.

for-mat (for´mat) *n.* A general style of a publication; the general form or layout of a publication. **format** *v.* In *computer science*, to produce data in a specified form.

for-ma-tion (for mā´shǝn) *n.* The act or process of forming or the state of being formed; the manner in which something is formed; a given arrangement, as of troops, as a square or in a column.

for-ma-tive (for´mǝ tiv) *adj.* Forming or having the power to form; of or pertaining to formation, growth, or development.

for-mer (for´mǝr) *adj.* Previous; preceding in place; being the first of two persons or things mentioned or referred to.

for-mer-ly *adv.* Previously.

form-fit-ting (form´fit´ing) *adj.* Closely following the contours of the body.

for-mi-da-ble (for´mi dǝ bl) *adj.* Extremely difficult; exciting fear by reason of size or strength. **-bly** *adv.*

form letter *n.* A standardized format of an impersonal letter sent to different people or to a large number of people.

for-mu-la (for´mū lǝ) *n., pl.* **formulas** *or* **formulae** A prescribed method of words or rules for use in a certain ceremony or procedure; a nutritious food for an infant in liquid form. *Math.* A combination or rule used to express an algebraic or symbolic form. *Chem.* A symbolic representation of the composition of a chemical compound. In *computer science*, a string of symbols that calculate to a value, as in a spreadsheet cell that calls for the total of the values in other specified cells, or that calculates to a logical true or false, as in a conditional branch command. **formulaic** *adj.*

for-mu-late (for´mū lāt´) *v.* To state or express as a formula. **formulation** *n.*

for-ni-ca-tion (for´nǐ kā´shǝn) *n.* Voluntary sexual intercourse between two unmarried people. **fornicator** *n.*

for-sake (for sāk´) *v.* To abandon or renounce; to give up. **forsaken** *adj.*

for-sooth (for sōth´) *adv.* In truth; certainly.

for-swear (for swâr´) *v.* To renounce emphatically or upon oath; to forsake; to swear falsely; to perjure oneself.

fort (fōrt) *n.* A fortified structure or enclosure capable of defense against an enemy; a permanent army post.

forte (fōrt´ē) *n.* An activity one does with excellence; a person's strong point;

the part of a sword blade between the middle and the hilt.

forth (fōrth) *adv.* Out into plain sight, as from seclusion; forward in order, place, or time.

forth-com-ing (fōrth´kum´ing) *adj.* Ready or about to appear or occur; readily available.

forth-right (fōrth´rīt´) *adj.* Direct; straightforward; frank. **forthrightly** *adv.* **forthrightness** *n.*

forth-with (fōrth´with´) *adv.* At once; promptly; immediately.

for-ti-fi-ca-tion *n.* The act of fortifying; something that fortifies, strengthens, or defends; a fortified place as a fort.

for-ti-fy (for´ti fī´) *v.* To strengthen and secure with military fortifications; to provide physical strength or courage to; to strengthen; to enrich food, as by adding vitamins, minerals, etc.

for-tis-si-mo (for tis´i mō´) *adv. Mus.* Very loudly, as a direction.

for-ti-tude (for´ti tōd´) *n.* Strength of mind in adversity, pain, or peril, allowing a person to withstand pain.

fort-night (fort´nīt´) *n.* A period of two weeks. **fortnightly** *adj. & adv.*

FOR-TRAN (for´tran) *n.* In *computer science*, a programming language for problems that are expressed in several different algebraic terms.

for-tress (for´tris) *n.* A fort.

for-tu-i-tous (for tō´i tus) *adj.* Occurring by chance; lucky; fortunate.

for-tu-nate (for´chǝ nit) *adj.* Brought about by good fortune; having good fortune. **fortunately** *adv.*

for-tune (for´chǝn) *n.* A hypothetical force that unpredictably determines events and issues favorably and unfavorably; success that results from luck; possession of material goods; a very large amount of money.

fortune hunter *n.* A person who seeks wealth through marriage.

for-tune-tell-er (for´chǝn tel´ǝr) *n.* A person who claims to predict the future. **fortune-telling** *n. & adj.*

for-ty *n. & adj.* Number equal to 4x10.

for-ty-nin-er (for´tē nī´nǝr) *n.* A United States pioneer in the 1849 California gold rush.

forty winks *n. Slang* A short nap.

for-um (fōr´um) *n., pl.* **forums** *or* **fora** A public marketplace in an ancient Roman city, where most legal and political business was transacted; a judicial assembly; a group discussion on any subject.

for-ward (for´wǝrd) *adj.* At, near, or toward a place or time in advance; overstepping the usual bounds in an insolent or presumptuous way; extremely unconventional, as in political opinions; socially advanced.

forward n. A player in football at the front line. **forward** v. To send forward or ahead; to help advance onward. **forwardly** adv. **forwardness** n.

forward pass n. Football An offensive pass thrown in the direction of the opponent's goal.

fos-sil (fos´il) n. The remains of an animal or plant of a past geologic age preserved in the rocks of the earth's surface; one that is outdated. **fossilization** n. **fossilize** v.

fos-ter (fo´stĕr) v. To give parental care to; to nurture; to encourage. **foster** adj. Giving or receiving parental care.

foster child n. A child supported financially and cared for by someone who is not the natural parent.

foster parent n. A person who financially supports and cares for a child who is not his own.

foul (foul) adj. Revolting to the senses; spoiled or rotten; covered with offensive matter; morally offensive; vulgar or obscene; unfavorable; dishonorable; indicating the limiting lines of a playing area. **foul** v. To physically contact or entangle; to become foul or dirty; to dishonor; to obstruct; to entangle; to make or hit a foul. **foul up** Slang To make a mistake. **foully** adv. **foulness** n.

fou-lard n. A soft, lightweight silk usu. decorated with a printed pattern.

foul ball n. A batted baseball that lands outside specified lines.

foul-mouthed adj. Using profane, vile, or obscene language.

foul play n. A violent act, often murder; an infringement of sporting rules.

found (found) v. To establish; to set up, often with funds to permit continuation and maintenance; to establish the basis or lay the foundation of; to melt metal and pour into a mold; to make by casting molten metal. **founder** n.

foun-da-tion (foun dā´shan) n. The act of founding or establishing; the basis on which anything is founded; an institution supported by an endowment; a cosmetic base for makeup.

foun-dry (foun´drē) n., pl. **foundries** An establishment where metal is cast.

fount (fount) n. A fountain; an abundant source.

foun-tain (foun´tan) n. A natural spring or jet of water coming from the earth; an artificially created spray of water; a basin-like structure from which such a stream comes; a point of origin or source.

fountain pen n. A pen having a reservoir of ink that automatically feeds the writing point.

four (fōr) n. The cardinal number that equals 3 + 1; anything consisting of four units. **four** adj. & pron.

four-fold adj. Consisting of four units; quadruple.

four-hand-ed adj. Involving four players, as a game of cards; engaged in by four people.

four–poster n. A bed having four tall posts, one at each corner, originally for the support of a canopy.

four-score (fōr´skōr´) adj. Being four times twenty; eighty.

four-teen (fōr´tēn´) n. The cardinal number that equals 13 + 1; anything consisting of fourteen units. **fourteen** adj. & pron. **fourteenth** n., adj. & adv.

fourth (fōrth) n. The ordinal number matching the number four in a series; the fourth forward gear of a transmission in a motor vehicle.

Fourth of July n. American Independence Day celebrated as a national holiday.

four–wheel adj. Automotive transmission in which all four wheels are linked to the source of driving power.

fowl (foul) n., pl. **fowl** or **fowls** A bird used as food or hunted as game, as the duck etc.; the edible flesh of a fowl. **fowl** v. To hunt or catch wild fowl.

fox (foks) n. A wild mammal having a pointed snout, upright ears, and a long bushy tail; the fur of a fox; a sly or crafty person. v. To outwit; to trick.

fox-hole (foks´hōl´) n. A shallow pit dug by a soldier as protection against enemy fire.

fox-hound (foks´hound´) n. A large dog breed developed for fox hunting.

fox-ing n. The pieces or piece of leather used to cover the upper front portion of a shoe.

fox terrier n. Small dog with a wiry or smooth white coat and dark markings.

fox trot n. A ballroom dance in 4/4 or 2/4 time consisting of a variety of rhythmic steps.

fox-y (fok´sē) adj. Like a fox; sly or crafty; sharp; cunning. Slang Very pretty. **foxily** adv.

foy-er (foi´ĕr) n. The public lobby of a hotel, theater, etc.; an entrance hall.

fpm abbr. Feet per minute.

fps abbr. Feet per second.

Fr abbr. Father (clergyman); French.

fra-cas (frā´kas) n. A noisy quarrel or disturbance; fight or dispute.

frac-tion (frak´shan) n. A small part; a disconnected part or fragment of anything. Mathematics An indicated quantity less than a whole number that is expressed as a decimal. Chem. A component of a compound separated from a substance by distilling.

frac-tion-al adj. Relating or pertaining to a fraction or fractions.

frac-ture (frak´chĕr) n. The act of

breaking; the state of being broken. *Med.* The breaking or cracking, as in a bone.

frag-ile (fraj´il) *adj.* Easily damaged or broken; frail; tenuous; flimsy. **fragilely** *adv.* **fragility** *n.*

frag-ment (frag´ment) *n.* A part detached or broken; part unfinished or incomplete. **fragment** *v.* To break into fragments.

frag-men-tal *adj. Geol.* Fragmentary; pertaining to rocks made up of fragments of older rocks.

frag-men-tary *adj.* Composed of fragments.

frag-men-tate *v.* To fragment.

fragmentation *n.* Broken into parts. In *computer science*, a condition wherein files on a disk are recorded to scattered rather than contiguous segments.

frag-ment-ed *adj.* Being reduced to fragments; lacking unity.

fra-grance *n.* The quality of being fragrant.

fra-grant (frā´grant) *adj.* Having an agreeable, especially sweet odor. **fragrantly** *adv.*

frail (frāl) *adj.* Delicate; weak; easily damaged. **frailly** *adv.* **frailness** *n.*

frame (frām) *v.* To put into a frame, as a picture; to build; to design; to adjust or adapt for a given purpose; to provide with a frame. *Slang* To incriminate so as to make a person appear guilty. **frame** *n.* Something made up of parts and joined together, such as a skeletal structure of a body or the timbers of a building; the pieces of wood or metal which surround a picture, photograph, or work of art; general structure; one exposure on a roll of film. In *computer science*, a window on a monitor screen that provides a view of information displayed by a program. **frame–up** *Slang* Actions which serve to make someone appear guilty whether he is not. **framer** *n.*

frame-work *n.* A structure composed of parts fitted together; the structure of ideas in a written composition.

fram-ing *n.* The act, process, or manner of constructing or contriving anything.

fran-chise (fran´chīz) *n.* A privilege or right granted to a person or group by a government; the constitutional right to vote; authorization to sell a manufacturer's products; the territory within which a privilege or immunity is authorized. **franchisee, -er** *n.*

fran-gi-ble (fran´ji bl) *adj.* Breakable.

frank (frangk) *adj.* Sincere and straightforward. **frank** *v.* To mark mail officially so that no charge is made for delivery. **frank** *n.* The right to send mail without charge; a signature or mark on mail indicating that mail can

be sent without charge; mail sent without charge. **frankly** *adv.*

frank-furt-er (frangk´fer ter) *n.* A smoked sausage made of beef or beef and pork; a hot dog.

frank-in-cense (frang´kin sens´) *n.* An aromatic gum resin obtained from African and Asian trees used as incense and in medicine.

Franklin, Benjamin *n.* (1706-1790) American statesman, scientist and inventor.

fran-tic (fran´tik) *adj.* Emotionally out of control with worry or fear. **frantically** *adv.*

fra-ter-nal (fra ter´nal) *adj.* Pertaining to or relating to brothers; of, pertaining to, or befitting a fraternity. *Biol.* Of or relating to a twin or twins that developed from separately fertilized ova. **fraternalism** *n.* **fraternally** *adv.*

fra-ter-ni-ty *n.* The relationship of a brother; a class of men associated for a common interest.

frat-er-nize (frat´er nīz´) *v.* To associate with others in a friendly way; to mingle intimately with the enemy, often in violation of military law. **fraternization** *n.*

frat-ri-cide (fra´tri sīd´) *n.* The killing of one's brother or sister; one who has killed his brother or sister. **-al** *adj.*

fraud (frod) *n.* A deliberate and willful deception perpetrated for unlawful gain; a trick or swindle; an impostor; a cheat.

fraud-u-lent (fro´ju lent) *adj.* Marked by or practicing fraud. **fraudulence** *n.* **fraudulently** *adv.*

fraught (frot) *adj.* Full of or accompanied by something specified.

fray (frā) *n.* A brawl, or fight; a heated argument or dispute. *v.* To wear out by rubbing; to irritate one's nerves.

fraz-zle (fraz´el) *v. Slang* To wear out; to completely fatigue. **frazzle** *n.*

freak (frēk) *n.* A seemingly capricious event; a whimsical quality or disposition. *Slang* A drug addict; a highly individualistic rebel; a person with an extreme physical abnormality; a fan or enthusiast. **freak out** To experience hallucinations or paranoia induced by a drug; to make or become highly excited. **freak, freakish, freaky** *adj.* **freakily** *adv.*

freck-le (frek´l) *n.* One of the small, brownish spots on the skin due to precipitation of pigment, usually increasing in number and intensity upon exposure to the sun.

free (frē) *adj.* Not imprisoned; not under obligation; politically independent; possessing political liberties; not affected by a specified circumstance or condition; exempt; costing nothing;

not being occupied or used; too familiar; forward; liberal, as with money. **free** *adv.* In a free way; without charge. **free** *v.* To set at liberty; to release or rid; to untangle. **freely** *adv.*

free-dom (frē'dom) *n.* The condition or state of being free; political independence; possession of political rights; boldness of expression; liberty; unrestricted access or use.

free enterprise *n.* A doctrine or type of economy under which private business is allowed to operate with minimal governmental control; capitalist economy.

free-hand *adv.* Drawn by hand without the assistance of any measuring or guiding instruments.

free lance (frēlans) *n.* One whose services are without long-term commitments to any one employer.

free-spoken *adj.* Speaking freely without reserve; outspoken.

free-standing (frē'stan'ding) *adj.* Standing alone without any support; free of any apparent support or attachments.

free trade *n.* International exchange between nations or states which is unrestricted.

freeze (frēz) *v.* To become ice or a similar solid through loss of heat; to preserve by cooling at an extremely low temperature; to become nonfunctional through the formation of ice or frost; to feel uncomfortably cold; to make or become rigid; to become suddenly motionless, rigid or inactive, as though through fear; to set prices at a certain level, to inhibit further use of. **freeze** *n.* An act of freezing or the state of being frozen; a cold snap.

freeze-dry (frēz'drī) *v.* To preserve by drying in a frozen state under a high vacuum. **freeze-dried** *adj.*

freezer (frē'zér) *n.* Anything that freezes or keeps cold; an insulated cabinet for freezing and storing perishable foods.

freight (frāt) *n.* A service of transporting commodities by air, land or water; the price paid for such transportation; a train that transports goods only. **freight** *v.* To carry as cargo.

freight-age *n.* Freight; the transportation of goods.

freight-er (frā'tér) *n.* A ship used for transporting cargo.

fren-zy (fren'zē) *n., pl.* frenzies A state of extreme excitement or violent agitation; temporary insanity or delirium.

fre-quen-cy *n.* The state of occurring often; the number of times an event is repeated.

fre-quent (frē'kwent) *adj.* Happening or appearing or reappearing often or

time after time. **frequent** *v.* To go to a place repeatedly. **frequenter** *n.* frequently *adv.*

fres-co (fres'kō) *n., pl.* -coes *or* -cos The art of painting on moist plaster with water-based paint; a picture so painted.

fresh (fresh) *adj.* Newly made, gathered, or obtained; not spoiled, musty, or stale; new; different; not soiled; pure and clean; having just arrived; refreshed; revived. *Slang* Impudent; disrespectful. **freshly** *adv.*

fresh-en *v.* To make fresh; to revive; renew.

fresh-wa-ter *adj.* Pertaining to water without salt.

fret (fret) *v.* To be anxious or irritated; to wear away; to make by erosion; to ripple water. **fret** *n.* An ornamental design, composed of repeated symmetric figures; a ridge of metal fixed across the fingerboard of a stringed instrument, as a guitar.

fret-ful *adj.* Irritable.

fret saw *n.* A small saw used to cut curved lines.

fret-work *n.* Ornamental work.

fri-a-ble (frī'a bl) *adj.* Easily crumbled or pulverized; brittle. **friableness** *n.*

fri-ar (frī'ér) *n.* A member of a mendicant Roman Catholic order.

fric-as-see (frik'a sē') *n.* A dish of meat or poultry stewed in gravy.

fric-tion (frik'shan) *n.* The rubbing of one surface or object against another; a conflict or clash. *Phys.* A force that retards the relative motion of two touching objects. **frictional** *adj.*

Fri-day (frī'dā) *n.* The sixth day of the week.

friend (frend) *n.* Someone who is personally well-known by oneself and for whom one holds warm regards; a supporter of a cause or group. **Friend** A member of the Society of Friends; a Quaker. **friendship** *n.*

friend-ly *adj.* Characteristic of a friend; like a friend; showing kindness and goodwill. **friendliness** *n.*

frieze (frēz) *n.* A decorative horizontal band along the upper part of a wall in a room.

frig-ate (frig'It) *n.* A square-rigged warship of the 17th to mid-19th centuries; U.S. warship smaller than a cruiser but larger than a destroyer.

fright (frīt) *n.* Sudden violent alarm or fear; a feeling of alarm. *Slang* Something very unsightly or ugly.

fright-ful *adj.* Causing intense fright or alarm. **frightfully** *adv.*

fright-en (frīt'en) *v.* To fill with fear; to force by arousing fear. **frightening** *adj.* **frighteningly** *adv.*

frig-id (frij'id) *adj.* Very cold; lacking warmth of feeling or emotional warmth;

sexually unresponsive. **frigidity** *n.*
frigidness *n.* **frigidly** *adv.*

frill (fril) *n.* A decorative ruffled or gathered border. *Slang* A superfluous item. **frilly** *adj.*

fringe (frinj) *n.* An edging that consists of hanging threads, cords, or loops.

fringe benefit *n.* Any employment benefit, such as paid holidays, pensions, or insurance, given in addition to salary.

frip-per-y (frip´e rē) *n., pl.* **fripperies** Showy and often cheap ornamentation; a pretentious display.

frisk (frisk) *v.* To skip or leap about playfully; to search someone for a concealed weapon by running the hands over the clothing quickly.

frit-ter (frit´ér) *v.* To squander or waste little by little. **fritter** *n.* A small fried cake made of plain batter, often containing fruits, vegetables, or fish.

fri-vol-i-ty *n.* The quality of being frivolous.

friv-o-lous (friv´o lus) *adj.* Trivial; insignificant; lacking importance; not serious; silly. **frivolousness** *n.* **frivolously** *adv.*

frizz (friz) *v.* To form into small, tight curls. **frizziness** *n.* **frizzy** *adj.*

friz-zly *adj.* Frizzed, as hair; very curly.

fro (frō) *adv.* Away from; back, as running to and fro.

frock (frok) *n.* A smock or loose-fitting robe; a robe worn by monks.

frog (frog) *n.* Any of various small, smooth-skinned, web-footed, largely aquatic, tailless, leaping amphibians; an ornamental braid, cord, or fastener; an arrangement of intersecting railroad tracks designed to permit wheels to pass over the intersection without difficulty; a perforated holder for flower stems. *Slang* Hoarseness in the throat.

frol-ic (frol´ik) *n.* Merriness; a playful, carefree occasion. *v.* To romp about playfully; to have fun. **frolicsome** *n.*

from (frum) *prep.* Starting at a particular time or place; used to indicate a specific point; used to indicate a specific source; used to indicate separation or removal; used to indicate differentiation, as in knowing right from left.

frond (frond) *n.* A large leaf, as of a tropical fern, usually divided into smaller leaflets.

front (frunt) *n.* The forward surface of an object or body; the area or position located before or ahead; a position of leadership; the area of action in a war; a field of activity for disguising objectionable or illegal activities; an apparently respectable person, group, or business used as a cover for illegal

or secret activities. *Meteor.* The line of separation between air masses of different temperatures. **frontal** *adj.* **frontally** *adv.*

front money *n.* Money paid in advance for a service or product that has been promised.

fron-tier (frun tēr´) *n.* A part of an international border or the area adjacent to it; an unexplored area of knowledge or thought. **frontiersman** *n.*

fron-tis-piece (frun´tis pēs´) *n.* An illustration that usually precedes the title page of a book or periodical.

front office *n.* The executive staff of an organization.

front-ward *adv.* Toward the front.

frost (frost) *n.* A feathery covering of minute ice crystals on a cold surface; the act or process of freezing. **frost** *v.* To cover with frost; to apply frosting to a cake. **frostily** *adv.* **frostiness** *n.*

frost-bite (frost´bit´) *n.* The local destruction of bodily tissue due to exposure to freezing temperatures, often resulting in gangrene.

froth (froth) *n.* A mass of bubbles on or in a liquid, resulting from agitation or fermentation; a salivary foam, as of an animal, resulting from disease or exhaustion; anything unsubstantial or trivial. **froth** *v.* To expel froth. **frothily** *adv.* **frothiness** *n.* **frothy** *adj.*

frou-frou (frö´frö´) *n.* A rustling sound, as of silk; a frilly dress or decoration.

fro-ward (frō´wérd) *adj.* Obstinate; contrary. **frowardly** *adv.*

frown (froun) *v.* To contract the brow as in displeasure or concentration; to look on with distaste or disapproval. **frowningly** *adv.* **frowning** *adj.*

frow-zy *or* **frow-sy** (frou´zē) *adj.* Appearing unkempt.

fro-zen (frō´zen) *adj.* Covered with, changed into, surrounded by, or made into ice; extremely cold, as a climate; immobilized or made rigid, as by fear; coldly reserved; unfriendly; kept at a fixed level, as wages; not readily available for withdrawal, sale, or liquidation, as from a bank.

fruc-tu-ous (fruk´chö us) *adj.* Fruitful; productive.

fru-gal (frö´gal) *adj.* Economical; thrifty. **frugality, frugalness** *n.* **frugally** *adv.*

fruit (fröt) *n., pl.* **fruit** *or* **fruits** The ripened, mature, seed bearing part of a flowering plant, as a pod or berry; the edible, fleshy plant part of this kind, as an apple or plum; the fertile structure of a plant that does not bear seeds; the outcome or result. **fruit** *v.* To produce or cause to produce fruit.

fru-i-tion (frö ish´an) *n.* Achievement or accomplishment of something worked for or desired; the state of bearing fruit.

frump-y (frump ē) *adj.* Unfashionable; dowdy. **frump, frumpiness** *n.*

frus-trate (frus´trāt) *v.* To keep from attaining a goal or fulfilling a desire; to thwart; to prevent the fruition of; to nullify. **frustration** *n.* **frustratingly** *adv.* **frustrating** *adj.*

fub-sy *adj.* To be chubby and squat.

fuch-sia (fū´sha) *n.* A chiefly tropical plant widely grown for its drooping, four-petaled flowers of purple, red, or white; a vivid reddish to purple color.

fuch-sine (fek´sin) *n.* A type of dye that is made by the oxidation of a mixture of aniline and toluidines which is a bright red.

fu-coid (fū´koid) *adj.* Pertaining to or being like seaweed or rock weeds.

fu-cose *n.* A type of aldose sugar.

fu-co-xan-thin *n.* A type of brown pigment occurring especially in the ova of brown algae.

fu-cus (fū´kus) *n.* A type of brown algae.

fud-dle (fud´l) *v.* To make someone or something confused.

fud-dy-dud-dy *n. pl.* **fuddy-duddies** (fud´ē dud´ē) An old-fashioned person.

fudge (fuj) *n.* A soft, cooked candy containing sugar, butter, and a flavoring, as chocolate. **fudge** *v.* To falsify; to adjust, make, or fit together in a clumsy way; to evade.

fuel (fū´el) *n.* A combustible matter consumed to generate energy, especially a material such as wood, coal, or oil burned to generate heat. **fuel** *v.* To take in or supply with fuel; stimulate, as an argument. **fueler** *n.*

fuel cell *n.* A kind of cell which will change the chemical energy of a fuel to an electrical energy.

fuel injection *n.* The forced spraying of fuel into the combustion chamber of an engine.

fuel oil *n.* An oil used for fuel, esp. one used as a substitute for coal.

fug (fug) *v.* To hang around or loll indoors in an atmosphere that is stuffy.

fu-ga-cious (fū gā´shus) *adj.* Lasting for only a short time. **fugacity** *n.*

fu-gal (fū´gal) *adj.* To be pertaining to the style of a musical fugue.

fu-gi-tive (fū´ji tiv) *adj.* Fleeing or having fled, as from arrest or pursuit. **fugitive** *n.* One who flees or tries to escape.

fu-gle *v.* To act as a model for proper behavior of soldiers. **fugleman** *n.*

fugue (fūg) *n. Mus.* A musical composition in which the theme is elaborately repeated by different voices or instruments; a psychological disturbance in which actions are not remembered after one returns to a normal state.

fu-ji *n.* A type of spun silk fabric that was first made in Japan.

-ful *adj. suffix* Having the qualities of something; to be filled with or full of.

ful-crum (fel´krum) *n.* The point on which a lever turns.

ful-fill *or* **ful-fil** (fel fil´) *v.* To convert into actuality; to effect; to carry out; to satisfy. **fulfillment** *n.*

ful-gent (ful´jent) *adj.* To be very bright or dazzling bright.

ful-gu-rant (fil´gur ant) *adj.* To be flashing like lightening flashes.

ful-gu-ra-tion *n.* The flashing as of lightning.

ful-gu-rite (ful´gū rīt) *n.* A type of tubular crust that is formed by the fusion of rock by lightning.

ful-gu-rous *adj.* To be giving off flashes like that of lightning.

fu-lig-i-nous (fū lij´i nus) *adj.* Being murky or to have a color that is dark.

full (fel) *adj.* To have in something the maximum amount that the thing is able to hold. **fullness** *n.*

full blood *n.* Pure extraction; an unmixed ancestry.

full moon *n.* A phase of the moon where the whole side of the disk is visible.

ful-mar (fel´mèr) *n.* A type of arctic seabird which is related to the petrels.

ful-mi-nate (ful´mi nāt) *v.* To condemn severely; to explode. **fulmination, fulminator** *n.*

ful-some (fel´som) *adj.* Offensively insincere. **fulsomely** *adv.* **-ness** *n.*

ful-vous (ful´vus) *adj.* Yellow; tawny.

fum-ble (fum´bl) *v.* To handle idly; to blunder, as mishandle a baseball or football. **fumble** *n.* The act of fumbling; a fumbled ball. **fumbler** *n.*

fume (fūm) *n.* An irritating smoke, gas, or vapor. **fume** *v.* To treat with or subject to fumes; to show or feel anger or distress.

fu-mi-gate (fū´mi gāt´) *v.* To subject to fumes in order to exterminate vermin or insects. **fumigation, fumigator** *n.*

fun *n.* That which is amusing or mirthful; entertaining; recreation or play, relaxing

func-tion (fungk´shan) *n.* The characteristics or proper activity of a person or thing; specific occupation, duty, or role; an official ceremony; something depending upon or varying with another. *Math.* A quantity whose value is dependent on the value of another. **function** *v.* To serve or perform a function as required or expected.

func-tion-al *adj.* Of or pertaining to functions; able to perform a regular function. **functionally** *adv.*

function code *n.* In *computer science*, any symbol or set of symbols that generates an instruction to the computer.

function keys (*abbr.* **Fn**) *n.* In *computer science*, where *n* equals a number, one of a set of ten or twelve keys that alone or in conjunction with either the Ctrl, Alt or Shift key execute commands in certain programs.

fund (fund) *n.* A source of supply; a sum of money or its equivalent reserved for a specific purpose. **fund** *v.* To convert into long-term arrangements for paying something off; to furnish or accumulate a fund for.

fun-da-men-tal (fun´d*a* men´tal) *adj.* Basic or essential; of major significance; anything serving as the primary origin; most important. **fundamental** *n.* **fundamentally** *adv.*

fu-ner-al (fū´nér *a*l) *n.* The service performed in conjunction with the burial or cremation of a dead person.

funeral director *n.* A person who manages funerals.

funeral home *n.* The establishment where a dead person is prepared for burial or cremation and for viewing of the body.

fu-ne-re-al *adj.* Pertaining to or relating to a funeral.

fun-gus (fung´gus) *n., pl.* **-gi** or **-guses** Any of numerous spore-bearing plants which have no chlorophyll, including yeasts, molds, mildews, and mushrooms. **fungous** *adj.* **fungal** *adj.*

fu-nic-u-lar (fū nik´ū lêr) *n.* A cable railway along which cable cars are drawn up a mountain, especially one with ascending and descending cars that counterbalance one another.

fun-nel (fun´el) *n.* A cone-shaped utensil having a tube for channeling a substance into a container. **funnel** *v.* To pass or cause to pass through a funnel.

fur *n.* The skin of certain animals, the hairy coating on such a skin; such skins that are used as a material for lining or trimming, or for entire garments.

fur-be-low (fer´be lō) *n.* A ruffle or frill on clothing; a piece of showy decoration or ornamentation.

fur-bish (fer´bish) *v.* To make bright, as by rubbing; to polish; to renovate.

fu-ri-ous (fer´e us) *adj.* Extremely angry; marked by rage or activity.

furl (ferl) *v.* To roll up and secure to something, as a pole or mast; to curl or fold.

fur-long (fer´long) *n.* A distance equal to approximately 201 meters or 230 yards.

fur-lough (fer´lō) *n.* Permission granted to be absent from duty, especially to members of the armed forces.

fur-nace (fer´nis) *n.* A large enclosure designed to produce intense heat.

fur-nish (fer´nish) *v.* To outfit or equip, as with fittings or furniture.

fur-ni-ture (fer´ni chêr) *n.* Movable articles, such as chairs and tables, used in a home, office, etc.

fu-ror (fūr´or) *n.* Violent anger; rage; great excitement; commotion; an uproar.

fur-row (fer´ō) *n.* A long, narrow trench in the ground, made by a plow or other tool; a deep wrinkle in the skin, especially of the forehead. **furrow** *v.*

fur-ther *adv.* At a more advanced point in time or space.

fur-ther-more *adv.* Moreover.

fur-ther-most *adj.* Most distant.

fur-tive (fer´tiv) *adj.* Done in secret; surreptitious; obtained underhandedly; stolen.

fu-ry (fūr´e) *n., pl.* **furies** Uncontrolled anger; turbulence; an angry or spiteful woman.

fuse (fūz) *n.* An electrical safety device containing a wire or strip of fusible metal that melts and interrupts the circuit's flow when the current exceeds a particular amperage; a mechanical, electrical, or electronic device used to detonate explosives, such as bombs or grenades.

fu-see or **fu-zee** (fū zē´) *n.* A large-headed friction match capable of burning in the wind; a colored signal flare used as a railroad signal.

fu-se-lage (fū´se lij) *n.* The central section of an airplane, containing the wings and tail assembly.

fu-si-ble *adj.* Capable of being melted.

fu-si-lade *n.* A quickly repeated or simultaneous discharge of a number of firearms.

fu-sion (fū´zhan) *n.* The act or procedure of melting together by heat; a blend produced by fusion; a nuclear reaction in which nuclei of a light element combine to form more massive nuclei, with the release of huge amounts of energy.

fuss *n.* An excessive display of restless activity.

fus-tian (fus´chan) *n.* A sturdy, stout cotton cloth. **fustian** *adj.* Pompous, pretentious language; bombastic.

fus-ti-gate *v.* To criticize.

fu-tile (fūt´il) *adj.* Ineffectual; being of no avail; without useful result; serving no useful purpose.

fu-ture (fū´chêr) *n.* The time yet to come; a prospective condition regarding advancement or success; the future tense or a verb form in the future tense.

fuzz (fuz) *n.* A mass of fine, loose particles, fibers, or hairs.

fuzz-y *adj.* Covered with fuzz; lacking in clarity.

FYI *abbr.* For your information.

G, g (jē) The seventh letter of the English alphabet. *Mus.* The fifth tone in the scale of C major. *Slang* One thousand dollars; a grand. *Physiol.* A unit of force equal to that due to the earth's gravity.

g *abbr.* Gravity, gram.

gab (gab) *v. Slang* To talk or chat idly.

gab-ble (gab´l) *v.* To speak rapidly or incoherently. **gabble** *n.*

gab-bro (gab´rō) *n.* A granular igneous rock. **gabbroic, gabbroid** *adj.*

gab-fest *n.* Informal gathering or meeting where people engage in prolonged, general talk.

ga-ble (gā´bl) *n. Arch.* The portion of a building enclosed by the sloping ends.

gad (gad) *v.* To wander about restlessly with little or no purpose. **gadder** *n.*

gad-a-bout (gad´a bout´) *n. Slang* One who goes about seeking excitement and fun.

gadg-et (gaj´it) *n. Slang* A small device or tool used in performing miscellaneous jobs, especially in the kitchen.

ga-doid (gā´doid) *adj.* Resembling or related to the cod family.

gad-o-lin-i-um (gad´o lin´ē um) *n.* A metallic element, silvery-white in color, of the rare-earth series, which is highly magnetic.

ga-droon (ga drōn´) *n.* The ornamental carving on a rounded molding.

gad-wall (gad´wal´) *n.* A grayish brown duck.

gaff (gaf) *n.* A sharp iron hook used for landing fish. *Naut.* A spar on the top edge of a fore-and-aft sail. *Slang* Abuse or harsh treatment. **gaff** *v.* To land or hook with a gaff; to deceive.

gaffe (gaf) *n.* A social blunder; mistake; a faux pas.

gaf-fer (gaf´ẽr) *n.* An old man; a lighting electrician.

gag (gag) *n.* Something, as a wadded cloth, forced into or over the mouth to prevent someone from speaking or crying out; an obstacle to or any restraint of free speech, such as by censorship. *Slang* A practical joke or hoax. **to pull a gag** To perform a practical joke on someone. **gag** *v.* To keep a person from speaking out by means of a gag; to choke on something.

ga-ga (gä´gä) *adj. Slang* Crazy; silly; wildly enthusiastic..

gage (gäj) *n.* Something that is given as security for an action to be performed; a pledge; anything, as a glove, thrown down as a challenge to fight or a challenge for combat.

gag-gle (gag´l) *n.* A flock of geese; a group; a cluster.

gag rule *n.* A law or rule that prevents discussion or expression of an opinion.

gag-ster *n.* A person who plays practical jokes.

gahn-ite *n.* A dark-colored mineral containing zinc and aluminum.

gai-e-ty (gā´i tē) *n., pl.* **gaieties** The state of being happy; cheerfulness; fun, festive activity.

gai-ly (gā´lē) *adj.* A gay or cheerful manner; showily or brightly.

gain (gān) *v.* To earn or acquire possession of something; to succeed in winning a victory; to develop an increase of; to put on weight; to secure as a profit; to improve progress; to draw nearer to.

gait (gāt) *n.* A way or manner of moving on foot; one of the foot movements in which a horse steps or runs.

gai-ter (gā´tẽr) *n.* A covering, as of leather or canvas, that covers the leg and extends from the knee to the instep; an old-fashioned shoe with a high top and elastic sides.

gal (gal) *n. Slang* A girl.

ga-la (gā´la) *n.* A festive celebration; party. **gala** *adj.*

ga-lac-tic (ga lak´tic) *adj.* Relating to a galaxy, especially the Milky Way.

ga-lac-tose (ga lak´tōs) *n.* The sugar typically occurring in lactose.

ga-la-go *n.* A nocturnal African primate with a long tail and long hind limbs enabling them to leap at great lengths.

ga-lah (ga lä´) *n.* A showy Australian cockatoo that is very destructive in wheat growing areas.

gal-an-tine (gal´an tēn´) *n.* A cold dish that consists of fish or meat that has been poached, stuffed, and covered with aspic.

ga-lax (gā´lax) *n.* An evergreen herb of the southeastern United States, whose leaves are widely used by florists.

gal-ax-y (gal´ak sē) *n., pl.* **galaxies** *Astron* Any of the very large systems of stars, nebulae, or other celestial bodies that constitute a universe; a brilliant, distinguished group or assembly. **Galaxy** The Milky Way.

gal-ba-num (gal´ba num) *n.* A greenish or brown aromatic, bitter gum resin used for medicinal purposes.

gale (gāl) *n. Meteor.* A very powerful wind stronger than a stiff breeze; an outburst, as of hilarity.

ga-le-na (ga lē´na) *n.* A metallic, dull gray mineral that is the principal ore of lead.

gal-i-ma-ti-as (gal´i mä´shē as) *n.* A confused mixture of words.

gal-i-ot *or* **gal-li-ot** *n.* A small galley or sailing ship, moved by oars and sails.

gall (gol) *n. Physiol.* The bitter fluid secreted by the liver; bile; bitterness of feeling; animosity; impudence; something that irritates. **gall** *v.* To injure the skin by friction; to chafe.

gal-lant (gal´ant) *adj.* Dashing in dress or appearance; majestic; stately; chivalrously attentive to women; courteous; having a fine appearance; courage; heroic. **gallantly** *adv.*

gal-lant-ry (gal´an trē) *n., pl.* **gallantries** Nobility and bravery; a gallant act.

gall-blad-der *or* **gall bladder** *n.* The small sac under the right lobe of the liver that stores bile.

gal-le-on (gal´ē on) *n.* A large, three-masted sailing ship.

gal-ley *n., pl.* **galleys** (gal´ē) A long medieval ship that was propelled by sails and oars; the long tray used by printers to hold set type; a printer's proof made from composed type, used to detect and correct errors.

gallic acid *n.* A slightly yellow crystalline acid found in plant galls and used as a developer in photography.

gal-li-gas-kins *n.* Very loose-fitting trousers of the 16th century.

gal-li-mau-fry (gal´i mo´frē) *n.* A hodgepodge; a jumbled mixture.

gal-li-nip-per *n.* A large mosquito.

gall-ing (gä´ling) *adj.* Being very irritated; annoying; vexing.

gal-li-um (gal´ē um) *n.* A silvery metallic element used in semiconductor technology and as a component of various alloys that melt at low temperatures, symbolized by Ga.

gal-li-vant (gal´i vant´) *v.* To roam about in search of amusement or pleasure; to flirt; to run about.

gal-lon (gal´on) *n.* A liquid measurement used in the United States, equal to 4 quarts; in Great Britain, a liquid measurement which equals 4 imperial quarts; a dry measurement that equals 1/8 bushel.

gal-loon (ga lön´) *n.* A trimming of lace, or embroidery with metallic threads.

gal-lows (gal´ōz) *n.* A framework of two or more upright beams and a cross-beam, used for execution by hanging.

gall-stone (gol´stōn´) *n. Pathol.* A small, hard concretion of cholesterol crystals that sometimes forms in the gall bladder or bile passages.

ga-loot (ga löt´) *n.* A strange or foolish person.

ga-lore (ga lōr´) *adj.* In great numbers; abundant; plentiful.

ga-losh (ga losh´) *n., pl.* **galoshes** A waterproof overshoe which is worn in bad weather.

ga-lumph (ga lumph´) *v.* To bump or gallop along clumsily.

gal-van-ic (gal van´ik) *adj.* Produced by or pertaining to galvanism; stimulating or shocking.

gal-va-nism (gal´va niz´um) *n.* Electricity that is produced by chemical action. *Med.* A therapeutic application of continuous electric current from voltaic cells.

gal-va-nom-e-ter (gal´va nom´i tèr) *n. Electr.* An apparatus for detecting the presence of an electric current and for determining its strength and direction.

gal-va-no-scope (gal´va no skōp´) *n.* An instrument used to detect the direction and presence of an electric current by the deflecting of a magnetic needle.

gam *n.* A school of whales.

gam-bit (gam´bit) *n.* In chess, an opening in which a piece is sacrificed for a favorable position; a maneuver that is carefully planned.

gam-ble (gam´bl) *v.* To take a chance on an uncertain outcome as in a contest or by buying a lottery number. **gamble** *n.* Any risky venture. **gambler** *n.*

gam-boge (gam bōj´) *n.* A gum resin that is orange to brown in color and is used as a yellow pigment.

gam-bol (gam´bol) *v.* To frolic, skip, or leap about in play. **gambol** *n.* Frolic; a playful leap or skip.

gambrel roof *n. Archit.* A ridged roof with the slope broken on each side, the lower slope steeper than the upper.

gam-bu-sia *n.* Any of various surface-feeding fishes which are stocked in fresh waters to eliminate mosquito larvae.

game (gām) *n.* A contest governed by specific rules; a way of entertaining oneself; amusement; a calculated way to do something; animals, fish, or birds that are hunted for sport or food.

gamely *adv.* In a courageous manner.

gam-e-tan-gi-um *n.* An organ or cell in which gametes are developed or produced.

gam-ete (gam´ēt) *n. Biol.* Either of two mature reproductive cells, an ovum or a sperm, which produce a zygote when united.

gam-in (gam´in) *n.* A homeless child who wanders the streets of a town or city.

gam-ma (gam´a) *n.* The third letter of the Greek alphabet. **gamma** *adj.* In the third position in the structure of a molecule.

gamma globulin *n. Biochem.* A globulin that is present in blood plasma and contains antibodies effective against certain infectious diseases.

gam-ma ray *n. Phys.* A radiation quantity or a photon emitted by a radioactive substance.

gam-mer (gam´ėr) *n.* An elderly woman.

gam-mon (gam´on) *n.* A cured ham; in the game of backgammon, a double victory in which a player removes all his pieces before the other player removes any.

gam-ut (gam´ut) *n.* The whole range;

series, or extent of anything.

gam-y (gā'mē) *adj.* Having the strong flavor of game, especially when slightly tainted; scandalous. **gaminess** *n.*

ga-nef (gā'nef) *n. Slang* Petty thief; rascal; an unscrupulous person.

gang (gang) *n.* A group of persons who are organized and work together or socialize regularly; a group of adolescent hoodlums or criminals. **gang up on** To attack as a group.

gan-gling (gang'gling) *adj.* Awkwardly tall and thin; lanky and loosely built.

gan-gli-on (gang'glē ǝn) *n., pl.* **ganglia** *Physiol.* A collection of nerve cells located outside the spinal cord or brain.

gan-grene (gang'grēn) *n. Pathol.* The death and decay of tissue in the body caused by a failure in the circulation of the blood supply. **gangrenous** *adj.*

gang-ster (gang'stėr) *n.* A member of a criminal gang; a racketeer; a mobster.

gap (gap) *n.* An opening or wide crack, as in a wall; a cleft; a deep notch or ravine in a mountain ridge, offering passage.

gape (gāp) *v.* To open the mouth wide, as in yawning; to stare in amazement with the mouth wide open; to become widely separated or open. **gape** *n.*

gar (gär) *n.* A fish having a spear-like snout and elongated body covered with bony plates; a garfish.

garb (gärb) *n.* Clothing; a particular way of dressing. **garb** *n.*

gar-bage (gär bij) *n.* Food wastes, consisting of unwanted or unusable pieces of meat, vegetables, and other food products; any unwanted or worthless material; trash

gar-ble (gär'bl) *v.* To mix up or confuse; to change or distort the meaning of with the intent to mislead or misrepresent. **garble** *n.* The act or process of garbling. **garbler** *n.*

gar-den (gär'den) *n.* A place for growing flowers, vegetables, or fruit; a piece of ground commonly used as a public recreation area. **garden** *v.* To work in or make into a garden. **garden** *adj.* Produced in a garden; referring to a garden. **gardener** *n.*

Garfield, James Abram *n.* (1831-1881) The twentieth president of the United States from March through September of 1881, assassinated.

gar-gan-tu-an (gär gan'chŏ ǝn) *adj.* Of enormous size; immense.

gar-gle (gär'gl) *v.* To force air from the lungs through a liquid held in the back of the mouth and throat. **gargle** *n.* A liquid preparation used to wash the mouth and throat. **gargle** *n.*

gar-goyle (gär'goil) *n.* A waterspout made or carved to represent a grotesque animal or human figure, projecting

from a gutter to throw rain away from the wall of a building.

gar-ish (gâr'ish) *adj.* Too showy and bright; gaudy. **garishly** *adv.*

gar-lic (gär'lik) *n.* A plant related to the onion with a compound bulb which contains a strong odor and flavor, used as a seasoning. **garlicky** *adj.*

garlic salt *n.* A condiment made of salt and ground dried garlic.

gar-ment (gär'ment) *n.* An article of clothing.

gar-ner (gär'nėr) *v.* To gather and store; to accumulate; to collect; to acquire.

gar-net (gär'nit) *n.* A dark red silicate mineral used as a gemstone and as an abrasive.

garnet paper *n.* An abrasive paper coated with crushed garnet.

gar-ni-er-ite *n.* A mineral consisting of hydrous nickel magnesium silicate; an important ore of nickel.

gar-nish (gär'nish) *v.* To add something to, as to decorate or embellish; to add decorative or flavorful touches to food or drink. **garnish** *n.*

gar-ret (gar'it) *n.* A room in an attic.

gar-ri-son (gar'i sǝn) *n.* The military force that is permanently placed in a fort or town; a military post.

gar-ron (gar'on) *n.* A small workhorse.

gar-ru-lous (gar'ǝ lus) *adj.* Given to continual talkativeness; chatty. very talkative. **garrulousness** *n.*

gar-ter (gär'tėr) *n.* A band or strap that is worn to hold a stocking in place; a band that holds up a sleeve. **garter**

garth (gärth) *n.* A small yard.

gas (gas) *n., pl.* **gases** A form of matter capable of expanding to fill a container and taking on the shape of the container; a combustible mixture used as fuel; gasoline; a gas used to produce an irritating, poisonous, or asphyxiating atmosphere. **gas** *v.* **gassy** *adj.*

gas-con (gas'kon) *n.* A boastful person.

gash (gash) *n.* A deep cut. **gash** *v.* To make a deep cut in.

gas-ket (gas'kit) *n. Mech.* A rubber seal or ring used between machine parts or around pipe joints to prevent leakage.

gas-o-hol *n.* A fuel blended from unleaded gasoline and ethanol.

gas-o-line (gas'ǝ lēn') *n.* A colorless, highly flammable mixture of liquid hydrocarbons made from crude petroleum and used as a fuel and a solvent.

gasp (gasp) *v.* To inhale suddenly and sharply, as from fear or surprise; to make labored or violent attempts to breathe. **gasp** *n.*

gas-tral (ga stral')*adj.* Relating to the stomach or digestive tract.

gas-trec-to-my *n.* The surgical removal

of the stomach or a part of it.

gas-tric (gas´trik) *adj.* Of or pertaining to the stomach.

gastric juice *n. Biochem.* The digestive fluid secreted by the stomach glands, containing several enzymes.

gastric ulcer *n. Pathol.* An ulcer formed on the stomach lining, often caused by excessive secretion of gastric juices.

gas-tri-tis (ga strī´tis) *n. Pathol.* Inflammation of the stomach lining.

gas-tro-en-ter-ol-o-gy (gas tro ent´e röl o jē) *n.* The medical study of the pathology and diseases of the stomach and intestines. **gastroenterologist** *n.*

gas-tro-in-tes-ti-nal *adj.* Relating to or affecting the stomach and intestines.

gas-tron-o-my (ga stron´o mē) *n.* The art of good eating. **gastronome** *n.* **gastronomic** *adj.* **gastronomical** *adj.*

gas-tro-scope *n.* An instrument for viewing the interior of the stomach.

gas-tro-vas-cu-lar *adj.* Functioning in both circulation and digestion.

gat (gat) *n. Slang* A pistol; short for Gatling gun.

gate (gāt) *n.* A movable opening in a wall or fence, commonly swinging on hinges, that closes or opens; a valve-like device for controlling the passage of gas or water through a conduit or dam; the total paid admission receipts or number of attendees at a public performance.

gath-er (gath´ér) *v.* To bring or come together into one place or group; to harvest or pick; to increase or gain; to accumulate; to fold or pleat a cloth by pulling it along a thread. **gather** *n.*

gath-er-ing *n.* The act of assembling; that which is gathered.

gauche (gōsh) *adj.* Socially awkward; clumsy; boorish. **gauchely** *adv.*

gau-cho (gow chō´) *n.* A cowboy of South America.

gaud *n.* An ornament or trinket.

gaud-y (gaw´dē) *adj.* Too decorated to be in good taste. **gaudiness** *n.*

gauge (gāj) *n.* A standard measurement, dimension, or capacity; an instrument used for measuring, testing, or registering; the distance between rails of a railroad; the diameter of the bore of a shotgun barrel. **gauge** *v.* To determine the capacity, contents or volume of; to estimate; to evaluate.

gaug-er *n.* A customs official who measures and inspects dutiable bulk goods.

gaunt (gont) *adj.* Thin and bony; haggard; gloomy or desolate in appearance.

ga-vage (ga väzh´) *n.* Forced feeding of nutrients into the stomach, by means of a flexible stomach tube and a force pump.

gave *v.* Past tense of give.

gav-el (gav´el) *n.* A mallet used to call for order or attention. **gavel** *v.*

ga-vi-al (gā´vē al) *n.* A large crocodile found in India, with long, slender jaws.

ga-votte (ga vot´) *n.* A dance performed by lifting the feet rather than sliding them. **gavotte** *v.*

gawk (gawk) *v.* To gape; to stare stupidly.

gay (gā) *adj.* Merry; happy and carefree; brightly ornamental or colorful; homosexual. **gay** *n.* A homosexual.

gaze (gāz) *v.* To look steadily or intently at something in admiration or wonder; to stare.

ga-zelle (ga zel´) *n.* A small, gracefully formed antelope of Asia and Africa, having curved horns and large eyes.

ga-zette (ga zet´) *n.* A newspaper; an official publication. **gazette** *v.* To publish or announce in a gazette.

gaz-et-teer (gaz´i tēr´) *n.* A dictionary consisting of geographical facts.

gaz-pa-cho (gaz pä chō) *n.* A cold soup made from vegetables, spices, oils, etc.

gds *abbr.* Goods.

ge-an-ti-cline (jē ant´ē klīn) *n.* A great upward fold of the earth's surface.

gear (gēr) *n.* A toothed wheel which interacts with another toothed part to transmit motion; an assembly of parts that work together for a special purpose; equipment. **gear** *v.* To regulate, match, or suit something.

gee (jē) *v.* A command given to horses or other work animals, directing them to turn right. **gee** *interj.* An expression of surprise or shock.

geese *n.* Plural of goose.

gee-zer (gēzér) *n. Slang* An old, odd, or eccentric man.

ge-gen-schein *n.* A faint, round patch of light sometimes seen in the sky at night.

Geiger counter (gī´gér koun´tér) *n. Phys.* An instrument used to measure, detect, and record cosmic rays and nuclear radiation.

gel (jel) *n. Chem.* A colloid that is in a more solid than liquid form. **gel** *v.*

geld (geld) *v.* To castrate or spay an animal, especially a horse.

gel-id (jel´id) *adj.* Very cold; frigid. .

gel-ig-nite (jel´ig nīt´) *n.* Dynamite with an absorbent base of potassium or sodium nitrate and some wood pulp.

gem (jem) *n.* A cut and polished precious or semiprecious stone; a person or thing that is highly treasured. **gem** *v.* To decorate with or as with gems.

gem-i-nate (jem´i nāt) *v.* To become paired or arrange in pairs.

gem-mip-a-rous *adj.* Reproducing by buds.

gem-mule (jem´ül) *n.* A small bud.

gem-ol-o-gy (je mol′o jē) *n.* The study of gems. **gemological** *adj.*

gems-bok *n.* A large antelope of southern Africa, strikingly marked and having long straight horns and a long tail.

gem-stone *n.* A mineral or petrified material which can be refined by cutting and polishing and used in jewelry.

gen *abbr.* Gender; general; generally.

gen-darme (zhän′därm) *n.* A policeman in France.

gen-der (jen′dèr) *n. Gram.* A member of a category, such as feminine, masculine, and neuter, into which words are divided and which determine agreement with or selection of modifiers or grammatical forms; the quality of being of the male or female sex.

gene (jēn) *n. Biol.* A functional hereditary unit which occupies a fixed location on a chromosome and controls or acts in the transmission of hereditary characteristics.

ge-ne-al-o-gy (jē′nē ol′o jē) *n., pl.* **genealogies** A record, table, or account showing the descent of a family, group, or person from an ancestor; the study of ancestry. **genealogical** *adj.*

gene mutation *n.* Alteration in an organism due to a chemical rearrangement within the molecules of a gene.

gen-er-a-ble *adj.* Capable of being generated or produced.

gen-er-al-i-za-tion (jen′ėr a lizā′shan) *n.* Something arrived at by generalizing, such as a broad, overall statement or conclusion.

gen-er-ate (jen′o rāt) *v.* To cause to be; to produce; to bring into existence, especially by a chemical or physical process. **generative** *adj.*

gen-er-a-tor (jen′e rā′tėr) *n. Mech.* A machine that changes mechanical energy into electrical energy.

gen-er-a-trix *n.* A point, line, or surface whose motion generates a line, surface, figure, or solid.

ge-ner-ic (je ner′ik) *adj.* Relating to or characteristic of an entire class or group; pertaining to a class or relating to a class of merchandise that does not have a trademark. **generically** *adv.*

gen-er-ous (jen′ėr us) *adj.* Sharing freely; abundant; overflowing. **generosity** *n.* **generously** *adv.*

gen-e-sis (jen′i sis) *n., pl.* **geneses** The act or state of originating. **Genesis** The first book of the Old Testament.

ge-net-ic (je net′ik) *adj.* Of or pertaining to the origin or development of something; of or relating to genetics.

genetic code *n. Biochem.* The biochemical basis of heredity that specifies the amino acid sequence in the synthesis of proteins and on which heredity is based.

ge-net-ics *n.* The science that deals with the hereditary and evolutionary differences and similarities of related organisms, as produced by the interaction of genes.

ge-ne-va (je nē′va) *n.* An alcoholic liquor flavored with juniper berries.

Ge-ne-va Con-ven-tion *n.* The international agreement signed in 1864 at Geneva which governs the wartime treatment of prisoners of war and of the wounded, sick, and the dead in battle.

gen-ial (je nē′al) *adj.* Cheerful, kind, pleasant and good-humored in disposition or manner. **geniality** *n.* **genially** *adv.*

gen-ic (jen′ik) *adj.* Pertaining to a gene or genes.

ge-nic-u-late (je nik′yu lat) *adj.* Bent at an angle like the knee.

ge-nie (jē′nē) *n.* A supernatural creature, capable of taking on human form, who does one's bidding.

gen-i-tal (jen′i tal) *adj.* Of or pertaining to the reproductive organs or the process of reproduction.

genitals (jen′i talz) *n., pl.* The external sexual organs. **genitalia** *n.*

gen-i-tive (jen′i tiv) *adj. Gram.* Indicating origin, source, or possession. **genitive** *n.* The genitive case.

gen-i-tor *n.* A male parent.

gen-i-to-u-ri-nar-y (jen′i tō yer′iner′ē) *adj. Anat.* Of or pertaining to the genital and urinary organs or their functions.

gen-ius (jēn′yus) *n., pl.* **geniuses** Exceptional intellectual ability or creative power; a strong, natural talent; a person who exerts powerful influence over another.

gen-o-cide (jen′o sīd′) *n.* The deliberate and systematic extermination or destruction of a political, racial, or cultural group.

ge-nome (je′nom) *n. Biol.* One of the two sets of chromosomes in a zygote.

gen-re *n.* A category of a specific artistic or literary accomplishment characterized by a particular form, technique, style, or subject matter.

gens (jenz) *n., pl.* **gentes** In ancient Rome, a clan that included families of the same name that have descended through the male line.

gent (jent) *n. Slang* A gentleman.

gen-teel (jen tēl′) *adj.* Elegant; refined or well-bred; polite; stylish or fashionable. **genteelly** *adv.*

gen-tile (jen′tīl) *n.* A person who is not a Jew, especially a Christian; among Mormons, of or relating to non-Mormons; a heathen or pagan.

gen-til-i-ty (jen til´i tē) *n.* The quality of being genteel; the members of the upper class; well-born or well-bred persons collectively.

gen-tle (jen´tl) *adj.* Moderate; not harsh, severe, rough, or loud; easily handled or managed; docile; not sudden or steep. **gentle** *v.* To tame; to calm. **gently** *adv.* **gentleness** *n.*

gen-try (jen´trē) *n.* People of good family or high social standing; the aristocracy; in England, the social class that is considered the upper ranks of the middle class.

gen-u-flect (jen´ū flekt´) *v.* To bend down on one knee, as in worship.

gen-u-ine (jen´ū in) *adj.* Real; authentic; not counterfeit or spurious; not hypocritical; sincere. **genuinely** *adv.*

ge-nus (jē´nus) *n., pl.* **genera** *Biol.* A group or category of plants or animals usually including several species that share certain specific characteristics.

geo- *prefix* Ground; earth; soil.

ge-o-cen-tric (jē´ō sen´trik) *adj.* Of or relating to the earth's center; formulated on the assumption that the earth is the center of the universe. **geocentrically** *adv.* **geocentrical** *adj.*

ge-o-chem-is-try (jē´ō kem´i strē) *n.* A branch of chemistry that deals with the chemical composition of the earth's crust. **geochemical** *adj.*

ge-ode (jē´ōd) *n. Geol.* A hollow rock having a cavity lined with crystals.

geodesic dome *n.* A vaulted or domed structure of lightweight straight elements that form interlocking polygons.

geodesic line (jē ō des´ik) *n. Math.* The shortest line between two fixed points on a sphere or other defined surface.

ge-od-e-sy (jē od´i sē) *n.* The geologic science dealing with the determination of the shape, area, and curvature of the earth. **geodesist** *n.* **geodetic** *adj.*

ge-og-no-sy (jē og´ne sē) *n.* That branch of geology that deals with the constituent parts of the earth, its description of land, air and water, its crust, and interior.

ge-og-ra-phy (jē og´ra fē) *n.* The science that deals with the earth's natural climate, resources, and population. **geographer** *n.* **geographic, geographical** *adj.* **geographically** *adv.*

ge-oid *n.* The surface around or within the earth which coincides with the mean sea level over the ocean and its extension under the continents.

ge-ol-o-gy (jē ol´o jē) *n., pl.* **geologies** The science that deals with the history, origin, and structure of the earth. **geologic, geological** *adj.*

ge-o-mag-net-ic *adj.* Relating to the earth's magnetism. **geomagnetism** *n.*

ge-om-e-ter *n.* A geometrid moth or its larva; a specialist in geometry.

ge-o-met-ric (jē´ō me´trik) *adj.* According to or pertaining to the rules and principles of geometry; increasing in a geometric progression.

geometric progression *n.* A sequence of numbers, as 4, 8, 16, 32 where each term is the product of a constant factor and the term that precedes it.

ge-om-e-trid *n.* A small, slender-bodied, delicate moth having broad wings, whose larvae are commonly called inchworms.

ge-om-e-try (jē om´i trē) *n.* The branch of mathematics that deals with the measurement, properties, and relationships of lines, angles, points, surfaces and solids.

ge-o-mor-phic *adj.* Relating to the form or surface features of the earth.

ge-o-mor-phol-o-gy *n.* The science that deals with the origin, development, and characteristics of the surface features of the earth.

ge-oph-a-gy *n.* The practice of eating earthy substances such as clay.

ge-o-phys-ics (jē´ō fiz´iks) *n.* The science of the earth and its relation to forces acting on it; it includes meteorology, magnetism, volcanology, and radioactivity.

ge-o-pol-i-tics (jē´ō pol´i tiks) *n.* The study of the influence of economic and geographical factors on the politics and policies of a nation or region.

geor-gette *n.* A fine transparent variety of silk crepe woven from hard-twisted yarns to give a dull pebbly surface.

Georgia *n.* A state located in the southeastern part of the United States; statehood January 2, 1788; state capital Atlanta.

ge-o-strat-e-gy *n.* A group of factors, geographical, political, and strategic, that are characteristic of a specific area.

ge-o-stroph-ic *adj.* Relating to the deflective force caused by the earth's rotation.

ge-o-tec-ton-ic *adj.* Relating to the structure, form, and arrangement of the earth's crust due to faulting or folding.

ge-o-ther-mal *or* **ge-o-ther-mic (jē´ō ther´mal)** *adj.* Relating to the internal heat of the earth.

ge-ot-ro-pism *n.* The tendency to turn gravitationally toward the earth.

ge-ra-ni-ol *n.* An unsaturated alcohol, chiefly used in soaps and perfumes.

ge-ra-ni-um (ji rā´nē um) *n.* A plant having rounded leaves and clusters of pink, red, or white flowers; a plant of the genus Pelargonium, with divided leaves and purplish or pink flowers.

ge-rar-di-a *n.* An herb belonging to the

figwort family, having showy purple, pink, or yellow flowers with distended bases.

ger-a-tol-o-gy *n.* The study that addresses the decline of life of animals threatened with extinction.

ger-bil (jer´bil) *n.* An animal of the rodent family found in the desert regions of Africa and Asia Minor, having long hind legs and a long tail; a popular pet.

ger-i-at-rics (jer´ē a´triks) *n.* The medical study that deals with the structural changes, diseases, physiology, and hygiene of old age. **geriatric** *adj.* **geriatrician** *n.*

germ (jerm) *n.* A small cell or organic structure from which a new organism may develop; a microorganism which causes disease. *Biol.* A reproductive cell.

Ger-man (jer´man) *n.* The language of Germany; an inhabitant or native of Germany.

ger-mane (jèr mān) *adj.* Relevant to what is being considered or discussed.

Ger-man-ic (jèr man´ik) *adj.* Relating to the language or customs of the Dutch, German, English, Afrikaans, Flemish, or Scandinavians.

ger-ma-ni-um (jèr mā´nē um) *n.* A grayish-white element widely used in electronics and optics, symbolized by Ge.

Ger-man meas-les *n. Med.* A contagious viral disease accompanied by sore throat, fever, and a skin rash; a disease capable of causing defects in infants born to mothers infected during the first stages of pregnancy.

German Shepherd *n.* A large breed of dog, which is often trained to help the police and the blind.

Germany *n.* A country in western Europe.

germ cell *n.* An egg or sperm cell.

ger mi cide (jer´mi sīd´) *n.* An agent used to destroy microorganisms or disease germs. **germicidal** *adj.*

ger-mi-nal (jer´mi nal) *adj.* Of or relating to a germ or germ cell; of or in the earliest stage of development.

ger-mi-nant *adj.* Having the ability to gradually grow and develop.

ger-mi-nate (jer´mi nāt´) *v.* To begin to grow, develop, or sprout. **germination** *n.* **germinative** *adj.*

germ plasm *n. Biol.* The part of the protoplasm of a germ cell containing the chromosomes and genes.

ger-on-tol-gy (jer´on tol´o jē) *n.* The study of the processes and phenomena of aging. **gerontological** *adj.* **gerontologic** *adj.* **gerontologist** *n.*

ger-ry-man-der (jer´i man˝dèr) *v.* To divide a voting area so as to advance unfairly the interests of a political party; to adjust or adapt to one's advantage.

ger-und (jer´und) *n. Gram.* A verb form that is used as a noun, such as *walking.*

ges-so (jes´ō) *n.* Plaster of Paris prepared with glue used in painting, etc.

gest (jest) *n.* A notable deed or feat.

ge-stalt (ge shält´) *n.* A pattern as a unified whole, with properties which cannot be derived by summation of its individual parts.

ge-sta-po (ge stä´pō) *n.* The secret police in Germany under the Nazi regime, known for its brutality.

ges-tate (jes´tāt) *v.* To conceive and gradually mature in the mind; to carry in the womb during pregnancy.

ges-ta-tion (je stā´shan) *n.* The carrying of a developing offspring in the uterus; pregnancy. **gestational** *adj.*

ges-tic *adj.* Pertaining to motions or gestures of the body.

ges-tic-u-late (je stik´ū lāt´) *v.* To make expressive or emphatic gestures, as in speaking. **gesticulation** *n.*

ges-ture (jes´chèr) *n.* A bodily motion, especially with the hands in speaking, to emphasize some idea or emotion. **gesture** *v.* To make gestures.

ge-sund-heit (ge zun˝hīt) *interj.* A German phrase used to wish good health to a person who has just sneezed.

GET In computer science, a program instruction to fetch data, a file or command from a non-contiguous source.

get (get) *v.* To come into possession of, as by receiving, winning, earning, or buying. **to get ahead** To attain success. **to get back at** To revenge oneself on. **to get by** To manage; to survive. **to get one's goat** To make somebody angry.

get-a-ble *adj.* Accessible; procurable; obtainable.

get-a-way (get´a wā´) *n.* The act of or instance of escaping by a criminal; a start, as of a race.

get-to-geth-er (get´ta geth´er) *n.* A small, informal family or social gathering.

get-up (get´up´) *n.* An outfit; a costume.

ge-um *n.* A perennial herb of the rose family with white, purple, or yellow flowers.

gew-gaw (gū´go) *n.* A little ornamental article of small value.

gey-ser (gī´zèr) *n.* A natural hot spring that intermittently ejects hot water and steam.

ghast-ly (gast´lē) *adj.* Horrible; terrifying; very unpleasant or bad; ghost-like in appearance; deathly pale.

ghat (gät) *n.* A broad flight of steps that leads down to the edge of a river.

gher-kin (ger´kin) *n.* A very small,

prickly cucumber pickled as a relish.

ghet-to (get´ō) n. A run-down section of a city in which a minority group lives because of poverty or social pressure.

ghost (gōst) n. The spirit of a dead person which is believed to appear to or haunt living persons; a spirit; a ghostwriter; a false, faint secondary television image.

ghost-ly adj. Pertaining to or relating to a ghost; suggestive of ghosts.

ghost town n. A town that once flourished but is now deserted.

ghost-writer n. A person hired to write for another person and to give credit for the writing or speaking to that other person.

ghoul (gōl) n. A person who robs graves; in Moslem legend, an evil spirit which plunders graves and feeds on corpses. **ghoulish** adj. **ghoulishly** adv.

GI (jē´ī´) n., pl. **GIs** or **GI's** An enlisted person in the United States armed forces. **GI** adj. In conformity with military regulations or customs. **GI** v. To clean or scrub in preparation for or as if for a military inspection. **GI** abbr. Government issue; general issue; gastrointestinal.

gi-ant (jī´ant) n. A legendary man-like being of supernatural size and strength; one of great power, importance, or size; large. **giant** adj.

giant powder n. A form of dynamite made of nitroglycerin and kieselguhr.

gib (gib) n. A thin plate of metal or other material to hold parts together or in place.

gib-ber (jib´ér) v. To talk or chatter incoherently or unintelligibly.

gib-ber-ish (jib´ér ish) n. Meaningless speech.

gib-bet (jib´it) n. A gallows. **gibbet** v. To execute by hanging on a gibbet.

gib-bon (gib´on) n. A slender, long-armed Asian ape.

gib-bous (gib´us) adj. The moon or a planet which is seen with more than half but not all of the apparent disk illuminated. **gibbously** adv. **gibbousness** n.

gibe (jīb) v. To ridicule or make taunting remarks. **gibe** n.

gib-let (jib´lit) or **giblets** n. The heart, liver, and gizzard of a fowl.

gid n. A disease of sheep caused by infestation of the brain caused with a larval tapeworm.

gid-dy (gid´ē) adj. Affected by a reeling or whirling sensation; dizzy; frivolous and silly; flighty. **giddily** adv. **giddiness** n.

gift (gift) n. Something that is given from one person to another; a natural aptitude; a talent.

gift-ed adj. The state of having a special ability.

gig (gig) n. A light, two-wheeled carriage drawn by one horse. **Naut.** A speedy, light rowboat; a spear with forks or prongs used for fishing. **Slang** A job, especially an engagement to play music. **Milit. Slang** A demerit; a punishment to military personnel.

gigabyte In computer science, one thousand million (one billion) bytes.

gi-gan-tic (jī gan´tik) adj. Of tremendous or extraordinary size; large; huge. **gigantically** adv.

gig-gle (gig´l) v. To laugh in high-pitched, repeated, short sounds. **giggle** n. **giggler** n. **giggly** adj.

gig-o-lo (jig´o lō) n. A man who is supported by a woman not his wife; a man who is paid to be an escort or dancing partner.

gigue (zhēg) n. A lively dance step.

Gila monster (hē´la mon´ster) n. A large, venomous lizard of the southwestern United States desert areas having an orange and black body.

gild (gild) v. To coat with a thin layer of gold; to brighten or adorn. **gild** v. To add unnecessary ornamentation. **gilded** adj. **gilder** n.

gild-ing n. A thin coating of gold leaf; a superficially attractive appearance.

gill (gil) n. Zool. The organ, of fishes and various other aquatic invertebrates, used for taking oxygen from water. **gill** n. A liquid measure that equals 1/4 pint.

gilt (gilt) adj. Covered with gold; of the color of gold. **gilt** n. A thin layer of gold or a gold-colored substance which is applied to a surface.

gilt-edge or **gilt-edged (gilt´ejd´)** adj. Of the highest value or the best quality.

gim-bals (jim´balz) n. A three-ringed device that keeps an object supported on its level, as the compass of a ship.

gim-crack (jim´krak´) n. A showy and useless object of little or no value.

gim-let (gim´lit) n. A small, sharp tool with a bar handle and a pointed, spiral tip which is used for boring holes.

gim-mal n. A series of interlocked rings.

gim-mick (gim´ik) n. A tricky feature that is obscured or misrepresented; a tricky device, especially when used dishonestly or secretly; a gadget. **gimmickry** n. **gimmicky** adj.

gimp (gimp) n. Slang A person who walks with a limp; a cripple. **gimp** v. **gimpy** adj.

gin (jin) n. An aromatic, clear alcoholic liquor distilled from grain and flavored with juniper berries; a machine used to separate seeds from cotton fibers; a snare or trap for game. **gin** v. To remove the seeds from cotton with a gin; to trap game in a gin.

gin-ger (jin´jèr) n. A tropical Asian plant that has a pungent, aromatic root, used in medicine and cooking. **ginger** v.

ginger ale n. An effervescent soft drink flavored with ginger.

ginger beer n. A sweet, nonalcoholic, effervescing drink flavored with ginger.

gin-ger-bread (jin´jèr bred) n. A dark, ginger and molasses flavored cake or cookie.

gin-ger-ly (jin´jèr lē) adv. Doing something very cautiously and carefully. **gingerliness** n. **gingery** adj.

gin-ger-snap (jin´jèr snap´) n. A brittle molasses and ginger cookie.

ging-ham (ging´am) n. A cotton fabric woven in solid colors and checks.

gin-gi-li (jin´ji lē) n. The sesame plant or its oil.

gin-gi-val adj. Referring to the gums.

gin-gi-vi-tis (jin´ji vī´tis) n. Pathol. Inflammation of the gums.

gink-go (gingk´gō) n., pl. **ginkgoes** A large Chinese shade tree cultivated in the United States, with edible fruit or nuts.

gin rummy n. A variety of the card game rummy.

gin-seng (jin´seng) n. An herb native to China and North America with an aromatic root believed to have medicinal properties.

Gip-sy (jip´sē) n. & adj. Variation of gypsy.

gi-raffe (ji raf´) n., pl. **giraffes** or **giraffe** The tallest of all mammals, having an extremely long neck and very long legs, living in Africa.

gir-an-dole n. Radiating and showy fireworks; an ornamented branched candlestick; a central jewel in a pendant.

gir-a-sol n. A variety of opal showing a reddish color when turned toward the light.

gird (gèrd) v. To surround, encircle, or attach with or as if with a belt.

gird-er (ger´dèr) n. A strong, horizontal beam, as of steel or wood, which is the main support in a building.

gir-dle (ger´dl) n. A cord, sash, or belt worn around the waist; a supporting undergarment to give support and to shape of the lower body. Anat. The pelvic arch of the body. **girdle** v.

girl (gerl) n. A female child or infant; a young, unmarried woman; any woman of any age; one's sweetheart. **girlish** adj. **girlishly** adv. **girlishness** n. **girlhood** n.

girl Friday n. A woman employee responsible for a variety of tasks.

girl friend n. A female friend; a regular or frequent female companion of a boy or man.

girl scout n. A member of the Girl Scouts of the United States; an organization for girls between 7 and 17 years of age.

girth (gerth) n. The circumference or distance around something; a strap that encircles an animal's body to secure something on its back, as a saddle.

gis-mo n. Slang A part or device whose name is unknown or forgotten; a gadget.

gist (jist) n. The central or main substance, as of an argument or question.

git-tern n. A medieval guitar strung with wire.

give (giv) v. To make a present of; to bestow; to accord or yield to another; to put into the possession of another; to convey to another; to donate or contribute; to apply; to devote; to yield as to pressure; to collapse; to furnish or provide; to deliver in exchange for pay. **give away** To hand over the bride to the bridegroom at a wedding ceremony. **give out** To collapse; to be exhausted. **give in** To surrender; to submit oneself. **give** n. **giver** n.

give–and–take n. To make a mutual exchange, as of conversation or opinions.

give-a-way (giv´awā´) n. Something that is given free as a premium; something that betrays, generally unintentionally

giv-en (giv´n) adj. Bestowed; presented; specified or assumed.

given name n. The name bestowed or given at birth or baptism.

give up v. To surrender; to cease to do; hand over; to abandon all hope, quit.

giz-zard (giz´èrd) n. The second stomach in birds, where partly digested food is finely ground.

gla-brous (glā´brus) adj. Biol. Having no hair or down; having a smooth surface. **glabrousness** n.

gla-cial (glā´shal) adj. Of or pertaining to, caused by, or marked by glaciers, extremely cold. **glacially** adv.

glacial epoch n. Geol. A portion of geological time when ice sheets covered the Northern Hemisphere.

gla-ci-ate v. To convert into or cover with a glacier; to produce glacial effects.

gla-cier (glā´shèr) n. A large mass of ice formed from compacted snow that moves slowly down mountains into valleys or across land surfaces.

gla-ci-ol-o-gy n. Any branch of geology dealing with snow or ice accumulation; geographical distribution, movement, or the effects of glaciers.

glad (glad) adj. Displaying, experiencing, or affording joy and pleasure; a state of being happy; being willing to help; grateful. **glad** n. Short for gladiolus.

glad-den (glad´n) v. To make glad.

glade (glād) n. A clearing in a forest or

woods.

glad hand *n*. A warm welcome to people you meet. **glad-hand** *v*.

glad-i-a-tor (glad´ē ā´têr) *n*. An ancient Roman slave, captive, or paid freeman who entertained the public by fighting, often to the death; one who is engaged in an intense struggle or controversy. **gladiatorial** *adj*.

glad-i-o-lus (glad´ē ō´lus) *n*., *pl*. **gladioli** *or* **gladioluses** A plant with fleshy bulbs, sword-shaped leaves, and spikes of colorful flowers.

glad-some (glad´som) *adj*. Giving cheer; showing joy. **gladsomely** *adv*. **gladsomeness** *n*.

glam-or-ize *or* **glam-our-ize** (glam´o rīz´) *v*. To make glamorous; to portray or treat in a romantic way.

glamour girl *n*. A woman considered to be beautiful who leads a glamorous life.

glam-our *or* **glam-or** (glam´êr) *n*. Alluring, fascinating charm. **glamorous** *adj*. **glamourous** *adj*.

glance (glans) *v*. To take a brief or quick look at something; to obliquely strike a surface at an angle and be deflected; to give a light, brief touch; to brush against. **glancing** *adj*. **glance** *n*.

gland (gland) *n*. *Anat*. Any of the body's organs that excrete or secrete substances.

glan-du-lar *adj*. Relating to or involving glands.

glare (glâr) *v*. To stare fiercely or angrily; to shine intensely; to dazzle. **glare** *n*. An uncomfortably harsh or bright light; angry look.

glar-ing (glâr´ing) *adj*. Shining with an extremely bright light; painfully obvious. **glaringly** *adv*. **glaringness** *n*.

glass (glas) *n*. A hard, amorphous, brittle, usually transparent material which is formed in a molten state and then hardened by rapid cooling; any substance made of or resembling glass; a mirror, tumbler, window pane, lens, or other material made of glass. **glasses** A pair of eyeglasses used as an aid to vision; glassware. **glass** *adj*. **glassy** *adj*.

glass blowing *n*. The art or process of shaping objects from molten glass by gently blowing air into them through a glass tube. **glassblower** *n*.

glass-ine *n*. A dense, translucent paper highly resistant to air, water, or oil.

glass-mak-er (glas´mā´kêr) *n*. A person who makes glass or glassware.

glass-ware *n*. Articles made of glass.

glass wool *n*. Glass fibers in a mass being used for thermal insulation and air filters.

glass -work *n*. The manufacture of glass and glassware; the fitting of glass; glazing; articles of glass.

glass-wort (glas´würt´) *n*. A succulent, leafless plant of the goosefoot family, living in salt water marshes as well as alkaline regions.

glau-co-ma (glo kō´ma) *n*. *Pathol*. A disease of the eye characterized by abnormally high pressure within the eyeball and gradual loss of vision.

glau-cous (glo´kus) *adj*. Yellowish green.

glaze (glāz) *n*. A thin, smooth coating, like the gloss applied on ceramics. **glaze** *v*. To become covered with a thin glassy coating of ice; to coat or cover with a glaze; to fit with glass, as to glaze a window. **glazer** *n*.

gla-zier (glā´zhêr) *n*. A person who sets glass. **glaziery** *n*.

glaz-ing (glā´zing) *n*. The process of furnishing or fitting with glass; the act of applying glaze.

gleam (glēm) *n*. A ray or beam of light; a glow. **gleam** *v*. To shine or emit light softly; to appear briefly but clearly. **gleamy** *adj*.

glean (glēn) *v*. To collect or gather facts by patient effort; to collect part by part; to pick bits of a crop left by a reaper. **gleaner** *n*.

glean-ings *n*. Things acquired a little at a time, or in slow stages; field leftovers.

glede *n*. A bird of prey.

glee (glē) *n*. Joy; merriment; gaiety; an unaccompanied musical composition. **gleeful** *adj*. **gleefully** *adv*.

glee club *n*. A singing group that is organized to sing short pieces of choral music.

gleet (glēt) *n*. An abnormal, transparent mucous discharge of the urethra, caused by gonorrhea.

glen (glen) *n*. A small, secluded valley.

glen-gar-ry (glen gar´ē) *n*. A woolen cap worn by the Scottish people.

glen plaid *n*. A twill pattern of checks.

gli-a-din *n*. Any simple protein found in gluten, from wheat and rye.

glib (glib) *adj*. Spoken easily and fluently; superficial. **glibly** *adv*. **glibness** *n*.

glide (glīd) *v*. To pass or move smoothly with little or no effort; to fly without motor power. **glidingly** *adv*. **glide** *n*.

glid-er (glī´dêr) *n*. One that glides; a swing gliding in a metal frame. *Aeron*. An aircraft without an engine, constructed to soar on air currents.

glim-mer (glim´êr) *n*. A faint suggestion; an indication; a dim unsteady light. **glimmer** *v*. To give off a faint or dim light.

glimpse (glimps) *n*. A momentary look.

glint *v*. To be reflected; to give off a flash or gleam. **glint** *n*. A brief, bright flash of light; a brief indication of recognition.

glis-sade (gli säd´) *n*. A gliding ballet step; a controlled slide in either a sitting or standing position, helps descend a steep, snowy, or icy incline.**-ssade** *v*.

glis-san-do (gli sän´dō) *n., pl.* **glissandi** *Mus.* A rapid passing from one tone to another by a continuous change of pitch.

glis-ten (glis´en) *v*. To shine softly as if reflected by light; to shine or glow with a luster. **glisten** *n*.

glitch (glich) *n*. A minor mishap or malfunction. *Elect.* A false signal caused by an unwanted surge of power.

glit-ter (glit´ėr) *n*. A brilliant sparkle; small bits of light-reflecting material used for decoration. **glitter** *v*. To sparkle with brilliance. **glittery** *adj.*

gloam-ing (glō´ming) *n*. Twilight; the dusk of early evening.

gloat (glōt) *v*. To express, feel, or observe with great malicious pleasure or self-satisfaction. **gloater** *n*. **gloatingly** *adv.*

glob (glob) *n*. A drop of something; a rounded, large mass of something.

glob-al (glō´bal) *adj.* Spherical; involving the whole world. **globalize** *v*.

globe (glōb) *n*. A spherical object; anything that is perfectly rounded; the earth; anything like a sphere, such as a fish bowl; a spherical representation of the earth, usually including geographical and political boundaries. **globular** *adj.*

globe-fish *n*. Fish with the capabilities to inflate themselves into a globular form.

globe-trotter *n*. One who travels all over the world.

glob-ule *n*. A very small particle of matter in the form of a ball.

glob-u-lin (glob´ū lin) *n. Biochem.* Any of a class of simple proteins found widely in blood, milk, tissue, muscle and plant seeds.

glo-chid-i-ate (glō kid´ē it) *adj.* Barbed at the tip; bearing barbs.

glom-er-ate (glom´ėr it) *adj.* Gathered into a round mass; conglomerated.

glom-er-ule (glom´e rŏl)´ *n*. A compact cluster, as of a single flower cluster that contains several flowers.

gloom (glōm) *n*. Partial or total darkness; depression of the mind or spirits. **gloomily** *adv.* **gloominess** *n*.

gloom-y *adj.* Partially or totally dark; low in spirits; lacking illumination.

glop (glob) *n. Slang* A messy mixture of food; something that is considered worthless.

glo-ri-fy (glōr´i fī)´ *v*. To worship and give glory to; to give high praise.

glo-ri-ole (glōr´ē ōl) *n*. A halo.

glo-ri-ous (glōr´ē us) *adj.* Magnificent; resplendent; delightful; illustrious; full of glory. **gloriously** *adv.*

glory (glōr´ē) *n., pl.* **glories** Distinction, praise or honor; exalted reputation; adoration and praise offered in worship; a wonderful asset; the height of one's triumph, achievement, or prosperity. **glory** *v*. To rejoice with jubilation.

gloss (glos) *n*. The sheen or luster of a polished surface; a deceptively or superficially attractive appearance; a note that explains or translates a difficult or hard to understand expression. **gloss** *v*. To cover over by falsehood in an attempt to excuse or ignore.

glos-sa-ry (glos´a rē) *n., pl.* **glossaries** A list of words and their meanings.

gloss-y (glos´ē) *adj.* Having a bright sheen; lustrous; superficially attractive. **glossy** *n*. A photo print on smooth, shiny paper. **glossily** *adv.* **-iness** *n*.

glost *n*. Ceramic glaze used on clay pottery.

glot-tis (glot´is) *n., pl.* **glottises** *or* **glottides** *Anat.* The opening or cleft between the vocal cords at the upper part of the larynx. **glottal** *adj.*

glove (gluv) *n*. A covering for the hand with a separate section for each finger; an oversized protective covering for the hand, as that used in baseball, boxing, or hockey. **glove** *v*. To protect the hand or any object with a covering like a glove; to provide with gloves; to catch a baseball in a hand protected by a glove. **gloved** *adj.*

glow (glō) *v*. To give off heat and light, especially without a flame; to have a bright, warm, ruddy color. **glow** *n*. A warm feeling of emotion. **glowing** *adj.*

glow-er (glou´ėr) *v*. To look sullenly or angrily at; to glare. **glower** *n*.

glow-ing (glō´ng) *adj.* Brilliantly luminous; experiencing feelings of heat or exuberance..

glow lamp *n*. Gas-discharged electric lamp in which electrons ionize a gas, emitting a glow.

glow-worm (glō´werm´) *n*. A European beetle; the luminous larva or grub-like female of an insect which displays phosphorescent light; the firefly.

glox-in-i-a (glok sin´ē a) *n*. A tropical South American plant with large, bell-shaped flowers.

glu-ca-gon *n*. A protein hormone that increases the content of sugar in the blood by increasing the rate of breakdown of glycogen in the liver.

glu-cose (glō´kōs) *n. Chem.* A substance less sweet than cane sugar, found as dextrose in plants and animals and obtained by hydrolysis; a yellowish to colorless syrupy mixture of dextrose, maltose, and dextrins with a small amount of water, used especially in making confectionery and in baking.

glue (glōō) *n.* Any of various adhesives in the form of a gelatin, made from animal substances, as bones or skins, and used to stick and hold items together. **glue** *v.* **gluey** *adj.*

glum (glum) *adj.* Moody and sullen. **glumly** *adv.* **glumness** *n.*

glut (glut) *v.* To feed or supply beyond capacity; to provide with a supply that exceeds demand. **glut** *n.* An oversupply; an overabundance.

glutamic acid *n.* An amino acid that occurs in plant and animal proteins, used in the form of a sodium salt substitute and flavor enhancer.

glu-ten (glōt´en) *n.* A mixture of plant proteins that is used as an adhesive and as a substitute for flour. **glutenous** *adj.*

glu-te-us *n.* The large muscles of the buttock.

glut-ton (glut´n) *n.* Someone who eats immoderately; one who has a large capacity for work or punishment.

glut-ton-ous *adj.* Marked by excessive eating; greedy. **gluttonously** *adv.*

gluttony *n.* The habit of eating and drinking excessively. **glutton** *n.*

glyc-er-ol (glis´e rōl´) *n.* *Chem.* A sweet, oily, syrupy liquid derived from fats and oils and used as a solvent, sweetener, antifreeze, and lubricant.

gly-co-pro-tein (glī´kō prō´tēn) *n.* A group of conjugated proteins containing a protein and a carbohydrate.

gly-co-side (glī´ko sīd´) *n.* *Chem.* Any of a group of carbohydrates which, when decomposed, produce glucose or other sugar.

glyph (glif) *n.* Any symbol that conveys meaning without using words; an ornamental channel carved on a column or frieze; a symbolic figure or character carved in relief.

gly-phog-ra-phy (gli fog´ra fē) *n.* Electrotype process where a plate having a raised surface appropriate for printing is made from an engraved plate.

glyp-tic *n.* The art of carving or engraving on precious gems or related stones.

glyp-to-dont *n.* An extinct mammal that resembled an armadillo.

G–man (jē´man´) *n., pl.* **G–men** An agent of the Federal Bureau of Investigation; a Government man.

gnarl (närl) *n.* A hard, protruding knot on a tree. **gnarled** *adj.*

gnash (nash) *v.* To grind or strike the teeth together, as in rage or pain.

gnat (nat) *n.* A small, winged insect, especially one that bites or stings.

gnat-catch-er *n.* Any of several American insectivorous birds, genus Polioptila.

gnath-ic (nath´ik) *adj.* Pertaining or relating to the jaw or jaws.

gnaw (naw) *v.* To bite or eat away with persistence; to consume or wear away. **gnawer** *n.*

gnaw-ing *n.* A constant, often severe, pain.

gneiss (nīs) *n.* A banded, coarse-grained rock with minerals arranged in layers.

gnome (nōm) *n.* In folklore, a dwarf-like creature who lives underground and guards precious metals and treasures.

gno-mon (nō´mon) *n.* An object that by, the position of its shadow, is an indicator of the hour of the day; a sundial.

GNP *abbr.* Gross national product.

gnu (nö) *n., pl.* **gnus** *or* **gnu** South African antelope with an ox-like head, curved horns, a long tail, and a mane.

go (gō) *v.* To proceed or pass along; to leave; to move away from; to follow a certain course of action; to function; to function correctly; to be in operation; to pass from one to another by award or lot; to have recourse; to resort to; to pass, as of time; to be abolished or given up; to pass to someone, as by a will. **go** *n.* An attempt; a try. **go back on** To abandon **go for** To try; to try to obtain. **go places** To be on the road to success. **go under** To suffer destruction or defeat; **on the go** Always busy.

goad (gōd) *v.* To drive cattle to move; to incite or arouse. **goad** *n.*

go–a-head (gō´a hed´) *n.* Permission; a signal to move ahead or proceed.

goal (gōl) *n.* A purpose; the terminal point of a race or journey; in some games, the area, space, or object into which participants must direct play in order to score.

goal-ie *n.* A goalkeeper.

goal-keep-er (gōl´kē pėr) *n.* The player responsible for defending the goal in hockey, soccer, and other games, preventing the ball or puck from passing over the goal for a score; a goal tender.

goal-post *n.* Two vertical poles with a crossbar which constitutes the goal line in some games, especially football..

goat (gōt) *n.* A horned, cud chewing mammal related to the sheep; a lecherous man. *Slang* One who is a scapegoat. **goatish** *adj.* **goatishly** adv.

goat-ee (gō tē´) *n.* A short, pointed beard on a man's chin.

goat-skin (gōt´skin´) *n.* The skin of a goat, often used for leather products.

gob (gob) *n.* A piece or lump of something. *Slang* A sailor.

gob-ble (gob´l) *v.* To eat and swallow food greedily; to take greedily; to grab.

gob-ble-dy-gook (gob´l dē gek´) *n.* *Informal* Wordy and often unintelligible language.

gob-bler (gob´lėr) *n.* A male turkey.

go–be·tween (gō'bi twēn') *n.* A person who acts as an agent between two parties.

gob·let (gob'lit) *n.* A drinking glass, typically with a base and stem.

gob·lin (gob'lin) *n.* In folklore, an ugly, grotesque creature said to be mischievous and evil.

go–bo (gō'bō) *n.* A dark screen to shield a television camera from light.

go–by (gō'bē) *n.* A small freshwater fish, often having the pelvic fins attached to form a ventral sucking cup enabling it to cling to rocks.

go–cart *n.* A small, gasoline-powered car, used for recreation or racing.

god (god) *n.* Someone considered to be extremely important or valuable; an image, symbol, or statue of such a being.

God (god) *n.* The Supreme Being; the ruler of life and the universe.

god–child (god'child') *n.* A child for whom an adult serves as sponsor at baptism, circumcision, and other rites.

god–daughter *n.* A female godchild.

god–dess (god'ĭs) *n.* A female of exceptional charm, beauty, or grace.

go–dev·il *n.* A small, gasoline car used on railroad tracks to transport workers and supplies.

god–father (god'fä thĕr) *n.* A man who sponsors a child at his or her baptism or other such ceremony.

god–for–sak·en (god'fĕr sā'ken) *adj.* In a remote desolate place.

god–head (god'hed') *n.* Godhood; divinity; the essential and divine nature of a god. **Godhead** Supreme being.

god–less (god'lĭs) *adj.* Not recognizing a god. **godlessness** *n.*

god–ly (god'lē) *adj.* Filled with love for God.

god–mother (god'muth ĕr) *n.* A woman who sponsors a child at his or her baptism or other such ceremony.

god–par–ent(god'pâr'ent) *n.* A godfather or godmother.

god–send (god'sĕnd') *n.* Something received unexpectedly that is needed or wanted.

god–son *n.* A male godchild.

God–speed (god'spēd') *n.* Best wishes for someone's venture or journey.

god–wit *n.* A long-billed wading bird related to snipes.

gof–fer *n.* An ornamental ruffled piece of lace used on women's clothing.

go–get–ter (gō'get'ĕr) *n.* An enterprising, aggressive person.

gog–gle (gog'l) *v.* To stare with bulging eyes.

gog–gles (gog'lz) *n.* Spectacles or eyeglasses to protect the eyes against dust, wind, sparks, and other debris.

go–ing (gō'ing) *n.* The act of moving, leaving, or departing; the condition of roads or ground that affects walking, riding, and other movement; a condition influencing activity or progress. **goings on** Actions or behavior that causes one to express disapproval.

goi–ter (goi'tĕr) *n. Pathol.* Any abnormal enlargement of the thyroid gland, visible as a swelling in the front of the neck. **goitrous** *adj.*

gold (gōld) *n.* A soft, yellow, metallic element that is highly ductile and resistant to oxidation; used especially in coins and jewelry; a precious metal; a bright, vivid yellow; money; the element symbolized by Au.

gold–en–rod (gōl'den rod') *n.* A North American plant with small yellow flowers; the state flower of Alabama, Kentucky, and Nebraska.

golden rule *n.* The principle of treating others as one wants to be treated.

gold standard *n.* The monetary system based on gold of a specified weight and fineness as the unit of value and exchange.

golf (golf) *n.* A game played outdoors with a hard ball and clubs, on a grassy course with 9 or 18 holes. **golfer** *n.*

gon–ad (gō'nad) *n. Anat.* The male or female sex gland where the reproductive cells develop; an ovary or testis. **gonadal, gonadial, gonadic** *adj.*

gon–do–la (gon'do la) *n.* A long, narrow, flat-bottomed boat propelled by a single oar or a motor and used on the canals of Venice. **gondolier** *n.*

gone (gon) *adj.* Past; bygone; dead; beyond hope; marked by faintness or weakness. **far gone** Exhausted; wearied; almost dead.

gon–er (go'nĕr) *n. Slang* One that is ruined, close to death, or beyond all hope of being saved.

gon–fa–lon (gon'fa lon) *n.* A banner hung from a cross piece and cut so as to end in streamers.

gong (gong) *n.* A heavy metal disk which produces a deep resonant tone when struck with a padded stick.

go–ni–om–e–ter *n.* An instrument used for measuring angles.

gon–o–coc–cus (gon'o kok'us) *n., pl.* **gonococci** The bacterium which causes gonorrhea. **gonococcic** *adj.*

gon–or–rhe–a (go'o rē'a) *n. Pathol.* A contagious venereal infection transmitted chiefly by sexual intercourse.

goo (gō) *n.* Any sticky substance.

goo–ber (gō'bĕr) *n. Regional* A peanut.

good (ged) *adj.* Having desirable or favorable qualities or characteristics; morally excellent; virtuous; well-behaved; tractable; proper; excellent in degree or quality; unspoiled; fresh; healthy; striking or attractive. **goods** Merchandise or wares; personal belongings; cloth; fabric. **for good** Forever; permanently.

Good Book *n.* The Bible.

good–by *or* **good–bye (ged˝bī´)** *interj.* Used to express farewell. **good-by, good-bye** *n.* A farewell; a parting word; an expression of farewell. **good-by, good-bye** *adj.* Final.

good fellow *n.* A good natured person.

good–for–nothing (ged´fer nuth´ing) *n.* A person of little worth or usefulness.

Good Friday *n.* The Friday before Easter, a day observed by Christians to commemorate the crucifixion of Jesus.

good–heart-ed (ged´här´tid) *adj.* Having a kind and generous disposition.

good–hu-mored *adj.* Having a cheerful temper or mood; amiable.

good-ness (ged´nis) *n.* The state or quality of being good; kindness; integrity.

good-will *n.* A desire for the well-being of others; the pleasant relationship between a business and its customers.

goof (göf) *n. Slang* A stupid or dull-witted person; a mistake. **goof** *v.* To blunder; to make a mistake.

goof–off *n.* A slacker; one who shuns responsibility or work. **goof-off** *v.* To be doing something else when there is work to be done.

gook (gek) *n. Slang* A slimy, sludgy, or dirty substance.

goon (gön) *n. Slang* A thug or hoodlum hired to intimidate or injure someone; a person hired to break strikes; a stupid person.

goose (gös) *n., pl.* **geese** A large water bird related to swans and ducks; a female goose. *Informal* A silly person.

go-pher (gö´fer) *n.* A burrowing North American rodent with large cheek pouches.

gore (gör) *v.* To stab or pierce. **gore** *n.* Clotted blood; a triangular or tapering piece of cloth in a sail or skirt.

gorge (gorj) *n.* A deep, narrow ravine; deep or violent disgust. **gorge** *v.* To eat or devour greedily. **gorger** *n.*

gor-geous (gor´jus) *adj.* Beautiful; dazzling; extremely beautiful; magnificent. **gorgeously** *adv.*

go-ril-la (go ril´a) *n.* A large African jungle ape, having a massive, stocky body, long arms, and tusk-like canine teeth. *Slang* A brutish person.

gorse (gors) *n.* A spiny plant bearing fragrant yellow flowers.

go-ry (gör´ē) *adj.* Covered or stained with blood; resembling gore.

gosh *interj.* An expression of surprise.

gos-hawk (gos´hok˝) *n.* A large, short-winged hawk formerly used in falconry.

gos-ling (goz´ling) *n.* A young goose.

gos-pel *or* **Gos-pel (gos´pel)** *n.* The teachings of Christ and the apostles; any information which is accepted as unquestionably true; any of the first four books of the New Testament.

gospel music *n.* American religious music based on simple folk melodies blended with rhythmic and melodic elements of spirituals and jazz.

gos-port *n.* A flexible one-way speaking tube used for communications between people in separate airplane cockpits.

gos-sa-mer (gos´a mèr) *n.* The fine film or strands of a spider's web **floating** in the air; anything sheer, **delicate**, light, or flimsy.

gos-san (gos´an) *n.* Decomposed rock or vein material of a reddish or rusty color, often forming a large part of the outcrop of an iron-bearing vein.

gos-sip (gos´ip) *n.* Idle, often malicious talk; a person who spreads sensational rumors or intimate facts. **gossip** *v.* To spread or engage in gossip. **gossiper** *n.* **gossipy** *adj.*

got *v.* Past tense of get.

gouache (gwäsh) *n.* A method of painting with opaque watercolors.

gouge (gouj) *n.* A chisel with a scoop-shaped blade used for wood carving; a groove or hole made with or as if with a gouge **gouge** *v.* To make a hole or groove with a gouge; to cheat, to charge exorbitant prices. **gouger** *n.*

gou-lash (gö´läsh) *n.* A stew made from beef or veal and vegetables seasoned chiefly with paprika.

gourd (görd) *n.* A vine fruit such as the pumpkin, squash, and cucumber; an inedible fruit with a hard rind, which can be used as a drinking or storage vessel when it is dried and hollowed.

gour-mand (ger´mand) *n.* A person who takes excessive pleasure in eating.

gour-met (ger´mä) *n.* Someone who appreciates and understands fine food and drink.

gout (gout) *n. Pathol.* A disease caused by a defect in metabolism and characterized by painful inflammation of the joints.

gov *abbr.* Government; governor.

gov-ern (guv´ern) *v.* To guide, rule, or control by right or authority; to control or guide the action of something; to restrain. **governable** *adj.*

gov-ern-ment (guv´ern ment) *n.* The authoritative administration of public policy and affairs of a nation, state or city; the system or policy by which a political unit is governed; any government territory, district, or area. **governmental** *adj.* **governmentally** *adv.*

gov-er-nor (guv´ĕr nĕr) *n.* Someone who governs, as the elected chief executive of a state in the United States; an official appointed to exercise political authority over a territory. *Mech.* A device which will automatically control the speed of a machine. **-ship** *n.*

govt *abbr.* Government.

gow-an *n.* A yellow or white field flower.

gown (goun) *n.* A woman's dress, especially for a formal affair; any long, loose-fitting garment; a robe worn by certain judges, officials, scholars, and clergymen.

grab (grab) *v.* To snatch or take suddenly; to take possession of by force or by dishonest means. *Slang* To capture the attention of someone or something. **grabber** *n.* **grabby** *adj.*

grab-ble *v.* To search with the hand; grope.

gra-ben (grä´ben) *n. Geol.* An elongated depression in the earth, caused by the downward pressure of two or more faults.

grace (grās) *n.* Seemingly effortless beauty, ease, and charm of movement, proportion, or form; a charming quality; an attractive characteristic. **graceful** *adj.* **gracefully** *adv.*

grace-less *adj.* Lacking of grace or any pleasing quality.

grace period *n.* A time, after the actual due date of a payment when one may make payment without penalties.

gra-cious (grā´shus) *adj.* Marked by having or showing kindness and courtesy; full of compassion; merciful. **graciously** *adv.* **graciousness** *n.*

grack-le (grak´l) *n.* Any of various American blackbirds having long tails and iridescent black plumage.

grad *abbr.* Graduate; graduated.

gra-date (grā´dāt) *v.* To shade into the next color or stage.

gra-da-tion (grā dā´shan) *n.* A gradual and orderly arrangement or progression according to quality, size, rank, or other value; the act of grading.

grade (grād) *n.* A step or degree in a process or series; a group or category; a level of progress in school, usually constituting a year's work; a letter or number indicating a level of achievement in school work; the degree to which something slopes, as a road, track, or other surface. *Milit.* Rank.

grade school *n.* Elementary school, usually from kindergarten to grade 5, 6, or 8.

gra-di-ent (grā´dē ent) *n.* A slope or degree of inclination. *Phys.* A rate of change in variable factors, as temperature or pressure.

gra-din (grā´din) *n.* One in a series of steps.

grad-u-al (graj´e al) *adj.* Moving or changing slowly by degrees; not steep or abrupt. **gradually** *adv.*

grad-u-ate (graj´ö āt´) *v.* To receive or be granted an academic diploma or degree upon completion of a course of study; to divide into categories, grades or steps. **graduate** *n.* A person who holds an academic degree; a container or beaker marked in units or degrees, used for measuring liquids.

graduate student A student who has received a college degree and is working toward an advanced or higher degree.

grad-u-a-tion (graj´ö ā´shan) *n.* The state of graduating; a commencement ceremony issuing diplomas or degrees.

gra-dus (grā´dus) *n.* A dictionary to assist in writing Greek or Latin verses.

graf-fi-to (gra fē´tö) *n., pl.* **graffiti** An inscription or drawing made on a public wall, subway train, rock, or any other surface.

graft (graft) *v.* To insert a shoot from a plant into another living plant so that the two will grow together as a single plant. *Surg.* To transplant a piece of tissue or an organ. **graft** *n.* Living tissue or skin used to replace damaged or destroyed tissue or skin; the act of acquiring or getting personal profit or advantage by dishonest or unfair means through one's public position.

gra-ham (grā´am) *n.* Whole wheat flour.

graham cracker *n.* A semisweet cracker made of whole wheat flour.

grail (grāl) *n.* The legendary cup used by Christ at the Last Supper; also called the *Holy Grail.*

grain (grān) *n.* A small, hard seed or kernel of cereal, wheat, or oats; the seeds or fruits of such plants as a group.

gral-la-to-ri-al *adj.* Pertaining to large, long-legged wading birds.

gram (gram) *n.* A metric unit of mass and weight equal to 1/1000 kilogram and nearly equal to one cubic centimeter of water at its maximum density.

gra-ma *n.* Any of several pasture grasses of the western United States.

gra-mer-cy *interj.* Used to express thanks; an exclamation of astonishment or sudden feeling of surprise.

gram-i-ci-din *n.* Germicide used against bacteria in local infections.

gra-min-e-ous *adj.* Like or relating to grass.

gram-i-niv-o-rous *adj.* Surviving on grains or similar food.

gram-mar (gram´ĕr) *n.* The study and description of the classes of words, their relations to each other, and their arrangement into sentences; the inflectional and syntactic rules of a language. **grammarian** *n.*

grammar checker In *computer science*, a program that inspects a file or document for grammatical errors, advises the user of the error and suggests alternatives.

gram-mat-i-cal *adj.* Relating to or conforming to the rules of grammar. **grammatically** *adv.*

gram mol-e-cule (gram′mo lek′ū lė) *n. Chem.* The quantity of a compound, expressed in grams, that is equal to the molecular weight of that compound.

gram-pus *n.* A large, marine mammal related to the whale family.

gran-a-ry (grā′na rē) *n., pl.* **granaries** A building for storing threshed grain; an area or region where grain grows in abundance.

grand (grand) *adj.* Large in size, extent, or scope; magnificent; of high rank or great importance; lofty; admirable; main or principal; highly satisfactory; excellent. **grand** *n. Slang* A thousand dollars. **grandly** *adv.* **grandness** *n.*

gran-deur (gran′jer) *n.* The quality or condition of being grand; splendor; magnificence.

gran-di-flo-ra *n.* A rose bush producing both single blooms and clusters of blooms on the same plant due to crossbreeding tea roses and floribunda.

gran-dil-o-quent (gran dil′o kwent) *adj.* Speaking in or characterized by a pompous or bombastic style.

gran-di-ose (gran′dē ōs′) *adj.* Impressive and grand; pretentiously pompous; bombastic. **grandiosely** *adv.*

grand jury *n.* A jury that listens to accusations against people and, if just cause exists, makes formal charges for trials.

grand mal (gran′mal′) *n. Pathol.* A form of epilepsy characterized by severe convulsions and loss of consciousness.

grand-moth-er (gran′muth′ėr) *n.* The mother of one's father or mother; a female ancestor.

grand opera *n.* A form of opera having a serious and complex plot with the complete text set to music.

grand-par-ent (gran′pâr′ent) *n.* A parent of one's mother or father.

grand piano *n.* A piano with the strings arranged horizontally in a curved, wooden case.

grand-son (gran′sun′) *n.* A son of one's son or daughter.

grand-stand (gran′stand′) *n.* A raised stand of seats, usually roofed, for spectators at a racetrack or sports event.

grange *n.* A farmhouse and the buildings around it; a granary.

grang-er-ize *v.* To illustrate a book using illustrations or prints taken from other sources.

gran-ite (gran′it) *n.* A hard, coarse-grained igneous rock composed chiefly of quartz, mica, and orthoclase, which is used for building material and in sculpture.

gran-ite-ware (gran′it wâr′) *n.* Ironware utensils coated with hard enamel.

gra-niv-o-rous (gra niv′ėr us) *adj.* Feeding on seeds or grain.

gran-ny *or* **gran-nie (gran′ē)** *n.* An old woman; a grandmother; a fussy person.

gra-no-la *n.* Rolled oats mixed with dried fruit and seeds and eaten as a snack.

gran-o-lith (gran′o lith) *n.* An artificial stone made of crushed granite and cement.

gran-o-phyre *n.* Igneous rocks in which the ground mass is chiefly a mixture of quartz and feldspar crystals.

Grant, Ulysses S. *n.* (1822-1885) The eighteenth president of the United States from 1869-1877.

grant (grant) *v.* To allow; to consent to; to admit something as being the truth; in law, to transfer property by a deed. **grant** *n.* That which is granted. **grantee, grantor** *n.*

grant–in–aid *n., pl.* **grants–in–aid** Financial support or subsidy for public use paid by a central government to local government for a public program or project.

gran-u-lar (gran′ū lėr) *adj.* The state of being composed of grains or containing grains or granules.

gran-u-lar (gran′ū lėr) *adj.* The state of being composed of grains or granules. **granularity** *n.*

gran-u-late (gran′ū lāt′) *v.* To make or form into granules or crystals; to become or cause to become rough and grainy.

gran-u-la-tion *n.* Tissue made up of minute projections of flesh that form in the process of healing.

gran-ule (gran′ūl) *n.* A very small grain or particle; part of a larger unit.

gran-u-lo-cyte *n.* A white blood cell whose cytoplasm containing granules.

gran-u-lo-ma (gran′ūlō′ma) *n.* A nodular growth of inflamed tissue associated with the process of infection.

grape (grāp) *n.* Any of numerous woody vines bearing clusters of smooth-skinned, juicy, edible berries, having a dark purplish blue, red, or green color, eaten raw or dried; also used in making wine.

graph (graf) *n.* A diagram representing the relationship between sets of things. In computer science, a chart that displays the relative magnitude of associated elements as bars, columns, or sections of a pie.

graph-eme *n.* The smallest written unit of an alphabet, a single letter as used to represent one phoneme as the *d* in *drop*.

graph-ic *or* **graph-i-cal (graf´ik)** *adj.* Describing in full detail; of or pertaining to drawings or blueprints, as in architecture. **graphically** *adv.*

graphic display In computer science, the depiction of graphic elements on a computer monitor screen.

graph-ite (graf´it) *n.* A soft black form of carbon having a metallic luster and slippery texture, used in lead pencils, lubricants, paints, and coatings. **graphitic** *adj.*

graph-i-tize *v.* To change into graphite, as part of the carbon in steel.

graph-ol-o-gy (gra fol´o jē) *n.* The study of handwriting for the purpose of analyzing a person's character or personality. **graphologist** *n.*

graph paper *n.* Paper ruled with lines for drawing graphs.

grap-nel (grap´nel) *n.* A small anchor with several flukes at the end.

grasp (grasp) *v.* To seize and grip firmly; to comprehend; to understand. **grasp** *n.* The power to seize and hold. **graspable** *adj.* **grasper** *n.*

grasp-ing (gras´ping) *adj.* Urgently desiring material possessions; greedy. **graspingly** *adv.* **graspingness** *n.*

grass (gras) *n.* Any of numerous plants having narrow leaves and jointed stems; the ground on which grass is growing. *Slang* Marijuana.

grate (grāt) *v.* To reduce, shred or pulverize by rubbing against a rough or sharp surface; to make or cause to make a harsh sound or a rasping noise. **grater** n. **grating** *adj.* **gratingly** *adv.*

grate (grāt) *n.* A framework or bars placed over a window or other opening; an iron frame to hold burning fuel in a fireplace or furnace.

grate-ful *adj.* The state of being thankful or appreciative for benefits or kindness; expressing gratitude. **gratefully** *adv.*

grat-i-cule (grat´i kūl´) *n.* The network of lines of latitude and longitude from which maps are drawn.

grat-i-fi-ca-tion *n.* The state of being gratified; that which affords pleasure, or enjoyment.

grat-i-fy (grat´i fī´) *v.* To give pleasure or satisfaction to; to fulfill the desires of; to indulge. **gratifying** *adj.*

gra-tin (grat´in) *n.* A brown crust formed on food cooked with a topping of crumbs or grated cheese.

grating (grā´ting) *n.* A grate.

grat-is (grat´is) *adv. & adj.* Without requiring payment; free.

grat-i-tude (grat´i tōd´) *n.* The state of appreciation and gratefulness; thankfulness.

gra-tu-i-tous (gra tö´i tus) *adj.* Given or obtained without payment; unjustified; unwarranted. **gratuitously** *adv.* **gratuitousness** *n.*

gra-tu-i-ty (gra tö´i tē) *n., pl.* **gratuities** A gift, as money, given in return for a service rendered; a tip.

grau-pel *n.* Granules of soft hail or sleet.

gra-va-men (gra vā´men) *n., pl.* **gravamens** *or* **gravamina** In law, the part of an accusation or charge weighing most heavily against the accused.

grave (grāv) *n.* A burial place for a dead body, usually an excavation in the earth. **grave** *adj.* Very serious or important in nature; filled with danger; critical. **grave** *v.* To sculpt or carve; to engrave. **gravely** *adv.* **graver** *n.*

grav-e (gräv ā´) *adj. Music* Solemn and slow.

grav-el (grav´el) *n.* Loose rock fragments often mixed with sand. *Pathol.* The deposit of sand-like crystals that form in the kidneys; also known as kidney stones.

grave-stone (grāv´stōn´) *n.* A stone that marks a grave; a tombstone.

grave-yard (grāv´yärd´) *n.* An area set aside as a burial place; a cemetery.

graveyard shift *n. Slang* A work shift that usually begins at midnight.

gra-vim-e-ter (gra vim´i tèr) *n.* An implement for determining specific gravity. **gravimetry** *n.*

grav-i-tate (grav´i tāt´) *v.* To be drawn as if by an irresistible force; to sink or settle to a lower level.

grav-i-ta-tion (grav´i tā´shan) *n. Physics* The force of attraction any two bodies exert towards each other. **gravitational, gravitative** *adj.* **gravitationally** *adv.*

grav-i-ty (grav´i tē) *n., pl.* **gravities** The gravitational force manifested by the tendency of material bodies to fall toward the center of the earth; gravitation in general; weight; importance, seriousness.

gra-vy (grā´vē) *n., pl.* **gravies** The juices exuded by cooking meat; a sauce made by seasoning and thickening these juices. *Slang* Money or profit which is easily acquired.

gray (grā) *n. & adj.* A neutral color between black and white; gloomy; dismal; having gray hair, characteristic of old age. **grayish** *adj.* **grayness** *n.*

gray matter *n.* The grayish-brown nerve tissue of the spinal cord and brain, consisting mainly of nerve cells and fibers; brains.

gray scale In *computer science*, a graduated series of dot patterns to depict various shades of gray on the monitor.

graze (grāz) *v.* To feed upon growing

grasses or herbage; to put livestock to feed on grass or pasturage; to brush against lightly in passing; to abrade or scrape slightly.

gra-zier (grā´zhèr) *n.* One who grazes cattle.

grease (grēs) *n.* Melted or soft animal fat; any thick fatty or oily substance, as a lubricant. **grease** *v.* To lubricate or coat with grease. **greasiness** *n.*

greasy spoon *n.* A small cheap restaurant.

great (grāt) *adj.* Very large in size or volume; prolonged in duration or extent; more than ordinary; considerable; remarkable; impressive; eminent; renowned; very good or first-rate; a generation removed from a relative. **greatly** *adv.* **greatness** *n.*

greave (grēv) *n.* An armor for the leg worn below the knee.

grebe (grēb) *n.* Any of various swimming and diving birds having partially webbed feet, a very short tail, and a pointed bill.

greed (grēd) *n.* Selfish desire to acquire more than one needs or deserves.

greed-y (grē´dē) *adj.* Excessively eager to acquire or gain something; having an excessive appetite for drink and food; gluttonous. **greedily** *adv.*

green (grēn) *adj.* Of the color between yellow and blue in the spectrum; not fully matured or developed; lacking in skill or experience. **green** *n.* A grassy plot or lawn, especially an area of closely mowed grass at the end of a golf fairway. **greenish** *adj.*

green-horn (grēn´horn˝) *n.* An inexperienced person; a beginner; a person who is easily fooled.

green-house (grēn´hous˝) *n.* An enclosed structure equipped with heat and moisture built for the cultivation of plants.

greet (grēt) *v.* To address someone in a friendly way; to welcome; to meet or receive in a specified manner. .

gre-gar-i-ous (gri gâr´ē us) *adj.* Habitually associating with others as in groups, flocks, or herds; enjoying the company of others; sociable. **gregariously** *adv.* **gregariousness** *n.*

greige (grāzh) *n.* Woven fabric in an unbleached undyed state.

grei-sen *n.* A crystalline rock composed chiefly of quartz and mica.

grem-lin (grem´lin) *n.* A mischievous elf said to cause mechanical trouble in airplanes.

gre-nade (gri nād´) *n.* A small explosive device detonated by a fuse and thrown by hand or projected from a rifle.

gren-a-dine (gren´a dēn´) *n.* A syrup made from pomegranates or red currants and used as a flavoring in mixed drinks.

grew *v.* Past tense of grow.

grey (grā) *n. & adj.* Variation of gray.

grey-hound (grā´hound´) *n.* One of a breed of slender, swift-running dogs with long legs.

grib-ble (grib´l) *n.* A small marine crustacean which destroys submerged timber.

grid (grid) *n.* An arrangement of regularly spaced bars; the system of intersecting parallel lines that divide maps, charts, and aerial photographs, used as a reference for locating points.

grid-dle (grid´l) *n.* A flat pan used for cooking.

grid-dle cake (grid´l kāk´) *n.* A pancake.

grid-i-ron (grid´īˊern) *n.* A metal framework used for broiling meat, fish, and other foods; a football field.

grief (grēf) *n.* Deep sadness or mental distress caused by a loss, remorse, or bereavement.

griev-ance (grē´vans) *n.* A real or imagined wrong which is regarded as cause for complaint or resentment; a complaint of unfair treatment.

grieve (grēv) *v.* To feel grief or sorrow.

griev-ous (grē´vus) *adj.* Causing grief, sorrow, anguish, or pain; causing physical suffering. **grievously** *adv.*

grif-fin *or* **grif-fon (grif´on)** *n.* In Greek mythology, a fabulous beast with a lion's body, an eagle's head, and wings.

grift *v. Slang* To obtain money by dishonest schemes, swindling, or cheating.

grig (grig) *n.* A lively young person.

grill (gril) *n.* A cooking utensil made from parallel metal bars; a gridiron; food cooked on a grill; a restaurant where grilled foods are a specialty. **grill** *v.* To broil on a grill.

gril-lage (gril´ij) *n.* A framework of lumber or steel for support in marshy soil.

grille *or* **grill (gril)** *n.* A grating with open metal work used as a decorative screen or room divider.

grilse *n.* A young, mature salmon returning from the sea to spawn for the first time.

grim (grim) *adj.* Stern or forbidding in appearance or character; unyielding; relentless; grisly; gloomy; dismal. **grimly** *adv.* **grimness** *n.*

grim-ace (grim´as) *n.* A facial expression of pain, disgust, or disapproval.

grime (grīm) *n.* Dirt, especially soot, clinging to or coating a surface. **griminess** *n.* **grimy** *adj.*

grin (grin) *v.* To smile broadly. **grin** *n.*

grind (grīnd) *v.* To reduce to fine particles; to sharpen, polish, or shape by friction; to press or rub together; to work or study hard. **grind** *n.* A person who works hard or who studies very hard.

grind-er (grīn′dẽr) n. One that grinds.

grind-stone (grīnd′stōn′) n. A flat, circular stone which revolves on an axle and is used for polishing, sharpening, or grinding.

grip (grip) n. A firm hold; a grasp; the ability to seize or maintain a hold; the mental or intellectual grasp; a suitcase. **grip** v. To grasp and keep a firm hold on; to capture the imagination or attention. **gripper** n. **grippingly** adv.

gripe (grīp) v. To cause sharp pain or cramps in the bowels; to anger; to annoy; to complain.

grippe (grip) n. Influenza. **grippy** adj.

gri-saille n. A method of decorating in single colors especially in various shades of gray, making objects appear as three-dimensional.

gris-ly (griz′lē) adj. Ghastly; gruesome.

grist (grist) n. Grain that is to be ground; a batch of such grain.

gris-tle (gris′l) n. Cartilage of meat.

grist-mill n. A mill for grinding grain.

grit (grit) n. Small, rough granules, as of sand or stone; having great courage and fortitude. **grit** v. To clamp the teeth together. **gritty** adj.

grits (grits) n. Coarsely ground hominy; coarse meal; eaten primarily in the southern states of the United States.

griz-zle (griz′l) v. To become or cause to become gray.

grizzly bear n. A large, grayish bear of western North America. Also called **grizzly**; pl. **grizzlies.**.

groan (grōn) v. To utter a deep, prolonged sound of or as of disapproval or pain. **groan** n. **groaningly** adv.

groat (grōt) n. A former British coin worth four pence; any grain without its hull; a tiny sum.

gro-cer (grō′sẽr) n. A storekeeper who deals in foodstuffs and various household supplies.

gro-cer-ies n. The merchandise sold in a grocery

gro-cer-y (grō sẽ rē) n., pl. groceries A store in which foodstuffs and household staples are sold.

grog (grog) n. Any alcoholic liquor, usually rum, mixed with water.

grog-gy (grog′ē) adj. Feeling dazed, weak, or not fully conscious, such as from a blow or exhaustion; drunk. **groggily** adv. **grogginess** n.

gro-gram (grog′ram) n. A loosely woven fabric of silk and mohair or silk and wool.

grog-shop n. A low-class barroom.

groin (groin) n. Anat. The crease or fold where the thigh meets the abdomen. Arch. The curved edge of a building formed by two intersecting vaults.

grom-met (grom′it) n. A reinforcing eyelet through which a rope, cord, or fastening may be passed. Naut. A ring of rope or metal used to secure the edge of a sail.

grom-well n. Any plant of the borage family having hairy herbs and smooth, stony nuts.

groom (grŏm) n. A person hired to tend horses; a stableman; a bridegroom. **groom** v. To make neat in appearance; to prepare for a particular position, as for a political office.

grooms-man (grŏmz′man) n., pl. **groomsmen** Best man at a wedding; any of a bridegroom's attendants.

groove (grŏv) n. A long, narrow channel or indentation; a fixed, settled habit or routine; a rut. **groove** v.

groovy (grō′vē) adj. Slang A state or condition of being wonderful; delightful.

grope (grōp) v. To feel about with or as with the hands, as in the dark; to look for uncertainly or blindly. **grope** n. **groper** n.

gros-beck (grōs′bĕk′) n. Any of several colorful birds related to the finch, with a stout, conical beak.

gros-grain (grō′grān′) n. A heavy, horizontally corded silk or rayon fabric, woven as a ribbon.

gross (grōs) adj. Exclusive of deductions; of or relating to the total amount received; excessively large or fat; lacking refinement or delicacy; coarse; vulgar. **gross** n. The entire amount without deduction; an amount that equals 12 dozen or 144 items. **gross** v **grossly** adv. **grossness** n.

gross national product n. The total market value of all goods and services produced by a nation in a year.

gross profit n. The total business receipts less cost of goods sold, before operating expenses and taxes are deducted.

gros-su-lar-ite n. A garnet of red, brown, yellow, green, or white.

gro-tesque (grō tĕsk′) adj. Distorted, incongruous or ludicrous in appearance or style; bizarre; outlandish. **grotesque, grotesqueness** n. **grotesquely** adv.

gro-tes-quer-y n. A grotesque representation; a group of absurdly represented characters.

grot-to (grot′ō) n., pl. **grottoes** or **grottos** A cave or cave-like structure.

grouch (grouch) n. An habitually irritable or complaining person. **grouchily** adv. **grouchiness** n. **grouchy** adj.

ground (ground) n. The surface of the earth; soil, sand, and other natural material at or near the earth's surface; the connecting of an electric current to the earth through a conductor.

ground (ground) v. Past tense of grind.

ground ball *n.* A batted baseball that bounds or rolls along the ground.

ground cherry *n.* A plant with round pulpy berries enclosed in a ribbed papery husk.

ground connection *n.* A grounding connection with the earth

ground cover *n.* A plant that forms a dense, extensive ground cover, often used to control erosion; the low-growing plants in a forest.

ground crew *n.* The mechanics who maintain and service an airplane.

ground glass *n.* Glass that has been treated so that it is not fully transparent.

ground hog *n.* A woodchuck.

Groundhog Day *n.* February 2, the day on which the groundhog either sees its shadow, predicting six more weeks of winter, or not, predicting an early spring.

ground ivy *n.* A trailing mint with rounded leaves and purple flowers.

ground-less (ground´lis) *adj.* Without foundation or basis.

ground plan *n.* A floor plan of a building; any first or basic plan.

ground rent *n.* Rent paid by a lessee for the use of land.

ground rule *n.* A basic rule; the rule in sports that modifies play on a particular field, course, or court.

grounds *n.* The land that surrounds a building; the basis for an argument, action or belief; the sediment at the bottom of a liquid, such as coffee.

ground sheet *n.* A waterproof cover to protect an area of ground, used under a sleeping bag.

ground swell *n.* Deep rolling of the sea, caused by a distant storm or gale.

ground wave *n.* A radio wave along the surface of the earth.

ground zero *n.* The point on the ground vertically beneath or above the point of detonation of an atomic bomb.

group (grōp) *n.* A collection or assemblage of people, objects, or things having something in common.

grou-per (grō´pér) *n.* A large fish related to the sea bass.

group-ie *n. Slang* A female follower of a rock group, especially when it is on tour.

group therapy *n.* Psychotherapy which involves sessions guided by a therapist and attended by several patients who discuss their problems.

grout (grout) *n.* A material used to fill cracks in masonry or spaces between tiles. **grout** *v.* **grouter** *n.*

grove (grōv) *n.* A small group of trees, lacking undergrowth.

grov-el (gruv´l) *v.* To lie or crawl face downward, as in fear; to act with abject humility. **groveler** *n.* **grovelingly** *adv.*

grow (grō) *v.* To increase in size, develop, and reach maturity; to expand; to increase; to come into existence; to be produced by natural processes; to increase gradually; to cause to grow; to cultivate. **grower** *n.*

growl (groul) *v.* To utter a deep, guttural, threatening sound, as that made by a hostile or agitated animal. **growl** *n.*

grown (grōn) *adj.* Fully matured; cultivated in a specified way, as in *home-grown.*

grown-up (grōn´up´) *n.* A mature adult.

growth (grōth) *n.* The act or process of growing; a gradual increase in size or amount. *Pathol.* An abnormal formation of bodily tissue, as a tumor.

growth factor *n.* A substance that enhances the growth of an organism.

growth stock *n.* The common stock of a company with potential increase in business and profits.

grub-stake (grub´stāl´) *n.* Funds and supplies furnished to a miner for a share of his findings until he can fend for himself.

grudge (gruj) *n.* A feeling of ill will, rancor, or deep resentment. **grudge** *v.* To be displeased, resentful, or envious of the possessions or good fortune of another person. **grudging** *adj.* **grudgingly** *adv.*

gru-el (grö´el) *n.* A thin liquid made by boiling meal in water or milk.

gru-el-ing (grö´e ling) *adj.* Very tiring; exhausting. **gruelingly** *adv.*

grue-some (grö´som) *adj.* Causing horror or fright or repulsion. **gruesomely** *adv.* **gruesomeness** *n.*

gruff (gruf) *adj.* Brusque and rough in manner; harsh in sound; hoarse. **gruffly** *adv.* **gruffness** *n.*

grum-ble (grum´bl) *v.* To complain in low, throaty sounds; to growl. **grumble** *n.* **grumbler** *n.*

grump-y (grum´pē) *adj.* Irritable and moody; ill-tempered. **grumpily** *adv.*

grun-gy *adj. Slang* Dirty, rundown, or inferior in condition or appearance.

grunt (grunt) *n.* The deep, guttural sound of a hog. **grunt** *v.*

grun-tle *v.* To put in a good mood.

gua-ca-mo-le (gwa´ka mō´lā) *n.* Mashed avocado seasoned with condiments.

gua-co (gwä´kō) *n.* A tropical climbing plant of America, whose leaves contain a substance that is used as an antidote for snake bites.

gua-neth-i-dine *n.* A drug used in treating severe high blood pressure.

gua-no (gwä´nō) *n.* The excrement of sea birds used as a fertilizer.

guar *abbr.* Guaranteed.

guar-an-tee (gar´an tē´) *n.* The promise or assurance of the durability or quality of a product; something held or given as a pledge or security. **guarantee** *v.* To assume responsibility for the default or debt of; to certify; to vouch for.

guar-an-tor (gar´an tor´) *n.* One who gives a guarantee or guaranty.

guar-an-ty (gar´an tē) *n., pl.* **guaranties** A pledge or promise to be responsible for the debt, duty, or contract of another person in case of default; something that guarantees.

guard (gärd) *v.* To watch over or shield from danger or harm; to keep watch as to prevent escape, violence, or indiscretion. **guard** *n.* A defensive position, as in boxing or fencing; in football, one of two linemen on either side of the center; in basketball, one of the two players stationed near the middle of the court; a device or piece of equipment that protects against damage, loss, or harm. **guarded** *adj.*

guard hair *n.* The coarse, long outer hair forming a protective coating over the soft underfur of certain animals.

guard-i-an (gär´dē an) *n.* One who is legally assigned responsibility for the care of the person and property of an infant, minor or person unable to do for himself because of physical or mental disability. **guardianship** *n.*

gub-ba *v. Slang* To tickle the neck area, especially of young children and babies. **gubba** *n.* The area that is tickled.

gu-ber-na-to-ri-al (gö¯bér natör´ē al) *adj.* Of or pertaining to a governor.

gudgeon (guj´on) *n.* A small European freshwater fish related to the carp.

gue-non (ge non´) *n.* A long-tailed arboreal African monkey.

guern-sey (gern´zē) *.,* A breed of brown and white dairy cattle.

guer-ril-la (ge ril´la) *n.* A member of an irregular military force that is capable of great speed and mobility, often operating behind enemy lines. **guerrilla** *adj.*

guess (ges) *v.* To make a judgment or form an opinion on uncertain or incomplete knowledge; to suppose; to believe.

guess-ti-mate (ges´ti māt´) *n. Slang* An estimate made without all the facts.

guest (gest) *n.* One who is the recipient of hospitality from another; a customer who pays for lodging.

guff (guf) *n. Slang* Nonsense or empty talk.

guf-faw (gu fo´) *n.* A loud burst of laughter. **guffaw** *v.*

guid-ance (gīd´ans) *n.* The act, process, or result of guiding or counseling.

guide *n.* One who leads or directs another, as in a course of action; a person employed to conduct others on trips, through museums, or on sightseeing tours. **guidable** *adj.*

guide-book (gīd´bek´) *n.* A handbook containing directions and other information for tourists and visitors.

guided missile *n. Mil.* An unmanned missile that can be controlled by radio signals while in flight.

guide-line *n.* Any suggestion, statement, or outline of policy or procedure; a rope or cord to guide a person over a difficult point.

guide-post *n.* A post to which a sign is attached for giving direction.

gui-don (gī´don) *n.* A small flag carried by a military unit as a unit marker.

guild (gild) *n.* An association of persons of the same trade or occupation.

guile *n.* Craft; duplicity; deceit.

guil-le-mot *n.* A bird of the auk family, native to the northern Atlantic coast.

guil-loche *n.* Architectural ornament composed of two or more strands interlacing or combining other patterns.

guil-lo-tine (gil´o ten´) *n.* An instrument of capital punishment in France, used for beheading condemned prisoners.

guilt (gilt) *n.* The condition or fact of having committed a crime or wrongdoing; the feeling of responsibility for having done something wrong.

guilt-less *adj.* A state or condition of being without guilt; innocent.

guilt-y (gil´tē) *adj.* Deserving of blame for an offense that has been committed; convicted of some offense; pertaining to, involving or showing guilt. **guiltily** *adv* **guiltiness** *n.*

guin-ea (gin´ē) *n.* Formerly, a British gold coin worth one pound and five pence.

guinea fowl (gin´ē foul) *n.* A widely domesticated bird of African origin with dark gray plumage speckled with white.

guinea hen *n* The female guinea fowl.

guinea pig (gin´ē pig) *n.* A small, domesticated rodent widely used for biological experimentation.

guinea worm *n.* A slender parasitic which can causes illness in man and animals

gui-pure (gi pur´) *n.* Heavy laces in which the pattern is connected by bars instead of worked on a net or a mesh ground.

guise *n.* External appearance in dress; garb; an assumed appearance.

gui-tar (gi tor´) *n.* A musical instrument with six strings, played by plucking or strumming.

gu-lar *adj.* Pertaining or relating to, or situated on, the throat.

gulch (gulch) *n.* A deep cleft or ravine caused by the action of water.

gulf (gulf) *n.* A large area of ocean or sea partially enclosed by land; a wide, impassable separation, as in social position or education.

gulf-weed *n.* A coarse branching olive-brown seaweed, found in tropical American waters.

gull (gul) *n.* A long-winged, web-footed sea bird, usually white and gray with a hooked upper mandible; a gullible person; one who is easily tricked.

gul-let (gul´it) *n. Pathol.* The passage from the mouth to the stomach; esophagus; the throat; the pharynx.

gul-li-ble (gul´i bl) *adj.* Easily cheated or fooled. **gullibility** *n.*, **gullibly** *adv.*

gul-ly (gul´ē) *n., pl.* **gullies** A ditch or channel cut in the earth by running water.

gulp (gulp) *v.* To swallow rapidly or in large amounts; to gasp or choke, as in nervousness; to swallow quickly or in large quantities. **gulp** *n.*

gum-mo-sis *n.* A plant disease that causes an abnormal gummy discharge.

gump-tion (gump´shan) *n. Slang* Boldness; initiative; enterprise; personal initiative; practical sense.

gum resin *n.* Various natural mixtures of gum and resin, extruded from certain plants.

gun (gun) *n.* A weapon made of a tube from which a projectile is thrown by the force of an explosion; a portable firearm. **gun** *v.* To shoot; to open up the throttle of an engine in order to accelerate. **gun for** To try to ruin, catch, or acquire.

gunk *n.* Obnoxious sticky material; greasy or messy material.

gun-smith (gun´smith´) *n.* A person who makes or repairs guns.

gur-gle (ger´gl) *v.* To flow in a broken, uneven current, making low, bubbling sounds. **gurgle** *n.* **gurgling** *adj.*

gur-nard *n.* A marine fish with a spiny head and three pairs of pectoral rays.

gush (gush) *v.* To flow or rush forth in volume and with sudden force; to be overly sentimental or enthusiastic. .

gush-er *n.* An oil well with a plentiful natural flow of oil; a person who gushes.

gus-set (gus´it) *n.* An insert in the seam of a garment or object to allow for expansion or to strengthen.

gust (gust) *n.* A sudden, violent rush of wind or air; a sudden outburst, as of emotion. **gust** *v.* **gustily** *adv.* **gustiness** *n.* **gusty** *adj.*

gus-ta-to-ry (gus´ta tō˝rē) *adj.* Of or pertaining to the sense of taste or the act of tasting.

gust-o (gus´tō) *n.* Hearty enjoyment or enthusiasm.

gut (gut) *n.* The alimentary canal or part of it; the prepared intestine of certain animals, used to make strings for musical instruments and tennis rackets.

gut *v.* To disembowel; to plunder.

gut-ta–per-cha *n.* A tough plastic from the latex of Malaysian trees that resembles rubber but has more resin and is used for electrical insulation and in dentistry.

gut-tate *adj.* Spotted, discolored by drops or drop-like spots.

guy (gī) *n. Slang* A man; a fellow.

guz-zle (guz´l) *v.* To drink greedily, continually, or to excess. **guzzler** *n.*

gym (jim) *n.* A gymnasium; an assortment of outdoor play equipment such as a seesaw, rings and a swing.

gym-no-spore *n.* A spore that does not have a protective covering.

gy-nan-dro-morph *n.* An abnormal individual exhibiting physical features characteristic of both sexes.

gy-nan-dry *n.* Hermaphroditism; the condition in an animal or plant where both male and female reproductive organs exist.

gy-ne-coid (jin´ekoid˝) *adj.* Having female characteristics; being typical of a woman.

gy-ne-col-o-gy (gī˝ne kol´o jē) *n.* The branch of medicine dealing with the female reproductive organs, female diseases, and female functions. **gynecological** *adj.* **gynecologist** *n.*

gyp (jip) *v. Informal* To swindle, cheat, or defraud. **gyp** *n.* A fraud. **gypper** *n.*

gyp-sum (jip´sum) *n.* A mineral, hydrous calcium sulfate, used to make plaster of Paris, gypsum plaster, and plasterboard.

gypsy moth *n.* A moth whose larvae are destructive to foliage.

gy-rate (jī´rāt) *v.* To rotate or revolve around a fixed point or axis; to move or turn in a spiral motion. **gyrate** *adj.* Coiled or winding about. **gyration** *n.* **gyrator** *n.* **gyratory** *adj.*

gyr-fal-con (jer´fol˝kon) *n.* A large falcon with color phases ranging from black to white.

gy-ro-com-pass (jī˝rō kum´pas) *n.* A compass that has a motor-driven gyroscope so mounted that its axis of rotation maintains a constant position with reference to the true or geographic north.

gy-ro-plane *n.* An airplane balanced and supported by the aerodynamic forces, such as a helicopter, having windmill-like wings that rotate horizontally.

gy-ro-scope (jī´ro skōp˝) *n.* A spinning wheel or disk whose spin axis maintains its angular orientation when not subjected to external torques. .

gy-ro-sta-bi-liz-er (jī˝ro stā´bi lī˝zėr) *n.* A gyroscopic instrument designed to reduce the rolling motion of ships.

gyve (jīv) *n.* A shackle for the legs. *v.* To chain; to shackle.

H, h (āch) The eighth letter of the English alphabet.

ha (hä) *interj.* An exclamation denoting joy, wonder, sudden emotion or surprise.

ha-ba-ne-ra (hä˝ba när´a) *n.* Cuban dance.

ha-be-as cor-pus (hā´bē as kor´pus) *n.* In law, a writ commanding a person to appear before a judge or court for the purpose of releasing that person from unlawful detention or restraint.

hab-er-dash-er (hab´ěr dash˝ěr) *n.* A person who deals in men's clothing and men's accessories.

hab-ile (hab´il) *adj.* Having skill; able.

ha-bil-i-ment (ha bil´i ment) *n.* Clothing characteristic of an office, rank, or occasion.

ha-bil-i-tate (ha bil´i tāt) *v.* To furnish money or equipment for development of a mine.

hab-it (hab´it) *n.* Involuntary pattern of behavior acquired by frequent repetition; manner of conducting oneself; an addiction; clothing that indicates membership or rank in a religious order or activity; *Biol.* the characteristic form of a plant or animal.

hab-it-a-ble (hab´i ta bel) *adj.* Suitable for habitation. **habitability, habitableness** *n.* **habitably** *adv.*

ha-bi-tant (hab´i tant) *n.* An inhabitant or settler; resident of a place.

hab-i-tat (hab´i tat˝) *n.* The region in which an animal or plant lives or grows, the place of residence of a person or group.

hab-i-ta-tion (hab´i tā´shan) *n.* A place of residence; a house or other dwelling where people or animals dwell.

hab-it-form-ing (hab´it for´ming) *adj.* Producing uncontrollable addiction.

ha-bit-u-al (ha bich´ö al) *adj.* Practicing by or acting according to habit; resorted to on a regular basis; regular. **habitually** *adv.* **habitualness** *n.*

ha-bit-u-ate (ha bich´ö āt˝) *v.* To make familiar; to accustom.

ha-chure (ha shur´) *n.* Shading used to denote surfaces in relief on a map.

ha-ci-en-da (hä˝sē en´da) *n.* A large estate or ranch in South American countries; the main building of a hacienda; a stock raising ranch.

hack (hak) *v.* To cut with repeated irregular blows; to manage successfully. *Computer Science* To look for ways to get past security on Internet sites to get at private data. **hack** *n.* A tool used for hacking; a rough, dry cough; a taxi or a taxi driver.

hack-er *n. Computer Science* A person who looks for ways to invade Internet sites to get private data or to damage the sites.

hack-le (hak´l) *n.* One of the long, slender, often narrow glossy feathers on the neck of a rooster; the hair on the back of the neck, especially of a dog, that rises in anger or fear.

hack-ney (hak´nē) *n.* A horse of medium size for ordinary driving or riding; a carriage or coach available for hire. **hackney** *v.* To make common or frequent use of.

had *v.* Past participle and past tense of have.

had-n't (had´nt) *contraction* Had not.

hae-ma-tox-y-lon (hē˝ma tok´si lon˝) *n.* A small, tropical American tree with thorns.

haf-ni-um (haf´nē um) *n.* A metallic element resembling zirconium chemically and is found in zirconium ores.

haft (haft) *n.* A handle of a weapon or tool.

hag (hag) *n.* A malicious, ugly old woman; a witch. **haggish** *adj.*

hag-gard (hag´ěrd) *adj.* A worn-out, exhausted, and gaunt look, as from hunger or fatigue; appearing wasted by suffering or want. **haggardly** *adv.*

hag-gle (hag´l) *v.* To argue or bargain on price or terms. *n.* The process or act of haggling someone. **haggler** *n.*

hag-i-og-ra-phy *n.* Biography of the lives of saints or revered persons; an idolizing biography. **hagiographer** *n.* **hagiographic, hagiographical** *adj.*

haik (hīk) *n.* An oblong piece of usually white clothing used to cover the head and body, used as an outer garment in northern Africa.

hai-ku (hī´kö) *n.* An unrhymed Japanese verse form, having three short unrhymed lines; a poem using this style.

hail (hāl) *n.* Precipitation of small, hard lumps of ice and snow; a hailstone; an exclamation, greeting, acclamation **hail** *v.* To pour down as hail; to call loudly in greeting or welcome; to shout with enthusiasm; to signal in order to draw attention.

hake (hāk) *n.* An edible marine food fish related to the cod.

ha-kim (hä kēm) *n.* A Muslim physician, ruler or governor.

ha-la-tion *n.* A light that spreads beyond its proper boundaries in a developed photographic image.

hal-cy-on (hal´sē on) *n.* A bird said to have the power of calming waves and winds during the winter solstice. **halcyon** *adj* Calm and tranquil; peaceful; prosperous.

hale (hāl) *adj.* Healthy and robust, free from disease; free from defect. **hale** *v.* To compel to obey. **haleness** *n.*

half (haf) *n., pl.* **halves** One of two equal parts into which a thing is divisible; part of a thing approximately

equal to the remainder; one of a pair.
half *adj.* Being one of two equal parts; being partial or incomplete.
half binding *n.* A style of binding books in which the back and corners are leather and the sides are paper or cloth.
half-breed (haf´brēd´) *n.* The offspring of an American Indian and a white person; offspring of parents from different races.
half–caste (haf´kast´) *n.* A person having one European and one Asian parent.
half–mast (haf´mast´) *n.* A point or position halfway down or less below the top of a ship mast, or flag pole; the position of a flag in respect for the dead. **half-mast** *v.* To hang a flag at half-mast.
half note *n. Mus.* A note with the time value equivalent to one half of a whole note.
hal-i-but (hal´i but) *n.* Any of the edible flat fishes of the North Atlantic or Pacific waters.
hal-ide (hal´īd) *n. Chem.* A binary compound formed by the direct union of a halogen with a more electropositive element or radical.
hal-ite (hal´īt) *n.* Large crystal or masses of salt; rock salt.
hal-i-to-sis (hal´ī tō´sis) *n.* A condition of having bad breath.
hal-le-lu-jah (hal´e lö´ya) *interj.* An expression of joy, praise, or jubilation.
hal-lu-ci-nate (ha-lö´si-nāt´) *v.* To affect with imaginary perceptions; to have a hallucination.
hal-lu-ci-na-tion (ha lö´si nā´han) *n.* An illusion of seeing something that is nonexistent; something one thinks is seen during a hallucination; a delusion.**hallucinatory** *adj.*
hal-lu-ci-no-gen (ha lö´si no jen´) *n.* A drug or other agent which causes hallucination. **hallucinogenic** *adj.*
hal-lu-ci-no-sis (ha-lö´si-nō´sis) *n. Psychi.* A mental disorder marked by hallucinations.
hal-lux (hal´uks) *n.* The innermost of the digits of the hind foot of air-breathing vertebrates; in man, the great toe.
hall-way (hol´wā´) *n.* A corridor; an entrance hall.
ha-lo (hā´lō) *n.* A ring of colored light surrounding the head; an aura of glory.
hal-o-gen (hal´o jen) *n.* Any of the group of nonmetallic elements including fluorine, chlorine, bromine, iodine, and astatine. **halogenous** *adj.*
hal-o-gen-ate (hal´o je-nāt´) *v. Chem.* To combine or treat with a halogen. **halogenation** *n.*
hal-o-ge-ton (hal o´je tan´) *n.* An annual herb of the goosefoot family found in western America.

hal-oid (hal´oid) *adj.* A substance that resembles common table salt in composition; formed by the mixture of a halogen and a metal.
hal-o-mor-phic (hal´o-mor´fik) *adj.* Influenced by the presence of an alkali or a neutral salt, or both.
hal-o-phile (hal´o fīl´) *n.* An organism that grows in a salty environment.
hal-o-phyte (hal´o-fīt´) *n.* A plant that grows in a salty soil.
halt (holt) *v.* To bring to a stop.
hal-ter (hol´têr) *n.* A rope or strap for leading or tying an animal; a noose for hanging a person; a woman's upper garment tied behind the neck and across the back.
hal-vah *n.* A flaky confection of sesame seeds in a base of syrup or honey.
halve (hav) *v.* To divide into two equal parts; to lessen by half; to share equally.
hal-yard (hal´yêrd) *n.* A rope for hoisting or lowering a sail, flag, or yard.
ham (ham) *n.* The meat of a hog's thigh; the back of the knee or thigh. **ham** *v.*
ham-burg-er (ham´ber´gêr) *n.* A patty of ground beef on a bun.
hame (hām) *n* One of two curved projections attached to the collar of a draft horse to which the traces are attached.
ham-let (ham´lit) *n.* A small rural village or town.
ham-mock (ham´ok) *n.* A hanging bed or couch of fabric or heavy netting, suspended from supports at each end.
ham-per (ham´pêr) *v.* To interfere with movement or progress. **hamper** *n.* A large receptacle, usually covered with a lid, used to store dirty laundry or to pack articles .
ham-string (ham´string´) *n.* Either of two tendons located at the back of the human knee; the large tendon at the back of the hock of four-footed animals. **hamstring** *v.* To cripple by cutting the hamstring; to frustrate.
ham-u-lus (ham´ū lus) *n.* A small hook or a hooked process.
hand (hand) *n.* The part of the arm below the wrist, consisting of the palm, four fingers and a thumb; a unit of measure, four inches, used especially to state the height of a horse; a pointer on a dial, as of a clock, meter, or gauge; the cards dealt to or held by a player in one round of a game; a manual laborer, worker, or employee. **hand** *v.* To give, offer, or transmit with the hand; direct with the hands.
hand-craft (hand´kraft´) *v.* To make or create an item by hand. **-ed** *adj.*
hand-cuff (hand´kuf´) *v.* To put handcuffs on; to make ineffective. **handcuffs** *n.* A pair of circular metal

shackles chained together that can be fastened around the wrists.

hand down v. To pass on in succession, from one relative to another; to deliver a court decision.

hand-i-cap (han´dē kap˝) n. A race or contest in which advantages or penalties are given to individual contestants to equalize the odds; any disadvantage that makes achievement unusually difficult; physical disability; an obstacle. **handicap** v. To give a handicap to.

hand-i-craft or **hand-craft (han´dē kraft˝)** n. Skill and expertise in working with the hands; an occupation requiring manual dexterity; skilled work produced by the hands.

hand-i-work (han´dē-würk˝) n. Work exhibiting the hand skills of its maker.

han-dle (han´dl) v. To touch, pick up, or hold with the hands; to represent; to trade or deal in. **handle, handler** n. **handleable** adj.

hand-made adj. Made by hand or by a hand process.

hand-maid or **hand-maid-en** n. A female maid or personal servant.

hand-some (han´som) adj. Very good-looking or attractive; very generous, as with money. **handsomely** adv. **handsomeness** n.

hand-to-mouth (hand´to mouth´) adj. Having barely enough to exist.

hand-writ-ing (hand´rī ting) n. Writing performed with the hand, especially cursive; the type of writing of a person. **handwriting on the wall** An omen of one's fate, usually unpleasant.

hand-y (han´dē) adj. Easy to use or reach; helpful or useful. **handiness** n.

hang (hang) v. To be attached to from above and unsupported from below; to fasten or be suspended so as to swing freely; to be put to death by hanging by the neck; to fasten or attach something, as a picture to a wall. **hang out** Slang To spend one's time in a particular place. **hang up** To end a telephone conversation by replacing the receiver on its cradle. **hang-up** A psychological or emotional problem; an obsession.

han-gar (hang´ér) n. A building for housing aircraft.

han-ger (hang´ér) n. A device from which something may be hung or on which something hangs.

hang-o-ver (hang´ō˝vér) n. Something remaining from what has passed; the effects of excessive alcohol intake.

hank (hangk) n. A loop, coil, or piece of hair, thread, or yarn.

han-ker (hang´kér) v. To have a yearning or craving for something. **-er,** n.

han-som (han´som) n. A two-wheeled covered carriage with the driver's seat elevated behind the cab.

Ha-nuk-kah or **Ha-nu-kah (hä´nu ka)** n. An eight-day Jewish holiday remembering the rededication of the Temple in Jerusalem.

hao-le (how´lē) n. A person who is not of the Hawaiian race, especially a Caucasian.

hap (hap) n. Chance or fortune.

hap-haz-ard (hap´haz˝érd) adj. Occurring by accident; happening by chance or at random; hit or miss. **haphazardly** adv. **haphazardness** n.

hap-less adj. Unfortunate; unlucky. **haplessly** adv. **haplessness** n.

hap-log-ra-phy (hap-log´ra-fē) n. The unintentional omission of a letter or letters in writing.

hap-ly (hap´lē) adv. By luck or chance; by accident; perhaps.

hap-pen (hap´n) v. To occur or come to pass; to take place; to discover by chance; to turn up or appear by chance.

hap-pen-ing (hap´e ning) n. A spontaneous event or performance; an important event.

hap-pen-stance (hap´en stans˝) n. An event occurring by chance.

hap-pi-ness (hap´ē-nis) n. The quality of being content; pleasure.

hap-py (hap´ē) adj. Enjoying contentment and well-being; glad, joyous, satisfied or pleased. **happily** adv.

happy-go-luck-y (hap´ē gō luk´ē) adj. Carefree and unconcerned.

hap-ten (hap´ten) n. A substance which reacts with an antibody only when they are together in a synthetic environment.

ha-rangue (ha rang´) n. A long, extravagant speech; a lecture.

ha-rass (har´us) v. To disturb or annoy constantly; to torment persistently. **harassment** n. **harasser** n.

har-bin-ger (här´bin´jér) n. A person that initiates or pioneers a major change; something that foreshadows what is to come.

har-bor (här´bér) n. A place of refuge or shelter; a bay or cove; an anchorage for ships. **harbor** v. To provide shelter; to entertain, as a feeling or thought. **harborage, harborer** n.

hard (härd) adj. Difficult to perform, endure, or comprehend; solid in texture or substance; resistant to cutting or penetration; containing salts which make lathering with soap difficult; high in alcoholic content. **hardness** n.

hard-boiled (härd´boild´) adj. Boiled or cooked in the shell to a hard or solid state.

hard copy n. In computer science, the printed information or data from a computer.

hard disk n. In computer science,

magnetic storage consisting of a rigid disk of aluminum coated with a magnetic recording substance; contained within a removable cartridge or mounted in the hard disk assembly of a microcomputer.

hard-en (här'den) v. To make or become hard or harder; to make or become physically or mentally tough; to make or become callous or unsympathetic.

har-di-hood (här'dē hed) n. Resolute courage; audacious boldness; vitality; vigor.

har-di-ment (här'dē ment) n. A bold deed.

Harding, Warren G. n. (1865-1923) The twenty-ninth President of the United States from 1921-1923, died in office.

hard-line (härd'līn') adj. Holding fast to a rigid principle; favoring forceful action.

hard-ware (härd'wâr') n. Manufactured machine parts; tools and utensils; the mechanical components of a computer installation.

har-dy (här'dē) adj. Bold and robust; able to survive very unfavorable conditions, as extreme cold; daring. **hardiness** n. **hardily** adv.

hare (hâr) n. Various mammals related to the rabbits but having longer ears and legs.

har-em (hâr'em) n. The women living in a Muslim residence; the living quarters of a harem.

har-i-cot (har'i-kō) n. A kind of thick mixture of meat and vegetables; the kidney bean or its pod or seed.

hark (härk) v. To listen closely.

har-le-quin (här'le kwin) n. A jester; a clown. **harlequin** adj. Patterned with vividly colored diamond shapes.

har-lot (här'lot) n. A prostitute.

harm (härm) n. Emotional or physical damage or injury. **harm** v. To cause harm to. **harmful** adj. **harmfully** adv.

har-mat-tan (här'ma-tan') n. A seasonal dust-laden wind occurring on the west coast of Africa.

harm-less (härm'lis) adj. Without harm; lacking ability to injure or harm.

har-mon-ic (här mon'ik) adj. Relating to musical harmony; in harmony; concordant. **harmonically** adv.

har-mon-i-ca (här mon'i ka) n. A small, rectangular musical instrument having a series of tuned metal reeds that vibrate with the player's breath.

har-mon-i-con (här-mon'i-kon) n. A harmonica or mouth organ.

har-mo-ni-ous (här mō'nē us) adj. Pleasing to the ear; characterized by agreement and accord; having components agreeably combined. **harmoniously** adv. **-ousness** n.

har-mo-nize (här'mo-nīz') v. To be in

harmony; to bring into agreement. *Mus.* To perform in harmony.

har-mo-ny (här'mo nē) n., pl. **harmonies** Complete agreement, as of feeling or opinion; an agreeable combination of component parts; pleasing sounds; a combination of musical tones into chords. **-izer** n.

har-ness (här'nis) n. The working gear, other than a yoke, of a horse or other draft animal.

harness racing n. A racing sport in which horses are harnessed to a two-wheeled sulky with a driver.

harp (härp) n. A musical instrument having a triangular upright frame with strings plucked with the fingers. **harp** v. To play a harp. **harp on** To write or talk about excessively. **harpist** n.

harp-si-chord (härp'si kord') n. A pianolike instrument whose strings are plucked by using quills or leather points connected to keys.

har-py (här'pē) n., pl. **harpies** A vicious woman; a predatory person.

har-ri-dan (har'i dan) n. A mean, hateful old woman.

har-ri-er (har'ē êr) n. A slender hawk with narrow wings that preys on small animals; a hunting dog; a cross-country runner.

Harrison, Benjamin n. (1833-1901) The twenty-third president of the United States from 1889-1893.

Harrison, William Henry n. (1773-1841) The ninth president of the United States from March 4th to April 4th 1841; died in office.

har-row (har'ō) n. A cultivating tool with sharp teeth and spikes for breaking up and smoothing soil. **harrow** v. To cultivate the soil with a harrow which is drawn across plowed soil to smooth.

har-row-ing adj. Causing distress.

har-ry (har'ē) v. To harass.

harsh (härsh) adj. Disagreeable; extremely severe. **harshness** n.

hart (härt) n. A fully grown male deer.

harte-beest (här'te bēst') n. A large African antelope.

har-um—scar-um (hâr'um skar'um) adj. Reckless; irresponsible.

har-vest (här'vist) n. The process or act of gathering a crop; the season or time for gathering crops. To reap; to obtain as if by gathering. **harvester** n.

harvest moon n. The full moon closest to the time of the September equinox.

has—been (haz'bin') n. One who has passed the period of his greatest effectiveness, achievement, or popularity.

ha-sen-pfef-fer (häsen fef'êr) n. A highly seasoned stew made from rabbit meat.

hasp (hasp) n. A clasp or hinged fastener that passes over a staple and is secured

by a pin, bolt, or padlock.
has-sle (has´l) *n. Slang* A type of quarrel or argument. **hassle** *v.*
has-sock (has´ok) *n.* A firm upholstered cushion used as a footstool.
haste (hāst) *n.* Speed; swiftness of motion or action; excessive eagerness to act. **haste** *v.* To make haste; to hurry.
has-ten (hā´sen) *v.* To act or move with haste or speed.
hast-y (hā´stē) *adj.* Rapid; swift; made or done with excessive speed. **hastily** *adv.* **hastiness** *n.*
hat (hat) *n.* A covering for the head, often with a crown and brim.
hatch (hach) *n.* A small opening or door, as in a ship's deck. **hatch** *v.* To bring forth, as young from an egg; to devise; to produce; to contrive secretly.
hatch-er-y (hach´e-rē) *n., pl.* **hatcheries** A place for hatching eggs such as fish or poultry eggs.
hate (hāt) *v.* To feel hostility or animosity toward; to dislike intensely. **hateful** *adj.* **hatefully** *adv.* **-fulness, hater** *n.*
hau-berk (haw´berk) *n.* A tunic of chain worn as defensive armor.
haugh-ty (haw´tē) *adj.* Arrogantly proud; disdainful. **haughtily** *adv.*
haul (hawl) *v.* To pull or draw with force; to move or transport, as in a truck or cart. **haul** *n.* The distance over which someone travels or something is transported; an amount collected at one time.
haul-age (haw´lij) *n.* The process or act of hauling; a charge for hauling.
haunch (hawnch) *n.* The hip; the buttock and upper thigh of a human or animal; the loin and leg of a four-footed animal.
haunt (hawnt) *v.* To appear to or visit as a ghost or spirit; to visit frequently; to linger in the mind. **haunting** *adj.*
hau-sen (haw´zn) *n.* A large white fish, an outstanding source for caviar.
haus-tel-lum (ho-stel´um) *n.* The sucking organ of insects, adapted to suck juices of plants or to suck blood.
haut-boi *or* **haut-boy** (hō´boi, ō´boi) *n.* An oboe; a double reed wind instrument made of wood.
haute couture *n.* Designers who create exclusive fashions for women.
hau-teur (hō ter´) *n.* A disdainful arrogance.
have (hav) *v.* To hold or own, as a possession or a property. **have to** Need to; must. **have had it** Suffered or endured all that one can tolerate.
have-lock (hav´lok) *n.* A cap with a flap that covers the neck, protecting the neck from sun.
ha-ven (hā´ven) *n.* A place that offers a safe refuge; a harbor or port; an inlet which provides a place for ships to anchor.
hav-er-sack (hav´er sak) *n.* A bag for

carrying supplies on a hike or march.
hav-oc (hav´ok) *n.* Mass confusion; widespread destruction; devastation.
haw (haw) *interj.* A hesitating sound made by a speaker who is groping for words. **haw** *v.* To hesitate in speaking; to falter in speaking.
Ha-wai-i *or* **Ha-wai-ian Is-lands** *n.* A state of the United States, which is an island group, located in the central Pacific, statehood August 21, 1959, state capital Honolulu.
hawk (hok) *n.* Any of several predatory birds with a short, hooked bill and strong claws for seizing small prey; one who advocates a warlike foreign policy; one having an aggressive attitude. **hawkish** *adj.* **hawkishly** *adv.*
haw-ser (ho´zer) *n.* A heavy cable or rope for towing or securing a ship.
haw-thorn (ho´thorn) *n.* A thorny shrub or tree bearing white or pink flowers and red fruit.
hay (hā) *n.* Alfalfa or grass that has been cut and dried for animal food.
hay-cock (hākok) *n.* A rounded pile of hay that is stacked and kept outdoors; a haystack.
Hayes, Rutherford Birchard *n.* (1822-1893) The nineteenth president of the United States from 1877-1881.
hay fever *n.* An acute allergy to certain airborne pollens, marked by severe irritation of the upper respiratory tract and the eyes.
hay-wire (hā´wier) *adj.* Broken; emotionally out of control; crazy.
haz-ard (haz´erd) *n.* A risk; chance; an accident; danger or source of danger. **hazard** *v.* To take a chance on; to venture. **hazardous** *adj.*
haze (hāz) *n.* A fog-like suspension of dust, smoke, and vapor in the air; a confused or vague state of mind. **haze** *v.* To harass with disagreeable tasks.
ha-zel (hā´zel) *n.* A small tree or shrub bearing edible brown nuts with smooth shells; a light brown or yellowish brown. **hazel** *adj.*
haz-y (hā zē) *adj.* Lacking clarity, vague. **hazily** *adv.* **haziness** *n.*
he (hē) *pron.* Third person singular masculine or generic pronoun used as the subject of a sentence.
he'd (hēd) *contr.* He had; he would.
he'll (hēl) *contr.* He will.
he's (hēz) *contr.* He has; he is.
he–man (hē´man) *n. Slang* A man marked by strength; a muscular man.
head (hed) *n.* The upper part of a human or animal body containing the brain, the principal nerve centers, the eyes, ears, nose and mouth. **headed** *adj.*
head-ache (hed´ak) *n.* A pain or ache in the head. *Slang* A bothersome problem. **headachy** *adj.*

head cold *n.* A common cold or viral infection that centers primarily in the nasal passages.

head-line (hed'līn') *n.* A title, caption, or summarizing words of a newspaper story or article printed in large type. **headline** *v.* To provide with a headline; to serve as the star performer.

head-note (hed'nōt') *n.* A prefixed note of explanation, such as a statement preceding the report of a legal case.

head wind (hed'wind') *n.* A wind blowing in the direction opposite the course of a ship or aircraft.

head-y (hed'ē) *adj.* Tending to intoxicate; affecting the senses; headstrong. **headily** *adv.* **headiness** *n.*

heal (hēl) *v.* To restore to good health; to mend. **healer** *n.*

health (helth) *n.* The overall condition or function of a living organism at a particular time; freedom from disease or defect. **healthful** *adj,* **healthfully** *adv.* **healthfulness** *n.*

heap (hēp) *n.* A haphazard assortment of things; a large number or quantity. **heap** *v.* To throw or pile into a heap.

hear (hēr) *v.* To perceive by the ear; to listen with careful attention; to be informed of; to listen to officially or formally, as in a court of law.

hear-ing (hēr'ing) *n.* One of the five senses; the range by which sound can be heard; an opportunity to be heard; in law, a preliminary examination of an accused person.

hearing aid *n.* An electronic device used to amplify the hearing of partially deaf persons.

heark-en (här'ken) *v.* To listen carefully.

hear-say (hēr'sā') *n.* Information heard from another; common talk; rumor.

hearse (hers) *n.* A vehicle for conveying a dead body to the place of burial.

heart (härt) *n.* The hollow, primary muscular organ of vertebrates which circulates blood throughout the body; the emotional center, such as in love, hate, consideration, or compassion; the most essential part of something.

heart-ache (härt'āk') *n.* Emotional grief; sorrow.

heart attack *n.* An acute malfunction or interrupted heart function.

heart-beat (härt'bēt')*n.* A pulsation of the heart, consisting of one contraction and one relaxation.

heart block *n.* An impairment of the ventricular beats of the heart.

heart-break (härt'brāk') *n.* Great sorrow; deep grief. **heartbreaking** *adj.* **heartbreakingly** *adv.*

heart-brok-en (härt'brōken) *a.* Deeply grieved; overcome by sadness.

heart-burn (härt'bern') *n.* A sensation of burning in the stomach and

esophagus, usually caused by excess acid in the stomach.

heart disease *n.* An abnormality of the heart or circulation.

heart-en (här'ten) *v.* To give courage to.

heart-felt (härt'felt') *adj.* Deeply felt; sincere.

hearth (härth) *n.* The floor of a fireplace or furnace; the stone that forms the front of a fireplace.

heart-y (här'tē) *adj.* Marked by exuberant warmth; full of vigor; nourishing; substantial. **heartily** *adv.* **heartiness** *n.*

heat (hēt) *n.* A quality of being hot or warm; a degree of warmth; depth of feeling; a period of sexual ardor in female animals. *Slang* Pressure or stress. **heat** *v.* To make or become warm or hot. **heater** *n.*

heath (hēth) *n.* An open tract of uncultivated wasteland covered with low-growing shrubs and plants.

hea-then (hē'then) *n.* A person or nation that does not recognize the God of Christianity, Judaism, or Islam; in the Old Testament, a Gentile; non-Jew. **heathen, heathenish** *adj.*

heath-er (heth'ér) *n.* A shrub that grows in dense masses and has small evergreen leaves and small pinkish flowers. **heather, heathery** *adj.*

heave (hēv) *v.* To raise or lift, especially forcibly; to hurl or throw. *Naut.* To push, pull, or haul, as by a rope. *Slang* To vomit. **heave** *n.* The act of throwing.

heav-en (hev'en) *n.* The sky; the region above and around the earth; the abode of God, the angels, and the blessed souls of the dead; a state or place of blissful happiness. **heavenliness** *n.* **heavenward** *adv. & adj.*

heav-en-ly (hev'en-lē) *adj.* Relating to heaven; celestial; delightful; holy.

heav-y (hev'ē) *adj.* Of great weight; very thick or dense; forceful; powerful; rough and violent, as stormy weather; of great significance; grave; painful, as bad news; oppressive.

heavy water *n.* Water that contains more than the usual hydrogen in its heavier isotopic form, deuterium, used for scientific experiments.

heb-do-mad (heb'do mad') n. A period of seven days.

he-be-phre-nia (hē'be frē'nē *a*) *n.* A schizophrenic reaction causing silliness, hallucinations and regression.

heb-e-tate (heb'i-tāt') *v.* To dull; to become dull or blunt.

He-brew (hēbrō) *n.* A member of a Semitic people claiming descent from Abraham, Isaac, and Jacob; the modern form of the language of the Hebrews.

heck (hek) *interj. & n. Slang* An

expression of disappointment, as in *oh heck.*

heck-le (hek´l) *v.* To badger or annoy, as with questions, comments, or gibes.

hec-tic (hek´tik) *adj.* Intensely active, rushed, or excited; marked by a persistent and fluctuating fever caused by a disease, such as tuberculosis; feverish; flushed.

hec-to-graph (hek´to graf˝) *n.* A machine for making copies of a drawing on a gelatin surface.

hec-tor (hek´tér) *n.* A bully; domineering person. **hector** *v.* To intimidate, to bully.

hed-dle (hed´l) *n.* A set of parallel cords or wires that guide warp threads in a loom.

hedge (hej) *n.* A boundary or fence formed of shrubs or low-growing trees; a means to guard against financial loss; a deliberately ambiguous statement.

he-don-ics *n.* Branch of ethics relating to pleasure. **hedonic** *adj.*

he-don-ism (hed´o niz˝um) *n.* The doctrine devoted to the pursuit of pleasure; the philosophy that pleasure is the principal good in life. **hedonist** *n.* **hedonistic** *adj.*

heed (hēd) *v.* To pay attention; to take notice of something. **heed** *n.* Attention. **heedful** *adj.* **heedfully** *adv.*

heed-less (hēd´lis) *adj.* Without heed; inconsiderate; careless.

heel (hēl) *n.* The rounded back part of the human foot under and behind the ankle; the part of a shoe supporting or covering the heel; a lower or bottom part; the crusty ends of a loaf of bread. **heel** *v.* To follow along at one's heels.

heft (heft) *n.* Weight; bulk; importance. **heft** *v.* To gauge or estimate the weight of by lifting; to lift up.

heft-y (hef´tē) *adj.* Bulky; heavy; sizable.

he-gem-o-ny (hi jem´o nē) *n.* Dominance or leadership, as of one country over another.

he-gi-ra (hi ji´ra) *n.* A journey or departure to flee an undesirable situation.

heif-er (hef´ér) *n.* A young cow, particularly one that has not produced a calf.

height (hīt) *n.* The quality of being high; the highest or most advanced point; the distance from the base of something; the apex; the distance above a specified level; altitude; the distance from head to foot.

height-en (hīt´en) *v.* To increase or become high in quantity or degree; to raise or lift.

Heimlich maneuver *n.* An emergency maneuver used to dislodge food from a choking person's throat; the closed fist is placed below the rib cage and

pressed inward to force air from the lungs upward.

hei-nous (hā´nus) *adj.* Extremely wicked; hateful or shockingly wicked. **heinously** *adv.* **heinousness** *n.*

heir (âr) *n.* A person who inherits another's property or title.

heir apparent *n.* An heir who is legally assured of his right to inherit if he survives his ancestor.

heir-ess *n.* A female heir, especially to a large fortune.

heir-loom (âr´lōm˝) *n.* A family possession handed down from generation to generation; an article of personal property acquired by legal inheritance.

heist (hist) *v.* To take from; to steal. **heist** *n.* A robbery.

he-li-an-thus (hē-lē-an´thus) *n.* Herbaceous plants, some of which are sunflowers.

hel-i-cal (hel´i kal) *adj.* Of or pertaining to the shape of a helix. **helically** *adv.*

hel-i-con (hel´i kon˝) *n.* A large, circular tuba that encircles the player's shoulder.

hel-i-cop-ter (hel´i kop˝tér) *n.* An aircraft propelled by rotors which can take off vertically rather than needing an approach or a rolling start.

he-li-o-cen-tric (hē˝lē-ō-sen´trik) *adj.* Referred to, measured or as seen from the sun's center.

he-lio-graph (hē´lē o graf˝) *n.* An apparatus for sending messages using the sun's rays reflected from a mirror.

he-li-o-trope (hē´lē-ō-trōp˝) *n.* A garden plant having small, fragrant, purple flowers.

he-li-um (hē´lē um) *n.* An extremely light, nonflammable, odorless, gaseous element, symbolized by He.

he-lix (hē´liks) *n.* Something that is spiral in form; a spiral line, as of wire winding around a tube; a coil.

hell *or* **Hell** (hel) *n.* The abode of the dead souls condemned to eternal punishment, a place of evil, torment, or destruction; great distress; anguish; a cause of trouble or misery. **hellish** *adj.* **hellishly** *adv.*

hel-lo (he lō´) *n.* An expression of greeting.

helm (helm) *n.* A wheel or steering apparatus for a ship; a position or any place of control or command.

hel-met (hel´mit) *n.* A protective covering for the head made of metal, leather, or plastic.

hel-minth (hel´minth) *n.* An intestinal worm, as the tapeworm.

helms-man (helmz´man) *n.* One who guides a ship.

hel-ot *n.* A serf; a slave. **helotry** *n.*

help (help) *v.* To assist or aid. **help** *n.*

Assistance; relief; one that assists; one hired to help. **helper** n. **helpful** adj.

help-ing (hel´ping) n. A single serving of food.

hel-ter–skel-ter (hel´tér skel´tér) adv. In a confused or hurried manner; in an aimless way. **helter-skelter** adj. Rushed and confused. **helter-skelter** n. Great confusion; a tumult.

helve (helv) n. A handle on a tool such as an axe or hatchet.

hem (hem) n. A finished edge of fabric folded under and stitched. **hem** interj. A sound made as in clearing the throat, used especially to attract attention or to fill a pause in speech. **hem** v. To fold under and stitch down the edge of. **hem in** to confine and surround.

he-mal (hē´mal) adj. Pertaining to the blood or blood vessels; noting, pertaining to, or situated on that side of the spinal column containing the heart and great blood vessels.

hem-an-gi-o-ma (hē man´jē o´ma) n. A benign tumor that occurs as a reddish elevated area on the skin.

hem-a-tin-ic (hem´a tin´ik) n. A medicine that tends to stimulate blood cell formation or increases the hemoglobin in the blood.

he-ma-tol-o-gy (hem´a tol´o jē) n. The branch of biological science that deals with blood and blood-generating organs. **hematologist** n.

he-ma-to-ma n. A tumor containing blood.

hem-i-cel-lu-lose (hem´i sel´ū lōs´) n. A natural carbohydrate less complex than cellulose, found mainly in the woody tissue of plants.

hem-i-cy-cle (hem´i sī´kl) n. A curved or half circle; a semicircular structure or building.

hem-i-ple-gia n. The paralysis of one half of the body or part of it resulting from injury to the motor center of the brain.

hem-i-sphere (hem´i sfēr´) n. A half sphere that is divided by a plane passing through its center; either symmetrical half of an approximately spherical shape; the northern or southern half of the earth divided by the equator or the eastern or western half divided by a meridian.

hem-line (hem´lin´) n. The line formed at the lower edge of a garment such as a skirt or dress.

he-mo-cy-to-me-ter (hē´mō sī tom´i tér) n. The instrument used in counting blood corpuscles.

he-mo-dy-nam-ics n. The branch of physiology that deals with the circulation of the blood.

he-mo-glo-bin (hē´mo glō´bin) n. The iron-containing respiratory pigment occurring in red corpuscles of vertebrates.

he-mo-ly-sin n. A substance which causes the dissolution of red blood cells.

he-mo-phil-i-a (hē´mo fil´ē a) n. Pathol. An inherited blood disease character-ized by severe, protracted, sometimes spontaneous bleeding.

hem-or-rhage (hem´ér ij) n. Bleeding, especially excessive bleeding. .

hem-or-rhoid (hem´o roid´) n. Pathol. A painful mass of dilated veins in swollen anal tissue. Also called *hemorrhoids* or *piles*.

he-mo-stat (hē´mo stat´) n. An agent that stops bleeding; a clamp-like instrument for preventing or reducing bleeding.

hemp (hemp) n. An Asian herb; hashish and marijuana are produced from the female plant and coarse fabrics and rope are made from the tough fibers of the male plant. **hempen** adj.

hem-stitch (hem´i stik´) n. The decorative border stitch used in sewing.

hen (hen) n. A mature female bird, especially an adult female domestic fowl.

hence (hens) adv. From this place or time; from this source.

hence-forth (hens´ förth´) adv. From this time on. Also *henceforward*.

hen-dec-a-gon (hen dek´a gon´) n. A plane figure with eleven sides and the same number of angles.

hen-e-quen (hen´e kin) n. A strong fiber obtained from the leaves of a tropical American plant, used for binder twine and course fabrics.

hen-na (hen´a) n. An Asian and North African ornamental tree bearing fragrant white or reddish flowers; a brownish red dye derived from henna leaves and used as a cosmetic dye; a strong reddish brown.

heno-the-ism (hen´o thē iz´um) n. The worship of one god although not denying the existence of other gods.

hep (hep) adj. Slang Knowledgeable about the styles or tends.

hep-a-rin (hep´a rin) n. Biochem A substance found especially in liver tissue having the power to slow or prevent blood clotting.

he-pat-ic (hi pat´ik) adj. Of or like the liver.

hep-a-ti-tis (hep´a tī´tis) n. Pathol. Inflammation of the liver causing jaundice.

hep-a-tize (hep´a tīz´) v. Pathol. To convert, as the spongy lung tissue, into liver-like tissue, caused by congestion.

hep-tad (hep´tad) n. A group of seven.

hep-ta-gon (hep´ta gon´) n. A polygon with seven angles and sides.

hep-tam-er-ous (hep tam´ér us) adj.

Containing seven parts.

her *pron.* The objective case and the possessive case of the feminine pronoun *she*.

her-ald (her´ald) *n.* A person who announces important news; one that comes before as a sign of what is to follow. **herald** *v.* To announce; to introduce. **heraldic** *adj.*

her-ald-ry (her´al drē) *n., pl.* **heraldries** The art or science of tracing genealogies and devising and granting coats of arms.

herb (erb) *n.* A soft-stemmed plant without woody tissue that usually withers and dies each year; an often pleasant-smelling plant.

her-ba-ceous (hcr bā´shus) *adj.* Like, or consisting of herbs; green and leaf-like.

herb-age (hur´bij) *n.* Herbs collectively; herbaceous vegetation; the succulent parts of herbaceous plants, as leaves and stems.

her-bal (hur´bal, ur´bal) *n.* A book on plants or herbs with reference to their medical properties.

herb-al-ist (hcr´ba list) *n.* One who gathers, grows, and deals in herbs.

her-bar-i-um (her bâr´ē um) *n., pl.* **herbariums** *or* **herbaria** A collection of dried plant specimens that are scientifically arranged for study; a place housing an herbarium.

her-bi-cide (er´bi sīd´) *n.* A chemical agent used to kill weeds.

her-bi-vore (her´bi vō´) *n.* A plant-eating animal.

her-biv-o-rous (her biv´er us) *adj.* Feeding chiefly on plant life or vegetables. **herbivorously** *adv.*

her-cu-le-an (hër´kü lē´an) *adj.* Of unusual size, force, or difficulty; having great strength.

herd (hërd) *n.* A number of cattle or other animals of the same kind, kept or staying together as a group; a large crowd of people. **herd** *v.* To bring together in a herd. **herdsman** *n.*

here (hēr) *adv.* In or at this place; in a present life or state.

here-af-ter (hēr af´tèr) *adv.* From now on; at some future time. **hereafter** *n.* Existence after death.

here-by (hēr bī´) *adv.* By means or by virtue of.

her-e-dit-a-ment (her´i dit´a ment) *n.* Any heritable property.

he-red-i-tar-y (he red´i ter´ē) *adj.* Passing or transmitted from an ancestor to a legal heir; having an inherited title or possession; genetically transmitted from parent to offspring.

he-red-i-ty (he´red´i tē) *n.* The genetic transmission of traits from parents to offspring.

here-in (hēr in´) *adv.* In or into this place.

here-of (hēr uv´) *adv.* Relating to or in regard to.

her-e-sy (her´i sē) *n., pl.* **heresies** A belief in conflict with orthodox religious beliefs; any belief contrary to set doctrine.

her-e-tic (her´i tik) *n.* A person holding opinions different from orthodox beliefs, especially religious beliefs.

here-to (hēr tō´) *adv.* To this matter, proposition, or thing.

here-with (hēr with´) *adv.* Together or along with this; hereby.

her-i-ta-ble (her´i ta bl) *adj.* Capable of being inherited. **heritably** *adv.*

her-i-tage (her´i tij) *n.* Property that is inherited; something handed down from past generations; a legacy.

herm (hèrm) *n.* Monument or statue, in the form of a square stone pillar, consisting of a head or bust.

her-maph-ro-dite (hèr maf´ro dīt´) *n.* A person, animal, or plant having both male and female reproductive organs. **hermaphroditic** *adj.*

her-me-neu-tics (hur´me nü´tiks) *n.* The art of interpretation of Bible scriptures.

her-met-ic *or* **her-met-i-cal (her met´ik)** *adj.* Tightly sealed against air and liquids; made impervious to outside influences. **hermetically** *adv.*

her-mit (hèr´mit) *n.* A person who lives in seclusion, often for religious reasons.

her-ni-a (hèr´nē a) *n.* The protrusion of a bodily organ, as the intestine, through an abnormally weakened wall that usually surrounds it; a rupture.

he-ro (hēr´ō) *n., pl.* **heroes** A person of outstanding valor; a figure in mythology and legend renowned for exceptional courage and fortitude.

he-ro-ic (hi rō´ik) *adj.* Relating or pertaining to heroes; impressive in power, size or extent; a great intensity; extreme. **heroically** *adv.*

heroic couplet *n.* A verse consisting of two rhyming lines of iambic pentameter.

her-o-in (her´ō in) *n.* A highly addictive narcotic derivative of morphine.

her-o-ine (her´ō in) *n.* A woman of heroic character; the principal female character in a story or play.

her-o-ism (her´ō iz´um) *n.* Heroic behavior.

her-on (her´on) *n.* A bird having a long slender bill, long legs, and a long neck.

her-pes (hèr´pēz) *n. Pathol.* A viral infection, characterized by small blisters on the skin or mucous membranes. **herpetic** *adj.*

her-pe-tol-o-gy (hèr´pi tol´o jē) *n.* The scientific study and treatment of reptiles and amphibians. **herpetologic, herpetological** *adj.* **herpetologically**

adv. **herpetologist** *n.*

her-ring-bone (her´ing bōn´) *n.* A pattern utilizing rows of short slanted parallel lines with connected rows slanting in the opposite direction.

herring gull *n.* The most common large gull in North America, living on both the seashore and inland waters.

hertz *n.* A unit of frequency equaling one cycle per second.

hes-i-tant (hez´i tant) *adj.* Given to hesitating; lacking decisiveness.

hes-i-tate (hez´i tāt´) *v.* To pause or to be slow before acting, speaking, or deciding; to be uncertain.

hes-i-ta-tion (hez´i tā´shan) *n.* The act of hesitating; a state of doubt or pausing.

het-er-o-chro-mat-ic (het´ér o krō mat´ ik) *adj.* Of or relating to or containing different colors; made up of different frequencies or wavelengths.

het-er-o-cy-clic (het´ér o sī´klik) *adj.* Relating to or characterized by an organic compound having a ring containing one or more atoms other than carbon.

het-er-o-dox (het´ér o doks´) *adj.* Not in accord with established beliefs or religious doctrine; holding unorthodox opinions or beliefs. **heterodoxy** *n.*

het-er-oe-cious (het´e rē´shus) *adj.* Of a parasite, passing through the different stages in the life cycle on often different hosts, as certain fungi.

het-er-on-o-my (het´e ron´o mē) *n.* Subordination to another.

het-er-o-nym (het´ér o nim´) *n.* A word having the same spelling as another but a different meaning and pronunciation.

het-er-o-plas-ty (het´ér o plas´tē) *n.* An operation in where lesions are repaired with grafted tissue taken from another organism or person.

het-er-o-sex-u-al (het´ér o sek´shö al) *adj.* Of or having sexual desire toward the opposite sex; involving different sexes. **heterosexuality** *n.*

het-er-o-sis (het´e rō´sis) *n.* An increased vigor or capacity for growth, often as the result of cross-breeding of plants or animals.

het-er-o-troph-ic (het´ér o trof´ik) *adj. Biol.* Using organic matter as a source of food.

het-er-o-zy-gote (het´ér o zī´gōt) *n.* A hybrid plant or animal that does not breed true because it contains at least one pair of genes with different characteristics.

heu-ris-tic (hū ris´tik) *adj.* Involving a teaching method that utilizes self-educating or a method of trial and error to improve performance.

hew (hū) *v.* To make or shape with or as if with an axe; to adhere strictly; to conform.

hex (heks) *n.* One held to bring bad luck; a jinx. **hex** *v.* To put under an evil spell; to bewitch.

hex-a-gon (hek´sa gon´) *n.* A polygon having six sides and six angles. **hexagonal** *adj.* **hexagonally** *adv.*

hex-a-gram (hek´sa gram´) *n.* A six-pointed starlike figure formed by placing two equilateral triangles concentrically with their sides parallel and on opposite sides of the center.

hex-am-e-ter (hek sam´i tér) *n.* A line of verse containing six metrical feet.

hex-a-pod (hek´sa pod´) *n.* Arthropods having six feet, comprising the true insects.

hey (hā) *interj.* An exclamation used to express surprise or joy and used to call attention to something.

hey-day (hā´dā´) *n.* A time of great power, prosperity or popularity; a peak.

hi-a-tus (hī ā tus) *n.* A gap, break, or lapse in time from which something is missing; a break; a break between shooting of television shows; a break in continuity.

hi-ba-chi *n., pl.* **hibachis (hē bä´chē)** A deep, portable charcoal grill used for cooking food.

hi-ber-nac-u-lum (hī´bér nak´ū lum) *n.* A shelter occupied during the winter by a dormant animal.

hi-ber-nal (hī bur´nal) *adj.* Relating to or belonging to the winter season; wintry.

hi-ber-nate (hī´bér nāt´) *v.* To pass the winter in an inactive, dormant, sleep-like state. **hibernation** *n.*

hick (hik) *n. Slang* A clumsy, unsophisticated country person. **hick** *adj.*

hick-o-ry (hik´o rē) *n., pl.* **hickories** A North American tree with a smooth or shaggy bark, hard edible nuts, and heavy, tough wood.

hid-den (hiden) *adj.* Out of sight; away from the public eye.

hide (hīd) *v.* To put or keep out of sight; to keep secret; to obscure from sight; to conceal oneself. **hide** *n.* The skin of an animal.

hid-e-ous (hid´ē us) *adj.* Physically repulsive; extremely ugly. **hideously** *adv.* **hideousness** *n.*

hi-dro-sis (hi drō´sis) *n.* Perspiration, especially the excretion of sweat due to drugs, or a disease characterized by sweating.

hi-er-ar-chy (hī´e rär´kē) *n., pl.* **hierarchies** An authoritative body or group of things or persons arranged in successive order; a ranked series of persons or things. **hierachic** *adj.*

hi-er-o-glyph (hī´ér o glif´) *n.* A symbol.

hi-er-o-glyph-ic (hī´ér o glif´ik) *n.* A

pictorial symbol representing an idea, object, or sound. **hieroglyphically** *adv.*

hi-er-o-phant (hī´ĕr o fant´) *n.* A priest in ancient Greece; one who interprets the rites of religion.

hi-fi (hī´fī´) *n.* High fidelity; electronic equipment capable of reproducing high fidelity sound. **hi-fi** *adj.*

hig-gle (hig´l) *v.* To bargain; to argue or haggle often over petty details.

high (hī) *adj.* Extending upward; located at a distance above the ground; more than normal in degree or amount; expensive.

higher education *n.* An education beyond the secondary level; college education.

high fidelity *n. Electronics* The reproduction of sound with minimal distortion, as on records or tapes.

high frequency *n.* A radio frequency in the band from three to thirty megacycles.

high-road (hī´rōd´) *n.* A main road; a direct or guaranteed method or course.

high–strung (hī´strung´) *adj.* Very nervous and excitable.

high tech *n.* An interior design that incorporates industrial materials or motifs; high technology.

high-way (hī´wā´) *n.* A main or principal road or thoroughfare of some length which connects towns and cities and is open to the public.

hi-jack *or* **high-jack** (hī´jak´) *v.* To seize illegally or steal while in transit; to coerce or compel someone; to commandeer a vehicle, especially an airplane in flight. **highjacker** *n.*

hike (hīk) *v.* To walk for a lengthy amount of time usually through rugged terrain or woods; to pull up clothing with a sudden motion. **hike** *n.* **hiker**

hi-lar-i-ous (hi lâr´ē us) *adj.* Boisterously happy or cheerful. **hilariously** *adv.* **hilarity** *n.*

hill (hil) *n.* A rounded elevation of the earth's surface, smaller than a mountain; a pile or heap; a small pile or mound, as of soil. **hill** *v.* To surround or cover with hills, as potatoes.

hill-ock (hil´ok) *n.* A small or low hill or mound. **hillocky** *adj.*

hill-top *n.* The summit or top of a hill.

hilt (hilt) *n.* The handle of a dagger or sword. **to the hilt** Fully; completely; thoroughly.

him (him) *pron.* The objective case of the masculine pronoun *he.*

hi-mat-i-on (hi mat´ē on´) *n.* A rectangular cloth draped over the left shoulder and body and worn as a garment in Greece.

him-self (him self´) *pron.* The identical male one; reflexive form of the third person masculine pronoun.

hind (hīnd) *adj.* Located at or toward the rear part; posterior.

hind-brain (hīnd´brān´) *n.* The posterior of the three primary divisions of the vertebrate brain including the pons, cerebellum, and medulla oblongata.

hin-der (hin´dĕr) *v.* To interfere with the progress or action of. **hinderer** *n.*

hind-most (hīnd´mōst´) *adj.* Farthest to the rear or back.

hin-drance (hin´drans) *n.* The act of hindering or state of being hindered.

hind-sight (hīnd´sīt´) *n.* Comprehension or understanding of an event after it has happened.

hinge (hinj) *n.* A jointed device which allows a part, as a door or gate, to swing or turn on another frame. **hinge** *v.* To attach by or to equip with a hinge or hinges; to be dependent on a single consideration or point.

hin-ny (hin´ē) *n.* The hybrid offspring of a stallion and female donkey.

hint (hint) *n.* An indirect indication or suggestion. **hint** *v.* To make something known by a hint.

hin-ter-land (hin´tĕr land´) *n.* A region remote from cities; an inland area adjacent to a coastal area.

hip (hip) *n.* The part of the human body that projects outward between the waist and thigh; the hip joint; the bright, red seed case of a rose. **hip** *adj. Slang* Said to be aware of or informed about current happenings.

hip-bone (hip´bōn´) *n.* The large, flat bone which forms a lateral half of the pelvis.

hip joint *n.* The joint between the hipbone and the thighbone.

hip-pie *or* **hip-py** (hip´ē) *n., pl.* **hippies** A young person who adopts unconventional dress and behavior along with the use of drugs to express withdrawal from middle class life and indifference to its values.

hire (hīĕr) *v.* To obtain the service of another for pay. **hirer** *n.*

hir-sute (hĕr´ōōt) *adj.* Covered with hair.

his (hiz) *pron.* The possessive case of the masculine or generic pronoun *he.*

His-pan-ic (hi span´ik) *adj.* Of or relating to the language, people, or culture of Spain or Latin America.

his-pid (his´pid) *adj.* Rough, shaggy, or covered with stiff bristles.

hiss (his) *n.* A sound resembling a prolonged, sibilant sound, as that of *sss.* **hiss** *v.* To emit such a sound as an expression of disapproval.

hist (hist) *interj.* A sibilant exclamation used to attract attention or command silence.

his-ta-mine (his´ta mēn´) *n. Biochem.* A white, crystalline compound that is found in plant and animal tissue, responsible for reducing blood pressure and having a dilating effect which plays a major role in reducing the symptoms of allergies. **histaminic** *adj.*

his-to-gen-e-sis (his´*to* jen´i sis) *n.* The origin, development, and formation of tissues.

his-tol-o-gy (hi stol´*o* jē) *n., pl.* **histologies** The study of the minute structures of animal and plant tissues as seen through a microscope.

his-tol-y-sis (hi stol´i sis) *n.* The dissolution and breaking down of bodily tissues.

his-tone (his´tōn) *n.* Any of a class of protein substances that, on hydrolysis, yield amino acids.

his-to-ri-an (hi stōr´ē *a*n) *n.* A person who specializes in the writing or study of history.

his-tor-ic (hi stor´ik) *adj.* Significant or famous in history; historical.

his-tor-i-cal (hi stor´i k*a*l) *adj.* Relating to or taking place in history; serving as a source of knowledge of the past; historic. **historically** *adv.*

his-to-ry (his´*to* rē) *n., pl.* **histories** Past events, especially those involving human affairs; an account or record of past events that is written in chronological order, especially those concerning a particular nation, people, activity, or knowledge; the study of the past and its significance.

hit (hit) *v.* To give a blow to; to strike with force; to come forcibly in contact with; to collide with; to inflict a blow on; to move or set in motion by striking; in baseball, to make a successful hit while at bat. **hitter** *n.*

hitch (hich) *v.* To fasten or tie temporarily, with a hook or knot. *Slang* To unite in marriage; to obtain a ride by hitchhiking. **hitch** *n.* A delay or difficulty. *Milit.* A period of time in the armed forces.

hitch-hike (hich´hīk˘) *v.* To travel by signaling and obtaining rides from passing drivers. **hitchhiker** *n.*

hith-er (hith´ér) *adv.* To this place. **hither** *adj.* Situated toward this side.

hith-er-to (hith´ér tö˘) *adv.* Up to now.

hive (hīv) *n.* A natural or man-made structure serving as a habitation for honeybees; a beehive.

hives (hīvz) *n., pl.* Any of various allergic conditions marked by itching welts.

ho (hō) *interj.* An exclamation expressing surprise; a call used to attract attention; exultation.

hoar (hōr) *adj.* Having white or gray hair; grayish or white, as with frost.

hoard (hōrd) *n.* The accumulation of something stored away for safekeeping or future use. **hoard** *v.* To amass and hide or store valuables, money, or supplies. **hoarder** *n.*

hoarse (hōrs) *adj.* Having a husky, gruff, or croaking voice. **hoarsely** *adv.*

hoars-en *v.* To become or make hoarse.

ho-at-zin (hō at´sin) *n.* A crested, olive-colored bird of South America, smaller than a pheasant and noted for the claws which grow out of its wings.

hoax (hōks) *n.* A trick or deception. **hoax** *v.* To deceive by a hoax. **hoaxer** *n.*

hob (hob) *n.* The projection at the side or interior of a fireplace used to keep things warm; an elf or hobgoblin.

ho-bo (hō´bō) *n., pl.* **hoboes** *or* **hobos** A vagrant who travels aimlessly about; a tramp.

hock (hok) *n.* The joint of the hind leg of a horse, ox, or other animal which corresponds to the ankle in man.

hock-ey (hok´ē) *n.* A game played on ice between two teams of skaters whose object is to drive a puck into the opponent's goal using curved wooden sticks; a similar kind of hockey played on a field with a small ball instead of a puck.

ho-cus-po-cus (hō´k*u*s pō´k*u*s) *n.* Any deception or trickery, as misleading gestures; nonsense words or phrases used in conjuring or sleight of hand.

hod (hod) *n.* A V-shaped trough held over the shoulder to carry loads, as bricks or mortar.

hodge-podge (hoj´poj˘) *n.* A jumbled mixture or collection.

Hodgkin's disease *n. Pathol.* A disease characterized by progressive enlargement of the lymph nodes, lymphoid tissue, and spleen, generally fatal.

hoe (hō) *n.* A tool with a long handle and flat blade used for weeding, cultivating, and loosening the soil. **hoe** *v.* **hoer** *n.*

hoe-down (hō´dou˘˘) *n.* A lively country square dance; party.

hog (hog) *n.* A pig, especially one weighing more than 120 pounds and raised for the market; a greedy, selfish, or dirty person. **hog** *v.* To take something selfishly; to take more than one's share. **hoggish** *adj.* **hoggishly** *adv.* **hoggishness** *n.*

ho-gan (hō´gon) *n.* A building made of logs and mud and used as a dwelling by the Navaho Indians.

hog-back (hag´bak˘) *n.* A sharply crested ridge of land with steeply sloping sides.

hoi pol-loi (hoi´ p*o* loi˘) *n.* The common people; the masses.

hoist (hoist) *v.* To haul or raise up. **hoist** *n.* A machine used for raising large objects.

ho-kum (hō´kum) *n.* Material introduced into a speech or a device used to evoke laughter or a desired audience response.

hold (hōld) *v.* To take and keep as in one's hand; to grasp; to possess; to put or keep in a particular place, position, or relationship; to suppress; to keep under control. **hold** *n.* A cargo storage area inside a ship or aircraft. **hold back** To withhold; retain. **hold down** To suppress. **hold in** To restrain or repress. **hold off** To keep from touching; to delay. **hold on** To continue, to endure, to cling to. **hold together** To remain united.

holding company *n.* A company which owns controlling stock or interest in securities of other companies.

hole (hōl) *n.* A cavity or opening in a solid mass or body. **hole** *v.*

hol-i-day (hol′i dā′) *n.* A day set aside by law to commemorate a special person or event; a day set aside for religious observance; a day free from work; any day of rest.

ho-li-ness (hō′lē nis) *n.* The state of being holy.

ho-lism (hō′lIz um) *n.* The theory that a living being has an identity other than the sum of its parts.

hol-land (hol′and) *n.* An unbleached, linen or cotton fabric used in the manufacture of window shades, clothing and bookbindings.

hol-lan-daise sauce (hol′an dāz′ sos) *n.* A creamy sauce made from butter, egg yolks, and lemon juice or vinegar.

hol-ler (hol′ér) *v.* To shout loudly; to yell. **holler** *n.*

hol-low (hol′ō) *adj.* Having a cavity or space within, concave or sunken; lacking significance or substance; not genuine; empty; meaningless. **hollowly** *adv.* **hollow** *n.*

hol-ly (hol′e) *n., pl.* **hollies** A tree or shrub that bears glossy spiny leaves and bright-red berries.

hol-ly-hock (hol′e hok′) *n.* A tall, cultivated plant of the mallow family, widely cultivated for its tall spikes of large, variously colored flowers.

hol-o-caust (hol′o kost′) *n.* A widespread or total destruction, especially by fire.

hol-o-graph (hol′o graf) *n.* A handwritten document, as a letter or will, signed by the person who wrote it. **holographic, holographical** *adj.*

ho-lo-gram (hō′lo gram) *n.* A three-dimensional picture made on a photographic plate without the use of a camera and viewed with coherent light from behind.

hol-o-type (hol′o tīp′) *n.* A single specimen selected for descriptive and taxonomical purposes to represent the entire species. **holotypic** *adj.*

Hol-stein (hōl′stīn) *n.* A breed of dairy cattle with black and white coloring.

hol-ster (hōl′stér) *n.* A leather case designed to hold a pistol or gun. **holstered** *adj.*

ho-ly (hō′lē) *adj.* Regarded as having divine power; sacred; spiritually pure.

Holy Communion *n.* The Christian rite during which the Eucharist is received.

Holy Ghost *n.* The third person of the Christian Trinity.

Holy Spirit *n.* The Holy Ghost.

ho-ly-stone (hō′lē stōn′) *n.* A soft sandstone used by seamen to scrub the decks of ships.

hom-age (hom′ij) *n.* Great respect or honor, especially when expressed publicly.

hom-burg (hom′berg) *n.* A man's felt hat having a stiff brim and high crown creased lengthwise.

home (hōm) *n.* The place where one resides; a place of origin; one's birthplace or residence during the formative years; a place one holds dear because of personal feelings or relationships; a place of security and comfort. **home** *n. & adj.*

home economics *n.* The study of the principles of home management.

ho-me-op-a-thy (hō′mē op′a thē) *n.* A system of treating a disease with minute doses of medicines that produce the symptoms of the disease being treated. **homeopath** *n.* **homeopathic** *adj.*

ho-me-o-sta-sis (hō′mē o stā′sis) *n. Biol.* A state of equilibrium that occurs between different but interdependent elements.

hom-i-cide (hom′i sīd′) *n.* The killing of one person by another; a person who kills another.

hom-i-let-ic (hom′i let′ik) *n.* Pertaining to the nature of a sermon.

hom-i-ly (hom′i lē) *n., pl.* **homilies** A sermon, particularly a discourse on moral behavior.

homing pigeon *n.* A pigeon trained to find its way home from great distances.

hom-i-ny (hom′i nē) *n.* Kernels of hulled and dried corn, often ground into a coarse white meal and boiled.

ho-mo-cer-cal (hō′mo sur′kal) *adj.* Having the lobes of the tail fin of approximately equal size, and the vertebral column ending near the base.

ho-mo-ge-ne-ous (hō′mo jē′nē us) *adj.* Of a similar nature or kind. **homogeneity, homogeneousness** *n.*

ho-mog-e-nize (ho moj′e nīz′) *v.* To process milk by breaking up fat globules and dispersing them uniformly. **homogenization,** *n.*

ho-mog-o-nous (ho mog′o nus) *adj.* Pertaining to a type of flower with equally long stamens and pistils.

ho-mo-graft (hō′mo graft′) *n.* A tissue taken from an individual and grafted to another of the same species.

hom-o-graph (ho′mo graf) *n.* A word that is identical to another in spelling, but different from it in origin and meaning.

ho-moi-o-ther-mal (hō moi´o thur´mal) *adj.* Having a relatively constant body temperature independent of the surroundings.

ho-mol-o-gate (ho mol´o gāt˝) *v.* To approve; to ratify.

ho-mol-o-gous (ho mol´o gus) *adj.* Related or similar in structure, nature, position, or value.

ho-mo-mor-phic(hō˝mo mar´fik,hom´o mar´ fik) *adj.* Having the same external form.

hom-o-nym (hom´o nim) *n.* A word that has the same sound and often the same spelling as another but a different meaning and origin.

hom-o-phone (hom´o fōn˝) *n.* One of two or more words that have the same sound but different spelling, origin, and meaning.

Ho-mo sa-pi-ens (hō´mō sā´pēenz) *n.* The scientific name for the humankind.

ho-mo-sex-u-al(hō˝mo sek´shō al) *adj.* Having sexual attraction or desire for persons of the same sex. **homosexual, homosexuality** *n.*

hon-cho *n., pl.* **honchos** The main person in charge; the boss; the manager.

hone (hōn) *n.* A fine-grained stone used to sharpen cutting tools, such as knives or razors. **hone** *v.* To perfect something; to sharpen.

hon-est (on´ist) *adj.* Not cheating, or stealing; free from fraud; truthful; honorable. **honestly** *adv.*

hon-es-ty (on´i stē) *n.* The quality of being honest; free from deceit or fraud; straightforwardness.

hon-ey (hun´ē) *n., pl.* **honeys** A sweet, sticky substance made by bees from the nectar gathered from flowers; sweetness. *Slang* Dear; darling.

hon-ey-bee (hun´ē bē˝) *n.* Any of various bees living in colonies and producing honey.

hon-ey-moon (hun´ē mōn˝) *n.* A trip taken by a newly married couple. **honeymoon** *v.* **honeymooner** *n.*

honk (hongk) *n.* The harsh, loud sound made by a goose; the sound made by an automobile horn. **honker** *n.*

hon-ky-tonk(hong´ē tongk˝) *n.* A cheap bar or nightclub.

hon-or (on´ẽr) *n.* High regard or respect; personal integrity; reputation; privilege; a title for mayors and judges. **honor** *v.* To accept something as valid; to treat with respect. **honorer** *n.*

hon-or-a-ble (on´ẽr a bl) *adj.* Worthy of esteem.

hon-o-rar-i-um (on´o râr´ē um) *n.* A payment or reward given in recognition for a service performed for which custom or propriety discourages a fixed fee.

hon-or-ar-y (on´o rer´ē) *adj.* Relating to an office or title bestowed as an honor, without the customary powers, duties, or salaries.

hon-or-if-ic (on´o rif´ik) *adj.* Granting honor; an expression of respect in addressing someone in a superior position.

honor system *n.* A system of management, whereby one is trusted to obey the regulations without supervision.

hood (hed) *n.* A covering for the head and neck, often attached to a garment; the movable metal hinged cover of an automobile engine.

-hood *suffix* The quality or state of; sharing a given quality or state.

hoof (hef) *n., pl.* **hooves** The horny covering of the foot in various mammals, as horses, cattle, and oxen. **hoof it** *v. Slang* To dance; to walk. **on the hoof** Alive; not butchered.

hook (hek) *n.* A curved or bent piece of metal used to catch, drag, suspend, or fasten something; in golf, a stroke that sends the ball curving to the left; in boxing, to strike with a short, swinging blow; in hockey, to check illegally with the hockey stick. *Naut. Slang* An anchor. **hook** *v. Slang* To cause to become dependent or addicted. **by hook or by crook** In one way or another. **hook, line, and sinker** Unreservedly; entirely. **to hook up with** To marry; to form an association.

hoo-li-gan (hö´li gan) *n.* A street hoodlum.

hoop (höp) *n.* A circular band of metal or wood used to hold staves of a cask or barrel together; in basketball, the basket.

hoop-la (höp´lä) *n. Slang* Noise and excitement.

hoot (höt) *n.* The loud sound or cry of an owl; *Slang* A very insignificant amount. **hooter** *n.* **hoot** *v.*

hoot-en-an-ny (höt´e nan´ē) *n., pl.* **hootenannies** An informal gathering of folk singers for a public performance.

Hoover, Herbert Clark *n.* (1874-1964) The thirty-first president of the United States from 1929-1933.

hop (hop) *n.* A perennial herb with lobed leaves and green flowers that resemble pine cones; the dried flowers of the plant, yielding an oil used in brewing beer. *Slang* A dance; a quick trip on a plane. **hop** *v.* To move by making short leaps on one foot; to move with light springing motions.

hope (hōp) *v.* To want or wish for something with a feeling of confident expectation. **to hope against hope** To continue hoping for something even

when it appears hopeless. **hopeful**
adj.& n. **hopefully** *adv.*

horde (hōrd) *adj.* A large crowd.

ho-ri-zon (ho ri´zon) *n.* The line along
which the earth and sky seem to meet;
the bounds or limit of one's knowledge,
experience or interest.

hor-mone (hor´mōn) *n. Physiol.* An
internal secretion carried by the
bloodstream to other parts of the body
where it has a specific effect.

horn (horn) *n.* A hard, bonelike,
permanent projection on the heads of
certain hoofed animals, as cattle, sheep,
or deer.

hor-net (hor´nit) *n.* Any of various social
wasps which can inflict a severe sting.

hor-o-loge (har´o lōj) *n.* A mechanism
for keeping time; an older timepiece,
as the sundial.

ho-rol-o-gy (ho rol´ojē) *n.* The science
of measuring time; the craft of making
devices to measure time.

hor-o-scope (hor´o skōp´) *n.* A chart or
diagram of the relative positions of the
planets and signs of the zodiac at a
certain time, as that of a person's birth,
used to predict the future.

hor-ren-dous (ha ren´dus) *adj.* Dreadful;
terrible.

hor-ri-ble (hor´i bl) *adj.* Shocking;
inducing or producing horror. *Informal*
Excessive; inordinate. **horribly** *adv.*

hor-rip-i-la-tion (ha rip´i lā´shan) *n.*
The standing on end of the hair as a
result of fear in dogs and cats.

hor-ror (hor´er) *n.* The painful, strong
emotion caused by extreme dread, fear,
or repugnance. *Informal* Something
that is disagreeable or ugly.

hors d'oeuvre (or derv´) *n.* An appetizer
served with cocktails before dinner.

horse (hors) *n.* A large, strong, hoofed
quadruped mammal with a long mane
and tail, used for riding and for pulling
heavy objects; a device that generally
has four legs, used for holding or
supporting something; in gymnastics,
a wooden block of wood four legs, used
for vaulting and other exercises.

horse-car (hars´kär´) *n.* A streetcar that
was formerly drawn by horses; a car
equipped for transporting horses.

horse-pow-er (hors´pow´ẽr) *n. Mech.*
A unit of power that is equal to 746
watts and nearly equivalent to the
gravitational unit that equals 550 foot-
pounds per second.

horst (horst) *n.* A block of the earth's
crust separated by faults from an
adjacent block.

hort *abbr.* Horticultural; horticulture.

hor-ti-cul-ture (hor´ti kul´chẽr) *n.* The
art or science of raising and tending
fruits, vegetables, flowers, or ornamental plants. **horticultural** *adj.* **horticul-**

turist *n.*

hor-tus sic-cus *n.* A collection of plant
specimens carefully dried and
preserved.

ho-san-na (hō zan´a) *interj.* Expression
to praise or glorify God.

hose (hōz) *n.. pl.* **hose** *or* **hoses** A sock;
a stocking; a flexible tube for carrying
fluids or gases under pressure. **hose**
v. To wash; to water; to squirt with a
hose.

ho-sel (hō´zel) *n.* The socket in the head
of a golf club that encloses the shaft.

ho-sier-y (hō´zhe rē) *n.* Stockings and
socks.

hos-pice (hos´pis) *n.* A lodging for
travelers or the needy often maintained
by a religious order.

hos-pi-ta-ble (hos´pi ta bl) *adj.* Treating
guests with warmth and generosity;
receptive. **hospitably** *adv.*

hos-pi-tal (hos´pi tal) *n.* An institution
where the injured or sick receive
medical, surgical, and emergency care.

host (hōst) *n.* One who receives or
entertains guests; one who provides
a room or building for an event or
function; a large number of people or
things. *Biol.* A living organism, as a
plant or an animal, in or in which a
parasite lives. **host** *v.*

hos-tage (hos´tij) *n.* A person held as
security that promises will be kept or
terms met by a third party.

hos-tel (hos´tel) *n.* A low-priced,
supervised lodging for young travelers.
hos-tel-ry *n.* An inn or hotel.

host-ess (hō´stis) *n.* A woman who
entertains socially; a woman who greets
patrons at a restaurant and escorts them
to their tables.

hos-tile (hos´til) *adj.* Of or relating to
an enemy; antagonistic. **hostilely** *adv.*

hos-til-i-ties (ho stil´i tēs) *n.* War; acts
of war

hos-til-i-ty (ho stil´i tē) *n., pl.* **hostilities**
Deep-seated opposition or hatred; war.

hot (hot) *adj.* At a high temperature;
having heat that exceeds normal body
temperature; sexually excited or
receptive; electrically charged, as a *hot*
wire. *Slang* Recently or illegally
obtained.

hot air *n. Slang* Idle talk.

hot-bed (hot´bed´) *n.* A glass-covered
bed of soil heated by fermenting
manure and used for raising seedlings;
an environment that is conductive to
rapid growth or development.

hot-el (hō tel´) *n.* A business that
provides lodging, meals, entertainment,
and other services for the public.

hour (our) *n.* A measure of time equal
to 60 minutes; 1/24th of a day; the time
of day or night.

hour-ly (our´lē) *adj.* Something that

happens or is done every hour.

house (hous) *n.* A building that serves as living quarters for one or more families; home; the shelter or refuge for a wild animal; a business firm; a legislative body of the U.S. government. **house** *v.* To provide work space or living space.

house of correction *n.* An institution where persons who have committed minor offenses are housed until they are released back into society.

hov-el (hev´el) *n.* A small dirty house.

hov-er (hev´ér) *v.* To remain suspended over something.

how (hou) *adv.* In what manner or way; to what effect; in what condition or state; for what reason; with what meaning.

how-dy *interj.* A word used to express a greeting. **howdy** *n.*

how-ev-er (hou ev´ér) *adv.* In whatever manner or way. *conj.* Nevertheless.

how-it-zer (hou´it sér) *n.* A short cannon that fires projectiles at a high trajectory.

howl (houl) *v.* To utter a loud, sustained, plaintive sound, as the wolf. **howl** *n.*

howl-er (hou´lêr) *n.* One that howls; a ridiculous or stupid blunder.

how-so-ev-er (hou´sō ev´ér) *adv.* To whatever degree or extent; in whatever way.

hua-ra-che (wa rä´chē) *n.* A sandal with a low heel and an upper made of interwoven leather thongs.

hub (hub) *n.* The center of a wheel; the center of activity.

hub-bub (hub´ub) *n.* Confusion; a tumult; uproar.

hub-cap *n.* The removable metal cap that covers the end of an axle, such as one used on the wheel of a motor vehicle.

hu-bris (hū´bris, hō´bris) *n.* Arrogance cause by inordinate pride.

huck-le-ber-ry (huk´l ber´ē) *n.* A type of bush, related to the blueberry and bearing glossy, blackish, usually acidic berries.

hud-dle (hud´le) *n.* A crowd together; in football, a brief meeting of teammates to prepare for the next play. **huddle** *v.* To nestle or crowd together; to confer.

hue (hū) *n.* A gradation of color; the attribute of a color that defines its place on the color spectrum; a particular color; a shade. **hued** *adj.*

huff (huf) *n.* A fit of resentment or of ill temper. **huff** *v.* To exhale or breathe heavily, as from excessive exertion. **huffily** *adv.* **huffiness** *n.* **huffy** *adj.*

hug (hug) *v.* To embrace; to hold fast; to keep, cling, or stay close to. **huggable** *adj.* **hugger** *n.*

huge (hūj) *adj.* Of great quantity, size, or extent. **hugely** *adv.* **hugeness** *n.*

hu-la (hō´la) *n.* A Hawaiian dance characterized by beautiful rhythmic movement of the hips and gestures with the hands.

hulk (hulk) *n.* A heavy, bulky thing; the body of an old ship no longer fit for service.

hulk-ing *adj.* Unwieldy or awkward.

hull (hul) *n.* The outer cover of a fruit or seed; the framework of a boat; the external covering of a rocket, spaceship, or guided missile.

hul-la-ba-loo (hul´a ba lō´) *n.* A confused noise; a great uproar.

hum (hum) *v.* To make a continuous low-pitched sound; to be busily active; to sing with the lips closed.

hu-man (hū´man) *adj.* Of, relating to, or typical of man; having or manifesting human form or attributes. **humanly** *adv.* **humanness** *n.*

hu-mane (hū mān´) *adj.* Marked by compassion, sympathy, or consideration for other people or animals; merciful.

hu-man-i-tar-i-an (hū man´i târ´ē an) *n.* A person who is concerned for human welfare, especially through philanthropy. **humanitarian** *adj.*

hu-man-oid (hū´ma noid´) *adj.* Of human form or characteristics.

hum-ble (hum´bl) *adj.* Marked by meekness or modesty; unpretentious; lowly. *v.* To make humble. **humbleness** *n.* **humbler** *n.* **humbly** *adv.*

hum-bug (hum´bug´) *n.* A misleading trick, hoax, fraud, or pretense; a person who seeks to deceive others; something foolish.

hum-drum (hum´drum´) *adj.* Boring; dull. **humdrum** *n.*

hu-mec-tant (hū mek´tant) *n.* A substance, as glycerol, that promotes moisture retention.

hu-mer-us (hū´mèr us) *n., pl.* **humeri** Long bone of the upper arm or forelimb extending from the shoulder to the elbow.

hu-mid (hū´mid) *adj.* Containing or characterized by a lot of moisture; damp.

hu-mid-i-fy (hū mid´i fī) *v.* To make humid or more moist. **humidifier** *n.*

hu-mid-i-stat (hū mid´i stat´) *n.* An instrument that controls or maintains the degree of humidity.

hu-mid-i-ty (hū mid´i tē) *n.* A moderate amount of wetness in the air; dampness.

hu-mi-dor (hū´mi dor´) *n.* A container used to keep cigars in which the air is kept properly humidified by a special device.

hu-mil-i-ate (hū mil´ē āt´) *v.* To reduce one's dignity or pride to a lower position. **humiliation, humility** *n.*

hum-ming-bird (hum´ing berd´) *n.* A

very small bird with narrow wings, long primary feathers, a slender bill, and an extensile tongue.

hum-mock (hum´ok) *n.* A rounded knoll or hill of snow or dirt. **hummocky** *adj.*

hu-mor (hū´mèr) *n.* Something that is or has the ability to be comical or amusing. *Physiol.* Fluid contained in the body such as blood or lymph. **humor, humorous** *adj.*

hu-mor-ist (hū´mèr ist) *n.* A person who has a sense of humor; one who uses humor to amuse others.

hump (hump) *n.* The rounded lump or protuberance, as on the back of a camel; a small hill. **over the hump** To be past the difficult or most critical state.

hu-mus (hū´drid) *n.* A complex material resulting from partial decomposition of plant or animal matter forming the organic portion of soil.

hunch (hunch) *n.* A strong, intuitive feeling about a future event or result. *v.* To bend into a crooked position or posture.

hunch-back (hunch´bak˘) *n.* A back deformed by a convex curvature of the spine, a person with this disorder.

hun-dred (hun´drid) *n.* The cardinal number equal to 10 x 10, symbol 100.

hun-ger (hung´gèr) *n.* A strong need or desire for food; a craving for food. **hunger** *v.* **hungrily** *adv.* **hungry** *adj.*

hunk-y-dor-y (hung´kē dōr˘ ē) *adj. Slang* All right; quite satisfactory; comfortable.

hunt (hunt) *v.* To search or look for food; to pursue with the intent of capture; to look in an attempt to find. **hunt** *n.*

hur-dle (hèr´dl) *n.* A portable barrier used to jump over in a race; an obstacle one must overcome. **hurdle** *v.* To leap over.

hur-dy-gur-dy (hèr´dē ger´dē) *n.* A musical instrument where the sound is produced by turning a crank.

hurl (hèrl) *v.* To throw something with great force; in baseball, to pitch. **hurl** *n.* **hurler** *n.*

hur-rah (hu rä´) *interj.* Used to express approval, pleasure, or exultation.

hur-ri-cane (her´i kān˘) *n.* A tropical cyclone with winds exceeding 74 miles per hour, usually accompanied by rain, thunder, and lightning.

hurricane lamp *n.* A lamp or candlestick with a glass chimney to protect the flame against wind.

hur-ry (her´ē) *v.* To move or cause to move with haste. *n.* The act of hurrying. **hurriedly** *adv.* **hurriedness** *n.*

hurt (hèrt) *v.* To experience or inflict with physical pain; to cause physical or emotional harm to; to damage. **hurtful** *adj.* **hurtfully** *adv.* **hurt** *n.*

hur-tle (hèr´tl) *v.* To move rapidly and

often noisily; to hurl with force..

hus-band (huz´band) *n.* A man who is married.

hus-band-ry (huz´ban drē) *n.* Agricultural cultivation, production of plants and animals, especially through scientific control and management.

hush (hush) *v.* To make or become quiet; to calm; to keep secret; to suppress. **hush** *n.* A silence.

husk (husk) *n.* The dry or membranous outer cover of certain vegetables, fruits, and seeds, often considered worthless.

hus-tings *n.* A platform used when making political speeches.

hus-tle (hus´el) *v.* To urge or move hurriedly along; to work busily and quickly. *Slang* To make energetic efforts to solicit business or make money. **hustle, hustler** *n.*

hut (hut) *n.* A small and simply constructed dwelling or shack a cabin.

hutch (huch) *n.* A enclosed area for confining small animals.

huz-zah, huz-za (hu zä´) *interj.* An expression of appreciation or approval.

hy-a-cinth (hī´a sinth) *n.* A bulbous plant that has a cluster of variously colored, highly fragrant, bell-shaped flowers.

hy-a-lite (hī´a līt˘) *n.* A colorless opal, sometimes whitish and sometimes transparent like glass.

hy-a-lu-ron-i-dase (hī´a lu ron´i dās˘) *n.* An enzyme that breaks down the molecules that hold cells together.

hy-brid (hī´brid) *n.* An offspring of two dissimilar plants or of two animals of different races, breeds, varieties, or species; something made up of mixed origin or makeup. **hybrid** *adj.*

hybrid computer A system which consists of a combination of analog and digital computer systems.

hy-brid-ize (hī´bri dīz˘) *v.* To cross, interbreed; to cause to form in a hybrid manner. **hybridization** *n.*

hy-da-tid (hī´da tid) *n.* A fluid-filled cyst that is formed in the bodies of men and certain animals by the tapeworm larva.

hy-dran-gea (hī drān´ja) *n.* A shrub cultivated for its showy clustered pink, white, or sometimes blue flowers.

hy-drant (hī´drant) *n.* A pipe with a valve and spout which supplies water from a main source.

hy-drate (hī´drāt) *n.* A chemical compound formed by the union of water with another substance in definite proportions. **hydrate** *v.* **hydration** *n.*

hy-drau-lic (hī dro´lik) *adj.* Operated, moved, or effected by the means of water; hardening or setting under water. **hydrau-lically** *adv.*

hy-drau-lics (hī dro´liks) *n. pl.* The scientific study that deals with practical applications of liquids in motion and the laws that govern their actions.

hy-dric (hī´drik) *adj.* Characterized by or pertaining to, containing, or requiring moisture.

hy-dro-elec-tric (hī´drō i lek´trik) *n.* Relating to the production of electricity by the use of waterpower.

hy-dro-foil (hī´dro foil´) *n.* A motorboat built with metal plates and fins attached by struts for lifting the hull clear of the water as speed is attained.

hy-dro-gen (hī´dro jen) *n.* A colorless, normally odorless, highly flammable gas that is the simplest and lightest of the elements, symbolized by H.

hy-dro-gen-ate (hī´dro je nāt´) *v.* To combine or treat with hydrogen.

hydrogen bomb *n.* A bomb that is extremely destructive, with an explosive power obtained from the rapid release of atomic energy.

hydrogen peroxide *n.* A colorless, unstable, liquid compound that is used as an antiseptic solution and as a bleach.

hy-dro-me-te-or (hī´drō mē´tē èr) *n.* Any of the various products formed by condensation of atmospheric water vapors, as rain, hail, or fog.

hy-dro-phil-ic (hī´dro fil´ ik) *a.* Having a strong attraction for water; having the ability of dissolving in water.

hy-dro-pho-bi-a (hī´dro fō´bē a) *n.* A fear of water; rabies. **-ic** *adj.*

hy-dro-phone (hī´dro fōn´) *n.* A device for locating causes and transmitting sound under water.

hy-dro-pon-ics (hī´dro pon´iks) *n.* The method of growing plants in chemical solutions instead of soil.

hy-dro-scope (hī´dro skōp´) *n.* A mirror device which enables a person to see at a considerable distance below the surface of the water.

hy-dro–ski (hī´drō skē´) *n.* A hydrofoil, affixed to the fuselage of a seaplane in order to accelerate speed during takeoffs.

hy-dro-sphere (hī´dro sfēr´) *n.* The water on the surface of the globe in oceans, lakes, and all other waters, and the water vapor in the atmosphere.

hy-dro-stat (hī´dro stat´) *n.* The electrical device that detects the presence of water, as from leakage.

hy-dro-tax-is (hī´dro tak´sis) *n.* The reflex movement by an organism in the direction of or away from water.

hy-dro-ther-a-py (hī´dro ther´ a pē) *n.* The scientific use of water in the treatment of disease.

hy-dro-ther-mal (hī´dro thèr´mal) *adj.* Referring or relating to heated water, esp. the action of heated water that dissolves or redistributes minerals.

hy-dro-tho-rax (hī´dro thōr´aks) *n.* The presence of excess serous fluid in the pleural cavities; especially the effusion that results from failing circulation of the heart or lungs. **hydrothoric** *adj.*

hy-drot-ro-pism (hī dro´tro piz˝um) *n. Biol.* A curving or growing toward or away from moisture.

hy-drous (hī´drus) *adj.* Containing water; containing water in a type of chemical union as in hydroxides or hydrates.

hy-drox-ide (hi drok´sī) *n. Chem.* A compound that is formed by the union of an element with one or more hydroxyl groups.

hydroxy acid *n. Chem.* An organic acid composed of a hydroxyl group and a carboxyl group that exhibits characteristics of an alcohol and an acid.

hy-drox-yl (hī drok´sil) *n. Chem.* A radical containing oxygen and hydrogen, found in alcohols, glycols, and hydroxides. **Hydroxylic** *adj.*

hy-dro-zo-an (hī dro zō an) *n.* Class of coelenterate aquatic marine animals.

hy-e-na (hīē´na) *n.* Any of several strong carnivorous mammals of Africa and Asia, with coarse hair and very powerful jaws, having nocturnal habits and feeding mostly on carrion.

hy-e-tal (hī´i tal) *adj.* Relating to rain and its distribution with reference to different regions.

hy-giene (hī´jēn) *n.* The science of the establishment and maintenance of good health and the prevention of disease. **hygienic** *adj.* **hygienically** *adv.*

hy-gi-en-ics (hī´jē en´iks) *n.* The science of cleanliness and cleanliness; hygiene.

hy-gro-graph (hī´gro graf´) *n.* An instrument used to record automatically the variations of moisture content of the atmosphere.

hy-grom-e-ter (hī grom´itèr) *n.* Instrument for measuring the degree of moisture of the atmosphere.

hy-gro-scope (hī´gro skōp´) *n.* Instrument for indicating the presence and approximate amount of moisture in the atmosphere.

hy-gro-ther-mo-graph (hī´gro thèr´mo graf´) *n. Meteor.* The instrument used to register both relative humidity and the temperature on one chart.

hy-la (hī´la) *n.* The tree frog.

hy-men (hī´men) *n.* The thin membrane that partly closes the external vaginal orifice.

hymn (him) *n.* A song of praise giving thanks to God; a song of joy.

hym-nal (him´nal) *n.* A book that contains hymns for worshiping.

hym-no-dy (him´no dē) *n.* The singing or composition of hymns; the collective hymns of a specific locality, era, or denomination. **hymnodist** *n.*

hym-nol-o-gy (him nol´o jē) *n.* The

study, classification, and history of old hymns; the composition of hymns; humns in general. **hymnological** adj.

hy-oid (hī'oid) adj. Referring or relating to the U-shaped movable bone between the root of the tongue and larynx.

hype v. Slang To put on; to stimulate; to promote or publicize extravagantly.

hy-per- pref. Excessive in anything that is performed or done.

hy-per-ac-tive (hī'pêr ak'tiv) adj. Excessively or abnormally active.

hyperbaric chamber n., Med. The airtight chamber that forces oxygen under pressure to a patient's heart and lungs.

hy-per-bo-le (hī per'bo lē) n. Deliberate exaggeration used to cause an effect, not to be taken literally. **hypobolic** adj.

hy-per-chro-mic a-ne-mi-a (hī'pêr kro'mik a nē'mē a) n. An anemia which has an increase in the hemoglobin and a reduction in the number of red blood cells.

hy-per-crit-i-cal (hī'pêr krit'i kal) adj. Being excessively critical.

hy-per-ga-my n. The act of marrying into an equal or higher social group.

hy-per-gly-ce-mia n. An excessive amount of sugar in the blood.

hy-per-gol-ic (hī'pêr ga'lik) adj. Referring to a rocket propellant that ignites upon contact of components without external aid.

hy-per-li-pe-mia n. The presence of excessive fat in the blood.

hy-perm-ne-sia n. The ability of having complete memory or recall of the past.

hy-per-os-to-sis n. An excessive thickening of bone tissue.

hy-per-pha-gia n. An abnormal desire for the consumption of food associated with injury to the hypothalamus.

hy-per-pnea n. Abnormally rapid breathing. **hyperpneic** adj.

hy-per-ten-sion (hi per ten'shan) n. The condition of abnormally high blood pressure especially in the arteries.

hy-per-ven-ti-la-tion n. An excessive rate of respiration leading to loss of carbon dioxide from the blood.

hy-per-vi-ta-min-osis n. An abnormal condition resulting from the excessive use of one or more vitamins.

hy-phen (hī'fen) n. A punctuation mark (-) used to show connection between the parts of a word. **hyphen** v.

hy-phen-ate (hī'fe nāt') v. To separate or join with a hyphen.

hyp-no-sis (hip nō'sis) n. pl. **hypnoses** A state that resembles sleep but is brought on or induced by another person whose suggestions are accepted by the subject.

hyp-not-ic (hip not'ik) adj. Inducing sleep. n. An agent, such as a drug, which induces sleep. **hypnotically** adv.

hyp-no-tize (hip'no tīz') v. To induce hypnosis; to be dazzled by; to be overcome by suggestion.

hy-po (hī'pō) n. pl. **hypos** Slang A hypodermic needle or syringe.

hy-po-chon-dri-a (hī'po kon'drē a) n. A mental depression accompanied by imaginary physical ailments.

hy-po-der-mic sy-ringe (hī'po dêr'mik) n. A syringe and hypodermic needle used for injecting a substance into one's body.

hy-po-gly-ce-mia n. An unusual decrease of sugar in the blood.

hy-po-ten-sion (hī'po ten'shan) n. A condition marked by unusually low blood pressure.

hy-pot-e-nuse (hī pot'e nŭs') n. That side of a right triangle which is opposite the right angle.

hy-po-thal-a-mus (hī'po thal'a mus) n. Anat. The part of the posterior section of the forebrain that composes the floor or base of the third ventricle.

hy-po-the-sis (hī poth'i sis) n. An assumption made in order to draw out and test the logical consequences.

hy-po-thet-e-cal (hī'po thet i cal) adj. Concerning a statement or idea that is not actual fact; theoretical.

hy-po-thy-roid-ism n. A condition which lowers the metabolic rate of the thyroid gland causing loss of vigor.

hy-po-xi-a (hī pok'sē a) n. A condition of a deficiency of oxygen reaching the tissues of the body.

hyp-sog-ra-phy (hip sog'rafē) n. The branch of geography which deals with the measurement of the varying elevations of the earth's surface.

hyp-som-e-ter (hip som'i têr) n. An instrument used to measure altitude by determining the boiling point of a liquid at the given height.

hyp-som-e-try (hip som'i trē) n. The measuring of elevations or altitudes, as related to sea level.

hy-rax (hī'raks) n. A small ungulate mammal with a thickset body, short legs and ears, and a rudimentary tail.

hys-sop (his'op) n. An aromatic herb from the mint family.

hys-ter-ec-to-my (his'te rek'to mē) n., pl. **hysterectomies** Surgery on a female which partially or completely removes the uterus.

hys-ter-ia (hi stēr'ē a) n. A psychological condition characterized by emotional excess and or unreasonable fear.

hys-ter-ic n. A person suffering from hysteria.

hys-ter-i-cal adj. Emotionally out of control. **hysterically** adv.

hys-ter-ics n. A fit of uncontrollable laughter or crying; hysteria.

I, i (ī) The ninth letter of the English alphabet; the Roman numeral for one. *n.* The self; the ego.

I (ī) *pron.* The person speaking or writing. *n.* The self; the ego.

i-amb *or* **i-am-bus** (ī´am) *n.* A metrical foot consisting of a short or unstressed syllable followed by an accented syllable. **iambic** *adj. & n.*

i-at-ric (ī at´rik) *adj.* Pertaining to medicine or a physician.

i-at-ro-gen-ic (ī a´tro jen´ik) *adj.* Induced inadvertently by a physician or his treatment. **iatrogenically** *adv.*

i-bex (ī´beks) *n.* An Old World mountain goat with long curved horns.

i-bi-dem (ib´i dem) *adv.* Used in footnotes to indicate a part of literary work that was just mentioned.

i-bis (ī´bis) *n.* A long-billed wading bird related to the heron and stork.

ice (īs) *n.* Solidly frozen water; a dessert of crushed ice which is flavored and sweetened. *Informal* Extreme coldness of manner. **ice** *v.* To change into ice; to cool or chill; to cover with icing. **icily** *adv.* **iciness** *n.* **icy** *adj.*

ice age *n. Geol.* A time of widespread glaciation.

ice cap (īs´kap´) *n.* An extensive perennial covering of ice and snow that covers a large area of land.

ice cream *n.* A smooth mixture of milk, cream, flavoring, sweeteners, and other ingredients, beaten and frozen.

ich-neu-mon (ik nö´mon) *n.* An animal that feeds on snakes and rodents; a mongoose.

ich-nite (ik´nīt) *n.* A fossil footprint.

ich-nog-ra-phy (ik nog´ra fē) *n.* The ground plan; the study or art of drawing ground plans.

ich-nol-o-gy (ik nol´o jē) *n.* The study of fossil footprints of animals.

ich-thy-oid (ik´thē oid´) *adj.* Exhibiting fish-like characteristics. **ichthyoid** *n.* A fish-like organism. **ichthyoidal** *adj.*

ich-thy-ol-o-gy (ik´thē ol´o jē) *n.* The zoological study of fishes. **ichthyo-logic, -yological** *adj.* **ichthologist** *n.*

ich-thy-or-nis (ik´thē ar´nis) *n.* An extinct bird with a genus of vertebrae like those of fish and with teeth.

ich-thy-o-sis (ik´thē ō´sis) *n.* A hereditary skin disorder represented by thick, scaly skin.

i-ci-cle (ī´si kl) *n.* A hanging spike of ice formed by dripping water that freezes.

i-ci-ly (ī´si lē) *adv.* In an icy manner; coldly, having no warmth.

i-ci-ness (ī´sē nis) *n.* The state of being very cold or icy.

ic-ing (ī´sing)*n.* A sweet preparation for frosting cakes and cookies.

i-con *or* **i-kon** (ī´kon) *n.* A Christian pictorial representation of Jesus Christ, the Virgin Mary, or other sacred figures. In computer science, a graphic image on a monitor screen that represents a directory, file, utility, etc. and that can be selected with a mouse click.

i-con-o-clasm (ī kon´o klaz´um) *n.* The attitude or practice of an iconoclast.

i-con-o-clast (ī kon´o klast´) *n.* One who opposes the use of sacred images; one who attacks traditional or cherished beliefs. **iconoclastic** *adj.*

i-co-nog-ra-phy (ī´ko nog´ra fē) *n.* A pictorial material illustrating a subject; a published work dealing with iconography.

i-co-nol-a-ter (ī´ko nol´a tèr) *n.* A person who worships images or icons.

i-con-o-scope (ī kon´o skōp´) *n.* A cathode ray tube in a television camera that converts light rays into electrical signals.

ic-ter-us (ik´tèr us) *n.* A yellow appearance of certain plants after being exposed to cold and excess moisture; jaundice.

ic-tus (ik´tus) *n. Pathol.* A stroke, seizure, or fit.

id (id) *n. Psych.* The unconscious part of the psyche associated with instinctual needs and drives.

I'd *contr.* I had; I should, I would.

I-da-ho *n.* A state located in the northwest part of the United States; statehood July 3, 1890; state capital Boise.

i-de-a (ī dē´a) *n.* Something existing in the mind; conception or thought; an opinion; a plan of action.

i-de-al (ī dē´al) *n.* A concept or imagined state of perfection; highly desirable; perfect; an ultimate objective; an honorable principle or motive. **ideal** *adj.* Conforming to absolute excellence.

i-de-ate (ī´dē āt´) *v.* To make an idea of something; to think.

i-de-a-tion (ī´dē ā´shan) *n.* The act of forming ideas.

i-dem (ī´dem) *pron. & adj.* The same; used to indicate a previously mentioned reference.

i-dem-po-tent (ī´dem pō´tent) *adj.* Pertaining to a mathematical quantity that is not zero when every positive power equals itself.

i-den-tic (ī den´tik) *adj.* Identical; constituting an expression in which governments follow precisely the same course.

i-den-ti-cal (ī den´ti kal) *adj.* Being the same; exactly equal or much alike; designating a twin or twins developed from the same ovum. **identically** *adv.*

i-den-ti-fi-a-ble (ī den´ti fī´a bl) *adj.* Having the capability of being identified or recognized. **-y** *adv.*

i-den-ti-fi-ca-tion (ī den´ti fi kā´shan) *n.* The act of identifying; the state of being identified; a means of identity.

i-den-ti-fy (ī den′ti fī) v. To recognize the identity of; to establish as the same or similar; to equate; to associate oneself with an individual or group.

i-den-ti-ty (ī den′ti tē) n. pl. **identities** The condition or state of being a specific person or thing and recognizable as such; the condition or fact of being the same as something else; individuality.

id-e-o-gram or **id-e-o-graph (id′ē o gram′)** n. A pictorial symbol used in a writing system to represent an idea or thing, as Chinese characters; a graphic symbol, as $ or %.

id-e-og-ra-phy (id′ē og′ra fē) n. A representation of some ideas by the use of graphic symbols.

i-de-o-log-i-cal (ī dē o loj′i kal) adj. Concerned with ideas.

i-de-ol-o-gist (ī dē ol′o gist) n. A supporter of a particular ideology.

ides (īdz) n. In the ancient Roman calendar, the fifteenth day of March, May, July, and October or the thirteenth day of the other months.

-i-din noun suffix A chemical compound that is related in structure to another compound.

id-i-o comb. form Personal; distinct; separate.

id-i-o-graph-ic (id′ē o graf′ik) adj. Pertaining to the concrete or unique.

id-i-o-lect (id′ē o′lekt) n. The speech pattern of an individual at a period of time in his life. **idiolectal** adj.

id-i-om (id′ē om) n. A form of expression having a meaning that is not readily understood from the meaning of its component words; the dialect of people or a region; a kind of language or vocabulary. **idiomaticness** n.

id-i-o-mat-ic (id′ē o mat′ik) adj. Pertaining to an idiom; being peculiar to a group.

id-i-o-mor-phic (id′ē o mar′fik) adj. To have the right or proper shape.

id-i-o-path-ic (id′ē a path′ik) adj. To be peculiar to an individual.

id-i-ot (id′ē ot) n. A mentally deficient person; an extremely foolish or stupid person.

id-i-ot-ic (id′ē ot′ik) adj. Showing of complete lack of thought or common sense by someone. **idiotically** adv. .

i-dle (īd′l) adj. Doing nothing; inactive; moving lazily; slowly; running at a slow speed or out of gear; unemployed or inactive. **idleness** n. **idler** n.

id-lesse (id′les) n. The state of being idle.

i-do-crase (ī′do krās′) n. A type of mineral which is a complex silicate of calcium, iron, magnesium, and aluminum.

i-dol (īd′ol) n. A symbol or representation of a god or deity that is worshiped; a person or thing adored.

i-dol-a-ter (ī dol′a tèr) n. One who worships idols; blind adoration; devotion.

i-dol-ize (īd′o līz′) v. To admire with excessive admiration or devotion; to worship as an idol. **idolization** n.

i-dyll or **i-dyl (īd′il)** n. A poem or prose piece about country life; a scene, event, or condition of rural simplicity; a romantic interlude. **idyllic** adj.

-ie suff. Little; dear.

if (if) conj. On the condition that; allowing that; supposing or granting that.

if-fy (if′ē) adj. Slang Marked by unknown qualities or conditions.

ig-loo (ig′lō) n. A dome-shaped Eskimo dwelling often made of blocks of snow.

ig-ne-ous (ig′nē us) adj. Geol. Relating to fire; formed by solidification from a molten magma.

ig-nes-cent (ig nes′ent) adj. Being capable of giving off sparks.

ignis fatuus (ig′nis fach′ō us) n. A type of light which will appear over marshy ground in the night; it is often attributable to the combustion of gas from organic matter that is decomposed.

ig-nite (ig nīt′) v. To start or set a fire; to render luminous by heat.

ig-ni-tion (ig nish′an) n. An act or action of igniting; a device or means for igniting the fuel mixture in an engine.

ig-no-min-i-ous (ig′no min′ē us) adj. Mark-ed by or characterized by shame or disgrace; dishonorable. **ignominiousness** n. **ignominiously** adv.

ig-no-min-y (ig′no min′ē) n. A disgraceful conduct or action; dishonor; shame.

ig-no-ra-mus (ig′no rā′mus) n. A totally ignorant person.

ig-no-rant (ig′nêr ant) adj. Lacking education or knowledge; not aware; lacking comprehension.

ig-no-ra-tio e-len-chi (ig′no rāt′ō ō i len′kī) n. An argument to prove or disprove something that is not an issue.

ig-nore (ig nōr′) v. To pay no attention to; to reject. **ignorable** adj.

i-gua-na (i gwä′na) n. A large, dark-colored , herbaceous tropical American lizard that is a food source for the native inhabitants.

i-guan-o-don (i gwä′no don′) n. A member of the genus of the gigantic herbivorous dinosaurs which are from the early Cretaceous period of England.

ike-ba-na (ik-ä bän′e) n. A Japanese art of arranging flowers that emphasizes balance and form.

-ile suffix Capable of; segment of.

il-e-i-tis (il′ē ī′tis) n. Inflammation of the ileum.

il-e-um (il´ē *u***m)** *n. pl.* **ilea** The lower part of the small intestine between the jejunum and the large intestine.

il-e-us (il´ē *u***s)** *n.* A functional obstruction of the bowel.

i-lex (ī´lex) *n.* A type of European evergreen; the genus of holly related shrubs.

il-i-ac (il´ē ak) *n.* Pertaining to the ilium.

Il-i-ad (il´ē ad) *n.* An epic in the Homeric tradition; a series of disastrous events.

il-i-um (il´ē *u***m)** *n.* The largest bone of each internal half of the pelvis.

ilk (ilk) *n.* Sort; kind.

ill (il) *adj.* Not healthy; sick; destructive in effect; harmful; hostile; unfriendly; not favorable; not up to standards. **ill** *adv.* In an ill manner; with difficulty; scarcely. **ill** *n.* Evil; injury or harm; something causing suffering.

I'll *contr.* I will; I shall.

ill–ad-vised (il´ad vīzd´) *adj.* Done without careful thought or sufficient advice.

il-la-tive (i lā´tiv) *n.* A word or phrase which introduces an inference. **illatively** *adv.* **illative** *adj.*

il-laud-a-ble (il lad´dabl) *adj.* To be deserving no praise. **illaudably** *adv.*

ill–bred *adj.* Ill-mannered; impolite; rude; raised improperly.

il-le-gal (i lē´gal) *adj.* Contrary to law or official rules; unlawful.

il-le-gal-ize (i lē´gal īz) *v.* To declare illegal. **illegalization** *n.*

il-le-git-i-mate (il´i jit´i mit) *adj.* Against the law; unlawful; born out of wedlock. **illegitimacy** *n.* **illegitimately** *adv.*

il-lic-it (i lis´it) *adj.* Not permitted by tradition or by law; unlawful.

il-lim-it-a-ble (i lim´i ta bl) *adj.* Incapable of being bounded or limited in any way. **illimitably** *adv.*

Il-lin-ois *n.* A state located in the central part of the northern United States; statehood December 3, 1818; state capital Springfield.

il-lite (il´īt´) *n.* A clay mineral that has essentially the crystal structure of muscovite. **illitic** *adj.*

il-lit-er-ate (i lit´ér it) *adj.* Unable to read and write; uneducated; having or showing a lack of knowledge of fundamentals on a particular subject. **illiteracy** *n.* **illiterately** *adv.*

ill–mannered *adj.* Lacking or showing a lack of good manners; rude.

ill–natured *adj.* Disagreeable or unpleasant disposition. **ill-naturedly** *adv.*

ill–ness (il´nis) *n.* Sickness; a state of being in poor health; the unhealthy condition of one's body or mind.

il-log-ic (i loj´ik) *n.* The state or quality of being illogical.

il-log-i-cal (i loj´i kal) *adj.* Contrary to the principles of logic; not logical.

illogicality *n.* **illogically** *adv.*

ill–tempered *adj.* Having or showing a cross temper or disposition.

ill–treat *v.* To treat someone or something improperly or cruelly. **l–treatment** *n.*

il-lu-mi-nate (il ü´me nāt) *v.* To give light; to make clear; to provide with under-standing; to decorate with pictures or designs; to be or to make spiritually or intellectually enlightened.

il-lu-mi-nism (il ü´me niz´em) *n.* A claim to a personal enlightenment which is not accessible to mankind in general.

il-lu-sion (i lö´zhan) *n.* A misleading perception of reality; an overly optimistic idea or belief; misconception; the action of deceiving; a misleading image presented to ones vision. **illusive, -usory, illusional** *adj.*

il-lus-trate (il´a strāt´) *v.* To explain or clarify, especially by the use of examples; to clarify by serving as an example; to provide a publication with explanatory features. **illustrator** *n.*

il-lus-tra-tion (il´es trā´shen) *n.* The act of illustrating; an example or comparison used to illustrate; a picture or graph to clarify text.

il-lus-tra-tive (il´es tre tiv) *adj.* Serving to illustrate. **illustratively** *adv.*

il-lus-tri-ous (i lus´trē us) *adj.* Greatly celebrated; renowned.

il-lu-vi-a-tion (il ü´vē ā´shen) *n.* A gathering of dissolved soil materials in an area as the result of lenching from another.

il-lu-vi-um (il ü´vē em) *n.* The material that is leached from one soil horizon to another soil horizon.

ill will *n.* Unfriendly or hostile feelings; malice.

I'm (īm) *contr.* I am.

im-age (im´ij) *n.* A representation of the form and features of someone or something; an optically formed representation of an object made by a mirror or lens; a mental picture of something imaginary. **image** *v.* To make a likeness of; to reflect; to depict vividly in language.

image enhancement In *computer science,* altering or improving a graphic image as art or a photograph by use of a computer program.

im-ag-ery (im´ij rē) *n. pl.* **imageries** Mental pictures; images existing in the imagination; figurative language.

im-ag-i-nar-y (i maj´i ner´ē) *adj.* Existing only in the imagination.

imaginary number *n.* A complex number whose imaginary part is not zero, as in $2 + 6i$. Where i is the symbol.

imaginary part *n.* The portion of a complex number which has an imaginary unit as a factor, such as the $3i$ in $7 + 3i$.

imaginary unit *n.* The positive square root of negative one (-1).

im-ag-i-na-tion (i maj´i nā´shan) *n.* The power of forming mental images of unreal or absent objects; such power used creatively; resourcefulness. **imaginative** *adj.* **imaginatively** *adv.*

im-ag-ine (im aj´in) *v.* To form a mental picture or idea of; to suppose; to guess.

imaging In computer science, to create or modify a graphic representation with the use of a computer.

i-ma-go (i mā´gō) *n. pl.* **imagoes** *or* **imagines** An insect in its sexually mature adult stage; the idealized image of self or another person.

i-mam (i mäm´) *n.* A prayer leader of Islam; rulers that claim descent from Muhammad.

im-bal-ance (im bal´ans) *n.* A lack of functional balance; defective coordination.

im-be-cile (im´bi sil) *n.* A mentally deficient person. **imbecilic** *adj.*

im-bibe (im bīb´) *v.* To drink; to take in. **imbiber** *v.*

im-bri-cate (im´bri kāt) *adj.* With edges overlapping in a regular arrangement, as roof tiles or fish scales.

im-bri-ca-tion (im´bri kā´shon) *adj.* A pattern which shows overlapping or a regular arrangement.

im-bro-glio (im brōl´yō) *n. pl.* **imbroglios** A complicated situation or disagreement; a confused heap; a tangle.

im-brue (im brü´) *v.* To drench something.

im-brute (im brüt´) *v.* To degrade someone to the level of that of a brute.

im-bue (im bū´) *v.* To saturate or penetrate, as with a stain or dye.

imdtly *abbr.* Immediately.

im-ip-ra-mine (im ip´re mēn˜) *n.* A kind of antidepressant drug.

im-i-ta-ble (im´et a bl) *adj.* Capable of worthy of imitation.

im-i-tate (im´e tāt) *v.* To copy the actions or appearance of another; to adopt the style of; to duplicate; to appear like

im-i-ta-tion (im e tā´shan) *n.* An act of imitating; something copied from an original. **imitation** *adj.*

im-i-ta-tive (im´e tāt´iv) *adj.* To be marked by imitation. **imitatively** *adv.*

im-mac-u-la-cy (im ak´ū le sē) *n.* The state of something being immaculate.

im-mac-u-late (im ak´ū lit) *adj.* Free from sin, stain, or fault; impeccably clean; without flaw.

im-mane (im ān´) *adj.* To be large or monstrous in character.

im-ma-nent (im´a nent) *adj.* Existing within; restricted to the mind; subjective; inherent. **immanency** *n.*

im-ma-nent-ism (im´a nent iz´em) *n.* A theory according to which God or other spirit is immanent in the world.

im-ma-te-ri-al (im´a tēr´ē al) *adj.* Lacking material body or form; of no importance or relevance. **immaterially** *adv.* **immaterialness** *n.*

im-ma-ture (im´a ter´) *adj.* Not fully grown; undeveloped; suggesting a lack of maturity. **immaturity** *n.*

im-meas-ur-a-ble (i mezh´ér a bl) *adj.* Not capable of being measured.

im-me-di-a-cy (i mē´dē a sē) *n. pl.* **immediacies** The quality of being immediate; directness; something of urgent importance.

im-me-di-ate (i mē´dē it) *adj.* Acting or happening without an intervening object, agent, or cause; directly perceived; occurring at once; close in time, location, or relation.

im-me-mo-ri-al (im´e mōr´ē al) *adj.* Beyond the limits of memory, tradition, or records. **immemorially** *adv.*

im-mense (i mens´) *adj.* Exceptionally large. **immensely** *adv.*

im-merge (im erj´) *v.* To plunge or immerse something or oneself into a medium such as water.

im-me-thod-i-cal (im´e thăd´i kol) *adj.* Not being methodical.

im-mi-grant (im´i grant) *n.* One who leaves his country to settle in another.

im-mi-grate (im´i grāt´) *v.* To leave one country and settle in another.

im-mi-nent (im´i nent) *adj.* About to happen. **imminence** *n.* **imminently** *adv.*

im-min-gle (im in´gl) *v.* To intermingle or to blend into something such as a group; to intermix.

im-mis-ci-ble (im is´i bl) *adj* To be incapable of attaining homogeneity or mixing.

im-mix (im iks´) *v.* To mix intimately; commingle. **im-mixture** *n.*

im-mo-bile (i mō´bil) *adj.* Not moving or incapable of motion **-bility** *n.*

im-mod-er-a-cy (im mad´er a sē) *adj.* The lack of moderation.

im-mod-er-ate (i mod´ér it) *adj.* Exceeding normal bounds.

im-mod-est (i mod´ist) *adj.* Lacking modesty; indecent; boastful. **immodestly** *adv.* **immodesty** *n.*

im-mo-late (im´o lāt´) *v.* To kill, especially by fire, as a sacrifice; to destroy completely. **immolator** *n.*

im-mor-al (im or´al) *adj.* Not moral.

im-mor-al-i-ty (im´o ral´i tē) *n. pl.* **immoralities** Lack of morality; an immoral act or practice.

im-mor-tal (i mort´l) *adj.* Exempt from death; lasting forever, as in fame. **immortal** *n.* A person of lasting fame.

im-mor-tal-ize (i mort´l īz) *v.* To make something immortal. **immortilizer** *n.*

im-mo-tile (im ōt´l) *adj.* Lacking motility; incapable of self movement.

im-mune (i mūn´) *adj.* Not affected or responsive; resistant, as to a disease.

im-mu-no-as-say (im´ū nō as´ā) *n.* An identification of a substance by the way it acts as an antigen.

im-mu-no-dif-fu-sion (im´ū nō dif füzhen) *n.* Separation of antigen complexes into parts by passing them through a semipermeable membrane.

im-mu-no-glob-u-lin (im´ū nō gläb´ū lin) *n.* A type of protein which is made up of heavy and light chains and is used as an antibody by the body.

immunol *abbr.* Immunology.

im-mu-no-sup-pres-sion (im´ū nō se presh´en) *n.* The suppression of the body's natural immune responses.

im-mu-no-ther-a-py (im´ū nō ther´e pē) *n.* The treatment of disease by the means of antigenic preparations or with antigens.

im-mure (i mūr´) *v.* To confine by or as if by walls; to build into a wall.

im-mu-ta-ble (i mū´ta bl) *adj.* Unchanging or unchangeable. **immutability** *n.* **immutably** *adv.*

imp (imp) *n.* A mischievous child.

im-pact (im´pakt) *n.* A collision; the impetus or force produced by a collision; an initial, usually strong effect. **impact** *v.* To pack firmly together; to strike or affect forcefully.

im-pair (im pâr´) *v.* To diminish in strength, value, quantity, or quality. **impairment** *n.* **impairer** *n.*

im-pan-el (im pan´el) *v.* To enroll on a panel; to select a jury.

im-par-a-dise (im par´e dīs) *v.* To enrapture.

im-par-i-ty (im par´itē) *n.* Disparity; inequality.

im-part (im pärt´) *v.* To grant; to bestow; to make known; to communicate. **impartment** *n.* **impartation** *n.*

im-par-tial (im pär´shal) *adj.* Not partial; unbiased; not favoring one over another. **impartiality** *n.*

im-part-i-ble (im pär´ti bl) *v.* Being not subject to partition. **impartibly** *adv.*

im-pass-a-ble (im pas´a bl) *adj.* Impossible to travel over or across. **impassableness** *n.* **impassably** *adv.*

im-passe (im´pas) *n.* A road or passage having no exit; a difficult situation with no apparent way out; a deadlock.

im-pas-si-ble (im pas´i bl) *adj.* Impervious to an injury; not to be moved by passion or sympathy; emotionless.

im-pas-sion (im pash´an) *v.* To arouse the passions of another.

im-paste (im pāst´) *v.* To make or form something into a crust or a paste

im-pas-to (im pas´tō) *n.* A kind of raised decoration on ceramic ware; a heavy layering of paint.

im-pa-tient (im pā´shent) *adj.* Unwilling to wait or tolerate delay; expressing irritation at having to wait; restlessly eager; intolerant. **impatiently** *adv.*

im-pawn (im pän´) *v.* To put or place something in pawn.

im-peach (im pēch´) *v.* To charge with misconduct in public office before a proper court of justice; to make an accusation against. **impeachment** *n.*

im-pec-ca-ble (im pek´abl) *adj.* Having no flaws; perfect; not capable of sin. **impeccably** *adv.* **impeccability** *n.*

im-ped-ance (im pēd´ans) *n.* A measure of the total opposition to the flow of an electric current, specifically in an alternating current circuit.

im-pede (im pēd´) *v.* To obstruct or slow down the progress of.

im-pel (im pel´) *v.* To spur to action; to provoke; to drive forward; to propel.

im-pend (im pend´) *v.* To hover threateningly; to be about to happen.

im-pend-ent (im pend´ent) *adj.* To be near at hand; imminent.

im-pen-e-tra-bil-i-ty (im pen´l tra bil´i tē) *n.* The inability of two parts of anything to occupy the same space at exactly the same time.

im-pen-e-tra-ble (im pen´i tra bl´) *adj.* Not capable of being penetrated; not capable of being seen through or understood; unfathomable.

im-pen-i-tent (im pen´i tent) *adj.* Not sorry; unrepentant. **impenitently** *adv.*

im-per-a-tive (im per´a tiv) *adj.* Expressing a command or request; empowered to command or control; compulsory. **imperative** *n.* **imperatively** *adv.*

im-per-cep-ti-ble (im´per sep´ta bl) *adj.* Not perceptible by the mind or senses; extremely small or slight. **imperceptibly** *adv.* **imperceptibility** *n.*

im-per-cep-tive (im´pēr sep´tiv) *adj.* Not being perceptive.

im-per-cip-i-ence (im´pēr sip´ē ens) *n.* The state of being imperceptive.

imperf *abbr.* Imperfect; imperforate.

im-per-fect (im per´fikt) *adj.* Not perfect; of or being a verb tense which shows an uncompleted or continuous action or condition. **imperfect** *n.* The imperfect tense. **imperfectly** *adv.*

im-per-fo-rate (im per´fēr it)) *adj.* To have no opening; lacking a normal opening.

im-pe-ri-al (im pēr´ē al) *adj.* Of or relating to an empire or emperor; designating a nation or government having dependent colonies; majestic; regal. **imperial** *n.* A pointed beard on the lower lip or chin. **imperially** *adv.*

im-per-il (im per´il) *v.* To put in peril; endanger.

im-pe-ri-ous (im pēr´ē us) *adj.* Commanding; domineering; urgent.

imperiousness *n*. imperiously *adv*.

im-per-ish-a-ble (im per´i sha bl) *adj*. Notperishable; permanently enduring.

im-pe-ri-um (im pēr´ē um) *n*. An absolute dominion; the right to employ the force of the state.

im-per-ma-nent (im per´ma nent) *adj*. Not permanent; not enduring; temporary; transient.

im-per-son-al (im per´so nal) *adj*. Having no personal reference or connection; showing no emotion or personality. impersonally *adv*.

im-per-son-ate (im per´so nāt´) *v*. To assume the character or manner of. impersonation *n*. impersonator *n*.

im-per-ti-nence (im pür´ti nens) *n*. The in-stance of impertinence; rudeness in actions or speech.

im-per-ti-nent (im per´ti nent) *adj*. Overly bold or disrespectful; not pertinent; irrelevant; rude.

im-per-turb-a-ble (im´pėr ter´ba bl) *adj*. Not easily perturbed or agitated. imperturbability *n*.

im-per-vi-ous (im per´vē us) *adj*. Incapable of being emotionally affected or influenced by argument. imperviously *adv*. imperviousness *n*.

im-pe-ti-go (im´pi tī´gō) *n* A contagious skin disease marked by pustules.

im-pe-trate (im´pi trāt´) *v*. To obtain something by a request.

im-pet-u-ous (im pech´ū us) *adj*. Marked by sudden action or emotion; impulsive. -ousness *n*. impetuously *adv*.

im-pe-tus (im´pi tus) *n*. A driving force; an incitement; a stimulus; momentum.

im-pi (im´pē) *n. pl.* impies, impis A brigade or large body of soldiers.

im-pi-ous (im´pē us) *adj* Not pious; irreverent; disrespectful. -ly *adv*.

imp-ish (im´pish) *adj*. Mischievous. impishly *adv*. impishness *n*.

im-pla-ca-ble (im plak´a bl) *adj*. Not capable of being placated or appeased. implacability *n*. implacably *adv*.

im-plant (im plant´) *v*. To set in firmly; to fix in the mind; to insert surgically. implant *n*. implantation *n*.

im-plau-si-ble (im plo´zi bl) *adj*. Difficult to believe; unlikely.

im-plead (im plēd´) *v*. To prosecute by law.

im-ple-ment (im´ple ment) *n*. A utensil or tool. implement *v*. To put into effect; to carry out; to furnish with implements. implementation *n*.

im-pli-cate (im´pli kāt´) *v*. To involve, especially in illegal activity; to imply.

im-pli-ca-tion (im´pli kā´shan) *n*. The act of implicating or state of being implicated; the act of implying; an indirect expression; something implied.

im-plic-it (im plis´it) *adj*. Contained in the nature of someone or something but not readily apparent; understood but not directly expressed; complete; absolute.

im-plode (im plōd´) *v*. To collapse or burst violently inward. implosive *adj*.

im-plore (im plōr´) *v*. To appeal urgently to; to entreat; to beg; to pray pervently. implorer *n*. imploringly *adv*.

im-plo-sion (im plō´shan) *n*. The action of bringing to a center. implosive *adj*.

im-ply (im plī´) *v*. To involve by logical inference; to express indirectly; to suggest.

im-po-lite (im´po līt) *adj*. Rude; uncivil. impoliteness *n*. impolitely *adv*.

im-pol-i-tic (im pol´i tik) *adj*. Not expedient; tactless. impolitically *adv*.

im-pon-der-a-ble (im pon´dėr a bl) *adj*. Incapable of being weighed or evaluated precisely. Imponderable n.

im-port (im pōrt´) *v*. To bring in goods from a foreign country for trade or sale; to mean; to signify; to be significant. import *n*. Something imported; meaning; significance; importance. importer *n*. importable *adj*.

im-por-tance (im pir´tans) *n*. The quality of being important; significance.

im-por-tant (im pir´tant) *adj*. Likely to determine or influence events; significant; having fame or authority; prominent. importantly *adv*.

im-por-tu-nate (im par´cha nit) *adj*. Urgent or persistent in pressing demands or requests; pertinacious. .

im-por-tune (im´ par tön´) *v*. To press with repeated requests; to harass or beset with solicitations; to beg or beg for urgently or persistently.

im-por-tu-ni-ty (im´par tö´ni tē) *n*. State of being importunate; persistence

im-pose (im pōz´) *v*. To enact or apply as compulsory; to obtrude or force oneself on another; to take unfair advantage; to palm off. imposer *n*

im-pos-si-ble (im pos´i bl) *adj*. Not capable of existing or happening; unlikely to take place or be done; unacceptable, difficult to tolerate or deal with. impossibility *n*. -ly *adv*.

im-post (im´pōst) *n*. A tax or duty.

im-pos-tor *or* im-pos-ter (im pos´tėr) *n*. One who assumes a false identity or title for the purpose of deception.

im-pos-tume (im pos´chüm´) *n*. A type of abscess.

im-pos-ture (im pos´chėr) *n*. Deception by the assumption of a false identity.

im-po-tent (im´po tent) *adj*. Without strength or vigor; having no power; ineffectual; incapable of sexual intercourse. impotence *n*. impotency *n*.

im-pound (im pound´) *v*. To confine in or as if in a pound; to seize and keep in legal custody; to hold water, as in a reservoir.

im-pov-er-ish (im pov´ĕr ish) v. To make poor; to deprive or be deprived of natural richness or fertility.

im-prac-ti-cal (im prak´ti kal) adj. Unwise to put into effect; unable to deal with practical or financial matters efficiently. **impracticality** n.

im-pre-cate (im pre kāt´) v. To utter curses or to invoke evil on someone or something.

im-preg-na-ble (im preg´na bl) adj. Incapable of being taken by force.

im-preg-nate (im preg´nāt) v. To make pregnant; to fertilize, as an ovum; to fill throughout; to saturate.

im-pre-sa-ri-o (im´pri sär´ē ō´) n. A theatrical manager or producer, especially the director of an opera company.

im-pre-scrip-ti-ble (im pri skrip´ti bl) adj. Not subject to prescription; referring to rights, not legally to be withdrawn or revoked.

im-press (im pres´) v. To apply or produce with pressure; to stamp or mark with or as if with pressure; to fix firmly in the mind; to affect strongly and usually favorably; to force into public service. **impress** n. The act of impressing; a mark made by impressing; a stamp or seal for impressing.

im-pres-sive (im pres´iv) adj. Making a strong impression; striking. **impressively** adv. **impressiveness** n.

im-pri-ma-tur (im´pri mä´tĕr) n. Official permission to print or publish; authorization.

im-pri-mis (im pri´mis) adv. In the first place.

im-print (im print´) v. To make or impress a mark or design on a surface; to make or stamp a mark on; to fix firmly in the mind. **imprint** n. A mark or design made by imprinting; a lasting influence or effect; a publisher's name, often with the date and place of publication, printed at the bottom of a title page.

im-pris-on (im priz´on) v. To put in prison. **imprisonment** n.

im-prob-a-ble (im prob´a bl) adj. Not likely to occur or be true. **improbability** n. **improbably** adv.

im-pro-bi-ty (im prō´bi tē) n. Lack of principle; dishonesty.

im-promp-tu (im promp´tö) adj. Devised or performed without prior planning or preparation. **impromptu** n. Something said or done without prior thought. **impromptu** adv. Offhandedly; extemporaneously.

improper fraction n. A fraction having a numerator larger than or the same as the denominator.

im-pro-pri-ate (im prō´prē āt´) v. To place valuables, such as the profits of church property, in the hands of a layman. **impropriate** adj.

im-pro-pri-e-ty (im´pro pri´i tē) n., pl. **improprieties** The quality or state of being improper; an improper act or remark.

im-prove (im pröv´) v. To make or become better; to increase something's productivity or value. **improvable** adj.

im-pro-vise (im´pro vīz´) v. To make up, compose, or perform without preparation; to make from available materials. **improviser** n.

im-pru-dent (im pröd´ent) adj. Not prudent; unwise. **imprudence** n.

im-pu-dent (im´pü dent) adj. Marked by rude boldness or disrespect.

im-pu-dic-i-ty (im´pü dis´i tē) n. Shamelessness; immodesty.

im-pugn (im pün´) v. To attack as false; to cast doubt on. **impugner** n.

im-puis-sance (im pü´i sans) n. Weakness; impotence.

im-puis-sant (im pü´i sant) adj. Being weak; powerless.

im-pulse (im´puls) n. A driving force or the motion produced by it; a sudden spontaneous urge; a motivating force; a general tendency. *Physiol.* A transfer of energy from one neuron to another.

im-pul-sive (im pul´siv) adj. Acting on im-pulse rather than thought; resulting from impulse; uncalculated. **impulsively** adv. **impulsiveness** n.

im-pu-ni-ty (im pü´ni tē) n. Exemption from punishment.

im-pure (im pür´) adj. Not pure; unclean; unchaste or obscene; mixed with another substance; adulterated; deriving from more than one source or style.

im-pute (im püt´) v. To attribute something, such as a mistake, to another; to charge.

in (in) prep. A function word that expresses inclusion or presence within a time, place, or circumstances. **in** abbr. Inch. **in** adv. Into a place, state, position, or a relationship; on the inside of a building.

in-a-bil-i-ty (in´a bil´i tē) n. A lack of sufficient power or capacity.

in ab-sen-tia (in´ ab sen chē a) adv. In the absence of.

in-ac-ces-si-ble (in´ak ses´i bl) adj. Not to be reached or approached. **inaccessibility** n. **inaccessibly** adv.

in-ac-cu-ra-cy (in ak´yĕr a sē) n. The state of being inaccurate. **inaccurately** adv.

in-ac-cu-rate (in ak´yĕr it) adj. Not correct; not according to the truth.

in-ac-tion (in ak´shan) n. The lack of activity or action.

in-ac-ti-vate (in ak´ti vāt´) v. To make someone or something inactive.

in-ac-tive (in ak´tiv) adj. Not active or

inclined to be active; out of current use or service. **inactively** *adv.* **inactivity** *n.* **inactiveness** *n.*

in-ad-e-qua-cy (in ad´e kwi sē) *n., pl.* **inadequacies** The instance of being inadequate; insufficiency.

in-ad-e-quate (in ad´e kwit) *adj.* Not adequate; deficient. **inadequately** *adv.*

in-ad-mis-si-ble (in´ad mis´i bl) *adj.* Not admissible; not proper to be allowed, admitted, or received.

in-ad-ver-tence (in´ad ver´tens) *n.* The action of something being inadvertent; an oversight or careless mistake.

in-ad-ver-tent (in´ad ver´tent) *adj.* Unintentional; accidental; inattentive. **inadvertently** *adv.*

in-ad-vis-a-ble (in´ad vī´za bl) *adj.* Not advisable; unwise. **inadvisability** *n.*

in-al-ien-a-ble (in äl´ya na bl) *adj.* Not capable of being given up or transferred. **inalienably** *adv.*

in-al-ter-a-ble (in al´tēr a bl) *adj.* Being not alterable. **inalterability** *n.*

in-am-o-ra-ta (in am´o rä´ta) *n.* The person with whom a person is in love.

in-and-in *adj. & adv.* Being in repeated generations of the same related stock families.

in-ane (i nän´) *adj.* Without sense or substance. **inanely** *adv.*

in-an-i-mate (in an´i mit) *adj.* Not having the qualities of life; not animated. **inanimately** *adv.*

in-a-ni-tion (in´a nish´an) *n.* Exhaustion, especially from malnourishment.

in-an-i-ty (i nan´i tē) *n., pl.* **inanities** The quality of being inane; the lack of substance, sense or ideas; senselessness; emptiness; silliness.

in-ar-gu-a-ble (in-är´gū e bl) *v.* Being not arguable. **inarguably** *adv.*

in-ar-tic-u-late (in´är tik´ū lit) *adj.* Not uttering or forming intelligible words or syllables; unable to speak; speechless; unable to speak clearly or effectively; unexpressed. **inarticulately** *adv.* **inarticulate-ness** *n.*

in-ar-ti-fi-cial (in är´ti fish´al) *adj.* Not artificial; natural.

in-ar-tis-tic (in´är tis´tik) *adj.* Not artistic; lacking artistic appreciation; uninformed on the principles of art.

in-as-much as (in´az much´az´) *conj.* Because of the fact that; since.

in-at-ten-tion (in´a ten´shan) *n.* The failure to pay attention.

in-at-ten-tive (in´a ten´tiv) *adj.* Not attentive; neglectful; heedless.

in-au-di-ble (in a´di bl) *adj.* Not audible; incapable of being heard.

in-au-gu-rate (in i´gū rāt´) *v.* To put into office with a formal ceremony; to begin officially. **inauguration** *n.*

in-aus-pi-cious (in´a spish´us) *adj.* Not auspicious; unlucky; unfavorable.

in-be-tween (in´bē twēn´) *adj.* Intermediate. **in-between** *n.* An intermediate or intermediary.

in between *adv. & prep.* Between.

in-bound (in´bound´) *adj.* Incoming.

in-bounds (in´bounds´) *adj.* Pertaining to putting the ball into play by throwing or passing it onto a court in the game of basketball.

in-breeding (in´brē´ding) *n.* The act of interbreeding individuals which are closely related in order to preserve desirable characteristics of the stock or thing being bred; as animals in the food chain.

in-cal-cu-la-ble (in kal´kya la bl) *adj.* Not calculable; indeterminate; unpredictable; very large. **incalculably** *adv.*

in-can-des-cent (in´kan des´ent) *adj.* Giving off visible light when heated; shining brightly; ardently emotional or intense.

in-can-ta-tion (in´kan tā´shan) *n.* A recitation of magic charms or spells; a magic formula for chanting or reciting.

in-ca-pa-ble (in kā´pa bl) *n.* Lacking the ability for doing or performing

in-ca-pac-i-tate (in´ka pas´i tāt´) *v.* To render incapable; to disable; in law, to disqualify. **incapacitation** *n.*

in-car-cer-ate (in kär´se rāt´) *v.* To confine; enclose.

in-car-na-tion (in´kär nā´shan) *n.* The act of incarnating or state of being incarnated; the embodiment of God in the human form of Jesus; one regarded as personifying a given abstract quality or idea.

in-cen-di-ar-y (in´sen dē´er´ē) *adj.* Causing or capable of causing fires; of or relating to arson; tending to inflame; inflammatory. **incendiary** *n.*

in-cense (in´sens) *n.* To make angry; to perfume with incense; to burn or offer incense. **incense** *n.* A substance, as a gum or wood, burned to produce a pleasant smell; the smoke or odor produced from incense.

in-cen-tive (in sen´tiv) *n.* Something inciting one to action or effort; a stimulus; a motive. **incentive** *adj.* Inciting to action; provocative.

in-cep-tion (in sept´) *n.* A beginning; an origin. **inceptive** *adj.*

in-cer-ti-tude (in ser´ti töd´) *n.* Uncertainty; lack of confidence; instability.

in-ces-sant (in ses´ant) *adj.* Occurring without interruption; continuous; ongoing. **incessantly** *adv.*

in-cest (in´sest) *n.* Sexual intercourse between persons so closely related that they are forbidden by law to marry. **incestuous** *adj.* **incestuously** *adv.*

inch (inch) *n.* A unit of measurement

equal to 1/12th of a foot. *v.* To move slowly.

in-ci-dence (in´si dens) *n.* The extent or rate of occurrence; the matter of being incident; falling upon; the range of influence.

in-ci-dent (in´si dent) *n.* An event; an event that disrupts normal procedure or causes a crisis.

in-ci-den-tal (in´si den´tal) *adj.* Occurring or likely to occur at the same time or as a result of something; minor; subordinate. **incidental** *n.* A minor attendant occurrence or condition.

in-cin-er-ate (in sin´e rāt´) *v.* To burn up. **incineration** *n.*

in-cip-i-ent (in sip´ē ent) *adj.* Just beginning to appear or occur. **incipience** *n.* **incipiently** *adv.*

in-cise (in sīz´) *v.* To make or cut into with a sharp tool; to carve into a surface; to engrave.

in-ci-sion (in sizh´an) *n.* The act of incising; a cut or notch, especially a surgical cut.

in-ci-sive (in sī´siv) *adj.* Having or suggesting sharp intellect; penetrating; cogent and effective; telling. **incisively** *adv.* **incisiveness** *n.*

in-ci-sor (in sī´zėr) *n.* A cutting tooth at the front of the mouth.

in-cite (in sīt´) *v.* To provoke to action. **incitement** *n.* **inciter** *n.*

in-clem-ent (in klem´ent) *adj.* Stormy or rainy; unmerciful. **inclemency** *n.*

in-clin-a-ble (in klī´na bl) *adj.* Having an inclination; favorably disposed.

in-cli-na-tion (in´kli nā´shan) *n.* An attitude; a disposition; a tendency to act or think in a certain way; a preference; a bow or tilt; a slope.

in-cline (in klīn´) *v.* To deviate or cause to deviate from the horizontal or vertical; to slant; to dispose or be disposed; to bow or nod; to cause to bend or lean. **incline** *n.* An inclined surface.

in-cli-nom-e-ter (in´kli nom´i tėr) *n.* An apparatus for indicating the direction of the earth's magnetic field in reference to the plane of the horizon.

in-clude (in klōd´) *v.* To have as a part or member; to contain; to put into a group or total. **included** *adj.*

in-clu-sion (in klō´zhan) *n.* The act or state of including; that which is included.

in-clu-sive (in klō´siv) *adj.* Embracing; comprehensive; including a great deal; covering the specified costs or limits. **inclusively** *adv.* In *computer science*, incorporating as part of the whole, such as the part of a formula in which terms or values joined by the reserved word *AND*, often enclosed by parenthesis, must both be considered in evaluating the formula. **inclusiveness** *n.*

in-co-er-ci-ble (in´kō ür´si bl) *adj.* Not coercible; incapable of being confined or controlled.

in-cog-ni-to (in kog´ni tō´) *adj.* Having a hidden or assumed identity; unknown. *adv.* With the real identity concealed. **incognito** *n.* A person who is in disguise.

in-cog-ni-zant (in kog´ni zant) *adj.* Lacking awareness.

in-co-her-ence (in´kō hēr´ens) *n.* The quality of being incoherent; something incoherent or disorganized.

in-co-her-ent (in´kō hēr´ent) *adj.* Lacking order, connection, or harmony; unable to think or speak clearly or consecutively. **incoherently** *adv.*

in-come (in´kum) *n.* Money or its equivalent received in return for work or as profit from investments.

income tax *n.* A tax on income earned by an individual or business.

in-com-ing (in´kum´ing) *adj.* Coming in or soon to come in.

in-com-men-su-ra-ble (in´ko men´shėr a bl) *adj.* Lacking a basis of comparison; utterly disproportionate.

in-com-men-su-rate (in´ko men´shėr it) *adj.* Not commensurate; disproportionate; inadequate.

in-com-mode (in´ko mōd´) *v.* To inconvenience; to disturb.

in-com-mu-ni-ca-ble (in´ko mū´ni ka bl) *adj.* Not communicable; incapable of being communicated; ineffable.

in-com-pa-ra-ble (in kom´pėr a bl) *adj.* Incapable of being compared; without rival. **incomparably** *adv.*

in-com-pat-i-ble (in´kom pat´a bl) *adj.* Not suited for combination or association; inconsistent. **incompatibility** *n.* **incompatibly** *adv.*

in-com-plete (in´kom plēt´) *adj.* Not complete; unfinished. **incompletely** *adv.* **incompleteness** *n.*

in-com-pre-hen-si-ble (in´kom pri hen´si bl) *adj.* Unable to be understood; unintelligible. **-ibility** *n.*

in-com-pre-hen-sion (in´kom pri hen´shan) *n.* Lack of understanding.

in-com-put-a-ble (in´kom pū´ta bl) *adj.* Incapable of being computed.

in-con-ceiv-a-ble (in´kon sē´va bl) *adj.* Not imaginable; unthinkable; impossible to understand. **inconceivably** *adv.*

in-con-clu-sive (in´kon klō´siv) *adj.* Having no definite result; indefinite.

in-con-den-sa-ble (in´kon den´sa bl) *adj.* Incapable of being condensed.

in-con-dite (in kon´dit) *adj.* Being put together badly; crude.

in-con-gru-i-ty (in´kong grö´i tē) *n. pl.* **incongruities** The quality or state of being incongruous; that which seems out of place.

in-con-gru-ous (in kong´grö us) *adj.* Not corresponding; disagreeing; made up of diverse or discordant elements; unsuited to the surroundings or setting; inappropriate. **incongruously** *adv.*

in-con-sec-u-tive (in˝kon sek´ū tiv) *adj.* Not successive.

in-con-se-quent (in kon´se kwent˝) *adj.* Not logical; irrelevant; disconnected. **inconsequently** *adv.*

in-con-se-quen-tial (in´kon se kwen´shal) *adj.* Without importance; petty. **inconsequentially** *adv.*

in-con-sid-er-a-ble (in´kon sid´ér a bl) *adj.* Not worthy of consideration; unimportant; trivial.

in-con-sid-er-ate (in´kon sid´ér it) *adj.* Not considerate for the feelings of others; thoughtless. **inconsiderately** *adv.* **inconsiderateness** *n.*

in-con-sis-tent (in´kon sis´tent) *adj.* Lacking firmness, harmony, or compatibility; incoherent in thought or actions; not consistent.

in-con-sol-a-ble (in´kon sō´la bl) *adj.* Not capable of being consoled; sad; brokenhearted. **inconsolably** *adv.*

in-con-so-nant (in kon´so nant) *adj.* Not in harmony; discordant.

in-con-spic-u-ous (in´kon spik´ū us) *adj.* Not readily seen or noticed. **inconspicuously** *adv.* **inconspicuousness** *n.*

in-con-stant (in kon´stant) *adj.* Likely to change; unpredictable; faithless; fickle. **inconstancy** *n.*

in-con-trol-la-ble (in´kon trō´la bl) *adj.* Uncontrollable; unmanageable.

in-con-ven-ience (in´kon ven´yens) *n.* The quality or state of being inconvenient; something inconvenient. **inconvenience** *v.* To cause inconvenience to; to bother.

in-con-vert-i-ble (in´kon vür´ta bl) *adj.* Incapable of being exchanged; currency that cannot be exchanged for that of another country.

in-con-vin-ci-ble (in´kon vin´si bl) *adj.* Incapable of being convinced.

in-cor-po-rate (in kor´pu rāt˝) *v.* To combine into a unified whole; to unite; to form or cause to form a legal corporation; to give a physical form to; to embody. **incorporation** *n.*

in-cor-rect (in´ko rekt´) *adj.* Not correct; inaccurate; not true; wrong; improper.

in-cor-rupt-i-ble (in´ko rup´ti bl) *adj.* Not capable of being corrupted morally; not subject to decay. **incorruptibility** *n.* **incorruptibly** *adv.*

in-cras-sate (in-kras´āt) *v.* To make thicker by evaporation or by adding another substance. **incrassate** *adj.*

in-crease (in krēs´) *v.* To make or become greater or larger; to have offspring; to reproduce. **increase** *n.* The act of increasing; the amount or

rate of increasing; something that is added. **increasingly** *adv.*

in-cred-i-ble (in kred´i bl) *adj.* Too unlikely to be believed; unbelievable; extraordinary; astonishing. **incredibility** *n.* **incredibly** *adv.*

in-cred-u-lous (in krej´u lus) *adj.* Skeptical; disbelieving; expressive of disbelief. **incredulity** *n.*

in-cre-ment (in´kre ment) *n.* An increase; something gained or added, especially one of a series of regular additions. **incremental** *adj.*

in-crim-i-nate (in krim´i nāt´) *v.* To involve in or charge with a wrongful act, as a crime. **incrimination** *n.*

in-cu-bus (in´kū bus) *n., pl.* **incubuses** *or* **incubi** An evil spirit believed to seize or harm sleeping persons; a nightmare; a nightmarish burden.

in-cul-cate (in kul´kāt) *v.* To impress on the mind by frequent repetition or instruction. **inculcation** *n.*

in-cul-pa-ble (in kul´pa bl) *adj.* Not culpable; free from guilt or blame.

in-cul-pate (in kul´pāt) *v.* To incriminate.

in-cum-bent (in kum´bent) *adj.* Lying or resting on something else; imposed as an obligation; obligatory; currently in office. **incumbent** *n.* A person who is currently in office. **incumbency** *n.*

in-cur (in ker´) *v.* To become liable or subject to, especially because of one's own actions. **incurrence** *n.*

in-cur-a-ble (in kür´a bl) *adj.* Unable to be cured by medical means.

in-cu-ri-ous (in kür´ē us) *adj.* Lacking interest; detached. **incuriously** *adv.*

in-cur-rent (in kür´ent) *n.* A current that flows inward.

in-cur-sion (in kür´zhan) *n.* A sudden hostile intrusion into another's territory.

in-cus (ing´kus) *n. pl.* **incudes** An anvil-shaped bone in the middle ear of mammals.

in-cuse (in kūz´) *v.* To form or impress by striking or stamping. **incuse** *n.*

in-da-mine (in´da mēn˝) *n.* Basic organic compounds which form blue and green salts, used to manufacture dyes.

in-debt-ed (in det´id) *adj.* Obligated to another, as for money or a favor; beholden. **indebtedness** *n.*

in-de-cent (in dē´sent) *adj.* Morally offensive or contrary to good taste. **indecency** *n.* **indecently** *adv.*

in-de-ci-pher-a-ble (in´di sī´fér a bl) *adj.* Not capable of being deciphered or interpreted; unreadable..

in-de-ci-sion (in´di sizh´an) *n.* Inability to make up one's mind; irresolution.

in-de-ci-sive (in´di sī´siv) *adj.* Without a clear-cut result; marked by indecision. **indecisively** *adv.* **indecisiveness** *n.*

in-de-clin-a-ble (in´di klī´na bl) *adj. Gram.* Not being inflected for case, number, etc..

in-dec-o-rous (in dek´er us) *adj.* Lacking good taste or propriety. **indecorously** *adv.* **indecorousness** *n.*

in-deed (in dēd´) *adv.* Most certainly; without doubt; in reality; in fact. **indeed** *interj.* Used to express surprise, irony, or disbe-lief.

in-de-fat-i-ga-ble (in´di fat´i ga bl) *adj.* Tireless. **indefatigably** *adv.*

in-de-fen-si-ble (in´di fen´si bl) *adj.* Incapable of being justified; not able to protect against a physical fight.

in-def-i-nite (in def´i nit) *adj.* Not decided or specified; vague; unclear; lacking fixed limits. **indefinitely** *adv.* **indefiniteness** *n.*

in-del-i-ble (in del´i bl) *adj.* Not able to be erased or washed away; permanent. **indelibility** *n.* **indelibly** *adv.*

in-del-i-cate (in del´i kit) *adj.* Lacking sensitivity; tactless or crude. **indelicacy** *n.* **indelicately** *adv.*

in-dem-ni-fy (in dem´ni fī´) *v.* To secure against hurt, loss, or damage; to make compensation for hurt, loss, or damage. **indemnification** *n.* **indemnifier** *n.*

in-dent (in dent´) *v.* To set in from the margin, as the first line of a paragraph; to notch the edge of; to serrate; to make a dent or depression in; to impress; to stamp. **indent** *n.* An indentation.

in-den-ture (in den´chèr) *n.* A legal deed or contract; a contract obligating one party to work for another for a specified period of time. **indenture** *v.* To bind into the service of another.

in-de-pend-ence (in´di pen´dens) *n.* The quality or state of being independent.

Independence Day *n.* July 4, a legal holiday in the United States, commemorating the adoption of the Declaration of In-dependence in 1776.

in-de-pend-ent (in´di pen´dent) *adj.* Politically self-governing; free from the control of others; not committed to a political party or faction; not relying on others, especially for financial support; providing or having enough income to enable one to live without working. **independent** *n.* One who is independent, especially a candidate or voter not committed to a political party. **independently** *adv.*

in--depth *adj.* Thorough; detailed.

in-de-scrib-a-ble (in´di skrī´ba bl) *adj.* Surpassing description; incapable of being described. **indescribably** *adv.*

in-de-struc-ti-ble (in´di struk´ti bl) *adj.* Unable to be destroyed.

in-de-ter-mi-na-ble (in´di tér´mi na bl) *adj.* Unable to determine as certain or fixed; not able to be decided.

in-de-ter-mi-nate (in´di tér´mi nit) *adj.* Not determined; not able to be determined; unclear or vague.

in-de-ter-min-ism (in´di tér´miniz´um) *n.* The theory maintaining that not every event has a cause; belief in free will.

in-dex (in´deks) *n., pl.* **indexes** *or* **indices** A list for aiding reference, especially an alphabetized listing in a printed work which gives the pages on which various names, places, and subjects are mentioned; something serving to guide or point out, especially a printed character calling attention to a paragraph or section.

index number *n.* A number which indicates change in a factor, as the cost of living, from one year or reference point chosen arbitrarily to another specified time.

index of refraction *n.* The quotient of the speed of light in a vacuum divided by the speed of light in a medium under consideration.

In-di-an-a (in´dē an a) *n.* A state located in the central part of the northern United States; statehood December 11, 1816; state capital Indianapolis.

Indian Ocean *n.* An ocean that extends from southern Asia to Antarctica and from eastern Africa to southeastern Australia.

in-di-cate (in´di kāt´) *v.* To point out; to show; to serve as a sign or symptom; to signify; to suggest the advisability of; to call for. **indicator** *n.*

in-dic-a-tive (in dik´a tiv) *adj.* Serving to indicate; of or being a verb mood used to express actions and conditions that are objective facts. **indicative** *n.* The indicative mood; a verb in the indicative mood. **indicatively** *adv.*

in-dict (in dīt´) *v.* To accuse of an offense; to charge; to make a formal accusation against by the findings of a grand jury. **indictable** *adj.* **indicter** *n.* **indictor** *n.* **indictment** *n.*

in-dif-fer-ence (in dif´ér ens) *n.* Lack of interest; apathy.

in-dif-fer-ent (in dif´ér ent) *adj.* Having no marked feeling or preference; impartial; neither good nor bad; without interest. **indifferently** *adv.*

in-di-gence (in´di jens) *n.* The condition of real hardship; poverty.

in-dig-e-nous (in dij´e nus) *adj.* Living or occurring naturally in an area; native.

in-di-gent (in´di jent) *adj.* Impoverished; needy.

in-di-ges-tion (in´di jes´chan) *n.* Difficulty or discomfort in digesting food.

in-dig-nant (in dig´nant) *adj.* Marked by or filled with indignation; showing displeasure. **indignantly** *adv.*

in-dig-na-tion (in´dig nā´shan) *n.* Anger aroused by injustice, unworthiness, or unfairness; feelings of disgust.

in-dig-ni-ty (in dig′ni tē) *n. pl.* **indignities** Humiliating treatment; something that offends one's pride.

in-di-go (in′di gō′) *n. pl.* **indigos** *or* **indigoes** A blue dye obtained from a plant or produced synthetically; a dark blue.

in-di-rect (in′di rekt′) *adj.* Not taking a direct course; not straight to the point. **indirection** *n.* **indirectly** *adv.*

in-dis-creet (in′di skrēt′) *adj.* Lacking sound judgment; imprudent; not discreet. **indiscreetly** *adv.*

in-dis-crete (in′di skrēt′) *adj.* Not consisting of distinct parts.

in-dis-cre-tion (in′di skresh′an) *n.* The condition of being indiscreet; want of discretion; lack of discretion.

in-dis-pose (in′di spōz′) *v.* To make or render unfit; to disqualify.

in-dis-posed *adj.* Mildly ill.

in-dis-tinct (in′di stingkt′) *adj.* Not distinct; not sharply outlined; blurred; not clear; confused. **indistinctly** *adv.*

in-dis-tinc-tive (in′di stingk′ tiv) *adj.* Without distinctive characteristics.

in-dite (in dīt′) *v.* To write; to compose; to put down in writing. **inditer** *n.*

in-di-vid-u-al (in′di vij′ō al) *adj.* Of, for, or relating to a single human being. **individually** *adv.* **individual** *n.*

in-di-vis-i-ble (in′di viz′i bl) *adj.* Not able to be divided.

in-doc-tri-nate (in dok′tri nāt′) *v.* To instruct in a doctrine or belief; to train to accept a system of thought uncritically. **indoctrination** *n.*

in-do-lent (in′do lent) *adj.* Disinclined to exert oneself; lazy. **indolence** *n.*

in-dom-i-ta-ble (in dom′i ta bl) *adj.* Incapable of being subdued or defeated.

in-door (in′dōr′) *adj.* Occurring inside a building or house rather than outdoors.

in-duce (in dōs′) *v.* To move by persuasion or influence; to cause to occur; to infer by inductive reasoning.

in-duce-ment (in dōs′ment) *n.* The act of inducing; something that induces.

in-duct (in dukt′) *v.* To place formally in office; to admit as a new member; to summon into military service.

in-duc-tile (in duk′til) *adj.* Not pliable; unyielding.

in-duc-tion (in duk′shan) *n.* The act of inducting or of being inducted; reasoning in which conclusions are drawn from particular instances or facts; the generation of electromotive force in a closed circuit by a magnetic field that changes with time; the production of an electric charge in an uncharged body by bringing a charged body close to it.

in-dulge (in dulj′) *v.* To give in to the desires of, especially to excess; to yield to; to allow oneself a special pleasure. **indulgent** *adj.* **indulger** *n.*

in-dul-gence (in dul′jens) *n.* The practice of indulging; an indulgent act.

in-du-rate (in′dü rāt′) *v.* To make stubborn; to make hardy; to become hard. **indurative** *adj.* **induration** *n.*

in-du-si-um (in dō′zē um) *n.* The covering or outgrowth of a fern.

in-dus-tri-al (in dus′trē al) *adj.* Of, relating to, or used in industry; involved in industrial products.

in-dus-tri-ous (in dus′trē us) *adj.* Working steadily and hard; diligent.

in-dus-try (in′du strē) *n., pl.* **industries** The commercial production and sale of goods and services; a branch of manufacture and trade; industrial management as distinguished from labor; diligence.

in-e-bri-ant (in e′brē ant) *n.* Anything that intoxicates.

in-e-bri-ate (in ē′brē at′) *v.* To make drunk; to intoxicate. **inebriate** *n.* **inebriated** *adj.* **inebriation** *n.*

in-ed-i-ble (in ed′i bl) *adj.* Not edible; not useful as food.

in-ed-it-ed (in ed′i tid) *adj.* Not edited; unabridged.

in-ef-fa-ble (in ef′a bl) *adj.* Beyond expression; indescribable.

in-ef-fec-tive (in′i fek′tiv) *adj.* Not producing intended or desired results; inefficient. **ineffectiveness** *n.*

in-ef-fi-ca-cy (in ef′i ka sē) *n.* Lack of the means or force to achieve the desired results.

in-ef-fi-cient (in′i fish′ent) *adj.* Wasteful of time, energy, or materials. **inefficiency** *n.* **inefficiently** *adv.*

in-el-e-gant (in el′e gant) *adj.* Not elegant; lacking in grace or refinement.

in-el-o-quent (in el′o kwent) *adj.* Not eloquent; not fluent in speech.

in-e-luc-ta-ble (in′i luk′ta bl) *adj.* Not capable of being avoided or overcome.

in-ept (in ept′) *adj.* Awkward or incompetent; not suitable. **ineptitude** *n.* **ineptness** *n.* **ineptly** *adv.*

in-e-qual-i-ty (in′i kwol′i tē) *n. pl.* **inequalities** The condition or quality of being unequal; the lack of evenness.

in-eq-ui-ty *n. pl.* **inequities** Injustice; unfairness.

in-e-qui-valve (in ē′kwi valv′) *adj.* Having valves unequal in size and form, used in reference to a bivalve mollusk.

in-ert (in ert′) *adj.* Not able to move or act; slow to move or act; sluggish; displaying no chemical activity.

in-er-tia (in er′sha) *n.* The tendency of a body to remain at rest or to stay in motion unless acted upon by an external force; resistance to motion or change. **inertial** *adj.* **inertially** *adv.*

in-es-cap-a-ble (in´e skä´pa bl) adj. That which is unavoidable.

in-es-sen-tial (in´i sen´shal) adj. Not necessary or essential.

in-es-ti-ma-ble (in es´ti ma bl) adj. Unable of being estimated or computed; too great to be fully appreciated.

in-ev-i-ta-ble (in ev´i ta bl) adj. Not able to be avoided or prevented. inevitability n. inevitably adv.

in-ex-cus-a-ble (in´ik skü´za bl) adj. Unpardonable; indefensible.

in-ex-haust-i-ble (in´ig zas´ti bl) adj. Not exhaustible; unfailing; tireless.

in-ex-ist-ence (in´ig zis´tens) n. Nonexistence.

in-ex-is-tent adj. Not existent.

in-ex-o-ra-ble (in ek´sèr a bl) adj. Not capable of being moved by entreaty; unyielding. inexorably adv.

in-ex-pe-di-ent (in´ik spē´dē ent) adj. Not expedient; inappropriate.

in-ex-pen-sive (in´ik spen´siv) adj. Not expensive; cheap.

in-ex-pe-ri-ence (in´ik spēr´ē ens) n. The lack of experience; without knowledge.

in-ex-pert (in eks´pèrt) adj. Unskilled.

in-ex-pi-a-ble (in eks´pē a bl) adj. Incapable of being expiated; unpardonable.

in-ex-pli-ca-ble (in eks´pli ka bl) adj. Not capable of being explained; unable to be interpreted. inexplicably adv.

in-ex-pli-cit (in´ik splis´it) adj. Not explicit; not clearly stated.

in-ex-pres-sive (in´ik spres´iv) adj. Not expressive; wanting in meaning.

in-ex-pug-na-ble (in´ik spug´na bl) adj. Cannot be overcome or taken by force; impregnable.

in-ex-tin-guish-a-ble (in ik sting´gwisha bl) adj. Not to be extinguished.

in ex-tre-mis (in ex trēm´is) adv. At the point of death.

in-fal-li-ble (in fal´i bl) adj. Not capable of making mistakes; not capable of failing; never wrong. infallibility n.

in-fa-mous (in´fa mus) adj. Having a very bad reputation; shocking or disgraceful. infamously adv.

in-fant (in´fant) n. A child in the first period of life; a very young child; in law, a minor.

in-fan-ti-cide (in fan´ti sīd´) n. The killing of an infant.

in-fan-ti-lism (in´fan ti liz˝um) n. Abnormal recurrence of childish characteristics; a lack of mature emotional development.

in-farct (in färkt´) n. An area of dead tissue caused by an insufficient supply of blood. infarcted adj. infarction n.

in-fat-u-ate (in fach´ū āt´) v. To arouse an extravagant or foolish love in. infatuated adj. infatuation n.

in-fect (in fekt´) v. To contaminate with disease-producing organisms; to transmit a disease to; to affect as if by contagion. infecter n.

in-fec-tion (in fek´shan) n. Invasion of a bodily part by disease-producing organisms; the condition resulting from such an invasion; an infectious disease.

in-fec-tious (in fek´shus) adj. Causing infection; communicable by infection, as diseases; contagious; catching.

in-fe-cund (in fē´kund) adj. Barren; not fruitful.

in-fe-lic-i-tous adj. Not happy; unfortunate; not apt, as in expression.

in-fe-lic-i-ty (in´fe lis´i tē) n. pl. infelicities The state of being unhappy.

in-fer (in fer´) v. To conclude by reasoning; to deduce; to have as a logical consequence; to lead to as a result or conclusion. inferable adj.

in-fer-ence (in´fèr ens) n. A conclusion based on facts and premises.

in-fe-ri-or (in fēr´ē èr) adj. Located under or below; low or lower in order, rank, or quality. inferiority n.

inferiority complex n. An acute sense of personal inferiority resulting in withdrawal from social contact or aggression.

in-fer-tile (in fèr´tfl) adj. Not fertile or fruitful; barren. infertility n.

in-fest (in fest´) v. To spread so as to be harmful or offensive, as a swarm of mosquitos. infestation n.

in-fi-del (in´fi del) n. One who has no religion; an unbeliever in a religion.

in-fi-del-i-ty (in´fi del´i tē) n., pl. infidelities The lack of faith or belief; unfaithfulness to a moral obligation; adultery.

in-fi-nite (in´fi nit) adj. Without boundaries; limitless; immeasurably great or large; in mathematics, greater in value than any specified number, however large; having measure that is infinite.

in-fin-i-tes-i-mal (in´fin i tes´i mal) adj. Immeasurably small. -lly adv.

in-fin-i-tive (in fin´l tiv) n. A verb form which expresses the meaning of the verb without specifying number or person; it can function as a noun, usually preceded by to.

in-fin-i-ty (in fin´i tē) n. pl. infinities The quality or state of being infinite; unbounded space, time, or amount; an inde-finitely large number.

in-firm (in ferm´) adj. Physically weak, especially from age; feeble; in law, not sound or valid.

in-fir-ma-ry (in fer´ma rē) n. pl. infirmaries An institution for the care of the sick or disabled.

in-flam-ma-ble (in flam´a bl) adj. Tending to catch fire easily; easily excited.

in-flam-ma-tion (in´flɑ mā´shɑn) *n.* Localized redness, swelling, heat, and pain in response to an injury or infection.

in-flam-ma-to-ry (in flam´ɑ tŏr´ē) *adj.* Tending to excite or anger, to inflame, anger. *Med.* Causing inflammation, usually accompanied by heat.

in-fla-tion (in flā´shɑn) *n.* The act or process of inflating; a period during which there is an increase in the monetary supply, causing a continuous rise in the price of goods. **-nary** *adj.*

in-flict (in flikt´) *v.* To cause to be suffered; to impose. **inflicter** *n.* **inflictor** *n.* **infliction** *n.*

in-flo-res-cence (in´flō res´ens) *n.* A characteristic arrangement of flowers on a stalk. **inflorescent** *adj.*

in-flu-ence (in´flō ens) *n.* The power to produce effects, especially indirectly or through an intermediary; the condition of being affected; one exercising indirect power to sway or affect. **influence** *v.* To exert influence over; to modify. **influential** *adj.*

in-flu-en-za (in´flō en´za) *n.* An acute, infectious viral disease marked by respiratory inflammation, fever, muscular pain, and often intestinal discomfort; the flu.

in-flux (in´fluks´) *n.* A stream of people or things coming in.

in-for-mal (in for´mɑl) *adj.* Not in usual form; unofficial; casual or relaxed.

in-form-ant (in for´mɑnt) *n.* One who discloses or furnishes information which should remain secret.

in-for-ma-tion (in´fŏr mā´shɑn) *n.* The news communicated by word or in writing; data or facts; knowledge gained from reading or instruction, or gathered in another way. In computer science, any data that can be stored, retrieved and manipulated by a computer.

information management In *computer science*, the systems and techniques involved in effectively compiling and manipulating useful data.

information processing In *computer science*, the manipulation of compiled data and the compilation of reports from the data.

information retrieval In *computer science*, descriptive of the techniques for accessing data from storage in the form or pattern that the user desires.

information theory *n.* The statistical study or theory that deals with the processes and efficiency of transmitted messages, as in a computer or telecommunications.

in-for-ma-tive (in for´mɑ tiv) *adj.* Providing information; instructive.

in-frac-tion (in frak´shɑn) *n.* A violation of a rule.

in-fran-gi-ble (in fran´ji bl) *adj.* Not capable of being broken into parts; unbreakable.

in-fra-son-ic (in´fra son´ik) *adj.* Producing or using frequencies below those of audible sound.

in-fra-struc-ture (in´fra struk´chèr) *n.* An underlying base or foundation; the basic facilities needed for the functioning of a system.

in-fre-quent (in frē´kwent) *adj.* Seldom; not occurring frequently; rare; occasional. **infrequently** *adv.*

in-fringe (in frinj´) *v.* To break a law; to violate; to encroach; to trespass.

in-fun-dib-u-lum (in´fun dib´ū lɑm) *n.* The funnel-shaped portion of the third ventricle in the brain that leads to the pituitary gland; the calyx of a kidney; the funnel-shaped abdominal opening of the fallopian tube.

in-fu-ri-ate (in fŭr´ē āt´) *v.* To make very angry or furious; to enrage. **infuriatingly** *adv.* **infuriation** *n.*

in-fuse (in fūz´) *v.* To pour into; introduce, instill or inculcate; to obtain a liquid extract by soaking a substance in water.

-ing *suffix* Used in forming nouns and adjectives from verbs showing activity or action; the result or a product of an action.

in-gem-i-nate (in jem´i nāt´) *v.* To repeat.

in-gen-ious (in jēn´yus) *adj.* Showing great ingenuity; to have inventive ability; clever. **ingeniously** *adv.*

in-ge-nu-i-ty (in´je nō´i tē) *n., pl.* **ingenuities** Cleverness; inventive skill.

in-gen-u-ous (in jen´ū us) *adj.* Frank and straightforward; lacking sophistication.

in-gest (in jest´) *v.* To take or put food into the body by swallowing. **ingestion** *n.* **ingestive** *adj.*

in-got (ing´got) *n.* A mass of cast metal shaped in a bar or block.

in-gre-di-ent (in grē´dē ent) *n.* An element that enters into the composition of a mixture; a part of anything.

in-gress (in´gres) *n.* A going in or entering of a building; an entrance. **ingression** *n.* **ingressive** *adj.*

in-grown (in´grōn´) *adj.* Growing into the flesh; growing abnormally within or into. **ingrowing** *adj.*

in-gur-gi-tate (in gur´ji tāt´) *v.* To swallow greedily or in great quantity.

in-hab-it (in hab´it) *v.* To reside in; to occupy as a home; where people live or work. **inhabitability** *n.* **inhabiter** *n.* **inhabitation** *n.* **inhabitable** *adj.*

in-hab-i-tant (in hab´i tant) *n.* A person who occupies a residence permanently, as distinguished from someone who visits.

in-hal-ant (in hā´lant) *n.* Something that

is inhaled. *adj.* Inhaling; used for inhaling.

in-hale (in´hāl´) *v.* To breathe or draw into the lungs, as air or tobacco smoke; the opposite of exhale.

in-her-ent (in hēr´ent) *adj.* Forming an essential element or quality of something. **inherently** *adv.*

in-her-it (in her´it) *v.* To receive something, as property, money, or other valuables, by legal succession or will. *n, Biol.* To receive traits or qualities from one's ancestors or parents. **inheritable** *adj.* **inheritor** *n.*

in-he-sion (in hē´zhαn) *n.* The fact of becoming a permanent part of something.

in-hib-it (in hib´it) *v.* To restrain or hold back; to prevent full expression. **inhibitor** *n.* **inhibiter** *n.* **inhibitive** *adj.*

in-hi-bi-tion (in´i bish´αn) *n.* The act of restraining, especially a self-imposed restriction on one's behavior; a mental or psychological restraint.

in-hos-pi-ta-ble (in hos´pi tα bl) *adj.* Not showing hospitality; not friendly or receptive; uninviting. **inhospitable-ness** *n.* **inhospitably** *adv.*

in-hu-mane (in´hū mān´) *adj.* Lacking compassion or pity; cruel. **-ly** *adv.*

in-hu-man-i-ty (in´hū man´i tē) *n. pl.* **inhumanities** The lack of compassion or pity; an inhumane or cruel act.

in-iq-ui-ty (i nik´wi tē) *n. pl.* **iniquities** The grievous violation of justice; wickedness; sinfulness. **iniquitous** *adj.*

in-i-tial (i nish´αl) *adj.* Of or pertaining to the beginning. **initial** *n.* The first letter of a name or word. **initial** *v.* To mark or sign with initials. **initially** *adv.*

initialize In *computer science,* to format a disk to accept data; to boot up a computer by loading the system files it needs to become functional.

in-i-ti-a-tive (i nish´ē α tiv) *n.* The ability to originate or follow through with a plan of action; the action of taking the first or leading step. *Govt.* The power or right to propose legislative measures.

in-ject (in jekt´) *v.* To force a drug or fluid into the body through a blood vessel or the skin with a syringe; to throw in or introduce a comment abruptly. **injection** *n.* **injectable** *adj.*

in-ju-di-cious (in´jō dish´us) *adj.* To act without discretion or sound judgment; unwise. **injudiciously** *adv.*

in-junc-tion (in jungk´shαn) *n.* An authoritative command or order; in law, a court order requiring a person to refrain from some specified action.

in-jure (in´jĕr) *v.* To cause physical harm, damage, or pain.

in-ju-ri-ous (in jer´ē us) *adj.* Causing injury, damage or hurt; slanderous; abusive. **injuriously** *adv.*

in-ju-ry (in´je rē) *n., pl.* **injuries** Damage or harm inflicted or suffered.

in-jus-tice (in jus´tis) *n.* The violation of another person's rights; an unjust act; a wrong; lack of fairness.

ink jet printer In *computer science,* a printer that forms images from tiny jets of ink sprayed on paper.

in-laid (in´lād´) *adj.* Ornamented with wood, ivory, or other materials embedded flush with the surface.

in--law (in´law) *n.* A relative by marriage.

in-lay (in´lā´) *v.* To set or embed something, as gold or ivory, into the surface of a decorative design. **inlay** *n.* An inlaid surface; a filling cemented into a tooth cavity.

in-let (in´let) *n.* A bay or stream that leads into land; a passage between nearby islands.

in-most (in´mōst´) *adj.* Farthest or deepest within; farthest from the surface or outside; secret, as feelings..

inn (in) *n.* A place of lodging where a traveler may obtain meals and lodging for the night.

in-nards (in´ĕrdz) *n.* The internal parts of the body; the inner parts of a machine.

in-nate (i nāt´) *adj.* Inborn and not acquired; having as an essential part; inherent. **innately** *adv.*

in-ner (in´ĕr) *adj.* Situated or occurring farther inside; relating to or of the mind or spirit; internal.

in-ner-vate (i nur´vāt) *v.* To supply with nerves or nervous energy.

in-ner-va-tion (i nur vā shun) *n.* The communicating of nervous energy by means of nerves; the stimulation of some part or organ through its nerves.

in-no-cent (in´o sent) *adj.* Free from sin, evil, or moral wrong; pure; legally free from blame or guilt; not maliciously intended; lacking in experience or knowledge; naive. **innocence** *n.*

in-no-vate (in´o vāt´) *v.* To introduce or begin something new. **innovative** *adj.* **innovator** *n.* **innovation** *n.*

in-nu-en-do (in´ū en´dō) *n. pl.* **innuendos** *or* **innuendoes** An indirect or oblique comment, suggestion or hint.

in-nu-mer-a-ble (i nŏ´mĕr α bl) *adj.* Too numerous; too much to be counted; countless. **innumerableness** *n.*

in-oc-u-late (i nok´ū lāt´) *v.* To introduce a mild form of a disease or virus to a person or animal in order to produce immunity. **inoculation** *n.*

in-op-er-a-ble (in op´ĕr α bl) *adj.* Unworkable; incapable of being treated or improved by surgery.

in-op-er-a-tive (in op´ĕr α tiv) *adj.* Not working; not functioning.

in-op-por-tune (in op´ĕr tŏn´) *adj.* Inappropriate; untimely; unsuitable.

in-or-di-nate (in ir´di nit) *adj.* Exceeding proper or normal limits; not regulated; unrestrained. **inordinately** *adv.*

in-or-gan-ic (in´ir gan´ik) *adj.* Not having or involving living organisms, their remains, or products.

in-os-cu-late (in os´ku lāt´) *v.* To unite into a continuous system by connecting open ends, as nerve fibers and arteries.

in-pa-tient (in´pā´shent) *n.* A patient admitted to a hospital for medical treatment.

in-per-so-nam (in pèr sō´nam) *adv.* Referring to a legal action against a person and not against specific things.

in-put (in´pŭt´) *n.* The amount of energy delivered to a machine; in computer science, information that is put into a data processing system. *Elect.* The voltage, current, or power that is delivered to a circuit. **input** *n.* In *computer science,* to supply data for processing.

input device In *computer science,* any equipment linked to the computer that enters source data, such as a keyboard, an optical scanner or a modem.

in-quest (in´kwest) *n.* A legal investigation into the cause of death.

in-quire (in kwïer´) *v.* To ask a question; to make an investigation. **inquirer** *n.*

in-quir-y (in kwïer´ē) *n. pl.* **inquiries** The act of seeking or inquiring; a request or question for information; a very close examination; an investigation or examination of facts or evidence.

in-quis-i-tive (in kwiz´i tiv) *adj.* Curious; probing; questioning. **inquisitively** *adv.*

in-sane (in sān´) *adj.* Afflicted with a mental disorder impairing a person's ability to function; showing the characteristics of a person who is not sane. **insanely** *adv.*

in-sa-tia-ble (in sā´sha bl) *adj.* Incapable of being satisfied. **insatiability, insatiableness** *n.* **insatiably** *adv.*

in-scribe (in skrïb´) *v.* To write, mark, or engrave on a durable surface; to enter a name in a register or on a formal list; to write a short note on a card. *Geometry* To enclose one figure in another so that the latter encloses the former. **inscriber** *n.*

in-sect (in sekt´) *n. Zool.* Any of a numerous class of small to minute winged arthropods with three pairs of legs, a segmented body, and usually two pairs of wings; a contemptible person.

in-se-cure (in´si kūr´) *adj.* Troubled by anxiety and apprehension; threatened; not securely guarded; unsafe; liable to break, fail, or collapse; precarious. **insecurely** *adv.* **insecurity** *n.*

in-sem-i-nate (in sem´i nāt´) *v.* To introduce semen into the uterus of; to make pregnant; to sow or implant seed.

in-sen-sate (in sen´sāt) *adj.* Showing a lack of humane feeling; unconscious; unable to experience sensations.

in-sen-si-ble (in sen´si bl) *adj.* Deprived of consciousness; unconscious; incapable of perceiving or feeling; unmindful; unaware. **insensibility** *n.*

in-sep-a-ra-ble (in sep´ér a bl) *adj.* Incapable of being separated or parted. **inseparability** *n.* **inseparably** *adv.*

in-sert (in sert´) *v.* To put in place; to set. **insert** *n.* In printing, something inserted or to be inserted. **-tion** *n.*

in-side (in´sïd´) *n.* The part, surface, or space that lies within. **insides** *n. pl.* The internal parts or organs. **inside** *adj.*

in-sid-er (in´sï´dér) *n.* One having special knowledge or access to confidential information.

in-sid-i-ous (in sid´ē us) *adj.* Cunning or deceitful; treacherous; seductive; attractive but harmful. **insidiously** *adv.*

in-sight (in´sït´) *n.* Perception into the true or hidden nature of things. **insightful** *adj.* **insightfully** *adv.*

in-sig-nif-i-cant (in´sig nif´i kant) *adj.* Lacking meaning importance, influence, or character; unimportant.

in-sin-cere (in´sin sēr´) *adj.* Not sincere; hypocritical. **insincerely** *adv.*

in-sin-u-ate (in sin´ū āt´) *v.* To suggest something by giving a hint; to introduce by using ingenious and sly means. **insinuating** *adv.*

in-sist (in sist´) *v.* To demand or assert in a firm way; to dwell on something repeatedly, as to emphasize. **insistence** *n.* **insist-ent** *adj.* **insistently** *adv.*

in-so-bri-e-ty (in´so brï´e tē) *n.* The lack of moderation; drunkenness.

in-so-far (in´so fär´) *adv.* To such an extent.

in-so-lent (in´so lent) *adj.* To be insultingly contemptuous in one's speech; overbearing. *n.* A rude disrespectful person. **insolently** *adv.*

in-sol-vent (in´sol´vent) *adj. In law,* unable to meet debts; bankrupt.

in-som-ni-a (in som´nē a) *n.* The chronic inability to sleep. **insomniac** *n.*

in-sou-ci-ant (in sö´sē ant) *adj.* Lighthearted and cheerful; unconcerned; not bothered. **insouciance** *n.*

in-spect (in spekt´) *v.* To examine or look at very carefully for flaws; to examine or review officially. **inspection** *n.*

in-spec-tor (in spek´tér) *n.* One who reviews or examines something critically.

in-spi-ra-tion (in´spi rā´shan) *n.* The stimulation within the mind of some idea, feeling, or impulse which leads to creative action; a divine or holy presence which inspires; the act of inhaling air. **inspirational** *adj.*

in-spire (in spīėr´) *v.* To exert or guide by a divine influence; to arouse and create high emotion; to exalt; to inhale; breathe in. **inspirer** *n.* **inspiringly** *adv.*

in-sta-bil-i-ty (in´sta bil´i tē) *n. pl.* **instabilities** Lacking stability.

installation In *computer science*, the process of setting up and configuring a computer system or program; the computer system so installed.

in-stall-ment (in stal´ment) *n.* One of several payments due in specified amounts at specified intervals.

in-stance (in´stans) *n.* An illustrative case or example; a step in proceedings. **instance** *v.* To illustrate.

in-stant (in´stant) *n.* A very short time; a moment; a certain or specific point in time. **instant** *adj.* Instantaneously; immediate; urgent.

in-stan-ta-ne-ous (in´stan tā´nē us) *adj.* Happening with no delay; instantly; completed in a moment.

in-stant-ly (in´stant lē) *adv.* Immediately; at once.

in-stead (in sted´) *adv.* In lieu of that just mentioned.

in-sti-gate (in´sti gāt´) *v.* To urge forward; to stir up; to foment; to provoke. **instigation** *n.* **instigator** *n.*

in-still (in stil´) *v.* To introduce by gradual instruction or effort; to pour in slowly by drops. **instillation** *n.*

in-stinct (in´stingkt) *n.* The complex and normal tendency or response of a given species to act in ways essential to its existence, development, and survival. **instinctive** *adj.* **instinctively** adv.

in-sti-tute (in´sti tōt´) *v.* To establish or set up; to find; to initiate; to set in operation; to start. **institute** *n.* An organization set up to promote or further a cause; an institution for educating.

in-sti-tu-tion (in´sti tō´shan) *n.* The principle custom that forms part of a society or civilization; an organization which performs a particular job or function, such as research, charity, or education; a place of confinement such as a prison or mental hospital. **institutionalize** *v.* **institutional** *adj.*

in-struct (in strukt´) *v.* To impart skill or knowledge; to teach; to give orders or direction. **instructive** *adj.*

in-struc-tion (in struk´shan) *n.* The act of teaching or instructing; important knowledge; a lesson; an order or direction. In *computer science*, a direction to the computer to set a parameter or execute an operation. **instruction format** In *computer science*, the syntax required by a particular program for issuing a command.

in-struc-tor (in struk´tér) *n.* One who

instructs; a teacher; a low-rank college teacher, not having tenure.

in-stru-ment (in´stru ment) *n.* A mechanical tool or implement; a device used to produce music; a person who is controlled by another; a dupe; in law, a formal legal document, deed, or contract.

in-stru-men-ta-tion (in´stru men tā´shan) *n.* The use of instruments or work performed with instruments. *n., Mus.* The arrangement of music for instruments.

in-sub-or-di-nate (in´su bor´di nit) *adj.* Not obedient; not obeying orders. **insubordinately** *adv.* **-tion** *n.*

in-sub-stan-tial (in´sub stan´shal) *adj.* Lacking substance or material nature; slight; imaginary; unreal; lacking firmness.

in-suf-fer-a-ble (in suf´ér a bl) *adj.* Not to be suffered; unendurable; intolerable.

in-suf-fi-cient (in´su fish´ent) *adj.* Inadequate; not enough. **insufficiently** *adv.* **insufficiency** *n.*

in-su-late (in´su lāt´) *v.* To isolate; to wrap or surround with nonconducting material in order to prevent the passage of heat, electricity, or sound into or out of; to protect with wrapping or insulation. **insulation** *n.* **insulator** *n.*

in-su-lin (in´su lin) *n., Biochem.* The hormone released by the pancreas, essential in regulating the metabolism of sugar; a preparation of this hormone removed from the pancreas of a pig or an ox, used in the treatment of diabetes.

in-sult (in´sult) *v.* To speak or to treat with insolence or contempt; to abuse verbally. **insult** *n.* An act or remark that offends someone. **insulter** *n.* **insulting** *adj.* **insultingly** *adv.*

in-sup-press-i-ble (in´su pres´i bl) *adj.* Incapable of being concealed or suppressed.

in-sur-ance (in shur´ans) *n.* Protection against risk, loss, or ruin; the coverage an insurer guarantees to pay in the event of death, loss, or medical bills; a contract guaranteeing such protection on future specified losses in return for annual payments; any safeguard against risk or harm.

in-sur-mount-a-ble (in´sér moun´ta bl) *adj.* Incapable of being overcome.

in-sur-rec-tion (in´su rek´shan) *n.* An open revolt against an established government. **insurrectionary** *adj. & n.* **insurrectional** *adj.* **-tionist** *n.*

in-sus-cep-ti-ble (in´su sep´ta bl) *adj.* Immune; incapable of being infected. **insusceptibility** *n.*

in-tact (in takt´) *adj.* Remaining whole and not damaged in any way.

in-take (in´tāk´) *n.* The act of taking in

or absorbing; the amount or quantity taken in or absorbed.

in-tan-gi-ble (in tan´ji bl) *adj.* Incapable of being touched; vague or indefinite to the mind. **intangibility** *n.* **intangibleness** *n.* **intangibly** *adv.*

in-te-ger (in´ti jër) *n.* Any of the numbers 1, 2, 3, etc., including all the positive whole numbers and all the negative numbers and zero; a whole entity.

in-te-gral (in´te gral) *adj.* Being an essential and indispensable part of a whole; made up, from, or formed of parts that constitute a unity.

integral calculus *n.* A branch of mathematical concerned with integrals and integration, their use in the solution of differential equations and problems that involve lengths, volumes, and areas.

in-te-grate (in´te grāt´) *v.* To make into a whole by joining parts together; to unify; to be open to people of all races or ethnic groups. **integration** *n.*

integrated circuit In *computer science*, an electronic device that contains a number of circuit elements working together.

integrated software In *computer science*, descriptive of applications that are able to share data; a program package that offers a combination of features, such as a word processor, spreadsheet, and database capability.

integrated system In *computer science*, a combination of computers and peripherals that are compatible.

in-teg-ri-ty (in teg´ri tē) *n.* Uprightness of character; honesty; the condition, quality, or state of being complete or undivided.

in-tel-lect (in´te lekt´) *n.* The power of the mind to understand and to accept knowledge; the state of having a strong or brilliant mind; a person of notable intellect.

in-tel-li-gent (in tel´i jent) *adj.* Having or showing intelligence.

in-tel-li-gi-ble (in tel´i ji bl) *adj.* Having the capabilities of being understood; understanding.

in-tem-per-ance (in tem´pêr ans) *n.* The lack of moderation, as in satisfying of the appetite or of one's passion for something; excess in anything.

in-tend (in tend´) *v.* To have a plan or purpose in mind; to design for a particular use. **intender** *n.*

in-ten-er-ate (in ten´e rāt´) *v.* To cause or to make something tender or softer than it was to begin with.

in-tense (in tens´) *adj.* Extreme in strength, effect, or degree; expressing strong emotion, concentration, or strain; profound. **intensely** *adv.* **-ness** *n.*

in-ten-si-fy (in ten´si fī´) *v.* To become

or make more intense or acute.

in-ten-si-ty (in ten´si tē) *n. pl.* **intensities** The quality of being intense or acute; a great effect, concentration, or force.

in-tent (in tent´) *n.* A purpose, goal, aim, or design. **intently** *adv.* **intentness** *n.*

in-ten-tion-al (in ten´shan al) *adj.* Deliberately intended or done. **intentionality** *n.* **intentionally** *adv.*

in-ter- (in ter´) *prefix.* Mutually; with each other; together; among or between.

in-ter-act (in´tër akt´) *v.* To act on each other or with each other. **-active** *adj.*

interactive system In *computer science*, a combination of computers and peripherals that are compatible.

interactive program In *computer science*, an application that responds to each user command as it is entered, then waits for the next command.

in-ter-breed (in´tër brēd´) *v.* To breed together by crossing one variety of plant or animal with another.

in-ter-cede (in´tër sēd) *v.* To argue or plead on another's behalf. **-er** *n.*

in-ter-cept (in´tër sept´) *v.* To interrupt the path or course of; to seize or stop.

in-ter-cep-tion (in´tër sep´shan) *n.* The state of being intercepted.

in-ter-change (in´tër chānj´) *v.* To put each in the place of another; to give and receive in return. **interchange** *n.* The intersection of a highway which allows traffic to enter or turn off without obstructing other traffic. **interchangeably** *adv.* **-er** *n.*

in-ter-change-a-ble (in´tër chānj´a bl) *adj.* To be capable of being interchanged with something; an alternate; **exchange. interchangeableness** *n.*

in-ter-clav-i-cle (in´tër klav´i kl) *n.* The bone which is located between the clavicles and in front of the sternum of reptiles. **interclavicular** *adj.*

in-ter-com (in´tër kom´) *n., Informal* A two-way communication system, as used in different areas of a home or business.

in-ter-con-nect (in´tër ka nekt´) *v.* To connect two or more things with one another. **interconnection** *n.*

in-ter-con-ti-nen-tal (in´tër kon´ti nen´tal) *adj.* Pertaining to or involving two or more continents.

in-ter-course (in´tër kōrs´) *n.* Mutual exchange between persons or groups; communication; sexual intercourse.

in-ter-cur-rent (in´tër kür´ent) *adj.* To be happening in the midst of a process.

in-ter-de-part-men-tal (in´tër dē´pärt men´tal) *adj.* To be involving or to be between different departments in a company or government. **-ally** *adv.*

in-ter-dis-ci-pli-nar-y (in´tër dis´i pli´nër ´ē) *adj.* To be involving or containing two or more artistic, academic, or scientific disciplines.

in-ter-est (in´tĕr ist) *n.* Curiosity or concern about something; that which is to one's benefit; legal or financial right, claim, or share, as in a business; a charge for a loan of money, usually a percent of the amount borrowed.

in-ter-est-ing (in´tĕr i sting) *adj.* Stimulating interest, attention, or curiosity. **interesting** *adv.*

in-ter-face (in´tĕr fās´) *n.* A surface forming a common boundary between adjacent areas; in *computer science*, the software or hardware connecting one device or system to another.

in-ter-fere (in´tĕr fēr´) *v.* To come between; to get in the way; to be an obstacle or obstruction. **interferer** *n.*

in-ter-fer-ence (in´tĕr fēr´ens) *n.* The process of interfering in something.

in-ter-file (in´tĕr fīl´) *v.* To place in or fit into an existing filc.

in-ter-flu-ent (in´tĕr flō´ent) *adj.* The flowing or intermingling into each other.

in-ter-fuse (in´tĕr fūz´) *v.* To make or to cause something to pass into another. **interfusion** *n.*

in-ter-gov-ern-men-tal (in´tĕr gov´ĕrn ment l) *adj.* To be happening between two or more governments.

in-ter-im (in´tĕr im) *n.* A time between events or periods. **interim** *adj.* Temporary.

in-te-ri-or (in tēr´ē ĕr) *adj.* Of, or contained in the inside; inner; away from the coast or border; inland; private; not exposed to view.

in-ter-ject (in´tĕr jekt´) *v.* To go between other parts or elements; to add something between other things. **interjector** *n.* **inter-jectory** *adj.*

in-ter-jec-tion (in´tĕr jek´shan) *n.* A word used as an exclamation to express emotion, as *Oh! Heavens! Super!*

in-ter-lay-er (in´tĕr lā´ĕr) *n.* The layer that is placed in between other layers.

in-ter-leaf (in´tĕr lēf´) *n. pl.* **interleaves** A blank sheet of paper that is bound or inserted between two other pages of a book.

in-ter-line (in´tĕr līn´) *v.* To mark or insert between the lines; to write between lines already written or printed.

in-ter-link (in´tĕr lĭngk´) *v.* To put togther or to link things together.

in-ter-lock (in´tĕr lok´) *v.* To join closely.

in-ter-lo-cu-tion (in´tĕr lə kū´shan) *n.* The interchange of speech with others; conversation; a dialogue or colloquy.

in-ter-lope (in´tĕr lōp´) *v.* To intrude or interfere in the rights of others.

in-ter-lude (in´tĕr lŏd´) *n.* A period of time that occurs in and divides some

longer process; light entertainment between the acts of a show, play, or other more serious entertainment.

in-ter-lu-nar (in´tĕr lō´nĕr) *adj.* To be pertaining to the interval that is between the new and old moon, where the moon is in-visible.

in-ter-me-di-ar-y (in´tĕr mē´dē er´ē) *n. pl.* **intermediaries** A mediator. **intermediary** *adj.* Coming between; intermediate.

in-ter-mez-zo (in´tĕr met´sō) *n.* The musical composition coming between the main sections or divisions of and extended musical work.

in-ter-min-a-ble (in tür´mi na bl) *adj.* To seem to have no end.

in-ter-min-gle (in´tĕr ming´gl) *v.* To blend or become mixed together.

in-ter-mis-sion (in´tĕr mish´an) *n.* A temporary interval of time between events or activities; the pause in the middle of a performance.

in-ter-mit (in´tĕr mit´) *v.* To cause something to cease for a certain amount of time.

in-ter-mit-tent (in´tĕr mit´ent) *adj.* Ceasing from time to time; coming at intervals.

in-tern (in tern´) *n.* A medical school graduate undergoing supervised practical training in a hospital. **intern** *v.* To confine as in wartime. **-ship** *n.*

in-ter-nal (in ter´nal) *adj.* Of or pertaining to the inside; pertaining to the domestic affairs of a country; intended to be consumed by the body from the inside.

internal storage In *computer science*, data storage that is built into, and directly accessible by, the computer.

in-ter-nal-ize (in ter´na līz) *adj.* To incorporate within oneself.

in-ter-na-tion-al (in´tĕr nash´a nal) *adj.* Pertaining to or involving two or more nations. **internationally** *adv.*

in-tern-ee (in´tern nē´) *n.* A person who is confined or interned.

internet In *computer science*, the information super highway connecting computers.

in-ter-nist (in´tür nist) *n.* A physician who is a specialist in internal medicine.

in-tern-ment (in tern´ment) *n.* The state of something being interned.

in-ter-nun-ci-o (in´tĕr nun´shē ō´) *adj.* The messenger who is between two parties.

in-ter-pel-late (in´tĕr pel´āt) *v.* To question; to call upon formally; to ask for an explanation of an official action.

in-ter-pen-e-trate (in´tĕr pen´l trāt´) *v.* To penetrate mutually; to penetrate between throughout, or within; to penetrate each other.

in-ter-per-son-al (in´tĕr pers´nel) *adj.*

To be relating to or pertaining to relations between people.

in-ter-plan-e-tar-y (in´tér plan´i ter´ē) *adj.* To be happening or operating between the planets.

in-ter-plant (in´tér plant´) *v.* To plant or place a crop between other crops.

in-ter-play (in´tér plā´) *n.* Action, movement, or influence between or among people.

in-ter-po-late (in ter´po lāt´) *v.* To insert between other things or elements; to change something by introducing additions or insertions. **interpolation** *n.* **interpolative** *adj.*

in-ter-pose (in´tér pōz´) *v.* To put between parts; to put in or inject a comment into a conversation or speech; to intervene. **interposer** *n.*

in-ter-pret (in ter´prit) *v.* To convey the meaning of something by explaining or restating; to present the meaning of something, as in a picture; to take words spoken or written in one language and put them into another language. **interpretable** *adj.* **interpretation, interpreter** *n.*

in-ter-pu-pil-lar-y (in´ter´pyü˝pi ler´ē) *adj.* To be located or extending between the pupils of one's eyes.

in-ter-ra-cial (in´tér rā´shal) *adj.* Between, among, or affecting different races.

in-ter-reg-num (in´tér reg´num) *n. pl.* **nums** An interval between two successive reigns; a break in continuity.

in-ter-re-late (in´tér ri lāt´) *v.* To have or bring into a mutual relationship. **interrelation, interrelationship** *n.*

in-ter-re-lat-ed (in´tér ri lāt´d) *adj.* To have a mutual relation with someone or something. **interrelatedly** *adv.*

in-ter-ro-gate (in ter´o gāt´) *v.* To question formally. **interrogation** *n.*

in-ter-rog-a-tive (in´te rog´a tiv) *adj.* Asking or having the form of a question. *n.* A word used to ask a question. **interrogatively** *adv.*

in-ter-rupt (in te rupt´) *v.* To break the continuity of something; to intervene abruptly while someone else is speaking or performing. **interrupter** *n.* **interruption** *n.* **interruptive** *adj.*

in-ter se (in´tér sā´) *adj. or adv.* To be between or among friends.

in-ter-sect (in´tér sekt´) *v.* To divide by cutting through or across; to form an intersection; to cross.

in-ter-sec-tion (in´tér sek´shan) *n.* A place of crossing; a place where streets or roads cross; in mathematics, the point common to two or more geometric elements.

in-ter-ses-sion (in´ter sesh en) *n.* The period that is between two academic sessions that can be used for brief,

concentrated courses.

in-ter-space (in´tér spās´) *n.* A space between things; an intervening space or interval. *v.* To fill a space

in-ter-sperse (in´tér spers´) *v.* To scatter among other things. **interspersion** *n.*

in-ter-sta-di-al (in´tér städ´ē el) *n.* The subdivision that is within a glacial stage and marking a temporary retreat of the ice.

in-ter-state (in´tér stāt´) *adj.* Between, involving, or among two or more states.

in-ter-stel-lar (in´tér stel´ér) *adj.* Among or between the stars.

in-ter-stice (in tür´stis) *n.* The small space between things.

in-ter-sti-tial (in´tér stish´al) *adj.* To be situated within a tissue or an organ.

in-ter-till (in´tér til´) *v.* To cultivate the ground between the rows of a crop.

in-ter-trop-i-cal (in´tér trop´i kal) *adj.* To be located between the tropics.

in-ter-twine (in´tér twīn´) *v.* To unite by twisting together.

in-ter-val (in´tér val) *n.* The time coming between two points or objects; a period of time between events or moments. *Mus.* The difference in pitch between two tones.

in-ter-vene (in´tér vēn) *v.* To interfere or take a decisive role so as to modify or settle something; to interfere with force in a conflict. **intervention** *n.*

in-ter-ven-or (in´tér vēn ér) *n.* A person who will intervene.

in-ter-ven-tion-ism (in´tér ven´shan izm) *n.* The practice of intervening in something. **interventionist** *n.*

in-ter-ver-te-bral (in´tér vertˊe bral) *adj.* To be situated between the vertebrae, such as a disk.

in-ter-view (in´tér vū´) *n.* A conversation conducted by a reporter to elicit information from someone; a conversation led by an employer who is trying to decide whether to hire someone. **interview** *v.* **interviewer** *n.*

in-ter-vi-vos (in´tér vē´vōs) *adj. & adv.* To be between living people; from one living person to another.

in-ter-vo-cal-ic (in´ter vō kal´ik) *n.* To be preceded and followed immediately by a vowel.

in-ter-weave (in´tér wēv´) *v.* To weave together; to intertwine.

in-ter-zon-al (in´tér zōn´l) *adj.* To be carried on between two or more zones.

in-tes-tate (in tes´tāt) *adj.* Having made no valid will; not disposed of by a will.

intestinal fortitude *n.* Stamina of a person; courage.

in-tes-tine *or* **intestines** (in tes´tin) *n., Anat.* The section of the alimentary canal from the stomach to the anus.

in-tim-a (in´ti ma) *n.* The covering of an organ which is the innermost and is made up of an endothelial layer and is backed by connective tissue.

in-ti-mate (in´ti mit) *adj.* Characterized by close friendship or association. **intimate** *n.* **intimately** *adv.* **intimacy** *n.* **intimateness** *n.*

in-tim-i-date (in tim´i dāt´) *v.* To make timid or fearful; to frighten; to discourage or suppress by threats or by violence. **intimidation** *n.*

in-tim-i-da-tor-y (in tim´i de´tŏr ¯e) *adj.* Tending to intimidate others.

in-tine (in tēn´) *n.* The layer that is innermost of a spore and is a cellular wall.

intitule (in tit´ūl) *v.* To give or furnish with a title.

intl *abbr.* International.

in-to (in´tŏ) *prep.* To the inside of; to a form or condition of; to a time in the midst of.

in-tol-er-a-ble (in tol´ėr a bl) *adj.* Not tolerable; unbearable. **intolerability** *n.* **intolerableness** *n.* **intolerably** *adv.*

in-tol-er-ant (in tol´ėr ant) *adj.* Not able to endure; not tolerant of the rights or beliefs of others; bigoted. **intolerance** *n.* **intolerantly** *adv.*

in-to-nate (in´tŏ nāt´) *v.* To utter something.

in-to-na-tion (in´tŏ nā´shan) *n.* The manner of speaking, especially the meaning and melody given to speech by changing levels of pitch.

in-tone (in tŏn´) *v.* To utter or recite in a monotone; to chant. **intoner** *n.*

in-tort (in tort´) *v.* To curl; to twist inward.

in-tor-tion (in tor´shan) *n.* A winding or twisting, usually inward, around an axis, as of a plant stem around a pole.

in to-to (in tŏ´tŏ) *adv.* Totally.

in-tox-i-cate (in tok´si kāt´) *v.* To make drunk; to elate or excite. **intoxicant** *n.* **intoxication** *n.*

in-tox-i-cat-ed (in tok´si kāt´d) *adj.* To be affected by alcohol.

in-tra- *prefix* Within.

in-tra-ar-te-ri-al (in´tra är tir´¯e al) *adj.* To be located or situated within an artery.

in-tra-car-di-ac (in´tra kär´dē ak) *adj.* To be occurring within a being's heart.

in-tra-cel-lu-lar (in´tra sel´ū lėr) *adj.* To be occurring within a cell or cells.

in-tra-cra-ni-al (in´tra krā nē al) *adj.* To be occurring within the skull.

in-trac-ta-ble (in trak´ta bl) *adj.* Hard to manage; difficult to cure or treat. **intractableness, intractability** *n.*

in-tra-cu-ta-ne-ous (in´tra kū tā´nē us) *adj.* To be occurring between the layers of a being's skin.

in-tra-der-mal (in´tra dür´mal) *adj.* To be done within the layers of a being's skin.

in-tra-mu-ral (in´tra mūr´al) *adj.* Taking place within a school, college, or institution; competition limited to a school community.

in-tra-mus-cu-lar (in´tra mus´kū lėr) *adj.* Within a muscle.

in-trans *abbr.* Intransitive.

in-tran-si-gence (in tran´si jens) *n.* The state of something being intransigent.

in-tran-si-gent (in tran´si jent) *adj.* Refusing to moderate a position; uncompromising or unbending. **intransigency** *n.* **intransigent** *n.*

in-tran-si-tive (in tran´si tiv) *adj.* To be not transitive. **intransitiveness** *n.*

in-trant (in trant´) *n.* A person who is entering or going into a learning institution.

in-tra-oc-u-lar (in´tra ok´ū lėr) *adj.* To be located within the eyeball.

in-tra-per-i-to-ne-al (in´tra per´e ton ē´al) *adj.* To be going into the peritoneal cavity of the body.

in-tra-per-son-al (in´tra per´son al) *adj.* To be taking place among the members of a population.

in-tra-pop-u-la-tion (in´tra pāp´ū lā´shan) *adj.* To be taking place between the members of a population.

in-tra-psy-chic (in´tra sī´kik) *adj.* Arising or occurring within the psyche, mind, or personality.

in-tra-spe-cif-ic (in´tra spi sif´ik) *adj.* Occurring among or within a species or involving the members of the same species.

in-tra-state (in´tra stāt´) *adj.* Within a state.

in-tra-u-ter-ine (in´tra ū´tėr in) *adj.* Within the uterus.

in-tra-vas-cu-lar (in´tra vas´kūler) *adj.* To be occurring within a vessel such as a blood vessel.

in-tra-ve-nous (in´tra vē´nus) *adj.* To be occurring within a vein. **intravenously** *adv.*

in-tra-vi-tam (in´tra vī´tam) *adj.* Happening during one's life; used on a living subject.

in-trep-id (in trep´id) *adj.* Courageous; unshaken by fear; bold. **intrepidly** *adv.* **intrepidness** *n.*

in-tri-ca-cy (in´tri ka sē) *n.* The state of something being intricate.

in-tri-cate (in´tri kit) *adj.* Having many perplexingly entangled parts or elements; complex; difficult to solve or understand. **intricately** *adv.*

in-tri-gant (in´tri gant) *n.* Someone or something that will intrigue.

in-trigue (in trēg´) *v.* To arouse the curiosity or interest; to fascinate; to plot; to conspire; to engage in intrigues. **intrigue** *n.* A secret or illicit love affair; a secret plot or plan. **intriguer** *n.*

in-tri-gu-ing (in tri´ging) *adj.* To be

engaging the interest of something or of someone to a marked degree.

in-trin-sic (in trin´sik) *adj.* Belonging to the true or fundamental nature of a thing; inherent. **intrinsically** *adv.*

in-tro-duce (in´tro dõs´) *v.* To present a person face to face to another; to make acquainted; to bring into use or practice for the first time; to bring to the attention of. **introductory** *adj.*

in-tro-duc-tion (in´tro duk´shan) *n.* A passage of a book that will introduce the story or the content of the book; something which introduces.

in-tro-gres-sion (in´tro gresh´en) *n.* The introduction of a gene from one gene complex to another gene complex.

in-tro-it (in´trõ it) *n.* A hymn or psalm sung at the beginning of a Roman Catholic Mass; a piece of music played at the be-ginning of a religious service.

in-tro-ject (in´tro jekt´) *n.* To unconsciously incorporate ideas into someone's personality.

in-tro-mis-sion (in´tro mish´in) *n.* The process of intromitting.

in-tro-mit (in´tro mit) *v.* To put something in; insert.

in-trorse (in trors´) *adj.* To be facing inward.

in-tro-spect (in´tro spekt´) *v.* To examine reflectively; to look into one's own feelings or thoughts. **introspection** *n.*

in-tro-ver-sion (in´tro vür´zhan) *n.* The state of being introverted.

in-tro-vert (in´tro vert´) *n.*, *Psychol.* A person who directs his interest to himself and not to friends or social activities. **introversive** *adj.* **-ed** *adj.*

in-trude (in trõd´) *v.* To thrust or push oneself in; to come in without being asked or wanted.

in-tru-sion (in trõ´zhan) *n.* The act of intruding.

in-tru-sive (in trõ´siv) *adj.* To be intruding where a person is not wanted or welcome. **intrusiveness** *n.* **-ly** *adv.*

in-tu-ba-tion (in´tü bã´shan) *n.* The act of placing a tube in a hollow organ or orifice. **intubate** *v.*

in-tu-it (in tõ´it) *v.* To understand through intuition. **intuitable** *adj.*

in-tu-i-tion (in´to ish´an) *n.* The direct knowledge or awareness of something without conscious attention or reasoning; knowledge that is acquired in this way. **intuitive** *adj.*

in-tu-i-tion-ism (in´to ish´a niz˝um) *n.* A type of doctrine that states that objects of one's perception are intuitively known to be real.

in-tu-mesce (in´tü mes´) *v.* To enlarge.

in-tu-mes-cence (in´tü mes´ns) *n.* The swelling or the bubbling that can be caused by heat. **intumescent** *adj.*

in-tus-sus-cept (in˝tus su sept´) *v.* To

undergo an intussusception.

in-tus-sus-cep-tion (in˝tus su sep´shan) *n.* The pulling or drawing in of something, such as with the intestines in one's body. **intussusceptive** *adj.*

in-u-lin (in´ü lin) *n.* A type of white polysaccharide which can be found in the sap of the roots of composite plants.

in-unc-tion (in´ungk´shan) *n.* The act of placing ointment on a body part.

in-un-date (in´un dãt´) *v.* To overwhelm with abundance or excess, as with work. **inundation** *n.* **inundatory** *adj.*

in-ure (in ür´) *v.* To become used to accepting something which is undesirable. **inurement** *n.*

in-u-tile (in ü´til) *adj.* To be unusable or useless.

in va-cu-o (in vak´ü õ´) *adv.* To be done in a vacuum.

in-vade (in vãd´) *v.* To enter by force with the intent to conquer or pillage; to penetrate and overrun harmfully; to violate; to encroach upon.

in vag-i-nate (in vaj´i nãt´) *v.* To sheathe something; to undergo an invagination.

in-va-lid (in´va lid) *n.* A chronically sick, bedridden, or disabled person.

in-val-id (in val´id) *adj.* Not valid; unsound; having no force; without legal force or void, as a contract. **invalidity** *n.* **invalidly** *adv.*

in-val-i-date (in val´i dãt´) *v.* To nullify; to make invalid. **invalidation** *n.* **invalidator** *n.*

in-va-lid-ism (in´va li diz˝um) *n.* A type of condition, which is chronic, of being an invalid.

in-val-u-a-ble (in val´ü a bl) *adj.* Priceless; of great value; to be of great help or use. **invaluably** *adv.*

in-var-i-a-ble (in vâr´ē a bl) *adj.* Constant and not changing.

in-var-i-ance (in vâr´ē ans) *n.* The state of being invariable; constancy.

in-va-sion (in vã´zhan) *n.* The act of invading; an entrance made with the intent of overrunning or occupying.

in-va-sive (in vã´siv) *adj.* To be characterized by or to be similar to military aggression; intruding..

in-vec-tive (in vek´tiv) *n.* To be characterized by abuse or insult. **invectively** *adv.*

in-veigh (in vã´) *v.* To angrily protest something. **inveigher** *n.*

in-vei-gle (in vã´gl) *v.* To win over by flattery. **inveiglement** *n.* **inveigler** *n.*

in-vent (in vent´) *v.* To devise or create by original effort or design.

in-ven-tion (in ven´shan) *n.* The act or process of inventing; a new process, method, or device conceived from study and testing.

in-ven-tive (in ven´tiv) *adj.* Skillful at invention or contrivance; ingenious.

inventively *adv.* **inventiveness** *n.*

in-ven-to-ry (in´ven tōr´ē) *n. pl.* **inventories** A list of items with descriptions and quantities of each; the process of making such a list.

in-ver-ness (in´vėr nes´) *n.* A type of loose belted coat with a cape.

in-verse (in vers´) *adj.* Reversed in order or sequence; inverted. **inverse** *n.* Something opposite. **inversely** *adv.*

in-ver-sion (in ver´zhan) *n.* The act of inverting or the state of being inverted; that which is inverted.

in-ver-sive (in ver´siv) *adj.* To be marked or characterized by inversion.

in-vert (in vert´) *v.* To turn upside down; to reverse the position, condition, or order of something. **invertible** *adj.*

in-vert-ase (in ver´tās) *n.* A type of enzyme which is capable of inverting sucrose.

in-ver-te-brate (in vûr´te brit) *adj.* Lacking a backbone or spinal column.

inverted comma *n.* A type of comma that is inverted to be upside down and is placed at the top of a line.

in-vert-er (in vert´ér) *n.* Someone or something that will invert.

in-vert-i-ble (in vert´i bl) *adj.* To be capable of being inverted.

invert sugar *n.* A type of dextrose that can be obtained from starch.

in-vest (in vest´) *v.* To use money for the purchase of stocks or property in order to obtain profit or interest; to place in office formally; to install; to make an investment. **investor** *n.*

in-ves-ti-gate (in ves´ti gāt´) *v.* To search or inquire into; to examine carefully. **investigative** *adj.* **investigation** *n.* **investigator** *n.*

in-ves-ti-ture (in ves´ti chèr) *n.* The ceremony or act of investing or installing someone in a high office.

in-vest-ment (in vest´ment) *n.* The act of investing money or capital to gain interest or income; property acquired and kept for future benefit.

in-vet-er-a-cy (in vet´ér a sē) *n.* The state of being persistent.

in-vet-er-ate (in vet´ér it) *adj.* To be confirmed in a habit. **inveterate** *adv.*

in-vi-a-ble (in vī´abl) *adj.* To be unable to survive. **inviability** *n.*

in-vid-i-ous (in vid´ē us) *adj.* To be causing animosity or discontent.

in-vig-o-rate (in vig´o rāt´) *v.* To give strength or vitality to. **invigoratingly** *adv.* **invigoration** *n.*

in-vin-ci-ble (in vin´si bl) *adj.* Incapable of being defeated. **invincibility** *n.*

in-vi-o-la-ble (in vī´o la bl) *adj.* Secure from profanation; safe from assault. **inviolability** *n.* **inviolably** *adv.*

in-vi-o-late (in vī´o lit) *adj.* Not violated. **inviolately** *adv.* **inviolateness** *n.*

in-vis-cid (in vis´id) *adj.* To have zero viscosity.

in-vis-i-ble (in viz´i bl) *adj.* Not capable of being seen; not visible; not open to view; hidden. **invisibility** *n.* **-ly** *adv.*

in-vi-ta-tion (in´vi tā´shan) *n.* The act of inviting; the means or words that request someone's presence or participation.

in-vi-ta-to-ry (in vī´ta tōr´ē) *adj.* Intending to invite; containing an invitation; to convey an invitation.

in-vite (in vīt´) *v.* To request the presence or participation of; to make a formal or polite request for; to provoke; to entice; to issue an invitation.

in-vi-tee (in vi tē´) *n.* The person who is being invited to something or somewhere.

in-vit-ing (in vīt´ing) *adj.* Tempting; attractive. **invitingly** *adv.*

in vi-tro (in vē´trō) *adv.* To be done outside the body, such as fertilization.

in vi-vo (in vē´vō) *adv.* To be in the living body of an animal or in a plant.

in-vo-cate (in´vo kāt´) *v.* To invoke someone or something into doing something.

in-vo-ca-tion (in´vo kā´shan) *n.* An appeal to a deity or other agent for inspiration, witness, or help; a prayer used at the opening of a ceremony or service.

in-voice (in´vois) *n.* An itemized list of merchandise shipped or services rendered, including prices, shipping instructions, and other costs; a bill. .

in-voke (in vōk´) *v.* To call upon for aid, support, or inspiration; to conjure. **invoker** *n.*

in-vol-u-cel (in vol´ū sel´) *n.* A small involucre often at the base of an individual flower or a small cluster of flowers.

in-vo-lu-cre (in´vo lō´kèr) *n.* One or more whorls of bracts that are situated below and close to a flower cluster or fruit.

in-vo-lu-crum (in´vo lü´krum) *n.* A type of surrounding sheath.

in-vol-un-tar-y (in vol´un ter´ē) *adj.* Not done by choice or willingly. **involun-tary** *n., Physiol.* Muscles which function with-out an individual's control. **involuntariness** *n.*

in-vo-lute (in´vo lōt´) *v.* To return to the former condition; to be cleared up.

in-vo-lu-tion (in´vo lō´shan) *n.* The process where something returns itself to its former condition or state.

in-volve (in volv´) *v.* To include as a part; to make a participant of; to absorb; to engross. **involvement** *n.*

in-volved (in volvd´) *n.* To be complex in an extreme manner; not easily understood.

in-vul-ner-a-ble (in vul′nĕr *a* bl) *adj.* To be immune to attack; impregnable; not able to be physically injured or wounded. **invulnerability** *n.* **invulnerably** *adv.*

in-wall (in wal′) *v.* To enclose within a wall. **inwall** *n.* interior wall.

in-ward (in′wĕrd) *adj.* Situated toward the inside, center, or interior; of or existing in the mind or thoughts. **inwardness** *n.*

in-weave (in wēv′) *v.* To interlace something.

in-wrought (in rot′) *adj.* To have the decoration worked in, such as with embroidery.

I/O In *computer science*, Input/Output.

I/O buffer In *computer science*, a portion of memory dedicated to the temporary storage of data received or to be sent by the computer- the buffer compensates for differences in communication speeds between devices the prevents the interruption of other operations.

I/O bus In computer science, a group of lines that carries signals between devices.

I/O port In computer science, the physical connector between the computer and its peripherals.

IOC *abbr.* International Olympic Committee.

i-o-date (i′o dāt′) *v.* To treat something with iodine. **iodation** *n.*

i-od-ic (i′od′ik) *adj.* To be pertaining to or containing iodine.

iodic acid *n.* An oxidizing solid that is formed by the oxidation of iodine.

i-o-dide (i′o dīd′) *n.* A type of iodine compound that has a more electropositive element.

i-o-din-ate (i′o din āt′) *v.* To cause a compound to combine with iodine.

i-o-dine (i′o din′) *n.* A grayish-black, corrosive, poisonous element, symbolized by I; a solution made up of iodine, alcohol, and sodium or potassium iodide used as an antiseptic.

i-o-dize (i′o dīz′) *v.* To treat something with iodine or to treat with an iodide.

i-o-do-form (i o′do form′) *n.* A type of yellow compound that has a penetrating, persistent odor and is used as an antiseptic dressing.

i-o-do-phor (i o′do for′) *n.* A type of complex iodine and organic compound that will release iodine gradually and is used as a disinfectant.

i-o-dous (i o′dus) *adj.* Pertaining to or containing iodine.

i-o-lite (i′o līt′) *n.* A mineral of a violet-blue color.

i-o moth (i′o moth′) *n.* A type of yellow American moth that has a large ocellated spot on both of its hind legs.

i-on (i′on) *n.*, *Physics* An atom or group of atoms which carries a positive or negative electric charge as a result of having lost or gained one or more electrons.

-ion *n.* *suffix* A process; a condition.

i-on-ize (i′on īz′) *v.* To convert completely or partially into ions. **ionizer** *n.* **ionization** *n.* **ionizable** *adj.*

i-on-o-sphere (i on o sfĕr′) *n.* An ionized region of the atmosphere; the earth's atmosphere beginning at an altitude of about 30 miles and a latitude of 300 miles above the earth's surface and extends upward approximately 200 miles.

i-o-ta (i ō′ta) *n.* The ninth letter in the Greek alphabet; a small amount.

I-o-wa (i ō′wa) *n.* A state which is located in the north central part of the United States.

ipecac (ip′e kak′) *n.* A type of South American creeping plant that has flowers which droop and is found in tropical areas; the extract from its roots that is used as an emetic and expectorant.

i-pro-ni-a-zid (i′pro nī′a zid) *n.* A type of derivative of isoniazid that was formerly used to treat tuberculosis.

ip-se dix-it (ip′sē dik′set) *n* A type of assertion that is made but not proven.

ip-si-lat-er-al (ip′si lat′ĕr al) *adj.* To be appearing on the same side of the body.

ip-so fac-to (ip′sō fak′tō) *adv.* By that very fact or act.

IQ *abbr.* Intelligence quotient.

i-ras-ci-ble (i ras′i bl) *adj.* Easily provoked to anger; quick-tempered. **irascibly** *adv.* **irascibility** *n.* **irascibleness** *n.*

i-rate (ī′rāt) *adj.* Raging; angry. **irately** *adv.* **irateness** *n.*

IRBM *abbr.* Intermediate range ballistic missile.

ire (īĕr) *n.* Anger; wrath

i-ren-ic (ī ren′ik) *adj.* To be operating toward peace.

ir-i-da-ceous (ir′l dā′shus) *adj.* To be pertaining to the iris family of flowers.

ir-i-des-cent (ir′i des′ent) *adj.* Displaying the colors of the rainbow in shifting hues and patterns. **iridescence** *n.*

i-rid-ic (i rid′ik) *adj.* To be pertaining to iridium or to the iris of the eye.

i-rid-i-um (i rid′ē um) *n.* A type of silver-white brittle and very hard metallic element of the platinum group.

ir-i-dos-mine (ir′i doz′min) *n.* A compound of iridium and osmium alloy, that often contains some platinum and rhodium.

i-ris (ī′ris) *n. pl.* **irises** or **irides** The pigmented part of the eye which regulates the size of the pupil by contracting and expanding around it.

Bot. A plant with narrow sword-shaped leaves and handsome flowers, as the gladiolus and crocus.

iris diaphragm *n.* Adjustable diaphragm made of thin opaque plates that is turned by a ring, so as to change the diameter of a central opening such as the aperture of a lens.

I-rish (ī´rish) *n.* Pertaining to Ireland and its people or their language.

Irish coffee *n.* A type of hot, sweetened coffee that contains Irish whiskey and whipped cream.

Irish confetti *n.* A brick, rock, or fragment of either, used as a missile.

Irish Gaelic *n.* The Celtic language that has been used in Ireland since the end of the medieval period.

I-rish-ism (ī´rish iz´im) *n.* A phrase or a word that is characteristic of the Irish.

Irish mail *n.* A child's toy with three or four wheels that is activated by a hand lever.

Irishman *n.* A male person who is native to or an inhabitant of Ireland.

Irish moss *n.* Red alga that has been dried and is used for thickening or emulsifying.

Irish setter *n.* A type of bird dog that has a chestnut or reddish coat.

Irish stew *n.* A type of stew that contains meat (lamb, beef, or mutton) onions, and potatoes.

Irish terrier *n.* A type of medium-sized terrier dog that was developed in Ireland and has a reddish wiry coat.

Irish whiskey *n.* A type of whiskey, mainly of barley, that is made in Ireland.

Irish wolfhound *n.* A very large hound that resembles the Scottish deerhound but is much stronger and larger.

Irish woman *n.* A female person who was born in Ireland or is of Irish descend.

irk (erk) *v.* To annoy or to weary someone or something.

irk-some (erk´sum) *adj.* Tending to annoy someone or something; aggravating.

i-ron (ī´ern) *n.* A type of heavy, malleable, ductile and magnetic element that is silver-white and will rust easily in moist air. **iron** *v.* To smooth with an iron.

Iron Age *n.* The most recent of three early stages of human progress, following the Stone Age and the Bronze Age.

i-ron-bound (ī´ern bound´) *adj.* Bound with iron; unyielding.

i-ron-clad (ī´ern klad´) *adj.* Covered with protective iron plates; strict; unbreakable.

iron curtain *n.* An impenetrable political and ideological barrier between the Soviet bloc and the rest of the world.

i-ron-er (ī´ern nèr) *n.* A person who irons things, such as clothing.

i-ron-fis-ted (ī´ern fis´tid) *adj.* To be ruthless and mean.

iron gray *n.* A type of color which is neutral and slightly greenish dark gray.

iron hand *n.* The rigorous control of someone or of something. **ironhandedness** *n.* **ironhanded** *adj.*

ironhearted *adj.* To be hardhearted and cruel.

iron horse *n.* The engine of a train.

i-ron-ic (ī ron´ik) *adj.* Marked by or characterized by irony. **ironical** *adj.*

i-ron-ing (ī´ern ing) *n.* The process or action of pressing or smoothing with a heated iron; clothes that have been ironed or are to be ironed.

i-ro-nist (ī´ro nist) *n.* A person who uses irony in developing of a literary work.

iron lung *n.* A tank which encloses the entire body with the exception of the head and regulates the respiration of a patient by alternately increasing and decreasing air pressure.

i-ron-ma-ster (ī´ern mä´stèr) *n.* The manufacturer of iron.

iron out *v.* To make harmonious or tolerable by modification of extremes.

i-ron-smith (ī´ern smith´) *n.* A person who works with iron, as a blacksmith.

i-ron-stone (ī´ern stōn´) *n.* A heavy, white, glazed pottery.

i-ron-ware (ī´ern wâr´) *n.* Utensils, tools, and other articles made of iron; hardware.

i-ron-work (ī´ern wurk) *n.* Any object that has been made from iron.

i-ro-ny (ī´ro nē) *n. pl.* **ironies** A literary device for conveying meaning by saying the direct opposite of what is really meant.

ir-ra-di-ance (i rä´dē ans) *n.* A ray of light or anything of such luster or splendor.

ir-ra-di-ate (i rä´dē ãt´) *v.* To subject to ultraviolet light, radiation, or similar rays. **irradiation** *n.* **irradiator** *n.*

ir-ra-tion-al (i rash´a nal) *adj.* Unable to reason; contrary to reason; absurd; in mathematics, a number which is not expressible as an integer or a quotient of integers. **irrationality** *n.* **irrationally** *adv.*

ir-rec-on-cil-a-ble (i rek´on sī´la bl) *adj.* Not willing or able to be reconciled. **irreconcilability** *n.* **irreconcilably** *adv.*

ir-re-cov-er-a-ble (i´ri kuv´ér a bl) *adj.* Incapable of being regained or recovered; not capable of being remedied or restored.

ir-re-cu-sa-ble (ir´i kū´za bl) *adj.* Not to be objected to.

ir-re-deem-a-ble (ir´i dē´ma bl) *adj.* Not capable of being recovered, bought back, or paid off; not convertible into coin.

ir-re-den-ta (ir´i den´ta) n. Any region whose people are connected ethnically or historically to one country or area, but who are forced to accept the political jurisdiction of another state.

ir-re-duc-i-ble (ir´i dö´si bl) adj. Incapable of being reduced or simplified; not reducible.

ir-ref-ra-ga-ble (i ref´ra ga bl) adj. Incapable of being disproved; undeniable. irrefragably n.

ir-re-fran-gi-ble (ir´i fran´ji bl) adj. Not to be violated; not to be broken.

ir-ref-ut-able (i ref´ū ta bl) adj. Cannot be disproved as truth. irrefutability n. irrefutably adv.

ir-reg-u-lar (i reg´ū lér) adj. Not according to the general rule or practice; not straight, uniform, or orderly; uneven. irregular n. One who is irregular. irregularity n.

ir-rel-a-tive (i rel´a tiv) adj. Not relative; without relationship; not related.

ir-rel-e-vant (i rel´e vant) adj. Not pertinent or related to the subject matter. irrelevantly adv. irrelevance n. irrele-vancy n.

ir-re-lig-ious adj. Lacking in religion; opposed to religion. irreligiously adv. irreligiousness n. irreligion n.

ir-re-me-di-a-ble (ir´i mē´dē a bl) adj. Incapable of being cured or remedied incurable.

ir-re-mis-si-ble (ir´i mis´a bl) adj. Unpardonable, as for sin.

ir-re-mov-a-ble (ir´i mö´va bl) adj. Not removable. irremovably adv.

ir-rep-a-ra-ble (i rep´ér a bl) adj. Unable to be set right or repaired. irreparability n. irreparably adv.

ir-re-peal-a-ble (ir´i pē´la bl) adj. Impossible to revoke or repeal.

ir-re-place-a-ble (ir´i plā´sa bl) adj. Unable to be replaced.

ir-re-press-i-ble (ir´l pres´i bl) adj. Impossible to hold back or restrain. irrepressibly n. irrepressibly adv.

ir-re-proach-a-ble (ir´i prö´cha bl) adj. Blameless; not meriting reproach. irreproachableness n. -ably adv.

ir-re-sist-i-ble (ir´i zis´ti bl) adj. Completely fascinating; impossible to resist. irresistibility n. -y adv.

ir-res-o-lu-ble (i re´zol´ū bl) adj. Admitting or having no explanation or solution.

ir-res-o-lute (i rez´o löt´) adj. Lacking resolution; indecisive; lacking firmness of purpose; hesitant. irresolutely adv. irresoluteness n.

ir-re-spec-tive (ir´i spek´tiv) adj. Regard-less of; not related to certain conditions. irrespective of prep. Without regard to anything.

ir-re-spon-si-bil-i-ty (ir´i spon´si bil´i tē) n. The quality of being irresponsible.

ir-re-spon-si-ble (ir´i spon´si bl) adj. Lacking in responsibility; not accountable. irresponsibly adv.

ir-re-spon-sive (ir´i spon´siv) adj. Unable to react or respond.

ir-re-triev-a-ble (ir´i trē´va bl) adj. Unable to be retrieved or recovered.

ir-rev-er-ence (i rev´ér ens) n. A lack of reverence; a disrespectful action.

ir-rev-er-ent (i rev´ér ent) adj. Lacking the proper respect. irreverently adv.

ir-re-vers-i-ble (ir´i ver´si bl) adj. Impossible to reverse. irreversibility n. irreversibly adv.

ir-rev-o-ca-ble (i rev´o ka bl) adj. Unable or incapable of being turned in the other direction; incapable of being repealed, annulled or undone. irrevocability n. irrevocably adv.

ir-ri-gate (ir´i gāt´) v. To water the land or crops artificially, as by means of ditches or sprinklers; to refresh with water. Med. To wash out with a medicated fluid or water. irrigation n. irrigator n. irrigational adj.

ir-ri-ta-ble (ir´i ta bl) adj. Easily annoyed; ill-tempered. Pathol. To respond abnormally to stimuli. irritability n. irritableness n.

ir-ri-tate (ir´i tāt´) v. To annoy or bother; to provoke; to be sore, chafed, or inflamed. irritant adj. & n. irritator n. irritation n. irritatingly adv.

ir-ri-ta-tive (ir´i tā´tiv) adj. Serving to excite or irritate; produced or accompanied by an irritant or irritation.

ir-rupt (i rupt´) v. To burst or rush in; to invade. irruption n. irruptive adj. irruptively adv.

IRS abbr. Internal Revenue Service.

is (iz) v. Third person, singular, present tense of the verb to be.

i-sa-gog-ic (ī´sa goj´ik) adj. To introduce one to the Bible pl isagogics n. The introductory study to the critical interpretation of the sacred writings of the Bible.

is-al-lo-bar (ī sai´o bär´) n. A line on a chart which connects the locations of equal change of atmospheric pressure.

is-ba (iz bä´) n. The Russian log hut.

is-che-mi-a (i skē´mē a) n. The tissue anemia that is localized due to an obstruction of the inflow of arterial blood.

is-chi-um (is´kēm um) n. pl. ischia The posterior bone of the pelvis at the hip joint of the body.

is-en-tro-pic (īs´en trö´pik) adj. To be related to constant entropy.

-ish suffix Of or belonging to a nationality or ethnic group; characteristic of; the approximate age of; the approximate time of; somewhat.

is-land (ī´lɑnd) *n*. A piece of land smaller than a continent, completely surrounded by water.

is-land-er(ī´lɑn dẽr) *n*. A person who makes his home on an island.

island universe *n*. Any galaxy other than the Milky Way.

isle (īl) *n*. A small island.

is-let (ī´lit) *n*. A small island.

-ism *suffix* Practice; process; a manner of behavior characteristic of person or thing; a system of principles.

is-n't (iz ᴐnt) *contr*. Is not.

iso-ag-glu-ti nin (ī´sō ɑ glŏt´i nin) *n*. A clotting agent from one individual organism, effective in the cells of other individuals of the same species.

is-o-bar (ī´so bär´) *n*. An imaginary line or a line drawn on a map connecting places on the surface of the earth where the barometric pressure is the same for a given time.

is-o-bath (ī´so bath´) *n*. An imaginary line, or a line drawn on a map, connecting points that have the same depth below sea level.

is-o-cli-nal (ī´so klīn´al) *adj*. To be having an equality of inclination.

is-o-cy-clic (ī´sō sī´klik) *adj*. Having a ring composed of atoms of only one element.

is-o-di-a-met-ric (ī´so dī´a me´trik)*adj*. Having equal axes or diameters; having a similar diameter throughout.

is-o-e-lec-tron-ic (ī´sō i lek tron´ik)*adj*. To have the same number of electrons.

is-o-gen-ic (ī´sō jen´ik) *adj*. To be characterized by having identical genes.

is-o-ge-o-therm (ī´so jē´o thurm´) *n*. The imaginary line under the earth's surface which passes through points with the same mean temperature.

is-o-gloss (ī´so glos´) *n*. A boundary line that divides areas which differ in a particular linguistic feature.

is-o-gon-ic (ī´so gon´ik) *adj*. Growing so that sizes of parts remain equivalent.

is-o-gram (ī´so gram´) *n*. A line on a map or chart showing all points having constant value in relation to any climatic variable.

is-o-late (ī´so lāt´) *v*. To set apart from the others; to put by itself; to place or be placed in quarantine. **isolation** *n*.

iso-la-tion-ism (ī´so lā´sha niz´um) *n*. A national policy of avoiding political or economic alliances or relations with other countries. **isolationist** *n*.

is-o-mer (ī´so mẽr) *n*. A compound having the same kinds and numbers of atoms as another compound but differing in chemical or physical properties due to the linkage or arrangement of the atoms.

isosceles triangle *n*. A triangle which

has two equal sides.

is-o-therm (ī´so therm´) *n*. A line on a map linking points that have the same temperature. **isothermal** *adj*.

is-o-tope (ī´so tōp´) *n*. Any of two or more species of atoms of a chemical element which contain in their nuclei the same number of protons but different numbers of neutrons.

is-o-trop-ic (ī´so trop´ik) *adj*. Having the same value in all directions.

is-sue (ish´ö) *n*. The act of giving out; something that is given out or published; a matter of importance to solve. *Med*. A discharge as of pus or blood. issue *v*. To come forth; to flow out; to emerge; to distribute or give out, as supplies. **issuable** *adj*.

it (it) *pron*. Used as a substitute for a specific noun or name when referring to places, things, or animals of unspecified sex; used to refer to the general state of something.

i-tal-ic (i tal´ik) *adj*. A style of printing type in which the letters slant to the right. **italics** *n. pl*. Italic typeface.

i-tal-i-cize (i tal´i sīz´) *v*. To print in italics.

itch (ich) *n*. A skin irritation which causes a desire to scratch; a contagious skin disease accompanied by a desire to scratch; a restless desire or craving. **itch** *v*. **itchiness** *n*. **itchy** *adj*.

-ite *suffix* A native or inhabitant of; an adherent of; a sympathizer or follower; a descendant of; a rock or mineral.

i-tem (ī´tem) *n*. A separately noted unit or article included in a category or series; a short article, as in a magazine.

i-tem-ize (ī´te mīz´) *v*. To specify by item; to list. **-er** *n*. **itemization** *n*.

it-er-ate (it´e rāt´) *v*. To state or do again; to repeat. **iteration** *n*.

i-tin-er-ant (ī tin´ẽr ᴐnt) *adj*. Traveling from place to place; wandering around.

i-tin-er-ar-y (ī tin´e rer´ē) *n. pl*. **itineraries** A scheduled route of a trip.

it'll (it´il) *contr*. It will; it shall.

it's (its) *contr*. It is; it has.

its (its) *adj*. The possessive case of the pronoun it.

-ity *n. suffix* Quality or state.

i-vied (ī´vēd) To be overgrown with ivy.

i-vo-ry (ī´vo rē) *n*. A hard, smooth, yellowish-white material which forms the tusks of elephants, walruses, and other animals; a yellow to creamy-white color. **ivories** The teeth; the keys on a piano. **ivory** *adj*.

i-vy (ī´vē) *n. pl*. **ivies** A climbing plant having glossy evergreen leaves.

-ization *suffix* The process, action, or result of doing a specified thing.

-ize *suffix* To cause to become or resemble.

iz-zard (iz´ẽrd) *n*. The letter Z.

J, j (jā) The tenth letter of the English alphabet.

JA *abbr.* Joint account; judge advocate.

jab (jab) *v.* To poke or thrust sharply with short blows; a rapid punch.

jab-ber (jab´ér) *v.* To speak quickly or without making sense.

jab-i-ru (jab´i rö´) *n.* A wading bird of the stork family, usually white in color.

jab-ot (zha bō´) *n.* A ruffle or decoration on the front of a blouse, dress, or shirt; a lace decoration that was formerly worn by men.

ja-cal (ha käl´) *n.* A small hut found in the southwestern United States and Mexico, with walls made of rows and rows of thin vertical poles filled in with mud.

jac-a-mar (jak´a mär´) *n.* A tropical, brilliantly colored, insectivorous bird of tropical America.

ja-ca-na (zhä´sa nä´) *n.* A small aquatic bird having long, straight claws that are adapted for walking on floating objects such as aquatic plants.

jac-a-ran-da (jak´a ran´da) *n.* A tall tropical tree; or the fragrant wood of such a tree.

jack-a-napes (jak´a näps) *n.* An impudent person, an impudent child.

jack-ass (jak´as´) *n.* A male donkey or ass; a stupid person or one who acts in a stupid fashion.

jack-boot (jak´böt´) *n.* A heavy military boot which reaches above the knee.

jack-daw (jak´do´) *n.* A glossy, black, crow-like bird.

jack-et (jak´it) *n.* A short coat worn by men and women; an outer protective cover for a book; the skin of a cooked potato **jacketed, jacketless,** *adj.*

Jackson, Andrew *n.* (1767-1845) The seventh president of the United States from 1829-1837.

jac-ti-ta-tion (jak´ti tā´shan) *n.* An untrue statement which is insulting to another.

jac-u-late (jak´ū lāt´) *v.* To throw outwards; to hurl.

jade (jād) *n.* A hard, translucent, green gem-stone, an old, worn-out, unmanageable horse; a mean old woman; hussy. **jade** *adj.* Worn-out; exhausted.

jad-ed (jā´did) *adj.* Tired; worn-out; bored.

jag (jag) *n.* A very sharp projection or point. *Slang* A binge or spree.

jag-ged *adj.* Having jags or sharp notches; serrated. **jaggedly** *adv.* **jaggedness** *n.*

jag-ger-y (jag´e rē) *n.* A brown sugar made from palm tree sap.

jag-uar (jag´wär) *n.* A large feline mammal of tropical America with a tawny coat and black spots.

ja-gua-run-di (jä´gwa run´dē) *n. pl.*

jaguarundis A type of wildcat that is short-legged and slender.

jai alai (hī´lī´) *n.* A game similar to handball in which players catch and throw a ball with long, curved, wicker baskets strapped to their arms.

jail (jāl) *n.* A place of confinement for incarceration.

ja-lop-y (ja lop´ē) *n. pl.* **jalopies** *Slang* An old, run-down automobile.

ja-lou-sie (jal´o sē´) *n.* A window, blind, or door having adjustable horizontal slats.

jam (jam) *v.* To force or wedge into a tight position; to apply the brakes of a car suddenly; to be locked in a position; to block; to crush. *Mus.* To be a participant in a jazz session. *Slang* To be in a difficult situation or to be crowded together, as of people, cars; a difficult situation. **jam** *n.* A pre-serve of whole fruit boiled with sugar.

jamb (jam) *n.* The vertical sidepiece of a door.

jam-ba-lay-a (jum´ba lī´a) *n.* A dish of rice that is cooked with vegetable, and various kinds of fish, meat, but usually shrimp or ham.

jam session *n.* An informal gathering of a group of jazz musicians, usually for their own enjoyment.

jan-gle (jang´gl) *v.* To make a harsh, unmusical sound; to dispute something in an angry way; to cause to become angry, tense or mad. **jangle** *n.* A discordant sound; a dispute or quarrel. **jangle, jangler** *n.*

jan-i-tor (jan´i tér) *n.* A person who cleans and cares for a building, office, school, apartment, etc. **janitorial** *adj.*

Jan-u-ar-y (jan´ū er´ē) *n.* The first month of the year, having thirty-one days.

jape (jāp) *v.* To joke; to make fun of or mock by words or actions. **jape, japer, japery** *n.*

Jap-o-nism (jap´oniz´um) *n.* To adapt to Japanese styles or methods; any manner-ism or trait that is characteristic of the Japanese.

jar (jär) *n.* A deep, cylindrical vessel with a wide mouth; a harsh sound. **jar** *v.* To strike against or bump into; to affect one's feelings unpleasantly.

jar-di-niere (jär´di ner´) *n.* A decorative pot or stand for flowers or plants; a garnish for meat made from cooked and diced vegetables.

jar-gon (jär´gon) *n.* The technical or specialized vocabulary used among members of a particular profession. a type of speech containing pretentious or unfamiliar words; unintelligible writing or speech; gibberish.

jas-mine *or* **jes-sa-mine** (jaz´min) *n.* A shrub with fragrant yellow or white flowers.

jas-per (jas´pėr) *n.* An opaque red, brown, or yellow variety of quartz, having a high polish and often used for jewelry and vases.

ja-to (jā´tō) *n.* A takeoff of an airplane which is assisted by an auxiliary rocket engine.

jaun-dice (jon´dis) *n., Pathol.* A diseased condition of the liver due to the presence of bile pigments in the blood and characterized by yellowish staining of the eyes, skin, and body fluids.

jaunt (jont) *n.* A short journey for pleasure. *v.* To make a short journey, trip, or excursion.

jaunting car *n.* A light weight, open air cart that has two seats, set back to back or facing each other, with an area in front for the driver.

jaun-ty (jon´tē) *adj.* Having a buoyantly carefree and self-confident air or manner about oneself. **jauntily** *adv.*

jave-lin (jav´lin) *n.* A light spear thrown as a weapon; a long spear with a wooden shaft, used in competitions of distance throwing.

jave-lin throw *v.* To wound or strike with a javelin.

jaw (jo) *n., Anat.* Either of the two bony structures forming the framework of the mouth and the teeth.

jaw-bone (jo´bōn´) *n.* One of the bones of the jaw, especially the lower jaw or mandible.

jazz (jaz) *n.* A kind of music which has a strong rhythmic structure and frequent syncopation and often involving ensemble and solo improvisation. *Slang* Lying and exaggerated talk; idle and foolish talk; liveliness. **jazz up** To make more interesting; to enliven. **jazzer** *n.* **jazzy** *adj.*

jazz band *n.* A musical band that plays jazz, and typically uses the saxophone, clarinet, piano, trombone, and drums.

jeal-ous (jel´us) *adj.* Suspicious or fearful of being replaced by a rival; resentful or bitter in rivalry; demanding exclusive love. **jealously** *adv.*

jeal-ous-y (jel´o sē) *n.* Envy; resentment against a rival or someone who possesses any coveted advantage.

Jefferson, Thomas *n.* (1743-1826) The third president of the United Stated from 1801-1809.

Je-ho-vah (ji hō´va) *n.* God, in the Christian translations of the Old Testament.

je-june (ji jön´) *adj.* Lacking in substance or nourishment; immature.

je-ju-num (ji jö´num) *n., Anat.* The part of the small intestine which extends from the duodenum to the ileum.

jel-ly (jel´ē) *n. pl.* **jellies** Any food preparation made with pectin or gelatin and having a somewhat elastic consis-

tency; a food made of boiled and sweetened fruit juice and juice and a filler or spread. **jelly** *v.* To make into jelly; to become or take the form of jelly; to become gelatinous; to assume or cause to assume definite form.

jen-net (jen´it) *n.* Name for a female donkey or a small Spanish horse.

jeop-ard-ize *v.* To put in jeopardy; to expose to loss or danger.

jeop-ard-y (jep´ėr dē) *n.* Exposure to loss or danger.

je-quir-i-ty (je kwir´i tē) *n.* The beans or seeds of the Indian licorice plant, black and scarlet in color, which contain abrin, a po-tent poison released when the seeds are broken open; the plant itself.

jer-e-mi-ad (jer´e mī´ad) *n.* A lament or prolonged complaint.

jerk (jerk) *v.* To give a sharp twist or pull to. **jerk** *n.* A sudden movement, as a tug or twist. *Physiol.* An involuntary contraction of a muscle resulting from a reflex action. *Slang* An annoying or foolish person. **jerky**, **jerkily** *adv.* **jerkiness** *n.*

jer-kin (jer´kin) *n.* A close-fitting jacket, usually sleeveless.

jerk-wa-ter (jerk´wo˘tėr) *adj.* Of little importance.

jer-o-boam (jer´o bō´am) *n.* An extra-large wine bottle.

jer-ry-build (jer´ē bild´) *v.* To build flimsily and cheaply. **jerrybuilt** *adj.*

jer-sey (jer´zē) *n. pl.* **jerseys** A soft ribbed fabric of wool, cotton, or other material; a knitted sweater, jacket, or shirt; fawn-colored, small dairy cattle which yield milk rich in butter fat.

Je-ru-sal-lem *n.* Capital of Israel.

jess (jes) *n.* A leather strap tied around each of the legs of a hawk, to which the falconer's leash is attached.

jest (jest) *n.* An action or remark intended to provoke laughter; a joke; a playful mood. **jester** *n.*

Jesus (jē´zus) *n.* The founder of Christianity, son of Mary and regarded in the Christian faith as Christ the son of God, the Messiah; also referred to as Jesus Christ or Jesus of Nazareth.

jet (jet) *n.* A sudden spurt or gush of liquid or gas emitted through a narrow opening; a jet airplane; a hard, black mineral which takes a high polish and is used in jewelry; a deep glossy black.

jet-ty (jet´ē) *n. pl.* **jetties** A wall, made by piling rocks or other material, which extends into a body of water to protect a harbor or influence the current; a pier.

Jew (jö) *n.* A descendant of the ancient Hebrew people; a person believing in Judaism.

jew-el (jö´el) *n.* A precious stone used for personal adornment; a person or

thing of very rare excellence or value.
jewel v. To furnish with jewels.
jew-el-er (jö´e lêr) n. A person who makes or deals in jewelry.
jew-fish (jö´fish) n. A large fish of the sea bass family, found in the tropical waters of the Atlantic Ocean.
Jew-ish (jö´ish) adj. Of, relating to, or resembling the Jews, their customs, or their religion. **Jewishness** n.
jib (jib) n., Naut. A triangular sail set on a stay extending from the outer end of a jib boom. **jib** v. To swing or shift from one side of a vessel to the other.
jibe (jïb) v. To sail a course so that a vessel shifts from one side to the other; to be in agreement or in harmony.
jif-fy (jif´ē) pl. **jiffies** A very short time.
jig (jig) n. Any of a variety of fast, lively dances; the music for such a dance. Mech. A device used to hold and guide a tool.
jig-ger (jig´ér) n. A small measure holding 1-1/2 oz. used for measuring liquor. Naut. A small sail in the stern of a sailing craft. Slang A small item which does not have a particular name.
jig-gle (jig´l) v. To move or jerk lightly up and down. **jiggle** n. A jerky, unsteady movement.
jig saw n. A saw having a slim blade set vertically, used for cutting curved or irregular lines.
jig-saw puz-zle n. A puzzle consisting of many irregularly shaped pieces which fit together and form a picture.
jilt (jilt) v. To discard a lover. **jilt** n. A woman who discards a lover.
jim-jams (jim´jamz) n., Slang. Feelings of nervousness; delirium tremors.
jim-my (jim´ē) n. pl. **jimmies** A short crowbar, used by a burglar. **jimmy** v. To force open or break into with a jimmy.
jin-go (jing´gō) n. Self-proclaimed patriot who advocates a tough, warlike foreign policy. **jingoish** adj.
jin-go-ism n. Extreme nationalism which is marked by a belligerent foreign policy. **jingoist** n. **jingoistic** adj.
jink (jingk) v. To move with agility; to make a quick, evasive turn.
jinn (jin) n. pl. **jinni** or **jinn** In Moslem legend, a spirit with supernatural powers.
jin-rik-i-sha (jin rik´sha) n. A two-wheeled vehicle used in the Orient, which is pulled by one or more men.
jinx (jingks) n., Slang A person or thing thought to cause bad luck; a period of bad luck.
jit-ter (jit´ér) v., Slang To be intensely nervous. **jittery** adj.
jit-ter-bug (jit´ér bug) n., Slang A lively dance or one who performs this dance. **jitterbug** v.

jit-ters n. Nervousness.
jive (jïv) n., Slang Jazz or swing music and musicians.
job (job) n. Anything that is done; work that is done for a set fee; the project worked on; a position of employment. **jobless** adj. **joblessness** n.
job-ber (job´ér) n. One who buys goods in bulk from the manufacturer and sells them to retailers; a person who works by the job; a pieceworker.
job-ber-y (job´e rē) n. Graft; dishonest use of a public office for private gain.
job-hold-er (job´hōl´dér) n. Someone who is working at a steady job.
job-hop-ping (job´hop´ing) n. The act of changing jobs at short intervals; often for better pay. **job-hopper** n.
job lot n. A mixed set of goods sold in a single deal, often at a reduced price.
job-name n. In computer science, a code that is assigned to a specific job instruction in a computer program, for the operator's use.
job processing In computer science, the execution of a particular task or series of tasks by the computer.
job work n. Work done by the job.
jock (jok) n., Slang A male athlete in college; a person who participates in athletics.
jock-ey (jok´ē) n. A person who rides a horse as a professional in a race; one who works with a specific object or device.
jo-cose (jō kōs´) adj. To be joking and jesting; causing laughter; merry; playful.
joc-u-lar (jok´ū lér) adj. Joking; playful. **jocularity** n. **Jocularly** adv.
joc-und (jok´und) adj. Cheerful; merry; suggestive of high spirits and lively mirthfulness. **jocundity** n.
jodh-pur (jod´pér) n. Riding breeches that are wide at the hips, narrow at the knees and fit tightly to the ankles.
jog (Jog) n. A slight movement or a slight shake; the slow steady trot of a horse, especially when exercising or participating in a sport; a projecting or retreating part in a surface or line. **jog** v. To shift direction abruptly; to exercise by running at a slow but steady pace. **jogger** n.
jog-gle (jog´l) v. To move or shake slightly. **joggle** n.
Johnson, Andrew n. (1808-1875) The seventeenth president of the United States from 1865-1869.
Johnson, Lyndon Baines n. (1908-1973) The thirty-sixth president of the United States from 1963-1969.
John the Baptist n. The baptizer of Jesus Christ.
join (join) v. To bring or put together so as to form a unit; to become a member

of an organization; to participate.

join-er (joi´nĕr) *n.* A person whose occupation is to build articles by joining pieces of wood; a cabinet maker; a carpenter.

joint (joint) *n.* The place where two or more things or parts are joined; a point where bones are connected. *Slang* A disreputable or shabby place of entertainment. **joint** *adj.* Marked by cooperation, as a joint effort; shared by two or more.

joint res-o-lu-tion *n.* A resolution that is approved by the two houses of a legislature, which becomes law when signed by the chief executive.

joist (joist) *n.* Any of a number of small parallel beams set from wall to wall to support a floor.

joke (jōk) *n.* Something said or done to cause laughter, such as a brief story with a punch line; something not taken seriously. **joke** *v.* To tell or play jokes. **jokingly** *adv.*

jok-er (jō´kèr) *n.* A person who jokes; a playing card, used in certain card games as a wild card; an unsuspected or unap-parent fact which nullifies a seeming advantage.

jol-li-fi-ca-tion *n.* Merrymaking; festivity.

jol-ly (jol´ē) *adj.* Full of good humor; merry. **jollity** *n.* **jolly** *v.*

jolt (jōlt) *v.* To knock or shake about. **jolt** *n.* A sudden bump or jar, as from a blow.

jon-quil (jong´kwil) *n.* A widely grown species of narcissus related to the daffodil, having fragrant white or yellow flowers and long narrow leaves.

jo-rum (jōr´um) *n.* A large drinking vessel.

josh (josh) *v., Slang* To make good-humored fun of someone; to tease; to joke.

joss (jos) *n.* A Chinese idol or image.

joss stick *n.* A stick of incense burnt by the Chinese.

jos-tle (jos´l) *v.* To make one's way through a crowd by pushing, elbowing, or shoving. **jostler** *n.*

jot (jot) *v.* To make a brief note of something. **jot** *n.* A tiny bit.

jounce (jouns) *v.* To bounce; to bump; to shake. **jounce** *n.* **jouncy** *adj.*

jour *abbr.* Journal; journalist.

jour-nal (jer´nal) *n.* A diary or personal daily record of observations and experiences; in bookkeeping, a book in which daily financial transactions are recorded. *Mech.* The part of an axle which rotates in or against a bearing.

jour-nal-ese (jer´na lēz´) *n.* The vocabulary and style of writing supposedly characteristic of most newspapers.

jour-nal-ism (jer´na liz´um) *n.* The occupation, collection, writing, editing, and publishing of newspapers and other periodicals. **journalist** *n.* **journalistic** *adj.* **journalistically** *adv.*

jour-ney (jer´nē) *n.* A trip from one place to another over a long distance; the distance that is traveled. **journey** *v.* to make a trip; to travel a long distance.

jour-neyman (jer´nē man) *n. pl.* **journey-men** A worker who has served an apprenticeship in a skilled trade.

jo-vi-al (jō´vē al) *adj.* Good-natured; good-humored; jolly. **joviality** *n.*

jowl (joul) *n.* The fleshy part of the lower jaw; the cheek. **jowly** *adj.*

joy (joi) *n.* A strong feeling of great happiness; delight; a state or source of contentment or satisfaction; anything which makes one delighted or happy. **joyful, joyless** *adj.* **joyfully** *adv.* **joyfulness** *n.* **joylessly** *adv.*

joy-ous (joi´us) *adj.* Joyful; causing or feeling joy. **joyously** *adv.*

joy stick *Slang* The control stick of an airplane or video game.

jub-bah (jub´ba) *n.* An outer garment worn in Muslin countries by both men and women, which is long and has sleeves.

ju-bi-lant (jō´bi lant) *adj.* Exultantly joyful or triumphant; expressing joy. **jubilance** *n.* **jubilantly** *adv.*

ju-bi-la-tion (jō´bi lā´shan) *n.* Rejoicing; exultation.

ju-bi-lee (jō´bi lē´) *n.* A special anniversary of an event; any time of rejoicing.

judge (juj) *v., Law* A public officer who passes judgment in a court. **judge** *v.* To decide authoritatively after deliberation.

judg-ment (juj´ment) *n.* The ability to make a wise decision or to form an opinion; the act of judging. *Law* The sentence or de-termination of a court.

ju-di-ca-ble (jō´di ka bl) *adj.* Able to be judged or tried.

ju-di-ca-to-ry (jō´di ka tōr´ē) *adj.* Pertaining to the administration of justice. **judicatory** *n.* A court of justice; a person or persons having judicial authority; processes used to administer justice.

ju-di-ca-ture (jō´di kā´chèr) *n.* The function of administration of justice; law, courts, or judges as a whole.

ju-di-cial (jō dish´al) *adj.* Pertaining to the administering of justice, to courts of law, or to judges; enforced or decreed by a court of law.

ju-di-cious (jō dish´us) *adj.* Having, showing, or exercising good sound judgment. **judiciously** *adv.* **-ness** *n.*

ju-do (jō´dō) *n.* A system or form of self-defense, developed from jujitsu in Japan in 1882, which emphasizes principles of balance and leverage.

ju-do-gi (jō dō´ gē) *n.* A loosely fitted white cotton costume, worn by judo wrestlers.

jug (jug) *n.* A small pitcher or similar vessel for holding liquids. *Slang* A jail.

ju-gal (jō´gal) *adj.* Relating to the bony arch of the cheek.

jug-ger-naut (jug´er not´) *n.* Any destructive force or object.

jug-gle (jug´l) *v.* To keep several objects continuously moving from the hand into the air; to practice fraud or deception.

ju-glan-da-ceous (jō´glan dā´shus) *adj.* Belonging to the tree family that includes walnuts and hickories.

jug-u-lar (jug´ū lēr) *adj., Anat.* Of or pertaining to the throat or the jugular vein.

jugular vein *n., Anat.* One of the large veins on either side of the neck.

ju-gu-late (jō´gū lāt) *v.* To use extreme measures in order to suppress disease; to slit the throat.

ju-gum (jō´ gum) *n.* In some insects, an area at the base of the forewings which locks the forewings and backwings together during flight.

juice (jōs) *n.* The liquid part of a vegetable, fruit, or animal. *Slang* Electric current. **juice** *v.*

juic-er (jō´sēr) *n.* A device for extracting juice from fruit.

juic-y (jō´sē) *adj.* Full of; abounding with juice; full of interest; richly rewarding, especially financially. **juiciness** *n.*

ju-jit-su (jō jit´sō) *n.* A Japanese system of using holds, throws, and stunning blows to subdue an opponent.

juke-box (jōk´boks´) *n.* A large, automatic, coin-operated record player equipped with push buttons for the selection of records.

ju-lep (jū´lip) *n.* A mint julep.

ju-li-enne (jō´lē en´) *adj.* Cut into thin strips. **julienne** *n.* A clear meat soup containing vegetables chopped or cut into thin strips.

Ju-ly (jū lī´) *n.* The seventh month of the year, having 31 days.

jum-ble (jum´bl) *v.* To mix in a confused mass; to throw together without order; to confuse or mix something up in the mind. **jumble** *n.*

jum-bo (jum´bō) *n.* A very large person, animal, or thing. **jumbo** *adj.* Very large.

jump (jump) *v.* To spring from the ground, floor, or other surface into the air by using a muscular effort of the legs and feet; to move in astonishment; to leap over; to increase greatly, as prices. *Informal* To attack by surprise. *Computer Science* To move from one set of instructions in a program to another set further behind or ahead.

jump-er (jum´pēr) *n.* One who or that which jumps; a sleeveless dress, usually worn over a blouse. *Electr.* A short wire used to bypass or join parts of a circuit.

jump-ing bean *n.* The seed of certain shrubs from Mexico which jumps about due to the movements of the larva inside.

jump seat *n.* An extra seat, often folding, found in a limousine or a taxicab.

jump shot *n.* In basketball, a shot made at the highest point of a jump.

jump-start *v.* To start an automobile by connecting a jumper cable from its battery to one of another automobile and turning the engine over.

jump suit *n.* Originally, a uniform for parachutists; now, any one-piece garment.

jump-y *adj.* Nervous; jittery.

jun-co (jung´kō) *n.* Any of various small birds of North America, having mainly gray plumage.

junc-tion (jungk´shan) *n.* The place where lines or routes meet, as roads or railways; the process of joining or the act of joining

junc-ture (jungk´chēr) *n.* The point where two things join; a crisis; an emergency; a point in time.

June (jūn) *n.* The sixth month of the year, having 30 days.

jun-gle (jung´gl) *n.* A densely covered land with tropical vegetation, usually inhabited by wild animals. **jungle** *adj.*

jungle fever *n.* A disease that is commonly found in tropical regions; a severe, recurring fever.

jun-ior (jōn´yēr) *adj.* Younger in years or rank, used to distinguish the son from the father of the same first name; the younger of two. **junior** *n.* The third year of high school or college.

ju-ni-per (jō´nī pēr) *n.* An evergreen shrub or tree of Europe and America with dark blue berries, prickly foliage, and fragrant wood.

junk (jungk) *n.* Discarded material, as glass, scrap iron, paper, or rags; a flat-bottomed Chinese ship with battened sails; rubbish; worthless matter. *Slang* Heroin, narcotics or dope.

jun-ket (jung´kit) *n.* A party, banquet, or trip; a trip taken by a public official with all expenses paid for by public funds; a custard-like dessert of flavored milk set with rennet. **junket** *v.*

junk-ie (jung´kē) *n., Slang* A drug addict that uses heroin.

jun-ta (hen´ta) *n.* A body of men or persons, as military officers, in power following a coup d'etat.

Ju-pi-ter (jō´pi tēr) *n., Astron.* The fifth planet from the sun; the largest planet in the solar system.

ju-ral (jur´al) *adj.* Pertaining to law;

legal; pertaining to rights and obligations.

ju-rat (jur´at) *n., Law* The description on an affidavit that states when, where, before whom, and by whom the affidavit was made.

ju-ra-to-ry (jur´a tŏr˝ē) *adj.* Referring to an oath.

ju-rid-i-cal (je rid´i k*a*l) *adj.* Of or pertaining to the law and to the administration of justice.

ju-ris-con-sult (jur˝is k*o*n sult´) *n.* An expert who gives opinions in cases of law.

ju-ris-dic-tion (jer˝is dik´sh*a*n) *n.* The lawful right or power to interpret and apply the law; the territory within which power is exercised.

ju-ris-pru-dence (jur˝is prŏd´ens) *n.* The record of court decisions that are the basis for the formal principles upon which laws are based; the science of law.

ju-ror (jer´ẽr) *n.* A person who serves on a jury.

ju-ry (jer´ē) *n. pl.* **juries** A group of legally qualified persons summoned to serve on a judicial tribunal to give a verdict ac-cording to evidence presented.

just (just) *adj.* Fair and impartial in acting or judging; morally right; merited; deserved; based on sound reason. **just** *adv.* To the exact point; precisely; exactly right. **justly** *adv.* **justness** *n.*

jus-tice (jus´tis) *n.* The principle of moral or ideal rightness; conformity to the law; the abstract principle by which right and wrong are defined; a judge.

justice of the peace *n.* A local magistrate having limited jurisdiction with authority to try minor cases, administer oaths, and perform marriages.

jus-ti-ci-a-ble (ju stish´ē *a* bl) *adj.* Expected to be settled by court action or within the legal system.

jus-ti-fi-a-ble (jus´ti fī *a* bl) *adj.* Able to be defended or proven to be right.

justified margin *n.* A typing or type-setting margin with all the characters at the ends of the lines vertically aligned.

jus-ti-fy (jus´ti fī´) *v.* To be just, right, or valid; to declare guiltless; to adjust or space lines to the proper length. **justifiably** *adv.* **justification** *n.*

jut (jut) *v.* To extend beyond the main portion; to project.

jute (jŏt) *n.* A tall, annual Asian herb of the linden family, yielding a strong, coarse fiber used to make sacking and rope.

ju-ve-nile (jō´ve n*i*l) *adj.* Young; youthful; not yet an adult. **juvenile** *n.* A young person; an actor who plays youthful roles; a child's book.

juvenile court *n.* A court which deals only with cases involving dependent, neglected, and delinquent children.

juvenile delinquent *n.* A person who is guilty of violations of the law, but is too young to be punished as an adult criminal; a young person whose behavior is out of control.

juvenile officer *n.* A police officer who specializes in investigating, prosecuting, and looking after juvenile delinquents.

ju-ve-nil-i-a (jō´ve nil´ē *a*) *n.* Works of art, such as writings or paintings, produced while young; any writings or artistic works intended to appeal to the young.

ju-ve-nil-i-ty (jō´ve nil´i tē) *n.* Youthful looks or actions; a childish act; behaving in an immature manner.

jux-ta-pose (juk˝sta pōz´) *v.* To put side by side; to place together. **juxtaposed** *adj.* **juxtaposition** *n.*

K

K, k (kā) The eleventh letter of the English alphabet.

K *abbr., Computer science* A unit of storage capacity equal to 1024 bytes.

ka-bob (k*a* bob´) *n.* Cubed meat and mushrooms, onions, and tomatoes placed on a skewer usually marinated, and broiled over an open fire.

ka-bu-ki (kä bö´kē) *n.* A traditional Japanese drama in which dances and songs are performed in a stylized fashion.

kaf-fee klatsch (kä´fä kläch˝) *n.* An informal get-together to drink coffee and talk.

kaf-ir (kaf´ẽr) *n.* A grain sorghum that is cultivated in dry areas having a tough leafy stalk and is used for fodder.

kai-nite (kī´nīt) *n.* A mineral that is used as a fertilizer and a source of magnesium and potassium.

ka-ka (kä´ka) *n.* A New Zealand parrot, having an olive-brown color.

ka-ka-po (kä˝kä pō´) *n.* A large parrot.

kale (kāl) *n.* A green cabbage having crinkled leaves which do not form a tight head.

ka-lei-do-scope (k*a* lī´d*o* skōp˝) *n.* A tubular instrument rotated to make successive symmetrical designs by using mirrors reflecting the changing patterns made by pieces of loose, colored glass at the end of a tube; a series of continuously changing colors; changing events or phases. **kaleidoscopic** *adj.* **kaleidoscopical** *adj.*

kaleyard school (kāl´yärd˝skōl) *n.* A school of writers from the 19th century who wrote about Scottish life in a very sentimental manner, using heavy dialect.

kal-mi-a (kal´mē *a*) *n*. An evergreen shrub of North America, having pink, white, or purple flowers.

kame (kām) *n*. A short ridge of gravel and sand that remains after glacial ice melts.

kam-ik (käm´ik) *n*. Boot made of sealskin, knee-high in length and worn in the eastern arctic regions.

ka-mi-ka-ze (kä´mi kä´zē) *n*. A Japanese pilot in World War II trained to make a suicidal crash; an aircraft loaded with ex-plosives used in a suicide attack.

kam-pong (käm´pong) *n*. A group of dwellings or a local village in countries that speak Malay.

kan-ga-roo (kang´g*a* rö´) *n. pl.* **kangaroos** *or* **kangaroo** Any of various herbivorous marsupials of Australia with short forelegs, large hind limbs capable of jumping, and a large tail.

kangaroo court *n*. A self-appointed, illegal court, usually marked by incompetence or dishonesty where the laws are deliberately totally disregarded or misinterpreted.

Kan-sas *n*. A state in the central United States; statehood January 29, 1861; state capital Topeka.

ka-o-lin *or* **ka-o-line** (kä´o lin) *n*. A fine clay which remains white after firing, used in ceramics and in manufacturing high quality porcelain.

ka-pok (kä´pok) *n*. A silky fiber manufactured from the fruit of the silk-cotton tree and used for stuffing cushions and life preservers, pillows, and sleeping bags and also used for insulation.

ka-put (kä pet´) *adj., Slang* Destroyed or out of order; something with no possibility of success.

kar-a-kul (kar´a kul) *n*. Any of a breed of fat-tailed sheep of central Asia, having a narrow body and coarse, wiry, brown fur.

kar-at (kar´*a*t) *n*. A unit of measure for the fineness of gold; a measure of weight for precious gems.

ka-ra-te (k*a* rä´tē) *n*. A Japanese art of self- defense, in which a person uses his elbows, feet, and knees in quick, damaging blows to his opponent.

ka-ross (k*a* ros´) *n*. Animal skins sewn together into the shape of a square and worn by natives; a throw rug made from animal skins.

kar-y-o-lymph (kar´ē *o* limf´) *n., Biol.* The transparent substance surrounding the nucleus of a cell.

kar-y-o-type (kar´ē *o* tīp´) *n*. The characteristics of the nucleus of a cell, including its size, form, and chromosome number.

ka-ty-did (kä´tē did) *n*. Any of various green insects related to grasshoppers and crickets having specialized organs on the wings of the male that make a shrill sound when rubbed together.

katz-en-jam-mer (kat´sen jam´ér) *n*. A feeling of uneasiness, worry, or nervousness that follows intoxication.

kau-ri (kou´rē) *n*. A New Zealand tree which is the source of valuable resin used in varnish and timber used in construction.

ka-va (kä-va) *n*. A pepper shrub from Polynesia; a beverage made from this shrub that can be intoxicating.

kay-ak (kī´ak) *n*. A watertight Eskimo boat, having a circular hole in the top for the occupant, and made from a light wooden frame with a sealskin cover.

kay-o (kā´ō´) *v*. To knock out an opponent, in boxing. **kayo** *n*. A knockout.

ka-zoo (k*a* zö´) *n*. A toy musical instrument with a paper membrane which vibrates simultaneously when a player hums into the tube.

ke-a (kā´*a*) *n*. A New Zealand parrot.

kedge (kej) *n*. A small anchor. **kedge** *v*. To pull a ship by the rope of an anchor.

keel (kēl) *n*. The central main stem on a ship or aircraft, which runs lengthwise along the center line from bow to stern, on which a frame is built upwards. **keel** *v*. To capsize. **keel over** To fall over suddenly; to turn upside down.

keel-age (kē´lij) *n*. A fee for mooring a ship in port.

keel-boat (kēl´bōt´) *n*. A boat used on rivers; a shallow boat used for freight.

keel-haul (kēl´hol´) *v*. To drag a person under the keel of a ship as a form of punishment.

keel-son (kēl´son) *n., Naut*. A structural member fastened above and parallel to the keel to give additional strength.

keen (kēn) *adj*. Having a sharp edge or point; acutely painful or harsh; intellectually acute; strong; intense. *Slang* Great. **keen** *v*. Wailing lament, especially for the dead. **keen** *v*. **keenly** *adv*. **keenness, keener** *n*.

keep (kēp) *v*. To have and hold; to not let go; to maintain, as business records; to know a secret and not divulge it; to protect and defend.

keep back *v*. To withhold things; to prevent one from coming forward.

keep-er (kē´pér) *n*. One who keeps, guards, or maintains something; a person who respects or observes a requirement; a device for holding something in place, as a latch, or clasp.

keep-ing (kē´ping) *n*. Charge or possession; conformity or harmony; maintenance or support.

keep off *v*. To fend or avert off. **keep**

off *v.* To stay back or remain at a distance.

keep-sake (kēp´sāk˘) *n.* A memento or souvenir; a token or remembrance of friendship.

keep up *v.* To persist in, sustain, or continue. To remain equal or even to; to stay informed; to continue without interruption.

kef (kāf) *n.* A tranquil and dreamy state; a narcotic.

keg (keg) *n.* A small barrel usually having the capacity of five to ten gallons; the unit of measure for nails which equals 100 pounds.

keg-ler (keg´lˇer) *n.* A bowler.

ke-loid (kē´loid) *n.* A scar formed from fibrous growth in the connective skin tissue.

kelp (kelp) *n.* Any large brown seaweed.

kel-pie (kel´pē) *n.* A sheep dog originally bred in Australia.

kemp *n.* A coarse hairlike fiber used in the making of carpet.

Kennedy, John Fitzgerald *n.* (1917-1963) The thirty-fifth president of the United States from 1961-1963; assassinated while in office.

ken-nel (ken´el) *n.* A shelter for or a place where dogs or cats are bred, boarded, or trained. **kennel** *v.*

ke-no (kē´nō) *n.* A game of chance resembling bingo; a lottery game.

kent-ledge (kent´lij) *n.* Ship ballast for a ship made of pig iron.

Ken-tuck-y *n.* A state located in the east central United States; statehood June 1, 1792; state capital Frankfort.

kep-i (kā´pē) *n.* A French military cap having a flat, round top and a visor.

ker-a-tin (ker´a tin) *n.* A fibrous protein which forms the basic substance of nails, hair, horns, and hooves.

ker-a-to-plas-ty (ker´a to plas˘tē) *n., Med.* An operation that replaces damaged corneal tissue with healthy corneal tissue. **keratoplastic** *adj.*

ker-a-to-sis (ker´a tō´sis) *n.* An area of skin overgrown with horny tissue.

ker-chief (ker´chif) *n.* A piece of cloth worn around the neck or on the head; scarf; a handkerchief.

kerf (kerf) *n.* A slit or notch made by a saw or other cutting tool; the place where a branch is cut across.

ker-mes (kor´mēz) *n.* A red dye consisting of the dried bodies of female scaled insects found in the Mediterranean area.

ker-mis (ker´mis) *n.* An annual fair of the Netherlands.

ker-nel (ker´nel) *n.* A grain or seed, as of corn, enclosed in a hard husk; the inner substance of a nut; the central, most important part. **kernally** *adj.*

ker-o-sene *or* **ker-o-sine** (ker´o sēn˘) *n.* An oil distilled from petroleum or coal and used for illumination.

ker-ri-a (ker´ē a) *n.* A shrub of Japan, having ridged, green stems and double or single flowers that are yellow in color.

ker-sey (ker´zē) *n.* A coarse cloth made from wool and cotton used mainly for rugged garments and outer wear.

ker-sey-mere (ker´zi mēr) *n.* A twill weave cloth made from fine wool; also cassimere.

ke-ryg-ma (ki rig´ma) *n.* The apostolic preaching of the life and teachings of Jesus Christ.

kes-trel (kes´trel) *n.* A small falcon that hovers in the air with its head in the direction of the wind, having a gray and brown plumage, common in Europe, inhabiting coasts, moors, and farms.

ketch (kech) *n.* A small sailing vessel with two masts, one large mainmast toward the bow of the ship, and a smaller mizzenmast in the direction of the stern but before the rudder.

ketch-up (kech´up) *n.* A thick, smooth sauce made from tomatoes. *Also catsup*

ke-tene (kē´tēn) *n.* A gas which is colorless and poisonous, having a penetrating odor.

ke-to (kē´tō) *adj.* Having or pertaining to a ketone.

ke-tol (kē´tol) *n.* Organic compound having both a ketone and alcohol group.

ke-tone (kē´tōn) *n.* An organic compound; used as a solvent; acetone. **ketonic** *adj.* **ketosis** *n.*

ket-tle (ket´l) *n.* A pot or vessel, usually made of metal, used for stewing or boiling liquids.

ket-tle-drum (ket´l drum˘) *n.* A musical instrument with a parchment head which can be tuned by adjusting the tension.

ket-tle of fish *n.* A mess; an awkward situation; matter of consideration.

key (kē) *n.* An object used to open a lock; button or level pushed on a keyboard of a typewriter, piano, etc; the crucial or main element; an island. **key** *v.*

key-board (kē´bôrd˘) *n.* A bank of keys, as on a piano, typewriter, or computer terminal. **keyboard** *v.* To set by means of a keyed typesetting machine; to generate letters by means of a word processor. **keyboarder** *n.*

key-note (kē´nōt˘) *n., Mus.* The first and harmonically fundamental tone of a scale; main principle or theme.

key-punch *n.* A machine operated from a keyboard that uses punched holes in tapes or cards for data processing systems. **keypunch** *v.* **keypuncher** *n.*

key-stroke *n.* A stroke of a key, as of a

typewriter or computer keyboard.

key-way (kē'wā') *n.* A slot cut in a wheel hub or shaft for the reception of a key.

key word *n.* A word having special significance in relation to other phrases, words, or concepts.

kg *abbr.* Kilogram.

khad-dar (kä'dēr) *n.* Cloth made from cotton.

khak-i (kak'ē) *n.* A yellowish brown or olive-drab color; a sturdy cloth which is khaki in color. **khakis** *n. pl.* A uniform of khaki cloth. **khaki** *adj.*

khan (kän) *n.* An Asiatic title of respect; a medieval Turkish, Mongolian or Tartar ruler. **khanate** *n.*

khe-dive (ke dēv') *n.* A ruler of Egypt from 1867 to 1914, governing as a viceroy of the sultan of Turkey.

ki *abbr.* Kiloliter.

kib-ble (kib'l) *n.* A bucket used in the shaft of a mine for hoisting ore.

kib-butz (ki buts') *n.* In Israel, a settlement or farm operated by a collective system.

kibe (kīb) *n.* An ulcerated chilblain, usually on the heel.

kib-itz (kib'its) *v., Slang* To look on and offer meddlesome advice to others. **kibitzer** *n.*

ki-bosh (kī'bosh) *n., Slang* Something that acts as a check or stop.

kick (kik) *v.* To strike something with a force by the foot. **kick in** To put in money. **kick out** To expel with force.

kick-back (kik'bak') *n.* A secret payment to a person who can influence a source of income; repercussion; a strong reaction.

kick-shaw (kik'shä') *n.* Something of little substance or value; a trinket.

kid (kid) *n.* A young goat; leather made from the skin of a young goat. *Slang* A child; youngster. **kid** *v.* To mock or tease playfully; to deceive for fun; to fool. **kiddish** *adj.*

kid-nap (kid'nap) *v.* To seize and hold a person unlawfully, often for ransom. **kidnapper** *n.* **kidnapping** *n.*

kid-ney (kid'ne) *n. pl.* **kidneys** Either of two organs situated in the abdominal cavity of vertebrates whose function is to keep proper water balance in the body and to excrete wastes in the form of urine.

kid-skin (kid'skin') *n.* A soft, pliable leather made from the skin of a young goat.

kidvid *n., Slang* Television programming for children.

kiel-ba-sa *n.* A smoked Polish sausage.

kier (kēr) *n.* A large-capacity tub or boiler used for bleaching and dyeing jobs.

kil-der-kin (kil'dēr kin) *n.* A measure of capacity of half a barrel; a vessel that holds this amount.

kill (kil) *v.* To put to death; to nullify; to cancel; to slaughter for food; to deprive of life; to neutralize or destroy the active qualities.

kil-lick (kil'ik) *n.* An anchor for a boat usually consisting of a stone secured by wood.

kil-li-fish (kil'ē fish') *n.* A fish found in the bays and rivers of N. America.

kill-joy (kil'joi') *n.* One who spoils the enjoyment of others.

kiln (kil) *n.* An oven or furnace for hardening or drying a substance, especially one for firing ceramics and pottery.

ki-lo (kil'ō) *n.* A kilogram.

kil-o-bit *n.* In Computer Science, one thousand binary digits.

kilobyte (KB) In Computer Science, one thousand bytes.

kil-o-cal-o-rie (kil'o kal'o rē) *n.* One thousand gram calories.

ki-lo-cy-cle (kil'o sī'kl) *n.* A unit equal to one thousand cycles; one thousand cycles per second.

kil-o-gram (kil'o gram') *n.* A measurement of weight in the metric system equal to slightly more than one third of a pound.

kil-o-li-ter (kil'o lē'tēr) *n.* Metric measurement equal to one thousand liters.

kil-o-me-ter (kil'o mē'tēr) *n.* Metric measurement equal to one thousand meters.

kil-o-ton (kil'o tun') *n.* One thousand tons; an explosive power equal to that of one thousand tons of TNT.

kil-o-volt (kil'o vōlt') *n.* One thousand volts.

kil-o-watt (kil'o wot') *n.* A unit of power equal to one thousand watts.

kil-o-watt–hour (kil'o wot'our') *n.* A unit of electric power consumption of one thousand watts throughout one hour.

kilt (kilt) *n.* A knee-length wool skirt with deep pleats, usually of tartan, worn especially by men in the Scottish Highlands.

kil-ter (kil'tēr) *n.* Good condition; proper or working order.

ki-mo-no (ko mō'no) *n.* A loose Japanese robe with a wide sash; a loose robe.

kin (kin) *n.* One's relatives by blood; relatives collectively.

ki-nase (kī'nās) *n.* A catalyst that assists in changing a zymogen into an enzyme.

kind (kīnd) *n.* A characteristic; a particular variety of sort.

kind (kīnd) *adj.* Of a friendly or good-natured disposition; coming from a good-natured readiness to please others.

kin-der-gar-ten (kin'dēr gär'ten) *n.* A school or class for young children from the ages of four to six to further their social, mental and physical development.

kin-der-gart-ner (kin´der gärt´ner) *n.* A child who attends kindergarten.

kind-heart-ed (kind´här´tid) *adj.* Having much generosity and kindness.

kin-dle (kin´dl) *v.* To ignite; to catch fire; to stir up; to arouse; to excite, as the feelings.

kind-less (kind´lis) *adj.* Mean, cruel, unkind, unfriendly. **kindlessly** *adv.*

kin-dling (kind´ling) *n.* Easily ignited material, such as sticks, wood chips, or paper, used to start a fire.

kind-ly (kind´lē) *adv.* A kind nature, disposition, or character; benevolent. **kindliness** *n.*

kind-ness (kind´nis) *n.* An act of good will; state or quality of being kind; a kind act.

kin-dred (kin´drid) *n.* A person's relatives by blood. **kindred** *adj.* Having a like nature; similar. **kindredness** *n.*

kin-e-mat-ics (kin´e mat´iks) *n.* The branch of dynamics that deals with motion, considered apart from force and mass. **kinematic** *adj.*

kin-e-scope (kin´i skōp´) *n.* A cathode-ray tube in a television set which translates received electrical impulses into a visible picture on a screen; a film of a television broad-cast.

ki-ne-sics (ki nē´siks) *n.* To study the relation-ship between communication and nonverbal body language. **kinesic** *adj.* **kinesically** *adv.*

ki-ne-si-ol-o-gy (ki nē´sē ol´o jē) *n.* Science that investigates organic and anatomy process in reference to human motion.

kin-es-the-sia (kin´is thē´zha) *n.* The sense of muscular movement or effort. **kinesthesis** *n.* **kinesthetic** *adj.*

ki-net-ic (ki net´ik) *adj.* Of, pertaining to, or produced by motion.

ki-net-ic art *n.* The type of modern abstract art that attempts to present or indicate a sense of motion.

kinetic theory *n, Physics* The theory of matter that hypothesizes that the minute particles of matter are constantly in very rapid random motion.

kin-folk (kin´fōk´) *n.* Relatives; family.

king (king) *n.* One who rules over a country; a male ruler; a playing card with a picture of a king; the main piece in the game of chess; a crowned checker in the game of checkers.

King James Bible *n.* An English translation of the Bible from Hebrew and Greek, published in 1611, authorized by King James I of England.

kink (kingk) *n.* A tight twist or knot-like curl; a sharp, painful muscle cramp; a mental quirk. **kink** *v.* To form or

cause to form a kink.

kink-a-jou (king´ka jö´) *n.* A tropical American mammal having large eyes, brown fur, and a long, prehensile tail.

kink-y *adj.* Tightly curled; sexually uninhibited. **kinkily** *adv.,* **-iness** *n.*

kin-ship(kin´ship) *n.* Family relationship; common blood bond.

kins-man (kinz´man) *n.* A blood relative, especially a male relative.

kins-wo-man (kinz´wum´an) *n.* A female blood relation.

ki-osk (kē osk´) *n.* A small building used as a refreshment booth or newsstand.

kip (kip) *n.* The untanned skin of a calf, a lamb and or an adult of any small breed; a bundle of such hides.

kip-per (kip´er) *n.* A salted and smoked herring or salmon. **kipper** *v.* To cure by salting, smoking, or drying.

kirk (kerk) *n.* The Presbyterian Church of Scotland as opposed to the Episcopal Church of Scotland.

kirsch (kersh) *n.* A brandy made from the fermented juice of black cherries.

kir-tle (ker´tl) *n.* A woman's long skirt or petticoat; a man's tunic or coat.

kis-met (kiz´mit) *n.* Fate; appointed lot.

kiss (kis) *v.* To touch two lips together in greeting; between two people.

kit (kit) *n.* A collection of tools, supplies, or items for a special purpose.

kitch-en (kich´en) *n.* A room in a house or building used to prepare and cook food.

kite (kīt) *n.* A light-weight framework of wood and paper designed to fly in a steady breeze at the end of a string; any of various predatory birds of the hawk family having long, usually forked tails.

kith (kith) *n.* Acquaintances or family.

kitsch (kich) *n.* Anything that is pretentious and in poor taste.

kit-ten (kit´en) *n.* A young cat. **kittenish** *adj.* **kittenishly** *adv.*

kit-ty (kit´ē) *n.* A small collection of objects or money; a young cat or kitten.

kit-ty–cor-nered (kit´ē kor´ner) *adj.* Diagonally; catty–cornered.

ki-va (kē´va) *n.* A Pueblo Indian chamber, used in ceremonies, often underground.

klatch *or* **klatsch (klach)** *n.* A social gathering devoted primarily to small talk and gossip.

klep-to-ma-ni-a (klep´to mä´nē a) *n.* Obsessive desire to steal or impulse to steal, especially without economic motive. **klep-tomaniac** *n.*

kloof (klöf) *n.* A ravine; gorge; deep mountain cleft.

kludge *n.* A computer system that is made up of poorly matched components.

klutz *n., Slang* A stupid or clumsy person. **klutziness** *n.* **klutzy** *adj.*

km *abbr.* Kilometer.

knack (nak) *n.* A natural talent; aptitude; dexterity.

knave (nāv) *n.* Tricky or dishonest person; a rascal. **knavish** *adj.* **knavishly** *adv.* **knavishness** *n.*

knead (nēd) *v.* To work dough into a uniform mass; to shape by or as if by kneading. **kneader, kneadability** *n.* **kneadable** *adj.*

knee (nē) *n.* The joint in the human body which connects the calf with the thigh.

kneel (nēl) *v.* To go down upon one's knees.

knell (nel) *v.* To sound a bell, especially when rung for a funeral; to toll. **knell** *n.* An act of knelling; a signal of disaster.

knick-ers (nik´ẽrz) *n.* *pl.* Short, loose-fitting pants gathered at the knee.

knick-knack (nik´nak˜) *n.* A trinket; trifling article.

knife (nīf) *n.* An instrument used to cut an item. **knife** *v.*

knish *n.* Baked or fried dough stuffed with meat, cheese, or potatoes.

knit (nit) *v.* To form by intertwining thread or yarn by interlocking loops of a single yarn by means of needles; to fasten securely; to draw together; to furrow the brow. **knitting** *n.*

knob (nob) *n.* A rounded protuberance; a lump; a rounded mountain; a rounded handle. **knobbed, knobby** *adj.*

knock (nok) *v.* To hit or strike with a hard blow; to criticize; to collide; to make a noise, as that of a defective engine. **knock out** To render unconscious.

knoll (nōl) *n.* A small, round hill; a mound.

knot (not) *n.* An intertwining of string or rope; a fastening made by tying together lengths of material, as string; a unifying bond, especially of marriage; a hard node on a tree from which a branch grows. *Naut.* A unit of speed, also called a nautical mile, which equals approximately 1.15 statute miles per hour. **knot** *v.* **knottiness** *n.*

knout (nout) *n.* A whip or scourge for flogging criminals. **knout** *v.*

know (nō) *v.* To perceive directly as fact or truth; to believe to be true; to be certain of; to be familiar with or have experience of. **knowable** *adj.*

know-how (nō´hou˜) *n.* Knowing how to do something.

know-ing (nō´ing) *adj.* To be astute; to know secret knowledge. **-ingly** *adv.*

knowl-edge (nol´ij) *n.* Acquainted with facts and areas of study; having ability to know facts, information.

knowl-edge-a-ble (nol´i ja bl) *n.* The state of being intelligent.

know-nothing (nō´nuth˜ing) *n.* An extremely stupid person.

knuck-le (nuk´l) *n.* On the finger; the joint of the finger. **knuckly** *adj.*

knuck-le-ball *n.* A pitch used in baseball that is a slow pitch.

knuck-le-bone (nuk´l bōn˜) *n.* The bone of the finger which forms the knuckle.

knuck-le-head (nuk´l hed˜) *n.* A person who is not very smart; dumb.

knuck-le joint *n.* A finger joint; a machine joint formed like a knuckle.

knur (ner) *n.* A lump or knot of a tree.

knurl (nürl) *n.* A ridge. **knurled, knurly** *adj.*

kohl (kōl) *n.* Dark powder used as cosmetics to darken under the eyes.

kohl-ra-bi (kōl rä´bē) *n.* *pl.* **kohlrabies** A variety of cabbage having a thick stem and eaten as a vegetable.

koi-ne (koi nā´) *n.* Any regional language or dialect which becomes the standard language of a larger region.

ko-la (kō´la) *n.* The tree which produces the kola nut.

ko-la nut *n.* The brownish nut used as a tonic or stimulant.

ko-lin-sky (ko lin´skē) *n.* A mink found in Asia.

kook (kök) *n.* *Slang* A crazy or eccentric person. **kookiness** *n.* **kooky** *adj.*

Ko-ran (kō rän´) *n.* The sacred book of Islam, accepted as containing the revelations made to Mohammed by Allah through the angel Gabriel.

ke-sher (kō´shẽr) *adj.* Serving food prepared according to Jewish dietary laws. *Slang* Appropriate; proper.

kow-tow (kou´tou´) *v.* To show servile deference.

kraal (kräl) *n.* A village of southern African natives; an enclosure for animals in southern Africa.

krill (kril) *n.* A small crustacean living in open ocean waters and an important food source for whales.

kryp-ton (krip´ton) *n.* A white, inert gaseous chemical used mainly in fluorescent lamps, symbolized by Kr.

ku-chen (kö´chen) *n.* Any coffee cake made with a sweetened yeast-dough.

ku-dos (kö´dōs) *n.* Acclaim or prestige resulting from notable achievement or high position; glory; recognition; renown.

kum-quat (kum´kwot) *n.* A small, round orange fruit having a sour pulp and edible rind; the tree bearing this fruit.

kwash-i-or-kor *n.* Severe malnutrition, especially in children, caused by protein deficiency.

kwh *abbr.* Kilowatt-hour.

ky-mo-graph (kī´mo graf˜) *n.* A device for graphically recording variations in motion or pressure; a blood pressure graph.

ky-pho-sis (kī fō´sis) *n.* Abnormal curving of the spine; hunchback.

L, l (el) *n*. The twelfth letter of the English alphabet; the Roman numeral for fifty.

lab (lab) *n*. Laboratory.

la-bel (lā´bel) *n*. Something that identifies or describes. **label** *v*. To attach a label to.

la-bi-al (lā´bē el) *adj*. Pertaining to or of the labia or lips.

la-bi-um (lā´bē um) *n*. *pl*. **labia** Any of the four folds of the vulva.

la-bor (lā´bèr) *n*. Physical or manual work done for hire. *Med*. The physical pain and effort involved in childbirth. *v*. To work; to progress with great effort. **laborer** *n*.

lab-o-ra-to-ry (lab´ro tōr´ē) *n*. *pl*. **laboratories** A place equipped for conducting scientific experiments, research, or testing; a place where drugs and chemicals are produced.

lab-ra-dor-ite (lab´ra da rīt´) *n*. A kind of plagioclase feldspar mineral, distinguished by its iridescent colors.

la-bret (lā btet) *n*. A decoration or ornament worn through a hole in the lip.

la-bur-num (la bur´nam) *n*. A small ornamental tree; from the legume family, grown for its yellow flowers.

lab-y-rinth (lab´e rinth) *n*. A system of winding, intricate passages; a maze. **labyrinthian** *adj*.

lab-y-rin-thine (lab´e rin then) *adj*. Resembling or related to a labyrinth.

lac (lak) *n*. The resinous secretion left on certain trees by the lac insect and used in making paints and varnishes.

lac-co-lith (lak´e lith) *n*. A body of igneous rock between beds of overlying strata that causes the formation of domes.

lac-er-ate (las´e rāt´) *v*. To open with a jagged tear; to wound the flesh by tearing. **laceration** *n*.

lac-er-a-tion (las e´rā shan) *n*. The act of tearing; a jagged tear caused by lacerating.

lach-es (lach´iz) *n*. Inexcusable delay in completing a duty or claiming a legal right.

lach-ry-mal *or* **lac-ri-mal** (lak´ri mal) Relating to or producing tears; relating to the glands that produce tears.

lach-ry-ma-to-ry (lak´ri ma tōr´ē) *n*. A small vase found in ancient tombs that is said to have held tears from mourners.

lach-ry-mose (lak´ri mō) *adj*. Tearful; crying; trying to provoke tears.

lack (lak) *n*. The deficiency or complete absence of something. *v*. To have little of something or to be completely without.

lack-a-dai-si-cal (lak´a dā´zi kal) *adj*. Lacking life, interest, or spirit;

melancholy. **lackadaisically** *adv*.

lack-a-day (lak´ a dā´) *interj*. Exclamation used to express sorrow or regret.

lack-ey (lak´ē) *n*. A male servant of very low status.

lack-lus-ter (lak´lus´tér) *adj*. Lacking sheen; dull.

la-con-ic (la kon´ik) *adj*. Short; concise, brief and to the point; expressing a great deal in a few words.

lac-quer (lak´êr) *n*. A transparent varnish which is dissolved in a volatile solution and dries to give surfaces a glossy finish. **lac-quer** *v*. **lacrimator**

lac-tase (lak´tās) *n*. An enzyme in intestinal juices in young mammals and in yeasts that catalyzes the production of galactose and glucose from lactose.

lac-tate (lak´tāt) *v*. To secrete or to milk. **lactation** *n*.

lac-te-al (lak´tēl) *adj*. Of, resembling, or like milk. *n*., *Anat*. Any of the lymphatic vessels carrying chyle from the small in-testine to the blood.

lac-tes-cent (lak tes´ent) *adj*. Being or becoming milky; producing milk.

lactic acid *n*. A limpid, syrupy acid that is present in sour milk, molasses, some fruits, and wines.

lac-tif-er-ous (lak´tif e res) *adj*. Producing milk or a milky liquid substances.

lac-tone (lak´tōn) *n*. Any of a class of cyclic esters derived from hydroxy acids.

lac-tose (lak´tōs) *n*. A white, odorless, crystalline sugar that is found in milk.

la-cu-na (la kū na) *n*. *pl*. **-nas, -nae** A space from which something is missing; a gap.

la-cu-nar (la kū´nêr) *n*. A ceiling with recessed panels.

la-cus-trine (lakus´trin) *adj*. Pertaining to a lake; living or formed in lakes, as various plants and animals.

lad (lad) *n*. A boy or young man.

lad-der (lad´êr) *n*. An implement used for climbing up or down in order to reach another place or area.

lade *v*. To load down, as with cargo or a burden; to dip or lift out.

lad-en (lād´en) *adj*. Heavily burdened; oppressed; weighed down; loaded.

la-di-da (lä´dē dä´) *adj*. An expression of ridicule aimed at pretentious or elegant manners.

la-dy (lā´dē) *n*. *pl*. **ladies** A woman showing refinement, cultivation, and often high social position; the woman at the head of a household; an address or term of reference for any woman.

lag (lag) *v*. To stray or fall behind; to move slowly; to weaken gradually. **lag** *n*. The process or act of retardation or falling behind; the amount or period of lagging.

lag-an (lag en) *n.* Something sunk at sea, but attached to a buoy in order to recover it.

la-ger (lä′gér) *n.* A light beer originated in Germany, which is brewed by slow fermentation and matured or aged under refrigeration.

lag-gard (lag erd) *adj.* Slow; backward; lagging. *n.* A person who lags behind everyone else; a loiterer.

lag-ging (lag′ing) *n.* A material used for thermal insulation; a plank used to prevent cave-ins of earth walls; a support during construction

la-gniappe (lan yap′) *n.* A small gift which is given to a purchaser by a storekeeper; anything given as an extra bonus.

la-goon (la gün) *n.* A body of shallow water separated from the ocean by a coral reef or sandbars. **lagoonal** *adj.*

la-i-cism (lā e siz em) *n.* A governmental system which is free from ecclesiastical in-fluence or jurisdiction.

laid *v.* Past tense of lay.

laid back *adj., Slang* Casual or relaxed in character.

lain *v.* Past tense of lie.

lair (leer) *n.* The den or bed of a wild animal. **lair** *v.* To lie in a lair; to place in a lair.

lais-sez–faire (le sā′faer) *n.* A policy stating that a government should exercise very little control in trade and industrial affairs; non-interference.

la-i-ty (lā′i tē) *n.* Laymen, the people of a religious group or faith as distinguished from clergy.

lake (lāk) *n.* A large inland body of either salt or freshwater.

lak-er (lā′kér) *n.* One connected or associated with lakes; a fish living in or taken from a lake.

lake trout *n.* Any of various species of trout found in freshwater lakes.

lam (lam) *v., Slang* To beat; to thrash; to run or flee quickly. **lam** *n., Slang* A trip to escape; the escape.

Lamaze method *n.* A method of childbirth in which the mother is prepared psychologically and physically to give birth without the use of drugs.

lamb (lam) *n.* A young sheep; the meat of a lamb used as food; a gentle person.

lam-baste or **lambast** (lam bāst′) *v., Slang* To thrash or beat.

lam-bent (lam′bent) *adj.* Lightly and playfully brilliant; flickering gently; softly radiant. **lambency** *n.*

lame (lām) *adj.* Disabled or crippled, especially in the legs or feet so as to impair free movement; weak; ineffective; unsatisfactory. **lamely** *adv.*

la-mel-la (la mel′a) *n. pl.* **lamellae** A thin flat plate or scale; one composing the thin plates of the gills of certain mollusks.

la-mel-li-branch (lamel′i brangk″) *n.* A species of mollusks, that include the oyster, mussel and clam.

la-ment (la ment′) *v.* To express sorrow; to mourn. *n.* An expression of regret or sorrow. **lamentable** *adj.*

lam-en-ta-tion (lam″en tā′shan) *n.* A wailing or expression of sorrow.

lam-i-na (lam′i na) *n. pl.* **laminae** *or* **laminas** A thin scale or layer. *Bot.* The blade or flat part of a leaf.

lam-i-nate (lam′i nāt′) *v.* To form or press into thin sheets; to form layers by the action of pressure and heat. **lamination** *n.* **laminated** *adj.*

lamp (lamp) *n.* A device for generating heat or light.

lamp-black (lamp′blak″) *n.* A black soot of very fine texture of pure carbon.

lamp-light-er (lamp′lī″tér) *n.* A person who lights street lamps; a torch or device for lighting lamps.

lam-poon (lam pün″) *n.* A satirical, but often humorous, attack in verse or prose, especially one that ridicules a group, person, or institution.

lam-prey (lam′prē) *n. pl.* **lampreys** An eel-like fish having a circular, suctorial mouth with rasping teeth and no jaw.

lam-ster (lam′stér) *n., Slang* A person who is fleeing from the law.

LAN In *computer science*, Local Area Network; a group of computers that are linked to share common programs, data, output devices, etc.

la-nate (lā′nāt) *adj.* Covered with a substance or growth that resembles wool.

lan-ce-o-late (lan′sē o lāt″) *adj.* Shaped like a lance head; widening above the base and tapering to the apex.

lanc-er (lan′sér) *n.* One such as a soldier who is armed with a lance.

lan-cet (lan′sit, län′sit) *n.* A small surgical instrument having a sharp pointed generally two-edged blade, used to open veins, abscesses or tumors.

lan-cet-ed (lan′si tid) *adj.* Characterized by lancet arches or lancet windows.

lancet window *n.* A narrow window characterized by a pointed apex.

lance-wood (lans′wud″) *n.* Elastic wood that is used for fishing rods and archery bows.

lan-ci-nate (lan′si nāt″) *v.* Pierce or stab; to tear. **lancination** *n.*

land (land) *n.* The solid, exposed surface of the earth as distinguished from the waters. **land** *v.* To arrive at a destination; to catch a fish; to get a new job.

land grant *n.* A grant of land made by a government, especially for railroads, roads, or agricultural colleges.

lane (lān) *n.* A small or narrow path between walls, fences, or hedges.

lang-syne (lang´zīn´) *n.* The time long ago; times past.

lan-guage (lang´gwij) *n.* The words, sounds, pronunciation and method of combining words used and understood by people.

lan-guet (lang´gwet) *n.* Something that resembles a tongue in shape, form or function.

lan-guid (lang´gwid) *adj.* Lacking in energy; drooping; weak. **languidly** *adv.* **languid-ness** *n.*

lan-guish (lang´gwish) *v.* To become weak; to be or live in a state of depression. **languisher** *n.* **-ment** *n.*

lan-guor (lang´gėr) *n.* Feebleness; physical exhaustion; listlessness; oppressive stillness. **languorous** *adj.* **languorously** *adv.*

la-ni-ar-y (lā´nē er´ē) *n. pl.* **laniaries** A canine tooth, of a carnivorous animal.

la-nif-er-ous (la nif´ėr us) *adj.* Woolly.

lank (langk) *adj.* Slender; lean.

lan-o-lin (lan´o lin) *n.* Wool grease obtained from sheep's wool and refined for use in ointments and cosmetics.

lan-tern (lan´tėrn) *n.* A portable light having transparent or translucent sides.

lantern jaw *n.* A thin, long and projecting lower jaw.

lanthanide series *n.* The series of rare elements of increasing atomic numbers that start with lanthanum and ending with lutetium.

lan-tha-num (lan´tha num) *n.* The white soft metallic element of the rare-earth series, that has a valence of three, and is allied to aluminum.

la-nu-gi-nose or **la-nu-gi-nous** (la nō´ji nōs´) *adj.* Downy; to be covered with down or fine soft hair.

la-nu-go (la nō´gō) *n., Biol.* A wooly or dense downy growth, as on the surface of a leaf or the hair that covers a newborn of some mammals.

lan-yard (lan´yėrd) *n.* A piece of rope or line used to secure objects on ships.

lap (lap) *n.* The surface of the upper thighs of the legs when a person is seated. **lap** *v.* To twist or wrap around; to enfold; to fold over; to lay a part above; to overlap.

lap-a-rot-o-my (lap´arot´o mē) *n.* The cutting of the abdominal wall.

lap board (lap´bōrd´) *n.* A thin board used on the lap as a writing surface or table.

la-pel (la pel´) *n.* The front part of a garment, especially that of a coat, that is turned back, usually a continuation of the collar.

lap-i-dar-y (lap´i der´ē) *n. pl.* **lapidaries** A craftsman who polishes, cuts, and engraves precious stones and or gems.

lap-i-date (lap´i dāt´) *v.* To pelt someone or something with stones; to stone to death.

la-pil-lus (la pil´us) *n.* A glassy volcanic fragment ejected during an eruption.

lap-in (lap´in) *n.* Rabbit fur that is sheared and dyed.

lapis lazuli *n.* A semiprecious stone that is azure blue in color, used in making jewelry

lap-pet (lap´it) *n.* A flap or fold on a headdress or on a garment.

lapse (laps) *n.* A temporary deviation or fall to a less desirable estate.

lap strake (lap´strāk´) *adj.* A boat, constructed with each plank overlapping the one below it.

laptop computer In *computer science*, a portable computer complete with monitor and keyboard as a unit, smaller in size than a desktop, larger than a notebook computer.

lar-ce-ny (lär´se nē) *n.* The unlawful taking of another person's property.

lard (lärd) *n.* The soft, white, solid or semi- solid fat obtained after rendering the fatty tissue of the hog.

lar-der (lär´dėr) *n.* A place, such as a pantry or room, where food is stored.

large (lärj) *adj.* Greater than usual or average in amount or size. **at large** To be free and not confined.

lar-gess or **lar-gesse** (lär jes´) *n.* Liberal or excessive giving to an inferior; generosity.

lar-go (lär´gō) *adv., Mus.* In a very slow, broad, and solemn manner.

lar-i-at (lar´ē at) *n.* A long, light rope with a running noose at one end to catch live-stock.

lark (lärk) *n.* A bird having a melodious ability to sing; a merry or carefree adventure.

lar-ri-kin (lar´i kin) *n. Slang.* A rough and rowdy person. *adj.* Disorderly; rough.

lar-rup (lar´up) *v.* To flog or whip. **larrup** *n.* A blow; whipping.

lar-va (lär´va) *n. pl.* **larvae** The immature, wingless, often worm-like form of a newly hatched insect; the early form of an animal that differs greatly from the adult, such as the tadpole. **larval** *adj.*

lar-vi-cide (lär´vi sid´) *n.* A chemical agent used to kill larvae.

la-ryn-ge-al (la rin´jē al) *adj.* Of or pertaining to the larynx. *n.* The sound made in the larynx.

lar-yn-gi-tis (lar´in ji´tis) *n.* Inflammation of the larynx.

lar-yn-gol-o-gy (lar´ing gol´o jē) *n.* The study or branch of medicine that deals with the larynx and its diseases.

lar-yn-got-o-my (lar˝ing got´o mē) *n.* The surgical removal of the larynx.

lar-ynx (lar´ingks) *n. pl.* **larynxes** The upper portion of the trachea which contains the vocal cords. **larynges** *adj.*

la-sa-gna *or* **la-sa-gne** (le zän ye) *n.* The traditional Italian dish of wide flat noodles baked with a sauce of tomatoes, meat, and cheese.

la-ser (lā´zer) *n.* A device which utilizes the natural oscillations of molecules or atoms between energy levels for generating coherent electromagnetic radiation in the visible, ultraviolet, or infrared parts of the spectrum.

laser disk In *computer science*, a storage disk that is read using laser technology.

laser printer In *computer science*, an electrostatic printer that uses laser technology to create images on paper.

lash (lash) *v.* To strike or move violently or suddenly; to attack verbally; to whip. *n.* Eyelash. **lasher** *n.*

lass (las) *n.* A young girl or woman.

las-si-tude (las´i tüd´) *n.* A condition of weariness; fatigue.

las-so (las´ō) *n. pl.* **-sos, -soes** A long rope or long leather thong with a running noose used to catch horses and cattle. **lasso** *v.*

last (last) *adj.* Following all the rest; of the final stages, as of life; worst; lowest in rank. **last** *adv.* After all others in sequence or chronology. **last** *v.* To continue. **last** *n.* A form in the shape of a foot used to hold a shoe while it is repaired or to shape a shoe as it is being made.

latch (lach) *n.* A device used to secure a gate or door, consisting of a bar that usually fits into a notch. **onto** To grab onto.

late (lāt) *adj.* Coming, staying, happening after the proper or usual time; having recently died. **lateness** *n.* **lately** *adv.*

la-tent (lāt´ent) *adj.* Not apparent or visible although present and capable of becoming; not manifested.

la-ter (lā´ter) *adv.* After the present; late in a greater degree.

lat-er-al (lat´er al) *adj.* Relating to or of the side. *n.* In football, an underhand pass thrown sideways or away from the line of scrimmage. **laterally** *adv.*

lat-er-ite (lat´e rīt´) *n.* A porous residual product of rock decay, reddish in color having heavy concentrations of iron and aluminum hydroxides.

la-tex (lā´teks) *n.* The milky, white fluid that is produced by certain plants, such as the rubber tree; a water emulsion of synthetic rubber or plastic globules used in paints and adhesives.

lath (lath) *n.* A thin, narrow strip of wood nailed to joists, rafters, or studding and used as a supporting structure for plaster.

lathe (lāth) *n.* A machine for holding material while it is spun and shaped by a tool.

lath-er (lath´er) *n.* A foam formed by detergent or soap and water.

lath-y (lath´ē) *adj.* Thin.

lat-i-cif-er-ous (lat´i sif´er us) *adj.* Containing latex, as in a plant cell.

lat-i-tude (lat´i tüd´) *n.* The angular distance of the earth's surface north or south of the equator, measured in degrees along a meridian; freedom to act and to choose.

lat-i-tu-di-nar-i-an(lat´i töd´inâr´ēan) *adj.* Permitting free and liberal thought and conduct, in religious beliefs.

lat-ten (lat´en) *n.* A brass-like alloy formed in thin sheets.

lat-ter (lat´er) *adj.* Being the second of two persons or two things.

laud (lod) *v.* To praise; to extol. **laudable** *adj.* **laudably** *adv.*

laud-a-ble (la´da bl) *adj.* Worthy of praise; commendable.

laud-a-to-ry (la´da tōr´ē) *adj.* Containing relating to or expressing praise. **laudative, laudatorily,** *adv.*

laugh (laf) *v.* To express or show joy, merriment, or amusement; to display ridicule or to show a degree of contempt; to become amused; to produce the sound of laughter; to express by laughing; to compel with laughter. **laugh** *n.* The sound expressing amusement, joy, or ridicule. **laugher** *n.* **laughingly** *adv.*

laugh-ter (laf´ter) *n.* The expression, sound, or act produced by laughing.

launch (lonch) *v.* To push or move a vessel into the water for the first time; to set a rocket or missile into flight; to put into operation.

laun-der (lon´der) *v.* To wash clothes or other materials in soap and water; to wash and iron. **launderer** *n.*

laun-dry (lon´drē) *n. pl.* **laundries** An establishment where laundering is done professionally; clothes or other articles to be or that have been laundered.

lau-re-ate (lor´ē it) *n.* A person honored for his accomplishment. **laureate** *v.*

lau-rel (lar´el) *n.* A small lauraceous evergreen tree having alternate leaves and small flowers.

la-va (lä´va) *n.* Molten rock which erupts or flows from an active volcano; the rock formed after lava has cooled and hardened.

lav-age (la väzh´) *n.* The washing out; the process of cleansing an organ by injection.

la-va-tion (la vā´shan) *n.* A cleansing or washing.

lav-a-to-ry (lav´a tōr´ē) *n. pl.* **-ies** A room with permanently installed washing and toilet facilities.

lave (lāv) v. To bathe; of a river or the sea, to flow along or against.

la-ver (lā´vèr) n. Any of several edible seaweeds or sea lettuce.

lav-ish (lav´ish) adj. Generous and extravagant in giving or spending. **lavisher** n. **lavishly** adv.

law (lo) n. A rule of conduct or action, recognized by custom or decreed by formal enactment, considered binding on the members of a nation, community, or group; a system or body of such rules.

law-ful (la´fùl) adj. To be in harmony with the law; allowed by law; agreeable to law; legitimate, rightful. **lawfully** adv. **lawfulness** n.

lawn (lon) n. A stretch of ground near a house, park, or building covered with grass that is mowed regularly.

law-ren-ci-um (lo ren´sē ùm) n. A short-lived radioactive element, symbolized by LR.

law-yer (lo´yèr) n. A person trained in the legal profession who acts for and advises clients or pleads in court.

lax (laks) adj. Lacking disciplinary control; lacking rigidity or firmness. **laxity** n. **laxness** n. **laxly** adv.

lax-a-tion (lak sā´shan) n. The state of being relaxed; a loosening.

lax-a-tive (lak´sa tiv) n. A medicine taken to stimulate evacuation of the bowels. **laxative** adj.

lax-i-ty (lak´si-tē) n. The state or quality or being lax or loose; looseness.

lay (lā) v. To cause to lie; to place on a surface; past tense of lie.

lay-er (lā´er) n. A single thickness, coating, or covering that lies over or under another. **layered** adj. **layer** v.

laz-ar (laz´ér) n. A person afflicted with a repulsive disease; a leper.

laz-a-ret-to (laz´a ret´ō) n. pl. **lazarettos** A hospital for patients afflicted with contagious diseases; a ship, building or hospital used for quarantine purposes.

laze (lāz) v. To pass time lazily; to lounge or relax. **laze** n.

laz-u-lite (laz´a līt´) n. An azure blue crystalline that is a phosphate of aluminum, magnesium and iron.

la-zy (lā´zē) adj. Unwilling to work; moving slowly; sluggish. **lazily** adv.

lea (lē) n. ,Poetic A grassy field or meadow.

leach (lēch) v. To cause a liquid to pass through a filter; to remove or wash out by filtering. **leachable** adj.

lead (lēd) v. To go ahead so as to show the way; to control the affairs or action of. **lead** n. A soft, malleable, heavy, dull gray metallic element symbolized by Pb, used in solder, paints, and bullets; a graphite stick used as the writing material in pencils; in printing, the thin strip of type metal used to provide space between printed lines.

lead poisoning (led poi´zo ning) n. Poisoning of a person's system by the absorption of lead or any of its salts.

lead time (lēd tīm) n. The amount of time required from the beginning of a process to the end results.

leaf (lēf) n. pl. **leaves** A flat out-growth from a plant structure or tree, usually green in color and functioning as the principal area of photosynthesis; a single page in a book. v. To turn the pages of a book. **leafless** adj. **leafy** adj.

league (lēg) n. An association of persons, organizations, or states for common action or interest; an association of athletic com-petition; an underwater measurement of distance that equals 3 miles or approximately 4.8 km.

leak (lēk) n. An opening, as a flaw or small crack, permitting an escape or entrance of light or fluid. **leaky**,

lean (lēn) v. To rest or incline the weight of the body for support; to rest or incline anything against a large object or wall; to rely or depend on; to have a tendency or preference for; to tend towards a suggestion or action. **lean** adj. having little or no fat; thin.

leap (lēp) v. To rise or project oneself by a sudden thrust from the ground with a spring of the legs; to spring, to jump. **leap** n. **leaper** n.

leap year n. A year containing 366 days, occurring every 4th year, with the extra day added to make 29 days in February

learn (lern) n. The process of acquiring knowledge, understanding, or mastery of a study or experience. **learner** n.

learn-ed (lur´nid) adj. Characterized by or associated with learning; acquired or obtained by study.

lease (lēs) n. A contract for the temporary use or occupation of property or premises in exchange for payment of rent. **lease** v.

leash (lēsh) n. A strong cord or rope for restraining a dog or other animal.

least-wise (lēst wīz) adv., Slang At least; at any rate.

leath-er (leth´ér) n. An animal skin or hide with the hair removed, prepared for use by tanning.

leave (lēv) v. To go or depart from; to permit to remain behind or in a specified place or condition; to forsake; to abandon; to bequeath, as in a will. **leave** n. Official permission for absence from duty.

leav-en (lev´en) n. An agent of fermentation, as yeast, used to cause batters and doughs to rise; any pervasive influence that produces a significant change.

leav-ing (lē´ving) n. Residue; something that is left. **leavings** Refuse or remains.

lec-i-thin (les´i thin) n. Any of a group of phosphorus containing compounds found in plant and animal tissues, commercially derived from egg yolks, corn, and soybeans, and used in the production of foods, cos-metics, pharmaceuticals, and plastics.

lec-tern (lek´tĕrn) n. A stand or tall desk, usually with a slanted top, on which a speaker or instructor may place books or papers.

lec-tion (lek´shɐn) n. A variant reading of a text or passage in a manuscript.

lec-ture (lek´chĕr) n. A speech on a specific subject, delivered to an audience for information or instruction. v. To give a speech or lecture; to criticize or reprimand.

led v. Past tense of lead.

ledge (lej) n. A narrow, shelf-like projection forming a shelf, as on a wall or the side of a rocky formation.

ledg-er (lej´ĕr) n. A book in which sums of money received and paid out are recorded.

leech (lēch) n. Any of various carnivorous or bloodsucking worms; a person who clings or preys on others.

leek (lēk) n. A culinary herb of the lily family, related to the onion, with a slender, edible bulb.

leer (lēr) n. A sly look or sideways glance expressing desire or malicious intent.

lee tide n. A tide running in the same direction in which the wind is blowing.

lee-ward (lē´wĕrd) adj., Naut. Pertaining to the side of a ship which is sheltered from the wind; opposite to windward. **leeward** n. A sheltered side.

lee-way (lē´wā´) n., Naut. The lateral drift of a plane or ship away from the correct course.

left (left) adj. Pertaining to or being on the side of the body that faces north when the subject is facing east.

left–hand (left´hand´) adj. Situated on or to the left; left-handed.

leg (leg) n. A limb or appendage serving as a means of support and movement in animals and man; a part or division of a journey or trip.

leg-a-cy (leg´a sē) n. pl. **-ies** Personal property, money, and other valuables that are bequeathed by will; anything that is handed down from an ancestor, predecessor, or earlier era.

le-gal (lē´gal) adj. Of, pertaining to, or concerned with the law or lawyers; some-thing based on or authorized by law. **legality** n. **-ization** n. **legalize** v.

le-ga-tion (li gā´shɐn) n. The official diplomatic mission in a foreign country, headed by a minister; the official residence or business premises of a diplomatic minister of lower rank than an ambassador.

le-ga-to (le gä´tō) adv., Music Smooth and flowing with successive notes connected. **legato** n.

leg-end (lej´end) n. An unverifiable story handed down from the past; a body of such stories, as those connected with a culture or people.

leg-i-ble (lej´i bl) adj. Capable of being read or deciphered. **legibility** n.

leg-is-la-tion (lej´is lā´shɐn) n. The act or procedures of passing laws; lawmaking; an officially enacted law.

leg-is-la-tive (lej´is lā´tiv) adj. Of or pertaining to legislation or a legislature; having the power to legislate.

leg-is-la-tor (lej´is lā´tĕr) n. A lawmaker; a member of a legislative body.

leg-is-la-ture (lej´is lā´chĕr) n. A body of persons officially constituted and empowered to make and change laws.

le-git-i-mate (li jit´imit) adj. Accordant with the laws and established rules or principles; to conform to accepted standards; born of parents legally married; of the regular type; genuine; in accordance with established laws or reasoning.

leg-ume (leg´ūm, li gūm´) n. A simple, one-cell, dried, dehiscent, fruit which splits along two seams that are attached to a ventral suture.

le-gu-min (li gū´min) n. A protein resembling casein, obtained from the seeds of leguminous plants.

leg-work n., Slang A chore, task, or gathering of information accomplished by going about on foot.

leis-ter (lē´stĕr) n. A barbed spear used to catch fish.

lei-sure (lē´zhŏr) n. The time of freedom from work or duty.

lei-sure-ly (lē´zhĕr lē) adv. Acting, without haste.

lem-nis-cus (lem nis´kʊs) n. A long band of nerve fibers of the brain.

lend (lend) v. To allow the temporary use or possession of something with the understanding that it is to be returned, to offer oneself as to a specific purpose.

length (lengkth) n. The linear extent of something from end to end, usually the longest dimension of a thing as distinguished from its thickness and width; the measurement of something to estimate distance. **lengthy** adj.

length-en (lengk´then) v. To make longer or to become longer.

length-wise (lengkth´wīz´) adv. & adj. Of or in the direction or dimension of length; longitudinally.

le-ni-ent (lē´nē ent) adj. Gentle, forgiving, and mild; merciful; undemanding; tolerant. **leniency** n.

len-i-tive (len´i tiv) *adj.* Having the ability to softening or moderate, as with medicines. **lenitive** *n.*

lens (lenz) *n.* In optics, the curved piece of glass or any other transparent substance that is used to refract light rays so that they converge or diverge to form an image; the transparent structure in the eye, situated behind the iris, which serves to focus an image on the retina.

lent (lent) *v.* Past tense of lend.

Lent (lent) *n.* The period of forty days, excluding Sundays, of fasting and penitence observed by many Christians from Ash Wednesday until Easter.

len-tan-do (len tän´dō) *adj.* In a slackening manner; getting slower.

len-ti-cel (len´ti sel) *n.* A pore in shape, in the bark of woody stems through which the gases are exchanged between the stem tissue and the atmosphere.

len-ti-go (len tī´gō) *n.* A freckle or a freckly condition.

len-til (len´til) *n.* A leguminous plant, having broad pods that contain edible seeds and leafy stalks used as fodder.

le-o-tard (lē´o tärd´) *n.* A close-fitting garment worn by dancers and acrobats.

lep-er (lep´ėr) *n.* One who suffers from leprosy.

lep-i-dop-ter-an (lep´i dop´tėr an) *n.* Any insects comprising the butterfly, moth, or skipper.

lep-i-dote (lep´i dōt´) *adj.* Covered with scurf or scurfy spots or scales.

lep-re-chaun (lep´re kon´) *n.* A mischief-making elf of Irish folklore, supposed to own hidden treasure.

lep-ro-sy (lep´ro sē) *n., Pathol.* A chronic communicable disease characterized by nodular skin lesions and the progressive destruction of tissue. **leprous** *adj.*

lep-ton (lep´ton) *n.* A small coin; small in mass, as an electron.

les-bi-an (lez´bē an) *n.* A homosexual woman. **lesbian** *adj.*

lese majesty *n.* An offense against a ruler or supreme power of state.

le-sion (lē´zhan) *n.* An injury; a wound; any well-defined bodily area where the tissue has changed in a way that is characteristic of a disease.

less (les) *adj.* Smaller; of smaller or lower importance or degree. **less** *prep.* With the subtraction of; minus.

-less *suffix* Without; lacking.

les-see (le sē´) *n.* One who leases a property.

less-en (les´en) *v.* To decrease or make smaller or less; to become smaller; to diminish.

les-son (les´on) *n.* An instance from which something is to be or has been learned; an assignment to be learned or studied as by a student.

les-sor (les´or) *n.* One who grants a lease to another.

let (let) *v.* To give permission; to allow. **let** *n.* An invalid stroke in a game such as tennis, that must be repeated because of some interruption or hindrance of playing conditions. **let's** (lets) *contr.* Let us.

le-thal (lē´thal) *adj.* Pertaining to or being able to cause death. **lethally** *adv.*

lethal gene *n.* A gene that may affect, prevent development, or cause death of an organism at any stage of its life.

le-thar-gic (le thär´jik) *adj.* Affected with or characterized by lethargy; sluggish; inclined to sleep; dull.

leth-ar-gy (leth´ėr jē) *n., Pathol.* A state of excessive drowsiness or abnormally deep sleep; laziness. **lethargic** *adj.*

let-ter (let´ėr) *n.* A standard character or sign used in writing or printing to represent an alphabetical unit or speech sound; a written or printed means of communication sent to another person.

let-up (let´up´) *n.* A pause or lessening of intensity.

leu-co-ma-ine (lōkō´ma ēn´) *n.* A poisonous nitrogen compound that is present in animal tissue as a by-product of metabolism.

leu-ke-mi-a (lü kē´mē a) *n., Pathol.* A generally fatal disease of the blood in which white blood cells multiply in uncontrolled numbers. **leukemic** *adj.*

le-vant-er (li van´tėr) *n.* A forceful wind that blows in an easterly direction.

le-vee (lev´ē) *n.* An embankment along the shore of a body of water, especially a river, built to prevent overflowing.

lev-el (lev´el) *n.* A relative position, rank, or height on a scale; a standard position from which other heights and depths are measured. *adj.* Balanced in height; even. *v.* To make or become flat or level. **leveler** *n.* **levelness** *n.*

level-headed (lev´el hed´id) *adj.* Showing good judgment and common sense. **level-headedness** *n.*

lev-i-gate (lev´i gāt´) *v.* To make a smooth paste; to rub or grind to a fine smooth powder.

lev-i-tate (lev´i tāt´) *v.* To rise and float in the air in apparent defiance of gravity. **levitation** *n.*

lev-i-ty (lev´i tē) *n. pl.* **-ies** Lack of seriousness; frivolity; lightness.

le-vo-ro-ta-tion (lē´vō rō tā´shan) *n.* Rotation toward the left; a counter-clockwise rotation or direction.

lev-y (lev´ē) *v.* To impose and collect by authority or force, as a fine or tax; to draft for military service; to prepare for, begin, or wage war. **levy** *n.*

lewd (lüd) *adj.* Preoccupied with sex; lustful. **lewdly** *adv.* **lewdness** *n.*

lex-i-cal (lek´si kal) *adj.* Pertaining or relating to words or vocabulary of a language, as distinguished from its construction and grammar.

lex-i-con (lek´si kon´) *n.* A dictionary; a vocabulary or list of words that relate to a certain subject, occupation, or activity. **lexical** *adj.*

li (lē) *n.* A Chinese linear unit of measure equivalent to about ⅓ mile or 0.5 kilometer.

li-a-bil-i-ty (lī´a bil´i tē) *n. pl.* -ies The condition or state of being liable; that which is owed to another.

li-a-ble (lī´a bl) *adj.* Legally or rightly responsible.

li-ai-son (lē´ā zon´) *n.* A communication, as between different parts of an armed force or departments of a government; a close connection or relationship; an illicit love affair.

li-ar (lī´ér) *n.* A person who tells falsehoods.

li-bel (lī´bel) *n., Law* A written statement in published form that damages a person's character or reputation.

lib-er-al (lib´ér al) *adj.* Characterized by generosity or lavishness in giving; abundant; ample; inclining toward opinions or policies that favor progress or reform, such as religion or politics. **liberalism** *n.* **liberality** *n.* **-lize** *v.*

liberal arts *n. pl.* Academic courses that include literature, philosophy, history, languages, etc., which provide general cultural information.

lib-er-ate (lib´e rāt´) *v.* To set free, as from bondage, oppression, or foreign control. **liberation** *n.*

lib-er-tar-i-an (lib´ér târ´ē an) *n.* A person who upholds the doctrine of the free will; one who advocates unrestricted liberty.

li-ber-ti-cide (li bur´ri sīd´) *n.* The destruction of liberty; a destroyer of liberty.

lib-er-tine (lib´ér tēn´) *n.* A person lacking moral or sexual restraint; one who leads a unscrupulous life.

lib-er-ty (lib´ér tē) *n. pl.* -ies The state of being free from oppression, tyranny, confinement, or slavery; freedom; in Navy terms, the permission to be absent from one's ship or duty for less that 48 hours.

li-bi-do (li bē´dō) *n.* One's sexual desire or impulse; the psychic energy drive that is behind all human activities. **libidinal** *adj.* **libidinous** *adj.*

li-brar-i-an (lī brer´ē en) *n.* A person in charge of a library; one who specializes in library work.

li-brar-y (lī´brer´ē) *n. pl.* **libraries** A collection of books, pamphlets, magazines, and reference books kept for reading, reference, or borrowing; a commercial establishment, usually in connection with a city or school, which lends or rents books.

lice *n.* Plural of louse.

li-cense (lī´sens) *n.* An official document that gives permission to engage in a specified activity or to perform a specified act. **licensee** *n.* **licenser** *n.*

li-cen-tious (lī sen´shus) *adj.* Lacking in moral restraint; immoral. **licentiously** *adv.* **licentiousness** *n.*

lic-it (lis´it) *adj.* Lawful. **licitly** *adv.*

lick (lik) *v.* To pass the tongue over or along the surface of. *Slang* To beat; to thrash.

lid (lid) *n.* A hinged or removable cover for a container; an eyelid. **lidded** *adj.*

li-dar (lī där) *n.* A radar system that emits pulsed laser light instead of microwaves.

lie (lī) *v.* To be in or take a horizontal recumbent position; to recline. *n.* A false or untrue statement.

liege (lēj) *n.* A feudal lord or sovereign. *adj.* Loyal; faithful.

lien (lēn) *n.* The legal right to claim, hold, or sell the property of another to satisfy a debt or obligation.

li-en-ter-y (lī´en ter´ē) *n.* A condition or type of diarrhea, where the food is discharged undigested.

lieu (lü) *n.* Place; instead of; in place of.

life (līf) *n. pl.* **lives** The form of existence that distinguishes living organisms from dead organisms or inanimate matter in the ability to carry on metabolism, respond to stimuli, reproduce, and grow.

life–support system *n.* A system giving a person all or some of the items, such as oxygen, water, food, and control of temperature, necessary for a person's life and health while in a spacecraft or while exploring the surface of the moon; a system used to sustain life in a critical health situation.

lift (lift) *v.* To raise from a lower to a higher position; to elevate; to take from; to steal. **lift** *n.* The act or process of lifting; force or power available for lifting; an elevation of spirits; a device or machine designed to pick up, raise, or carry something; an elevator.

lift-off (lift´of´) *n.* The vertical take off or the instant of takeoff of an aircraft or spacecraft.

lig-a-ment (lig´a ment) *n.* A tough band of tissue joining bones or holding a body organ in place. **ligamentous** *adj.*

li-gate (lī´gāt) *v.* To tie with a ligature.

lig-a-ture (lig´a chér) *n.* Something, as a musical cord, that is used to bind; a thread used in surgery; something that unites or connects; a printing character that combines two or more letters.

light (līt) *n.* Electromagnetic radiation that can be seen by the naked eye; brightness; a source of light; spiritual illumination; enlightenment; a source of fire, such as a match. *adj.* Having light; bright; of less force, quantity, intensity, weight, than normal; having less calories or alcoholic content; dizzy; giddy. **light** *v.* **lightness** *n.*

light–year *or* **light year** (līt´yēr´) *n.* A measure equal to the distance light travels in one year, approximately 5.878 trillion miles.

lig-ne-ous (lig´nē us) *adj.* Of or resembling wood; woody.

lig-ni-fy (lig´ni fī´) *v.* To make or become woody or wood-like.

lig-nin (lig´nin) *n.* An organic substance associated with cellulose that forms the woody cell walls of plants.

lg-nite (lig´nīt) *n.* A brownish-black soft coal, especially one in which the texture of the original wood is distinct.

lig-no-cel-lu-lose (lig´nō sel´ū lōs¯) *n.* An association of lignin and cellulose that contains the essential part of woody cell walls and the fibrous tissue in plants.

lig-ro-in (lig´rō in) *n.* A volatile, flammable fraction of petroleum used as a solvent.

like (līk) *adj.* Of the same form, appearance, kind, character, or amount. *n.* A counter-part one that is like a another; the match or equal.

li-lac (lī´lak) *n.* A shrub widely grown for its large, fragrant purplish or white flower cluster; a pale purple. **lilac** *adj.*

lilt (lilt) *n.* A light song; a rhythmical way of speaking.

lil-y (lil´ē) *n. pl.* **lilies** Any of various plants bearing trumpet-shaped flowers; a plant similar or related to the lily, as the water lily.

limb (lim) *n.* A large bough of a tree; an animal's appendage used for movement or grasping; an arm or leg.

lim-bate (lim´bāt) *adj.* Bordered, in color as a leaf or flower with one color surrounded by an edging of another.

lim-ber (lim´bér) *adj.* Bending easily; pliable; moving easily; agile. **limber** *v.* To make or become limber.

lim-bo *or* **Lim-bo** (lim´bō) *n.* The abode of souls kept from entering Heaven; a place or condition of oblivion or neglect.

lime (līm) *n.* A tropical citrus tree with evergreen leaves, fragrant white flowers, and edible green fruit; calcium oxide.

lim-er-ick (lim´ér ik) *n.* A humorous verse of five lines.

lime-stone (līm´stōn´) *n.* A form of sedimentary rock composed mainly

of calcium carbonate which is used in building and in making lime and cement.

lim-it (lim´it) *n.* A boundary; a maximum or a minimum number or amount; a restriction on frequency or amount. *v.* To restrict; to establish bounds or boundaries. **able** *adj.*

lim-i-ta-tion (lim´i tā´shan) *n.* The instance or act of limiting; that which limits; a certain period of time that limits.

limn (lim) *v.* To describe; to depict by drawing. **limner** *n.*

li-mo-nite (lī´mo nīt´) *n.* A natural iron oxide used as an ore of iron.

lim-ou-sine (lim´o zēn´) *n.* A luxurious large vehicle; a small bus used to carry passengers to airports and hotels.

limp (limp) *v.* To walk lamely. *adj.* Lacking or having lost rigidity; not firm or strong. **limply** *adv.* **limpness** *n.*

lim-pid (lim´pid) *adj.* Transparently clear. **limpidity** *n.* **limpidly** *adv.*

lin-age (lī´nij) *n.* The number of printed or written lines on a page.

linch-pin (linch´pin´) *n.* A locking pin inserted through a shaft to keep a wheel from slipping off.

Lincoln, Abraham *n.* (1809-1865) The sixteenth president of the United States from 1861-1865.

lin-den (lin´den) *n.* Any of various shade trees having heart-shaped leaves.

line (līn) *n.* A mark made with a pencil, pen, or other writing tool, on a surface; the spoken words of a play; a short written note. *Math.* The shortest distance between two points. **line-up** A line of persons formed for the purpose of inspection or identification; the members of a team who take part in a game; a group of television programs that are aired sequentially.

lin-e-age (lin´ē ij) *n.* A direct line of descent from an ancestor.

lin-e-a-ment (lin´ē a ment) *n.* A contour, shape, or feature of the body and especially of the face.

lin-e-ar (lin´ē ér) *adj.* Of, pertaining to, or resembling a line; long and narrow.

linear acceletator *n., Phys.* A device for accelerating charged particles in a straight line by successive impulses from a series of electric fields.

lin-en (lin´en) *n.* Thread, yarn, or fabric made of flax; household articles, such as sheets and pillow cases, made of linen or a similar fabric. **linen** *adj.*

line of sight *n.* The imaginary line that extends from the viewer's eye to the distant point to which he is looking.

ling (ling) *n.* Any of various marine food fishes related to the cod.

lin-ger (ling´gér) *v.* To be slow in parting or reluctant to leave; to be slow to act;

to procrastinate. **lingerer** *n*. **-ingly** *adv*.

lin-ge-rie (län´zhe rā´) *n*. Women's undergarments.

lingo (ling´gō) *n. pl.* **goes** Language that is unfamiliar; a specialized vocabulary.

lin-gual (ling´gwǝl) *adj*. Relating or pertaining to the tongue; relating to the surface of the tooth laying next to the tongue.

lin-guist (ling´gwist) *n*. One who is fluent in more than one language; a person specializing in linguistics.

lin-i-ment (lin´i ment) *n*. A liquid or semi-liquid medicine applied to the skin.

li-nin (lī´nin) *n., Biol*. The substance that forms the net-like formation which connects the chromatin granules in a cell nucleus.

lin-ing (lī´ning) *n*. A material which is used to cover an inside surface.

link (lingk) *n*. One of the rings forming a chain; something in the form of a link; a tie or bond; a cuff link. *v*. To connect by or as if by a link or links.

link-age (ling´kij) *n*. The act or process of linking; a system of connecting structures.

linked documents In *computer science*, records or files that are connected so that data from one will be automatically entered in another, such as billing records that are automatically added to the accounts receivable file.

linking verb *n., Gram.* A verb which links a subject to the predicate of a sentence: as *become, be, feel, seem*.

links (lingks) *n. pl.* A golf course.

link-work (lingk´wurk´) *n*. Work that is composed of links, as a chain.

li-no-le-um (li nō´lē um) *n*. A floor covering consisting of a surface of hardened linseed oil and a filler, as wood or powdered cork, on a canvas or burlap backing.

lin-seed (lin´sēd´) *n*. The seed of flax used in paints and varnishes.

linsey-woolsey (lin´zē wǒl´zē) *n* A coarse, sturdy fabric of wool and linen or cotton.

lin-stock (lin´stok´) *n*. A staff with a fork tip and formally used to hold a lighted match.

lin-tel (lin´tel) *n*. A horizontal beam across the top of a door which supports the weight of the structure above it.

lint-er (lin´tér) *n*. A machine used to remove fibers that remain on cotton seeds after the first ginning.

li-pase (lī´pās, lip´ās) *n., Biochem.* An enzyme, that occurs in the liver and pancreas that accelerates the breaking down of fats into fatty acids and glycerin.

li-pid (lī´pid) *n., Biochem.* Substances of an organic material, including sterols, fats, and waxes, that are insoluble in water but are able to be metabolized.

lip-oid (lip´oid) *adj., Biochem.* Resembling fat.

liq-ue-fac-tion (lik´we fak´shǝn) *n*. The act of making liquid or becoming liquid.

liq-ue-fy (lik´ we fī´) *v*. To convert or reduce to a liquid state.

li-queur (li ker´) *n*. A sweet alcoholic beverage flavored with fruit, spices or nuts; a cordial.

liq-ui-date (lik´wi dāt´) *v*. To settle a debt by payment or other settlement; to close a business by settling accounts and dividing up assets; to get rid of, especially to kill. **liquidation** *n*.

liq-uor (lik´ér) *n*. A distilled alcoholic beverage; a liquid substance, as a watery solution of a drug.

lisle (līl) *n*. A fine, tightly twisted cotton thread.

lisp (lisp) *n*. A speech defect or mannerism marked by lisping. **lisp** *v*. To mispronounce the s and z sounds, usually as th.

lis-some (lis´om) *adj*. Nimble. **lissomely** *adv*. **lissomeness** *n*.

list (list) *n*. A series of numbers or words; a tilt to one side. **list** *v*.

list-ed (lis´tid) *adj*. Set down or to make a list, as a telephone number.

lis-ten (lis n) *v*. To monitor or tune in to conversation or a broadcast.

list-ing (lis´ting) *n*. The act or process of making or putting in a list; the entry on a list; a directory.

list-less (list´lis) *adj*. Lacking energy or enthusiasm. **listlessly** *adv*.

lit (lit) *abbr*. Literary; literature.

lit-a-ny (lit´e nē) *n. pl.* **litanies** A prayer in which phrases, recited by a leader are alternated with answers from the congregation.

li-tchi or **li-chee** (lē´chē) *n*. A Chinese tree, bearing edible fruit; the fruit of the tree.

lit-er-a-cy (lit´ér a nē) *n*. The state or quality of being literate, having the skills of reading and writing.

lit-er-al (lit´ér al) *adj*. Conforming to the exact meaning of a word; concerned primarily with facts; without embellishment or exaggeration. **literally** *adv*.

lit-er-ar-y (lit´e rer´ē) *adj*. Pertaining to literature; appropriate to or used in literature; of or relating to the knowledge of literature. **literarily** *adv*.

lit-er-ate (lit´ér it) *adj*. Having the ability to read and write; showing skill in using words. **literacy** *n*. **literate** *n*.

lit-er-a-ture (lit´ér a chér) *n*. Printed material, as leaflets for a political campaign; written words of lasting excellence.

li-tharge (lith´ärj) *n.* The yellowish-red oxide of lead, that is used for glazing earthenware.

lithe (līth) *adj.* Bending easily; supple. **lithely** *adv.* **litheness** *n.*

li-thi-a-sis (li thī´a sis) *n., Pathol.* The formation of stony solid concretions in any part of the body, as in the gallbladder.

lith-ic (lith´ik) *adj.* Pertaining or relating to or consisting of stone; *Pathol.* Pertaining to stones in the body, as in the bladder.

lith-i-um (lith´ē um) *n.* A metallic element, the lightest metal know.

li-thog-ra-phy (li thog´ra fē) *n.* A printing process in which a flat surface is treated so that the ink adheres only to the portions that are to be printed. **lithograph** *n. & v.* **lithographer** *n.* **lithographic** *adj.* **lithographical** *adj.*

li-thol-o-gy (li thol´o jē) *n.* The microscopic study and classification of rocks.

lith-o-marge (lith´o märj´) *n.* A compact clay.

lith-o-sphere (lith´o sfēr´) *n.* The crust or outer surface of the solid earth, thought to be approximately 50 miles thick.

lit-i-gate (lit´i gāt´) *v.* To conduct a legal contest by judicial process. **litigant** *n.* **litigation** *n.* **litigator** *n.*

lit-mus (lit´mus) *n.* A blue powder obtained from lichens which turns red in acid solutions and blue in alkaline solutions, used as an acid-base indicator.

lit-ter (lit´ėr) *n.* A covered and curtained couch, mounted on shafts and used to convey a single passenger; a stretcher used to carry a sick or injured person; material used as bedding for animals; the offspring at one birth of a multiparous animal; an accumulation of waste material. **litter** *v.* **litterer** *n.*

lit-tle (lit´l) *adj.* Small in size or extent; not large; short in time; small in amount or quantity.

Little Dipper *n.* Ursa Minor.

lit-to-ral (lit´ėr al) *adj.* Relating to or existing on a shore. *n.* A shore.

lit-ur-gy (lit´ėr jē) *n. pl.* **-ies** A prescribed rite or body of rites for public worship. **liturgical** *adj.*

liv-a-ble (liv´abl) *adj.* Endurable; suitable for living in.

live (liv) *v.* To have life; to be alive; capable of performing vital functions; to remain effective; not to perish; to pass through or spend life in a particular manner.

live (līv) *adj.* Being in life, living, or alive; of or pertaining to life or living beings.

liv-er (liv´ėr) *n.* The large, very vascular, glandular organ of vertebrates which secretes bile.

live-stock (līv´stok´) *n.* Farm animals raised for human use.

live wire *n., Slang* An energetic person.

liv-id (liv´id) *adj.* Discolored from a bruise; very angry.

liv-ing (liv´ing) *n.* The act or condition of being alive; one who or that which lives; manner or course of life.

load (lōd) *n.* A mass or weight that is lifted or supported; anything, as cargo, put in a ship, aircraft, or vehicle for conveyance; something that is a heavy responsibility; a burden. **loader** *n.* **loading** *n.* **load** *v.*

load-ed (lō´did) *adj.* Intended to trick or trap. *Slang* Drunk; rich.

loaf (lōf) *n. pl.* **loaves** A food, especially bread, that is shaped into a mass. To spend time in idleness.

loam (lōm) *n.* Soil that consists chiefly of sand, clay, and decayed plant matter.

loan (lōn) *n.* Money lent with interest to be repaid; something borrowed for temporary use. *v.* To lend.

loath (lōth) *adj.* Averse.

loathe (lōth) *v.* To dislike intensely.

loath-ing (lō´thing) *n.* Intense dislike; abhorrence.

loath-some (lōth´som) *adj.* Arousing disgust. **loathsomely** *adv.*

lob (lob) *v.* To hit or throw in a high arc; to move in an arc. **lob** *n.*

lob-by (lob´ē) *n. pl.* **lobbies** A foyer, as in a hotel or theater; a group of private persons trying to influence legislators. **lobbyist** *n.* **lobby** *v.*

lobe (lōb) *n.* A curved or rounded projection or division, as the fleshy lower part of the ear. **lobar** *adj.*

lo-bot-o-my (lō bot´o mē) *n. pl.* **lobotomies** Surgical severance of nerve fibers by incision into the brain.

lob-ster (lob´stėr) *n.* Any of several large, edible marine crustaceans with five pairs of legs, the first pair being large and claw- like.

lob-ule (lob´ūl) *n.* A small lobe; a subdivision of a lobe. **lobular** *adj.*

lo-cal (lō´kel) *adj.* Pertaining to, being in, or serving a particular area or place.

lo-cale (lō kal´) *n.* A locality where a particular event takes place; the setting or scene, as of a novel.

lo-cate (lō´kāt) *v.* To determine the place, position, or boundaries of; to look for and find; to establish or become established; to settle. **locator** *n.*

lo-ca-tion (lō kā´shan) *n.* The process or act of locating; a place where something is or can be located; a site outside a motion picture or television studio where a movie is shot.

loch (lok) *n.* A lake.

lock (lok) *n.* A device used, as on a door,

to secure or fasten; a part of a waterway closed off with gates to allow the raising or lowering of boats by changing the level of the water; a strand or curl of hair. **lock** v.

lo-co (lō´kō) adj., Slang Insane.

lo-co-mo-tion (lō´ko mō´shan) n. The act or power of moving from place to place.

lo-co-mo-tive (lō´ko mō´tiv) n. A self-propelled vehicle that is generally electric or diesel-powered and is used for moving railroad cars.

lo-co-weed (lō´kō wēd´) n. Any of several plants found throughout the western and central United States which are poisonous to livestock.

loc-u-late (lok´ūlāt´) adj., Biol. Composed or divided into cells or loculi.

lo-cus (lō´kus) n. pl. **lo-ci** or **lo-ca** A place; locality; the center of activity.

lo-cust (lō´kust) n. Any of numerous grasshoppers which often travel in swarms and damage vegetation; any of various hard-wooded leguminous trees, such as carob, black locust, or honey locust.

lo-cu-tion (lōkū´shan) n. A particular form of a phrase; a style of verbal expression.

lode-star (lōd´stär) n. The North Star, used as reference point or guiding star.

lodge (loj) n. A house, such as a cabin, used as a temporary or seasonal dwelling or shelter; an inn; the den of an animal, such as a beaver; a local chapter of a fraternal organization; the meeting hall of such a chapter.

lod-i-cule (lod´i kūl) n., Bot. One of the delicate membranous scales at the base of a grass.

loft (loft) n. One of the upper, generally unpartitioned floors of an industrial or commercial building, such as a warehouse; an attic; a gallery in a church or hall.

log (lag, log) n. A bulky piece of timber either from a branch or a tree trunk. The record of a ship or aircraft travel.

loge (lōzh) n. A small compartment, especially a box in a theater; a small partitioned area, as a separate forward section of a theater mezzanine or balcony.

log-gi-a (loj´a) n. A roofed but open arcade along the front of a building; an open balcony in a theater.

log-ic (loj´ik) n. The science dealing with the principles of reasoning, especially of the method and validity of deductive reasoning; something that forces a decision apart from or in opposition to reason.

log-i-cal (loj´i kal) adj. Relating to; or in accordance with logic; something

marked by consistency of reasoning. **logically** adv.

log in or **log on** In computer science, to type the password that allows access to the computer.

lo-gi-on (lō´gē on´) n. pl. **logions** or **logia** Traditional saying attributed to Jesus.

lo-gis-tics (lō jis´tiks) n. The methods of procuring, maintaining, and replacing material and personnel, as in a military operation. **logistic** adj.

log-jam (lag´jam´) n. A jumble or group of logs wedged together in a river; deadlock.

lo-gom-a-chy (lō gom´a kē) n. pl. **logomachies** A dispute over or about words; a verbal disagreement

lo-go-type (lo´go tīp´) n. Identifying symbol for a company or publication.

log-roll (lag´rōl´) v. To promote successfully passage of a bill; rolling of logs in water.

lo-gy (lō´gē) adj. Something marked by sluggishness. **loginess** n.

loin (loin) n. The area of the body located between the ribs and pelvis; a cut of meat from an animal.

loin-cloth (loin´kloth´) n. A cloth worn about the loins.

loins (loinz) n. The thighs and groin; the reproductive organs.

loi-ter (loi´tér) v. To stay for no apparent reason; to dawdle or delay.

loll (lol) v. To move or act in a lax, lazy or indolent manner; to hang loosely or laxly. **loller** n.

lol-ly-gag (lol ē gag) v., Slang To fool around.

lo-ment (lō´ment) n., Bot. A dry indehiscent one-cell fruit, produced from a single ovary, which separates at maturity into numerous segments.

lone (lōn) adj. Single; isolated; sole; unfrequented.

lone-ly (lōn´lē) adj. Being without companions; dejected from being alone.

lon-er (lō ner) n. A person who avoids the company of others.

long (lang, long) adj. Having a greater length than usual; considerable extent, not short; unusually great; prolonged past the usual time. n. A long length of time; a long sounding syllable.

long abbr. Longitude.

long distance n. The service handling by telephone communications; calls between a location and out of state or out of country. **long distance** adv. Connecting distant places; over a long distance.

long division n., Math. Arithmetical division, where several steps are involved in finding the answer, in which all steps are indicated in writing.

lon-gev-i-ty (lon jev´i tē) n. Long duration; length or duration of life; long continuance; length of service.

lon-gi-tude (lon´ji tüd´) n. The angular distance that is east and west of the prime meridian at Greenwich, England.

lon-gi-tu-di-nal (lon´ji tüd´i nal) adj. Of or relating to the length; relating to longitude. **longitudinally** adv.

lon-gueur (lang gur´) n. A tedious section passage in a book.

look (lek) v. To examine with the eyes; to see; to glance, gaze, or stare at. **look** n. The act of looking; the physical appearance of something or someone.

loom (lüm) v. To come into view as a image; to seem to be threatening. n. A machine used for interweaving thread or yarn to produce cloth.

loon (kön) n. An idle or worthless man; a crazy person; a fish-eating diving bird of the northern hemisphere.

loo-ny or **loo-ney (lü´ne)** n. Crazy; foolish.

loop (lüp) n. A circular length of line folded over and joined at the ends; a loop-shaped pattern, figure, or path. **loop** v. To form into a loop; to join, fasten, or encircle with a loop.

loop-hole (lüp´hôl´) n. A means of escape; a legal way to circumvent the intent of a law.

loose (lüs) adj. Not tightly fastened; not confined or fitting; free.

loose end n. Something left unattached or hanging loose; unfinished business.

loose-jointed (lös´join´tid) adj. Having loose joints of unusually free movement.

loos-en (lös´en) v. To make looser, or less firm, compact, or tight; to relax.

loot (lüt) n. Goods, usually of significant value, taken in time of war; goods that have been stolen. **loot** v. To plunder; to steal. **looter** n.

lop (lop) v. To remove branches from; to trim; to cut off with a single blow.

lope (lôp) v. To run with a steady gait. **lope** n. **lopper** n.

lop-eared (lop´ërd´) adj. Having ears that droop or hang down.

lop-sid-ed (lop´sī´did) adj. Larger or heavier on one side than on the other; tilting to one side. **lopsidedly** adv.

lo-qua-cious (lō kwā´shus) adj. Talkative; given to excessive or continual talking; **loquaciously** adv.

lo-quat (lō´kwot, lō´kwat) n. A small Asian evergreen tree.

lo-ran (lôr´an) n. A system by which a navigator determines the position of his airplane or ship based in part on the measurement of arrival times and signals sent out by ground stations.

Lord (lord) n. God. A man having dominion and power over other people; the owner of a feudal estate.

lore (lôr) n. Traditional fact; knowledge

that has been gained through education or experience.

lor-gnon (lor nyon´) n. A pair of eyeglasses or opera glasses.

lorn (larn) adj. Forsaken; abandoned; desolate.

lose (loz) v. To mislay; to fail to keep; misplace. **loser** n.

loss (los) n. The suffering or damage used by losing; someone or something that is lost. **losses** pl. Killed, wounded, or captured soldiers; casualties.

loss ratio n. The ratio between insurance premiums and insurance losses in a given period of time.

lost (lost) adj. Unable to find one's way.

lot (lot) n. Fate; fortune; a parcel of land having boundaries; a plot.

lo-ta (lō´ta) n. A small spherical water vessel of copper or brass used in India.

lo-tic (lō´tic) adj. Living in or related to actively moving water.

lo-tion (lō´shan) n. A liquid medicine for external use on the hands and body.

lot-ter-y (lot´e rē) n. pl. -ies A contest in which winners are selected by a random drawing.

lot-to (lot´ō) n. A game of chance that resembles bingo.

loud (loud) adj. Marked by intense sound and high volume. **loudly** adv.

Lou-is-i-an-a n. A state located in the south central part of the United States, statehood April 30, 1812, state capital Baton Rouge.

lounge (lounj) v. To move or act in a lazy, relaxed manner. n. A room, as in a hotel or theater, where people may wait; a couch. **lounger** n.

loupe (löp) n. A small magnifying glass, that attaches to eyeglasses, or is held close to the eye for viewing an object up close.

louse (lous) n. pl. lice A small, wingless sucking and biting insect that lives on various animals as well as human beings. Slang A contemptible person.

louse up v., Slang. To botch or mess up.

lous-y (lou´zē) adj. Lice- infested. Slang Mean; poor; inferior; abundantly supplied. **lousily** adv.

lout (lout) n. An awkward, stupid person. **loutish** adj.

lou-ver or **lou-vre (lü´vėr)** n. An opening in a wall fitted with movable, slanted slats which let air in, but keep precipitation out; one of the slats used in a louver. **louvered** adj.

love (luv) n. Intense affection for another arising out of kinship or personal ties; a strong feeling of attraction resulting from sexual desire; enthusiasm or fondness; a score of zero in tennis. **love** v. **lovable** adj. **loving** adj.

low (lō) adj. Not high; being below or under normal height, rank, or level;

depressed or lacking in health or vigor; soft in pitch; small in number; cheap in price. **low** *v.* To moo, as a cow.

low-er (lō´ér) *adj.* Relatively low in position; in a position considered inferior to others in value or rank; located beneath or under something. **lower** *v.* To make lower in position; to reduce the value of.

low-er–case (lō´ér kās´) *adj.* Having as its typical form a, b, c, or u, v, w rather than A, B, C, or U,V, W.

lowest common denominator *n.* The least common multiple of the denominators of a set of fractions.

low frequency *n.* A radio-wave frequency between 30 and 300 kilohertz.

low-key (lō´kē´) *adj.* Restrained.

low-land (lō´land) *n.* Land that is lower than the adjacent neighboring country; level or low country.

low–lev-el (lō´lev´el) *adj.* Being of minor importance; done, placed or occurring at a low level.

low–pres-sure (lō´presh´ér) *adj.* Having or operation under a low degree of steam or water pressure.

low profile *n.* A deliberately inconspicuous lifestyle or posture.

low–ten-sion (lō´ten´shan) *adj.* Having a low voltage; built to be used at low voltage.

lox (loks) *n.* Smoked salmon; liquid oxygen.

loy-al (loi´al) *adj.* Faithful in allegiance to one's country and government; faithful to a person, cause, ideal, or custom. **loyalty** *n.*

loy-al-ist (loi´ al ist) *n.* One who is or remains loyal to a political cause, party, government, or sovereign.

loz-enge (loz´inj) *n.* Small medicated candy, normally having the shape of a lozenge.

LSD (el´es´dē´) *n.* Lysergic acid diethylamide, a hallucinogenic drug that induces psychotic symptoms, producing changes in thought, perception, mood, and behavior.

lu-au (lü´ ou´) *n.* A traditional Hawaiian feast.

lub-ber (lub´ér) *n.* An awkward, clumsy or stupid person; an inexperienced sailor.

lu-bri-cant (lü´bri kant) *n.* A material, as grease or oil, applied to moving parts to reduce friction.

lu-carne (lö kärn´) *n.* A window set vertically in a steeple.

lu-cid (lü´sid) *adj.* Easily understood; mentally clear; rational; shining. **lucidity** *n.* **lucidness** *n.* **lucidly** *adv.*

luck (luk) *n.* Good fortune; the force or power which controls odds and which brings good fortune or bad fortune. **lucky** *adj.* **luckily** *adv.* **luckiness** *n.*

lu-cra-tive (lü´kra tiv) *adj.* Producing profits or great wealth. **lucratively** *adv.*

lu-cre (lü´kér) *n.* Money; profit.

lu-cu-brate (lü´kü brāt´) *v.* To study or work laboriously.

lu-di-crous (lü´di krus) *adj.* Amusing or laughable through obvious absurdity; ridiculous. **ludicrously** *adv.*

luff (luf) *v.* To turn a sailing vessel toward the wind.

lug (lug) *n.* An ear-like handle or projection used as a hold; a tab. **lug** *v.* To carry with difficulty.

luge (lüzh) *n.* A small sled similar to a toboggan which is ridden in a supine position and used in competitions like the Olympics..

lug-gage (lug´ij) *n.* Something that is lugged, especially suitcases or a traveler's baggage.

lu-gu-bri-ous (le gü´brē us) *adj.* Mournful; dejected; especially exaggeratedly or affectedly so. **lugubriously** *adv.* **lugubriousness** *n.*

luke-warm (lük´worm´) *adj.* Mildly warm; tepid; unenthusiastic; soothing. **lukewarm-ly** *adv.*

lull (lul) *v.* To cause to rest or sleep; to cause to have a false sense of security. **lull** *n.* A temporary period of quiet.

lul-la-by (lul´a bi´) *n. pl.* **lullabies** A song to lull a child to sleep.

lum-ba-go (lum bā´gō) *n.* Painful rheumatic pain of the muscles and tendons of the lumbar region.

lum-bar (lum´bér) *adj.* Part of the back and sides between the lowest ribs and the pelvis.

lum-ber (lum´bér) *n.* Timber, sawed or split into boards. *v.* To walk clumsily.

lu-mi-nar-y (lu´mi ner ē) *n. pl.* **-ies** A celestial body, as the sun; a notable person.

lu-mi-nes-cence (lü´mi nes´ens) *n.* An emission of light without heat, as in fluorescence.

lu-mi-nous (lü´mi nus) *adj.* Emitting or reflecting light; bathed in steady light; illuminated; easily understood; clear. **luminously** *adv.*

luminous paint *n.* A paint that glows in the dark.

lum-mox (lum´uks) *n.* A clumsy oaf.

lump (lump) *n.* A projection; a protuberance; a swelling, as from a bruise or infection. **lump** *v.* To group things together.

lum-pen (lum´pen *adj.* Relating to groups of people who have been uprooted from their normal routine or economic status.

lump-ish (lum´pish) *adj.* Stupid or dull. **lumpishly** *adv.* **lumpiness** *n.*

lump-y (lum´pē) *adj.* Covered or full of lumps.

lu-na-cy (lü´na sē) *n. pl.* **lunacies**

Insanity.

lu-nar (lü´nèr) *adj.* Of, relating to, caused by the moon.

lunar eclipse *n.* An eclipse where the moon passes partially or wholly through the umbra of the earth's shadow.

lu-nate (lö´nāt) *adj.* Having the form or shape like the half-moon; crescent-shaped.

lu-na-tic (lü´na tĭk) *n.* A crazy person.

lunatic fringe *n.* Members of a political or extremist expressing extreme or eccentric views.

lunch (lunch) *n.* A meal served between breakfast and supper.

lunch-eon (lun´chon) *n.* A lunch.

lunch-room (lunch´röm¨) *n.* Room in a school, business or establishments where individual may eat lunch.

lung (lung) *n.* One of the two spongy organs that constitute the basic respiratory organ of air breath-ing vertebrates.

lunge (lunj) *n.* A sud-den forward movement. **lunge** *v.*

lu-pine (lö´pĭn) *adj.* To be wolf-like; wolfish.

lu-pu-lin (lö´pŭ lĭn) *n.* A yellow powder that is obtained from hops and used as a sedative.

lu-pus (lü´pus) *n.* A bacterial disease of the skin.

lurch (lürch) *v.* To heave something to one side.

lure (ler) *n.* A decoy; something appealing; an artificial bait to catch fish. **lure** *v.* To attract or entice with the prospect of reward or pleasure.

lu-rid (lür´id) *adj.* Sensational; shining with a fiery glare; fierce passion. **luridly** *adv.* **luridness** *n.*

lurk (lerk) *v.* To lie in concealment, as in an ambush.

lus-cious (lush´us) *adj.* Very pleasant to smell or taste; appealing to the senses. **lusciously** *adv.* -ness *n.*

lush (lush) *adj.* Producing luxuriant growth or vegetation. *Slang* An alcoholic. **lushly** *adv.* **lushness** *n.*

lust (lust) *n.* Intense sexual desire; an intense longing; a craving. **lustful** *adj.*

luster (lus´tèr) *n.* A glow of reflected light; sheen; brilliance or radiance; brightness. **lustrous** *adj.* **lusterless** *adj.*

lus-ter-ing (lus´tèr ing) *n.* The process that gives a luster to cloth.

lus-ter-ware (lus´tèr wâr¨) *n.* A glossy and often iridescent piece of pottery.

lust-ful (lust´ful) *adj.* Having a strong desire for sexual satisfaction.

lus-trate (lus´trāt) *v.* To purify by a ceremony.

lus-trous (lus´trus) *adj.* Characterized by sheen; bright; luminous. **lustrously** *adv.* **lustrousness** *n.*

lust-y (lus´tē) *adj.* Vigorous; healthy; robust; lively. **lustily** *adv.*

lusus naturae (lö´sus na tür´ē) *n.* An abnormally formed animal, person, or plant; a freak of nature.

lu-tan-ist (löt´a nist) *n.* A person who plays the lute.

lute (lüt) *n.* A medieval musical stringed instrument with a fretted fingerboard, a pear-shaped body, and a bent neck.

lute-string (löt´string) *n.* A glossy silk fabric formerly used for women's ribbons and dresses.

lu-te-ti-um *or* **lu-te-ci-um (lü tē´shē um)** *n.* A silvery rare-earth metallic element symbolized by Lu.

lux-ate (luk´sāt) *v.* To dislocate a limb, as a shoulder, arm, or hip.

lux-u-ri-ant (lug zher´ē ant) *adj.* Growing or producing abundantly; lush; plentiful. **luxuriance** *n.*

lux-u-ri-ate (lug zher´ē āt) *v.* To enjoy luxury or abundance; to grow abundantly; pleasure.

lux-u-ry (luk´sha rē) *n.* *pl.* -ies Something desirable but costly or hard to get; something which adds to one's comfort or pleasure but is not absolutely necessary; sumptuous surroundings or living.

ly-can-thro-py (lī kan´thro pē) *n.* An insanity where the patient supposes himself to be a wolf; the delusional trans-formation of a human into the form of a wolf.

ly-ce-um (lī sē´um) *n.* A hall where public programs are presented; an organization which sponsors such programs as lectures and concerts.

lye (lī) *n.* A powerful caustic solution yielded by leaching wood ashes; po-tassium hydroxide; sodium hydroxide.

ly-ing-in (lī´ing in¨) *n.* Confinement in childbirth.

lymph node *n.* A roundish body of lymphoid tissue; lymph gland.

lym-pho-ma (lim¨fo´ma) *n. pl.* **lympho-mas** *Pathol.* A tumor located in the lymphoid tissue.

lynch (linch) *v.* To execute without authority or the due process of law.

lynx (lingks) *n.* A wildcat. **lynx-eyed** *adj.* Having acute eyesight.

lyre (līèr) *n.* A harp-like stringed instrument of Ancient Greece.

lyr-ic (lir´ik) *adj.* Concerned with thoughts and feelings; romantic; appropriate for singing. *n.* A lyric poem. **lyrics** The words of a song. **lyrical** *adj.* **lyrically** *adv.*

lysergic acid diethylamide *n.* An organic compound which induces psychotic symptoms similar to those of schizo-phrenia; LSD.

ly-sis (lī´sis) *n., Med.* The gradual decline of a disease.

M, m (em) The thirteenth letter of the English alphabet; the Roman numeral for 1,000.

m *abbr.* Mile.

ma (mä) *n., Slang* Mother.

ma'am (mam) *n.* Madam.

mac *n.* An address for a man whose name is unknown.

ma-ca-bre (ma kab´re) *adj.* Suggesting death and decay.

mac-ad-am (ma kad´am) *n.* Pavement for roads consisting of layers of compacted, broken stone, usually cemented with asphalt and tar.

mac-a-ro-ni(mak´a rō´nē) *n.* Dried pasta made into short tubes and prepared as food.

ma-caw (ma ko´) *n.* Any of various tropical American parrots with long tails, brilliant plumage, and harsh voices.

mac-e-doine (mas´i dwän´) *n.* A jellied salad; mixture of diced vegetables or fruits.

mace (mās) *n.* An aromatic spice made by grinding the cover of the nutmeg.

mac-er-ate (mas´e rāt´) *v.* To make a solid substance soft by soaking in liquid; to cause to grow thin. **macer-ater** *or* **macerator** *n.* **maceration** *n.*

ma-chet-e (ma shet´e) *n.* A large, heavy knife with a broad blade, used as a weapon.

mach-i-nate (mak´i nāt´) *v.* To plot. **machination** *n.* **machinator** *n.*

ma-chine (ma shēn´) *n.* A device or system built to use energy to do work; a political organization. *v.* To produce precision tools.

ma-chin-ist (ma shē´nist) *n.* One skilled in the operation or repair of machines.

ma-chis-mo *n.* An exaggerated sense of masculinity **macho** *Slang* Exhibiting machismo.

ma-cho *adj., Slang* Exhibiting machismo.

mack-er-el (mak´ér el) *n.* A fish with dark, wavy bars on the back and a silvery belly, found in the Atlantic Ocean.

mack-le (mak´l) *n.* To become blurred.

ma-cle *n.* The double crystal of a diamond.

mac-ra-me (mak´ra mā´) *n.* The craft or hobby of tying knots into a pattern.

macro In *computer science*, a set of computer instructions that are executed by a single command or a hot key combination.

mac-ro-bi-ot-ic *adj.* Relating to or being on an extremely restricted diet to promote longevity, consisting mainly of whole grain, vegetables and fish.

mac-ro-cosm *n.* A large scale model of something that is smaller. **-ic** *adj.*

mac-ro-cyte *n.* A red blood cell that is larger than normal. **macrocytic** *adj.,*

mac-ro-graph *n.* A drawing or photograph that is at least life-size or larger.

ma-crog-ra-phy *v.* To investigate something by the use of the naked eye.

ma-cron *n.* A short mark (-) placed over a vowel to indicate the pronunciation as a long sound.

ma-cron (mā´kron) *n.* A mark (-) placed over a vowel to indicate a long sound.

mac-ro-scop-ic *or* **macroscopical (mak´-ro skop´ik)** *adj.* Large enough to be seen by the naked eye. **macroscopical, macroscopically** *adv.*

mac-u-la (mak´ū la) *n.* A discolored spot on the skin, an anatomical spot. **macular** *adj.*

mad (mad) *adj.* Angry; afflicted with a mental disorder; insane.

mad-am (mad´am) *n.* A title used to address a married woman; used without a name as a courtesy title when addressing a woman.

mad-cap *adj.* Impulsive, rash or reckless; hare brained.

mad-den *v.* To craze; to enrage; to make mad. To become mad.

mad-ding *adj.* Behaving senselessly; acting mad, inducing madness.

made (mād) *v.* Past tense of make. *adj.* Constructed not natural; invented or construct-ed.

mad-e-moi-selle *n.* An unmarried French girl or woman.

made-to-order *adj.* Custom-made.

made-up (mād´up´) *adj.* Fabricated; invented; having makeup on.

mad-house (mad´hous´) *n. Slang* A place of confusion and disorder.

Madison, James *n.* (1751-1836) The fourth president of the United States from 1809-1817.

mad-man *n.* A lunatic.

mad-ness *n.* The state of being mad; extreme excitement.

mad-ri-gal (mad´ri gal) *n., Music* An unaccompanied song, usually for four to six voices, developed during the early Renaissance.

mael-strom (māl´ntrom) *n.* Any irresistible or dangerous force, a whirlpool of the coast of Norway.

maes-tro (mī´strō) *n.* A person mastering any art, but especially a famous conductor of music.

mag-a-zine(mag´a zēn´) *n.* A publication with a paper cover containing articles, stories, illustrations and advertising; the part of a gun which holds ammunition ready for feeding into the chamber.

ma-gen-ta (ma jen´ta) *n.* A purplish-red color.

mag-got (mag´ot) *n.* The legless larva of any of various insects, as the housefly, often found in decaying matter.

mag·ic (maj´ik) *n.* The art which seemingly controls natural events and forces by means of supernatural agencies. **magic** *adj.* **magical** *adj.*

magician *n.* A person who is skilled in magic and performs magic.

mag·is·te·ri·al *adj.* Pertaining to the office or a magistrate; arrogant; pompous; authoritative.

mag·is·trate (maj´i strāt´) *n.* A civil officer with the power to enforce the law.

mag·ma (mag´ma) *n.* *pl.*-mas -mata *or Geol.* The molten rock beneath the earth's surface from which igneous rocks are formed.

Magna Carta (mag´na kär´ta) *n.* The Great Charter of English liberties which the barons forced King John to sign in June 1215; any document constituting a guarantee of rights and privileges.

mag·nan·i·mous (mag nan´i mus) *adj.* Generous in forgiving insults or injuries. **magnanimity** *n.* **magnanimousness** *n.* **magnanimously** *adv.*

mag·nate (mag´nāt) *n.* A person notable or powerful, especially in business.

mag·ne·sia (mag nē´zha) *n.,* *Chem.* A light, white powder used in medicine as an antacid and laxative.

mag·ne·si·um (mag nē´zē um) *n.* A light, silvery metallic element which burns with a very hot, bright flame and is used in lightweight alloys, symbolized by Mg.

mag·net (mag´nit) *n.* A body having the property of attracting iron and other magnetic material. **magnetism** *n.*

magnetic field *n.* The area in the neighborhood of a magnet or of an electric current, marked by the existence of a detectable magnetic force in every part of the region.

mag·ne·to (mag nē´tō) *n.* A small alternator which works by means of magnets that are permanently attached, inducing an electric current for the spark in some engines.

mag·ne·tom·e·ter (mag´ni tom´i tèr) *n.* An instrument used for measuring the direction and intensity of magnetic forces.

mag·ne·to·sphere (mag nē´to sfēr´) *n.* *Physics.* A region of the upper atmosphere extending from about 500 to several thousand km above the surface, forming a band of ionized particles trapped by the earth's magnetic field.

mag·ni·fi·ca·tion *n.* The act of magnifying; magnified reproduction.

mag·nif·i·cent (mag nif´i sent) *adj.* Having an extraordinarily imposing appearance; beautiful; outstanding; exceptionally pleasing.

mag·ni·fy (mag´ni fī´) *v.* To increase in size; to cause to seem more important or greater; to glorify or praise someone or something. **magnification** *n.*

mag·nil·o·quent (mag nil´o kwent) *adj.* Speaking or spoken in a lofty and extravagant manner. **magniloquence** *n.* **magniloquently** *adv.*

mag·ni·tude (mag´ni tōd´) *n.* Greatness or importance in size or extent. *Astron.* The relative brightness of a star expressed on a numerical scale, ranging from one for the brightest to six for those just visible.

mag·no·lia (mag nōl´ya) *n.* An ornamental flowering tree or shrub with large, fragrant flowers of white, pink, purple, or yellow.

Magnolia State *n.* Nickname of the state of Mississippi.

mag·num (mag´num) *n.* A wine bottle holding about two quarts or approximately 2/5 gallon.

mag·num o·pus *n.* A great work of art; literary or artistic masterpiece; the greatest single work of an artist, writer, or other creative person.

mag·pie (mag´pī´) *n.* Any of a variety of large, noisy bird found the world over having long tapering tails and black and white plumage.

ma·ha·ra·ja *or* **ma·ha·ra·jah (mä´harä´ja)** *n.* A king or prince who rules an Indian state.

ma·ha·ra·ni *or* **ma·ha·ra·nee (mä´harä´nē)** *n.* The wife of a maharajah.

ma·hat·ma (ma hät´ma) *n.* In some Asian religions, a person venerated for great knowledge; a title of respect.

ma·hog·a·ny (ma hog´a nē) *n.* *pl.* -ies Any of various tropical trees having hard, reddish-brown wood, much used for cabinet work and furniture.

maid (mād) *n.* A young unmarried woman or girl; a female servant.

mail (māl) *n.* Letter, printed matter, or parcel handled by the postal system. *v.* To send something through the mail; to put in a mailbox for delivery.

mail-box *n.* A box used to deposit mail waiting for delivery and collection; a box at a private residence that receives mail.

mail order *n.* Goods which are ordered and sent by mail.

maim (mām) *v.* To disable or to deprive of the use of a body part; to impair.

main (mān) *adj.* Being the most important part of something. *n.* A large pipe used to carry water, oil, or gas. **mainly** *adv.*

Maine *n.* A state located in the northeastern corner of the United States; statehood March 15, 1820; state capital Augusta.

main·tain (mān tān´) *v.* To carry on or to keep in existence; to preserve in a desirable condition. **maintenance** *n.*

maj-es-ty (maj´i stē) *n., pl.* **-ties** Stateliness; dignity. **majestic** *adj.*

ma-jor (mā´jėr) *adj.* Greater in importance, quantity, number, or rank.

ma-jor-i-ty (ma jor´i tē) *n. pl.* **-ies** The greater number of something; more than half; the age at which a person is considered to be an adult, usually 21 years old; a number of voters in agreement; a political party group with the most votes.

majority rule *n.* A majority vote that consists of at least one vote over half of the total.

make (māk) *v.* To cause something to happen; to create; to provide, as time; to manufacture a line of goods. *n.* A brand name, as a make of a car. **with** To carry off. **hay** To take advantage of a given opportunity in the early stages. **bones** To perform unhesitating. **make away** *v.* **make** *n.* **maker** *n.*

make–be-lieve (māk´bi lēv´) *n.* A pretending to believe. *v.* To pretend.

make–up (māk´up´) *n.* The manner in which something is formed together or assembled; constructions; the qualities of physical or mental constitution; cosmetics. *v.* To invent a story.

mal-ad-min-is-ter *v.* To conduct dishonestly. **maladministration** *n.*

mal-a-droit (mal´a droit´) *adj.* Lacking skill; awkward; clumsy. **maladroitly** *adv.* **maladroitness** *n.*

mal-a-dy (mal´a dē) *n. pl.* **-ies** A chronic disease or sickness.

mal-aise (ma lāz´) *n.* The vague discomfort sometimes indicating the beginning of an illness.

mal-a-prop-ism (mal´a prop iz´um) *n.* A foolish misuse of a word. **malaprop, malapropian** *adj.*

mal-ap-ro-pos (mal´ap ro pō´) *adj.* Not appropriate. **malapropos** *adv.*

ma-lar-i-a (ma lâr´ē a) *n., Pathol.* The infectious disease introduced into the blood by the bite of the infected female anopheles mosquito and characterized by cycles of fever, chills, and profuse sweating.

ma-lar-key (ma lär´kē) *n., Slang* Foolish or insincere talk; nonsense.

mal-con-tent (mal´kon tent´) *adj.* Unhappy with existing conditions or affairs. **malcontent** *n.*

mal de mer *n.* Seasickness.

male (māl) *adj.* Of or belonging to the sex that has organs to produce spermatozoa. *Bot.* A plant with stamens but no pistil. *n.* A male person or animal. **maleness** *n.*

mal-e-dic-tion (mal´i dik´shan) *n.* A curse; execration. **maledictory** *adj.*

mal-e-fac-tor (mal´e fak´ter) *n.* A person

who commits a crime or an unlawful act; a criminal. **malefaction** *n.*

ma-lef-i-cent *n.* Harmful; doing evil or wrong. **maleficence** *n.*

ma-lev-o-lent (ma lev´o lent) *adj.* Full of spite or ill will for another; malicious. **malevolence** *n.*

mal-for-ma-tion (mal´for mā´shan) *n.* Defective structure or form.

mal-func-tion (mal fungk´shan) *n.* Failure to function correctly.

mal-ice (mal´is) *n.* The direct intention or desire to harm others. *Law* The willfully formed design to injure another without just reason or cause.

ma-lign (ma līn´) *v.* To speak slander or evil of. **maligner** *n.*

ma-lig-nant (ma lig´nant) *adj., Pathol.* Of or relating to tumors and abnormal or rapid growth, and tending to metastasize; opposed to benign; causing death or great harm. **malignancy** *n.* **malignity** *n.* **malignantly** *adv.*

ma-lin-ger (ma ling gėr) *v.* To pretend injury or sickness so as to avoid responsibility or work. **malingerer** *n.*

mall (mol) *n.* A walk or other shaded public promenade; a street with shops, restaurants, and businesses which is closed to vehicles.

mal-le-a-ble (mal´ē a bl) *adj.* Able to be bent, shaped, or hammered without breaking; capable of being molded, altered, or influenced. **malleability** *n.* **malleableness** *n.* **malleably** *adv.*

mal-le-us (mal´ē us) *n., Anat.* The club-shaped bone of the middle ear or the largest of three small bones; also called the hammer.

mal-nour-ished (mal´ner´isht) *adj.* Undernourished.

mal-nu-tri-tion (mal´nū trish´an) *n.* Insufficient nutrition.

mal-o-dor *n.* An offensive stench; odor.

mal-oc-clu-sion (mal´o klō´zhan) *n.* Improper alignment of the teeth.

mal-o-dor-ous (mal ō´dėr us) *adj.* Having a disagreeable or foul odor.

mal-po-si-tion *n., Pathol* Wrong position as of a fetus in the uterus or a body organ.

mal-prac-tice (mal prak´tis) *n.* Improper treatment of a patient by his doctor during surgery or treatment which results in damage or injury; failure to perform a professional duty in a proper, careful, or correct fashion, resulting in injury, loss, or other problems.

malt (molt) *n.* Grain, usually barley, used chiefly in brewing and distilling; an alcoholic beverage.

mal-tose (mol´tōs) *n.* A white, crystalline sugar found in malt.

mal-treat (mal trēt´) *v.* To treat badly, unkindly, or roughly. **-ment** *n.*

mal-ver-sa-tion *n.* Improper behavior

in a position of trust.

ma-ma (mam´a) n. Mother.

mam-bo (mäm´bō) n. A dance resembling the rumba of Latin America.

mam-mal (mam´al) n. Any member of a class whose females secrete milk for nourishing their young, including man.

mam-ma-ry gland (mam´a rē) n. The milk-producing organ of the female mammal, consisting of small cavity clusters with ducts ending in a nipple.

mam-mog-ra-phy n. An x-ray examination of the breast for early detection of cancer.

mam-moth (mam´oth) n. An extinct, early form of elephant whose tusks curved upwards and whose body was covered with long hair; any thing of great or huge size.

man (man) n. pl. men An adult or fully-grown male; the human race; Husband; an expression of pleasure or surprise.

man-a-cle (man´a kl) n. A device for re-straining the hands; handcuffs.

man-age (man´ij) v. To direct or control the affairs or use of; to organize. **manageability** n. **manageable** adj.

man-age-ment n. The act of directing, or managing for a purpose; administration; a group of managers.

man-date (man´dāt) n. An authoritative order or command. Law A judicial order issued by a higher court to a lower one. **mandate** v.

man-da-to-ry (man´da tōr´ē) adj. Required by, having the nature of, or relating to a mandate; obligatory.

man-di-ble (man´di bl) n. The lower jaw bone. Biol. Either part of the beak of a bird. **mandibular** adj.

man-do-lin (man´do lin) n. A musical instrument having a pear-shaped body and a fretted neck.

man-drake (man´drāk) n. A plant having purplish flowers and a branched root sometimes resembling the human form.

man-drel or **mandril (man´drel)** n. A spindle or shaft on which material is held for working on a lathe.

ma-nege (ma nezh´) n. The art of training and riding horses; the performance of a horse so trained.

ma-neu-ver (ma nö´věr) n., Milit. A planned strategic movement or shift, as of warships, or troops; any planned, skillful, or calculated move. **maneuverability** n. **maneuverable** adj.

man-ga-nese (mang´ga nēs´) n. A hard, brittle, gray-white metallic element which forms an important component of steel alloys, symbolized by Mn.

mange (mänj) n. A contagious skin disease of dogs and other domestic animals caused by parasitic mites and marked by itching and hair loss.

man-ger (mān´jěr) n. A trough or box which holds livestock feed.

man-gle (mang´gl) v. To disfigure or mutilate by bruising, battering, or crushing; to spoil. **mangler** n.

ma-ni-a (mā´nē a) n. An extraordinary enthusiasm or craving for something; intense excitement and physical over activity, often a symptom of manic depressive psychosis.

-mania suffix Unreasonable or intense desire or infatuation with.

ma-ni-ac (mā´nē ak´) n. A violently insane person. **maniac** adj.

man-ic–de-pres-sive (man´ik di pres´iv) adj. Of a mental disorder characterized by alternating periods of manic excitation and depression.

man-i-cot-ti n. Pasta shaped like a tube, filled with meat or ricotta cheese and served with hot tomato sauce.

man-i-cure (man´i kūr) n. The cosmetic care of the hands and finger nails. **manicure** v. **manicurist** n.

man-i-fest (man´i fest´) adj. Clearly apparent; obvious. v. To display, reveal or show. n. A list of cargo or passengers. **manifestly** adv.

man-i-fes-ta-tion (man´i fe stā´shan) n. The act or state of being manifest; making clear to the understanding; display; that which reveals; a person who participates in public demonstrations.

man-i-fes-to (man´i fes´tō) n. pl. -toes or -tos A public or format explanation of principles or intentions, usually of a political nature

man-i-fold (man´i fōld´) adj. Having many and varied parts, forms, or types; having an assortment of features. Mech. A pipe with several or many openings, as for the escaping of exhaust gas. **manifoldly** adv. **manifoldness** n.

man-i-kin or **mannikin (man´i kin)** n. A little man; a dwarf; a mannequin.

ma-nip-u-late (ma nip´ū lāt´) v. To handle or manage shrewdly and deviously for one's own profit. **manipulation** n. **manipulator** n.

manned (mand) adj. Operated by a human being.

man-ne-quin (man´e kin) n. A life-sized model of a human figure, used to fit or display clothes; a woman who models clothes.

man-ner (man´ěr) n. The way in which something happens or is done; an action or style of speech; one's social conduct and etiquette. **mannered** adj.

man-ner-ism (man´e riz´um) n. A person's distinctive behavioral trait or traits. **mannerist** n.

man-ner-ly (man´ěr lē) adj. Well-behaved; polite. **mannerliness** n.

ma-nom-e-ter (ma nom´i těr) n. An instrument used to measure pressure, as of gases or liquids. **manometric** *adj.*

man-or (man´ẽr) *n.* A landed estate; the house or hall of an estate.

man-que *adj.* Lacking fulfillment; frustrated.

man-sard (man´särd) *n., Archit.* A curved roof with the lower slope almost vertical and the upper almost horizontal.

manse (mans) *n.* The house of a clergyman.

man-sion (man´shan) *n.* A very large, impressive house.

man-size *or* **man-sized** (man´sīzd) *Slang* Quite large.

man-slaugh-ter (man´slo´tẽr) *n., Law* The unlawful killing without malice of a person by another.

man-slay-er *n.* One who murders or kills a human being.

man-ta (man´ta) *n.* A rough-textured cotton fabric; any of several very large fishes having large, very flat bodies with wing-like fins.

man-teau (man´tō) *n. pl.* -teaus *or* -teaux A robe or cloak.

man-tel *also* **mantle** (man´tl) A shelf over a fireplace; the ornamental brick or stone around a fireplace.

man-til-la (man til´a) *n.* A light scarf worn over the head and shoulders by women in Latin America and Spain.

man-tis (man´tis) *n. pl.* **mantises** *or* **mantes** A tropical insect with a long body, large eyes, and swiveling head, which stands with its forelegs folded as if in prayer.

man-tle (man´tl) *n.* A loose-fitting coat which is usually sleeveless; something that covers or conceals; a device consisting of a sheath of thread, used in gas lamps to give off brilliant illumination when heated by a flame. **mantle** *v.*

man-u-al (man´ū al) *adj.* Used or operated by the hands. *n.* A small reference book which gives instructions on how to operate or work something. **manually** *adv.*

man-u-fac-ture (man´ū fak´chẽr) *v.* To make a product; to invent or produce something. **manufacturer** *n.*

ma-nure (ma ner´) *n.* The fertilizer used to fertilize land, obtained from animal dung. **manure** *v.*

man-u-script (man´ū skript´) *n.* A typed or written material copy of an article, book, or document, which is being prepared for publication.

many (men´ē) *adj.* A mounting to a large or indefinite number or amount.

man-y-sid-ed *adj.* Having many aspects or sides, talents or capabilities.

map (map) *n.* A plane surface representation of a region. *v.* To plan anything in detail. **mapmaker** *n.* **mapper** *n.*

maple (mā´pl) *n.* A tall tree having lobed leaves and a fruit of two joined samaras; the wood of this tree, amber-yellow in color when finished and used for furniture and flooring.

maple sugar *n.* Sugar made from the sap of the maple tree.

maple syrup *n.* The refined sap of the sugar maple.

mar *v.* To scratch or deface; to blemish; to ruin; to spoil.

mar-a-bou (mar´a bö´) *n.* A stork of Africa, whose soft down is used for trimming women's garments.

ma-ra-ca (ma rä´ka) *n.* A percussion instrument made from gourds containing dried beans or pebbles.

mar-a-schi-no (mar´a skē´nō) *n.* A cherry preserved in a cordial distilled from the fermented juice of the small wild cherry and flavored with cracked cherry pits.

mar-a-thon (mar´a thon´) *n.* A foot race of 26 miles, usually run on the streets of a city; any contest of endurance.

mar-ble (mär´bl) *n.* A limestone which is partly crystallized and irregular in color. *v.* To contain sections of fat, as in meat. **marbles** A game played with balls of glass. A person's common sense or sanity.

march (märch) *v.* To walk with measured, regular steps in a solemn or dignified manner. *Mus.* A musical composition.

March (märch) *n.* The third month of the year, containing 31 days.

mare (mâr) *n.* The female of the horse and other equine animals.

ma-re (mär´a) *n. pl., Astron.* Any of the dark areas on the surface of the moon.

mare clausum *n.* The body of water that is controlled by one nation.

ma-re li-be-rum *n.* A body of water that is available to all nations for travel and navigation.

mar-ga-rine (mär´jẽr in) *n.* A butter substitute made from vegetable oils and milk.

mar-gin (mär´jin) *n.* The edge or border around the body of written or printed text; the difference between the selling price and cost of an item.

mar-gi-na-li-a *n. pl.* The notes in the margin of a book.

mar-i-jua-na *or* **marihuana** (mar´l wä´na) *n.* Hemp; the dried flower tops and leaves of this plant, capable of producing disorienting or hallucinogenic effects when smoked in cigarettes or ingested.

ma-ri-na (ma rē´na) *n.* A docking area for boats, furnishing moorings and supplies for small boats.

mar-i-nade (mar´i nād´) *n.* A brine made

from vinegar or wine and oil with various herbs and spices for soaking meat, fowl, or fish before cooking.

mar-i-nate (mar´i nāt´) v. To soak meat in a marinade.

ma-rine (ma rēn´) adj. Of, pertaining to, existing in, or formed by the sea. n. A soldier trained for service on land and at sea. **Marine** A member of the Marine Corps.

mar-i-tal (mar´i tal) adj. Pertaining to marriage. **maritally** adv.

mar-i-time (mar´i tīm´) adj. Located or situated on or near the sea; pertaining to the sea and its navigation and commerce.

mark (märk) n. A visible impression, trace, dent, or stain; an identifying seal, inscription, or label.

mar-ket (mär´kit) n. The trade and commerce in a certain service or commodity; a public place for purchasing and selling merchandise; the possible consumers of a particular product. v. To sell. **marketability** n.

mar-ma-lade (mär´ma lād´) n. A preserve made from the pulp and rind of fruits.

ma-roon (ma rōn´) v. To put ashore and abandon on a desolate shore. n. A dull purplish red.

mar-que-try (mär´ki trē) n. Inlaid work of wood or ivory used for decorating furniture.

mar-quis (mär´kwis) n. The title of a nobleman ranking below a duke.

mar-qui-sette (mär´ki zet´) n. A fabric of cotton, silk, nylon, or a combination of these, used in curtains, clothing, and mosquito nets.

mar-riage (mar´ij) n. The state of being married; wedlock; the act of marrying or the ceremony entered into by a man and woman so as to live together as husband and wife. **marriageability** n. **marriageable** adj.

mar-row (mar´ō) n. The soft, vascular tissue which fills bone cavities; the main part or essence of anything.

mar-row-bone n. A bone that is rich in marrow.

mar-ry (mar´ē) v. To take or join as husband or wife; to unite closely.

Mars (märz) n. The 4th planet from the sun.

marsh (märsh) n. An area of low, wet land; a swamp. **marshy** adj.

mar-su-pi-al (mär sŏ´pē al) n. An animal, such as a kangaroo, koala, or opossum, which has no placenta, but which in the female has an abdominal pouch with teats to feed and carry the offspring.

mar-tial (mär´shal) adj. Of, pertaining to, or concerned with war or the military life.

martial arts n. pl. Oriental arts of self-defense, such as karate or judo, which are practiced as sports.

martial law n. Temporary rule by military forces over the citizens in an area where civil law and order no longer exist.

mar-tin (mär´tin) n. A bird of the swallow family with a tail that is less forked than that of the common swallow.

mar-ti-ni (mär tē´nē) n. pl. -nis A cocktail of gin and dry vermouth, served with an olive or lemon peel.

mar-tyr (mär´tèr) n. A person who would rather die than renounce his religious principles; one making great sacrifices to advance a cause, belief, or principle. **martyrdom** n.

mar-vel (mär´vel) n. Anything causing surprise, wonder, or astonishment.

mar-vel-ous or marvellous (mär´ve lus) Informal Excellent; very good, admirable. **marvelously** adv.

Mary-land n. A state located on the eastern coast of the United States; statehood April 28, 1788; state capital Annapolis.

mar-zi-pan (mär´zi pan´) n. A confection of grated almonds, sugar, and egg whites.

mas-car-a (ma skar´a) n. A cosmetic preparation used for coloring or darkening the eyelashes.

mas-cot (mas´kot) n. A person, animal, or object thought to bring good luck.

mas-cu-line (mas´kū lin) adj. Of or pertaining to the male sex; male; the masculine gender.

ma-ser (mā´zèr) n., Physics One of several devices which are similar to the laser but which operate with microwaves rather than light.

mask (mask) n. A covering used to conceal the face in order to disguise or protect. v. To hide or conceal.

mas-o-chism (mas´o kiz´um) n. A condition in which sexual gratification is marked by pleasure in being subjected to physical pain or abuse. **masochist** n. **masochistic** adj.

mas-quer-ade (mas´ke rād´) n. A costume party in which the guests are masked and dressed in fancy costumes. v. To disguise oneself.

mass (mas) n. A body of matter that does not have definite shape but is relatively large in size; physical volume; the measure of a body's resistance to acceleration.

Mass or mass (mas) n. A celebration in the Roman Catholic and some Protestant churches; the service including this celebration.

Mass-a-chu-setts n. A state located in the northeastern part of the United

States; statehood February 6, 1788; state capital Boston.

mas-sa-cre (mas´a kèr) n. The indiscriminate and savage killing of human beings in large numbers. **massacre** v.

mas-sage (ma säzh´) n. The manual or mechanical manipulation of the skin to improve circulation and to relax muscles. **massage** v.

mas-seur (ma ser´) n. A man who gives massages.

mas-seuse (ma sös´) n. A woman who gives massages.

mas-sive (mas´iv) adj. Of great intensity, degree, and size. **massively** adv. **massiveness** n.

mast (mast) n. The upright pole or spar which supports the sails and running rigging of a sail boat.

mas-tec-to-my (ma stek´to mē) n. pl. -ies The surgical removal of breast.

mas-ter (mas´tèr) n. A person with control or authority over others; one who is exceptionally gifted or skilled in an art, science, or craft; the title given for respect or in address. v. To learn a skill, craft, or job; to overcome defeat. **mastership** n.

mas-ti-cate (mas´ti kāt´) v. To chew.

mas-to-don (mas´to don´) n. A large, extinct mammal which resembles an elephant.

mas-toid (mas´toid) n., Anat. The nipple shaped portion at the rear of the temporal bone behind the ear.

mas-tur-ba-tion (mas´tèr bā´shan) n. The act of stimulating the sexual organs by hand or other means without sexual intercourse. **masturbate** v.

mat (mat) n. A flat piece of material made of fiber, rubber, rushes, or other material and used to cover floors; the border around a picture, which serves as a contrast between the picture and the frame.

match (mach) n. Anything that is similar or identical to another; a short, thin piece of wood or cardboard with a specially treated tip which ignites as a result of friction. v. To equal; to oppose successfully. **matchable** adj.

mate (māt) n. A spouse; something matched, joined, or paired with another; in chess, a move which puts the opponent's king in-jeopardy. Naval A petty officer. **mate** v.

ma-te-ri-al (ma tēr´ē al) n. The substance from which anything is or may be composed or constructed of; anything that is used in creating, working up, or developing something.

ma-ter-nal (ma ter´nal) adj. Relating to a mother or motherhood; inherited from one's mother.

ma-ter-ni-ty (ma ter´ni tē) n. The state of being a mother; the qualities of a mother; the department in a hospital for the prenatal and postnatal care of babies and their mothers.

math (math) n. Mathematics.

math-e-mat-ics (math´e mat´iks) n. The study of form, arrangement, quantity, and magnitude of numbers and operational symbols. **mathematical** adj. **mathematician** n.

mat-i-nee (mat´i nā´) n. An afternoon performance of a play, concert, movie, etc.

mat-ri-cide (ma´tri sīd´) n. The killing of one's own mother; one who kills his mother. **matricidal** adj.

ma-tric-u-late (ma trik´ū lāt´) v. To enroll, or to be admitted into a college or university. **matriculation** n.

mat-ri-mo-ny (ma´tri mō´nē) n. The condition of being married; the act, sacrament, or ceremony of marriage. **matrimonial** adj. **matrimonially** adv.

ma-trix (mā´triks) n., pl. **matrixes** or **matrices** Something within which something else develops, originates, or takes shape; a mold or die.

ma-tron (mā´tron) n. A married woman or widow of dignity and social position; the woman supervisor in a prison. **matronly** adv. **matronliness** n.

mat-ter (mat´èr) n. Something that makes up the substance of anything; that which is material and physical, occupies space, and is perceived by the senses; something that is sent by mail; something that is written.

mat-u-rate (mach´e rāt´) v. To ripen or mature. **maturation** n.

ma-ture (ma tēr´) adj. Completely developed; at full growth; something as a bond at a bank, that is due and payable. **mature** v. **maturely** adv.

mat-zo (mät´sa) n. pl. -zos or -zot A large, flat piece of unleavened bread eaten during Passover.

maud-lin (mod´lin) adj. Overly sentimental; tearfully and overwhelmingly emotional.

maun-der (mon´dèr) v. To wander or talk in an incoherent manner.

mau-so-le-um (mo´so lē´um) n. pl. -leums or -lea A large and stately tomb.

mauve (mōv) n. A purplish rose shade; a moderately reddish to gray purple.

mav-er-ick (mav´èr ik) n. An unbranded or orphaned calf or colt. Slang A person who is unorthodox in his ideas or attitudes.

mawk-ish (mo´kish) adj. Disgustingly sentimental; sickening or insipid. **mawkishly** adv. **mawkishness** n.

max abbr. Maximum.

max-i n. A floor-length garment, such as a skirt or coat.

max-il-la (mak sil´a) n, pl. -lae or -las

The upper jaw or jawbone.

max-im (mak´sim) *n.* A brief statement of truth, general principle, or rule of conduct.

max-i-mize (mak´si mĭz´) *v.* To increase as greatly as possible; to intensify to the maximum.

max-i-mum (mak´si mum) *n. pl.* -mums *or* -ma The greatest possible number, measure, degree, or quantity.

may (mā) *v.* To be permitted or allowed; used to express a wish, purpose, desire, contingency, or result.

May (mā) *n.* The fifth month of the year, having 31 days.

may-be (mā´bē) *adv.* Perhaps; possibly.

may-hem (mā´hem) *n., Law* The offense of injuring a person's body; any situation brought on by violence, confusion, noise, or disorder.

may-on-naise (mā´o nāz´) *n.* A dressing for salads, made by beating raw egg yolk, oil, lemon juice or vinegar, and seasonings.

may-or (mā´ér) *n.* The chief magistrate of a town, borough, municipality, or city. **mayoral** *adj.* **mayoralty** *n.*

maze (māz) *n.* A complicated, intricate network of passages or pathways; a labyrinth; a state of uncertainty, bewilderment, or perplexity. **maze** *v.*

McKinley, William. (1843-1901) The twenty-fifth president of the United States from 1897- 1901; assassinated.

me (mē) *pron.* The objective case of the pronoun I.

mead (mēd) *n.* An alcoholic beverage made from fermented honey and water with yeast and spices added.

mead-ow (med´ō) *n.* A tract of grassland used for grazing or growing hay.

mea-ger *or* **mea-gre** (mē´gér) *adj.* Thin; lean; deficient in quantity, richness, vigor, strength or fertility. **meagerly** *adv.* **meagerness** *n.*

meal (mēl) *n.* The edible seeds of coarsely ground grain; any powdery material; the food served or eaten at one sitting at certain times during the day; the time or occasion of taking such food. **mealy** *adj.*

mean (mēn) *v.* To have in mind as a purpose or intent; to be of a specified importance or significance. *adj.* Poor or inferior in appearance or quality. *n.* The middle point. **means** The method or instrument by which some end is or may be accomplished; the available resources.

me-an-der (mē an´dèr) *v.* To wander about without a certain course or a fixed direction. **meander** *n.*

mean-ing (mē´ning) *n.* That which is meant or intended; the aim, end, or purpose; the significance; an interpretation. **meaningful** *adj.* **-fulness** *adj.*

mean-time (mēn´tīm´) *n.* The time or period between or during the intervening time.

mean-while (mēn´hwīl´) *adv.* During the intervening time.

mea-sles (mē´zelz) *n.* A contagious viral disease usually occurring in children, characterized by the eruption of red spots.

mea-sly (mē´zlē) *adj., Slang* Very small; meager.

meas-ure (mezh´ér) *n.* The range, dimension, extent, or capacity of anything. *Mus.* The group of beats marked off by regularly recurring primary accents; the notes and rests between two successive bars on a musical staff. *v.* To determine the range, dimension, extent, volume, or capacity of anything. **measurable** *adj.* **measurably** *adv.* **measurer** *n.*

meat (mēt) *n.* The flesh of an animal which is used as food; the core or essential part of something..

me-chan-ic (me kan´ik) *n.* A person skilled in the making, operation, or repair of machines or tools.

me-chan-i-cal (me kan´i kal) *adj.* Involving or having to do with the construction, operation, or design of tools or machines; produced or operated by a machine. **mechanically** *adv.*

mechanical drawing *n.* A drawing done with the aid of squares, compasses, or other instruments.

med-al (med´al) *n.* A small piece of metal with a commemorative image or inscription which is presented as an award.

med-al-ist (med´a list) *n.* A person who designs, collects, or makes medals; one who has been awarded or received a medal.

me-dal-lion (me dal´yan) *n.* A large circular or oval medal which is used as a decorative element.

med-dle (med´l) *v.* To interfere or participate in another person's business or affairs. **meddler** *n.* **meddlesome** *adj.*

med-i-a (mē´dē a) *n. pl.* The instruments of news communication, as radio, television, and newspapers.

me-di-al (mē´dē al) *adj.* Pertaining to or situated in the middle; ordinary.

me-di-an (mē´dē an) *n.* Something that is halfway between two different parts. *adj.* Relating to or constituting the median of a set of numbers.

median strip *n.* The strip which divides highway traffic lanes which are going in opposite directions.

me-di-ate (mē´dē āt´) *v.* To help settle or reconcile opposing sides in a dispute. **mediation** *n.* **mediator** *n.*

med-ic (med´ik) *n. Slang* A physician

or intern; a medical student; in the armed forces, a corpsman or enlisted person trained to give first aid.

med-i-cal (med´i kal) *adj.* Relating to the study or practice of medicine.

medical examiner *n.* A physician who is authorized by a governmental body to ascertain causes of death.

med-i-cine (med´i sin) *n.* Any agent or substance used in the treatment of disease or in the relief of pain; the science of diagnosing and treating disease; the profession of medicine.

me-di-e-val *or* **mediaeval (mē´dēē´val)** *adj.* Like or characteristic of the Middle Ages.

me-di-o-cre (mē´dēō´kėr) *adj.* Common; fair; undistinguished.

med-i-tate (med´i tāt´) *v.* To be in continuous, contemplative thought; to think about doing something. **meditative** *adj.* **meditation** *n.*

me-di-um (mē´dē um) *n. pl.* **-dia** *or* **-ums** Something which occupies a middle position between two extremes; the means of communicating information or ideas through publishing, radio, or television

med-ley (med´lē) *n.* A mixture or confused mass of elements; a jumble. *Music* A musical composition made up of parts of different songs.

me-dul-la (mi dul´a) *n., Anat.* The center of certain vertebrate structures, such as bone marrow.

medulla oblongata (mi dul´a ob´longgä´ ta) *n.* The mass of nerve tissue found at the base of the brain, controlling bodily functions such as breathing and circulation.

meek (mēk) *adj.* Showing patience and a gentle disposition; lacking spirit or backbone; submissive. **meekly** *adv.*

meet (mēt) *v.* To come upon; to encounter; to come into conjunction or contact with someone or something; to cope or deal with; to handle; to fulfill an obligation or need.

meet-ing (mē´ting) *n.* An assembly or gathering of persons; a coming together.

meg-a-bucks *n., Slang* One million dollars; a lot of money.

megabyte (MB) In *computer science,* one million bytes.

meg-a-hertz *n. pl.* **-hertz** *Physics.* One million cycles per second, used as a radio-frequency unit.

meg-a-lo-ma-ni-a (meg´a lō mā´nēa) *n.* A mental disorder marked by fantasies of power, wealth, or omnipotence. **mega-lomaniac** *n.* **megalomaniacal** *adj.*

meg-a-lop-o-lis (meg´a lop´o lis) *n.* A very large urban complex.

meg-a-phone (meg´a fōn´) *n.* A

funnel-shaped device which is used to amplify or direct the voice.

meg-a-ton (meg´a tun´) *n.* One million tons; the unit equal to the explosive power of one million tons of TNT.

meg-a-watt (meg´a wot´) *n.* A unit of electrical power equal to one million watts.

mel-an-cho-li-a (mel´an kō´lē a) *n. Psychi.* A mental disorder of great depression of spirits and excessive brooding without apparent cause.

mel-an-chol-y (mel´an kol´ē) *adj.* Excessively gloomy or sad.

me-lange (mā länzh´) *n.* A medley or mixture.

mel-a-nin (mel´a nin) *n., Biochem.* The brownish-black pigment which is contained in animal tissues, as the hair and skin.

mel-a-nism (mel´a niz´um) *n.* An abnormally dark pigmentation of the skin.

mel-a-no-ma (mel´a nō´ma) *n., pl.* **-mas** *or*-**mata** A dark-colored tumor or malignant mole.

meld (meld) *v.* In pinochle and other card games, to declare or announce a combination of cards for inclusion in one's total score. *n.* The card or combination of cards declared for a score.

me-lee (mā´lā) *n.* The confused and tumultuous mingling of a crowd.

mel-io-rate (mel´ya rāt´) *v* To cause to improve or to make better. **meliorative** *&* *n.* **melioration** *n.*

mel-lif-er-ous (me lif´er us) *adj.* Producing or bearing honey.

mel-lo *adj.* Sweet and soft; rich and full flavored; rich and soft in quality, as in sounds or colors.

me-lo-di-ous (me lō´dē us) *adj.* Characterized by a melody; tuneful; pleasant to hear. **melodiously** *adv.*

mel-o-dra-ma (mel´o dr´ä´ma) *n.* A very dramatic presentation which is marked by suspense and romantic sentiment; sensational and highly emotional language or behavior. **melodramatic** *adj.* **melodramatically** *adv.*

mel-o-dy (mel´o dē) *n. pl.* **-ies** An agreeable succession of pleasing sounds. **melodic** *adj.* **melodically** *adv.*

mel-on (mel´on) *n.* The large fruit of any of various plants of the gourd family, as the watermelon.

melt (melt) *v.* To change from a solid to a liquid as a result of pressure or heat.

melt-down *n.* The melting of a nuclear-reactor core.

mem-ber (mem´bėr) *n.* A person who belongs to a society, party, club, or other organization. *Biol.* An organ or part of an animal or person's body, especially a limb.

mem-ber-ship (mem´ber ship´) n. The state or fact of being a member.

mem-brane (mem´brān) n. A thin, pliable, sheet-like layer of tissue which covers body surfaces and separates or connects body-parts. **membranous** adj.

me-men-to (me men´tō) n. pl. -tos or -toes A keepsake.

mem-o (mem´ō) n. A memorandum.

mem-oir (mem´wär) n. Personal records or reminiscences; an autobiography.

mem-o-ra-ble (mem´er a bl) adj. Worth remembering or noting.

mem-o-ran-dum (mem´o ran´dum) n. pl. -dums or-da A brief, informal note written as a reminder.

me-mo-ri-al (me mōr´ē al) n. Something that serves to keep in remembrance, as a person or event. adj. Perpetuating remembrance. **memorialize** v.

Memorial Day n. The holiday that recognizes members of the armed forces killed in wars, celebrated on the last Monday in May.

mem-o-rize (mem´o rīz´) v. To commit something to memory. **memorization** n. **memorizer** n.

mem-ory (mem´o rē) n. pl. -ries The mental function or capacity of recalling or recognizing something that has been previously learned or experienced.

men n. pl. The plural of man.

men-ace (men´is) n. Something or someone who threatens; an annoying person. menace v. **menacingly** adv.

me-nar-che n. The beginning or the first occurrence of menstruation.

mend (mend) v. To fix; to repair; to correct.

men-da-cious (men dā´shus) adj. Prone to lying; deceitful; untrue; false. **mendaciously** adv. **mendacity** n.

men-de-le-vi-um (men´de lē´vē um) n. A short-lived radioactive element of the actinide series, symbolized by Md.

me-ni-al (mē´nē al) adj. Relating to a household servant or household chores requiring little responsibility or skill.

men-in-gi-tis (men´in jī´tis) n., Pathol. An inflammation of the membranes which enclose the brain and spinal cord.

me-ninx (mē´ningks) n. pl. **meninges** The membrane which encloses the spinal cord and brain. **meningeal** adj.

men-o-pause (men´o poz´) n., Physiol. The time of final menstruation, occurring normally between the ages of 45 and 50. **menopausal** adj.

men-ses (men´sēz) n. pl. The blood and dead cell debris which are discharged from the uterus through the vagina by women who are not pregnant; menstruation, occurring at monthly intervals between puberty and menopause.

men-stru-ate (men´strō āt´) v. To discharge the menses, approximately every 28 days. **menstrual** adj.

men-stru-a-tion (men´strō ā´shan) n. Physiol. The process, act, or periodical flow of bloody fluid from the uterus, also called period.

-ment suffix The result or product of achievement; action; process.

men-tal (men´tal) adj. Relating to or of the mind. **mentally** adv.

mental deficiency n. Subnormal intellectual development, marked by deficiencies ranging from impaired learning ability to social incompetence.

men-tal-i-ty (men tal´i tē) n. pl. -ies Mental faculties or powers; mental activity; habit of mind.

men-thol (men´thōl) n., Chem. The white, waxy crystalline alcohol which is obtained from and has the odor of peppermint oil. **mentholated** adj.

men-tion (men´shan) v. To refer to incidentally, in passing, or briefly. **mentionable, mentioner** adj.

men-tor (men´tér) n. A wise and trusted person.

men-u (men´ū) n. A list of food or dishes available at a restaurant; in computer science, a list of options displayed on the screen from which the operator may choose.

me-ow (mē ou´) n. The cry of a cat.

me-phi-tis (me fi´tis) n. A sickening or foul smell; a stench emitted from the earth.

mer-can-tile (mer´kan tēl´) adj. Of or relating to merchants, trading, or commerce.

mer-ce-nar-y (mer´se ner´ē) n. A person who is concerned only with making money and obtaining material gain; a person paid to serve as a soldier in a foreign country. **mercenary** adj.

mer-chan-dise (mer´chan dīz´) n. Commodities or goods that are bought and sold. v. To buy and sell.

mer-chant (mer´chant) n. A person who operates a retail business for profit.

mer-chant-man (mer´chant man) n. A ship used for commercial shipments.

mer-cu-ry (mûr´kū rē) n. A silvery, metallic, liquid element used in thermometers and barometers, symbolized by Hg.

mer-cy (mer´sē) n. pl. -ies Compassionate and kind treatment. **merciful** adj. **merciless** adj. **mercifully** adv. .

mere (mēr) adj. Absolute; no more than what is stated. **merest** adj. **merely** adv.

merge (merj) v. To unite or bring together as one; in computer science, to combine two or more files into one, retaining the internal order of both.

merger (mer´jér) n. The act of combining two or more corporations into one.

me-ringue (me rang´) *n.* A mixture of stiffly beaten egg whites and sugar, used as a topping for cakes and pies or baked into crisp shells.

mer-it (mer´it) *n.* A characteristic act or trait which is worthy of praise. **merit** *v.* To earn; to be worthy of.

mer-i-toc-ra-cy *n. pl.* **-ies** A system which bases advancement on ability or achievement.

mer-i-to-ri-ous (mer´i tōr´ē us) *adj.* Deserving honor, praise or reward.

mer-ry (mer´ē) *adj.* Delightful; gay; entertaining; festive; happy; joyous. **merrily** *adv.* **merriness** *n.*

mer-ry–go–round (mer´ē gō round´) *n.* A circular, revolving platform often with benches and animal figures, usually found in circuses and amusement parks.

me-sa (mā´sa) *n.* A flat-topped hill or small plateau with steep sides.

mesh (mesh) *n.* Open spaces in a thread, wire or cord net; something that entraps or snares; the fitting or coming together of gear teeth for transmitting power.

mes-mer-ize (mez´me rīz´) *v.* To hypnotize or put into a trance.

mes-quite (me skēt´) *n.* A thorny, deep-rooted shrub or small tree which grows in the southwestern United States and in Mexico.

mess (mes) *n. pl.* **messes** A disorderly or confused heap; a jumble; a dish or portion of soft or liquid food; a meal eaten by a group of persons, usually in the military.

mes-sage (mes´ij) *n.* Any information, command, or news transmitted from one person to another.

mes-sen-ger (mes´en jėr) *n.* A person who carries a message or does an errand for another person or company.

Mes-si-ah (mi si´a) *n.* The anticipated or expected king of the Jews; Jesus Christ.

mess-y *adj.* Untidy; upset; dirty; lacking neatness. **messily** *adv.* **messiness** *n.*

me-tab-o-lism (me tab´o liz´um) *n.* The chemical and physical changes in living cells which involve the maintenance of life. **metabolic** *adj.*

meta-car-pus (met´a kär´pus) *n.* The part of the forefoot or hand which connects the bones of the toes or fingers to the ankle or wrist.

met-a-gal-ax-y (met´a gal´ak sē) *n.* The universe; the entire system of galaxies.

metal (met´al) *n.* One of a category of opaque, fusible, ductile, and typically lustrous elements. **metallic** *adj.*

met-al-lur-gy (met´a lėr´jē) *n.* The technology and science which studies methods of extracting metals from their ores and of preparing them for use. **metallurgical** *adj.* **metallurgist** *n.*

met-a-mor-pho-sis (met´a mor´fo sis) *n.* The transformation and change in the structure and habits of an animal during normal growth, as the metamorphosis of a tadpole into a frog. **metamorphism** *n.* **metamorphose** *v.*

met-a-phor (met´a for´) *n.* A figure of speech in which the context demands that a word or phrase not be taken literally, such as 'the sun is smiling'; a comparison which doesn't use *like* or *as.*

me-tas-ta-sis (me tas´ta sis) *n.* A spread of cancer cells from the original tumor to one or more additional sites within the body. **metastasize** *v.*

met-a-tar-sus (met´a tär´sus) *n. pl.* **-si** The part of the human foot which forms the instep and contains five bones between the ankle and the toes; the hind foot of four-legged animals.

me-te-or (mē´tēėr) *n.* A moving particle in the solar system which appears as a trail or streak in the sky as it comes into contact with the atmosphere of the earth.

me-te-or-ic (mē´tē or´ik) *adj.* Of or relating to a meteor or meteors; resembling a meteor in speed, brilliance, or brevity.

me-te-or-ite (mē´tē o rīt´) *n.* A stony or metallic mass of a meteor which reaches the earth after partially burning in the atmosphere.

me-te-or-ol-o-gy (mē´tē o rol´ojē) *n.* The science concerned with the study of weather, weather conditions and weather forecasting. **meteorological** *adj.* **meteorologic** *adj.* **meteorologically** *adv.* **meteorologist** *n.*

me-ter (mē´tėr) *n.* The arrangement of words, syllables, or stanzas in verse or poetry; a measure equaling 39.37 inches.

meth-a-done (meth´a dōn´) *n.* A man made narcotic used in the treatment of heroin addiction.

meth-ane (meth´an) *n.* A colorless, odorless flammable gas used as a fuel, a product of the decomposition of organic matter.

meth-a-nol (meth´a nōl´) *n.* A colorless, odorless flammable alcohol that is used as an antifreeze, as a fuel, and as a raw material in chemical synthesis.

me-thinks (mi thingks´) *v.* It seems to me.

meth-od (meth´od) *n.* A manner, a process, or the regular way of doing something; the orderly arrangement, development, or classification. **methodical** *adj.* **methodically** *adv.*

meth-yl (meth´il) *n.* An alkyl radical derived from methane which occurs in several organic compounds.

me-tic-u-lous (me tik´ū lus) *adj.* Very precise; careful; concerned with small details. **meticulously** *adv.*

me-tis (mā tēs´) *n.* A person of mixed blood, usually of French and Indian ancestry.

met-ric (me´trik) *adj.* Of or relating to the metric system. **metrical** *adj.* Pertaining to rhythm. **metrication** *n.*

metric system *n.* A decimal system of weights and measures based on the meter as a unit of length and the kilogram as a unit of mass, originated in France around 1790.

met-ro (me´trō) *n.* A subway system for transportation.

met-ro-nome (me´tro nōm´) *n.* An instrument designed to mark time by means of a series of clicks at exact intervals. **metronomic** *adj.*

me-trop-o-lis (me trop´o lis) *n.* A large or capital city of a state, region, or country. **metropolitan** *adj.*

mew (mū) *n.* A hideaway; a secret place.

mez-za-nine (mez´a nēn´) *n.* A low story between two main stories of a building; the lowest balcony in a theater.

mice *pl. n.* The plural of mouse.

Mich-i-gan *n.* A state located in the on the northern border of the central United States; statehood January 26, 1837; state capital Lansing.

mi-crobe (mī´krōb) *n.* A germ, plant, or animal so small that is can be seen only with the aid of a microscope.

mi-cro-ceph-a-ly *n.* A condition of abnormal smallness of the head, usually associated with mental defects.

mi-cro-cir-cuit *n.* An electronic circuit composed of very small components.

mi-cro-com-put-er *n.* A computer which uses a microprocessor.

mi-cro-film (mī´kro film´) *n.* A film used to photograph printed matter at a greatly reduced size.

micro-or-gan-ism(mī´krōor´ganiz´um) *n.* An organism too small to see without the aid of a microscope.

mi-cro-phone (mī´kro fōn´) *n.* An instrument which converts acoustical waves into electrical signals and feeds them into a recorder, amplifier or broadcasting transmitter.

mi-cro-proc-es-sor *n.* In *computer science*, a semiconductor processing unit which is contained on an integrated circuit chip.

mi-cro-scope (mī´kro skōp´) *n.* An optical instrument consisting of a lens or combination of lenses, used to produce magnified images of very small objects.

mi-cro-scop-ic (mī´kro skop´ik) *adj.* Too small to be seen by the eye alone. **microscopical** *adv.*

mi-cro-sur-ger-y *n.* Surgery performed by means of a microscope and laser beam. **microsurgical** *adj.*

mi-cro-wave (mī´krō wāv´) *n.* A very short electromagnetic wave.

mid (mid) *adj.* In the middle or center; central.

mid-den *n.* A refuse heap or dunghill.

mid-dle (mid´l) *adj.* Being equally distant from extremes or limits; the central. *n.* Anything which occupies a middle position; the waist.

midg-et (mij´it) *n.* A very small person.

mid-i *n., Slang* A dress, skirt, or coat which extends to the calf.

midst (midst) *n.* The central or middle part or position; a person positioned among others in a group.

miff (mif) *n.* Ill humor; displeasure. **miff** *v.*

might (mīt) *n.* Force, power, or physical strength. *v.* To indicate a present condition contrary to fact; to ask permission politely.

might-y (mī´tē) *adj.* Showing or having great power.

mi-graine (mī´grān) *n.* A condition of severe, recurring headaches often accompanied by nausea.

mi-grant (mī´grant) *n.* A person who moves from one place to another to find work in the fields.

mi-grate (mī´grāt) *v.* To move from one place to another or from one climate to another. **migration** *n.* **migrational** *adj.* **migratory** *adj.*

mike (mīk) *n., Slang* Microphone.

mil (mil) *n.* A unit of measure equal to 1/1000 of an inch, used in measuring wire.

mild (mild) *adj.* Gentle in manner, behavior, or disposition; not severe or extreme. **mildly** *adv.* **mildness** *n.*

mil-dew (mil´dō´) *n.* A fungal growth which is usually white in color.

mile (mīl) *n.* A unit of measurement equaling 5,280 feet.

mil-i-tant (mil´i tant) *adj.* Engaged in warfare or combat; aggressive. .

mil-i-ta-rize (mil´i ta rīz´) *v.* To train or equip for war.

mil-i-tar-y (mil´i ter´ē) *adj.* Of or related to arms, war, or soldiers. *n.* A nation's armed forces. **militarily** *adv.*

milk (milk) *n.* A whitish fluid produced by the mammary glands of all mature female mammals as a source of food for their young. *v.* To draw milk from the breast or udder. *Slang* To take advantage of every possibility in a given situation. **milky** *adj.*

Milky Way (mil´kē) *n.* The broad, luminous galaxy in which the solar system is located.

mill (mil) *n.* A building housing machinery for grinding grain into meal or flour; any of various machines which grind, crush, or press; a unit of money which equals 1/1000 of a United States dollar. **mill** v. To grind. **miller** A person who operates, works, or owns a grain mill; a moth whose wings are covered with a powdery substance.

mil-li-ner (mil´i nêr) n. Someone who designs, sells, or makes women's hats.

mil-lion (mil´yon) n. A very large number equal to 1,000 x 1,000. **million** adj.

mil-lion-aire (mil´ya nâr´) n. A person whose wealth is estimated at $1,000,000 or more.

mime (mīm) v. To act a part or performance without using words. n. An actor who portrays a part, emotion, or situation using only gestures and body language. **mimer** n.

mim-e-o-graph (mim´ē o graf´) n. A duplicating machine that makes duplicates of typed or drawn information from a stencil through which ink is pressed.

mim-ic (mim´ĭk) v. To imitate another person's behavior or speech.

mince (mins) v. To cut or chop something into small pieces.

mind (mīnd) n. The element of a human being which controls perception, thought, feeling, memory, and imagination. v. To obey; to take care of; to bring; to remember; to object to.

mine (mīn) n. A pit or underground excavation from which metals or coal can be uncovered and removed. The one that belongs to me. **miner** n.

mine pron. The one that belongs to me.

mine-lay-er n. A navy ship used to lay underwater mines.

min-er-al (min´êr al) n. A solid inorganic substance, such as silver, diamond, or quartz, which is taken from the earth. **mineral** adj. **mineralize** v.

min-e-stro-ne (min´i strō´nē) n. A very thick vegetable soup that may contain pasta and beans.

min-gle (ming´gl) v. To mix or come together. **mingler** n.

min-i-a-ture (min´ē a chêr) n. A copy or model of something that has been greatly reduced in size.

min-i-com-put-er n. In computer science, a computer designed on a very small scale.

min-i-mize v. To reduce something to a minimum.

min-i-mum (min´i mum) n. pl., -ums or -uma The least, smallest, or lowest amount, degree, number, or position.

min-is-ter (min´i stêr) n. The pastor of a Protestant church; a high officer of state who is in charge of a governmental division.

mink (mingk) n. pl. **mink** or **minks** A semiaquatic animal of the weasel family whose thick, lustrous fur is used for making fur coats.

Min-nes-o-ta n. A state located in the north central part of the United States; statehood May 11, 1858; state capital St. Paul.

min-now (min´ō) n. A small, freshwater fish used as bait.

mi-nor (mī´nêr) adj. Not of legal age; lesser in degree, size or importance.

mi-nor-i-ty (mi nor´i tē) n. pl. -ies The smaller in number of two groups making a whole; a part of the population that differs, as in race, sex, or religion.

min-ster (min´stêr) n. A large cathedral or church.

min-strel (min´strel) n. A medieval traveling musician or poet.

mint (mint) n. A place where coins are made by a government; any of a variety of aromatic plants used for flavoring; candy flavored by such a plant.

min-u-end (min´ū end´) n. A number of quantity from which another is to be subtracted.

min-u-et (min´ū et´) n. A slow, stately dance.

mi-nus (mī´nus) prep. Reduced, by subtraction. n. The minus sign (-); a negative number.

mi-nus-cule (min´u skūl´) n. Small in size; a lowercase letter.

min-ute (min´it) n. The unit of time which equals 60 seconds.

mi-nute (mī nōt´) adj. Extremely small in size.

mir-a-cle (mir´a kl) n. A supernatural event or happening regarded as an act of God.

mi-rage (mi räzh´) n. An optical illusion in which nonexistent bodies of water with reflections of objects are seen.

mire (mīer) n. Soil or heavy mud.

mir-ror (mir´êr) n. A polished surface which reflects light, forming the image of an object.

mirth (merth) n. Merriment or joyousness expressed by laughter.

mis- prefix Wrong, bad, or ill.

mis-ad-ven-ture (mis´ad ven´chêr) n. An unlucky mishap; a misfortune.

mis-an-thrope (mis´an thrōp´) n. Someone who hates mankind.

mis-ap-pre-hend (mis´ap ri hend´) v. To understand something incorrectly; to misunderstand.

mis-ap-pro-pri-ate (mis´a prō´prēat) v. To embezzle money; to use wrongly for one's own benefit.

mis-car-riage (mis kar´ij) n. The premature birth of a fetus from the uterus.

mis-ce-ge-na-tion (mis´i je nā´shan) n. The marriage between two people of different races.

mis-cel-la-ne-ous (mis´e lā´nē us) adj. Consisting of a mixed variety of parts, elements, or characteristics.

mis-chance (mis chans´) n. Bad luck or mishap.

mis-chief (mis´chif) n. Behavior which causes harm, damage, or annoyance.

mis-chie-vous (mis´chi vus) adj. Tending to behave in a play fully annoying way. **mischievously** adv.

mis-ci-ble (mis´i bl) adj., Chem. Capable of being mixed.

mis-con-ceive (mis´kon sēv´) v. To misunderstand the meaning. **misconceiver** n. **misconception** n.

mis-con-duct (mis kon´dukt) n. Improper conduct or behavior; bad management.

mis-count (mis kount´) v. To count incorrectly; to miscalculate.

mis-cre-ant (mis´krē ant) n. A person who is involved in criminal or evil acts; a heretic. **miscreant** adj.

mis-cue (mis kū´) n. An error; a mistake.

mis-deed (mis dēd´) n. A wrong or improper act; an evil deed.

mis-de-mean-or (mis´di mē´nėr) n., Law A crime less serious than a felony.

mis-er (mī´zėr) n. A person who hoards money; a person who lives a meager life in order to hoard his money.

mis-er-a-ble (miz´ėr a bl) adj. Very uncomfortable or unhappy; causing misery. **miserably** adv.

mis-er-y (miz´e rē) n. A state of great unhappiness, distress, or pain.

mis-feed n. In *computer science*, the failure of paper or other media to pass through a printer or other device properly.

mis-fit (mis fit´) n. A person who is not adjusted to his environment; anything which does not fit correctly.

mis-for-tune (mis for´chan) n. Bad luck or fortune.

mis-giv-ing (mis giv´ing) n. A feeling of doubt.

mis-guide (mis gīd´) v. To guide incorrectly; to misdirect. **misguidance** n. **misguidedly** adv.

mis-han-dle (mis han´dl) v. To handle clumsily; to manage inefficiently.

mis-hap (mis´hap) n. An unfortunate accident; bad luck.

mish-mash (mish´mash´) n. A jumble or hodgepodge.

mis-in-ter-pret (mis´in ter´prit) v. To understand or explain incorrectly. **misinterpretation** n.

mis-judge (mis juj´) v. To make a mistake in judgment **misjudgment** n.

mis-lay (mis lā´) v. To lose; to put something in a place and not remember where.

mis-lead (mis lēd´) v. To lead in a wrong direction; to deliberately deceive. **misleader** n. **misleading** adj.

mis-no-mer (mis nō´mėr) n. A wrong or inappropriate name.

mis-pro-nounce (mis´pro nouns´) v. To pronounce a word incorrectly.

mi-sog-a-my (mi sog a mē) n. Hatred of marriage.

mi-sog-y-ny (mi soj´i nē) n. Hatred of women.

mis-place (mis plās´) v. To mislay; to put in a wrong place.

mis-rep-re-sent (mis´rep ri zent´) v. To represent wrongly, misleadingly, or falsely. **misrepresentation** n.

mis-rule (mis röl´) n. Misruling; the condition of being misruled; disorder.

Miss (mis) n. The proper title for an unmarried woman or girl. v. To fail to hit, reach, or make contact with something; to omit; to feel the absence or loss of.

mis-shape (mis shāp´) v. To deform; to shape badly; to distort. **misshapen** adj.

mis-sile (mis´il) n. An object that is thrown or shot at a target.

mis-sion (mish´an) n. An instance or the act of sending; an assignment or task to be carried out.

mis-sion-ar-y (mish´a ner´ē) n. pl. -ies A person sent to do religious or charitable work, usually in a foreign country.

Miss-i-ssip-pi n. A state located in the south central part of the United States; statehood December 10, 1817; state capital Jackson.

Miss-ou-ri n. A state located in the central part of the United States; statehood August 10, 1821; state capital Jefferson City.

mis-spell (mis spel´) v. To spell a word incorrectly. **misspelling** n.

mis-take (mi stāk´) n. A wrong statement, action, or decision. **mistaken** adj. **mistakable** adj. **mistakably** adv.

Mis-ter (mis´tėr) n. A courtesy title used before a man's name, abbreviated as Mr.

mis-tle-toe (mis´l tō´) n. A parasitic plant with thick leaves, small yellowish flowers and white berries.

mis-treat (mis trēt´) v. To treat badly or wrongly. **mistreatment** n.

mis-tress (mis´tris) n. A woman having authority, ownership, or a position of control; a woman having a sexual relationship with a man who is not her husband.

mis-tri-al (mis trī´al) n. A trial that is invalid because of an error during the procedure.

mis-trust (mis trust´) v. To have doubt; to lack trust in something or someone. **mistrust** n. **mistrustful** adj.

mis-un-der-stand (mis´un dėr stand´) v. To interpret incorrectly; to fail to understand. **misunderstanding** n.

mite (mīt) *n.* A very small insect; a small amount of money.

mi-ter (mī'tér) *n.* A joint made by cutting two pieces at an angle and then fitting them together.

mit-i-gate (mit'i gāt') *v.* To make or become less severe or painful.

mi-to-sis (mī tō'sis) *n. pl.* **mitoses** A process of cell division in which chromatin divides into chromosomes.

mitt (mit) *n.* A women's glove that covers the wrist and hand, leaving the fingers exposed; in baseball, a glove for a catcher or first baseman made in the style of a mitten.

mix (miks) *v.* To blend or combine into one; to come or bring together.

mixed number *n.* A number representing the sum of an integer and a fraction, such as 5 1/2.

mix-ture (miks'chèr) *n.* The state of being mixed; the process or act of mixing; a combination of two or more substances.

mix-up (miks'up') *n.* An instance or state of confusion.

mo *abbr.* Money order; mail order.

moan (mōn) *n.* A very low, dull sound indicative of pain or grief. *v.* To make a moan.

moat (mōt) *n.* A deep and wide trench surrounding a castle, usually filled with water.

mob (mob) *n.* A large, unruly crowd. *v.* To overcrowd.

mo-bi-lize (mō'bi līz') *v.* To put into motion; to make ready as in preparing an Army. **mobilization** *n.*

moc-ca-sin (mok'a sin) *n.* A heelless shoe or slipper made of a soft leather.

mo-cha (mō'ka) *n.* An Arabian coffee of superior quality; a flavoring with coffee, often used with chocolate.

mock (mok) *v.* To treat with contempt or scorn; to imitate a mannerism or sound closely; to mimic. *adv.* In an insincere manner. *n.* An imitation; a copy. **mockingly** *adv.*

mock-er-y (mok'e rē) *n. pl.* **-ies** Insulting or contemptuous action or speech; a subject of laughter or sport; a false or counterfeit appearance; something that's ridiculous.

mock-he-ro-ic (mok'hi rō'ik) *n.* A satirical imitation of the heroic manner or style.

mock-up *or* **mock-up** (mok'up') *n.* A model of a structure used for study, testing, or demonstration.

mod *n.* A modern and unusual style of dress. *adj.* Modern.

mode (mōd) *n.* A way or method of doing something; a particular manner or form; the value or score that occurs most frequently in a set of data; the current fashion or style, as in dress.

mod-el (mod'el) *n.* A small representation of an object; a pattern that something will be based on; a design or type; one serving as an example; one who poses for an artist or photographer. **model** *v.* **modeler** *n.*

modem In Computer Science, modulator/demodulator; a device for translating digital signals to telephone signals and back, used to communicate between computers via telephone lines.

mod-er-ate (mod'ér it) *adj.* Not excessive; tending toward the mean or average extent or quality; opposed to extreme political views.

mod-ern (mod'érn) *adj.* Typical of the recent past or the present; advanced or up-to-date. **modern** *n.* **modernity** *n.* **modernly** *adv.*

mod-ern-ize (mod'ér nīz') *v.* To make or become modern. **-ation** *n.*

mod-est (mod'ist) *adj.* Placing a moderate estimate on one's abilities or worth; retiring or reserved; limited in size or amount. **modesty** *n.*

mod-i-cum (mod'i kum) *n.* A small amount.

mod-i-fy (mod'I fī') *v.* To alter; to make different in character or form; to change to less extreme; to moderate. **modified** *adj.* **modifiable** *adj.* **modification** *n.*

mod-ish (mō'dish) *adj.* Fashionable. **modishly** *adv.* **modishness** *n.*

mo-diste (mō dēst') *n.* A person dealing in fashionable clothing for women.

mod-u-late (moj'u lāt') *v.* To soften; to temper; to vary the intensity of. *Music* To change from one key to another; to vary the tone or intensity of. **modulation** *n.* **modulator** *n.* **modulative** *adj.* **modulatory** *adj.*

mod-ule (moj'öl) *n.* One of a series of standardized components which work together in a system. *Electr.* A self-contained subassembly of electronic components, as a computer stage; the self-contained area of a spacecraft for performing a particular task. **modular** *adj.*

mod-us op-er-an-di (mō'dus op'eran'dī) *n.* A method of operating or proceeding.

mod-us vi-ven-di (mō'dus vi ven'dī) *n.* A compromise which avoids difficulties.

mo-gul (mō'gul) *n.* A very great or important person; a small hill or bump of ice and snow on a ski slope.

mo-hair (mō'hâr') *n.* The fabric or yarn made from the silky hair of the Angora goat.

Mo-ham-med *n.* The Arab founder of Islam.

moi-e-ty (moi'e tē) *n.* A half; any portion; part or share.

moil (moil) *v.* To work hard; to drudge.

moi-re (mwä rā´) *n.* Fabric, especially silk or rayon having a wavy pattern.

moist (moist) *adj.* Slightly wet; damp; saturated with moisture or liquid. **moistly** *adv.* **moistness** *n.*

mois-ten (moi´sen) *v.* To make or become moist or slightly wet. **moistener** *n.*

mois-ture (mois´chėr) *n.* Liquid diffused or condensed in a relatively small quantity; dampness. **moisturize** *v.*

mol (mōl) *abbr.* Molecular; molecule.

mo-lar (mō´lėr) *n.* A grinding tooth which has a broad surface for grinding food, located in the back of the mouth. **molar** *adj.*

mo-las-ses (mo las´iz) *n.* A thick, dark syrup produced when sugar is refined.

mold (mōld) *n.* A superficial, often woolly growth produced on damp or decaying organic matter or on living organisms; a fungus that produces such a growth; crumbling, soft, pliable earth suited to plant growth; distinctive nature or character; the frame on or around which an object is constructed; a cavity in which an object is shaped; general shape; form. **mold** *v.*

mole (mōl) *n.* A pigmented spot or mark on the human skin; a small, insectivorous mammal that lives mostly underground and has an arrow snout, small eyes, and silky fur; a large wall of stone or masonry used as a breakwater or pier.

mo-lec-u-lar (mo lek´ū lėr) *adj.* Of, relating to, or caused by molecules.

molecular biology *n.* The branch of biology dealing with the structure and development of biological systems which are studied in terms of their molecular constituents.

mol-e-cule (mol´e kūl´) *n.* The simplest structural unit into which a substance can be divided and still retain its identity.

mo-lest (mo lest´) *v.* To bother, annoy, or persecute; to accost sexually. **molestation** *n.* **molester** *n.*

mol-li-fy (mol´i fī´) *v.* To make less angry; to soften; to make less intense or severe. **mollification** *n.*

mol-lusk *or* **mol-lusc** (mol´usk) *n.* Any of various largely marine invertebrates, including the edible shellfish.

mol-ly-cod-dle (mol´ē kod´l) *v.* To spoil by pampering; to coddle.

molt (mōlt) *v.* To cast off or shed an external covering, as horns, feathers, or skin, which is periodically replaced by new growth. **molt** *n.*

mol-ten (mōl´ten) *adj.* Transformed to liquid form by heat.

mo-lyb-de-num (mo lib´de num) *n.* A hard, gray metallic element used to harden steel alloys, symbolized by Mo.

mo-men-tar-i-ly (mō´men târ´ilē) *adv.*

For just a moment; soon; from moment to moment.

mo-men-tar-y (mō´men ter´ē) *adj.* Lasting just a moment; occurring presently or at every moment.

mo-men-tous (mō men´tus) *adj.* Of great importance or consequence; significant. **momentously** *adv.* **-ness** *n.*

mo-men-tum (mō men´tum) *n., pl.* **-ta** *or* **-tums** A property of a moving body which determines the length of time required to bring it to rest when under the action of a constant force.

mon-arch (mon´ärk) *n.* A person who reigns over a kingdom or empire; a large orange and black butterfly. **monarchic** *adj.* **monarchical** *adj.*

mon-as-ter-y (mon´a ster´ē) *n. pl.* **-ies** A house for persons under religious vows. **monasterial** *adj.*

mo-nas-tic (mo nas´tik) *adj.* Of, relating to, or typical of monasteries, monks, or life in monasteries.

mo-nas-ti-cism (mo nas´ti siz´um) *n.* The monastic lifestyle or system.

mon-au-ral (mon är´al) *adj.* Of or relating to a system of transmitting or recording sound by techniques in which one or more sources are channeled into one carrier.

mon-e-tar-y (mon´i ter´ē) *adj.* Of or relating to money or how it is circulated. **monetarily** *adv.*

mon-ey (mun´ē) *n.* Anything which has or is assigned value and is used as a medium of exchange.

mon-ey-lend-er *n.* Someone whose business is lending money to others with interest.

mon-ger (mung´gėr) *n.* One who attempts to stir up or spread something that is undesirable; one who deals.

mon-goose (mong´gōs´) *n. pl.* **-ses** A chiefly African or Asian mammal which has the ability to kill venomous snakes.

mon-grel (mung´grel) *n.* An animal or plant, especially a dog, produced by interbreeding.

mo-ni-tion (mō nish´an) *n.* A caution or warning, as for an impending danger.

mon-i-tor (mon´i tėr) *n.* A student assigned to assist a teacher; a receiver used to view the picture being picked up by a television camera; the image being generated by a computer.

mon-i-to-ry (mon´i tōr´ē) *adj.* Giving a caution or conveying a warning.

monk (mungk) *n.* A man who is a member of a religious order and lives in a monastery. **monkish** *adj.*

mon-o-n Mononucleosis.

mon-o-chro-mat-ic (mon´o krōmat´ik) *adj.* Of, consisting of, or having one color. **monochromatically** *adv.*

mon-o-cle (mon´o kl) *n.* An eyeglass for

one eye.

mon-o-cot-y-le-don (mon´o kot´/lĕd´on) *n.* Any of various plants having a single embryonic seed leaf appearing at germi-nation. **monocotyledonous** *adj.*

mo-noc-u-lar (mo nok´ū lĕr) *adj.* Of, relating to, or having one eye.

mo-nog-a-my (mo nog´a mē) *n.* Marriage or sexual relationship with only one person at a time. **monogamist** *n.* **monogamous** *adj.*

mon-o-gram (mon´o gram´) *n.* A design consisting of one or more initials.

mon-o-graph (mon´o graf´) *n.* A scholarly pamphlet or book on a particular and usually limited subject. **monographic** *adj.*

mon-o-lin-gual (mon´o ling´gwal) *adj.* Knowing only one language.

mon-o-lith (mon´o lith) *n.* A single block of stone, as one used in architecture or sculpture. **monolithic** *adj.*

mon-o-logue *or* **mon-o-log** (mon´o log´) *n.* A speech by one person which precedes conversation; a series of jokes and stories delivered by a comedian. **monologist** *n.*

mon-o-ma-ni-a (mon´o mā´nē a) *n.* A pathological obsession or mental disorder in which a person is totally obsessed with a single idea. **monomaniac** *n.* **monomaniacal** *adj.*

mo-no-mi-al (mō nō´mē al) *n.* An algebraic expression consisting of only one term. **monomial** *adj.*

mon-o-nu-cle-ar (mon´o nō´klē ĕr) *adj.* Having only one nucleus.

mon-o-nu-cle-o-sis (mon´o nō´klēo´sis) *n.* An infectious disease marked by an abnormal increase white blood cells caused by a virus.

mon-o-nu-cle-o-tide *n.* A compound containing one molecule each of a phosphoric acid, a pentose, and either a purine or pyrimidine base.

mon-o-phon-ic (mon´o fon´ik) *adj.* Having only one part; a solo voice with accompaniment, as a piano.

mon-o-plane (mon´o plan´) *n.* An aircraft with one wing or one set of wings.

mo-nop-o-ly (mo nop´o lē) *n. pl.,* **-ies** Exclusive ownership or control, as of a service or commodity, by a single group, person, or company; a group, person, or company having a monopoly; exclusive possession; a service or commodity controlled by a single group. **monopolist** *n.* **monopolization** *n.* **monopolistic** *adj.* **monopolize** *v.*

mon-o-rail (mon´o rāl´) *n.* A single rail serving as a track on which a wheeled vehicle can travel; a vehicle that travels on such a rail.

mon-o-so-di-um glu-ta-mate (mon´o sō´dēum glō´ta māt´) *n.* Sodium glutamate used as a seasoning,

abbreviated as MSG.

mon-o-syl-la-ble (mon´o sil´a bl) *n.* A word of one syllable. **monosyllabic** *adj.* **monosyllabically** *adv.*

mon-o-the-ism (mon´o thē iz´um) *n.* The belief that there is just one God. **monotheist** *n.* **monotheistic** *adj.*

mon-o-tone (mon´o tōn´) *n.* The utterance of sounds, syllables, or words in a single unvarying tone.

mo-not-o-nous (mo not´o nus) *adj.* Spoken in a monotone; lacking in variety. **monotonously** *adv.*

mon-ox-ide (mon ok´sīd) *n.* An oxide that contains one oxygen atom per molecule.

Monroe, James *n.* (1758-1831). The fifth president of the United States from 1817-1825.

mon-soon (mon sön´) *n.* A periodic wind, especially in the Indian Ocean and southern Asia; the season of the monsoon in India and parts of Asia.

mon-ster (mon´stĕr) *n.* An animal or plant having an abnormal form or structure; an animal, plant, or object having a frightening or deformed shape; one unusually large for its kind. **monstrosity** *n.* **monstrousness** *n.* **monstrous** *adj.* **monstrously** *adv.*

mon-tage (mon tazh´) *n.* A composite picture made by combining several separate pictures or parts of several pictures; a rapid succession of images in a motion picture, designed to illustrate an association of ideas.

Mon-tan-a *n.* A state located in the northwestern United States; statehood November 8, 1889; state capital Helena.

month (munth) *n.* One of the twelve divisions of a calendar year.

month-ly (munth´lē) *adj.* Occurring, done, or payable each month. *n.* A publication issued once a month. **monthly** *adv.*

mon-u-ment (mon´ū ment) *n.* An object, such as a statue, built as a memorial to a person or an event; a burial vault; an area set aside for public use by a government because of its aesthetic, historical, or ecological significance.

mon-u-men-tal (mon´ū men´tal) *adj.* Serving as or similar to a monument; massive; extremely important.

mooch (mōch) *v., Slang* To acquire by begging; to steal. **moocher** *n.*

mood (mōd) *n.* A conscious yet temporary state of mind or emotion; the prevailing spirit; a verb form or set of verb forms inflected to show the understanding of the person speaking regarding the condition expressed.

mood-y (mō´dē) *adj.* Subject to moods, especially depression; gloomy.

moon (mōn) *n.* The earth's only natural

satellite; a natural satellite which revolves around a planet. v. To dream.

moon shot n. The launching of a spacecraft to the moon or its vicinity.

moor (mer) v. To make fast with cables, lines, or anchors. n. An expanse of open, rolling, infertile land.

moose (mōs) n. pl. moose A very large North American deer having a large broad muzzle.

moot (mŏt) v. To bring up as for debate or discussion; to argue. adj. Open to debate; having no legal significance.

mope (mōp) v. To be uncaring or dejected; to move in a leisurely manner.

mo-raine (mo rān') n. An accumulation of earth and stones carried and finally deposited by a glacier.

mor-al (mŏr'al) adj. Of or pertaining to conduct or character from the point of right and wrong; teaching a conception of right behavior. n. The lesson to be learned from a story, event, or teaching. **morals** Standards of right and wrong.

mo-rale (mo ral') n. An individual's state of mind with respect to the tasks he or she is expected to perform; esprit decorps.

mor-al-ist (mor'a list) n. Someone concerned with moral principles and questions; someone who practices morality. **moralism** n. **moralistic** adj.

mo-ral-i-ty (mo ral'i tē) n. pl. -ies The quality of being morally right; moral behavior.

mo-rass (mo ras') n. A marsh or bog; low-lying wet, soft ground; something which hinders or overwhelms.

mor-a-to-ri-um n. pl. -iums or -ia A temporary pause in activity; an authorization given legally to a debtor to suspend payments for a period of time.

mo-ray (mŏr'ā) n. Any of various marine eels found usually in tropical waters.

mor-bid (mor'bid) adj. Of, pertaining to, or affected by disease; suggesting an unhealthy mental state of being; gruesome. **morbidity** n. **morbidness** n. **morbidly** adv.

mor-da-cious (mor dā'shus) adj. Violent in action; prone to biting.

mor-dant (mor'dant) adj. Biting and caustic in thought, manner, or style. **mordancy** n. **mordantly** adv.

more (mŏr) adj. Greater number, size, or degree; additional. n. An additional or greater number, degree, or amount. adv. To a greater extent or degree; in addition. pron. Additional things or persons.

mo-rel (mo rel') n. An edible mushroom having a sponge-like cap or hood.

more-o-ver (mŏr ō'vėr) adv. Furthermore; besides.

mo-res (mŏr'āz) n. pl. The moral customs and traditional customs of a social group.

morgue (morg) n. A place in which dead bodies are kept until claimed or identified; the reference file at a newspaper or magazine office.

mor-i-bund (mor'i bund') adj. Approaching extinction; at the point of death. **moribundity** n.

morn (morn) n. Morning.

morn-ing (mor'ning) n. The early part of the day; the time from midnight to noon.

morning star n. A planet seen in the eastern part of the sky just before or at sunrise.

mo-roc-co (mo rok'ō) n. A soft, textured leather made of goatskin.

mo-ron (mŏr'on) n. An adult exhibiting an intelligence equal to that of a seven to twelve year old child; a very stupid person. **moronic** adj. **moronically** adv.

mo-rose (mo rōs') adj. Having a sullen disposition; marked by gloom. **morosely** adv. **moroseness** n.

mor-pheme (mor'fēm) n. A meaningful unit which cannot be divided into smaller meaningful parts. **morphemic** adj. **morphemically** adv.

mor-phi-a (mor'fē a) n. Morphine.

mor-phine (mor'fēn) n. A highly addictive narcotic derived from opium which can be used as either a sedative or to dull pain.

mor-phol-o-gy (mor fol'o jē) n. The study of the form and structure of living organisms, considered separate from function; the study and description of word formation in a language. **morphological** adj. **morphologically** adj. **morphologist** n.

mor-ris (mor'is) n. An old English folk dance.

mor-row (mor'ō) n. The next day.

mor-sel (mor'sel) n. A small piece or quantity of food; a tasty dish.

mor-tal (mor'tal) adj. Having caused or about to cause death; fatal; subject to death; very tedious or prolonged; unrelentingly hostile; of, relating to, or connected with death. n. A human being. **mortally** adv.

mor-tal-i-ty (mor tal'i tē) n. pl. -ies The state or condition of being mortal; the death rate; deaths.

mor-tar (mor'tėr) n. A strong vessel in which materials can be crushed or ground with a pestle; a muzzle-loading cannon for firing shells at short ranges and at high angles; a mixed building material, as cement with sand and water, which hardens and is used with masonry or plaster.

mor-tar-board (mor'tėr bōrd') n. A square-board with a handle, for holding mortar; an academic cap topped by a stiff, flat square.

mort-gage (mor´gij) *n.* A temporary conveyance of property to a creditor as security for the repayment of a debt; a contract or deed defining the terms of a mortgage. *v.* To pledge or transfer by means of a mortgage. **mortgagee** *n.* **mortgagor** *n.*

mor-ti-cian (mor tish´an) *n.* An undertaker.

mor-ti-fy (mor´ti fi´) *v.* To destroy the strength or functioning of; to subdue or deaden through pain or self-denial; to subject to severe humiliation; to become gangrenous. **mortification** *n.*

mor-tise (mor´tis) *n.* A usually hollowed out rectangular hole in a piece of wood which receives a tenon of another piece to form a joint.

mor-tu-ar-y (mor´chŏ er´ē) *n.* *pl.* **-ies** A place in which dead bodies are temporarily held until burial or cremation.

mo-sa-ic (mō zā´ĭk) *n.* A decorative inlaid design of small pieces, as of colored glass or tile, in cement. **mosaic** *adj.*

mo-sey (mō´zē) *v.,* *Slang* To move slowly; to shuffle along.

mosque (mosk) *n.* A Moslem house of worship.

mos-qui-to (mo skē´tō) *n.* *pl.* **-toes** *or* **-tos** Any of various winged insects of which the females suck the blood of animals or humans.

mosquito net *n.* A fine net or screen to keep out mosquitoes.

moss (mos) *n.* Delicate, small green plants which of ten form a dense, mat-like growth. **mossiness** *n.*

moss-back (mos´bak´) *n.* An old-fashioned person.

moss rose *n.* An old-fashioned garden rose which has a glandular, mossy calyx and flower stalk.

most (mōst) *adj.* The majority of. *n.* The greatest amount. *pron.* The largest part or number. *adv.* In or to the highest degree.

most-ly (mōst´lē) *adv.* For the most part; principally.

mot (mō) *n.* A short, witty saying.

mote (mōt) *n.* A particle, as of dust; a speck of dust.

mo-tel (mō tel´) *n.* A temporary, roadside dwelling for motorists with rooms opening directly onto a parking area.

mo-tet (mō tet´) *n.* A polyphonic vocal composition, based on a religious text and usually sung without accompaniment.

moth (moth) *n.* A usually nocturnal insect having antennae that are often feathered, duller in color and with wings smaller than the butterflies.

moth-ball (moth´bol´) *n.* A ball, usually of camphor, used to repel moths from clothing during storage. **in mothballs** A condition of protective storage.

moth-eat-en (moth´ēt´en) *adj.* Partially eaten by moths; in a state of disrepair.

moth-er (muth´ér) *n.* A female parent; one who holds a maternal relationship toward another; an old or elderly woman; a woman in a position of authority. *adj.* Of, relating to, or being a mother. *v.* To give birth to; to care for or protect like a mother. **motherhood** *n.* **motherliness** *n.*

mother-board *n.* In *computer science,* the primary circuit board in a computer.

mother-in-law (muth´ér in lo´) *n.* The mother of one's spouse.

mother-land (muth´ér land´) *n.* The country or land of one's birth.

moth-er-of-pearl (muth´ór ov perl´) *n.* The pearly iridescent internal layer of a mollusk shell.

mo-tif (mō tēf´) *n.* An underlying main element or theme that recurs in a musical, artistic, or literary work.

mo-tile (mōt´il) *adj.* Exhibiting or capable of movement.

mo-tion (mō´shan) *n.* The act or process of changing position; a purposeful movement of the body or a bodily part; a formal proposal or suggestion that action be taken. **motionless** *adj.*

motion picture *n.* A sequence of filmed pictures that gives the illusion of continuous movement, when projected on a screen.

motion sickness *n.* Dizziness; nausea brought on by motion as traveling by land or water.

mo-ti-vate (mō´ti vāt´) *v.* Causing to act.

mo-tive (mō´tiv) *n.* Something, as a need or desire, which causes a person to act; a musical motif. *adj.* Causing or having the power to cause motion.

mot-ley (mot´lē) *adj.* Composed of a variety of components.

mo-tor (mō´tér) *n.* Any of various devices which develop energy or impart motion. *adj.* Imparting or producing motion, driven by or equipped with a motor; of, relating to or designed for motor vehicles; of, relating to, or involving muscular movement. *v.* To travel or transport by motor vehicle.

motor-bike (mō´tér bīk´) *n.* A small motorcycle.

mo-tor-boat (mō´tér bōt´) *n.* A boat propelled by an internal-combustion engine or an electric motor.

mo-tor-cade (mō´tér kād´) *n.* A procession of motor vehicles.

mo-tor-car (mō´tér kär´) *n.* An automobile.

mo-tor-cy-cle (mō´tér sī´kl) *n.* A two-wheeled automotive vehicle. **motorcycle** *v.* **motorcyclist** *n.*

motor home *n.* A motor vehicle built on a truck frame and equipped to provide a self-contained home during travel.

mo-tor-ize (mō´to riz´) *v.* To equip with a motor; to supply with motor-propelled vehicles. **motorization** *n.*

mo-tor-man (mō´tèr man) *n.* An operator of a locomotive engine, streetcar, or sub-way train.

motor scooter *n.* A small two-wheeled vehicle similar to a scooter but having a low-powered gasoline engine.

motor vehicle *n.* A motor-powered vehicle which travels freely without the need for rails.

mot-tle (mot´l) *v.* To mark or be marked with spots or streaks of different colors or shades; to blotch. *n.* A blotch.

mot-to (mot´ō) *n. pl.* -toes *or* -tos A sentence, phrase, or word expressing purpose, character, or conduct; an appropriate phrase inscribed on something.

moue (mö) *n.* A grimace, as of disapproval or disdain.

mound (mound) *n.* A small hill of earth, sand, gravel or debris; the slightly elevated ground in the middle of a baseball diamond on which the pitcher stands.

mount (mount) *v.* To rise or ascend; to get up on; climb upon; to increase in amount or extent; to organize and equip; to launch and carry out. *n.* A horse or other animal used for riding; a support to which some-thing is fixed.

moun-tain (moun´tin) *n.* A land mass that rises above its surroundings and is higher than a hill.

mountain ash *n.* Any of various deciduous trees bearing clusters of small white flowers and orange-red berries.

moun-tain-eer (moun´ta nēr´) *n.* An inhabitant of a mountainous region; one who climbs mountains for sport. **mountaineer** *v.*

mountain goat *n.* A long-haired Rocky Mountain goat.

mountain laurel *n.* A low-growing evergreen shrub with poisonous leaves and clusters of pink or white flowers.

mountain lion *n.* A large wildcat; puma.

moun-tain-ous (moun´ta nus) *adj.* Of or relating to a region with many mountains.

moun-tain-side (moun´tan sīd´) *n.* The side of a mountain.

moun-tain-top (moun´tan top´) *n.* The top of a mountain.

moun-te-bank (moun´te bangk´) *n.* A quack doctor; a false and boastful pretender; a charlatan.

Mountie Mounty *n.* A member of the Canadian Mounted Police.

mount-ing (moun´ting) *n.* A supporting frame or structure of an article.

mourn (mōrn) *v.* To express grief; to feel grief or sorrow; to follow the religious customs and rituals surrounding the death of a loved one.

mouse (mous) *n., pl.* **mice** A small rodent that frequents human habitations; a timid person.

mousse (mös) *n.* A light frozen dessert.

mouth (mouth) *n., pl.* **mouths** The bodily opening through which nutrients are taken.

mouth-off *v.* To speak disrespectfully.

mouth-to-mouth (mouth´tō mouth´) *adj.* Pertaining to a method of artificial resuscitation.

move (mōv) *v.* To set in motion; to change one's place or location; to make a recommendation in a formal manner. **movable** *adj.* **moveable** *adj.*

move-ment (mōv´ment) *n.* The act of moving; a part of a musical composition; an excretion of the bowels.

mov-er *n.* One that moves; a person employed to help in moving the contents of a home or business.

mov-ie (mō´vē) *n.* A motion picture; motion picture industry.

mow (mō) *v.* To cut down, as with a machine. *n.* The part of the barn where hay or grain is stored. **mower** *n.*

moz-za-rel-la *n.* A soft white cheese with a mild flavor.

Mr *abbr.* Mister.

Mrs *abbr.* Mistress.

Ms *abbr.* A form of address used for a woman when her marital status is irrelevant or unknown.

much (much) *adj.* In great amount, quantity, degree, or extent. *adv.* To a great extent. *n.* Something impressive.

mu-ci-lage (mū´si lij) *n.* A sticky substance that is similar to plant gums.

muck (muk) *n.* Moist farmyard manure; moist, sticky soil or filth. *v.* To dirty with or as with muck. **mucky** *adj.*

muck-rake (muk´rāk´) *v.* To search out and publicly expose real or apparent misconduct on the part of well-known persons. **muckraker** *n.*

mu-co-sa (mū kō´sa) *n.* A mucous membrane.

mu-cous (mū´kus) *adj.* Of, pertaining to, or secreting mucus.

mucous membrane *n.* A membrane secreting mucus which lines bodily channels that come into contact with air.

mu-cus (mū´kus) *n.* The viscous liquid secreted by glands by the mucous membrane.

mud (mud) *n.* A mixture of water and earth. *Slang* A slanderous remark. **muddy** & *v.* **muddily** *adv.*

mud-dle (mud´l) *v.* To make muddy; to mix up or confuse; to make a mess of;

to think or act in a confused way. **muddler** *n.*

mud-guard (mud´gärd´) *n.* A piece of material applied to a wheel well to prevent mud from splashing onto a vehicle.

mud-sling-er *n.* One who makes malicious statements or charges against a political opponent. **mudslinging** *n.*

muff (muf) *n.* An arm, tubular covering for the hands; a bungling performance. *v.* To handle awkwardly; to act or do something stupidly or clumsily.

muf-fin (muf´in) *n.* A soft, cup-shaped bread that is cooked in a muffin pan and often served hot.

muf-fle (muf´l) *v.* To wrap up so as to conceal or protect; to deaden the sound of; to suppress.

muf-fler (muf´lêr) *n.* A scarf worn around the neck; a device which deadens noise, especially one forming part of the exhaust system of an automotive vehicle.

mug (mug) *n.* A large drinking cup; a person's face; a photograph of someone's face. *v.* To make funny faces; to assault viciously, usually with the intent to rob. **mugger** *n.*

mug-gy (mug´ē) *adj.* Warm, humid and sultry. **muggily** *adv.* **mugginess** *n.*

mug-wump (mug´wump´) *n.* A defector from the Republican Party in 1884; anyone who acts independently, especially in politics.

muk-luk (muk´luk) *n.* A boot made from the skin of seals or reindeer, worn by Eskimos; a slipper that resembles a mukluk.

mu-lat-to (mu lat´ō) *n. pl.* **-tos** *or* **-toes** A person with one white parent and one black parent; a person of mixed black and white ancestry.

mul-ber-ry (mul´ber´ē) *n.* Any of several trees having an edible, berry-like fruit.

mulch (mulch) *n.* A loose protective covering, as of sawdust or compost, or wood chips spread on the ground to prevent moisture evaporation, to protect roots from freezing, and to retard the growth of weeds. **mulch** *v.*

mulct (mulkt) *n.* A financial penalty or fine. *v.* To punish by fining; to obtain by fraud or theft.

mule (mūl) *n.* A hybrid animal that is the offspring of a female horse and a male ass. *Slang* A stubborn person. **mulish** *adj.* **mulishly** *adv.*

mule deer *n.* A long-eared deer of western North America, heavier built and larger than the white-tail deer.

mule-foot *adj.* Having a solid foot; not cleft.

mule-skinner *n.* A muleteer.

mu-le-teer (mū´le tēr´) *n.* A person who drives mules.

mu-ley (mū´lē) *adj.* Naturally without horns.

mull (mul) *v.* To mix or grind thoroughly; to ponder; to think about.

mul-lah (mul´a) *n.* A Muslim leader and clergyman.

mul-lein (mul´en) *n.* A plant having yellow flowers and downy leaves.

mul-let (mul´it) *n.* An edible marine and freshwater fish.

mul-li-gan stew (mul´i gan) *n.* A stew made of various vegetables and meats.

multi- *prefix* Much, many, multiple; more than two.

mul-ti-dis-ci-plin-ary *adj.* Using or related to a combination of several disciplines for a common cause.

mul-ti-far-i-ous (mul´ti fâr´ē us) *adj.* Having much diversity. **-ously** *adv.*

mul-ti-form (mul´ti form´) *adj.* Having many appearances or forms. **multiformity** *n.*

mul-ti-lane *adj.* Having several lanes.

mul-ti-lat-er-al (mul´ti lat´ér al) *adj.* Having many sides; involving or participated in by more than two parties or nations. **multilaterally** *adv.*

mul-ti-lin-gual (mul´ti ling´gwal) *adj.* Expressed in several languages.

mul-ti-mil-lion-aire (mul´tē mil´yanâr´) *n.* A person whose fortune is worth many millions of dollars.

mul-ti-na-tion-al *adj.* Involving or relating to several countries.

mul-tip-a-rous *adj.* Producing more than one at a birth.

mul-ti-ple (mul´ti pl) *adj.* Relating to or consisting of more than one individual, part, or element. *Math.* A number into which another number can be divided with no remainders.

multiple-choice (mul´ti pl chois´) *adj.* Offering several answers from which the correct one is to be chosen.

multiple sclerosis *n.* A degenerative condition marked by patches of hardened tissue in the spinal cord or the brain.

multi-plex (mul´ti pleks) *n.* A communications system in which two or more messages can be transmitted simultaneously on the same circuit. **multiplex** *v.* **multiplexor** *n.*

mul-ti-pli-ca-tion (mul´ti plikā´shan) *n.* The mathematical operation by which a number indicates how many times another number is to be added to itself.

mul-ti-plic-i-ty (mul´ti plis´i tē) *n. pl.* **-ies** A large number or variety.

mul-ti-pli-er (mul´ti plī´ér) *n.* A number that is or is to be multiplied by another number.

mul-ti-ply (mul´ti plī´) *v.* To increase in amount or number; to combine by multiplication.

mul-ti-sense *adj.* Having several meanings.

mul-ti-stage (mul´ti stāj´) *adj.* Consisting of propulsion units which operate in turn.

mul-ti-tude (mul´ti töd´) *n.* A very large amount or number. **multitudinous** *adj.*

mul-ti-vi-ta-min *n.* A pill containing several vitamins that are essential to health.

mum (mum) *adj.* Silent, not speaking.

mum-ble (mum´bl) *v.* To speak or utter in a low, confused manner. **mumble** *n.* **mumbler** *n.*

mum-ble-ty-peg (mum´bl tē peg´) *n.* A game in which players try to throw a knife from various positions so that the blade will stick into the ground.

mum-bo jum-bo (mum´bō jum´bō) *n.* A complicated or obscure ritual; a confusing and complicated language or activity.

mum-mer (mum´ẽr) *n.* A performer who acts in a pantomime.

mum-mery (mum´e rē) *n., pl.* -ies A hypocritical or ridiculous ceremony.

mum-mi-fy (mum´i fī´) *v.* To dry and embalm a mummy; to cause to shrivel and dry up. **mummification** *n.*

mum-my (mum´ē) *n. pl.* -ies A body embalmed or treated for burial in the manner of the ancient Egyptians.

mumps (mumps) *n., pl.* An acute, contagious viral disease marked by fever and swelling of the salivary glands.

mun *abbr.* Municipal; municipality.

munch (munch) *v.* To chew noisily. **muncher** *n.*

mun-dane (mun dān´) *adj.* Pertaining to or relating to the world; characterized by the ordinary and practical. **mundanely** *adv.*

mu-nic-i-pal (mū nis´i pal) *adj.* Relating to or typical of a municipality; having self-government in local affairs. **municipally** *adv.* **municipality** *n.*

mu-nif-i-cent (mū nif´i sent) *adj.* Very liberal in giving; lavish. **munificence** *n.* **munificently** *adv.*

mu-ni-tions *n. pl.* Guns and ammunition. **munition** *v.*

mu-ral (mer´al) *n.* A painting created on a wall. **muralist** *n.*

mur-der (mer´dẽr) *n.* The crime of unlawfully killing a person. *Slang* Something very dangerous, difficult, or uncomfortable. *v.* To kill a person unlawfully and with premeditated malice. **murderer** *n.*

mur-der-ous (mer´dẽr us) *adj.* Intending or having the purpose or capability of murder. **murderously** *adv.*

murk (merk) *n.* Darkness; gloom. **murkily** *adv.* **murkiness** *n.*

mur-mur (mer´mẽr) *n.* A low, indistinct, and often continuous sound; a gentle or soft utterance. **murmur** *v.*

mur-mur-ous *adj.* Characterized by murmurs. **murmurously** *adv.*

Murphy bed (mer´fē bed) *n.* A bed which folds into a closet.

mur-rain (mer´in) *n.* A plague affecting plants or domestic animals.

mur-rey (mer´ē) *n.* Mulberry colored; purplish-black.

mus *abbr.* Museum; musical; musician.

muscae volitantes A condition of spots before the eyes due to cells and cell fragments in the vitreous humor and lens.

mus-cle (mus´l) *n.* Bodily tissue which consists of long cells that contract when stimulated. **muscle** *v.*

mus-cle-bound (mus´l bound´) *adj.* Having muscles which are overdeveloped and lack the capacity to flex fully, usually caused by too much exercise.

mus-cu-lar (mus´kū lẽr) *adj.* Relating to or consisting of muscle; brawny; having well-developed muscles. **muscularity** *n.*

muscular dystrophy *n.* A noncontagious hereditary disease characterized by gradual but irreversible muscular deterioration.

mus-cu-la-ture (mus´kū la chẽr) *n.* The muscles of an animal's body.

muse (mūz) *n.* A state of deep thought.

mu-sette (mū zet´) *n.* A small bagpipe having a soft, sweet tone or sound; a small bag with a shoulder strap.

mush (mush) *n.* A thick porridge of corn meal boiled in water or milk; soft matter. **mushiness** *n.* **mushy** *adj.*

mush-room (mush´röm) *n.* A fungus having an umbrella-shaped cap on a stalk. *v.* To grow or multiply quickly.

mu-sic (mu´zik) *n.* Organized tones in sequences and combinations which make up a continuous composition. **musical** *adj.*

music box *n.* A box enclosing an apparatus which produces music when activated.

mu-si-cian (mū zish´an) *n.* A composer or performer of music. **musicianly** *adj.* **musicianship** *n.*

mu-si-col-o-gy (mū´zi kol´o jē) *n.* The scientific and historical study of music. **musicological** *adj.* **musicologist** *n.*

musk (musk) *n.* A substance with a strong, powerful odor which is secreted by the male musk deer. **muskiness** *n.* **musky** *adj.*

mus-keg (mus´keg) *n.* A bog formed by moss, leaves, and decayed matter resembling peat.

mus-ket (mus´kit) *n.* A heavy, large-caliber shoulder gun with a long barrel.

musk-mel-on (musk´mel´on) *n.* A sweet

melon having a rough rind and juicy, edible flesh.

musk-rat (musk´rat´) *n.* A rodent of North America with brown fur.

Mus-lim (muz´lim) *n.* A follower of Islam. **Muslim** *adj.*

mus-lin (muz´lin) *n.* A plain-woven, sheer, or coarse fabric.

muss (mus) *v.* To make messy or untidy. *Slang* A confused conflict.

mus-sel (mus´el) *n.* A freshwater bivalve mollusk.

must (must) *v.* To be forced to; to have to; to be obligated to do something; to be necessary to do something. *n.* A requirement; absolute; something indispensable.

mus-tache *also* **moustache** *n.* The hair growing on the human upper lip, especially on the male upper lip.

mus-tang (mus´tang) *n.* A wild horse of the western plains.

mus-tard (mus´terd) *n.* A condiment or medicinal preparation made from the seeds of the mustard plant.

mustard gas *n.* An irritating liquid chemical used as a war gas.

mus-ter (mus´ter) *v.* To come or bring together; to convene; to bring or call forth. *n.* The act of examining or inspecting critically.

mustn't *contr.* Must not.

mus-ty (mus´tē) *adj.* Moldy or stale in odor or taste. **mustily** *adv.*

mu-ta-ble (mū´ta bl) *adj.* Prone to or capable of change. **mutability** *n.* **mutableness** *n.*

mu-tant (mūt´ant) *n.* An individual or organism which differs from the parental strain as a result of mutation.

mu-tate (mū´tāt) *v.* To undergo or cause to undergo mutation. **mutative** *adj.*

mute (mūt) *adj.* Unable to speak. *n.* A person who cannot speak. **mutely** *adv.*

mu-ti-late (mūt´i lāt´) *v.* To deprive of an essential part, as a limb of the body; to maim or cripple; to make imperfect. **mutilation** *n.* **mutilator** *n.*

mu-ti-ny (mūt´i ne) *n. pl.* **-ies** Open revolt against lawful authority. **mutineer** *n.* **mutinous** *adj.*

mutt (mut) *n., Slang* A mongrel; a dog of mixed breed.

mut-ter (mut´ėr) *v.* To speak or utter in a low voice; to grumble; to complain.

mut-ton (mut´on) *n.* The flesh of a fully grown sheep, used for food.

mu-tu-al (mū´chö al) *adj.* Having the same relationship; received and directed in equal amounts.

mutual fund *n.* An investment company which invests its shareholders' money in diversified ways.

muu-muu *n.* A dress which hangs loosely, originally given to the native women of Hawaii by missionaries.

muz-zle (muz´l) *n.* The projecting mouth of certain animals; the open end or mouth of an implement such as the barrel of a gun. **muzzler** *n.*

my (mī) *adj.* Relating to or of myself or one. *interj.* Used to express surprise, dismay, or pleasure.

my-ce-li-um (mī sē´lē um) *n. pl.* **-lia** A mass of interwoven filaments which form the main growing structure of a fungus. **mycelial** *adj.*

my-col-o-gy (mī kol´o je) *n.* A branch of botany; the scientific study of fungi. **mycological** *adj.* **mycologist** *n.*

my-e-li-tis *n.* An inflammation of the spinal cord or bone marrow.

my-elo-ma *n.* A tumor of the bone marrow.

myo-car-dio-graph (mī´o kär´dēograf´) *n.* A recording tool which traces the action of the heart muscles.

myo-car-di-um *n.* The muscular layer of the heart, located in the middle of the heart wall. **myocardial** *adj.*

my-o-pia (mī ō´pē a) *n.* A visual defect in which visual images come to a focus in front of the retina of the eye rather than on the retina, causing fuzzy images. **myopic** *adj.* **myopically** *adv.*

myr-tle (mer´tl) *n.* An evergreen shrub.

my-self (mī self´) *pron.* The one identical with me; used reflexively; my normal, healthy state or condition.

mys-te-ri-ous (mi stēr´ē us) *adj.* Relating to or being a mystery; impossible or difficult to comprehend. **mysteriously** *adv.* **mysteriousness** *n.*

mys-ter-y (mis´te rē) *n. pl.* **-ies** Something not understood; a problem or puzzle; an enigma; a Christian sacrament.

mys-tic (mis´tik) *adj.* Relating to mystics, mysticism, or mysteries. *n.* A person practicing or believing in mysticism. **mystical** *adj.* **mystically** *adv.*

mys-ti-cism (mis´ti siz´um) *n.* The spiritual discipline of communion with God or the spirit world.

mys-ti-fy (mis´ti fī) *v.* To perplex, to bewilder. **mystification** *n.*

myth (mith) *n.* A traditional story dealing with supernatural ancestors; a person or thing having only an unverifiable or imaginary existence. **mythical** *adj.* **mythic** *adj.* **mythically** *adv.*

my-thol-o-gy (mi thol´o jē) *n. pl.* **-ies** A body of myths dealing with gods and heroes. **mythological** *adj.* **mythologist** *n.*

my word *interj.* An expression of astonishment or surprise.

myx-e-de-ma *n.* A disease that is caused by the decreased activity of the thyroid gland and marked by the loss of mental and physical vigor; dry skin and hair. **myxedematous** *adj.*

N, n (en) The fourteenth letter of the English alphabet.

nab (nab) v. Slang To seize; to arrest; to catch suddenly.

na-celle (na sel´) n. The housing of an airplane that usually contains the engine.

na-dir (nā´dèr) n. The lowest point.

nag (nag) v. To bother by scolding or constant complaining. **nag** n. A worthless horse. **nagging** adj.

na-ga-na (na gä´na) n. A disease of horses caused by flies.

na-iad (nā´ad) n., Mythol. A nymph presiding over and living in springs, brooks, and fountains.

na-ive (nä ēv´) adj. Simple and trusting; not sophisticated. **naively** adv.

na-ked (nā´kid) adj. Without clothes on the body; nude; exposed; uncovered. **nakedly** adv. **nakedness** n.

nam-by-pam-by (nam´bēpam´bē)adj. Weak; indecisive; lacking in substance or character.

name (nām) n. A title or word by which something or someone is known. v. To give a name. **namable** n.

name-sake (nām´sāk´) n. A person named after someone with the same name.

nap (nap) n. A short rest or sleep, often during the day. v. The surface of a piece of leather or fabric.

na-palm (nā´päm) n. A mixture of aluminum soaps used in jelling gasoline for use in bombs or by flame throwers.

nape (nāp) n. The back of the neck.

na-per-y (nāp´e rē) n. Linens in general that are used for domestic purposes.

naph-tha (naf´tha) n. A volatile, colorless, liquid, that is used especially as a solvent or fuel.

na-pi-form (nāpi form´) adj. Having the globular shape of a turnip.

nap-kin (nap´kin) n. A cloth or soft paper, used at the dinner table for wiping the lips and fingers.

na-po-le-on (na pō´lē an) n. A pastry of several flaky layers filled with custard cream.

nap-py (nap´ē) n. pl. **nappies.** A small rimless, shallow serving.

na-prap-a-thy (na prap´a thē) n. A system of treatment of a disease, that is based on the theory that an illness is caused by dis-ordered connective tissues, and that using massage, manipulation, and dietary measures, healing is achieved.

nar-cis-sus (när sis´us) n. A widely grown type of bulbous plant which includes the jonquil, narcissus, and daffodil.

nar-co-ma-ni-a (när´o mä´nē a) n. The abnormal craving for a narcotic.

nar-co-sis (när kō´sis) n. A deep drug-induced state of stupor or unconsciousness.

nar-cot-ic (när kot´ik) n. A drug which dulls the senses, relieves pain, and induces a deep sleep; if abused, it can become habit-forming and cause convulsions or comas.

nard (närd) n. An aromatic medical, ointment that is obtained from the rhizomes of an East Asian plant.

nar-is (nâr´is) n,. pl. **nares** The nasal passage or opening; the nostril.

nar-rate (nar´rāt) v. To tell a story or give a description in detail. **-tion** n.

nar-row (nar´ō) adj. Slender or small in width; of less than standard width. **narrowly** adj. **narrowness** n.

narrow–mind-ed (nar´ō mīn´did) adj. Lacking sympathy or tolerance.

nar-y (nâr´ē) adj. Never a; not a; not; not one.

na-sal (nā´zal) adj. Of or pertaining to the nose; producing a nasal speech sound.

na-sal-ize (nā´za līz´) v. To produce or speak in a nasal manner.

nas-tic (nas´tik) adj., Bot. Relating to the movement of a plant part, as a result of changing cellular pressure on the surface.

na-stur-tium (na ster´shim) n. A five-petaled garden plant usually having red, yellow, or orange flowers.

nas-ty (nas´tē) adj. Dirty, filthy, or indecent; unpleasant. **nastily** adv.

na-tal (nāt´al) adj. Pertaining to or associated with birth.

na-tant (nāt´ant) adj. Swimming or floating; in or on water.

na-ta-tion (nā tā´shan) n. The act or part of swimming. **natator** n. A swimmer.

na-ta-to-ri-al (nā´ta tōr´ē al) adj. Pertaining to, adapted for, or characterized by swimming.

na-ta-to-ri-um (nā´ta tōr´ē um) n. pl. **natatoriums** An indoor swimming pool.

na-tes (nā´tēz) n. pl. The buttocks.

na-tion (nā´shan) n. A group of people made up of one or more nationalities under one government. **national** adj.

na-tion-al (nash´a nal) adj. Pertaining or relating to a nation or people; maintained by a nation as an independent political unit; devoted totally to one's own nation, welfare, and interests; to be patriotic.

na-tion-al-i-ty (nash´a nal´i tē) n. The fact or condition of belonging to a nation.

na-tive (nā´tiv) n. A person born in a country or place. adj. Belonging to one by nature or birth.

na-tiv-ism (nā´ti viz´um) n. The policy of protecting and favoring native inhabitants from immigrants.

na-tiv-i-ty (na tiv´i tē) n. Birth, circumstances, or conditions; the birth of
Christ.

nat-ro-lite (na´tro līt´) n. A hydrolous
silicate of sodium and aluminum, that
occurs occasionally in white, needle-
shaped crystals.

na-tron (nā´tron) n. Native carbonate
of soda found in solution found in some
mineral springs and lakes, used in
previous times as an embalming agent.

nat-ty (nat´ē) adj. Tidy; neatly dressed;
of a neat appearance.

nat-u-ral (nach´ĕr al) adj. Produced or
existing by nature; not artificial. Mus.
A note that is not sharp or flat.
naturalness, naturally adv.

na-ture (nā´chĕr) n. The universe and
its phenomena; kind, sort, or type;
one's own character or temperament.

naught (not) n. Nothing; the number 0;
zero.

naugh-ty (no´tē) adj. Unruly; not proper;
ill-behaved. naughtily adv.

nau-se-a (no´zē a) n. An upset stomach
with a feeling that one needs to vomit.
nauseous adj. nauseate v. nauseat-
ingly adv.

nau-se-ate (na´ze āt´) v. To feel nausea
or be sick to ones stomach; to be
inclined to vomit.

nau-seous (na´shus) adj. Disgusting;
nauseating; to cause a feeling of nausea.
nauseously adv. nauseousness n.

nau-ti-cal (no´ti kal) adj. Pertaining to
ships or seamanship. nautically adv.

na-val (nā´val) adj. Of or relating to
ships; maritime.

na-vel (nā´vel) n. A small mark or scar
on the abdomen where the umbilical
cord was attached.

na-vic-u-lar (na vik´ū lĕr) adj. Having
the shape of a boat. n. The bone of the
ankle or wrist.

nav-i-gate (nav´i gāt´) v. To plan the
course of a ship or aircraft; to steer a
course. navigator n. navigation.

nav-i-ga-tion (nav i gā´shun) n. The act
or science of navigating ships; the
science of determining the location,
speed, destination, and direction of
airplanes and other crafts and moving
them from place to place.

na-vy (nā´vē) n. One of a nation's
organizations for defense; a nation's
fleet of ships; a very dark blue.

neap tide (nēp) n. A tide in the minimum
range which occurs during the first and
third quarter of the moon or twice a
month.

near (nēr) adv. At, to, or within a short
time or distance. adj. Closely or
intimately related. nearness n.

near-by (nĕr´bī´) adj. & adv. Close by;
near at hand; adjacent.

near-sight-ed (nĕr´sī´tid) adj. Able to
see clearly at short distances only.

neat (nēt) adj. Tidy and clean; free from
disorder and dirt. Slang Great, fine,
or wonderful. neatly adv. neatness n.

neb-bish (neb´ish) n. A timid, ineffectual
person.

Neb-ras-ka n. A state located in the
central part of the United States;
statehood March 1, 1867; state capital
Lincoln.

neb-u-lize (neb´ū liz´) v. Reduce to fine
spray .

neb-u-lous (neb´ū lus) adj. Confused
or vague; hazy, cloudy, or misty.

nec-es-sar-y (nes´i ser´ē) adj. Unavoidable; required; essential; needed.

ne-ces-si-tate (ne ses´i tāt´) v. To make
necessary; to oblige; to require; to force
or be forced.

ne-ces-si-ty (ne ses´i tē) n. pl. -ies The
condition of being necessary; the
condition making a particular course
of action necessary; a requirement;
something inevitable.

neck (nek) n. The part of the body which
connects the head and trunk; a narrow
part or projection, as of land, a stringed
instrument, or bottle. v. To caress and
kiss.

ne-crol-o-gy (ne krol´o jē) n. pl. ne-crol-
o-gies A death notice or list of the most
recent dead.

nec-tar (nek´tĕr) n. A good-tasting
beverage; a sweet fluid in various
flowers, gathered by bees to help make
honey.

nec-tar-ine (nek´ta rēn´) n. A variety
of the common peach, whose fruit at
maturity is smooth like a plum.

nee (nā) n. Birth, the surname a woman
was born with.

need (nēd) n. The lack of something
desirable, useful, or necessary;
misfortune or poverty; a necessity.

nee-dle (nēd´l) n. A slender, pointed steel
implement which contains an eye
through which thread is passed. v. To
tease.

need-n't (nēd´ant) Need not.

ne-far-i-ous (ni fār´e us) adj. Extremely
wicked; despicable.

ne-gate (ni gāt´) v. To nullify; to deny;
to rule out. negation n.

neg-a-tive (neg´a tiv) adj. Expressing
denial or disapproval; not positive. n.
In photography, a negative photo.
negatively adj. negativeness n.

neg-a-tron (neg´a tron´) n. An electron.

neglect (ni glekt´) v. To ignore; to pay
no attention to; to fail to perform.

neg-li-gee (neg´li zhā´) n. A woman's
loose fitting dressing gown.

neg-li-gence (neg´li jens) n. The act or
condition of being negligent, an act
of being habitually neglectful.

neg-li-gent (neg´li jent) adj. To neglect

what needs to be done; neglectful.

ne-go-ti-a-ble (ni gō´shē a bl) *adj.* Capable of being negotiated.

ne-go-ti-ate (ni gō´shē ãt´) *v.* To confer with another person to reach an agreement; to accomplish successfully.

ne-gus (nēgus) *n.* A beverage made of wine, hot water, sugar, lemon and nutmeg or other spices.

neigh (nã) *v.* To make the cry of a horse.

neigh-bor (nã´bêr) *n.* One who lives near another; fellowman. **neighboring** *adj.*

neigh-bor-hood (nã´bêr hed´) *n.* A section or small region that possesses a specific quality; the people living in such a region.

nei-ther (nē´thêr) *adj.* Not one or the other. *pron.* Not the one or the other. *conj.* Not either; also not.

nek-ton (nek´ton) *n.* Free-swimming aquatic animals in the middle depths of the sea, that are independent of wave patterns and cur-rents.

nem-a-to-cyst (nem´a to sist) *n.* A minute stinging apparatus of coelenterate animals, that is used in kill its prey.

ne-o-clas-sic (nē´ō klas´ik) *adj.* Pertaining to a renewal of a classic style, as literature.

neo-dym-i-um (nē´ō dim´ē um) *n.* A metallic element of the rare-earth group, symbolized by Nd.

ne-ol-o-gism (nē ol´o jiz´um) *n.* A new word or phrase; that is often disapproved of because of its newness.

ne-o-my-cin (nē´ō mī´sin) *n.* An antibiotic, developed from microorganisms, and used in a variety of local skin infections.

ne-on (nē´on) *n.* An inert gaseous element used in lighting fixtures, symbolized by Ne.

ne-o-nate (nē´o nãt´) *n.* A newborn child less than a month old.

ne-o-na-tol-o-gy *n.* The medical study of the first 60 days of a baby's life.

neo-phyte (nē´o fīt´) *n.* A novice; a beginner.

ne-o-plasm (nē´o plaz´um) *n.* A tumor tissue serving no physiologic function.

ne-ot-e-ny (nē ot´e nē) *n.* The achievement of sexual maturity during the larval stage.

neph-e-line (nef´e li nit´) *n.* A heavy, dark-colored rock of volcanic origin.

neph-ew (nef´ū) *n.* The son of one's sister, brother, sister-in-law, or brother-in-law.

ne-phrid-i-um (ne frid´ē um) *n. pl.* nephridia A primitive excretory organ or structure in annelids, mollusks, and other invertebrates, like the kidney and functioning in some cases in reproduction.

neph-rite (nef´rīt) *n.* A white to dark green variety of actinolite, a form of jade.

ne-phrit-ic *adj.* Relating to the kidneys; afflicted with an inflammation of the kidneys.

nep-o-tism (nep´o tiz´um) *n.* The act of showing favoritism to relatives or friends in the work force. **nepotist** *n.*

nep-tu-ni-um (nep tõ´nē um) *n.* A radioactive metallic element, symbolized by Np.

ne-rit-ic (ne rit´ik) *adj.* Of or pertaining to the region of shallow water immediately adjoining the seacoast.

nerve (nerv) *n.* The bundles of fibers which convey sensation and originate motion through the body. *Slang* Impudent.

nerve cell *n.* Any of the cells constituting the cellular element of nerve tissue; neuron.

nerv-ous (ner´vus) *adj.* Affecting the nerves or the nervous system; agitated; worried. **nervously** *adv.* **-ness** *n.*

nervous breakdown *n.* Nervous exhaustion; emotional or mental weakness, that results from extended mental strain.

nervous system *n., Physiol.* The body system that coordinates, regulates, and controls the various internal functions and responses to stimuli.

ner-vure (nûr´vūr) *n.* The vein of a leaf.

nes-cience (nesh´ens) *n.* The lack of knowledge; ignorance

nest (nest) *n.* A place, shelter, or home built by a bird to hold its eggs and young.

nes-tle (nes´l) *v.* To settle snugly; to lie close to. **nestler** *n.*

nest-ling (nest´ling) *n.* A young bird still living in the nest.

net (net) *n.* A meshed fabric made of cords, ropes, threads, or other material knotted or woven together; the profit, weight, or price which remains after all additions, subtractions, or adjustments have been made.

neth-er (neth´ér) *adj.* Situated below or beneath.

net-tle (net´l) *n.* A plant having toothed leaves covered with stinging hairs. *v.* To provoke; to sting.

net-work (net´werk´) *n.* A system of interlacing tracks, channels, or lines; an interconnected system; a group of broadcasting stations.

network server In *computer science*, a computer that stores and manages programs and data for other computers in the network.

neu-ral (ner´al) *adj.* Relating to a nerve or the nervous system.

neu-ral-gia (ne ral´ja) *n.* Pain that occurs along the course of a nerve.

neu-ri-lem-ma (nur´i lem´a) *n.* The delicate plasma membrane sheath of a nerve fiber.

neu-ri-tis (ne rī'tis) n. An inflammation of a nerve which causes pain, the loss of reflexes, and muscular decline.

neu-ro-cir-cu-la-to´-ry (nur¯o sur'kū la tōr¯ē) adj. Pertaining to the circulatory and nervous systems of the human body.

neu-ro-fi-bril (nūr'o fi'bril) n., Anat. The minute fibrils in the nerve cells.

neu-ro-gen-ic (nūr'o jen'ik) adj., Med. Beginning in a nerve or the nerve tissue.

neu-rog-li-a (nū rog'lē a) n. The delicate connective tissue that binds together and supports the necessary parts of the nervous tissue.

neu-rol-o-gy (ne rol'o jō) n. The medical and scientific study of the nervous system and its disorders. **neurological** adj. **neurologist** n.

neu-ro-ma (nū rō'ma) n. pl. **neuromas** Pathol. A tumor or mass that is growing from or comprised of nerve tissue.

neu-ron or neu-rone (ner' on) n., Anat. A granular cell nerve which is the main functional unit of the nervous system.

neu-rop-ter-an (nū rop'tér an) n. Insects having two pairs of net-like membranous wings.

neu-ro-sis (ne rō'sis) n. Any one of various functional disorders of the mind or emotions having no physical cause. **neurotic** adj. **neurotically** adv.

neu-ro-tox-ic (nūr¯o tok'sik) adj. Poisonous to nerves or to nerve tissue such as the brain.

neu-ter (nō'tér) adj. Neither feminine nor masculine. n. A castrated animal.

neu-tral (nō'tral) adj. Not supporting either side of a debate, quarrel, or party; a color which does not contain a decided hue Chem. Neither alkaline nor acid. **neutrality** n. **neutrally** adv.

neu-tral-ize (nō'tra līz') v. To make or declare neutral.

neu-tri-no (nū trē'nō) n. Phys. The uncharged elementary particle having a mass nearing zero.

neu-tron (nō'tron) n. An uncharged particle in the nucleus of an atom present in all atomic nuclei except the hydrogen nucleus.

Ne-va-da n. A state located in the western part of the United States; statehood October 31, 1864; state capital Carson City.

nev-er (nev'ér) adv. Not ever; absolutely not.

nev-er-more (nev'ér mōr') adv. Never again.

nev-er–nev-er (nev'ér nev'ér) adj. Imaginary.

nev-er-the-less (nev'ér the les') adv. Nonetheless; however.

ne-vus (nē'vus) n., pl. **nevi** A congenital pigmented mark, or blemish; a birthmark.

new (nō) adj. Not used before; unaccustomed; unfamiliar. **newness** n.

New Deal n. The legislative and social programs of President F. D. Roosevelt designed for relief, economic recovery, and social security during the 1930's.

New Hampshire n. A state located in the northeastern part of the United States; statehood June 21, 1788; state capital Concord.

New Jersey n. A state located on the eastern coast of the United States; statehood December 18, 1787; state capital Trenton.

New Mexico n. A state located in the southwestern part of the United States; statehood January 6, 1912; state capital Santa Fe.

news (nōz) n. pl. Current happenings; matter considered newsworthy.

news-pa-per (nōz'pā'pér) n. A weekly or daily publication which contains recent news and information.

New Testament n. The second part of the Christian Bible containing the Gospels, Acts, Epistles, and the Book of Revelation.

New Year's Day n. January 1st, the first day of the year.

New York n. A state located on the eastern coast of the United States; statehood July 26, 1788; state capital Albany.

next (nekst) adj. Immediately following or proceeding; nearest in space or position.

nex-us (nek'sus) n. pl. **nexus** A connected group; connection; connector; a linked series.

nib-ble (nib'l) v. To bite a little at a time; to take small bites. **nibble, nibbler** n.

nic-co-lite (nik'o līt') n. A pale copper-red mineral with a metallic luster that consists mainly of nickel arsenide.

nice (nīs) adj. Pleasing; enjoyable; polite and courteous; refined. **nicely** adv.

ni-ce-ty (nī'si tē) n. pl. **niceties** A delicate point; a fine destination. The characteristic of being nice; precision.

niche (nich) n. A recess or alcove in a wall, usually used for displays.

nick (nik) n. A small chip or cut on a surface; the final critical moment.

nick-el (nik'el) n. A hard, silver, metallic element used in alloys and symbolized by Ni; a United States coin worth five cents.

nick-name (nik'nām') n. The familiar form of a proper name, expressed in a shortened form. **nickname** v.

nic-o-tine or nicotin (nik'o tēn') n. A poisonous alkaloid found in tobacco and used in insecticides and medicine.

nic-ti-tate (nik´ti tāt´) v. To wink.

ni-dic-o-lous (nī dik´o lus) adj. Sharing the nest of another; raised for a time in a nest.

ni-dif-u-gous (nī dif´ū gus) adj. Indicating a bird that leaves a nest soon after it is hatched.

ni-dus (nīdus) n. A nest or breading place; a place where insects deposit their eggs.

niece (nēs) n. A daughter of one's sister or brother or one's sister-in-law or brother-in- law.

ni-el-lo (nē el´ō) n. The art of decorating silver plates with incised designs filled with a black metallic composition.

nig-gle (nig´l) v. To triffle; to find fault in a petty way; to work ineffectively.

nigh (nī) adv. Near in relationship, time, or space.

night (nīt) n. The time between dusk and dawn or the hours of darkness.

night blindness n. A condition of the eyes where the visual capacity is reduced in faint or dim light.

ni-gres-cent (nī gres´ent) adj. Blackish; a shade of black. **nigrescence** n.

nig-ri-tude (nig´ri tŏd´) n. Complete darkness.

ni-gro-sine (nī´gro sēn´) n. A blue-black dye that is used commercially as a dyeing agent.

ni-hil-ism (nī´i liz˝um) n. An extreme form of skepticism where traditional values and beliefs are unfounded; the total disbelief in religion or moral obligations and principles.

nil (nil) v. Nothing.

nill (nil) v. To be unwilling.

nim-ble (nim´bl) adj. Marked by a quick, light movement; quick-witted. **nimbleness** n. **nimbly** adv.

nim-bo-stra-tus (nim˝bō strātus) n. pl. **nimbostratus** Meteor. A low, dark gray cloud often producing rain.

nin-com-poop (nin´kom pŏp´) n. A silly or stupid person.

nine (nīn) n. The cardinal number that is equal to 8+1. **nine** adj. & pron.

nin-ny (nin´ē) n. pl. **ninnies** A fool; a simpleton.

ni-non (nē non´) n. A smooth sheer fabric, as chiffon, used for curtains, and women's clothing.

ni-o-bi-um (nī ō´bē um) n. A gray, metallic element used in alloys, symbolized by Nb.

nip (nip) v. To pinch, bite, or grab something. n. A pinch, bite, or grab; a sharp, stinging feeling caused by cold temperatures. **nipper** n.

ni-pa (nē´pa) n. A fruit-bearing palm; a shelter made from the leaves of the nipa palm.

nip-ple (nip´l) n. The small projection of a mammary gland through which

milk passes; an artificial teat usually made from a type of rubber which a bottle-fed baby nurses.

nip-py (nip´ē) adj. Inclined to be biting cold, as chilly weather.

Ni-sei (nē´sā´) n. A native American of Japanese ancestry.

ni-sus (nīsus) n., pl. **nisus** Endeavor; effort; striving; an impulse.

nit (nit) n. The egg of a louse or other similar parasitic insects.

nit-id (nit´id) adj. Bright; shining; lustrous.

nit–pick (nit´pik´) v. Slang To be overly critical with unimportant details.

ni-trate (nī´trāt) n. Chem. A salt or ester of nitric acid; potassium or sodium nitrate, used as a fertilizer.

ni-tro-gen (nī´tro jen) n. A nonmetallic gaseous element which is essential to life, symbolized by N.

nitrogen balance n. Equivalent of the intake and loss of nitrogen in an organism or in soil.

ni-tro-glyc-er-in (nī´tro glis´ér in) n. A highly flammable, explosive liquid, used to make dynamite and in medicine, to dilate blood vessels.

nit-wit (nit´wit´) n. A stupid person.

ni-val (nīval) adj. Pertaining to snow.

nix (niks) n. A water spirit usually small and either good or bad.

Nixon, Richard M. n. (1913-1994) The thirty-seventh president of the United States from 1969-1974; resigned August 9, 1974 due to Watergate scandal.

no (nō) adv. Used to express rejection, disagreement, or denial; not so; not at all.

no-bel-i-um (nō bē´lē um) n. A radioactive element, symbolized by No.

Nobel prize (nō bel´ prīz) n. An award given to people with achievements in literature, economics, medicine, and other fields, established by the last will and testament of Alfred Nobel.

no-bil-i-ty (nō bil´i tē) n. The state or quality of being noble; the rank or status of a noble.

no-ble (nō´bl) adj. Morally good; superior in character or nature; of high quality or class. n. A person of rank or noble birth. **nobleman** ,-**ness** n.

no-blesse (nō bles´) n. Nobility; person of noble rank collectively.

noblesse oblige n. The obligation of people of wealth and social position to behave with honor and generosity.

no-bod-y (nō´bod´ē) pron. Not anybody; no person.

no-cent (nō sent) adj. Harmful; hurtful, or injurious.

noc-tur-nal (nok ter´nal) adj. Pertaining to or occurring during the night; active at night and quiet during the daylight hours. **nocturnally** *adv.*

noc-u-ous (nok´ū us) *adj.* Harmful; injurious.

nod (nod) *n.* A quick downward motion of the head as one falls off to sleep; a downward motion of the head indicating acceptance or approval. *v.* To move the head down and then up again.

node (nōd) *n.* A swollen or thickened enlargement; a knot.

nod-ule (noj´ōl) *n.* A little knot or lump.

no-dus (nō´dus) *n.* A difficult situation.

no-el (nō el´) *n.* A Christmas carol.

no-et-ic (nō et´ik) *adj.* Pertaining to the mind or intellect.

nog (nog) *n.* A wooden peg or block; a strong ale.

nog-gin (nog´in) *n.* A small mug or cup; a small quantity of a beverage.

no-how (nō´hou´) *adv.* In no way or manner; not at all.

noil (noil) *n.* A short fiber of wool, cotton, or silk often separated during combing and separately spun into yarn.

noise (noiz) *n.* A sound which is disagreeable or loud; in computer science, un-wanted data in an electronic signal.

noi-some (noi´som) *adj.* Offensive to the sense of smell; noxious; harmful.

nois-y (noi´zē) *adj.* Making an excessive amount of noise; abounding in or attended with noise.

no-mad (nō´mad) *n.* A member of a group of people who wander from place to place. **nomadic** *adj.* **nomadism** *n.*

nom de guerre (nom´ de gâr´) *n.* An assumed name under which one pursues a profession.

no-men-cla-tor (nōmen klā´tėr) *n.* An inventor of names.

no-men-cla-ture (nō´men klā´chér) *n.* The set of names used to describe the elements of art, science, and other fields.

nom i nal (nom´i ndl) *adj.* Of or relating to something that is in name or form only. **nominally** *adv.*

nom-i-nate (nom´i nāt´) *v.* To select a candidate for an elective office; to appoint or designate to a position. **nomination, nominator** *n.*

nom-i-nee (nom´i nē´) *n.* A person nominated for a position or office.

no-mism (nō´miz um) *n.* Conduct based on moral or religious beliefs.

no-mol-o-gy (nō mol´ojē) *n.* The science of the formulation of law; the science that deals directly with the laws of reason.

non- *prefix* Not.

non-a-bra-sive (non´a brā´siv) *adj.* Not causing wear by friction.

non-ab-sorb-ent (non´ab sor´bent) *adj.* Unable to absorb liquids.

non-ac-cept-ance (non´ak sep´tans) *n.* Failure to accept.

non-ad-he-sive (non´ad hē´siv) *adj.* Not having the quality to adhere.

non-ad-min-is-tra-tive (non´ad min´l strā´ tiv) *adj.* Not pertaining to the executive staff of an organization.

non-a-ge-nar-i-an (non´a je nâr´ēan) *adj.* A person between the ages of 90 and 100 years.

non-a-gon (non´a gon´) *n.* A geometric figure with nine sides and nine angles.

non-al-co-hol-ic (non´al ko ho´lik) *adj.* Not containing alcohol.

non-ap-pear-ance (non´a pēr´ans) *n.* The failure to appear.

non-be-liev-er (non´bi lē´vėr) *n.* One who does not believe; a person who does not believe in God.

non-cha-lant (non´sha länt´) *adj.* Giving an effect of casual unconcern. **nonchalance** *n.* **nonchalantly** *adv.*

non-col-le-gi-ate (non´kolē´jIt) *adj.* Not belonging to a college.

non-com-bus-ti-ble (non´kom bus´ti bl) *adj.* Not easily ignitable.

non-com-mu-ni-ca-ble (non´ka mū´i ka bl) *adj.* Not transmissible through personal contact, as a disease.

non compos men-tis (non kom´pos men´tis) *adj.* Mentally unbalanced; not of sound mind.

non-con-duc-tor (non´kon duk´tėr) *n.* A substance which conducts with difficulty or in a very small degree, such as electricity, heat, or sound.

non-con-form-ist (non´kon for´mist) *n.* One who does not feel compelled to follow or accept traditions.

non-con-tagious (non´kon ta´jus) *adj., Med.* Of a disease, not transmissible by contact.

non-co-op-er-a-tion (non´kō op´e rā shan) *n.* Failure to cooperate with an individual, party, or organization.

non-cor-ro-sive (non´ko rō´sive) *adj.* Unable to corrode, as certain acids.

non-de-duct-i-ble (non´di dukt´i bl) *adj.* Unable to subtract.

non-de-script (non´di skript´) *n.* A person or something not easily classed or described.

non-de-struct-ive (non´di stuk´tiv) *adj.* Not causing destruction, or ruin.

non-dis-tinc-tive (non´di stingk´tiv) *adj.* Not distinctive.

none (nun) *adj.* Not any; not one.

non-ef-fec-tive (non´i fek´tiv) *adj.* Without the necessary power to cause or produce effect.

non-en-ti-ty (non en´ti tē) *n. pl.* **nonentities** Nonexistence; something that does not exist.

non-es-sen-tial (non´isen´shal) *adj.* Not essential; not absolutely necessary. *n.*

An unnecessary person or thing.

non-ex-empt (nun'ig zempt') *adj.* Not exempt from liability.

non-sense (non'sens) *n.* Something that seems senseless or foolish; something which is very unimportant.

non seq-ui-tur (non sek'wi tér) *n.* An inference that does not follow as the logical result of what has preceded it.

non-sex-ist *adj.* Not discriminating on the basis of gender.

noo-dle (nöd'l) *n.* A flat strip of dried dough made with eggs and flour. *Slang* The head.

nook (nek) *n.* A corner, recess, or secluded place.

noon (nön) *n.* The middle of the day; 12: 00 o'clock.

noose (nös) *n.* A loop of rope secured by a slipknot, allowing it to decrease in size as the rope is pulled.

nor (nor) *conj.* Not either; or not.

norm (norm) *n.* A rule, model, or pattern typical for a particular group.

nor-mal (nor'mal) *adj.* Ordinary, average, usual; having average intelligence; standard. **normalcy, normality** *n.* **normally** *adv.*

north (north) *n.* The direction to a person's left while facing east.

North Carolina *n.* A state located in the southeastern part of the United States; statehood November 21, 1789; state capital Raleigh.

North Dakota *n.* A state located in the north central part of the United States; statehood November 2, 1889; state capital Bismarck.

nose (nöz) *n.* The facial feature containing the nostrils; the sense of smell. *v.* To discover by smell.

no-sol-o-gy (nö sol'o jē) *n. pl.* **nosologies** A systematic list of diseases; the branch of medical science that deals with the grouping of diseases.

nos-tal-gia (ne stal'ja) *n.* A yearning to return to the past. **nostalgic** *adj.*

nos-tril (nos'tril) *n.* The external openings of the nose.

nos-trum (nos'trum) *n.* A secret remedy for a medical condition.

nos-y *or* **nos-ey** (nö'zē) *adj.* Snoopy; inquisitive; prying.

not (not) *adv.* In no manner; used to express refusal or denial.

no-ta-ble (nö'ta bl) *adj.* Remarkable, distinguished. *n.* A person or thing which is notable. *v.* To acknowledge and certify as a notary public. **-ly** *adv.*

notary public *n.* A person who is legally authorized as a public officer to witness and certify documents.

no-ta-tion (nö tā'shan) *n.* A process or system of figures or symbols used in specialized fields to represent quantities, numbers, or values.

notch (noch) *n.* A v-shaped indentation or cut. **notch** *v.*

note (nöt) *n.* A record or message in short form. *Mus.* A tone or written character.

not-ed (nö'tid) *adj.* Famous; well-known.

note-wor-thy (nöt'wür'thē) *adj.* Significant; worthy of observation or attention. **noteworthily** *adv.*

noth-ing (nuth'ing) *n.* Not anything; no part or portion. *adv.* In no way; not at all.

no-tice (nö'tis) *n.* An announcement; a notification. *v.* To give notice; to become aware of. **noticeable** *adj.*

no-ti-fi-ca-tion (nö'ti fi kā'shan) *n.* The act of notifying; a notice in words of writing; anything which gives information.

no-ti-fy (nö'ti fī') *v.* To give notice of; to announce. **notifier, notification** *n.*

no-tion (nö'shan) *n.* An opinion; a general concept; an idea. *pl.* Small useful articles, as thread or buttons.

no-tion-al (nö'sha nal) *adj.* Referring to or expressing ideas, concepts.

no-to-ri-ous (nö tör'ē us) *adj.* Having a widely known and usually bad reputation.

not-with-stand-ing (not'with stan'ding) In spite of. *adv.* Nevertheless; anyway. *conj.* Although.

nou-gat (nö'gat) *n.* A confection made of sugar, honey, or corn syrup, contains nuts and fruit pieces.

noun (noun) *n.* A word which names a person, place, or thing.

nour-ish (ner'ish) *v.* To furnish with the nutriment and other substances needed for growth and life; to support. **nourishing** *adj.* **nourishment** *n.*

nour-ish-ment (nûr'ish ment) *n.* Food, the act of nourishing.

nou-veau riche (nö'vö rēsh') *n.* A person who has recently become rich.

no-va (nö'va) *n. pl.* **-vae** *or* **-vas** A star which flares up and fades away after a few years or months.

nov-el (nov'el) *n.* An inventive narrative dealing with human experiences; a book. **novelist** *n.*

nov-el-ty (nov'el tē) *n. pl.* **-ies** Something unusual or new.

No-vem-ber (nö vem'bér) *n.* The 11th month of the calendar year, having 30 days.

nov-ice (nov'is) *n.* A person who is new and unfamiliar with an activity or business.

now (nou) *adv.* At the present time; immediately.

now-a-days (nou'a dāz') *adv.* At the present time.

no-way (nö'wā') *adv.* Not at all.

no-where (nö'hwâr') *adv.* Not in or at any place.

nox-ious (nok'shus) *adj.* Harmful;

obnoxious; corrupt.

noz-zle (noz´l) *n*. A projecting spout or vent of something.

nu-ance (nö´äns) *n*. A gradation or variation by which a color passes from the lightest possible shade to its darkest shade.

nub (nub) *n*. A knob; a small piece or lump.

nub-bin (nub´in) *n*. A small piece.

nu-bile (nö´bil) *adj*. Suitable or ready for marriage; of the right age for marriage.

nu-bi-lous (nö´bi lus) *adj*. Cloudy; foggy; vague.

nu-cha (nö´ka) *n. pl.* **nuchae** The nape of the neck.

nu-cle-ar (nö´klē ér) *adj*. Pertaining to and resembling a nucleus; relating to atomic energy.

nuclear force *n*. The powerful and explosive interaction between the nucleons which holds the atomic nuclei together.

nu-cle-ase (nö´klē ās´) *n*. An enzyme which breaks down nucleic acids.

nu-cle-ate (nö´klē it) *v*. To form into a nucleus; to gather round or form a nucleus. *adj*. Having a nucleus.

nu-cle-on (nö´klē on´) *n., Phys.* An elementary particle of the atomic nucleus, a proton or neutron.

nu-cle-on-ics *n. pl.* The science dealing with the practical application of nuclear physics.

nu-cle-us (nö´klē us) *n*. The main element around which all other elements group; the central core of an atom.

nude (nöd) *adj*. Unclothed; naked. **nudity, nudism** *n*.

nu-di-cau-lous (nö´di ko´lus) *adj., Bot.* having leafless stems.

nu-ga-to-ry (nö´ga tōr´ē) *adj*. Trifling; worthless; inoperative.

nudge (nuj) *v*. To poke or push gently.

nug-get (nug´it) *n*. A lump, as of precious metal.

nui-sance (nö sans) *n*. A source of annoyance or inconvenience.

null (nul) *adj*. Invalid; having no value or consequence. **nullification** *n*.

nul-li-fy (nul´i fī´) *v*. To counteract.

numb (num) *adj*. Lacking physical sensation; paralyzed or stunned. **numb** *v*. **numbness** *n*.

num-ber (num´bér) *n*. A word or symbol which is used in counting or which indicates how many or which one in a series.

nu-men (nö´min) *n. pl.* **numina** A divine spiritual force or influence, one thought to dwell within an object.

nu-mer-al (nö´mér al) *n*. A symbol, figure, letter, word, or a group of these which represents a number.

nu-mer-a-tion (nö´me rā´shan) *n*. The act of numbering or calculating.

nu-mer-a-tor (nö´me rā´tér) *n*. The term in mathematics indicating how many parts are to be taken; the number in a fraction which appears above the line.

nu-mer-ous (nö´mér us) *adj*. Consisting or made up of many units, things, or individuals.

num-mu-lar (num´ūlér) *adj*. Characterized by circular lesions.

nun (nun) *n*. A woman who has joined a religious group and has taken vows to give up worldly goods and never to marry.

nup-tial (nup´shal) *adj*. Of or pertaining to a wedding. **nuptials** *n. pl.* A wedding.

nurse (ners) *n*. A person who is specially trained to care for disabled or sick persons. **nurse** *v*. To feed a baby from a mother's breast; to provide care to a sick or disabled person.

nur-ture (ner´chér) *n*. The upbringing, care, or training of a child. **nurture** *v*. **nurturer** *n*.

nut (nut) *n*. A hard-shelled fruit or seed which contains an inner, often edible kernel. *Slang* A person who does crazy or silly things.

nu-ta-tion (nö tā´shan) *n*. The involuntary nodding of the head.

nu-tri-ent (nö´trē ent) *n*. A substance which nourishes. **nutrient** *adj*.

nu-tri-tion (nö trish´an) *n*. The process by which a living being takes in food and uses it to live and grow. **nutritive, nutritional** *adj*. **nutritionally** *adv*. **nutritionist** *n*.

nu-tri-tious (nö trish´us) *adj*. Containing or serving as nourishment.

nuts (nuts) *adj., Slang* Foolish, crazy.

nuz-zle (nuz´l) *v*. To gently rub against something with the nose; to cuddle.

nyc-ta-lo-pi-a (nik´ta lō´pē a) *n*. A condition of the eyes where the sight is good during day or bright light but abnormally poor at night or in dim light; night blindness.

ny-lon (nī´lon) *n*. A strong, elastic material; yarn or fabric made from nylon. *pl.* **nylons** Stockings made of nylon.

nymph (nimf) *n*. Nature goddesses who lived in woods, rivers, and trees; various immature insects, especially the larva which undergoes incomplete metamorphosis.

O

O, o (ō) The 15th letter of the English alphabet.

O (ō) *n*. A word used before a name when addressing that person; an interjection.

oaf (ōf) *n*. A stupid or clumsy person.

oar (ōr) *n*. A long pole, flat at one end, used in rowing a boat.

oasis (ō ā´sis) *n*., *pl*. **oases** A fertile section in the desert which contains water; anything that can provide refuge.

oat (ōt) *n*. A cultivated cereal grass whose grain or seed is used as food for humans as well as animals.

oath (ōth) *n*. A solemn promise in the name of God or on a Bible that a person will speak only the truth.

oat-meal (ōt´mēl´) *n*. A cooked cereal food made from rolled oats.

ob-du-rate (ob´de rit) *adj*. Stubborn; hard-hearted; not giving in.

o-be-di-ent (ō bē´dē ent) *adj*. Obeying or willing to do what one is told.

ob-e-lisk (ob´e lisk) *n*. A tall, four-sided stone pillar which slopes from a pointed top.

o-bese (ō bēs´) *adj*. Very fat. **obesity** *n*.

o-bey (ō bā´) *v*. To carry out instructions; to be guided or controlled; to follow directions. **obeyer** *n*.

o-bit-u-ar-y (ō bich´ō er´ē) *n*. *pl*. **-ies** A published announcement that a person has died, often containing a short biography of the person's life.

ob-ject (ob jekt´) *v*. To voice disapproval; to protest. Something that is visible or can be touched. A word in a sentence which explains who or what is acted upon.

ob-jec-tion (ob jek´shan) *n*. A feeling of opposition or disagreement, etc.; the reason for a disagreement.

ob-jec-tive (ob jek´tiv) *adj*. Pertaining to or dealing with material objects rather than mental concepts. *n*. Something that one works toward, a goal; a purpose. **objectivity** *n*.

ob-la-tion (o blā´shan) *n*. A religious offering or the act of sacrifice; that which is offered.

ob-li-ga-tion (ob´li gā´shan) *n*. A promise or feeling of duty; something one must do because one's conscience or the law demands it; a debt which must be repaid.

o-blige (o blīj´) *v*. To constrain; to put in one's debt by a service or favor; to do a favor. **obliger** *n*. **obligingly** *adv*.

o-blique (o blēk´) *adj*. Inclined; not level or straight up and down; slanting; indirect. **obliqueness** *n*. **obliquity** *n*.

o-blit-er-ate (o blit´e rāt´) *v*. To blot out or eliminate completely; to wipe out. **obliteration** *n*. **obliterator** *n*

o-bliv-i-on (o bliv´ē an) *n*. The condition of being utterly forgotten; the act of forgetting.

ob-liv-i-ous (o bliv´ē us) *adj*. Not aware or conscious of what is happening; unmindful. **obliviously** *adv*.

ob-long (ob´long´) *adj*. Rectangular; longer in one direction than the other;

normally, the horizontal dimension; the greater in length. **oblong** *n*.

ob-nox-ious (ob nok´shus) *adj*. Very unpleasant; repugnant.

o-boe (ō´bō) *n*. A double reed, tube-shaped woodwind instrument. **oboist** *n*.

ob-scene (ob sēn´) *adj*. Indecent; disgusting. **obscenity** *n*.

ob-scure (ob skūr´) *adj*. Remote; not clear; faint. *v*. To make dim; to conceal by covering. **obscurity** *n*.

ob-ser-va-tion (ob´zer vā´shan) *n*. The act of observing something; that which is observed; a judgment or opinion. **observational** *adj*.

ob-ser-va-to-ry (ob zer´vatōr´ē) *n*. *pl*. **-ies** A building or station furnished with instruments for studying the natural phenomenon; a high tower affording a panoramic view.

ob-serve (ob zerv´) *v*. To pay attention; to watch. **observable** *adj*. **observant** *adj*. **observably** *adv*. **observer** *n*.

ob-sess (ob ses´) *v*. To preoccupy the mind with an idea or emotion; to be abnormally preoccupied. **-ion** *n*.

ob-so-lete (ob´so lēt´) *adj*. No longer in use; out-of-date; no longer current. **obsolescence** *n*. **obsolescent** *adj*.

ob-sta-cle (ob´sta kl) *n*. An obstruction; anything which opposes or stands in the way of.

ob-ste-tri-cian (ob´sti trish an) *n*. A physician who specializes in the care of a woman during pregnancy and childbirth.

ob-stet-rics (ob ste´triks) *n*. The branch of medicine which deals with pregnancy and childbirth.

ob-sti-nate (ob´sti nit) *adj*. Stubbornly set to an opinion or course of action; difficult to control or manage; hardheaded. **obstinacy** *n*. **-ately** *adv*.

ob-strep-er-ous (ob strep´ér us) *adj*. Noisy, unruly, or boisterous in resistance to advice or control. **obstreperously** *adv*. **-ness** *n*.

ob-struct (ob strukt´) *v*. To block, hinder or impede. **obstructor** *n*. **-tion** *n*.

ob-tain (ob tān´) *v*. To acquire or gain possession of. **obtainable** *adj*.

ob-trude (ob trōd´) *v*. To thrust forward without request or warrant; to call attention to oneself.

ob-tuse (ob tōs´) *adj*. Lacking acuteness of feeling; insensitive; not distinct or clear to the senses, as pain or sound. *Bot*. Rounded or blunt at the end, as a petal or leaf.

ob-vi-ate (ob´vē āt´) *v*. To counter or prevent by effective measures; to provide for.

ob-vi-ous (ob´vē us) *adj*. Easily seen, discovered, or understood.

oc-ca-sion (o kā´zhan) *n*. The time an event occurs; the event itself; a celebration. v. To bring about; to cause.

oc-ca-sion-al (o kā´zha nal) adj. Appearing or occurring irregularly or now and then; intended, made, or suitable for a certain occasion; incidental.

oc-cip-i-tal bone (ok sip´i tal) n., Anat. The bone which forms the back of the skull.

oc-cult (o kult´) adj. Concealed. n. The action or influence of supernatural agencies or secret knowledge of them.

oc-cu-pan-cy (ok´kū pan sē) n. The state or act of being occupied; the act of holding in possession; the time or term during which something is occupied.

oc-cu-pa-tion (ok´ū pā´shan) n. A job, profession, or vocation; a foreign military force which controls an area.

oc-cu-py (ok´ū pī´) v. To take and retain possession of; to live in. occupier n.

oc-cur (o ker´) v. To suggest; to have something come to mind; to happen.

o-cean (ō´shan) n. An immense body of salt water which covers 3/4 of the earth's surface; one of the oceans.

o'clock (o klok´) adv. Of, or according to the clock.

oc-ta-gon (ok´ta gon´) n. A polygon with eight angles and eight sides. octagonal octagonally adv.

oc-tave (ok´tiv) n., Music A tone on the eighth degree above or below another tone.

Oc-to-ber (ok tō´bér) n. The 10th month of the calendar year, having 31 days.

oc-to-ge-nar-i-an (ok´to je när´ēan) n. A person between 80 and 90 years.

oc-to-pus (ok´to pus) n. pl. -es or -pi A cephalopod with a sac-like body and eight tentacles containing double rows of suckers.

oc-u-lar (ok´ū lêr) adj. Of or relating to the eye; perceived or done by the eye.

OD n., Slang An overdose of a drug; one who has taken an overdose. v. To overdose; to die from an overdose.

odd (od) adj. Unusual; strange; singular; left over; not even. oddly adv.

odds (odz) n. An equalizing advantage given to a weaker opponent; a ratio between the probability against and the probability for something happening or being true.

ode (ōd) n. A lyric poem usually honoring a person or event.

o-dom-e-ter (ō dom´i tér) n. A device in a vehicle used to measure distance traveled. odometry n.

o-dor (ō´dér) n. A smell; a sensation which occurs when the sense of smell is stimulated.

od-ys-sey (od´i sē) n. A long voyage marked by many changes of fortune; a spiritual quest.

of (uv) prep. Proceeding; composed of; relating to; at a distance from.

off (of) adv. From a position or place; no longer connected or on. adj. Canceled. prep. Away from.

of-fend (o fend´) v. To make angry; to arouse resentment; to break a law; to insult. offender n.

of-fense (o fens´) n. A violation of a duty, rule, or propriety; the act of causing dis-pleasure; the act of assaulting or attacking; in football and other sports, the team having possession of the ball.

of-fen-sive (o fen´siv) adj. Disagreeable; causing resentment; insulting.

of-fer (o´fêr) v. To present for acceptance or rejection; to present as an act of worship; to make available; to present in order to satisfy a requirement.

of-fice (o´fis) n. A place where business or professional duties are conducted; an important job, duty, or position.

of-fi-cial (o fish´al) adj. Something derived from proper authority. n. One who holds a position or office; a person who referees a game such as football, basketball, or soccer. officially adv.

of-fi-ci-ate (o fish´ē at´) v. To carry out the duties and functions of a position or office.

of-ten (o´fen) adv. Frequently; many times.

oh (ō) Used to express surprise, fear, or pain.

O-hi-o n. A state in the north central section of the United States; statehood March 1, 1803; state capital Columbus.

ohm (ōm) n. A unit of electrical resistance equal to the resistance of a conductor in which one volt produces a current of one ampere.

oil (oil) n. Any of various substances, usually thick, which can be burned or easily melted; a lubricant. v. To lubricate.

oint-ment (oint´ment) n. An oily substance used on the skin as an aid to healing or to soften the skin.

Ok-la-ho-ma n. A state in the south central part of the United States; statehood November 16, 1907; state capital Oklahoma City.

ok-tane (ok´tān) n. Any of several hydrocarbon compounds which occur in petroleum.

old (ōld) adj. Having lived or existed for a long time; of a certain age.

old–fash-ioned (ōld´fash´ond) adj. Pertaining to or characteristic of former times or old customs; not modern or up-to-date.

Old Glory n. The flag of the United States of America.

Old Testament n. The first of two parts of the Christian Bible, containing the history of the Hebrews, the laws of Moses, writings of the prophets, and the Scriptures of Judaism.

ol-fac-tory (ol fak´to rē) *adj.* Pertaining to the sense of smell.

oli-gar-chy (ol´i gär´kē) *n., pl.* **-ies** A government controlled by a small group for corrupt and selfish purposes; the group exercising such control.

ol-ive (ol´iv) *n.* A small oval fruit from an evergreen tree with leathery leaves and yellow flowers, valuable as a source of oil.

om-buds-man (om´bŏdz man´) *n.* **-men** A government official appointed to report and receive grievances against the government.

om-e-let *or* **om-e-lette (om´e lit)** *n.* A dish made from eggs and other items, such as bacon, cheese, and ham, and cooked until set.

o-men (ō´men) *n.* A phenomenon which is thought of as a sign of something to come, whether good or bad.

om-i-nous (om´i nus) *adj.* Foreshadowed by an omen or by a presentiment of evil; threatening.

o-mis-sion (ō mish´an) *n.* The state or act of being omitted; anything neglected or left out.

o-mit (ō mit´) *v.* To neglect; to leave out; to overlook.

om-ni-bus (om´ni bus´) *n.* A public vehicle designed to carry a large number of people; a bus. *adj.* Covering a complete collection of objects or cases.

om-nip-o-tent (om nip´o tent) *adj.* Having unlimited or infinite power or authority.

om-nis-cient (om nish´ent) *adj.* Knowing all things; having universal or complete knowledge.

om-niv-or-ous (om niv´ĕr us) *adj.* Feeding on both vegetable and animal substances; absorbing everything. **omnivorously** *adv.*

on (on) *prep.* Positioned upon; indicating proximity; indicating direction toward; with respect to. on *adv.* In a position of covering; forward.

once (wuns) *adv.* A single time; at any one time. *conj.* As soon as.

on-col-o-gy (ong kol´o jē) *n.* The study of tumors. **oncological, oncologic** *adj.*

one (wun) *adj.* Single; undivided. *n.* A single person; a unit; the first cardinal number (1).

oneself *pron.* One's own self.

one–sid-ed (wun´sī´did) *adj.* Partial to one side; unjust. **one-sidedness** *n.*

on–line (on´līn´) *adj., computer science* Controlled directly by a computer.

on-ly (ōn´lē) *adj.* Sole; for one purpose alone. *adv.* Without anyone or anything else. *conj.* Except; but.

on-to (on´tŏ) *prep.* To a position or place; aware of.

o-nus (ō nus) *n.* A burden; a responsibility or duty which is difficult or unpleasant; the blame.

on-ward (on´wĕrd) *adv.* Moving forward in time or space. **onwards** *adj.*

on-yx (on´iks) *n.* A gemstone; a chalcedony in layers of different colors.

oo-dles (ŏd´lz) *n., pl. Slang* A great or large quantity.

ooze (ōz) *n.* A soft deposit of slimy mud on the bottom of a body of water; muddy or marshy ground; a bog. *v.* To flow or leak slowly; to disappear little by little.

o-pal (ō´pal) *n.* A translucent mineral composed of silicon, often marked with an iridescent play of colors.

o-paque (ō pāk´) *adj.* Not transparent; dull; obscure. **opacity** *n.* **-ness** *n.*

o-pen (ō´pen) *adj.* Having no barrier; not covered, sealed, locked, or fastened. **open** *n.* A contest for both amateurs and professionals. **open** *v.* To begin or start. **openness** *n.* **openly** *adv.*

open–and–shut (ō´pen an shut´) *adj.* Easily settled; simple to decide.

op-er-a (ō´pĕr a) *n.* Drama having music as a dominant factor, an orchestral accompaniment, acting, and scenery.

op-er-ate (op´e rāt´) *v.* To function, act, or work effectively; to perform an operation, as surgery. **operative** *adj.*

op-er-a-tion (op´e rā´shan) *n.* The process of operating; the system or method of operating; a series of acts to effect a certain purpose; a process; a procedure performed on the human body with surgical instruments to restore health; various mathematical or logical processes.

oph-thal-mol-o-gy (of´thal mol´o jē) *n.* A branch of medical science dealing with diseases of the eye, its structure, and functions.

o-pin-ion (o pin´yan) *n.* A judgment held with confidence; a conclusion held without positive knowledge.

o-pi-um (ō pē um) *n.* A bitter, highly addictive drug; a narcotic.

op-po-nent (o pō´ nent) *n.* An adversary; one who opposes another.

op-por-tune (op´ĕr tŏn´) *adj.* Occurring at the right or appropriate time. **opportunist** *n.* **opportunely** *adv.*

op-por-tu-ni-ty (op´ĕr tŏ´ni tē) *n., pl.* **opportunities** A favorable position; a chance for advancement.

op-pose (o pōz´) *v.* To be in direct contention with; to resist; to be against. **opposable** *adj.* **opposition** *n.*

op-po-site (op´o zot) *adj.* Situated or placed on opposing sides.

op-press (o pres´) *v.* To worry or trouble the mind; to weigh down; to burden as if to enslave. **oppression** *n.*

op-ti-cal (op´ti kal) *adj.* Pertaining to

sight; constructed or designed to assist vision. **optically** *adv.*

op-ti-cian (op tish´an) *n.* A person who makes eyeglasses and other optical articles.

op-ti-mism (op´ti miz´um) *n.* A doctrine which emphasizes that everything is for the best.

op-ti-mum (op´ti mum) *n., pl.* **optima** The degree or condition producing the most favorable result. *adj.* Conducive to the best result.

op-tion (op´shan) *n.* The act of choosing or the power of choice; a choice.

op-tion-al *adj.* Left to one's decision; elective; not required.

op-tom-e-try (op tom´i trē) *n.* The occupation or profession of examining the eyes and prescribing corrective lenses.

op-u-lence (op´ū lens) *n.* Wealth in abundance; affluence.

or (or) *conj.* A word used to connect the second of two choices or possibilities, indicating uncertainty.

-or *suffix* Indicating a person or thing which does something.

or-a-cle (or´u kl) *n.* A seat of worship where ancient Romans and Greeks consulted the gods for answers; a person of unquestioned wisdom.

o-ral (ōr´al) *adj.* Spoken or uttered through the mouth; taken or administered through the mouth. **orally** *adv.*

oral contraceptive *n.* A pill containing hormones, taken monthly to prevent pregnancy.

o-rate (ō rāt´) *v.* To speak in an elevated manner.

orb (orb) *n.* A globe or sphere.

or-bit (or´bit) *n.* The path of a celestial body or a manmade object. *v.* To revolve or move in an orbit; to circle.

or-chard (or´chèrd) *n.* Land that is devoted to the growing of fruit trees.

or-ches-tra (or´ki stra) *n.* A group of musicians performing together on various instruments. **orchestral** *adj.*

or-dain (or dān´) *v.* To appoint as a minister, priest, or rabbi by a special ceremony; to decree.

or-deal (or dēl´) *n.* A painful or severe test of character or endurance.

or-der (or´dèr) *n.* A condition where there is a logical arrangement or disposition of things; sequence or succession; method; an instruction for a person to follow; a request for certain objects. *v.* To command; to demand.

orderly (or´dèr lē) *adj.* Neat, tidy.

or-di-nance (or´di nans) *n.* A command, rule, or order; a law issued by a municipal body.

or-di-nar-y (or´di ner´ē) *adj.* Normal; having no exceptional quality; common; average; plain.

ore (ōr) *n.* A natural underground substance, as a mineral or rock, from which valuable matter is extracted.

o-reg-a-no (o reg´a nō´) *n.* A bushy perennial herb of the mint family, used as a seasoning for food.

Or-e-gon (or´e gon) *n.* A state in the northwestern part of the United States; statehood February 14, 1859; state capital Salem.

or-gan-dy *or* **or-gan-die** (or´gan dē) *n.* A translucent, stiff fabric of cotton or silk.

or-gan-ic (or gan´ik) *adj.* Effecting or pertaining to the organs of an animal or plant. **organically** *adv.*

or-gan-i-za-tion (or´ga ni zā´shan) *n.* The state of being organized or the act of organizing; a group of people united for a particular purpose.

or-gan-ize (or´ga nīz´) *v.* To assemble or arrange with an orderly manner; to arrange by planning.

or-gasm (or´gaz um) *n.* *Physiol.* Intensive emotional excitement; the culmination of a sexual act.

o-ri-ent (ōr´ē ent´) *v.* To determine the bearings or right direction with respect to another source.

or-i-fice (or´i fis) *n.* An opening through which something may pass; a mouth.

or-i-gin (er´i jin) *n.* The cause or beginning of something; the source; a beginning place.

o-rig-i-nal (o rij´i nal) *adj.* Belonging to the first or beginning. *n.* A new idea produced by one's own imagination; the first of a kind. **originality** *n.*

or-na-ment (or´na ment) *n.* A decoration. *v.* To adorn or beautify. **ornamen-tal** *adj.* **ornamentation** *n.*

or-nate (or nāt´) *adj.* Excessively ornamental; elaborate; showy, as a style of writing.

or-phan (or´fan) *n.* A child whose parents are deceased. **orphanage** *n.*

or-ris (or´is) *n.* Any of several species having a fragrant root and used in medicine, perfumes, and cosmetics.

or-tho-don-tics (or´tho don´tiks) *n.* The branch of dentistry dealing with the correction and prevention of irregularities of the teeth.

or-tho-dox (or´tho doks´) *adj.* Following established traditions and beliefs, especially in religion.

or-tho-pe-dics *or* **or-tho-pae-dics** (or´ thōpē´diks) *n.* A branch of surgery that deals with correcting skeletal deformities.

os-cil-late (os´i lāt) *v.* To swing back and forth with regular motion, as a pendulum. **oscillation** *n.* **oscillator** *n.*

os-mi-um (oz´mē um) *n.* A hard but brittle metallic element symbolized as OS.

os-mo-sis (oz mō'sis) n. The tendency of fluids separated by a semipermeable membrane to pass through it and become mixed and equal in strength.

os-ten-ta-tion (os'ten tā'shan) n. The act of displaying pretentiously in order to excite.

osteo n., comb. form Bone; pertaining to the bones.

os-te-op-a-thy (os'tē op'a thē) n. A medical practice based on the theory that diseases are due chiefly to abnormalities of the body, which can be restored by manipulation of the parts by therapeutic measures.

os-teo-po-ro-sis n. A disorder causing gradual deterioration of bone tissue, usually occurring in older women.

os-tra-cize (os'tra sīz') v. To exile or exclude from a group; to shut out.

oth-er (uth'ér) adj. Additional; alternate; different from what is implied or specified. other pron. A different person or thing.

oth-er-wise (uth'ér wīz') adv. Under different conditions of circumstances.

ot-ter (ot'ér) n., pl. otter or otters Web-footed aquatic mammals, related to the weasel.

ouch (ouch) n. & interj. An exclamation to express sudden pain.

ought (ot) v. Used to show or express a moral duty or obligation; to be advisable or correct.

ounce (ouns) n. A unit of weight which equals 1/16 of a pound.

our (our) adj. Of or relating to us ourselves. our pron. The possessive case of the pronoun we.

oust (oust) v. To eject; to remove with force.

out (out) adv. Away from the center or inside. adj. Away. n. A means of escape. prep. Through; forward from.

out-break (out'brāk') n. A sudden outburst; an occurrence.

out-cast (out'kast') n. A person who is excluded; a homeless person.

out-come (out'kum') n. A consequence or result.

out-let (out'let) n. An exit.

out-line (out'līn') n. A rough draft showing the main features of something. outline v.

out-put (out'pet') n. Production or yield during a given time.

out-stand-ing (out'stan'ding) adj. Excellent; prominent; unsettled, as a bill owed; projecting.

o-val (ō'val) adj. Having the shape of an egg; an ellipse.

o-va-ry (ō'va rē) n., pl. -ies One of the pair of female reproductive glands.

o-va-tion (ō vā'shan) n. An enthusiastic display of approval for a person or a performance; applause.

ov-en (uv'en) n. An enclosed chamber used for baking, drying, or heating.

o-ver (ō'vér) prep. Above; across; upon. adv. Covering completely; thoroughly; again; repetition. adj. Higher; upper. prefix Excessive, as overcrowded.

over-act (ō'vér akt') v. To act in an exaggerated way.

over-all (ō'vér ol') adj. Including or covering everything; from one side or end to another; generally. n. Pants with a bib and shoulder straps.

over-con-fi-dence (ō'vér kon'fi dens) n. Extreme or excessive confidence.

over-do (ō'vér dō') v. To do anything excessively; to overcook.

over-dose (ō'vér dōs') n. To take an excessive dose of medication, especially narcotics.

over-due (ō'vér dō') adj. Past the time of return or payment.

overload n. In computer science, a condition that can cause a crash, due to an attempt to transfer more data than memory can hold or transferring data faster than the CPU can process it.

over-ride (ō'vér rīd') v. To disregard; to take precedence over; to declare null and void.

over-sight (ō'vér sīt') n. A mistake made inadvertently.

overt (ō vert') adj. Open to view.

overwrite v. In computer science, to save information to storage already occupied, obliterating the old data.

o-void (ō'void) adj. Having the shape of an egg.

ov-u-late (ō'vū lāt') n. To discharge or produce eggs from an ovary.

o-vum (ō'vum) n. pl. ova The female reproductive cell.

owe (ō) v. To be in debt for a certain amount; to have a moral obligation.

owl (oul) n. A predatory nocturnal bird, having large eyes, a short, hooked bill, and long powerful claws. owlish adj.

own (ōn) adj. Belonging to oneself. own v. To possess; to confess; to admit; to have, as property. owner n.

ox (oks) n., pl. oxen A bovine animal used domestically in much the same way as a horse; an adult castrated bull.

ox-ide (ok'sīd) n. A compound of oxygen and another elements.

ox-y-gen (ok'si jen) n. A colorless, odorless, tasteless gaseous element essential to life, symbolized by O.

oys-ter (oi'stér) n. An edible marine mollusk having an irregularly shaped shell.

oyster bed n. A breading area or place for oysters.

o-zone (ō'zōn) n. A pale-blue gas formed of oxygen with an odor like chlorine, formed by an electrical discharge in the air. Slang Fresh air.

P, p (pē) The 16th letter of the English alphabet.

pab-u-lom (pan´ū lʉm) *n.* Type of food such as an absorbable solution.

pa-ca (pä´kʌ) n. A large brown with white spots, rodent from Central and South America.

pace (pās) *n.* A person's step in walking or the length of a person's step; stride; the gait of a horse in which the legs on the same side are moved at the same time. **pacer** *n.*

pace-mak-er (pās´mā´kėr) *n.* The person who sets the pace for another in a race; a surgically implanted electronic instrument used to stabilize or stimulate the heartbeat.

pa-chi-si (pʌ chē´zē) *n.* Another name for the game Parcheesi; ancient board game played with dice.

pach-y-derm (pak´i dûrm˝) *n.* A group of animals including the elephant, the rhinoceros, and hippo; animals having thick skins. **pachydermal** *adj.*

Pa-cif-ic (pʌ sif´ik) *n.* The largest ocean on the earth, extending from North & South America westward to Asia and Australia.

pa-cif-i-ca-tion (pas´i fi kā´shʌn) *n.* The state of something being pacified or calmed.

pac-i-fism (pas´i fiz˝um) *n.* The policy dealing with the establishment of universal peace between all nations; opposition to violence or war as a means of settling problems or disputes.

pac-i-fy (pas´i fī) *v.* To quiet or soothe anger or distress; to calm.

pack (pak) *n.* A bundle; a group or number of things tied or wrapped up; a full set of associated or like things, such as a pack of cards; a group of wolves or wild dogs that hunt together. *v.* To put things together in a trunk, box, or suitcase, to put away for storage. **packing** Material used to make a tight connection, as in steam pipes.

package (pak´ij) *n.* Something tied up, wrapped or bound together.

pack-et (pak´ĭt) *n.* A type of parcel or package that is small in size and can be used to carry or hold small items.

pact (pakt) *n.* An agreement between nations, groups, or people.

pad (pad) *n.* Anything stuffed with soft material and used to protect against blows; a cushion; a drawing or writing tablet of paper gummed together at one edge; the cushion-like part of the foot on some animals, as the dog. *Slang* A person's home. *v.* To stuff, line, or protect with soft material; to extend or lengthen something by inserting unnecessary matter; to travel by foot in a soft and nearly inaudible way.

pad-ding (pad ing) *n.* The material, as cotton, or synthetic fibers, which is used for the purpose of protecting something.

pad-dle (pad´l) *n.* A broad-bladed implement usually made from wood, used to steer and propel a small boat; a tool used for mixing, turning, or stirring; a small wooden, rounded racket used in table tennis. **paddle** *v.*

pad-dy (pad´ē) *n.* Land usually in China, which is flooded with water and used for the purpose of growing rice.

pad-lock (pad´lok) *n.* A detachable lock, having a pivoted u-shaped hasp which can be inserted through a ring and then locked. **padlock** *v.*

pa-dre (pä´ drä) *n.* A title used in Spain and Italy for a priest.

pa-dro-ne (pʌ drō´nē) *n.* The person who is master of a vessel; the owner or operator of a business; an innkeeper.

pad-u-a-soy (paj´ö ʌ soi˝) *n.* A corded, rich silk fabric.

pae-an (pē´ʌn) *n.* A song of praise or joy.

pae-do-gen-e-sis (pē´dʌ jen´i sis) *n.* The reproduction by immature animals.

pae-on (pē´on) *n.* A type of metrical foot that is made up of four syllables, one long and three short.

pa-gan (pā´gʌn) *n.* A person who does not acknowledge God in any religion; a heathen. **pagan** *adj.* **paganism** *n.*

page (pāj) *n.* A person hired to deliver messages or run errands; one side of the leaf of a book or letter. In *computer science*, a unit of memory used by the computer to manipulate data in storage; a single sheet of output from the printer. **page** *v.* To call or summon a person.

pag-eant (paj´ent) *n.* An elaborate exhibition or spectacular parade for public celebration; anything having a showy appearance.

pag-eant-ry (paj´en trē) *n.* A type of exhibition that is showy; a spectacle.

pag-i-nate (paj´i nāt˝) *v.* To number or to place numbers on a page showing the order in which they should be placed in order to read.

pa-go-da (pʌ gō´dʌ) *n.* A sacred Buddhist tower, built as a memorial or shrine.

paid *v.* Past tense of pay.

pail (pāl) *n.* A cylindrical container usually having a handle; a bucket.

pail-ful (pāl´fül˝) *adj.* The total amount that a pail is able to hold.

pail-lasse (pal yas˝) *n.* A type of mattress that is filled with wood shavings and can be used under another mattress for support.

pail-lon (pä yän˝) *n.* A type of metallic foil which is used for the purpose of enamel work.

pain (pān) *n.* The unpleasant feeling

resulting from injury or disease; any distress or suffering of the mind; sorrow. v. To cause or experience pain.

pain-kill-er (pān kil´ér) n. Medication that relieves pain. **painkilling** adj.

pains-tak-ing (pānz´tā´king) adj. To be given to taking pains; done with carefulness and diligence.

paint (pānt) n. A mixture of colors or pigments which are spread on a surface as protection or as a decorative coating; makeup for the face, as rouge. v. To apply paint to a surface; the practice of using paint to express oneself on canvas. **painter** n. **painting** n.

paint-ing (pān´ting) n. The piece of art that is made by a painter and can be hung on one's wall for decoration.

pair (pâr) n. pl. **pairs** or **pair** Two things which are similar and used together; something made of two parts which are used together; two persons or animals which live or work together.

pais-ley (pāz´lē) adj. To have colors that are bright and patterned into a design which is typical of paisley.

pa-ja-mas (pa jäm´az) n. pl. A loose fitting garment for sleeping, consisting of a jacket and pants.

pal (pal) n. A good friend.

pal-ace (pal´is) n. The royal residence of a sovereign, as of a king; a mansion.

pal-a-din (pal´a din) n. One who is an eminent hero.

pa-laes-tra (pa les´tra) n. A type of school of ancient Greece that was used to teach athletics.

pal-at-a-ble (pal´a ta bl) adj. Pleasant to the taste; agreeable to one's feelings or mind.

pal-a-tal (pal´a tal) adj. To be pertaining or to be related to the palate.

pal-ate (pal´it) n. The muscular tissue at the roof of a person's mouth, opposite the tongue; sense of taste.

pa-la-tial (pa lā´shal) adj. Pertaining to a palace. **palatialness** n.

pal-a-tine (pal´a tīn´) adj. To be related to the palate of one's mouth. n. A lord invested with royal privileges within his territory.

pa-lav-er (pa lav´ér) n. A type of discussion; superfluous talk.

pale (pāl) n. The pointed stake of a fence; a picket; an area that is enclosed within bounds. adj. Having a whitish or lighter than normal complexion; pallid; weak.

pa-le-eth-nol-o-gy (pā´lē eth nol´o jē) n. A part or branch of ethnology which deals with the earliest human races known.

pa-le-o-bot-a-ny (pā´lē ō bot´a nē) n. A study of plants which are discovered in their fossilized state or condition.

pa-le-og-ra-phy (pā´lē og´ra fē) n. The study of ancient writings. **paleog-**

raphically adv. **paleographer** n.

pa-le-o-lith (pā´lē o lith) n. A stone implement that is from the Paleolithic period.

pa-le-on-tol-o-gy (pā´lē on tol´o jē) n. The study and the science which deals with ancient life and how they lived.

pa-le-o-zo-ol-o-gy (pā´lē ō zō ol´o jē) n. The science or the study of the fossil animals.

pal-ette (pal´it) n. A thin oval board with a hole for the thumb, on which an artist lays and mixes colors.

pal-frey (pol´frē) n. A type of small horse that is used by a lady.

pal-imp-sest (pal´imp sest´) n. A piece of writing paper from which something has been erased and another writing has been written over, leaving the first faintly visible.

pal-in-drome (pal´in drōm´) n. A word, number, or sentence which reads the same backward or forward, such as toot or 1991.

pal-ing (pā´ling) n. A type of fence which is made from pales or pickets.

pal-in-gen-e-sis (pal´in jen´i sis) n. The regeneration or the rebirth of someone or something. **palingenetically** adv.

pal-i-node (pal´i nōd´) n. A poem that contains something from a previous piece; a recantation. **palinodist** n.

pal-i-sade (pal´i sād´) n. A fence made of stakes for protection. **palisade** v.

pall (pol) n. A heavy cloth used to cover a bier or coffin; a very gloomy atmosphere.

pal-la-di-um (pa lā´dē um) n. A silvery-white metallic element symbolized by Pd.

pal-let (pal´it) n. A wooden platform on which material for freight shipments can be moved or stored.

pal-li-al (pal´ē al) adj. To be related to or pertaining to pallium.

pal-li-ate (pal´ē āt´) v. To conceal something with an excuse.

pal-lid (pal´id) adj. Deficient in color; lacking sparkle.

pal-lor (pal´ér) n.Lacking color.

palm (päm) n. The inner area of the hand between the fingers and wrist; any of a large group of tropical evergreen trees, having an unbranched trunk with a top or crown of fan-like leaves. v. To hide something small in or about the hand.

pal-mar (pal´mèr) adj. To be located or situated in the palm of one's hand.

pal-met-to (pal met´ō) n. A type of palm tree that has fan-shaped leaves. *Palmetto* The nickname for the state of South Carolina.

palm-is-try (pä´mi strē) n. The practice of fortune telling by the configurations of the palms of the hands.

palmitic acid *n.* A type of fatty acid that is used for the making of soap.

pal-mi-tin (pal′mi tin) *n.* A type of colorless compound that is found in palm oil and can be used in the making of soap.

palm-y (pä′mē) *adj.* To be prosperous.

pal-my-ra (pal mī′ra) *n.* A type of palm that is used for the making of stiff brushes.

pal-o-min-o (pal′o mē′nō) *n.* A type of horse that has a coat which is golden in color and a mane that is flaxen.

pal-pa-ble (pal′pa bl) *adj.* To be capable of being touched or felt by someone or something; easily detected; obvious; plain. **palpably** *adv.* **palpability** *n.*

pal-pate (pal′pāt) *v.* To check something through the use of touch, such as a doctor would examine a patient.

pal-pe-bral (pal′pe bral) *adj.* To be located near the eyelid of someone or something.

pal-pus (pal′pus) *n.* A type of organ found on certain insects and is used for the purpose of sensing.

pal-sy (pol′zē) *n. pl.* -ies Paralysis; the loss of ability to control one's movements. **palsy** *v.*

pal-ter (pol′tė) *v.* To haggle over something, such as the price of a good.

pal-try (pol′trē) *adj.* To be worthless or inferior. **paltriness** *n.*

pa-lu-dal (pa löd′al) *adj.* To be related to or referring to a marsh.

pal-u-drine (pal′ū drēn′) *n.* A type of drug which is used for the purpose of treating malaria in people.

pam-pas (pam′paz) *n.* The grassy plains that can be found in South America

pam-per (pam′pėr) *v.* To treat with extreme care.

pam-pe-ro (päm pâr′ō) *n.* The strong and cold wind that blows in the pampas of South America and coming from the Andes mountain chain.

pam-phlet (pam′flit) *n.* A brief publication which is not permanently bound

pan (pan) *n.* A type of vessel that is usually made of metal and is used for the cooking of foods over heat.

pan-a-ce-a (pan′a sē′a) *n.* A remedy for all diseases, difficulties, or ills; a cure-all.

pa-nache (pa nash′) *n.* A type of showy plume that is worn on a cap.

pan-cake (pan′kāk′) *n.* A thin, flat cake made from batter and fried on a griddle, served with butter, powdered sugar, syrup, and other toppings.

pan-chro-mat-ic (pan′krō mat′ik) *adj.* To be sensitive to the light of all of the colors.

pan-cra-ti-um (pan krā′shē a) *n.* A type of gymnastic context that was held in ancient Greece and contained a combination of wrestling and boxing.

pan-cre-as (pan′krē as) *n., Anat.* A large, irregularly shaped gland situated behind the stomach which releases digestive enzymes and produces insulin. **pancreatic** *adj.*

pan-cre-at-ec-to-my (pan′krēt omē) *n.* The surgical removal of any part or all of the pancreas.

pan-de-mo-ni-um (pan′de mō′nē um) *n.* A place marked with disorder and wild confusion; disorder; confusion.

pan-der *or* **panderer** (pan′dėr) *n.* A go-between in sexual affairs; a pimp; one who profits from the base desires or passions of others. *v.* To act as a panderer for someone.

pan-dit (pan′dėt) *n.* A man who is respected highly.

pan-dow-dy (pan dou′dē) *n.* A type of deep-dish pie that has been made with apples.

pan-e-gry-ic (pan′i jir′ik) *n.* A type of writing about a person that praises them.

pan-el (pan′el) *n.* A flat, rectangular piece of material, often wood, which forms a part of a surface; a group of people selected to participate in a discussion group or to serve on a jury. **panelist** *n.* **panel** *v.*

pan-eling (pan′el ing) *n.* A type of wood that has been made into panels and is used to cover walls for decoration.

pan-e-tel-la (pan′i tel′a) *n.* A type of cigar that has one end that is slender.

pang (pang) *n.* A sudden and sharp pain that does not last for very long.

pan-go-lin (pang gō′lin) *n.* A type of scaled mammal that has a pointed tail and eats ants, found in Africa.

pan-han-dle (pan′han′dl) *n.* A projecting strip of land that is not a peninsula, such as the state of Texas.

pan-ic (pan′ik) *n.* A sudden unreasonable fear which overpowers. *v.* To cause or to experience panic. **panicky** *adj.*

pan-ic-strick-en (pan′ik strik′en) *adj.* To be overcome by great fear.

panne (pan) *n.* A type of light-weight velvet.

pan-nier (pan′yėr) *n.* One of a pair of large baskets which are carried on either side of an animal or over a person's back.

pan-ni-kin (pan′i kin) *n.* A small cup or pan.

pan-o-cha (pa nō′cha) *n.* A type of sugar that has a course grade and can be found in Mexico.

pan-o-ply (pan′o plē) *n. pl.* -lies The complete equipment of a warrior, including his armor and weapons.

pan-o-ram-a (pan′o ram′a) *n.* An unlimited or complete view in all directions of what is visible.

pan-sy (pan´zē) *n.* A garden plant with flowers bearing blossoms in a variety of colors.

pant (pant) *v.* To breathe in rapid or short gasps; to yearn. *n.* A short breath.

pan-ta-lets (pan´ta lets´) *n.* A type of underpants that are long and have a fringed bottom.

pan-tech-ni-con *n.* A type of storehouse that is used to store furniture.

✓**pan-the-ism** (pan´thē iz´um) *n.* The belief that the laws and forces of nature are all manifestations of God. **pantheist** *n.* **pantheistic** *adj.*

pan-the-on (pan´thē on´) *n.* A type of building or temple that was built in order to honor all the gods.

pan-ther (pan´thėr) *n.* A black leopard in its unspotted form. **pantheress** *n.*

pan-ther-ess (pan´thėr is) *n.* The female panther.

pan-to-mime (pan´to mīm´) *n.* Communication done solely by means of facial and body gestures. *v.* To express or act in pantomime.

pan-to-then-ic ac-id (pan´to then´ik as´id) *n.* A type of vitamin belonging to the B complex that promotes cell growth.

pan-try (pan´trē) *n.* A closet or room for the storage of food, dishes, and other kitchen items.

pants (pants) *n.* Trousers; underpants.

pan-zer (pan´zėr) *n.* A type of German tank.

pap (pap) *n.* A soft food for invalids or babies.

pa-pa-cy (pā´pa sē) *n.* The dignity or jurisdiction of a pope; a pope's term in office.

pa-pa-in (pa pā´ in) *n.* A type of enzyme that is found in the juice of the unripe fruit of the papaya tree.

pa-pa-ya (pa pä´ya) *n.* A type of tropical tree that will yield melon-like fruits.

pa-per (pā´pėr) *n.* A substance made of pulp from wood and rags, formed into sheets for printing, wrapping and writing.

pa-per-back (pā´pėr bak´) *n.* A book with its cover made of paper.

pa-pier--ma-che (pā´pėr ma shā) *n.* A material consisting of paper mixed with glue or paste which can be molded when wet and becomes hard when dry.

pap-il-lo-ma (pap´i lō´ma) *n.* A type of benign tumor that exists on mucous membranes or the skin.

pa-poose (pa pös´) *n.* A North American Indian child or baby.

pa-pri-ka (pa prē´ka) *n.* A dark red seasoning powder made by grinding red peppers.

Pap test *n.* A test in which a smear of bodily secretion from the uterus is examined for the early detection of cancer.

pap-ule (pap´ūl) *n.* A type of elevation in the skin that does not contain pus, but is inflammatory. **papular** *adj.*

pa-py-rus (pa pī´rus) *n.* A reed-like plant used as paper in early Egypt, to write upon.

par-a-bi-o-sis (par´a bī ō´sis) *n.* The joining or fusion of two separate organisms, such as Siamese twins.

par-a-ble (par´a bl) *n.* A short, fictitious story which illustrates a moral lesson.

par-a-chute (par´a shŏt´) *n.* A folding umbrella-shaped apparatus of light fabric used to make a safe landing after a free fall from an airplane. **-ist** *n.*

pa-rade (pa rād´) *n.* An organized public procession; a march. **parader** *n.*

par-a-di-chlor-ben-zene (par´a dīklôr´ ben´zēn) *n.* A white compound used as an insecticide.

par-a-dise (par´a dīs´) *n.* A state or place of beauty, bliss or delight; heaven. **paradisiac** *adj.* **paradisiacal** *adj.*

par-a-dox (par´a doks´) *n.* A statement which seems opposed to common sense or contradicts itself, but is perhaps true. **paradical** *adj.*

par-aes-the-sia (par´is thē´zha) *n.* An abnormal sensation, as the prickling of the skin.

par-af-fin (par´a fin) *n.* A white, waxy sub-stance derived from petroleum and used to make lubricants, candles, and sealing materials. **paraffin** *v.*

par-a-gen-e-sis (par´a jen´i sis) *n.* A type of formation of minerals where they are too close together and impact on one another's development. **paragenetic** *n.* **paragenetically** *adv.*

par-a-go-ge (par´a gō´jē) *n.* An addition of a letter or syllable to the end of a word that is incorrect.

par-a-gon (par´a gon´) *n.* A pattern or model of excellence or perfection.

par-a-graph (par´a graf´) *n.* A section of a composition dealing with a single idea, containing one or more sentences with the first line usually indented.

par-al-de-hyde (pa ral´de hīd´) *n.* A type of colorless liquid that can be used in medicine as a hypnotic.

par-al-lel (par´a lel´) *adj.* Moving in the same direction but separated by a distance, as railroad tracks. *n.* A parallel curve, line, or surface; a comparison; one of the imaginary lines which circle the earth paralleling the equator and mark the latitude. In computer science, descriptive of operations that occur simultaneously. **parallelism** *n.*

parallel bars *n.* One pair of bars that are horizontal and supported by uprights.

par-al-lel-o-gram (par´a lel´o gram´) *n.* A four-sided figure having parallel opposite sides which are equal.

parallel interface n. In *computer science*, a multichannel interface that allows the transfer of a full computer word at one time.

parallel port v. In *computer science*, a connection on the computer for communicating with a peripheral device, such as a printer.

pa-ral-o-gism (pa ral´o jiz´um) n. A type of argument that is fallacious.

pa-ral-y-sis (pa ral´i sis) n., pl. **paralyses** Complete or partial loss of the ability to feel sensation or to move.

par-a-lyze (par´a līz´) v. To cause to be inoperative or powerless.

par-a-mat-ta (par´a mat´a) n. A type of light twilled fabric that can be used for the making of dresses.

par-a-med-ic (par´a med´ik) n. A person trained to give emergency medical treatment until a doctor is available.

par-am-ne-sia (par´am nē´zha) n. The illusion of remembering things that have not yet been experienced.

parameter n. In *computer science*, a limit or characteristic, as of a program or operating system. *Math.* A term in a mathematical expression.

par-a-mount (par´a mount´) adj. Superior to all others in rank, importance, and power.

par-a-mour (par´a mür) n. An unlawful lover.

pa-rang (pä´räng) n. A type of knife that is large and heavy.

par-a-noi-a (par´a noi´a) n. Mental insanity marked by systematic delusions of persecution or grandeur.

par-a-noid (par´a noid´) adj. To be marked by paranoia.

par-a-nor-mal (par´a nor´mal) adj. To be supernatural in character.

par-a-pet (par´a pit) n. A type of covering or wall that is used to protect the soldiers from the attacks of the enemy in front of them.

par-a-pher-na-lia (par´a fèr nāl´ya) n. Personal effects or belongings, the apparatus or articles used in some activities; equipment.

par-a-phrase (par´a frāz´) v. To put something written or spoken into different words while retaining the same meaning.

par-a-phras-tic (par´a fras´tik) adj. To be making or forming a paraphrase.

par-a-ple-gi-a (par´a plē´jē a) n. The paralysis of the lower trunk and of both legs.

par-a-site (par´a sīt´) n. Biol. An organism which lives, grows, feeds, and takes shelter in or on another organism; a person depending entirely on another without providing something in return.

par-a-sit-i-cide (par´a sit´i sīd´) n. A

type of agent that is used to destroy parasites.

par-a-si-tize (par´a si tīz´) v. To live upon another object as a parasite.

par-a-sol (par´a sol´) n. A small umbrella used as protection from the sun.

par-a-thi-on (par´a thī´on) n. A type of insecticide that is very poisonous.

parathyroid gland n. The four glands that are located in or near the thyroid gland and are used for the control of calcium in the blood.

par-a-troops (par´a trö´ps) n. Troops which are equipped and trained to parachute behind enemy lines.

par-a-ty-phoid (par´a tī´foid) n. A type of very infectious bacterial disease that has symptoms which are like those of typhoid fever.

par-boil (pär´boil´) v. To precook something in boiling water.

par-cel (pär´sel) n. A wrapped package; a bundle; a portion or plat of land.

parch (pärch) v. To become very dry from intense heat; to become dry from thirst or the lack of water.

parch-ment (pärch´ment) n. Goatskin or sheepskin prepared with a pumice stone and used as a material for writing or drawing.

par-don (pär´don) v. To forgive someone for an offense; in law, to allow a convicted person freedom from the penalties of an office or crime. **pardonable** adj. **pardonably** adv.

pare (pâr) v. To cut away or remove the outer surface gradually. **parer** n.

par-e-go-ric (par´e gor´ik) n. A medication used to relieve stomach pains.

par-ent (pâr´ent) n. A mother or father; a forefather; an ancestor; a source.

par-ent-age (pâr´en tij) n. The origin or birth of someone.

par-en-ter-al (pa ren´tèr al) adj. To be introduced into the body by means other than the digestive tract.

pa-ren-the-sis (pa ren´thi sis) n., pl. **parentheses** One of a pair of curved lines ( ) used to enclose a qualifying or explanatory remark.

pa-re-sis (pa rē´sis) n. A type of paralysis that is incomplete and affecting only movement. **paretic** adj.

par-fleche (pär´flesh) n. The hide of an animal that has been dried upon a frame, such as the buffalo.

par-get (pär´jit) v. To cover something with plaster.

pa-ri-ah (pa rī´a) n. A person who is thought of as an outcast.

pa-ri-e-tal (pa rī´i tal) adj. Referring to the two bones of the skull which form the side and the top.

par-ing (pâr´ing) n. The action of cutting or of paring a piece of a vegetable off, such as with a potato.

par-ish (par´ish) *n.* In association with the Roman Catholic Church, the district under the charge of a priest; the members of a parish.

par-i-ty (par´i tē) *n.* Equal in amount, character, or status; the fact of having borne children.

park (pärk) *n.* A tract of land used for recreation. **park** *v.* To leave something temporarily in a parking garage or lot, as a car.

par-ka (pär´ka) *n.* A cloth jacket with an attached hood.

par-lia-ment (pär´li ment) *n.* The assembly which constitutes the law making body of various countries, as the United Kingdom.

par-lia-men-ta-ry *adj.* To be relating or pertaining to a parliament.

par-lor (pär´lėr) *n.* A room for entertaining visitors or guests; a business offering a personal service, as beauty parlor, ice cream parlor, or funeral parlor.

par-lous *adj.* To be dangerous; clever.

pa-ro-chi-al (pa rō´kē al) *adj.* Belonging to a local parish; having to do with a parish.

pa-ro-chi-al-ism (pa rō´kē a liz˝um) *n.* A condition or state of being parochial.

parochial school *n.* A type of school which is maintained by the parish.

par-o-dy (par´o dē) *n., pl.* **-ies** A composition, song, or poem which mimics another in a ridiculous way.

pa-rol (pa rōl´) *n.* An oral statement.

pa-role (pa rōl´) *n.* The conditional release of a prisoner before his sentence expires. **parole** *adj.*

parotid gland *n.* A type of salivary gland that is located in front of each ear.

pa-rot-i-di-tis (pa rot´i dī´tis) *n.* The swelling and inflammation of the parotid glands.

par-ox-ysm (par´ok siz˝um) *n.* A violent attack or outburst; a spasm.

par-quet (pär kā) *n.* A main floor of the theater which will extend back from the orchestra pit.

parquet circle *n.* Those seats which are located at the rear of the main floor in a theater.

parr (pär) *n.* A type of salmon when it is young and has not yet entered the salt waters.

par-ri-cide (par´i sīd´) *n.* One who murders his mother or father; the crime of murdering parents. **parricidal** *adj.*

par-rot (par´ot) *n.* A brightly colored, semitropical bird with a strong, hooked bill. **parrot** *v.* To imitate or repeat.

par-rot-fish (par´ot fish˝) *n.* A type of fish that is tropical and has bright colors.

par-ry (par´ē) *v.* To avoid something;

to turn aside. **parry** *n.*

parse (pärs) *v.* To identify the parts of speech in a sentence and to indicate their relationship to each other.

par-si-mo-ny (pär´si mō˝nē) *n.* Extreme reluctance to use one's resources or to spend money. **parsimonious** *adj.* **parsimoniously** *adv.*

pars-ley (pärs´lē) *n.* An herb with curly leaves which is used for seasoning and garnishing.

par-son (pär´son) *n.* A pastor or clergyman.

parsonage (pär´so nij) *n.* The home provided by a church for its parson.

part (pärt) *n.* A segment, portion, or division of a whole; a component for a machine; the role of a character, as in a play; the line which forms where the hair is parted by combing or brushing. **part** *v.* To leave or go away from; to be separated into pieces; to give up control or possession.

par-take (pär tāk´) *v.* To have a share or part; to take; to take a part in something.

par-tial (pär´shal) *adj.* Incomplete; inclined to favor one side more than the other. **partiality** *n.* **partially** *adv.*

par-tic-i-pate (pär tis´i pāt´) *v.* To join in or share; to take part. **participant** *n.* **participation** *n.* **participator** *n.*

par-ti-cle (pär´ti kl) *n.* A very small piece of solid matter. *Gram.* A group of words, such as articles, prepositions, and conjunctions which convey very little meaning but help to connect, specify, or limit the meanings of other words.

par-tic-u-lar (pėr tik´ū lėr) *adj.* Having to do with a specific person, group, thing, or category; noteworthy; precise.

part-ing (pär´ting) *n.* A division; a separation; the place where a division or separation occurs. *adj.* Done, given, or said on departing.

par-ti-tion (pär tish´an) *n.* A separation or division. *v.* To divide. In computer science, as on a disk for file management or for processing a database sort.

part-ner (pärt´nėr) *n.* One who shares something with another.

part-ner-ship (pärt´nėr ship) *n.* Two or more persons who run a business together and share in the profits and losses.

par-tridge (pär´trij) *n.* A plump or stout-bodied game bird.

par-ty (pär´tē) *n. pl.* **-ies** A group of persons who gather for pleasure or entertainment; a group of persons associated together for a common purpose; a group which unites to promote or maintain a policy, a cause, or other purposes, as a political group; *n.* in law, a person or group of people involved in a legal proceeding.

pass (pas) *v.* To proceed; to move; to transfer; to go away or come to an end; to get through a course, trial or test; to approve; to vote for; to give as an opinion or judgment; to hit or throw a ball to another player. **pass** *n.* A ticket or note that allows a person to come and go freely. **come to pass** To happen. **pass away** To die or cease to live. **pass over** To leave out, to ignore.

pas-sage (pas´ij) *n.* The act of going, proceeding, or passing; the enactment by a legislature of a bill into law; a small portion or part of a whole book or speech; something, as a path or channel, through, over or along which something else may pass.

pas-sen-ger (pas´en jér) *n.* One who travels in a vehicle, car, plane, boat, or other conveyance.

pas-sion (pash´an) *n.* A powerful feeling; lust; sexual desire; an outburst of strong feeling; violence or anger. **Passion** The suffering of Christ which followed the Last Supper to the time of his death. **passionless** *adj.* **passionate** *adj.*

pas-sive (pas´iv) *adj.* Not working, acting, or operating; inactive; acted upon, influenced, or affected by something external. *Gram.* Designating the form of a verb which indicates the subject is receiving the action. **passively** *adv* **passivity** *n.* **-ness** *n.*

Pass-o-ver (pas´ō´vér) *n.* The Jewish holiday which commemorates the Exodus from Egypt.

pass-port (pas´pórt) *n.* An official permission issued to a person allowing him to travel out of this country and to return; a document of identification.

past (past) *adj.* Having to do with or existing at a former time. **past** *n.* Before the present time; a person's history or background. **past** *adv.* To go by. **past** *prep.* After; beyond in time; beyond the power, reach, or influence.

paste (pāst) *n.* A mixture usually made from water and flour, used to stick things together; dough used in making pastry; a brilliant glass used in imitating precious stones. **paste** *v.*

pas-tel (pa stel´) *n.* A crayon made of ground pigments; a drawing made with crayons of this kind. **pastel** *adj.* Pale and light in color or shade.

pas-teur-i-za-tion (pas´che rī´zér) *n.* The process of killing disease-producing microorganisms by heating the liquid to a high temperature for a period of time.

pas-time (pas´tīm´) *n.* Spending spare time in a pleasant way; a diversion.

pas-tor (pas´tér) *n.* A Christian clergyman in charge of a church or congregation.

past participle *n.* A participle used with reference to actions and conditions in the past.

pas-try (pā´strē) *n.* Food made with dough or having a crust made of dough, as pies, tarts, or other desserts.

pas-ture (pas´chér) *n.* An area for grazing of domestic animals. **pastured** *v.* **pasturing** *v.* **pasturage** *n.*

pat (pat) *v.* To tap lightly with something flat. *n.* A soft, caressing stroke.

patch (pach) *n.* A piece of fabric used to repair a weakened or torn area in a garment; a piece of cloth with an insignia which represents an accomplishment. *v.* To repair or put together hastily. **patchy** *adj.* **patchable** *adj.*

pat-ent (pat´ent) *n.* A governmental protection assuring an inventor the exclusive right of manufacturing, using, exploiting, and selling an invention. **patent** *adj.* Evident; obvious. **patentee, patency** *n.* **patently** *adv.*

pa-ter-nal (pa ter´nal) *adj.* Relating to or characteristic of a father; inherited from a father. **paternally** *adv.*

path (path) *n.* A track or course; a route; a course of action or life. In *computer science,* the course followed by the computer in seeking programs and files.

pa-thet-ic (pa thet´ik) *adj.* A rousing pity, tenderness, or sympathy.

pa-thol-o-gy (pa thol´o je) *n.* The science that deals with facts about diseases, their nature and causes. **pathologic** *adj.* **pathological** *adj.* **pathologist** *n.*

pa-thos (pā´thos) *n.* A quality in a person that evokes sadness or pity.

pa-tience (pā´shens) *n.* The quality, state, or fact of being patient; the ability to be patient.

pa-tient (pā´shent) *adj.* Demonstrating uncomplaining endurance under distress. *n.* A person under medical care.

pa-tri-arch (pā´trē ärk´) *n.* The leader of a tribe or family who rules by paternal right; a very old and revered man. **patriarchal** *adj.* **patriarchy** *n.*

pa-tri-ot (pā´trē ot) *n.* A person who loves and defends his country. **patriotic** *adj.* **patriotically** *adv.* **patriotism** *n.*

pa-trol (pa trōl´) *n.* Walking around an area for the purpose of maintaining or observing security; a person or group carrying out this action. **patrol** *v.*

pa-tron (pā´tron) *n.* A person who fosters, protects, or supports some person, enterprise, or thing; a regular customer. **patroness** *n.*

pat-sy (pat´sē) *n., pl.* **patsies** *Slang* A person who is taken advantage of.

pat-tern (pat´érn) *n.* Anything designed or shaped to serve as a guide in making something else; a sample. **pattern** *v.* To make according to a pattern.

pat-ty (pat′ē) *n., pl.* **patties** A small, flat piece of chopped meat.

pau-per (po′pėr) *n.* A very poor person who depends on charity. **pauperism** *n.* **pauperize** *v.*

pause (poz) *v.* To linger, hesitate, or stop for a time. **pause** *n.*

pave (pāv) *v.* To surface with gravel, concrete, asphalt, or other material.

pa-vil-ion (pa vil′yon) *n.* A large, roofed structure used for shelter.

paw (po) *n.* The foot of an animal. **paw** *v.* To handle clumsily or rudely.

pawn (pon) *n.* Something given as security for a loan; a hostage; a chessman of little value. **pawn** *v.*

pay (pā) *v.* To give a person what is due for a debt, purchase, or work completed; to compensate; to suffer the consequences.

pay-ment (pā′ment) *n.* The act of paying.

pay-roll (pā′rōl) *n.* The amount of money to be paid to a list of employees.

PC *abbr. & n.* In *computer science,* personal computer, a microcomputer originally designed for individual use at home or in business.

pea (pē) *n.* A round edible seed contained in a pod and grown on a vine.

peace (pēs) *n.* A state of physical or mental tranquillity; calm; serenity; the absence of war; the state of harmony between people. **peaceable** *adj.* **peaceful** *adj.* **peaceably** *adv.*

peak (pēk) *n.* A projecting edge or point; the summit of a mountain; the top. **peak** *v.* To bring to the maximum.

peal (pēl) *n.* The ring of bells; the long, loud sound of thunder or laughter. **peal** *v.* To ring.

pea-nut (pē′nut′) *n.* A nut-like seed which ripens underground; the plant bearing this nut.

pearl (perl) *n.* A smooth, rounded deposit formed around a grain of sand in the shell of various mollusks, especially the oyster; anything which is precious, rare, or fine. **pearly** *adj.*

peas-ant (pez′ant) *n.* A farmhand or rustic workman; an uneducated person of the lowest class. *Slang* Uneducated or uncouth.

peat (pēt) *n.* The black substance formed when plants begin to decay in wet ground, as bogs. **peaty** *adj.*

peb-ble (peb′l) *n.* A small, smooth stone. *v.* To treat, as to give a rough texture.

pe-can (pi kän′) *n.* A large tree of the central and southern United States with an edible oval, thin-shelled nut.

peck (pek) *v.* To strike with the beak; to eat without any appetite, taking only small bites. **peck** *n.* A measure which equals 1/4 of a bushel.

pec-tin (pek′tin) *n.* A complex carbohydrate found in ripe fruits and used in making jelly. **pectic** *adj.*

pe-cu-liar (pi kūl′yėr) *adj.* Odd; strange. **peculiarity** *n.* **peculiarly** *adv.*

ped-al (ped′al) *n.* A lever usually operated by the foot. **pedal** *v.*

ped-dle (ped′l) *v.* To travel around in an attempt to sell merchandise.

ped-es-tal (ped′i stal) *n.* A support or base for a statue. **pedestal** *v.* To set on or provide with a pedestal.

pe-des-tri-an (pe des′trē an) *n.* A person traveling by foot.

pe-di-at-rics (pē′dē a′triks) *n.* The branch of medicine dealing with the care of children and infants. **pediatric** *adj.* **pediatrician** *n.*

ped-i-cure (ped′i kūr′) *n.* The cosmetic care of the toenails and feet.

ped-i-gree (ped′i grē′) *n.* A line of ancestors, especially of an animal of pure breed.

ped-i-ment (ped′i ment) *n.* A broad, triangular architectural or decorative part above a door.

pe-dom-e-ter (pe dom′i tėr) *n.* An instrument which indicates the number of miles one has walked.

pe-dun-cle (pi dung′kl) *n. Biol.* A stalk-like support in some plants and animals.

peek (pēk) *v.* To look shyly or quickly from a place of hiding; to glance.

peel (pēl) *n.* The natural rind or skin of a fruit. *v.* To pull or strip the skin or bark off; to remove in thin layers. *Slang* To undress. **peeler** *n.*

peep (pēp) *v.* To utter a very small and weak sound, as of a young bird.

peer (pēr) *v.* To look searchingly; to come partially into one's view. **peer** *n.* An equal; a member of the British nobility, as a duke or earl.

pee-vish (pē′vish) *adj.* Irritable in mood; cross. **peevishly** *adv.* **peevishness** *n.*

peg (peg) *n.* A small pin, usually of wood or metal; a projecting pin on which something may be hung. *Slang* An artificial leg, often made of wood.

pei-gnoir (pän wär′) *n.* A woman's loose fitting dressing gown.

pe-koe (pē′kō) *n.* A superior black tea made from young or small leaves.

pel-let (pel′it) *n.* A small round ball made from paper or wax; a small bullet or shot.

pelt (pelt) *n.* The skin of an animal with the fur.

pel-vis (pel′vis) *n., pl.* **pelvises** *or* **pelves** The structure of the vertebrate skeleton which rests on the lower limbs, supporting the spinal column.

pen (pen) *n.* An instrument used for writing.

pe-nal (pēn′al) *adj.* Of or pertaining to punishment or penalties.

pen-al-ty (pen′al tē) *n., pl.* **penalties** The

legal punishment for an offense or crime; something which is forfeited when a person fails to meet a commitment; in sports, a punishment or handicap imposed for breaking a rule.

pen-ance (pen´ans) *n.* A voluntary act to show sorrow or repentance for sin.

pen-cil (pen´sil) *n.* A writing or drawing implement made from graphite. *v.* To make, write, or draw with a pencil.

pend-ing (pen´ding) *adj.* Not yet decided; imminent. *prep.* During; until.

pen-du-lous (pen´ja lus) *adj.* Hanging downward so as to swing; wavering.

pen-du-lum (pen´ja lum) *n.* A suspended object free to swing back and forth.

pen-e-trate (pen´i trāt´) *v.* To force a way through or into; to pierce; to enter; to pass through something. **penetrable** *adj.* **penetrating** *adj.* **penetration** *n.*

pen-guin (pen´gwin) *n.* A web-footed, flightless, marine bird of the southern hemisphere.

pen-i-cil-lin (pen´i sil´in) *n.* A powerful antibiotic derived from mold and used to treat certain types of bacterial infections.

pen-in-su-la (pe nin´sa la) *n.* A piece of land projecting into water from a larger land mass. **peninsular** *adj.*

pe-nis (pē´nis) *n., pl.* **penises** The male sex organ; the male organ through which urine leaves the body.

pen-i-tent (pen´i tent) *adj.* Having a feeling of guilt or remorse for one's sins or misdeeds; sorry. **penitence** *n.*

Penn-syl-va-ni-a *n.* A state located in the mideastern part of the United States; statehood December 12, 1787; state capital Harrisburg.

pen-ny (pen´ē) *n., pl.* **pennies** A United States coin worth 1/10th of a dollar or one cent ($.01).

pen sion (pen´shan) *n.* The amount of money a person receives regularly after retirement. **pension** *v.* To pay a person his pension.

pen-sive (pen´siv) *adj.* Involved in serious, quiet reflection; causing melancholy thought. **pensively** *adv.*

pen-ta-gon (pen´ta gon´) *n.* Any object or building having five sides and five interior angles. **Pentagon** The five-sided office building in Arlington, Va. which houses the Defense Department.

peo-ple (pē´pl) *n., pl.* **people** Human beings; a body of persons living in the same country, under the same government, and speaking the same language; one's relatives or family.

pep-per (pep´ér) *n.* A strong, aromatic condiment. *v.* To pelt or sprinkle.

pep-tic (pep´tik) *adj.* Pertaining to or aiding digestion.

per an-num (pér an´um) *adv.* For, by, or in each year; annually.

per-cale (pér kāl´) *n.* A closely woven cotton fabric.

per cap-i-ta (pér kap´i ta) *adj. & adv.* Of each individual.

per-ceive (pér sēv´) *v.* To become aware of by the senses; to understand; to feel or observe. **perceivable** *adj.*

per-cent-age (pér sen´tij) *n.* The rate per hundred; a part or proportion in relation to a whole. *Slang* Profit; advantage.

per-cept (per´sept) *n.* A mental impression of something perceived; the immediate knowledge obtained from perceiving.

perch (perch) *n.* A place on which birds rest or light; any place for standing or sitting; a small, edible freshwater fish having tender white meat.

per-cip-i-ent (pér sip´ent) *adj.* Having the power of perception. **percipience** *n.* **percipiency** *n.*

per-co-late (per´ko lāt´) *v.* To pass or cause to pass through a porous substance; to filter. **percolation** *n.*

per-cus-sion (pér kush´an) *n.* The sharp striking together of one body against another; the striking of a cap in a firearm. *Music* An instrument which makes music when it is struck, as a drum or cymbal.

per-en-ni-al (pe ren´ē al) *adj.* Lasting from year to year; perpetual. *n.* A plant which lives through the winter and blooms again in the spring.

per-fect (per´fikt) *adj.* Having no defect or fault; flawless; accurate; absolute. *v.* To make perfect. **perfectly** *adv.*

per-form (pér form´) *v.* To execute or carry out an action; to act or function in a certain way; to give a performance or exhibition. **performable** *adj.* **performer, performance** *n.*

per-fume (per´fūm) *n.* A fragrant substance which emits a pleasant scent; one distilled from flowers.

per-haps (pér haps´) *adv.* Possibly; maybe; not sure.

per-i-gee (per´i jē´) *n.* The point of an orbit when a satellite of the earth is closest to the earth; the lowest part of an orbit.

per-il (per´il) *n.* A source of danger; exposure to the chance of injury; danger. **perilous** *adj.* **perilously** *adv.*

pe-ri-od (pēr´ē od) *n.* An interval of time marked by certain conditions; an interval of time that is regarded as a phase in development; menstruation; the punctuation mark (.) which indicates the end of a sentence or an abbreviation.

pe-riph-er-y (pe rif´e rē) *n., pl.* -ies The outer part, boundary, or surface.

peripheral *n.* In *computer science*, a

device that is connected to a computer and controlled by it.

peripheral program *n.* In *computer science*, a utility; a program that adds to the capabilities of a computer or another program, such as a memory manager or grammar checker.

per-ish (per´ish) *v.* To ruin or spoil; to suffer an untimely or violent death.

per-i-win-kle (per´i wing´kl) *n.* Any of several edible marine snails; a trailing evergreen plant with blue and sometimes white flowers.

per-jure (per´jer) *v.* To give false testimony while under oath. -**jury** *n.*

per-ma-nent (per´ma nent) *adj.* Continuing in the same state; lasting indefinitely; enduring. **permanent** *n.* A hair wave which gives long lasting curls or body to the hair. **permanence, permanency** *n.* **permanently** *adv.*

permanent memory *n.* In *computer science*, a storage medium, such as a computer disk, that retains its memory when power is off.

per-me-ate (per´mē āt´) *v.* To spread through; to pervade; to pass through the pores. **permeation** *n.*

per-mis-sion (per mish´an) *n.* The act of permitting something; consent.

per-mit (per mit´) *v.* To consent to; to allow. *n.* An official document giving permission for a specific activity.

per-ni-cious (per nish´us) *adj.* Very harmful; malicious. **perniciously** *adv.*

per-ox-ide (pe rok´sīd) *n. Chem.* Oxide containing the highest proportion of oxygen for a given series; a chemical used with other ingredients to bleach the hair.

per-pen-dic-u-lar (per´pen dik´ū ler) *adj.* Being at right angles to the plane of the horizon. *Math.* Meeting a plane or given line at right angles. **perpendicular** *n.* **perpendicularity** *n.*

per-pe-trate (per´pi trāt´) *v.* To perform; to commit; to be guilty. **perpetration** *n.* **perpetrator** *n.*

per-pet-u-al (per pech´ö al) *adj.* Lasting or continuing forever or an unlimited time. **perpetually** *adv.*

per-plex (per pleks´) *v.* To confuse or be confused; to make complicated. **perplexing** *adj.* **perplexingly** *adv.*

per-se-cute (per´se kūt´) *v.* To harass or annoy persistently; to oppress because of one's religion, beliefs, or race. **persecution** *n.* **persecutor** *n.*

per-se-vere (per´se vēr´) *v.* To persist in any purpose or idea; to strive in spite of difficulties or obstacles. **perseverance** *n.* **perseveringly** *adv.*

per-sim-mon (per sim´on) *n.* A tree having reddish-orange, edible fruit.

per-sist (per sist´) *v.* To continue firmly despite obstacles; to endure. **persis-**

tence *n.* **persistency** *n.* **persistent** *adj.*

per-son (per´son) *n.* A human being; an individual; the personality of a human being. *Law* Any human being, corporation, or other entity having legal rights and duties.

per-son-al (per´so nal) *adj.* Belonging to a person or persons; of the body or person; relating to oneself; done by oneself.

per-son-nel (per´so nel´) *n.* The body of people working for a business or service.

per-spec-tive (per spek´tiv) *n.* A painting or drawing technique in which objects seem to have depth and distance.

per-spi-ra-tion (per´spi rā shan) *n.* The salty fluid excreted from the body by the sweat glands.

per-spire (per spīer´) *v.* To give off perspiration.

per-suade (per swād´) *v.* To cause to convince or believe by means of reasoning or argument. **persuader** *n.* **persuasiveness** *n.* **persuasive** *adj.*

per-tain (per tān´) *v.* To relate to; to refer to; to belong as a function, adjunct or quality; to be appropriate or fitting.

per-ti-na-cious (per´ti nā´shus) *adj.* Adhering firmly to an opinion, belief, or purpose; stubbornly persistent. **pertinaciously** *adv.* **pertinacity** *n.*

per-ti-nent (per´ti nent) *adj.* Relating to the matter being discussed; or the matter at hand.

per-turb (per terb´) *v.* To disturb, make anxious, or make uneasy; to cause confusion. **perturbation** *n.*

per-vade (per vād´) *v.* To spread through every part of something; to permeate.

per-ver-sion (per ver´zhan) *n.* The act of being led away from the accepted course; a deviant form of sexual behavior.

per-vert (per vert´) *v.* To lead away from the proper cause; to use in an improper way. *n.* A person practicing or characterized by sexual perversion. **perverted** *adj.* **pervertible** *adj.*

pes-si-mism (pes´i miz´um) *n.* The tendency to take a gloomy view of affairs or situations and to anticipate the worst. **pessimist** *n.* **pessimistic** *adj.*

pest (pest) *n.* A person or thing which is a nuisance; an annoying person or thing; a destructive insect, plant, or animal.

pes-ter (pes´ter) *v.* To harass with persistent annoyance; to bother.

pes-ti-cide (pes´ti sīd´) *n.* A chemical substance used to destroy rodents, insects, and pests. **pesticidal** *adj.*

pes-ti-lence (pes´ti lens) *n.* A widespread and often fatal infectious disease, as bubonic plague or cholera.

pet-al (pet´al) *n. Bot.* One of the leaf-like parts of a flower.

pe-tite (pe tēt´) *adj.* Small in size; little.

pet-it four (pet´ē fōr´) *n., pl.* petit fours A small decorated cake.

pe-ti-tion (pe tish´an) *n.* A solemn request or prayer; a formal written request addressed to a group or person in authority. **petitioner** *n.*

pet-ri-fy (pe´tri fī´) *v.* To convert into a stony mass; to make fixed or immobilize, as in the face of danger or surprise. **petrification** *n.*

pe-tro-le-um (pe trō´lē um) *n.* An oily, thick liquid which develops naturally below the ground surface, used in products such as gasoline, fuel oil, and kerosene.

pew (pū) *n.* A row of bench-like seats for seating people in church.

pew-ter (pū´ter) *n.* An alloy of tin with copper, silver-gray in color and used for tableware and kitchen utensils.

pfen-nig *n., pl.* -nigs *or* -nige A small coin of Germany, equal to one hundredth of a Deutschemark.

phal-lus (fal´us) *n., pl.* -li *or* -luses A representation of the penis, often as a symbol of generative power.

phan-tasm (fan´taz um) *n.* The creation of an imaginary image; a fantasy; a phantom. **phantasmal** *adj.*

phan-tom (fan´tom) *n.* Something which exists but has no physical reality; a ghost.

phar-ma-cy (fär´ma sē) *n., pl.* pharma-cies A place of business which specializes in preparing, identifying, and disbursing drugs; a drugstore.

phar-ynx (far´ingks) *n., pl.* -ynges *or* -ynxes The part of the throat located between the palate and the esophagus, serving as a passage for air and food.

phase (fāz) *n.* Any decisive stage in development or growth. *Astron.* One of the forms or appearances of a planet.

pheas-ant (fez´ant) *n.* A long-tailed game bird noted for the beautiful plumage of the male.

phe-nom-e-non (fi nom´e non´) *n., pl.* phenomena *or* phenomenons Something that can be observed or perceived; a rare occurrence. *Slang* An outstanding person with remarkable power, ability, or talent.

phi-lan-der (fi lan´dēr) *v.* To make love without feeling or serious intentions.

phi-lat-e-ly (fi lat´e lē) *n.* The collection and study of postage stamps and postmarked material. **philatelic** *adj.*

phil-har-mon-ic (fil´här mon´ik) *adj.* Pertaining to a symphony orchestra.

phi-los-o-phy (fi los´o fē) *n. pl.* -ies The logical study of the nature and source of human knowledge or human values; the set of values, opinions, and ideas of a group or individual.

pho-bi-a (fō´bē a) *n.* A compulsive fear of a specified situation or object.

phone (fōn) *n.* A telephone. **phone** *v.* To call or communicate by telephone.

phon-ic (fon´ik) *adj.* Pertaining to sounds in speech; using the same symbol for each sound. **phonetics** *n.*

pho-no-graph (fō no graf´) *n.* A machine which uses a needle to reproduce sound from a grooved disc or record.

pho-ny (fō´nē) *adj. Informal* Counterfeit; fraudulent; not real or genuine.

phos-phate (fos´fāt) *n., Chem.* A salt or phosphoric acid which contains mostly phosphorus and oxygen.

phos-pho-rus (fos´fer us) *n.* A highly flammable, poisonous, nonmetallic element used in safety matches, symbolized by P.

pho-to (fō´tō) *n. Slang* A photograph.

pho-to-cop-y (fō´to kop´ē) *v.* To reproduce printed material using a photographic process. **photocopier** *n.* **photocopy** *n.*

pho-to-graph (fō´to graf´) *n.* A picture or image recorded by a camera and then reproduced on a photosensitive surface.

pho-to-stat (fō´to stat´) *n.* A trademark for a camera designed to reproduce documents and graphic material.

pho-to-syn-the-sis (fō´to sin´thi sis) *n. Biochem.* The chemical process by which plants use light to change carbon dioxide and water into carbohydrates, releasing oxygen as a byproduct.

phrase (frāz) *n. Gram.* A brief or concise expression which does not contain a predicate.

phre-nol-o-gy (fri nol´o jē) *n.* The study of or the theory that the conformation of the human skull indicates the degree of intelligence and character.

phys-i-cal (fiz´i kal) *adj.* Relating to the human body apart from the mind or emotions; pertaining to material rather than imaginary subjects. *n.* A medical exam to determine a person's physical condition. **physically** *adv.*

phy-si-cian (fi zish´un) *n.* A person licensed to practice medicine.

phys-ics (fiz´iks) *n.* The scientific study which deals with energy, matter, motion, and related areas of science.

phys-i-ol-o-gy (fiz´ē ol´o jē) *n., pl.* -ies The study of living animals, plants, and their activities and functions; the vital functions and processes of an organism. **physiological** *adj.*

phys-i-o-ther-a-py (fiz´ē ō ther´apē) *n.* The treatment of disease or physical defects by the use of heat and massage.

pi-an-o (pē an´ō) *n.* A musical instrument with a manual keyboard and felt-covered hammers which produce musical tones when struck upon steel wires.

pi-az-za (pē az´a) *n.* A public square or an open area in an Italian town or city.

pi-ca (pī´ka) *n.* A printer's type size of 12 points, equal to about 1/6 inch; a typewriter type size with 10 characters to an inch.

pic-co-lo (pik´o lō) *n.* A small flute with a brilliant sound pitched an octave above the flute.

pick (pik) *v.* To select or choose from a number or group

pick-et (pik´it) *n.* A pointed stake driven into the ground as support for a fence; a person positioned outside of a place of employment during a strike. *Mil.* A soldier posted to guard a camp.

pick-le (pik´l) *n.* A cucumber preserved in a solution of brine or vinegar. *Slang* A troublesome situation.

pic-nic (pik´nik) *n.* An outdoor social gathering where food is provided usually by the people attending.

pic-ture (pik´chèr) *n.* A visual representation on a surface, which is printed, drawn or photographed; the mental image or impression of an event or situation.

piece (pēs) *n.* An element, unit, or part of a whole; a musical or literary work. *Slang* A firearm.

piece-meal (pēs´mēl´) *adv.* Gradually, bit by bit.

pier (pēr) *n.* A structure extending into the water, used to secure, protect, and provide access to vessels.

pierce (pērs) *v.* To penetrate or make a hole in something; to force into or through. **piercing** *adj.*

Pierce, Franklin *n.* (1804-1869) The fourteenth president of the United States from 1853-1857.

pi-e-ty (pī´i tē) *n., pl.* **pieties** Devoutness toward God.

pig (pig) *n.* A cloven-hoofed mammal with short legs, bristly hair, and a snout for rooting; the edible meat of a pig; pork. *Slang* A greedy or gross person.

pig-ment (pig´ment) *n.* A material used as coloring matter, suitable for making paint. *Biol.* Any substance such as melanin and chlorophyll which imparts color to vegetable tissue or animals.

pile (pīl) *n.* A quantity of anything thrown in a heap; a massive or very large building or a group of buildings.

pil-fer (pil´fèr) *v.* To steal in little quantities; to steal items of little value.

pil-grim (pil´grim) *n.* A person who travels to a sacred place; a wanderer. **Pilgrims** The English Puritans who founded the Plymouth colony in New England in the year 1620.

pill (pil) *n.* A small tablet containing medicine which is taken by mouth; someone or something which is disagreeable but must be dealt with.

pill An oral contraceptive drug taken by women.

pil-lar (pil´èr) *n.* A freestanding column which serves as a support.

pil-low (pil´ō) *n.* A cloth case filled with feathers or other soft material, used to cushion the head during sleep.

pi-lot (pī´lot) *n.* A person who is licensed to operate an aircraft; someone who is trained and licensed to guide ships in and out of port. *v.* To act or serve as a pilot.

pi-men-to (pi men´tō) *n.* A sweet pepper used as a stuffing for olives or as a relish.

pimp (pimp) *n.* A person who arranges customers for prostitutes in exchange for a share of their money.

pim-ple (pim´pl) *n.* A small eruption of the skin, having an inflamed base. **pimpled** *adj.* **pimply** *adj.*

pin (pin) *n.* A small, stiff piece of wire with a blunt head and a sharp point, used to fasten something, usually temporarily; one of the rounded wooden clubs serving as the target in bowling.

pin-a-fore (pin´a fōr´) *n.* A sleeveless apron-like garment.

pin-cers (pin´chèrz) *n.* An implement having two handles and a pair of jaws working on a pivot, used to hold objects.

pinch (pinch) *v.* To squeeze between a finger and thumb causing pain or discomfort; to be miserly. *n.* The small amount that can be held between the thumb and forefinger.

pink (pingk) *n.* Any of various plants related to the carnation, having fragrant flowers; a light or pale hue of crimson; the highest or best possible degree.

pin feed In *computer science*, a device that feeds a continuous form through a printer by engaging a series of holes along the edges of the form.

pin-na-cle (pin´a kl) *n.* The highest peak; a sharp point; a pointed summit.

pint (pīnt) *n.* A liquid or dry measurement equal to half of a quart or two cups.

pin-to (pin´tō) *n. pl.* **-tos** *or* **-toes** A horse with spots; a spotted bean of the southwestern United States.

pin-wheel (pin´hwēl´) *n.* A toy with revolving paper or plastic fastened to a stick; a fireworks display featuring a revolving wheel of colored flames.

pin-worm (pin´werm´) *n.* A nematode parasite which infests the human intestines and rectum.

pi-o-neer (pī´o nēr´) *n.* One of the first settlers of a new region or country; the first developer or investigator in a new field of enterprise, research, or other endeavor.

pi-ous (pī´us) *adj.* Reverently religious; devout. **piously** *adv.* **piousness** *n.*

pipe (pīp) *n.* A hollow cylinder for conveying fluids; a small bowl with a hollow stem for smoking tobacco. *Music* A tubular flute.

pipe-line (pīp´līn´) *n.* A pipe used to transfer gas or oil over long distances; a means for conveying information.

pique (pēk) *n.* A feeling of resentment or irritation.

pirated software *n.* In *computer science*, programs obtained outside of normal or legal channels.

pis-ta-chi-o (pi stash´ē ō´) *n.* A small tree of western Asia; the edible fruit from this tree.

pis-til (pis´til) *n.* The seed-producing female reproductive organ of a flower.

pis-tol (pis´tol) *n.* A small handheld firearm.

pis-ton (pis´ton) *n.* Mech. A solid cylinder fitted in a larger cylinder, moving back and forth under liquid pressure.

pit (pit) *n.* An artificial or manmade hole in the ground; a slight indentation in the skin, as a scar from the chicken pox; an area for refueling or repair at a car race; the stone in the middle of some fruit, as peaches. *Slang* **the pits** Anything at its worst.

pith (pith) *n. Bot.* The sponge-like soft tissue at the center of the branch or stem of many plants.

pit-i-ful (pit´i ful) *adj.* Evoking or meriting pity. **pitifully** *adv.*

pit-y (pit´ē) *n. pl.* **pities** A feeling of compassion or sorrow for another's misfortune. **pity** *v.* To turn.

piv-ot (piv´ot) *n.* A thing or person upon which development, direction, or effect depends. **pivot** *v.* To turn.

pixel *n.* In *computer science*, a picture element; a basic component of a computer screen display.

piz-za (pēt´sa) *n.* An Italian food consisting of a doughy crust covered with tomato sauce, cheese, and other toppings and then baked.

place (plās) *n.* A region; an area; a building or location used for a special purpose; the position of something in a series or sequence. **place** *v.* To put in a particular order or place.

place-ment (plās´ment) *n.* The act of being placed; a business or service which finds positions of employment for applicants.

pla-cen-ta (pla sen´ta) *n., pl.* **-tas** *or* **-tae** *Anat.* The vascular, membranous structure which supplies a fetus with nourishment before its birth.

plague (plāg) *n.* Anything that is troublesome. *Pathol.* A highly contagious and often fatal epidemic disease, as the bubonic plague.

plaid (plad) *n.* A rectangular wool cloth or garment, usually worn by men and women, having a crisscross or checkered design.

plain (plān) *adj.* Level; flat; clear; open, as in view; not rich or luxurious; not highly gifted or cultivated. **plainly** *adv.*

plain-tiff (plān´tif) *n.* A person who brings suit.

plan (plan) *n.* A scheme or method for achieving something; a drawing to show proportion and relationship to parts. **plan** *v.* To have in mind as an intention or purpose.

plane (plān) *n.* A tool for smoothing or leveling a wood surface. *Geom.* A surface as a straight line that joins any two points on it. *Slang* Airplane.

plan-et (plan´it) *n. Astron.* A celestial body which is illuminated by light from the star around which it revolves.

plan-e-tar-i-um (plan´i târ´ē um) *n. pl.* **-iums** *or* **-ia** A device for exhibiting celestial bodies as they exist at any time and for any place on earth.

plank (plangk) *n.* A broad piece of wood; one of the issues or principles of a political platform.

plant (plant) *n.* A living organism belonging to the vegetable kingdom, having cellulose cell walls. *v.* To place a living organism in the ground for growing; to place so as to deceive or to spy.

plaque (plak) *n.* A flat piece, made from metal, porcelain, ivory, or other materials, engraved for mounting; the bacteria deposit which builds up on the teeth.

plas-ma (plaz´ma) *n.* The clear fluid part of blood, used for transfusions.

plas-ter-board (plas´tér bôrd´) *n.* A building material of layered gypsum bonded to outer layers of paper.

plas-tic (plas´tik) *adj.* Pliable; capable of being molded. **plastic** *n.* A synthetically made material which is molded and then hardened into objects.

plastic surgery *n.* Surgery dealing with the restoration or repair of deformed or destroyed parts of the body or skin.

pla-teau (pla tō´) *n.* An extensive level of elevated land; a period of stability.

plat-form (plat´form) *n.* Any elevated or raised surface used by speakers or by other performers or for display purposes; a formal declaration of principles or policy of a political party.

plat-i-num (plat´i num) *n.* A silver-white, metallic element, corrosive resistant, used in jewelry; symbolized by Pt.

plat-ter (plat´ér) *n.* A large, oblong, shallow dish for serving food.

plau-si-ble (plo´zi bl) *adj.* Seeming to

be probable; appearing to be trustworthy or believable.

play (plā) v. To entertain, as in recreation; to take part in a game; to perform in a dramatic role; to perform with a musical instrument; in fishing, to allow a hooked fish to tire itself out; to pretend to do something. n. A dramatic presentation.

pla-za (plä´za) n. An open-air market place or square; a shopping mall.

plea (plē) n. An urgent request; in law, an allegation made by either party in a law suit.

plea bargaining v. Making a pretrial agreement to plead guilty to a lesser charge if a more serious one will be dropped.

plead (plēd) v. To argue for or against something in court; to ask earnestly.

pleas-ant (plez´ant) adj. Giving or promoting the feeling of pleasure; very agreeable. **pleasantly** adv.

please (plēz) v. To make happy; to give pleasure; to be the will or wish of; to prefer.

pleas-ur-a-ble (plezh´ér a bl) adj. Pleasant; gratifying.

pleas-ure (plezh´ér) n. A feeling of satisfaction or enjoyment; one's preference or wish.

pleat (plēt) n. A fold in a cloth made by doubling the cloth back and fastening it down.

plebe (plēb) n. A freshman or first year student at the United States Naval Academy.

pledge (plej) n. A solemn promise; a deposit of something as security for a loan; a promise to join a fraternity; a person who is pledged to join a fraternity. v. To promise or vow.

plen-ti-ful (plen´ti ful) adj. Having great abundance. **plentifully** adv.

plen-ty (plen´tē) n. An ample amount; prosperity or abundance.

pleu-ra (pler´a) n. pl. **pleurae** Anat. The membranous sac which covers the inside of the thorax membrane, which covers the lungs.

pli-a-ble (plī´a bl) adj. Flexible; easily controlled or persuaded. **pliability** n. **pliableness** n. **pliably** adv.

pli-ers (plī´érz) n. A pincers-like tool used for holding, bending, or cutting.

plight (plīt) n. A distressing circumstance, situation, or condition.

plod (plod) n. To walk in a heavy, slow way.

plot (plot) n. A small piece of ground usually used for a special purpose; the main story line in a piece of fiction; a plan; an intrigue; a conspiracy. v. To represent something by using a map or chart; to scheme secretly.

plow (plou) n. An implement for breaking up or turning over the soil. v. To dig out. Slang To hit with force.

pluck (pluk) v. To remove by pulling out or off; to pull and release the strings on a musical instrument. Slang To swindle. **plucker** n.

plug (plug) n. Anything used to stop or close a hole or drain. Electr. A two-pronged device attached to a cord and used in a jack or socket to make an electrical connection. **plug** v. Slang To advertise favorably; to give a recommendation or a piece of publicity for someone.

plum-age (plö´mij) n. The feathers of a bird.

plumb (plum) n. A lead weight tied to the end of a string, used to test the exact perpendicular line of something.

plumb-er (plum´ér) n. A person who repairs or installs plumbing in a home or business.

plumb-ing (plum´ing) n. The profession or trade of a plumber; the connecting of pipes and fixtures used to carry water and waste.

plume (plöm) n. A feather used as an ornament.

plun-der (plun´dèr) v. To deprive of goods or property in a violent way.

plunge (plunj) v. To thrust or cast something, as into water; to submerge; to descend sharply or steeply.

plunk (plungk) v. To put down or place suddenly; to pluck or strum a banjo.

plu-ral (pler´al) adj. Consisting of or containing more than one. **plural** n.

plus (plus) n. The symbol (+) which indicates addition; increase; extra quantity.

plu-to-ni-um (plö tō´nē um) n. A radioactive metallic element symbolized by Pu.

ply (plī) v. To mold, bend, or shape. n. A layer of thickness; the twisted strands of thread, yarn, or rope.

ply-wood (plī´wed´) n. A structural material consisting of thin layers of wood which have been glued and pressed together.

pneu-mo-nia (ne mōn´ya) n. An inflammation caused by bacteria, virus of the lungs, or irritation.

poach (pōch) v. To cook in a liquid just at the boiling point; to trespass on another's property with the intent of taking fish or wild game. **poacher** n.

pock-et (pok´it) n. A small pouch within a garment, having an open top and used for carrying items. v. To put in or deposit in a pocket.

pod (pod) n., Bot. A seed vessel, as of a bean or pea. Aeron. A separate and detachable compartment in a spacecraft.

po-di-a-try n. Professional care and treatment of the feet.

po-di-um (pō´dē um) *n., pl.* **-ia** *or* **-iums** A small raised platform for an orchestra conductor or a speaker.

po-em (pō´im) *n.* A composition in verse with language selected for its beauty and sound.

po-et (pō´it) *n.* A person who writes poetry.

po-et-ry (pō´i trē) *n.* The art of writing stories, poems, and thoughts into verse.

poin-set-ti-a (poin set´ē ə) *n.* A tropical plant having large scarlet, pink, or white leaves, used in Christmas decorations.

point (point) *n.* The sharp or tapered end of something; a mark of punctuation, as a period (.); a geometric object which does not have property or dimensions other than location; a degree, condition, or stage; a particular or definite spot in time. **point** *v.* To aim; to indicate direction by using the finger.

point and click *v.* In *computer science*, to select an object by moving the mouse cursor to it, then pressing and releasing the mouse button.

poise (poiz) *v.* To bring into or hold one's balance. **poise** *n.* Equilibrium; self-confidence; the ability to stay calm in all social situations.

poi-son (poi´zon) *n.* A substance which kills, injures, or destroys. **poisoner** *n.* **poisonous** *adj.*

poke (pōk) *v.* To push or prod at something with a finger or other implement.

pok-er (pō´kėr) *n.* A card game, played by two or more people in which the players bet on the cards dealt to them.

po-lar (pō´lėr) *adj.* Having to do with the poles of a magnet or sphere; relating to the geographical poles of the earth.

po-lar-ize (pō´la rīz´) *v.* To cause something to vibrate in an exact pattern; to break up into opposite groups.

pole (pōl) *n.* Either of the two ends of the axis of a sphere, as the earth, the two points called the North and South Poles, where the axis of the earth's rotation meets the surface; a long, slender rod.

po-lice (pə lēs´) *n.* A division or department organized to maintain order; the members of such a department. **police** *v.* To patrol; to enforce the law and maintain order.

po-liceman (pə lēs´man) *n.* A member of the police force. **policewoman** *n.*

pol-i-cy (pol´i sē) *n., pl.* **policies** Any plan or principle which guides a person's or group's decision making.

pol-i-o-my-e-li-tis (pō´lē ōmī´e li´tis) *n.* Inflammation of the spinal cord causing paralysis; also polio.

pol-ish (pol´ish) *v.* To make lustrous and smooth by rubbing; to become refined or elegant.

po-lite (pə līt´) *adj.* Refined, mannerly, and courteous.

po-lit-i-cal (pə lit´i kal) *adj.* Concerned with or pertaining to government; involved in politics.

pol-i-ti-cian (pol´i tish´an) *n.* A person active in governmental affairs or politics.

pol-i-tics (pol´i tiks) *n.* The activities and methods of a political party.

Polk, James Knox *n.* (1795-1849) The eleventh president of the United States from 1845-1849.

poll (pōl) *n.* The recording of votes in an election; a public survey taken on a given topic. In *computer science*, an I/O function that scans transmission lines to check their status and ascertain when data is to be sent or received. **poll** *v.* To vote.

pol-len (pol´en) *n.* The yellow dust-like powder which contains the male reproductive cells of a flowering plant.

pol-lute (pə lōt´) *v.* To contaminate; to make unclear or impure; to dirty.

po-lo (pō´lō) *n.* A game played on horseback in which players try to drive a wooden ball through the opposing team's goal using long-handled mallets.

po-lo-ni-um (pə lō´nē um) *n.* A radioactive metallic element symbolized by PO.

pol-ter-geist (pōl´tėr gīst´) *n.* A mischievous spirit which makes noise.

pol-y-es-ter (pol´ē es´tėr) *n.* A strong lightweight synthetic resin used in fibers.

pol-y-gon *n.* A closed figure bounded by straight lines.

pol-y-graph (pol´ē graf) *n.* A machine designed to record different signals given off by the body, as respiration, blood pressure, or heartbeats; may be used to detect a person who could be lying.

pol-y-he-dron (pol´ē hē´dron) *n., pl.* **-dra** *or* **-drons** *Geom.* A solid bounded by polygons.

pom-pa-dour (pom´pa dōr´) *n.* A hairstyle which is puffed over the forehead.

pomp-ous (pom´pus) *adj.* A showing or appearance of dignity or importance.

pond (pond) *n.* A body of still water, smaller in size than a lake.

pon-der (pon´dėr) *v.* To think about very carefully; to meditate.

pon-der-ous (pon´dėr us) *adj.* Massive; having great weight.

pon-tiff (pon´tif) *n.* A pope.

po-ny (pō´nē) *n., pl.* **-ies** A small horse.

pool (pōl) *n.* A small body of water; the collective stake in gambling games.

poor (per) *adj.* Lacking possessions and

money; not satisfactory; broke; needy; destitute.

pop (pop) *v.* To cause something to burst; to make a sharp, explosive sound. *Slang* Soda. **popper** *n.*

pope (pōp) *n.* The head of the Roman Catholic Church.

pop-lar (pop´lêr) *n.* A rapid growing tree having a light, soft wood.

pop-u-lar (pop´ū lêr) *adj.* Approved of; widely liked; suited to the means of the people.

pop-u-la-tion (pop´ū lā´shan) *n.* The total number of people in a given area, country, or city.

por-ce-lain (pōr´se lin) *n.* A hard, translucent ceramic which has been fired and glazed.

porch (pōrch) *n.* A covered structure forming the entrance to a house.

por-cu-pine (por´kū pīn´) *n.* A clumsy rodent covered with long sharp quills.

pore (pōr) *v.* To ponder or meditate on something. **pore** *n.* A minute opening, as in the skin.

pork (pōrk) *n.* The edible flesh of swine. *Informal* Favors given by a government for political reasons and not public necessity.

por-no *n.*, *Slang* Pornography.

por-nog-ra-phy (por nog´ra fē) *n.* Pictures, films, or writing which deliberately arouse sexual excitement.

por-poise (por´pos) *n.* An aquatic mammal with a blunt, rounded snout.

port (pōrt) *n.* A city or town with a harbor for loading and unloading cargo from ships; the left side of a ship; a dark red, sweet, fortified wine. In *computer science*, any of the connections to a computer that allow the transfer of data.

port-a-ble (pōr´ta bl) *adj.* Capable of being moved easily.

por-ter (pōr´têr) *n.* A person hired to carry baggage.

port-fo-li-o (pōrt fō´lē ō´) *n.* A carrying case for holding papers, drawings, and other flat items.

port-hole (pōrt´hōl´) *n.* A small opening in the side of a ship providing light and ventilation.

por-tion (pōr´shan) *n.* A section or part of a whole; a share. **portion** *v.* To allot; to assign.

por-tray (pōr trā´) *v.* To represent by drawing, writing, or acting.

pose (pōz) *v.* To place or assume a position, as for a picture.

po-si-tion (po zish´an) *n.* The manner in which something is placed; an attitude; a viewpoint; a job; employment. *v.* To place in proper order.

pos-i-tive (poz´i tiv) *adj.* Containing, expressing, or characterized by affirmation; very confident; absolutely certain; not negative. **positively** *adv.* **positiveness** *n.*

pos-se (pos´ē) *n.* A deputized group or squad.

pos-ses-sion (po zesh´an) *n.* The fact or act of possessing property; the state of being possessed, as by an evil spirit.

pos-ses-sive (po zes´iv) *adj.* Having a strong desire to possess; not wanting to share. *n.* The noun or pronoun case which indicates ownership.

pos-si-ble (pos´i bl) *adj.* Capable of being true, happening, or being accomplished. **possibility** *n.* **possibly** *adv.*

post (pōst) *n.* An upright piece of wood or metal support; a position or employment. **post** *v.* To put up information in a public place. **post** *prefix* After; later than; behind.

post-age (pō´stij) *n.* The charge or fee for mailing something.

pos-te-ri-or (po stēr´ē êr) *adj.* Located in the back. *n.* The buttocks.

post-mor-tem (pōst mor´tem) *adj.* The examination of a body after death; an autopsy.

post-pone (pōst pōn´) *v.* To put off; to defer to a later time. **postponable** *adj.* **postponement** *n.* **postponer** *n.*

post-script (pōst´skript) *n.* A short message added at the end of a letter.

pos-ture (pos´chêr) *n.* The carriage or position of the body.

pot (pot) *n.* A rounded, deep container used for cooking and other domestic purposes. *Slang* A large sum of money which is shared by all members of a group; marijuana. **potful** *n.*

po-tas-si-um (po tas´ē um) *n.* A silvery-white, highly reactive metallic element symbolized by K.

po-ta-to (po tā´tō) *n.*, *pl.* **potatoes** A thick, edible, underground tuber plant native to America.

po-tent (pōt´ent) *adj.* Having great strength or physical powers; having a great influence on the mind or morals; sexually competent.

po-ten-tial (po ten´shal) *adj.* Possible, but not yet actual; having the capacity to be developed. *Electr.* The potential energy of an electric charge that depends on its position in an electric field.

pot-pour-ri (pō´pe rē´) *n.* A mixture of sweet-smelling dried flower petals and spices, kept in an airtight jar.

pot-ter-y (pot´e rē) *n.*, *pl.* **-ies** Objects molded from clay and fired by intense heat; place where objects are made.

pouch (pouch) *n.* A small bag or other container for holding or carrying money, tobacco, and other small articles. *Zool.* The sac-like structure in which some animals carry their young.

poul-try (pōl´trē) *n.* Domestic fowl as ducks and hens, which are raised for eggs or meat.

pound (pound) *n., pl.* **pound** A measure of weight equal to sixteen ounces; a public enclosure where stray animals are fed and housed. To strike repeatedly or with force; to throb or beat violently or rapidly. **pound** *v.*

pov-er-ty (pov´ĕr tē) *n.* The condition or state of being poor and needing money.

POW (pē´ō´dub´l ū´) *abbr.* Prisoner of war.

pow-der (pou´dĕr) *n.* A dry substance which has been finely ground or pulverized; dust; an explosive, such as gunpowder. *v.* To dust or cover.

pow-er-ful (pou´ĕr ful) *adj.* Possessing energy or great force; having authority.

power of attorney *n.* A legal document in which one person gives another the authority to act for him.

power surge *n.* In *computer science,* a sudden increase in electrical energy that can damage a computer's system and files.

power up *n.* In *computer science,* to turn on a piece of equipment.

prac-ti-cal (prak´ti kal) *adj.* Serving an actual use or purpose; inclined to act instead of thinking or talking about something; useful.

pract-ice (prak´tis) *n.* A custom or habit of doing something. **practice** *v.* To work at a profession; to apply; to put into effect; to exercise or rehearse.

prai-rie (prâr´ē) *n.* A wide area of level or rolling land with grass and weeds but no trees.

praise (prāz) *v.* To express approval; to glorify.

prank (prangk) *n.* A mischievous, playful action or trick. **prankster** *n.*

pra-seo-dym-i-um (prā´zē ō dim´ōum) *n.* A metallic element of the rare-earth group, symbolized by Pr.

prawn (pron) *n.* An edible shrimp-like crustacean found in both salt and fresh water.

pray (prā) *v.* To address prayers to God; to ask or request.

prayer (prâr) *n.* A devout request; the act of praying; a formal or set group of words used in praying.

praying mantis *n.* An insect which holds its front legs folded as if in prayer.

preach (prēch) *v.* To advocate; to proclaim; to deliver a sermon. **preacher** *n.* **preachment** *n.* **preachy** *adj.*

pre-am-ble (prē´am bl) *n.* An introduction to something, as a law, which states the purpose and reasons for the matter which follows.

pre-cau-tion (pri ko´shan) *n.* A measure of caution or care taken in advance to guard against harm.

pre-cede (pri sēd´) *v.* To be or go before in time, position, or rank.

prec-e-dent (pres´i dent) *n.* An instance which may serve as a rule or example in the future.

pre-cept (prē´sept) *n.* A rule, order, or commandment meant to guide one's conduct.

pre-cinct (prē´singkt) *n.* An electoral district of a county, township, city, or town; an enclosure with definite boundaries.

pre-cious (presh´us) *adj.* Having great worth or value; beloved; cherished.

pre-cip-i-ta-tion (pri sip´i tā´shan) *n.* Condensed water vapor which falls as snow, rain, sleet or hail. *Chem.* The act of causing crystals to separate and fall to the bottom of a liquid.

pre-cip-i-tous (pri sip´i tus) *adj.* Very steep; marked with very steep cliffs.

pre-cise (pri sīs´) *adj.* Exact; definite; strictly following rules; very strict.

pre-ci-sion (pri sizh´un) *n.* Exactness; the quality of being precise; accuracy.

pre-clude (pri klōd´) *v.* To shut out; to make impossible; to prevent.

pre-co-cious (pri kō´shus) *adj.* Showing and developing skills and abilities very early in life.

pre-con-ceive (prē´kon sēv´) *v.* To form a notion or conception before knowing all the facts. **preconception** *n.*

pre-da-cious (pri dā´shus) *adj.* Living by preying on other animals.

pred-a-tor (pred´a tèr) *n.* A person who lives or gains by stealing from another person; an animal that survives by killing and eating other animals.

pre-des-ti-na-tion (pri des´ti nā´shan) *n.* Destiny; fate; the act by which God has predestined all events.

pred-i-ca-ble (pred´i ka bl) *adj.* Capable of being predicated to foretell.

pred-i-cate (pred´i kāt´) *n. Gram.* The word or words which say something about the subject of a clause or sentence; the part of a sentence which contains the verb. *v.* To establish.

pre-dict (pri dikt´) *v.* To tell beforehand; to foretell; to forecast. **predictability** *n.* **predictable** *adj.* **predictably** *adv.*

pre-dom-i-nant (pri dom´i nant) *adj.* Superior in strength, authority, number, or other qualities.

pree-mie *n. Slang* A baby born before the expected due date.

pre-empt (prē empt´) *v.* To take or get hold of before someone else; to take the place of; to do something before someone else has a chance to do it. **preemption** *n.* **preemptive** *adj.*

pre-fab-ri-cate (prē fab´ri kāt´) *v.* To construct in sections beforehand.

pref-ace (pref´is) *n.* The introduction

at the beginning of a book or speech.

pre-fect (prē'sekt) *n.* A high administrative official. **prefecture** *n.*

pre-fer (pri fer') *v.* To select as being the favorite; to promote; to present.

pref-er-ence (pref'ĕr ens) *n.* A choice; a special liking for anything over another. **preferential** *adj.*

pre-fix (prē fïks') *v.* To put at the beginning; to put before.

preg-nant (preg'nant) *adj.* Carrying an unborn fetus; significant.

pre-his-tor-i-cal (prē'hi stor'ik) *adj.* Of or related to the period before recorded history.

pre-judge (prē juj') *v.* To judge before one knows all the facts. -ment *n.*

prej-u-dice (prej'a dis) *n.* A biased opinion based on emotion rather than reason; bias against a group, race, or creed.

pre-lim-i-nar-y (pri lim'i ner'ē) *adj.* Leading up to the main action.

prel-ude (prel'ūd) *n.* An introductory action. *Music* The movement at the beginning of a piece of music.

pre-ma-ture (prē'ma ter') *adj.* Occurring or born before the natural or proper time. **prematurely** *adv.*

pre-med-i-tate (pri med'i tāt') *v.* To plan in advance or beforehand.

pre-mi-er (pri mēr') *adj.* First in rank or importance. *n.* The chief executive of a government. **premiership** *n.*

pre-mi-um (prē'mē um) *n.* An object offered free as an inducement to buy; the fee or amount payable for insurance; an additional amount of money charged above the nominal value.

pre-na-tal (prē nāt'al) *adj.* Existing prior to birth.

pre-oc-cu-py (prē ok'ū pī') *v.* To engage the mind or attention completely.

prep (prep) *Slang* Preparatory school; preparation.

prep-a-ra-tion (prep'a rā'shan) *n.* The process of preparing for something.

pre-par-a-to-ry (pri pâr'a tōr'ē) *adj.* Serving as preparation.

pre-pare (pri pâr') *v.* To make ready or qualified; to equip. **preparedly** *adv.*

pre-pay (prē pā') *v.* To pay for in advance.

pre-pon-der-ate (pri pon'de rāt') *v.* To have superior importance, weight, force, influence, or other qualities. **preponderance** *n.* **preponderancy** *n.* **preponderantly** *adv.*

prep-o-si-tion (prep'o zish'an) *n. Gram.* A word placed in front of a noun or pronoun to show a connection with or to something or someone.

pre-pos-ter-ous (pri pos'tĕr us) *adj.* Absurd; ridiculous; beyond all reason.

prep-pie (prep ē) *n. Slang* A student

attending a prep school; a young adult who behaves and dresses very traditionally.

pre- *prefix* Earlier or prior to something; in front.

preprocessing *n.* In *computer science*, configuring data before entering it into a program, such as converting spreadsheet rows to comma separated values for entering into a database.

pre-rog-a-tive (pri rog'a tiv) *n.* The unquestionable right belonging to a person.

pres-age (pres'ij) *n.* An omen or indication of something to come; a premonition. **presage** *v.*

pre-school (prē'skōl') *adj.* Of or for children usually between the ages of two and five. **preschooler** *n.*

pre-scribe (pri skrïb') *v.* To impose as a guide; to recommend.

pre-scrip-tion (pri skrip'shan) *n. Medical* A physician's written order for medicine.

pres-ence (prez'ens) *n.* The state of being present; the immediate area surrounding a person or thing; poise.

pres-ent (prez'ent) *adj.* Now going on; not past or future. *Gram.* Denoting a tense or verb form which expresses a current state or action. **present** *v.* To bring into the acquaintance of another; to introduce; to make a gift of. **present** *n.* A gift. **presently** *adv.* Currently.

pres-en-ta-tion (prez'en tā'shan) *n.* A formal introduction of one person to another; something presented, as an exhibition, show, or product.

pre-serv-a-tive (pri zer'va tiv) *adj.* Keeping something from decay or injury. **preservative** *n.*

pre-serve (pri zerv') *v.* To save from destruction or injury; to prepare food to prevent spoilage or decay.

preserves *n.* Fruit which has been preserved with sugar.

pre-side (pri zīd') *v.* To have a position of authority or control; to run or control a meeting.

pres-i-dent (prez'i dent) *n.* The chief executive officer of a government, corporation, or association. **presidency** *n.* **presidential** *adj.*

press (pres) *v.* To act upon or exert steady pressure or force; to squeeze out or extract by pressure; to smooth by heat and pressure; to iron clothes. **press** *n.* A machine used to produce printed material.

pres-sure (presh'ĕr) *n.* The act of or the state of being pressed; a constraining moral force; any burden, force, painful feeling, or influence; the depressing effect of some-thing hard to bear.

pres-tige (pre stēzh') *n.* Importance based on one's past reputation and achievements.

pres-to (pres´tō) *adv, Music* Very fast and quick; at once.

pre-sume (pri zöm´) *v.* To take for granted; to take upon oneself without permission; to proceed overconfidently. **presumable** *adj.* **presumably** *adv.* **presumer** *n.*

pre-sump-tion (pri zump´shan) *n.* Arrogant conduct or speech; something that can be logically assumed true until disproved.

pre-tend (pri tend´) *v.* To make believe; to act in a false way. **pretender** *n.*

pre-tense (pri tens´) *n.* A deceptive and false action or appearance; a false purpose.

pre-ten-tious (pri ten´shus) *adj.* Having or making claims to worth, excellence, etc.; showy.

pre-text (prē´tekst) *n.* A motive assumed in order to conceal the true purpose.

pret-ty (prit´ē) *adj.* Pleasant; attractive; characterized by gracefulness; pleasing to look at. *Slang* **sitting pretty** In a favorable position; good circumstances. **prettify** *v.* **prettily** *adv.*

pret-zel (pret´sel) *v.* A hard, cooked dough usually twisted in a knot and sprinkled with salt.

pre-vail (pri vāl´) *v.* To succeed; to win control over something; to predominate. **prevailer** *n.* **prevailingly** *adv.*

pre-vent (pri vent´) *v.* To keep something from happening; to keep from doing something.

pre-ven-tive *or* **preventative (pri ven´tiv)** *adj.* Protecting or serving to ward off harm, disease, or other problems.

pre-view *or* **prevue (prē´vū´)** *n.* An advance showing or viewing to invited guests.

pre-vi-ous (pre´vē us) *adj.* Existing or occurring earlier. **previously** *adv.*

price (pris) *n.* The set amount of money expected or given for the sale of something.

prick (prik) *n.* A small hole made by a sharp point. **prick** *v.* To pierce something lightly.

pride (prid) *n.* A sense of personal dignity; a feeling of pleasure because of something achieved, done, or owned.

priest (prēst) *n.* A clergyman in the Catholic church who serves as mediator between God and His worshipers.

pri-ma-ry (prī´mer ē) *adj.* First in origin, time, series, or sequence; basic; fundamental.

prime (prīm) *adj.* First in importance, time, or rank. *n.* A period of full vigor, success, or beauty. **prime** *v.* To make ready by putting something on before the final coat, as to prime wood before painting.

prim-i-tive (prim´i tiv) *adj.* Of or pertaining to the beginning or earliest time; resembling the style or manners of an earlier time. **primitive** *n.*

primp (primp) *v.* To dress or arrange with superfluous attention to detail.

prin-ci-pal (prin´sipal) *adj.* Chief; most important. **principal** *n.* The headmaster or chief official of a school; a sum of money invested or owed which is separate from the interest.

prin-ci-ple (prin´si pl) *n.* The fundamental law or truth upon which others are based; a moral standard.

print (print) *n.* An impression or mark made with ink; the design or picture which is transferred from an engraved plate or other impression. **print** *v.* To stamp designs; to publish something in print, as a book or magazine.

printer fonts *n.* In *computer science*, type fonts built into a printer or a printer cartridge.

Print Screen key *n.* In *computer science*, the function key that commands the computer to copy the data on the monitor screen to the printer.

print-out (print´out´) *n.* In *computer science* the output of a computer printed on paper.

pri-or (prī´ér) *adj.* Previous in order or time.

pri-or-i-ty (prī or´i tē) *n.* Something which takes precedence; something which must be done or taken care of first.

prism (priz´um) *n.* A solid figure with triangular ends and rectangular sides, used to disperse light into a spectrum.

pris-on (priz´on) *n.* A place of confinement where people are kept while waiting for a trial or while serving time for breaking the law; jail. **prisoner** *n.*

pri-vate (prī´vit) *adj.* Secluded or removed from the public view; secret; intimate, owned or controlled by a group or person rather than by the public or government.

priv-i-lege (priv´i lij) *n.* A special right or benefit granted to a person.

prize (prīz) *n.* An award or something given to the winner of a contest; something exceptional or outstanding.

pro (prō) *n.* An argument in favor of or supporting something. *Slang* A professional or an expert in a given field.

prob-a-bil-i-ty (prob´a bil´i tē) *n., pl.* **-ies** The state or quality of being probable; a mathematical statement or prediction of the odds of something happening or not happening.

prob-a-ble (prob´a bl) *adj.* Likely to become a reality, but not certain or proved. **probably** *adv.*

pro-bate (prō´bāt) *n.* The act of legally

proving that a will is genuine.

pro-ba-tion (prō bā´shan) *n*. A period used to test the qualifications and character of a new employee; the early release of law breakers who must be under supervision and must report as requested to a probation officer.

probe (prōb) *n*. An instrument used for investigating an unknown environment; a careful investigation or examination.

prob-lem (prob´lem) *n*. A perplexing situation or question; a question presented for consideration, solution, or discussion. **problem** *adj*. **-matic** *adj*.

pro-ce-dure (pro sē´jėr) *n*. A certain pattern or way of doing something; the normal methods or forms to be followed.

pro-ceed (pro sēd´) *v*. To carry on or continue an action or process. *Law* To begin or institute legal action.

proc-ess (pros´es) *n*. The course, steps, or methods toward a desired result. *Law* Any judicial request or order. In *computer science*, the sequence of operations which gives a desired result. **process** *v*. To compile, compute, or assemble data.

processing *n*. In *computer science*, data manipulation by the computer.

pro-ces-sion (pro sesh´an) *n*. A group which moves along in a formal manner; a parade.

pro-ces-sion-al (pro sesh´a nal) *n*. A hymn sung during a procession; the opening of a church service. **processional** *adj*. Relating to a procession.

pro-ces-sor (pros´es or) *n*. In *Computer Science*, the central unit of a computer which processes data.

pro-claim (prō klām´) *v*. To announce publicly.

proc-la-ma-tion (prok´la mā´shan) *n*. An official public declaration or announcement.

pro-cras-ti-nate (prō kras´ti nāt´) *v*. To put off, defer, or postpone to a later time. **procrastination** *n*. **-tor** *n*.

proc-tor (prok´tėr) *n*. A person in a university or college whose job it is to see that order is maintained during exams. **proctorial** *adj*.

pro-cure (prō kūr´) *v*. To acquire; to accomplish.

prod (prod) *v*. To arouse mentally; to poke with a pointed instrument. **prod** *n*. A pointed implement used to prod or poke.

prod-i-gal (prod´i gal) *adj*. Wasteful expenditure of money, strength, or time; extravagant. **prodigal** *n*. One who is a spendthrift or is wasteful.

pro-duce (pro dōs´) *v*. To bear or bring forth by a natural process; to manufacture; to make; to present or bring into view. **producer** *n*.

prod-uct (prod´ukt) *n*. Something produced, manufactured, or obtained *Math*. The answer obtained by multiplying.

pro-duc-tion (pro duk´shan) *n*. The process or act of producing; something produced, as a play.

pro-fane (pro fān´) *adj*. Manifesting disrespect toward sacred things; vulgar.

pro-fess (pro fes´) *v*. To admit or declare openly; to make an open vow.

pro-fes-sor (pro fes´ėr) *n*. A faculty member of the highest rank in a college or university; a highly skilled teacher.

pro-fes-sion-al (pro fesh´a nal) *adj*. Having to do with a job or profession; referring to or engaging in an occupation, usually a sport for money rather than for fun.

pro-fi-cient (pro fish´ent) *adj*. Highly skilled in a field of knowledge. **proficiency** *n*. **proficiently** *adv*.

pro-file (prō´fīl) *n*. The outline of a person's face or figure as seen from the side; a short biographical sketch indicating the most striking characteristics.

prof-it (prof´it) *n*. The financial return after all expenses have been accounted for. *v*. To gain an advantage or a financial reward. **profitable** *adj*.

pro-found (pro found´) *adj*. Deeply held or felt; intellectually penetrating.

pro-fuse (pro fūs´) *adj*. Extravagant; giving forth lavishly; overflowing. **profusely** *adv*. **profuseness** *n*.

prog-e-ny (proj´e nē) *n*., *pl*. **-ies** One's offspring, children, or descendants.

prog-no-sis (prog nō´sis) *n*., *pl*. **prognoses** A prediction of the outcome and course a disease may take.

pro-gram (prō´gram) *n*. Any prearranged plan or course; a show or performance, as one given at a scheduled time. In *computer science*, a sequence of commands which tell a computer how to perform a task or sequence of tasks. **program** *v*.

programmable *adj*. In *computer science*, descriptive of a device whose function can be altered by the user.

programmable mouse *n*. In *computer science*, a mouse whose buttons may be assigned a command or series of commands, usually in conjunction with key combinations.

programmer *n*. In *computer science*, an individual who creates or alters routines for a computer.

programming language *n*. In *computer science*, a precise system of vocabulary and syntax for writing instructions for the computer.

prog-ress (prog´res) *n*. Forward motion or advancement to a higher goal; an advance; steady improvement.

pro-hib-it (prō hib´it) v. To forbid legally; to prevent.

pro-ject (proj´ekt´) n. A plan or course of action; a proposal; a large job. v. To give an estimation on something.

pro-jec-tile (pro jek´til) n. Anything hurled forward through the air.

pro-jec-tion (pro jek´shan) n. The act or state of being projected; the state or part that sticks out.

pro-lif-er-ate (prō lif´e rāt´) v. To grow or produce with great speed, as cells in tissue formation.

pro-logue (prō´log) n. An introductory statement at the beginning of a poem, song, or play.

pro-long (pro long´) v. To extend or lengthen in time.

prom-e-nade (prom´e nād´) n. An unhurried walk for exercise or amusement; a public place for such a walk, as the deck of a ship.

prom-i-nent (prom´i nent) adj. Jutting out; widely known; held in high esteem.

pro-mis-cu-ous (pro mis´kū us) adj. Lacking selectivity or discrimination, especially in sexual relationships.

prom-ise (prom´is) n. An assurance given that one will or will not do something; a pledge. **promise** v.

promissory note n. A written document or agreement that contains a promise to pay a debt to a particular person by a specified date or on demand.

prom-on-to-ry (prom´on tōr´ē) n. A projecting rock that extends into the sea.

pro-mote (pro mōt´) v. To raise to a higher rank or position; to work on behalf of. **promotion** n.

pro-mot-er (pro mō´tēr) n. A person who encourages; one who aids in promoting a financial understanding; a person who starts or sets up a business venture.

prompt (prompt) adj. Arriving on time; punctual; immediate. **prompt** v. To suggest or inspire. **prompt** n. In computer science, a cursor; a highlight on the monitor screen that indicates where the next character will be entered; a program query or instruction.

promp-ti-tude (promp´ti tōd´) n. Promptness.

prom-ul-gate (prom´ul gāt´) v. To proclaim; to make known to the public.

prone (prōn) adj. Lying flat; face down. **pronely** adv. **proneness** n.

prong (prong) n. A pointed, projecting part, as the end of a sharp instrument or the end of an antler.

pro-nom-i-nal (prō nom´inal) adj. Sharing the nature of a pronoun.

pro-noun (prō´noun´) n. Gram. A word which can be used in the place of a noun or noun phrase.

pro-nounce (pro nouns´) v. To deliver officially; to articulate the sounds. **pronunciation** n.

pro-nounce-ment (pro nouns´ment) n. Act of pronouncing a word or letter; a decision.

pron-to (pron´tō) adv. Quickly; promptly.

proof (prōf) n. The establishment of a fact by evidence; the act of showing that something is true; a trial impression from the negative of a photograph. **proof** v. To proofread; to mark and make corrections.

prop (prop) n. A support to keep something upright. v. To sustain.

prop-a-gate (prop´a gāt´) v. To reproduce or multiply by natural causes; to pass on qualities or traits.

pro-pel (pro pel´) v. To thrust or cause to move forward; to motivate.

prop-er (prop´ēr) adj. Appropriate; especially adapted or suited; conforming to social convention; correct.

proper adjective n. An adjective whose form is obtained from that of a proper noun.

proper fraction n. A fraction with a larger denominator than numerator.

prop-er-ly (prop´ēr lē) adv. In a suitable manner; fitly; correctly.

proper noun n. A noun denoting a specific person, place, or thing which is capitalized.

prop-er-ty (prop´ēr tē) n., pl. **properties** Any object of value owned or lawfully acquired, as real estate; a piece of land. **propertied** adj.

proph-e-cy (prof´i sē) n., pl. **-ies** A prediction made under divine influence.

proph-et (prof´it) n. One who delivers divine messages; one who foretells the future. **prophetess** n.

pro-pi-ti-ate (pro pish´ē āt´) v. To win the good will of, to stop from being angry. **pro-pitiation** n.

pro-po-nent (pro pō´nent) n. One who supports or advocates a cause.

pro-por-tion (pro pōr´shan) n. The relation of one thing to another in size, degree, or amount. v. To adjust or arrange with balance and harmony. **proportional** adj.

pro-por-tion-ate adj. In proportion; a true comparative relation.

pro-pose (pro pōz´) v. To present or put forward for consideration or action; to suggest someone for an office or position; to make an offer; to offer marriage. **proposal** n.

prop-o-si-tion (prop´o zish´an) n. A scheme or plan offered for consideration; a subject or idea to be proved or discussed. **proposition** v. To make a sexual suggestion.

pro-pri-e-tor (pro prī´i tėr) n. The person who owns property and has the exclusive title or legal right.

pro-pri-e-ty (pro prī´i tē) n., pl. **proprieties** The quality or state of being proper in accordance with recognized principles or usage.

pro-pul-sion (pro pul´shan) n. The act or process of propelling. **-sive** adj.

pro-pul-sis n. The outward protuberance of an organ.

pro-rate (prō rāt´) v. To distribute or divide proportionately. **proration** n.

pro-scribe (prō skrīb´) v. To banish; to outlaw; to prohibit.

prose (prōz) n. Ordinary language, speech, or writing which is not poetry.

pros-e-cute (pros´e kūt´) v. To carry on. Law To bring suit against a person; to seek enforcement for legal process. **prosecution** n.

pros-pect (pros´pekt) n. Something that has the possibility of future success; a possible customer. v. To explore. **prospective** adj. **prospectively** adv.

pros-per (pros´pėr) v. To be successful; to achieve success. **prosperous** adj.

pros-tate (pros´tāt) n. A small gland at the base of the male bladder.

pros-ti-tute (pros´ti tŏt´) n. One who sells the body for the purpose of sexual intercourse.

pros-trate (pros´trāt) adj. Lying with the face down to the ground. **prostrate** v. To overcome; to adopt a submissive posture. **prostrative** adj.

pro-tect (pro tekt´) v. To guard or shield from attack or injury; to shield. **protective** adj. **protectively** adv.

protected field n. In computer science, a block of text, formula, etc. that cannot be altered.

protected files n. In computer science, read-only files; computer memory that may be read, but cannot be altered.

pro-tein (prō´tēn) n. Biochem. Any of a very large group of highly complex nitrogenous compounds occurring in living matter and composed of amino acids which are essential for tissue repair and growth.

pro-test (pro test´) v. To make a strong formal objection; to object to. n. The act of protesting. **protester** n.

pro-to-col (prō´to kol´) n. The code and rules of diplomatic and state etiquette. In computer science, the rules governing the transfer of data between a computer and peripherals or another computer.

pro-ton (prō´ton) n. Physics A unit of positive charge equal in magnitude to an electron.

pro-tract (prō trakt´) v. To extend in space; to protrude.

pro-trude (prō trŏd´) v. To project; to thrust outward. **protrusion** n.

proud (proud) adj. Showing or having a feeling that one is better than the others; having a feeling of satisfaction; having proper self-respect or proper self-esteem.

prove (prōv) v. To show with valid evidence that something is true. **provable** adj. **provably** adv.

prov-erb (prov´erb) n. An old saying which illustrates a truth. **Proverbs** The book contained in the Bible which has many sayings supposed to have come from Solomon and others.

pro-vide (pro vīd´) v. To supply or furnish with what is needed.

pro-vi-dence (prov´i dens) n. The supervision of God over his people.

pro-vi-sion (pro vizh´an) n. A supply of food or needed equipment.

pro-voke (pro vōk´) v. To cause to be angry; to annoy. **provocation** n.

prox-i-mate (prok´si mit) adj. Immediate; direct; close.

prox-y (prok´sē) n., pl. **proxies** The authority, usually written, to act for another.

prude (prōd) n. A person who is very modest, especially in matters related to sex. **prudery** n. **prudishness** n.

pru-dent (prōd´ent) adj. Cautious; discreet; managing very carefully.

psalm (säm) n. A sacred hymn, taken from the Book of Psalms in the Old Testament.

psal-tery (sol´tėr ē) n. A type of musical instrument that was used many years ago.

pseu-do (sö´dō) adj. Being counterfeit or fake.

pseu-do-nym (sö´do nim) n. A name that is a fake. **pseudonymous** adj.

psi (sī) n. The twenty-third letter that is found in the Greek alphabet.

psil-o-cy-bin (sil´o sī´bin) n. Hallucinogenic compound from a fungus.

pso-ri-a-sis (so rī´a sis) n. Pathol. A noncontagious, chronic, inflammatory skin disease characterized by reddish patches and white scales.

psych (sī´kē) v. Slang To prepare oneself emotionally or mentally; to outwit or outguess.

psy-chas-the-ni-a (sī´kas thē´nē a) n. A type of emotional disorder that is caused by morbid fears.

psych-e-del-ic (sī´ki del´ik) adj. Causing extraordinary alterations in the consciousness of a person.

psy-chi-a-trist (si kī´a trist) n. A person who is a specialist in the field of psychiatry.

psy-chi-a-try (si kī´a trē) n. The branch of medicine which deals with the diagnosis and treatment of mental disorders.

psychic 337 pugnacious

psy-chic (sī'kik) adj. Cannot be explained by natural or physical laws. n. A person who communicates with the spirit world.

psy-cho-a-nal-y-sis (sī'kō a nal'i sis) n. The way of studying and analyzing one's subconscious thoughts.

psy-cho-an-a-lyst (sī'kō an'a list) n. The person who has been trained and is qualified to practice psychoanalysis on others.

psy-cho-bi-ol-o-gy (sī'kō bī ol'o jē) n. The science of the study of the relationships between the body and the mind.

psy-cho-gen-e-sis (sī'kō jen'i sis) n. The development of the mind.

psy-chol-o-gy (sī kol'o jē) n., pl. -gies The science of emotions, behavior, and the mind. psychologist n.

psy-cho-path (sī'kō path') n. A person suffering from a mental disorder characterized by aggressive antisocial behavior. psychopathic adj.

ptar-mi-gan (tär'mi gan) n. A type of species of grouse that has feathered feet and can be located in the cold regions.

PT boat (pē'tē'bōt) n. A type of small vessel of the navy.

pter-i-dol-o-gy (ter'i dol'o jē) n. The section or part of botany concerned with the study of ferns.

pter-o-dac-tyl (ter'o dak'til) n. A type of flying reptile that is now extinct and is believed to have lived thousands of years ago.

pter-o-saur (ter'o sor') n. A type of flying reptile that is now extinct.

pto-maine (tō'mān) n. A type of compound that can be very poisonous and is produced by an animal.

pto-sis (tō'sis) n. The drooping of a body organ. ptotic adj.

pty-a-lin (tī'a lin) n. A type of enzyme found in saliva of man and used to digest starch into maltose and dextrin.

pty-a-lism (tī'a liz'um) n. The excessive production of saliva in one's mouth.

pub (pub) n. A type of tavern.

pu-ber-ty (pū'bér tē) n. The stage of development in which sexual reproduction can first occur; the process of the body which culminates in sexual maturity. pubertal adj. puberal adj.

pu-ber-u-lent (pū ber'ū lent) adj. To be covered or to have down.

pu-bes-cence (pū bes'ens) n. The arrival of the stage of puberty in a person.

pubis (pū'bis) n. The part of the bone that forms the pelvis which is located in the front.

pub-lic (pū'bik) adj. Pertaining to or affecting the people or community; for everyone's use; widely or well known.

pub-li-can (pub'li kan) n. A person who collects taxes in a town or city; any collector of public revenues.

pub-li-ca-tion (pub'li kā'shan) n. The business of publishing; any pamphlet, book, or magazine.

public defender n. The attorney who defends someone without charging them because they cannot afford to hire an attorney for themselves.

public domain n. Public property; a published work whose copyrights have expired.

public house n. A type of inn.

pub-li-cist (pub'li sist) n. A press or publicity agent; a person who is a specialist in public relations; a specialist on international law.

pub-lic-i-ty (pu blis'i tē) n. The state of being known to the public; common knowledge.

pub-lic-ly (pub'lik lē) adv. Public manner; without concealment.

public property n. The property which is owned by the public.

public sale n. A type of sale which is made after a public notice.

pub-lish (pub'lish) v. To print and distribute a book, magazine, or any printed matter to the public. publishable adj.

pub-lish-er (pub'li shér) n. A person who will publish the works of others as in books.

puce (pūs) adj. To be a reddish brown.

puck (puk) n. A hard rubber disk used in playing ice hockey.

pud-dle (pud'l) n. A small pool of water.

pu-den-cy (pud'en sē) n. The modesty of someone.

pudg-y (puj'ē) adj. To be fat and short.

pueb-lo (pweb'lō) n. A type of village of grouped houses that can be found in New Mexico, used by the Pueblo Indians of North America.

pu-er-ile (pū'ér il) adj. To be childish in character and actions.

pu-er-per-al (pū ûr'pér al) adj. To be related to childbirth.

puff (puf) n. A brief discharge of air or smoke. v. To breathe in heavy breaths.

puff adder n. A type of large African viper that will puff up its body when it becomes agitated.

puff-ball (puf'bol') n. A type of fungus that is rounded and will discharge its spores in a mass of smoke.

puff-er (puf'ér) n. A person or something that puffs.

puff-er-y (puf'e rē) n. A type of praise which is very exaggerated.

puf-fin (puf'in) n. A type of sea bird that has a red bill and can be found in the North Atlantic regions.

pug (pug) n. A type of dog which looks like a small bulldog.

pug-na-cious (pug nā'shus) adj. Being

inclined to fight. **pugnaciousness** n.

pug-ree (pug´rē) n. A type of turban that is worn to keep the rays of the sun off one's head.

pu-is-sance (pū´i sans) n. Might; strength.

puke (pūk) v. To throw up or vomit food.

puk-ka (puk´a) adj. To be good.

pull (pel) v. To apply force; to cause motion toward or in the same direction of; to remove from a fixed place.

pul-let (pül´it) n. A young chicken.

pull-o-ver (pül´ō´vėr) n. A type of clothing that is put on the body by pulling it over the head.

pul-lu-late (pul´ya lāt´) v. To send off or forth buds.

pul-mo-nar-y (pul´mo ner´ē) adj. To be referring to the lungs.

pulmonary artery n. The artery which is going from the heart to the lungs and is carrying unoxygenated blood.

pulmonary vein n. A vein which comes from the lungs to the heart and is carrying the blood which has received oxygen in the lungs and is ready to be pumped through the rest of the body.

pulp (pulp) n. The soft juicy part of a fruit; a moist mass; inexpensive paper.

pul-pit (pel´pit) n. The elevated platform lectern used in a church from which a service is conducted.

pulp-wood (pulp´wüd´) n. A type of soft wood which is found in the pine and spruce, and it is used for the purpose of making paper.

pul-sate (pul´sāt) v. To beat rhythmically. **pulsation** n. **pulsator** n.

pul-sa-tile (pul´sa til) adj. To be throbbing.

pul-sa-tion (pul sā´shan) n. The action or the process of beating.

pul-sa-tor (pul´sā tėr) n. Something which will pulsate, such as the heart.

pulse (puls) n., Physiol. The rhythmical beating of the arteries caused by the action of the heart. **pulse** v.

pul-sim-e-ter (pul sim´i tėr) n. A type of device that is used to measure the rate and the strength of one's pulse.

pul-ver-a-ble (pul´vėr a bl) adj. To be capable of being changed or reduced to dust.

pul-ver-ize (pul´ve rīz´) v. To be reduced to dust or powder by crushing.

pul-ver-u-lent (pul ver´ya lent) adj. To be made up of fine powder.

pul-vil-lus (pul vil´us) n. A type of cushion-like mass that is found on the feet of certain insects.

pu-ma (pū´ma) n. A type of large cat that is tawny in color and is located in North and South America.

pump (pump) n. A mechanical device for moving a gas or liquid. v. To raise with a pump; to obtain information

through persistent questioning.

pum-per-nick-el (pum´pėr nik´el) n. A type of coarse bread that is made from rye.

pump-kin (pump´kin) n. A large, edible yellow-orange fruit having a thick rind and many seeds.

punch (punch) n. A tool used for perforating or piercing; a blow with the fist; a drink made of an alcoholic beverage and a fruit juice or other nonalcoholic beverage. v. To use a punch on something; to hit sharply with the hand or fist.

pun-cheon (pun´chon) n. A type of tool used to punch holes into something.

pun-chi-nel-lo (pun´chon) n. A person who is grotesque.

punching bag n. A type of leather bag that is stuffed and used to punch on for practice.

punc-tate (pungk´tāt) adj. To be ending with a point; marked with dots, that are variously scattered over a surface.

punc-til-i-ous (pungk til´ē us) adj. To be formal in one's behavior.

punc-tu-al (pungk´chö al) adj. Prompt; arriving on time.

punc-tu-ate (pungk´chö āt´) v. To mark words or written material with punctuation; to give or show emphasis.

punc-ture (pungk´chėr) v. To prick or pierce with a pointed instrument. n. The act or effect of puncturing.

pun-gent (pun´jent) adj. Sharp or acrid in smell or taste.

pun-ish (pun´ish) v. To subject a person to confinement or impose a penalty for a crime.

punishment (pun´ish ment) n. A penalty which is imposed for breaking the law or a rule.

pun-ster (pun´stė) n. A person who likes to make puns.

punt (punt) n. A narrow, long, flat-bottomed boat; in football, a kick of a football dropped from the hands. v. To kick a football.

pun-ty (pun´tē) n. A rod that is made of iron and is used for the making of glassworks.

pu-ny (pū´nē) adj. To be weak and underdeveloped; insignificant or petty.

pup (pup) n. A puppy, young dog, or the young of other animals.

pu-pa (pū´pa) n. The stage in the development of an insect that is between the larva and the adult stage.

pupil (pū´pil) n. A person who attends school and receives instruction by a teacher.

pu-pil-age (pū´pi laj) n. The state of being a pupil.

pup-pet (pup´it) n. A small figure of an animal or person which is manipulated by hand or by strings. **puppeteer** n.

pup-py (pup´ē) *n.* The young of a dog.

pup tent *n.* A type of tent that sleeps only a few people.

pur-blind (pür´blīnd´) *adj.* To be lacking in insight. **purblindness** *n.*

pur-chase (per´chas) *v.* To receive by paying money as an exchange.

pure (pür) *adj.* Free from anything that damages, weakens, or contaminates; innocent; clean. **pureness** *n.*

pur-ga-tive (pür´ga tiv) *n.* A type of medicine that is used to clean the bowels in preparation for surgery.

purge (perj) *v.* To make clean; to free from guilt or sin; to rid of anything undesirable, as unwanted persons. *Med.* To cause or induce emptying of the bowels. **purge** *n.*

pu-ri-fy (pür´i fī´) *v.* To make clean or pure. **purification** *n.* **purifier** *n.*

pu-ri-ty (pür´i tē) *n.* The quality of being pure; freedom from guilt or sin.

pur-ple (per´pl) *n.* A color between red and violet. **purplish** *adj.*

pur-port (per´pört) *v.* To give the appearance of intending; to imply, usually with the intent to deceive.

pur-pose (per´pos) *n.* A desired goal; an intention. **purposeful** *adj.* **purposeless** *adj.* **purposely** *adv.*

purr (per) *n.* The low, murmuring sound characteristic of a cat. **purr** *v.*

purse (pers) *n.* A small pouch or bag for money; a handbag; a pocketbook; the sum of money offered as a prize.

pur-sue (per sö´) *v.* To seek to achieve; to follow in an attempt to capture.

pur-suit (per söt´) *n.* The act of pursuing an occupation.

pur-vey (per vā´) *v.* To supply provisions as a service. **purveyance** *n.*

pus (pus) *n.* A yellowish secretion formed in infected tissue which contains bacteria.

push (pesh) *v.* To move forward by exerting force; to force oneself through a crowd; to sell illegally. *Slang* To sell illegal drugs.

pus sy (pü´ē) *adj.* To be containing or to be filled with pus.

pus-tu-late (pus´cha lāt´) *v.* To cause blisters.

put (pet) *v.* To cause to be in a location; to bring into a specific relation or state; to bring forward for debate or consideration, as to put up for. **down** To humiliate.

pu-ta-tive (pü´ta tiv) *adj.* Commonly supposed.

pu-tre-fy (pü´tre fī´) *v.* To cause to decay; to decay. **putrefaction** *n.*

putt (put) *n.* In golf, a light stroke made on a putting green to get the ball into the hole.

puz-zle (puz´l) *v.* To bewilder; to confuse. *n.* A toy, board game, or word game which tests one's patience and skills.

pyg-my (pig´mē) *n. pl.* **-ies** A very small person or animal; a dwarf.

py-lon (pī´lon) *n.* A tower serving as a support for electrical power lines.

py-or-rhe-a (pī´o rē´a) *n., Pathol.* Inflammation of the gums and sockets of the teeth. **pyorrheal** *adj.*

py-ral-i-did *n.* A type of moth that has a slender body.

pyr-a-mid (pir´a mid) *n.* A solid structure with a square base and sides which meet at a point.

pyre (pī´er) *n.* A pile of combustible material for burning a dead body.

py-ro-ma-ni-a (pī´ro mā´nē a) *n.* A compulsion to set fires.

py-rom-e-ter (pī rom´ter) *n.* A type of device that can measure very high temperatures. **pyrometrically** *adv.*

py-rope (pī´rōp) *n.* A type of deep-red garnet.

py-ro-pho-bi-a (pī´ro fō´bē a) *n.* A fear of fire that is considered to be abnormal.

py-ro-phor-ic (pī´ro for´ik) *adj.* To be highly flammable.

pyr-rhic (pir´ik) *n.* A metrical foot containing two short syllables.

pyr-rhu-lox-i-a (pir´a lok´sē a) *n.* A type of gray grosbeak that has a rose-colored breast and crest.

py-thon (pī´thon) *n.* A large nonvenomous snake which crushes its prey.

py-u-ri-a (pī ür´ē a) *n., Pathol.* The condition where there is pus in the urine.

pyx-ie (pik´sē) *n.* A type of evergreen plant located in the eastern United States.

pyx-is (pik´sis) *n.* A small box, used by the Romans to hold jewelry.

Q

Q, q (kū) The seventeenth letter of the English alphabet.

qat *n.* A small plant found in Africa, the fresh leaf is chewed for a stimulating effect.

qi-vi-ut *n.* Yarn spun from the fine, soft hair of the musk ox.

qt. *abbr.* Quart.

quad-ran-gle (kwod´rang´gl) *n., Math* A plane figure with four sides and four angles.

quad-rant (kwod´rant) *n.* A quarter section of a circle, subtending or enclosing a central angle of 90 degrees.

qua-draph-o-ny *n.* The recording of sound using four transmission channels.

quad-rate (kwod´rit) *adj.* Being square or almost square.

qua-drat-ics (kwo drat´iks) *n.* A branch of algebra concerned with equations.

quad-ra-ture *n.* An arrangement of two

celestial bodies with a separation of 90 degrees.

qua-dren-ni-um (kwo dren´ē *u*m) *n.* A period consisting of four years.

quad-ri-cen-ten-ni-al *n.* An anniversary celebrating 400 years.

quad-ri-ceps (kwod´ri seps´) *n.* The muscle located in the front of the thigh.

qua-dri-ga *n.* A chariot pulled by four horses abreast.

qua-drille *n.* A square dance with five or six figures executed by four couples.

quad-ril-lion (kwo dril´yon) *n.* A thousand trillions; one followed by fifteen zeros.

quad-ri-par-tite *adj.* Consisting of four persons or parts.

quad-ri-ple-gic *n.* A person who is paralyzed in both arms and both legs.

qua-dru-ma-na *n.* A group of primates distinguished by hand-shaped feet.

quad-ru-ped (kwod´re ped´) *n.* Any animal having four feet.

quad-ru-ple (kwo drö´pl) *adj.* Consisting of four parts; multiplied by four.

qua-dru-plet (kwo drup´lit) *n.* One of four infants born at the same time.

qua-dru-pli-cate (kwo drö´pli kit) *n.* Consisting of four identical parts.

quag-ga (kwag´a) *n.* A wild ass of Africa related to the zebras.

quag-mire (kwag´mīēr´) *n.* An area of soft muddy land that gives way underfoot; a marsh.

qua-hog (kwo´hog) *n.* A clam found in the Atlantic Ocean.

quail (kwāl) *n. pl.* A small game bird, about the same size as the pigeon.

quaint (kwānt) *adj.* Pleasing in an old-fashioned, unusual way.

quake (kwāk) *v.* To shake or tremble violently.

quak-er (kwā´kėr) *n.* The religious sect called the Society of Friends.

qual-i-fi-ca-tion An act of qualifying; the ability, skill, or quality which makes something suitable for a given position.

qualifier *n.* In *computer science*, a symbol or set of symbols in a formula that limits or clearly defines an element.

qual-i-fy (kwol´i fī´) *v.* To prove something able; restrict; limit; modify.

qual-i-ty (kwol´i tē) *n., pl.* qualities A distinguishing characteristic; a high degree of excellence.

qualm (kwäm) *n.* A sudden feeling of sickness; sensation of uneasiness.

quan-da-ry (kwon´da rē) *n.* A state of perplexity.

quan-ti-ty (kwon´ti tē) *n.* Number; amount; bulk; weight; a portion; as a large amount.

quan-tum (kwon´tum) *n., pl.* quanta An amount or quantity.

quar-an-tine (kwor´an tēn´) *n.* A period of enforced isolation for a specified period of time used to prevent the spread of a contagious disease.

quar-rel (kwor´el) *n.* An angry disagreement; a dispute. quarrel *v.* To find fault with; to dispute or debate.

quarrier (kwor´ē ėr) *n.* A person who works in a stone quarry.

quar-ry (kwor´ē) *n., pl.* quarries An animal hunted for food; an open pit or excavation from which limestone or other material is being extracted.

quart (kwort) *n.* A unit of measurement equaling four cups.

quartan (kwor´tan) *n.* Something happening every four days.

quar-ter (kwor´tėr) *n.* One of four equal parts into which anything may be divided; a place of lodging, as a barracks; a United States coin equal to 1/4 of a dollar.

quar-ter-back (kwor´tėr bak´) *n. football* The offensive player who directs the plays for his team.

quarterdeck *n.* The part of a deck used for ceremonial and official use only.

quarter horse *n.* A horse capable of high speed and great endurance.

quarterly *adj.* Payable at intervals of three months.

quar-ter-mas-ter (kwor´tėr mas´tėr) *n.* The officer in charge of supplies for army troops; a navy officer who steers a ship and handles signaling equipment.

quar-tet (kwor tet´) *n.* A musical composition for four voices or instruments; any group or set of four.

quartz (kworts) *n.* A hard, transparent crystallized mineral.

qua-sar (kwā´sär) *n.* One of the most distant and brightest bodies in the universe, which emits immense quantities of radio waves.

quash (kwosh) *v.* To nullify or suppress by judicial action.

quay (kē) *n.* A landing place beside water for loading and unloading ships.

quea-sy (kwē´zē) *adj.* Nauseated; sick. **queasiness** *n.*

que-bra-cho *n.* A tree of the sumac family, which has hard wood found in South America.

queen (kwēn) *n.* The wife of a king; a woman sovereign or monarch; in chess, the most powerful piece on the board, which can move any number of squares in any direction; the fertile female in a colony of social insects.

quell (kwel) *v.* To put down with force; to quiet; to pacify.

quench (kwench) *v.* To extinguish or put out; to cool metal by thrusting into water; to drink to satisfy a thirst.

quer-cit-ron *n.* A large oak tree rich in tannin used in dyeing and tanning.

quer-u-lous (kwer´a lus) *adj.* Complaining or fretting; expressing complaints.

que-ry (kwĕr´ē) n. An injury; a question. v. To question. In computer science, a request for data as a record or set of records from a database.

query language n. In computer science, formal notation for requesting specific data, as from a database.

quest (kwest) n. A search; pursuit; an expedition to find something.

ques-tion (kwes´chan) n. An expression of inquiry which requires an answer; a problem; an unresolved matter; the act of inquiring or asking. **question** v. To ask; to inquire.

ques-tion-able adj. Being in doubt; not certain or sure.

question mark n. A mark of punctuation, (?), used in writing to indicate a question.

ques-tion-naire (kwes´cha nâr´) n. A written series of questions to gather statistical information often used for a survey.

queue (kū) n. In computer science, a sequence of stored programs or data on hold for processing. **queue** v. To form a line; to stand in line.

quib-ble (kwib´l) v. To raise trivial objection. **quibble** n. **quibbler** n.

quiche n. Unsweetened custard baked in a pastry shell, usually with vegetables or seafood.

quick (kwik) adj. Moving swiftly; occurring in a short time; responding, thinking, or understanding something rapidly and easily. **quickly** adv.

quick-en adj. To become faster; to increase in pace.

quick-temp-ered (kwik´tem´pėrd) adj. Being easily angered or upset.

quick-wit-ted (kwik´wit´ld) adj. Being quick to understand something.

quid (kwid) n. A small portion of tobacco; a cow's cud.

qui-es-cent (kwē es´ent) adj. Being in a state of quiet repose.

qui-et (kwī´it) adj. Silent; making very little sound; still; tranquil; calm. **quiet** v. To become or make quiet. **quiet** n. The state of being quiet.

quill (kwil) n. A strong bird feather; a spine from a porcupine; a writing instrument made from a long feather.

quilt (kwilt) n. A bed coverlet made of two layers of cloth with a soft substance between and held in place by lines of stitching. v. To sew or stitch together.

quince n. A fruit resembling a yellow apple used to make marmalade, etc.

quin-i-dine n. An alkaloid used in treating cardiac rhythm irregularities.

qui-nine (kwī´nīn) n. Chem. A very bitter, colorless, crystalline powder used in the treatment of malaria.

quin-quen-ni-al adj. Happening or being done every five years.

quin-sy (kwin´zē) n. Pathol. A severe inflammation of the tonsils, which is accompanied by fever.

quin-tes-sence (kwin tes´ens) n. The most essential and purest form of anything.

quin-tet (kwin tet´) n. A musical composition written for five people; any group of five.

quin-til-lion (kwin til´yon) n. A thousand quadrillions, one followed by eighteen zeros.

quin-tu-ple (kwin tö´pl) adj. Increased five times; multiplied by five; consisting of five parts. **quintuple** v. To make five times larger.

quip (kwip) n. A sarcastic remark.

quire (kwī´ėr) n. Twenty-five sheets of paper removed from a complete ream of paper; a set of all the sheets of paper necessary to form a book.

quirk (kwerk) n. A sudden, sharp bend or twist; a personal mannerism.

quis-ling (kwiz´ling) n. A person who is a traitor, working against his own country from within.

quit (kwit) v. To cease; to give up; to depart; to resign or leave a job or position.

quite (kwit) adv. To the fullest degree; really; actually; to a great extent.

quittance n. A document which releases someone from an obligation.

quiv-er (kwiv´ėr) v. To shake with a trembling motion. n. The arrows used in archery; the case holding the arrows.

quix-ot-ic (kwik sot´ik) adj. Extravagantly romantic, impractical.

quiz (kwiz) v. To question, as with an informal oral or written examination.

quo-rum (kwôr´um) n. The number of members needed in order to validate a meeting.

quo-ta (kwō´ta) n. An allotment or proportional share; a proportion or share required from each person, state, or group in order to meet a certain number required.

quo-ta-tion (kwō tā´shun) n. The exact quoting of words as a passage; the stated current price.

quotation mark n. One of a pair of punctuation marks " " or ' ' around a direct quote.

quote (kwōt) v. To repeat exactly what someone else has previously stated; to state the price of an item.

quo-tid-i-an (kwō tid´ē an) adj. Occurring or recurring daily.

quo-tient (kwō´shent) n. Math. The amount or number which results when one number is divided by another.

QWERTY keyboard n. In computer science, a keyboard with letters arranged the same as those on a typewriter.

R, r (är) The eighteenth letter of the English alphabet.

ra-ba-to (ra bä´tö) *n.* A wide lace-edged collar of the early 17th century.

rab-bet (rab´it) *n.* A recess or groove along the edge of a piece of wood cut to fit another piece to form a joint. *v.* To join the edges of in a rabbet joint.

rab-bi (rab´ī) *n.* An ordained leader of Jews; the leader and teacher of a Jewish congregation. **rabbinic** *adj.*

rab-bin-ate *n.* The dignity of a rabbi.

rab-bit (rab´it) *n.* A burrowing mammal related to but smaller than the hare.

rab-ble (rab´l) *n.* A disorderly crowd; a disordered jumble. **rabble** *v.*

rab-ble-ment *n.* A rabble; a tumult.

rab-ble-rous-er (rab´l rou´zêr) *n.* A person who stirs masses of people to riot; a demogogue.

rab-id (rab´id) *adj.* Affected with rabies; mad; furious. **rabidly** *adv.*

ra-bies (rä´bëz) *n.* An acute, infectious viral disease of the central nervous system, often fatal, which is transmitted by the bite of an infected animal.

rac-coon (ra kön´) *n., pl.* **raccoons, raccoon** A nocturnal mammal with a black, mask-like face and a black and white ringed, bushy tail.

race (räs) *n.* A contest which is judged by speed; any contest, such as a race for an elective office. **race** *v.* **racer** *n.*

race (räs) *n.* The zoological division of the human population having common origin and physical traits, such as hair form and pigmentation; a group of people having such common characteristics or appearances.

ra-ceme (rä sëm´) *n.* A type of plant bearing flowers along its stalk. **racemose** *adj.*

rac-er (rä´sêr) *n.* A person who takes part in a race; one who runs in a race.

ra-chis (rä´kis) *n.* A type of axial structure.

ra-cial (rä´shal) *adj.* A characteristic of a race of people. **racially** *adv.*

rac-ism (rä´siz um) *n.* A thought or belief that one race is better than another race. **racist** *n.* One who believes that one race is better than another race.

rack-et *or* **racquet** *n.* A lightweight bat-like object with netting stretched over an oval frame, used in striking a tennis ball or a shuttlecock.

ra-clette *n.* A Swiss dish with cheese melted over a fire then scraped onto bread or potatoes.

rac-on-teur *n.* One who is skilled in the act of telling stories.

rac-y (rä´së) *adj.* Having a spirited or strongly marked quality; slightly improper or immodest. **racily** *adv.*

ra-dar (rä´där) *n.* A system which uses radio signals to detect the presence of an object or the speed the object is traveling.

ra-dar as-tron-o-my *n.* Astronomy that deals with investigations of the celestial bodies of the solar system by comparing characteristics of reflected radar waves with characteristics of ones transmitted from earth.

ra-dar-scope (rä´där sköp´) *n.* A screen or oscilloscope that serves as a visual indicator in a radar receiver.

rad-dled *adj.* Being in a state of confusion; broken down; worn; lacking composure.

ra-di-al (rä´dë al) *adj.* Pertaining to or resembling a ray or radius; developing from a center axis.

ra-di-ance (rä´dë ans) *n.* The quality of being shiny; the state of being radiant; relating or emitting to radiant heat.

ra-di-ant (rä´dë ant) *adj.* Emitting rays of heat or light; beaming with kindness or love; projecting a strong quality.

ra-di-ant en-er-gy *n.* The energy traveling as a wave motion.

ra-di-ant heat *n.* Heat that is transmitted by radiation.

ra-di-a-tion (rä´dë ä´shan) *n.* An act of radiating; the process of emitting radiant energy in the form of particles or waves. **radiative** *adj.*

ra-di-a-tor (rä´dë ä´tér) *n.* Something which radiates; a system of pipes for heating or cooling external or internal substances.

rad-i-cal (rad´i kal) *adj.* Proceeding from a foundation or root; drastic; making extreme changes in views, conditions, or habits; carrying convictions or theories to their fullest application. **radically** *adv.* **radicalness** *n.*

rad-i-cate *v.* To take root.

rad-i-cle (rad´i kl) *n.* The lower part of a plant embryo or seedling.

ra-di-o (rä´dë ö´) *n.* The technique of communicating by radio waves; the business of broadcasting programmed material to the public via radio waves.

ra-di-o-ac-tiv-i-ty *n. Phys.* A spontaneous emission of electromagnetic radiation, as from a nuclear reaction.

ra-di-o-chem-is-try *n.* The part of chemistry that deals with radioactive bodies. **radiochemical** *adj.*

ra-di-o-fre-quen-cy (rä´dë ö frē´kwen sē) *n.* A frequency which is above 15,000 cycles per second that is used in radio transmission.

ra-di-o-gram (rä´dë ö gram´) *n.* A type of radiograph.

ra-di-o-graph *n.* A picture made by rays from a radioactive substance. **-ic** *adj.* **radiographically** *adv.*

ra-di-o-lar-o-an *n.* A member of the group of minute marine protozoans having an amoeboid body.

ra-di-o-lo-ca-tion *n.* The finding of the location of something using of radar.

ra-di-ol-o-gy (rā´dē ol´o jē) *n.* A science which deals with rays from a radioactive substance and their uses for medical diagnosis. **radiologist** *n..*

ra-di-o-lu-cen-cy *n.* The state of being permeable to radiation.

ra-di-o-pho-to *n.* A picture transmitted via radio.

ra-di-o-sonde *n.* A miniature radio transmitter with instruments for broadcasting the humidity, pressure, and temperature.

rad-ish (rad´ish) *n.* The pungent, edible root of the radish plant.

ra-di-um (rā´dē um) *n.* A radioactive metallic element symbolized by Ra.

ra-di-us (rā´dē us) *n., pl.* **radii** *or* **radiuses** A line from the center of a circle to its surface or circumference.

ra-dix *n.* The origin of something; a root.

ra-dome *n.* A plastic housing which protects the antenna assembly on an airplane.

ra-don (rā´don) *n.* A heavy, colorless, radioactive gaseous element symbolized by Rn.

rad-u-la (raj´e la) *n.* The chitinous band in a mollusk's mouth that is used to break up its food. **radular** *adj.*

raff (raf) *n.* The rabble of a group or town; riffraff.

raf-fi-a (raf´ē a) *n.* A fiber from an African palm tree used for making baskets, hats, and other woven articles.

raf-fi-nose (raf´i nōs´) *n.* A slightly sweet sugar obtained commercially from cotton seed meal.

raff-ish (raf´ish) *adj.* Something marked by crudeness or flashy vulgarity. **raffishly** *adv.* **raffishness** *n.*

raf-fle (raf´l) *n.* A game of chance; a lottery in which one buys chances to win something.

raf-fle-si-a *n.* A type of plant that has foul-smelling flowers and appears to be stemless.

raft (raft) *n.* A floating structure made from logs or planks and used for water transportation.

rag (rag) *n.* A cloth which is useless and sometimes used for cleaning purposes.

ra-ga (rä´ga) *n.* Ancient melodic patterns in Indian music.

rage (rāj) *n.* Violent anger; intense feelings. **raging** *adj.*

rag-gle (rag´l) *n.* A small groove cut in masonry.

rag-i (rag´ē) *n.* East Indian cereal grass used as a staple food in the Orient.

rag-lan (rag´lan) *n.* A loose fitting coat with extra wide sleeves.

raglan sleeve *n.* A sleeve with slanted seams from the underarm to the neck.

rag-man *n.* A person who collects objects which have been discarded by others.

ra-gout (ra gü´) *n.* A highly seasoned meat and vegetable dish with a thick sauce.

raid (rād) *n.* A sudden invasion or seizure. **raid** *v.*

rail (rāl) *n.* A horizontal bar of metal, wood, or other strong material supported at both ends or at intervals; the steel bars used to support a track on a railroad.

rail-ler-y *n.* A teasing that is good-humored.

rail-road *n.* A road having a line of rails providing a track for cars propelled by a locomotive. **railroader** *n.*

railroad worm *n.* A fruit fly larva.

rail-split-ter *n.* A person who chops logs into fence rails.

rai-ment (rā´ment) *n.* Garments.

rain (rān) *n.* The condensed water from atmospheric vapor, which falls to earth in the form of drops.

rain-bow (rān´bō´) *n.* An arc that contains bands of colors of the spectrum and is formed opposite the sun and reflects the sun's rays, usually visible after a light rain shower.

rain forest *n.* A tropical woodland that has an annual rainfall of at least 100 inches.

rain-wear *n.* Waterproof clothing.

raise (rāz) *v.* To cause to move upward; to build; to make greater in size, price, or amount; to increase the status; to grow; as plants; to rear as children; to stir one's emotions; to obtain or collect, as funds or money.

raised (rāzd) *adj.* Being elevated.

rai-sin (rā´zin) *n.* A grape dried for preservation and eating.

ra-ja (rä´ja) *n.* An Indian prince or chief.

ral-len-tan-do (rä´len tän´dō) adj. In music, a gradual decrease in tempo.

ral-ly (ral´ē) *v.* To call together for a common cause. **rally** *n.* A rapid recovery, as from depression, exhaustion, or any setback; in a meeting whose purpose is to rouse or create support, an automobile race over public roads at average speeds between checkpoints over a route unfamiliar to the participants.

ram (ram) *n.* A male sheep; an implement used to drive or crush by impact; to cram or force into place.

RAM *abbr.* Random access memory.

ram-ble (ram´bl) *v.* To stroll or walk without a special destination in mind; to talk without sequence of ideas. **ramble** *n.* **ramblingly** *adv.*

ram-bler *n.* A climbing rose with small flowers in large clusters.

ram-bunc-tious (ram bungk´shus) *adj.* Rough or boisterous; unruly.

ram-bu-tan *n.* A bright red spiny fruit

found on the soapberry plant.

ram-e-kin (ram´e kin) n. A dish made of cheese with bread crumbs or eggs baked in a mold; a baking dish.

ra-men-tum (ra men´tum) n. A type of scaly material that adheres to the leaves and the stems of certain ferns.

ra-met n. A member of a clone.

ra-mie (ram´ē) n. A perennial plant with strong fibers used in the manufacture of clothing.

ram-i-form (ram´i form˘) adj. To have the shape of a branch.

ram-i-fy (ram´i fī´) v. To send forth branches.

ra-mose (rā´mōs) adj. To have branching.

ramp (ramp) n. An incline which connects two different levels; movable staircase allows passengers to enter or leave an aircraft.

ram-page (ram pāj´) n. A course of destruction or violent behavior. **rampage** v. To storm about in a rampage. **rampageous** adj.

ram-pan-cy (ram´pan sē) n. The state or quality of being rampant.

ram-pant (ram´pant) adj. Acting or growing without control; wild in actions; extravagant; standing on the hind legs and elevating both forelegs. **rampantly** adv.

ram-part (ram´pärt) n. An embankment raised as a fortification or barrier.

ram-pi-on n. A tuberous root bellflower with leaves which can be used in salads.

ram-rod (ram´rod´) n. A metal rod used to drive or plunge the charge into a muzzle-loading gun or pistol; the rod used for cleaning the barrels of a rifle or other firearm.

ram-shack-le (ram´shak´l) adj. Likely to fall apart from poor construction or maintenance.

rams-horn (ramz´horn´) n. A snail used in an aquarium as a scavenger.

ram-til n. A tropical herb grown for its oil seeds.

ram-u-lose (ram´ya lōs´) adj. To have small branches.

ranch (ranch) n. A large establishment for raising cattle, sheep, or other livestock; a large farm that specializes in a certain crop or animal.

ran-cid (ran´sid) adj. Having a rank taste or smell. **rancidness** n.

ran-cor (rang´kėr) n. Bitter ill will. **rancorous** adj. **rancorousness** n.

ran-dom (ran´dom) adj. Done or made in a way that has no specific pattern or purpose; to select from a group whose members all had an even chance of being chosen. **randomly** adv.

ran-dom-iz-a-tion n. An arrangement to simulate a chance distribution.

rang v. Past tense of ring.

range (rānj) n. An area over which anything moves; an area of activity; a tract of land over which animals such as cattle and horses graze; an extended line or row especially of mountains; an open area for shooting at a target; large cooking stove with burners and oven; the limits of a series. **range** v. To arrange in a certain order; to extend or proceed in a particular direction.

range finder n. Instrument that is used in gunnery to determine the distance to a target.

rang-er (rān´jėr) n. A person who is hired to tend the public forests.

rang-y (rān´jē) adj. To be adapted for moving around. **ranginess** n.

ra-ni (rā´nē) n. A Hindu queen.

ra-nid n. A large family of frogs.

rank (rank) n. A degree of official position or status. **rank** v. To place in order, class, or rank. **rank** adj. A strong and disagreeable odor, smell, or taste. **rankly** adv. **rankness** n.

ran-kle (rang´kl) v. To cause anger or deep bitterness.

ran-sack (ran´sak) v. To search or plunder through every part of something.

ran-som (ran´som) n. The price demanded or paid for the release of a kidnaped person; the payment for the release of a person or property detained. **ransom** v.

rant (rant) v. To talk in a wild, excited loud way. **ranter** n.

ran-u-la (ran´ū la) n. A type of cyst that can occur under the tongue due to a blockage in a duct.

rap (rap) v. To talk with people with similar interest and problems.

ra-pa-cious adj. Living on prey seized alive; taking by force; plundering.

rape (rāp) n. The crime of forcible sexual intercourse; abusive treatment.

rap-id (rap´id) adj. Having great speed; completed quickly or in a short time. **rapidity** n. **rapidness** n.

rap-id–fire adj. Pertaining to firing shots in close succession to one another.

rap-id trans-it n. The train system that runs within a city and in the area around it.

ra-pi-er (rā´pē ėr) n. A long, slender, straight sword with two edges.

rap-ine (rap´in) n. The forcible taking of another's property.

rap-pa-ree n. An Irish soldier or bandit.

rap-pee (ra pē´) n. A snuff made from dark tobacco leaves.

rap-pel (ra pel´) n. A descent from a cliff using a rope under one thigh, across the back and over the opposite shoulder.

rap-pi-ni (rap skal on) n. An immature turnip plant used for its greens.

rap-port (ra pōr´) *n.* A harmonious relationship.

rap-proche-ment (rä prosh män´) *n.* The establishment of cordial relations.

rap-scal-ion (rap skal´yon) n. A rascal.

rapt (rapt) *adj.* Deeply absorbed or carried away with something and not noticing anything else. **raptness** *n.*

rap-tor (rap´tōr) *n.* A bird of prey.

rap-to-ri-al (rap tōr´ē al) adj. Having the ability to seize prey.

rap-ture (rap´chér) *n.* An experience of being carried away by emotion. **rapturous** *adj.* **rapturously** *adv.*

rare (râr) *adj.* Scarce; infrequent; often held in high esteem or admiration because of infrequency. **rareness** *n.*

rare-bit (râr´bit) *n.* A dish made of cheese poured over toast or crackers.

rar-e-fy *v.* To make thin or less dense.

rare-ly *adv.* Seldom; not often.

rar-ing *adj.* Being full of eagerness and enthusiasm.

rar-i-ty *n.* The quality of something being rare.

ras-bo-ra (raz bōr´a) *n.* A breed of brightly colored fish often kept in tropical aquariums.

ras-cal (ras´kal) *n.* A person full of mischief; a person who is not honest.

ras-cal-i-ty *n.* Behavior which is mischievous.

rash (rash) *adj.* Acting without consideration or caution. *n.* A skin irritation or eruption caused by an allergic reaction.

rash-er *n.* A thin slice of bacon; a portion of several slices of bacon.

ra-so-ri-al (ra sōr´ē al) *adj.* Scratching the ground in search of food.

rasp *n.* A file with coarse raised and pointed projections. **rasp** *v.* To scrape or rub with a coarse file; to utter something in a rough, grating voice. **rasper** *n.*

rasp-ber-ry (raz´ber´ē) *n.* A small edible fruit, red or black in color and having many small seeds. *Slang* Contemptuous sound made by expelling air with the tongue between the lips in order to make a vibration.

rasp-y (ras´pē) *adj.* Grating; irritable.

ras-ter *n.* An area onto which an image is reproduced in a kinescope.

rat-a-fia (rat´a fē´a) *n.* A liqueur flavored with kernels of fruit and almonds.

rat-a-tat (rat´a tat´) *n.* A sharp tapping, or repeated knocking.

ratch-et (rach´it) *n.* A mechanism consisting of a pawl that allows a wheel or bar to move in one direction only.

rate (rāt) *n.* The measure of something to a fixed unit; the degree of price or value; a fixed ratio or amount. **rate** *v.* To appraise.

ra-tel (rāt´el) *n.* An African nocturnal carnivorous mammal resembling a badger.

rate of ex-change *n.* The amount of one currency which equals the given amount of another.

rathe (rāth) *adj.* To be before the normal time.

rath-er (rath´ér) *adv.* Preferably; with more reason or justice; more accurate or precise.

rat-i-cide (rat´i sīd´) *n.* A material that is used to kill rats.

rat-i-fy (rat´i fī´) *v.* To approve something in an official way.

ra-ti-ne (rat´i nā´) *n.* A nubby ply yarn made by twisting a thick and a thin yarn under pressure.

rat-ing (rā´ting) *n.* A relative evaluation or estimate of something.

ra-tio (rā´shō) *n., pl.* **ratios** The relationship between two things in amount, size, degree, expressed as a proportion.

ra-ti-o-ci-na-tion (rash´ē os´i nā´shan) *n.* A reasoned train of thought.

ra-tion (rash´an) *n.* A fixed portion or share. **ration** *v.* To provide or allot in rations. **rationing** *n.*

ra-tion-al (rash´a nal) *adj.* Having the faculty of reasoning; being of sound mind. **rationality** *n.* **rationally** *adv.*

ra-tion-ale *n.* An explanation of principles, opinions, beliefs, or phenomena.

ra-tio-nal-ize *v.* To provide plausible but not truthful reasons for conduct.

ra-toon (ra tön´) *v.* To grow or sprout up from the root.

rat race *n.* A strenuous activity or rush.

rat-tan (ra tan´) *n.* An Asian palm whose stems are used to make wicker works.

rat-teen *n.* A woolen fabric which is coarse in texture.

rat-tle (rat´l) *v.* To make a series of rapid, sharp noises in quick succession; to talk rapidly; chatter. **rattle** *n.* A baby's toy made to rattle when shaken.

rat-tle-brain (rat´l brān´) *n.* A thoughtless person. **rattlebrained** *adj.*

rat-tle-trap (rat´l trap´) *n.* Something that is rickety or noisy; an old car.

rat-ty (rat´ē) *adj.* Shabby; unkempt.

rau-cous (ro´kus) *adj.* Loud and rowdy; having a rough, hoarse sound; disorderly. **raucously** *n.*

raun-chy *adj.* Being dirty, slovenly.

rau-wol-fi-a *n.* A type of shrub which is used as a source of the drug reserpine.

rav-age (rav´ij) *v.* To bring on heavy destruction; devastate. **ravagement, ravager** *n.*

rave (rāv) *v.* To speak incoherently; to speak with enthusiasm. **rave** *n.* The act of raving.

rav-el (rav´el) *v.* To separate fibers or

threads; to unravel. **ravel** *n.* A loose thread; something tangled.

ra-ven (rā´ven) *n.* A large bird, with shiny black feathers. **raven** *adj.* Of or relating to the glossy sheen or color of the raven.

rav-en-ing *adj.* To be hunting in order to devour something.

rav-en-ous (rav´e nus) *adj.* Being very hungry and eager for food.

rav-in (rav´n) *n.* Something seized as prey.

ra-vine (ra vēn) *n.* A deep gorge with steep sides in the earth's surface, usually created by flowing water.

rav-ing (rav´ ing) *adj.* An incoherent, wild, or extravagant outburst.

rav-i-o-li (rav´ē ō´lē) *n.* A small piece of dough filled with meat or cheese served in a tomato sauce.

rav-ish (rav´ish) *v.* To seize and carry off; to rape. **ravishment, ravisher** *n.*

rav-ish-ing *adj.* Unusually striking.

raw (ro) *adj.* Uncooked; in natural condition; not processed; inexperienced; damp, sharp, or chilly. **rawly** *adv.* **rawness** *n.*

raw material *n.* Material that is existing in its natural form.

ray (rā) *n.* A thin line of radiation or light; a small trace or amount; one of several lines coming from a point.

ray-on (rā´on) *n.* A synthetic cellulose yarn; any fabric made from such yarn.

raze (rāz) *v.* To destroy or demolish.

ra-zor (rā´zér) *n.* A sharp cutting instrument used especially for shaving.

razz (raz) *v. Slang* To heckle; to tease.

raz-zle-daz-zle (raz´l daz´l) *n.* A state of complete confusion.

re- *prefix* Again, anew, or reverse action.

reach (rēch) *v.* To stretch out; to be able to grasp. **reach** *n.* The act of stretching out. **reachable** *adj.* **reacher** *n.*

re-act (rē akt´) *v.* To act in response to. *Chem.* To undergo a chemical change; to experience a chemical reaction; to move in a reverse direction; to cause to react.

re-ac-tant (rē ak´tant) *n.* Substance which enters into and is altered by the course of a chemical reaction.

re-ac-tion (rē ak´shan) *n.* The mental or bodily response to an activity; the process or act of reacting; the action that is induced by vital resistance to another action; exhaustion caused by excessive exertion or stimulation; an emotional disorder forming a person's response to his life; the force that a body exerts when encountering force from another body in the opposite direction; a chemical change; the state resulting from an interaction of chemical entities.

re-ac-tion-ar-y *adj.* Marked by, or relating to political reaction.

re-ac-ti-vate *v.* To activate something again. **reactively** *adv.* **reactiveness** *n.* **reactivity** *n.*

re-ac-tor (rē ak´tér) *n.* A person, object, device, or substance which reacts to something.

read (rēd) *v.* To visually go over something, as a book, and to understand its meaning; to learn or be informed; to perceive something in a meaning which may or may not actually be there; to become acquainted with or look at the contents; to recognize the nature of by observing outward expression or signs.

read-i-ly (red´i lē) *adv.* Without hesitation; without a lot of difficulty.

read-ing *n.* An interpretation of something; the act of reading; a particular interpretation or version; the indication of a state of affairs.

read-out (rēd´out´) *n.* In *computer science*, the process of removing information from a computer and displaying it in an understandable form; the process of reading something; the radio transmission of pictures or information from a space vehicle either immediately upon acquisition or by tape recording playback.

read-y (red´ē) *adj.* Prepared for use or action; quick or prompt. **readiness** *n.*

read-y-made *n.* Something made beforehand for sale to the public; something that is lacking individuality or originality.

Reagan, Ronald Wilson *n.* (1911-) The fortieth president of the United States from 1981-1989.

re-a-gent (rē ā´jent) *n.* Any substance which causes a chemical reaction.

re-ag-gre-gate *v.* To reform into a whole. **reaggregate, reaggregation** *n.*

re-al (rē´al) *adj.* Something which is existing, genuine, true, or authentic. *Law* Property which is regarded as permanent, fixed, or immovable; not illusory, artificial, or fraudulent.

real estate *n.* The property in land and buildings.

re-al-gar *n.* An orange-red mineral consisting of arsenic sulfide with a resinous luster.

re-a-li-a (rē ā´lē a) *n.* Objects used to relate classroom teaching to the real life of people studying.

re-al-ism (rē´a liz´um) *n.* Concern with actual facts and things as they really are. **realist** *n.* **realistic** *adj.*

re-al-i-ty (rē al´i tē) *n. pl.* **realities** The fact or state of being real or genuine; an actual situation or real event; something that is neither dependent nor derivative but exists necessarily.

re-al-ize (rē´a līz´) *v.* To understand

correctly; to make real; to make or cause to seem real. **realizable** *adj*. **realizer, realization** *n*.

re-al-ly (rē´a lē) *adv*. Actually; truly; indeed; unquestionably.

realm (relm) *n*. A scope or field of any power or influence.

re-al-po-li-tik *n*. Politics that are based on material and practical factors and not on ethical or theoretical objectives.

real-valued *adj*. Using only real numbers for values.

ream (rēm) *n*. A quantity of paper containing 500 sheets; a huge amount. **ream** *v*. To widen the opening of something; to shape a hole by reaming.

reap (rēp) *v*. To harvest a crop with a sickle or other implement; to cut with a scythe, sickle, or other harvesting machine.

reap-er (rē´pėr) *n*. A machine used to reap grain; one who reaps.

reap-hook *n*. An implement that is held by the hand and has a hook-shaped blade used in reaping grain.

rear (rēr) *n*. The back. **rear** *adj*. Of or at the rear. **rear** *v*. To raise up on the hind legs; to raise as an animal or child; to erect by building something.

rea-son (rē´zon) *n*. A statement given to confirm or justify a belief, promise, or excuse; the ability to decide things, to obtain ideas, to think clearly, and to make logical and rational choices and decisions. **reason** *v*. To discuss something logically. **reasoning** *adj*.

rea-son-a-ble (rē´zo na bl) *adj*. Moderate; rational; not excessive or extreme. **reasonableness** *n*.

re-as-sur-ance *n*. The act of reassuring, reinsurance.

re-as-sure (rē´a sher´) *v*. To restore confidence. **reassuringly** *adv*.

reave *v*. To carry away. **reaver** *n*.

re-bar-ba-tive *adj*. The act of being repellent. **rebarbatively** *adv*.

re-bate (rē´bāt) *n*. A deduction allowed on items sold; a discount; money which is returned to the purchaser from the original payment. **rebate** *v*. To return part of the payment. **rebater** *n*.

reb-be *n*. A Jewish spiritual leader.

re-bec *n*. An ancient musical instrument with a pear-shaped body and slender neck.

re-bel (ri bel´) *v*. To refuse allegiance; to resist any authority; to react with violence; to take arms against a government.

re-bel-lion (ri bel´yon) *n*. An organized uprising to change or overthrow an existing authority.

re-bel-lious (ri bel´yus) *adj*. Engaged in rebellion; relating to a rebel or rebellion; characteristic of a rebellion. **rebelliously** *adv*. **rebelliousness** *n*.

re-birth (rē berth´) *n*. A revival or renaissance; reincarnation; spiritual regeneration.

re-bound (ri bound´) *v*. To spring back; to recover from a setback or frustration; to gain possession of a rebound ball in basketball. **rebound** *n*. Recoil.

re-bo-zo *n*. A long scarf worn by Mexican women.

re-broad-cast (rē brod´kast´) *v*. To repeat or broadcast again at a later time or date. **rebroadcaster** *n*.

re-buff (ri buf´) *v*. To refuse abruptly; to snub.

re-build (rē bild´) *v*. To restore or make extensive changes to a building; to reconstruct; remodel.

re-buke (ri būk´) *v*. To reprimand; to criticize sharply; to turn back. **rebuke** *n*. Strong disapproval.

re-bus (rē´bus) *n*. A riddle using words or syllables whose names resemble the intended words or syllables in sound.

re-but (ri but´) *v*. To try and prove someone wrong by argument or evidence; to contradict by formal argument.

re-but-tal *n*. An argument that rebuts.

re-but-ter (ri but´ėr) *n*. The reply of a defendant to the plaintiff's surrejoinder.

re-cal-ci-trant (ri kal´si trant) *adj*. Being difficult to handle or operate.

re-cal-cu-late (rē kal´kū lāt´) *v*. To calculate again to discover an error or formulate new conclusions.

re-ca-les-cence *n*. An increase in temperature occurring while cooling metal.

re-call (ri kol´) *v*. To order or summon to return to ask for something to be returned; so that defects can be fixed or repaired; to remember; to recollect. **recallability** *n*. **recallable** *adj*.

re-cant (ri kant´) *v*. To formally admit that a previously held belief was wrong by making public confession; to withdraw; renounce. **recantation** *n*.

re-cap (rē´kap´) *v*. To restore an old tire; to review or summarize something. **recappable** *adj*.

re-cap-i-tal-i-za-tion *n*. A revision of the capital structure of a corporation.

re-ca-pit-u-la-tion *n*. A concise summary; the third section of a sonata.

re-cast (rē kast´) *v*. To cast new people in a play; to cast once again.

re-cede (ri sēd´) *v*. To move back; as flood water; to withdraw from an agreement; to grow less or smaller.

re-ceipt (ri sēt´) *n*. The written acknowledgment of something received. **receipts** An amount of money received.

re-ceiv-ables (ri sē´va blz) *n*. The amount of money received.

re-ceive (ri sēv´) *v*. To take or get something; to greet customers or guests; to accept as true or correct; to assimilate through senses.

re-ceiv-er (ri sē´vėr) *n.* A person that receives something.

re-cen-sion (ri sen´shan) *n.* A revision of a text.

re-cent (rē´sent) *adj.* Happening at a time just before the present; relating to a short time ago. **recently** *adv.* **recentness** *n.*

re-cep-ta-cle (ri sep´ta kl) *n.* Anything which holds something; an electrical outlet designed to receive a plug.

re-cep-tion (ri sep´shan) *n.* The act or manner of receiving something; a formal entertainment of guests, as a wedding reception.

re-cep-tion-ist (ri sep´sha nist) *n.* An employee who greets callers and answers the telephone for a business.

re-cep-tive (ri sep´tiv) *adj.* Able to receive; open and responsive to ideas. **receptively** *adv.* **receptivity** *n.*

re-cep-tor (ri sep´tėr) *n.* A group of cells that receive stimuli.

re-cess (ri ses´) *n.* A break in the normal routine of something; a depression or niche in a smooth surface.

re-ces-sion (ri sesh´an) *n.* The act of receding; withdrawal; a period or time of reduced economic activity.

re-ces-sion-al (ri sesh´a nal) *n.* A musical piece at the conclusion of a service. **recessive** *adj.* Having a tendency to go backward. **recessively** *adv.*

re-charge *v.* To restore the active materials in a battery; to make a new attack. **recharger** *n.* **rechargeable** *adj.*

re-cheat *n.* A hunting call on a horn to assemble the hounds.

re-cid-i-vism *n.* A tendency to relapse into a previous mode of behavior.

rec-i-pe (res´i pē) *n.* The directions and a list of ingredients for preparing food.

re-cip-i-ent (ri sip´ē ent) *n.* A person who receives.

re-cip-ro-cal (ri sip´ro kal) *adj.* To return the same way.

reciprocal pronoun *n.* A pronoun to denote mutual action between members in a plural subject.

re-cip-ro-cate (ri sip´ro kāt´) *v.* To give and return mutually, one gift or favor for another. **reciprocator** *n.*

re-cip-ro-ca-tion *n.* A mutual exchange; an alternating motion. **-tive** *adj.*

rec-i-proc-i-ty *n.* Mutual exchange of privileges; the state of being reciprocal.

re-cit-al (ri sīt´al) *n.* A performance given by an individual musician or dancer. **recitalist** *n.*

rec-i-ta-tion *n.* An instance of repeating aloud; a student's oral reply to questions.

re-cite (ri sīt´) *v.* To repeat something from memory; give an account of

something in detail. **reciter** *n.*

reck-less (rek´lis) *adj.* State of being careless and rash when doing something. **-ness** *n.* **-ly** *adv.*

reck-on (rek´on) *v.* To calculate; to compute; to estimate; to consider; to assume. **reckon with** Take into consideration.

re-claim (ri klām´) *v.* To redeem; to reform; to recall; to change to a more desirable condition or state.

rec-la-ma-tion (rek´la mā´shan) *n.* The state of being reclaimed.

re-cline (ri klīn´) *v.* To assume a prone position.

re-clos-able *adj.* Capable of being shut or closed again.

rec-luse (rek´lōs) *n.* A person who chooses to live in seclusion.

rec-og-ni-tion (rek´og nish´an) *n.* An acknowledgment which is formal; the action of recognizing something; special attention or notice.

re-cog-ni-zance (ri kog´ni zans) *n.* An amount of money which will be forfeited for a nonperformance of an obligation.

rec-og-nize (rek´og nīz´) *v.* To experience or identify something or someone as having been known previously; to be appreciative. **recognizable** *adj.* **recognizably** *adv.*

re-coil (ri koil´) *v.* To fall back or to rebound; to spring back under pressure.

rec-ol-lect (rek´o lekt´) *v.* To remember or recall to the mind. **recollection** *n.*

rec-om-mend (rek´o mrnd´) *v.* To suggest to another as desirable; advise. **recommendation** *n.* **-able** *adj.*

re-com-mit (rē´ko mit´) *v.* To refer back to; to entrust or consign again. **recommitment** *n.* **recommittal** *n.*

rec-om-pense (rek´om pens´) *v.* To reward with something for a service.

re-com-pose (rē´kom pōz´) *v.* To restore the composure of. **recomposition** *n.*

rec-on-cile (rek´on sīl´) *v.* To restore a friendship after an estrangement. **reconcilably** *adv.* **reconcilable** *adj.* **reconciler** *n.* **reconcilement** *n.*

rec-on-dite (rek´on dīt´) *adj.* Being obscure. **reconditely** *adv.*

re-con-di-tion (rē´kon dish´an) *v.* To return to a good condition.

re-con-firm (rē´kon ferm´) *v.* Confirm something again. **reconfirmation** *n.*

re-con-nais-sance (ri kon´i sans) *n.* An observation of territory such as that of the enemy.

re-con-noi-ter (rē´ko noi´tėr) *v.* To survey a region.

re-con-sid-er (rē´kon sid´ėr) *v.* To think about again with a view to changing a previous action or decision. **reconsideration** *n.*

re-con-sti-tute *v.* To restore to a former condition. reconstitution *n.*

re-con-struct *v.* To build something again. reconstructible, -tive *adj.*

re-con-struc-tion (rē'kon struk'shan) *n.* Something which has been reconstructed or rebuilt.

re-con-ver-sion *n.* Returning back to the previous or original state.

re-con-vey *v.* To return back to a previous position or owner. reconveyance *n.*

re-cord (ri kord') *v.* To write down for future use or permanent reference; to preserve sound on a tape or disk for replay; a phonograph record. record *n.* Information which is recorded and kept permanently.

re-cord-er (ri kor'dér) *n.* A person who records things such as official transactions.

re-cord-ing (ri kor'ding) *n.* The act of making a transcription of sounds.

re-count (rē kount') *v.* To tell the facts; narrate or describe in detail; to count again. recount *n.* A second count to check the results of the first count.

re-coup (ri köp') *v.* To be reimbursed; to recover. recoupable *adj.*

re-course (rē'kōrs) *n.* A turning to or an appeal for help; a source of help.

re-cov-er (ri kuv'ér) *v.* To regain something which was lost; to be restored to good health. *Law* To obtain a judgment for damages. recoverability *n.* recoverable *adj.* recoverer *n.*

re-cov-er-y (ri kuv'e rē) *n.* The power to regain something.

rec-re-ant (rek'rē ant) *adj.* Cowardly; unfaithful.

re-cre-ate (rē'krēāt') *v.* To create again; to form in the imagination. recreative *adj.* recreatable *adj.* recreative *adj.*

rec-re-a-tion (rek'rē ā'shan) *n.* Refreshment of body and mind; a pleasurable occupation or exercise.

re-crim-i-nate *v.* The retaliatory charging of another. recriminatory, recriminative *adj.* recrimination *n.*

re-cru-desce (rō'krū des') *v.* To break out; become raw again.

re-cruit (ri krōt') *v.* To enlist someone for military or naval purposes; to look for someone as for a service or employment. *n.* A newly enlisted person. recruiter, recruitment *n.*

rec-tal (rek'tal) *adj.* Referring to the rectum of the body. rectally *adv.*

rec-tan-gle (rek'tang'gl) *n.* A parallelogram with all right angles. rectangular *adj.* rectangularity *n.*

rec-ti-fi-er (rek'ti fī'ér) *n.* That which rectifies something. rectifiable *adj.*

rec-ti-fy (rek'ti fī') *v.* To make correct. *Chem.* To purify by repeated distillations. *Electr.* To make an alternating current a direct current. -fication *n.*

rec-ti-lin-ear (rek'ti lin'ē ér) *adj.* Made up of or indicated by straight lines; bounded by straight lines. -ly *adv.*

rec-ti-tude (rek'ti tōd') *n.* Rightness in principles and conduct; correctness.

rec-to (rek'tō) *n.* The right hand page of a book.

rec-tor (rek'tér) *n.* A member of the clergy in charge of a parish; a priest in charge of a congregation, church, or parish; the principal or head of a school or of a college. rectorate *n.* rectorial *adj.* rectorship *n.*

rec-to-ry (rek'to rē) *n.* The rector's residence.

rec-trix *n.* The quill feathers of a bird's tail that are important in controlling flight.

rec-tum (rek'tum) *n.,* Anat. The lower terminal portion of the large intestine connecting the colon and anus.

re-cum-bent (ri kum'bent) *adj.* Lying down or reclining. recumbently *adv.*

re-cu-per-ate (ri kö'pe rāt') *v.* To regain strength or to regain one's health; to recover from a financial loss. recuperation *n.* recuperative *adj.*

re-cur (ri ker') *v.* To happen, to return, or to appear again. recurrence *n.*

re-cur-rent (ri kür'ent) *adj.* Happening time after time. recurrently *adv.*

re-cu-san-cy *n.* The refusal to accept established authority.

re-cy-cle *v.* To return to an earlier usable condition. recyclable *adj.*

red (red) *n.* Having the color which resembles blood, as pigment or dye which colors red.

re-dact (ri dakt') *v.* To adapt for publication. redactional *adj.*

red carpet *n.* A greeting reserved for very important people.

Red Cross *n.* An organization which helps people in need, collects and preserves human blood for use in emergencies, and responds with help in time of disaster.

rede (rēd) *v.* To advise or counsel.

re-dec-o-rate (rē dek'o rāt') *v.* To change in appearance; to refurbish. redecorator *n.* redecoration *n.*

re-deem (ri dēm') *v.* To buy back; to pay off; to turn something in, as coupons or rain checks and receive something in exchange. redeemable *adj.*

re-de-fine (*v.* To examine with a view to change. redefinition *n.*

re-demp-tion (ri demp'shan) *n.* The act of redeeming; rescue; ransom; that which redeems; salvation.

re-demp-tion-er (ri demp'shan ér) *n.* An immigrant to America who obtained passage by becoming a servant.

re-demp-tive (ri demp'tiv) *adj.* Relating to redemption.

re-de-ploy (rē'di ploi') *v.* To move men

and equipment from one location to another.

re-de-scribe *v.* To give a more updated version of something.

re-de-sign (rē'di zīn') *v.* To change or revise the appearance or function of something.

re-de-vel-op-ment *n.* The renovation of a rundown area.

red-in-gote (red'ing gōt) *n.* A fitted double-breasted coat with wide flat cuffs and collar worn by men in the 18th century.

red ink *n.* A business loss.

red-in-te-grate (red in'te grāt') *v.* To restore to a former sound state.

re-di-rect (rē'di rekt') *v.* To change the course of. **redirection** *n.*

re-dis-trib-ute (rē'di strib'ūt) *v.* To spread to different areas. **redistributive** *adj.* **redistribution** *n.*

re-double *v.* To make something twice in size or amount.

re-doubt (ri dout') *n.* A small enclosed fortification.

re-doubt-a-ble *adj.* To be dreaded. **redoubtably** *adv.*

re-dound (ri dound') *v.* To have an effect on something.

red pencil *v.* To correct; to censor.

re-dress (ri dres') *v.* To put something right; to remedy. **redresser** *n.*

red tide *n.* The presence of large numbers of dinoflagellates in seawater which is fatal to many forms of marine life.

re-duce (ri dōs') *v.* To decrease; lessen in number, degree, or amount; to put into order; to lower in rank; to lose weight by dieting. **reducer** *n.* **-ible** *adj.*

re-duc-tion (ri duk'shan) *n.* The state of being reduced.

re-dun-dant (ri dun'dant) *adj.* Exceeding what is necessary; repetitive. **redundantly** *adv.* **redundancy** *n.*

re-du-pli-cate (ri dō'pli kāt') *v.* To repeat something. **reduplication** *n.* **reduplicatively** *adv.*

re-ech-o *v.* To reverberate again.

reed (rēd) *n.* Tall grass with a slender stem, which grows in wet areas; a thin tongue of wood, metal, cane, or plastic; placed in the mouthpiece of an instrument to produce sounds by vibrating. **reediness** *n.* **reedy** *adj.*

reed-buck *n.* An African antelope.

re-ed-u-cate *v.* To train again through education; rehabilitate. **-ation** *n.*

reef (rēf) *n.* A chain of rocks, coral, or sand at or near the surface of the water.

reef knot *n.* A square knot used on a sail.

reek (rēk) *v.* To emit vapor or smoke; to give off a strong offensive odor.

reel (rēl) *n.* A device which revolves on an axis and is used for winding up or letting out fishing line, rope, or other string-like material; a lively and fast dance; a bobbin for sewing thread.

re-e-lect (rē'i lekt) *v.* The act of electing someone again for an office.

re-em-pha-size (rē em'fa sīz') *v.* To stress something or an idea again.

re-em-ploy (rē'em ploi') *v.* To rehire someone who previously worked for you.

re-en-act (rē'en akt') *v.* To perform again; to repeat the actions of a previous event.

re-en-list *v.* To enlist or join a group or an armed force again. **-ment** *n.*

re-en-ter (rē en'tér) *v.* To enter a room or area again.

re-en-try (rē en'trē) *n.* The return of a space craft after a mission into outer space.

reeve (rēv) *n.* A medieval English manor officer responsible for overseeing feudal obligations.

re-ex-am-ine (rē'ig zam'in) *v.* Examine something or someone another time or again. **reexamination** *n.*

re-fer-to-ry (ri fek'to rē) *n.* The place in colleges where students dine.

re-fer (ri fer') *v.* To direct for treatment, information, or help; to classify within a general category or cause.

ref-e-ree *n.* A person who supervises a game, making sure all the rules are followed.

ref-er-ence (ref'ér ens) *n.* The act of referring someone to someplace or to something.

reference mark *n.* A mark, such as an asterisk, to direct the reader's attention to a footnote.

ref-er-en-dum (ref'e ren'dum) *n.* A public vote on an item for final approval or for rejection.

ref-er-ent (ref'ér ent) *n.* What is referred to, such as a person; the thing that a word or sign stand for. **referent** *adj.*

re-fill (rē fil') *v.* To fill something with an item again. **refillable** *adj.*

re-fine (ri fīn') *v.* To purify by removing unwanted substances or material; to improve. **refined** *adj.* **refinement** *n.*

re-fin-er-y (ri fī'ne rē) *n.* A place or location which is used for the purpose of refining products, such as sugar.

re-fin-ish *v.* The act of putting a new surface onto something, such as wood.

re-fit (rē fit') *v.* To repair something.

re-flect (rē flekt') *v.* To throw back rays of light from a surface; to give an image, as from a mirror; to ponder or think carefully about something. **reflection, reflectiveness** *n.*

re-flec-tom-e-ter (rē'flek tom'i tér) *n.* A device for measuring radiant energy.

re-flec-tor *n.* Something which is able to reflect things, such as light.

re-flex (rē'fleks) *adj.* Turning, casting, or bending backward. **reflex** *n.* An involuntary reaction of the nervous system to a stimulus.

re-flex-ive (ri flek'siv) *adj.* A relation that exists between an entity and itself. **reflexiveness** *n.* **reflexivity** *n.*

re-flex-ol-o-gy *n.* The science of behavior of simple and complex reflexes.

re-flo-res-cent *adj.* Blooming again.

re-flow *v.* To flow back again.

re-fo-cus (rē fō'kus) *v.* To change the direction of.

re-forge (rē fōrj') *v.* To make over.

re-form (ri form') *v.* To reconstruct, make over, or change something for the better; improve; to abandon or give up evil ways. **reformer** *n.* **-ed** *adj.*

reformat *v.* In *computer science*, to change the style of text; to convert a file for use by a different application.

re-for-ma-to-ry *n.* A jail-like institution for young criminals.

re-fract (ri frakt') *v.* The deflecting of something, such as a ray of light. **refractive** *adj.*

re-frac-to-ry *adj.* Unmanageable; obstinate; difficult to melt; resistant to heat. **refractory** *n.* Something which does not change significantly when exposed to high temperatures. **refractorily** *adv.*

refractory period *n.* The period immediately following the response of a muscle before it recovers to make a second response.

re-frain (ri frān') *v.* To hold back; to keep oneself from following a passing impulse. **refrain** *n.* A recurring phrase at the end of each stanza of a poem or song.

re-fresh (ri fresh') *v.* To freshen something again; to restore strength. **refreshing** *adj.* **refresher** *n.*

re-fresh-ment (ri fresh'ment) *n.* Something which will refresh someone, such as a cold drink or snack.

re-frig-er-a-tor *n.* A piece of storage equipment which chills food and other materials.

re-fu-el (rē fū'el) *v.* To put fuel into something again; take on additional fuel.

ref-uge *n.* Shelter or protection from harm; any place one may turn for relief or help.

ref-u-gee (ref'ū jē') *n.* A person who flees to find safety. **refugeeism** *n.*

re-ful-gent (ri ful'jent) *n.* State of being radiant or putting off a bright light.

re-fund (ri fund') *v.* To return or pay back; to reimburse. **refundable** *adj.*

re-fur-bish *v.* To make clean; to renovate. **refurbisher, refurbishment** *n.*

re-fus-al (ri fū'zal) *n.* The denial of something which is demanded.

re-fuse (ri fūz') *v.* To decline; to reject; to deny.

re-fute (ri fūt') *v.* To overthrow or to disprove with the use of evidence. **refutable** *adj.* **refutably** *adv.* **-er** *n.*

re-gain (ri gān') *v.* To recover; to reach again.

re-gal (ri gāl') *adj.* Of or appropriate for royalty. **regally** *adv.*

re-gale (ri gāl') *v.* To entertain or delight; to give pleasure.

re-ga-li-a (ri gā'lē a) *n.* Something which represents royalty such as a scepter.

re-gard (ri gärd') *v.* To look upon closely; to consider; to have great affection for. **regard** *n.* Careful attention or thought; esteem or affection. **regards** Greetings or good wishes.

re-gard-less *adj.* State of being careless or showing no regard towards something or someone.

re-gat-ta (ri gat'a) *n.* A boat race.

re-gen-cy (rē'jen sē) *n., pl.* **-ies** The jurisdiction or office of a regent.

re-gen-er-ate *v.* To reform spiritually or morally; to make or create anew; to refresh or restore.

re-gent (rē'jent) *n.* One who rules and acts as a ruler during the absence of a sovereign, or when the ruler is underage.

reg-i-cide *n.* A person who kills a king.

re-gime (re zhem') *n.* An administration.

reg-i-men (rej'i men') *n.* Government control; therapy; a systematic plan to improve the health.

reg-i-ment *n.* A military unit of ground troops which is composed of several battalions. **regimental** *adj.*

re-gion (rē'jun) *n.* An administrative, political, social, or geographical area.

re-gion-al (rēja nal) *adj.* Typical of or pertaining to a geographic region; limited to a particular region.

reg-is-ter (rej'i ster) *n.* Something which contains names or occurrences; a book of public records.

reg-is-tered (rej'i sterd) *adj.* Recorded with the owner's name; recorded on the basis of pedigree of an animal.

reg-is-trar *n.* The person who keeps a register; an office of an educational institution which is in charge of registration, keeping academic records, and evaluating credentials.

reg-is-tra-tion *n.* An act of recording things or names.

reg-is-try *n.* The nationality of a ship in a register; an official record book.

reg-let (reg'lit) *n.* A narrow strip of molding.

re-gress *v.* To return to a previous state or condition. **regressor** *adj.* **-ive** *n.*

re-gres-sion *n.* The progressive decline of a disease; a shift toward a lower state; gradual loss of memory and acquired skills. **regressive** *adj.*

re-gret (ri gret´) *v.* To feel disappointed or distressed about; to be sorry for. **regret** *n.* A sense of loss or expression of grief; a feeling of sorrow. **regretta-bly, regretfully** *adv.* **regrettable, regretful** *adj.*

re-group (rē grōp´) *v.* To reorganize after a setback in an activity.

reg-u-lar *adj.* Usual; normal; customary; conforming to set principles, proce-dures, or discipline; well-ordered; not varying. **regularity** *n.* **regularly** *adv.*

reg-u-lar-ize (reg´ya lāt´) *v.* To conform to laws, rules, and customs.

reg-u-late (reg´ya lāt´) *v.* To adjust to a specification or requirement; to bring order or authority. **regulative** *adj.* **regulatory** *adj.* **regulator** *n.*

reg-u-la-tion *n.* A rule that is set down in order to govern an area or people.

reg-u-lus (reg´a lus) *n.* A star in the constellation Leo.

re-gur-gi-tate (ri g *v.* To pour something forth. **regurgitation** *n.*

re-ha-bil-i-tate *v.* To restore to a former state by education and therapy. **rehabilitation** *n.* **rehabilitative** *adv.*

re-hash (rē hash´) *v.* To rework or go over old material; to discuss again.

re-hears-al *n.* The act of practicing for a performance; a practice session.

re-hu-man-ize *v.* To restore to a full life; restore human rights and dignity.

re-hy-drate (rē hī´drāt) *v.* To return fluid lost due to dehydration.

reichs-mark *n.* A German coin.

reign (rān) *n.* The period in time when the monarch rules over an area.

re-im-burse (rē´im bers´) *v.* To repay; to make restitution. **-ment** *n.*

rein (rān) *n.* One of a pair of narrow, leather straps attached to the bit of a bridle and used to control a horse.

re-in-car-na-tion *n.* The state of rebirth in new forms of life.

re-in-force (rē´in fōrs´) *v.* To support; to strengthen with additional people or equipment. **reinforcement** *n.*

re-in-state (rē´in stāt´) *v.* To restore something to its former position or condition. **reinstatement** *n.*

re-in-te-grate *v.* To reunite with something.

re-in-vent *v.* To remake something that has already been invented.

re-in-vest (rē´in vest´) *v.* To invest money in additional securities.

re-in-vig-o-rate *v.* To restore vigor.

re-is-sue (rē ish´ö) *v.* To make available again.

re-it-er-ate *v.* To say or do something over and over again. **reiteration** *n.*

re-ject (ri jekt´) *v.* To refuse; to discard as useless. **reject** *n.* **rejection** *n.*

re-jec-tion *n.* The process in which the body rejects an organ transplant or tissue.

re-joice *v.* To fill with joy; to be filled with joy. **rejoicer** *n.* **rejoicingly** *adv.*

re-joic-ing (ri jois´ing) *n.* An occasion or expression of joy.

re-join *v.* To respond or to answer someone.

re-ju-ve-nate (ri jō´ve nāt´) *v.* To restore to youthful appearance or vigor. **rejuvenation** *n.*

re-kin-dle (rē kin´dl) *v.* To inflame something again. **rekindler** *n.*

re-lapse (ri laps´) *v.* To fall back or revert to an earlier condition. **relapser** *n.*

re-late (ri lāt´) *v.* To tell the events of; to narrate; to bring into natural association. **relater** *n.* **relatable** *adj.*

re-lat-ed *adj.* To be in the same family; connected to each other by blood or marriage.

re-la-tion (ri lā´shan) *n.* The relationship between people by marriage or blood lines; a person one is related to.

re-la-tion-ship (ri lā´shan ship´) *n.* A connection by blood or family; kinship; friendship; a natural association.

rel-a-tive (rel´a tiv) *adj.* Relevant; connected; considered in comparison or relationship to other. **relative** *n.* A member of one's family. **relatively** *adv.*

rel-a-tiv-i-ty (rel´a tiv´i tē) *n.* A condition or state of being relative.

re-lax (ri laks´) *v.* To make loose or lax; to relieve something from effort or strain; to become less formal or less reserved. **relaxation** *n.*

re-lax-a-tion (rē´lak sā´shan) *n.* A period of recreational activity or pastime.

re-laxed *adj.* Being at rest or ease. **relaxedly** *adv.* **relaxedness** *n.*

re-lay (rē´lā) *n.* A race in which a fresh team replaces another. **relay** *v.* To pass from one group to another.

re-lease *v.* To set free from confinement; to unfasten; to free; to relinquish a claim on something. *n.* A release from an obligation. **releaser** *n.*

rel-e-gate (rel´e gāt´) *v.* To banish someone or something. **relegation** *n.*

re-lent (ri lent´) *v.* To soften in temper, attitude, or determination; to slacken. **relentless, relentlessness** *adj.*

rel-e-vant (rel´e vant) *adj.* Related to matters at hand. **relevantly** *adv.*

re-li-a-ble (ri lī´a bl) *adj.* Dependable; capable of being relied upon.

re-li-ance (ri lī´ans) *n.* Confidence and trust; something which is relied upon.

re-li-ant (ri lī´ant) *adj.* State of being confident or having reliance.

re-lic (rel´ik) *n.* Something which is very old; a keepsake; an object whose cultural environment has disappeared.

re-lic-tion *n.* The recession of water from land leaving it permanently uncovered.

re-lief (ri lēf´) *n.* Anything which decreases or lessens anxiety, pain, discomfort, or other unpleasant conditions or feelings.

re-lieve *v.* To lessen or ease pain, anxiety, embarrassment, or other problems; to release or free from a duty by providing a replacement. **reliever** *n.*

re-lig-ion *n.* An organized system of beliefs, rites, and celebrations centered on a supernatural being; belief pursued with devotion. **religious** *adj.*

re-li-gi-ose *adj.* Being excessively religious.

re-lin-quish (riling´kwish) *v.* To release something or someone; withdraw from; to give up. **relinquishment** *n.*

rel-i-quary (rel´i kwer´ē) *n.* A shrine in which sacred relics are kept.

re-lish (rel´ish) *v.* Pleasure; a spicy condiment taken with food to lend it flavor.

re-live(rē liv´) *v.* To experience something again in the imagination or fantasy.

re-lo-cate *v.* To move to another area; establish in another place. **-tion** *n.*

re-luct (ri lukt´) *v.* To revolt; to feel opposition.

re-luc-tance *n.* An unwillingness; opposition by a magnetic substance to magnetic flux.

re-luc-tant (ri lik´tant) *adj.* Unwilling, not yielding. **reluctation** *n.*

re-lume (ri lōm´) *v.* To light again.

re-ly (ri lī´) *v.* To trust or depend; to have confidence in someone.

re-main (ri mān´) *v.* To continue without change; to stay after the departure of others.

re-main-der (ri mān dèr) *n.* Something left over. *Math* The difference which remains after division or subtraction.

re-make *v.* To revise an old movie, etc.

re-mand (ri mand´) *v.* To order back; to send to another court or agency for further action; to return to custody pending trial.

re-man-u-fac-ture *v.* To make into a new product. **remanufacturer** *n.*

re-mark (ri märk´) *n.* A brief expression or comment; to take notice; to observe; to comment.

re-mark-a-ble *adj.* Extraordinary.

re-match (rē´mach) *n.* A second contest between the same contestants or teams.

rem-e-di-a-ble (ri mē´dē a bl) *adj.* Being able to be remedied.

re-me-di-al (ri mē´dē al) *adj.* Concerned with the correction of study habits.

rem-e-dy (rem´i dē) *n., pl.* remedies A therapy or medicine which relieves pain; something which corrects an error or fault. **remedy** *v.* To cure or relieve a disease; to rectify.

re-mem-ber *v.* To bring back or recall to the mind; to retain in the mind carefully; to keep a person in one's thoughts; to recall a person to another as a means of greetings. **remember-ability, rememberer** *n.* **-erable** *adj.*

re-mem-brance *n.* Something which is remembered by someone.

re-mex (rē´meks) *n.* A quill feather in the wing of a bird. **remigial** *adj.*

re-mil-i-ta-rize *v.* To equip again with military installations.

re-mind (ri mīnd´) *v.* To cause or help to remember. **reminder** *n.*

rem-i-nisce (rem´i nis´) *v.* To recall the past things which have happened.

rem-i-nis-cence *n.* The practice or process of recalling the past. **reminiscent** *adj.*

re-mint *v.* To make old coins into a new coins by melting down the old coins.

re-mise (ri mīz´) *v.* To grant or release a claim to.

re-miss *adj.* Lax in performing one's duties; negligent. **remissness** *n.*

re-mis-sion *n.* A forgiveness; act of remitting; a temporary state of a disease when it doesn't progress; forgiveness.

re-mit (ri mit´) *v.* To send money as payment for goods; to forgive, as a crime or sin; to slacken, make less violent, or less intense.

re-mit-tance (ri mit´ans) *n.* A sum of money sent to reduce a debt.

re-mit-tent *adj.* Marked by periods of abatement and increase of symptoms.

rem-nant (rem´nant) *n.* A small piece or a scrap of something; an unsold end of a material.

re-mod-el *v.* To reconstruct something making it like new; to alter the structure of a building or house.

re-mon-e-tize (rē mon´i tīz´) *v.* To restore to use as legal tender.

re-mon-strance *n.* Statement of reasons against an idea or something.

re-mon-strate *v.* Giving strong reasons against an act or an idea. **remonstra-tive** *adj.* **remonstration** *n.*

re-morse (ri mors´) *n.* Deep moral regret for past misdeeds. **remorseful** *adj.* **remorsefully** *adv.* **remorsefulness** *n.*

re-mote *adj.* Distant in time, space, or relation. **remotely** *adv.* **-ness** *n.*

remote access *n.* In *computer science,* ability of a computer to connect and interact with a computer or peripheral that is not in the immediate area.

re-mount (rē mount´) *v.* To mount something again.

re-mov-a-ble (ri mō´va bl) *adj.* Being able to be removed.

re-mov-al *n.* The change of a site or place; the act of removing from a post.

re-move (ri mōv´) *v.* To get rid of; to extract; to dismiss from office; to change one's business or residence. *n.* An act of moving. **removable** *adj.*

re-mu-da (ri mŏo´da) *n.* A herd of horses from which the horses to be used for the day are chosen.

re-mu-ner-ate (ri mū´ne rāt´) *v.* Pay an equivalent for a service; to reward. **remunerator, remuneration** *n.*

ren-ais-sance *n.* A revival or rebirth; the humanistic revival of classical art, literature, and learning in Europe which occurred during the 14th through the 16th centuries.

re-nal *adj.* Of or relating to the kidneys.

re-nas-cence (ri nas´ens) *n.* A revival or a rebirth.

re-na-ture *v.* To restore to an original condition.

ren-con-tre (ren kon´tér) *n.* A hostile contest between forces or individuals.

ren-coun-ter (ren koun´tér) *v.* A casual meeting; a duel; a debate.

rend (rend) *v.* To remove from with violence; to split.

ren-der *v.* To give or make something available; to submit or give; to represent artistically; to liquify or melt fat by means of heat. **rendering** *n.* **renderable** *adj.*

ren-dez-vous *n.* A meeting place that has been prearranged; an appointment made between two or more people. *v.* To meet at a particular time and place.

ren-di-tion (ren dish´an) *n.* An interpretation or a translation.

ren-dzi-na *n.* A grayish brown intrazonal soil developed in grassy regions of high humidity; a rich limey soil.

ren-e-gade (ren´e gād´) *n.* A person who rejects one allegiance for another; an outlaw; a traitor. **renegade** *adj.*

re-nege (ri nig´) *v.* To fail to keep one's word. **reneger** *n.*

re-new (ri nö´) *v.* To make new or nearly new by restoring; to resume.

re-ni-tent (ri nīt´ent) *adj.* Resisting pressure; opposed.

ren-net (ren´it) *n.* An extract taken from a calf's stomach and used to curdle milk for making cheese.

ren-nin (ren´in) *n.* An enzyme that coagulates milk used in making cheese.

re-nom-i-nate (rē nom´i nāt´) *v.* To nominate for a succeeding term.

re-nounce (ri nouns´) *v.* To reject something. **renouncement** *n.*

ren-o-vate (ren´o vāt´) *v.* To return or to restore to a good condition; to make new. **renovation, renovator** *n.*

re-nown (ri noun´) *n.* The quality of being widely honored. **renowned** *adj.*

rent (rent) *n.* The payment made for the use of another's property. *v.* To obtain occupancy in exchange for payment. **rental** *n.* **rentable** *adj.*

re-nun-ci-a-tion (ri nun´sē ā´shan) *n.* Renouncing. **renunciative** *adj.*

re-o-pen (rē ō´pen) *v.* To resume again,

as a discussion or session.

re-or-der (rē or´dér) *n.* An order for more of the same kind as previously ordered.

re-or-gan-i-za-tion (rē´organīzā´shan) *n.* The process of reorganizing something.

rep (rep) *n. Slang* Representative. *v.* To represent.

re-pack-age *v.* To wrap into a more efficient and attractive form.

re-pair (ri pâr´) *v.* To restore to good or usable condition; to renew; refresh.

re-pand (ri pand´) *adj.* Having a slightly wavy margin.

rep-a-ra-ble *adj.* Being able to be corrected.

rep-a-ra-tion (rep´a rā´shan) *n.* The act of repairing something.

re-par-a-tive (ri par´a tiv) *adj.* Able to make amends.

rep-ar-tee *n.* A quick, witty response or reply; an interchange of clever retorts.

re-pass (rē pas´) *v.* To pass through again.

re-past (ri past´) *n.* Something taken as food; food which comprises a meal.

re-pa-tri-ate (rē pātrē āt´) *v.* To go back to one's own country; to return to the country of one's origin. **-ation** *n.*

re-pay (ri pā) *v.* To pay back money; to compensate; to do something in return.

re-peal (ri pel´) *v.* To withdraw officially; to rescind; to revoke. **repealable** *adj.* **repeal** *n.* **repealer** *n.*

re-peat (ri pēt´) *v.* To utter something again; to do an action again.

re-peat-ed *adj.* Recurring again and again.

re-peat-er (ri pē´tér) *n.* Something or someone which repeats.

re-pel (ri pel´) *v.* To discourage; to force away; to create aversion.

re-pel-lent (ri pel´ent) *adj.* Able to repel; tending to drive away or ward off.

re-pent (ri pent´) *v.* To feel regret for something which has occurred; to change one's sinful way. **repentance** *n.* **repentant** *adj.* **repenter** *n.*

re-per-cus-sion (rē´pér kush´an) *n.* An unforeseen effect produced by an action.

rep-er-toire (rep´ér twär´) *n.* The accomplishments or skills of a person.

rep-er-to-ry *n.* A collection of things.

re-pe-tend *n.* A repeated sound or refrain.

rep-e-ti-tion (rep´i tish´an) *n.* The act of doing something over and over again; the act of repeating.

re-pine *v.* To feel discontent; to complain.

re-place *v.* To return something to its previous place. **replaceable** *adj.* **replacement** *n.* **replacer** *n.*

re-plant *v.* To provide with new plants; to move plants to a new location.

re-play *v.* To play something again.

re-plen-ish (ri plen´ish) *v.* To add to

something to replace what has gone or been used. **replenisher** *n*. -ment *n*.

re-plete (ri plēt´) *adj*. Having plenty; abounding; full. **repleteness** *n*.

re-ple-tion (ri plē´shan) *n*. An act of eating too much food.

rep-li-ca (rep´li ka) *n*. A reproduction or copy of something. **replicate** *v*.

re-ply (ri plī´) *v*. To give an answer to either verbally or in writing. **reply** *n*.

re-port (ri pōrt´) *n*. A detailed account; usually in a formal way. **report** *v*. To tell about; to make oneself available; to give details of. **reportable** *adj*.

report card *n*. The report of a student's progress in school submitted to the parents for review.

re-pos-al (ri pō´zal) *n*. An act or action of reposing.

re-pose (ri pōz´) *n*. The act of being at rest. *v*. To lie at rest. **reposeful** *adj*.

re-pos-it (ri poz´it) *v*. To put something back into place.

re-po-si-tion (rē´po zish´an) *n*. The state of something being repositioned.

re-pos-i-tor-y *n*. The location where things may be placed for preservation, a side altar in a Catholic church.

re-pos-sess (rē´po zes´) *v*. To restore ownership of something.

re-pow-er *v*. To return power anew to something or someone.

rep-re-hend (rep´ri hend´) *v*. To show or express disapproval of. **reprehension** *n*. **reprehensible** *adj*.

rep-re-hen-sive (rep´ri hen ziv) *adj*. To be conveying reproof.

rep-re-sent *v*. To stand for something; to serve as the official representative for.

rep-re-sent-a-tion *n*. The act of representing. **representational** *adj*.

rep-re-sent-a-tive *n*. A person or thing serving as an example or type. *adj*. Of or relating to government by representation; typical. **representatively** *adv*.

re-press (ri pres´) *v*. To restrain; hold back; to remove from the conscious mind. **repressive** *adj*. **repressibility** *n*. **repression** *n*. **repressiveness** *n*.

re-prieve (ri prēv´) *v*. To postpone punishment; to provide temporary relief. **reprieve** *n*. A temporary suspension of an execution.

rep-ri-mand (rep´ri mand) *v*. To censure severely; rebuke. **repripand** *n*.

re-print (rē print´) *n*. An additional printing of a book exactly as the previous one. **reprint** *v*. **reprinter** *n*.

re-pri-sal *n*. Retaliation with intent to inflict injury in return for injury received; a sum of money paid in restitution.

re-prise (ri prīz´) *v*. To take back by force.

re-proach (ri prōch´) *v*. To blame; to

rebuke. **reproachful** *adj*.

rep-ro-bate (rep´ro bāt´) *adj*. The state of being morally depraved. **reprobate** *v*. To condemn as unacceptable or evil.

re-pro-cess *v*. To treat in a special way in preparation for reuse.

re-pro-duce (rē´pro dōs´) *v*. To produce an image or copy. *Biol*. To produce an offspring; to recreate or produce again. **reproducer** *n*. **reproducible** *adj*. **reproduction** *n*. **reproductive** *adj*.

re-pro-gram *v*. To rewrite an existing pro-gram for a computer.

re-proof (ri prōf´) *n*. A censure.

re-prove (ri prōv´) *v*. To tell or express a disapproval of something.

rep-tile *n*. A cold-blooded, egg-laying vertebrate, as a snake, lizard, or turtle.

re-pub-lic (ri pub´lik) *n*. A political unit or state where representatives are elected to exercise the power.

Republican Party *n*. One of the two political parties in the United States.

re-pu-di-ate (ri pū´dē āt´) *v*. To cast away; to refuse to pay something.

re-pugn (ri pūn´) *v*. To offer resistance.

re-pug-nance (ri pug´nans) *n*. The state or condition of being opposed.

re-pug-nant (ri pug´nant) *adj*. Distasteful; repulsive; offensive.

re-pulse (ri puls´) *v*. To repel or drive back; to repel or reject rudely; to disgust or be disgusted. **repulsion** *n*.

re-pul-sive (ri pul´siv) *adj*. State of causing aversion. **repulsively** *adj*.

rep-u-ta-ble (rep´ū ta bl) *adj*. Considered to be honorable; held in high esteem. **reputably** *adv*. **reputability** *n*.

rep-u-ta-tion *n*. The commonly held evaluation of a person's character.

rep-ute (ri pūt´) *v*. To account or to consider something. **reputedly** *adj*.

re-quest *v*. To ask for something.

re-qui-em (rek´wē em) *n*. The Roman Catholic mass for a deceased person.

re-quire (ri kwī´ér) *v*. To demand or insist upon. **requirement** *n*.

req-ui-site (rek´wi zit) *adj*. Absolutely needed; necessary.

req-ui-si-tion (rek´wi zish´an) *n*. A request; a demand by one government to another for release of prisoners.

re-quite (ri kwīt´) *v*. To reward; to repay someone. **requiter** *n*.

rere-dos (rēr´dos) *n*. An ornamental screen or partition wall behind an altar.

re-run (rē run) *n*. A television show which is shown again.

re-sale (rē´sā) *n*. The act of selling something again. **resalable** *adj*.

re-scind (ri sind´) *v*. To repeal; to void. **rescinder** *n*. **rescindment** *n*.

res-cue (res´kū) *v*. To free from danger. *n*. An act of deliverance. **rescuer** *n*.

re-search *n*. A scientific or scholarly investigation. *v*. To carefully seek out.

re-sec-tion (ri sek´shan) n. The surgical removal of a action of an organ.

re-se-da (rl sē´da) n. An herb of the mignonette family with greyish-green leaves.

re-sem-ble (ri zem´bl) v. To have similarity to something.

re-send v. To send back.

re-sent (ri zent´) v. To feel angry about. resentful adj. resentment n.

res-er-va-tion (rez´ér vā´shan) n. The act of keeping something back.

re-serve (ri zerv´) v. To save for a special reason; to set apart; to retain; to put off. n. Something that is saved for a future point in time; the portion of a country's fighting force kept inactive until called upon.

re-serve-clause n. A clause in an athlete's contract which gives the club the exclusive rights of the athletes services until he is traded or released.

res-er-voir (rez´ér vwär´) n. A body of water stored for the future; large reserve; a supply.

reset In computer science, to command a return to an original state; to restart the computer.

re-shape (rē shāp´) v. To give new form to.

re-side (ri zīd´) v. To dwell permanently; to exist as a quality or attribute; live in or at. residence n.

res-i-den-cy (rez´i den sē) n. A period of training in a medical field.

res-i-due (rez´i dö´) n. Matter remaining after treatment or removal of a part; some-thing which remains.

re-sign v. To give up; to submit to something as being unavoidable; to quit.

res-ig-na-tion n. A formal notification stating the resignation of one's job, etc.

re-sil-ience (ri zil´yens) n. The ability to recover from a shock without permanent aftereffects.

res-in n. A plant substance from certain plants and trees used in varnishes and lacquers. resinous n.

re-sist (ri zist´) v. To work against or actively oppose; to withstand. -ible adj.

re-sist-er n. A person who is opposed to the policies of the government.

re-sis-tor (ri zis´tér) n. An electrical device used in an electric circuit for protection or current control.

res-ju-di-ca-ta n. A matter decided on its merits by a court and not subject to litigation again between the same parties.

res-o-lute (rez´o löt´) adj. Coming from or characterized by determination. resolutely resolution n.

re-solve (ri zolv´) v. To make a firm decision on something; to find a solution. resolvable adj. -lution n.

res-o-nance n. The increase of sound by the vibration of other bodies.

res-o-na-tor (rez´o nā´tér) n. A device for increasing sounds of a musical instrument.

re-sort (ri zort´) v. To go frequently or customarily. n. A place, or recreation, for rest and for a vacation.

re-sound (ri zound´) v. To be filled with echoing sounds; to reverberate; to ring or sound loudly. resounding adj.

re-source (rē´sōrs) n. A source of aid or support which can be drawn upon if needed. resources n. One's available capital or assets. resourceful adj.

re-spect (ri spekt´) v. To show consider-ation or esteem for; to relate to. n. Courtesy or considerate treatment. respectful adj. respectability n.

res-pi-ra-tion n. The process or act of inhaling and exhaling; the act of breathing; the process in which an animal or person takes in oxygen from the air and releases carbon dioxide. respirator n. respiratory adj.

re-spire (ri spīér´) v. To inhale and exhale air; take in oxygen.

res-pi-rom-e-ter n. An instrument for studying the extent and character of respiration.

res-pite (res´pit) n. A temporary postponement.

re-splen-dent (ri splen´dent) adj. Having a shining appearance. -ly adj.

re-spond (ri spond´) v. To answer or reply; to act when prompted by something or someone.

re-sponse (ri spons´) n. A reply; the act of replying. responsive adj.

re-spon-si-ble adj. Trustworthy; in charge; having authority; being answerable for one's actions or the actions of others. responsibility n.

re-spon-sum n. A formal opinion from a rabbinic authority to a submitted question or problem.

rest (rest) n. A cessation of all work, activity, or motion. Mus. An interval of silence equal in time to a note of same value. v. To stop work; to place or lay. restful adj. rester n. -fully adv.

res-tau-rant (res´tér ant) n. A place which serves meals to the public.

res-tau-ran-teur (res´tér a tür´) n. The owner of a restaurant.

res-ti-tu-tion (res´ti tö´shan) n. The act of restoring something to its rightful owner; compensation for injury, loss, or damage.

res-tive (res´tiv) adj. Nervous or impatient because of a delay; resisting control. restively adv. restiveness n.

re-store (ri stōr´) v. To bring back to a former condition or original state; to make restitution of. restoration n.

re-strain (ri strān´) v. To hold back or be held back; to control, limit, or restrict. **restrainer** n. **restraint** n.

restraining order n. A legal document issued to keep a situation unchanged.

re-strict (ri strikt´) v. To confine within limits. **restriction** n. **restrictive** adj. **restrictively** adv.

re-sult (ri zult´) v. To happen or exist in a particular way. n. The consequence of an action, course, or operation.

re-sume (rizōm´) v. To start again after an interruption. **resumption** n.

res-u-me (rez´e mā´) n. A summary of one's personal history, background, work, and education.

re-su-pi-nate (ri sö´pi nāt´) adj. To bend backward to an inverted position.

res-ur-rec-tion n. The act of Christ rising from the dead.

re-sus-ci-ate (ri sus´i tāt) v. To return to life; to revive; give mouth-to-mouth breathing technique to help a person to start breathing again. **resuscitation, resuscitator** n.

re-tail n. The sale of goods or commodities to the public. v. To sell to the consumer. **retail** adj. **retailer** n.

re-tain (ri tān´) v. To hold in one's possession; to remember; to employ someone, as for his services.

re-tain-er n. A person or thing that retains; a fee paid for one's services.

re-tal-i-ate (ri tal´ē āt´) v. To seek revenge against someone. **-tion** n.

re-tard (ri tard´) v. To delay or slow the progress of. **retardant** n. & adj.

re-tar-da-tion n. A condition in which mental development is slow or delayed; a condition of mental slowness.

re-ten-tion (ri ten´shan) n. The act or condition of being retained.

re-ten-tive adj. Having the capacity of retaining knowledge with ease.

ret-i-cent (ret´i sent) adj. Doing uncommunicative in speech; reserved.

re-tic-u-late (ri tik´ya lit) v. To divide or construct as to form a network.

ret-i-na (ret´i na) n. pl. **-nas, nae** The light sensitive membrane lining the inner eyeball connected by the optic nerve to the brain. **retinal** adj.

re-tire (ri tīēr´) v. To depart for rest; to remove oneself from the daily routine of working. Baseball To put a batter out. **retirement, retiree** n.

re-tired (ri tīēd´) adj. No longer working at one's profession.

re-tir-ing adj. Being shy or withdrawn.

re-tort (ri tort´) n. A witty or cutting reply to another person.

re-touch (rē tuch´) v. To alter a negative to produce a more desirable picture.

re-trace (ri trās´) v. To go back over.

re-tract (ri trakt´) v. To draw back or to take back something that has been

said. **retractable** adj. **retraction** n.

re-tral adj. Toward the back.

re-tread (rē tred´) v. To replace the tread of a worn tire. **retread** n.

re-treat n. The act of withdrawing from danger; a time of study, prayer, and meditation in a quiet, isolated location.

ret-ri-bu-tion (re´tri bū´shan) n. An act of getting revenge against another person. **retributively** adv. **-tive** adj.

re-trieve (ri trēv´) v. To regain; to find something and carry it back. **retrievable** adj. **retrieval** n.

ret-ro-ac-tive adj. Taking effect on a date prior to enactment; extending to a prior time. **retroactively** adv.

ret-ro-grade (re´tro grād´) adj. Moving backward; contrary to normal order.

ret-ro-gres-sion n. A reversal in development from a higher to a lower state.

ret-ro-pack n. A system of rockets on a spacecraft which produce thrust used to reduce speed.

ret-ro-re-flec-tor n. A device that reflects radiation.

ret-ro-rock-et n. A rocket on an airplane or spacecraft which produces thrust in the opposite direction to the motion of the craft for deceleration.

ret-ro-spect (re´tro spekt´) n. A review of things in the past. **retrospectively** adv. **retrospective** adj.

re-turn v. To come back to an earlier condition; to reciprocate. n. The act of sending, bringing, or coming back. **returns** n. A yield or profit from investments; a report on the results of an election. **returnable** adj. **returnee, re-un-ion (rēūn´yan)** n. A reuniting; the coming together of a group which has been separated for a period of time.

re-us-able (rē ū´za bl) adj. Capable of using something over and over again.

re-val-u-ate (rē val´ū āt´) v. To increase the value of something.

re-val-ue (rē val´ū) v. To reappraise something as jewelry.

re-vamp (rē vamp´) v. Patch or reconstruct some thing again.

re-veal (ri vēl´) v. To disclose or make known; to expose or bring into view.

rev-eil-le (rev´e lē) n. The sounding of a bugle used to awaken soldiers in the morning.

rev-el (rev´el) v. To take great delight in. **reveler** n.

rev-e-la-tion (rev´e lā´shan) n. An act of or something revealed; a manifestation of divine truth. **Revelation** The last book in the New Testament.

re-venge (ri venj´) v. To impose injury in return for injury received. **revengeful** adj. **revenger** n.

rev-e-nue (rev´en´ū) n. Income returned by an investment.

re-verb *n.* An echo effect produced electronically in recorded music.

re-vere (ri vēr´) *v.* To honor and respect.

re-ver-sal (ri ver´sal) *n.* An act of over throwing a legal proceeding or judgment.

re-verse (ri vers´) *adj.* Turned backward in position. *n.* The opposite of something; a change in fortune usually from better to worse; change or turn to the opposite direction; to transpose or exchange the positions of. *Law* To revoke a decision. **reverser** *n.*

re-vert (ri vert´) *v.* To return to a former practice or belief. **reversion** *n.*

re-view (ri vū´) *v.* To study or look over something again; to give a report on. *n.* A reexamination; a study which gives a critical estimate of something.

re-vile (ri vīl´) *v.* To use verbal abuse.

re-vise (ri vīz´) *v.* To look over something again with the intention of improving or correcting it. **reviser, revision** *n.*

re-vi-tal-ize (rē vīt´a līz´) *v.* To give new life or energy to. **revitalization** *n.*

re-viv-al (ri vī´val) *n.* The act or condition of reviving; the return of a film or play which was formerly presented; a meeting whose purpose is religious reawakening.

re-vive (ri vīv´) *v.* To restore, refresh, or recall; to return to consciousness or life. **revivable** *adj.* **reviver** *n.*

re-voke (ri vōk´) *v.* To nullify or make void by recalling. **revocation** *n.*

re-volt (ri vōlt´) *n.* To try to overthrow authority; to fill with disgust.

rev-o-lu-tion (rev´o lö´shan) *n.* The act or state of orbital motion around a point; the abrupt overthrow of a government; a sudden change in a system.

re-volve (ri volv´) *v.* To move around a central point; to spin; to rotate.

re-volv-ing charge ac-count (ri vol´ving) *n.* A charge account in which payment is made in monthly installments.

re-vue (ri vū´) *n.* A musical show consisting of songs, dances, skits, and other similar entertainment.

re-ward (ri word´) *n.* Something given for a special service. *v.* To give a reward.

rhab-do-man-cy (rab´do man´sē) *n.* The discovery of things that are concealed in the ground by the use of a divining rod.

rham-na-ceous (ram nā´shus) *adj.* To be pertaining to or belonging to the buckthorn family of plants.

rhap-sod-ic (rap sod´ik) *adj.* To have the characteristics of a rhapsody.

rhap-so-dist (rap´so dist) *n.* A person who speaks in a rhapsodical way or manner.

rhap-so-dize (rap´so dīz´) *v.* To recite rhapsodies.

rhap-so-dy (rap´so dē) *n. pl.* **-ies** An excessive display of enthusiasm.

rhat-a-ny (rat´a nē) *n.* A type of South American shrub whose roots are used as an astringent.

rhe-ni-um (rē´nē um) *n.* A metallic element symbolized by Re.

rhe-ol-o-gy (rē ol´o jē) *n.* The study of the behavior of a liquid matter.

rhe-om-e-ter (rē om´i tér) *n.* A type of device that is used for measuring the flow of liquids.

rhe-sus (rē´sus) *n.* A light-brown monkey that is used for laboratory tests.

rhe-tor (rē´tér) *n.* One who is an orator.

rhet-o-ric (ret´ér ik) *n.* Effective expression in writing or speech; language which is not sincere.

rhe-tor-i-cal (ri tor´i kal) *adj.* To be involving rhetoric. **rhetoricalness** *n.*

rhetorical question *n.* A kind of question that is used for an effect and no answer is expected.

rhet-o-ri-cian (ret´o rish´an) *n.* A person who writes elaborate prose.

rheum (röm) *n.* A fluid that is discharged from the mucus glands of the body.

rheumatic fever *n.* A severe infectious disease that is characterized by the swelling of the heart lining and the heart valves.

rheu-ma-tism (rö´ma tiz´um) *n.* A kind of inflammation that affects the joints and muscles of the body and can be very pain-ful.

Rh fac-tor *n.* A substance found in the red blood cells of 85% of all humans; the presence of this factor is referred to as RH positive; the absence as RH negative.

rhi-nal (rīn´al) *adj.* To be referring to the nose.

rhi-ni-tis (rī nī´tis) *n.* An inflammation that occurs in the nose or the membranes of the nose.

rhi-noc-er-os (rī nos´ér os) *n.* A very large mammal with one or two upright horns on the snout found in Africa and Asia. **rhinocerotic** *adj.*

rhi-zan-thous (rī zan´thus) *adj.* To be bearing very short-stemmed flowers.

rhi-zo-bi-um (rī zō´bē um) *n.* A type of bacteria that is important in maintaining the soil's fertility.

rhi-zo-ceph-a-lan (rī´zō sef´a lan) *n.* A kind of crustacean that lives off a host and causes the host to lose its ability to reproduce.

rhi-zoid (rī´zoid) *n.* The hair-like structure that provides a root for ferns and mosses.

rhi-zome (rī´zōm) *n.* A subterranean plant stem thickened by deposits of reserve food material which produces shoots above and roots below.

rhi-zo-mor-phous (rī´zō mor´fus) *adj.*
To be shaped like a root.

rhi-zo-pus (rī´zō pus) *n.* A type of mold
fungus.

rho-da-mine (rō´da mēn´) *n.* A red dye.

Rhode Island *n.* A state located in the
northeastern part of the United States;
statehood May 29, 1790; state capital
Providence.

rho-di-um (rō´dē um) *n.* A metallic
element symbolized by Rh.

rho-do-chro-site (rō´do krō´sīt) *n.* A
kind of mineral that is made of
manganese car-bonate and is pink in
color.

rho-do-den-dron (rō´do den´dron) *n.*
A variety of cultivated shrubs and trees
with showy flowers and evergreen
leaves.

rho-do-lite (rōd´o līt´) *n.* A type of garnet
that is rose-red in color.

rho-do-ra (rō dōr´a) *n.* A shrub found
in Canada and New England having
delicate pink flowers produced before
the leaves in spring.

rhom-boid (rom´boid) *n.* A parallelogram where the angles are oblique and
adjacent sides are unequal. -ble *adj.*

rhom-bus (rom´bus) *n.* A four sided
figure whose sides are equal in length.

rhon-chus (rong´kus) *n.* A type of rale
that occurs in the bronchial tubes of
the airway.

rhu-barb (rō´bärb) *n.* A garden plant
with large leaves and edible stalks used
for pies.

rhyme (rīm) *n.* A word having a sound
similar to another. **rhymer** *n.*

rhy-thm (rith´um) *n.* Music, speech, or
movements which are characterized
by equal or regularly alternating beats.
rhythmic, rhythmical *adv.*

rhyth-mics (rith´miks) *n.* The science
of rhythms.

ri-al-to (rē al´tō) *n.* The theater district.

ri-ant (rī´ant) *adj.* To be smiling; happy.

rib (rib) *n.* One of a series of curved
bones enclosed in the chest of man
and animals. *Slang* To tease.

rib-ald (rib´ald) *adj.* To be using
indecent humor.

rib-band (rib´band´) *n.* A narrow strip
used in ship building to hold frames
in position during construction.

rib-bon (rib´on) *n.* A narrow band or
strip of fabric, such as satin, used for
trimming.

rib-bon fish (rib´on fish´) *n.* A kind of
marine fish that has a long and flat
body.

ri-bo-fla-vin (rī´bō flā´vin) *n.* A B
complex vitamin that is found in milk,
leafy vegetables, and liver.

rice (rīs) *n.* A cereal grass grown
extensively in warm climates.

ric-er (rī´ser) *n.* A kitchen utensil thru
which soft foods are pressed in order
to produce strings about the diameter
of rice grain.

rich (rich) *adj.* Having great wealth; of
great value; satisfying and pleasing
in voice, color, tone, or other qualities;
extremely productive; as soil or land.

rich-es (rich´iz) *n.* One's wealth.

rich-ly (rich´lē) *adv.* To be done in a rich
manner or way.

Richter scale *n.* An instrument which
measures a seismic disturbance such
as an earth-quake with 1.5 being the
smallest and 8.5 being a very
devastating earthquake.

ri-cin (rī´sin) *n.* A white powder that is
poisonous and is used to cause the
agglutination of the red corpuscles.

rick-ets (rik´its) *n.* A childhood disease
which is caused by lack of inadequate
sunlight or vitamin D resulting in
severely deformed bones.

rick-ett-si-a (ri ket´sē a) *adj.* A
microorganism that is passed from
arthropods to humans.

rick-et-y (rik´i tē) *adj.* To be ready to
fall apart or fall down. **ricketiness** *n.*

rick-rack (rik´rak´) *n.* A zigzag braid
used in trimming.

rick-sha (rik´sho´) *n.* A small 2-wheeled
vehicle that is pulled by one man and
that originated in Japan.

ric-o-chet (rik´o shā´) *n.* A glancing blow
off a flat surface.

ri-cot-ta *n.* A white whey cheese of Italy
resembling cottage cheese.

ric-tus (rik´tus) *n.* An opening.

rid (rid) *v.* To make free from anything
objectionable. **ridable** *adj.*

rid-dance (rid´ans) *n.* The getting rid
of something or someone that is
unwanted.

rid-dle (rid´l) *v.* To perforate with
numerous holes. **riddle** *n.* A puzzling
problem or question which requires
a clever solution.

ride (rīd) *v.* To travel in a vehicle or on
an animal; to sit on and drive, as a
motorcycle. **ride for a fall** To flirt with
danger. **ride high** To experience great
success. **ride roughshod over** To treat
with abuse.

ridge (rij) *n.* A long, narrow crest; a
horizontal line formed where two
sloping surfaces meet. **ridge** *v.*

ridge-pole (rij´pōl´) *n.* Timber located
at the top of a roof which is horizontal.

rid-i-cule (rid´i kūl´) *n.* Actions or words
intended to make a person or thing the
object of mockery. **ridiculer** *n.*

ri-dic-u-lous (ri dik´ū lus) *adj.* To be
causing derision or ridicule; to be
laughable. **ridiculousness** *n.*

ri-dot-to *n.* A place of entertainment in
masquerade popular in the 18th century
England.

rife (rīf) *adj.* State of being abundant or abounding. **rifely** *adv.*

rif-fle (rif´l) *n.* Rippled water which is caused by a ridge.

rif-fler *n.* A small scraping tool.

riff-raff (rif´raf´) *n.* The rabble; low persons in society; a disreputable person.

ri-fle (rī´fl) *n.* A firearm having a grooved bore designed to be fired from the shoulder.

ri-fle-man (rī´fl man) *n.* A person skilled in the shooting of a rifle.

ri-fling (rī´fling) *n.* The act of putting or cutting spiral grooves in the barrel of a gun.

rift (rift) *n.* A fault; disagreement; a lack of harmony; a shallow place in a stream.

rig (rig) *v.* To outfit with necessary equipment. *n.* The arrangement of sails, masts, and other equipment on a ship; the apparatus used for drilling water or oil wells.

rig-a-doon (rig´a dön´) *n.* A lively dance of the 17th and 18th century.

rig-a-to-ni (rig´a tō´nē) *n.* A curved macaroni with fluted edges.

rig-ging (rig´ing) *n.* The lines used aboard a ship in working sails and supporting masts and spars; ropes, etc. used to support and manipulate scenery in the theater.

right (rīt) *adj.* In accordance with or conform able to law, justice, or morality; proper and fitting; properly adjusted, disposed, or placed; orderly; sound in body or mind. *n.* The right side, hand, or direction; the direction opposite left. *adv.* Immediately; completely; according to justice, morality, or law.

right angle *n., Geom.* An angle of 90 degrees; an angle with two sides perpendicular to each other.

right-eous (rī´chus) *adj.* Free from guilt; morally right; acting in accordance with moral or divine law. **righteousness** *n.*

right tri-an-gle *n.* A type of triangle where one angle is 90 degrees.

right wing *n.* One who is a member of a conservative political party. **right-winger** *n.* **rightwing** *adj.*

rig-id (rij´id) *adj.* Not bending; inflexible; severe; stern. **-ity** *n.* **-ness** *n.*

ri-gid-i-fy (ri jid´i fī´) *v.* To make something rigid. **rigidification** *n.*

rig-ma-role (rig´ma rōl´) *n.* A mean less or complex procedure.

rig-or (rig´ér) *n.* The condition of being rigid or stiff; stiffness of temper; harshness. **rigorous , rigorously** *adv.*

rig-or-ism (rig´o riz´um) *n.* A strictness in practice.

rig-or mor-tis (rig´ér mor´tis) *n.* The rigidity of muscles occurring after death.

rile (rīl) *v.* To make angry.

rill-et (ril´it) *n.* A small brook.

rim (rim) *n.* The outer edge or border of something; the outer part of a wheel joined to the hub on a car. **rimless** *adj.*

rime (rīm) *n.* An accumulation of granular ice on the windward sides of exposed objects formed from super-cooled fog or clouds.

ri-mose (rī´mōs) *adj.* To be filled with fissures. **rimosity** *n.* **rimosely** *adv.*

rim-rock (rim´rok´) *n.* An overlying strata of rock on a plateau that outcrops to form a vertical face.

rind (rīnd) *n.* A tough outer layer which may be taken off or peeled off.

rin-der-pest (rin´dèr pest´) *n.* A kind of contagious disease that affects the ruminant animals.

ring (ring) *n.* A circular mark, line, or object; a small circular band worn on a finger; a group of persons acting together; especially in an illegal way. *v.* To make a clear resonant sound, as a bell when struck. *n.* The sound made by a bell.

ring-lead-er (ring´lē´dèr) *n.* The person who is the leader of a group, usually one that will violate the law.

ring-let (ring´lit) *n.* A small curl of hair.

ring-mas-ter (ring´mas´tèr) *n.* The person in charge of performances in the circus.

ring-worm (ring´werm´) *n., Pathol.* A contagious skin disease caused by fungi and marked by discolored, ring-shaped, scaly patches on the skin.

rink (ringk) *n.* A smooth area covered with ice used for hockey or ice-skating; a smooth wooden surface for roller-skating.

rinse (rins) *v.* To wash lightly with water. *n.* The act of rinsing; a hair coloring or conditioning solution. **rinsed** *v.*

rins-ing (rin´sing) *n.* The action or act of a person who rinses.

ri-ot (rī´ot) *n.* A wild and turbulent public disturbance. *Slang* An irresistibly amusing person. **riotous** *adj.* **-er** *n.*

rip (rip) *v.* To tear apart violently; to move violently or quickly. *n.* A torn place. **rip-off** To steal.

ri-par-i-an (ri pâr´ē an) *adj.* To be located on the bank by water, such as a lake.

rip cord *n.* A cord which, when pulled, releases a parachute from its pack.

rip cur-rent *n.* A strong surface current flowing outward from shore which results from the return flow of waves.

ripe (rīp) *adj.* Fully developed or aged; mature. **ripeness** *n.*

rip-en (rī´pen) *v.* To age; to develop to maturity.

ri-poste (ri pōst´) *n.* A quick return thrust

used in fencing; a verbal outbreak.

rip-per (rip´ĕr) *n.* A machine used to break up rock, ore, etc.

rip-ping (rip´ing) *adj.* To be pertaining to the tearing of something.

rip-ple (rip´l) *v.* To cause to form small waves on the surface of water; to waver gently. **rippler** *n.*

rip rap (rip´rap´) *n.* A foundation wall of stones thrown together in random fashion.

rip–roar-ing *adj.* To be noisy and loud.

rip tide (rip´tid´) *n.* Water made rough by the meeting of opposite tides and currents.

rise (riz) *v.* To move from a lower position to a higher one; to extend upward; to meet a challenge or demand. *n.* The act of going up or rising; an elevation in condition or rank.

ris-er (ri´zĕr) *n.* A person who rises; the upright part of a stairway.

ris-i-bil-i-ty (riz´i bil´i tē) *n.* The ability to laugh.

ris-i-ble (riz´i bl) *adj.* Being inclined to or causing laughter.

ris-ing (ri´zing) *adj.* To be growing in height; to be more active.

risk (risk) *n.* A chance of suffering or encountering harm or loss; danger; a person who is a hazard to an insurer.

risk-y (ris´kē) *adj.* To be hazardous or full of risk. **riskiness** *n.*

ri-sot-to (ri so´tō) *n.* Rice cooked in meat stock, seasoned with cheese.

rite (rit) *n.* A formal religious ceremony; any formal custom or practice.

rit-u-al (rich´ō al) *n.* A prescribed method for performing a religious ceremony. *adj.* Pertaining to or practiced as a rite. **ritualism** *n.* **-ly** *adv.*

ritz-y (rit´sē) *adj.* To be fashionable; having a high fashion.

ri-val (ri´val) *n.* One who strives to compete with another; one who equals or almost equals another.

ri-val-ry (ri´val rē) *n.* Competition.

rive (riv) *v.* To tear or to rip. **river** *n.*

riv-er (riv´ĕr) *n.* A relatively large natural stream of water, usually fed by another body of water.

river bed (riv´ĕr bed´) *n.* The channel thru which the river flows.

riv-er-ine (riv´e rin´) *adj.* To be caused or formed by a river.

riv-er-weed (riv´ĕr wēd´) *n.* A type of submerged freshwater plant.

ri-vet (riv´it) *n.* A metal bolt that is used to secure two or more objects.

riv-u-let (riv´ū lit) *n.* A small stream.

roach back *n.* A back that is curved.

road (rōd) *n.* A public highway used for vehicles, people, and animals; a path or course; a course toward the achievement of something.

road-a-bil-i-ty (rō´da bil´i tē) *n.* In reference to a car, its ability to ride over all types of roads.

road show *n.* A theatrical show given by a traveling troupe on tour.

roam (rōm) *v.* To travel aimlessly or without a purpose. **roamer** *n.*

roan (rōn) *n.* The color of a horse; a sheepskin tanned with sumac.

roar (rōr) *v.* To utter a deep prolonged sound of excitement; to laugh loudly; a boisterous outcry. **roar** *n.* **roarer** *n.*

roar-ing (rōr´ing) *n.* A loud sound or cry that is given off by something.

roast (rōst) *v.* To cook meat by using dry heat in an oven. *n.* A cut of meat.

roast-er (rō´stĕr) *n.* A person that roasts.

rob (rob) *v.* To take property unlawfully from another person. **robber** *n.*

ro-hand *n.* A piece of woven yarn used to fasten the sail to a spar.

rob-ber (rob´ĕr) *n.* A person who steals from others.

rob-ber fly *n.* A large predatory fly.

rob-ber-y (rob´e rē) *n.* The act of larceny from a person by violence or threat.

robe (rōb) *n.* A long loose garment usually worn over nightclothes; a long flowing garment worn on ceremonial occasions.

ro-ble (rō´blä) *n.* Type of white oak tree that is found mainly in California.

ro-bot (rō´bot) *n.* A machine capable of performing human duties.

ro-bot-ics *n.* In *computer science*, the development of machines that performan human tasks.

ro-bot-ize (rō´bo tiz´) *v.* To make something automatic. **robotization** *n.*

ro-bust (rō bust´) *adj.* Full of strength and health; rich; vigorous. **robustly** *adv.* **robustness** *n.*

ro-bus-tious (rō bus´chus) *adj.* To be sturdy or strong. **robustiousness** *n.*

roc-am-bole (rok´am bōl´) *n.* One type of garlic that is cultivated.

rock (rok) *n.* A hard naturally formed material. *Slang* One who is dependable. **rock** *v.* To move to and fro.

rock-et (rok´it) *n.* A device propelled with the thrust from a gaseous combustion. *v.* To move rapidly.

rocket plane *n.* An airplane propelled by rockets.

rock-et-ry (rok´i trē) *n.* The study of rockets.

rock-fish (rok´fish´) *n.* The striped bass.

rock-oon (rok´ōn) *n.* A research rocket carried by a balloon to a high altitude and then fired.

rock salt *n.* Salt that is artificially prepared in large crystals, sometimes used in the preparation of ice cream made at home.

rock-y (rok´ē) *adj.* Unsteady or unstable; full of rocks. **rockiness** *n.*

rod (rod) *n.* A straight stick growing from

a tree or bush; a pole with a line attached for fishing. **rodlike** *adj.*

rode *v.* Past tense of ride.

ro-dent (rōd´ent) *n.* A mammal, such as a rat, mouse, or beaver having large incisors used for gnawing.

ro-den-ti-cide (rō den´ti sīd´) *n.* A material that is used to destroy rodents.

ro-de-o (rō´dē ō´) *n.* A public show, contest, or demonstration of ranching skills, as riding and roping.

rod-o-mon-tade (rō´do mon tād´) *n.* Boasting that is vain.

roe (rō) *n.* The eggs of a fish.

roent-gen-o-gram (rent´ge no gram´) *n.* Type of photograph which is made with the use of x-rays.

roent-gen-o-ther-a-py (rent´genōther´ apē) *n.* Kind of medical treatment using x-rays.

rogue (rōg) *n.* A scoundrel or dishonest person; a mischievous or playful person. **roguishness** *n.* **roguishly** *adv.*

roil (roil) *v.* To make one angry.

role (rōl) *n.* The position or character that an actor or actress plays.

roll (rōl) *v.* To move in any direction by turning over and over; to sway or rock from side to side, as a ship; to make a deep prolonged sound as thunder. *n.* A list of names. *Slang* A large amount of money.

rol-lick (rol´ik) *v.* To frolic about.

rolling mill *n.* A type of mill where metal is rolled into sheets.

roll up *v.* To collect items together.

ROM Read Only Memory; In *computer science*, memory, as on a compact disk, that can be accessed, but cannot be altered.

ro-maine (rō mān´) *n.* Type of lettuce that has narrow leaves.

ro-mance (rō mans´) *n.* A love affair, usually of the young, characterized by ideals of devotion and purity; a fictitious story filled with extravagant adventures. **romance** *n.*

Roman numeral *n.* The letter of the Roman system of numbering still used in formal contexts, as: I=1, V=5, X=10, L=50, C=100, D=500, M=1000.

ro-man-tic (rō man´tik) *adj.* Very amorous; referring to romance.

romp (romp) *v.* To run, play, or frolic in a carefree way.

ron-dure (ron´jèr) *n.* A form that is gracefully curved.

rood (rōd) *n.* A measurement of land which equals 1/4 acre; a cross or crucifix.

roof (rōf) *n.* The top or covering of a house or other building keeping the elements of weather out. **rooflike** *adj.*

roof garden *n.* The garden that can be found on top of a building.

roof-ing (rō´fing) *n.* The supplies and material that are used to cover a roof.

rook-ie (rek´ē) *n.* An untrained person; a novice or inexperienced person.

room (rōm) *n.* A section or area of a build-ing set off by partitions or walls. *v.* To occupy or live in a room.

room-er (rō´mèr) *n.* Person who rents a room from someone and pays rent.

room-mate (rōm´māt´) *n.* A person who will share the same room with another.

Roosevelt, Franklin Delano *n.* (1882-1945) The thirty-second president of the United States from 1933-1945.

Roosevelt, Theodore *n.* (1858-1919) The twenty-sixth president of the United States from 1901-1909.

roost (rōst) *n.* A place or perch on which birds sleep or rest. **Roost** *n.* To settle into a roost or place of nest.

roost-er (rō´stèr) *n.* The male chicken.

root (rōt) *n.* The part of a plant which grows in the ground. *Math* A number when multiplied by itself, will produce a given quantity. **root** *v.* To search or rummage for something; to turn up the earth with the snout, as a hog.

root out *v.* To discover something.

root rot *n.* A plant disease which is recognized by the decaying of it's roots.

root-y (rō´tē) *adj.* To have a lot of roots.

rope (rōp) *n.* A heavy cord of twisted fiber. **know the ropes** To be familiar with all of the conditions at hand.

ro-que-laure *n.* A knee-length coat that was worn in the 18th and 19th centuries.

ror-qual (ror´kwal) *n.* Large whale.

ro-sa-ry (rō´za rē) *n. pl.* **-ies** A string of beads for counting prayers; a series of prayers.

rose (rōz) *n.* A shrub or climbing vine having sharp prickly stems and variously colored fragrant flowers.

ro-se-ate (rō´zē it) *adj.* To be of a deep pink color. **roseately** *adv.*

rose-bud (rōz´bud´) *n.* The state of the rose just before it blooms.

rose fever *n.* The allergy that is associated to rose pollen.

ro-se-o-la (rō zē´o la) *n.* A rash that is rose colored and appearing on the skin.

Rosh Hashanah (rōsh´ ha shä´na) *n.* The Jewish New Year.

ros-i-ly (rō´zi lē) *adv.* In a cheerful manner; with a rosy color.

ros-in-weed (roz´in wēd´) *n.* A sunflower-like plant that is found in North America.

ros-ter (ros´tèr) *n.* A list of names.

ros-y (rō´zē) *adj.* To be pink, like the color of roses. **rosiness** *n.*

rot (rot) *v.* To break down or decompose.

ro-ta-ry (rō´ta rē) *adj.* Turning or designed to turn; of or relating to axial rotation.

ro-tate (rō´tāt) *v.* To turn on an axis; to

alternate something in sequence. **rotation** n. **rotator** n. **rotatory** adj.

rote (rōt) n. Repetition of sounds.

ro-te-none (rōt´e nōn´) n. Type of compound that is used as an insecticide.

ro-tis-ser-ie (rō tis´e rē) n. A rotation device with spits for roasting food.

ro-tor (rō´tèr) n. A rotating part of a mechanical device.

rot-ten (rot´en) adj. Decomposed; morally corrupt; very bad.

rot-ten-stone (rot´en stōn´) n. Type of soft stone that is used for polishing brass.

rot-ter (rot´ẽr) n. A really bad person.

ro-tund (rō tund´) adj. Plump; rounded.

ro-tun-da (rō tun´da) n. A building that is round having a domed roof.

rouge (rōzh) n. A cosmetic coloring for the cheeks.

rough (ruf) adj. Having an uneven surface; violent or harsh. **rough** n. The part of a golf course with tall grass. **rough** v. To treat roughly. **roughly** adv. In a very rude manner; approximately.

rough-age (ruf´ij) n. Material that is coarse in texture.

rough-and-ready (ruf´an red´ē) adj. Crude in method but effective in action.

rou-leau (rō lō´) n. A trimming for hats that is rolled.

rou-lette (rō let´) n. A gambling game in which players bet on which slot a small ball will land in.

round (round) adj. Curved; circular; spherical. **round** v. To become round; to surround. **round** adv. Throughout; prescribed duties, places, or actions.

rouse (rouz) v. To awaken or stir up.

rout (rout) v. To dig something up, such as a root.

route (rōt) n. A course of travel. **route** v. To send in a certain direction.

rou-tine (rō tēn´) n. Activities done regularly. **routine** adj. Ordinary.

rove (rōv) v. To wander over a wide area. **rover** n. **roving** adj.

row (rō) n. A number of things positioned next to each other; a continuous line. **row** v. To propel a boat with oars.

row-dy (rou´dē) n. A person who is disorderly. **rowdily** adv. **-iness** n.

roy-al (roi´al) adj. Relating to a king or queen.

roy-al-ist (roi´a list) n. A person who supports the king.

roy-al-ty n. pl. **royalties** Monarchs and their families; a payment to someone for the use of his invention, copyright, or services.

R.S.V.P. abbr. Respondez s'il vous plait; please reply.

rub (rub) v. To move over a surface with friction and pressure; to cause to become worn or frayed.

rub-ber (rub´ẽr) n. A resinous elastic material obtained from the coagulated and processed sap of tropical plants or produced synthetically. **-bery** adj.

rubber cement n. A type of adhesive that is liquid and made of rubber.

rub-ber-ize (rub´e rīz´) v. Coat or cover something with rubber.

rubber plant n. Type of plant that is found in East India and yields rubber.

rubber stamp n. A type of rubber plate which is coated with ink and used for the purpose of leaving prints on paper or other objects.

rub-bish (rub´ish) n. Worthless trash; nonsense.

rub-ble (rub´l) n. The pieces of broken material or stones.

rub-down (rub´doun´) n. A type of quick and brisk massage.

ru-be-fa-cient (rō´he fā´shent) n. A type of substance which will turn the area of skin it is applied to red.

ru-hel-la (rō bel´a) n. The German measles.

ru-bel-lite (rō bel´it) n. A red gem stone.

ru-be-o-la (rō bē´o la) n. The German measles. **rubeoloid** adj. **rubeolar** adj.

ru-bi-cund (rō´bi kund´) adj. State of being of a red color or hue.

ru-bid-i-um (rō bid´ē um) n. A silvery, highly reactive element symbolized by Rb.

ru-bi-ous (rō´bē us) adj. Being red in color.

ru-bric (rō´brik) n. A heading, title, or initial letter of a manuscript which appears in red. **rubrically** adv. **-al** adj.

ru-bri-cate (rō´bri kāt´) v. To color something red. **rubricator** n.

ru-by (rō´bē) n. pl. **-ies** A deep-red precious stone. **rubylike** adj.

ru-by glass n. Type of red glass.

ru-by spi-nal n. A gem stone, red in color.

ruche (rōsh) n. Piece of crimped fabric which is used to trim a woman's clothes.

ruck-sack (ruk´sak´) n. A knapsack that is carried by hikers.

ruck-us n., Slang A noisy uproar, or com-motion.

rud-der (rud´ẽr) n., Naut. A broad, flat, hinged device attached to the stern of a boat used for steering.

ru-di-ment (rō´di ment) n. A first step, element, skill, or principle. Biol. An undeveloped organ. **-tariness** n.

rue (rō) v. To repent.

rue-ful (rō´ful) adj. To be causing sorrow or remorse. **ruefully** adv.

ru-fes-cent (rō fes´ent) adj. To be red in color or tint. **rufescence** n.

ruff (ruf) n. A stiff collar which has pleats in it.

ruffed grouse n. A bird, like the chicken, and living in North America having a fan-haped tail and tufted feathers at the neck.

ruf-fi-an (ruf´ē an) *n.* A lawless, rowdy person. **ruffianly** *adj.* **ruffianism** *n.*

ruf-fle (ruf´l) *n.* A pleated strip or frill; a decorative band. *v.* To disturb or destroy the smoothness.

ru-fous (rō´fus) *adj.* To be red in color or tint.

rug (rug) *n.* A heavy textile fabric used to cover a floor.

ru-ga (rō´ga) *n.* A wrinkle or fold in something.

rug-ged (rug´id) *adj.* Strong; rough; having an uneven or rough surface. **ruggedness** *n.* **ruggedly** *adv.*

ru-gose (rō´gōs) *adj.* To be filled with folds and wrinkles. **rugous** *adj.*

ru-in (rō´in) *n.* Total destruction. **ruin** *v.* To destroy. **ruination** *n.* **-ous** *adj.*

rule (rōl) *n.* Controlling power; an authoritative direction or statement which regulates the method of doing something; a standard procedure. **rule** *v.* To have control over; to make a straight line using a ruler; to be in command.

rule out *v.* To omit something.

rul-er (rō´lèr) *n.* A straight edge used for measuring; a person who rules as a sovereign.

rul-ing (rō´ling) *n.* A type of decision which is handed down by a judge in a trial.

rum (rum) *n.* A type of liquor made from molasses and is distilled.

rum-ble (rum´bl) *v.* To make a heavy, continuous sound. *n.* A long, deep rolling sound.

ru-men (rō´min) *n.* The first stomach of ruminant animals, such as a cow or goat.

ru-mi-nant (rō´mi nant) *n.* A cud-chewing animal; as a cow, deer, sheep, or giraffe; an animal which chews something which was swallowed. **ruminantly** *adv.*

ru-mi-nate (rō´mi nāt´) *v.* To chew a cud; to ponder at length. **rumination** *n.* **ruminative** *adj.* **ruminator** *n.*

rum-mage (rum´ij) *v.* To look or search thoroughly by digging or turning things over; to ransack.

ru-mor (rō´mèr) *n.* An uncertain truth which is circulated from one person to another; gossip. **rumor** *v.* To spread by rumor.

rump (rump) *n.* The fleshy hind quarter of an animal; the human buttocks.

rum-ple (rum´pl) *v.* To form into creases or folds; to wrinkle.

rum-pus (rum´pus) *n.* A loud noise or disturbance.

rumpus room *n.* A type of room which is used for parties.

run (run) *v.* To hurry busily from place to place; to move quickly in such a way that both feet leave the ground for a portion of each step; to make a rapid journey; to be a candidate seeking an office; to drain or discharge. *Law* To be effective, concurrent with. **run** *n.* A speed faster than a walk; a streak, as of luck; the continuous extent or length of something; an outdoor area used to exercise animals. In baseball, the method of scoring a point by running the bases and returning to home plate.

run-a-way (run´a wā´) *n.* A person who leaves home without telling anyone where they are going and does not plan on coming back.

rung (rung) *n.* A bar or board which forms a step of a ladder.

run-nel (run´el) *n.* A small stream.

run-ner–up (run´èr up´) *n.* A contestant who finishes second in a competition.

runt (runt) *n.* The smallest animal in a litter. **runty** *adj.* **runtiness** *n.*

run time In *computer science*, the period required for a computer to perform a particular task, such as a mail merge.

rup-ture (rup´chèr) *n.* A state of being broken; the act of bursting.

ru-ral (rer´al) *adj.* Pertaining to the country or country life. **ruralist** *n.*

ru-ral-ize (rer´a līz´) *v.* The act of moving to or living in the country or the rural area. **ruralization** *n.*

rural route *n.* A mail route which runs through the country.

rush (rush) *v.* To move quickly; to hurry; to be in a hurry. **rushy** *adj.*

rust (rust) *n.* Ferric oxide which forms a coating on iron material exposed to moisture and oxygen; deterioration through neglect. **rust** *v.* To form rust.

rus-tic (rus´tik) *adj.* Characteristic of country life. **rustic** *n.* A simple person.

rus-tle (rus´l) *v.* To move making soft sounds, such as those made by leaves of a tree.

rut (rut) *n.* An indented track made by the wheels of vehicles.

ru-ta-ba-ga (rō´ta bā´ga) *n.* A vegetable of the mustard family which makes an underground white tuber.

ruth (rōth) *n.* Grief; sorrowful for another.

ru-the-ni-um (rō thē´nē um) *n.* A metallic element symbolized by Ru.

ruth-ful (rōth´ful) *adj.* To be mournful.

ruth-less (rōth´lis) *adj.* Merciless.

ru-ti-lant (rōt´i lant) *adj.* To have a glow that is reddish in color or tine.

rut-ty (rut´ē) *adj.* A state of having many ruts.

rye (rī) *n.* A cultivated cereal grass used to make flour and whiskey.

rye whiskey *n.* Whiskey distilled from rye.

S, s (ess) The nineteenth letter of the English alphabet.

sab-bat (sab´at) *n.* The midnight assembly of the diatomists.

Sab-ba-tar-i-an *n.* A person who observes the Sabbath on Saturday.

Sab-bath *n.* The seventh day of the week; sundown on Friday to sundown on Saturday; a day set aside as the day of worship for Jews and some Christians; Sunday, the first day of the week, a day set apart as the day of worship by most Christians.

sab-bat-i-cal (sa bat´ik) *adj.* To be relating to the Sabbath.

saber–toothed tiger *n.* A type of extinct cat which was characterized by the great development of the upper canines.

sa-bin *n.* Unit of acoustic absorption.

sa-ble (sā´bl) *n.* A carnivorous mammal having soft, black or dark fur.

sa-ble-fish (sā´bl fish˝) *n.* A type of large spiny-finned fish which is grey or black and of the Pacific coast.

sa-bot (sab´ō) *n.* The kind of wooden shoe which is worn by the people in various European countries.

sab-o-tage (sab´o täzh˝) *n.* An act of malicious destruction, intended to obstruct production of war material by the opposing side.

sab-o-teur *n.* A person who commits sabotage.

sac (sak) *n., Biol.* A membranous pouch in an animal or plant, containing a liquid.

sa-ca-huis-te *n.* A kind of forage grass that has long linear leaves.

sac-cade *n.* A type of small, rapid, and jerky movement of the eye.

sac-cate (sak´it) *adj.* To have the form of a pouch.

sac-cha-rate *n.* A compound of sugar usually with a bivalent metal.

sac-char-i-fy *v.* To break some compound into a simple sugar.

sac-cha-rim-e-ter *n.* A kind of device which is used for the purpose of measuring the amount of sugar in a solution.

sac-cha-rin (sak´a rin) *n.* A white, crystal-line sugar powder used as a non-caloric sugar substitute.

sac-cha-rine (sak´a rin) *adj.* Pertaining to or like sugar.

sac-cha-roi-dal *adj.* Being of fine granular texture.

sac-cha-rom-e-ter *n.* A type of hydrometer that has a special scale.

sac-cu-lar *adj.* To be resembling a sac.

sac-cu-late *adj.* To be formed of a series of saccular expansions.

sac-cule *n.* A chamber which is the smaller of the membranous labyrinth of the ear.

sac-er-do-tal (sas˝é dōt´al) *adj.* Pertaining to the priesthood or priests.

sa-chem (sa´chem) *n.* A kind of North American Indian chief.

sa-chet (sa shā´) *n.* A small bag of a sweet smelling powder used to scent clothes.

sack (sak) *n.* A strong bag for holding articles. *Slang* Dismissal from a position or job; sleeping bag or bed.

sacque (sak) *n.* A type of infant jacket that is short and fastens at the neck.

sa-cral *adj.* Pertaining to the sacrum.

sac-ra-ment (sak´ra ment) *n. Eccl.* A formal Christian rite performed in a church, as a baptism. **Sacrament** The consecrated bread and wine of the Eucharist; the Lord's Supper.

sac-ra-ment-al *adj.* The use of the sacramental acts or rites.

sa-crar-i-um *n.* An ancient Roman shrine which holds sacred articles.

sa-cred (sā´krid) *adj.* Dedicated to worship; holy. **sacredly** *adv.*

sac-ri-fice (sak´ri fīs´) *n.* The practice of offering something, as an animal's life, to a deity. **sacrifice** *v.* To give up something of value for something else. **sacrificial** *adj.*

sa-cro-il-i-ac *adj.* Pertaining to the region of juncture of the sacrum and the ilium.

sa-crum *n.* The section or part of the vertebral column which is directly connected with the pelvis and in man is made up of five fused vertebrae.

sad (sad) *adj.* Marked by sorrow; unhappy; causing sorrow; deplorable. **sadly** *adv.* **sadness** *n.*

sadden *v.* To become or to make sad.

sad-dle (sad´l) *n.* A seat for a rider, as on the back of a horse or bicycle; a cut of meat which includes the backbone. **saddle** *v.* To put a saddle on; to load down; to burden.

saddlebag *n.* A covered pouch which is put across the back of the horse.

saddle leather *n.* A type of leather which is made from the hide of cattle that is vegetable-tanned and used for making saddles.

saddle roof *n.* A type of roof having one ridge and two gables.

sad-i-ron (sad´īern) *n.* A type of flatiron which is pointed at both ends.

sa-dism (sad´iz um) *n. Psychol.* A condition in which sexual gratification comes from inflicting pain on others; cruelty. **sadistic** *adj.*

sad sack *n.* A kind of person who is inept.

sa-fa-ri (sa fär´ē) *n., pl.* **safaris** A trip; a hunting expedition in Africa.

safe (sāf) *adj.* Secure from danger, harm, or evil; unharmed; not likely to cause harm. **safe** *n.* A strong metal container used to protect and store documents or money. **safely** *adv.*

safe–conduct *n.* The protection which

is given to a person that is passing through a military zone.

safe–deposit box *n.* A box which can be found in a bank and used for the purpose of protecting the valuables of the one who uses it.

safe-guard *n.* A kind of precautionary measure.

safety belt *n.* A type of belt that is used to prevent a person from injury or falling.

saf-ra-nine *n.* Any of the various mixtures of safranine salts which are used in dyeing.

saf-role *n.* A type of poisonous ether that is used for perfuming and flavoring.

sag *v.* To droop; to sink from pressure or weight; to lose strength; decline in amount.

sa-ga (sä′ga) *n.* A long heroic story.

sa-ga-cious (sa gā′shus) *adj.* Being of keen penetration and judgment.

sag-a-more (sag′a mōr′) *n.* The subordinate chief of the Algonquian Indians who are of the north Atlantic coast.

sage (sāj) *n.* A person recognized for judgment and wisdom. **sage** *adj.*

sagebrush *n.* A type of North American low shrubs with a bitter juice and odor.

sag-ger (sag′ér) *n.* A type of box which is made of fireclay.

sag-it-tal *adj.* Pertaining to the suture between the parietal bones of the skull.

sag-it-tate (saj′i tāt′) *adj.* To be shaped like an arrowhead.

sa-go *n.* A type of powdered starch that is made from the pith of a sago palm.

sa-gua-ro *n.* A type of arborescent cactus which grows in the southwestern United States and Mexico.

said (sed) *v.* Past tense of say.

sail (sāl) *n.* A strong fabric used to catch the wind and cause a ship to move; a trip on a sailing vessel or boat. **sail** *v.* To travel on a sailing vessel.

sail-board A type of small flat sailboat made for two passengers.

sail-boat *n.* A type of boat which is propelled with a sail.

sail-cloth *n.* A type of canvas which is used for making sails.

sail-er *n.* A boat which has specified sailing qualities.

sail-fish *n.* A type of pelagic fish that has a large dorsal fin.

sailor *n.* The person that sails or works on a boat or ship.

sain-foin (sān′foin) *n.* A type of herb that has pink flowers.

saint (sānt) *n.* A person of great purity who has been officially recognized as such by the Roman Catholic Church; a person who has died and is in heaven.

sake (sāk) *n.* Motive or reason for doing something.

sal-a-ble (sā′la bl) *adj.* Fit to be sold.

sa-la-cious *adj.* To be appealing to sexual desire. **salaciousness** *n.*

sal-ad (sal′ad) *n.* A dish usually made of green vegetables, fruit, or meat tossed with dressing.

sal-a-man-der (sal′a man′dér) *n.* A lizard-like amphibian with porous, scaleless skin.

sa-la-mi (sa lä′mē) *n.* A spiced sausage made of beef and pork.

sa-la-ry (sal′a rē) *n., pl.* **salaries** A set compensation paid on a regular basis for services rendered or hours served. **salaried** *adj.*

sale (sāl) *n.* An exchange of goods for a price; disposal of items at reduced prices. **salable** *adj.*

sa-lep *n.* The dried tubers of various Old World orchids.

sal-er-a-tus *n.* A kind of leavening agent.

sales *adj.* Pertaining to selling.

sales tax *n.* A tax which is placed on the sale of goods.

sal-i-cin (sal′i sin) *n.* A bitter white glucoside that is found in the bark of willows.

sa-lic-y-late *n.* The ester of salicylic acid.

sa-li-ence *n.* The state of being salient.

sa-li-ent (sā′lē ent) *adj.* Projecting beyond a line; conspicuous.

sa-li-tian *n.* Any of the group of amphibians which consists of frogs, toads, and tree toads.

sa-lim-e-ter *n.* Type of hydrometer for indicating a percentage of salt in a solution.

sa-li-nize *v.* To impregnate with salt.

sa-li-nom-e-ter *n.* A type of instrument used for the purpose of measuring salt in a solution.

sa-li-va (sa lī′va) *n.* Tasteless fluid secreted in the mouth which aids in digestion.

sal-i-var-y *adj.* Pertaining to saliva or the glands of the body that secrete saliva.

sal-i-vate *v.* To produce or make an abnormal flow of saliva.

Salk vaccine (salk′ vak sēn′) *n.* A vaccine used to immunize against polio.

sal-low (sal′ō) *n.* A type of Old World broad-leaved willow.

sal-ly *n., pl.* **sallies** A sudden rush to launch an assault.

sal-ma-gun-di *n.* A kind of salad plate made with eggs, meats, and vegetables.

sal-mi *n.* A ragout of roasted game that is stewed in a rich sauce.

salm-on (sam′on) *n., pl.* **salmon** *or* **salmons** A large game fish with pinkish flesh.

sal-mon-el-la *n.* A type of aerobic rod-shaped bacteria that causes food poisoning.

sal-mo-nel-lo-sis *n.* A disease that is

caused by salmonellae.

sal-mo-nid *n.* A member of the family of elongated soft-finned fishes.

sa-lon (sa lon´) *n.* A large drawing room; a business establishment pertaining to fashion.

sa-loon (sa lōn´) *n.* A place where alcoholic drinks are sold; a barroom.

sa-loop (sa lōp´) *n.* A hot drink which is made from sassafras and dried tubers of orchids.

sal-pa *n.* An oceanic tunicate which is found to be abundant in warm seas.

sal-pin-gian *adj.* Pertaining to or relating to a fallopian or eustacian tube.

sal-pin-gi-tis *n.* The swelling or inflammation of a fallopian tube or a eustachian tube.

sal-si-fy *n.* A type of European biennial herb that has an edible root.

sal soda *n.* A crystalline hydrated sodium carbonate.

salt (solt) *n.* A white crystalline solid, mainly sodium chloride, found in the earth and sea water, used as a preservative and a seasoning. **salt** *adj.* Containing salt. **salt** *v.* To season or preserve with salt. **salty** *adj.*

sal-ta-tion (sal tā´shan) *n.* The process of jumping or leaping.

sal-ta-to-ri-al *adj.* To be adapted for leaping.

sal-ta-to-ry *adj.* Pertaining to dancing.

sal-tine (sol tēn´) *n.* A crisp cracker which is sprinkled with salt.

salt-pe-ter (solt´pē´tèr) *n.* Potassium nitrate.

sa-lu-bri-ous (sa lō´brē us) *adj.* To be promoting well-being or health.

sa-lu-ki *n.* A type of northern African and Asiatic breed of hunting dogs.

sal-u-tar-y (sal´ū ter´ē) *adj.* Wholesome; healthful; beneficial.

sal-u-ta-tion (sal´ū tā´shan) *n.* An expression; a greeting of good will, as used to open a letter.

sa-lu-ta-to-ri-an *n.* A student that usually has the second highest rank in the class; based on grade scores.

sa-lu-ta-to-ry *adj.* Pertaining to a salutation.

sa-lute (sa lōt´) *v.* To show honor to a superior officer by raising the right hand to the forehead. **salute** *n.* An act of respect or greeting by saluting.

salv-a-ble *adj.* Capable of being salvaged; reuseable.

sal-vage (sal´vij) *n.* Act of rescuing a ship, its cargo, or its crew; property which has been saved. **salvage** *v.* To save from destruction; to rescue.

sal-va-tion (sal vā´shan) *n.* The means which effect salvation; the deliverance from the effects of sin.

salve (sav) *n.* A medicated ointment to soothe the pain of a burn or wound.

sal-ver (sal´vèr) *n.* A type of tray which is used for serving food and drinks.

sal-ver-form *adj.* Being tubular with a spreading limb.

sal-vi-a *n.* Type of herbs of the mint family that have a two-lipped open calyx.

sal-vif-ic *adj.* Having the intent to save.

sal-vo (sal´vō) *n., pl.* **salvos** *or* **salvoes** The discharge of a number of guns at the same time.

sal volatile *n.* A solution of ammonium carbonate in alcohol.

SAM *abbr.* Surface-to-Air Missile.

Sa-mar-i-tan (sa mar´i tan) *n.* A person who is ready to help others in need.

sa-mar-i-um (sa mâr´ē um) *n.* A metallic element symbolized by Sm.

sam-ba *n.* A type of Brazilian dance.

sam-bar *n.* A large Asiatic deer that has long, coarse hair on its neck.

sam-bo *n.* A type of international wrestling with judo techniques.

same (sām) *adj.* Identical; exactly alike; similar; not changing. **same** *pron.* The very same one or thing.

sa-mite (sam´īt) *n.* A silk fabric with interwoven gold or silver threads.

sam-o-var *n.* A type of Russian urn used to boil water for making tea.

samp *n.* A coarse hominy.

sam-phire (sam´fī ér´) *n.* A common glasswort that is sometimes pickled.

sam-ple (sam´pl) *n.* A portion which represents the whole. **sample** *v.* To try a little.

sam-pler (sam´plèr) *n.* A person who collects or examines samples.

sample room *n.* the room where samples of product are stored or displayed.

sam-shu *n.* An alcoholic liquor distilled in China from millet or rice.

sam-u-rai *n.* The warrior aristocracy of Japan.

san-a-to-ri-um (san´a tōr´ē um) *n. pl.* **sanatoriums** An institution for treating chronic diseases.

sanc-ti-fy (sangk´ti fī´) *v.* To make holy. **sanctification** *n.*

sanc-ti-mo-ni-ous *adj.* To be possessing sanctity. **sanctimoniousness** *n.*

sanc-ti-mo-ny *n.* A hypocritical holiness.

sanc-tion (sangk´shan) *n.* Permission from a person of authority; a penalty to ensure compliance. **sanction** *v.* To officially approve an action.

sanc-tu-ar-y (sangk´chö er´ē) *n., pl.* **sanctuaries** A sacred, holy place, as the part of a church, where services are held; a safe place; a refuge.

sanc-tum *n.* A place which is sacred.

sand (sand) *n.* Fine grains of disintegrated rock found in deserts and on beaches; a light tan color. **sand** *v.* To smooth or polish with sandpaper; to sprinkle or toss sand.

san-dal (san´dal) *n.* A shoe which is fastened to the foot by straps attached to the sole; a low shoe or slipper with an ankle strap.

san-dar-ac (san´da rak˝) *n.* A resin that is aromatic and brittle obtained from the African sandarac tree.

sand-cast (sand´kast) *v.* To make a casting by pouring the metal into a mold which is made of sand.

sand dollar *n.* A flat circular sea urchin that lives in shallow water on the sandy bottom.

sand-glass *n.* A type of instrument for measuring the passing of time with the running of sand through it.

sand-pa-per *n.* A type of paper that is covered on one side with sand used for the purpose of smoothing rough edges.

sand-wich (sand´wich) *n.* Two or more slices of bread between which a filling, such as cheese or meat, is placed.

sane (sān) *adj.* Having a healthy, sound mind; showing good judgment. **sanely** *adv.* **sanity** *n.*

san-ga-ree (sang˝ga rē) *n.* An iced drink of wine, beer, ale, or liquor which has been garnished with nutmeg.

sang-froid (sän frwä´) *n.* A self-possession or imperturbability.

san-gui-nar-ia *n.* The roots and rhizome of the bloodroot which can be used as an emetic or an expectorant.

san-guine (sang´gwin) *adj.* To be relating to the blood. **sanguinely** *adv.*

san-guin-e-ous *adj.* Pertaining to bloodshed; consisting of blood.

san-guin-o-lent *adj.* To be tinged by blood or to contain blood.

san-guin-o-pu-ru-lent *adj.* Containing us and blood in the discharge.

san-i-cle *n.* A type of plants that are held to have healing powers.

san-it *abbr.* Sanitation; sanitary.

san-i-tar-i-an *n.* One who is a specialist in sanitary science and the public health.

san-i-tar-i-ly *adv.* Doing something in a sanitary manner or way.

san-i-tar-y (san´i ter˝ē) *adj.* Free from bacteria or filth which endanger health. **sanitary** *n.*

san-i-tate *v.* To make a thing sanitary; clean.

san-i-ta-tion (san˝i tā´shan) *n.* The process of making something sanitary.

san-i-tize (san´i tīz´) *v.* To make sanitary; to make clean or free of germs.

san-i-ty *n.* The state of being sane.

sank *v.* Past tense of sink.

san-nup (san´up) *n.* An American Indian male who is married.

sans-cu-lotte *n.* One who is considered to be from a lower class and lacking culture or refinement.

san-se-vie-ria *n.* A member of the group of tropical herbs of the lily family that yield a strong fiber.

sap (sap) *n.* The liquid which flows or circulates through plants and trees. *v.* To weaken or wear away gradually. *Slang* A gullible person; fool.

sa-pi-ent (sā´pē ent) *adj.* Wise.

sap-phire (saf´īer) *n.* A clear, deep-blue gem, used in jewelry.

sar-casm (sär´kaz um) *n.* An insulting or mocking statement or remark. **sarcastic** *adj.* **sarcastically** *adv.*

sar-dine (sär dēn´) *n.* A small edible fish of the herring family, canned in oil, mustard, or tomato sauce.

sar-don-ic (sär don´ik) *adj.* Scornful; mockingly cynical.

sa-ri (sär´ē) *n.* A garment consisting of a long piece of lightweight material wrapped around the body and over the shoulder of Hindu women.

sar-sa-pa-ril-la (sas´pa ril´a) *n.* The dried root of a tropical American plant, which is used as flavoring.

sash (sash) *n.* A band worn over the shoulder or around the waist.

sass (sas) *n. Slang* Rudeness; a disrespectful manner of speech. **sass** *v.* To talk with disrespect.

sas-sa-fras (sas´a fras˝) *n.* The dried root of a North American tree, used as flavoring.

Sa-tan (sāt´an) *n.* The devil.

sat-el-lite (sat´e līt˝) *n.* A natural or man-made object which orbits a celestial body.

sat-in (sat´in) *n.* A smooth, shiny fabric made of silk, nylon, or rayon, having a glossy face and dull back.

sat-ire (sat´ī er) *n.* The use of mockery, sarcasm, or humor in a literary work to ridicule or attack human vice.

sat-is-fac-tion (sat´is fak´shan) *n.* Anything which brings about a happy feeling; the fulfillment of a need, appetite, or desire; a source of gratification. **satisfactory** *adj.*

sat-u-rate (sach´a rāt´) *v.* To make completely wet; to soak or load to capacity. **saturable** *adj.* **-tion** *n.*

sat-yr (sā´tēr) *n. Myth.* A Greek woodland god having a human body and the legs, horns, and ears of a goat.

sauce (sos) *n.* A liquid or dressing served as an accompaniment to food.

sau-cer (so´sēr) *n.* A small shallow dish for holding a cup.

sau-er-kraut (sour´krout´) *n.* Shredded and salted cabbage cooked in its own juices until tender and sour.

sau-na (sou´nä) *n.* A steam bath in which one is subjected to heat produced by water poured over heated rocks.

sau-sage (so´sij) *n.* Chopped meat, usually pork, which is highly seasoned, stuffed into a casing, and cooked.

sav-age (sav´ij) *adj.* Wild; not domesticated; uncivilized; brutal. **savage** *n.* A vicious or crude person. **-ery** *n.*

save (sāv) *v.* To rescue from danger, loss, or harm; to prevent waste or loss; to keep for another time in the future; to be delivered from sin. **saver** *n.*

sav-ior (sāv´yėr) *n.* One who saves.

sa-voir-faire (sav´wär fâr´) *n.* Social skill; the ability to say and do the right thing.

sa-vor (sā´vėr) *n.* The taste or smell of something. **savor** *v.* To have a particular smell; to truly enjoy. **-y** *adj.*

saw (so) *n.* A tool with a sharp metal blade edged with teeth-like points for cutting. **saw** *v.* Past tense of *see*; to cut with a saw.

sax-o-phone (sak´so fōn´) *n.* A brass wind instrument having finger keys and a reed mouthpiece.

say (sā) *v.* To speak aloud; to express oneself in words; to indicate; to show. **say** *n.* The chance to speak; the right to make a decision.

scab (skab) *n.* The stiff and crusty covering which forms over a healing wound. *Slang* One who continues to work while others are on strike.

scab-bard (skab´ėrd) *n.* A type of sheath for a bayonet or a dagger.

scab-ble *v.* To dress something, such as stone, with a rough furrowed surface.

scab-by *adj.* To be diseased with scab.

sca-bies (skā´bēz) *n.* A contagious skin disease characterized by severe itching, caused by a mite under the skin.

sca-bi-o-sa *n.* A type of herb of the teasel family

sca-brous (skab´rus) *adj.* To be rough to the touch. **scabrousness** *n.*

scad (skad) *n.* A type of caragid fish.

scaf fold (skaf´ọld) *n.* A temporary support of metal or wood erected for workers who are building or working on a large structure.

scaf-fold ing *n.* A system of scaffolds.

scal-a-ble *adj.* Able to be scaled.

sca-lar *adj.* To have an uninterrupted series of steps such as a staircase.

sca-lar-i-form *adj.* To be like or resembling a ladder.

scal-a-wag (skal´a wag´) *n.* Rascal.

scald (skold) *v.* To burn with steam or a hot liquid; to heat a liquid to a temperature just under boiling.

scale (skāl) *n.* A flat plate which covers certain animals, especially fish and reptiles; a device for weighing; a series of marks indicating the relationship between a map or model and the actual dimensions. *Music* A sequence of eight musical notes in accordance with a specified scheme of intervals.

scale–down *n.* A kind of reduction that

is according to a fixed ratio.

sca-lene (skā lēn´) *adj.* Having three sides that are unequal in length.

scale-pan *n.* A kind of pan which is used for the purpose of weighing things.

scal-er (skā´lėr) *n.* Someone or something that scales an object.

scale–up *n.* The increase that is according to a ratio which is fixed.

scall (skol) *n.* A type of scabby disorder which can occur on the skin.

scal-lion *n.* A type of onion that will form a thick basal part but without a bulb.

scal-lop (skol´op) *n.* A marine shellfish with a fan-shaped, fluted bivalve shell; the fleshy edible muscle of the scallop.

scalp (skalp) *n.* The skin which covers the top of the human head where hair normally grows. **scalp** *v.* To tear or remove the scalp from. *Slang* To buy or sell something at an inflated price.

scal-pel (skal´pel) *n.* A small, straight knife with a narrow, pointed blade, used in surgery.

scalp lock *n.* A tuft of the hair on the crown of an otherwise shaved head.

scamp (skamp) *n.* A tricky person.

scamp-er *v.* To run playfully about.

scamp-i *n.* A type of large shrimp that is prepared with a garlic sauce.

scan (skan) *v.* To examine all parts closely; to look at quickly; to analyze the rhythm of a poem. *Electron.* To move a beam of radar in search of a target. **scanner** *n.*

scan-dal (skan´dal) *n.* Something which brings disgrace when exposed to the public; gossip.

scan-dal-ize (skan´da līz´) *v.* To offend someone in a moral sense.

scan-dal-mon-ger (skan´dal mon˝gėr) *n.* One who circulates scandal.

scan-dal-ous *adj.* Being offensive to morality. **scandalously** *adv.*

scan-dal sheet *n.* A magazine or newspaper, based on gossip or scandal

scan-dent *adj.* To be characterized by a climbing means of growth; such as a vine.

scan-di-um (skan´de um) *n.* A metallic element symbolized by Sc.

scanner *n.* In *computer science*, an optical device for reading hard copy and translating it to digital data.

scant (skant) *adj.* Not plentiful or abundant; inadequate; give out sparingly. **scantily** *adv.*

scant-ling (skant´ling) *n.* The dimensions of material used in building, as the wood or brick.

scant-y (skan´tē) *adj.* To be somewhat less than is normal; lacking; meager.

scape (skāp) *n.* The shaft of a column; shaft of a feather. **scape** *v.* means of escape; a mistake.

scape-goat *n.* A person bearing a blame

for others.

scape-goat-ing *n.* The act of casting blame on an innocent individual.

scape-grace (skāp´grās¯) *n.* A rascal.

scaph-oid *adj.* To be shaped like a boat.

scap-u-la (skap´ū la) *n.,, pl.* **-lae** One pair of large, flat, triangular bones which form the back of the shoulder.

scap-u-lar *adj.* To be pertaining to or related to the scapula or the shoulder.

scar (skär) *n.* A permanent mark which remains on the skin after a sore or injury has healed. **scar** *v.*

scar-ab *n.* The scarabaeid beetle.

scar-a-bae-id *n.* A stout-bodied beetle.

scarce (skârs) *adj.* Not common or plentiful; rare. **scarceness** *n.*

scarce-ly *adv.* Being done by a slight margin.

scar-ci-ty *n.* The state of being scarce.

scare (skâr) *v.* To become scared or to frighten someone suddenly.

scarf (skärf) *n.* A wide piece of cloth worn around the head, neck, and shoulders for warmth.

scarf-skin (skärf´skin¯) *n.* The skin which forms the cuticle of the nail.

scar-i-fi-ca-tion *n.* The marks which can be made by scarifying.

scar-i-fy (skar´i fī¯) *v.* To make small cuts into the skin. **scarifier** *n.*

scar-i-ous (skâr´ē us) *adj.* To be membranous in texture.

scar-la-ti-na (skär´la tē´na) *n.* A mild form of scarlet fever.

scar-let (skär´lit) *n.* A bright or vivid red.

scarlet fever *n.* A communicable disease caused by streptococcus and character-ized by a sore throat, vomiting, high fever, and a rash.

scar tissue *n.* A connective tissue that forms a scar and is made mostly of fibroblasts.

scar-y (skâ´ē) *adj.* To be able to scare; to be easily scared.

scathe (skäth) *v.* To assail something with withering denunciation.

scath-ing (skā´thing) *adj.* To be bitterly severe. **scathingly** *adv.*

scat-ter (skat´ér) *v.* To spread around; to distribute in different directions.

scat-ter-brain *n.* A heedless person.

scat-ter-ing (skat´ér ing) *n.* The process of something being scattered.

scatter pin *n.* A pin which is worn for decoration on one's clothes.

scatter rug *n.* A small rug.

scav-enge *v.* To salvage something from being discarded; to take away from an area.

scav-en-ger (skav´in jèr) *n.* An animal, as a vulture, which feeds on decaying or dead animals or plant matter.

sce-na *n.* A solo vocal that consists of a recitative.

sce-nar-i-o (si när´ē ō´) *n.* A synopsis of a dramatic plot.

sce-nar-ist (si när´ist) *n.* A person who creates and writes a scenario.

scend (send) *v.* To heave up under the influence of a natural force.

scene (sēn) *n.* A view; the time and place where an event occurs; a public display of temper; a part of a play.

scene dock *n.* An area or space which is near the stage in a theater and is used for the storage of the scenery.

scen-er-y *n.* Painted screens or other accessories that are used with a play.

scent (sent) *n.* A smell; an odor. *v.* To smell; to give something a scent.

scent-ed *adj.* To have a smell or odor.

scep-ter (sep´tér) *n.* A rod or staff carried by a king or queen as a sign of authority.

sch *abbr.* School.

scha-den-freu-de *n.* The enjoyment that is obtained through the troubles of others.

sched-ule (skej´ōl) *n.* A list or written chart which shows the times at which events will happen, including a plan given for work and specified deadlines; a timetable of events.

schee-lite (shā´līt) *n.* A type of mineral that consists of the tungstate of calcium and is a source of tungsten.

sche-ma (skē´ma) *n.* A presentation which is diagrammatic.

sche-mat-ic *adj.* To be pertaining to a schema. **schematically** *adv.*

scheme (skēm) *n.* A plan of action; an orderly combination of related parts; a secret plot. **schemer** *n.*

schil-ler (shil´ér) *n.* A type of bronzy iridescent luster.

schism (siz´um) *n.* A formal separation from a religious body.

schis-mat-ic (siz mat´ik) *n.* The person who creates schism.

schis-ma-tize *v.* To take part in schism.

schist *n.* A type of metamorphic rock that has a closely foliated structure.

schis-tose *adj.* To be pertaining to schist rock.

schiz-o-carp *n.* A type of dry compound fruit that will split at its maturity.

schiz-ont *n.* A type of multinucleate sporozoan that will reproduce by schizogony.

schle-miel *n.* An unlucky bungler.

schlie-ren *n.* Irregularly, shaped masses in a rock such as streaks, which differ in texture from the main mass.

schmo *n.* A foolish or boring person; a jerk; naive.

schnapps *n.* A type of distilled liquors or spirits.

schnau-zer *n.* A dog that has a long head, small ears, and a wiry coat.

schnit-zel (shnit´sel) *n.* A type of

garnished and seasoned veal cutlet.

schnor-rer n. A person who wheedles other people into supplying his or her wants; one who solicits unjustified help from others.

schnoz-zle n. *Slang* The nose. *Yiddish*

schol-ar (skol´ẽr) n. A student with a strong interest in learning.

schol-ar-ly (skol´ẽr lē) adj. Being suitable to learned persons.

schol-ar-ship n. A grant of money which is given to a students to enable them to go to school.

scho-las-tic (sko las´tik) adj. Pertaining to schools. **scholastically** adv.

scho-li-um n. A comment which is marginal.

school (skōl) n. A place for teaching and learning; a group of persons devoted to similar principles.

school age n. The time of one' life when one is able to attend school and required to do so by the law.

school board n. The board of people who are in charge of public schools.

school-book n. A textbook which is used for the schoolwork done in schools.

school-room (skōl´rŏm´) n. A classroom that is used for teaching.

school-time n. The time that is designated for the beginning of a session of school.

schoon-er (skō´nẽr) n. A sailing vessel with two or more masts.

Schwann sell n. A type of cell of the neurilemma of the fiber of the nerve.

sci-ae-nid n. A carnivorous marine percoid fish, such as the croaker.

sci-at-ic (sī at´ik) adj. Being located near the hip area of the body.

sciatic nerve n. The largest nerve of the body that runs down both legs.

sci-ence (sī´ens) n. The study and theoretical explanation of natural phenomena in an orderly way; knowledge acquired through experience. **scientific** adj. **scientist** n.

sci-en-tism n. The attitudes that are typical of the natural scientist.

sci-fi abbr. Science fiction.

scil-la n. A type of Old World herb of the lily family that has pink, blue, or white flowers.

scim-i-tar (sim´i tẽr) n. A type of saber that is made of a curved blade and is used by the Turks and the Arabs.

scin-til-late (sin´ti lāt´) v. To give off or emit quick flashes. **scintillator** n.

scir-rhus n. A type of malignant tumor that has a preponderance of fibrous tissue.

scis-sion (sizh´an) n. The process of splitting or cutting.

scis-sors (siz´ẽrz) n. A cutting tool consisting of two blades joined and pivoted so that the edges are close to each other.

scler-a n. A dense fibrous white outer coat that will enclose the eyeball except the section which is covered by the cornea.

scler-ite (sklẽr´īt) n. A type of hard chitinous plate or piece.

scle-ro-der-ma (sklẽr´o dur´ma) n. A disease of the skin that causes thickening of the subcutaneous tissues.

scle-rom-e-ter n. A device which is used for the purpose of determining the hardness of something.

scle-ro-pro-tein n. A type of protein that can be found in the skeletal and the connective tissues of the body.

scle-ro-sis (skli rō´sis) n. A hardening of a part of the body, as an artery.

scle-rot-ic adj. Pertaining to the sclera.

scler-o-ti-za-tion n. The state of being sclerotized, usually referring to the cuticle of an insect.

scler-o-tized adj. Being made hard by a substance other than chitin.

scoff n. The expression of derision or scorn. **scoffer** n.

scold (skōld) v. To accuse or reprimand harshly.

sco-lex (skōleks) n. A head of the tapeworm either in the larval or adult stage of its life.

sco-li-o-sis (skō´lē ō´sis) n. The lateral curvature of the spine. **scoliotic** adj.

sconce (skons) n. A wall bracket for holding candles.

scoop (skōp) n. A small, shovel-like tool. *Slang* An exclusive news report released ahead of ones competition. **scoop** v. To lift up or out.

scoot (skōt) v. To go suddenly and quickly.

scope (skōp) n. The range or extent of one's actions; the space to function or operate in.

-scope suff. A device for seeing or discovering.

sco-pol-a-mine (sko pŏl´a mēn´) n. A kind of poisonous alkaloid that can be found in the roots of some plants belonging to the nightshade family; used as a sedative, mydriatic or truth serum.

scor-bu-tic adj. To be like or resembling scurvy. **scorbutically** adv.

scorch (skorch) v. To burn slightly, changing the color and taste of something; to parch with heat.

scorched adj. To be discolored by scorching.

scorch-er (skor´chẽr) n. *Slang* A very hot day.

score (skōr) n. A numerical record of total points won in a game or other contest; the result of an examination; a grouping of twenty items; a written musical composition which indicates the part to be performed by each person; a groove made with a pointed tool. **score** v. To achieve or win; to arrange a musical score for.

score-board n. A board which is used to display the score of a game.

score-card n. A card which is used for the recording of the score in a game.

sco-ria n. A refuse from the melting of metals. **scoriaceous** adj.

scorn (skorn) n. Contempt; disdain. **scorn** v. To treat with scorn; to reject with contempt.

scorn-ful adj. Being full of scorn.

scor-pae-nid n. A member of the group or family of marine spiny-finned fishes, having large mouths and sharp teeth.

scor-pi-oid adj. Curved or circular at the end like the tail of the scorpion.

scor-pi-on (skor´pē ǝn) n. An arachnid having an upright tail tipped with a poisonous sting.

Scor-pi-us n. The southern constellation that is located partly in the Milky Way and next to Libra.

sco-ter n. A sea duck of the northern coasts of Europe and North America.

scot-free adj. To be totally free from harm or penalty.

sco-to-ma n. A dark spot in the visual field.

scoun-drel n. A villain or a robber.

scour (skour) v. To clean by rubbing with an abrasive agent; to clean thoroughly. **scourer** n.

scout (skout) v. To observe activities in order to obtain information. **scout** n. A person whose job is to obtain information; a member of the boy scouts or girl scouts.

scow (skou) n. A large barge with a flat bottom and square ends used to transport freight, gravel, or cargo.

scowl (skoul) v. To make an angry look; to frown. **scowl** n.

scrab-ble (skrab´l) v. To scratch about frantically, as if searching for something. **scrabble** n. **scrabbler** n.

scrag v. To kill or to execute by hanging.

scrag-gly (skrag´lē) adj. Messy; irregular.

scram v. To go away at once.

scram-ble v. To move with panic.

scrap (skrap) n. A small section or piece. **scrap** v. To throw away waste.

scrap-book (skrap´bük´) n. A book that contains miscellaneous items.

scrape (skrāp) v. To rub a surface with a sharp object in order to clean. Slang An embarrassing situation.

scra-pie n. A kind of viral disease of sheep where they become itchy, excited, excessively thirsty, weak, and eventually a paralysis occurs.

scratch (skrach) v. To mark or make a slight cut on; to mark with the fingernails. **scratch** n. The mark made

by scratching; a harsh, unpleasant sound. Slang Money

scratch test n. A test for allergic susceptibility that involves placing an extract of an allergy producing substance into a scratch on the skin.

scrawl (skrol) n. To write or draw quickly and often illegibly. **scrawl** n.

scraw-ny (skro´nē) adj. Very thin; skinny. **scrawniness** n.

screak v. To make or produce a shrill noise.

scream (skrēm) v. To utter a long, sharp cry, as of fear or pain. **scream** n. A long piercing cry. Slang A very funny person.

scree (skrē) n. A gathering of stones lying on a slope.

screech (skrēch) v. To make a shrill, harsh noise.

screech owl n. A type of owl that has a tuft of feathers on its head.

screed n. A piece of writing that is informal.

screen (skrēn) n. A movable object used to keep something from view, to divide, or to decorate; a flat reflecting surface on which a picture is projected. **screen** v. To keep from view.

screen saver n. In computer science, a screen blanker that displays a random, moving pattern on the screen.

screen test n. A type of short film sequence testing the abilities of a prospective movie actor.

screw (skrö) n. A metal piece that resembles a nail, having a spiral thread which is used for fastening things together; a propeller on a ship. **screw** v. To join by twisting. **screw up** To make a mess of.

scrib-ble v. To write without thought.

scribe (skrīb) n. A person whose profession is to copy documents and manuscripts.

scrib-er n. A sharp tool for the purpose of making marks in material to be cut.

scrieve v. To move along smoothly.

scrim (skrim) n. A type of durable cotton fabric used for clothing and curtains.

scrim-mage (skrim´ij) n. In football, a practice game. **scrimmage** v.

scrimp (skrimp) v. To make something too small or short.

scrim-shaw (skrim´sho´) n. The art of carving designs on whale ivory or whalebone.

scrip n. A type of small wallet; money; a receipt.

script n. The written text of a play; document.

scrip-tur-al adj. According to a sacred writing. **scripturally** adv.

scrip-ture (skrip´chér) n. A sacred writing. **Scriptures** The Bible.

script-writ-er n. A person who writes

screenplays and other scripts.

scriv-en-er *n*. A public copyist; writer.

scrod (skrod) *n*. A type of young fish such as the haddock or the cod.

scrof-u-la (skrof´ū la) *n*. A tuberculosis of the lymph glands.

scrof-u-lous *adj*. To be affected with scrofula.

scroll (skrōl) *n*. A roll of parchment or similar material used in place of paper.

scroll-work *n*. An ornamentation that is characterized by scrolls.

scrooge *n*. A type of person who is miserly.

scro-tum (skrō´tum) *n., pl.* **scrota** The external sac of skin which encloses the testes. **scrotal** *adj*.

scrounge *v*. To collect by foraging.

scrub (skrub) *v*. To clean something by rubbing. *Slang* To cancel.

scrub-land *n*. An area of land which has been covered with scrub.

scruff *n*. The region on the back of the neck.

scrump-tious (skrump´shus) *adj. Slang* Delightful.

scru-ple (skrö´pl) *n*. A principle which governs one's actions.

scru-pu-los-i-ty *n*. The state of being scrupulous.

scru-pu-lous (skrö´pū lus) *adj*. Having moral integrity. -ly *adv*.

scru-ta-ble (skrö´ta bl) *adj*. To be able to be deciphered.

scru-ti-nize *v*. To look at or to examine something very carefully.

scru-ti-ny *n*. An inspection of something.

sct *abbr*. Scout.

scu-ba (skö´ba) *n*. An apparatus used by divers for underwater breathing; from the initials for Self-Contained Underwater Breathing Apparatus.

scuba diver *n*. One who swims under the water with the use of scuba gear.

scud *v*. To move or to go quickly.

scuff (skuf) *v*. To drag or scrape the feet while walking. **scuff** *n*.

scuf-fle (skuf´l) *v*. To struggle in a confused manner. **scuffle** *n*.

scuffle hoe *n*. A type of hoe which has both edges sharpened.

scull (skul) *n*. An oar mounted at the stern of a boat, which is moved back and forth to produce forward motion.

scul-ler-y (skul´e rē) *n*. A room used for storing and cleaning dishes.

scul-lion *n*. A type of kitchen helper.

scul-pin (skul´pin) *n*. A type of large-headed scaleless fish.

sculpt *v*. To carve; to make a sculpture.

sculp-tor (skulp´tér) *n*. A person who creates statues from clay, marble, or other material.

sculp-ture (skulp´chér) *n*. The art of processing a hard or soft material into another form, such as a statue.

scum (skum) *n*. A thin layer of waste matter floating on top of a liquid.

scum-ble *v*. To make something less brilliant by covering it with a thin coat of color.

scurf (skerf) *n*. Flaky dry skin; dandruff.

scur-ril-i-ty *n*. The state of being scurrilous.

scur-ri-lous *adj*. To be vulgar and evil.

scur-ry (sker´ē) *v*. To move quickly; to scamper.

scur-vy *n*. A type of disease that is caused by the lack of ascorbic acid and is characterized by bleeding gums and bleeding into the skin.

scut *n*. A tail which is short and erect.

scu-tage *n*. A kind of tax that is levied on a tenant of a knight's land in the place of service for the military.

scutch *v*. To separate flax or hemp from their woody fibers.

scute *n*. An external horny plate.

scu-tel-late (skū tel´it) *adj*. To be resembling scutellum.

scu-tel-lum (skū tel´um) *n*. A small shield-shaped plant structure.

scut-tle *n*. A small opening with a movable lid in the hull of a ship. **scuttle** *v*. To deliberately sink a boat or other floating object by making holes in the bottom or sides.

scy-pho-zo-an (sī fo zō´an) *n*. A type of coelenterates of the group of jellyfish lacking a true polyp.

scythe (sīth) *n*. A tool with a long handle and curved, single-dged blade, used for cutting hay, grain and grass.

sea *n*. The body of salt water which covers most of the earth; a large body of salt water.

seacoast *n*. Land that borders the sea.

seal (sēl) *n*. A device having a raised emblem, displaying word or symbol, used to certify a signature or the authenticity of a document; a tight closure which secures; a large aquatic mammal with a sleek body and large flippers; the fur or pelt of a seal. **seal** *v*. To close tightly; to mark with a seal, to hunt seals. **sealant** *n*.

sea level *n*. The level of the sea's surface, used as a standard reference point in measuring the height of land or the depth of the sea.

seam (sēm) *n*. The line formed at the joint of two pieces of material.

sear (sēr) *v*. To wither or dry up; to shrivel; to burn or scorch.

search (serch) *v*. To look over carefully; to find something; to probe.

sea-son (sē´zon) *n*. One of the four parts of the year: spring, summer, fall or autumn, and winter; a time marked by particular activities or celebrations. **season** *v*. To add flavorings or spices; to add interest or enjoyment; to age.

seat (sēt) *n.* A place or spot, as a chair, stool, or bench, on which to sit; the part of the body used for sitting; the buttocks. **seat** *v.*

se-cede (si sēd´) *v.* To withdraw from an organization. **secession** *n.*

se-clude (si klōd´) *v.* To isolate; to keep apart.

sec-ond (sek´ond) *n.* A unit of time equal to 1/60 of a minute; a very short period of time; an object which does not meet first class standards. *Math.* Unit of measure equal to 1/60 of a minute of angular measurement.

sec-on-dar-y (sek´on der´ē) *adj.* Not being first in importance; inferior; pertaining to high school.

se-cret (sē´krit) *n.* Knowledge kept from others; a mystery. **secretly** *adv.* **secret** *n.* **secrecy** *n.*

sec-re-tary (sek´ri ter´ē) *n. pl.* **secretaries** A person hired to write and keep records for an executive or an organization; the head of a government department. **secretarial** *adj.*

se-crete (si krēt´) *v.* To produce and give off; to release or discharge.

sec-tion (sek´shan) *n.* A part or division of something; a separate part. **section** *v.* To divide or separate into parts.

sec-tor (sek´tėr) *n.* An area or zone in which a military unit operates; the part of a circle bounded by two radii and the arc they cut. **sector** *v.*

sec-u-lar (sek´ya lėr) *adj.* Relating to something worldly; not religious.

se-cure (si kūr´) *adj.* Safe and free from doubt or fear; sturdy or strong; not likely to fail. **secure** *v.* To tie down, fasten, lock, or otherwise protect from risk or harm; to ensure. **securely** *adv.*

se-cu-ri-ty (si kūr´i tē) *n., pl.* **securities** The state of being safe and free from danger or risk; protection; an object given to assure the fulfillment of an obligation; in *computer science*, the prevention of unauthorized use of a device or program.

se-dan (si dan´) *n.* A closed automobile with a front and back seat.

se-date (si dāt´) *adj.* Serene and composed. **sedate** *v.* To keep or be kept calm through the use of drugs. **sedative** *n.* A medicine to calm or help one to sleep.

sed-i-ment (sed´i ment) *n.* Material which floats in or settles to the bottom of a liquid. **sedimentary** *adj.*

se-duce (si dös´) *v.* To tempt and draw away from proper conduct; to entice one to have sexual intercourse. **seducer** *n.* **seduction** *n.* **seductive** *adj.*

see (sē) *v.* To have the power of sight; to understand; to experience; to predict; to imagine. **see red** To be extremely angry.

seed (sēd) *n.* A fertilized plant ovule with an embryo, capable of producing an offspring. **seed** *v.* To plant seeds; to remove the seeds from.

seek (sēk) *v.* To search for; to try to reach; to attempt. **seeker** *n.*

seem (sēm) *v.* To appear to be; to have the look of. **seeming** adj.

seep (sēp) *v.* To leak or pass through slowly. **seepage** *n.*

seer (sē ėr) *n.* A person who predicts the future.

see-saw (sē´so´) *n.* A board supported in the center which allows children to alternate being up and down.

seg-ment (seg´ment) *n.* Any of the parts into which a thing is divided. **segment** *v.* To divide. **-ation** *n.*

seg-re-gate (seg´re gāt´) *v.* To separate or isolate from others.

seg-re-ga-tion (seg´re gā´shan) *n.* The act of separating people based on the color of their skin.

seine (sān) *n.* A fishing net having weights on one edge and floats on the other.

seize (sēz) *v.* To grasp or take possession forcibly.

sel-dom (sel´dom) *adv.* Not often.

se-lect (si lekt´) *v.* To choose from a large group; to make a choice. **selection**, **select** *n.* **selector** *n.*

se-le-ni-um (si lē´nē um) *n.* An element symbolized by Se.

self (self) *n., pl.* **selves** The complete and essential being of a person; personal interest, advantage or welfare.

self–de-fense (self´di fens´) *n.* The act of defending oneself or one's belongings.

sell (sel) *v.* To exchange a product or service for money; to offer for sale.

se-man-tics (si man´tiks) *n.* The study of word meanings and the relationships between symbols and signs.

sem-a-phore (sem´a fōr´) *n.* A system for signaling by using flags, lights or arms in various positions.

se-men (sē´men) *n.* Secretion of the male reproductive system, thick and whitish in color, containing sperm.

se-mes-ter (si mes´tėr) *n.* One of two periods of time in which a school year is divided.

sem-i-an-nu-al (sem´ē an´ū al) *adj.* Occurring twice a year.

sem-i-co-lon (sem´i kō´lon) *n.* A punctuation mark (;) having a degree of separation stronger than a comma but less than a period.

sem-i-nar (sem´i när´) *n.* A course of study for students engaged in advanced study of a particular subject.

sem-i-nar-y (sem´i ner´ē) *n., pl.* **-ies** A school that prepares ministers, rabbis, or priests for religious careers.

sen-ate (sen´it) *n.* The upper house of a legislature. **Senate** The United States upper house.

send (send) *v.* To cause something to be conveyed from one place to another; to dispatch.

se-nile (sē´nīl) *adj.* Having a mental deterioration often associated with old age. **senility** *n.*

sen-ior (sēn´yėr) *adj.* Being the older of two; of higher office or rank; referring to the last year of high school or college. **senior** *n.* One who is older or of higher rank.

sen-ior-i-ty (sēn yor´i tē) *n.* Priority over others based on the length of time or service.

sen-sa-tion (sen sā´shan) *n.* An awareness associated with a mental or bodily feeling; something causing a condition of strong interest.

sense (sens) *n.* Sensation; feeling; the physical ability which allows a person to be aware of things around him; the five senses; taste, smell, touch, sight, and hearing; an ethical or moral attitude, the meaning of a word; sense *v.* To feel through the senses; to have a feeling about.

sen-si-bil-i-ty (sen´si bil´i tē) *n., pl.* -ies The ability to receive sensations.

sen-si-ble (sen´si bl) *adj.* Capable of being perceived through the senses; sensitive; having good judgment.

sen-si-tive (sen´si tiv) *adj.* Capable of intense feelings; affected by the emotions or circumstances of others; tenderhearted; of or relating to secret affairs of state. **sensitively** *adv.* **sensitivity** *n.* **sensitiveness** *n.*

sen-sor (sen´sėr) *n.* A device which responds to a signal.

sen-su-al (sen´shö al) *adj.* Preoccupied with the gratification of the senses. **sensually** *adv.* **sensualist** *n.* **sensuality** *n.* **sensuous** *adj.*

sent *v.* Past tense of send.

sen-tence (sen´tens) *n.* A series of words arranged to express a single complete thought; a prison term for a convicted person, determined by a judge or jury. **sentence** *v.* To impose or set the terms of punishment.

sen-ti-ment (sen´ti ment) *n.* Feelings of affection; an idea, an opinion, a thought, an attitude based on emotion rather than reason.

sen-ti-men-tal (sen´ti men´tal) *adj.* Emotional; affected by sentiment.

sen-ti-nel (sen´ti nel) *n.* A guard.

se-pal (sē´pal) *n.* One of the leaves which forms a calyx in a flower.

sep-a-rate (sep´a rāt´) *v.* To divide or keep apart by placing a barrier between; to go in different directions; to set apart from others. **separate** *adj.* Single; individual.

sep-a-ra-tion (sep´a rā´shan) *n.* The process of separating or being separated; an interval which separates.

Sept *abbr.* September.

September *n.* The ninth month of the calendar year, having 30 days.

se-quel (sē´kwel) *n.* A new story which follows or comes after an earlier one and which uses the same characters.

se-quence (sē´kwens) *n.* A set arrangement; a number of connected events; the regular order; the order in which something is done. **sequential** *adj.*

ser-e-nade (ser´enäd´) *n.* Musical expression of romantic love.

se-rene (se rēn´) *adj.* Calm; peaceful.

serf (serf) *n.* A slave owned by a lord during the Middle Ages.

serge (serj) *n.* A twilled, durable woolen cloth.

ser-geant (sär´jent) *n.* A noncommissioned officer who ranks above a corporal but below a lieutenant.

se-ri-al (sēr´ē al) *adj.* Arranged in a series with one part presented at a time.

se-ries (sēr´ēz) *n.* A number of related items which follow one another.

se-ri-ous (sōr´ē us) *adj.* Sober; grave; not trivial; important. **seriously** *adv.*

ser-mon (ser´mon) *n.* A message or speech delivered by a clergyman during a religious service.

ser-pent (ser´pent) *n.* A snake.

ser-rate (ser´it) *adj.* Having sharp teeth; having a notched edge

se-rum (sēr´um) *n., pl.* **serums** *or* **sera** The yellowish fluid part of the blood which remains after clotting; the fluid extracted from immunized animals and used for the prevention of disease.

ser-vant (ser´vant) *n.* One employed to care for someone or his property.

serve (serv) *v.* To take care of; to wait on; to prepare and supply; to complete a term of duty; to act in a certain capacity; to start the play in some sports. **serve** *n.* The manner of serving or delivering a ball.

server *n.* In computer science, a computer that stores and manages programs and data for other computers in a network.

serv-ice (ser´vis) *n.* Help given to others; a religious gathering; the military; a set of dishes or utensils. **service** *v.* To repair; to furnish a service to something or someone.

ses-a-me (ses´a mē) *n.* A tropical plant and its edible seeds.

ses-sion (sesh´an) *n.* A meeting or series of meetings; a meeting set for a specific purpose; the period during the day or year during which a meeting takes place.

set (set) *v.* To put or place; to cause to do; to regulate; to adjust; to arrange;

to place in a frame or mounting; to go below the horizon; to establish or fix. **set** *n.* A group of things which belong together; a piece of equipment made up of many pieces; a young plant. **set** *adj.* Established; ready.

set-ting (set´ing) *n.* The act of placing or putting something somewhere; the scenery for a show or other production; the place where a novel, play, or other fictional work takes place; a jewelry mounting.

set-tle (set´l) *v.* To arrange or put in order; to restore calm or tranquillity to; to come to an agreement on something; to resolve a problem or argument; to establish in a new home or business.

sev-en (sev´en) *n.* The cardinal number 7, which is 6 + 1. **seven** *adj. & pron.* **seventh** *adj. & n.*

sev-er (sev´ér) *v.* To cut off or separate. **severance** *n.*

sev-er-al (sev´ér al) *adj.* Being more than one or two, but not many; separate.

se-vere (si vēr´) *adj.* Strict; stern; hard; not fancy; extremely painful; intense. **severely** *adv.* **severity** *n.*

sew (sō) *v.* To fasten or fix; to make stitches with thread and needle.

sew-age (sō´ij) *n.* The solid waste material carried away by a sewer.

sew-er (sō´ér) *n.* A conduit or drain pipe used to carry away waste.

sex (seks) *n.* One of two divisions, male and female, into which most living things are grouped; sexual intercourse.

sex-tet (seks tet´) *n.* A group of six people or things; music written for six performers.

shab-by (shab´ē) *adj.* Worn-out; ragged. **shabbily** *adv.* **shabbiness** *n.*

shack (shak) *n.* A small, poorly built building.

shack-le (shak´l) *n.* A metal band locked around the ankle or wrist of a prisoner; anything that restrains or holds. *v.* To restrain with shackles.

shade (shād) *n.* A shadow that will gather with the coming of darkness; a comparative darkness due to the interception of the rays of the sun by an object.

shad-ing *n.* A filling up with color within outlines to give the object a three-dimensional shape or look.

shad-ow (shad´ō) *n.* An area from which light is blocked. **shadow** *v.* To cast or throw a shadow on.

shad-y (shā´dē) *n.* Being sheltered or protected from the rays of the sun.

shaft (shaft) *n.* A long, narrow part of something; a beam or ray of light; a long, narrow underground passage; a tunnel; a narrow, vertical opening in a building for an elevator.

shag *n.* A long matted fiber.

shag-gy (shag´ē) *adj.* To be covered with long, matted, or coarse hair.

shak-a-ble *n.* Being capable of being shaken.

shake (shāk) *v.* To move or to cause a back-and-forth or up-and-down motion; to tremble; to clasp hands with another, as to welcome or say farewell; to upset or disturb. **shaky** *adj.*

sha-ko (shak´ō) *n.* A stiff military hat that has a plume and high crown.

shale *n.* A fissile rock which is made by the consolidation of mud or clay having a finely stratified structure.

shale oil *n.* A type of dark oil which is obtained from oil shale by heating.

shall (shal) *v.* To expect to; to plan to; used to express future tense; to indicate promise or a command.

shal-loon *n.* The twilled fabric of wool which is used for linings of coats.

shal-lop *n.* A type of small boat that can be propelled with oars or sails.

shal-lot (sha lot´) *n.* A type of perennial herb that resembles an onion and is used for seasoning.

shal-low (shal´ō) *adj.* Not deep; lacking intellectual depth.

sham (sham) *n.* A person who is not genuine but pretends to be; a cover for pillows. **sham** *v.* To pretend to have or feel something.

sham-ble (sham´bl) *v.* To walk while dragging one's feet. **shambles** A scene or state of complete destruction.

sham-bling *adj.* Characterized with or by slow awkward movements.

shame (shām) *n.* A painful feeling of embarrassment or disgrace brought on by doing something wrong; dishonor; disgrace; a disappointment.

shame-faced (shām´fāst´) *adj.* To be showing shame. **shamefacedness** *n.*

shame-ful (shām´ful) *adj.* Arousing feelings of shame within someone.

shame-less (shām´lis) *adj.* Showing a lack of shame. **shamelessness** *n.*

sham-poo (sham pö´) *n.* A soap used to cleanse the hair and scalp; a liquid preparation used to clean upholstery and rugs; the process of cleaning with shampoo. **shampoo** *v.*

shang-hai (shang´hī) *v.* To put someone on board a ship with the help of a drug.

shank (shangk) *n.* The portion of the leg between the ankle and the knee; a cut of meat from the leg of an animal, such as a lamb.

shap-a-ble *n.* To be capable of being shaped.

shape (shāp) *n.* The outline or configuration of something; the form of a human body; the condition of something; the finished form in which something may appear. *v.* To cause to take a particular form.

shape-less (shāp′lĭs) *adj.* To have no real or definite shape; without shape.

shape-ly (shāp′lē) *adj.* To have a pleasant or pleasing shape to the form.

shard (shärd) *n.* A fragment of a substance which is brittle.

share (shâr) *n.* A part or portion given to or by one person; one of equal parts, as the capital stock in a corporation. **share** *v.* To divide or distribute portions.

share-hold-er *n.* A person who holds a share in a piece of property.

shark (shärk) *n.* A large marine fish which eats other fish and is dangerous to man; a greedy, crafty person.

shark-skin *n.* The skin or hide of the shark that ismade into leather goods.

sharp (shärp) *adj.* Having a thin edge or a fine point; capable of piercing or cutting; clever; quick-witted; intense; painful.**sharp** *n. Music* A note raised half a tone above a given tone. **sharpness** *n.* **sharply** *adv.*

sharp-tongued (shärp–tŭngd′) *adj.* To have bitter or harsh speech.

shat-ter (shăt′ér) *v.* To burst suddenly into pieces.

shave (shāv) *v.* To remove a thin layer; to cut body hair, as the beard, by using a razor; to come close to. *n.* The act of shaving.

shawl (shol) *n.* An oblong or square piece of fabric worn over the head or shoulders.

she (shē) *pron.* A female previously indicated by name.

shear (shēr) *v.* To trim, cut, or remove the fleece or hair with a sharp instrument; to clip. **shearer** *n.*

sheath (shēth) *n.* A cover or case for a blade, as a sword.

sheath-bill (shēth′bĭl′) *n.* A white shore bird that has a horny sheath on the base of the upper mandible.

sheave *n.* A wheel that is grooved.

shed (shed) *v.* To pour out or cause to pour; to throw off without penetrating; to cast off or leave behind, esp. by a natural process. **shed** *n.* A small building for shelter or storage.

shed-der *n.* Something that sheds something such as skin.

sheen (shēn) *n.* Luster.

sheep (shēp) *n., pl.* **sheep** A cud-chewing thick-fleeced mammal, widely domesticated for meat and wool; a meek or timid person.

sheer (shēr) *adj.* Very thin; almost transparent; complete; absolute; very steep, almost perpendicular.

sheet (shēt) *n.* A large piece of cloth for covering a bed; a single piece of paper; a continuous, thin piece of anything.

sheet metal *n.* A type of metal that is in the form of a sheet.

shelf (shelf) *n. pl.* **shelves** A flat piece of wood, metal, plastic, or other rigid material attached to a wall or within another structure, used to hold or store things; something which resembles a shelf, as a ledge of rocks.

shelf ice *n.* An ice sheet that starts on land and continues out to sea and out to where it rests on the floor of the ocean.

shell (shel) *n.* The hard outer covering of certain organisms; something light and hollow which resembles a shell; the framework of a building under construction; a case containing explosives which are fired from a gun. *v.* To remove the shell from.

shel-lac (she lak′) *n.* A clear varnish used to give a smooth, shiny finish to furniture and floors. *Slang* To defeat decisively.

shel-ter (shel′tér) *n.* Something which gives protection or cover. **shelter** *v.* To give protection.

shelve (shelv) *v.* To put aside; to place on a shelf.

shelv-ing *n.* The degree of sloping of something.

shep-herd (shep′érd) *n.* A person who takes care of a flock of sheep; a person who takes care of others.

shepherd's pie *n.* A type of pie that is made with meat and has a mashed potato crust.

sher-bet (sher′bĭt) *n.* A sweet frozen dessert made with fruit juices, milk or water, egg white, and gelatin.

sher-iff (sher′if) *n.* A high ranking law-enforcement officer.

sher-ry (sher′ē) *n.* A type of wine of Spanish origin that has a nutty taste.

shield (shēld) *n.* A piece of protective metal or wood held in front of the body; anything which serves to conceal or protect; a badge. **shield** *v.*

shield law *n.* The law that protects journalists from being forced to reveal confidential sources.

shift (shift) *n.* A group of people who work together, a woman's loose-fitting dress. **shift** *v.* To change direction or place, to change or move the gears in an automobile.

shill *n.* A person or thing that acts as a decoy.

shim-mer (shim′ér) *v.* To shine with a faint sparkle. **shimmery** *adj.*

shin (shin) *n.* The front part of the leg from the knee to the ankle. *v.* To climb a rope or pole by gripping and pulling with the hands and legs.

shin-bone *n.* The tibia in the lower leg.

shin-dig *n.* A party or social gathering.

shine (shin) *v.* To give off light; to direct light; to make bright or glossy; to polish shoes. *n.* Brightness.

shin-er (shī′nér) *n.* A black eye.

shin-gle (shing´gl) *n*. A thin piece of material used to cover a roof or sides of a house. **shingle** *v*.

shin-gles (shing´glz) *n. Pathol.* An acute, inflammatory viral infection, characterized by eruptions along a nerve path.

shin-ing *adj*. To be reflecting light.

shin-splints *n*. The inflammation and injury to the muscles of the lower leg due to run-ning on hard surfaces.

ship (ship) *n*. A large vessel for deep-water travel or transport. *v*. To send or transport.

ship-board *n*. A side of a ship.

ship-borne *adj*. To be designed to be carried or transported by a ship.

ship-build-er *n*. A person who builds ships. **shipbuilding** *n*.

ship-ment (ship´ment) *n*. The process of shipping goods from one port to another.

ship-worm *n*. A marine clam that will burrow into the wharf and wooden ships causing damage to them.

ship-wreck (ship´rek´) *n*. The loss of a ship; destruction; ruin. *v*. To destroy; wreck.

ship-wright *n*. The carpenter who is skilled in the repair and construction of ships.

shire (shi´ér) *n*. The administrative division such as a county.

shire town *n*. The town in which is located a court of jurisdiction.

shirt (shert) *n*. A garment worn on the upper part of the body.

shirt-ing (shür´ting) *n*. The fabric which can be used to make shirts.

shirt-maker *n*. A person who is capable of making shirts.

shirt-tail *n*. The section of the shirt which falls below the waist in the back.

shiv-er (shiv´ér) *v*. To tremble or shake with excitement or chill.

shoal (shōl) *n*. Large group.

shoat *n*. A hog less than one year old.

shock (shok) *n*. A sudden blow or violent impact; an unexpected, sudden upset of mental or emotional balance; a serious weakening of the body caused by the loss of blood pressure or sudden injury. **shock** *v*. To cause great surprise, disgust, or outrage; to give an electric shock.

shock absorber *n*. A device which is used for absorbing the energy of impulses to something.

shock-er (shok´ér) *n*. Something that produces shock.

shod *adj*. To be equipped with a shoe.

shoe (shō) *n*. An outer cover for a foot; the part of a brake which presses against the drum or wheel to slow or stop the motion. *v*. To put on shoes.

shoot (shōt) *v*. To kill or wound with a missile, as a bullet, fired from a weap-on; to discharge or throw rapidly; to push forward or begin to grow by germinating.

shooting star *n*. A meteor that appears in the sky as a temporary streak of light.

shop (shop) *n*. A small business or small retail store; a place where certain goods are produced. **shop** *v*. To visit a store in order to examine or buy things. **shopper** *n*.

shop-keep-er *n*. A person who runs a store.

shop-lift (shop´lift´) *v*. To take something from a store without paying for it. **shoplifting** *n*.

shore (shōr) *n*. The land bordering a body of water.

shore-line *n*. A line or location where a body of water and the shore meet.

short (short) *adj*. Having little height or length; less than normal in distance, time, or other qualities; less than the needed amount. **shorts** Underpants or outer pants which end at the knee or above. **shortage** A lack in the amount needed. **short-change** To give less than the correct amount, as change for money. **short circuit** An electrical malfunction.

short-cut *n*. A type of route that is more direct than the one that is usually taken.

short-en-ing (shor´te ning) *n*. A fat, such as butter, used to make pastry rich and light.

short-fall (short´ fol) *n*. The failure to accomplish a goal.

short-hand (short´hand´) *n*. A type of writing where words and phrases are represented by symbols.

short-lived (short´livd´) *adj*. Not lasting long or living long.

short-sight-ed (short´si´tid) *adj*. To be missing or lacking one's foresight.

shot (shot) *n*. The discharging of a gun, rocket, or other device; an attempt; a try; an injection; a photograph. *Slang* Useless; ruined.

should (shed) *v*. Past tense of *shall*.

shoul-der (shōl´dér) *n*. The part of the body located between the neck and upper arm; the side of the road. *v*. To use the shoulder to push or carry something; to take upon oneself.

should-n't (shed´ant) *contr*. Should not.

shout (shout) *v*. To yell. *n*. A loud cry.

shouting distance *n*. A short distance.

shove *v*. To push something or someone in a manner that may be rough.

shov-el (shuv´el) *n*. A tool with a long handle and a scoop, used for picking up material or digging. **shovel** *v*. To move, dig, push, or scoop up.

show (shō) *v*. To put within sight; to point out; to explain; to put on display. *n*. A display; a movie, play or similar entertainment.

show bill *n*. A poster which may be used for advertising purposes.

show-er (shou'ẽr) *n*. A short period of rain; a party with gifts given in honor of someone; a bath with water spraying down on the bather. **shower** *v*. To take a shower; to be generous; to pour down. **showery** *adj*.

shrap-nel (shrap'nel) *n. pl.* **shrapnel** A large shell containing metal fragments; fragments of metal that are exploded with great force.

shred (shred) *n*. A narrow strip or torn fragment; a small amount. *v*. To rip, tear, or cut into shreds.

shrew (shrö) *n*. A small mouse-like mammal, having a narrow, pointed snout.

shriek (shrēk) *n*. A loud, sharp scream or noise. **shriek** *v*.

shrill (shril) *adj*. A high-pitched, sharp sound.

shrimp (shrimp) *n., pl.* **shrimp** *or* **shrimps** A small, edible shellfish.

shrine (shrīn) *n*. A place for sacred relics; a place considered sacred because of an event or person associated with it.

shrink (shringk) *v*. To make or become less or smaller; to pull back from; to flinch. *Slang* A psychiatrist.

shroud (shroud) *n*. A cloth in which a body is wrapped for burial. *v*. To cover.

shrub (shrub) *n*. A woody plant which grows close to the ground and has several stems beginning at its base.

shrug (shrug) *v*. To raise the shoulders briefly to indicate doubt or indifference. **shrug** *n*.

shuck (shuk) *n*. The outer husk that covers an ear of corn. **shuck** *v*.

shud-der (shud'ẽr) *v*. To tremble uncontrollably, as from fear.

shut-fle (shuf'l) *v*. To drag or slide the feet; to mix together in a haphazard fashion; to rearrange or change the order of cards. **shuffle** *n*.

shun (shun) *v*. To avoid deliberately.

shut (shut) *v*. To move a door, drawer, or other object to close an opening; to block an entrance; to lock up; to cease or halt operations.

shut-tle (shut'l) *n*. A device used to move thread in weaving; a vehicle, as a train or plane, which travels back and forth from one location to another.

shy (shī) *adj*. Bashful; timid; easily frightened. *v*. To move suddenly from fear. **shyly** *adv*. **shyness** *n*.

si-al-a-gogue *n*. A kind of agent that will promote the flow of saliva.

si-al-ic *adj*. Pertaining to the light rock which is rich in alumina and silica.

Siamese twin *n*. One of a pair of twins that are united at some part of the body with the other twin.

sib-ling (sib'ling) *n*. One of two or more children from the same parents.

sick (sik) *adj*. In poor health; ill; nauseated; morbid. **sickness** *n*.

sick bay *n*. A room on a ship that can be used as a hospital.

sick-en (sik'en) *v*. To become sick.

sick-en-er (sik'e nẽr) *n*. Something that disgusts or sickens.

sick-le (sik'l) *n*. A tool with a curved blade attached to a handle, used for cutting grass or grain.

sick leave *n*. The absence from one's work that is permitted due to an illness.

sick-le cell *n*. An abnormal red blood cell which will take the shape of a crescent.

sickle feather *n*. A long curved tail feather of the cock.

sick-ly *adj*. To be somewhat unwell.

side (sīd) *n*. A surface between the front and back or top and bottom of an object; either surface of a flat object; the part to the left or right of a vertical axis; the right or left portion of the human body; the space beside someone or something; an opinion or point of view which is the opposite of another. **side** *v*. To take a stand and support a particular side. *adj*. Supplementary; peripheral.

side-band *n*. A band of frequencies that are produced by modulation.

side effect *n*. The secondary effect.

side-glance *n*. A look that is directed to the side.

side issue *n*. The issue that is apart from the main point.

si-de-re-al (sī dēr'e al) *adj*. To be pertaining to the stars.

sid-er-ite *n*. A type of ferrous carbonate that is an iron ore.

sid-er-it-ic *adj*. Pertaining to siderite.

side-split-ting *adj*. To be very funny.

side-step *v*. To step to the side.

side stroke *n*. A swimming stroke swimmers do on their sides.

side-ward *adj*. To move toward the side.

SIDS *abbr*. Sudden Infant Death Syndrome; unexpected death of a seemingly healthy baby, occurring during sleep in the first four months of life.

siege (sēj) *n*. The action of surrounding a town or port in order to capture it; a prolonged sickness.

si-er-ra (sē er'a) *n*. A rugged chain of mountains or hills.

si-es-ta (sē es'ta) *n*. A rest; short nap.

sie-va bean *n*. A type of bean which is closely related to the lima bean.

sieve (siv) *n*. A meshed or perforated device which allows small particles to pass through but which holds back larger particles; a device for separating liquids from solids.

sieve plate *n*. A wall which is perforated located at the end of one of the cells that make up a sieve tube.

sieve tube *n.* A type of tube that is made of thin-walled cells.

sift (sift) *v.* To separate coarse particles from small or fine ones by passing through a sieve. **through** To carefully examine. *v.* **sifter** *n.*

sigh (sī) *v.* To exhale a long, deep breath, usually when tired, sad, or relieved.

sight (sīt) *n.* The ability to see with the eyes; the range or distance one can see; a view; a device mounted on a firearm used to guide the eye or aim.

sighted *adj.* To have sight.

sight gag *n.* A comic episode where the effect is created by a camera shot rather than by the words.

sight-less *adj.* Lacking or missing the sense of sight. **sightlessness** *n.*

sight-ly (sīt´lē) *adj.* To be pleasing to the sight. **sightliness** *n.*

sight-see (sīt´sē) *v.* To travel about and see sights that are of interest.

sig-il (sij´il) *n.* A word that is supposed to have occult power in magic.

sig-ma (sig´ma) *n.* The 18th letter in the Greek alphabet.

sig-moid *adj.* To be curved in two directions.

sign (sīn) *n.* A piece of paper, wood, metal, etc., with information written on it; a gesture that tells or means something. *v.* To write one's name.

sig-nal (sig´nal) *n.* A sign which gives a warning; the image or sound sent by television or radio. **signal** *v.* To make or send a signal to.

sig-nal-ize (sig´na līz´) *v.* To make signals to someone. **signalization** *n.*

sig-nal-man *n.* A person who works with signals or signals others.

sig-na-ture (sig´na chèr) *n.* The name of a person, written by that person; a distinctive mark which indicates identity. *Music* A symbol indicating the time and key.

sig-net *n.* A type of seal which is used to give personal authority to a document or papers instead of using a signature.

signet ring *n.* A type of ring that is engraved with a signet.

sig-ni-fi-a-ble *adj.* Being represented with a symbol or a sign of some sort.

sig-nif-i-cance (sig nif´i kans) *n.* The quality of being important; the meaning of something which is considered important.

sig-ni-fi-er *n.* Something that signifies.

sig-ni-fy (sig´ni fī´) *v.* To express or make known by a sign; to indicate. **signification** *n.* **significant** *adj.*

sign in *v.* To record the arrival of someone at a particular time by the signing of a list or the punching of the time

clock.

sign language *n.* A means of communicating by using hand gestures; the language of deaf people.

sign manual *n.* The signature of a king which is on a royal grant and is placed at the top or beginning of the document.

sign off *v.* To tell or to announce the end of a program or of a broadcast.

sign on *v.* To tell or to announce the beginning of a broadcast for the day.

si-gnor *n.* An Italian man.

si-gno-ra *n.* An Italian woman.

si-gno-ri-na (sēn´yo rē´na) *n.* Italian woman who is not yet married.

sign out *v.* To tell of one's departure by signing a list depicting when a person left.

sign-post *n.* A post that bears signs on it for the use of giving directions.

sike (sīk) *n.* A type of stream which is small in size.

si-lage (sīlij) *n.* The fodder which is converted into feed for livestock.

si-lence (sī´lens) *n.* The state or quality of being silent; quiet. *v.* To quiet.

si-lenc-er (sī´len sèr) *n.* Someone or something which will cause silence.

si-lent (sī´lent) *adj.* Making no sound; not speaking; mute; an unpronounced letter, as the "g" in *gnat*.

si-lents *n.* A kind of motion picture in which there is not a spoken dialogue.

silent treatment *n.* The act of ignoring another person completely.

sil-hou-ette (sil´ö et´) *n.* The outline of something, as a human profile, filled in with a solid color, as black; the outline of an object. **silhouette** *v.*

sil-i-con (sil´i kon) *n.* The second most common chemical element, found only in combination with another substance, symbolized as Si.

silicone rubber *n.* A type of rubber that is made from silicone elastomers and is flexible over a wide range of different temperatures.

silk (silk) *n.* A soft, thread-like fiber spun by silkworms; thread or fabric made from silk. **silken** *adj.* **silky** *adj.*

silk-a-line *n.* A type of cotton fabric with a smooth finish like that of silk.

silk cotton *n.* A type of silky covering that can be found on the seeds of various silk cotton trees.

silk–cotton tree *n.* A type of tropical tree that has large fruits with the seeds covered by silk cotton.

silk gland *n.* The gland that will produce the fluid which is excreted in filaments and then hardens into silk when it comes into contact with air.

silk oak *n.* An Australian timber tree that has mottled wood which is used for the purpose of making cabinets.

silk stocking *n.* A person who is dressed

in a fashionable manner.

silk-worm *n.* A type of larva that spins a large amount of silk in its cocoon.

sill (sil) *n.* The horizontal support that forms the bottom part of the frame of a window or door.

sil-ly (sil'ē) *adj.* Foolish; lacking good sense, seriousness, or substance.

si-lo (sī'lō) *n.* A tall, cylindrical structure for storing food for farm animals; an underground shelter or storage for guided missiles.

silt *n.* A deposit of soil and sediment that is often caused by a river.

silt-stone *n.* A type of stone which is composed of silt.

sil-va *n.* The trees of a country or region.

sil-ver (sil'vér) *n.* A soft, white metallic element used in tableware, jewelry, and coins, symbolized by Ag. *v.* To coat with silver. *adj.* Of the color silver.

silver age *n.* A period in history that is secondary to the gold age.

silver bell *n.* A type of tree located in the southeastern United States that is grown for its bell-shaped flowers.

sil-ver-ber-ry *n.* A type of shrub which is found in North America and is related to the buffalo berry.

silver fir *n.* A fir that has leaves that are silver-colored underneath.

sil-ver-fish *n.* A small wingless insect which eats clothing and paper.

silver fox *n.* A color phase of the red fox when the coat is white.

silver hake *n.* A type of hake that is found off the New England coast and is used as an important food fish.

silver lining *n.* A hopeful prospect.

silver maple *n.* A type of maple of North America that has leaves which are silvery white beneath.

sil-vern *adj.* To be made of silver.

silver paper *n.* A metallic paper, such as tinfoil, with a silver-like coating.

silver perch *n.* A type of fish with a silvery in color, resembling perch.

sil-ver-sides *n.* A fish that has a silver stripe down both sides of its body.

sil-ver-smith *n.* A person who makes goods and articles out of silver.

sil-ver-y *adj.* To have a musical tone which is clear and soft.

sil-vics *n.* A study of the characteristics and ecology of forest trees.

sim-i-lar (sim'i lér) *adj.* Almost the same, but not identical.

sim-i-lar-i-ty *n.* The state of two things or people being like or similar.

sim-i-le (sim'i lē) *n.* A structure of speech which is used to compare two things that are often unlike.

sim-mer (sim'ér) *v.* To cook just below boiling; to be near the point of breaking, as with emotion.

simmer down *v.* To calm.

si-mo-nize *v.* To polish something with wax.

si-moom *n.* A dry wind from the African and Asian deserts.

sim-ple (sim'pl) *adj.* Easy to do or understand; not complicated; ordinary; not showy; lacking intelligence or education. **simply** *adv.*

simple closed curve *n.* A type of curve that does not intersect itself.

simple fraction *n.* A type of fraction where the denominator and the numerator are of whole numbers.

simple motion *n.* A type of motion that is in a straight line.

sim-plic-i-ty (sim plis'i tē) *n.* The state of being easy to understand; naturalness; sincerity.

sim-pli-fy (sim'pli fī') *v.* To make easy or simple. **simplification** *n.*

sim-u-late (sim'ū lāt') *v.* To have the appearance, effect, or form of. **simulation** *n.* **simulator** *n.*

sim-u-lat-ed rank *n.* The status of a civilian that is equal to a military rank.

si-mul-ta-ne-ous *adj.* Occurring at exactly the same time. **-ly** *adv.*

sin (sin) *n.* The breaking of a religious law or a law of God. *v.* To do something which is morally wrong.

since (sins) *adv.* At a time before the present. **since** *prep.* During the time later than; continuously from the time when something occurs.

sin-cere (sin sēr') *adj.* Honest; not deceitful; genuine; true. **-ly** *adv.*

sin-cip-i-tal *adj.* To be pertaining to the sinciput.

sin-ci-put *n.* The upper half or section of the skull.

sine *n.* A function in trigonometry.

sine qua non *n.* Something which is indispensable.

sin-ful *adj.* Being tainted with sin.

sing (sing) *v.* To use the voice to make musical tones; to make a humming or whistling sound. **singer** *n.*

singe (sinj) *v.* To slightly burn the surface of something; to remove feathers.

sin-gle (sing'gl) *adj.* Of or referring to only one, separate; individual; unmarried. *n.* A separate, individual person or item; a dollar bill; in baseball, a hit that allows the batter to progress to first base.

single-breasted *adj.* To have a center closing that has one row of buttons.

single cross *n.* The first generation hybrid between two selected lines.

sin-gle file *n.* A line where the people are one right behind each other.

single-handed *adj.* To be done by one person. **single-handedly** *adv.*

sin-gle-minded *adj.* To have one overriding purpose.

sin-gle-ness *n.* State of being single.

sin-gu-lar (sing´gū lèr) *adj.* Separate; one; extraordinary; denoting a single unit, thing or person.

sin-gu-lar-i-ty (sing´gū lar´i tē) *n.* A unit that is separate.

sin-gu-lar-ize *v.* To make something singular.

sin-is-ter (sin´i stèr) *adj.* To be evil or causing evil. **sinisterness** *n.* **-ly** *adv.*

sink (singk) *v.* To submerge beneath a surface; to go down slowly; to become less forceful or weaker. **sink** *n.* A basin for holding water, attached to a wall and connected to a drain.

sink-er *n.* A weight that is used for the purpose of sinking a fishing line into the water.

sink-hole *n.* A type of hollow depression where drainage collects.

si-nol-o-gy *n.* A study of the Chinese and the culture, history, and language. **sinological** *adj.* **sinologist** *n.*

sin-u-ate (sin´ū it) *adj.* Having a margin with indentations. **sinuately** *adv.*

sin-u-ous (sin´ū us) *adj.* To be marked with strong lithe movements.

si-nus (sī´nus) *n., Anat.* A body cavity; one of eight air spaces in the bones of the face which drain into the nasal cavity.

si-nus-i-tis *n.* The swelling and inflammation of the sinuses of the skull.

sip (sip) *v.* To drink in small amounts.

si-phon (sī´fon) *also* **syphon** *n.* A tube through which liquid from one container can be drawn into another by forced air pressure. **siphon** *v.*

si-pho-no-phore *n.* A type of free-swimming hyfrozoans that are transparent and have specialized zooids.

sip-pet (sip´it) *n.* A small piece of toast used for garnishing.

sir (ser) *n.* A respectful term used when addressing a man.

sir-dar (sèr där´) *n.* The person who holds a responsible position in India.

si-ren (sī´ren) *n.* A whistle which makes a loud wailing noise as a warning; a seductive woman.

si-re-ni-an *n.* A type of aquatic herbivorous mammal, such as the manatee.

sir-loin (sür´loin) *n.* The cut of meat that is from the hindquarter.

sis-ter (sis´tèr) *n.* A female having the same parents as another; a woman in membership with others, as in a church group or sorority. **-ly** *adj.*

sis-ter-hood *n.* Women who have a close relationship.

sis-trum *n.* A type of percussion instrument used in ancient Egypt.

sit (sit) *v.* To rest the body with the weight on the buttocks; to cover eggs for hatching; to pose for a portrait.

si-tar *n.* An Indian lute that has a long neck and varying number of strings.

site (sīt) *n.* A location of planned buildings.

sit-ting (sit´ing) *n.* An act of one that sits.

sitting duck *n.* A defenseless target.

sit-u-a-tion *n.* A way in which something or someone is placed, with its surroundings. **situationally** *adv.*

six (siks) *n.* The cardinal number 6, after five and before seven.

six-fold (siks´fōld) *adj.* To have six members.

six-pack *n.* Packaging for six cans so that they can be bought together.

six-penny nail *n.* A type of nail that is about two inches in length.

six-teen (siks´tēn´) *n.* The cardinal number 16; which is 15 + 1.

siz-a-ble (sī´za bl) *adj.* Large in size or dimensions.

size (sīz) *n.* The measurement or dimensions of something; a sticky substance used to glaze walls before applying wallpaper. **size** *v.*

siz-ed *adj.* To have a size which is specified.

siz-zle (siz´l) *v.* To make a hissing sound, as of fat frying. **sizzle** *n.*

sizzler *n.* The one that will sizzle.

skald *n.* Ancient Scandinavian poet.

skat *n.* A kind of three-handed game of cards where each player bids for the privilege to attempt any of the several contracts.

skate (skāt) *n.* A device with blades or rollers which attaches to the shoe and allows one to glide over ice or roll over a wooden or cement surface; a shoe for skating. **skater** *n.*

skate-board *n.* A narrow piece of wood with wheels attached.

ska-tole *n.* A foul smelling substance which is found in the intestines.

ske-dad-dle *v.* To leave or to run away from something or someone.

skeet *n.* The sport of trapshooting where the targets are made of clay and thrown in a way which resembles the manner in which birds fly.

skee-ter *n.* A type of iceboat that has one sail.

skein (skān) *n.* A piece of thread which is wound onto a reel.

skel-e-tal *adj.* Pertaining to or relating to the skeleton.

skel-e-ton (skel´i ton) *n.* The framework of bones that protects and supports the soft tissues and organs.

skel-e-ton-ize *v.* To reduce something to skeleton form.

skeleton key *n.* A key that is filed in order to be able to open many locks which can be used as a master key.

skep (skep) *n.* A type of hive that is doomed and has been made of twisted straw.

skep-sis *n.* A philosophic doubt as to the reality of something.

skep-tic (skep´tik) *n.* A person who doubts or questions. **skepticism** *n.* **skeptical** *adj.* **skeptically** *adv.*

sker-ry *n.* A island which is rocky.

sketch (skech) *n.* A rough drawing or outline; a brief literary composition.

sketch-book *n.* A book which is used for the purpose of sketching things.

skew (skü) *v.* To turn or slant. **skew** *n.* A slant.

skew-bald *adj.* To be marked with spots of white or another color or colors.

skew curve *n.* A type of curve which is three-dimensional and does not lie in the same plane or single plane.

skew-er *n.* A piece of metal used as a pin for the purpose of fastening foods together in order to broil them on a grill

skew lines *n.* Type of lines which are straight and do not intersect and are not located within the same plane.

skew-ness *n.* The lack of symmetry or of straightness of an object such as a line or curve.

ski (skē) *n., pl.* **skis** One of a pair of long, narrow pieces of wood worn on the feet for gliding over snow or water. **ski** *v.* **skier** *n.*

ski-a-gram *n.* The figure which is formed by shading the outline of a shadow that is created by the figure.

ski boot *n.* A rigid boot which is attached to the ski and is used to hold the ski on the foot.

skid (skid) *v.* To slide to the side of the road; to slide along without rotating.

skid-der *n.* A person who uses a skid or who skids.

skid-dy *adj.* Being likely to cause skidding.

skid road *n.* A type of road where logs are skidded along.

skill (skil) *n.* Ability gained through practice; expertise. **skilled** *adj.*

skiff (skif) *n.* A type of small and light sailing ship.

ski-ing (skē´ing) *n.* The sport of jumping and moving on skis

ski jump *n.* Jump is made by one who is wearing skis off of a large ramp.

ski lift *n.* A conveyor used to bring the skiers to the top of a hill.

skill (skil) *n.* Ability gained through practice; expertise.

skilled (skild) *adj.* To have acquired a skill for something.

skil-let (skil´it) *n.* A type of pot that has feet and is used for the purpose of cooking foods on the hearth.

skill-ful (skil´ful) *adj.* To be displaying a skill. **skillfully** *adv.*

skil-ling (skil´ing) *n.* Type of old Scandinavian unit of value, such as a coin.

skill-less (skil´lis) *adj.* To have no skill for anything. **skillessness** *n.*

skim (skim) *v.* To remove the top layer; to remove floating matter; to read over material quickly; to travel over lightly and quickly. **skimmer** *n.*

ski mask *n.* A type of face covering that is made of fabric and can be worn while one is skiing for protection from the elements.

skim milk *n.* A type of milk where the cream has been taken out.

skim-ming (skim´ing) *n.* The substance or that which is skimmed from a liquid.

skimp (skimp) *v.* To economize; to hold back. **skimpy** *adj.*

skin (skin) *n.* The tough, outside covering of man and some animals; the outside layer of a vegetable or fruit; the fur or pelt of an animal. **skin** *v.* **skinless** *adj.*

skin-deep *adj.* To be as deep as the skin; very thin.

skin diving *n.* A sport that involves swim-ming under the water without a breathing device.

skin-flint (skin´flint) *n.* A type of person who would extort or save money any way that is possible.

skin game *n.* A game that involves a trick or swindling of a person.

skin graft *n.* A section of the skin that is removed from one area and placed in an area where the skin has been removed or damaged.

skin grafting *n.* The process of placing or making a skin graft.

skin-head (skin´hed) *n.* A person whose hair is very short.

skink *v.* To serve alcoholic drinks.

skink-er *n.* One who serves liquor.

skin-ner (skin´ér) *n.* A person who deals or sells skins.

skin-ny (stin´e) *adj.* To be lacking a sufficient amount of flesh on the body, making one look thin.

skin-tight (skin´tit) *adj.* To be closely fitted to one's body.

skip (skip) *v.* To move in light jumps or leaps; to go from one place to another, missing what is between. **skip** *n.*

skip-jack *n.* A type of fish that will jump above the surface of the water.

ski pole *n.* The pole used in skiing to push the skier along the snow.

skirl (skürl) *n.* The high shrill sound which is produced by a bagpipe.

skir-mish *n.* A small and minor fight.

skirt (skert) *n.* A piece of clothing that extends down from the waist. **skirt** *v.* To extend along the boundary; to avoid the issue.

skirt-ing (skür´ting) *n.* The fabric which is suitable for making skirts.

ski run *n.* The trail which is used for the sport of skiing.

skit (skit) *n.* A type of humorous story.

ski tow *n.* A conveyor used to bring skiers

to the top of the hill.

skit-tish (skit'ish) *adj.* To be frightened easily.

skiv-er (skī'vėr) *n.* A type of thin leather that is made from sheepskin.

ski-wear *n.* The clothing that is used while one is skiing to keep warm.

skulk *v.* To conceal something out of fear; to move in a furtive way. **skulk** *n.* A person who skulks around.

skull (skul) *n.* The bony part of the skeleton which protects the brain.

skull-cap (skul'kap˘) *n.* A type of cap that is close-fitting.

skull practice *n.* A type of meeting for a discussion or the exchanging of ideas.

skunk (skungk) *n.* A black mammal with white streaks down its back; which sprays an unpleasant smelling liquid when annoyed or frightened.

skunk cab-bage *n.* A type of herb that has a very foul odor and is found in the eastern part of North America.

sky (skī) *n. pl.* **skies** The upper atmosphere above the earth; the celestial regions.

sky blue *n.* A color which may range from light blue to pale blue.

sky-cap *n.* A person who has the job of handling the luggage at an airport.

sky-div-ing *n.* The sport of jumping out of an airplane while it is flying in the air.

sky-ey (skīē) *adj.* Pertaining to or resembling the sky.

sky-high (skī'hī) *adv. or adj.* To be located high in the air; to do in a manner which is exorbitant.

ski-lark *n.* A type of lark which is large in size and is especially noted for its song.

sky-light *n.* The light of the sky; a window in the roof to admit natural light.

sky-line *n.* The outline of a building or other very large object against the sky.

sky-phos (skī'fos) *n.* A type of drinking vessel that was used in ancient Greece and had two handles.

sky-scrap-er (skīskrā˘pėr) *n.* A type of building which is very tall and therefore seems to scrape the sky.

sky-ward *adj.* To be moving toward the sky.

sky-way (skī'wā˘) *n.* The route which is used by airplanes.

sky-write *v.* To write letters or words in the sky.

sky-writ-ing *n.* The writing which is formed in the sky with the use of smoke.

slab (slab) *n.* A thick piece or slice.

slab-sid-ed *adj.* To have sides which are flat.

slack (slak) *adj.* Not taut or tense; sluggish; lacking in strength. *v.* To

make slack. *n.* A part of something which hangs loose. **slacks** Long pants or trousers.

slack-baked *n.* To be underdone.

slack-en *v.* To slow something down.

slack-er *n.* One who shirks an obligation.

slain *v.* Past tense of slay.

sla-lom *n.* A type of skiing where the skier zig-zags down the hill between upright obstacles such as flags.

slam (slam) *v.* To shut with force; to strike with a loud impact. **slam** *n.* A loud noise produced by an impact.

slan-der (slan'dėr) *n.* A false statement that deliberately does harm to another's reputation. **slanderous** *adj.*

slang (slang) *n.* Informal language that contains made-up words or common words used in a different or uncommon way.

slant (slant) *v.* To lie in an oblique position; to slope; to report on something giving only one side or viewpoint. *n.* An incline or slope.

slap (slap) *n.* A sharp blow with an open hand. **slap** *v.*

slap-hap-py *adj.* To be recklessly foolish.

slap shot *n.* The shot which is taken in ice hockey that is made with a swinging stroke.

slap-stick *n.* A type of comedy that stresses or contains horseplay and silly expressions.

slash (slash) *v.* To cut with a fast sweeping stroke; to reduce or limit greatly. *n.* A long cut.

slash-ing *n.* The process of slashing something. **slashingly** *adv.*

slash pine *n.* A type of southern pine which is a source of lumber and of turpentine.

slat *n.* A narrow piece of wood.

slate (slāt) *n.* A fine grained rock that splits into thin layers, often used as a writing surface or roofing material.

slate black *n.* A color that is purplish black.

slat-er *n.* A person who slates.

slath-er *v.* To spread something in a thick manner onto something else.

slat-ing *n.* The work that is done by a slater.

slat-tern-ly (slat'ėrn lē) *adj.* To be dirty because of neglect.

slat-y *adj.* To have the characteristic of slate.

slaugh-ter (slo'tėr) *v.* To kill livestock for food; to kill in great numbers. *Slang* To soundly defeat. **slaughterer** *n.* **slaughterous** *adj.*

slaugh-ter-house *n.* A place where one butchers or slaughters animals.

slave (slāv) *n.* A person held against his will and made to work for another.

slave ant *n.* A type of ant that is enslaved by the slave-making ant of the colony.

slave driver n. A person who is the supervisor of slaves.

slave-hold-er n. A person who is the owner of the slaves.

slav-ish (slā´vish) adj. Pertaining to the characteristics of a slave.

slay (slā) v. To kill or to destroy something in a violent manner.

sleave (slēv) v. To separate something such as silk fibers into filaments.

sleave silk n. A type of floss silk that is easily separated into filaments.

sled (sled) n. A vehicle with runners, used to travel on snow or ice.

sled dog n. A type of dog which has been trained to pull a sledge.

sledge n. A kind of vehicle that has low runners and is used for the purpose of transporting loads over the snow and is pulled by dogs.

sledge-ham-mer n. A type of hammer which is very heavy and must be wielded with both hands.

sleek (slēk) adj. Smooth and shiny; neat and trim. **sleekly** adv. **-ness** n.

sleep (slēp) n. A natural state of rest for the mind and body. **sleep** v.

sleeping bag n. The bag which is lined and is used for sleeping.

sleep-ing car n. A car of a train that has accommodations allowing a person to sleep.

sleeping pill n. A type of drug which is taken to help a person fall asleep.

sleep-less adj. Being not able to get to sleep. **sleeplessness** n.

sleep out v. To sleep away in a place that is not one's home.

sleep-walk-er n. A person who is able to walk while still asleep.

sleep-y (slē´pē) adj. Pertaining to sleep; needing sleep.

sleet (slēt) n. Rain that is partially frozen; a combination of snow and rain. **sleet** v. **sleety** adj.

sleeve (slēv) n. The part of a garment which covers the arm; a case for something.

sleeve-let n. A kind of covering which is worn on the forearm in order to protect the clothing from dirt and wear.

sleigh (slā) n. A vehicle mounted on runners, usually pulled over ice and snow by horses.

sleigh bell n. A type of bell that is attached to a sleigh.

slen-der (slen´dèr) adj. Slim; inadequate in amount. **slenderly** adv.

slept v. Past tense of sleep.

sleuth n. A detective.

slew n. A large amount of something.

slice (slīs) n. A thin cut; a portion or share; in sports, a ball in flight that curves off to the right of its target. v. To cut into slices. **slicer** n.

slice bar n. A type of steel bar that has a flat blade used for chipping.

slick (slik) adj. Smooth and slippery; quick; smart; clever; attractive for the present time but without quality or depth. n. Water with a thin layer of oil floating on top.

slick-en-side n. A striated surface that is produced on a rock by moving along a fault.

slick-er (slik´er) n. A raincoat made of yellow oilcloth.

slide (slīd) v. To move smoothly across a surface without losing contact. n. The act of sliding; a slanted smooth surface usually found on playgrounds; a transparent picture which can be projected on a screen; a small glass plate for examining specimens under a microscope.

slid-er n. Something that slides.

slide valve n. A kind of valve which opens and closes something such as a passageway.

slide-way n. The way which something slides.

slid-ing seat n. The rower's seat which will slide aft and fore.

slight (slīt) adj. Minor in degree; unimportant. v. To ignore. **slightly** adv.

slight-ing adj. To be characterized by disrespect. **slightingly** adv.

slim (slim) adj. Slender; meager; not much. **slimness** n.

slime (slīm) n. A wet, slippery substance. **slimy** adj.

slim-ming adj. To be giving the appearance or effect of slenderness.

sling (sling) n. A piece of material, as leather, or a strap which secures something; a piece of fabric worn around the neck used to support an injured hand or arm; a weapon made of a strap, used to throw a stone.

sling-shot n. A type of v-shaped device which has an elastic band and is used to propel objects such as rocks through the air.

slink-y (sling´ke) adj. To be sinuous and sleek in moving.

slip (slip) v. To move in a smooth, quiet way; to fall or lose one's balance. Slang To become less active or alert. **slip** n. The action of slipping; the place between two piers used for docking a boat; a woman's undergarment; a small piece of paper; a portion of a plant used for grafting.

slip-case (slip´kās´) n. A type of container that has one end open in order to slide books into for protection.

slip-cov-er n. A type of cover that can be slipped on and off of something.

slip-knot n. A knot that will slip along the rope of which it is made.

slip-o-ver n. A type of garment that will slip on and off with ease.

slip-page n. The process of slipping.

slip-pery (slip´e rē) adj. To cause something to slip. **slipperiness** n.

slip–sheet v. To put in or to insert a slip sheet between other sheets.

slip sheet n. A type of paper that is put between newly printed sheets.

slip-sole n. A type of thin insole.

slip stitch n. A stitch which is used for concealing folded edges in sewing.

slip up v. Make a blunder or mistake.

slit v. To cut an opening into something.

slit n. A narrow opening or cut into something.

slith-er (slith´ẽr) v. To slide or slip in an indirect manner; to move like a snake. **slithery** adj.

slit trench n. A trench which is narrow and is used as shelter in a battle from shell fragments.

sliv-er (sliv´ẽr) n. A thin, narrow piece of something that has been broken off.

slob (slob) n. One who is slovenly.

slob-ber (slob´ẽr) v. To dribble from the mouth. **slobber** n.

sloe gin n. A type of sweet liquor made of grain spirits, flavored with plums.

slog v. To plod along slowly and heavily.

slo-gan (slō´gan) n. A phrase used to express the aims of a cause.

slo-gan-ize v. To use something as a slogan.

sloop (slōōp) n. A type of boat with one mast which is rigged fore-and-aft.

slop (slop) n. A tasteless liquid food.

slop chest n. The store which is on a merchant ship and supplies the crew with goods such as tobacco.

slope (slōp) v. To slant upward or downward. n. An upward or downward incline, as a ski slope.

slop jar n. A type of pail that is large in size and is used for the purpose of receiving and holding the waste water from a washbowl.

slop-py adj. To be wet so that it spatters easily.

slosh (slosh) v. To splash in a liquid, as water. **sloshy** adj.

slot (slot) n. A narrow, thin groove or opening. Slang A place or scheduled time for an event.

slot-back n. The offensive halfback in the game of football that lines up behind and between the tackle and the offensive end.

sloth (sloth) n. Laziness; a slow mammal found in South America.

sloth-ful adj. To be inclined to sloth. **slothfulness** n.

slouch (slouch) n. A drooping or sagging posture; a lazy person. v. To sit or walk with poor posture.

slouch hat n. A kind of hat that has a wide flexible brim.

slouch-y adj. To be lacking good posture.

slouchiness n.

slough n. The skin which is cast off from a snake as he sheds it.

slo-ven (sluv´en) n. A person who is habitually negligent of cleanliness.

slov-en-ly (sluv´en lē) adj. To be untidy as in one's personal appearance.

slow (slō) adj. Moving at a low rate of speed; requiring more time than usual; not lively; sluggish; not interesting. adv. At less speed; in a slow manner. **slow** v. To make slower.

slow–foot-ed adj. To be moving at a slow pace. **slow-footedness** n.

slow-poke n. A person who is slow.

slow–witted adj. To be mentally slow.

sludge n. A mass which is slushy.

slue v. To cause something to skid.

slug (slug) n. A slow animal related to the snail; a bullet or a lump of metal. v. To strike forcefully with the fist or a heavy object.

slug-fest n. A type of fight which is marked by the exchange of blows that are heavy.

slug-gard (slug´ẽrd) n. A person who is habitually lazy. **sluggardly** adj.

slug-ger n. A person who strikes with heavy blows such as a fighter.

slug-gish adj. To be slow to respond to a treatment or to a stimulation. **sluggishness** n. **sluggishly** adv.

sluice (slōōs) n. A man-made ditch used to move water; a sloping trough used for floating logs. v. To wash with flowing water.

sluice-way (slōōs´wā) n. A channel which is artificial and into which water is admitted from a sluice.

slum (slum) n. A crowded urban neighborhood marked by poverty.

slum-ber (slum´bẽr) v. To sleep; to doze. n. Sleep. **slumberer** n.

slum-ber-ous (slum´bė us) adj. Being able to induce slumber.

slumber party n. A type of overnight gathering usually of girls at someone's house.

slum-my adj. To be pertaining to a slum.

slump (slump) v. To fall or sink suddenly. **slump** n.

slung v. Past tense of sling.

slur (slẽr) v. To slide over without careful consideration; to pronounce unclearly. n. An insult. Music Two or more notes connected with a curved line to indicate they are to be slurred.

slurp (slẽrp) v. To make or produce a sucking noise while one is drinking.

slur-ry (slẽr´ē) n. A type of watery mixture of matter which is insoluble.

slush (slush) n. Melting snow; snow which is partially melted. **slushy** adj.

slut (slut) n. A woman of bad character; a prostitute. **sluttish** adj.

sly (slī) adj. Cunning; clever; sneaky;

underhanded. **slyly** adv. **slyness** n.

sly-boots n. A person who is sly.

sm abbr. Small.

smack (smak) v. To slap; to press and open the lips with a sharp noise. n. The act or noise of slapping something. adv. Directly.

smack-ing (smak'ing) adj. Lively.

small (smol) adj. Little in size, quantity, or extent; unimportant. **small** n. The part that is less than the other.

small ale n. A weak ale that is brewed with little malt and is a cheap drink.

small arm n. A firearm which can be fired while it is held in the hands.

small change n. The coins of a low denomination; thingsof little value.

small-clothes n. The close-fitting knee breeches which were worn in the 18th century.

small–fry adj. Pertaining to a child.

small hours n. Early morning hours.

small intestines n. The section of the intestines which is located between the colon and the stomach.

small-mouth bass n. Type of black bass which can be found in clear lakes and rivers.

small-pox (smol'poks') n. An acute, contagious disease marked by high fever and sores on the skin.

small–scale adj. To be small in scope.

small–sword n. A light tapering sword that is used for thrusting in fencing.

small talk n. A casual conversation.

smalt-ite n. A type of white or grey mineral which is an arsenide of nickel and cobalt.

smal-to n. A type of colored glass that can be used for mosaic work.

smarm-y adj. Smug; self-satisfied.

smart (smärt) adj. Intelligent; clever. **smart-ly** adv. **smartness** n.

smart-en v. To make someone smarter.

smart-weed n. A polygonums that has a strong acid juice.

smash (smash) v. To break into small pieces; to move violently, as to shatter; to ruin. **smash** n. The pound or act of crashing. **smashing** adj.

smat-ter v. To speak with a superficial knowledge.

smaze n. The combination of smoke and haze that is similar to smog in its appearance only.

smear (smēr) v. To spread or cover with a sticky, oily, or moist substance. Slang To discredit one's reputation.

smear-y adj. Marked with smears.

smell (smel) v. To notice an odor by means of the olfactory sense organs. n. An odor; the ability to perceive an odor; the scent of something.

smel-ly (smel'ē) adj. To have an odor.

smelt (smelt) v. To heat metals or their ores to a high temperature in order to

obtain pure metallic constituents.

smelt-er n. Something or someone that smelts.

smew (smū) n. A bird of northern Europe and Asia; the male of this species has a white crest.

smid-gen (smij'en) n. A small amount.

smi-lax n. A type of twinning plant which has ovate bright green cladophylls.

smile (smīl) n. A grin; a facial expression in which the corners of the mouth turn upward, indicating pleasure. **smile** v.

smirch (smürch) v. To make something stained or dirty.

smirk (smerk) v. To smile in a conceited way. **smirk** n. **smirker** n.

smite (smīt) v. To hit with great force using the hand.

smith (smith) n. One who repairs or shapes metal.

smith-er-y n. The art of a smith.

smith-son-ite n. A type of zinc which is white.

smock (smok) n. A loose-fitting garment worn as a protection for one's clothes while working. v. To gather fabric into very small pleats or gathers.

smock frock n. An outer garment which is loose-fitting and is worn by workmen.

smog (smog) n. A mixture of smoke and fog. **smoggy** adj.

smoke (smōk) n. A cloud of vapor released into the air when something is burning. **smoke** v. To preserve or flavor meat by exposing it to smoke. **smoky** adj.

smoke-house n. A place or building where meat and fish are cured by using smoke.

smoke jumper n. A type of forest fighter who will parachute to the area of a fire that may have become hard to reach by land.

smoke out v. To force or drive out with the use of smoke.

smoke-stack n. The chimney through which gases and smoke are able to be discharged.

smoke tree n. A type of shrubby tree belonging to the sumac family.

smok-ing jack-et n. A type of jacket which is worn by the man at home.

smolder (smōl'der) v. To burn slowly without flame and with little smoke.

smolt n. A young sea trout or salmon.

smooth (smooth) adj. Not irregular; flat; without lumps, as in gravy; without obstructions or impediments. adv. Evenly. v. To make less difficult; to remove obstructions.

smooth-en v. To make a thing smooth.

smooth-y n. A type of person who has manners which are greatly polished.

smor-gas-bord (smor'gas bōrd') n. A buffet meal with a variety of foods to choose from.

smother (smuth´ér) *n*. Failure to receive enough oxygen to survive. *v*. To conceal; to be overly protective.

smudge (smuj) *v*. To soil by smearing with dirt. *n*. A dirty mark or smear; a fire made to fill the air with smoke in order to protect fruit trees from frost.

smug (smug) *adj*. Complacent with oneself; self-satisfied. **smugly** *adv*. **smugness** *n*.

smug-gle (smug´l) *v*. To import or export goods illegally without paying duty fees. **smuggler** *n*.

smug-ly *adv*. To be done in a smug manner.

smut *n*. A type of matter or substance which will soil something.

smut-ty *adj*. To be tainted or soiled by smut. **smittiness** *n*.

SMV *abbr*. Slow moving vehicle.

snack (snak) *n*. A small amount of food taken between meals. **snack** *v*.

snack bar *n*. An eating place for the public that serves snacks at a counter.

snaf-fle *n*. A jointed bit used with a bridle.

sna-fu *v*. To be someone in a confused state.

snag (snag) *n*. A stump or part of a tree that is partly hidden under the surface of water; a pull in a piece of fabric. *v*. To tear on a rough place. *Slang* To catch unexpectedly; to snatch.

snail (snāl) *n*. A gastropod mollusk that can live in a spiral shell.

snail-paced *adj*. To be moving at a slow pace.

snake (snāk) *n*. Any of a large variety of scaly reptiles, having a long tapering body; an untrustworthy person.

snake-bite *n*. A bite of a snake on the skin.

snake charmer *n*. A person who exhibits his power to charm a snake.

snake-mouth *n*. A type of bog orchid that is located in eastern N. America and Japan and has pink flowers.

snake-skin *n*. The leather that has been pre-pared from the skin of a snake.

snake-weed (snā´kēd´) *n*. A plant that is associated with snakes and used in the treatment of snake bites.

snak-y *adj*. Entwined with snakes.

snap (snap) *v*. To break suddenly with a sharp, quick sound; to fly off under tension; to snatch something suddenly.

snap back *n*. A type of football snap; a sudden recovery.

snap bean *n*. A type of bean which is grown for its pods that are broken and cooked.

snap-drag-on *n*. A type of plant of the figwort family and having white, yellow, or crimson flowers.

snap-per (snap´ér) *n*. A type of fish found in warm seas.

snapper-back *n*. In the game of football, a center.

snap-pish (snap´ish) *adj*. To be given to curt irritable speech.

snap-shot *n*. A type of photograph which is made by an amateur with a small camera.

snare (snâr) *n*. Anything that entangles or entraps; a trap with a noose, used to catch small animals.

snare drum *n*. A type of drum that has snares stretched across the lower end.

snarl (snärl) *v*. To speak in an angry way; to cause confusion; to tangle or be tangled. *n*. A growl.

snatch (snach) *v*. To seize or grasp something suddenly. *n*. The act of taking something; a brief or small part.

snatch block *n*. A type of block which can be opened on one side in order to get the bight of a rope.

snaz-zy *adj*. To be flashily attractive.

sneak (snēk) *v*. To act or move in a quiet, sly way. *n*. A person who acts in a secret, underhanded way.

sneak-ing *adj*. To be characteristic of a sneak. **sneakingly** *adv*.

sneak pre-view *n*. An advance showing of a motion picture.

sneak thief *n*. A type of thief that will steal whatever he can without using violence.

sneak-y *adj*. To be marked by shiftiness.

sneer (snēr) *v*. To express scorn by the look on one's face.

sneeze (snēz) *v*. To expel air from the nose suddenly and without control. **sneeze** *n*.

sneeze-wort *n*. A type of strong-scented herb found in Eurasia.

snee-zy *adj*. To be causing sneezing.

snick *v*. To cut at something slightly.

snide (snīd) *adj*. To be unworthy of esteem; malicious.

sniff *v*. To inhale through the nose in short breaths with a noise; to show scorn. **sniff** *n*. **sniffer** *n*.

sniff-ish *adj*. Expressing an attitude.

snif-ter *n*. A type of drink of liquor that has been distilled.

snig-gle *n*. To try to catch an eel by putting the baited hook into the place where they hide.

snip (snip) *v*. To cut off in small pieces and with quick strokes. **snip** *n*.

snipe (snīp) *n*. *pl*. **snipe** *or* **snipes** A bird with a long bill which lives in marshy places. *v*. To shoot at people from a hidden position. **sniper** *n*.

snip-pet (snip´it) *n*. A small part or thing.

snips *n*. A type of hand shears that can be used for the purpose of cutting metal.

sniv-el (sniv´l) *v*. To whine with snuffling.

snob (snob) *n.* A person who considers himself better than anyone else and who looks down on those he considers to be his inferiors.

snob-ber-y *n.* A snobbish conduct.

snob-bish (snob´ish) *adj.* Being like a snob.

snood (snöd) *n.* A type of band that can be worn on a woman's hair.

snook (snök) *n.* A type of fish that is large and can be used as food or for sport.

snook-er *n.* A type of pool which is played with six colored balls and fifteen red balls.

snoop (snöp) *v., Slang* To prowl or spy. *n.* One who snoops.

snoop-y *adj.* To be given to snooping.

snoot (snöt) *n.* An expression of contempt.

snooze (snöz) *n.* To sleep for a short amount of time.

snore (snör) *v.* To breath with a harsh noise while sleeping. **snorer** *n.*

snor-kel (snor´kel) *n.* A tube that extends above the water, used for breathing while swimming face down.

snort (snort) *n.* To force air through the nostrils with a loud, harsh noise. *Slang* To inhale a narcotic through the nose.

snort-er *n.* Someone or something that snorts.

snout (snout) *n.* A nose of an animal such as a swine.

snout beetle *n.* A type of beetle that has a head which has projected into a snout.

snow (snö) *n.* Vapor that forms crystals in cold air and falls to earth in white flakes. **snow** *v.* To fall like snow. *Slang* To deceive.

snow-ball *n.* A rounded mass of snow that is pressed together.

snow-blind (snö´blind) *adj.* To be affected with snow blindness.

snow bound (snö´bound) *adj.* To be blocked in by a large snowfall.

snowfall *n.* The precipitation falling as snow.

snow-mo-bile (snö´ma bēl) *n.* A vehicle used for traveling on snow.

snub (snub) *v.* To treat with contempt or in an unfriendly way. **snub** *n.*

snub-ber (snub´ér) *n.* Someone who snubs.

snuff (snuf) *v.* To draw air in through the nostrils. **snuff** *n.*

snuff-box (snuf´boks) *n.* A type of small box that can be used for holding snuff.

snuff-er *n.* A type of device used for dropping and holding the snuff of a candle.

snuf-fle *v.* To breathe through a nose that is obstructed producing a sniffing sound.

snug (snug) *adj.* Warm, pleasant, comfortable and safe.

snug-gle (snug´l) *v.* To curl up to someone in an affectionate manner.

so (sö) *adv.* To a degree or extent as a result; likewise; also; indeed. *conj.* In order that; therefore.

soak (sök) *v.* To pass through something with the use of pores. **soaker** *n.*

soak-age (sök´äj) *n.* The amount of liquid that is gained through absorption.

soap (söp) *n.* A cleansing agent made of an alkali and a fat, and used for washing. *v.* To rub with soap.

soap-ber-ry (söp´ber´e) *n.* A type of tropical woody plant.

soap-box (söp´boks) *n.* A platform that is used by an informal orator.

soap bubble *n.* A type of hollow globe which is formed by blowing a small film of soapsuds.

soap-less *adj.* Containing no soap.

soap plant *n.* A type of plant which has a part that can be used in the place of soap.

soap-y (sö´pē) *adj.* To be covered or smeared with soap.

soar (sör) *v.* To glide or fly high without any noticeable movement; to rise higher than usual.

sob (sob) *v.* To weep with short, quick gasps.

so-ber (sö´bér) *adj.* Not drunk or intoxicated; serious; solemn; quiet. **soberly** *adv.* **soberness** *n.*

soc-cer (sok´ér) *n.* A game in which two teams of eleven people each try to kick a ball into the goal of the opposing team.

so-cia-ble (sö´sha bl) *adj.* Capable of friendly social relations; enjoying the company of others. **sociably** *adv.*

so-cial (sö´shal) *adj.* Having to do with people living in groups; enjoying friendly companionship with others. *n.* An informal party or gathering.

so-cial-ism (sö´sha liz um) *n.* A system in which people as a whole, and not individuals, control and own all property.

so-ci-e-ty (so sī´i tū) *n., pl. -ies* People working together for a common purpose; companionship.

so-ci-ol-o-gy (sö sē ol´o jē) *n.* The study of society and the development of human society. **sociologic** *adj.* **sociological** *adj.*

sock-et (sok´it) *n.* A hollow opening into which something is fitted.

Soc-ra-tes *n.* Greek philosopher.

so-da (sö´da) *n.* Sodium carbonate; a flavored, carbonated drink.

sod-den (sod´en) *adj.* Completely saturated; very wet; lacking in expression.

so-di-um (sö´dē um) *n.* A metallic element symbolized by Na.

sod-om-y (sod´o mē) *n.* Anal sexual

intercourse.

so-fa (sō´fa) *n.* An upholstered couch with arms and a back.

soft (soft) *adj.* Not stiff or hard; not glaring or harsh; mild or pleasant; gentle in sound.

soft-ball (soft´bol´) *n.* A game played on a smaller diamond than baseball, with a larger, softer ball.

soft-ware (soft´wâr´) *n.* In *computer science*, data, as routines, programs and languages, which is essential to the operation of computers.

sog-gy (sog´ē) *adj.* Saturated with a liquid or moisture.

sol-ace (sol´is) *n.* Comfort in a time of trouble, grief, or misfortune.

so-lar (sō´lèr) *adj.* Relating to or connected with the sun; utilizing the sun for power or light; measured by the earth's movement around the sun.

so-lar-i-um (sō lâr´ē um) *n. pl.* **-ia** *or* **-ums** A glassed-in room exposed to the sun's rays.

solar system *n.* The sun and the planets, asteroids, etc. that orbit it.

sol-der (sod´ér) *n.* Any alloy, as lead or tin, which is melted and used to mend or join other pieces of metal. **solder** *v.* To join with solder.

sol-dier (sōl´jèr) *n.* An enlisted person who serves in the military.

sole (sōl) *n.* The bottom of a foot or shoe; single, the only one; a flat fish very popular as seafood.

sol-emn (sol´em) *adj.* Very serious; characterized by dignity; sacred. **solemnity** *n.* **solemnness** *n.*

so-lic-it (so lis´it) *v.* To try to obtain; to ask earnestly; to beg or entice a person persistently. **solicitation** *n.*

sol-id (sol´id) *adj.* Having a definite firm shape and volume; having no crevices; not hollow; having height, weight and length; without interruption; reliable, sound and upstanding. *n.* A solid substance. **solidification** *n.* **-ify** *v.*

sol-i-taire (sol´i târ´) *n.* A single gemstone set by itself; a card game played by one person.

sol-i-tude (sol´i tōd´) *n.* The act of being alone or secluded; isolation.

so-lo (sō´lō) *n.* A musical composition written for and performed by one single person or played by one instrument.

sol-stice (sol´stis) *n.* Either of the two times in a twelve month period at which the sun reaches an extreme north or south position.

sol-u-ble (sol´ū bl) *adj.* Capable of being dissolved; able to be solved or explained. **solubility** *n.* **solubly** *adv.*

solve (solv) *v.* To find the answer to. **solvable** *adj.*

som-ber (som´bér) *adj.* Dark; gloomy; melancholy.

some (sum) *adj.* Being an indefinite number or quantity; unspecified. *pron.* An undetermined quantity. *adv.* An approximated degree. **somebody** A person unknown. **somehow** In a way. **someday** *adv.* At an unspecified future time.

som-er-sault (sum´ér solt´) *n.* The act or acrobatic stunt in which one rolls the body in a complete circle, with heels over head.

som-nam-bu-lism (som nam´bya liz´um) *n.* The act of walking during sleep. **somnambulant** *adj.*

son (sun) *n.* A male offspring.

so-na-ta (so nä´ta) *n.* An instrumental composition with movements contrasting in tempo and mood but related in key.

song (song) *n.* A piece of poetry put to music; the act or sound of singing.

son-ic (son´ik) *adj.* Pertaining to sound or the speed of sound.

son-net (son´it) *n.* A poem made up of fourteen lines.

soon (sön) *adv.* In a short time; in the near future; quickly.

soot (set) *n.* The black powder generated by incomplete combustion of a fuel, such as coal or wood.

soothe (söth) *v.* To make comfortable; to calm.

sop (sop) *v.* To soak up a liquid; to absorb. *n.* Anything softened by a liquid; something given as a conciliatory offering.

soph-o-more (sof´o mōr´) *n.* A second year college or high school student.

so-pran-o (so pran´ō) *n.* The highest female singing voice.

sor-cery (sor´se rē) *n.* The use of supernatural powers.

sor-did (sor´did) *adj.* Filthy, very dirty; morally corrupt.

sore (sōr) *adj.* Tender or painful to the touch, as an injured part of the body; severe or extreme. *n.* A place on the body which has been bruised, inflamed, or injured in some way. **sorely** *adv.*

sor-ghum (sor´gum) *n.* A cane-like grass grown for its sweet juices and used as fodder for animals; the syrup prepared from the sweet juices.

so-ror-i-ty (so ror´i tē) *n. pl.* **-ies** A social organization for women.

sor-rel (sor´el) *n.* Any of several herbs with sour tasting leaves, used in salads.

sor-row (sor´ō) *n.* Anguish; mental suffering; an expression of grief. **sorrowful** *adj.* **sorrowfully** *adv.*

sor-ry (sor´ē) *adj.* Feeling or showing sympathy or regret; worthless.

sort (sort) *n.* A collection of things having common attributes or similar qualities. *v.* to arrange according to class, kind, or size.

sor-tie (sor´tē) *n., Mil.* An attack on enemy forces; a combat mission flown by an aircraft.

SOS (es´ō´es´) *n.* A call for help; the international distress signal; a call made when a rescue is needed, especially by a ship or plane.

souf-fle (sŏ flā´) *n.* A fluffy dish made of egg yolks, whipped egg whites, and other ingredients, served as a main dish or sweetened as a dessert.

sought *v.* Past tense of seek.

soul (sōl) *n.* The spirit in man that is believed to be separate from the body and is the source of a person's emotional, spir-itual, and moral nature. *Slang* A spirit or attitude derived from Blacks and their culture.

sound (sound) *n.* A sensation received by the ears from air, water, noise, and other sources. **sound** *v.* To make a sound; to make noise. **sound** *adj.* Free from flaw, injury, disease, or damage. **soundly** *adv.*

soup (sŏp) *n.* A liquid food made by boiling meat and/or vegetables, in water.

sour (sour) *adj.* Sharp to the taste; acid; unpleasant; disagreeable. *v.* To become sour or spoiled. **sourly** *adv.*

source (sōrs) *n.* Any point of origin or beginning; the beginning or place of origin of a stream or river.

source data In *computer science*, data that has been entered into the computer for manipulation.

south (south) *n.* The direction opposite of north. *adv.* To or towards the south. *adj.* From the south. **southerly** *adj.* & *adv.* **southern** *adj.* **southerner** *n.*

South Carolina A state located in the southeastern part of the United States; statehood May 23, 1788; state capital Columbia.

South Dakota *n.* A state located in the central northwestern part of the United States; statehood November 2, 1889; state capital Pierre.

south paw (south´po´) *n.* A left-handed person. **southpaw** *adj.*

South Pole *n.* The southern most part of the earth.

south-west (south´west´) *n.* The direction between south and west.

sou-ve-nir (sŏ´ve nēr´) *n.* An item kept as a remembrance of something or someplace.

sov-er-eign (sov´rin) *n.* A ruler with supreme power; a monarch. *adj.* Possessing supreme authority.

sow (sō) *v.* To scatter seeds on the ground for growth. *n.* A female pig.

space (spās) *n.* The unlimited area in all directions in which events occur and have relative direction; an interval of time; the area beyond the earth's atmosphere.

spade (spād) *n.* A tool with a flat blade used for digging; a heavy shovel.

spa-ghet-ti (spa get´ē) *n.* Long thin pasta.

span (span) *n.* The extent of space from the end of the thumb to the end of the little finger of a spread hand; the section between two limits or supports. *v.* To extend across.

span-iel (span´yel) *n.* A dog with large drooping ears and short legs.

spank (spangk) *v.* To strike or slap the buttocks with an open hand as a means of punishment.

spare (spâr) *v.* To refrain from injuring, harming or destroying; to refrain from using; to do without. **spare** *n.* An extra, as a spare tire.

spark (spärk) *n.* A glowing or incandescent particle, as one released from a piece of burning wood or one produced by means of friction. **spark** *v.* To give off sparks.

spar-kle (spär´kl) *v.* To emit or reflect light.

spar-row (spar´ō) *n.* A small bird with grayish or brown plumage.

sparse (spärs) *adj.* Scant; thinly distributed. **sparsely** *adv.* **sparsity** *n.*

spasm (spaz´um) *n.* An involuntary muscle contraction.

spat-ter (spat´ér) *v.* To splash or scatter a liquid.

spat-u-la (spach´a la) *n.* A kitchen utensil with a flexible blade for mixing soft substances.

spawn (spon) *n.* The eggs of fish or other water animals, as oysters or frogs. *v.* To lay eggs.

speak (spēk) *v.* To utter words; to express a thought in words.

speak-er (spē´kèr) *n.* A person who speaks, usually before an audience.

spear (spēr) *n.* A weapon with a long shaft and a sharp pointed head. *v.* To strike, pierce, or stab with a spear.

spear-mint (spēr´mint´) *n.* A plant yielding an aromatic oil; flavoring.

spe-cial-ist (spesh´u list) *n.* A person, such as a doctor, who devotes his practice to one particular field.

spe-cial-ize (spesh´a līz´) *v.* To focus one's efforts or interests in one field of activity or study.

spec-i-men (spes´ i men) *n.* A sample; a representative of a particular thing.

speck (spek) *n.* Small particle; a spot.

speckle *v.* To cover or dot with specks.

spec-ta-cle (spek´ta kl) *n.* A public display of something strange and unusual. **spectacles** Eyeglasses.

spec-trum (spek´trum) *n. Physics* The band of colors produced when light is passed through a prism or by other means, separating the light into different wave lengths.

spec-u-late (spek´ū lāt´) v. To reflect and think deeply; to take a chance on a business venture in hopes of making a large profit. **speculation** n.

speech (spēch) n. The ability, manner, or act of speaking; a talk before the public. **speechless** adj.

speed (spēd) n. Rate of action or movement; quickness; rapid motion. Slang A drug used as a stimulant.

spell (spel) v. To say out loud or write in proper order the letters which make up a word; to relieve. n. The state of being controlled by magic; a short period of time; a time or period of illness; an attack.

spell-bind v. To fascinate or hold as if by magic.

spell checker In Computer Science, a feature in some word processors that checks and corrects spelling in a document.

spend (spend) v. To give out; to use up; to pay; to exhaust.

sperm (sperm) n. The male cell of reproduction; semen. **spermatic** adj.

sphere (sfēr) n., Math A round object with all points the same distance from a given point; globe, ball, or other rounded object. **spherical** adj.

sphinx (sfingks) n., pl. **sphinxes** or **sphinges** An ancient Egyptian figure having the head of a man, male sheep, or hawk and the body of a lion; a very mysterious person.

spice (spīs) n. A pungently aromatic plant used as flavoring in food, as nutmeg, cinnamon, pepper, or curry.

spi-der (spī´dèr) n. An eight-legged arachnid with a body divided into two parts that spins webs used to capture and hold its prey.

spike (spīk) n. A large, thick nail; a pointed metal piece on the sole of a shoe to prevent slipping, as on a sports shoe. **spike** v.

spill (spil) v. To allow or cause something to flow or run out of something, often accidentally. **spill** n.

spin (spin) v. To draw out fibers and twist into thread; to run something around and around; to resolve. Slang A short drive or ride in an auto. **spinner** n.

spin-ach (spin´ich) n. A widely cultivated plant with dark green leaves which are used in salads.

spin-dle (spin´dl) n. A rod with a slit in the top and a piece of wood at the other end, used to hold thread or yarn; a needle-like rod mounted on a base, used to hold papers.

spine (spin) n. The spinal column; the backbone; the back of a bound book, inscribed with the title.

spin-ster (spin´stèr) n. An unmarried woman; an old maid.

spir-it (spir´it) n. The vital essence of man, considered divine in origin; the part of a human being characterized by personality and self-consciousness; the mind; a supernatural being, as an angel.

spir-i-tual (spir´i chö al) adj. Of the nature of spirit; relating to religion; sacred. n. A religious song originating among the Blacks of the southern United States. **spirituality** n.

spite (spīt) n. Hatred or malicious bitterness; a grudge; ill will. **spite** v. **spiteful** adj. **spitefully** adv.

spitz (spits) n. A small dog with a tail which curls over its back.

splash (splash) v. To spatter a liquid; to wet or soil with liquid; to make a splash. **splash** n. **splashy** adj.

splash-down (splash´doun´) n. The landing of a missile or spacecraft in the ocean.

spleen (splēn) n. Anat. A highly vascular, flattened organ which filters and stores blood, located below the diaphragm.

splen-did (splen´did) adj. Illustrious; magnificent.

splice (splīs) v. To join together by wearing, overlapping, and binding the ends.

splint (splint) n. A device used to hold a fractured or injured limb in the proper position for healing. **splint** v.

splotch (sploch) n. A discolored and irregularly shaped spot.

splutter (splut´èr) v. To make a slight, short spitting sound. **splutter** n.

spoil (spoil) v. To destroy the value, quality, or usefulness; to overindulge as to harm the character. **spoils** n.

spoke (spōk) n. One of the rods that serve to connect and support the rim of a wheel. v. Past tense of speak.

spokes-man (spōks´man) n. One who speaks on behalf of another.

sponge (spunj) n. Any of a number of marine creatures with a soft, porous skeleton which soaks up liquid. v. To clean with a sponge. **spongy** adj.

spon-sor (spon´sèr) n. A person who is responsible for a debt or duty of another; a business that finances a television or radio program that in turn advertises its product. **-ship** n.

spon-ta-ne-ous (spon tā´nē us) adj. Done from one's own impulse without apparent external cause. **spontaneity** n. **spontaneously** adv.

spoof (spöf) n. A deception; nonsense.

spook (spōk) n., Slang A ghost. v. To scare or frighten. **spooky** adj.

spool (spöl) n. A small cylinder for holding thread, tape or wire.

spoon (spön) n. An eating or cooking utensil; a shiny metallic fishing lure.

Slang To make love, as by kissing.

spo-rad-ic (spŏ rad´ĭk) *adj.* Occurring occasionally or at irregular intervals.

spore (spōr) *n., Bot.* The reproductive single-celled structure produced by nonflowering plants; any cell capable of developing into a new organism, seed, or germ.

sport (spōrt) *n.* An interesting diversion; a particular game or physical activity with set rules; a person who leads a fast life. **sport** *adj.* Relating or pertaining to sports.

sport-ing (spōr´tĭng) *adj.* Of or relating to risk taking or gambling; displaying sportsmanship.

sports-man-ship (spōrts´man ship´) *n.* Fair play; the ability to win or lose graciously.

spot (spot) *n.* A small area that differs in size, portion, or color; a dangerous or difficult situation. **spot** *v.*

spot-light (spot´lĭt´) *n.* A powerful light thrown directly at one area.

spouse (spous) *n.* One's husband or wife; a marriage partner.

spout (spout) *v.* To pour out forcibly, as under pressure; to cause to shoot forth. *Slang* To orate pompously.

sprain (sprān) *n.* A wrenching or twisting of a muscle or joint.

sprawl (sprol) *v.* To sit or lie in an ungraceful manner; to develop haphazardly. **sprawl** *n.* **sprawler** *n.*

spray (sprā) *n.* A liquid dispersed in a fine mist or droplets. *v.* To disperse or send forth in a spray. **sprayer** *n.*

spread (spred) *v.* To unfold or open fully; to apply or distribute over an area; to force apart; to extend.

spreadsheet *n.* In *computer science*, a document with data, arranged in rows and columns, that can be adjusted for the entry of additional data and manipulated for reporting.

spree (sprē) *n.* An excessive indulgence in an activity; a binge.

spright-ly (sprit´lĕ) *adj.* Vivacious, lively. **sprightliness** *n.*

Spring-field *n.* The capital of the state of Illinois.

sprin-kle (spring´kl) *v.* To scatter in small particles or drops; to rain in small drops. **sprinkle** *n.*

sprint (sprint) *n.* A short, fast race.

sprock-et (sprok´ĭt) *n., Mech.* A tooth-like projection from the rim of a wheel.

spruce (sprŏs) *n.* An evergreen tree with needle-like foliage, cones, and soft wood.

spry (sprī) *adj.* Quick; brisk; energetic.

spud (spud) *n., Slang* A potato.

spur (sper) *n.* A sharp, projecting device worn on a riders boot, used to nudge a horse. *v.* To urge on.

sput-nik (spet´nik) *n.* An unmanned Soviet earth satellite.

sput-ter (sput´ẽr) *v.* To throw off small particles in short bursts; to speak in an agitated manner.

spu-tum (spū´tum) *n. pl.* **-ta** Saliva or mucus that is expectorated.

spy (spī) *n., pl.* **spies** A secret agent who obtains information; one who watches other people secretly.

squab *n.* A type of fledgling bird.

squab-ble (skwob´l) *v.* To engage in a petty argument. **squabble** *n.*

squad (skwod) *n.* A small group organized to perform a specific job.

squad car *n.* A type of police car.

squad-ron (skwod´ron) *n.* A naval unit that has two or more divisions.

squa-lene *n.* An acyclic hydrocarbon that is widely distributed in nature.

squal-id (skwol´id) *adj.* Marked by degradation from poverty or neglect.

squall (skwol) *v.* To cry out.

squa-lor *n.* The state of being squalid.

squa-ma-tion *n.* A state of being scaly or having an arrangement of scales.

squa-mo-sal (skwa mō´sal) *adj.* Pertaining to the membrane bone of the skull.

squa-mous (skwä´mus) *n.* To be consisting of scales. **squamously** *adv.*

squamous cell *n.* A type of cell which is derived from squamous epithelium.

squan-der (skwon´dẽr) *v.* To spend extra vagrantly or wastefully.

square (skwâr) *n.* A parallelogram with four equal sides; an implement having a T or L shape used to measure right angles. *v. Math.* To multiply a number by itself. *Slang* An unsophisticated person.

square deal *n.* A fair trade.

square knot *n.* A kind of knot that is comprised of two reverse half-knots.

square root *n.* A number which when multiplied by itself gives the given number.

squat (skwot) *v.* To sit on the heels; to crouch; to settle on a piece of land in order to obtain legal title. **-ter** *n.*

squaw (skwo) *n.* An American Indian woman.

squawk (skwok) *v.* To protest something in a loud manner.

squeak (skwēk) *v.* To utter a sharp, penetrating sound. **squeak** *n.* **-y** *adj.*

squeal (skwēl) *v.* To produce or to make a shrill cry. **squealer** *n.*

squea-mish (skwē´mish) *adj.* Easily shocked or nauseated. **-ly** *adv.*

squea-mish-ness *n.* State of being squeamish.

squee-gee (skwē´jē) *n.* A tool having a stout rubber blade across a wooden handle, used to wash windows.

squeeze (skwēz) *v.* To press together; to extract by using pressure; to hug.

squeg v. To oscillate in a manner which is irregular.

squelch (skwelch) n. The process or act of suppressing. squelchy adv.

squib (skwib) n. A firecracker that does not explode.

squid (skwid) n. A type of 10-armed cephalopod that has a tapered body.

squig-gle (skwig) n. A short wavy line or twist.

squil-la (skwil´a) n. A type of stomatopod crustacean that digs into mud.

squinch v. To make something more compact.

squint (skwint) v. To view something through partly closed eyes; to close the eyes in this manner. squint n.

squint–eyed adj. To have eyes that squint.

squire (skwī´ẽr) n. An old-fashioned title for a rural justice of the peace, lawyer, or judge; a man who escorts a woman; a young man who ranks just below a knight.

squire-ar-chy (skwīẽr´är kē) n. The gentry.

squirm (skerm) n. To twist the body in a wiggling motion. squirm v.

squir-rel (skwer´el) n. A rodent with gray or brown fur, having a long bushy tail and dark eyes. squirrel v.

squir-rel cage n. A type of cage that is used for small animals and has a rotatable cylinder for exercising.

squir-rel-ly (squir rel y) adj. To be odd.

squirt (skwert) v. To eject in a thin stream or jet; to wet with a squirt. n. The act of squirting.

squirting cucumber n. A type of plant of the Mediterranean that belongs to the gourd family and will burst to eject its seeds when it is ripe.

squish-y adj. To be soft and damp.

sta-bi-lize (stā´bi līz´) v. To make firm; to keep from changing. stabilization n. stabilizer n.

sta-ble (stā´bl) n. A building for lodging and feeding horses or other farm animals. adj. Standing firm and resisting change.

stac-ca-to (sta kä´tō) adj. Music Marked by sharp emphasis.

stack (stak) n. A large pile of straw or hay; any systematic heap or pile; a chimney. stack v. To fix cards so as to cheat.

sta-di-um (stā´dē um) n., pl. stadia A large structure for holding athletic events or other large gatherings.

staff (staf) n. pl. staffs or staves A pole or rod used for a specific purpose; the people employed to assist in the day-to-day affairs of running a business, organization, or government. Mil. A group of people on an executive or advisory board. Music The horizontal lines on which notes are written. staff v.

stag-nant (stag´nant) adj. Not flowing; standing still; foul from not moving; inactive. stagnate v.

stair (stâr) n. A step or a series of steps.

staircase (stâr´kās) n. A series or a flight of steps that connect one level to another.

stake (stāk) n. A bet placed on a game of chance; a sharpened piece of wood for driving into the ground. stake v.

stale (stāl) adj. Having lost freshness; deteriorated; lacking in interest; dull; inactive.

stale-mate (stāl´māt´) n. A position in chess when a player cannot move without placing his king in check.

stalk (stok) n. Main axis of a plant. v. To approach in a stealthy manner.

stall (stol) n. An enclosure in a barn, used as a place to feed and confine animals; a sudden loss of power in an engine; a booth used to display and sell. v. To try to put off doing something; to delay.

stal-lion (stal´yan) n. An uncastrated, fully grown male horse.

sta-men (stā´men) n. pl. stamens Bot. The pollen-producing organs of a flower.

stam-i-na (stam´i na) n. Physical or moral endurance.

stam-mer (stam´ẽr) v. To make involuntary halts or repetitions of a sound or syllable while speaking. .

stamp (stamp) v. To put the foot down with force; to imprint or impress with a die, mark, or design. n. The act of stamping; the impression or pattern made by a stamp; a postage stamp.

stam-pede (stam pēd´) n. A sudden rush of panic, as of a herd of horses or cattle. v. To cause a stampede.

stance (stans) n. The posture or position of a standing person or animal.

stand (stand) v. To be placed in or maintain an erect or upright position; to take an upright position; to remain unchanged; to maintain a conviction; to resist. n. The act of standing; a device on which something rests; a small booth for selling or displaying items.

stand-ard (stan´dẽrd) n. A model which stands for or is accepted as a basis for comparison. standard adj.

stand-ing (stan´ding) n. A status, reputation, or achievement; a measure of esteem. adj. Unchanging; stationary; not moving.

sta-ple (stā´pl) n. A principle commodity grown in an area; a major element; a metal fastener designed to hold materials such as cloth or paper.

star (stär) n., Astron. A self-luminous body that is a source of light; any of the celestial bodies that can be seen in the night sky; a symbol having five or six points resembling a star.

star-board (stär´bĕrd) *n. & adj. & adv.* The right side of a ship or boat.

starch (stärch) *n.* Nutrient carbohydrates that are found in foods such as rice and potatoes. *v.* To stiffen clothing by using starch. **starchiness** *n.* **starchy** *adj.*

stare (stâr) *v.* To look with an intent, direct gaze. **stare** *n.* **starer** *n.*

stark (stärk) *adj.* Bare; total; complete; forbidding in appearance. **starkly** *adv.*

star-ling (stär´ling) *n.* A common black or brown bird.

star-tle (stär´tl) *v.* To cause a sudden surprise; to shock. **startle** *n.*

starve (stärv) *v.* To suffer or die from not having food; to suffer from the need of food, love, or other necessities.

state (stāt) *n.* A situation, mode, or condition of something; a nation; the governing power or authority of; one of the subdivisions or areas of a federal government, as the United States. *v.* To make known verbally.

stat-ic (stat´ik) *adj.* Not moving. *n.* A random noise heard on a radio.

sta-tion (stā´shan) *n.* The place where someone or something is directed to stand; a scheduled stopping place; the place from which radio and television programs are broadcast.

sta-tion-ar-y (stā´sha ner´ē) *adj.* Not movable; unchanging.

sta-tion-er-y (stā´sha ner´ē) *n.* Writing paper and envelopes.

sta-tis-tic (sta tis´tik) *n.* An estimate using an average or mean on the basis of a sample taken; numerical data.

stat ue (stach´ū) *n.* A form sculpted from wood, clay, metal, or stone.

stave (stāv) *n.* A narrow piece of wood used in forming part of a container, as a barrel. **stave** *v.*

stay (stā) *v.* To remain; to pause; to maintain a position, to halt or stop; to postpone or delay an execution. *n.* A short visit.

stead (stĕd) *n.* The position, place, or job of another.

stead-fast (stĕd´fast´) *adj.* Not changing or moving; firm in purpose; true; loyal. **steadfastly** *adv.* **-ness** *n.*

stead-y (stĕd´e) *adj.* Firmly placed, fixed or set; not changing; constant; uninterrupted.

steal (stēl) *v.* To take another person's property; to move in a sly way; to move secretly. *Baseball* To take a base without the ball being hit. *Slang* A real bargain.

steam (stēm) *n.* Water in the form of vapor; the visible mist into which vapor is condensed by cooling. **steam** *v.* **steamy** *adj.*

steel (stēl) *n.* A various mixture of iron, carbon, and other elements; a strong

material that can be shaped when heated. **steely** *adj.*

stem (stem) *n.* The main stalk of a plant; the main part of a word to which prefixes and suffixes may be added. *v.* To stop or retard the progress or flow of something.

sten-cil (sten´sil) *n.* A form cut into a sheet of material, as cardboard or plastic, so that when ink or paint is applied, the pattern will reproduce on paper or another material.

ste-nog-ra-phy (ste nog´ra fē) *n.* The skill of writing in shorthand. **stenographer** *n.* **stenographic** *adj.*

step (step) *n.* A single completed movement in walking, dancing, or running; the distance of such a step; the part of a ladder that one places the feet on in ascending or descending. *Music* A musical scale; a degree.

ste-re-o (ster´ē ō´) *n.* A record player with stereophonic sound. **stereo** *adj.*

ste-reo-phon-ic (ster´ē o fon´ik) *adj.* Relating to or giving a three-dimensional effect of auditory perspective.

ster-e-o-type (ster´ē o tīp´) *n.* A conventional opinion or belief; a metal printing plate.

ster-ile (ster´il) *adj.* Free from microorganisms; sanitary; unable to reproduce.

ster-ling (ster´ling) *n.* An alloy of 92.5% silver and another metal, as copper.

stern (stern) *adj.* Inflexible; harsh. *n.* The rear of a boat or ship. **-ly** *adv.*

ster-num (ster´num) *n. pl* **-nums** *or* **-na** A long, flat bone located in the chest wall, connecting the collarbones and the cartilage of the first seven pairs of ribs. **sternal** *adj.*

steth-o-scope (steth´o skōp´) *n.* An instrument used to listen to the internal sounds of the body.

stew (stōō) *v.* To cook slowly; to simmer; to boil. *n.* A dish of stewed meat and potatoes. *Slang* To worry.

stew-ard (stōō´erd) *n.* A manager of another's financial affairs; a person responsible for maintaining household affairs; a male attendant on an airplane or ship. **-ess** *n.* **-ship** *n.*

stick (stik) *n.* A slender piece of wood; a club, rod, or walking stick. *v.* To put a hole in something; to pierce; to cling; to become jammed.

stiff (stif) *adj.* Not flexible; not easily bent; awkward. *n. Slang* A dead body.

sti-fle (stī´fl) *v.* To suffocate; to cut off; to suppress; to keep back.

stig-ma (stig´ma) *n. pl.* **-mata** *or* **-mas** A mark of disgrace. **stigmata** The part of a flower where pollen is deposited at pollination; wounds resembling the crucifixion scars of Jesus Christ.

still (stil) *adj.* Silent; calm; peaceful; until

now or another time. *adv.* Nevertheless. **still** *v.* **stillness** *n.*

still-birth (stil´berth´) *n.* The birth of a dead fetus.

stilt (stilt) *n.* One of a pair of long poles with foot supports, used for walking.

stim-u-lant (stim´ū lant) *n.* An agent which arouses or accelerates physiological activity.

stim-u-late (stim´ū lāt´) *v.* To excite to a heightened activity; to quicken. **stimulation** *n.*

stim-u-lus (stim´ū lus) *n.* Something that excites to action.

sting (sting) *v.* To prick with something sharp; to feel or cause to feel a smarting pain; to cause or feel sharp pain, either physical or mental. *n.* The act of stinging; the injury or pain caused by the stinger of a bee or wasp. **-er** *n.*

stin-gy (stin´jē) *adj.* Not giving freely; cheap.

stink (stingk) *v.* To give off a foul odor that is highly offensive.

stip-u-late (stip´ū lāt´) *v.* To settle something by agreement; to establish conditions of agreement. **-tion** *n.*

stir (ster) *v.* To mix a substance by moving round and round; to agitate or provoke. **stirrer** *n.*

stitch (stich) *n.* In sewing, a single loop formed by a needle and thread; the section of loop of thread, as in sewing. *v.* To join with a stitch.

stock (stok) *n.* A supply of goods kept on hand; animals living on a farm; a share in ownership, as in a company or corporation; the raw material or the base used to make something. *v.* To provide with stock. *adj.* Regular, common, or typical.

stock-ade (sto kād´) *n.* Barrier placed around a fort for protection.

stock-ing (stok´ing) *n.* A knitted covering for the foot.

stock-y (stok´ē) *adj.* Short and plump; built sturdily.

stole (stōl) *n.* A long, narrow scarf that is usually worn around a woman's shoulders, as a mink stole. *v.* Past tense of steal.

stom-ach (stum´ak) *n., Anat.* The organ into which food passes from the esophagus; one of the primary organs of digestion. *v.* To tolerate or stand; to put up with.

stone (stōn) *n.* Rock; compacted earth or mineral matter; a gem or jewel; the seed or pit of certain fruits. *Med.* A hard rock that forms inside a body organ, as the kidney. **stoned** To be overcome by an excessive amount of alcohol or drugs.

stood *v.* Past tense of stand.

stool (stōl) *n.* A seat without a backrest and arms; a small version of this on which to rest the feet; a bowel movement.

stoop (stöp) *v.* To bend the body forward and downward from the waist. *n.* A porch attached to a house.

stop (stop) *v.* To cease; to halt; to refrain from moving, operating, or acting; to block or obstruct; to visit for a short time. *v.* A location where a bus, train, or other means of mass transportation may pick up or drop off passengers.

stor-age (stōr´ij) *n.* The act of storing or keeping; in *computer science*, the part of a computer in which all information is held; the memory.

store (stōr) *n.* A business offering merchandise for sale; a supply to be used in the future. *v.* To supply; to accumulate.

stork (stork) *n.* A large, wading bird.

storm (storm) *n.* An atmospheric condition marked by strong winds with rain, sleet, hail, or snow. **storm** *v.* To attack with a powerful force.

sto-ry (stōr´ē) *n. pl.* **-ies** A narration of a fictional tale or account; a lie; a level in a building or house.

stout (stout) *adj.* Strong; sturdy; substantial; courageous. **stoutly** *adv.*

stove (stōv) *n.* An apparatus in which oil, electricity, gas, or other fuels are consumed to provide the heat for cooking.

stow (stō) *v.* To pack or put away.

strad-dle (strad´l) *v.* To sit or stand with the legs on either side of something; to favor both sides of an issue.

straight (strāt) *adj.* Being without bends, angles, or curves; upright; erect; honest; undiluted; unmodified; heterosexual. *n.* In poker, a numerical sequence of five cards not of the same suit. **straightly** *adv.* **straightness** *n.*

strain (strān) *v.* To stretch beyond a proper limit; to injure by putting forth too much effort; to pass through a sieve to separate small particles from larger ones.

strait (strāt) *n.* A narrow passageway which connects two bodies of water.

strand (strand) *n.* Land that borders a body of water; one of the threads that are twisted together to form a rope. *v.* To leave in a difficult situation.

strange (strānj) *adj.* Not previously known or experienced; odd; peculiar; inexperienced; alien. **strangely** *adv.*

stran-ger (strān´jėr) *n.* A person unknown; unrecognized; a newcomer; an alien.

stran-gle (strang´gl) *v.* To kill by choking. **strangler** *n.*

strap (strap) *n.* A long, narrow strip of leather or other material used to secure objects. **strap** *v.*

strat-e-gy (strat´i jē) *n. pl.* **-ies** The

skillful planning and managing of an activity. **strategic** *adj.* **strategist** *n.*

stra-tum (strā´tum) *n. pl.* **-ta** *or* **-tums** A horizontal layer, as of the earth's crust.

straw (stro) *n.* A stalk of dried and threshed grain; a slender, plastic or paper straw used to suck up a liquid. **straw** *adj.* Yellowish brown color.

straw-ber-ry (stro´ber´ē) *n.* A low plant with white flowers and red fruit; the fruit of this plant.

stray (strā) *v.* To roam or wander. *n.* A lost or wandering animal or person. *adj.* Lost. **strayer** *n.*

streak (strēk) *n.* A narrow stripe or line that is different from the surrounding area; a run of good or bad luck. **streak** *v.* To rush or move rapidly; to make a streak.

stream (strēm) *n.* A small body of flowing water; a steady or continuous succession or procession. *v.* To flow in or like a stream.

street (strēt) *n.* A public thoroughfare in a town or city with buildings on either or both sides.

strength (strengkth) *n.* The quality of being strong; power in general; degree of concentration or potency.

strength-en (strengk´then) *v.* To grow strong or stronger.

stren-u-ous (stren´ū us) *adj.* Necessitating or characterized by vigorous effort or exertion. **strenuously** *adv.*

stress (stres) *n.* Special significance; an emphasis given to a specific syllable, word, action, or plan; strain or pressure.

stretch (strech) *v.* To extend fully; to extend forcibly beyond proper limits; to prolong. *n.* The state or act of stretching. **stretchable** *adj.* **-y** *adj.*

strew (strö) *v.* To scatter about.

strick-en (strik´en) *adj.* Suffering, as from an emotion, illness, or trouble.

strict (strikt) *adj.* Holding to or observing rules exactly; imposing absolute standards. **-ly** *adv.* **ness** *n.*

stride (strīd) *v.* To walk with a long, sweeping step. **stride** *n.*

strike *v.* To hit with the hand; to ignite, as with a match; to afflict suddenly with a disease; to discover; to conclude or make; to stop working as a protest against something or in favor of rules or demands presented to an employer.

string *n.* A strip of thin twine, wire, or catgut used on stringed musical instruments; a series of related acts, items, or events; in Computer Science, data arranged in an ascending or descending sequence according to a command within the data.

strin-gent (strin´jent) *adj.* Of or relating to strict requirements; marked by obstructions or scarcity.

strip *v.* To take off the outer layer or covering; to divest of rank; to remove one's clothes; to rob; to perform a striptease. **strip** *n.* **stripper** *n.*

stripe *n.* A streak, band, or strip of a different color or texture; a piece of material or cloth worn on the sleeve of a uniform to indicate rank, award, or service..

stroke (strōk) *n.* The movement of striking; a sudden action with a powerful effect; a single movement made by the hand or as if by a brush or pen. *Path.* A sudden interruption of the blood supply to the brain. *v.* To pass the hand over gently.

stroll (strōl) *v.* To walk in a slow, leisurely way. **stroll** *n.*

strong (strong) *adj.* Exerting or possessing physical power; durable; difficult to break. **strongly** *adv.*

stron-ti-um (stron´shē um) *n.* A metallic element symbolized by Sr.

struc-ture (struk´chér) *n.* A construction made up of a combination of related parts. **structure** *v.* **-ral** *adj.*

strug-gle (strug´l) *v.* To put forth effort against opposition. **struggle** *n.* **struggler** *n.* **strugglingly** *adv.*

strych-nine (strik´nin) *n.* An extremely poisonous alkaloid derived from certain plants, used to kill rodents and as a neural stimulant.

stub (stub) *n.* A short, projecting part; the short end of something after the main part has been removed or used. **stub** *v.*

stub-born (stub´érn) *adj.* Inflexible; difficult to control, handle, or manage. **stubbornness** *n.*

stuc-co (stuk´ō) *n. pl.* **-coes** *or* **-cos** Fine plaster used to coat exterior walls and to decorate interior walls.

stud (stud) *n.* An upright post, as in a building frame, to which sheets of wallboard or paneling are fastened; a small removable button used as an ornament; a male horse used for breeding. **stud** *v.*

stu-dent (stöd´ent) *n.* A person who studies at a school or college.

stu-di-o (stö´dē ō´) *n.* The place of work for an artist, photographer, or other creative person; a place for filming movies.

stud-y (stud´ē) *n. pl.* **-ies** The process of ap-plying the mind to acquire knowledge.

stum-ble (stum´bl) *v.* To trip and nearly fall over something; to come upon unexpectedly. **stumble** *n.*

stump (stump) *n.* The part of a tree which remains after the top is cut down. *v.* To puzzle or be puzzled; to walk heavily; to campaign.

stun (stun) *v.* To render senseless by or

as if by a blow.

stu-pen-dous (stō pen´dus) *adj.* Astonishing or highly impressive. **stupendousness** *n.* **stupendously** *adv.*

stu-pid (stō´pid) *adj.* Slow in apprehension or understanding. **-ity** *n.*

stur-dy (ster´dē) *adj.* Possessing robust strength and health. **sturdily** *adv.* **sturdiness** *n.*

stur-geon (ster´jen) *n.* A large freshwater fish highly valued as a source of caviar.

stut-ter (stut´ér) *v.* To speak with involuntary repetitions of sound.

sty (stī) *n. pl.* **sties** An inflammation of the edge of an eyelid.

style (stīl) *n.* A method, manner, or way of performing, speaking, or clothing; elegance, grace, or excellence in performance or appearance.

suave (swäv) *adj.* Ingratiating; smoothly pleasant in manner.

sub- (sub) *prefix.* Beneath, under, or below.

sub (sub) *abbr.* Substitute.

sub-con-scious (sub kon´shus) *adj.* Below the level of consciousness.

sub-due (sub dö´) *v.* To bring under control by influence, training, persuasion or force.

sub-ject (sub´jikt) *n.* The word in a sentence that defines a person or thing; a person who is under the control of another's governing power. *v.* To subdue or gain control over.

sub-jec-tive (sub jek´tiv) *adj.* Taking place within, relating to or proceeding from an individual's emotions or mind. **-ly** *adv.* **-tivity** *n.*

sub-ma-rine (sub´ma rēn´) *adj.* Operating or existing beneath the surface of the sea. *n.* A ship that travels underwater. **submariner** *n.*

sub-merge (sub merj´) *v.* To plunge under the surface of the water. **submergible** *adj.* **submergence** *n.*

sub-mit (sub mit´) *v.* To give in to or surrender to another's authority. **submission** *n.* **submittal** *n.*.

sub-or-di-nate (su bor´di nit) *adj.* Being of lower class or rank; minor; inferior. **subordinate** *v.* **-nation** *n.*

sub-poe-na (su pē´na) *n.* A legal document requiring a person to appear in court for testimony.

sub-se-quent (sub´se kwent) *adj.* Following in time, place, or order. **subsequently** *adv.*

sub-side (sub sīd´) *v.* To move to a lower level; to become less intense.

sub-sid-i-ar-y (sub sid´ē er´ē) *adj.* Providing assistance in a lesser capacity. **subsidiary** *n.*

sub-si-dy (sub´si dē) *n., pl.* **-dies** Financial aid granted directly to a private commercial enterprise from the government.

sub-sist (sub sist´) *v.* To have continued existence.

sub-soil (sub´soil) *n.* The layer of earth that is below the surface soil.

sub-stance (sub´stans) *n.* Matter or material of which anything consists.

sub-sti-tute (sub´sti töt´) *n.* Something or someone that takes the place of another. **substitute** *v.*

sub-ten-ant (sub ten´ant) *n.* A person who rents property from a tenant.

sub-ter-ra-ne-an (sub´te rā´nē an) *adj.* Located or occurring underground.

sub-ti-tle (sub´tīt´l) *n.* An explanatory title, as in a document, book, etc.; a written translation that appears on a foreign motion picture screen.

sub-tract (sub trakt´) *v.* To deduct or take away from.

sub-trop-i-cal (sub trop´i kal) *adj.* Pertaining to regions adjacent to the tropics.

sub-urb (sub´erb) *n.* A residential community near a large city.

sub-way *n.* An underground electric-powered train, usually used as a means of transportation.

suc-ceed (suk sēd´) *v.* To accomplish what is attempted; to come next or to follow.

suc-cess (suk ses´) *n.* Achievement of something intended or desired; attaining wealth, fame, or prosperity.

suc-ces-sion (suk sesh´an) *n.* The act or process of following in order; sequence; series; the order, sequence, or act by which something changes hands.

suc-ces-sive (suk ses´iv) *adj.* Following in order or sequence. **successively** *adv.* **successiveness** *n.*

suc-cu-lent (suk´u lent) *adj.* Juicy; full of juice or sap. **succulence** *n.* .

such (such) *adj.* Of this or that kind or thing; a great degree or extent in quality. *pron.* Of a particular degree or kind; a person or thing of such.

suck (suk) *v.* To pull liquid into the mouth by means of a vacuum created by the lips and tongue. **suck** *n.*

su-crose (sö´krōs) *n.* Sugar obtained from the sugar beet or sugar cane.

suc-tion (suk´shan) *n.* The process or act of sucking.

sud-den (sud´en) *adj.* Happening very quickly; most often without warning or notice; sharp; abrupt; marked by haste. **suddenly** *adv.* **suddenness** *n.*

suds *n.* Bubbles or soapy water. *Slang* Beer.

suede (swād) *n.* Leather with a soft, napped finish.

su-et (sö´it) *n.* The hard fat around the kidney and loins of sheep.

suf-fer (suf´ér) *v.* To feel pain or distress; to sustain injury or damage.

suf-fi-cient (su fish´ent) *adj.* As much

as is needed or desired. **-ciency** *n.*

suf-fix (suf'iks) *n.* A form affixed to the end of a word.

suf-fo-cate (suf'o kāt') *v.* To kill by depriving something or someone of oxygen. **suffocation** *n.*

sugar (sheg'ẽr) *n.* A sweet, water soluble, crystalline carbohydrate.

sug-gest (sug jest') *v.* To give an idea for action or consideration; to imply; hint or intimate.

sug-ges-tion (sug jes'chan) *n.* The act of suggesting; a slight insinuation; hint.

su-i-cide (sō'i sid') *n.* The act of taking one's own life. **suicidal** *adj.*

suit (sōt) *n.* A set of articles, as clothing, to be worn together; in cards, one of the four sets: spades, hearts, clubs, and diamonds, that make up a deck. **suit** *v.* To meet the requirements of; to satisfy.

sul-fur *also* **sul-phur** (sul'fẽr) *n.* A light, yellow, nonmetallic element occurring naturally in both combined and free form, used in matches, gunpowder and medicines.

sulk (sulk) *v.* To be sullenly silent.

sul-len (sul'en) *adj.* Ill-humored, melancholy; gloomy; depressing.

sul-try (sul'trē) *adj.* Hot and humid; muggy.

sum (sum) *n.* The result obtained by adding; the whole amount, quantity, or number; summary.

sum-ma-ry (sum'a rē) *n. pl.* **summaries.** Giving the sum or substance. *adj.* A statement covering the most important points or topics. **summarily** *adv.*

sum-mer (sum'ẽr) *n.* The warmest of the four seasons, following spring and coming before autumn. **summery** *adj.*

sum-mit (sum'it) *n.* The top and highest point, degree, or level.

sum-mons (sum'onz) *n., pl.* **summonses** An order or command to perform a duty; a notice to appear at a certain place and time.

sun (sun) *n.* The star around which other planets of the solar system orbit; the energy, visible light, and heat, that is emitted by the sun.

Sun-day *n.* The Christian holy day; the first day of the week.

sun-down (sun'doun') *n.* The time of day the sun sets.

sunk-en (sung'ken) *adj.* Submerged or deeply depressed in.

su-per (sō'pẽr) *adj.* Exceeding a norm; in excessive intensity or degree; surpassing most others; superior in rank, status or position; excellent. *n., Slang* Superintendent of a building.

su-perb (se perb') *adj.* Of first-rate quality. **superbly** *adv.*

su-per-fi-cial (sō'pẽr fish'al) *adj.* Pertaining to a surface; concerned only

with what is not real.

su-pe-ri-or (su pēr'ē ẽr) *adj.* Of higher rank, grade, or dignity. *n.* A person who surpasses another in rank or excellence. **superiority** *n.* **superiorly** *adv.*

su-per-la-tive (su per'la tiv) *adj.* Of the highest degree of excellence; pertaining to the degree of comparison of an adverb or adjective that shows extreme extent or level. **superlatively** *adv.*

su-per-nat-u-ral *adj.* An order of existence beyond the natural world; pertaining to a divine power.

su-per-sede (sō'pẽr sēd') *v.* To take the place of; to set aside.

su-per-son-ic (sō'pẽr son'ik) *adj., Aero.* Characterized by a speed greater than that of sound.

su-per-sti-tion (sō'pẽr stish'an) *n.* A belief held, despite evidence that it is irrational; a belief, resulting from faith in magic or chance. **superstitious** *adj.*

su-per-vise (sō'pẽr vīz') *v.* To have charge in directing the work of other people. **supervision** *n.* **supervisor** *n.*

sup-per (sup'ẽr) *n.* The last or evening meal of the day.

sup-ple-ment (sup'le ment) *n.* A part that compensates for what is lacking. **supplementary** *adj.* **-al** *adj.*

sup-ply (su plī') *v., n. pl.* **-plies** To provide with what is needed; to make available. **supplier** *n.*

sup-port (su pōrt') *v.* To bear or hold the weight of; to tolerate; to give assistance or approval. *n.* The act of supporting. **supportive** *adj.*

sup-pose (su pōz') *v.* To think or assume as true; to consider probable. **supposed** *adj.* **supposedly** *adv.*

sup-pos-i-to-ry (su poz'i tōr'ō) *n. pl.* **-ries** A medication, in solid form, that melts when inserted into the body cavity, as the rectum.

su-preme (su prēm') *adj.* Of the highest authority, rank, or power.

sur-charge (ser'chärj') *n.* An extra fee added to the cost of something; to overcharge.

sure (sher) *adj.* Firm and sturdy; being impossible to doubt; inevitable; not liable to fail. **surer** *adj.* **surest** *adj.*

surge (serj) *v.* To increase suddenly. *n.* A large swell of water. In Computer Science, an increase in electrical current that may damage the computer or its memory.

sur-geon (ser'jon) *n.* A physician who practices surgery.

sur-ger-y (ser'je rē) *n. pl.* **-ies.** The branch of medicine in which physical deformity or disease is treated by an operative procedure.

surge suppresser In *computer science*, a device that protects the computer and peripherals from power surges.

sur-mise (sėr mīz´) v. To guess; to conjecture.

sur-mount (sėr mount´) v. To overcome; to be at the top.

sur-name (ser´nām´) n. A person's family's last name.

sur-pass (sėr pas´) v. To go beyond the limits of; to be greater than.

sur-plus (ser´plus) n. An amount beyond what is needed.

sur-prise (sėr prīz´) v. To come upon unexpectedly or suddenly; to cause to feel astonished. **surprise** n. **sur-priser** n. **surprisingly** adv.

sur-ren-der (su ren´dėr) v. To give up or yield possession or power. n. The act of surrendering.

sur-rey (ser´ē) n. pl. -reys. A four-wheeled, horse-driven carriage.

sur-ro-gate (ser´o gāt) n. A person who puts himself in the place of another.

sur-round (su round´) v. To extend around all edges of something; to enclose or shut in.

sur-veil-lance (sėr vā´lans) n. Close observation kept over one, especially as a suspect.

sur-vey (sėr vā´) v., n. pl. -veys. To examine in detail; to determine area, boundaries, or position and elevation of a section of the earth's surface.

sur-vive (sėr vīv´) v. To continue to exist; to outlast; to outlive. -al n.

su-shi n. A Japanese dish of thin slices of fresh, raw fish.

sus-pect (su spekt´) v. To have doubt or dis-trust; to have a suspicion or inkling of someone or something. **suspect** n.

sus-pend (su spend´) v. To bar from a privilege for a certain time, as a means of punishment; to hang so as to allow free movement.

sus-pense (su spens´) n. The feeling of being insecure or undecided, resulting from uncertainty.

sus-pi-cion (su spish´an) n. The instance of suspecting something wrong without proof. **suspicious** adj. -**ciously** adv.

sus-tain (su stān´) v. To hold up and keep from falling; to suffer or undergo an injury.

su-ture (sö´chėr) n. The stitching together or joining the edges of an incision or cut. **suture** v.

swab (swäb) n. A small stick with a wad of cotton on both ends, used to apply medication. Slang A sailor.

swad-dle (swäd´l) v. To wrap closely, using a long strip of flannel or linen.

swal-low (swäl´ō) v. To cause food to pass from the mouth to the stomach; to retract or take back, as words spoken. n. The act of swallowing.

swap (swäp) v. To trade something for something in return. **swap** n.

swarm (sworm) n. A large number of insects, as bees; a large group of persons or things. **swarmer** n.

swat (swät) v. To hit something with a sharp blow.

swatch (swäch) n. A strip of cloth cut off a larger piece, used as a sample.

swath (swoth) n. The area or width of grass cut by a machine. **swathe** v.

sway (swā) v. To move or swing from right to left or side to side; to exert influence or control. n. Dominating power.

swear (swâr) v. To make an affirmation under oath. **swearer** n.

sweat (swet) v. To excrete a salty moisture from the pores of the skin. Informal To work hard; to cause to sweat. Slang Being impatient; having anxiety.

sweat gland n., Anat. One of the tubular glands that secrete sweat externally through pores.

sweep (swēp) v. To touch lightly; to remove or clear away with a brush or broom; to move with an even action.

sweet (swēt) adj. Having a sugary, agreeable flavor; arousing pleasant emotions; a beloved or dear person.

swell (swel) v. To increase in size or bulk; to grow in volume. n. The process, effect, or act of swelling; a continuous wave that is long and billowing. Informal Fine; smart.

swel-ter (swel´tėr) v. To suffer from extreme heat.

swerve (swerv) v. To turn aside from the regular course.

swift (swift) adj. Moving with great speed; accomplished or occurring quickly. **swiftly** adv. **swiftness** n.

swim (swim) v. To move oneself through water by moving parts of the body, as arms, head, and legs.

swin-dle (swin´dl) v. To cheat out of property or money; to practice fraud. **swindle** n. **swindler** n.

swine (swīn) n. pl. **swine** A hoofed mammal with a snout, related to pigs and hogs; a low, despicable person.

swing (swing) v. To move freely back and forth; to hang or to be suspended. n. The act of a swing; a seat that hangs from chains or ropes. Music Jazz played by a large band and developed by using simple harmonic patterns. **swinger** n.

swirl (swerl) v. To move with a whirling, rotating motion. **swirly** adj.

switch (swich) n. A small, thin, flexible stick, twig or rod. Electr. A device for opening or closing an electric circuit; to shift to another train track by using a switch; to exchange.

swiv-el (swiv´el) n. A coupling device, ring, or pivot that allows attached parts to move freely. **swivel** v.

sword (sōrd) *n.* A weapon with a long, pointed cutting blade.

syc-a-more (sik´a mōr´) *n.* A North American tree that is used widely for shade.

sy-cee *n.* The silver money which was once used in China.

sy-co-ni-um *n.* A type of fleshy fruit where the ovaries are borne in an enlarged receptacle.

sy-co-phan-cy *n.* The behavior of a sycophant.

sy-co-phant *n.* A self-seeking flatterer.

sy-co-phan-tic *adj.* Pertaining to a sycophant. **sycophantically** *adv.*

sy-co-sis *n.* An inflammatory disorder of the hair follicles.

syl-la-bar-y *n.* A listing of syllables.

syl-lab-ic *adj.* Pertaining to or denoting syllables.

syl-la-bic-i-ty *n.* The state of being a syllable.

syl-la-ble (sil´a bl) *n., Phonet.* A word or part of one that consists of a single vocal impulse, usually consisting of one or more vowels or consonants.

syl-la-bub *n.* A type of desert that is made by curdling milk with an acid such as wine.

syl-la-bus *n.* An outline of a course of study.

syl-lo-gism (sil´o jiz´um) *n.* An argument with a major premise, a minor premise and a conclusion that is logically drawn from the premises. **syllogistic** *adj.*

syl-lo-gist *n.* A person who applies syllogistic reasoning.

sylph *n.* A slender woman who is very graceful. **sylphlike** *adj.*

sylph-id *n.* A diminutive sylph.

syl-van *adj.* To be living or located in the woods.

syl-va-nite *n.* A kind of mineral which will often occur in crystals.

sym-bi-ont *n.* An organism that is living in symbiosis.

sym-bi-o-sis *n.* A living together in close union of two dissimilar organisms.

sym-bol (sim´bol) *n.* Something that stands for or represents something else. **symbolic** *adj.* **symbolical** *adj.*

sym-bol-ism *n.* The practice of using symbols.

sym-bol-ist *n.* A person who is skilled in the interpretation of symbols.

sym-bol-iz-a-tion *n.* An instance of symbolizing.

sym-bol-ize *v.* To serve as a symbol of or for something.

sym-bol-o-gy *n.* The interpretation of a symbol or symbols.

sym-met-ri-cal *adj.* Involving symmetry. **symmetricalness** *n.*

sym-me-trize *v.* To make something symmetrical in form or size.

sym-me-try (sim´i trē) *n. pl.* -tries

Balance in form, size, and position of parts that are on two sides of an axis.

sym-pa-thet-ic (sim´pa thet´ik) *adj.* Having or showing kindness or sympathy for others. **sympathetically** *adv.* **sympathize** *v.*

sympathetic nervous system *n.* Part of the body's nervous system which when stimulated will decrease muscle tone and constriction of the blood vessels and will depress secretions.

sympathetic vibration *n.* The vibration which is produced in a body by another body.

sym-pa-thin *n.* The substance which is produced by the sympathetic nerve endings in the body.

sym-pa-thize *v.* To respond to someone or something with sympathy.

sym-pa-tho-lyt-ic *adj.* To be tending to oppose physiological results of the sympathetic nervous activity.

sym-pa-tho-mi-met-ic *adj.* To be able to simulate the sympathetic nervous system in effect and action.

sym-pa-thy (sim´pa thē) *n. pl.* -thies Mutual understanding or affection during a time of sadness or loss.

sym-pat-ric (sim pa´trik) *adj.* To be happening or occurring in the same area.

symphonic poem *n.* An extended composition for a symphony orchestra in a freer form than a symphony.

sym-pho-ni-ous (sim fō´nē us) *adj.* To be agreeing such as in sound.

sym-pho-nist *n.* One who composes or writes symphonies.

sym-pho-ny (sim´fo nē) *n., pl.* -nies A large orchestra with wind, percussion and string sections. -nic *adj.*

sym-phy-se-al *adj.* Pertaining to or related to a symphysis.

sym-po-di-al *adj.* To be involving the formation of a main axis from a secondary axis. **sympodially** *adv.*

sym-po-si-arch *n.* The person who will preside over a symposium.

sym-po-si-um *n.* A gathering or meeting where several specialists will give short speeches on a topic or on subjects which are related.

symp-tom (simp´tom) *n.* A sign of change in a body's functions or appearance.

symp-tom-at-ic *adj.* To be having the characteristics of a particular disease but arising from something else.

symp-tom-at-ol-ogy *n.* The part of medical science that deals with symptoms of a disease or diseases.

syn *abbr.* Synonymous; synonym.

syn-aes-the-sis *n.* The harmony of opposing impulses which are produced by a piece of art.

syn-a-gogue (sin´a gog´) *n.* A place for

Jewish worship and prayer.

syn-a-loe-pha (sin″a lē′fa) n. A reduction to one syllable of two vowels of syllables which are adjacent.

syn-apse (sin′aps) n. A point where a nervous impulse passes from one neuron to the next neuron.

syn-ar-thro-di-al adj. Pertaining to or related to a synarthrosis.

syn-ar-thro-sis (sin″är thrō′sis) n. A joining of bones that is immovable and is united by fibrous connective tissues.

syn-car-pous adj. To have the carpels of gynoecium to unite in a compound ovary.

syn-chro-mesh adj. To be designed for effecting synchronized gear shifting.

syn-chro-nism(sing′kro niz″um)n. The state of being synchronous.

syn-chro-ni-za-tion (sing″kro ni zā′shan) n. A result of synchronizing.

syn-chro-nize (sing′kro nīz′) v. To take place at the same time.

syn-chro-nous adj. To be existing at precisely the same time.

syn-chro-ny n. A synchronistic treatment or occurrence.

syn-cli-nal adj. Inclined down from opposite directions then meeting.

syn-co-pate (sing′ko pāt′) v. To produce by a synscope. **syncopator** n.

syn-co-pated (sing′kopā′tid) adj. To be exhibiting syncopation.

syn-cret-ism n. A combination of different beliefs or practices.

syn-cy-ti-um n. The multinucleate mass made of protoplasm which is formed from the fusion or the joining of cells.

syn-det-ic adj. To be marked by a conjunctive. **syndetically** adv.

syn-dic n. A type of municipal magistrate in other countries.

syn-di-cate (sin′di kit) n. An organization set up to carry out business transactions; a company that sells materials for simultaneous publication at several of different locations.

syn-drome (sin′drōm) n. A set of concurrent symptoms that indicate or characterize a disorder or disease.

syn-e-col-o-gy n. A section or branch of ecology which deals with the development, structure, and distribution of ecological communities.

syn-eph-rine n. A type of crystalline sympathomimetic amine.

syn-er-gism n. Cooperative action of independent units that improves the total results. **synergistic** adj.

syn-er-gy n. Combined action.

syn-o-nym (sin′o nim) n. A word that means the same or nearly the same as another. **synonymous** adj.

syn-op-sis (si nop′sis) n. pl. -ses A shortened statement or narrative.

syn-os-to-sis n. The joining or the union of bones which are separate to form a single bone.

sy-no-vi-al (si nō′vē a) adj. Pertaining to or relating to synovia, a lubricating substance that resembles the white of a egg.

sy-no-vi-tis (sin″ovī′tis) n. The inflammation or the swelling of a synovial membrane.

syn-tax (sin′taks) n. The way in which words are put together or arranged to form sentences and phrases. **syntactic** adj. **syntactical** adj.

syn-the-sis (sin′thi sis) n., pl. A production of a substance by the joining of chemical elements.

syn-the-size v. To produce or to make with synthesis.

syn-thet-ic adj. To be involving synthesis. **synthetically** adv.

syph-i-lis (sif′i lis) n. An infectious venereal disease transmittable by direct contact and usually progressing in severity.

syph-i-lol-o-gist n. One who specializes in the treatment and the diagnosis of syphilis.

syph-i-lol-o-gy n. Med. The study and treatment of the disease syphilis.

sy-ringe (si rinj′) n. A medical instrument used to inject or draw fluids from the body. **syringe** v.

sy-rin-go-my-el-ia n. A progressive chronic disease of the spinal cord associated with muscle atrophy, spasticity, and sensory disturbances.

syr-up (sir′up) n. A thick, sweet liquid, used as a topping for food.

sys-tal-tic (si stol′tik) adj. To be marked by regular dilatation and contraction.

sys-tem (sis′tem) n. A planned method of doing something; the human body or related parts of the body that perform vital functions; an orderly arrangement. **systematic** adj. **systematically** adv.

system backup n. In computer science, a reserved copy of all of the program and data files in a computer; a second set of hardware that can replace the primary hardware in the event of equipment failure.

system resources n. In computer science, all of the elements unique to a particular computer system, as peripheral devices, type of CPU, memory, etc.

system software n. In computer science, the programs that control the operation of the computer and its peripherals.

sys-to-le (sis′to lē′) n. Physiol. The regular rhythmic contraction of the heart that pumps blood through the aorta and pulmonary artery.

sy-zy-gy n. A configuration of three celestial bodies in one gravitational system such as the moon, the sun, and earth when an eclipse is taking place.

T, t (tē) The twentieth letter of the English alphabet.

tab (tab) *n.* A strip, flap, or small loop that projects from something. *Slang* A bill or total, as for a meal. In computer science, a tabulator; a user-defined position on a text line to which the cursor can be advanced with a single key stroke; to move by activating the *tab* key.

tab-ard (tabĕrd) *n.* A type of sleeveless coat that is worn as a tunic by a knight over the top the armor.

tab-by (tab´ē) *n.* A type of domestic cat that has a coat which is mottled and striped.

tab-er-na-cle (tab´ĕr nak´l) *n.* A portable shelter or structure used by the Jews during their journey out of Egypt; a place of worship.

ta-bes (tāb´bēz) *n.* The wasting that comes with or is accompanying a chronic disease.

tabes forsalis *n.* A type of syphilitic disorder that affects the nervous system and is marked with wasting, incoordination, and pain.

ta-bla (tab´la) *n.* A type of drum which is usually used in pairs of different sizes in the Hindu music.

ta-ble (tā´bl) *n.* An article of furniture having a flat top, supported by legs; a collection of related signs, values, or items. **table** *v.* To put off or postpone the discussion of something until another time.

tab-leau (tab´lō) *n. pl.* **tableaux** *or* **tableaus** A vivid representation; a stage scene rep-resented by motionless and silent people who stand in an appropriate arrangement.

ta-ble-land *n.* An area of land which is flat and is elevated, such as a table.

tab let (tab´lit) *n.* A pad used for writing; a thin, flat piece of stone or wood which is fit for or has an inscription.

table tennis *n.* A type of game that is like lawn tennis and is played on a table top with a plastic ball and wooden paddles.

ta-ble-top (tā´bl top´) *n.* A top of a table.

ta-ble-ware (tā´bl wār´) *n.* The utensils such as forks, knives, and plates that are used on the table to eat food with.

table wine *n.* A type of wine that is served with the food and does not have more that 14 percent alcohol.

tab-loid (tab´loid) *n.* A small newspaper with news reported by means of pictures and concise reporting.

ta-boo (ta bō´) *n.* A custom or rule against doing, using, or mentioning something. *adj.* Forbidden by social authority, convention, or custom.

ta-bor (tā´bĕr) *n.* A type of small drum that has one head made of calf skin.

tab-o-ret (tab´rit) *n.* A type of cylindrical seat that is without a back or arms.

tab-u-lar (tab´ū lĕr) *adj.* Pertaining to or arranged in a table or list. **-ly** *adv.*

tabula rasa *n.* A person's mind in its hypothetical empty state before receiving an impression from the outside.

tab-u-late (tab´ū lāt´) *v.* To put something in a tabular form. **tabulation** *n.*

tab-u-la-tor (tab´ū lā´tĕr) *n.* Something or someone that tabulates.

ta-chom-e-ter (ta kom´i tĕr) *n.* An instrument for measuring velocity and speed.

tach-y-car-dia (tak´i kär´dē a) *n.* A rapid heart beat.

tach-y-lyte (tak´i līt´) *n.* A type of black basalt, glossy in appearance.

ta-chym-e-ter (ta kim´i tĕ) *n.* A device that is used to determine bearings or distances quickly.

tac-it (tas´it) *adj.* Understood; expressed or implied nonverbally; implicit. **tacitly** *adv.* **tacitness** *n.*

tac-i-turn *adj.* To be temperamentally disinclined to speak or talk.

tack (tak) *n.* A small, short nail with a flat head; a sewing stitch used to hold something temporarily; the changing of a sailboat from one direction to another. *v.* To attach or fasten with tacks; to change the direction in which a sailboat is going. **tacker** *n.*

tack-board *n.* A type of board that can be made of cork and used for the purpose of tacking notices up.

tack claw *n.* A small tool used to remove tacks.

tack-i-fy *v.* To cause or to make something tacky. **tackifier** *n.*

tack-ily *adv.* To be done in a tacky manner.

tack-i-ness *n.* The state of being tacky.

tack-le (ta´kl) *n.* Equipment used for fishing or other sports or occupations; an apparatus of ropes and pulley blocks for pulling and hoisting heavy loads; in football, a position on a football team; the lineman between the guard and end. **tackle** *v.* **tackler** *n.*

tack-y (tak´ē) *adj.* Slightly sticky; shabby; lacking style or good taste; flashy.

ta-co (tä´kō) *n., pl.* **-cos** A type of Mexican or Spanish food made of a tortilla folded over with a filling inside.

tac-o-nite *n.* A type of flint-like rock which can be considered a low-grade iron ore.

tact (takt) *n.* Having the ability to avoid what would disturb or offend someone. **tactful** *adj.* **tactfully** *adv.* **-fulness** *n.*

tac-tic (tak´tik) *n.* A way or method of working toward a goal; the art of using strategy to gain military objectives or other goals. **tactical** *adj.* **tactician** *n.*

tac-tics (tak´tiks) *n., pl.* The art of maneuvering forces in combat or war.

tac-til-i-ty *n.* The responsiveness of someone or something to stimulation of the sense of touch. **tactile** *adj.*

tact-less *adj.* To be marked by a lack of tact. **tactlessness** *n.* **tactlessly** *adv.*

tad (tad) *n.* A small boy; an insignificant degree or amount.

tad-pole (tad´pōl´) *n.* The early stage in the growth of a frog or toad during which it breathes by external gills, has a long tail, and lives in the water; a polliwog.

tae-ni-a-sis *n.* A type of disease that can be caused by tapeworms.

taf-fe-ta (taf´i ta) *n.* A stiff, smooth fabric of rayon, nylon, or silk.

taf-fe-tized *adj.* To have a finish that is crisp in nature.

taff-rail (taf´rāl´) *n.* The rail around the stern of a boat or ship.

taf-fy (taf´ē) *n.* A type of candy which is boiled and is made of brown sugar and is pulled until it becomes porous.

taf-i-a (taf´ē a) *n.* A type of rum of West India that is made from distilled sugar cane juice.

Taft, William Howard *n.* (1857-1930) The twenty-seventh president of the United States from 1909-1913.

tag (tag) *n.* A piece of plastic, metal, paper, or other material that is attached to something in order to identify it; a children's game in which one child is "it" and tries to catch another child, who then becomes "it." **tagger** *n.*

tag-along *n.* The person that follows the lead of another person.

tag-board *n.* A type of cardboard that is used for the making of shipping tags.

tag end *n.* A random bit.

tag up *v.* To touch the base one is occupying in the game of baseball before advancing after a fly ball is caught.

tah-sil-dar (ta sēl där´) *n.* One who is a revenue officer in the country of India.

tai-ga *n.* The moist subarctic forest which begins where the tundra ends and contains firs and spruces.

tail (tāl) *n.* The posterior extremity, extending from the end or back of an animal. **tails** *n., pl.* The opposite side of a coin from heads; formal evening dress for men. **tail** *v.* To follow or keep close watch on someone; to connect end to end.

tail-gate (tāl´gāt´) *n.* The hinged gate at the back of a truck or automobile for loading and unloading. *v.* To follow very closely in a car.

taille (tāl) *n.* A type of tax that was levied by a French king on his subjects or the land that they held in their possession.

tai-lor (tā´lēr) *n.* One whose profession is making, mending, and altering clothing. **tailor** *v.* To adapt for a specific purpose.

tai-lored (tā´lērd) *adj.* Made by a tailor.

tail-or-ing (tā´lēr ing) *n.* The occupation of a tailor.

tail-spin (tāl´spin´) *n.* An emotional collapse.

taint (tānt) *v.* To spoil, contaminate, or pollute. *n.* A blemish or stain.

take (tāk) *v.* To seize or capture; to get possession of; to receive, swallow, absorb, or accept willingly; to attack and surmount; to move, convey, or conduct to a different place; to require; to choose or pick. *Slang* To cheat; to subtract. **take** *n.* The process of acquiring; the total receipts for admission at an event.

take back *v.* To make or state a retraction of something such as a statement.

take in *v.* To receive as a lodger; to encompass something within the limits of some-thing else.

take on *v.* To deal with something or someone.

talc (talk) *n.* A soft, fine-grained, smooth mineral used in making talcum powder.

talcum powder *n.* A type of powder that is made of talc and an antiseptic.

tale (tāl) *n.* A story or recital of relating events that may or may not be true; a malicious or false story; gossip.

tal-ent (tal´ent) *n.* The aptitude, disposition, or characteristic ability of a person. **talented** *adj.*

talent scout *n.* A person who discovers and recruits people with talent for a specialized activity or field.

ta-ler *n.* A silver coin which was issued by German states in the 15th to the 19th centuries.

talk (tok) *v.* To communicate by words or speech; to engage in chatter or gossip. **talk** *n.* A speech or lecture, usually given to a group of people. *Slang* To boast; to brag. **talker**, **talkativeness** *n.* **talkative** *adj.*

talk-y (to´kē) *adj.* To be containing or having too much talk in something.

tall (tol) *adj.* Of greater than average height; of a designated or specified height; imaginary, as a tall tale.

tal-lage (tal´ij) *n.* A fee that is paid a lord for his feudal tenant.

tall-boy (tol´boi´) *n.* A type of chest of drawers where the top section is smaller than the lower section.

tal-low (tal´ō) *n.* Hard fat rendered from sheep or cattle, used to make candles, lubricants, and soap. **tallow** *adj.*

tal-ly (tal´ē) *n., pl.* **tallies** A record or counting of money, amounts, or scores. **tally** *v.* To agree with; to reckon or a score; to count.

tal-ly-man (tal´ē man) *n.* The person who checks or has a record of counting.

tal-on (tal´on) *n.* A long, curved claw found on birds or animals, used to kill or capture prey. **taloned** *adj.*

ta-lus *n.* The slope which is formed by the gathering or accumulation of rock debris.

ta-ma-le (ta mä´lē) *n.* The meat that is seasoned with chili and then is rolled into a cornmeal dough and is steamed.

tam-bour (tam´būr) *n.* A type of frame that can be used for the purpose of embroidering.

tam-bou-rine (tam´bo rēn´) *n.* A percussion instrument made of a small drum with jingling metal disks around the rim.

tame (tām) *adj.* Not wild or ferocious; domesticated or manageable. **tame** *v.* To make docile or calm. **tamely** *adv.* **tamer** *n.* **tameness** *n.*

tame-less (tām´lis) *adj.* Being unable to be tamed.

tam-per (tam´pèr) *v.* To change, meddle, or alter something; to use corrupt measures to scheme. **tamperproof** *adj.*

tan (tan) *v.* To cure a hide into leather by using chemicals. *Slang* To spank a child. **tan** *n.* A brownish skin tone caused by exposure to the sun.

tan-a-ger *n.* A type of American passerine bird which can be found in the woodlands.

tan-bark *n.* A type of bark that is rich in tannin and is used in the tanning process.

tan-dem (tan´dem) *n.* Any arrangement that involves two or more things, animals or persons arranged one behind the other.

tang (tang) *n.* A sharp, distinct taste, smell, or quality; a slender shank that projects from a tool and connects to a handle.

tan-ge-lo *n.* The hybrid that is between a tangerine and a pomelo or grapefruit.

tan-gent (tan´jent) *n.* A line that touches a curved line but does not intersect or cross it; a sudden change from one course to another. **tangency** *n.*

tan-ger-ine (tan´je rēn) *n.* A small citrus fruit with an easily peeled orange skin, resembling an orange.

tan-gi-ble (tan´ji bl) *adj.* Capable of being appreciated or felt by the sense of touch; capable of being realized. **tangibleness, tangibility** *n.*

tan-gle (tang´gl) *v.* To mix, twist, or unite in a confused manner making separation difficult. **tanglement** *n.*

tangled *adj.* To be in a state of disorder. **tangly** *adj.* To be full of tangles.

tan-go (tang´gō) *n.* A ballroom dance with long, gliding steps. **tango** *v.*

tan-gram *n.* A type of Chinese puzzle that is made by cutting a square of material into different shapes, such as five triangles, a rhomboid, and a square and they are able to be combined in different figures.

tank (tangk) *n.* A large container for holding or storing a gas or liquid. .

tankage *n.* The contents of a tank.

tan-nage (tan´ij) *n.* A process of tanning something.

tan-nery *n.* The place where tanning is done.

tan-ning (tan´ing) *n.* The browning of the skin with an exposure to the sun.

tan oak *n.* A type of evergreen oak that will yield tan bark.

tan-tal-ic (tan tal´ik) *adj.* To be pertaining to tantalum.

tan-ta-lite (tan´ta lit´) *n.* The mineral that is made of dark oxide of iron, tantalum, manganise, and columbium.

tan-ta-lize (tan´ ta liz´) *v.* To tease or tempt by holding or keeping something just out of one's reach. **-ingly** *adv.*

tan-ta-liz-ing (tan´tu līz´) *adj.* To have a quality that stimulates an interest.

tan-ta-lum (tan´ta lūm) *n.* A metallic element symbolized by Ta.

tan-ta-mount (tan´ta mount´) *adj.* To be equivalent in effect, significance, or value.

tan-ta-ra (tan´tèr a) *n.* A blare of the horn or trumpet.

tan-trum (tan´trum) *n.* A fit; an outburst or a rage of bad temper.

tan-yard *n.* The part of the tannery that is used to house the tanning vats.

tan-za-nite *n.* A type of mineral that is a blue variety of zoisite.

tap (tap) *v.* To strike repeatedly, usually while making a small noise; to strike or touch gently; to make secret contact with something; in medicine, to remove fluids from the body. **tapper** *n.*

tape backup In *computer science*, a reserve copy of computer programs and data on magnetic tape.

tap dance *n.* A type of step dance that is tapped out by the means of shoes that have metal taps on them.

tape (tāp) *n.* A narrow strip of woven fabric; a string or ribbon stretched across the finish line of a race.

tape measure *n.* A strip of cloth or other material that is marked off in units of measure and is used to measure things.

ta-per (tā´pèr) *n.* A very slender candle. *v.* To become gradually smaller or thinner at one end.

ta-per-er *n.* The person who bears or carries a taper in a religious procession.

tap-es-tried *adj.* To be decorated with tapestry.

tap-es-try (tap´i strē) *n. pl.* **-ies** A thick fabric woven with designs and figures.

ta-pe-tum *n.* The layer of the nutritive cells that is found in the sporogenous tissue.

tape-worm (tāp´wŭrm˝) *n.* A type of cestode worm that is parasitic and found in the intestine of animals and man.

tap-i-o-ca (tap´ē ō´kᵃ) *n.* A bead-like substance used for thickening and for puddings.

ta-pis *n.* The tapestry material that is used for table coverings and hangings.

tappet hen *n.* A hen that is crested.

tap-ping *n.* Process where something is tapped.

tap-root *n.* A root that will grow vertically downward and has other lateral roots.

taps (taps) *n. pl., Milit.* A bugle call that signals lights out, also sounded at memorial and funeral services.

tap-ster (tap´stĕr) *n.* The person who is hired to dispense liquors in a barroom.

tar (tär) *n.* A black bituminous viscous liquid that is made or obtained by the destructive distillation of organic matter.

tar-an-tel-la (tar´ᵃn telᵃ) *n.* A type of folk dance of Italy.

ta-ran-tu-la (tᵃ ran´chᵃ lᵃ) *n.* A type of spider which is hairy and slow and not poisonous to man.

ta-rax-a-cum (tᵃ rak´sᵃ kᵘm) *n.* A dried root of the dandelion which can be used as a tonic and diuretic.

tar-dy (tär´dē) *adj.* Late; not on time. tardily, tardiness *n.*

tare (târ) *n.* An element which is undesirable.

targe *n.* A type of light shield.

tar-get (tär´git) *n.* An object marked to shoot at; an aim or goal. In computer science, objective, as a file or device to which data is to be transmitted, or a directory to which a file is to be copied or saved.

target date *n.* A date which has been set for the completion of something.

tar-iff (tar´if) *n.* Duty or tax on merchandise coming into or going out of a country.

tar-la-tan (tär´lᵃ tan) *n.* A type of cotton fabric that is heavily sized for stiffness.

tarn (tärn) *n.* A type of steep-banked mountain pool.

tar-nish (tär´nish) *v.* To become discolored or dull; to lose luster; to spoil. tarnish, tarnishable *adj.*

ta-ro *n.* A type of plant of the arum family that is grown in the tropics for its root stocks which can be eaten.

tar-ok *n.* The card game that was popular in Europe and Asia was played with a deck of 40, 52, or 56 cards.

tar-pau-lin (tär pa´lin) *n.* A sheet of waterproof canvas used as a protective covering.

tar-ra-gon (tar´ᵃ gon˝) *n.* A type of European wood that is grown for its aromatic foliage.

tar-ry (tar´ē) *v.* To linger, delay, or hesitate.

tar-sal *adj.* To be pertaining to the tarsus.

tar-si-er *n.* A type of nocturnal mammal of East India which is related to the lemurs.

tar-sus (tär´sᵘs) *n.* A bone of the foot or hand which makes up the ankle or the wrist.

tart (tärt) *adj.* Sharp; sour; cutting, biting in tone or meaning. -ly, tartness *n.*

tar-tan (tär´tan) *n.* A plaid fabric pattern of Scottish origin. tartan *adj.*

tar-tar (tär´tĕr) *n.* The reddish, acidic, crust-like deposit which forms as grape juice turns to wine; a hard deposit which forms on the teeth, composed of secretions, food, and calcium salts.

task (task) *n.* A bit of work, usually assigned by another; a job. In computer science, a job assigned to the computer.

task-mas-ter *n.* A person who imposes labor upon another person.

tasse *n.* An overlapping plate in a suit of armor which will make a short skirt below the waist.

tas-sel (tas´el) *n.* An ornamental decoration made from a bunch of string or thread.

taste (tāst) *n.* The ability to sense or determine flavor in the mouth; a personal liking or disliking. *v.* To test or sense flavors in the mouth. tasteless, tasteful *n.*

tasty *adj.* To have a taste which is pleasing. tastiness *n.*

ta-ta-mi *n.* The straw matting which is used as a covering for the floor in the Japanese home.

tat-ter (tat´ĕr) *n.* A torn scrap of cloth. *v.* To become or make ragged.

tat-ter-de-ma-lion (tat´ĕr di māl´yon) *n.* One who is dressed in clothing that is ragged.

tat-ting (tat´ing) *n.* A type of handmade lace.

tat-tle (tat´l) *v.* To reveal the secrets of another by gossiping. tattler *n.*

tat-too (ta tö´) *n.* A permanent design or mark made on the skin by pricking and inserting an indelible dye.

tat-ty *adj.* To be frayed.

taught (tot) *v.* Past tense of teach.

taunt (tont) *v.* To mock or insult someone.

taupe *n.* A color which is a brownish gray.

tau-rine (tor´ēn) *adj.* To be pertaining to a bull.

taut (tot) *adj.* Tight; emotionally strained. tautly *adv.* tautness *n.*

tau-tog *n.* A type of fish that is found along the Atlantic coast of the United States.

tau-tol-o-gy (ta'tol'o jē) *n., pl. -ies* Redundancy; a statement which is an unnecessary repetition of the same idea.

tau-to-mer-ic *adj.* To be pertaining to tautomerism.

tav-ern (tav'ĕrn) *n.* An inn; an establishment or business licensed to sell alcoholic drinks. **taverner** *n.*

tav-ern-er *n.* A person who runs a tavern.

taw *v.* To dress such as skins by a dry process. **taw** *n.* A playing marble.

taw-dry (to'drē) *adj.* To be gaudy in appearance. **tawdriness** *n.*

taw-pie *n.* A person who is foolish.

tax (taks) *n.* A payment imposed and collected from individuals or businesses by the government. *v.* To strain. **taxable** *adj.* **taxation** *n.* **taxer** *n.*

tax-ex-empt (taks'ig zempt) *adj.* Exempted from tax; bearing tax-free interest on federal or state income.

tax evasion *n.* The failure, which is deliberate, to pay taxes.

tax-i (tak'sē) *v.* To move along the ground or water surface on its own power before taking off.

tax-i-cab (tak'sē kab') *n.* A vehicle for carrying passengers for money.

tax-i-der-my (tak'si dur'mē) *n.* The art or profession of preparing, stuffing, and mounting animal skins.

tax-i stand *n.* The place where a taxi will park while the driver waits for a passenger.

tax-pay-er (taks'pā'ĕr) *n.* A person who pays a tax.

tax shelter *n.* A credit or allowance that reduces taxes on current earnings for an individual investor or corporation.

tax stamp *n.* The stamp which is placed on something to show that the tax for it has been paid.

Taylor, Zachary *n.* (1784-1850) The twelfth president of the United States from 1849-1850.

tea (tē) *n.* A small tree or bush which grows where the climate is very hot and damp; a drink made by steeping the dried leaves of this shrub in boiling water.

teach (tēch) *v.* To communicate skill or knowledge; to give instruction or insight. **teaching** *n.*, **teachability** *n.*, **teachable-ness** *n.*, **teachable** *adj.*

teach-er (tē'chĕr) *n.* A person who teaches; one who instructs.

teachership *n.* A position of teaching.

teacher's pet *n.* A student in the class who gets the special attention of the teacher.

teaching aid *n.* The device which is used to help reinforce the classroom instructions.

teak *n.* A type of tall tree of East India that can be used for shipbuilding.

teal blue *n.* A color which is a dark greenish blue.

team (tēm) *n.* Two or more players on one side in a game; a group of people trained or organized to work together; two or more animals harnessed to the same implement. *v.* To join or work together.

teammate *n.* A person who is on a team with others.

team-ster (tēm'stĕr) *n.* A person who drives a team of animals or a vehicle as an occupation.

tea party *n.* A gathering that takes place in the afternoon where tea is served.

tear (tĕr) *n.* A fluid secreted by the eye to moisten and cleanse. *v.* To cry.

tear (tār) *v.* To become divided into pieces; to separate; to rip into parts or pieces; to move fast; to rush. *n.* A rip or torn place.

tear-down *n.* The process of taking something apart.

tear-ful *adj.* To be accompanied by tears.

tear gas *n.* A type of gaseous substance that will blind the eyes with tears.

tear jerker *n.* A story that is pathetic.

tea-room *n.* A type of room in a restaurant that is designed for the female clientele.

tea rose *n.* A type of rose that descends from the Chinese rose.

tear-stain *n.* The streak that is left by a tear. **tearstained** *adj.*

tear up *v.* To remove or to damage something.

teary *adj.* To be stained with tears.

tease (tēz) *v.* To make fun of; to bother; to annoy; to tantalize. *n.* A person who teases. **teaser** *n.*, **teasingly** *adv.*

teasel *n.* A type of herb which is prickly and is used in the wool industry.

teat *n.* The protuberance that milk flows out of.

tech-ne-tium (tek nē'shē um) *n.* A metallic element symbolized by Tc.

tech-noc-ra-cy *n.* Government by a society that is shaped by the impact of technology.

tech-ni-cal (tek'ni kal) *adj.* Expert; derived or relating to technique; relating to industry or mechanics.

tech-ni-cal-i-ty (tek'ni kal'i tē) *n.* The state of something being technical.

tech-ni-cian *n.* A person who is a specialist in the technical details of a subject.

tech-nique (tek nēk') *n.* A technical procedure or method of doing something.

tech-no-crat *n.* A person who is a member of a technocracy.

tech-no-crat-ic *adj.* To be pertaining to a technocracy.

technol *abbr.* Technology.

tech-nol-o-gist *n.* A person who is a specialist in technology.

tech-nol-o-gy (tek nol′o jē) *n., pl.* *-ies* The application of scientific knowledge to serve man in industry, commerce, medicine and other fields.

tec-ton-ic (tek ton′ik) *adj.* To be pertaining to the deformation of the crust of the earth. **tectonically** *adv.*

tec-ton-ics *n.* The art of construction and building of things, such as a building.

ted (ted) *v.* To turn and scatter something, such as grass for drying purposes.

ted-der (ted′ér) *n.* Someone or something that teds.

teddy bear *n.* A type of bear that is stuffed and used as a child's toy.

te-di-ous (tē′de us) *adj.* Boring; taking a longtime. **tediously** *adv.*

tedium *n.* The state of being tedious.

tee (tē) *n.* A peg used to hold a golf ball on the first stroke toward a hole or goal post; a peg used to support a football during a field goal attempt. **teed off**

teem (tem) *v.* To abound; to be full of; to swarm or crowd.

teen-ag-er (tēn′ā′jèr) *n.* A young adult who is in the teen years of life, such as 13 to 19 years old.

teens (tēnz) *n.* *pl.* The ages between 13 and 19; the years of one's life between 13 and 19.

tee-ter (tē′tér) *v.* To move about in an unsteady manner.

teeth *n.* *pl.* The plural of tooth.

teethe (tēth) *v.* To grow one's teeth.

teeth-er *n.* An object which can be used by babies while they are cutting teeth.

teff *n.* A type of grass which is grown for its grain in Africa.

tel-e-cast (tel′ē kast′) *n.* A television broadcast. **telecast** *v.*

tel-e-com-mu-ni-ca-tion *n.* The communication between two points which are a great distance away from each other.

tel-e-course *n.* A school course which can be taught over the television.

tel-e-film *n.* A movie or picture which has been made or produced for television.

tel-e-gram (tel′e gram) *n.* A message sent or received by telegraph.

tel-e-graph (tel′e graf) *n.* A system for communicating; a transmission sent by wire or radio. *v.* To send messages by electricity over wire. **telegraphist, telegrapher** *n.* **telegraphic** *adj.*

te-le-ost *n.* The group of fishes that have a bony skeleton. **teleostean** *adj.*

te-lep-a-thy (te lep′a thē) *n.* Communication by means of mental processes rather than ordinary means. **-ic** *n.*

tel-e-phone (tel′e fōn′) *n.* A system or device for transmitting conversations

by wire. **telephone** *v.* **telephoner** *n.*

telephone number *n.* The number which has been given to a person and one is able to call this person with this number.

tel-e-phon-ic (tel′e fon′ik) *adj.* To be able to convey sound.

tel-e-pho-to (tel′ē fō′tō) *adj.* Relating to a camera lens which produces a large image of a distant object.

tel-e-pho-to (tel′e fō′tō) *adj.* Relating to a camera lens which produces a large image of a distant object.

tel-e-pho-to-graph-ic *adj.* To be pertaining to the process of telephotography.

tel-e-play (tel′e plā′) *n.* A type of play which has been written for the television.

tel-e-scope (tel′i skōp′) *n.* An instrument which contains a lens system which makes distant objects appear larger and nearer. **telescopic** *adj.*

tel-e-sis *n.* The progress which is directed and planned in an intelligent manner.

tel-e-thon (tel′e thon′) *n.* A long telecast used to raise money for a worthy cause.

tel-e-vise (tel′e vīz′) *v.* To broadcast some show with the use of a television.

tel-e-vi-sion (tel′e vizh′an) *n.* Reception and transmission of images on a screen with sound; the device that reproduces television sounds and images.

tel-ex *n.* Teletype communications by means of automatic exchanges.

te-lio-spore *n.* A type of chlamydospore that is thick-walled and in its final stage in the life cycle of the rust fungus.

tell (tel) *v.* To relate or describe; to command or order. **-ing, tellable** *n.*

tell-er *n.* A person who will relate or tell.

tell-tale *n.* The device for recording something.

tel-lu-ri-an (te lūr′ē an) *adj.* To be pertaining to the earth.

tel-lu-ri-um (te lur′ē um) *n.* An element symbolized by Te.

tel-lu-rom-e-ter *n.* The device that will measure a distance with the use of microwaves.

tel-lu-rous (tel′yer us) *adj.* To be pertaining to tellurium.

tem-per (tem′pér) *n.* The state of one's feelings. *v.* To modify something, making it flexible or hard.

tem-per-a-ment (tem′pér a ment) *n.* Personality; a characteristic way of thinking, reacting, or behaving.

tem-per-ance (tem′pér ans) *n.* Moderation; restraint; moderation or abstinence from drinking alcoholic beverages.

tem-per-ate (tem′ér it) *adj.* Avoiding extremes; moderate. **temperately** *adj.*

tem-per-a-ture (tem′pér a cher) *n.* A measure of heat or cold in relation to the body or environment; an elevation in body temperature above the normal 98.6 degrees Fahrenheit.

tem-pest (tem´pist) *n.* A severe storm, usually with snow, hail, rain, or sleet.

tem-ple (tem´pl) *n.* A place of worship; the flat area on either side of the forehead.

tem-po (tem´po) *n. pl.* **-pos** *or* **-pi** *Mus.* The rate of speed at which a musical composition is to be played.

tem-po-rar-y (tem´po rer´e) *adj.* Lasting for a limited amount of time; not permanent.

temporary storage In *computer science*, the computer's main memory; the area that holds program and data files that are active.

tempt (tempt) *n.* To encourage or draw into a foolish or wrong course of action; to lure. **temptation** *n.*

ten (ten) *n.* The cardinal number equal to 9 + 1; the number before eleven.

te-na-cious (to nā´ shus) *adj.* Persistent; stubborn. **tenaciousness** *n.*

ten-ant (ten´ant) *n.* A person who pays rent to occupy another's property. **tenantless** *adj.* **tenantable** *adj.*

Ten Commandments *n.* The ten rules of moral behavior which were given to Moses by God.

tend (tend) *v.* To be inclined or disposed; to be directed; to look after.

ten-den-cy (ten´den sē) *n. pl.* **-ies** A disposition to act or behave in a particular way; a particular direction, mode, outcome, or direction.

ten-der (ten´dér) *adj.* Fragile; soft; not hard or tough; painful or sore when touched. **tender** *n.* Something offered as a formal bid or offer; compassionate; a supply ship. **tender** *v.* To make an offer to buy or purchase; to present, as a resignation. **tenderly** *adv.* **tenderhearted** *adj* **tenderness** *n.*

ten-der-loin (ten´dér loin´) *n.* A cut of tender pork or beef.

ten-don (ten´dòn) *n.* A band of tough, fibrous tissues that connect a muscle and bone.

ten-dril (ten´dril) *n.* A thread-like part of a climbing plant which attaches itself to a support. **tendriled** *adj.*

Ten-nes-see *n.* A state located in the eastern part of the United States; statehood June 1, 1796; state capital Nashville.

ten-nis (ten´is) *n.* A sport played with a ball and racket by 2 or 4 people on a rectangular court.

ten-or (ten´ér) *n.* An adult male singing voice, above a baritone.

tense (tens) *adj.* Taut or stretched tightly; nervous; under strain. **tense** *v.*

ten-sion (ten´shan) *n.* The condition of stretching or the state of being stretched. **tensional** *adj.* **-less** *adj.*

tent (tent) *n.* A portable shelter made by stretching material over a supporting framework.

ten-ta-cle (ten´ta kl) *n.* A long, unjointed, flexible body part that projects from certain invertebrates, as the octopus. **tentacular** *adj.* **-ed** *adj.*

ten-ta-tive (ten´ta tiv) *adj.* Experimental; subject to change; not definite.

ten-ure (ten´yèr) *n.* The right, state, or period of holding something, as an office or property. **tenurial, tenured** *adj.* **tenurially** *adv.*

te-pee (tā´pē) *n.* A tent made of hides or bark used by the Indians of North America.

tep-id (tep´id) *adj.* Lukewarm. **tepidly** *adv.* **tepidness** *n.*

te-qui-la *n.* A type of Mexican liquor.

te-ral *n.* A type of wide-brimmed felt hat that is worn by the people in subtropical areas.

ter-a-to-log-i-cal *adj.* To be abnormal in structure of growth.

ter-a-to-ma *n.* A type of tumor that is made up of a heterogeneous mixture of the tissues. **teratomatous** *adj.*

ter-bi-um (tùr´bē üm) *n.* A metallic element of the rare-earth group symbolized by Th.

ter-cen-ten-a-ry (ter sen´te ner´ē) *n. pl.* **-ries.** The time span of 300 years; a 300th anniversary. **tercentenary** *adj.*

ter-cet *n.* A group of three lines of verse.

ter-e-binth (ter´e binth) *n.* A type of European tree that belongs to the sumac family and yields turpentine.

ter-e-bin-thine (ter´e bin´thin) *adj.* To be pertaining to or resembling turpentine.

te-rete *adj.* To be almost cylindrical but to be tapering at both ends.

ter-gi-ver-as-tion *n.* The evasion of a clear-cut statement.

ter-gum (tùr´gum) *n.* A plate of an rthropod that is a dorsal section.

ter-i-ya-ki *n.* A Japanese dish where the ingredients are marinated in soy sauce then grilled.

term *n.* A phrase or word; a limited time or duration; a phrase having a precise meaning. *Math* The quantity of two numbers either added together or subtracted.

ter-mi-nal (ter´mi nal) *adj.* Of, forming, or located at the end; final. *n.* A station at the end of a bus line, railway, or airline; in Computer Science, the instrument through which data enters or leaves a computer.

ter-mi-nate (tùr´mi nāt´) *v.* To bring to a conclusion or end; to finish; to fire someone from a job. **termination** *n.*

ter-mite (tee´mit) *n.* The winged or wingless insect which lives in large colonies feeding on wood.

ter-race (ter´as) *n.* An open balcony or

porch; a level piece of land that is higher than the surrounding area; a row of houses built on a sloping or raised site.

ter-ra cot-ta *n.* A hard, baked clay used in ceramic pottery.

ter-rain (*te* rān´) *n.* The surface of an area, as land.

ter-ra-pin (ter´*a* pin) *n.* An edible turtle of North America, living in both fresh and salt water.

ter-res-tri-al (*te* res´trē *a*l) *adj.* Something earthly; not heavenly; growing or living on land.

ter-ri-ble (ter´*i* bl) *adj.* Causing fear or terror; intense; extreme; horrid; difficult. **terribly** *adv.* **-ness** *n.*

ter-ri-er (ter´ē ėr) *n.* A very active small dog, originally bred by hunters to dig for burrowing game, now kept as a family pet.

ter-rif-ic (*te* rif´ik) *adj.* Terrifying. *Informal* Excellent; causing amazement.

ter-ri-fy (ter´i fī´) *v.* To fill with fear or terror; to frighten; to menace. **terrified** *adj.* **terrifying** *adj.*

ter-ri-to-ry (ter´i tōr´ē) *n. pl.* **-ies** An area, usually of great size, which is controlled by a particular government; a district or area assigned to one person or group. **territorial** *adj.*

ter-ror (ter´ėr) *n.* Extreme fear; one who causes terror.

ter-ror-ism *n.* The state of being terrorized or the act of terrorizing; the use of intimidation to attain one's goals or to advance one's cause.

terse (ters) *adj.* Brief; using as few words as possible without loss of force or clearness. **tersely** *adv.* **terseness** *n.*

test (test) *n.* An examination or evaluation of something or someone; an examination to determine one's knowledge, skill, intelligence or other qualities. **tester** *n.* In computer science, to subject to diagnostics or sample problems to ascertain that a hardware device or program is working properly.

tes-ta-ment (tes´*ta* ment) *n.* A legal document which states how one's personal property is to be distributed upon his death. **Testament** One of the two sections of the Bible; the Old Testament and the New Testament.

tes-tate (tes´tāt) *adj.* Having left a valid will.

test data In *computer science*, data whose output is known for a particular formula or routine.

tes-ti-fy (tes´ti fī´) *v.* To give evidence while under oath; to serve as proof.

tes-ti-mo-ni-al (tes´ti mō´nē *a*l) *n.* A formal statement; a gift, dinner, reception, or other sign of appreciation given to a person as a token of esteem.

tes-ti-mo-ny (tes´ti mō´nē) *n. pl.* **-ies** A solemn affirmation made under oath; an outward expression of a religious experience.

tes-tis (tes´tis) *n. pl.* **testes** The sperm producing gland of the male.

test run In *computer science*, to operate with test data to confirm the validity of a formula or routine.

test tube *n.* A thin glass tube closed at one end, used in biology and chemistry.

test-tube baby *n.* A baby conceived outside of the womb by fertilizing an egg removed from a woman and then returning the fertilized egg to the womb.

tet-a-nus (tet´*a* nus) *n., Pathol* An often fatal disease marked by muscular spasms, commonly known as lockjaw.

teth-er (teth´ėr) *n.* A rope or chain which fastens an animal to something but allows limited freedom to wander within its range.

Tex-as *n.* A state located in the south central part of the United States; statehood December 29, 1845; state capital Austin.

text (tekst) *n.* The actual wording of an author's work distinguished his from notes; the main part or body of a book. In computer science, the body of a document; any set of character and symbols that conveys a message. **textual** *adj.* **textually** *adv.*

text-book (tekst´bek´) *n.* A book used by students to prepare their lessons.

text editor In *computer science*, a basic program for altering text without formatting.

tex-tile (teks´til) *n.* A cloth made by weaving; yarn or fiber for making cloth.

tex-ture (teks´chėr) *n.* The look, surface, or feel of something; the basic makeup. **textural** *adj.* **texturally** *adv.*

thal-li-um (thal´ē um) *n.* A metallic element resembling lead, symbolized by Tl.

than (than) *conj.* In comparison with or to something.

thank (thangk) *v.* To express one's gratitude; to credit.

thank-ful (thangk´ful) *adj.* Feeling or showing gratitude; grateful. **thankfully** *adv.* **thankfulness** *n.* **thankless** *adj.*

thanks (thangks) *n. pl.* An expression of one's gratitude.

Thanksgiving Day *n.* A United States holiday, set apart as a legal holiday for public thanksgiving, celebrated on the fourth Thursday of November.

that (that) *adj. pl.* **those** The person or thing present or being mentioned. Used to introduce a clause stating what is said.

thatch (thach) *n.* Grass, straw, or similar material used to make a roof. **thatch**

overlay or cover with or as if with thatch.

thaw (tho) v. To change from a frozen state to a liquid or soft state; to grow warmer; to melt. **thaw** n.

the-a-tre (thē´a tėr) n. A building adapted to present dramas, motion pictures, plays, or other performances; a performance.

the-at-ri-cal (thē a´tri kal) adj. Extravagant; designed for show, display, or effect. **theatricals** n.

the definite adj. or article Used before nouns and noun phrases as a determiner, designating particular persons or things. adv. Used to modify words in the comparative degree; by so much; by that much.

theft (theft) n. The act or crime of stealing; larceny.

their (thâr) adj. & pron. The possessive case of they; belonging to two or more things or beings previously named.

the-ism (thē´iz um) n. The belief in the existence of God. **theist, theistic** adj.

them (them) pron. The objective case of they.

theme (thēm) n. The topic or subject of something. Mus. A short melody of a musical composition. **thematic** adj.

them-selves (them selvz´) pron. Them or they; a form of the third person plural pronoun.

then (then) adv. At that time; soon or immediately. adj. Being or acting in or belonging to or at that time.

thence (thens) adv. From that place, event, fact, or origin.

the-oc-ra-cy (thē ok´ra sē) n. pl. -ies Government by God or by clergymen who think of themselves as representatives of God. **theocrat** n.

the-ol-o-gy (thē ol´o´jē) n. pl. -ies The religious study of the nature of God, beliefs, practices, and ideas. **-ian** n.

the-o-rize (thē´o rīz´) v. To analyze theories. **theoretician** n. **theorization** n. **theorizer** n. **theorist** n.

the-o-ry (thē´o rē) n. pl. -ies A general principle or explanation which covers the known facts; an offered opinion which may possibly, but not positively, be true.

ther-a-peu-tics (ther´a pū´tiks) n. The medical treatment of disease.

ther-a-py (ther´a pē) n. pl. -ies The treatment of certain diseases; treatment intended to remedy an undesirable condition. **therapist** n.

there (thâr) adv. In, at, or about that place; toward, into, or to. **thereabouts** adv. **thereafter** adv. **thereby** adv. **therefore** adv. **-from** adv. **therein** adv.

ther-mal (ther´mal) adj. Having to do with or producing heat.

ther-mom-e-ter (thėr mom´i tėr) n. A glass tube containing mercury which rises and falls with temperature changes. **thermometric** adj.

ther-mo-plas-tic (ther´mo plas´tik) adj. Pliable and soft when heated or warm but hard when cooled.

ther-mo-stat (ther´mo stat´) n. A device that automatically responds to temperature changes and activates equipment such as air conditioners and furnaces to adjust the temperature to correspond with the setting on the device. **thermostatic** adj.

the-sau-rus (thi so´us) n. pl. -ruses or -ri A book which contains synonyms.

these pron. The plural of this.

the-sis (thē´sis) n. pl. -ses A formal argument or idea; a paper written by a student that develops an idea or point of view.

they (thā) pron. The two or more beings just mentioned.

they'd (thād) contr. They had.

they'll (thal) contr. They will.

they're (thâr) contr. They are.

they've (thāv) contr. They have.

thick (thik) adj. Having a heavy or dense consistency; having a considerable extent or depth from one surface to its opposite. Slang Excessive. **thickly** adv. **thickness** n. **thicken** v.

thief (thēf) n. pl. thieves A person who steals.

thieve (thēv) v. To take by theft.

thigh (thī) n. The part of the leg between the hip and the knee of man.

thim-ble (thim´bl) n. A small cap-like protection for the finger, worn while sewing. **thimbleful** n.

thin (thin) adj. Having very little depth or extent from one side or surface to the other; not fat; slender. v. To make or become thin. **thinly** adv. **-ness** n.

thing (thing) n. Something not recognized or named; an idea, conception, or utterance; a material or real object. **things** n. One's belongings.

think (thingk) v. To exercise thought; to use the mind; to reason and work out in the mind; to visualize. **thinkable** adj. **thinker** n.

third (therd) n. Next to the second in time or place; the last in a series of three. Mech. The 3rd forward gear in an automobile, truck, tractor, or other vehicle.

thirst (therst) n. An uncomfortably dry feeling in the throat and mouth accompanied by an urgent desire for liquids. **thirsty** adj.

this (this) pron. pl. these The person or thing that is near, present, or just mentioned; the one under discussion.

this-tle (this´l) n. A prickly plant usually producing a purplish or yellowish flower.

thith-er (thith´ẽr) *adv.* To that place; there; on the farthest side.

thong (thong) *n.* A narrow strip of leather used for binding.

tho-rax (thõr´aks) *n. pl.* **-raxes** *or* **-races** The section or part of the human body between the neck and abdomen, supported by the ribs and breastbone.

tho-ri-um (thõr´ē um) *n.* A radioactive metallic element symbolized by Th.

thorn (thorn) *n.* A sharp, pointed, woody projection on a plant stem. **thorniness** *n.* **thorny** *adj.*

thor-ough (ther´ō) *adj.* Complete; intensive; accurate; very careful; absolute. **-ness** *n.* **thoroughly** *adv.*

thor-ough-bred (ther´ōbred´) *adj.* Being of a pure breed of stock.

thor-ough-fare (ther´ō fâr´) *n.* A public highway, road or street.

those *adj. & pron.* The plural of that.

though (thō) *adv.* Nevertheless; in spite of.

thought (thot) *n.* The process, act, or power of thinking; a possibility; an idea. **thoughtful** *adj.* **thoughtless** *adj.*

thou-sand (thou´zand) *n.* The cardinal number equal to 10 X 100.

thrash (thrash) *v.* To beat or strike with a whip; to move violently about; to defeat. **thrasher** *n.*

thread (thred) *n.* A thin cord of cotton or other fiber; the ridge going around a bolt, nut or screw. *v.* To pass a thread through, as to thread a needle.

thread-bare (thred´bâr´) *adj.* Shabby.

threads *n. pl., Slang* Clothes.

threat (thret) *n.* An expression or warning of intent to do harm; anything holding a possible source of danger. **threaten** *v.* **threatener** *n.*

thresh (thresh) *v.* To separate seed from a harvested plant mechanically; to strike severely.

thresh-old (thresh´ōld) *n.* A horizontal piece of wood or other material which forms a doorsill; a beginning point.

threw *v.* Past tense of throw.

thrice (thrīs) *adv.* Three times.

thrift (thrift) *n.* The careful use of money and other resources. **thriftily** *adv.* **thriftiness** *n.* **thrifty** *adj.*

thrill (thril) *n.* A feeling of sudden intense excitement, fear, or joy. **thrilling** *adj.* **thrillingly** *adv.*

thrive (thrīv) *v.* To prosper; to be healthy; to do well in a position.

throat (thrōt) *n.* The front section or part of the neck containing passages for food and air.

throb (throb) *v.* To beat, move, or vibrate in a pulsating way; to pulsate.

throm-bo-sis (throm bō´sis) *n. pl.* **-ses** The development of a blood clot in a blood vessel or in the heart cavity.

throng (throng) *n.* A large group or crowd. *v.* To crowd around or into.

throt-tle (throt´l) *n.* The valve which controls the flow of fuel to an engine. *v.* To control the speed or fuel with a throttle.

through (thrō) *prep.* From the beginning to the end; in one side and out the opposite side. *Slang* Completed; finished.

through-out (thrō out´) *prep., adv.* In every place; everywhere; at all times.

throw (thrō) *v.* To toss or fling through the air with a motion of the arm; to hurl with force. *Slang* To entertain, as to throw a party. **throw up** To vomit. **throw out** To discard something.

thru (thrō) *prep., adv., & adj.* Through.

thrush (thrush) *n.* A small songbird having a brownish upper body and spotted breast.

thrust (thrust) *v.* To push; to shove with sudden or vigorous force. *n.* A sudden stab or push.

thru-way *or* **throughway (thrō´wā´)** *n.* A major highway; an expressway.

thud (thud) *n.* A heavy, dull thumping sound.

thug (thug) *n.* A tough or violent gangster. **thuggish** *adj.*

thumb (thum) *n.* The short first digit of the hand; the part of the glove that fits over the thumb. *v.* To browse through something quickly. *Slang* To hitchhike.

thump (thump) *n.* A blow with something blunt or heavy. **thump** *v.*

thun-der (thun´dẽr) *n.* The loud explosive sound made as air is suddenly expanded by heat and then quickly contracted again.

thun-der-show-er (thun´dẽr shou´ẽr) *n.* A brief rainstorm with thunder and light-ning.

thus (thus) *adv.* In this or that way; therefore.

thwack (thwak) *v.* To strike hard, using something flat.

thwart (thwort) *v.* To prevent from happening; to prevent from doing something. *n.* A seat positioned crosswise in a boat.

thy (thī) *adj.* Pertaining to oneself; your.

thyme (tīm) *n.* An aromatic mint herb whose leaves are used in cooking.

thy-roid (thī´roid) *adj., Anat.* Pertaining to the thyroid gland. *n.* The gland in the neck of man that produces hormones which regulate food use and body growth.

thy-rox-ine (thī rok´sēn) *n.* A hormone secreted by the thyroid gland.

ti-a-ra (tē ar´a) *n.* A bejeweled crown in the form of a half circle and worn by women at formal occasions.

tick (tik) *n.* One of a series of rhythmical tapping sounds made by a clock; a small bloodsucking parasite, many of which are carriers of disease.

tick-et (tik´it) *n.* A printed slip of paper or cardboard allowing its holder to enter a specified event or to enjoy a privilege; a list of candidates who represent a political party.

tick-le (tik´l) *v.* To stroke lightly so as to cause laughter; to amuse or delight. **tickle** *n.* **tickler** *n.*

tidal wave *n.* An enormous rise of destructive ocean water caused by a storm or earth-quake.

tid-bit (tid´bit´) *n.* A choice bit of food, news, or gossip.

tide (tid) *n.* The rise and fall of the surface level of the ocean which occurs twice a day due to the gravitational pull of the sun and moon on the earth.

tid-ings (ti´dingz) *n. pl.* News; information about events.

ti-dy (ti´dē) *adj.* Well arranged; neat; orderly. *v.* To make orderly and neat. **tidily** *adv.* **tidiness** *n.*

tie (ti) *v.* To secure or bind with a rope, line, cord or other similar material; to make secure or fasten with a rope; to make a bow or knot in; to match an opponent's score. *n.* A string, rope, cord or other material used to join parts or hold something in place; a necktie; a beam that gives structural support. **tie** A device, as timber, laid crosswise to support train tracks.

tier (tēr) *n.* A layer or row placed one above the other. **tiered** *adj.*

ti-ger (ti´gér) *n.* A large carnivorous cat having tawny fur with black stripes.

tight (tit) *adj.* Set closely together; bound or securely firm; not loose; taut; difficult. *adv.* Firmly

tight-en (tit´en) *v.* To become or make tighter. **tightener** *n.*

tile (til) *n.* A thin, hard, flat piece of plastic, asphalt, baked clay, or stone used to cover walls, floors, and roofs. *v.* To cover with tile.

till (til) Until; unless or before. *v.* To cultivate; to plow. *n.* A small cash register or drawer for holding money.

tilt (tilt) *v.* To tip, as by raising one end. *n.* The state of tilting or being tilted.

tim-ber (tim´bér) *n.* Wood prepared for building; a finished piece of wood or plank.

timber line *n.* The height on a mountain beyond which trees cannot grow.

time (tim) *n.* A continuous period measured by clocks, watches, and calendars; the period or moment in which something happens or takes place. *adj.* Of or pertain-ing to time; pertaining to paying in, installments. *Slang* A period of imprisonment.

time–shar-ing *n.* The joint ownership of property with each individual sharing the use of the property.

time tri-al *n.* A race or competition where each participant is timed individually over a set distance.

tim-id (tim´id) *adj.* Lacking self-confidence; shy.

tin (tin) *n.* A white, soft, malleable metallic element, symbolized by Sn; a container made of tin. *adj.* Made of tin.

tinc-ture (tingk´chèr) *n.* A tinge of color; an alcohol solution of some medical substance. *v.* To tint.

tin-der (tin´dèr) *n.* A readily combustible substance or material used for kindling.

tine (tin) *n.* A narrow pointed spike or prong, as of a fork or antler.

tinge (tinj) *v.* To impart a faint trace of color; to tint. *n.* As light trace of added color.

tin-gle (ting´gl) *v.* To feel a stinging or prickling sensation. **tingle** *n.* **-ly** *adj.*

tin-kle (ting´kl) *v.* To produce a slight, sharp series of metallic ringing sounds.

tin-ny (tin´ē) *adj.* Pertaining to or composed of tin.

tin-sel (tin´sel) *n.* Thin strips of glittering material used for decorations.

tint (tint) *n.* A slight amount or trace of color. *v.* To color.

ti-ny (ti´nē) *adj.* Minute; very small.

tip (tip) *v.* To slant from the horizontal or vertical. *n.* Extra money given as an acknowledgment of a service; a gratuity; a helpful hint.

tip-ple (tip´l) *v.* To drink an alcoholic beverage to excess.

tip-sy (tip´sē) *adj.* Partially intoxicated. **tipsiness** *n.*

ti-rade (ti´rād) *n.* A long, violent speech or outpouring, as of censure.

tire (tièr) *v.* To become or make weary; to be fatigued; to become bored. *n.* The outer covering for a wheel, usually made of rubber, serving to absorb shock and to provide traction.

tire-less *adj.* Untiring. **tirelessly** *adv.*

tis-sue (tish´ö) *n., Biol.* Similar cells and their products developed by plants and animals; a soft, absorbent piece of paper, consisting of two layers.

ti-ta-ni-um (ti tā´nē um) *n.* A metallic element symbolized by Ti.

tithe (tith) *n.* A tenth of one's income given voluntarily for the support of a church. **tithe** *v.* **tither** *n.*

tit-il-late (tit´i lāt´) *v.* To excite or stimulate in a pleasurable way. **titillating** *adj.* **titillative** *adj.*

ti-tle (tit´l) *n.* An identifying name of a book, poem, play, or other creative work; a name or mark of distinction indicating a rank or an office; in law, the evidence giving legal right of possession or control of something; in sports, a championship. *v.* To give a title or name to.

to (tō) *prep.* Toward, opposite or near; in contact with; as far as; used as a function word indicating an action, movement, or condition suggestive of movement; indicating correspondence, dissimilarity, similarity, or proportion; indicating the one for which something is done or exists. *adv.* In the state, direction, or condition.

toast (tōst) *v.* To heat and brown over a fire or in a toaster. *n.* Sliced bread browned in a toaster. **toasty** *adj.*

to-bac-co (to bak´ō) *n.* A tropical American plant widely cultivated for its leaves, which are prepared in various ways, as for chewing or smoking.

to-bog-gan (to bog´an) *n.* A long sled-like vehicle without runners, having long thin boards curved upwards at the forward end. **tobogganist** *n.* **toboggan** *v.*

to-day (to dā´) *adv.* On or during the present day. *n.* The present time, period, or day.

tod-dle (tod´l) *v.* To walk unsteadily with short steps.

toddler *n.* A small child learning to walk.

tod-dy (tod´ē) *n. pl.* -ies A drink made with hot water, sugar, spices, and liquor.

toe (tō) *n.* One of the extensions from the front part of a foot; the part of a stocking, boot or shoe that covers the toes. *v.* To kick, reach, or touch with the toe or toes.

tof-fee (to´fē) *n.* A chewy candy made of butter and brown sugar.

to-geth-er (te geth´ér) *adv.* In or into one group, mass, or body; regarded jointly; in time with what is happening or going on. **togetherness** *n.*

toggle In *computer science,* a switch that may be in either of two states; to select one of two options.

toil (toil) *v.* To labor very hard and continuously. *n.* A difficult task.

toi-let (toi´lit) *n.* A porcelain apparatus with a flushing device, used as a means of disposing body wastes.

to-ken (tōk´en) *n.* A keepsake; a symbol of authority or identity; a piece of imprinted metal used in place of money. *adj.* Done as a pledge or indication.

tol-er-ate (tol´e rāt´) *v.* To put up with; to recognize and respect the opinions and rights of others; to endure; to suffer. **toleration** *n.* **tolerance** *adj.*

toll (tōl) *n.* A fixed charge for travel across a bridge or along a road. *v.* To sound a bell in repeated single, slow tones.

to-ma-to (to mā´tō) *n. pl.* -toes A garden plant cultivated for its edible fruit; the fruit of such a plant.

tomb (tōm) *n.* A vault for burying the dead; a grave.

tomb-stone (tōm´stōn´) *n.* A stone used to mark a grave.

tom-cat (tom´kat´) *n.* A male cat.

to-mor-row (to mor´ō) *n.* The day after the present day. *adv.* On the day following today.

ton (tun) *n.* A measurement of weight equal to 2,000 pounds. *Slang* A large amount.

tone (tōn) *n.* A vocal or musical sound that has a distinct pitch, loudness, quality, and duration; the condition of the body and muscles when at rest. *v.* To change or soften the color.

tongs (tongz) *n. pl.* An implement with two long arms joined at one end, used for picking up or lifting.

tongue (tung) *n.* The muscular organ attached to the floor of the mouth, used in tasting, chewing, and speaking; anything shaped like a tongue, as the material under the laces or buckles of a shoe.

ton-ic (ton´ik) *n.* A medicine or other agent used to restore health; in music, the first note of a scale. *Slang* Flavored carbonated soda.

to-night (to nīt´) *n.* This night; the night of this day; the night that is coming. *adv.* On or during the present or coming night.

ton-sil (ton´sil) *n.* One of a pair of tissue similar to lymph nodes, found on either side of the throat.

ton-sil-lec-to-my (ton´si lek´to mē) *n.* The surgical removal of tonsils.

too (tō) *adv.* Also; as well; more than is needed.

tool (tōl) *n.* An implement used to perform a task; anything needed to do one's work. *v.* To make or shape with a tool.

tooth (tōth) *n. pl.* teeth One of the hard, white structures rooted in the jaw and used for chewing and biting; the small, notched, projecting part of any object, such as a gear, comb or saw. **toothless** *adj.*

top (top) *n.* The highest part or surface of anything; a covering or lid; the above ground part of a rooted plant; the highest degree; a toy having a symmetric body with a tapered end upon which it spins.

to-paz (tō´paz) *n.* A gemstone, usually yellow in color.

top-coat (top´kōt´) *n.* An outer coat.

To-pe-ka *n.* The capital of the state of Kansas.

top-ic *n.* The subject discussed in an essay, thesis, speech or other discourse; the theme.

to-pog-ra-phy (to pog´ra fē) *n. pl.* -ies A detailed description of a region or place; a physical outline showing the features of a region or place.

top-ple (top'l) *v.* To fall; to overturn.

top-sy-tur-vy (top'sē ter'vē) *adv.* With the top side down; upside down. *adj.* In a con-fused state. *n.* Confusion.

To-rah (tōr'a) *n.* The body of law and wis-dom contained in Jewish Scripture and oral tradition; a parchment scroll that contains the first five books of the Old Testament.

torch (torch) *n.* A stick of resinous wood which is burned to give light; any portable device which produces hot flame. *Slang* To set fire to.

tor-ment (tor'ment) *n.* Extreme mental anguish or physical pain; a source of trouble or pain. *v.* To cause terrible pain; to pester, harass, or annoy. **tormentingly** *adv.* **tormentor** *n.*

tor-na-do (tor nā'dō) *n., pl.* **tornados** *or* **tornadoes** A whirling, violent windstorm accompanied by a funnel-shaped cloud that travels a narrow path over land; a whirlwind.

tor-pe-do (tor pē'dō) *n., pl.* **torpedoes** A large, self-propelled, underwater missile launched from a ship, containing an explosive charge.

tor-pid (tor'pid) *adj.* Having lost the power of motion or feeling; dormant. **torpidity** *n.* **torpidly** *adv.*

tor-rent (tor'ent) *n.* A swift, violent stream; a raging flood. **torrential** *adj.*

tor-rid (tor'id) *adj.* Parched and dried by the heat. **torridly** *adv.*

tor-sion (tor'shan) *n.* The act or result of twisting; the stress produced when one end is held fast and the other turned.

tor-so (tor'sō) *n. pl.* **-sos** *or* **-si** The trunk of the human body.

tort (tort) *n., Law* A wrongful act requiring compensation for damages.

tor-toise (tor'tos) *n.* A turtle that lives on the land; a person or thing regarded as slow.

tor-tu-ous (tor'chö us) *adj.* Marked by repeated bends, turns, or twists; devious. **tortuousness** *n.*

tor-ture (tor'chèr) *n.* The infliction of intense pain as punishment; something causing anguish or pain. *v.* To subject or cause intense suffering; to wrench or twist out of shape. **torturer** *n.* **torturously** *adv.*

toss (tos) *v.* To fling or throw about continuously; to throw up in the air. *n.* A throw.

tot (tot) *n.* A young child; a toddler.

to-tal (tōt'al) *n.* The whole amount or sum; the entire quantity. *adj.* Absolute; complete. **total** *v.* **totally** *adv.*

to-tal-i-tar-i-an *adj.* Characteristic of a government controlled completely by one party; exercising complete political control. **totalitarian** *n.*

tote (tōt) *v.* To carry something on one's arm or back. *n.* A load.

to-tem (tō'tem) *n.* An animal or plant regarded as having a close relationship to some family clan or group; a representation or symbol.

tot-ter (tot'ér) *v.* To walk unsteadily; to shake or sway as if about to fall.

tou-can (tō'kan) *n.* A brightly colored tropical bird having a very large thin bill.

touch (tuch) *v.* To allow a part of the body, as the hands, to feel or come into contact with; to hit or tap lightly; to eat or drink; to join; to come next to; to have an effect on; to move emotionally. *n.* An instance or act of touching; the feeling, fact, or act of touching or being touched; a trace; a tiny amount; a method, manner, or style of striking the keys of an instrument with a keyboard. **touchable** *adj.*

tough (tuf) *adj.* Resilient and strong enough to withstand great strain without breaking or tearing; strong; hardy; very difficult; difficult to cut or chew. *n.* An unruly person; a thug. **toughly** *adv.* **toughness** *n.*

tou-pee (tō pā) *n.* A small wig piece worn to cover a bald spot on one's head.

tour (ter) *n.* A trip with visits to points of interest; a journey; a period or length of service at a single place or job. **tourism** *n.* **tourist** *n.*

tour-na-ment (ter'na ment) *n.* A contest involving a number of competitors for a title or championship.

tour-ni-quet (ter'ni kit) *n.* A device used to temporarily stop the flow of blood through an artery.

tou-sle (tou'zl) *v.* To mess up; to disarrange.

tout (tout) *v.* To solicit customers. *Slang* In horse racing, a person who obtains information on racehorses and sells it to bettors. **touter** *n.*

tow (tō) *v.* To drag or pull, as by a chain or rope. *n.* An act of being pulled; a rope or line for pulling or dragging; coarse broken flax, hemp, or jute liber prepared for spinning.

to-ward *or* **towards** (tōrd) *prep.* In the direction of; just before; some what before; regarding; with respect to.

tow-el (tou'el) *n.* An absorbent piece of cloth used for drying. **towel** *v.*

tow-er (tou'èr) *n.* A very tall building or structure; a skyscraper; a place of security or defense. **towering** *adj.*

town (toun) *n.* A collection of houses and other buildings larger than a village and smaller than a city.

town-ship (toun'ship) *n.* A subdivision of a county having corporate powers of municipal government.

tox-e-mi-a (tok sē'mē a) *n., Pathol.*

Blood poisoning; a condition in which the blood contains toxins.

tox-ic (tok´sik) *adj.* Relating to a toxin; destructive, deadly, or harmful.

tox-in (tok´sin) *n.* A poisonous substance produced by chemical changes in plant and animal tissue.

toy (toi) *n.* An object designed for the enjoyment of children; any object having little value or importance; a small trinket; a bauble; a dog of a very small breed. *v.* To amuse or entertain oneself.

trace (träs) *n.* A visible mark or sign of a thing, person, or event; something left by some past agent or event. **trace** *v.* To follow the course or track of; to copy by drawing over the lines visible through a sheet of transparent paper; to decorate with line patterns. **traceable** *adj.* **traceably** *adv.* **tracer** *n.*

track (trak) *n.* A mark, as a footprint, left by the passage of anything; a regular course; a set of rails on which a train runs; a circular or oval course for racing or walking. **track** *v.* To follow the trail of footprints of. **trackable** *adj.* **tracker** *n.*

trackball In computer science, a hand held device, similar to a mouse, but with a fixed base holding a sphere that is manipulated to move the cursor.

tract (trakt) *n.* An extended area, as a stretch of land. *Anat.* An extensive region of the body, one comprising body organs and tissues that together perform a specialized function.

trac-tion (trak´shan) *n.* The act of drawing, as a load over a surface; the state of being drawn or pulled; rolling friction that prevents a wheel from skidding over the surface on which it runs.

trac-tor (trak´tér) *n.* A diesel or gasoline-powered vehicle used in farming to pull another piece of machinery.

tractor feed In *computer science*, a device that feeds a continuous form through a printer by engaging a series of holes along the deep edges of the form; same as *pin feed* or *sprocket feed*.

tractor trailer *n.* A large truck having a cab and no body, used to pull large trailers.

trade (träd) *n.* A business or occupation; skilled labor; a craft; an instance of selling or buying; a swap. **trade** *v.* **tradeable** *adj.* **trader** *n.*

trade-mark (träd´märk´) *n.* A brand name which is legally the possession of one company and cannot be used by another. **trademark** *v.*

trade–off *n.* A compromise of possibilities when all cannot be attained at the same time; a surrender of one

consideration in order to obtain another.

tra-di-tion (tra dish´an) *n.* The doctrines, knowledge, practices, and customs passed down from one generation to another. **traditional** *adj.* **-ally** *adv.*

tra-duce (tra dös´) *v.* To betray. **traducement** *n.* **traducer** *n.*

traf-fic (traf´ik) *n.* The passage or movement of vehicles; trade, buying and selling; the signals handled by a communications system. **-ker** *n.*

trag-e-dy (traj´i dē) *n. pl.* **-ies** An extremely sad or fatal event or course of events; a story, play, or other literary work which arouses terror or pity by a series of misfortunes or sad events.

trail (trāl) *v.* To draw, drag, or stream along behind; to follow in the tracks of; to follow slowly behind or in the rear; to let hang so as to touch the ground. *n.* Something that hangs or follows along behind; a rough path through a wooded area.

trail-er (trā´lêr) *n.* One who trails; a large vehicle that transports objects and is pulled by another vehicle.

train (trān) *n.* The part of a long gown that trails behind the wearer; a long moving line of vehicles or persons; a group of railroad cars. *v.* To instruct so as to make skillful or capable of doing something; to aim; to direct. **trainable** *adj.* **trainer** *n.* **training** *n.* **trainee** *n.*

trait (trāt) *n.* A quality or distinguishing feature, such as one's character.

trai-tor (trā´tér) *n.* A person who betrays his country, a cause, or another's confidence.

tra-jec-to-ry (tra jek´to rē) *n. pl.* **-ies** The curved line or path of a moving object.

tram-mel (tram´el) *n.* A long, large net used to catch birds or fish; something that impedes movement. **trammeler** *n.* **trammel** *v.*

tramp (tramp) *v.* To plod or walk with a heavy step. *n.* A homeless person or vagrant who travels about aimlessly.

tram-ple (tram´pl) *v.* To tread heavily; to stomp; to inflict injury, pain, or loss by heartless or brutal treatment. **trample** *n.* **trampler** *n.*

tram-po-line (tram´po lēn´) *n.* A canvas device on which an athlete or acrobat may perform. **trampolinist** *n.*

trance (trans) *n.* A stupor, daze, mental state, or condition, such as produced by drugs or hypnosis.

tran-quil (trang´kwil) *adj.* Very calm, quiet, and free from disturbance. **tranquilly** *n.* **tranquillity** *n.* **-ize** *v.*

trans-act (tran sakt´) *v.* To perform, carry out, conduct, or manage business in some way. **transact, transactor** *n.* **transactional** *adj.*

transaction file In *computer science*, a record of recent transactions, used to update a master file, such as a recording of daily sales used to update the sales account , receivables, cash account, inventory, etc.

tran-scend (tran send´) *v.* To pass beyond; to exceed; to surpass. **transcendent** *adj.* **transcendence** *n.*

tran-scribe (tran skrīb´) *v.* To make copies of something; to adopt or arrange.

tran-script (tran´skript) *n.* A written copy.

trans-crip-tion (tran skrip´shǝn) *n.* The process or act of transcribing.

trans-fer (trans fer´) *v.* To remove, shift, or carry from one position to another. In computer science, to move data or files from one location , storage device, or computer to another. **transferable** *adj.* **transference** *n.*

trans-fig-ure (trans fig´yer) *v.* To change the outward appearance or form; to exalt; to glorify. **transfiguration** *n.*

trans-fix (trans fiks´) *v.* To pierce; to hold motionless, as with terror, awe or amazement. **transfixion** *n.*

trans-form (trans form´) *v.* To change or alter completely in nature, form or function. **transformable** *adj.* **transformation** *n.* **transformer** *n.*

trans-fuse (trans fūz´) *v.* To transfer liquid by pouring from one place to another. *Med.* To pass blood from the blood vessels of one person into the vessels of another. **transfusion** *n.* **transfuser** *n.*

trans-gress (trans gres´) *v.* To go beyond the limit or boundaries; to sin against or violate. **transgression** *n.* **transgressor** *n.* **transgressive** *adj.*

tran-sient (tran´shent) *adj.* Not staying or lasting very long; moving from one location to another. In computer science, temporary, as a file that is created by a program while it is processing, then deleted when processing is completed.

tran-sit (tran´sit) *n.* Passage or travel from one point to another; an instrument for surveying that measures horizontal and vertical angles.

trans-late (trans lāt´) *v.* To change from one language to another while retaining the orig-inal meaning; to explain. In computer science, to change signals to a different format, as from analog to digital; to adapt data files to a format that can be read by a different program. **translation** *n.* **translator** *n.*

trans-lu-cent (trans lō´sent) *adj.* Diffusing and admitting light but not allowing a clear view of the object.

trans-mis-sion (trans mish´ǝn) *n.* The act or state of transmitting. *Mech.* The gears and associated parts of an engine which transmit power to the driving wheels of an automobile or other vehicle. In *computer science*, the transfer of signals between parts of a computer system.

transmission speed *n.* In *computer science*, the rate at which data can be sent and received.

trans-mit (trans mit´) *v.* To dispatch or convey from one thing, person, or place to another. **transmissible** *adj.* **transmittable** *adj.* **transmitter** *n.*

trans-mute (trans mūt´) *v.* To change in nature, kind, or substance.

tran-som (tran´sǝm) *n.* A small, hinged window over a doorway; the horizontal crossbar in a window.

trans-par-ent (trans pâr´en sē) *adj.* Admitting light so that images and objects can be clearly viewed; easy to understand; obvious. In computer science, descriptive of computer processing that is taking place in the background , not under the direct supervision of, or apparent to, the user. Seen through or easily detected. **transparency** *n.* **transparently** *adv.*

tran-spire (tran spīer´) *v.* To give off waste products through plant or animal pores in the form of vapor; to happen; to take place. **transpiration** *n.*

trans-plant (trans plant´) *v.* To remove a living plant from where it is growing and plant it in another place; to remove a body organ from one person and implant it in the body of another, as a heart or a kidney transplant, to remove skin from one area of the body and move it to another area of the body, as a skin graft. **transplant** *n.* **transplantable** *adj.*

trans-port (trans pört´) *v.* To carry or move from one place to another. *n.* A vessel or ship used to carry military supplies and troops; the process or act of transporting. **transportation** *n.*

trans-pose (trans pōz´) *v.* To reverse the place or order of. *Mus.* To perform or write music in a key different from the one it was originally written in.

trans-sex-u-al *n.* A person whose sex has been changed surgically.

trap (trap) *n.* A device for holding or catching animals; *v.* To catch in a trap; to place in an embarrassing position. *Slang* The mouth.

tra-peze (tra pēz´) *n.* A short horizontal bar suspended by two ropes, used for acrobatic exercise or stunts.

trau-ma (trou´ma) *n. pl.* -mas *or* -mata A severe wound caused by a sudden physical injury; an emotional shock causing lasting and substantial damage to a person's psychological develop-ment.

tra-vail (tra vāl´) n. Strenuous mental or physical exertion; labor in childbirth. v. To undergo the sudden sharp pain of childbirth.

trav-el (trav´el) v. To journey or move from one place to another. n. The process or act of traveling. **-er** n.

tra-verse (trav´ers) v. To pass over, across, or through. n. A path or route across; something that lies across something else. **-sable** adj., **-al** n.

trawl (trol) n. A strong fishing net which is dragged through water.

tray (trā) n. A flat container having a low rim, used for carrying, holding, or displaying something.

treach-er-ous (threch´er us) adj. Disloyal; deceptive; unreliable. **treacherously** adv. **treachery** n.

tread (tred) v. To walk along, on, or over; to trample. n. The act or manner of treading; the part of a wheel which comes into contact with the ground.

trea-son (trē´zon) n. Violation of one's allegiance to a sovereign or country, as giving or selling state secrets to another country or attempting to overthrow the government. **treasonable** adj. **treasonous** adj.

treas-ure (trezh´er) n. Hidden riches; something regarded as valuable. v. To save and accumulate for future use; to value.

treasurer (trezh´er er) n. A person having charge and responsibilities for funds.

treas-ur-y (trezh´a rē) n. pl. **-ies** A place where public or private funds are kept. **Treasury** The executive department of the United States Government in charge of collection, management, and expenditure of public revenue.

treat (trēt) v. To behave or act toward; to regard in a given manner; to provide entertainment or food for another at one's own expense or cost. n. A pleasant surprise; something enjoyable which was unexpected. **treatable** adj.

treat-ment (trēt´ment) n. The manner or act of treating; medical care.

treb-le (treb´l) adj. Multiplied by three; having three. Mus. Performing or having the highest range, part, or voice. n. A high-pitched sound or voice.

tree (trē) n. A tall woody plant, usually having a single trunk of considerable height; a diagram resembling a tree, as one used to show family descent. Slang To get the advantage of something. In computer science, a graphic representation of a directory structure showing the directories that branch from the root directory, then their subdirectories, etc. **tree** v.

tre-foil (trē´foil) n. Any of various plants having three leaflets with red, purple, yellow, or pink flowers.

trek (trek) v. To make a slow and arduous journey. **trek** n. **trekker** n.

trel-lis (trel´is) n. A lattice work frame used for supporting vines and other climbing plants.

trem-ble (trem´bl) v. To shake involuntarily, as with fear or from cold; to express or feel anxiety. **tremble** n. **trembler** n. **trembly** adj.

tre-men-dous (tri men´dus) adj. Extremely huge, large, or vast. Slang Wonderful.

trem-or (trem´er) n. A quick, shaking movement; any continued and involuntary trembling or quavering of the body.

trench (trench) n. A ditch; a long, narrow excavation in the ground. v. To cut deep furrows for protection. **trencher** n.

trend (trend) n. A general inclination, direction, or course; a fad. v. To have a specified direction. **-setter** n.

Tren-ton n. The capital of the state of New Jersey.

tres-pass (tres´pas) v. To infringe upon another's property; in law, to invade the rights, property, or privacy of another without consent or knowledge.

tri-al (trī´al) n. In law, the examination and hearing of a case before a court of law in order to determine the case; an attempt or effort; an experimental treatment or action to determine a result. adj. Pertaining to or of a trial; performed or used during an experiment or test.

tri-an-gle (trī´ang´gl) n., Geom. A plane figure bounded by three sides and having three angles. **triangular** adj.

tribe (trīb) n. A group of people composed of several villages, districts, or other groups which share a common language, culture, and name.

trib-u-la-tion (trib´ū lā´shan) n. Great distress or suffering caused by oppression.

trib-ute (trib´ūt) n. An action of respect or gratitude to someone; money or other goods given by one country to another showing obedience and insuring against invasion.

tri-ceps (trī´seps) n., Anat. The large muscle at the back of the upper arm.

trick (trik) n. An action meant to fool, as a scheme; a prank; a feat of magic. v. To deceive or cheat. **tricky** adj.

trick-er-y (trik´e rē) n. Deception.

trick-le (trik´l) v. To flow in droplets or a small stream. **trickle** n.

tri-cy-cle (trī´si kl) n. A small vehicle having three wheels, propelled by pedals.

tri-dent (trīd´ent) n. A long spear with three prongs, used as a weapon.

tried (trīd) *adj.* Tested and proven reliable or useful.

tri-en-ni-al (trī en´ē al) *adj.* Happening every third year; lasting for a time period of three years. **triennial** *n.* **triennially** *adv.*

tri-fle (trī´fl) *n.* Something of little value or importance; a dessert made with cake, jelly, wine, and custard. *v.* To use or treat without proper concern.

trig-ger (trig´ĕr) *n.* A lever pulled to fire a gun; a device used to release or start an action. *v.* To start.

trill *n.* A tremulous utterance of successive tones. *v.* To utter with a fluttering sound.

tril-lion (tril´yon) *n.* The cardinal number equal to one thousand billion.

trim (trim) *v.* To clip or cut off small amounts in order to make neater; to decorate. *adj.* Neat. **trim** *n.*

tri-ni-tro-tol-u-ene (trī nī´trōtol´ū ēn´) *n.* A very powerful explosive, abbreviated as TNT.

trin-ket (tring´kit) *n.* A small piece of jewelry.

tri-o (trē´ō) *n.* A set or group of three.

trip (trip) *n.* Travel from one place to another; a journey; a loss of balance. *v.* To stumble. *Slang* A hallucinatory effect induced by drugs.

tripe (trīp) *n.* The stomach lining of oxen or similar animals, used as food. *Slang* Nonsense.

trip-le (trip´l) *adj.* Having three parts. *v.* To multiply by three; in baseball, a three-base hit.

trip-let (trip´lit) *n.* One of three born at the same time.

trip-li-cate (trip´li kāt´) *n.* A group of three identical things. **triplicate** *v.*

tri-pod (trī´pod) *n.* A three-legged stand or frame.

trite (trīt) *adj.* Used too often; common.

tri-umph (trī´umf) *v.* To be victorious. *n.* A victory. **triumphant** *adj.*

triv-i-al (triv´ē al) *adj.* Insignificant; of little value or importance; ordinary

trol-ley (trol´ē) *n.* A streetcar powered by electricity from overhead lines; a small container or basket used to convey material, as in an underground tunnel or mine.

trom-bone (trom bōn´) *n.* A brass musical instrument, larger and lower in pitch than a trumpet.

troop (trōp) *n.* A group or assembly of people or animals; a group of Boy Scouts or Girl Scouts having an adult leader; a military unit. **trooper** *n.*

tro-phy (trō´fē) *n. pl.* -ies A prize or object, such as a plaque, awarded to someone for his success, victory, or achievement.

trop-ic (trop´ik) *n.* Either of two imaginary parallel lines which constitute the Torrid Zone. **Tropics** The very warm region of the earth's surface that lies between the Tropic of Cancer and the Tropic of Capricorn. **tropical** *adj.*

tro-po-sphere (trop´o sfēr´) *n.* The lowest atmosphere between the earth's surface and the stratosphere.

trot (trot) *n.* The gait of a horse or other four-footed animal, between a walk and a run, in which the hind leg and opposite front leg move at about the same time.

troth (troth) *n.* Good faith; the act of pledging one's fidelity. **troth** *v.*

trou-ble (trub´l) *n.* Danger; affliction; need; distress; an effort; physical pain, disease or malfunction. *v.* To bother; to worry; to be bothered; to be worried. **troubler** *n.* **troublingly** *adv.*

troubleshoot In *computer science,* to attempt to locate the source of a hardware or software problem and correct it.

trough (trof) *n.* A long, narrow, shallow container, especially one that holds food or water for animals.

troupe (trōp) *n.* A group, especially of the performing arts. **troupe** *v.*

trou-sers (trou´zĕrz) *n. pl.* An outer garment that covers the body from the waist down.

trout (trout) *n.* A freshwater game or food fish.

trowel (trou´el) *n.* A flat-bladed garden tool with a pointed blade, used for digging. **trowel** *v.* **troweler** *n.*

tru-ant (trö´ant) *n.* A person who is absent from school without permission.

truce (trös) *n.* An agreement to stop fighting; a cease-fire.

truck (truk) *n.* An automotive vehicle used to carry heavy loads; any of various devices with wheels designed to move heavy loads; garden vegetables for sale. **trucker** *n.*

trudge (truj) *v.* To walk heavily; to plod.

true (trö) *adj.* In accordance with reality or fact; not false; real; loyal; faithful. *adv.* Truthfully. **truly** *adv.*

Truman, Harry S. *n.* (1884-1972) The thirty-third president of the United States from 1945-1953.

trump (trump) *n.* In cards, a suit of any cards which outrank all other cards for a selected period of time.

trum-pet (trum´pit) *n., Mus.* A brass instrument having a flared bell, valves, and a mouthpiece. *v.* To proclaim something loudly.

truncate In computer science, to shorten by eliminating less significant parts, as by rounding off a decimal number or eliminating leading zeros in the number.

trunk (trungk) *n.* The main part of a tree;

the human body, excluding the head, arms and legs; a sturdy box for packing clothing, as for travel or storage; the long snout of an elephant. **trunks** Men's clothing worn for swimming or athletics.

truss (trus) v. To fasten or tie securely. *Med.* A support or device worn to keep a hernia in place.

trust (trust) n. Confidence or faith in a person or thing; care or charge. *Law* The confidence or arrangement by which property is managed and held for the good or benefit of another person. v. To have confidence or faith in; to believe; to expect; to entrust; to depend on.

truth (trōth) n., pl. **truths** The facts corresponding with actual events or happenings; sincerity or honesty. **truthful** adj. **truthfully** adv. **truthfulness** n.

try (trī) v. To make an attempt; to make an effort; to strain; to hear or conduct a trial; to place on trial. **trying** adj.

tsp abbr. Teaspoon.

tub (tub) n. A round, low, flat-bottomed, vessel often with handles on the side, as one used for washing.

tu-ba (tō´ba) n. A large, brass wind instrument having a low pitch.

tube (tōb) n. A hollow cylinder, made of metal, rubber, glass or other material, used to pass or convey something through. **tube** adj. **tubal** adj.

tu-ber (tō´bér) n. The underground stem of certain plants, as the potato, with buds from which new plants arise.

tu-ber-cu-lo-sis n. A contagious lung disease of humans and animals caused by bacteria; abbreviated as TB.

tuck (tuk) n. A flattened fold of material, usually stitched in place. v. To sew or make a tuck in material; to put in a safe place; to make secure.

tuft (tuft) n. A small cluster of feathers, threads, hair, or other material fastened or growing closely together.

tug (tug) v. To strain and pull vigorously. n. A hard pull; a strong force.

tu-i-tion (tō ish´an) n. Payment for instruction, as at a private school or college.

tu-lip (tō´lip) n. A bulb-type plant, having upright cup-like blossoms.

tum-ble (tum´bl) v. To fall or cause to fall; to perform acrobatic rolls, somersaults, and similar maneuvers; to mix up; to turn over and over. **tumbler** n. **tumble** n.

tum-ble-down (tum´bl doun´) adj. Ramshackle; in need of repair.

tu-mor (tō´mér) n., *Pathol.* A swelling on or in any part of the body; an abnormal growth which may be malignant or benign.

tu-mult (tō´mult) n. The confusion and noise of a crowd; a riot; any violent commotion. **tumultuous** adj.

tu-na (tō´na) n. pl. -na or -nas Any of several large marine food fish.

tune (tōn) n. A melody which is simple and easy to remember; agreement; harmony. v. To adjust. **tunable** adj. **tunably** adv.

tu-nic (tō´nik) n. A loose garment extending to the knees, worn by ancient Romans and Greeks.

tun-nel (tun´el) n. An underground or underwater passageway. **tunnel** v.

tur-ban (ter´ban) n. A Moslem headdress that consists of a long scarf wound around the head.

tur-bine (ter´bin) n. A motor having one or more rotary units mounted on a shaft, which are turned by the force of gas or a liquid.

tur-bu-lent (ter´bya lent) adj. Marked by a violent disturbance. **turbulence** n. **turbulently** adv.

tu-reen (te rēn´) n. A large dish, often covered, used to serve soup or stew.

turf (terf) n. A layer of earth with its dense growth of grass and matted roots. *Slang* Home territory or ground.

tur-key (ter´kē) n. A large game bird of North America, having a bare head and extensible tail; the meat of this bird. *Slang* A failure.

tur-moil (ter´moil) n. A state of confusion or commotion.

turn (tern) v. To move or cause to move around a center point; to revolve or rotate; to transform or change; to move so that the bottom side of something becomes the top and the top becomes the bottom.

turn-buck-le (tern´buk´l) n. A metal coupling, used to regulate the distance between two metal rods or wires.

turn-down (tern´doun´) n., *Slang* A rejection or refusal.

tur-nip (ter´nip) n. An edible root from the mustard family of plants.

turn-over (tern´ō´vér) n. The process or act of turning over; an upset; a change or reversal; the number of times merchandise is bought, sold, and restocked in a certain period of time; the number of people hired in a given period of time to replace those who have left.

tur-pen-tine (ter´pen tīn´) n. The thick sap of certain pine trees; a clear liquid manufactured from this sap, used to thin paint.

tur-quoise (ter´koiz) n. A blue-green gemstone; a light bluish-green color.

tur-ret (ter´it) n. A small ornamental tower on a building; a raised, usually rotating, section of a ship, tank, or plane where the gunner sits.

tur-tle (ter'tl) *n.* A scaly-skinned animal having a soft-body covered with a hard shell into which the head, legs, and tail can be retracted.

tusk (tusk) *n.* A long, curved tooth, as of an elephant or walrus.

tus-sle (tus'l) *n.* A hard fight or struggle with a problem or person. **tussle** *v.*

tu-tor (tö'tër) *n.* A person who teaches another person privately. *v.* To teach, coach, or instruct privately.

tutorial In *computer science*, an adjunct to a program that teaches the user how to use each program.

tut-ti–frut-ti (tö'tē frö'tē) *n.* An ice cream flavor that contains different types of can-died fruits.

tu-tu (tö'tö) *n.* A very short ballet skirt.

tux-e-do (tuk sē'dö) *n.* A semiformal dress suit worn by men.

twang (twang) *n.* A sharp, ringing sound like that of a violin or other stringed instrument. *v.* To cause or make a twang.

tweak (twēk) *v.* To pinch and twist sharply. **tweak** *n.*

tweed (twēd) *n.* A coarse woolen fabric, woven in two or more colors. **tweeds** Clothing made of tweed.

tweez-ers (twē'zërz) *n. pl.* A small, pincer-like implement used to grasp or pluck small objects.

twelve (twelv) *n.* The cardinal number equal to 11 + 1.

twen-ty (twen'tē) *n.* The cardinal number equal to 19 + 1 or 2 X 10.

twice (twīs) *adv.* Double; two times.

twid-dle (twid'l) *v.* To turn or twirl in an aimless way.

twig (twig) *n.* A small branch which grows from a larger branch on a tree.

twi-light (twi'līt') *n.* The soft light of the sky between sunset and complete darkness.

twill (twil) *n.* A weave that produces the parallel rib on the surface of a fabric.

twin (twin) *n.* One of two persons born at the same time to the same mother; one of two similar persons or things. *adj.* Having two similar or identical parts.

twine (twin) *v.* To weave or twist together. *n.* A strong cord or thread made by twisting many threads together.

twinge (twinj) *n.* A sudden, sharp pain; a brief emotional or mental pang.

twin-kle (twing'kl) *v.* To gleam or shine with quick flashes; to sparkle.

twirl (twerl) *v.* To rotate or cause to turn around and around. **twirl** *n.*

twist (twist) *v.* To wind two or more pieces of thread, twine, or other materials together to make a single strand; to curve; to bend; to distort or change the meaning of; to injure and wrench. *n.* The act of twisting.

twit (twit) *v.* To tease about a mistake. *n.* A taunting reproach.

twitch (twich) *v.* To move or cause to move with a jerky movement. *n.* A sudden tug.

two (tö) *n.* The cardinal number of 1 + 1; the second in a sequence.

two-bit (tö'bit') *adj.* Insignificant. **bits** Twenty-five cents. **faced** Double-dealing. **twofold.** Being double as much or as many.

two–time (tö'tim') *v., Slang* To be unfaithful to. **two-timer** *n.*

ty-coon (ti kön') *n., Slang* A business person of wealth and power.

tyke (tik) *n.* A small child.

Tyler, John *n.* (1790-1862) The tenth president of the United States from 1841-1845.

type (tip) *n.* A class or group of persons or things; letters, numbers, and other symbols typewritten on paper or another surface; in printing, the piece of plastic, metal, or wood having the character or characters that are printed; a model or example of. **type** *v.* To identify according to some sort of classification; to typewrite. **typecast** *v.* To use more than once or repeatedly in the same kind of role.

type-face (tip'fās') *n.* A style or design of printing type.

type-set-ter (tip'set'ër) *n.* A person who arranges or sets type. **typesetting** *n.*

ty-phoid (ti'foid) *n., Pathol.* An acute, infectious disease caused by germs in drink or food, resulting in high fever and intestinal hemorrhaging.

ty-phoon (ti fön') *n.* A tropical hurricane, especially one in the western part of the Pacific Ocean.

typ-i-cal (tip'i kal) *adj.* Exhibiting the characteristics of a certain class or group. **typically** *adv.*

typ-i-fy (tip'i fi') *v.* To be characteristic or typical of; to show all the traits or qualities of a group. **typification** *n.* **typifying** *adj.*

typ-ist (ti'pist) *n.* The operator of a typewriter.

ty-po (ti'pö) *n., Slang* An error in typewriting or in setting type; any printed error which was not the fault of the author.

ty-ran-no-sau-rus (ti ran'o sor') *n.* A large, flesh-eating dinosaur which walked on its hind legs.

tyr-an-ny (tir'a nē) *n.* Harsh, absolute, and unfair rule by a government, king or other ruler.

ty-rant (ti'rant) *n.* An absolute, unjust, or cruel ruler; one who exercises power or control unfairly.

ty-ro *also* **ti-ro (tirö)** *n.* A novice or a beginner.

U, u (ū) The twenty-first letter of the English alphabet.

ubiq-ui-none *n.* The quinone which is able to function as an electron transfer agent in the Kreb's cycle.

ubiq-ui-tous (ū bik′wi tus) *adj.* To be everywhere at the same point in time.

ubiq-ui-ty (ū bik′wi tē) *n.* A presence in many places or locations at the same time.

ud-der (ud′er) *n.* The milk-producing organ pouch of some female animals, having two or more teats.

ugh (öch) Used to express disgust or horror.

ug-li-fy (ug′li fī) v. To make something or someone ugly.

ug-ly (ug′lē) *adj.* Offensive; unpleasant to look at.

ug-some *adj.* To be loathsome.

uh *interj.* To express hesitation.

uh–huh *interj.* Used for the purpose of showing or indicating agreement.

uhf *abbr.* Ultra high frequency.

uh-lan (ö′län) *n.* Part of a body of the Prussian light cavalry that was originally modeled on Tartar lancers.

uin-ta-ite *n.* A type of black asphalt which can be found especially in Utah.

ukase *n.* The proclamation by a Russian government that has the force of law.

u-ku-le-le (ū′kǎ lā′lē) *n.* A small, four-stringed musical instrument, originally from Hawaii.

ula-ma *n.* Body of mullahs.

-u-lar *adj., suffix* To be relating to.

ul-cer (ul′sèr) *n.* A festering, inflamed sore on a mucous membrane or on the skin that results in the destruction of the tissue. **ulcerous** *adj.*

ul-cero-gen-ic *adj.* To be tending to develop into an ulcer.

-ule *n., suffix* Small or little one.

-u-lent *adj., suffix* That abounds in.

ulex-ite *n.* A kind of mineral that occurs in loose fibers that is able to transmit light lengthwise with very little diminished intensity.

ul-lage (ul′ij) *n.* That amount a container lacks from being full.

ul-na (ul′na) *n., Anat.* One of the two bones of the forearm.

-u-lose *n., suffix* Ketose sugar.

ulot-ri-chous (ū lo′ti kus) *adj.* To have crisp or woolly hair.

-u-lous *adj., suffix* Being slightly.

ul-ster (ul′stèr) *n.* A type of long loose overcoat that is of Irish origin and is made of heavy material.

ul-te-ri-or (ul tēr′ē ér) *adj.* To be located or situated on the further side of something or someone.

ultima *n.* A last syllable of a word.

ul-ti-ma ra-tio *n.* A final argument or the last resort to a problem or discussion.

ul-ti-mate (ul′ti mit) *adj.* Final; ending; most extreme; maximum; most.

ul-ti-ma-tum (ul′ti mä′tum) *n. pl* -tums, -ta   A final demand, proposal, or choice, as in negotiating.

ul-ti-mo (ul′ti mō′) *adj.* To be happening or occurring in the month which precedes the present.

ul-ti-mo-gen-i-ture (ul′ti mō jen′i chèr) *n.* The system of inheritance where the youngest boy succeeds to the estate.

ultra *adj.* To be going beyond others.

ul-tra- (ul′tra) *prefix* Beyond the scope, range, or limit of something.

ul-tra-ba-sic *adj.* To be extremely basic. **ultrabasic** *n.*

ul-tra-cen-trif-u-gal *adj.* Pertaining to being obtained by the means or methods of ultra-centrifuge.

ul-tra-cen-tri-fuge (ul′tra sen′tri füj′) *n.* A kind of high speed centrifuge that is able to sediment colloidal and other small particles.

ul-tra-con-ser-va-tive (ul′tra kon sür′va tiv) *adj.* To be extremely cautious.

ul-tra-fash-ion-able *adj.* Being up-to-date with fashions and customs.

ul-tra-fiche *n.* A type of microfiche whose microimages are of printed matter which has been reduced 90 times or more.

ul-tra-fil-tra-tion *n.* The act of filtrating small particles through a membrane and holding back the larger particles.

ul-tra-high *adj.* To be exceedingly high.

ul-tra-ism (ul′tra iz′um) *n.* An example of radicalism. **ultraist** *n. or adj.*

ul-tra-lib-er-al *adj.* To be very liberal. **ultraliberal** *n.*

ul-tra-ma-rine (ul′tra ma rēn′) *adj.* To be situated beyond the sea or the ocean.

ul-tra-mi-cro *adj.* To be referring or dealing with something which is smaller than micro.

ul-tra-mi-cro-scope (ul′tra mī′kro sköp′) *n.* A type of instrument used for the purpose of viewing objects which are too small to be viewed through a regular microscope.

ul-tra-mi-cro-scop-ic *adj.* Being too small in size to be viewed with a regular microscope.

ul-tra-mi-cro-tome *n.* A type of microtome that is made or designed to cut very thin sections off of something for the purpose of examining it. **ultramicrotomy** *n.*

ul-tra-mil-i-tant *adj.* To be very militant. **ultramilitant** *n.*

ul-tra-min-ia-ture *adj.* Extremely small; below miniature; tiny.

ul-tra-mod-ern (ul′tra mod′èrn) *adj.* Extremely advanced or modern in style or ideas.

ul-tra-na-tion-al-ism *n.* An excessive devotion to national interests.

ul-tra-pure *adj.* To be of the utmost purity. **ultrapurely** *adv.*

ul-tra-se-cret *adj.* To be highly secret.

ul-tra-short *adj.* To be short in duration.

ul-tra-son-ic (ul´tra son´ik) *adj.* Relating to sound frequencies inaudible to humans. **ultrasonically** *adv.*

ul-tra-son-ics *n.* The science of the ultrasonic happenings and phenomena.

ul-tra-so-phis-ti-cat-ed *adj.* To be very sophisticated.

ult-ra-sound *n.* The vibrations of the same physical nature as sound.

ul-tra-vi-o-let (ul´tra vī´o lit) *adj.* Producing radiation having wave lengths just shorter than those of visible light and longer than those of x-rays.

ultra vires *adv.* Beyond the scope of legal authority.

ul-u-lant *adj.* To have a howling sound or noise. **ululation** *n.*

ul-u-late *v.* To howl like a wolf of dog; to wail very loud.

um-ber *n.* A moderate brown color.

um-bil-i-cal *adj.* Pertaining to the navel.

umbilical cord *n.* The structure by which a fetus is attached to its mother, serving to supply food and dispose of waste.

um-bil-i-cate *adj.* To be depressed such as the navel in appearance.

um-bil-i-cus (um bil´i kus) *n.* A little depression occurring in the abdominal wall where the umbilical cord was attached to the embryo.

um-bles (um´belz) *n.* Entrails of an animal such as a deer which used to be used as food.

um-bo (um´bō) *n.* The elevation of the tympanic membrane of the ear.

um-bra *n.* The conical shadow that excludes all light from the given source.

um-brage (um´brij) *n.* A reason for doubt.

um-bra-geous *adj.* To be filled with shadows. **umbrageousness** *n.*

um-brel-la (um brel´a) *n.* A collapsible frame covered with plastic or cloth, held above the head as protection from sun or rain.

umi-ak (ō´mē ak´) *n.* An open flat bottom Eskimo boat propelled with broad paddles.

ump *v., Slang* To act or to behave as an umpire such as in the game of baseball.

um-pir-age *n.* An act of umpiring.

um-pire (um´pī èr) *n.* In sports, the person who rules on plays in a game. *v.* To act as an umpire.

ump-teen (ump´tēn´) *adj., Slang* An indefinitely large number.

un- *prefix* The reverse or opposite of an act; removal or release from.

un-a-bat-ed *adj.* To be not abated.

un-able (un ā´bl) *adj.* Not having the mental capabilities.

un-abridged *adj.* To be the most complete of a group or of a class.

un-ac-cept-able (un´ak sep´ta bl) *adj.* To be not welcome. **unacceptably** *adv.*

un-ac-com-mo-dat-ed (un´a kom´o dā´tid) *adj.* To be not accommodated.

un-ac-com-pa-nied *adj.* Alone; without a companion. *Mus.* Solo.

un-ac-count-a-ble (un´a koun´ta bl) *adj.* Without an explanation; mysterious; not responsible. **unaccountably** *adv.*

un-ac-cus-tomed (un´a kus´tomd) *adj.* Not used to or in the habit of; not ordinary.

un-adorned (un´a dornd´) *n.* Being without decorations.

un-adorn-ment *n.* The state of being unadorned.

un-adul-ter-at-ed *adj.* To be pure.

un-ad-vised (un´ad vīzd´) *adj.* To do something or an action without consideration.

un-af-fect-ed (un´a fek´tid) *adj.* Not being affected in any way by something or someone.

un-af-fec-tion-ate *adj.* Without or lacking affection.

un-al-loyed (un´a loid´) *adj.* To be not alloyed; pure.

un-al-ter-able (un ol´tèr a bl) *adj.* Incapable of being changed. **unalterableness** *n.*

un-am-biv-a-lent *adj.* Being not ambivalent. **unambivalently** *adv.*

un-an-chor *v.* To remove or to loosen for an anchor, as a boat.

un-anes-the-tized *adj.* Not having been subject to the anesthetic.

u-na-nim-i-ty *n.* The state of being unanimous.

u-nan-i-mous (ū nan´i mus) *adj.* Agreed to completely; based on the agreement of all. **unanimously** *adv.*

un-an-tic-i-pat-ed *adj.* To be not anticipated. **unanticipatedly** *adv.*

un-apol-o-get-ic *adj.* To be put forward without an apology.

un-ap-peas-able *adj.* Not to be appeased.

un-ap-proach-able (un´a prō´cha bl) *adj.* To be physically inaccessible.

un-apt (un apt´) *adj.* Not likely.

un-armed (un ermd´) *adj.* Lacking means for protection.

un-ar-tic-u-lat-ed *adj.* To be not carefully reasoned before something is done.

una-ry *adj.* To consist of a single item.

un-a-shamed (un´a shāmd´) *adj.* To be without guilt. **unashamedly** *adv.*

un-as-sail-a-ble (un´a sā´la bl) *adj.* Being not liable to attack.

un-as-ser-tive (un´a sür´tiv) *adj.* Not being assertive.

un-as-sist-ed (un´a sis´tid) *adj.* To be made without being assisted by another.

un-as-sum-ing (un´a sö´ming) *adj.*

Modest and not showy.

un-at-tach-ed (un´a tacht´) *adj*. Not engaged, going steady, or married.

un-at-trac-tive *adj*. Not attractive or pretty; dull.

un-a-vail-ing (un´a vā´ling) *adj*. To be not availing.

un-a-void-able (un´a void´a bl) *adj*. Inevitable; unstoppable. **avoidably** *adv*.

un-a-ware (un´a wâr´) *adj*. Not realizing. **unawareness** *n*. **unawarely** *adv*.

un-backed *adj*. To be lacking aid or support from another.

un-bal-ance (un bal´ans) *v*. To put someone or something out of balance.

un-bal-anced (un bal´anst) *adj*. Not in balance.

un-bar-bered *adj*. To have unkempt long hair.

un-barred *adj*. Not being fixed or secured with a bar.

un-be *v*. To cease to have being.

un-bear-a-ble (un bâr´a bl) *adj*. Not possible to endure; intolerable.

un-beat-able (un bēt´a bl) *adj*. To be possessing unsurpassable qualities.

unbeaten *adj*. Being not pounded.

un-be-com-ing (un bi kum´ing) *adj*. Unattractive; not pleasing; not proper, polite or suitable for the situation or occasion. **unbecomingness** *n*.

un-be-known *or* **un-be-knownst** (un´bin-ōnst´) *adj*. Not known; without one's knowledge.

un-be-lief *n*. The skepticism in the matters such as one's religious faith.

un-be-liev-able (un´bi lēv´a bl) *adj*. Incredible; hard to accept; not to be believed. **unbelievably** *adv*.

un-be-liev-er (un´bi lē´vér) *n*. A person who does not believe certain things as being true.

un-belt-ed *adj*. To not be belted or furnished with a belt.

un-bend (un bend´) *v*. To make something straight. **unbendable** *adj*.

un-bend-ing (un ben´ding) *adj*. To not bend.

un-bi-ased *adj*. To be not biased.

un-bib-li-cal *adj*. To be unsanctioned by the Bible.

un-bid-den (un bid´en) *adj*. To be not bidden.

un-bind (un bīnd´) *v*. To take or remove a band from something or from someone.

un-blessed (un blest) *adj*. To be not blessed.

un-blind-ed *adj*. Existing free from illusion.

un-blink-ing *adj*. Not showing any emotions such as crying.

un-block *v*. To free something from being blocked by something else.

un-bod-i-ed (un bod´ēd) *adj*. To have no body.

un-bolt (un bōlt´) *v*. To unfasten with the withdrawal of a bolt such as with a lock on a door.

un-born (un born) *adj*. To be existing without birth.

un-bo-som (un bŭz´om) *v*. To disclose or tell the thoughts of oneself to another.

un-bound (un bound´) *adj*. Being free or not fastened to anything or by anything.

un-brace (un brās´) *v*. To detach as if removing a brace or a band from something or someone.

un-braid *v*. To take apart grouped strands of hair or cloth.

un-branched (un brancht´) *adj*. To have no or be without branches.

un-bred (un bred´) *adj*. Being not taught.

un-bri-dle *v*. To free from or to unfasten a bridle.

un-bro-ken (un brō´ken) *adj*. Being not violated or broken; being in one piece.

un-buck-le (un buk´l) *v*. To loosen or remove the buckle of something such as a belt.

un-budg-ing *adj*. Unable to be moved or changed.

un-build (un bild) *v*. To take down such as a house.

un-bun-dle *v*. To price or place something separately.

un-bur-den (un bŭr´den) *v*. To relieve from a burden; to free from fears or problems.

un-but-tered *adj*. Being without butter.

un-cage *v*. To set something or someone free from a cage or the object that holds them.

un-cal-cu-lat-ed *adj*. Not thought about or out before it occurs.

un-called for (un kåld´fâr´) *adj*. Not necessary or needed; not requested.

un-can-did *adj*. Not honest.

un-can-ny (un kan´ē) *adj*. Strange, odd, or mysterious; exceptional. **uncannily** *adv*. **uncanniness** *n*.

un-cap (un kap´) *v*. To remove covering or lid of something.

un-caused *adj*. Having no cause or reason.

un-ceas-ing *adj*. To never cease or end. **unceasingly** *adv*.

un-cel-e-brat-ed *adj*. Not being famous or well-known.

un-cer-e-mo-ni-ous (un´ser e mō´nē us) *adj*. To be informal; not ceremonious.

un-cer-tain (un ser´tan) *adj*. Doubtful; not sure; not known; hard to predict.

un-cer-tain-ty (un sür´tan tē) *n*. The state of being uncertain or unsure.

un-change-able (un chān´ja bl) *adj*. To be not changing. **-ableness** *n*.

un-changed *adj*. Having nothing new or different.

un-char-ac-ter-is-tic *adj*. Being not

typical.

un-charged (un chärjd´) *adj*. Not being charged with something.

un-char-i-ta-ble (un char´i ta bl) *adj*. To be lacking in charity. -ness *n*.

un-chart-ed (un chär´tid) *adj*. Not plotted such as on a map.

un-chiv-al-rous *adj*. Not being chivalrous. **unchivalrously** *adv*.

un-choke *v*. To unblock an obstruction such as a piece of food in the throat.

un-ci-al (un shē al) *n*. A style of writing used in Greek and Latin manuscripts.

un-ci-form (un´si form´) *adj*. To be hook shaped.

un-ci-nar-ia *n*. A type of parasitic worm in the shape of a hook; hookworm.

un-ci-nate (un´si nit) *adj*. To be bent at the end or the tip.

un-cir-cum-cised (un sür´kum sīzd´) *adj*. Being spiritually impure.

un-civ-il (un siv´il) *adj*. Being not civil.

un-civ-i-lized (un siv´i lizd´) *adj*. Without culture or refinement; without an established cultural and social way of living.

un-clamp *v*. To remove the clamp off of something.

un-clar-i-ty *n*. A lack of clarity.

un-clasp (un klasp´) *v*. To remove the clasp of or open the clasp of something.

un-clas-si-cal *adj*. Not being classical.

un-clas-si-fied *adj*.To not be subject to a security classification.

un-cle (ung´kl) *n*. The brother of one's mother or father; the husband of an aunt.

un-clean (un klēn´) *adj*. Immoral; dirty; not decent

un-clench (un klench´) *v*. To open something from a clenched position.

un-climb-a-ble *adj*. Unable to be climbed. **unclimbableness** *n*.

un-cloak (un klōk´) *v*. To remove a cover from

un-closed *adj*. Not being settled.

un-clothe (un klōth´) *v*. To uncover or undress.

un-cloud-ed *adj*. Not being covered by clouds. **uncloudedly** *adv*.

un-clut-ter (un klut´ér) *v*. To take clutter from an area; to make neat.

un-cof-fin *v*. To take out of a coffin.

un-coil (un koil´) *v*. To release from a coiled state; to unwind.

un-coined (un koind´) *adj*. Not being minted.

un-com-fort-a-ble (un kumf´ta bl) *adj*. Disturbed; not at ease physically or mentally; causing discomfort.

un-com-mit-ted (un´ko mit´id) *adj*. Not being committed to something or to someone.

un-com-mon (un kom´on) *adj*. Rare; odd; unusual; extraordinary. -ly *adv*.

un-com-mu-ni-ca-ble *adj*. Being unable to communicate something.

un-com-mun-i-ca-tive (un´ko mū´ni kā´tiv) *adj*. Not able to give information about something.

un-com-pas-sion-ate *adj*. Being unfeeling; not compassionate.

un-com-pet-i-tive *adj*. Being unable to compete in a competition or sport.

un-com-plain-ing*adj*. Notcomplaining. **uncomplainingly** *adv*.

un-com-pli-cat-ed *adj*. To be not complex or complicated; simple.

un-com-pli-men-ta-ry (un´kom pli men´ta rē) *adj*. Not being complimentary.

un-com-pre-hend-ing (un´kom pli men´ta rē) *adj*. To be lacking in understanding of something.

un-com-pro-mis-ing (un kom´pro mī´zing) *adj*. Firm; unwilling to give in or to compromise.

un-con-cern (un´kon sern´) *n*. Lack of interest; disinterest; indifference.

un-con-cerned *adj*. The state of not having any interest in something or someone. **unconcernedly** *adv*.

un-con-di-tion-al (un´kon dish´a nal) *adj*. Without conditions or limits.

un-con-di-tioned *adj*. Not subject to conditioning.

un-con-form-a-ble (un´kon for´ma bl) *adj*. Not conforming to anything such as ideals.

un-con-for-mi-ty *n*. The lack of conformity.

un-con-ge-nial *adj*. Not being compatible to something or to someone.

un-con-ge-nial-i-ty *n*. The state of being uncongenial.

un-con-quer-a-ble (un kong´ke a bl) *adj*. Being unable to be conquered by someone.

un-con-scio-na-ble (un kon´sha na bl) *adj*. To be not guided by the conscience. **unconscionability**, *n*.

un-con-scious (un kon´shus) *adj*. Not mentally aware; done without thought; not on purpose.

un-con-sid-ered (un´kon sid´erd) *adj*. To be not worth considering.

un-con-sol-i-dat-ed *adj*. To be arranged loosely.

un-con-sti-tu-tion-al (un´kon sti tō´sha nal) *adj*. Contrary to the constitution or the basic laws of a state or country.

un-con-straint *adj*. To be free from constraint.

un-con-trol-la-ble (un´kon trō´la bl) *adj*. To exist free from the control of another.

un-con-ven-tion-al (un´kon ven´sha nal) *adj*. Not in accordance with convention.

un-con-vinc-ing *adj*. To not be convincing. **unconvincingly** *adv*.

un-cool *adj*. To be lacking or without assurance.

un-cork (un kork´) v. To release from a container that has been sealed with a cork.

un-cou-ple (un kup´l) v. To release or disconnect from railroad cars.

un-couth (un kōth´) adj. Acting or speaking crudely, unrefined; clumsy or awkward. **uncouthness** n.

un-cov-er (un kuv´ér) v. To remove the cover from something; to disclose.

un-cre-at-ed (un˝krē ā´tid) adj. To not exist because of creation.

un-crit-i-cal (un krit´i kal) adj. To be lacking in discrimination.

un-cross v. To remove or to change something from a crossed position.

un-crown v. To remove the crown from someone such as a king.

un-crum-ple v. To return something to its original smooth condition.

un-crush-a-ble adj. Not being able to be crushed by something or by someone.

unc-tion n. An ointment which is used for the purpose of anointing an injury.

unc-tu-ous (ungk´chö us) adj. To be smooth in texture; have organic matter and be easily workable.

un-curl (un kürl´) v. To straighten something from a curled position.

un-cut (un kut´) adj. Not being cut into.

un-cyn-i-cal adj. Not being cynical.

un-daunt-a-ble adj. To be incapable of being daunted.

un-daunt-ed (un don´tid) adj. Being courageously resolute. **-ly** adv.

un-de-bat-a-ble adj. Being not subject to debate. **undebatably** adv.

un-de-cid-ed (un˝di sī´did) adj. Unsettled; having made no firm decision; open to change. **-edly** adv.

undecylenic acid n. Type of acid that is found in perspiration.

un-de-fend-ed adj. Being not defended or protected.

un-dem-o-crat-ic adj. To not be agreeing with the ideals of the democratic party.

un-de-mon-stra-tive (un˝de mon´stra tiv) adj. Being restrained in the expression of one's feelings or emotions. **undemonstrativeness** n.

un-de-ni-a-ble (un´di nī´a bl) adj. Not open to doubt or denial; not possible to contradict. **undeniably** adv.

un-der (un´dér) prep. Below, in place or position; in a place lower than another; less in degree, number, or other quality; inferior in rank, quality, or character; during the reign or period; in accordance with. **under** adv. In; in a position underneath or below something; less than the required amount; insufficient.

under (un´dér) prefix Location beneath or below; lower in importance or rank, degree or amount.

un-der-a-chiev-er (un˝dér a chē´vér) n. A kind of student that fails to achieve his or her scholastic potential.

un-der-act (un˝dér akt´) v. To perform something in a feeble manner.

un-der-ac-tiv-i-ty n. A low level of activity which is thought of as not being normal.

un-der-age (un˝dér āj´) adj. Being less than legal age.

un-der-arm (un´dér ärm) n. The armpit.

un-der-bel-ly (un´dér bel´ē) n. The parts or sections of the body which are low.

un-der-bid (un˝dér bid´) v. To bid for something at a level which is too low.

un-der-bred (un˝dér bred´) adj. Being of an inferior breed.

un-der-brush (un´dér brush´) n. Small bushes, vines, and plants that grow under tall trees.

un-der-bud-get-ed adj. To be provided with a budget which is inadequate.

un-der-car-riage (un´dér kar´ij) n. The landing gear of an airplane.

un-der-charge (un˝dér chärj´) v. To charge too little for something that one buys.

un-der-class (un˝dér klas´) n. The class which is lower such as in high school.

un-der-class-man (un˝dér klas´man) n. A person who is a member of the freshman class in high school.

un-der-clothes (un´dér klōz´) n. Clothes worn next to the skin; underwear.

un-der-coat (un´dér kōt) n. A jacket which can be worn under another jacket.

un-der-coating n. A kind of waterproof coating which is applied to the underside of cars for the prevention of rusting and other types of wear.

un-der-cover (un˝dér kuv´ér) adj. To be executed in a secret manner; engaged in spying for one's country, etc.

un-der-croft (un˝dér kroft´) n. A type of room which is subterranean.

un-der-cur-rent (un´dér kür´ent) n. The current that is located below the surface currents in the water.

un-der-cut v. To sell something at a price which is lower than the competitor's price to get the business of the one being offered the price.

un-der-de-vel-oped (un˝dér di vel´apt) adj. Not fully mature or grown; lacking modern communications and industry.

un-der-de-vel-op-ment n. The state of being underdeveloped.

un-der-do (un˝dér dö) v. To do something less thoroughly than one is able to do it.

un-der-done (un˝dér dun´) adj. To be not completely cooked.

un-der-dress n. A piece of clothing which is made to be worn under the dress of a woman when the dress is sheer.

un-der-ed-u-cat-ed *adj.* Being educated poorly.

un-der-em-ployed *adj.* To have less than adequate employment.

un-der-es-ti-mate (un´dĕr es´ti māt´) *v.* To place or to put a value or price on something which is too low.

un-der-feed (un´dĕr fēd´) *v.* To feed someone or something too little food.

un-der-foot(un´dĕr fot´)*adj.* Underneath or below the feet; being so close to one's feet as to be in the way.

un-der-fur (un´dĕr für´) *n.* A thick and soft fur that is lying under the long and coarse hair of a mammal.

un-der-gar-ment (un´dĕr gär´ment) *n.* A kind of garment that is made to be worn under another piece of garment, such as underwear.

un-der-gird (un´dĕr gürd´) *v.* To make the foundation of something.

un-der-glaze (un´dĕr glāz´) *adj.* Suitable for applying before glaze is applied to something.

un-der-go (un´dĕr gō´) *v.* To have the experience of; to be subjected to.

un-der-grad-u-ate (un´dĕr graj´ū it) *n.* A college or university student studying for a bachelor's degree.

un-der-ground (un´dĕr ground´) *adj.* A channel or space which is subterranean. *n.* A group which functions outside of the law.

un-der-ground-er *n.* The member of the underground.

un-der-growth *n.* A type of growth which is found growing on the floor of the forest.

un-der-hand (un´dĕr hand´) *adj.* Done deceitfully and secretly; sly; sneaky. **underhandedly** *adv.*

un-der-hung *adj.* To have an underhung jaw; protruding or projecting beyond the upper jaw.

un-der-insured *adj.* Being not sufficiently insured.

un-der-laid (un´dĕr lād´) *adj.* To be placed beneath something.

un-der-lay (un´dĕr lā) *v.* To cover the bottom of something.

un-der-let (un´dĕr let) *v.* To be below the real value.

un-der-lie (un´dĕr li´) *v.* To be at the basis of something.

un-der-line (un´dĕr lin´) *v.* To draw a line directly under something.

un-der-ling (un´dĕr ling) *n.* The person who is under the orders of another person.

un-der-lip (un´dĕr lip´) *n.* The lower lip of a person's mouth.

un-der-ly-ing (un´dĕr li´ing) *adj.* To be lying below something.

un-der-manned *adj.* Being inadequately staffed.

un-der-mine (un´dĕr mīn´) *v.* To weaken; to make less strong.

un-der-most (un´dĕr mōst´) *adj.* The lowest in position.

un-der-neath (un´dĕr nēth´) *adv.* Beneath or below; on the under side; lower. **underneath** *prep.* Under; below.

un-der-nour-ished *n.* To be supplied with less than the minimum amount of the needed food. **undernourishment** *n.*

un-der-nu-tri-tion *n.* The lacking or deficient bodily nutrition which is due to inadequate food intake.

un-der-paid *adj.* To receive less than enough or adequate pay.

un-der-pants (un´dĕr pants´) *n.* The pants that are worn under another garment.

un-der-part *n.* An auxiliary part or section.

un-der-pass (un´dĕr pas´) *n.* A road or walk that goes under another.

un-der-pin (un´dĕr pin´) *v.* To strengthen the foundation of something.

un-der-pin-ning (un´dĕr pin´ing) *n.* The material which is used for the support of a structure.

un-der-play (un´dĕr plā´) *v.* To act with restraint.

un-der-plot *n.* A kind of dramatic plot in a play that is subordinate to the main action or plot.

un-der-powered *adj.* To be driven by an engine that is not sufficiently powered.

un-der-priv-i-leged (un´dĕr priv´i lijd) *adj.* Deprived of economic and social advantages.

un-der-pro-duc-tion *n.* A type of production which is unable to satisfy the demand.

un-der-pro-duc-tive *adj.* Being unable to produce something adequately.

un-der-proof *adj.* To be containing less alcohol than the proof spirit.

un-der-rate (un´dĕr rat´) *v.* To rate or value below the true worth.

un-der-re-port *v.* To report something as being less than it actually is.

un-der-ripe (un´dĕr rip´) *adj.* To be insufficiently ripe.

un-der-sat-u-rat-ed *adj.* To be less than normally saturated or wet with a liquid.

un-der-score (un´dĕr skōr´) *v.* To emphasize. **underscore** *n.*

un-der-sea (un´dĕr sē´) *adj.* Being carried under the sea or under the surface of the sea.

un-der-sec-re-tar-i-at *n.* The staff which is under the secretary.

un-der-sell (un´dĕr sel´) *v.* To sell for less than a competitor.

un-der-side (un´dĕr sīd´) *n.* The side or part on the bottom.

un-der-stand (un´dĕr stand´) *v.* To comprehend; to realize; to know the feelings and thoughts of.

un-der-stand-a-ble (un´dèr stan´da bl) *adj.* Able to sympathize or comprehend. **understandably** *adv.*

un-der-state (un´dèr stāt´) *v.* To make too little of the actual situation. **understatement** *n.*

un-der-stood (un´dèr sted´) *adj.* Agreed upon by all.

un-der-stud-y (un´dèr stud´ē) *v.* To learn, another person's part or role in order to be able to replace him if necessary. **under-study** *n.*

un-der-take (un´dèr tāk´) *v.* To set about to do a task; to pledge oneself to a certain job; to attempt. **-taking** *n.*

un-der-tak-er (un´dèr tā´kèr) *n.* A person who prepares the dead for burial.

un-der-tone (un´dèr tōn´) *n.* A low, quiet voice; a pale or subdued color visible through other colors.

un-der-tow (un´dèr tō´) *n.* The underwater current which runs in the opposite direction of the surface current.

un-der-wa-ter (un´dèr wä´tèr) *adj.* Occurring, happening or used beneath the surface of the water.

un-der-write (un´dèr rīt´) *v.* To sign or write at the end of something; to finance; to assume a risk by means of insurance. To assume responsibility for; to undertake to pay a written pledge of money. **underwriter** *n.*

un-de-sir-a-ble (un´di zī´èr a bl) *adj.* Offensive; not wanted. **-ly** *adv.*

un-do (un dö´) *v.* To cancel; to reverse; to loosen or unfasten; to open a package.

un-done *adj.* Not finished; unfastened; ruined.

un-du-late (un´ja lāt´) *v.* To move from side to side with a flowing motion; to have a wavy shape. **undulation** *n.*

un-dy-ing (un dī´ing) *adj.* Without end.

un-earth (un erth´) *v.* To dig up from the earth; to find or discover.

unearthly (un erth´lē) *adj.* Strange; not from this world.

un-eas-y (un ē´zē) *adj.* Feeling or causing distress or discomfort; embarrassed; awkward; uncertain. **uneasily** *adv.*

un-em-ployed (un´em ploid´) *adj.* Without a job; without work. **-ment** *n.*

un-en-thu-si-as-tic *adj.* Not being excited about something.

un-e-qual (un ē´kwal) *adj.* Not even; not fair; not of the same size or time; lacking sufficient ability.

un-equiv-o-cal *adj.* Being clear; having no doubt.

un-es-sen-tial *adj.* Not being important.

un-e-ven (un ē´ven) *adj.* Not equal; varying inconsistency or form; not balanced.

un-e-vent-ful (un´i vent´ful) *adj.* Lacking insignificance; calm.

un-expect-ed (un´ik spek´tid) *adj.* Surprising; happening without warning. **unexpectedly** *adv.*

un-fail-ing (un fā´ling) *adj.* Constant, unchanging.

un-fair (un fār´) *adj.* Not honest; marked by a lack of justice. **unfairly** *adv.*

un-faith-ful (un fāth´ful) *adj.* Breaking a promise or agreement; without loyalty; guilty of adultery.

un-fa-mil-iar (un´fa mil´yér) *adj.* Not knowing; strange; foreign.

un-fath-om-able *adj.* Being unable to comprehend.

un-fa-vor-able (un fā´vèr a bl) *adj.* Undesired; harmful.

un-feel-ing (un fē´ling) *adj.* Without sympathy; hardhearted; without sensation. **unfeelingly** *adv.*

un-fin-ished *adj.* At loose ends; not completed.

un-fit (un fit´) *adj.* Not suitable; not qualified; in poor body or mental health.

un-fold (un fōld´) *v.* To open up the folds of and lay flat; to reveal gradually. **unfoldment** *n.*

un-fore-seen (un´fōr sēn´) *adj.* Not anticipated or expected.

un-for-get-ta-ble (un´fèr get´a bl) *adj.* Impossible or hard to forget; memorable. **unforgettably** *adv.*

un-for-tu-nate (un for´cha nit) *adj.* Causing or having bad luck, damage, or harm. *n.* A person who has no luck.

un-found-ed (un foun´did) *adj.* Not founded or based on fact; groundless; lacking a factual basis.

un-friend-ly (un frend´lē) *adj.* Showing a lack of kindness; not friendly; not favorable.

un-furl (un ferl´) *v.* To unroll or unfold; to open up or out.

un-fur-nished (un fer´nisht) *adj.* Without furniture.

un-god-ly (un god´lē) *adj.* Wicked; evil; lacking reverence for God.

un-grate-ful (un grāt´ful) *adj.* Not thankful; showing no appreciation.

un-guent (ung´gwent) *n.* A healing or soothing salve; ointment.

un-hap-py (un hap´ē) *adj.* Sad; without laughter or joy; not satisfied or pleased. **unhappily** *adv.* **unhappiness** *n.*

un-healthy *adj.* Sickly; not enjoying good health.

un-heard (un herd´) *adj.* Not heard; not listened to.

un-heard-of (un herd´uv´) *adj.* Not known or done before; without precedent.

un-ho-ly *adj.* Wicked.

un-hook (un hek´) *v.* To release or undo from a hook.

un-hur-ried *adj.* At a leisurely pace. **unhurriedly** *adv.*

u-ni-corn (ū′ni kårn′) *n.* A mythical animal resembling a horse, with a horn in the center of its forehead.

u-ni-cy-cle (ū′ni sī′kl) *n.* A one wheeled vehicle with pedals.

unidentified flying object *n.* A flying object that cannot be explained or identified, abbreviated as UFO.

uni-fac-to-ri-al *adj.* Controlled by a single gene.

u-ni-form (ū′ni form′) *n.* Identical clothing worn by the members of a group to dis-tinguish them from the general population. **uniformly** *adv.*

uniform spacing In *computer science,* a type of font in which everyday character occupies exactly the same space regardless of the width of the character itself.

u-ni-fy (ū′ni fī′) *v.* To come together as one; to unite.

uni-lat-er-al *adj.* Affecting only one side of a subject.

uni-lin-ear *adj.* Developing in a series of stages from primitive to advanced.

un-in-hab-It-ed *adj.* Not lived in; empty.

un-in-ter-est-ed (un in′tèr i stid) *adj.* Having no interest or concern in; not interested.

un-ion (ūn′yon) *n.* The act of joining together of two or more groups or things; a group of countries or states joined under one government; a marriage; an organized body of employees who work together to upgrade their working conditions and wages. **Union** The United States, especially the federal government during the Civil War.

u-nip-ar-ous (ū nip′ér us) *adj.* Having produced one egg or offspring at a time.

u-nique (ū nēk′) *adj.* Unlike any other; sole.

u-ni-sex *adj.* Adaptable and appropriate for both sexes.

u-ni-son (ū′ni son) *n.* In music, the exact sameness of pitch, as of a tonal harmonious agreement.

u-nit (ū′nit) *n.* Any one of several parts regarded as a whole; an exact quantity that is used as a standard of measurement; a special section or part of a machine.

u-ni-tar-i-an (ū′ni târ′ē an) *n.* A member of a denomination that believes the deity exists in one person.

u-nite (ū nīt′) *v.* To join or come together for a common purpose.

United Nations *n.* An international organization formed in 1945; comprised of nearly all the countries of the world whose purpose is to pro-mote security, economic development, and peace.

unit rule *n.* A ruling which allows a delegation to a Democratic national convention to cast its entire vote as a unit by majority vote.

u-ni-ty (ū′ni tē) *n. pl.* **unities** The fact or state of being one; accord; agreement; harmony.

u-ni-valve (ū′ni valv′) *n.* A mollusk having a one-piece shell, such as a snail.

u-ni-ver-sal (ū′ni ver′sal) *adj.* Having to do with the world or the universe in its entirety.

u-ni-verse (ū′ni vers′) *n.* The world, stars, planets, space, and all that is contained.

u-ni-ver-si-ty (ū′ni ver′si tē) *n. pl.* **universities** An educational institution offering undergraduate and graduate degrees in a variety of academic areas.

un-just (un just′) *adj.* Not fair; lacking justice or fairness. **unjustly** *adv.*

un-kempt (un kempt′) *adj.* Poorly groomed; messy; untidy.

un-kind (un kind′) *adj.* Harsh; lacking in sympathy, concern, or under-standing. **unkindly** *adj.* **-ness** *n.*

un-known (un nōn′) *adj.* Strange; unidentified; not known; not familiar or famous. **unknown** *n.*

un-lead-ed (un led′id) *adj.* Containing no lead.

un-like (un līk′) *adj., prep* Dissimilar; not alike; not equal in strength or quantity.

un-lim-it-ed (un lim′i tid) *adj.* Having no boundaries or limitations.

un-load (un lōd′) *v.* To take or remove the load; to unburden; to dispose or get rid of by selling in volume.

un-lock (un lok′) *v.* To open, release, or unfasten a lock; open with a key.

un-loose (un lōs′) *v.* To loosen or undo; to release.

un-luck-y (un luk′ē) *adj.* Unfortunate; having bad luck; disappointing or unsuitable. **unluckily** *adv.*

un-manned (un mand′) *adj.* Designed to operate or be operated without a crew of people.

un-mask *v.* To reveal the truth of one's identity; to expose.

un-men-tion-a-ble (un men′sha na bl) *adj.* Improper or unsuitable.

un-mis-tak-a-ble (un′mi stā′ka bl) *adj.* Very clear and evident; understood; obvious. **unmistakably** *adv.*

un-mor-al (un mor′al) *adj.* Having no moral knowledge.

un-nat-u-ral (un nach′ér al) *adj.* Abnormal or unusual; strange; artificial.

un-nec-es-sar-y (un nes′i ser′ē) *adj.* Not needed; not appropriate.

un-nerve (un nerv′) *v.* To frighten; to upset.

un-num-bered (un num′bèrd) *adj.*

Countless; not identified by number.

un-oc-cu-pied (un ok'ya pīd') *adj.* Empty; not occupied.

un-pack (un pak') *v.* To remove articles out of trunks, suitcases, boxes, or other storage places.

un-pleas-ant (un plez'ant) *adj.* Not agreeable; not pleasant. **unpleasantly** *adv.* **unpleasantness** *n.*

un-pop-u-lar (un pop'ya lėr) *adj.* Not approved or liked. **unpopularity** *n.*

un-pre-dict-a-ble (un'pri dik'ta bl) *adj.* Not capable or being foretold; not reliable. **unpredictably** *adj.*

un- *prefix* The reverse or opposite of an act; removal or release from.

un-pre-pared (un'pri pârd') *adj.* Not equipped or ready.

un-pro-fes-sion-al (un'pro fesh'a nal) *adj.* Contrary to the standards of a profession; having no professional status.

un-prof-it-a-ble (un prof'i ta bl) *adj.* Showing or giving no profit; serving no purpose.

un-qual-i-fied (un kwol'i fīd') *adj.* Lacking the proper qualifications; unreserved.

un-ques-tion-a-ble *adj.* Being indisputable.

un-rav-el (un rav'el) *v.* To separate threads; to solve; to clarify; to come apart.

un-re-al (un rē'al) *adj.* Having no substance or reality.

un-rea-son-a-ble (un rē'zo na bl) *adj.* Not according to reason; exceeding all reasonable limits.

un-re-lent-ing *adj.* Not weakening in vigor or determination.

un-re-li-a-ble (un'ri lī'a bl) *adj.* Unable to be trusted; not dependable.

un-re-served (un'ri zervd') *adj.* Done or given without reserve; unlimited.

un-re-strained (un'ri strānd') *adj.* Not held back, forced, or affected.

un-ripe *adj.* Immature, not ready to harvest. **unripeness** *n.*

un-ruf-fled *adj.* Serene and calm in the face of setbacks.

un-ru-ly (un rö'lē) *adj.* Disorderly; difficult to subdue or control.

un-sat-is-fac-to-ry (un'sat is fak'to rē) *adj.* Unacceptable; not pleasing.

un-sa-vor-y *adj.* Disagreeable; morally offensive.

un-screw (un skrö') *v.* To loosen or unfasten by removing screws from.

un-scru-pu-lous (un skrö'pya lus) *adj.* Without morals, guiding principles, or rules. **unscrupulously** *adv.* **unscrupulousness** *n.*

un-seat (un sēt') *v.* To cause to lose one's seat; to force out of office.

un-seg-re-gat-ed *adj.* Being free from racial segregation.

un-sel-fish (un sel'fish) *adj.* Willing to share; thinking of another's well being before one's own. **unselfishly** *adv.* **unselfish- ness** *n.*

un-set-tle (un set'l) *v.* To cause to be upset or excited; to disturb. **-ed** *adj.*

un-sheathe (un shēth') *v.* To draw a sword from a sheath or other case.

un-sight-ly (un sīt'lē) *adj.* Not pleasant to look at; ugly.

un-skilled (un skild') *adj.* Having no skills or training in a given kind of work.

un-skill-ful (un skil'ful) *adj.* Lacking in proficiency. **unskillfully** *adv.*

un-sound (un sound') *adj.* Having defects; not solidly made; unhealthy in body or mind. **unsoundly** *adv.*

un-speak-a-ble (un spē'ka bl) *adj.* Of or relating to something which cannot be expressed or described. **-ably** *adv.*

un-sta-ble (un stā'bl) *adj.* Not steady or firmly fixed; having the tendency to fluctuate or change.

un-stead-y (un sted'ē) *adj.* Not secure; unstable; variable. **unsteadily** *adv.* **unsteadiness** *n.*

un-sub-stan-tial (un'substan'shal) *adj.* Lacking strength, weight, or solidity; unreal.

un-suit-a-ble (un sö'ta bl) *adj.* Unfitting; not suitable; not appropriate for a specific circumstance. **unsuitably** *adv.*

unswerving *adj.* Being loyal and steady.

un-tan-gle (un tang'gl) *v.* To free from snarls or entanglements.

un-thank-ful (un thangk'ful) *adj.* Ungrateful.

un-think-a-ble (un thing'ka bl) *adj.* Unimaginable.

un-ti-dy (un tī'dē) *adj.* Messy; showing a lack of tidiness. **untidily** *adv.*

un-tie (un tī') *v.* To unfasten or loosen; to free from a restraint or bond.

un-til (un til') *prep.* Up to the time of. *conj.* To the time when; to the degree or place.

un-time-ly (un tīm'lē) *adj.* Premature; before the expected time.

un-told (un tōld') *adj.* Not revealed; not told; inexpressible; cannot be described or revealed.

un-touch-a-ble (un tuch'a bl) *adj.* Cannot be touched; incapable of being obtained or reached.

un-true (un trö) *adj.* Not true; contrary to the truth; not faithful; disloyal.

un-used (un ūzd') *adj.* Not put to use; never having been used.

un-u-su-al (un ū'zhö al) *adj.* Not usual; uncommon. **unusually** *adv.* **-ness** *n.*

un-ut-ter-a-ble (un ut'ėr a bl) *adj.* Incapable of being described or expressed; unpronounceable.

un-veil (un vāl') *v.* To remove a veil from; to uncover; to reveal.

un-war-y (un wâr´ē) adj. Not cautious or careful; careless.

un-wa-ver-ing (un wā´ver ing) adj. Steady; not moving; steadfast.

un-whole-some (un hōl´som) adj. Unhealthy; morally corrupt or harmful.

un-will-ing (un wil´ing) adj. Reluctant; not willing. **unwillingly** adv.

un-wind (un wīnd´) v. To undo or reverse the winding of; to untangle.

un-wise (un wīz´) adj. Lacking good judgment or common sense. **-ly** adv.

un-wor-thy (un wer´thē) adj. Not deserving; not becoming or befitting; lacking merit or worth; shameful.

up (up) adv. From a lower position to a higher one; on, in, or to a higher level, position, or place; to a greater degree or amount; in or into a specific action or an excited state, as they stirred up trouble; to be even with in time, degree, or space, as up to date; under consideration, as up for discussion; in a safe, protected place, as vegetables are put up in jars; totally, completely, as the building was burned up; in baseball, at bat or, **as up to bat**. up front To be honest.

up and running In *computer science,* descriptive of computers and peripherals that are on line and functioning properly.

up-beat (up´bēt´) n., *Mus.* The relatively unaccented beat preceding the down beat. **upbeat** adj. Optimistic; happy.

up-bring-ing (up´bring´ing) n. The process of teaching and rearing a child.

up-com-ing (up´kum´ing) adj. About to take place or appear.

up-date (up dāt´) v. To revise or bring up-to-date; to modernize. In *computer science,* to add or alter data to reflect the most recent information available.

up-grade (up´grād´) v. To increase the grade, rank, or standard of. n. An upward slope.

up-hold v. To support.

up-hol-ster (up hōl´ster) v. To cover furniture with fabric covering, cushions, and padding. **upholsterer** n. **upholstery** n.

up-keep (up´kēp´) n. The cost and work needed to keep something in good condition.

up-lift (up lift´) v. To raise or lift up; to improve the social, economic, and moral level of a group or of a society.

up-on (u pon´) adv., prep. On.

up-per (up´er) adj. Higher in status, position or location. **upper** n. The part of a shoe to which the sole is attached. *Slang* A drug used as a stimulant. **case** The large or capital case of letters.

up-per–class (up´er klas´) adj. Economically or socially superior.

up-per-class-man (up´er klas´man) n.

A junior or senior at a high school or college.

up-right (up´rīt´) adj. Having a vertical direction or position; honest. **upright** n. Something standing vertically, such as a beam in a building.

up-ris-ing (up´rī´zing) n. A revolt; a rebellion; an insurrection.

up-roar (up´rōr´) n. A confused, loud noise; a commotion.

up-root (up rōt´) v. To detach completely by pulling up the roots. **uprooter** n.

up-set (up set´) v. To capsize; to turn over; to throw into confusion or disorder; to overcome; to beat unexpectedly. **upset** adj. Capsized; overturned; distressed; troubled.

up-stage (up´stāj´) adj. & adv. Toward or at the back part of a stage. *Slang* To steal the show or scene from.

up-stairs (up´stârz´) adv. Up one or more flights of stairs. **upstairs** adj. Situated on the upper floor.

up-stand-ing (up stan´ding) adj. Straightforward; honest; upright.

up-start (up´stärt´) n. One who has risen quickly to power or wealth, especially one who is conceited.

up-stream (up´strēm´) adv. Toward the origin of a stream; against the current.

up-tight adv. Nervous, tense, or anxious.

up time In *computer science,* the period that a computer is on line and functioning properly.

up–to–date (up´to dāt´) adj. Most current or recent; appropriate to the present time.

up-town (up´toun´) adv. Toward or in the upper part of town. n. The upper part of town or city. **uptown** adv.

up-ward or **up-wards** adv. From a lower position to or toward a higher one. **upward** adj. Directed toward a higher position.

u-ra-ni-um (ū rā´nē um) n. A hard, heavy, shiny metallic element that is radioactive, used especially in research and in nuclear weapons and fuels, symbolized by U.

ura-nog-ra-phy n. The science concerned with the description of the heavens and the celestial bodies.

ura-nom-e-try (ūr´a nom´i trē) n. A chart of celestial bodies.

U-ra-nus n. The seventh planet of the solar system in distance from the sun.

ur-ban (er´ban) adj. Pertaining to a city or having characteristics of a city; living or being in a city. **urbanite** n.

ur-ban-ol-o-gy n. The study dealing with the problems of a city such as education, politics, planning, etc.

urge (erj) v. To encourage, push, or drive; to recommend persistently and strongly. n. An influence, impulse, or force.

ur-gent (er´jent) adj. Requiring immediate attention. **urgency** *n.* **-ly** *adv.*

urine (ūr´in) *n.* In man and other mammals, the yellowish fluid waste produced by the kidneys.

us (us) *pron. pl.* The objective case of we; used as an indirect object, direct object, or object of a preposition.

us-a-ble *or* **useable** (ū´za bl) *adj.* Fit or capable of being used. **usably** *adv.*

us-age (ū´sij) *n.* The way or act of using something; the way words are used.

use (ūz) *v.* To put into action; to employ for a special purpose; to employ on a regular basis; to exploit for one's own advantage. *n.* The state or fact of being used; the act or way of using something; the reason or purpose for which something is used; the function of something; the occupation or utilization of property. **used** *adj.* **useful** *adj.* **useless** *adj.*

user friendly In *computer science*, descriptive of a computer system or program that is intuitive, making it easier to use.

ush-er (ush´ér) *n.* A person who directs people to the correct seats in a theater. *v.* To show or escort someone to a place; to go before as a representative or sign of something that comes later.

u-su-al (ū´zhō al) *adj.* Ordinary or common; regular; customary. **usually** *adv.* **usualness** *n.*

u-surp (ū serp´) *v.* To take over by force without authority. **usurpation** *n.*

usu-ry *n.* An exorbitant rate of interest charged to a borrower.

Ut-ah *n.* A state located in the western part of the United States, statehood January 4, 1896, state capital Salt Lake City.

u-ten-sil (ū ten´sil) *n.* A tool, implement, or container, especially one for the kitchen.

u-ter-ine (ū´tér in) *adj.* Referring to birth by the same mother but by a different father.

u-ter-us (ū´tér us) *n.* An organ of female mammals within which young develop and grow before birth. **uterine** *adj.*

utilities In *computer science*, computer programs that improve performance or productivity of the computer or the user.

u-til-i-ty (ū til´i tē) *n. pl.* **-ies** The state or quality of being useful; a company which offers a public service, as water, heat, or electricity.

u-til-ize (ūt´i līz´) *v.* To make, put to use.

ut-most (ut´mōst´) *adj.* Of the greatest amount or degree; most distant.

u-to-pi-a (ū tō´pē a) *n.* A condition or place of perfection or complete harmony and peace.

ut-ter (ut´ér) *v.* To say or express verbally; to speak. *adv.* Absolute; complete. **utterly** *adv.* **utterance** *n.*

ut-ter-most *n.* To do or perform to our highest ability.

u-vu-la (ū´vya la) *n.* The fleshy projection which hangs above the back of the tongue. **uvular** *adj.*

ux-or-i-cide (uk sōr´i sīd´) *adj.* Murder of a wife by her husband.

V

V, v (vē) The twenty-second letter of the English alphabet; the Roman numeral for the number 5.

va-cant (vā´kant) *adj.* Empty; not occupied; without expression or thought.

va-cate (vā´kāt) *v.* To leave; to cease to occupy.

va-ca-tion (vā kā´shan) *n.* A period of time away from work for pleasure, relaxation, or rest. *v.* To take a vacation.

vac-ci-nate (vak´si nāt´) *v.* To inject with a vaccine so as to produce immunity to an infectious disease, as measles or smallpox.

vac-ci-na-tion (vak´si nā´shan) *n.* The inoculation with a vaccine.

vac-cine (vak sēn´) *n.* A solution of weakened or killed microorganisms, as bacteria or viruses, injected into the body to produce immunity to a disease.

vac-u-um (vak´ū um) *n. pl.* **vacuums** *or* **vacuua** A space which is absolutely empty; a void; a vacuum cleaner. **vacuum** *v.* To clean with a vacuum cleaner.

vag-a-bond (vag´a bond´) *n.* A homeless person who wanders from place to place; a tramp; a wanderer.

va-gar-y (*va* gâr´ē) *n. pl.* **-ies** An eccentric or capricious action or idea.

va-gi-na (*va* jī´na) *n. pl.* **vaginas, vaginae** *Anat.* The canal or passage extending from the uterus to the external opening of the female reproductive system.

vaginitis (vaj´i ni´tis) *n.* An inflammation of the vagina.

va-grant (vā´grant) *n.* A person who wanders from place to place. *adj.* Roaming from one area to another without a job. **vagrancy** *n.*

vague (vāg) *adj.* Not clearly expressed; not sharp or definite. **vaguely** *adv.*

vain (vān) *adj.* Conceited; lacking worth or substance; having too much pride in one-self.

val-ance (val´ans) *n.* A decorative drapery across the top of a window.

vale (vāl) *n.* A valley.

val-e-dic-to-ri-an (val´l dik tōr´ē an) *n.* The student ranking highest in a graduating class, who delivers a speech at the commencement.

val-en-tine (val´en tīn´) *n.* A card or gift

sent to one's sweetheart on Valentine's Day, February 14th.

val-et (val'it) *n.* A man who takes care of another man's clothes and other personal needs; a hotel employee who attends to personal services for guests.

val-iant (val'yant) *adj.* Brave; exhibiting valor. **valiance, valor** *n.*

val-id (val'id) *adj.* Founded on facts or truth. *Law* Binding; having legal force. **validity, validate** *n.*

val-ley (val'e) *n. pl.* **-leys** Low land between ranges of hills or mountains.

val-or (val'er) *n.* Bravery. **valorous** *adj.* **valorously** *adv.*

val-u-a-ble (val'u *a* bl) *adj.* Of great value or importance; having a high monetary value; having a worthy quality or value. **valuableness** *n.*

val-ue (val'u) *n.* The quality or worth of something that makes it valuable; material worth; a principle regarded as worthwhile or desirable. *Math* A calculated numerical quantity. *v.* To estimate the value or worth of; to regard very highly; to rate according to importance, worth, or usefulness.

valve (valv) *n.* The movable mechanism which opens and closes to control the flow of a substance through a pipe or other passageway. *Anat.* A membranous structure in a vein or artery that prevents or slows the backward movement of fluid. **valveless** *adj.*

va-moose (va mös') *v., Slang* To leave in a hurry.

van (van) *n.* A large closed wagon or truck.

va-na-di-um (va nã'dē *um*) *n.* A metallic element symbolized by V.

Van Buren, Martin *n.* (1782-1862) The eighth president of the United States from 1837-1841.

van-dal-ism (van'da liz'um) *n.* The malicious defacement or destruction of private or public property.

vane (vãn) *n.* A metal device that turns in the direction the wind is blowing; a thin rigid blade of an electric fan, propeller, or windmill.

va-nil-la (va nil'*a*) *n.* A flavoring extract used in cooking and baking; prepared from the vanilla bean.

van-ish (van'ish) *v.* To disappear suddenly; to drop out of sight; to go out of existence.

van-i-ty (van'i tē) *n. pl.,* **-ies** Conceit; extreme pride in one's ability, possessions, or appearance.

van-tage (van'tij) *n.* A superior position; an advantage.

va-por (vã'pēr) *n.* Moisture or smoke suspended in air, as mist or fog. **vaporish, vaporous** *adj.* **vaporize** *v.*

var-i-able (vâr'ē *a* bl) *adj.* Changeable; tending to vary; inconstant. *n.* A quantity or thing which can vary. In *computer science*, a symbol or code that represents a value that changes during processing. **variably** *adv.*

var-i-ance (vâr'ē ans) *n.* The state or act of varying; difference; conflict.

var-i-a-tion (vâr'ē ā'shan) *n.* The result or process of varying; the degree or extent of varying. *Mus.* A different form or version of a given theme, with modifications in rhythm, key, or melody.

var-i-e-gat-ed (vâr'ē *e* gāt'tid) *adj.* Having marks of different colors.

va-ri-e-ty (va rī'i tē) *n.* The state or character of being varied or various; a number of different kinds; an assortment.

var-i-ous (vâr'ē us) *adj.* Of different kinds. **variousness** *n.*

var-mint (vär'mint) *n., Slang* A troublesome animal; an obnoxious person.

var-nish (vär'nish) *n.* A solution paint used to coat or cover a surface with a hard, transparent, shiny film. *v.* To put varnish on.

var-si-ty (vär'si tē) *n. pl. -ies* The best team representing a college, university, or school.

var-y (vâr'ē) *v.* To change; to make or become different; to be different; to make of different kinds.

vas-cu-lar (vas'kya lēr) *adj., Biol.* Having to do with vessels circulating fluids, as blood.

va-sec-to-my (va sek'to mē) *n. pl -ies* Method of male sterilization involving the surgical excision of a part of the tube which conveys semen.

vast (vast) *adj.* Very large or great in size. **vastly** *adv.* **vastness** *n.*

veg-e-ta-ble (vej'ta bl) *n.* A plant, as the tomato, greenbeans, lettuce, raised for the edible part. *adj.* Resembling a vegetable in activity; passive; dull.

veg-e-tar-i-an (vej'i tär'ē an) *n.* A person whose diet is limited to vegetables only. Consuming only plant products. **vegetarianism** *n.*

ve-hi-cle (vē'i kl) *n.* A motorized device for transporting goods, equipment, or passengers; any means by which something is transferred, expressed, or applied.

veil (vãl) *n.* A piece of transparent cloth worn on the head or face for concealment or protection; anything that conceals from view. *v.* To cover or conceal, as with a veil.

vein (vãn) *n., Anat.* A vessel which transports blood back to the heart after passing through the body; one of the branching support tubes of an insect's wing; a long wavy, irregularly colored streak, as in marble, or wood. **vein** *v.*

ve-lour (ve ler') n. A soft velvet-like woven cloth having a short, thick nap.

vel-vet (vel'vit) n. A fabric made of rayon, cotton, or silk, having a smooth, dense pile. **velvety** adj.

vend-er (ven'dèr) n. A person who sells, as a peddler.

ven-det-ta (ven det'a) n. A fight or feud between blood-related persons, involving revenge killings.

ven-er-a-ble (ven'ér a bl) adj. Meriting or worthy of respect by reason of dignity, position, or age.

venereal disease n. A contagious disease, as syphilis, or gonorrhea, which is typically acquired through sexual intercourse.

ven-i-son (ven'i son) n. The edible flesh of a deer.

ven-om (ven'om) n. A poisonous substance secreted by some animals, as scorpions or snakes, usually transmitted to their prey or an enemy through a bite or sting. **venomous** adj.

ve-nous (vē'nus) adj. Of or relating to veins. Physiol. Returning blood to the heart after passing through the capillaries, supplying oxygen for the tissues, and becoming charged with carbon dioxide. **venously** adv.

ven-ti-late (ven'ti lāt') v. To expose to a flow of fresh air for refreshing, curing, or purifying purposes

ven-ture (ven'chèr) n. A course of action involving risk, chance, or danger, especially a business investment. v. To take a risk.

ven-ue (ven'ō) n. The place where a crime or other cause of legal action occurs; the locale of a gathering or public event.

verb (verb) n. The part of speech which expresses action, existence, or occurrence.

ver-bal (ver'bal) adj. Expressed in speech; expressed orally; not written; relating to or derived from a verb. n. An adjective, noun, or other word which is based on a verb and retains some characteristics of a verb. **verbally** adv. **verbalize** v.

ver-ba-tim (vèr bā'tim) adv. Word for word.

ver-be-na (vèr bē'na) n. An American garden plant having variously colored flower clusters.

verge (verj) n. The extreme edge or rim; margin; the point beyond which something begins. v. To border on.

ver-min (ver'min) n. pl. **vermins** A destructive, annoying animal which is harmful to one's health.

Ver-mont n. A state located in the northeastern part of the United Sates; statehood March 4, 1791; state capital Montpelier.

ver-sa-tile (ver'sa til) adj. Having the capabilities of doing many different things; having many functions or uses.

verse (vers) n. Writing that has a rhyme; poetry; a subdivision of a chapter of the Bible. v. To make verse; to tell or celebrate in verse; to familiarize by close association or study.

ver-sion (ver'zhan) n. An account or description told from a particular point of view; a translation from another language, especially a translation of the Bible; a form or particular point of view; a condition in which an organ, such as the uterus, is turned; manual turning n. Of a fetus in the uterus to aid delivery. **versional** adj.

ver-so (ver'sō) n. pl. **-sos** The left-hand page.

ver-sus (ver'sus) prep. Against; in contrast to; as an alternative of.

ver-te-bra (ver'te bra) n. pl. **-brae, -bras** One of the bony or cartilaginous segments making up the spinal column.

ver-tex (ver'teks) n. pl. **-es, -tices** The highest or top most point; the pointed top of a triangle, opposite the base; the point at which two lines meet to form an angle.

ver-ti-cal (ver'ti kal) adj. In a straight up-and-down direction; being perpendicular to the plane of the horizon or to a primary axis; upright.

ver-y (ver'ē) adv. To a high or great degree; truly; absolutely; exactly; actually; in actual fact.

ves-per (ves'pèr) n. An evening prayer service; a bell to call people to such a service.

ves-sel (ves'el) n. A hollow or concave utensil, as a bottle, kettle, container, or jar; a hollow craft designed for navigation on water, one larger than a rowboat. Anat . A tube or duct for circulating a bodily fluid.

vest (vest) n. A sleeveless garment open or fastening in front, worn over a shirt.

ves-tige (ves'tij) n. A trace or visible sign of something that no longer exists. **vestigial** adj. **vestigially** adj.

ves-try (ves'trē) n. pl. **vestries** A room in a church for meetings and classes.

vet (vet) n., Slang A veterinarian; a veteran.

vet-er-an (vet'èr an) n. A person with a long record or experience in a certain field; one who has served in the military.

Veterans Day n. A day set aside to commemorate the end of World War I in 1918, celebrated on November 11th of each year; national holiday.

vet-er-i-nar-i-an (vet'èr i nâr'ēan) n. One who is trained and authorized to give medical treatment to animals.

vet-er-i-nar-y (vet'èr i ner'ē) adj.

Pertaining to or being the science and art of prevention and treatment of animals.

ve-to (vē'tō) *n. pl.* **vetoes** The power of a government executive, as the President or a governor, to reject a bill passed by the legislature. *v.* To reject a bill passed by the legislature.

vex (veks) *v.* To bother; or annoy; to torment.

vexed *adj.* Annoyed by something.

VGA In *computer science*, video graphics array; a standard for high resolution display on a color monitor screen.

vi-a (vī'a) *prep.* By way of; by means of.

vi-a-duct (vī'a dukt') *n.* A bridge, resting on a series of arches, carrying a road or railroad.

vi-al (vī'al) *n.* A small, closed container used especially for liquids.

vi-brate (vī'brāt) *v.* To move or make move back and forth or up and down.

vice (vīs) *n.* An immoral habit or practice; evil conduct. *prefix* One who takes the place of another.

vice-ge-rent *n.* A substitute for someone having his or her powers to make decisions on their behalf.

vi-ce ver-sa (vī'se ver'sa) *adv.* With the order or meaning of something reversed.

vi-cin-i-ty (vi sin'i tē) *n. pl.* **-ies** The surrounding area or district; the state of being near in relationship or space.

vi-cious (vish'us) *adj.* Dangerously aggressive; having the quality of immorality; unpleasantly intence. **viciously** *adv.* **viciousness** *n.*

vie tim (vik'tim) *n.* A person who is harmed or killed by another; a living creature which is slain and offered as sacrifice; one harmed by circumstance or condition. **victimize** *v.*

vic-tor (vik'tér) *n.* A person who conquers; the winner.

vic-to-ri-ous (vik tōr'ē us) *adj.* Being the winner in a contest. **-ously** *adv.*

vic-to-ry (vik'to rē) *n. pl.* **-ies** A defeat of those on the opposite side.

vid-e-o (vid'ē ō') *adj.* Being, related to, or used in the reception or transmission of television.

video card In *computer science*, a board in the computer that controls the display on the monitor.

video disc *n.* A disc containing recorded images and sounds which may be played on a television set.

video game *n.* A computerized game displaying on a display screen, controlled by a player or players.

video terminal *n., computer science* A computer device having a cathode-ray tube for displaying data on a screen.

vie (vī) *v.* To strive for superiority.

view (vū) *n.* The act of examining or seeing; a judgment or opinion; the range or extent of one's sight; something that is kept in sight. *v.* To watch or look at attentively; to consider.

vig-il (vij'il) *n.* A watch with prayers kept on the night before a religious feast; a period of surveillance.

vig-or (vig'ér) *n.* Energy or physical strength; intensity of effect or action.

vile (vīl) *adj.* Morally disgusting, miserable, and unpleasant. **vilely** *adv.*

vil-la (vil'a) *n.* A luxurious home in the country; a country estate.

vil-lage (vil'ij) *n.* An incorporated settlement, usually smaller than a town.

vil-lain (vil'an) *n.* An evil or wicked person; a criminal; an uncouth person. **villainous** *adj.* **villainy** *n.*

vin-di-cate (vin'di kāt') *v.* To clear of suspicion; to set free; to provide a defense or justification for. **-tion** *n.*

vin-dic-tive (vin dik'tiv) *adj.* Showing or possessing a desire for revenge; spiteful.

vine (vīn) *n.* A plant whose stem needs support as it climbs or clings to a surface.

vin-e-gar (vin'e gér) *n.* A tart, sour liquid derived from cider or wine and used in flavoring and preserving food.

vin-tage (vin'tij) *n.* The grapes or wine produced from a particular district in one season.

vi-nyl (vī'nil) *n.* A variety of shiny plastics, similar to leather, often used for clothing and for covering furniture.

vi-o-la (vē ō'la) *n.* A stringed instrument, slightly larger and deeper in tone than a violin.

vi-o-late (vī'o lāt') *v.* To break the law or a rule; to disrupt or disturb a person's privacy. **violation** *n.*

vi-o-lence (vī'o lens) *n.* Physical force or activity used to cause harm, damage, or abuse. **violent** adj.

vi-o-let (vī'o lit) *n.* A small, low-growing plant with blue, purple, or white flowers; a purplish-blue color.

vi-o-lin (vī'o lin') *n.* A small stringed instrument, played with a bow.

vi-per (vī'pér) *n.* A poisonous snake; an evil or treacherous person.

vir-gin (ver'jin) *n.* A person who has never had sexual intercourse. *adj.* In an unchanged or natural state.

Vir-gin-ia *n.* A state located in the eastern part of the United States; statehood June 25, 1788; state capital Richmond.

vir-ile (vir'il) *adj.* Having the qualities and nature of a man; capable of sexual performance in the male. **virility** *n.*

vir-tu (ver tö') *n.* The love or knowledge of fine objects of art.

virtual memory In *computer science,*

an extension of the computer's main memory in disk storage.

vir-tue (ver´chŏ) *n.* Morality, goodness or uprightness; a special type of goodness. **virtuous** *adj.* **-ly** *adv.*

vi-rus (vī´rus) *n.* Any of a variety of microscopic organisms which cause diseases. In *computer science*, unauthorized instructions in the computer that disrupt its normal operation.

vi-sa (vē´za) *n.* An official authorization giving permission on a passport to enter a specific country.

vis-cid (vis´id) *adj.* Sticky; having an adhesive quality.

vise (vīs) *n.* A tool in carpentry and metal work having two jaws to hold things in position. **vise** n.

vis-i-bil-i-ty (viz´i bil´i tē) *n.* *pl.* **-ies** The degree or state of being visible; the distance that one is able to see clearly.

vis-i-ble (viz´i bl) *adj.* Apparent; exposed to view.

vi-sion (vizh´an) *n.* The power of sight; the ability to see; an image created in the imagination; a supernatural appearance.

vis-it (viz´it) *v.* To journey to or come to see a person or place. *n.* A professional or social call. *Slang* To chat. **visitor, visitation** *n.*

vi-sor (vī´zėr) *n.* A brim on the front of a hat which protects the eyes from glare, the sun, wind, and rain.

vi-su-al (vizh´ŏ al) *adj.* Visible; relating to seeing or sight.

vi-tal (vīt´al) *adj.* Essential to life; very important. **vitally** *adv.*

vital signs *n.* *pl., Med.* The pulse rate, body temperature, blood pressure, and respiratory rate of a person.

vi-ta-min (vī´ta min) *n.* Any of various substances which are found in foods and are essential to good health.

vit-re-ous (vi´trē us) *adj.* Related to or similar to glass.

vit-ri-fy (vi´tri fī´) *v.* To convert into glass or a substance similar to glass, by heat and fusion.

vi-va-cious (vi vā´shus) *adj.* Filled with vitality or animation; lively.

viv-id (viv´id) *adj.* Bright; brilliant; intense; having clear, lively, bright colors; realistic. **vividly** *adv.*

viv-i-fy (viv´l fī´) *v.* To give life to. **vivification** *n.*

vo-cab-u-lar-y (vŏ kab´ya ler´ē) *n.* A list or group of words and phrases, usually in alphabetical order; all the words that a person uses or understands. In *computer science*, the collection of reserved words that are acceptable for use in a particular programming language.

vo-cal (vŏ´kal) *adj.* Of or related to the

voice; uttered by the voice; to speak freely and loudly. *n.* A vocal sound.

vocal cords *n.* *pl.* The lower of two folds or bands in the throat which produce sound when made tighter or loosened when air is breathed out while speaking or singing.

vo-ca-tion (vŏ kā´shan) *n.* A career, occupation, or profession.

vo-cif-er-ate (vŏ sif´e rāt´) *v.* To utter or cry out loudly; to shout. **vociferation** *n.* **vociferous** *adj.* **vociferously** *adv.*

vod-ka (vod´ka) *n.* A colorless liquor of neutral spirits distilled from fermented rye or wheat mash.

vogue (vŏg) *n.* The leading style or fashion; popularity. **vogue** *adj.*

voice (vois) *n.* The sounds produced by speaking; the ability or power to produce musical tones. *v.* To express; to utter; to give voice.

void (void) *adj.* Containing nothing; empty; not inhabited; useless; vain; without legal force or effect; null. *n.* Empty space; the quality or state of being lonely. *v.* To make void; to discharge; to emit.

voile (voil) *n.* A fine, soft, sheer fabric used for making light clothing and curtains.

vol-ley (vol´ē) *n.* *pl.* **-leys** A simultaneous discharge of a number of missile weapons; the shooting or eruption of similar things at one time; in the game of tennis, a shot in which the ball is hit before touching the ground.

volt-age (vōl´tij) *n.* The amount of electrical power, given in terms of the number of volts.

vol-ume (vol´ūm) *n.* The capacity or amount of space or room; a book; a quantity; the loudness of a sound.

volume label In *computer science*, the name given to a hard or floppy disk to identify it.

vol-un-tar-y (vol´an ter´ē) *adj.* Done cooperatively or willingly; from one's own choice.

vol-un-teer (vol´un tēr´) *n.* One who offers himself for a service of his own free will. *adj.* Consisting of volunteers. *v.* To offer voluntarily.

vo-lup-tuous (vo lup´chŏ us) *adj.* Full of pleasure; delighting the senses; sensuous; luxury. **voluptuousness** *n.*

vom-it (vom´it) *v.* To eject contents of the stomach through the mouth. *n.* The food or matter ejected from the stomach by vomiting.

voo-doo (vŏ´dŏ) *n.* A religious cult derived from African ancestor worship; a cure or spell resulting from magical powers. **voodooism** *n.*

vo-ra-cious (vŏ rā´shus) *adj.* Having a large appetite; insatiable. **-ly** *adv.*

vote (vōt) *n.* The expression of one's choice by voice, by raising one's hand, or by secret ballot. *v.* To express one's views. **voteless** *adj.* **voter** *n.*

vo-tive (vō'tiv) *adj.* Performed in fulfillment of a vow or in devotion.

vouch (vouch) *v.* To verify or support as true; to guarantee. **voucher** *n.*

vow (vou) *n.* A solemn pledge or promise, especially one made to God; a marriage vow. *v.* To make a vow.

vow-el (vou'el) *n.* A sound of speech made by voicing the flow of breath within the mouth; a letter representing a vowel, as a, e, i, o, u, and sometimes y.

voy-age (voi'ij) *n.* A long trip or journey.

vul-gar (vul'gėr) *adj.* Showing poor manners; crude; improper; immoral or indecent. **vulgarity** *n.*

vul-ner-a-ble (vul'nėr a bl) *adj.* Open to physical injury or attack. **vulnerability** *n.* **vulnerably** *adv.*

vul-ture (vul'chėr) *n.* A large bird of the hawk family, living on dead animals; a greedy person; one who feeds on the mistakes or bad luck of others.

W

W, w (dub'l ū') The twenty-third letter of the English alphabet.

wacky *adj.* Amusingly or absurdly irrational. **wackiness** *n.*

wad (wod) *n.* A small crumpled mass or bundle; a soft plug used to hold shot or gunpowder charge in place. *Slang* A large roll of money. **wad** *v.*

wad-able *adj.* Capable of being wadded.

wad-ding *n.* Wads or materials for making wads; a sheet of loose fibers that is used for stuffing or padding.

wad-dle (wod'l) *v.* To walk with short steps and swing from side to side. **waddle** *n.* **waddler** *n.*

wade (wād) *v.* To walk through a substance as mud or water which hampers one's steps.

wader *n.* A person that wades; a name for high top waterproof boots.

wae-sucks *interj.* A Scottish phrase used to express pity.

wa-fer (wā'fėr) *n.* A small, thin, crisp cracker, cookie, or candy.

waf-fle (wof'l) *n.* Pancake batter cooked in a waffle iron.

waft (waft) *v.* To drift or move gently, as by the motion of water or air.

waft-age *n.* The state or act of being wafted.

waf-ture *n.* A wavelike motion.

wag (wag) *v.* To move quickly from side to side or up and down. *n.* A playful, witty person. **waggish** *adj.*

wage (wāj) *n.* A payment of money for labor or services. *v.* To conduct.

wage earner *n.* A person who works for a salary or wages.

wage level *n.* The approximate position of wages at any given time.

wag-on (wag'on) *n.* A four-wheeled vehicle used to transport goods; a station wagon; a child's four-wheeled cart with a long handle.

wa-hi-ne *n.* A Polynesian girl or woman.

waif (wāf) *n.* An abandoned, homeless, or lost child; a piece of property found without the owner; a stray animal.

wail (wāl) *n.* A loud, mournful cry or weep. *n.* To make such a sound.

waist (wāst) *n.* The narrow part of the body between the thorax and hips; the middle part or section of something which is narrower than the rest.

wait (wāt) *v.* To stay in one place in expectation of; to await; to put off until a later time or date; to be ready or prepared. *n.* A time of waiting.

wait-er (wā'tėr) *n.* A man who serves food at a restaurant.

wait-ress (wā'tris) *n.* A woman who serves food at a restaurant.

waive (wāv) *v.* To forfeit of one's own free will; to postpone or dispense with.

waiv-er *n.* The act of intentionally abandoning a privilege or right.

wake (wāk) *v.* To come to consciousness, as from sleep. *n.* A vigil for a dead body; the surface turbulence caused by a vessel moving through water.

walk (wok) *v.* To move on foot over a surface; to pass over, go on, or go through by walking; in baseball, to advance to first base after four balls have been pitched. **walker** *n.*

walk-ie-talk-ie *n.* A battery-operated radio transmitting and receiving set.

wall (wol) *n.* A vertical structure to separate or enclose an area. *v.* To provide or close up, as with a wall.

wal-la-by (wol'a bē) *n.* A small or medium sized kangaroo.

wal-lah *n.* A person who performs a specific service or duty.

wal-let (wol'It) *n.* A flat folding case for carrying paper money.

wal-lop (wol'op) *n.* A powerful blow; an impact. *v.* To move with disorganized haste. **walloper** *n.*

wall-pa-per (wol'pā'pėr) *n.* Decorative paper for walls, usually having a colorful pattern.

Wall Street *n.* The street in New York City where the New York Stock Exchange is located.

wal-nut (wol'nut) *n.* An edible nut with a hard, light-brown shell; the tree on which this nut grows.

waltz (wolts) *n.* A ballroom dance in 3/4 time; music for a waltz. *v.* To dance a waltz; to advance successfully and easily.

wam-pum (wom´*pum*) *n*. Polished shells, once used as currency by North American Indians. *Slang* Money.

wand (wond) *n*. A slender rod used by a magician.

wan-der (won´dèr) *v*. To travel about aimlessly; to roam; to stray.

wane (wān) *v*. To decrease in size or extent; to decrease gradually. *n*. A gradual deterioration.

wan-gle (wang´gl) *v*. To resort to devious methods in order to obtain something wanted. **wangler** *n*.

want (wont) *v*. To wish for or desire; to need; to lack; to fail to possess a required amount; to hunt in order to apprehend. *n*. The state of lacking a required or usual amount. **wanting** *adj*.

war (wor) *n*. An armed conflict among states or nations; a state of discord; the science of military procedures.

ward (word) *n*. A section in a hospital for certain patients requiring similar treatment; a person under protection or surveillance. *v*. To keep watch over someone or some thing.

ware (wâr) *n*. Manufactured items of the same general kind; items or goods for sale.

ware-house (wâr´hous´) *n*. A large building used to store merchandise.

warm (worm) *adj*. Moderate heat; neither hot or cold; comfortably established; marked by a strong feeling; having pleasant feelings.

warn (worn) *v*. To give notice or inform beforehand; to call to one's attention; to alert.

warp (worp) *v*. To become bent out of shape; to deviate from a proper course. *n*. The condition of being twisted or bent; threads running down the length of a fabric.

war-rant (wor´ant) *n*. A written authorization giving the holder legal power to search, seize, or arrest. *v*. To provide a reason; to give proof. **warrantable** *adj*. **warrantor** *n*.

war-ri-or (wor´ē ér) *n*. One who fights in a war or battle.

war-y (wâr´ē) *adj*. Marked by caution; alert to danger.

wash (wosh) *v*. To cleanse by the use of water; to remove dirt; to move or deposit as if by the force of water. *n*. A process or instance of washing; a group of soiled clothes or linens.

Wash-ing-ton *n*. A state located in the northwestern part of the United States, statehood November 11, 1889, state capital Olympia.

Washington, George *n*. (1732-1799) The first president of the United States from 1789-1797.

was-n't (wuz´ant) Was not.

wasp (wasp) *n*. Any of various insects,

having a slim body with a constricted abdomen, the female capable of inflicting a painful sting.

waste (wāst) *v*. To be thrown away; to be available but not used completely. *n*. A barren region; the instance of wasting; useless material produced as a by-product. *Slang* To destroy or murder. **wasteful** *adj*. **waster** *n*.

watch (woch) *v*. To view carefully; to guard; to keep informed. *n*. The act of staying awake to guard or protect; a small timepiece worn on the wrist, designed to keep the correct time of day.

watch-ful (woch´ful) *adj*. Carefully observant or attentive. **watchfully** *adv*.

watch-man (woch´man) *n*. A person hired to keep watch; a guard.

wa-ter (wo´tèr) *n*. The clear liquid making up oceans, lakes, and streams; the body fluids as tears or urine. *v*. To pour or spray water on something or someone; to give water to drink; to weaken or dilute with water.

water power *n*. The power of energy produced by swift-moving water.

wa-ter-proof (wo´tèr prôf´) *adj*. Capable of preventing water from penetrating. *v*. To make or treat in order to make waterproof. *n*. A material or fabric which is waterproof.

wa-ter-shed *n*. The raised area between two regions that divides two sections drained by different river sources.

wa-ter-way (wo´tèr wā´) *n*. A navigable body of water; a channel for water.

watt (wot) *n*. A unit of electrical power represented by current of one ampere, produced by the electromotive force of one volt.

wave (wāv) *v*. To move back and forth or up and down; to motion with the hand. *n*. A swell or moving ridge of water; a curve or curl, as in the hair.

wa-ver (wā´vèr) *v*. To sway unsteadily; to move back and forth; to weaken in force. **waver** *n*. **waveringly** *adv*.

wax (waks) *n*. A natural yellowish substance made by bees, solid when cold and easily melted or softened when heated. **waxy** *adj*.

way (wā) *n*. A manner of doing something; a tendency or characteristic; a habit or customary manner of acting or living; a direction; freedom to do as one chooses.

way-lay (wā´lā´) *v*. To attack by ambush; to rob.

way-ward (wā´wèrd) *adj*. Unruly; unpredictable.

we (wē) *pron*. Used to refer to the person speaking and one or more other people.

weak (wēk) *adj*. Having little energy or strength; easily broken; having inadequate skills; not reasonable or convincing. **weakness** *n.* **weakly** *adv.*

wealth (welth) *n.* An abundance of valuable possessions or property; all goods and resources having monetary value.

wealth-y (wel´thē) *adj.* Having much wealth or money; abundant; rich.

wean (wēn) *v.* To accustom an infant or small child to food other than a mother's milk or bottle.

weap-on (wep´on) *n.* A device used in fighting a war; advice which can be used to harm another person.

wear (wâr) *v.* To have on or put something on the body; to display. *n.* The act of wearing out or using up; the act of wearing, as clothing. **-able** *adj.*

wea-ri-some (wēr´ē som) *adj.* Tedious, boring or tiresome.

wea-ry (wēr´ē) *adj.* Exhausted; tired; feeling fatigued. *v.* To make or become tired; to become fatigued. **wearily** *adv.*

wea-sel (wē´zel) *n.* A mammal with a long tail and short legs; a sly, sneaky person.

weath-er (weth´ér) *n.* The condition of the air or atmosphere in terms of humidity, temperature, and similar features. *v.* To become worn by the actions of weather; to survive.

weath-er-man (weth´ér man´) *n.* A man who reports or forecasts the weather.

weather vane *n.* A device that turns, indicating the direction of the wind.

weave (wēv) *v.* To make a basket, cloth, or other item by interlacing threads or other strands of material. **weaver** *n.*

web (web) *n.* A cobweb; a piece of interlacing material which forms a woven structure; something constructed as an entanglement; a thin membrane that joins the toes of certain water birds.

wed (wed) *v.* To take as a spouse; to marry.

we'd (wēd) *contr.* We had; we should.

wed-ding (wed´ing) *n.* A marriage ceremony; an act of joining together in close association.

wedge (wej) *n.* A tapered, triangular piece of wood or metal used to split logs, to add leverage, and to hold something open or ajar. *v.* To force or make something fit tightly.

wed-lock (wed´lok) *n.* Marriage; the state of being married.

Wed-nes-day *n.* The fourth day of the week.

weed (wēd) *n.* An unwanted plant which interferes with the growth of grass, vegetables, or flowers.

week (wēk) *n.* A period of seven days, beginning with Sunday and ending with Saturday; the time or days normally spent at school or work.

week-day (wēk´dā´) *n.* Any day of the week except Saturday or Sunday.

week-end (wēk´end´) *n.* The end of the week from the period of Friday evening through Sunday evening.

week-ly (wēk´lē) *adv.* Every week; once a week. *adj.* Taking place or done every week of or relating to a week.

weep (wēp) *v.* To shed tears; to express sorrow, joy, or emotion; by shedding tears; to cry. **weeper** *n.*

weigh (wā) *v.* To determine the heaviness of an object by using a scale; to consider carefully in one's mind; to be of a particular weight; to oppress or burden.

weight (wāt) *n.* The amount that something weighs; heaviness; a heavy object used to hold or pull something down; an over-powering force; the quality of a garment for a particular season. *v.* To make heavy.

weight-y (wā´tē) *adj.* Burdensome; important.

weird (wērd) *adj.* Having an extraordinary or strange character. **weirdly** *adv.*

weird-o *n.*, *Slang* A person who is very strange.

wel-come (wel´kom) *v.* To extend warm hospitality; to accept gladly. *adj.* Received warmly. *n.* A greeting upon one's arrival.

weld (weld) *v.* To unite metallic parts by applying heat and sometimes pressure, allowing the metals to bond together. *n.* A joint formed by welding.

wel-fare (wel´fâr´) *n.* The state of doing well; governmental aid to help the disabled or disadvantaged.

well (wel) *n.* A hole in the ground which contains a supply of water; a shaft in the ground through which gas and oil are obtained. *adj.* Being in good health; in an agreeable state.

we'll (wel) *contr.* We will; we shall.

well-be-ing (wel´bē´ing) *n.* The state of being healthy, happy, or prosperous.

well-done (wel´dun´) *adj.* Completely cooked; done properly.

well-groomed (wel´grōmd´) *adj.* Clean, neat, and properly cared for.

well known (wel´nōn´) *adj.* Widely known.

well-man-nered *adj.* Polite; having good manners.

well-mean-ing (wel´mē´ning) *adj.* Having good intentions.

well-to-do (wel´to dō´) *adj.* Having more than enough wealth.

welsh (welsh) *v.*, *Slang* To cheat by avoiding a payment to someone; to neglect an obligation. **welsher** *n.*

welt (welt) *n.* A strip between the sole and upper part of a shoe; a light swelling on the body, usually caused by a blow to the area. *v.* To hit severly.

wel-ter-weight (wel´tér wāt´) *n.* A boxer weighing between 136 and 147 pounds.

went *v*. Past tense of go.

wept *v*. Past tense of weep.

were (wer) *v*. Past tense and subjunctive form of be.

we're (wēr) *contr*. We are

were-n't (wernt) *contr*. Were not.

west (west) *n*. The direction of the setting sun; the direction to the left of a person standing north. *adj*. At, of, or from the west. *adv*. To or toward the west.

West Virginia *n*. A state located in the eastern part of the United States; statehood June 20, 1863; state capital Charleston.

whack (hwak) *v*. To strike with a hard blow, to slap. *n*. An attempt.

whale (hwāl) *n*. A very large mammal resembling a fish which lives in salt water. *Slang* An outstanding or impressive example.

wharf (hworf) *n*. A pier or platform built at the edge of water so ships can load and unload.

what (hwut) *pron*. Which one; which things; which type or kind. *adv*. In which way. *adj*. Which particular one.

what-ev-er (hwut ev´ẽr) *pron*. Everything or anything. *adj*. No matter what. *Slang* Which thing or things.

what's *contr*. What is.

wheat (hwēt) *n*. A grain ground into flour, used to make breads and similar foods.

wheel (hwēl) *n*. A circular disk which turns on an axle; an apparatus having the same principles of a wheel; something which resembles the motion or shape of a wheel. *v*. To move on or as if by wheels; to turn around a central axis; to rotate, pivot, or turn around.

whelk (hwelk) *v*. Any of various large water snails, sometimes edible.

when (hwen) *adv*. At what time; at which time. *pron*. What or which time. *conj*. While; at the time that; although.

whence (hwens) *adv*. From what source or place; from which.

when-ev-er (hwen ev´ẽr) *adv*. At any time; when. *conj*. At whatever time.

where (hwâr) *adv*. At or in what direction or place; in what direction or place.

where-a-bouts (hwâr´a bouts´) *adv*. Near, at, or in a particular location. *n*. The approximate location.

where-as (hwâr az´) *conj*. It being true or the fact; on the contrary.

where-by (hwâr bī´) *conj*. Through or by which.

wher-ev-er *adv*. In any situation or place.

whet (hwet) *v*. To make sharp; to stimulate.

wheth-er (hweth´ẽr) *conj*. Indicating a choice; alternative possibilities; either.

whet-stone (hwet´stŏn´) *n*. A stone used to sharpen scissors, knives, and other implements.

whew (hwū) *n*., *interj*. Used to express relief; or tiredness.

whey (hwā) *n*. The clear, water-like part of milk that separates from the curd.

which (hwich) *pron*. What one or ones; the one previously; whatever one or ones; whichever. *adj*. What one; any one of.

which-ev-er (hwich ev´ẽr) Any; no matter which or what.

whiff (hwif) *n*. A slight puff; a light current of air; a slight breath or odor.

while (hwīl) *n*. A length or period of time. *conj*. During the time that; even though; at the same time; although.

whim (hwim) *n*. A sudden desire or impulse.

whim-per (hwim´pẽr) *v*. To make a weak, soft crying sound. **whimper** *n*.

whim-si-cal (hwim´zi kal) *adj*. Impulsive; erratic; light and spontaneous.

whine (hwīn) *v*. To make a squealing, plaintive sound; to complain in an irritating, childish fashion.

whin-ny (hwin´ē) *v*. To neigh in a soft gentle way.

whip (hwip) *v*. To spank repeatedly with a rod or stick; to punish by whipping; to move in a motion similar to whipping or beating. *n*. A flexible stick or rod used to herd or beat animals; a dessert made by whipping ingredients; the utensil used to do so. *Slang* To overcome. **whipper** *n*.

whip-lash (hwip´lash´) *n*. An injury to the spine or neck caused by a sudden jerking motion of the head.

whir (hwer) *v*. To move with a low purring sound.

whirl (hwerl) *v*. To rotate or move in circles; to twirl; to move, drive, or go very fast. *n*. A rapid whirling motion.

whisk (hwisk) *v*. To move with a sweeping motion; to move quickly or lightly. *n*. A sweeping movement; a utensil used in cooking; to stir.

whisk-er (hwis´kẽr) *n*. The hair that grows on a man's face; the long hair near the mouth of dogs, cats, and other animals. **whiskers** A man's beard.

whis-key (hwis´kē) *n*. An alcoholic beverage distilled from rye, barley, or corn.

whis-per (hwis´pẽr) *v*. To speak in a very low tone; to tell in secret. *n*. A low rustling sound; the act of whispering.

whis-tle (hwis´l) *v*. To make a clear shrill sound by blowing air through the teeth, through puckered lips, or through a special instrument. *n*. A device used to make a whistling sound.

white (hwīt) *n*. The color opposite of black; the part of something that is white or light in color, as an egg or the eyeball; a member of the Caucasian group of people. *adj*. Having a light color; pale; pure; blameless, without sin.

White House n. The official residence of the President of the United States, located in Washington, D.C.

whither (with´er) v. To dry up or wilt from a lack of moisture; to lose freshness or vigor.

whit-tle (hwit´l) v. To cut or carve off small shavings from wood with a knife; to remove or reduce gradually.

whiz (hwiz) v. To make a whirring or buzzing sound, a projectile passing at a high rate of speed through the air. *Slang* A person having notable expertise, as with a computer.

who (hö) pron. Which or what certain individual, person, or group; referring to a person previously mentioned.

who'd contr. Who would; who had.

who-ev-er (hö ev´ér) pron. Whatever person; all or any persons.

whole (höl) adj. Complete; having nothing missing; not divided or in pieces; a complete system or unity; everything considered. *Math* Not a fraction. **wholeness** n.

whole-sale (höl´säl´) n. The sale of goods in large amounts to a retailer. adj. Relating to or having to do with such a sale. v. To sell wholesale.

whole-some (höl´som) adj. Contributing to good mental or physical health. **wholesomely** adv. **wholesomeness** n.

whole wheat (höl´hwēt´) adj. Made from the wheat kernel with nothing removed.

who'll contr. Who shall; who will.

whol-ly (hö´lē) adv. Totally; exclusively.

whom (höm) pron. The form of who used as the direct object of a verb or the object of a preposition.

whom-ev-er (höm ev´ér) pron. The form of whoever used as the object of a preposition or the direct object of a verb.

whooping cough (hö´ping kaf) n. An infectious disease of the throat and breathing passages in which the patient has spasms of coughing often followed by gasps for breath.

whoosh (hwösh) v. To make a rushing or gushing sound, as a rush of air.

whop-per (hwop´ér) n. Something of extra ordinary size. *Slang* A lie.

who's contr. Who is; who has.

whose (höz) pron. Belonging to or having to do with one's belongings. adj. Relating to *which* or *whom*.

why (hwi) adj. For what reason or purpose. conj. The cause, purpose, or reason for which. interj. Expressing surprise or disagreement.

wick (wik) n. The soft strand of fibers which extends from a candle or lamp and draws up the fuel for burning.

wick-er (wik´ér) n. A thin, pliable twig

used to make furniture and baskets.

wick-et (wik´it) n. A wire hoop in the game of croquet; a small door, window, or opening used as a box office.

wide (wid) adj. Broad; covering a large area; completely extended or open. adv. Over a large area; full extent.

wide-spread (wid´spred´) adj. Fully spread out; over a broad area.

wid-ow (wid´ō) n. A woman whose husband is no longer living.

wid-ow-er (wid´ō ér) n. A man whose wife is no longer living.

width (width) n. The distance or extent of something from side to side.

wield (wēld) v. To use or handle something skillfully; to employ power effectively.

wie-ner (wē´nér) n. A frankfurter; a hot dog.

wife (wif) n. A married female.

wig (wig) n. Artificial or human hair woven together to cover baldness or a bald spot on the head.

wig-gle (wig´l) v. To squirm; to move with rapid side-to-side motions.

wig-wam (wig´wom) n. An Indian dwelling place.

wild (wild) adj. Living in a natural, untamed state; not occupied by man; not civilized; strange and unusual. adv. Out of control. n. A wilderness region not cultivated or settled by man.

wil-der-ness (wil´dér nis) n. An unsettled area; a region left in its uncultivated or natural state.

wild-life (wild´lif´) n. Animals and plants living in their natural environments.

will (wil) n. The mental ability to decide or choose for oneself; strong desire or determination; a legal document stating how one's property is to be distributed after death. v. To bring about by an act of a will; to decide as by decree; to give or bequeath something in a will.

Wilson, Woodrow n. (1856-1924) The twenty-eighth president of the United States from 1913-1921.

wilt (wilt) v. To cause or to become limp; to lose force; to deprive of courage or energy.

win (win) v. To defeat others; to gain victory in a contest; to receive. n. Victory; the act of winning. **-ner** n.

winch (winch) n. An apparatus with one or more drums on which a cable or rope is wound, used to lift heavy loads.

wind (wind) n. A natural movement of air. v. To become short of breath.

wind instrument (wind´in´stru ment) n. A musical instrument which produces sound when a person forces his breath into it.

wind-pipe (wind´pip´) n. The passage in the neck used for breathing; the trachea.

wine (wīn) n. A drink containing 10-15% alcohol by volume, made by fermenting grapes.

wing (wing) n. One of the movable appendages that allow a bird or insect to fly; one of the airfoils on either side of an aircraft, allowing it to glide or travel through the air. v. To move as if on wings; to fly.

win-ning (win´ing) adj. Defeating others; captivating. n. Victory.

win-some (win´som) adj. Very pleasant; charming.

win-ter (win´tèr) n. The coldest season, coming between autumn and spring. adj. Relating to or typically of winter.

wipe (wīp) v. To clean by rubbing; to take off by rubbing. n. The act or instance of wiping.

Wis-con-sin n. A state located in the north central part of the United States; statehood May 29, 1848; state capital Madison.

wis-dom (wiz´dom) n. The ability to understand what is right, true, or enduring; good judgment; knowledge.

wise (wīz) adj. Having superior intelligence; having great learning; having a capacity for sound judgment marked by deep understanding.

wish (wish) v. To desire or long for something; to command or request. n. A longing or desire.

wish-ful (wish´ful) adj. Having or expressing a wish; hopeful. -fully adv.

wisp (wisp) n. A tuft or small bundle of hay, straw, or hair; a thin piece.

wit (wit) n. The ability to use words in a clever way; a sense of humor.

witch (wich) n. A person believed to have magical powers; a mean, ugly, old woman.

with (with) In the company of; near or alongside; having, wearing or bearing; in the judgment or opinion of; containing; in the possession or care of; supporting; among; occurring at the same time. v. To take away or back; to retreat.

with-draw (with dro´) v. To take away; to take back; to remove; to retreat.

with-hold (with hōld´) n. To hold back or keep.

with-out (with out´) adv. On the outside; not in possession of. prep. Something or someone lacking.

with-stand (with stand´) v. To endure.

wit-ness (wit´nis) n. A person who has seen, experienced, or heard something; something serving as proof or evidence. v. To see or hear something; to give proof or evidence of; to give testimony.

wit-ty (wit´ē) adj. Amusing or cleverly humorous.

wiz-ard (wiz´èrd) n. A very clever person; a person thought to have magical powers. Slang One with amazing skill.

wob-ble (wob´l) v. To move unsteadily from side to side, as a rocking motion.

woe (wō) n. Great sorrow or grief; misfortune.

wok n. A convex metal cooker for stir frying food.

woke v. Past tense of wake.

woman (wem´an) n. The mature adult human female; a person who has feminine qualities.

womanhood (wem´an hed´) n. The state of being a woman.

womb (wōm) n. The uterus; the place where development occurs.

won (wun) v. Past tense of win.

won-der (wun´dèr) n. A feeling of amazement or admiration. v. To feel admiration; to feel uncertainty.

won-der-ment (wun´dèr ment) n. A feeling or state of amazement.

won-drous (wun´drus) adj. Wonderful; marvelous.

won't (wōnt) contr. Will not.

won-ton n. A noodle dumpling filled with minced pork and served in soup.

wood-en (wed´en) adj. Made of wood; resembling wood; stiff; lifeless; lacking flexibility. woodenly adv.

wool (wel) n. The soft, thick hair of sheep and other such mammals; a fabric made from such hair.

word (werd) n. A meaningful sound which stands for an idea; a comment; a brief talk; an order or command. v. To express orally. wording n.

word processing n. A system which produces typewritten documents with automated type and editing equipment.

work (werk) n. The action or labor required to accomplish something; employment; a job; a project or assignment; something requiring physical or mental effort. v. To engage in mental or physical exertion; to labor to have a job; to arrange.

work-man-ship (werk´man ship´) n. The skill or art of a craftsman; the quality given to something in the process of making it.

work-out (werk´out´) n. A period of strenuous exercise.

world (werld) n. The planet Earth; the universe; the human race; a field of human interest or effort.

worldly (werld´lē) adj. Interested in pleasure rather than religious or spiritual matters.

worm (werm) n. A small, thin animal having a long, flexible, rounded or flattened body. Slang A crude person.

worn (wōrn) adj. Made weak or thin from use; exhausted.

wor-ry (wer´ē) v. To be concerned or troubled; to tug at repeatedly; to annoy;

to irritate. *n.* Distress or mental anxiety.

wor-ship (wer´ship) *n.* Reverence for a sacred object; high esteem or devotion for a person. *v.* To revere; attend a religious service.

worst (werst) *adj.* Bad; most inferior; most disagreeable. *adv.* In the worst degree.

worth (werth) *n.* The quality or value of something; personal merit; the quantity that can be purchased for a certain amount of money.

wor-thy (wer´thē) *adj.* Valuable or useful; deserving admiration or honor.

would-n't (wed´nt) *contr.* Would not.

wound (wönd) *n.* A laceration of the skin. *v.* To injure by tearing, cutting, or piercing the skin.

wow (wou) *interj.* An expression of amazement, surprise, or excitement.

wran-gle (rang´gl) *v.* To quarrel noisily.

wrap (rap) *v.* To fold in order to protect something; to encase or enclose. *n.* A coat, shawl, or other outer protection. *Slang* To finish doing something, to finish producing or making something.

wrath (rath) *n.* Violent anger or fury.

wreak (rēk) *v.* To inflict punishment upon another person.

wreath (rēth) *n.* A decorative ring-like form of intertwined flowers, bows, and other articles.

wrest (rest) *v.* To twist or pull away in a violent way. *n.* A forcible twist.

wres-tle (res´l) *v.* To struggle with an opponent in order to pin him down. *n.* The instance of wrestling.

wretch (rech) *n.* An extremely unhappy person; a miserable person.

wrig-gle (rig´l) *v.* To squirm; to move by turning and twisting.

wring (ring) *v.* To squeeze and twist by hand or machine; to press together.

wrin-kle (ring´kl) *n.* A small crease on the skin or on fabric. *v.* To have or make wrinkles.

wrist (rist) *n., Anat.* The joint of the body between the hand and forearm; the part of a sleeve which encircles the wrist.

writ (rit) *n., Law* A written court document directed to a public official or individual ordering a specific action.

write (rīt) *v.* To form symbols or letters; to form words on a surface; to communicate by writing; to earn a living by writing books.

writhe (rīth) *v.* To twist, as in pain; to suffer greatly with pain.

writ-ing (rī´ting) *n.* A book or other written work; handwriting; the process of forming letters into words; the occupation of a writer.

wrong (rong) *adj.* Incorrect; against moral standards; not suitable; immoral; unsuitable; in appropriate. *n.* An act which is wicked or immoral. *v.* To do

wrong; to injure or hurt. **wrongly** *adv.*

wrote *v.* Past tense of write.

wrought (rot) *adj.* Fashioned; formed; beatened or hammered into shape.

wrung *v.* Past tense of wring.

Wy-o-ming *n.* A state located in the western part of the United States; statehood July 10, 1890; state capital Cheyenne.

X

X, x (eks) The twenty-fourth letter of the English alphabet.

xan-thate (zan´thāt) *n.* Ester or slat of a xanthic acid.

xan-thic (zan´thik) *adj.* The color yellow or all colors that tend toward the color yellow when relating to flowers.

xan-thin (zan´thin) *n.* A carotinoid pigment that is soluble in alcohol.

xan-thine (zan´thēn) *n.* A crystalline nitrogen compound, closely related to uric acid, found in blood, urine, and certain plant and animal tissues.

xan-tho-chroid (zan´tho kroid´) *adj.* Pertaining to the light-complexioned Caucasoid race.

xan-tho-ma (zan thō´ma) *n.* A skin condition of the eyelids marked by small, yellow, raised nodules or plates.

X chro-mo-some (eks´krō´mo sōm) *n.* The sex female chromosome, associated with female characteristics; occurs paired in the female and single in the male chromosome pair.

xe-bec (zē´bek) *n.* A small vessel with three masts having both lateen and square sails.

xe-nic *adj.* Relating to, or employing a culture medium that contains one or more unidentified organisms.

xe-non (zē´non) *n.* The colorless, odorless gaseous element found in small quantities in the air, symbolized by Xe.

xe-no-phile *n.* One attracted to foreign people, styles, manners, etc.

xen-o-phobe (zen´o fōb´) *n.* A person who dislikes, fears, and mistrusts foreigners or anything stranger.

xe-rarch (zērärk) *adj.* Originating or developing in a dry place.

xe-ric (zēr´ik) *adj.* Relating to or requiring only a small amount of moisture. **xeric-ally** *adv.*

xe-roph-i-lous (zi rof´i lus) *adj.* Tolerant or characteristic of xeric environments.

xe-roph-thal-mi-a (zēr´of thal´mē a) *n.* An itching soreness of the eyes that is caused by an insufficient amount of vita-min A.

xe-ro-phyte (zēr´o fīt´) *n.* A plant that can live in a surrounding of extreme heat and drought. **xerophytic** *adj.* **xerophytically** *adv.* **xerophytism** *n.*

X-Ra-di-a-tion *n.* Treatment with

X-rays.

X ray (eks´rā´) *n*. Energy that is radiated with a short wavelength and high penetrating power; a black and white negative image or picture of the interior of the body.

x–sec-tion *n*. Cross section of something. **x–sectional** *adj*.

xy-lo-phone (zī´lo fōn´) *n*. A musical instrument consisting of mounted wooden bars which produce a ringing musical sound when struck with two small wooden hammers. **xylophonist** *n*.

xy-lose (zī´lōs) *n*., *Chem*. A crystalline aldose sugar.

xy-lot-o-mous (zīlot´o mus) *adj*. Capable of cutting or boring wood.

Y

Y, y (wī) The twenty-fifth letter of the English alphabet.

yacht (yot) *n*. A small sailing vessel powered by wind or motor, used for pleasure cruises. **yacht** *v*.

yak (yak) *n*. A long haired ox of Tibet and the mountains of central Asia.

yam (yam) *n*. An edible root; a variety of the sweet potato.

Yan-kee (yang´kē) *n*. A native of the northern United States. **Yankee** *adj*.

yap (yap) *v*. To bark in a high pitched, sharp way. *Slang* To talk in a relentless, loud, or stupid manner.

yard (yärd) *n*. A unit of measure that equals 36 inches or 3 feet; the ground around or near a house or building.

yard goods *n*. Fabric that is sold by the yard.

yard-man (yärd´man) *n*. A person employed as a worker in a railroad yard.

yard-mas-ter (yärd´mas˝tèr) *n*. A person in charge of a railroad yard.

yard-stick (yärd´stik´) *n*. A graduated measuring stick that equals 1 yard or 36 inches.

yarn (yarn) *n*. Twisted fibers, as of wool, used in knitting or weaving. *Slang* An involved tale or story.

yawn (yon) *v*. To inhale a deep breath with the mouth open wide. **yawner** *n*.

yawn-ing (yo´ning) *adj*. Expressing tiredness by a yawn.

Y-Chro-mo-some (wī´krō˝mo sōm) *n*. The sex chromosome associated with male characteristics.

ye (yē) *pron*. You, used especially in religious contexts, as hymns.

yea (yā) *adv*. Yes; indeed; truly.

yeah *adv*., *Slang* Yes.

year (yēr) *n*. A period of time starting on January 1st and continuing through December 31st, consisting of 365 days or 366 days in a leap year, which occurs every four years.

year-book (yēr´bük˝) *n*. A book printed each year giving facts about the year; a book printed each year for a high school, college, etc.

year-ling (yēr´ling) *n*. An animal that is one year old.

year-ly (yēr´lē) *adj*. Pertaining to something that happens, appears, or comes once a year, every year.

yearn (yern) *v*. To feel a strong craving.

year–round *adj*. Lasting or continuing for an entire year.

yeast (yēst) *n*. Fungi or plant cells used to make baked goods rise or fruit juices ferment.

yell (yel) *v*. To cry out loudly. *n*. A loud cry; a cheer to show support for an athletic team.

yel-low (yel´ō) *n*. The bright color of a lemon; the yolk of an egg. *v*. To make or become yellow. *adj*. Of the color yellow. *Slang* Cowardly.

yellow fever *n*. An acute infectious disease of the tropics, spread by the bite of a mosquito.

yelp *n*. A quick, sharp, shrill cry, as from pain.

yen (yen) *n*. An intense craving or longing.

yeo-man (yō´man) *n*. The owner of a small farm; a petty officer who acts as a clerk.

yeo-man-ly *n*. The rank of a yeoman; befitting a yeoman.

Yeoman's service *n*. Useful, good, or substantial service.

yes (yes) *adv*. To express agreement or consent.

yes-ter-day (yes´tèr dē) *n*. The day before today; a former or recent time. *adv*. On the day before the present day.

yes-ter-year *n*. Time just recently past; last year.

yet (yet) *adv*. Up to now; at this time; even now; more so. *conj*. Nevertheless.

yet-i *n*. The abominable snowman.

yew (ū) *n*. An evergreen tree having poisonous flat, dark-green needles and poisonous red berries.

yield (yēld) *v*. To bear or bring forward; to give up the possession of something; to give way to. *n*. An amount that is produced; the act of producing.

yield-ing (yēl´ding) *adj*. Ready to yield, comply, or submit; unresisting. **yieldingly** *adv*.

yo-del (yōd´el) *v*. To sing in a way so that the voice changes from normal to a high shrill sound and then back again.

yo-ga (yō´ga) *n*. A system of exercises which helps the mind and the body in order to achieve tranquillity and spiritual insight.

yo-gurt (yō´gèrt) *n*. A thick custard-like

food made from curdled milk and often mixed with fruit.

yoke (yōk) n. A wooden bar used to join together two oxen or other animals working together; the section of a garment fitting closely around the shoulders. v. To join in with a yoke.

yolk (yōk) n. The yellow nutritive part of an egg.

Yom Kip-pur (yom kip´ẽr) n. The Jewish holiday observed with fasting and prayer for the forgiveness of sins.

you (ū) pron. The person or persons addressed.

you all (ū ol´) pron., Slang y'all A southern variation used for two or more people in direct address.

you'd (ūd) contr. You had; you would.

you'll (ūl) contr. You will; you shall.

young (yung) adj. Of or relating to the early stage of life; not old. n. The offspring of an animal. **youngster** n.

your (yer) adj. Belonging to you or yourself or the person spoken to.

you're (ūr) contr. You are.

your-self (yer self´) pron. A form of you for emphasis when the object of a verb and the subject is the same.

youth (ūth) n. The appearance or state of being young; the time of life when one is not considered an adult; a young person.

you've (ūv) contr. You have.

yowl (youl) v. To make a loud, long cry or howl. **yowl** n.

yt-ter-bi-um (i ter´bē um) n. A metallic element of the rare-earth group symbolized by Yb.

yt-tri-um (i´trē um) n. A metallic element symbolized by Y.

yuc-ca (yuk´a) n. A tropical plant having large, white flowers and long, pointed leaves.

yule (ūl) n. Christmas.

yule-tide (ūl´tīd´) n. The Christmas season.

Z.

Z, z (zē) The twenty-sixth letter of the English alphabet.

za-ny (zā´nē) n. pl. -nies A clown; a person who acts silly or foolish. adj. Typical of being clownish. **zaniness** n. **zannily** adv.

zap v., Slang To destroy; to do away with.

zeal (zēl) n. Great interest or eagerness.

zeal-ot (zel´ot) n. A fanatical person; a fanatic.

zeal-ous (zel´us) adj. Full of interest; eager; passionate. **zealously** adv.

ze-bra (zē´bra) n. An African mammal of the horse family having black or brown stripes on a white body.

zeph-yr (zef´ẽr) n. A gentle breeze.

ze-ro (zēr´ō) n. pl. -ros, -roes The number or symbol "0"; nothing; the point from which degrees or measurements on a scale begin; the lowest point. v. To aim, point at, or close in on. adj. Pertaining to zero; nonexisting.

zest (zest) n. Enthusiasm; a keen quality. **zestful** adj. **zestfully** adj. **zesty** adj.

zig-zag (zig´zag´) n. A pattern with sharp turns in alternating directions. adv. To move in a zigzag course or path.

zilch n., Slang Nothing; zero.

zil-lion (zil´yon) n., Slang An extremely large number.

zinc (zingk) n. A bluish-white crystalline metallic element, used as a protective coat-ing for steel and iron, symbolized by Zn.

zip (zip) n. To act or move with vigor or speed. v. To move with energy, speed, or facility; to open or close with a zipper. Slang Energy; zero; nothing.

zip code n. The system to speed the delivery of mail by assigning a five digit number, plus four to each postal delivery location in the United States.

zip-per (zip´ẽr) n. A fastener consisting of two rows of plastic or metal teeth that are interlocked by means of sliding a tab.

zir-co-ni-um (zẽr kō´nē um) n. A metallic element symbolized by Zr.

zit n., Slang A pimple.

zo-di-ac (zō´dē ak´) n. The celestial sphere; the unseen path followed through the heavens by the moon, sun, and most planets; this area divided into twelve parts or twelve astrological signs, each bearing the name of a constellation.

zone (zōn) n. An area or region set apart from its surroundings by some characteristic.

zoo (zö) n., pl. zoos A public display or collection of living animals.

zo-ol-o-gy (zō ol´o jē) n. The science that deals with animals, animal life, and the animal kingdom, **zoologist** n.

zoom (zöm) v. To move with a continuous, loud, buzzing sound; to move upward sharply; to move toward a subject with great speed.

zuc-chi-ni (zö kē´nē) n. pl. -ni A summer squash that is long and narrow and has a dark-green, smooth rind.

zy-mol-o-gy (zī mol´o jē) n. The branch of science dealing with ferments and fermentation. **zymologic** n.

zy-mo-scope (zī´mo skōp) n. An instrument that measures yeast's fermenting power.

zy-mot-ic (zī mot´ik) adj. Relating or pertaining to fermentation.

zy-mur-gy (zī´mer jē) n. The chemistry dealing with the fermentation process.